CENSUS OF POPULATION 1950

PREFACE

This volume presents statistics on the number of inhabitants and the characteristics of the population of the State, its counties, standard metropolitan areas, urban places, and other constituent areas The data are based upon tabulations from the Seventeenth Decennial Census of the population of the United States, its Territories and possessions, conducted as of April 1, 1950 Provision for the Seventeenth Decennial Census was made in the act providing for the Fifteenth and subsequent decennial censuses, approved June 18, 1929, as amended

The major portion of the information compiled from the Census of Population of 1950 is contained in Volume I, *Number of Inhabitants*, and in Volume II, *Characteristics of the Population* These final volumes first appeared in the form of three series of State bulletins Series P–A, 'Number of Inhabitants", Series P–B, ' General Characteristics"; and Series P–C, "Detailed Characteristics "

Final Population Volumes I and II are assembled as follows.

Population Volume I comprises the Series P–A bulletins, thereby providing in a single publication the distribution of the Nation's inhabitants among and within the States and the Territories, possessions, etc

Population Volume II comprises all three series of bulletins (Series P–A, P–B, and P–C) This volume is divided into a United States Summary part, a part for each State, and parts for the Territories and possessions, each part comprising the three bulletins for that area All reports for a given State are thereby made available within a single binding. The three bulletin series (P–A, P–B, and P–C) represent Chapters A, B and C of the corresponding State part of Population Volume II

The materials presented here were prepared under the supervision of Howard G Brunsman, Chief, Population and Housing Division, and Dr Henry S Shryock, Jr , Assistant Chief for Population Statistics, with the assistance of Edwin D Goldfield, Program Coordinator, and Charles Merzel They were prepared by Dr Paul C Glick, Chief, Social Statistics Section, assisted by Severn Provus, Emanuel Landau, Elizabeth A Larmon, and Arthur F Grube, Dr Henry D Sheldon, Chief, Demographic Statistics Section, assisted by Charles P Brinkman, Tobia Bressler, Robert L Rowland, and Suzanne F Bershad, Gertrude Bancroft, Coordinator for Manpower Statistics, assisted by Max Shor, Herman P Miller, Lillian Palenius, and Leon R Paley, and David L Kaplan, Chief, Occupation and Industry Statistics Section, assisted by Claire Casey, Dorothy S Hayden, Elsie K Goodman, and William J Milligan

The compilation of the statistics was under the direction of Robert B Voight, Assistant Chief for Operations, assisted by Morton A Meyer, Milton D Lieberman, E Richard Bourdon, Edward I Lober, Mary E Ivins, Eva Tolchinsky, Lillian I Hoffman, and Martin Frishberg Sampling procedures were under the direction of Joseph Steinberg, Chief, Statistical Sampling Section, assisted by Joseph Waksberg The technical editorial work and planning were under the supervision of Mildred M Russell, assisted by Dorothy M Belzer.

The collection of the information on which these statistics were based was under the supervision of Lowell T Galt, then Chief, Field Division, with the assistance of Jack B Robertson, John M Bell, Leon S Geoffrey, and Harold Nisselson The geographic work, including the delineation of special types of urban territory and the preparation of maps, was under the supervision of Clarence E Batschelet, Chief, Geography Division with the assistance of Dr Robert C. Klove, Dr Vincent M Throop, and William T Fay The tabulations were under the supervision of C F Van Aken, Chief, Machine Tabulation Division, with the assistance of Morton Boisen, and Howard T Jenkins Robert H Brooks of the Administrative Service Division was responsible for printing arrangements

In addition to those of the present staff, important contributions to the general planning of the 1950 Census were made by the late J C Capt, Director of the Census until his retirement on August 17, 1949, and Dr Philip M Hauser, Acting Director until March 9, 1950

December 1952

U S CENSUS OF POPULATION: 1950

Volume

- I Number of Inhab tants (comprising Series P-A billetins)
- II Characteristics of the Population (comprising Series P-A, P-B, and P-C pulletins)
- III Census Tract Statistics (comprising Series P-D bulletins)
- IV Special Reports Employment Characteristics, Occupational and Industrial Characteristics, Characteristics of Families, Mar.tal Status, Institutional Population, Nativity and Parentage, Non-white Population of Race, Persons of Spanish Surrame, Puerto Ricans in Continental United States, State of Birth, Mobility of the Population Characteristics by Size of Place, Education, Fertility

U. S CENSUS OF HOUSING. 1950

Volume

- I General Characteristics (comprising Series H-A pulletins)
- II Nonfarm Housing Characteristics (comprising Series H-B bulletins)
- III Farm Housing Characteristics
- IV Residential Financing
- V Block Statistics (comprising Series H-E bulletins)

Housing statistics for census tracts are included in the Population Series P-D bulletins

POPULATION VOLUME II

This volume comprises 54 parts, as listed below

2	Alabama
3	Arizona
4	Arkansas
5	California
6	Colorado
7	Connecticut
8	Delaware
9	District of Columbia
10	Florida
11	Georgia
12	Idaho
13	Illinois
14	Indiana
15	Iowa
16	Kansas
17	Kentucky
18	Louisiana
19	Maine

20. Maryland

1 United States Summary

41	THE SOCIAL TRADECTOR
22	Michigan
23	Minnesota
24	Mississippi
25	Missouri
26	Montana
27	Nebraska
28	Nevada
	New Hampshire
30	New Jersey
31	New Mexico
32	New York
33	North Carolina
34	North Dakota
35.	Ohio
36	Okiahoma
37	Oregon
38	Pennsylvania
39	Rhode Island
40	South Carolina

21 Massachusetts

42	Tennessee	
43	Texas	
44	Utah	
45	Vermont	
46	Virginia	
47	Wasnington	
48	West Virginia	
49	Wisconsin	
50	Wyoming	
51-	-54 Territories and po together)	ossession

41 South Dakota

50 Wyoming

51-54 Territories and possessions (bound together)

51 Alaska

52 Hawan

53 Puerto Rico

54 American Samoa, Canal Zone,
Guam, Virgin Islands of the
United States

CONTENTS

INTRODUCTION

	Page		Page
General	X1	Defiritions and explanations—Continued	
Published data for nonwhite population	71	Citizensnip	771
Availability of unpublished data	ζ,	Marital status and married couples.	\VI.
		Household and family	XVI
Population trends	M	Relationship to head of household.	XVII
		Residence in 1949	XIX
Definitions and explanations	711	Country of birth of foreign-born white	272
Usual place of residence	X111	School enrollment	217
Completeness of enumeration	X 111	Year of school in which enrolled and years of	
Urban and rural residence	2.111	school completed	7/
Urbanized areas	X1V	Employment status	ZZ.
Types of places	XIV	Hours worked during census week	XX.11
Farm population—rural and urban	λlV	Weeks worked in 1949	XXII
Rural-nonfarm population	VIZ	Occupation, industry, and class of worker	XXII
Standard metropolitan areas	714	Income	XXVI
Quality of data for small areas	XV		
Medians	V	Reliability of sample data	x/v ii
Race and color	XV1	Sample design	X/AII
Age	XVI	Sampling variability	X/AII
Nativity	XV1	Ratio estimates	XXXX

TABLES

[See list of tables preceding each chapter]

Chapter A Number of inhabitants (Tables 1-9)

Chapter B General characteristics (Tables 10-50)
Chapter C Detailed characteristics (Tables 51-94)

Corrections of errors discovered after the State bulletins were issued are listed on page xxxi

GENERAL CHARACTERISTICS

SUBJECTS

SUBJECTS PRESENTED BY TYPE OF AREA AND TABLE NUMBER

[Sex not indexed separately as practically all tables include distributions by sex]

Subject	State: Total	State: Urban-rural	Standard metropolitan areas, urbanized areas, and urban places of 10,000 or more	Urban places of 2,500 to 10,000	Places of 1,000 to 2,500	Counties: Total	Counties: Rural nonfarm	Counties: Rural farm
	Table	*Table*	*Table*	*Table*	*Table*	*Table*	*Table*	*Table*
Summary	10	10	10	11		12		
Age	15	15	33	38	40	41	48	49
By color	15	15	33	[1] 38		41	[1] 48	49
1940–1950	15	15	33			41		
By color	15	15						
1880–1950, by color	16							
Citizenship	17	17	34			42		
1930–1950	17							
Class of worker of employed persons	28	28	35	39		43		
By color	[1] 28a	[1] 28a	36			44		
1940–1950	29							
Country of birth	24	24	[2] 34a	[4] 38		[2] 42		
Education								
School enrollment, by age	18	18	34			42		
1910–1950	19							
Years of school completed	20	20	34	38		42	48	49
By color	20	20	[1] 36			[1] 44	48a	[1] 49a
1940–1950	20							
Families, unrelated individuals, and households	22	22	34			42		
Income in 1949 of families and unrelated individuals	32	32	37	39		45	[3] 46	
By color	[1] 32a	[1] 32a	[1] 37a			[1] 45a		
Industry of employed persons	30	30	35	39		43		
By color	[1] 30a	[1] 30a	[1] 36			[1] 44		
1940–1950	31							
Institutional population	22	22	34			42		
Labor force								
Employment status	25	25	35	39		43	48	49
By color	25	25	36			44	[1] 48a	[1] 49a
1940–1950	27							
Labor force, 1940–1950, and gainful workers 1920–1930, by color	26							
Marital status	21	21	34	38		42		
By color	21	21	[1] 36			[1] 44		
1940–1950	21							
Married couples	22	22	34			42		
By color			[1] 36			[1] 44		
Nativity	17	17	34	38		42	48	49
1930–1950	17							
Occupation								
Experienced civilian labor force	28	28						
Employed persons	28	28	35	39		43	48	49
By color	[1] 28a	28a	[1] 36			[1] 44	[1] 48a	[1] 49a
1940–1950	29							
Experienced unemployed persons	28	28	35			43		
Race	14	14	34, [4] 47	38	40	42, [4] 47	48	49
1880–1950	14							
Residence in 1949	23	23	34			42		
By color	[1] 23	[1] 23						
Urban-rural residence								
Rural-farm population in places of 1,000 to 2,500					40			
Urban-farm population	13	13	34			42		
1930–1950, by color	13	13						
1950 population based on old urban-rural definition	13	13				50	50	50
By age and color	15	15				50	50	50
For urban-farm population	13	13				50		

[1] For Southern States only
[2] Southern States excluded
[3] For urban and rural nonfarm parts of counties combined
[4] For selected cities and counties

SUBJECTS PRESENTED BY TYPE OF AREA AND TABLE NUMBER

[Sex not indexed separately, as all tables include distribution by sex]

Subject	State: Total	State: Urban-rural	Standard metropolitan areas: 250,000 or more	Standard metropolitan areas: 100,000 to 250,000	Cities: 250,000 or more	Cities: 100,000 to 250,000	Cities: 50,000 to 100,000
AGE cross-classified with—	*Table*	*Table*	*Table*	*Table*	*Table*	*Table*	*Table*
Citizenship by color	[illegible]				55	55	
Color by single years of age	51	32			71		
Education							
Kindergarten enrollment, by single years of age and color [1]	6	61			61	6	
School enrollment by single years of age and color [1]	62	52			62	62	
School enrollment by single years of age 1940–1950	62						
Year of school in which enrolled, by single years of age and color	63	63			63	63	
Years of school completed for persons 5 to 24 years old by single years of age and color [1]	64	64	64		64		
Years of school completed for persons 5 to 24 years old by single years of age 1940–1950	64						
Years of school completed for persons 25 years old and over, by color [1]	65	65	65	65	65	65	
Years of school completed for persons 25 years old and over 1940-1950	65						
Income	89	[2] 89	89				
Industry of employed persons	82		82				
Labor force							
Employment status by color [1]	66	66	66	66	66	66	
Employment status by hours worked, school enrollment and color	71	71	71				
Labor force status, by marital status and color	70	70	70	70			
Labor force status 1940–1950	69						
Status of employed persons	67	67	67	67	67	67	
Status of persons not in the labor force by color [1]	68	68	68	68	68	68	
Marital status and presence of spouse by color	57	57	57	57	57	57	
Marital status, 1890–1950	56						
Nativity by color	54						
Nativity of the white population	53	53	53	53	53	53	
Nativity of the white population by single years of age	51				51		
Occupation of employed persons by color [1]	76		76				
Quasi household population by color [1]	60	60	60	60			
Race	53	53	53	53	53	53	
Relationship to household head by color	58	58	58	58			
OCCUPATION cross-classified with—							
Age of employed persons, by color [1]	76		76				
Class of worker of employed persons	77		77	77			
Detailed occupation of the experienced civilian labor force and of employed persons	73		73	73	73	73	
Detailed occupation of employed persons, 1940–1950	74						
Income of the experienced civilian labor force	78		78				
Industry of employed persons (major occupation group only)	84		84				
Occupation of the experienced civilian labor force and of employed persons		75					75
Race of employed persons	77		77	77			
INDUSTRY cross-classified with—							
Age of employed persons	82		82				
Class of worker of employed persons	83		83	83			
Detailed industry of the experienced civilian labor force and of employed persons	79		79	79	79	79	
Detailed industry of employed persons 1940–1950	80						
Income of the experienced civilian labor force	86		86				
Industry of employed persons							81
Occupation of employed persons (major occupation group only)	84		84				
Race of employed persons	83		83	83			
Weeks worked in 1949 by the experienced civilian labor force	85		85				
TOTAL INCOME IN 1949 OF PERSONS cross-classified with—							
Age	89	[2] 89	89				
Class of worker of the experienced civilian labor force	92	[2] 92	92				
Family status	90	[2] 90	90				
Income, by color [1]	88	88					88
Industry of the experienced civilian labor force	86		86				
Occupation of the experienced civilian labor force	78		78				
Race	87	[2] 87	87	87	87	87	
Type of income	93	[2] 93	93				
Weeks worked in 1949	91	[2] 91	91				
OTHER SUBJECTS							
Quasi household population, by color [1]	59	59	59	59	59	59	
Quasi household population, 1940–1950	59						
Relationship to household head by color [1]	59	59	59	59	59	59	
Relationship to household head, 1940–1950	59						
Wage or salary income of the experienced labor force in 1949	94		94		94	94	
Wage or salary income of the experienced labor force, 1939–1949	94						
Weeks worked in 1949, by labor force status	72		72	72			

[1] Statistics by color shown for areas containing 50 000 nonwhite inhabitants or more; for urban rural areas, separate statistics by color shown for Southern States only.

[2] For urban and rural-nonfarm parts of States combined.

Characteristics of the Population

GENERAL

The major portion of the information on the population of this State, compiled from the Censuses of Population and Housing of 1950, is presented in this volume It contains three chapters previously published as separate bulletins Chapter A recapitulates the statistics on the distribution of the total population within the State (originally published in the Series P-A bulletin and in Volume I), Chapter B presents statistics on the general characteristics of the population of the various political subdivisions of the State, such as counties and cities, as well as of standard metropolitan areas and urbanized areas (originally published in the Series P-B bulletin), and Chapter C presents data on the detailed characteristics of the population of the larger areas within the State (originally published in the Series P-C bulletin)

The major part of this volume is devoted to the presentation of information on the characteristics of the population Statistics on the general characteristics contained in Chapter B include data on urban-rural residence age, sex, race, nativity, citizenship, country of birth school enrollment years of school completed, marital status, residence in 1949, employment status, occupation industry, class of worker, and family income In Chapter C, information on most of these characteristics is presented again but in greater detail The statistics in Chapter C include cross-classifications of age with race, nativity, citizenship marital status relationship to household head, education, and employment status, the occupational and industrial attachments of the labor force, and personal income The general content of the tables in Chapter B and Chapter C is indicated in the charts on pp viii and ix

Additional reports are also planned on such subjects as mobility of the population, characteristics of families and households, nativity and parentage, institutional population, characteristics of the nonwhite population by race, and characteristics of the labor force These special reports will relate mainly to the United States and regions In some cases, a few tables for States and other large areas will also be included

Statistics on the number of inhabitants as shown in Chapter A in this volume are all based on complete counts of the population Similarly, the statistics on the general characteristics of the population presented in Chapter B are based on complete counts except in the case of those characteristics, such as school enrollment and income, that were reported for only 20 percent of the population For Chapter C, only the tabulations relating to occupation and industry are based on complete counts, all the other tabulations are confined to the 20-percent sample Because of sampling variability, differences may be expected between figures obtained from a complete count and the corresponding figures based on the 20-percent sample Furthermore, differences between figures for corresponding items in different tables may arise because they were prepared from separate tabulations The resources available did not permit a full adjustment of small processing differences, whereas in earlier censuses such adjustments were made

In the Series P-A, P-B, and P-C bulletins, the tables were numbered in such a way as to provide a continuous series when bound together in this volume Thus tables 1 to 9 present data on the number of inhabitants for this State, tables 10 to 50 present the data on general characteristics of the population, and tables 51 to 94 present the data on detailed characteristics

PUBLISHED DATA FOR NONWHITE POPULATION

In Chapter B, there are a number of tables for the South in which additional information on the characteristics of the nonwhite population is presented These tables—28a, 30a, 32a, 37a, 45a, 48a, and 49a—present statistics on occupation industry, income and other subjects for the State and areas within the State Most of the foreign-born white population is to be found outside the South Tables 34a and 42a present statistics on country of birth of the foreign-born white in the North and West These basic differences between the South and other regions are also recognized in tables 36, 38, 44, and 50 in which the content for Southern States is somewhat different from the content for the Northern and Western States

In Chapter C, statistics for the nonwhite population are presented for all areas with a relatively large nonwhite population regardless of the region in which they are located Statistics on marital status, relationship to head of household, education, employment status, and occupation are presented by age for the nonwhite population for those States, standard metropolitan areas, and cities that had 50,000 or more nonwhite inhabitants in 1950 For Southern States, separate data on nonwhite persons are also presented for those urban, rural-nonfarm, and rural-farm parts of the State having 50,000 or more nonwhite inhabitants (In most of the Northern and Western States relatively few nonwhite persons live in rural areas)

Selected statistics are also presented in Chapter C for the population classified by race (white Negro, and other races) for all States and for standard metropolitan areas, and, in some cases, cities with a total population of 100,000 or more These data include separate distributions by age occupation, industry, and income

AVAILABILITY OF UNPUBLISHED DATA

For urban places smaller than 10,000 inhabitants, and for the urban and rural parts of counties, only part of the tabulated data are published in Chapter B A complete listing of tabulated, but unpublished statistics for these areas is contained in the publication, U S Bureau of the Census, *U S Censuses of Population and Housing 1950, Key to Published and Tabulated Data for Small Areas*, Washington, D C, 1951[1]

Some of the detailed statistics tabulated for large areas in connection with the preparation of Chapter C are not being published for example, separate data for each standard metropolitan area and city of 100,000 or more, and certain statistics for the nonwhite population A complete description of these unpublished data can be obtained upon request

The tabulated, but unpublished, statistics can be made available upon request for the cost of transcription or consolidation If enumeration district data are desired copies of maps showing enumeration district boundaries can also be furnished, usually at nominal cost Requests for such unpublished material should be addressed to the Director, Bureau of the Census, Washington 25, D C

---

[1] Address purchase orders to the Superintendent of Documents U S Government Printing Office, Washington 25, D C Price 30 cents

POPULATION TRENDS

The State.—The greater part of the area now constituting Louisiana was organized in 1804 as the Territory of Orleans It included at that time the Baton Rouge District—that part of the present State lying east of the Mississippi River—but excluded the southwestern part of the present State—that part lying west of the Louisiana Purchase boundary In 1812 all the present area of Louisiana except the Baton Rouge District was admitted to the Union as the eighteenth State, and upon the addition of the District a few days later Louisiana assumed its present boundaries Its population on April 1 1950, according to the Seventeenth Census, was 2,683,516 The State has a land area of 45,162 square miles In 1950 there was an average of 59.4 inhabitants per square mile as compared with an average of 52.3 in 1940 Among the States Louisiana ranked twenty-first in population and thirty-first in land area

In 1820, the first year in which it was enumerated as a State in a Federal census Louisiana had a population of 153,407 (table 1) In 1950, 130 years later, its population was more than 17 times as large. The 1900 population of 1,381,625 was nine times as large as the population in 1820 The rates of population growth in the twentieth century ranged from 8.6 percent for the decade 1910 to 1920 to 19.9 percent for the previous decade The numerical increase of 319,636 between 1940 and 1950 was the largest in the history of the State and represented a gain of 13.5 percent over the 2,363,880 persons enumerated in 1940

Urban and rural population.—The 1950 urban population of Louisiana comprised 1,471,696 persons, or 54.8 percent of the population of the State (table 1) The urban population was living in the 72 urban places in the State and in other territory included in the urban-fringe areas of the Baton Rouge, New Orleans, and Shreveport Urbanized Areas

The rural population of Louisiana comprised 1,211,820 persons or 45.2 percent of the population of the State (table 1) Of the rural population, 134,762 persons, or 11.1 percent, were living in 66 incorporated places and 20 unincorporated places of 1,000 to 2,500 inhabitants (table 2)

Urban population according to new and old definitions.—According to the new urban-rural definition, the 1950 urban population of Louisiana included the following (*1*) The 1,363,789 persons in the 66 incorporated places of 2,500 inhabitants or more, (*2*) the 26,449 inhabitants of the 6 specially delineated unincorporated places of 2,500 or more, and (*3*) the 81,458 persons living in other territory included in the Baton Rouge, New Orleans, and Shreveport Urbanized Areas Since there were no areas urban under special rule in Louisiana according to the old definition, the population of the first element comprised the urban population under the old definition The population of the remaining elements—107,907—represents the gain in the urban population which resulted from the change in definition (See section below on "Urban and rural residence")

Trends of urban and rural population.—Trends in the urban and rural population can be examined only on the basis of the old definition On this basis, the urban population more than tripled between 1900 and 1950, rising from 366,288 to 1,363,789 (table 1) The largest numerical increase as well as the most rapid rate of growth in the urban population over the 50-year period came in the decade 1940 to 1950, when an increase of 383,350, or 39.1 percent was recorded The proportion of the population of the State living in urban territory nearly doubled between 1900 and 1950 rising from 26.5 to 50.8 percent

The rural population of Louisiana rose from 1,015,337 in 1900 to 1,383,441 in 1940 Between 1940 and 1950, however the rural population declined for the first time in the history of the State The decline of 63,714 or 4.6 percent, between 1940 and 1950 brought the rural population to 1,319,727

Parishes.—The parishes in Louisiana ranged in size from Cameron with a population of 6,244 to Orleans with a population of 570,445 (table 5) Between 1940 and 1950, 34 of the 64 parishes increased in population The most rapid rate of increase was experienced in Jefferson Parish, in which the population more than doubled All but 3 of the 34 parishes which increased in population between 1940 and 1950 were among the 57 which had gained in the previous decade

Minor civil divisions.—To the primary divisions into which parishes are divided, the Bureau of the Census applies the general term "minor civil divisions" The minor civil divisions in Louisiana are called police jury wards (Orleans Parish which is coextensive with New Orleans city, is not divided into police jury wards) The incorporated cities (other than New Orleans) towns and villages form subdivisions of the minor civil divisions in which they are located

Table 6 shows statistics on the population of each parish by minor civil divisions for the last three censuses The population of each incorporated city, town, village, or unincorporated place is shown in *italics* under the population of the police jury ward in which it is located When an incorporated or unincorporated place lies in two or more minor civil divisions, the population of the several parts is shown in table 6 in the appropriate parishes and minor civil divisions, and each part is designated by "part" Figures on the total population of such places are given in table 7 Unincorporated places are designated by "uninc" Changes between the 1940 Census and the 1950 Census in the boundaries of the areas listed are shown in notes to table 6. For changes in boundaries prior to the 1940 Census see reports of the Sixteenth Census (1940), *Population*, Vol I pp 435–441 and reports of earlier censuses

Incorporated and unincorporated places.—In 1950 there were 224 places in Louisiana incorporated as cities, towns, or villages and 26 unincorporated places of 1,000 inhabitants or more There were 1,313,237 persons living in the incorporated places 140,448 of whom were in the 158 places of fewer than 2,500 inhabitants The 20 unincorporated places of 1,000 to 2,500 inhabitants accounted for 30,567 of the 57,016 persons living in unincorporated places

Urbanized areas.—There were three urbanized areas in Louisiana Of the 948,840 persons living in the urbanized areas, 823,280 were in the central cities of the areas and 125,560 in the urban-fringe areas The urban-fringe areas included a population of 44,102 in five incorporated places and 81,458 in the unincorporated parts (tables 2 and 9)

DEFINITIONS AND EXPLANATIONS

The definitions of the pertinent concepts used in the 1950 Census are given below Several of these definitions differ from those used in 1940 The changes were made after consultation with users of census data in order to improve the statistics, even though it was recognized that comparability would be adversely affected In many cases, the new definitions were tested in connection with the Current Population Survey, and, where feasible, measures of the impact of the change on the statistics were developed This survey, covering a sample of 25,000 households throughout the country, has been in operation since April 1940 and has provided national estimates of the employment status of the population (*Current Population Reports*, Series P–57, "The Monthly Report on the Labor Force") The distribution of employed workers by major occupation group is included each quarter in this series, and statistics on other subjects, such as mantal status, school enrollment, migration, and moome, are collected in the Current Population Survey and published annually in other series of Current Population Reports

USUAL PLACE OF RESIDENCE

In accordance with Census practice dating back to 1790, each person enumerated in the 1950 Census was counted as an inhabitant of his result place of residence or usual place of abode, that is, the place where he lives and sleeps most of the time. This place is not necessarily the same as his legal residence, voting residence, or domicile, although, in the vest majority of cases, the use of these different bases of classification would produce identical results.

In the application of this rule, persons were not always counted as residents of the places in which they happened to be found by the census enumerators. Persons in continental United States and Hawaii in places where guests usually pay for quarters (hotels, etc.) were enumerated there on the night of April 11, and those whose usual place of residence was elsewhere were allocated to their homes. Visitors found staying in private homes, however, were not ordinarily interviewed there. In addition, information on persons away from their usual place of residence was obtained from other members of their families, landladies, etc. If an entire family was expected to be away during the whole period of the enumeration, information on it was obtained from neighbors. A matching process was used to eliminate duplicate reports for persons who reported for themselves while away and were also reported by their families at home.

Persons in the armed forces quartered on military installations were enumerated as residents of the States, counties, and minor civil divisions in which their installations were located. Members of their families were enumerated where they actually resided in the 1950 Consus, college stidents living away from home were considered residents of the communities in which they were residing while attending college, whereas in 1940, as in most previous censuses, they were generally enumerated at their parental homes This change affects the comparability of the 1950 and 1940 figures on education of persons of college age in States and local areas Comparability of the statistics on other subjects may also be affected for areas containing large colleges or universities

In 1950 the crews of vessels of the American Merchant Marine in harbors of the United States were counted as part of the population of the ports in which their vessels were berthed on April 1, 1950. In 1940 such persons were treated as part of the population of the port from which the vessel operated. Inmates of institutions, who ordinarily lived there for long periods of time, were counted as inhabitants of the place in which the institution was located, whereas patients in general hospitals, who ordinarily have short stays, were counted at, or allocated to, their homes. All persons without a usual place of residence were counted where they were anumerated

COMPLETENESS OF ENUMERATION

The degree of completeness of enumeration has always been a matter of deep concern to the Bureau of the Census, and, in the course of its history, a number of devices have been developed to aid in securing adequate coverage. These devices include the special procedures for the enumeration of transients and infants, urging notifications from persons who believed that they may not have been enumerated, and the early announcement of population counts in local areas to make possible the thorough investigation of compliants as to the accuracy of the count. In the 1950 Census earlier procedures were strengthened and additional procedures were introduced. Adequate handling of the problem of underenumeration involves not only the development of techniques in order to insure satisfactory coverage but also methods of measuring the completeness of coverage.

Prior to 1950, no method had been devised to give an over-all direct measure of the completeness of enumeration of the total appointance. For the most part, discussion in census reports was confined to qualitative statements based on various kinds of evidence. Some quantitative measures were developed, however. For example, the underenumeration of enidren inner 5 had been estimated for recent censuses by comparisons of census counts with survivors of births in the preceding five years. Such comparisons indicate that the total understatement in the published figure for this age group was about \$10,000 in the 1950 Census, according to a provisional estimate, and about \$60,000 in the 1940 Census, the corresponding percentages were 4.8 and 7.6, respectively.

In the 1950 Census the population of all ages was re-enumerated on a sample basis in a carefully conducted post-enumeration survey tous permitting a direct check on a case-by-case basis of the actual enumeration. The results of this survey indicate a net underenumeration in the census count of the total population of the United States of about 2,100,000, or 14 percent

URBAN AND RURAL RESIDENCE

According to the new definition that was adopted for use in the 1950 Census, the urban population comprises all persons living in (a) places of 2,500 inhabitants or more incorporated as cities, boroughs, and villages, (b) incorporated towns of 2,500 inhabitants or more except in New England, New York, and Wisconsin, where "towns" are simply minor civil divisions of counties, (c) the densely settled urban fringe, including both incorporated and unincorporated areas, around cities of 50,000 or more, and (d) unincorporated places of 2,500 inhabitants or more outside any urban fringe. The remaining population is classified as rural. According to the old definition, the urban population was limited to all persons living in incorporated places of 2,500 inhabitants or more and in areas (usually minor civil divisions) classified as urban under special rules relating to population size and density

In both definitions, the most important component of the urban territory is the group of incorporated places having 2,590 inhabitants or more A definition of urban territory restricted to such places would exclude a number of equally large and densely settled places, merely because they were not incorporated places Under the old definition, an effort was made to avoid some of the more obvious omissions by the inclusion of the places classified as urban under special rules. Even with these rules, however, many large and closely built-up places were excluded from the urban territory To improve the situation in the 1950 Census, the Bureau of the Census set up, in advance of enumeration, boundaries for urban-fringe areas around cities of 50,000 or more and for unincorporated places outside urban fringes All the population residing in urban-fringe areas and in unincorporated places of 2,500 or more is classified as urban according to the 1950 definition (Of course, the incorporated places of 2,500 or more in these fringes are urban in their own right) Consequently, the special rules of the old definition are no longer necessary Although the Bureau of the Census has employed other definitions in the course of its bistory, the statistics on the Although the Bureau of the Census has employed population by urban and rural residence shown for years prior to 40 are in substantial accordance with the 1940 definition 1950 statistics on urban-rural residence presented in this volume are in accordance with the new definition unless otherwise specified m a given table

Basic characteristics for urban and rural areas classified according to the old urban-rural definition are presented for the State in tables 13 and 15 and for counties in table 50. The 1950 figures presented in table 15 on age by color for persons in the rural-farm and rural-nonfarm population under the old urban-rural definition are partly estimated, since the detailed age by color distribution was not tabulated for the farm and nonfarm parts of the areas that are urban under the new definition but were rural under the old definition.

TIRBANIZED AREAS

is indicated above, one of the components of urban territory under the new definition of urban-rural residence is the urban fringe. Areas of this type in combination with the cities which their surround have been defined in the 1950 Census as urbanized areas.

Each interior area contains at least one city with 50 000 unabitants or more in 1940 or according to a special census taken since 1940. Fach unranized area also includes the surrounding ciose visetified incorporated places and unincorporated areas that comprise its urbail frings. The boundaries of these frings areas were established to conform as nearly as possible to the actual to marries of thickly estilled territory, usually claracterized by a closely spaced sirect pattern. The territory of an urbanized area may reclassified into moorporated parts and numnorporated parts. (See urbanized area maps which follow table 9 in Chapter A.)

An arbanized area also may be divided into central city or cities and uroan finge as defined below

Central cities — Although an urbanized area may coi tain more than one city of 50,000 or more, not all cities of this size are necessarily central cities. The largest city of an area is always a certral city. In addition, the second and third most populous cities in the area may qualify as central cities provided they have a population of at least one-third of that of the largest city in the area and a minimum of 25,000 inhabrants. The names of the right dual urbanized areas indicate the central cities of the area. The sole exception to this rule is found in the New York—Northeastern New Jerse. Urbanized Area, the contral cities of which are New York City, Jersey Uti. and Newark.

Urban fringe—The urban fringe includes that part of the urbanized area which is outside the central city or cities. The following types of areas are embraced if they are contiguous to the central city or cities or if they are contiguous to any area already included in the urban fringe.

- 1 Incorporated places with 2,500 inhabitants or more in 1940 or at a subsequent special cersus conducted prior to 1950
- 2 Incorporated places with fewer than 2,500 inhabitants containing an area with a concentration of 100 dwelling units or more with a density in this concentration of 500 units or more per square mile. This density represents approximately 2,000 persons per square mile and normally is the minimum found associated with a closely spaced street pattern.
- 3 Unincorporated territory with at least 500 dwelling units per square mile
- 4 Territory devoted to commercial, industrial, transportational, recreational, and other purposes functionally related to the central city.

Also included are ovelying noncontiguous areas with the required dwelling unit density located within 1½ miles of the main contiguous urbanized part, measured along the shortest connecting highway, and other outlying areas within one-half mile of such noncontiguous areas which meet the minimum residential density vale.

TYPES OF PLACES

The term "place 'refers to a concentration of population regardless of legally prescribed limits, powers, or functions. Thus some areas laving the legal powers and functions characteristic of incorporated places are not recognized as places.

Incorporated places —In a majority of instances, however, the legally prescribed in its of incorporated places serve to define concentrations of population Of the 18,548 places recognized in the 1950 Census, 17,118 are incorporated as cities, towns, villages, or boroughs. In New England, New York, and Wisconsin, however, towns, although they may be incorporated, are minor ovil divisions or counties and are not considered as places. Similarly, in the States in which townships possess powers and functions identical with those of villages, the township is not classified as place. Although areas of this type are not recognized.

as places, their densely settled portions may be recognized as unincorporated places or as a part of a 1 urban fringe

Unincorporated places —In addition to incorporated places the 1950 Census recognizes 4,430 unincorporated places. These unincorporated places, which contain neavy concentrations of population, are recognized as places by virtue of their physical recognition, possible, the Bureau of the Census has defined ooundaries for all unincorporated places of 1,000 inhabitants or more which lie outside the urban fringes of cities or 50,000 inhabitants or more Because local practice as to incorporation varies considerably from one part of the country to another, some States have very few if any such unincorporated places and others have a great many Although their are also unincorporated places within the urban fringe, it was not feasible to establish boundaries for such places, and, therefore, they are not separately iountified

Urban places—In the 1950 Census urban places comprise incorporated and unincorporated places of 2,500 inhabitants or more Bossuse incorporated places of fewer than 2,500 which lie in the urban fringe are not recognized as urban places and because unincorporated places of 2,500 or more are not identified in the urban fringe, the total population of urban places is somewhat less than the total urban population

FARM POPULATION-RURAL AND URBAN

The farm population for 1950 as for 1940 and 1930, includes all persons living on farms without regard to occupation. In determining farm and nonfarm residence in the 1950 Census, however, certain special groups were classified otherwise than in earlier censuses. In 1950, persons living on what might have been considered farm land were classified as nonfarm if they paid cash rent for their homes and yards only. A few persons in institutions, summer camps, "motels," and tourist camps were classified as farm residents in 1940, whereas in 1950 all such persons were classified as nonfarm. For the United States as a whole, there is evidence from the Current Population Survey that the farm population in 1950 would have been about 9 percent larger had the 1940 procedure been used

In most tables, data by farm residence are presented for the rural-farm population only, since virtually all of the farm population is located in rural areas Only 12 percent of the farm population lived in urban areas in 1950 Figures on the urban-farm population are shown in tables 13, 34, 42, and 50

RURAL NONFARM POPULATION

The rural-nonfarm population includes all persons living outside urban areas who do not live on farms. In 1940 and earlier, persons living in the suburbs of cuties constituted a large proportion of the rural-nonfarm population. The effect of the new urban-rural definition has been to change the classification of a considerable number of such persons to urban. The rural-nonfarm population is, therefore, somewhat more homogeneous than under the old definition. It still comprises, however persons hiving in a variety of types of residences, such as isolated nonfarm homes in the open country, villages and hamlets of fewer than 2,500 inhabitants, and some of the fringe areas surrounding the smaller incorporated places

STANDARD METROPOLITAN AREAS

Origin and Purpose

If has long been recognized that, for many types of social and commit analysis, it is necessary to consider as a unit the entire population in and around the city whose activities form an integrated social and economic system. Prior to the 1950 Census, aceas of this type had been defined in somewhat different ways by various agencies. Leading examples were the metropolitan districts of the Census of Population, the industrial areas of the Census of Manufactures, and the labor market areas of the Bureau

of Employment Securit. The usefulness of data pubushed for any of these areas was similed by this lack of comparability

Accordingly, the Bureau of the Census in cooperation with a number of other Federa, agencies, under the leadersh p of the Budget, established ine "standard metropolitan area" so that a wide variety of statistical data might be presented on a uniform basis. Since counties instead of minor civil divisions are used as the basic component of standard metropolitan areas except in the New England States, it was felt that many more kinds of statistics could be compiled for them than for metropolitan districts. These new areas supersede not only the metropolital districts but also the industrial areas and certain other similar areas used by other Federal agencies.

Definitions

Except in New England, a standard metropolitan area is a county or group of contiguous cointies which contains at least one city of 50,000 mhabitants or more. In addition to the county, or counties, containing such a city, or cities, contiguous counties are included in a standard metropolitan area if secording to certain criteria they are essentially metropolitan in character and socially and economically integrated with the central city. For a description of the standard metropolitan areas in this State, if any, see p xxx.

Criteria of metropolitan character—These criteria relate primarily to the character of the county as a place of work or as a home for concentrations of nonagricultural workers and their dependents Specifically, these criteria are.

- 1 The county must (a) contain 10,000 nonagreultural workers, or (b) contain 10 percent of the ronagr cultural workers working in the standard metropolutan area, or (c) have at least one-half of its population reading in minor civil divisions with a population density of 150 or more per square mile and contiguous to the central city
- 2 Nonagricultural workers must constitute at least twothirds of the total number of employed persons of the county

Criteria of integration.—The criteria of integration relate primarily to the extent of economic and social communication between the outlying counties and the central county as indicated by such items as the following

- 1 Fifteen percent or more of the workers residing in the contiguous county work in the county containing the largest city in the standard metropolitan area, or
- 2 Twenty-five percent or more of the persons working m the contiguous county reside in the county containing the largest city in the standard metropolitan area, or
- 3 The number of telephone calls per month to the county containing the largest city of the standard metropolitan area from the contiguous county is four or more times the number of subsenbers in the contiguous county

Areas in New England —In New England, the city and town are administratively more important than the county, and data are compiled locally for such minor civil divisions. Here towns and cities were the units used in defining standard metropolitan areas, and some of the criteria set forth above could not be applied in their place, a population density criterion of 150 or more persons per square mile, or 100 or more persons per square mile where strong integration was evident, has been used

Central crites — Although there may be several crites of 50,000 or more in a standard metropolitan area, not all are necessarily central crites. The largest city in a standard metropolitan area is the principal central city. Any other city of 25,000 or more within a standard metropolitan area having a population amounting to one-third or more of the population of the principal city is also a central city. However, no more than three cities have been defined as central cities of any standard metropolitan area. The name of every central city is included in the name of the area, with the exception that in the case of the New York-Northeastern New Jersey Standard Metropolitan Area, "Jersey City" and "Newark"

are not part of the name. Data for standard metropolitan areas located in two or more States are presented in the report for the Srate containing the principal central city.

Difference Between Standard Metropolitan Areas and Metropolitan Districts

Since the metropolitan district was outli up from minor civil divisions and ance the standard metropolitan area is usually composed of whole counties, the standard metropolitan area ordinarily includes a larger territory than the corresponding metropolitan district. There are, however, cases in which parts of the metropolitan district, as defined in 1940 an one fall within any standard metropolitan area. It is also true that in a number of cases single metropolitan districts of 1940 have been split into two standard metropolitan areas. Many metropolitan districts would have been changed, of course, had they been brought up to date for 1950

In general then, the two kinds of areas are not comparable Since metropolitar districts were defined almost wholly in terms of censity and standard metropolitan areas include whole counties selected on the basis of more complicated criteria, the population density of the standard metropolitan areas is considerably lower on the average and shows more variation from one area to another Differences between the two types of areas are relatively small in New England, and would have been even less had the metropolitan districts peer brought up to date.

Difference Between Standard Metropolitan Areas and Urbanized Areas

The standard metropolitan area can be characterized as the metropolitan community as distinguished from both the legal city and the physical city. Standard metropolitan areas are larger than urpanized areas and in most cases contain an entire urbanized area However, in a few instances, the fact that the boundaries of standard metropolitan areas are determined by county lines, and those of urbanized areas by the pattern of urban growth, means that there are small segments of urbanized areas which he outside standard metropolitan areas In general then, urbanized areas represent the thickly settled urban core of the standard metropolitan areas, with the exceptions noted above Because of discontinuities in land settlement, there are also some cases in which a single standard metropolitan area contains two urbanized The lists of urbanized areas and of standard metropolitan areas areas also differ somewhat because the former nad to be established for cities of 50,000 or more before 1950, whereas the latter were established for cities of 50 000 or more as determined in the 1950 Census

QUALITY OF DATA FOR SMALL AREAS

Data for the smaller areas represent the work of only a few enumerators (often only one or two) The misinterpretation by an enumerator of the instructions for a particular item may, therefore, have an appreciable effect on the statistics for a very small community—e g, places of less than 10,000 inhabitants and particularly places of less than 2,500 inhabitants—even though it would have a negligible effect upon the figures for a large area

MEDIANS

Medians are presented in connection with the data on age, years of school completed, and meome which appear in this volume. The median is the value which divides the distribution into two equal parts—one-half of the cases falling below this value and one-half of the cases exceeding this value. In the computation of medians, cases for which the information was not reported are omitted. The median income for families and unrelated individuals is based on the total number reporting, including those reporting no income. The median income for persons is based on the distribution of those reporting \$1 or more

RACE AND COLOR

Definitions

The concept of race as it has been used by the Bureau of the Census is derived from that which is commonly accepted by the general public as reflected in the action of legislative and judicial bodies of the country It does not, therefore, reflect clear-cut definitions of biological stock, and several categories obviously refer to nationalities Although it lacks scientific precision, it is doubtful whether efforts toward a more scientifically acceptable definition would be appreciably productive, given the conditions under which census enumerations are carried out The information on race is ordinarily not based on a reply to questions asked by the enumerator but rather is obtained by observation Enumerators were instructed to ask a question when they were in doubt Experience has shown that reasonably adequate identification of the smaller "racial" groups is made in areas where they are relatively numerous but that representatives of such groups may be misclassified in areas where they are rare

Color —The term "color" refers to the division of population into two groups white and nonwhite The group designated as "nonwhite" consists of Negroes, Indians Japanese, Chinese, and other nonwhite races Persons of Mexican birth or ancestry who were not definitely Indian or of other nonwhite race were classified as white in 1950 and 1940 In the 1930 publications, Mexicans were included in the group 'Other races," but the 1930 data published in this report have been revised to include Mexicans in the white population

Negro —In addition to full-blooded Negroes, this classification also includes persons of mixed white and Negro parentage and persons of mixed Indian and Negro parentage unless the Indian blood very definitely predominates or unless the individual is accepted in the community as an Indian

American Indian.—In addition to full-blooded Indians, persons of mixed white and Indian blood are included in this category if they are enrolled on an Indian reservation or agency roll Also included are persons of mixed Indian blood if the proportion of Indian blood is one-fourth or more, or if they are regarded as Indians within the community Indians living in Indian Territory or on reservations were not included in the population until 1890

Other races —Separate statistics are given in this volume for Japanese and Chinese The category "All other" includes Filipinos, Koreans, Asiatic Indians, etc

Mixed Parentage

Persons of mixed parentage are classified according to the race of the nonwhite parent and mixtures of nonwhite races are generally classified according to the race of the father

In 1950, for the first time, an attempt was made to identify persons of mixed white, Negro, and Indian ancestry living in certain communities in the eastern United States in a special category so they might be included in the categories "Other races" and "All other" rather than being classified white, Negro, or Indian This identification was accomplished with varying degrees of success, however These groups are not shown separately, but they are included in the "nonwhite" total The communities in question are of long standing and are locally recognized by special names, such as "Siouian" or "Croatan," "Moor," and "Tunica" In previous censuses, there had been considerable variation in the classification of such persons by race

AGE

Definitions

The age classification is based on the age of the person at his last birthday as of the date of enumeration, that is, the age of the person in completed years The enumerator was instructed to obtain the age of each person as of the date of his visit rather than as of April 1, 1950

Assignment of Unknown Ages

When the age of a person was not reported, it was estimated on the basis of other available information such as marital status, school attendance, employment status, age of other members of the family, and type of household Age was estimated by this procedure in the 1950 Census for 0 19 percent of the population of the United States This method of assigning unknown ages on the basis of related information was used for the first time in the 1940 Census when estimates of age were made for 0 16 percent of the population of the United States In previous censuses, with the exception of 1880, persons of unknown age were shown in a separate category The summary totals for "14 years and over" and "21 years and over" for earlier censuses presented in this volume include all persons of "unknown age" since there is evidence that most of the persons for whom age was not reported were in the age classes above these limits

Errors in Age Statistics

A considerable body of evidence exists which indicates that age is misreported in several characteristic ways and that certain age groups are less completely enumerated than others in censuses A comparison of age distributions from the 1950 Census with age distributions based on figures from the 1940 Census and brought up-to-date from official records of births, deaths and migration, suggests that this generalization is also true for the 1950 Census This comparison shows that, for the United States as a whole, there appears to be an underenumeration of children under 5 of approximately 4 8 percent as compared with about 7 6 percent in 1940 Males between the ages of 18 and 24 also appear to have been relatively underenumerated Likewise, there appears to be a deficit of persons in the age range 55 to 64 years, which, however, is more than offset by an excess over the number expected in the age group 65 years old and over

In addition to errors in the statistics for broad-age groups arising from underenumeration and the misstatement of age, there is a tendency to report age in multiples of 5 This tendency is apparent in statistics for single years of age in which the frequencies for single years ending in 0 and 5 are frequently greater than those for the two adjoining years This type of misreporting presumably occurs in situations in which the respondent, in the absence of specific knowledge as to his exact age or the age of the person for whom he is reporting, gives an approximate figure The returns also exaggerate the number of centenarians, particularly among nonwhite persons In general, the degree of inaccuracy in reported ages is greater for adults than for children

NATIVITY

In this volume, the population is classified according to place of birth into two basic groups, native and foreign born A person born in the United States or any of its Territories or possessions is counted as native Also included as native is the small group of persons who, although born in a foreign country or at sea, were American citizens by birth because their parents were American citizens Since the Republic of the Philippines was established as an independent country in 1946, persons living in the United States who had been born in the Philippine Islands were classified as foreign born in the 1950 Census whereas in earlier censuses they had been classified as native The small number of persons for whom place of birth was not reported were assumed to be native

Because of the declining numerical importance of the foreign-born population, nativity has not been used so extensively for cross-classifications in 1950 as in earlier censuses Information on the nativity and parentage of the white population and country of origin of the foreign white stock will be published in a special report The distribution of the separate nonwhite races by nativity and more detailed data on the foreign-born nonwhite population will be presented in a later publication

CITIZENSHIP

The classification of the population by citizenship embraces two major categories, citizen and alien. Citizens are subdivided into native and naturalized. It is assumed that all natives are citizens of the United States. In addition to the citizen and alien categories, there is a third group, made up of foreign-born persons for whom no report on citizenship was obtained, designated "citizenship not reported." Since it is likely that most of these persons are aliens, they are often included with "alien" in summary figures for total aliens.

MARITAL STATUS AND MARRIED COUPLES

Definitions

Marital status.—In the 1950 Census data on marital status are based on replies to the question "Is he now married, widowed, divorced, separated, or [has he never [been] married?" The classification refers to the status at the time of enumeration. Persons classified as "married" comprise, therefore, both those who have been married only once and those who remarried after having been widowed or divorced. Persons reported as separated or in common-law marriages are classified as married. Those reported as never married or with annulled marriages are classified as single. Since it is probable that some divorced persons are reported as single, married, or widowed, the census returns doubtless understate somewhat the actual number of divorced persons who have not remarried.

In some tables, the category "Married" is further divided into "Married, spouse present" and "Married, spouse absent." In the office processing, this classification was made for a 20-percent sample of the data collected. A person is classified as "married, spouse present" if the person's husband or wife was reported as a member of the household or quasi household in which the person was enumerated, even though he or she may have been temporarily absent on business or vacation, visiting, in a hospital, etc., at the time of the enumeration. The number of married men with wife present who are classified as heads of households is the same as the number of wives of heads of households shown in the tables on relationship to head of household, except for differences arising from sampling variation or from methods used in processing the data. The number shown as not head of household is the same as the number of married couples without own household, except for differences arising from processing methods used.

Persons reported as separated are included in the group designated as "Married, spouse absent." Separated persons include those with legal separations, those living apart with intentions of obtaining a divorce, and other married persons permanently or temporarily estranged from their spouse because of marital discord. The group "Other married, spouse absent" includes married persons employed and living for several months at a considerable distance from their homes, those whose spouse was absent in the armed forces, in-migrants whose spouse remained in another area, husbands or wives of inmates of institutions, and all other married persons (except those reported as separated) whose place of residence was not the same as that of their spouse.

Differences between the number of married men and the number of married women arise from spouses having their usual residences in different areas, from differences in the completeness of enumeration of married men and women, and from response and processing errors.

Married couple.—A married couple is defined as a husband and his wife enumerated as members of the same household or quasi household. As indicated above, this classification was made for a 20-percent sample of the data collected. Married couples are classified as "with own household" if the husband is head of the household. Other married couples, classified as "without own household," may be living in households as relatives of the head or as lodgers or employees, or they may be living in quasi households such as large rooming houses or hotels.

Comparability

The category "Separated" was included in the question on marital status for the first time in 1950. Previously the question included the categories single, married, widowed, and divorced. This change may have made the number of persons reported as divorced somewhat smaller in 1950 than it would have been under the earlier procedure.

In 1950, as in previous censuses, marital status was not reported for a small number of persons. For such persons marital status was estimated in 1950 and 1940 on the basis of age and the presence of spouse or children. Because of the methods used in 1950, however, some persons who would have been classified as single under the 1940 procedure were classified as "married, spouse absent" or "widowed" in 1950.

To obtain the marital status distribution of the population 14 years old and over for 1890 to 1930 it has been necessary to assume that the small number of persons under 15 years old classified as married, widowed, divorced, or with marital status not reported were 14 years old.

HOUSEHOLD AND FAMILY

Definitions

Household.—A household includes all the persons who occupy a house, an apartment or other group of rooms, or a room, that constitutes a dwelling unit. In general, a group of rooms occupied as separate living quarters is a dwelling unit if it has separate cooking equipment or a separate entrance; a single room occupied as separate living quarters is a dwelling unit if it has separate cooking equipment or if it constitutes the only living quarters in the structure. A household includes the related family members and also the unrelated persons, if any, such as lodgers, foster children, wards, or employees who share the dwelling unit. A person living alone in a dwelling unit or a group of unrelated persons sharing the same dwelling unit as partners is also counted as a household. The count of households excludes groups of persons living as members of a quasi household (see below).

The average population per household is obtained by dividing the population in households by the number of households. It excludes persons living in quasi households.

Quasi household.—A quasi household is a group of persons living in quarters not classified as a dwelling unit, for example, in a house with at least five lodgers, or in a hotel, institution, labor camp, or military barracks.

Family.—A family, as defined in the 1950 Census, is a group of two or more persons related by blood, marriage, or adoption and living together; all such persons are regarded as members of one family. The number of families was determined from the number of persons classified as heads of families; this classification was made for a 20-percent sample of the data collected. A family may comprise persons in either a household or a quasi household. If the son of the head of the household and the son's wife are members of the household they are treated as part of the head's family. A lodger and his wife who are not related to the head of the household, or a resident employee and his wife living in, are considered as a separate family, however. Thus, a household may contain more than one family. A household head living alone or with nonrelatives only is not regarded as a family. Some households, therefore, do not contain a family.

The average population per family is obtained by dividing the population in families by the number of families. In Chapter B, the population in families includes, in addition to family members, the small number (about 145,000) of unrelated individuals under 14 years old who had not been tabulated separately at the time this report was prepared.

Unrelated individual.—Unrelated individuals are those persons (other than inmates of institutions) who are not living with any relatives. In the office processing this classification was made for a 20-percent sample of the data collected. An unrelated individual may be (a) a household head living alone or with nonrelatives only, (b) a lodger or resident employee with no relatives in the household, or (c) a member of a quasi household who has no relatives living with him. Thus a widow who occupies her house alone or with one or more persons not related to her, a roomer not related to anyone else in the dwelling unit, a maid living as a member of her employer's household but with no relatives in the household, and a resident staff member in a hospital living apart from any relatives are all examples of unrelated individuals.

Institutional population.—The institutional population includes those persons living as inmates in such places as homes for delinquent or dependent children, homes and schools for the mentally or physically handicapped, places providing specialized medical care, homes for the aged, prisons, and jails. Staff members and their families are not included in the institutional population. Inmates of institutions are not counted as "unrelated individuals," largely because statistics on "unrelated individuals" are more useful to consumers of data on labor force, income, and housing statistics if they exclude such inmates.

The number of inmates of institutions is shown in the tables in Chapter B. Inmates 14 years old and over are shown in certain employment status tables in Chapters B and C and in table 90 on income in Chapter C.

Family status.—In table 90, persons 14 years old and over are classified into the categories family head, wife, or other relative of family head, unrelated individual, and inmate of institution. This classification differs from that in tables 58 and 59 which pertains to relationship to household head (see below).

Comparability

Earlier census data.—Minor changes in the instructions for identifying dwelling units in 1950 as compared with 1940 may have affected to a slight extent the increase in households between the two dates. For example, in the 1940 Census the occupants of a lodginghouse were regarded as constituting a quasi household if the place included 11 or more lodgers; in the 1950 Census the criterion was reduced to 5 or more lodgers. As a result of this change, the number of quasi households probably doubled in many areas. In general, however, the number of households and the number of occupied dwelling units in the 1950 Census may be regarded as comparable with the number of "families," "private households," and occupied dwelling units as shown in the census reports for 1930 and 1940.

In the 1950 Census, the number of households and the number of occupied dwelling units were identical by definition; small differences between these numbers appear in the published reports, however, because the data for the Population and the Housing reports were processed independently.

The term "family" as used in the 1950 Census is not comparable with that used by the Bureau of the Census before 1947. The new definition excludes the large number of household heads with no relatives in the household who would have been classified as families under the old definition. On the other hand, the new definition includes the small number of groups of mutually related lodgers or employees in households and of mutually related persons in quasi households who would not have been classified as families under the old definition. The net effect has been to reduce the number of families.

In certain Population and Housing reports of the 1940 Census, the average population per household included the relatively small number of persons living in quasi households. Such persons were excluded in calculating the average population per household shown in the present volume.

The coverage of the institutional population in the 1950 Census is somewhat more inclusive than that in the 1940 Census. For example, patients in tuberculosis sanataria were included in 1950 but not in 1940. Furthermore, the identification of certain other types of institutions, such as nursing, convalescent, and rest homes, was probably improved in 1950 by the use of lists of such places compiled from welfare agencies.

Current Population Survey.—Estimates of the number of households and of the number of families for the United States as a whole are published annually from the Current Population Survey. The estimates based on this survey for March 1950 were higher than the figures obtained from the census in April 1950. These differences may be attributed to such factors as sampling variability, methods used in weighting the sample figures, and differences between the interviewers with respect to training and experience.

RELATIONSHIP TO HEAD OF HOUSEHOLD

Definitions

Head of household.—One person in each household is designated as the "head." The number of heads, therefore, is equal to the number of households. The head is usually the person regarded as the head by the members of the household. Married women are not classified as heads if their husbands are living with them at the time of the census.

Wife.—The total number of females shown under the heading "wife" is ordinarily somewhat less than the total number of married women with husband present since the category "Wife" in the relationship tables includes only wives of heads of households. As indicated in the section on "Marital status," the number of "wives" is directly comparable with data in the marital status tables on the number of married men with wife present who are heads of households. Either of these figures may be used to indicate the number of "husband-wife households."

Child.—This category includes sons and daughters, stepchildren, and adopted children of the head regardless of their age or marital status. It excludes sons-in-law and daughters-in-law and, of course, any children of the head no longer living in the household.

Grandchild.—This category comprises all persons living in the household who are sons, daughters, stepchildren, or adopted children of a child of the head.

Parent.—This class comprises both parents and parents-in-law of the head if living in the household.

Other relative.—This group includes such relatives of the head as sons-in-law, sisters-in-law, nephews, brothers, aunts, grandparents, cousins, and great-grandchildren, if these are members of the household.

Lodger.—All persons in households who are not related to the head, except resident employees and their families, are counted as lodgers. Among these persons are lodgers, roomers, and boarders, and their relatives residing in the same household. Also included are partners, foster children, and wards.

Resident employee.—This category consists of all employees of the head of the household who usually reside in the household with their employer (mainly cooks, maids, nurses, and hired farm hands), and their relatives residing in the same household. In 1940, relatives of resident employees living in the same household were shown as lodgers.

Head of quasi household.—Heads of quasi households are usually managers or officers in institutions, hotels, lodginghouses, and similar establishments. If the landlady in a roominghouse reported herself as the head but her husband was a member of the quasi household, he was designated as head for consistency with the treatment of married heads and wives of heads of households. The number of heads of quasi households also represents the number of quasi households.

RESIDENCE IN 1949

Definitions

The data on residence in 1949 were derived from answers to several questions asked of a 20-percent sample of persons of all ages The first question was, "Was he living in this same house a year ago?" Those persons who were not living in the same house were asked, "Was he living in this same county a year ago?" and if not, "What county and State was he living in a year ago?"

Residence in 1949 is the usual place of residence one year prior to the date of enumeration As indicated by the categories of table 23, residence in 1949 was used in conjunction with residence in 1950 to determine the extent of mobility of the population Persons who had changed residence from 1949 to 1950 were classified into two groups according to their 1949 residence, viz, "Different house same county" and "Different county or abroad" Residence abroad includes residence in all foreign countries and all Territories and possessions of the United States The group whose 1949 residence was "Same house as in 1950" includes all persons 1 year old and over who were living in the same house on the date of enumeration in 1950 as on the date one year prior to enumeration Included in this group are persons who had never moved during the 12 months as well as persons who had moved but by 1950 had returned to their 1949 residence Persons 1 year old and over for whom complete and consistent information regarding residence in 1949 was not collected, are included in the group "Residence not reported"

The number of persons who were living in different houses in 1950 and 1949 is somewhat less than the total number of moves during the year Some persons in the same house at the two dates had moved during the year but by the time of enumeration had returned to their 1949 residence Other persons made two or more progressive moves Furthermore, persons in a different house in the same county may actually have moved between counties during the year but by 1950 had returned to the same county of residence as that in 1949

Comparability

A similar set of questions on mobility was first asked in the 1940 Census These questions, however, applied to residence five years earlier rather than one year earlier

For the United States as a whole, figures from the Current Population Survey of March 1950 on residence in March 1949 and figures on this same subject from the 1950 Census as of April 1, 1950, indicate appreciable differences both in the proportion of persons who were living in a different house in 1949 and in 1950 and in the proportion of migrants, that is, persons who were living in a different county in 1949 and 1950 The figures from the Current Population Survey indicate a greater extent of total mobility (any change of usual residence) than those from the census but a relatively smaller extent of migration These differences apparently arise from the somewhat different periods covered by the two sets of figures, the different methods used in collecting and processing the data, and sampling variability Furthermore, members of the armed forces are largely excluded from the Current Population Survey

COUNTRY OF BIRTH OF FOREIGN-BORN WHITE

Definitions

The statistics on this subject are based on the respondent's answer to the question, "What State (or foreign country) was he born in?" In case questions arose in the interview involving changes in international boundaries, the enumerator was instructed to decide on the basis of the international boundaries as of April 1, 1950 In coding and editing the list of countries used was that officially accepted by the United States as of April 1, 1950

In view of the numerous changes in boundaries which have occurred in Europe in the period of time during which statistics on country of birth have been collected by the Bureau of the Census, and the fact that many foreign-born persons at any given census are likely to report in terms of the boundaries at the time of their birth or emigration or in accordance with national preferences, there may have been considerable departure from the rule specified in the instructions

Comparability

In 1940 the classification of the population by country of birth was based on the political boundaries of January 1, 1937 The corresponding 1930 data are based on the political boundaries of that year, which were, in most respects, identical with those of January 1, 1937

For the censuses from 1850 to 1900, figures on country of birth are shown for the total foreign-born population From 1910 to 1940 however, this item is presented for the foreign-born white only Although the 1950 statistics on country of birth are presented only for the foreign-born white population in this report, subsequent reports will contain information on the country of birth of the nonwhite population

SCHOOL ENROLLMENT

Definitions

The data on school enrollment were derived from answers to the question, "Has he attended school at any time since February 1?" This question was asked of a 20-percent sample of persons under 30 years of age

"Regular" schools—In the instructions to the enumerators enrollment was defined as enrollment in "regular" schools only Such schools are public private, or parochial schools, colleges, universities, or professional schools, either day or night—that is, those schools where enrollment may lead to an elementary or high school diploma, or to a college, university, or professional school degree Enrollment could be full time or part time

If a person was enrolled in such a school subsequent to February 1, 1950 he was classified as enrolled even if he had not actually attended school since that date For example, he may not have attended because of illness

If a person was receiving regular instruction at home from a tutor and if the instruction was considered comparable to that of a regular school or college the person was counted as enrolled Enrollment in a correspondence course was counted only if the course was given by a regular school such as a university, and the person received credit thereby in the regular school system

Kindergarten—Children enrolled in kindergarten were reported separately in 1950 and were not counted as enrolled in school The statistics on kindergarten enrollment were tabulated only for children 5 and 6 years old Nursery schools were not regarded as kindergartens or schools

Schools excluded—Persons enrolled in vocational, trade, or business schools were excluded from the enrollment figures unless such schools were graded and considered a part of a regular school system Persons receiving on-the-job training in connection with their work were not counted as enrolled in school Persons enrolled in correspondence courses other than those described above were not counted as enrolled in school

Editing of 1950 Data

In 1950, as in prior censuses, persons for whom there was no report as to school enrollment are not shown separately In both 1940 and 1950, the editing rules were determined largely on the basis of information on ages of compulsory attendance as compiled by the U S Office of Education Additional information used included other items on the schedule and results of Current Population Surveys showing the enrollment rates for various age groups In general, persons 5 through 17 years of age not reporting on school enrollment were treated as enrolled, whereas those 18 through 29 years old were considered not enrolled

Comparability

Earlier census data.—The corresponding question in the Censuses of 1910, 1920, and 1930 applied to a somewhat longer period, the period since the preceding September 1. The census dates were April 15 in 1910, January 1 in 1920, and April 1 in 1930. Furthermore in these censuses the question was not restricted as to the kind of school the person was attending.

In 1940 the question referred to the period from March 1 to the date of the enumeration, which began on April 1. There are indications that in some areas the schools closed early (i. e., before March 1) for such reasons as lack of funds, flood conditions, or crop sowing. For such areas the enrollment rates would, therefore, have been relatively low. In order to insure more complete comparability among areas in 1950, it was therefore considered advisable to increase the reference period to that between February 1 and the time of the enumeration.

In 1950, for the first time in a decennial census, kindergarten enrollment was separately identified. In earlier censuses no specific instructions were given about kindergarten and, therefore enrollment figures for children 5 and 6 years old undoubtedly included some children enrolled in kindergarten.

As mentioned in the section on "Usual place of residence," college students were enumerated in 1950 at their college residence whereas in previous years they were generally enumerated at their parental home. This change in procedure should not have affected the comparability of the 1950 and 1940 national totals on school enrollment, but it may affect the comparability of 1950 and 1940 figures on school enrollment at college age for some States and local areas.

Current Population Survey.—In each year starting with 1945, the Census Bureau has collected statistics on school enrollment for the United States as a supplement to the Current Population Survey for October. The basic definitions used in these supplements are the same as those of the 1950 Census. The figures are not strictly comparable, however, because the supplement is taken in October rather than in April and relates to enrollment in the current term. Although the April 1950 Census figures and the October 1949 survey figures on enrollment both pertain to the same school year, 1949–1950, the April 1950 figures may be properly compared with those for October 1949 only if some allowance is made (*a*) for those persons who left school between October 1949 and February 1950, either by dropping out or graduation; and (*b*) for those persons who entered school after October.

For younger children, particularly those 5 and 6 years old, a comparison of October and April enrollments is misleading. Many school systems operate under the policy of permitting children to start the first grade only if they have attained a certain age by the beginning of the school year. This requirement maximizes enrollments for these ages in the fall, whereas by April many children have attained the given age but are not yet enrolled.

Data from school systems.—Data on school enrollment are also collected and published by Federal, State, and local governmental agencies. These data are obtained from reports of school systems and institutions of higher learning and are only roughly comparable with the enrollment data collected by the Bureau of the Census by household interviews. The census enrollment figures tend to be lower, largely because they refer to shorter time periods and count a person only once, although he may attend more than one school during the reporting period.

YEAR OF SCHOOL IN WHICH ENROLLED AND YEARS OF SCHOOL COMPLETED

Definitions

The data on year of school in which enrolled were derived from the answers to the first of the following two questions, and those on years of school completed from the combination of answers to both questions (*a*) "What is the highest grade of school that he has attended?" and (*b*) "Did he finish this grade?" These questions were asked of a 20-percent sample of persons of all ages.

The questions on educational attainment applied only to progress in "regular" schools, as defined in the section on "School enrollment."

Highest grade of school attended.—The question called for the highest grade attended, regardless of "skipped" or "repeated" grades, rather than the number of full school years which the person had spent in school.

In some areas in the United States, the school system has, or used to have, 7 years of elementary school rather than the more conventional 8 years. For the sake of comparability, persons who had progressed beyond a 7-year elementary school system were treated as though they had progressed beyond the usual 8-year system. Junior high school grades were translated into their elementary or high school equivalents.

In the case of persons whose highest grade of attendance was in a foreign school system, the enumerator was instructed to obtain the approximate equivalent grade in the American school system or, if that were too difficult to determine, the number of years the person had attended school. Persons whose highest level of attendance was in an ungraded school were treated in similar fashion. Persons whose highest level of training was by a tutor and whose training was regarded as qualifying under the "regular" school definition were also given the approximate equivalent in the regular school system.

Completion of highest grade.—The second question on educational attainment was to be answered "Yes" if the person had completed the full grade. If the person was still attending school in that grade, had completed only a half grade, or had dropped out of or failed to pass the last grade attended, the required answer was "No." In the case of persons who failed to report on completion of the grade, those classified as enrolled were assumed not to have finished and those not enrolled were assumed to have finished.

Comparability

Year of school in which enrolled and years of school completed.—In the present volume, the year of school in which enrolled is shown for enrolled persons 5 to 29 years old and the years of school completed are shown for all persons 5 years old and over.

For 1950, statistics on educational attainment for persons enrolled in school are shown in terms of the school year in which they were enrolled, whereas in the 1940 reports statistics were shown in terms of the highest grade they had completed. The present procedure was adopted because it provides statistics in a form that should be generally more useful to those interested in school systems.

Generally, for persons enrolled in school the grade in which they were enrolled is one grade higher than the highest grade completed. Data from a preliminary sample of the 1950 Census, however, indicate that by the time of the census enumeration, about 15 percent of the "enrolled" population 5 to 20 years old had completed the same grade in which they had been enrolled. This apparent contradiction occurs because the question on enrollment referred to "any time since February 1" whereas the completion question referred to the date of enumeration. Thus, highest grades of school completed for the enrolled population obtained by subtracting one grade from the grade in which enrolled must be considered only approximately correct.

The 1940 Census reports included data on highest grade of school completed for the population 5 to 24 years old not enrolled in school. As a result of the facts noted above, similar data for 1950 could only be approximated. Two steps would be involved. First, one grade should be deducted from the grade in which enrolled (as given in table 63) in order to approximate the highest grade completed for persons enrolled in school, second, the number of enrolled persons who have completed a given grade should be subtracted from the total number of persons who have completed the grade (as given in table 64).

Quality of 1940 and 1950 data.—In 1940 a single question was asked on highest grade of school completed. Previous censuses

Data from a preliminary semple of the 1950 Census for persons of elementary and high school ages show larger proportions in 1950 than it 1940 in both the modal grade and the next lower grade for a part.cular age and smaller proportions r each of the first two grades above the mode. It seems reasonable to assume that, as a result of the change in questionnaire des gr, there was also relatively less exaggeration in educationa, attainment ir 1950 than in 1940 ever for older persons

Median School Years

Median educational attainment (. e , either median year of school in which carolled or median school years completed) as expressed in terms of a continuous series of numbers For example, the fourth year of high school is indicated by 12 and the first year of college by 13 For the sake of comparability, the first year of high school is uniformly represented by 9, although, as previously noted, there are some areas with only 7 years of elementary

The procedure used in both 1950 and 1940 for calculating the median years of school completed makes allowance for the fact that many persons reported as having completed a given full s. nool year have also completed part of the next higher grade. It is assumed, for example, that persons who reported six full years of school completed had actually completed 6 5 grades At the time of enumeration, persons enrolled in school had propably completed somewhat more than one-half grade beyond their last full year, on the average, whereas persons who nad left school had probably completed less than one half year beyond their last full year, on the average A similar procedure was followed in the computation of the median school year in which enrolled

EMPLOYMENT STATUS

Definitions

Census week -The 1950 data on employment status pertain to the calendar week preceding the enumerator's visit This wock, defined as the "census week," is not the same for all respondents, because not all persons were enumerated during the same week The majority of the population was enumerated during the first The 1940 data refer to a fixed week for all persons, nalf of April March 24 to 30, 1940, regardless of the date of enumeration

Employed -Employed persons comprise all civilians 14 years old and over who, during the census week, were either (a) "at work"-those who did any work for pay or profit, or worked without pay for 15 hours or more on a family farm or in a family business, or (b) "with a job but not at work"—those who did not work and were not looking for work but had a job or business from which they were temporarily absent because of vacation, illness, industrial dispute, bad weather, or lay off with definite instructions to return to work within 30 days of layoff. Also included as "with a job" are persons who had new jobs to which they were scheduled to report within 30 days

Unemployed -Persons 14 years old and over are classified as unemployed if they were not at work during the census week but were (ther looking for work or would have been looking for work except that (a) they were temporarily ill, (b) they expected to return to a job from which they had been laid off for an indefinite period, or (c) they believed no work was available in their community or in their line of work Since no specific questions dentifying persons in these last three groups were included on the census schedule, it is likely that some persons in these groups were not returned by the census enumerators as unemployed

ployed persons are separated in some tables into new workers and experenced workers When information on the senedule was psufficient for this distinction to be made, the unemployed person was classified as an experienced worker, since the great majority of persons seeking work have had previous work experience

Labor force -The labor force includes all persons classified as employed or usemp'oved, as described above, and also members of the armed forces persons on active duty with the United States A-my, Air Force Navy, Marine Corps, or Coast Guard "civilian labor force comprises the employed and unemployed components of the labor force." The "experienced labor force." consists of the armed lordes, employed workers and the unemployed with pre lows ork experience. The 'experienced civilian appropriate comprises the two latter groups.

Not in labor force - - Persons not in the labor force comprise ail civil ans 14 years of age and over who are not classified as en ployed or an employed including persons doing only incidental unpaid 'amily work 'less than 15 hours during the cersus week) sons not in the labor force are further classified in this report into the following caregories

1 Keeping house — Persons primarily occupied with their home housework

2 Unable to tore—Persons who cannot work because of a long-term physical or montal illness or disability. There is some evidence, however, that some persons were reported as 'unable to work' who were only temporaryly all or who, although elderity, were not permanently quasabled.

3. Immales of sustituious — Persons other than staff members and ther fam.hes, hving in unstatutions (See definition of institutional population on page xvin) Staff members of institutional and their families are classified into employment status categories on the same basis as are persons hving outside of institutions

4 Other and not reported—Persons in this general category include the following two groups which were combined for the purpose of this report

tude the following two groups which were combined for the pose of this report

a Persons not in the labor force other than those keeping house, unable to work, or in institutions. This group includes students, the retured, those too old to work, the voluntarily die, and seasonal workers for whom the census week fell in an "off" season and who were not reported as unemployed b Persons for whom information on employment status was not reported. Although the number of porsons classified as "not reported" was not tabulated separately for this report, it is estimated on the basis of preliminary data that the funther in this group is approximately. I milison for the United States as a whole, or about 1 percent of the total United States apopulation 14 years old and over. Analysis of the characteristics (sex, age, color, marital status, school enrollment, and urban-rural residence) of persons in this group suggests that approximately half a million might have been added to the labor force had the necessary information been obtained. There may be considerable variation from State to State, however, in the proportion of persons altasified as "not reported" and, within this group, in the number who mild the proposition of the province of the control of the province of the control of th

Basis for Classification

The employment status classification is based primarily on a series of interrelated "sorter" questions designed to identify, in this sequence (a) Persons who worked at all during the census reek, (b) those who did not work but were looking for work, and (c) those who neither worked nor looked for work but had a job or business from which they were temporarily absent. The four questions used for this purpose are described below

1 "What was this person doing most of lest week—working, keeping house, or something else!" This question was designed to classify persons according to their major activity and to identify the large number of full-time workers. Persons unable to work at all because of physical or mental disabilities were also identified

here 2 "Did this person do any work at all last week, not counting work around the house?" The question was asked of all persons except taose reported in the presions question as working or unable to work. It was designed to mentify persons working partitude or intermittently in audition to their major activity.

2 "Wise this person looking for work" Asset of persons replying in the previous question that they did not work at all, this dietion served to obtain a count of the unempto ed.

4 "Even though he didn" work lost week, does he have a job or ossiness?" Persons temporarily absent from their job or ossiness were identified by means of this question, which was asked of perso is neither working nor looking for work.

Problems in Classification

('lassification of the population by employment status is always Some of the concepts are difficult to apply, but, subject to error more important for certain groups, the complete information needed is not always obtained. For example, housewives, students, and semiretired persons, who are in the labor force on only a part-time or intermittent basis, may fail to report that they are employed or looking for work unless carefully questioned. In many cases, enumerators may assume that such persons could not be in the labor force and will omit the necessary questions As a result, the statistics will understate the size of the labor force and overstate the number of persons not in the labor force | See also paragraph below on "Current Population Survey"

Comparability

Statistics on gainful workers -The data on the labor force for 1940 and 1950 are not exactly comparable with the statistics for gainful workers presented in this report for 1920 and 1930 because of differences in definition "Gainful workers" were persons reported as having a gainful occupation, that is, an occupation in which they earned money or a money equivalent, or in which they assisted in the production of marketable goods, regardless of whether they were working or seeking work at the time of the A person was not considered to have had a gainful occupation if his work activity was of hmited extent In contrast, the labor force 19 defined on the basis of activity during the census week only and includes all persons who were employed, unemployed, or in the armed forces in that week Certain classes of persons, such as retired workers, some inmates of institutions, incapacitated workers, and seasonal workers neither working nor seeking work at the time of the census, were frequently included among gainful workers, but, in general, such persons are On the other hand, the census not muluded in the labor force included in the labor force for 1940 and 1950 persons seeking work without previous work experience, that is, new workers At the time of the 1920 and 1930 Censuses such new workers were probably, for the most part, not reported as gainful workers

In 1920, the census date was January 1, whereas in 1930, 1940 and 1950 it was April 1 For this additional reason, the number of gainful workers reported for 1920, especially in agricultural areas, may not be altogether comparable with the statistics for later years

1940 Census - During the period 1940 to 1950 various changes were developed in the questionnaires and in interviewing techniques, designed to obtain a more nearly complete count of the labor force 2 Although the changes in questionnaire design were incorporated into the 1950 Census schedule and interviewing techniques were stressed in training, the quality of the 1950 statistics does not appear to have been much improved relative to that for 1940 by these measures

The 1940 data for employed persons in this volume vary in some cases from the figures originally published in the 1940 reports The appropriate 1940 figures for the employed shown in the present report have been adjusted to exclude the estimated number of men in the armed forces at that time This was done to achieve comparability with the 1950 employed total which is limited to

Statistics for persons on public emergency work in 1940 were originally published separately, but in this report they have been combined with those for persons seeking work in the figures on unemployed for 1940

Current Population Survey -The estimated size of the civilian labor force in the United States based on the Current Population Survey is about 5 percent above the corresponding figure from the 1950 Census An investigation of the reason for the dis-crepancy is being conducted Examination of the census returns for a sample of households that were also included in the Current Population Survey for April 1950 indicates that although differences of all kinds were found, on balance, the Current Population Survey enumerators, who are much more experienced than were the temporary census enumerators, reported more completely the employment or unemployment of teen-agers and of women 25 years old and over This difference is reflected in higher labor force participation rates and unemployment rates for those groups and a more accurate reporting of persons employed in industries, such as agriculture, trade, and personal services, where part-time or occasional work is widely prevalent. These are the groups for whom variability in response is relatively great in labor force sur-On the other hand, the differences were at a minimum for men and young women—the major components of the "full-time"

It may be estimated on the basis of this analysis that perhaps 3 percent of the total population 14 years old and over in April 1950 were actually in the labor force but were classified outside the labor force in the census returns This percentage will vary from State to State and between one population group and another. For example, misclassification was somewhat greater for nonwhite than for white persons

Other data -Because the 1950 Census employment data were obtained by household interview, they differ from statistics based on reports from individual business establishments, farm enterprises, and certain government programs The data based on household interviews provide information about the work status of the whole population, without duplication Persons employed at more than one job are counted only once as employed and are classified according to the job at which they worked the greatest number of hours during the census week In statistics based on reports from business and farm establishments, on the other hand persons who work for more than one establishment may be counted more than once Moreover, other data, unlike those presented here, generally exclude private household workers, unpaid family workers, and self-employed persons, and may include workers less than 14 years of age An additional difference arises from the fact that persons with a job but not at work are included with the employed in the statistics shown here, whereas only part of this group is likely to be included in employment figures based on establishment payroll reports Furthermore, the nousehold re-ports include persons on the basis of their place of residence regardless of where they work, whereas establishment reports relate persons to their place of work regardless of where they live the two types of data may not be comparable for areas where a significant number of workers commute to or from other areas

For a number of reasons, the unemployment figures of the Bureau of the Census are not directly comparable with the published figures for unemployment compensation claims or claims for veterans' readjustment allowances Certain persons such as private household and government workers are generally not eligible for unemployment compensation Further, the place where claims are filed may not necessarily be the same as the place of residence of the unemployed worker In addition, the qualifications for drawing unemployment compensation differ from the definition of unemployment used by the Census Bureau For example, persons working only a few hours during the week and persons with a job but not at work are sometimes eligible for unemployment compensation but are classified by the Census Bureau as employed

³ Sec U 8 Bureau of the Census Current Population Reports, Labor Force Employment and Unemployment in the United states 1940 to 1946 Series P-50 No 2 September 1947

HOURS WORKED DURING CENSUS WEEK

The data on hours worked were derived from answers to the question "How man; hours did be work last week?" asked of persons who reported they had worked during the weck prior to their enumeration. The statistics refer to the number of hours actually worked during the census week and not necessarily to the number usually worked or the scheduled number of hoirs. For persons working at more than one job, the figures relate to the combined number of hours worked at all jobs during the week. The data on nours worked presented in Chapter C provide a broad classification of voung employed persons into full-time and partitime workers. The proportion of persons who worked only a small number of hours is probably understated because such persons were omitted from the labor force count more frequently than were full-time workers.

WEEKS WORKED IN 1949

Definitions

The statistics on weeks worked are based on replies to the question, "Last year, in how many weeks did this person do any work at all, not counting work around the house." This question was asked of a 20-percent sample of persons 14; cars old and over The data pertain to the number of different weeks during 1949 in which a person did any work for pay or profit (including paid vacations and sick leave) or worked without pay on a family farm or in a family business. Weeks of active service in the armed forces are also included. If is probable that the number of persons who worked in 1949 is understated, because there is some tendency for respondents to forget intermittent or short periods of employment.

Comparability

In 1950, no dustinction was made between a part-time and a full-time workweek, whereas in 1940 the enumerator was instructed to convert part-time work to equivalent full-time weeks. A full-time week was defined as the number of hours locally regarded as full time for the given occupation and industry. Further differences are that, in the 1940 reports, the data were shown for wage and salary workers only and were published in terms of months rather than weeks.

OCCUPATION, INDUSTRY, AND CLASS OF WORKER

In the 1950 Census of Population, information on occupation, industry, and class of worker was collected for persons in the experienced civilian labor force. All three items related to one specific job held by the person. For an employed person, the information referred to the job he held during the census week if he was employed at two or more jobs, the job at which he worked the greatest number of hours during the census week was reported. For an experienced unemployed person, the information referred to the last job he had held.

The classification systems used for the occupation and industry data in the 1950 Census of Population are described below. These systems were developed in consultation with many individuals, private organizations, and government agencies, and, in particular, the Joint Committee on Occupational Classification (sponsored by the American Statistical Association and the United States Bureau of the Budget)

Occupation

The occupation information presented here was derived from answers to the question, "What kind of work was he doing?"

Classification system—The occupational classification system developed for the 1950 Census of Population is organized into 12 major groups, which form the basis for the occupation data in Chapter B of this volume. The system consists of 469 items, 270 which are specific occupation categories, the remainder are subgroupings (mainly on the basis of industry) of 13 of the occu-

parion categories. For the detailed occupation tables in Chapter C, certain of the categories were combined, and the detailed occupation list used here consists of 446 items stables 73 and 74. The composition of each of the detailed categories is shown in the publication, U.S. Bureau of the Census, 1950 Cersus of Population Classified Invites of Occupations and Industries, Washington, D.C., 1950

In the presentation of occupation data for cities of 50,000 to 100 000 in Chapter C, as well as in the cross-classifications of occupation by urban-tural residence, ago, race, class of worker, and moome, intermediate occupational c assifications of 158 items for males and 67 items for females have been used (tables 75 to 78). Those intermediate classifications represent selections and combinations of the .tems in the detailed system — listing of the relationships between the two levels of classification can be octained by writing to the Director, Bureau of the Cersus, Washington 25, D C. This listing will also appear in the United States surmourly part of Volume II

In the separation of "Managers, officials, and proprietors (nec)" by class of worker into salaried and self-employed components, the small number of unpaid family workers in this occupation is included it the self-employed component. Since the data presented in the occupation tables refer only to civitans, the category 'Members of the armed forces' shown in table 73 is limited to experienced unemployed persons whose last job was as a member of the armed forces.

Relation to DOT classification — The occupational classification of the Population Census is generally comparable with the system used in the Disciourly of Occupational Titles (DOT). The two systems, however, are designed to meet different needs and to be used under different occuminationes. The DOT system is designed to ment primarily for employment service needs, such as placement and counseling, and is ordinarily used to classify very detailed occupational information obtained in an interview with the worker immself. The census system, on the other hand, is designed for statistical purposes and is ordinarily used in the classification of limited occupational descriptions obtained in an interview with a member of the worker's family. As a result, the DOT system is much more detailed than the census system, and it also calls for many types of distinctions which cannot be made from census information.

Industry

The industry information presented here was derived from answers to the question, "What kind of business or industry was he working in?"

Classification system—The industrial classification system developed for the 1950 Census of Population consists of 148 categories, organized into 13 major groups. For the detailed industry tables in Chapter C of this volume a few of the categories were combined, and the detailed industry list used here consists of 146 categories (tables 79 and 80). The composition of each of the detailed categories is shown in the publication, U S Bureau of the Census, 1950 Census of Population, Classified Index of Occupations and Industries, Washington, D C, 1950

Although certain of the industry data in Chapter B are limited to the 13 major groups, most of the industry data in Chapter B are based on a condensed classification of 41 groups — Furthermore, in Chapter C, an intermediate classification of 77 categories has been used in the presentation of industry data for cities of 50,000 to 100,000, as well as in the cross-classifications of industry by age, race, class of worker, major occupation group, weeks worked, and income (tables 81 to 86)—Both the 41-item and 77-item classifications represent selections and combinations of the categories in the detailed system—The relationships among these three levels of classification are shown in list A

³ See U S Department of Labor, Bureau of Employment Security, Dictionary of Occupational Pules Second Edition, Vols I and II, Washington D C 1949

LOUISIANA

List A —RELATIONSHIPS AMONG CONDENSED, INTERMEDIATE, AND DETAILED INDUSTRIAL CLASSIFICATION SYSTEMS USED IN THE 1950 CENSUS OF POPULATION

n arcmi.eses if third column are code Jesignst ons in the Standard Industrial Classification are text for explanation]

Cordened class fication—II items	intermediate class firstion.—77 items	Detailed classification—148 items
Agretitur	Agriec l'ure	Agriculture (01 07 exc 0713)
Fures and Liberies -	Forestry and fishence	Frestry (08) Fisheries (09)
M _{II} r : g	(Cos runing. Crude per oleur and natural gas extraction Min ng and quarrying except (ue)	Coal mining (11, 12) Cride petroleum and natural gas extraction (13) (Motal mining (10) Nonmetallu mining and quarrying except fuel (14)
Constitution	· Construction	Construct on (10 i7)
In the and lumber and wood products .	Logging Sawmils planing mills, and mill work Miscellaneous wood, products Furnit re and fixtures.	Logains (241) Sawmils plaring mills and mill work (242, 243) Visco laneous wood products (244, 249) Fur nature and fixtures (25)
Pr mary metal industries	[Primary non and steel industries Primary non-errous industries	[Blast furnaces steel works and rolling mills (331) Other primary iron and steel industries (332–339) Primary iron sindustries (333–336 –332)
Fabricated wetal and: strus (no. not specifical	Fan icated metal industries (incl. not specified metal)	1 ebrusated steel products (19 exc 194 341-349, 344 exc 3444 346 348 449-3498) 18brusated nonferrous metal products (3444 3463 347 3489 3496, 349 3496) 18brusated notal industries
Machinery except electrical	Machinery, except electrical	Ameultural machinery and tractors (352) Office and store machines and datases (357) Micellaneous machinery (351 333-356, 359 359)
Electrical unchinery equipment and supplies	Flectrical machiners, equipment and supplies.	Electrical machinery, equipment, and supplies (36)
Motor values and motor veh de equipment	Motor vericles and motor vehicle equipment	Motor chicles and motor vehicle equipment (371)
Transi ortation equipment exe motor vehica -	Aircra I and parts Ship and boat building and repairing Railroad and miscellamous transportation equipment	A-tursft and parts (172) Enip and boat building and repa mm. (375) Raili oad and m-seellaneous transportation equipment (874–375, 379)
	Glass and glass products	Glass and glass products (321-323) [Ce nent and concrete gypsum, and plaster products (324, 327)
Other curable goods	Strine and diay products	Class and glass products (322-323) (Che nert and connecte symptoms, and plaster products (324, 227) (Structural class products (325) (Structural class class (325) (Nacchiacowa "analizatoring and sitres (35))
	All other durab a goods	Photographic equipment and supplies (886) - Watches, clocks and disckwork operated devices (387) Misculaneous manufacturing industries (29)
Food and kindred products	Meat products Baker, products	Meat products (201) Bakery products (205)
,	Other food industries	Conjugated Serving frame, verstables and sea foods (208, Grau mill predicts (992, 204) (Confectionery and estated products (207) Beverage industries (208) [Miscellaneous food on paraticular during the confection of the confectio
	Knitting mills Yarn, thread, and tabric n. hs	Knitting mills (225) Yern thread and sabric mills (221 224)
Textile mill products	O her textile mill products.	Knitting mills (22a) yaru, throad, and fabric mills. (22i–224) (Dysing and finaling earlies, except kint goods (22f) (Carpets, rugs, and other floor or ordings (22f) (Miscellamous earlie mill products (22f–22f)
Apparel and other fabricated textile products	Appaiel and other fabricated textile products.	[Apparel and recessories (23 exc 239) Miscellaneous fabricated textile products (239)
Princing publishing and allied industries.	Printing publishing and allied industries.	Printing publishing and albed industries (27)
Themsels and allied products	Chemicals and allied products	Syntuctic fibes (2825) Drugs and medicaires (283) Paritie, arnichres and related products (285) Misseriameous onemicals and allied products (281 282 evc 2825 284 226-239)
	Tobacco manufactures Paper and allied products	Tobacco manufactures (21) [Pulp, paper and paperboard mills (261) [Pagerboard contamor and boxes (267)
Other nondurable goods	Petroleum and coal products	Miscellaneous pape and pulp products (264-266 209) (Petroleum rufning (291) Miscellaneous petroleum and coal products (23-exc 201) Rubber products (30)
TOTAL WAY SALVEY	Rubber products Footwear, except ruober Lea her and leatner products except (ootwear	Miscellaneous perforein and coal products (25-0x 251) Rubber products (30) Footwar, elept rubber (313-314) I eliher tamped curred and finished (311) Loather products, evopt footwar (312, 33-317-119)
Not specified in anu-inturing radiustries	No spec Col man incoming manstres	Not specified manufacturing industries 3
Pailroads and re Iway on rest service	Rulroads and railway express service	Reliroads and raffw by express service (40)
turking survice and worel ousing	fruck ng wer lee and warehousing.	(Trucking service (421, 428) Warehousing and storum (422-425, 420)
	(%-reof rall-ways and bus lines Water transportation 4h transportetion	Street railways and bus lines (41, 43 exc 483) Water transportation (44)
Prior transportation -	All o her trusportation	Ar transportation (15) (Taxical service (463) (Petroloum and gasoline pipe lines (46) (Services uncidental to transportation (4")
'eleco-nmun.ca 10ns	1 elecor munications	[Telephone (wire and n io) (481) Felegriph (vire and nath.) (48 evc 461)
See foo-notes at end of table		(Transkt et 11 (v n.g g.r.g L3(H2)) (48 646 481)

List A —RELATIONSHIPS AMONG CONDENSED, INTERMEDIATE AND DETAILED INDUSTRIAL CLASSIFICATION SYSTEMS USED IN THE 1950 CENSUS OF POPULATION—Con

Condensed classification—41 items	Intermediate classification—" thems	Detailed classification—148 items
Utilities and solutary services	Bleckrie and eas ut likes h a'er supple, san a'y sir lees and other tale es	Electric aght and power (49) chestro-gas studies (468) (les and kears supply systems (692 498) (sate maps) (see 1997) (other and not specified utattics 2 (47)
2 a a a		
Wholesale trade	W holesde arare.	Motor vrbioles and et a pages 1.501, 4110 Drass, chemicals, and luifer products (502, 1112) Drass, godds erd apparel (503, 5113, 1527) Prog pools erd apparel (503, 5113, 1527) Poon and related products (502, 60), 511, 6133 CI34 014) Electrical goods berdewie, and plumbang equipment (509, 501, 6116) Machinery equipment, and suspiles (508, 5118, 5119) Petrolauro products (5127) Petrolauro products (
Food & dairy products stores and milk retaining.	Food and days products stores and Theresh	(Food stores except dairy products (54 exc 545)
		Darry products stores and milk retailing (545)
Eating and drinking places	Eating and drinking places	Esting and drinking places (58)
	General merchandise and five and ten cent stores	General merchandise stores (53 exc 533) Five and tencent stores (533)
	Apparel and accessories stores	Appare, and accessories stores except shoe stores (56 evc. 536) Shoe stores (568)
Other retail trade	Furniture, home curnishings and equipment stores. Motor vehicles and acressories retailing Gusoline service stations Drug stores	Firmiture and housefurnishings stores (571) [Household appl area and radio stores (572) [Motor vehicles and accessories retailing (55 exc 554) [Gasoline Graves stations (554)
	Hardware, farm implement, & building material retailing	Drig stores (\$91) Hardware and furn implement stores (\$25) Lumber and building ma erial retailing (\$2 exc o25) Liquor stores (\$92) Retail florats (\$992)
	All other rotail trade	Jeetan normats (3992) Jewelry stores (357) Fael and noe retailing (598) Miscellaneous retail stores (593–598, 599 exc 5992) Not specified retail trade 3
		(Banking and credit agencies (60, 61)
Finance, insurance and real estate	Banking and other finance	Security and commodity brokerage, and investment companies (6:
	(Insurance and real estate	Insurance (63, 64) Real estate a (60) Real estate insurance law offices \$ (66)
Business services	Business serv ces_	(Advertising (731) Accounting auditing and bookkeeping services (787) (Miscellaneous business services (732-736, 739)
Repair services	Automobile repair services and garages Miscellaneous repair services	Automobile repair services and garages (*5) Miscellaneous repair services (76).
Private households	Private households	Private households (88)
Hotels and lodging places	Hotels and lodging places	Hotels and lodging places (70)
Other personal services	Landering, cleaning, and dyeing services All other personal services	Laundering, cleaning, and dyeing services (721, 722-7277) (Dressmaking shops (727-17) (Shee repair shops (725) (Miscellaneous personal services (723-724, 726-729)
Entertainment and recreation services	Entertainment and recreation services	Radio broadcasting and television (77) Thesters and motion pictures (78, 792) Bowling alleys and billiard and pool parlors (793) Miscellaneous entertainment and recreation services (791 744-794 799)
Medical and other health services	Medical and other health services	(Medical and other health services, except hospitals (80 exc 806)
Educational services, government	Educational services, government	Hospitals (895) Educational services, government Educational services private (82 84)
Other professional and related services	Welfare, religious, and mambership organizations Legal engineering, and misc. professional services	(Wellare and religious services (864, 857) (Nonprofit membership organ astiona (861-865, 889) (Leval services (81) (Engineering and architectural services (801) (Miscellaneous professional and related services (89 exc 891)
	Cocies originations and writer brosessories act alone	
Public administration	Postal service.	[Miscellaneous professional and related services (89 exc 891) Postal service Federal public administration [State public administration Local public administration

Note See Executive Office of the President Bureau of the Budget, Standard Industrial Classification Manual Vol I, Manufacturing Industrias, Part 1 (November 1945 edition), and Vol II, Nonmanufacturing Industrias (May 1949 edition), Washington, D. C.

¹ Components of SIC categories SW2and Sales are allocated between "Other primary ron and steel industries" and "Frimary nonferrous industries" on a ferrous nonferrous basis

1 Components of SIC categories SW2and Sales are allocated between "Other primary ron and steel industries" and "Frimary nonferrous industries" on a ferrous nonferrous basis

1 In the Population Census system, not appendix "exterposition structure which were not sufficiently precise for allocation to a special category within the group

1 "Electric light and power and "Electric-gas utilities" are combined into a single category in the Volume II tables on detailed industry

1 "Electric light and power and "Electric-gas utilities" are combined into a single category in the Volume II tables on detailed industry

2 Components of SIC categories 50% small 51% are allocated by type of merchandles to the appropriate "Population Census wholesale trade category, wherever possible

Diresmaking shops are showed-insuranceasis office." Secret combined into a single category in the Yolume II tables on detailed industry

1 Secret for explanation of basic difference between SIC and Population Census in classification of governments workers.

Relation to Standard Industrial Classification—List A shows for each Population Census category the code designation of the similar category or categories in the Standard Industrial Classification (SIC). This relationship is presented here for general information purposes only and does not imply complete comparability. The SIC, which was developed under the sponsorship of the United States Bureau of the Budget, is designed for the classification of industry reports from establishments. These reports are, by their nature and degree of detail, considerably different from industry reports obtained from household enumerations such as the Population Census. As a result, many distinctions called for in the SIC cannot be observed in the Population Census. Furthermore, the needs which the Population Census data are designed to meet frequently differ from the needs which the establishment data meet. Perhaps the most basic difference between the two systems is in the allocation of government workers. The SIC classifies all government agencies in a single major group, whereas the Population Census industrial classification system allocates them among the various groups according to type of activity, as explained in the next paragraph.

Definition of "Public administration"—The major group "Public administration" includes only those activities which are uniquely governmental functions, such as legislative and judicial activities and most of the activities in the executive agencies. Government agencies engaged in educational and medical services and in activities commonly carried on also by private enterprises, such as transportation and manufacturing, are classified in the appropriate industrial category. For example, persons employed by a hospital are classified in the "hospitals" category, regardless of whether they are paid from private or public funds. The total number of government workers appears here in the data on class of worker, of particular significance in this connection is the cross-classification of industry by class of worker (table 83).

Relation to certain occupation groups—In the Population Census classification systems, the industry category "Agriculture" is somewhat more inclusive than the total of the two major occupation groups, "Farmers and farm managers" and "Farm laborers and foremen." The industry category includes, in addition to all persons in these two major occupation groups, (a) other persons employed on farms, such as truck drivers, mechanics, and bookkeepers, and (b) persons engaged in agricultural activities other than strictly farm operation, such as crop dusting or spraying, cotton ginning, and landscape gardening. Similarly, the industry category "Private households" is somewhat more inclusive than the major occupation group "Private household workers." In addition to the housekeepers, laundresses, and miscellaneous types of domestic workers covered by the major occupation group, the industry category includes persons in occupations such as chauffeur and secretary, if they work for private households.

Class of Worker

The class-of-worker information, as noted above, refers to the same job as does the occupation and industry information. The allocation of a person to a particular class-of-worker category is basically independent, however, of the occupation or industry in which he worked. The classification by class of worker consists of four categories which are defined as follows:

1. *Private wage and salary workers*—Persons who worked for a private employer for wages, salary, commission, tips, pay-in-kind, or at piece rates.

2. *Government workers*—Persons who worked for any governmental unit (Federal, State, or local), regardless of the activity which the particular agency carried on.

3. *Self-employed workers*—Persons who worked for profit or fees in their own business, profession, or trade, or who operated a farm either as an owner or tenant. Included here are the owner-operators of large stores and manufacturing establishments as well as small merchants, independent craftsmen and professional men, farmers, peddlers, and other persons who conducted enterprises of their own. Persons paid to manage businesses or farms owned by other persons or by corporations, on the other hand, are classified as private wage and salary workers (or in some few cases as government workers).

4. *Unpaid family workers*—Persons who worked without pay on a farm or in a business operated by a member of the household to whom they are related by blood or marriage. The great majority of unpaid family workers are farm laborers.

The relatively small number of persons for whom class of worker was not reported has been included among private wage and salary workers unless there was evidence on the census schedule that they should have been classified in one of the other class-of-worker categories.

Quality of Data

The omission from the labor force of an appreciable number of workers (mainly youths, women, and part-time workers), as explained in the section on "Employment status," has probably resulted in some understatement in many of the occupation, industry, and class-of-worker figures. Another factor to be considered in the interpretation of these data is that enumerators sometimes returned occupation and industry designations which were not sufficiently specific for precise allocation. One cause may have been the enumerator's carelessness or his lack of knowledge of how to describe a particular job on the census schedule. Another possible cause was lack of adequate knowledge about the worker's job on the part of the housewife or other person from whom the enumerator obtained the information. Indefinite occupation and industry returns can frequently be assigned, however, to the appropriate category through the use of supplementary information. For example, in the case of occupation, the industry return on the census schedule is often of great assistance. In the case of indefinite industry returns, helpful information can frequently be obtained from outside sources regarding the types of industrial activity in the given area. The basic document used in the allocation of the schedule returns of occupation and industry to the appropriate categories of the classification systems is the publication, U S Bureau of the Census, *1950 Census of Population, Alphabetical Index of Occupations and Industries*, Washington, D C, 1950.

It can be expected that the application of detailed occupational and industrial classifications to approximately 60 million workers will be subject to some error. Although the number of misclassifications probably does not have any serious effect on the usefulness of most of the data, there are a few cases where relatively small numbers of erroneous returns may produce what might be regarded as a serious misstatement of the facts. These cases relate mainly to the numbers of women and children shown in occupations which are unusual for such persons, and to the government workers shown in industries that are ordinarily not carried on by government agencies. Some of the more obvious misclassifications have been adjusted, but it was not possible to perform a complete review of the data for small discrepancies.

Comparability

1940 Census data—The changes in schedule design and interviewing techniques for the labor force questions, as explained in the section on "Employment status," do not affect comparability between 1940 and 1950 for most of the occupation, industry, and class-of-worker categories. There is evidence, however, that for the categories which include relatively large proportions of female unpaid family workers ("Farm laborers, unpaid family workers," "Agriculture," and "Unpaid family workers"), the 1940 data are sometimes understated by an appreciable amount relative to 1950.

For experienced unemployed persons the 1950 occupation data are not comparable with the data shown in the 1940 Third Series bulletins. The occupation data for public emergency workers (one of the two component groups of the unemployed in 1940) refer to "current job," whereas the "last job" of the unemployed was reported in 1950.

The occupational and industrial classification systems used in 1940 are basically the same as those of 1950. There are a number of differences, however in the title and content for certain items, and in the degree of detail shown for the various major groups A complete analysis of classification differences between 1940 and 1950 is in preparation The 1940 classification system for class of worker is comparable with the 1950 classification system

The 1940 occupation and industry data shown in this volume include adjustments which take account of the differences between the 1940 and 1950 classification systems These adjustments were based mainly on estimates developed from figures for the country as a whole, rather than from a detailed evaluation of the various classification differences in each State

In addition, satisfactory numerical information was not always available on the effect of some classification changes, even on a national level Furthermore, there were certain differences between the 1940 and 1950 coding and editing procedures which could not be measured statistically Caution should be exercised, therefore, in interpreting small numerical changes Caution should also be exercised with regard to large relative increases in the numbers of women engaged in occupations which are unusual for women Although it is certainly true that women have expanded the range of their occupational activities during the last decade, the figures shown here may, in some cases, tend to overstate this expansion because more intensive checking of questionable returns of this type was performed in 1940 than in 1950, this is particularly true of the railroad occupations

The 1940 data on occupation, industry, and class of worker shown in this volume have been revised to eliminate members of the armed forces, in order to achieve comparability with the 1950 figures for the employed which are limited to civilians In the occupation tables of the 1940 reports, the armed forces were mainly included in the major group "Protective service workers" In the industry tables, the armed forces were all included in the major group "Government" In the class-of-worker tables, the armed forces were all included in the category "Government workers" (or in the total "Wage or salary workers")

The 1940 major occupation group figures presented in Chapter C of this volume may differ in some cases from the corresponding figures presented in Chapter B The revised figures shown in Chapter C were developed by a more detailed analysis of the 1940–1950 classification differences than were the figures in Chapter B

1930 and earlier census data—Prior to 1940, the census data on the economically active population referred to "gainful workers" rather than to "labor force" The differences between these two concepts are described in the section on "Employment status" The effects of this variation in approach on the various occupation and industry categories are virtually impossible to measure For most categories, the number of gainful workers is probably equivalent to the number of persons in the experienced civilian labor force For certain categories, particularly those with relatively large numbers of seasonal workers, the gainful worker figures are probably somewhat greater than the labor force figures

The occupational and industrial classification systems used in the 1930 Census and earlier censuses were markedly different from the 1950 systems The relationship between the present and earlier systems is being analyzed, and the results of the study will be made available by the Census Bureau For information on occupation and industry data from 1930 and earlier censuses, see the publication, U S Bureau of the Census, Sixteenth Census Reports Population *Comparative Occupation Statistics for the United States, 1870 to 1940,* Washington, D C, 1943

Other data—Comparability between the statistics presented in this volume and statistics from other sources is frequently affected by the use of different classification systems, as well as by many of the factors described in the paragraphs on comparability with Current Population Survey data and other data in the section on "Employment status"

INCOME

Definitions

Components of income—Income, as defined in the 1950 Census, is the sum of money received from wages or salaries, net income (or loss) from self-employment, and income other than earnings The figures in this report represent the amount of income received before deductions for personal income taxes, social security, bond purchases, union dues, etc

Receipts from the following sources were not included as income money received from the sale of property, unless the recipient was engaged in the business of selling such property, the value of income "in kind" such as food produced and consumed in the home or free living quarters withdrawals of bank deposits, money borrowed, tax refunds, gifts and lump-sum inheritances or insurance payments

Information was requested of a 20-percent sample of persons 14 years of age and over on the following income categories (*a*) The amount of money wages or salary received in 1949, (*b*) the amount of net money income received from self-employment in 1949, and (*c*) the amount of other money income received in 1949 If the person was the head of a family, these three questions were repeated for the other family members as a group in order to obtain the income of the whole family The composition of families is as found at the time of interview, although the time period covered by the income statistics is the calendar year 1949 Specific definitions of these three categories are as follows

1 *Wages or salary*—This is defined as the total money earnings received for work performed as an employee It includes wages, salary, armed forces pay, commissions, tips, piece-rate payments, and cash bonuses earned

2 *Self-employment income*—This is defined as net money income (gross receipts minus operating expenses) from a business, farm, or professional enterprise in which the person was engaged on his own account or as an unincorporated employer Gross receipts include the value of all goods sold and services rendered Expenses include the costs of goods purchased, rent, heat, light, power, depreciation charges, wages and salaries paid, business taxes, etc

3 *Income other than earnings*—This includes money income received from sources other than wages or salary and self-employment, such as net income (or loss) from rents or receipts from roomers or boarders, royalties, interest, dividends, and periodic income from estates and trust funds, pensions, veterans' payments, armed forces allotments for dependents, and other governmental payments or assistance, and other income such as contributions for support from persons who are not members of the household, alimony, and periodic receipts from insurance policies or annuities

Statistics on the income of families and unrelated individuals are presented in Chapter B Unrelated individuals are shown by the amount of their own income, for family groups, however, the combined incomes of all members of each family are treated as a single amount In Chapter C, data are presented for all persons 14 years of age and over, tabulated by the amount of their own income

Quality of the Income Data

The figures in this census, as in all field surveys of income, are subject to errors of response and nonreporting In most cases the schedule entries for income are based not on records but on memory, usually that of the housewife The memory factor in data derived from field surveys of income probably produces underestimates, because the tendency is to forget minor or irregular sources of income Other errors of reporting are due to misunderstanding of the income questions or to misrepresentation

A possible source of understatement in the figures on family income was the assumption in the editing process that there was no other income in the family when only the head's income was reported It is estimated that this assumption was made for about 5 percent of the families This procedure was adopted in order to make maximum use of the information obtained In the large majority of the fully reported cases the head's income constituted all or most of the total family income.

The income tables in Chapter B include in the lowest income group (under $500) those families and unrelated individuals who were classified as having no 1949 income, as defined in the census. For the country as a whole, about 6 percent of the families and unrelated individuals were reported as having no income. Many of these were living on income "in kind," savings or gifts, or were newly created families or families in which the sole breadwinner had recently died or left the household. A relatively large proportion, however, probably had some money income which was not recorded in the census.

Although the 1950 Census income data are subject to these limitations, they appear to be of about the same quality as those obtained from the Current Population Survey, which has provided a consistent series of national estimates of the distribution of consumer income each year since 1944.

Comparability

1940 Census data.—In 1940 all persons 14 years of age and over were asked to report (*a*) the amount of money wages or salary received in 1939 and (*b*) whether income amounting to $50 or more was received in 1939 from sources other than money wages or salaries. Comparable wage or salary income distributions for 1940 and 1950 are presented in table 94 of this report. All of the other 1950 Census income data shown in this report relate to total money income and are more inclusive than are the statistics from the 1940 Census.

Income tax data.—For several reasons, the income data shown in this report are not directly comparable with those which may be obtained from statistical summaries of income tax returns. Income as defined for tax purposes differs somewhat from the Bureau of the Census concept. Moreover, the coverage of income tax statistics is less inclusive because of the exemptions of persons having small amounts of income. Furthermore, some of the income tax returns are filed as separate returns and others as joint returns and, consequently, the income reporting unit is not consistently either a family or a person.

Bureau of Old Age and Survivors Insurance wage record data.—The wage or salary data shown in this report are not directly comparable with those which may be obtained from the wage records of the Bureau of Old Age and Survivors Insurance for several reasons. The coverage of the wage record data for 1949 is less inclusive than the 1950 Census data because of the exclusion of the wages or salaries of such groups as domestic servants, farm laborers, governmental employees, and employees of nonprofit institutions. Furthermore, no wages or salaries received from any one employer in excess of $3,000 in 1949 are covered by the wage record data. Finally, as the Bureau of the Census data are obtained by household interviews, they will differ from the Old Age and Survivors Insurance wage record data which are based upon employers' reports.

Office of Business Economics State income payments series.—The Office of Business Economics of the Department of Commerce publishes data on the aggregate income received by the population in each State. If the aggregate income were estimated from the income distributions shown in this report, it would be smaller than that shown in the State income payments series for several reasons. The Bureau of the Census data are obtained by household interview, whereas the State income payments series is estimated largely on the basis of data derived from business and governmental sources. Moreover, the definitions of income are different. The State income payments series includes some items not included in the income data shown in this report, such as income in kind, the value of the services of banks and other financial intermediaries rendered to persons without the assessment of specific charges, and the income of persons who died or emigrated prior to April 1, 1950. On the other hand, the Bureau of the Census income data include contributions for support received from persons not residing in the same living quarters.

RELIABILITY OF SAMPLE DATA

SAMPLE DESIGN

Some of the data in the tables which follow are indicated by asterisks or by headnotes as being based on information asked of a representative 20-percent sample of the population. A separate line was provided on the population schedules for each person enumerated, with every fifth line designated as a sample line. Within each enumeration district, the schedules were divided approximately equally among five versions. On each version the sample constituted a different set of lines so that each line on the schedule was in the sample on one of the five versions. The persons enumerated on these sample lines were asked all of the pertinent sample questions.[4]

Although the procedures used did not automatically insure an exact 20-percent sample of persons in each locality, they were unbiased and for large areas the deviation from 20 percent was expected to be quite small. Small biases, however, arose when the enumerator failed to follow his sampling instructions exactly. These biases were usually in the direction of a slight under-representation of adult males, particularly heads of households, with the result that the sample of all persons was very slightly under 20 percent. In the United States as a whole, the proportion of the total population enumerated in the sample was 19.95 percent, the proportion of household heads 19.73 percent, and the proportion of all other persons 20.04 percent. The proportion of the total population in the sample, by regions, was 19.94 percent in the Northeast, 19.93 in the North Central, 19.97 in the South, and 19.96 in the West. Among States, the proportions in the sample ranged from 19.86 percent to 20.00 percent.[5]

Estimates of the number of persons with specified characteristics based on sample data have in all cases been obtained by multiplying the number of persons in the sample with these characteristics by five. Estimates of percentages have been obtained in each case by using the sample values for both the numerator and denominator.

SAMPLING VARIABILITY

The figures based on the 20-percent sample are subject to sampling variability which can be estimated from the standard errors shown in tables A and B. These tables do not reflect the effects of the biases mentioned above. The standard error is a measure of sampling variability. The chances are about 2 out of 3 that the difference due to sampling variability between an estimate and the figure that would have been obtained from a complete count of the population is less than the standard error. The amount by which the standard error must be multiplied to obtain other odds deemed more appropriate can be found in most statistical textbooks. For example, the chances are about 19 out of 20 that the difference is less than twice the standard error, and 99 out of 100 that it is less than 2½ times the standard error.

Illustration. Let us assume that for a particular city with a population of 100,000 table 62 shows that there were an estimated

[4] In 19 counties of Michigan and Ohio, the sample consisted basically of every fifth household and the pertinent sample questions were directed to all persons in the household. A household sample of this type was used as an experiment to determine the feasibility of such samples in future censuses of population.

[5] In the experimental areas of Michigan and Ohio biases due to the underenumeration of household heads did not exist, although some other small problems arose, because some enumerators made errors in the selection of the sample in institutions.

900 persons 10 years of age who were enrolled in school (90 percent of the 1,000 in this age group) Table A shows that the standard error for an estimate of 900 in areas with 100,000 inhabitants is about 70 Consequently, the chances are about 2 out of 3 that the figure which would have been obtained from a complete count of the number of persons 10 years of age who are enrolled in school in this city differs by less than 70 from the sample estimate It also follows that there is only about 1 chance in 100 that a complete census result would differ by as much as 175, that is, by about 2½ times the number given in the table Table B shows that the standard error of the 90 percent on a base of 1,000 is 2 percent For most estimates, linear interpolation will provide reasonably accurate results [6]

The standard errors shown in Tables A and B are not directly applicable to differences between two sample estimates These tables are to be applied differently in the three following types of differences

1 The difference may be one between a sample figure and one based on a complete count, e g, arising from comparisons between 1950 data and those for 1940 or earlier years The standard error of a difference of this type is identical with the variability of the 1950 estimate

2 The difference may be one between two sample estimates, one of which represents a subclass of the other This case will usually occur when a residual of a distribution is needed For example, an estimate of the number of persons 7 to 13 years of age not enrolled in school can be obtained by subtracting the estimate of the number enrolled as shown in table 18 from the sample estimate of the total number in that age group Tables A and B can be used directly for a difference of this type, with the difference considered as a sample estimate

3 The standard error of any other type of difference will be approximately the square root of the sum of the squares of the standard error of each estimate considered separately This formula will represent the actual standard error quite accurately for the difference between estimates of the same characteristic in two different areas, or for the difference between separate and uncorrelated characteristics in the same area. If, however, there is a high positive correlation between the two characteristics, the formula will overestimate the true standard error

Some of the tables present estimates of medians (e g, median years of school completed, median income) as well as the corresponding distributions The sampling variability of estimates of medians depends on the distribution upon which the medians are based [7]

[6] A closer approximation of a standard error in table A may be obtained by using $2.1(x)\sqrt{\frac{1}{x}-\frac{9}{T}}$ where x is the size of the estimate and T is the total population of the area, in table B, the approximation is $2.1\sqrt{\frac{P(1-P)}{y}}$ where P is the percentage being estimated and y the size of the base For example, the approximation provided by the above formula of the standard error of an estimate of 100,000 (x) in an area with a total population of 150,000 (T) is 420, linear interpolation would yield about 295

[7] The standard error of a median based on sample data may be estimated as follows If the estimated total number reporting the characteristic is N, compute the number $N/2-\sqrt{N}$ Cumulate the frequencies in the table until the class interval which contains this number is located By linear interpolation, obtain the value below which $N/2-\sqrt{N}$ cases lie In a similar manner, obtain the value below which $N/2+\sqrt{N}$ cases lie If information on the characteristic had been obtained from the total population, the chances are about 2 out of 3 that the median would lie between these two values The chances will be about 19 out of 20 that the median will be in the interval computed similarly but using $\frac{N}{2}\pm2\sqrt{N}$ and about 99 in 100 that it will be in the interval obtained by using $\frac{N}{2}\pm2.5\sqrt{N}$

RATIO ESTIMATES

It is possible to make an improved estimate of an absolute number (improved in the sense that the standard error is smaller) whenever the class in question forms a part of a larger group for which both a sample estimate and a complete count are available This alternative estimate is particularly useful when the characteristic being estimated is a substantial part of the larger group when the proportion is small, the improvement will be relatively minor The improved estimate (usually referred to as a "ratio estimate") may be obtained by multiplying a percentage based on sample data by the figure which represents the complete count of the base of the percentage

The effect of using ratio estimates of this type is, in general, to reduce the relative sampling variability from that shown for an estimate of a given size in table A to that shown for the corresponding percentage in table B Estimates of these types are not being published by the Bureau of the Census because of the much higher cost necessary for their preparation than for the estimates derived by multiplying the sample result by five

TABLE A.—STANDARD ERROR OF ESTIMATED NUMBER

[Range of 2 chances out of 3]

Estimated number	Population of area[1]							
	1,000	10,000	25,000	100,000	250,000	1,000,000	5,000,000	15,000,000
50	10	10	10	10	10	10	10	[illegible]
100	20	20	20	20	20	20	20	20
250	30	30	30	30	30	30	30	30
500	30	50	50	50	50	50	50	50
1,000	20	60	60	70	70	70	70	70
2,500		90	100	100	100	100	100	100
5,000		110	130	140	140	150	150	150
10,000		60	160	200	200	210	210	210
15,000			170	240	250	250	250	250
25,000			90	290	310	320	330	330
50,000				340	420	450	460	460
75,000				310	480	550	560	560
100,000				180	520	620	650	650
250,000					200	910	1,010	1,030
500,000						1,070	1,390	1,440
1,000,000						570	1,870	2,000
2,500,000							2,400	3,010
5,000,000							1,290	3,550
10,000,000								4,060
15,000,000								2,220

[1] An area is the smallest complete geographic area to which the estimate under consideration pertains Thus the area may be the State, city, county, standard metropolitan area, urbanized area, or the urban or rural portion of the State or county The rural-farm or rural-nonfarm population of the State or county, the nonwhite population, etc., do not represent complete areas

TABLE B.—STANDARD ERROR OF ESTIMATED PERCENTAGE

[Range of 2 chances out of 3]

Estimated percentage	Base of percentage							
	500	1,000	2,500	10,000	25,000	100,000	500,000	5,000,000
2 or 98	1.3	0.9	0.6	0.3	0.2	0.1		
5 or 95	2.0	1.4	0.9	0.5	0.3	0.1	0.1	
10 or 90	2.8	2.0	1.2	0.6	0.4	0.2	0.1	
25 or 75	4.0	2.8	1.8	0.9	0.6	0.3	0.1	
50	4.6	3.3	2.1	1.0	0.7	0.3	0.1	

W

LOUISIANA

STANDARD METROPOLITAN AREAS AND CONSTITUENT PARTS

The Baton Rouge Standard Metropolitan Area comprises East Baton Rouge Parish.

The New Orleans Standard Metropolitan Area comprises Jefferson, Orleans, and St. Bernard Parishes.

The Shreveport Standard Metropolitan Area comprises Caddo Parish.

LIST OF CORRECTIONS

This volume has been prepared primarily by assembling and binding the statistical portion of previously issued bulletins which constituted preprinted chapters. This publication plan was adopted to conserve public funds. The corrections appearing below represent changes which would ordinarily have been made if the volume had been prepared by reprinting the contents of the bulletins.

Table	Page (prefix 18)	Item	Change From—	Change To—
5	[illegible]	Change name of Terrebone Parish to Terrebonne		
6	10	EAST BATON ROUGE PARISH [illegible] reference 14 to Baton Rouge city, add to footnote 14 "Parts of old police jury wards 3, 6, [illegible], and [illegible] annexed to Baton Rouge city in 1949."		
6	12	WEBSTER PARISH Change designation of Dowline from town to village, change footnote accordingly		
8	14	Delete New Orleans from headnote listing of incorporated places of 5,000 or more which [illegible] wards. The following tabulation presents the 1950 population of New Orleans by wards		

New Orleans	570,445	Ward 9	72,069
Ward 1	[illegible],375	Ward 10	2[illegible] 761
Ward 2	19 783	Ward 11	26,972
Ward 3	25,026	Ward 12	33,684
Ward 4	[illegible],49[illegible]	Ward 13	26,5[illegible]
Ward 5	31,5[illegible]3	Ward 14	28,9[illegible]9
Ward 6	15,3[illegible]1	Ward 15	27,06[illegible]
Ward 7	[illegible]0,400	Ward 16	1[illegible],07[illegible]
Ward 8	42,044	Ward 17	30,288

Table	Page (prefix 18)	Item	Change From—	Change To—
[illegible]	2[illegible]	URBAN FARM, 1950, old urban definition Total, the State		
		All classes, total	[illegible],337	3 286
		Increase 1940 to 1950 Number	-23[illegible]	-281
		Percent	-[illegible] 4	-7 9
		White	[illegible],544	2,5[illegible]2
		Nonwhite	793	[illegible]4
		Male		
		All classes, total	1,765	1,741
		White	1,3[illegible]6	1,349
		Nonwhite	[illegible]99	39[illegible]
		Female		
		All classes, total	1,572	1,54[illegible]
		White	1,178	1,16[illegible]
		Nonwhite	394	38[illegible]
42	80	POINTE COUPEE PARISH, Years of school completed Female, 25 years old and over High school, 4 years	2,345	345

NUMBER OF INHABITANTS

Louisiana

LIST OF TABLES

[Page numbers listed here omit the State prefix number which appears as part of the page number for each page. The prefix for this State is 18]

Table	Page
1.—Population of Louisiana, urban and rural: 1810 to 1950	5
2—Population in groups of places according to size 1950	5
3 —Population in groups of places according to size 1900 to 1950	6
4 Population of incorporated places of 10,000 or more from earliest census to 1950	7
5 - Area and population of parishes, urban and rura: 1930 to 1950.	8
6.—Population of parishes by mmor civil divisions; 1930 to 1950	9
 Population of all incorporated places and of unincorporated places of 1,000 or more. 1950 and 1940. 	13
8 — Population of incorporated places of 5,000 or more, by wards: 1950	14
9.—Population of urbanized areas: 1950	14

Targe-scale copies of this map may be purchased from Superintendent of Documents, U S Government Pruring Office, Washington 25, D C

Table 1.—POPULATION OF LOUISIANA, URBAN AND RURAL 1810 TO 1950

[For description of new and old urban definitions, see text Minus sign (−) denotes decrease]

Census date	The State: Population	The State: Increase over preceding census: Number	The State: Increase over preceding census: Percent	Urban territory: Number of urban places[1]	Urban territory: Population	Urban territory: Increase over preceding census: Number	Urban territory: Increase over preceding census: Percent	Rural territory: Population	Rural territory: Increase over preceding census: Number	Rural territory: Increase over preceding census: Percent	Percent of total: Urban	Percent of total: Rural
New urban definition, 1950 (Apr 1)	2,683,516	319,636	13 5	72	[2] 1,471,696	----	----	1,211,820	----	----	54.8	45 2
Old urban definition												
1950 (Apr 1)	2,683,516	319,636	13 5	65	1,363,789	383 350	39 1	1,319,727	−63,714	−4.6	50 8	49 2
1940 (Apr 1)	2,363,880	262,287	12 5	54	980,439	146,907	17 6	1,383,441	115,380	9 1	41 5	58.5
1930 (Apr 1)	2,101,593	303,084	16 9	48	833,532	205 369	32 7	1,268,061	97,715	8.3	39 7	60 3
1920 (Jan 1)	1,798,509	142,121	8 6	38	628,163	131 647	26 5	1,170,346	10,474	0 9	34.9	65 1
1910 (Apr 15)	1,656,388	274,763	19 9	26	496,516	130,228	35.6	1 159,872	144,535	14 2	30 0	70.0
1900 (June 1)	1,381,625	263,037	23.5	15	366,288	82,443	29 0	1,015,337	180,594	21 6	26 5	73.5
1890 (June 1)	1,118,588	178,642	19 0	9	283,845	44,455	18 6	834,743	134,187	19 2	25 4	74.6
1880 (June 1)	939 946	213,031	29 3	6	239,390	36,867	18 2	700,556	176,164	33 6	25 5	74.5
1870 (June 1)	726,915	18,913	2 7	3	202,523	17,497	9 5	524,392	1,416	0.3	27 9	72 1
1860 (June 1)	708,002	190,240	36.7	4	185,026	50,556	37 6	522,976	139,684	36 4	26 1	73 9
1850 (June 1)	517,762	165,351	46.9	3	134,470	29,070	27 6	383,292	136,281	55 2	26.0	74.0
1840 (June 1)	352,411	136,672	63.4	2	105,400	59,318	128.7	247,011	77,354	45 6	29 9	70 1
1830 (June 1)	215,739	62,332	40 6	1	46,082	18,906	69 6	169,657	43,426	34.4	21 4	78.6
1820 (Aug 7)	153,407	76,851	100 4	1	27,176	9,934	57 6	126,231	66,917	112.8	17 7	82 3
1810 (Aug 6)	[3] 76,556	----	----	1	17,242	----	----	59,314	----	----	22.5	77 5

[1] According to the new urban definition, the urban population comprises persons residing in urban territory but not necessarily in an urban place, which is defined as an incorporated place of 2,500 or more, or an unincorporated place of 2,500 or more located outside an urbanized area. Under the old definition, incorporated places of 2,500 or more and places urban under special rule are classified as urban places There were no places urban under special rule in Louisiana.

[2] Includes 81,458 persons in urban territory outside of urban places.

[3] *Population of the Territory of Orleans*

Table 2.—POPULATION IN GROUPS OF PLACES ACCORDING TO SIZE· 1950

Type of area and size of place	Number of places	Population	Percent of total population	Percent of total
The State	----	2,683,516	100 0	----
Urban, total	([1])	1,471,696	54.8	100 0
Within urbanized areas	----	948,840	35.4	64.5
Central cities, total	3	823 280	30 7	55 9
Cities of 500,000 to 1,000,000	1	570,445	21 3	38 8
Cities of 250,000 to 500,000	----	----	----	----
Cities of 100,000 to 250,000	2	252,835	9 4	17 2
Cities of 50,000 to 100,000	----	----	----	----
Cities under 50,000	----	----	----	----
Urban fringes, total	----	125,560	4 7	8 5
Incorporated places of 2,500 or more	5	44,102	1 6	3.0
Incorporated places of 10,000 to 25,000	2	29,283	1 1	2 0
Incorporated places of 5,000 to 10,000	1	8,328	0 3	0 6
Incorporated places of 2,500 to 5,000	2	6,491	0 2	0 4
Incorporated places under 2,500	----	----	----	----
Unincorporated territory	----	81,458	3 0	5 5
Outside urbanized areas	64	522,856	19 5	35 5
Places of 25,000 to 50,000	4	148,298	5 5	10 1
Places of 10,000 to 25,000	8	103,656	3 9	7 0
Urban, total—Con				
Outside urbanized areas—Con				
Places of 5,000 to 10,000	22	160,335	6.0	10 9
Places of 2,500 to 5,000	30	110,567	4.1	7 5
Rural total	----	1,211,820	45 2	100 0
Places under 2,500	178	180,015	6.7	14 9
Places of 2,000 to 2,500	16	35,852	1.3	3 0
Places of 1,500 to 2,000	28	47,235	1 8	3 9
Places of 1,000 to 1,500	42	51,675	1 9	4.3
Places under 1,000	92	45,253	1 7	3 7
Other rural territory	----	1,031,805	38 4	85 1
Urbanized areas, total	3	948,840	35 4	100 0
Areas of 500,000 to 1,000,000	1	659,768	24 6	69 5
Areas of 250,000 to 500,000	----	----	----	----
Areas of 100,000 to 250,000	2	289,072	10 8	30. 5
Areas of 50,000 to 100,000	----	----	----	----

[1] There were 72 places of 2,500 or more

NUMBER OF PLACES	72	66	54	48	88	26	15
Trhan territory	1	1		~			
Places of 200.05 o 100.000 Places of 15.000 to 30.000 Places of 20.000 to 30.000 Places of 20.000 to 30.000 Places of 20.000 to 30.000	4 10 23 32	2 4 10 22 27	1 3 5 18 28	1 2 4 1I 29	1 1 4 8 24	1 1 4 5 15	1 2 4 8 89
Rural territory.	178	158	156	162	45	39	25
Places o: 1,089 to 2 500 Places t ader 1,000	86 92	92	58 98	53 109	117	107	64
Carolistre smarrary Places of 200 000 or more Places of 250,000 or more Places of 1,000 or more	1 1 3 3 7 17 17 40 72	1 1 3 8 7 17 39 66	1 1 2 5 10 28 54	1 1 2 4 8 19 48	1 1 2 2 6 14 38	1 1 2 6 11 26	1 1 1 1 2 7 7
рори аточ						400 810	356, 238
Urhan territory	1,471,696	1, 363, "89	980, 439 980, 439	883 532 888, 532	628, 163 628 163	496, 516	356 288
Places of 2 500 or more	1, 390, 238 570, 445	1, 363 789 570, 44o	494, 537	458, 762	387 219	439,075	287, 104
Places of 100 000 to 250,000	252, 835	252, 885	98, 167				
Planes of 30,000 to 100,000 P-aves of 25,00 to 26,000 Finuses o 10,000 to 2e,000 Planese o 6,000 to 10,000 Pheses of 2,000 to 10,000 Pher urean territory	148 298 132 939 168 663 117 058 81, 458	148, 298 132, 939 160 345 98, 927	90 094 79, 647 123, 378 94, 616	76, 605 56 757 67, 480 72, 564 101 314	43, 974 65, 035 52, 377 79 638	28, 015 47, 768 29, 491 52 167	27, 282 24 o71 27, 881
Bural territory	1,211,820	1,319 727	1 383 441	1 268 061	1, 170 346	1, 159, 872	1,015,337
Piaces of 1 000 to 2,000 Piaces unde 1 000 .	184, 762 45, 253 1 031, 80o	45 253	\$9,728 51,511 1 242 207	78, 415 -5, 639 1, 134, 007	68, 213 60, 842 1, 041, 291	5", 116 n2, 686 1, 050, 0"0	35 590 30, 378 949, 364
Cannilative summary	570, 445 570 445 823 280 823, 280 971, 578 1 104, 517 1, 273, 180 1, 390, 289	823 280	494, 58" 494, 537 592, 704 682 798 762, 415 885, 823 980, 439	458 762 458 762 535 417 592 174 659 651 32, 218 833, 532	387, 219 387, 219 387, 219 387, 219 431, 098 406, 118 548, 025 628, 168	339 075 339,075 339 07, 367,090 414,8,8 444,349 496,516	287, 104 287, 104 287, 104 287, 104 314, 986 338, 907 366, 288
PERCENT OF TOTAL POPULATION							
Lrban territory	54.8		41 5	39 7	34 9	30 0	26.5
Flaces of 2,000 or more Flaces of 20,000 to 1000,000. Pleces of 20,000 to 50,000	51 8 21 8	50 8 21 3	20 9	21 8	21 3	20 5	20 8
Places of 100,000 to 20,000 Places of 50,000 to 20,000	9 4						
Places of 25,000 to 50,000	5 0	5 5 5 0	3.4	2 7	2 4 3 6	1 7 2 9 1 8	2.0
Places of 5 000 to 10,000	4.4	8 0 3 7	0 2 4 0	3 5 4 8	2 0	1 8 3 1	1 2
Other urban territory.	45 1		\$8.5	GO 3	G5 1	70,0	78.1
Places of 1 000 to 2,500. Places under 1 000 Other rural term ory	- 35 (1 1 38.4	3.9	3 8 2 2		3 8 3 4 57 9	3 4 3 2 68 4	
Cumulative summary. Places of 500 000 or more. Places of 250 000 or more Places of 100 000 or more	21. 21. 30 30 30.	21 3 21 3	20 9 20 9	2) 8	21 5	20.6	20
Places of 50 000 or more.	30	30 7	20 9 25 1	21 8 25 5	21 5 21 2 21 0 24 0 27 6	20 5	20 20
P-aces of 25 000 or more. Places of 1,0000 or more Places of 5,000 or more Places of 2,400 or more	35. 2 41 2 47 51 8	21 3 7 30 7 7 30 7 2 36 2 41 2 47 1 8 00 8	25 1 28.9 32 8 87 5 41 5	21 8 21 8 25 5 29 2 31 4 84 8 39 7	24 0 27 6 30 5 34 9	20. 6 20 6 20 5 22 2 25 0 26. 8	20 20 20 20 20 22 22. 24.

Table 4.—POPULATION OF INCORPORATED PLACES OF 10,000 OR MORE FROM EARLIEST CENSUS TO 1950

[Minus sign (−) denotes decrease]

Incorporated place and census year	Population	Increase over preceding census: Number	Increase over preceding census: Percent
Alexandria city			
1950	34,913	7,847	29.0
1940	27,066	4,041	17.6
1930	23,025	5,515	31.5
1920	17,510	6,297	56.2
1910	11,213	5,565	98.5
1900	5,648	2,787	97.4
1890	2,861	1,061	58.9
1880	1,800	582	47.8
1870	1,218	−243	−16.6
1860	1,461	789	117.4
1850	672		
Bastrop town			
1950	12,769	6,143	92.7
1940	6,626	1,505	29.4
1930	5,121	3,905	321.1
1920	1,216	362	42.4
1910	854	67	8.5
1900	787		
1890	(1)		
1880	822	301	57.8
1870	521	40	8.3
1860	481		
Baton Rouge city			
1950	125,629	90,910	261.8
1940	34,719	3,990	13.0
1930	30,729	8,947	41.1
1920	21,782	6,885	46.2
1910	14,897	3,628	32.2
1900	11,269	791	7.5
1890	10,478	3,281	45.6
1880	7,197	699	10.8
1870	6,498	1,070	19.7
1860	5,428	1,523	39.0
1850	3,905	1,636	72.1
1840	2,269		
Bogalusa city			
1950	17,798	3,194	21.9
1940	14,604	575	4.1
1930	14,029	5,784	70.2
1920	8,245		
Bossier City town			
1950	15,470	9,684	167.4
1940	5,786	1,783	44.5
1930	4,003	2,909	265.9
1920	1,094	319	41.2
1910	775		
Crowley city			
1950	12,784	3,261	34.2
1940	9,523	1,867	24.4
1930	7,656	1,548	25.3
1920	6,108	1,009	19.8
1910	5,099	885	21.0
1900	4,214	3,794	903.3
1890	420		
Gretna city			
1950	13,813	2,934	27.0
1940	10,879	1,295	13.5
1930	9,584	2,387	33.2
1920	7,197		
Houma city			
1950	11,505	2,453	27.1
1940	9,052	2,521	38.6
1930	6,531	1,371	26.3
1920	5,160	136	2.7
1910	5,024	1,812	56.4
1900	3,212	1,932	150.9
1890	1,280	196	18.1
1880	1,084	491	82.8
1870	593	164	38.2
1860	429		
Lafayette city			
1950	33,541	14,331	74.6
1940	19,210	4,575	31.3
1930	14,635	6,780	86.3
1920	7,855	1,463	22.9
1910	6,392	3,078	92.9
1900	3,314	1,208	57.4
1890	2,106		
Lake Charles city			
1950	41,272	20,065	94.6
1940	21,207	5,416	34.3
1930	15,791	2,703	20.7
1920	13,088	1,639	14.3
1910	11,449	4,769	71.4
1900	6,680	3,238	94.1
1890	3,442	2,604	310.7
1880	838		
Monroe city			
1950	38,572	10,263	36.3
1940	28,309	2,281	8.8
1930	26,028	13,353	105.3
1920	12,675	2,466	24.2
1910	10,209	4,781	88.1
1900	5,428	2,172	66.7
1890	3,256	1,186	57.3
1880	2,070	121	6.2
1870	1,949		
1860	(1)		
1850	435		
New Iberia city			
1950	16,467	2,720	19.8
1940	13,747	5,744	71.8
1930	8,003	1,725	27.5
1920	6,278	−1,221	−16.3
1910	7,499	684	10.0
1900	6,815	3,368	97.7
1890	3,447	738	27.2
1880	2,709	1,237	84.0
1870	1,472		
New Orleans city			
1950	570,445	75,908	15.3
1940	494,537	35,775	7.8
1930	458,762	71,543	18.5
1920	387,219	48,144	14.2
1910	339,075	51,971	18.1
1900	287,104	45,065	18.6
1890	242,039	25,949	12.0
1880	216,090	24,672	12.9
1870	191,418	22,743	13.5
1860	168,675	52,300	44.9
1850	116,375	14,182	13.9
1840	102,193	56,111	121.8
1830	46,082	18,906	69.6
1820	27,176	9,934	57.6
1810	17,242		
Opelousas city			
1950	11,659	2,679	29.8
1940	8,980	2,681	42.6
1930	6,299	1,862	42.0
1920	4,437	−186	−4.0
1910	4,623	1,672	56.7
1900	2,951	1,379	87.7
1890	1,572	−104	−6.2
1880	1,676	130	8.4
1870	1,546	760	96.7
1860	786		
Ruston town			
1950	10,372	3,265	45.9
1940	7,107	2,707	61.5
1930	4,400	1,011	29.8
1920	3,389	12	0.4
1910	3,377	2,053	155.1
1900	1,324	557	72.6
1890	767		
Shreveport city			
1950	127,206	29,039	29.6
1940	98,167	21,512	28.1
1930	76,655	32,781	74.7
1920	43,874	15,859	56.6
1910	28,015	12,002	75.0
1900	16,013	4,034	33.7
1890	11,979	3,970	49.6
1880	8,009	3,402	73.8
1870	4,607	2,417	110.4
1860	2,190	462	26.7
1850	1,728		
West Monroe town			
1950	10,302	1,742	20.4
1940	8,560	1,994	30.4
1930	6,566	4,326	193.1
1920	2,240	1,113	98.8
1910	1,127	352	45.4
1900	775	328	73.4
1890	447		

[1] Not returned separately

Table 5 -- AREA AND POPULATION OF PARISHES, URBAN AND RURAL 1930 TO 1950

[""gires in "fa...cs are shown only for those parishes where change in definition affects given and rural classification. Minus sign (-) denotes decrease Percent not shown where base as less than 100]

ering I			ST EAL		Tetal por	ulation			Jros	n populat	lon	Ru	ral populat	ЮД	Percent	urban
Parish	Map refer- ence (ree p. 18-2)	Land ares in square milts, 1950	195	Per square _nuc	1940	1930	Percent :	1930 to 1940	1950	1940	Percent increase	1950	1940	Percent increase	1950	1940
The State Old urban defi-		45, 162	2, 683, 516	59 4	2 363, 880	2, 101 593	13 5	12 5	1,471,696	980, 489		1, 211, 820 1 518, 727	1, 389, 441	4 8	54 8 o0.8	. 41
cad.8	H-4 G-3 H-8 I-8 E-5	862 775 300 857 826	47, 050 18 535 22 387 17 278 38, 031	71 1 24 3 74 6 48 4 46 0	46, 260 17 540 21 210 18, 541 39 256	39 326 15,261 18 438 15 990 34 926	7 4 5 5 -6.8 -3.1	17 6 14 9 15 1 10 0 12 4	22, 166 5 598 4, 150 8.301	14 497 3 933 3,889 3,675	52 9 42 3 6 7	24 884 13 23" 18 23" 17 278 29 730	31 768 13 607 17 326 18 541 35 681	-21 7 -2 7 5 3 -3 8 -15 7	47 1 20 7 18. 5	31 22 19
esaregard erville ossier Old urben defindion ando. Old urben definition alcasieu	G-2 B-8 A-2 A-1 H-2	1, 18 ₂ 826 841 	17 766 19 105 40 139 176, 547 89, 635	15 0 23 1 47 7 198 1 81 2	14, 847 23, 933 33, 162 150, 208	14, 569 23, 789 28 388 124, 670 41, 968	19 7 -20 2 21.0 17 5	1 9 0 6 16.8 20.5	16,779 16,779 18,470 133,429 127 208 64 691 63 702	3 750 5,780 98.107 27,905	54 6 167 4 29 6	11 967 19 105 23 360 24,689 43,118 48 241 24,944 36,833	11 097 23 988 27, 876 52, 056	7 8 -20 2 -9 9 -5 2 -5 9	32 6 41 8 88 0 75 6 78 1 72 2 50 9	17 68
alossieu Old zroan defination aldwell ameron atanoula lanborue oncordia	C-5 I-1 D-6 A-3 D-7	550 1, 44 732 766 709	10 293 6 244 11, 834 25 063 14, 398	18.7 4.3 16.2 32.7 20.3	12 046 7, 203 14 618 29 855 14, 562	10, 480 6, 054 12 401 32 285 12, 778	-14 8 -13 3 -19 0 -16 1 -1 1	10 5 19.0 17 4 -7 5 14 0	7 789 9 847	3, 497 2 857	122 7 34 7	10 293 6 244 11 834 17 274 10 551	12.046 7, 203 14, 618 26 358 11 70e	-14 6 -13 3 -19 0 -34 5 -9 9	31 1 26 7	11
De So'o Lest Baton Rouge Old u-ban depantion Last Carroll Last Februana Lyangeline	C-1 G-8 A-7 G-8 G-5	898 482 432 454 672	24 398 158 236 16, 302 19, 133 31, 629	27 3 342 0 37 7 42 1 47 1	81 803 88, 415 19 023 18, 039 30, 497	31 016 68, 208 15 815 17 449 20 483	-23.3 79 0 -14.3 6.1 3.7	29 6 29 6 20 3 3 4 19 7	4,440 135 767 120,629 4,123 6 772 6,633	4, 065 54. 7.9 8 7.1 5 384 3, 721	9 2 261 8 11 1 25 8 78 3	19 958 22, 469 55 607 12 179 12, 361 24, 996	27, 738 58 896 16 312 12 656 26 776	-28 0 -59 8 -20 5 -2 3 -6 6	18 2 85 8 79 4 20 8 35 4 2_ 0	1: 5: 1: 2: 1:
rankim Frant beris bervals 1	C-6 E-4 I-7 H-7 C-4	648 670 598 626 583	29 376 14 203 40, 059 26, 760 15, 434	45 3 21 3 68 1 42 6 26 5	32 382 15 933 37, 188 27, 721 17, 807	30 830 10,709 28 192 24,638 13,808	-9 3 -10 5 -2 5 -13 3	6 1 1 4 81 9 12 8 29 0	3, 655 21, 159 5 747 3 097	2, 884 17 109 5, 049 2 639	29 0 28 7 13 8 17 4	25 721 14 268 18 900 21 008 12,387	20, 548 15 983 20 074 22 672 15, 168	-13 0 -10 5 -5 8 -7 4 -18 7	12.4 52.8 21.5 20.1	44 1: 1-
efferson Ola urban definuion efferson Davisalsye'te afourche Old urban definution a Salle	I-10 H-3 H-5 I-9	658 283 1, 157	103, 878 26, 298 57, 743 42 209	254 0 40 0 204 0 36.5	50, 427 24, 191 43 941 38, 615	19 765 38 827 82, 419	106. 0 - 8. 7 31 4 9 3 - 16. 0	26 0 22 4 13 2 19 1 6 1	92 216 81 070 12,512 38 541 10 550 7,780	16 871 7, 343 19 210 5, 851	95 8 70 4 74.6	11, 658 72, 808 13, 786 24, 202 81, 659 54, 478 2, 717	\$4 506 16 848 24 731 \$\$ 764 10,959	1.0 7 -18 2 -2 1 5 2 16 0	88. 8 99 9 47 6 58 1 25. 0 18 3	8 3 4
Lincoln. Livingston Madison Morahouse Natchitoches	B-4 H-9 B-7 A-6 C-3	489 865 682 804 1, 297	25, 782 20, 054 17, 451 32, 038 38 144	55 0 30 2 26 4 39 8 29 4	24, 790 17, 790 18, 443 27, 571 40, 997	22, 822 18, 200 14 829 23, 689 38, 477	4.0 12.7 -5 4 16.2 -7 0	8 6 -2 3 24 4 16 4 6 5	7,768 12,709 9,914	7, 107 5, 712 6 626 6, 812	45 9 35 9 92 7 45 5	15 410 20 054 9 693 19 269 28 230	17, 583 17 790 12 731 20 945 34 185	-12 9 12 7 -23 9 -8 0 -17 4	40 2 	2 2 2
Orleans Ouachita Plaquemines Conte Coupee Rapides	G-6 E-4	199 642 984 564 1, 329	570 445 74, 713 14, 239 21, 841 90 648	2866 6 116 4 14 5 38 7 68 2	494, 537 59, 168 12, 318 24, 004 73, 370	408, 762 54 337 9 608 21 007 65, 455	15.3 26.3 10.6 -9.0 23.5	7 8 8 9 28 2 14.3 12 1	570, 445 48, 874 2, 818 41, 336	494, 537 36, 869 31, 363	15 3 32 6 31 8	25 839 14 239 19 023 49 312	42,007	15 9 15 6 -20 8 17 4	100 0 65.4 12 9 45.6	100
Red River Richland Shine St Bernard Old urban definition It Charles Old urban definition	I-12	413 576 1,029 510	12, 113 26, 672 20, 880 11, 087	29 3 46 3 20 3 21 7	15, 881 28, 829 23, 586 7, 280	16, 078 26, 874 24, 110 6, 5.2	-23 7 -7 5 -11 5 52 8	-1 2 9 3 -2.2 1 8	3, 138 2, 643 3, 868			12, 113 23, 534 20, 880 8, 444 1' 087 9, 997 18 368	28 829 23, 588 7 680	-28 7 -18 4 -11 5	11 8 23.8 25 2	
t Helena t James t John the Baptist Old urban definition t Landry t Martin 1	G-9 I-9 I-10 G-5 H-6 I-10	420 249 225 980 721	9, 018 15 834 14 861 - 78, 476 26, 303	21. 5 61 6 66. 0 84 4 36 6	9, 542 16, 596 14, 766 71, 481 26, 394	8 492 15, 338 14, 078 60 0~4 21 767	-5 5 -7 6 0 6 -9 8 -0 2	12 4 8.2 4.9 19.0 21 3	4, 465 19 848 4, F14	14, 222 3, 501	39 5 31 8	9, 013 15 334 10 396 14 861 58, 633 21, 739	16, 596 14, 766 57, 209	-5 5 -7 6 0 8 2 4 -5 0	30 0 25 3 17 5	1
t Mary. t Tammany. angipahoa. ensas errebone. Old urban definition.	J-6 G-10 G-10 C-7 J-8	605 908 803 623 1, 391	35, 848 26, 988 33, 218 13, 209 43 328	59 3 29 7 66.3 21 2 31 1	31, 458 23, 621 45 519 1c 940 35 880	29, 397 20, 929 48 227 15, 096 29, 816	14. 0 14. 2 18. 9 -17 1 20. 8	7 0 12.9 -1 5 5 6 20 3	18. o22 8. o7 14. 904 16, 314 11, 505	11, 243 6, 987 10 034 9, 062	64 7	17 326 18, 411 38 314 13, 209 27 014 51, 823	16, 637 35 485 15, 940	-14.3 10.7 8.0 -17.1	31 8 28 0 37 7 26 6	2 2 2
Inion ermillon ermon ashfigton ebster	A-4 I-5 E-3 G-10 A-3	906 1, 224 1, 360 665 626	19, 141 35, 929 18 974 38, 371 35, 704	21 1 30 2 14 0 57 7 57 0	20 948 37, 750 19, 142 34, 443 33, 676	20 731 33,684 20 047 29 904 29 458	-8.6 -2.2 -0.9 11.4 6.0	1 0 12 1 -4 5 15 2 14 3	18 900 4 670 17, 798 13, 170	9 510 2 829 14, 604 9, 499	46. 2 65 1 21 9 38 6	19 141 23 029 14 304 20 573 22, 384	28, 240 16, 313	-8.6 -18.5 -12.3 3.7 -6.8	37 6 24 6 46 4 36.9	2 1 4 2
est Baton Rouge est Carroll est Feliciana		201 356 410 950	11, 738 17, 248 10, 169 16, 119	58 4 48.4 24.8 17 0	11 268 19 202 11 720 16 923	9 716 13,895 10,924 14,766	-10 4 -13 2 -4 8	15 9 38.6 7 3 14 6	3, 097 5, 929	4, 512		8, 641 17 248 10, 169 10, 490	11,720	-23 3 -10 4 -13 2 -15 5	26. 4 34. 9	

¹ Part of St Martin annexed to Iberville in 1946

Table 6.-POPULATION OF PARISHES BY MINOR CIVIL DIVISIONS 1930 TO 1950

N	1	-			-						
Pansh and mmor civil d vision	1950	1940	1930	Pansh and minor civa di islor.	1950	1940	1530	Parish and minor ci le vis.on	i950	1940	1930
Acadıa Parısh		46 260	89, 326	Beauregard Parsh.	17,766	14,847	14,589	Caldwell Parish	10,293	12,046	10 43
P. ard 1 1 Payne 'own 1 Ward 2 Ward 2 Ward 3 Church Point town Ward 4 Tota 11/lage.	8 871 6, 485 3, 596 7 902 2 897 5, 222 1 162	7 970 4 974 4 809 7 606 1,892 6,572	7, 163 8 710 4 338 5 173 1 087 5 732	Ward 1 Ward 2 Mirry ille town Ward 3 De Ridder cuy 1 Ward 4 Ward 4	2 K94 1 995 9 819 5 799 614	1 302 2 437 1,916 6 671 5 750	587 2 883 2 586 2 994 5 747 498	Ward 1 Ward 210 Ward 3 Ward 3 Ward 4 Olarks (urine) Col.implic rillage E	99" 964 1,079 8,128 1 545 920	1 194 1 048 1 251 5,700	1, 21 1, 07 1, 19 4 51
Tota 114age. **Pard 5. **Estherwood village. **Mermentau village. **Mermentau village. **Mermentau village. **Mermentau village. **Ward 6! **Crowley city. **Ward 7.	3 698 247	1 000 4,034 571 748 12 075 9 588	897 3 816 579 594 10 155 7 855	Ward 6 Ward 7 Ward 8 Breaville Parish	1 035 946 650 19 105	1 233 1 .02 1 005 42 23, 988	985 940 9:3 -7= 23,789	Ward 8 Ward 4 Ward 4 Clarks (wrine) Columber village * Columber village * Ward 6 Ward 6 Ward 6 Ward 7 Ward 7 Ward 9 Ward 9 Ward 10	464 464 182 367 560 212 350	407 772 282 487 606 833 478	45 66 17 34 55 37
Allen Parish	2, 561	3,194	2, 949	Ward 16	3 774	1 701	5 029 808	Cameron Parish	6 244	7 203	6 05
Ward 1 Oberium milage Ward 2 Frender tearn	3 269 1 544 4,240	2,932 962 3 767 1,410 641	2 75° 790 2,907 968 737	Ward 1 t Arcadia town t Ward 2 t Bryceland vuluage t Gibbland town. W.rd 3 Bieni ille zillage. Ward 4	1,370	4 307 189 1 098 1,884 857	4 259 176 1,690 2,121 381	Ward 1 Cow Island Ward 2 Grand Chence Ward 3, Cameron Ward 4 Grand Lake Ward 5, Johnsons Bayot.	904 2 276 1 012 380	808 1 070 2, 100 1 472 393	94 96 1 42 1,34
Ward 3 Recres village 1 Ward 1 Ward 51	108	1,480	1,370	Ward 4 Pringgold town 5 Ward 7 Castor t Hage	5,226 1 007 1 866	6, 607 1, 006 2 372	5,758 6,8 2,280	Ward 8 Hackberry	1, 208	1,350	12,45
Ward 5 2 Elizabeth (uninc.)	9 432 1 118 5 598	8,720	7,490		1,923 1,187	2, 01-6	2 453 1 479		_	1.051	82
Ascension Parish		21 215	18, 438	Ward 7 Saline village	357	1, 042 381	346	Ward 1. Ward 2. Ward 3		2 921 730 826	2,88 40 1,18
Ward 1 Port Barrow-Smoke Bend	2, 924	2 799	2, 315	Bossier Parish Ward 1	40, 139 3 574	33, 162 4, 118	28, 388 5, 431	Hort sonburg tillage	1,618 544 4 317	2 281 453 5 075	1, 94 45 3 52
Ward 2. Ward 3	1,619 933 4,150 4,160 1,068	1 146 3 889 5 889	1,008 3 788 5 788	Ward 1' Bossier City town (part)' Benton rillage Bossier City town (part)' Benton rillage	23 831 15 2.9	15, 337 519 0 788	9 938	Ward 6 Jonesville tour Ward 7 Claiborne Parish	1, 246 25, 963	# 080 -, 784 29, 855	1,18 1,58 33,28
Denatasonula catg. Ward 4. Ward 5. Ward 6. Ward 7. Gonzales wilage Ward 8. Ward 9. Ward 10.	1,008 1,583 490 4,328 1,648 2 408	1 307 1,668 -77 3,523 867 2,573	1,088 1,507 798 2,873 468 2,238	Ward 3 Plan Dealing town Ware 4 Ward 5 Ward 6 Hanghon village	4 927 1 821 1 417 1,710 4,680	5 383 1, 685 1, 857 1 812 2, 660	5.341 1. 18 2 208 1 680 3,760	Ward 1 Ward 2 Ward 3.11 Haynesville town 1	1 886 1 772 6 256 5 040	2 365 2 414 6 602 2,418	2, 59 3 05 7 88 2, 54
Ward 9 Ward 10	1,520	1,437 2,006	2, 238 199 2, 320	Caddo Parish	501 1"6, 847	150, 203	124, 670	Ward 4	1, 518 2, 106 487	2 543 2,713 491	2 52 3 26 48
Assumption Parish	17, 278	18,541	15 990	Ward 1	4 300 8,370	6, 468	8 38 ⁻ 7 653	Ward 6 Ward 7 11	1 425 7,613	2,818 7,505 8,407	2 67 6, 86
Ward 1 Ward 2 Wurd 3 Ward 4	1,162 1,086 548 1 122	1,289 1,243 716 1 276	1,084 1,109 689 1 187	Ward 1 Ward 2 Oil City village * Visum town Ward 8 Morningsport town Ward 4 Shrevoport city *	2 436 7 896 709	\$ 460 4,924 718	1 646 4,889 808	Ward 4 Ward 5 Athens wifags Ward 8 Ward 7 Homer town 1 Ward 8 Ward 8 Junction City (part) 11	1,749 2,008 482 113	3, 497 2, 744 658 86	2 66 75
Ward 4. Ward 5. Ward 6. Napoleoneille town.	3 128 3 447 1 860	3 824 1 301	2,988 3 504 1 180	Ward 4 !	187, 368 187, 206	106 439 98, 167	82 053 70 05e	Concordia Parish	14,298	14, 562	12,77
Ward 9 3. Avoyelles Parish.	2 830 2,692 1 754 38,031	8 874 2, 788 39, 256	3 153 2, 331 34 926	Ward 5	4 350 2,370 3 094 4,369 4 435	4, 631 2 489 1, 915 6, 147 7 203	4 857 3 287 2,157 6 110 2 207	Ward 1 Ward 2 Ward 8. Ward 4. Ward 4. Vidais town Ward b Ward 7 Perriday town 7 Wrd 9 12 Perriday town 7 Wrd 9 12	228 87 106 503 2 829 1,641	303 280 113 762 2 712 1 718	131 131 1 04 2 27 1,14
Ward 1	1 604	1 852	1 513	Calcasieu Parish		56, 506	41, 963	Ward b	730 5 43b	875 6, 202	4 13

Markmille town 4 Ward 8	7 441 5 655 3 043 1,459 2,235 1 325 2,925 550	6 441 1 811 2 925 1 158 2,502 1 446 3,162	5,530 1,527 3,221 1,007 2,449 1,219 2,905	Ward 3 'Ward 3 ' Ward 3 ' Cosport (usine). Lake Charles city ' Ward 4 ' Meplescood , name). Sulphur tours '' We't lake tourn '' We't lake tourn '' We'd S		926 1 961 31 900 21 207 9, 459	636 1 753 21,466 15,791 0 690	Perridgy town '9 Ward 8 19 Ward 9 10 19 Ward 10 19 Ward 11 19 Cleyton cillage 19 Ward 12 13	5, 847 1, 983 1, 006 348 1, 584 667 271	8 857 1,548 1,380 1,409	
Ward 6 Moreauville village (part) Ward 7 Simmesport village	3,452	4,001	2,73b	Sulphur town 9	5 996	\$ 504	1,888	De Soto Parish	24,398	81 803	31,01
Ward 8 Moreauville village (part) Plauchenille village Ward 9. Cotton-port town Energreen town Burtise town Burks town	4, 321 285 277 4, 686 1, 534	5, 233 495 367 4, 902 1, 196 384 6, 792 3 075	5 288 350 866 4,411 1,015 298 5,375 2 404	Ward 6. De Quivey town. Ward 7. Vinton con	6 314 8 857 4,166 8 607	1,835 4 907 5,252 3 565 1 787 1,963	2,012 4 640 5 589 4,220 1 989 1 546	Ward 1 Lorgerred village Ward 2 Ward 3 Ward 4 Manefield city 3 Monefield city 3 Ward 4 Ward 4	1,968 284 2 511 2 273 8,310 4,440 876 1,972	3,116 263 3 881 3 639 8 004 4 065 435 3,043	3 \$2 8 73 3, 24 7, 80 5, 8* 46 2 \$0

^{1942,} and 1945. mexed to ward 2 since 1940 Part of ward 1 sinexed to Arcadia town in 1949 Ringgold town returned as a I BRAUKE-ARD - Parts of word 3 annexed to De Ridder cty in 1941, 1442, and 1945.

BREWING - Part of ward 1 sunexed to Arcadia town in 1949 Ringsold town returned as a "flags in 1940"

Black - Part of ward 1, including part of Bryceland Unilsee, annexed to ward 2 in 1941 1942

Basser City town annexed part of ward 1 in 1944 and parts of ward 5 in 1941 1942

CARDO - OOL City vinige moorpowsted in 1949 Part of ward 4 annexed to ward 8 and part of ward 8 annexed to 4 ward 5 in 1949

CARDO - OOL City vinige moorpowsted in 1949 Part of ward 4 annexed to ward 8 annexed to 4 ward 8 annexed to 8 annexed to 8 investment of ward 4 annexed to 8 investment of ward 8 8 investmen

¹ OLIBORNE — Parts of ward 3 annexed to mappen use the many raises want a managed to mard 7 in 1946. Ward 11 organized from parts of wards 7 and 8 in 1941 Ward 12 organized from parts of wards 10 in 1942. Clayton village incorporated in 1948.

11 De Soro — Mansfeld dity, returned in 1940 as a town, annexed part of ward 4 in 1947.

Table 6 -- POPULATION OF PARISHES BY MINOR CIVIL DIVISIONS 1930 TO 1950-Con

									-	-	-
Parisi and minore vii a vision	1930	1940	1930	Parish

Table 6.—POPULATION OF PARISHES BY MINOR CIVIL DIVISIONS: 1930 TO 1950—Con.

Parish and minor civil division	1950	1940	1930
De Soto Parish—Con.			
Ward 6	2,357	3,468	3,699
Grand Cane village	280	377	398
Ward 7	2,.90	3,497	3,347
Ward 8	2,811	3,155	2,746
Logansport town	1,270	1,222	1,030
East Baton Rouge Parish[14]	158,236	88,415	68,208
Ward 1	125,629	34,719	30,729
Baton Rouge city	125,629	34,719	30,729
Ward 2	24,309	---	---
Baker village[14]	763	---	---
Zachary town	1,0.2	780	626
Ward 3	8,298	---	---
East Carroll Parish	16,302	19,023	15,815
Ward 1[15]	1,719	1,906	1,871
Ward 2[15]	2,830	3,332	3,316
Ward 3	7,186	7,491	5,558
Lake Providence town	4,123	3,711	2,867
Ward 4	441	563	680
Ward 5	1,517	2,480	2,395
Ward 6[15]	979	1,446	980
Ward 7[15]	1,630	1,803	1,015
East Feliciana Parish	19,133	18,039	17,449
Ward 1	1,15.	1,910	2,249
Slaughter town	290	306	327
Ward 2	1,701	1,868	2,237
Ward 3	8,263	6,433	5,380
Jackson town	6,772	5,384	3,969
Ward 4	1,493	1,384	1,567
Norwood village[16]	214	---	---
Ward 5	2,982	2,779	2,152
Clinton town	1,383	998	708
Ward 6	1,182	1,274	1,231
Ward 7	1,058	1,210	1,276
Ward 8	1,297	1,166	1,357
Evangeline Parish	31,629	30,497	25,483
Ward 1[17]	15,153	13,556	10,641
Ville Platte town[17]	6,633	3,721	1,722
Ward 2	4,262	4,611	3,212
Basile village	1,572	1,132	408
Ward 3	7,155	7,542	6,829
Mamou village	2,254	1,879	800
Ward 4	2,234	2,024	1,780
Ward 5	2,825	2,964	3,021
Franklin Parish	29,376	32,382	30,530
Ward 1	3,427	3,641	4,168
Wisner village	798	617	692
Ward 2	3,601	4,422	3,989
Gilbert village	452	498	406
Ward 3	3,783	3,648	3,149
Ward 4	2,717	3,029	2,971
Ward 5	2,090	2,372	2,321
Ward 6	2,604	3,035	3,188
Baskin village	117	330	4 6
Ward 7	7,598	7,585	6,583
Winnsboro town	3,655	2,834	1,965
Ward 8	1,468	1,837	1,808
Ward 9	2,478	2,813	2,358
Grant Parish	14,263	15,933	15,709
Ward 1	3,427	3,510	3,291
Colfax town	1,651	1,354	1,141
Ward 2	2,106	2,071	3,402
Ward 3	1,668	1,745	1,447
Dry Prong village[18]	377	---	---
Ward 4	430	608	441
Ward 5	1,130	2,463	3,901
Georgetown village[18]	355	---	---
Ward 6	904	1,015	900
Ward 7	2,441	2,700	2,267
Montgomery town	695	495	383
Ward 8	2,157	1,821	---
Pollock town	421	3.7	376

Parish and minor civil division	1950	1940	1930
Iberia Parish	40,059	37,183	28,192
Ward 1, Patoutville	2,501	2,290	2,137
Weeks Island (uninc.)	1,499	---	---
Ward 2, Isle Piquante	1,505	2,135	1,740
Ward 3, Belle Place	1,491	1,784	1,292
Ward 4, Fausse Pointe	2,728	3,179	2,703
Loreauville village	478	490	441
Ward 5, Coteau	1,606	1,926	2,329
Ward 6[19]	20,654	15,934	9,881
New Iberia city[19]	16,467	13,747	8,003
Ward 7, Petite Anse	1,617	1,920	1,520
Delcambre town (part)[19]	667	583	272
Ward 8[19]	6,140	5,865	4,570
Jeanerette town[19]	4,692	3,362	2,228
Ward 9	1,817	2,150	2,020
Iberville Parish[20]	26,750	27,721	24,638
Ward 1	5,853	6,167	4,729
White Castle town	1,839	1,692	1,499
Ward 2[20]	5,068	4,410	3,741
Plaquemine town (part)[20]	1,659	879	785
Ward 3	3,530	3,479	3,656
Plaquemine town (part)	3,530	3,479	3,656
Ward 4	1,301	1,811	1,540
Ward 5	1,687	1,733	1,552
Ward 6	2,418	2,555	2,176
Turnerville (uninc.)	1,048	---	---
Ward 7	2,235	1,998	2,276
Grosse Tete village	548	382	303
Ward 8	3,337	3,348	3,435
Plaquemine town (part)	558	691	685
Ward 9	1,821	2,217	1,533
Maringouin village	898	708	518
Jackson Parish	15,434	17,807	13,808
Ward 1	1,199	1,778	1,700
Eros village	195	289	225
Ward 2	8,397	7,534	4,639
Hodge village	1,386	1,4.5	1,367
Jonesboro town[21]	3,097	2,339	1,949
Ward 3	2,080	2,958	2,543
Quitman village	204	218	207
Ward 4	530	1,227	827
Ward 5	515	744	686
Ward 6	1,368	1,997	2,045
Ward 7	1,345	1,569	1,318
Chatham town	833	605	391
Jefferson Parish	103,873	50,427	40,032
Ward 1	6,455	4,202	3,688
Gretna city (part)	6,311	4,121	2,987
Ward 2	3,090	2,722	2,679
Gretna city (part)	2,881	2,624	2,679
Ward 3	8,292	6,212	5,323
Gretna city (part)	4,621	4,134	3,908
Ward 4	28,940	13,973	11,345
Westwego town	8,328	4,992	3,987
Ward 5	1,161	941	949
Ward 6	3,938	3,545	2,651
Grand Isle (uninc.)	1,190	---	---
Ward 7	16,209	4,587	3,414
Ward 8	27,067	10,263	6,517
Ward 9[22]	10,721	3,982	3,466
Harahan village	3,394	1,082	892
Kenner town[22]	5,535	2,375	2,440
Jefferson Davis Parish	26,298	24,191	19,765
Ward 1	3,960	3,445	3,099
Lake Arthur town	2,849	2,131	1,662
Ward 2	10,689	8,086	5,364
Jennings city	9,663	7,343	4,036
Ward 3	1,245	1,427	1,571
Ward 4	2,621	2,469	2,230
Elton town	1,434	901	742
Ward 5	1,284	1,042	1,201
Ward 6	3,798	3,452	3,029
Welsh town	2,410	1,822	1,514
Ward 7	844	1,286	1,333
Ward 8	1,359	1,391	1,599
Ward 9	518	493	336

Parish and minor civil division	1950	1940	1930
Lafayette Parish	57,743	43,941	38,827
Ward 1[23]	4,128	3,516	3,323
Duson village (part)	556	334	267
Lafayette city (part)[23]	123	---	---
Scott village (part)	472	308	234
Ward 2	3,343	3,753	4,347
Duson village (part)	151	129	129
Ward 3[23]	37,792	23,258	17,809
Lafayette city (part)[23]	33,418	19,210	14,635
Ward 4	901	1,208	1,251
Ward 5	2,183	2,230	2,279
Broussard village	1,237	791	806
Ward 6	4,062	4,413	4,201
Carencro village	1,587	914	684
Ward 7	1,404	1,423	1,346
Ward 8	2,194	2,074	2,074
Scott village (part)	276	104	110
Ward 9	1,788	2,076	2,197
Youngsville village	769	647	538
Lafourche Parish[24]	42,209	38,615	32,419
Ward 1	2,261	1,756	1,543
Ward 2[24]	9,432	---	---
Thibodaux city[24]	7,730	5,851	4,442
Ward 3	4,500	---	---
Raceland (uninc.) (part)	1,350	---	---
Ward 4	3,056	---	---
Larose (uninc.) (part)	368	---	---
Lockport town[24]	1,388	877	660
Ward 5	2,429	---	---
Ward 6	2,908	---	---
Ward 7	3,868	---	---
Raceland (uninc.) (part)	370	---	---
Ward 8	577	---	---
Ward 9	1,517	---	---
Larose (uninc.) (part)	125	---	---
Ward 10	11,266	---	---
Golden Meadow (uninc.)	2,820	---	---
Larose (uninc.) (part)	799	---	---
La Salle Parish	12,717	10,959	11,668
Ward 1	271	333	260
Ward 2	4,165	3,647	3,846
Olla village	1,115	691	740
Tullos town	792	589	707
Urania (uninc.)	1,004	---	---
Ward 3	2,244	2,462	3,593
Ward 4[25]	4,784	3,083	2,984
Jena town	1,438	946	1,007
Ward 5[25]	760	735	506
Ward 6[25]	147	297	229
Ward 7	346	402	250
Lincoln Parish	25,782	24,790	22,822
Ward 1	14,685	9,995	7,672
Ruston town	10,372	7,107	4,400
Ward 2	1,324	1,977	1,870
Ward 3	2,568	3,041	3,364
Ward 4	2,066	2,989	3,054
Choudrant village	390	438	494
Ward 5	1,311	1,926	2,281
Ward 6	2,005	1,853	1,908
Dubach town	703	749	603
Ward 7	645	1,145	989
Ward 8	1,178	1,894	1,684
Livingston Parish	20,054	17,790	18,206
Ward 1	1,684	1,582	1,494
Ward 2[26]	5,152	4,690	4,533
Denham Springs town	2,053	1,233	1,002
Ward 3	1,148	1,153	948
Ward 4	2,768	2,813	2,879
Ward 5	1,180	1,545	1,293
Ward 6	2,222	2,155	2,123
Ward 7	956	989	919
Ward 8	876	846	610
Ward 9	1,832	1,485	2,834
Ward 10	509	532	573
Ward 11[26]	1,727	---	---
Walker village	500	424	521

[14] EAST BATON ROUGE.—Parish redistricted in 1940; comparative figures shown wherever possible. Baker village incorporated in 1944.
[15] EAST CARROLL.—Part of ward 7 annexed to ward 1 in 1940. Parts of ward 6 annexed to wards 2 and 7 in 1940 and 1943, respectively.
[16] EAST FELICIANA.—Norwood village incorporated in 1948.
[17] EVANGELINE.—Part of ward 1 annexed to Ville Platte town in 1947.
[18] GRANT.—Dry Prong village incorporated in 1947. Georgetown village incorporated in 1949.
[19] IBERIA.—Parts of ward 6 annexed to New Iberia city in 1942, 1946, 1948, and 1950. Delcambre town returned in 1940 as a village. Part of ward 8 annexed to Jeanerette town in 1949.
[20] IBERVILLE.—Part of St. Martin Parish, having no population in 1950, annexed to Iberville Parish in 1946 but not assigned to any ward. Part of ward 2 annexed to Plaquemine town in 1948.
[21] JACKSON.—Part of ward 2 annexed to Jonesboro town in 1947.
[22] JEFFERSON.—Part of ward 9 annexed to Kenner town since 1940.
[23] LAFAYETTE.—Parts of wards 1 and 3 annexed to Lafayette city in 1950, and part of ward 3 annexed in 1941.
[24] LAFOURCHE.—Parish redistricted in 1941; comparative figures shown wherever possible. Thibodaux city, returned in 1940 as a town, annexed parts of ward 2 in 1945. Lockport town returned in 1940 as a village.
[25] LA SALLE.—Parts of ward 5 annexed to wards 4 and 6 in 1942.
[26] LIVINGSTON.—Part of ward 2, including Walker village, taken to form ward 11 in 1947.

Table 6.—POPULATION OF PARISHES BY MINOR CIVIL DIVISIONS: 1930 TO 1950—Con.

Parish and minor civil division	1950	1940	1930
Madison Parish	17,451	18,443	14,829
Ward 1	496	711	796
Mound village (part)	76	98	---
Ward 2 [27]	1,327	1,714	2,014
Delta village (part)	160	189	---
Mound village (part)	89	107	---
Ward 3	794	2,09	996
Ward 4 [27]	10,774	9,546	6,929
Tallulah village [27]	7,758	5,712	3,952
Ward 5	808	1,490	1,310
Ward 6	1,442	1,838	1,308
Ward 7	975	1,227	943
Ward 8	840	758	467
Morehouse Parish	32,038	27,571	23,689
Ward 1	1,039	1,378	666
Ward 2	993	1,016	780
Ward 3	1,138	912	1,265
Ward 4 [28]	14,336	8,836	6,599
Bastrop town [28]	12,769	6,626	5,121
Ward 5	3,173	3,968	3,088
Oak Ridge village	287	378	260
Ward 6	4,183	4,577	4,018
Mer Rouge village	784	718	669
Ward 7	780	963	971
Ward 8	2,164	2,274	2,238
Collinston village	546	488	478
Ward 9	406	400	469
Ward 10	3,526	3,652	3,565
Bonita village	504	522	507
Natchitoches Parish	38,144	40,997	38,477
Ward 1 [29]	14,222	11,262	8,464
Natchitoches city [29]	9,914	6,812	4,547
Ward 2	2,849	3,100	3,611
Goldonna village	864	256	260
Ward 3	1,637	2,205	2,234
Ward 4	4,037	4,521	4,8 3
Campti village	1,014	1,004	999
Ward 5	3,712	4,241	4,357
Marthaville town	181	213	---
Ward 6 [29]	1,159	1,525	1,301
Provencal village	500	355	388
Ward 7	650	2,157	1,394
Ward 8	606	995	1,243
Ward 9	5,242	7,255	7,605
Ward 10	2,980	3,705	3,455
Orleans Parish	570,445	494,537	458,762
New Orleans city	570,445	494,537	458,762
Ouachita Parish	74,713	59,168	54,337
Ward 1	3,064	3,358	3,569
Ward 2	1,825	2,015	2,263
Ward 3	20,504	15,857	15,250
Monroe city (part)	17,488	13,962	13,684
Ward 4	1,425	1,516	1,742
Ward 5 [30]	20,012	14,433	1 760
Brownsville (uninc.)	2,207	---	---
Highland Park–Splane Place (uninc.)	1,665	---	---
West Monroe city [30]	10,302	8,560	6,566
Ward 6	2,214	2,163	2,214
Ward 7	1,117	1,711	1,711
Ward 8	1,192	1,135	1,109
Ward 9	680	795	1,019
Ward 10 [30]	22,671	16,325	13,610
Monroe city (part) [30]	21,184	14,607	12,844
Plaquemines Parish	14,239	12,318	9,608
Ward 1	970	854	---
Ward 2	702	807	---
Ward 3	1,356	1,232	---
Ward 4	380	461	---
Ward 5	1,713	1,439	---
Ward 6	1,335	931	---
Ward 7	763	816	---
Ward 8	248	227	---
Ward 9	3,317	2,466	---
Potash–Port Sulphur (uninc.)	1,205	---	---
Ward 10	3,476	3,035	---
Buras–Triumph (uninc.)	1,799	---	---

Parish and minor civil division	1950	1940	1930
Pointe Coupee Parish	21,841	21,004	21,007
Ward 1	1 6 0	2,433	---
Ward 2	1,983	2,765	---
Ward 3	1,176	1,590	---
Ward 4	2,158	2,393	---
Morganza village	817	744	606
Ward 5	1,865	1,949	---
Ward 6	429	927	---
Ward 7	1,500	1,630	---
Ward 8	3,165	3,114	---
Ward 9	4,889	4,243	---
New Roads town	2,818	2,255	1,473
Ward 10	3,148	2,954	---
Rapides Parish	90,648	73,370	65,455
Ward 1, Alexandria [31]	41,307	30,291	26,983
Alexandria city [31]	34,913	27,066	23,025
Ward 2, Lamourie	4,470	4,623	[illegible]
Woodworth village [31]	392	---	---
Ward 3, Cheneyville	5,406	6,132	5,895
Cheneyville town	918	913	835
Lecompte town	1,443	1,311	1,247
Ward 4, Spring Hill	5,027	4,958	5,524
Forest Hill village	365	318	304
Glenmora town	1,556	1,152	1,675
McNary village	267	151	21
Ward 5, Henderson	1,915	2,062	2,113
Ward 6, Calcasieu	1,726	1,519	1,085
Ward 7, Cotile [31]	4,574	4,614	4,131
Boyce town [31]	981	782	820
Ward 8, Rapides	2,221	2,602	2,805
Ward 9, Pineville	13,863	7,781	8,284
Pineville city [31]	6,423	4,297	3,612
Ward 10, Rigolette	7,139	4,775	3,764
Tioga village	393	1,300	528
Ward 11	3,300	3,014	---
Red River Parish	12,113	15,881	16,078
Ward 1 [32]	4,169	4,322	3,567
Coushatta town [32]	1,788	1,289	909
Ward 2	933	1,231	1,511
Ward 3	1,715	2,691	2,774
Ward 4	1,486	1,861	1,967
Ward 5	907	1,131	1,174
Ward 6	1,449	2,535	2,644
Ward 7	776	1,145	1,248
Ward 8	618	960	1,193
Richland Parish	26,672	28,829	26,374
Ward 1	5,786	5,505	5,403
Delhi town	1,861	1,192	1,408
Ward 2 [33]	10,401	10,677	7,942
Rayville town [33]	3,138	2,412	2,076
Ward 3	2,344	2,855	2,791
Ward 4	2,519	3,108	3,283
Ward 5	2,881	3,762	4,447
Mangham town [33]	554	572	714
Ward 6	1,103	1,399	1,448
Ward 7	834	1,223	1,059
Sabine Parish	20,880	23,586	24,110
Ward 1, Middle Creek	2,344	3,045	4,081
Ward 2, Toro	1,080	1,555	1,465
Ward 3, Negreet	1,088	1,715	1,731
Ward 4, Many	6,643	5,559	6,021
Many town	1,681	1,471	1,339
Ward 5, Bayou Scie	2,576	2,586	2,453
Zwolle town (part)	706	695	440
Ward 6, San Patricio	1,597	1,909	2,023
Converse village (part)	265	262	291
Noble village	258	258	268
Ward 7, Bayou San Miguel	1,879	2,231	2,416
Pleasant Hill town	856	737	807
Ward 8, Little Bayou Scie	1,861	1,874	1,696
Zwolle town (part)	849	805	824
Ward 9	721	960	987
Ward 10	791	1,049	1,237
Converse village (part)	46	52	---
St. Bernard Parish	11,087	7,280	6,512
Ward 1	2,856	1,067	1,029
Ward 2	801	915	912
Chalmette (uninc.) (part)	305	---	---
Ward 3	1,509	705	437
Chalmette (uninc.) (part)	1,392	---	---

Parish and minor civil division	1950	1940	1930
St. Bernard Parish—Con.			
Ward 4	363	844	671
Ward 5 [34]	1,857	1,454	1,360
Ward 6 [34]	1,45	584	289
Ward 7	1,806	1,638	1,414
St. Charles Parish	13,363	12,321	2 111
Ward 1	1,537	2,010	1,939
Ward 2	2,214	2,408	2,096
Ward 3	4,203	3,134	3,734
Norco–Goodhope (uninc.)	3,396	---	---
Ward 4	3,047	2,533	1,825
Ward 5	2,062	2,146	2,517
St. Helena Parish	9,013	9,542	8,492
Ward 1	798	981	1,146
Ward 2	2,124	2,064	1,817
Greensburg town (part)	345	571	362
Ward 3	549	1,584	1,166
Greensburg town (part)	78	18	---
Ward 4	1,544	1,551	1,528
Ward 5	2,035	2,159	1,772
Ward 6	963	1,273	1,063
St. James Parish	15,334	16,596	15,338
Ward 1	1,291	1,456	1,633
Remy (uninc.)	1,054	---	---
Ward 2	1,008	1,324	1,114
Ward 3	915	1,280	1,163
Ward 4	961	1,067	1,058
Ward 5	1,056	1,118	1,078
Ward 6	1,653	1,796	1,723
Ward 7	2,405	2,720	2,261
Ward 8	1,624	1,621	1,4 1
Ward 9 [35]	4,391	4,205	3,837
Gramercy village [35]	1,164	---	---
Lutcher town [35]	2,198	2,167	1,481
St. John the Baptist Parish	14,861	14,766	14,078
Ward 1	1,358	1,500	1,435
Ward 2	1,276	1,430	1,152
Ward 3	1,281	1,678	1,670
Ward 4	3,830	3,241	2,870
Laplace (uninc.)	2,352	---	---
Ward 5	4,499	4,466	3,744
Reserve (uninc.)	4,465	---	---
Ward 6	2,617	2,451	3,207
Garyville (uninc.)	1,850	---	---
St. Landry Parish	78,476	71,481	60,074
Ward 1 [36]	26,714	21,336	16,474
Opelousas city [36]	11,659	8,980	6,299
Port Barre village (part) [36]	44	---	---
Ward 2	7,566	6,693	7,513
Grand Coteau village	1,108	662	580
Sunset village	1,080	630	590
Ward 3	5,921	6,435	5,188
Arnaudville village (part)	790	524	417
Leonville village	514	461	408
Ward 4 [36]	10,971	10,845	11,504
Krotz Springs village	866	650	449
Melville town	1,901	1,828	1,541
Palmetto village	257	111	408
Port Barre village (part) [36]	1,022	850	674
Ward 5	6,685	7,418	8,142
Washington town	1,291	1,264	1,004
Ward 6	16,604	13,374	11,253
Eunice town	8,184	5,242	3,597
Ward 7	3,955	5,380	---
St. Martin Parish [37]	26,353	26,394	21,767
Ward 1	7,381	6,919	5,374
St. Martinville town	4,614	3,501	2,455
Ward 2 [37]	404	797	2,221
Ward 3	4,477	4,829	3,732
Parks village	460	400	409
Ward 4	6,949	6,364	5,238
Breaux Bridge town	2,492	1,668	1,399
Ward 5	6,679	6,710	5,172
Arnaudville village (part)	88	118	64
Ward 6	463	775	---

[27] MADISON.—Delta village returned in 1940 in ward 2 only; that part of Delta village in ward 1 had no population in 1950. Parts of ward 4 annexed to Tallulah village in 1942, 1944, 1945, and 1949.
[28] MOREHOUSE.—Parts of ward 4 annexed to Bastrop town in 1950.
[29] NATCHITOCHES.—Part of ward 6 annexed to ward 1 in 1946. Parts of ward 1 annexed to Natchitoches city in 1946, 1947, 1949, and 1950.
[30] OUACHITA.—Part of ward 5 annexed to West Monroe city in 1940. Parts of ward 10 annexed to Monroe city in 1948, 1949, and 1950.
[31] RAPIDES.—Parts of ward 1 annexed to Alexandria city in 1942, 1943, 1944, 1945, 1946, 1949, and 1950. Woodworth village incorporated in 1943. Part of ward 7 annexed to Boyce town in 1946. Pineville city returned in 1940 as a town.
[32] RED RIVER.—Part of ward 1 annexed to Coushatta town since 1940.
[33] RICHLAND.—Part of ward 2 annexed to Rayville town in 1948. Mangham town returned in 1940 as a village.
[34] ST BERNARD.—Part of ward 5 annexed to ward 6 in 1947.
[35] ST JAMES.—Part of ward 9 annexed to Lutcher town in 1948. Gramercy village incorporated in 1947.
[36] ST LANDRY.—Part of ward 1 annexed to Opelousas city in 1949. Port Barre village returned in 1940 as in ward 4 only.
[37] ST MARTIN.—Part of ward 2 annexed to Iberville Parish in 1946.

Table 6.—POPULATION OF PARISHES BY MINOR CIVIL DIVISIONS: 1930 TO 1950—Con.

Parish and minor civil division	1950	1940	1930
St. Mary Parish	35,848	31,458	29,397
Ward 1	2,577	2,702	2,416
Ward 2	1,466	2,119	1,748
Ward 3 [38]	9,753	10,260	9,046
Franklin town [38]	*6,144*	*4,274*	*3,271*
Ward 4	2,222	2,331	2,502
Ward 5	2,484	2,440	3,25
Patterson town	*1,938*	*1,800*	*2,206*
Ward 6	10,626	7,723	7,396
Morgan City	*9,759*	*6,969*	*5,985*
Ward 7	1,291	1,250	1,209
Ward 8	2,885	2,265	1,829
Berwick town	*2,619*	*1,906*	*1,279*
Ward 9	631	368	-
Ward 10 [38]	1,913	-	-
Baldwin town [38]	*1,188*	*924*	*822*
St. Tammany Parish	26,988	23,624	20,929
Ward 1	1,903	1,838	1,527
Madisonville town	*861*	*915*	*837*
Ward 2	2,968	2,672	2,338
Folsom town [39]	*166*	-	-
Ward 3	6,744	5,853	4,622
Covington town	*5,113*	*4,123*	*3,208*
Ward 4	2,228	2,101	1,667
Mandeville town	*1,368*	*1,326*	*1,069*
Ward 5	1,308	1,268	1,384
Ward 6	1,276	1,441	1,752
Ward 7	1,289	929	900
Ward 8	2,133	2,089	1,470
Pearl River village	*697*	*612*	*254*
Ward 9	5,806	4,477	4,248
Slidell town	*3,464*	*2,864*	*2,807*
Ward 10	1,033	956	1,021
Abita Springs town	*559*	*528*	*471*
Tangipahoa Parish	53,218	45,519	46,227
Ward 1	4,084	3,689	3,479
Kentwood town	*2,417*	*1,804*	*1,726*
Tangipahoa village	*852*	*519*	*304*
Ward 2	1,568	1,595	1,648
Ward 3	8,051	7,448	8,429
Amite City town	*2,804*	*2,499*	*2,536*
Roseland town	*1,038*	*878*	*1,189*
Ward 4	2,718	2,651	1,998
Ward 5	3,031	2,875	1,586
Ward 6	8,480	8,737	9,405
Independence town	*1,606*	*1,498*	*1,700*
Ward 7	23,382	17,487	18,553
Hammond city	*8,010*	*6,033*	*6,072*
Ponchatoula town	*4,090*	*4,001*	*2,898*
Ward 8	1,454	1,037	1,129
Tensas Parish	13,209	15,940	15,096
Ward 1	1,375	1,785	2,298
Ward 2	3,200	3,992	3,076
Newellton village	*1,280*	*789*	*627*
Ward 3 [40]	3,123	3,988	4,308
St Joseph town [40]	*1,218*	*1,096*	*884*
Ward 4	936	1,131	819
Ward 5	364	427	478
Ward 6	2,755	2,771	2,341
Waterproof town	*1,180*	*598*	*420*
Ward 7	1,456	1,846	1,776
Terrebonne Parish	43,328	35,880	29,816
Ward 1	2,933	2,610	2,017
Ward 2 [41]	1,668	2,239	1,966
Ward 3 [41]	22,558	13,307	9,299
Bayou Cane (uninc.)	*2,212*	-	-
Coteau (uninc.)	*1,214*	-	-
Daigleville (uninc.)	*4,809*	-	-
Houma city	*11,505*	*9,052*	*6,531*
Ward 4 [41]	3,353	4,744	3,857
Ward 5	1,319	1,391	1,295
Ward 6	2,594	2,399	1,880
Ward 7	4,079	3,612	3,136
Ward 8	1,995	2,350	3,422
Ward 9 [41]	1,212	1,723	1,419
Ward 10	1,617	1,505	1,525
Union Parish	19,141	20,943	20,731
Ward 1 [42]	3,580	3,248	2,948
Farmerville town [42]	*2,173*	*1,428*	*1,137*
Ward 2 [42]	2,600	2,766	2,936
Marion village [42]	*685*	*481*	*444*
Ward 3	2,615	3,305	3,333
Ward 4 [42]	3,486	3,932	3,545
Bernice town [42]	*1,524*	*1,071*	*965*
Ward 5	1,676	2,102	2,238
Ward 6	1,238	1,679	1,630
Ward 7	821	864	817
Ward 8	1,187	1,127	1,118
Ward 9	805	927	947
Ward 10	1,043	1,093	1,219
Junction City (part) [42]	*401*	*269*	*294*
Vermilion Parish	36,929	37,750	33,684
Ward 1, Lake Peigneur	4,320	4,734	4,014
Delcambre town (part) [43]	*796*	*672*	*368*
Erath town	*1,514*	*1,408*	*895*
Ward 2, Prairie Gregg	1,575	2,083	2,133
Ward 3 [43]	12,183	9,673	6,883
Abbeville city [43]	*9,338*	*6,672*	*4,356*
Ward 4, Broussard Cove	1,833	2,408	2,875
Maurice village	*335*	*320*	*330*
Ward 5, Queue Tortue	2,061	3,212	3,563
Ward 6, Cow Island	2,191	2,813	2,817
Ward 7, Moutons Cove	1,667	2,380	2,358
Ward 8, Gueydan	4,129	4,208	3,989
Gueydan town	*2,041*	*1,506*	*1,313*
Ward 9 [43]	6,970	6,179	5,052
Kaplan town [43]	*4,562*	*2,838*	*1,953*
Vernon Parish	18,974	19,142	20,047
Ward 1 [44]	7,185	5,297	5,474
Leesville town [44]	*4,670*	*2,829*	*3,291*
Newllano village [44]	*277*	-	-
Ward 2	2,886	3,074	3,578
Hornbeck town	*524*	*481*	*491*
Ward 3	1,482	1,644	1,675
Ward 4	1,108	1,143	2,467
Ward 5	2,115	2,558	2,392
Ward 6	1,213	2,721	4,461
Ward 7	2,023	1,547	-
Rosepine village	*334*	*407*	*214*
Ward 8	962	1,168	-
Washington Parish	38,371	34,443	29,904
Ward 1	1,274	1,315	1,390
Ward 2	1,683	2,009	1,866
Ward 3	4,153	3,375	2,324
Franklinton town	*2,348*	*1,579*	*965*
Ward 4	20,758	17,227	15,691
Bogalusa city	*17,798*	*14,604*	*14,029*
Washington Parish—Con.			
Ward 5	2,116	1,902	1,404
Varnado village	*306*	*310*	*204*
Ward 6	1,686	1,898	1,629
Ward 7	2,849	2,520	2,076
Angie village	*230*	*187*	*207*
Ward 8	2,692	2,809	2,244
Ward 9	1,160	1,388	1,280
Webster Parish	35,701	33,676	29,458
Ward 1	2,947	3,818	4,395
Ward 2 [45]	11,716	10,785	6,943
Cotton Valley town [45]	*1,188*	-	-
Springhill town [45]	*3,383*	*2,822*	*1,546*
Ward 3	4,647	4,242	4,015
Doyline town [45]	*1,170*	-	-
Ward 4	14,104	11,615	10,916
Minden city	*9,787*	*6,677*	*5,623*
Sibley town	*629*	*405*	*422*
Ward 5	2,390	3,215	3,189
West Baton Rouge Parish	11,738	11,263	9,716
Ward 1	962	1,085	1,013
Addis village	*605*	*492*	*425*
Ward 2	1,996	1,897	1,689
Brusly Landing village	*493*	*483*	*345*
Ward 3	4,048	3,026	2,381
Port Allen town	*3,097*	*1,898*	*1,524*
Ward 4	1,719	1,596	1,341
Ward 5	1,516	1,901	1,565
Ward 6	654	909	912
Ward 7	843	849	815
West Carroll Parish	17,248	19,252	13,895
Ward 1	2,266	2,435	2,139
Epps village	*308*	*391*	-
Ward 2	3,171	3,417	2,379
Ward 3	4,154	4,756	3,021
Ward 4	5,157	5,730	4,164
Oak Grove town	*1,795*	*1,654*	*1,241*
Ward 5	2,500	2,914	2,142
West Feliciana Parish	10,169	11,720	10,924
Ward 1	1,192	1,233	1,029
St Francisville town	*936*	*821*	*850*
Ward 2	646	770	931
Ward 3	1,544	1,741	1,440
Ward 4	658	867	915
Ward 5	504	656	1,049
Ward 7	3,554	3,898	3,106
Ward 8	487	785	826
Ward 9	566	749	581
Ward 10	973	1,241	1,046
Winn Parish	16,119	16,923	14,766
Ward 1 [46]	7,558	6,418	5,032
Winnfield town [46]	*5,629*	*4,512*	*3,721*
Ward 2	1,394	1,321	1,366
Ward 3	1,191	1,762	1,715
Sikes village [46]	*342*	-	-
Ward 4	629	824	665
Ward 5	1,158	1,515	1,362
Ward 6	741	974	1,012
Ward 7	1,465	1,919	1,782
Dodson village	*375*	*442*	*436*
Ward 8	1,046	1,155	930
Ward 9	374	488	455
Ward 10	543	547	448

[38] ST MARY —Part of ward 3, including Baldwin town, taken to form ward 10 in 1948 parts of ward 3 annexed to Franklin town in 1940 and 1948
[39] ST TAMMANY —Folsom town incorporated prior to 1940, but not previously reported
[40] TENSAS —Parts of ward 3 annexed to St Joseph town in 1944 1949, and 1950
[41] TERREBONNE —Parts of wards 2, 4, and 9 annexed to ward 3 in 1948
[42] UNION —Part of ward 1 annexed to Farmerville town in 1948 Part of ward 2 annexed to Marion village in 1949 Part of ward 4 annexed to Bernice town in 1949 For population of Junction City Ark, see footnote to table 7
[43] VERMILION —Delcambre town returned in 1940 as a village. Parts of ward 3 annexed to Abbeville city in 1944, 1945, and 1947 Abbeville city returned in 1940 as a town Parts of ward 9 annexed to Kaplan town in 1944, 1947, and 1950
[44] VERNON —Part of ward 1 annexed to Leesville town in 1948 Newllano village incorporated in 1942
[45] WEBSTER —Part of ward 2 annexed to Springhill town in 1945 Cotton Valley and Doyline towns incorporated in 1944 and 1948, respectively
[46] WINN —Part of ward 1 annexed to Winnfield town in 1947 Sikes village incorporated in 1946

Table 7.—POPULATION OF ALL INCORPORATED PLACES AND OF UNINCORPORATED PLACES OF 1,000 OR MORE: 1950 AND 1940

["Uninc." designates an unincorporated place. Figures for 1940 not available for unincorporated places and places incorporated subsequent to Apr. 1, 1940. Specific unincorporated places inside urbanized areas not separately identified and therefore not listed in this table. For 1930 population of incorporated places see table 6]

City, town, village, or unincorporated place	Parish	1950	1940
Abbeville	Vermilion	9,338	6,672
Abita Springs	St Tammany	659	528
Addis	West Baton Rouge	505	492
Alexandria	Rapides	34,913	27,066
Amite City	Tangipahoa	2,804	2,499
Angie	Washington	230	187
Arcadia	Bienville	2,241	1,601
Arnaudville	St Landry / St Martin	872	64[illegible]
Athens	Claiborne	487	491
Baker	East Baton Rouge	762	----
Baldwin	St Mary	1 38	984
Basile	Evangeline	1,572	1,132
Baskin	Franklin	117	330
Bastrop	Morehouse	12,769	6,626
Baton Rouge	East Baton Rouge	[1] 125,629	34,719
Bayou Cane (uninc.)	Terrebonne	2,212	----
Benton	Bossier	741	519
Bernice	Union	1,524	1,071
Berwick	St Mary	2,619	1,906
Bienville	Bienville	445	357
Bogalusa	Washington	17,798	14,604
Bonita	Morehouse	504	422
Bossier City	Bossier	15,470	5,786
Boyce	Rapides	981	732
Breaux Bridge	St Martin	2,492	1,668
Broussard	Lafayette	1,237	791
Brownsville (uninc.)	Ouachita	2,207	----
Brusly Landing	West Baton Rouge	493	433
Bryceland	Bienville	123	139
Buras-Triumph (uninc.)	Plaquemines	1,799	----
Bunkie	Avoyelles	4,666	3,575
Campti	Natchitoches	1,014	1,004
Carencro	Lafayette	1,587	914
Castor	Bienville	171	244
Chalmette (uninc.)	St Bernard	1,695	----
Chatham	Jackson	833	605
Cheneyville	Rapides	918	913
Choudrant	Lincoln	395	438
Church Point	Acadia	2,897	1,892
Clarks (uninc.)	Caldwell	1,345	----
Clayton	Concordia	657	----
Clinton	East Feliciana	1,383	998
Colfax	Grant	1,651	1,854
Collinston	Morehouse	546	482
Columbia	Caldwell	920	[1] 840
Converse	Sabine	311	314
Coteau (uninc.)	Terrebonne	1,214	----
Cottonport	Avoyelles	1,534	1,196
Cotton Valley	Webster	1,188	----
Coushatta	Red River	1,788	1,289
Covington	St Tammany	5,113	4,123
Crowley	Acadia	12,784	9,523
Daigleville (uninc.)	Terrebonne	4,809	----
Delcambre	Iberia / Vermilion	1,463	1,255
Delhi	Richland	1,861	1,192
Delta	Madison	150	183
Denham Springs	Livingston	2,053	1,233
De Quincy	Calcasieu	3,837	3,252
De Ridder	Beauregard	5,799	3,750
Dodson	Winn	375	442
Donaldsonville	Ascension	4,150	3,880
Doyline	Webster	1,170	----
Dry Prong	Grant	377	----
Dubach	Lincoln	705	749
Duson	Lafayette	707	463
Elizabeth (uninc.)	Allen	1,113	----
Elton	Jefferson Davis	1,434	901
Epps	West Carroll	308	391
Erath	Vermilion	1,514	1,408
Eros	Jackson	195	289
Estherwood	Acadia	547	539
Eunice	St Landry	8,184	5,242
Evergreen	Avoyelles	382	384
Farmerville	Union	2,173	1,428
Ferriday	Concordia	3,847	2,857

City, town, village, or unincorporated place	Parish	1950	1940
Folsom	St Tammany	166	----
Forest Hill	Rapides	265	302
Franklin	St Mary	6,144	4,274
Franklinton	Washington	2,342	1,579
Garyville (uninc.)	St John the Baptist	1,8[illegible]0	----
Georgetown	Grant	3[illegible]	----
Gibsland	Bienville	[illegible]085	1,023
Gilbert	Franklin	452	428
Glenmora	Rapides	1,50[illegible]	1,452
Golden Meadow (uninc.)	Lafourche	2,820	----
Goldonna	Natchitoches	364	256
Gonzales	Ascension	1,642	857
Gosport (uninc.)	Calcasieu	8,318	----
Gramercy	St James	1,84[illegible]	----
Grand Cane	De Soto	286	377
Grand Coteau	St Landry	1,103	662
Grand Isle (uninc.)	Jefferson	1,190	----
Grayson	Caldwell	455	407
Greensburg	St Helena	423	389
Gretna	Jefferson	13,813	10,879
Grosse Tete	Iberville	5[illegible]8	302
Gueydan	Vermilion	2,041	1,506
Hammond	Tangipahoa	8,010	6,033
Harahan	Jefferson	3,394	1,082
Harrisonburg	Catahoula	544	422
Haughton	Bossier	501	409
Haynesville	Claiborne	3,040	2,[illegible]18
Highland Park-Splane Place (uninc.)	Ouachita	1,665	----
Hodge	Jackson	1,386	1,445
Homer	Claiborne	4,749	3,497
Hornbeck	Vernon	424	481
Houma	Terrebonne	11,505	9,052
Independence	Tangipahoa	1,606	1,496
Iota	Acadia	1,162	1,000
Iowa (uninc.)	Calcasieu	1,125	----
Jackson	East Feliciana	6,772	5,384
Jeanerette	Iberia	4,692	3,362
Jena	La Salle	1,438	946
Jennings	Jefferson Davis	9,663	7,343
Jonesboro	Jackson	3,097	2,639
Jonesville	Catahoula	[illegible],904	2,080
Junction City [2]	Claiborne / Union	514	355
Kaplan	Vermilion	4,[illegible]02	2,538
Kenner	Jefferson	5,535	2,375
Kentwood	Tangipahoa	2,417	1,854
Kinder	Allen	2,003	475
Krotz Springs	St Landry	806	630
Lafayette	Lafayette	33,541	19,210
Lake Arthur	Jefferson Davis	2,849	2,131
Lake Charles	Calcasieu	41,272	21,207
Lake Providence	East Carroll	4,123	3,711
Laplace (uninc.)	St John the Baptist	2,352	----
Larose (uninc.)	Lafourche	1,286	----
Lecompte	Rapides	1,443	1,311
Leesville	Vernon	4,670	2,829
Leonville	St Landry	514	451
Lockport	Lafourche	1,388	877
Logansport	De Soto	1,270	1,222
Longstreet	De Soto	224	263
Loreauville	Iberia	478	490
Lutcher	St James	2,198	2,167
McNary	Rapides	267	1[illegible]1
Madisonville	St Tammany	861	915
Mamou	Evangeline	2,254	1,379
Mandeville	St Tammany	1,368	1,326
Mangham	Richland	554	572
Mansfield	De Soto	4,440	4,065
Mansura	Avoyelles	1,439	1,138
Many	Sabine	1,681	1,474
Maplewood (uninc.)	Calcasieu	2,671	----
Maringouin	Iberville	898	708
Marion	Union	685	481
Marksville	Avoyelles	3,635	1,811
Marthaville	Natchitoches	121	243

City, town, village, or unincorporated place	Parish	1950	1940
Maurice	Vermilion	385	420
Melville	St Landry	[illegible]861	828
Mermentau	Acadia	630	571
Mer Rouge	Morehouse	784	713
Merryville	Beauregard	1,383	1,216
Minden	Webster	9,787	6,677
Monroe	Ouachita	38,572	28,309
Montgomery	Grant	695	4[illegible]5
Mooringsport	Caddo	709	748
Moreauville	Avoyelles	835	815
Morgan City	St Mary	9,759	6,969
Morganza	Pointe Coupee	817	744
Morse	Acadia	679	742
Mound	Madison	105	145
Napoleonville	Assumption	1,260	1,301
Natchitoches	Natchitoches	9,914	6,812
New Llano	Vernon	277	----
Newellton	Tensas	1,280	789
New Iberia	Iberia	16,467	13,747
New Orleans	Orleans	[illegible]70,4[illegible]	494,53[illegible]
New Roads	Pointe Coupee	2,8[illegible]8	2,255
Noble	Sabine	238	238
Norco-Goodhope (uninc.)	St Charles	3,360	----
Norwood	East Feliciana	414	----
Oakdale	Allen	5,598	3,933
Oak Grove	West Carroll	1,786	1,654
Oak Ridge	Morehouse	287	373
Oberlin	Allen	1,544	962
Oil City	Caddo	422	----
Olla	La Salle	[illegible]115	691
Opelousas	St Landry	11,659	8,980
Palmetto	St Landry	457	444
Parks	St Martin	460	460
Patterson	St Mary	1,938	1,800
Pearl River	St Tammany	637	612
Pineville	Rapides	6,423	4,297
Plain Dealing	Bossier	1,321	1,085
Plaquemine	Iberville	5,747	5,049
Plaucheville	Avoyelles	277	307
Pleasant Hill	Sabine	856	787
Pollock	Grant	421	317
Ponchatoula	Tangipahoa	4,090	4,001
Port Allen	West Baton Rouge	3,097	1,398
Port Barre	St Landry	1,066	850
Port Barrow-Smoke Bend (uninc.)	Ascension	1,019	----
Potash-Port Sulphur (uninc.)	Plaquemines	1,255	----
Quitman	Jackson	204	212
Raceland (uninc.)	Lafourche	2,025	----
Rayne	Acadia	6,485	[illegible],9[illegible]4
Rayville	Richland	3,138	2,412
Reeves	Allen	106	120
Remy (uninc.)	St James	1,06[illegible]	----
Reserve (uninc.)	St John the Baptist	4,465	----
Ringgold	Bienville	1,007	1,006
Robeline	Natchitoches	350	355
Roseland	Tangipahoa	1,038	873
Rosepine	Vernon	334	407
Ruston	Lincoln	10,372	7,107
St. Francisville	West Feliciana	936	821
St Joseph	Tensas	1,218	1,096
St Martinville	St Martin	4,611	3,501
Saline	Bienville	357	381
Scott	Lafayette	688	407
Shreveport	Caddo	127,206	98,167
Sibley	Webster	623	405
Sikes	Winn	342	----
Simmesport	Avoyelles	1,510	1,215
Slaughter	East Feliciana	290	306
Slidell	St Tammany	3,464	2,864
South Mansfield	De Soto	276	433
Springhill	Webster	3,383	2,822
Sulphur	Calcasieu	5,996	3,504
Sunset	St Landry	1,080	630
Tallulah	Madison	7,758	5,712
Tangipahoa	Tangipahoa	352	319

[1] Corrected figure; see footnote 10, table 6.
[2] Population of Junction City in Union County, Ark.: 1,013 in 1950; 797 in 1940; 814 in 1930.

Table 7.—POPULATION OF ALL INCORPORATED PLACES AND OF UNINCORPORATED PLACES OF 1,000 OR MORE 1950 AND 1940—Con

City, town, village, or unincorporated place	Parish	1950	1940	City, town, village, or unincorporated place	Parish	1950	1940	City, town, village, or unincorporated place	Parish	1950	1940
Thibodaux	Lafourche	7,730	5,851	Vivian	Caddo	2,426	2,460	White Castle	Iberville	1,839	1,692
Tioga	Rapides	338	1,300	Walker	Livingston	500	424	Winnfield	Winn	5,629	4,512
Tullos	La Salle	732	589	Washington	St Landry	1,291	1,264	Winnsboro	Franklin	3,655	2,834
Turnerville (uninc)	Iberville	1,048	-	Waterproof	Tensas	1,180	592	Wisner	Franklin	738	617
Urania (uninc)	La Salle	1,004	-	Weeks Island (uninc)	Iberia	1,499		Woodworth	Rapides	392	---
Varnado	Washington	306	315	Welsh	Jefferson Davis	2,416	1,822	Youngsville	Lafayette	769	647
Vidalia	Concordia	1,641	1,318	Westlake	Calcasieu	1,871	-	Zachary	East Baton Rouge	1,542	730
Ville Platte	Evangeline	6,633	3,721	West Monroe	Ouachita	10,302	8,560				
Vinton	Calcasieu	2,597	1,787	Westwego	Jefferson	8,328	4,992	Zwolle	Sabine	1,555	1,600

Table 8.—POPULATION OF INCORPORATED PLACES OF 5,000 OR MORE, BY WARDS 1950

[Other incorporated places of 5,000 or more (Abbeville, Alexandria, Baton Rouge, Bogalusa, De Ridder, Gretna, Hammond, Houma, Jennings, Lafayette, Lake Charles, Minden, Monroe, Morgan City, Natchitoches, New Iberia, New Orleans, Oakdale, Shreveport, Thibodaux, and West Monroe cities; Bastrop, Bossier City, Covington, Eunice, Franklin, Jackson, Kenner, Plaquemine, Rayne, Ville Platte, Westwego, and Winnfield towns, and Tallulah village) have no wards]

City or town and ward	Population	City or town and ward	Population	City or town and ward	Population	City or town and ward	Population	City or town and ward	Population
Crowley city	12,784	**Opelousas city**	11,659	**Pineville city**	6,423	**Ruston town**	10,372	**Sulphur town**	5,996
Ward 1	5,243	Ward 1	1,801	Ward 1	1,183	Ward 1	833	Ward 1	1,054
Ward 2	1,064	Ward 2	3,014	Ward 2	2,476	Ward 2	1,892	Ward 2	2,238
Ward 3	3,199	Ward 3	3,433	Ward 3	1,272	Ward 3	5,105	Ward 3	1,447
Ward 4	3,278	Ward 4	3,321	Ward 4	1,492	Ward 4	2,542	Ward 4	1,257

Table 9.—POPULATION OF URBANIZED AREAS 1950

Area	Population
BATON ROUGE URBANIZED AREA	
The area	138,864
Baton Rouge city	125,629
Outside city	13,235
The urbanized area includes the following minor civil division and parts of minor civil divisions	
East Baton Rouge Parish (part)	135,767
Police jury ward 1	125,629
Baton Rouge city	125,629
Police jury ward 2 (part)	10,138
West Baton Rouge Parish (part)	3,097
Police jury ward 3 (part)	3,097
Port Allen town	3,097
NEW ORLEANS URBANIZED AREA	
The area	659,768
New Orleans city	570,445
Outside city	89,323
The urbanization area includes the following parish and parts of minor civil divisions	
Jefferson Parish (part)	86,680
Police jury ward 1 (part)	6,311
Gretna city (part)	6,311
Police jury ward 2 (part)	2,881
Gretna city (part)	2,881
Police jury ward 3 (part)	7,980
Gretna city (part)	4,621

Area	Population
NEW ORLEANS URBANIZED AREA—Con.	
Jefferson Parish (part)—Con	
Police jury ward 4 (part)	25,094
Westwego town	8,328
Police jury ward 7 (part)	15,897
Police jury ward 8 (part)	25,123
Police jury ward 9 (part)	3,394
Harahan village	3,394
Orleans Parish	570,445
New Orleans city	570,445
St Bernard Parish (part)	2,643
Police jury ward 1 (part)	2,622
Police jury ward 2 (part)	21
SHREVEPORT URBANIZED AREA	
The area	150,208
Shreveport city	127,206
Outside city	23,002
The urbanized area includes the following parts of minor civil divisions	
Bossier Parish (part)	16,779
Police jury ward 1 (part)	251
Bossier City town (part)	251
Police jury ward 2 (part)	16,528
Bossier City town (part)	15,219
Caddo Parish (part)	133,429
Police jury ward 4 (part)	133,429
Shreveport city	127,206

URBANIZED AREA MAPS

The three urbanized areas located in Louisiana, for which statistics are shown in table 9 are depicted in the following maps The shaded areas, in combination comprise the urbanized area To assist in locating the exact external boundaries of the area.

each pouldary feature (street acgment, political boundary, or other) has been assigned a number. The boundary segments thus numbered are snown on the map and the features to which trey apply are presented in the following key

KEY TO NUMBERED BOUNDARY SEGMENTS

Baton Rouge Urbanized Area

Main urbanized part: (1) East Baton Rouge-West Baton Rouge Main urbanized part: (1) East Baton Rouge-West Baton Rouge parish nne, (2) Devil's Swamp, (3) extension of Mills Ave and Mills Ave, (4) Avenue "D," (5) Elmer Ave, (6) L & A R R, (7) Sapsucker St., (8) Scenic Highway (U S Highways 61 and 65), (9) Thomas Rd (State Highway 882), (10) Baker Highway (Seotland Ave), (11) Baker Lane, (12) Giddens Rd (Giobons Lane), (13) Blount Rd, (14) Catherine St. (Amanda St.), (15) Frogress Rd, (16) Scenic Highway (U S Highways 61 and 65), (17) Rosenwald Rd, (18) Y & M V R R, (19) Y & M V R R, spur, (20) Rosenwald Rd,

(21) property line of Harding Field, (22) Blount Rd, (23) Plank Rd, (24) Badley Rd, (25) Airbase Ave, (26) Harding Blvd, (27) Seeme Highway (U. 8 Highways 61 and 65), (28) Y & M V R R, (29) property line of Mengal Co. (30) Seeme Highway (U. 8 Highways 61 and 65), (31) 75th Ave and 75th Ave extension, (32) Monte Sano Bayou, (33) corporate limits of Baton Rouge, (34) corporate limits of Port Allen, (35) corporate limits of Baton Baton Rouge

Outlying urbanized part: (36) Plank Rd., (37) Ford St., (38) Apperson St., (39) Cadillac St. (40) White St. (41) Page St., (42) Mitchell St. (43) Peerless St., (44) Apperson St., (45) Monarch

New Orleans Urbanized Area

Main urbanized part (1) Corporate limits of New Orleans, (2) St Claude Ave (St Bernard's Highway), (3) Southern R R spur and Southern R R spur extension, (4) corporate (19) extension of unnamed road and unnamed road, (20) Baratana Rd (State Highway 30),

(21) Belle Terre Rd (Bekon Rd) and Belle Terre Rd exten-(21) Belle Terre Rd (Bekon Rd) and Belle Terre Rd extension, (22) Majronne Canal, (23) extension of Victory Dr and Victory Dr, (24) corporate limits of Westwego, (25) corporate limits of New Orleans, (26) Ward 4-Ward 7 line, (27) U S Highway 90 (28) Jefferson Highway (U S Highway 55, State Highway 1), (29) drainage ditch (30) extension of Cross St and Cross St, (31) 2d St, (32) Belt Line R R, (33) Ward 7-Ward S line (34) unnamed canal, (35) Arline Highway, (36) Rose Ave, (37) Canal 5, (38) Manson Ave (39) Airline Highway, (40) Cleary

(41) Bauvis St., (42) drainage ditch, (43) Canal 5, (44) extension of St. Rene St., (45) Arnoult Rd., (46) 47th St. and 47th St. extension, (17) Athania Parkwar (48) 44th St., (49) Ridgelake Dr., (50) 45th St. (1da St.), (51) Metairie Lawn Dr., (52) Calloude St., (53) Labarre Rd., (54) Canal 4, (55) drainage canal, (56) extension of Socrates St. and Socrates St., (57) Helois Ave. and Helois Ave. extension, (58) Canal 3, (59) Bonnabel Blvd., (60) Regroup St. Feronia St ,

(61) Onon Ave, (62) Pomona St. (63) Phosphor Ave, (64) Canal 3, (65) Lake Pontchartram Ave, (66) Hollygrove St., (67) Canal 3, (63) Lake Fortena train Ate, (60) Honggrove of 101/10/10 Myrtle St, (71) Carrollton St, (72) Canal 3, (73) corporate units of New Orleans, (74) Dubun St, (75) Carroll Canal (Canal 21, (76) extension of Choctaw St, Choctaw St, and extension of Choctaw St , (77) Lake Pontanartrain

Outlying urbanized parts (78) U.S. Highway 90, (79) State Highway 430 (Old Spanish Trail), (80) levee of the Mississippi River, (81) property line of W.A. Ransom Lumber Co., (82) levee of the Mississippi River, (83) corporate limits of Harahan, (84) Jefferson Highway (U.S. Highway 65, State Highway 1), (85) Levee of the Mississippi River, (83) Corporate limits of Harahan, (84) Jefferson Highway (U.S. Highway 65, State Highway 1), (85) Hines St, (86) Rhomberg Ave (Rhombers Ave), (87) Meirose St, (88) Evans Ave, (89) Butler St, (90) Edwards Ave

Shreveport Urbanized Area

(1) Corporate limits of Bossier City, (2) C B. R. R., (3) North-side Dr and Northside Dr extension, (4) L & A R R., (5)

side Dr and Northside Dr extension, (4) L & A R R, (5) corporate limits of Bossier City, (6) private road, (7) property line of Southern Acid & Sulphur Co., (8) I C R R, (9) drainage canal, (10) property line of Cities Service Oil Co., (11) private road, 12) Dime Overland Highway (U S Highway 80) (13) Jacquelyn St, (14) Bobbie St. (15) Waller Ave, (16) corporate limits of Bossier City, (17) corporate limits of Shreveport, (18) St. Vincent St., (19) T & P R R, (20) Linwood Ave, (21) West 85th St, (22) Welsh Ave., (23) West 82d St., (24) corporate limits of Shreveport, (25) Walace Ave and Wallace Ave extension, (26) Vernon St. (27) 4th Ave (Urion Ave.), (28) corporate limits of Shreveport, (29) Hollywood Ave., (31) Wagner Ave., (32) Jewella Rd, (33) Ward 4-Ward 7 line, (34) Murry St., (35) Henry St. (36) Cemetery Rd. (37) corporate limits of Shreveport, (38) Dilg Dr., (39) Lake Shore Dr., (42) Mooringsport Rd. (North Market St.), (43) corporate limits of Shreveport (41) K C 8 & T & P R R, (22) Moreoport Rd. (North Market St.), (43) corporate limits of Shreveport of Shreveport

LOUISIANA
BATON ROUGE URBANIZED AREA

NUMBER OF INHABITANTS

18-17

NEW ORLEANS URBANIZED AREA—SECTION 1

NEW ORLEANS URBANIZED AREA—SECTION 3

LOUISIANA SHREVEPORT URBANIZED AREA

GENERAL CHARACTERISTICS

Louisiana

LIST OF TABLES

[Page numbers listed here omit the State prefix number which appears as part of the page number for each page. The prefix for this State is 18]

Tabl	THE STATE Summary	Page	Table STANDARD METROPOLITAN AREAS URBANIZED AREAS Page AND URBAN PLACES OF 10,000 OR MORE
10 -	Summary of population characteristics for the State (_rban and rural), standard metropolitan areas, urban zed sreas,		33 —Agc b. color and -ea for standard metrops standards., in Lantzed areas, and inhun maces of 13/-20 or more 1930 44
	and urban places of 10 000 or more 1959 Summary of population characteristics, for urban places 1950	23	34 -Genural anamacteristics of the population, for standard metro- poultail sites urbanized areas and iroan places of 10 000 or more 1900.
	Summary of population characteristics, for parishes 1550	25	35 — Economic characteristics of the propuletion, by sex, for standard metropolitan areas - rbanized areas and urban places of 10 900 or more 1950 — 51
	(Figures for 1950 are presented according to new and cid urban definitions) Race by sex for the State, tybun and rural 1950, and for the	26	do —Coaracteristics of the monwhite population for standard metropolitan areas urbanized steas, and urban places of
15 -	State 1880 to 1940	26	37—Income in 1949 of families and unrelated individuals for standard metropolitan areas, urbs ized areas, and trben
	old urban (letinitions) -Age by color and sex, for the State 1880 to 1950 -Citizen ship and nativity of the population 2, years old and over	27 30	r laces or 10,000 or more 1950 56 37a - Ircome ur 1949 or nonwhite fam.les and unrelated and aduals, for standard metropolitan areas, urner zed aras, and urban
	tor the State, urban and rural, 1930 and for the State 1940 and 1930	32	plases of 10.000 or more 1950 57
19 —	urban and rural 1950 -School enrollment by age, for the State 1930 to 1950 -Years of school completed by persons 25 years old and over	32 32	PARISHES AND PLACES OF LESS THAN 10 000
21 -	by color and by sex for the State urban and rural, 1 '50, and for the State 1940	32	38 Gereral characteristics of the population, for urban places of 2,500 to 10 000 1950 58
22 -	and for the State 1940 -Married couples, families households, and in-titutional ponulation, for the State urban and rural 1950	24	39 —Economic characterist os of the population by sex for urban places of 2,500 to 10,000 1950 61
	-Residence in 1919, by color, for the State, urban and rural 1950 -Country of birth of foreign-born population, for the State,	34	40 —Race, age, and rual-farm population, by sex, for places of 1 000 to 2 500 1950
	uroan and rural, 1980, and for the State, 1860 to 1940 Economic Statistics	4	41 —Age by color and sex, for parking 1950 67 42 — Genumal characteristics of the population for marking 1950 78
	-Employment status by color and sex for the State urban and urral 1950	35	43 — Economic characteristics of the population, by sev, for parishes 1950.
	1920 by colo. and sex, for the StateEurployment status by color and sex, for the State 1950 and	36	44 — Characteristics of the norwhite population, for parisines 1950. 90 45 — Injoune in 1949 of families and unrelated individuals, for parishes 1950. 950.
28 ~	1940	36	45a -Income in 1940 o nonwhite families and unrelated ind viduals, for purishes 1950
28a	State, urban and rural 1950 Class of we ket and major occupation group of employed white	37	46 —Income in 1949 of 1 rban and rural-nonfarm families and unre- lated individuals, for purishes 1950 ————————————————————————————————————
29 -	and nonwhite persons by sex, for the State, urban and rural 1950 -Class of worker and major occupation group of employed	38	47 —Ind ans Japanese and Chinose, by sex, for selected punshes and cities 1950.
30 —	persons, nv sex for the State 1950 and 1940 -Industry group of employed persons by sex, for the State uroan and riral 1950	39	18—Characteristics of the rural-nonfarm population for parishes 1950
	-Industry group of employed white and nonwhite persons for the State urban and rural 1950	40	oarishes 1950
	-Industry group of employed persons by sex for the State 1950 and 1940	41	1950 106 49a - Characteristics of the rural-farm nonwhite population for
	State, urban and rural 1959	42	patishes 1950
	individuals for the State, urban and rural 1930	43	color, and sex for selected parishes 1950

Table 10 —SUMMARY OF POPULATION CHARACTERISTICS, FOR THE STATE URBAN AND RURAL, STANDARD METROPOLITAN AREAS, URBANIZED AREAS AND URBAN PLACES OF 10 000 OR MORE 1950

[Asterisk (*) denotes statistics based on 20-percent sample Minus sign (−) denotes decrease Percent not shown where less than 0.1 For complete-count items, percent and median not shown where base is less than 100 for sample items percent and median not shown where base is less than 500 For additional statistics for [illegible] shown in this table see tables 33 to 37]

Area	Total population — Number	Percent increase 1940 to 1950	Median age years	Percent 65 years old and over	Percent non white	Persons per household	Married couples — Percent without own household*	Persons 1 year old and over — Percent in same house 1949 and 1950*	Persons [illegible] 7 years old — Percent in school*	Persons 25 yrs. old and over — Median school years completed*	Persons 14 years old and over — Number in labor force	Male — Percent in labor force	Female — Percent in labor force	Civilian labor force — Percent unemployed	Employed — Percent engaged in manufacturing	Families and unrelated individuals — Median income* (dollars)	Percent having incomes less than $2,000*
The State	2,68[illegible]	[illegible]	25.[illegible]	6.[illegible]	32.[illegible]	3.6[illegible]	[illegible]7	80.5	79	[illegible]	[illegible],626	75.5	2[illegible].6	4.6	15.[illegible]	[illegible],810	[illegible]3.9
Urban	1,47[illegible],[illegible]96	[illegible]	[illegible]	6.4	30.[illegible]	[illegible]	7.[illegible]	[illegible]	82.[illegible]	8.[illegible]	[illegible]	[illegible]	[illegible]	[illegible]3	16.2	[illegible]	[illegible]0
Rural nonfarm	[illegible]44,36[illegible]	[illegible]7	[illegible]9	7.4	[illegible]	[illegible]	[illegible]	[illegible]	[illegible]4	6.5	[illegible]168,[illegible]	[illegible]	[illegible]	5.3	20.[illegible]	[illegible],460	6[illegible].8
Rural farm	[illegible] 455	[illegible]3.2	[illegible]6	6.[illegible]	4[illegible]	4.[illegible]	[illegible]8	[illegible]2	[illegible]	[illegible]6.[illegible]	[illegible],406	[illegible]	[illegible]	1.5	[illegible]5	1,[illegible]6	74.7
STANDARD METROPOLITAN AREAS																	
Baton Rouge	[illegible]58,236	7[illegible]	26.3	[illegible]	3[illegible]	[illegible]4[illegible]	[illegible]	76.3	83.6	[illegible]8	[illegible]58,9[illegible]	[illegible]8	[illegible]	4.9	2[illegible].4	[illegible],[illegible]18	4[illegible].0
New Orleans	68[illegible],4[illegible]	[illegible]	30.0	6.7	29.3	3.36	9.[illegible]	80.[illegible]	82.[illegible]	8.5	275,[illegible]	78.8	[illegible]	6.0	15.7	2,33[illegible]	42.9
Shreveport	[illegible]6 [illegible]47	17	[illegible]8.[illegible]	[illegible]8	27.[illegible]	3.[illegible]	8.[illegible]	[illegible]2	84.4	9.[illegible]	[illegible]0,090	[illegible]	[illegible]	[illegible]0	11.3	2,157	4[illegible]
URBANIZED AREAS																	
Baton Rouge	[illegible]38,[illegible]	[illegible]	26.3	[illegible]	3[illegible]	3.44	6.[illegible]	75.[illegible]	83.[illegible]	10.2	[illegible] 2[illegible]0	78.3	31.3	[illegible]9	23.7	2,699	[illegible]9.[illegible]
New Orleans	[illegible]9,768	[illegible]	[illegible]	5.7	29.0	3.35	9.[illegible]	80.[illegible]	83.[illegible]	8.6	2[illegible]	7[illegible]	31.3	6.0	15.0	2,342	42.7
Shreveport	1[illegible]0,[illegible]	[illegible]	28.[illegible]	6.2	32.5	3.3[illegible]	8.4	7[illegible].8	83.8	10.[illegible]	62,69[illegible]	81	3[illegible]	3.2	1[illegible]	2,396	42.7
URBAN PLACES																	
Alexandria	[illegible],9[illegible]	29.0	2[illegible]	[illegible]7	[illegible]5	3.30	7.[illegible]	78.[illegible]	[illegible]4	8.7	[illegible]3,668	76.8	34.0	5.[illegible]	[illegible]9	2,012	49.8
Bastrop	1[illegible],7[illegible]9	92	[illegible]	[illegible]	3[illegible]	3.4[illegible]	[illegible]	[illegible]	87.[illegible]	[illegible]9	4,717	[illegible]8	27.5	[illegible]8	4[illegible].9	2,38[illegible]	40.3
Baton Rouge	125,629	26[illegible]	26.9	4.4	28.0	[illegible]1	[illegible]	75.[illegible]	85.2	10.6	4[illegible]	7[illegible].3	32.[illegible]	[illegible]	23	2,8[illegible]	38.2
Bogalusa	17,[illegible]98	[illegible]	26.9	5.4	32	3.45	[illegible]4	83.[illegible]	8[illegible]	[illegible]	6,3[illegible]	77.4	27.2	[illegible]2	40.2	2,1[illegible]	[illegible]4
Bossier City	15,470	167.4	[illegible]0	[illegible]0	1[illegible]	[illegible]24	[illegible]9	[illegible]	53.0	1[illegible]	[illegible],86[illegible]	85.9	26.6	[illegible]	10.8	3,039	28.2
Crowley	12,784	34.2	26.[illegible]	6.7	2[illegible]	3.47	[illegible]6	8[illegible]	[illegible]4.7	[illegible]9	[illegible]21[illegible]	70.[illegible]	25.[illegible]	7.5	[illegible]8	1,812	5[illegible].6
Gretna	13,813	2[illegible]	28.3	6.1	26.8	3.4[illegible]	7.4	84.1	81.6	7.5	5,12[illegible]	79.1	26.[illegible]	[illegible]7	26.3	2,284	41.8
Houma	11,505	[illegible]	26.[illegible]	6.[illegible]	[illegible]6.0	3.6[illegible]	[illegible]	80.8	82.6	[illegible]8	4,187	81.9	25.7	5.5	10.3	[illegible],565	38.2
Lafayette	33,54[illegible]	74.6	25.4	4.9	2[illegible].8	3.48	6.4	[illegible]	77.2	[illegible]9	[illegible]2,384	[illegible]2.3	[illegible]	4.4	8.7	1,898	52.[illegible]
Lake Charles	41,272	[illegible]4.[illegible]	2[illegible]	4.9	27.[illegible]	3.39	[illegible]0	[illegible]8	83.8	[illegible]0	16,413	81.7	30.7	[illegible]	20.3	2,825	3[illegible].2
Monroe	38,[illegible]	[illegible]	29.4	6.9	4[illegible].3	3.24	[illegible]9	74.[illegible]	8[illegible].5	8.[illegible]	16,101	78.3	37.8	[illegible]	11.6	[illegible],93[illegible]	5[illegible].5
New Iberia	16,467	19.8	27.[illegible]	6.[illegible]	2[illegible].0	3.[illegible]1	6.1	80.9	[illegible]	7.7	5,979	77.3	28.3	[illegible]6	7.7	2,449	4[illegible].3
New Orleans	570,44[illegible]	15.3	30.9	7.[illegible]	32.0	3.31	9.8	81.4	82	8.6	233,979	[illegible]8.3	3[illegible].2	[illegible]	[illegible]4.2	2,25[illegible]	44.4
Opelousas	[illegible]1,[illegible]5[illegible]	29.8	2[illegible].6	6.[illegible]	4[illegible]	3.[illegible]3	[illegible]6	85.3	[illegible]3.9	[illegible]	3,755	70.1	2[illegible]	2.5	10.[illegible]	1,727	55.2
Ruston	10,372	45.9	24.4	6.6	[illegible]0	[illegible]31	[illegible]7	[illegible]2.1		[illegible]9	3,[illegible]4	57.0	33.[illegible]	1.7	[illegible]0	1,39[illegible]	6[illegible]
Shreveport	127,206	29.6	29.5	[illegible]7	3[illegible].2	[illegible]28	[illegible]	7[illegible]	83.[illegible]	[illegible]2	[illegible],396	80.8	37.1	3.2	1[illegible]	2,326	4[illegible]
West Monroe	10,302	20.4	28.8	5.5	20.4	[illegible]31	6.[illegible]	[illegible]		9.[illegible]	4,[illegible]	81.[illegible]	34.9	3.3	21.2	2,650	3[illegible].6

[1] Based on old urban definition
[2] 1940 figures not available

Table 11 —SUMMARY OF POPULATION CHARACTERISTICS, FOR URBAN PLACES 1950

[Asterisk (*) denotes statistics based on 20-percent sample Minus sign (−) denotes decrease Percent not shown where less than 0.1 For complete-count items, percent and median not shown where base is less than 100 for sample items percent and median not shown where base is less than 500 For additional statistics for places of 10,000 and over see tables 33 to 37 for places of 2,500 to 10,000 see tables 38 and 39]

Urban place	Total population — Number	Percent increase 1940 to 1950	Median age (years)	Percent 65 years old and over	Percent non-white	Persons 25 years old and over — Median school years completed*	Persons 14 years old and over — Number in labor force	Male — Percent in labor force	Female — Percent in labor force	Civilian labor force — Percent unemployed	Employed — Percent engaged in manufacturing	Families and unrelated individuals — Median income* (dollars)	Percent having incomes less than $2 000*
Abbeville	9,338	40.0	2[illegible].8	7.2	16.1	5.7	3,110	[illegible]0.8	25.0	[illegible]1	8.8	1,600	59.3
Alexandria	34,913	29.0	29.3	[illegible]7	41.[illegible]	8.7	[illegible]3,668	76.8	34.0	5.4	11.9	2,012	49.8
Amite City	2,804	12.2	29.7	9.3	30.[illegible]	9.[illegible]	1,025	[illegible]4.3	30.2	2.5	15.2	1 838	55.0
Bastrop	12,769	92.7	25.9	[illegible]	34.[illegible]	[illegible]9	4,717	79.8	27.5	6.8	43.9	2,38[illegible]	40.3
Baton Rouge	125 629	26[illegible].8	26.9	4.4	28.0	10.6	49,152	[illegible]6.3	32.2	4.5	23.7	2,85[illegible]	38.2
Berwick	2,619	37.4	25.0	6.3	13.7	6.5	85[illegible]	81.7	16.9	9.1	14.6	2,406	41.1
Bogalusa	17 798	21.9	26.9	5.4	32.3	8.1	6,350	77.4	27.2	5.2	40.2	2,112	47.4
Bossier City	15,470	167.4	26.0	3.0	16.1	[illegible]1.6	5,865	85.9	26.6	4.1	10.8	3,039	28.2
Bunkie	4,666	30.5	26.3	6.[illegible]	27.2	7.7	[illegible],58[illegible]	76.9	25.0	6.1	[illegible].2	[illegible],921	51.9
Church Point	2 897	53.1	23.9	[illegible].9	13.7	4.9	[illegible]29	74.9	2[illegible].7	4.6	4.9	1,519	59.9
Covington	5,113	24.0	28.3	9.7	32.3	8.[illegible]	1,658	70.5	25.1	2.4	12.9	1,500	64.8
Crowley	12,784	34.2	26.1	6.[illegible]	26.[illegible]	6.9	4,211	70.5	25.9	[illegible].5	13.8	1 812	5[illegible].6
Daigleville (uninc.)	4,809	([1])	21.4	[illegible].2	18.8	5.6	[illegible],485	81.8	1[illegible].9	6.5	18.2	1,937	51.8
De Quincy	3,837	18.0	28.4	5.8	22.2	8.1	[illegible],425	80.[illegible]	23.0	2.5	19.2	2,523	38.4
De Ridder	5,799	54.6	28.[illegible]	7.3	29.7	8.2	2,[illegible]32	[illegible]6.4	25.8	4.7	26.9	1,[illegible]64	54.9
Donaldsonville	4,150	6.7	28.[illegible]	8.7	37.8	7.6	[illegible],394	[illegible]3.1	25.8	9.3	12.1	1,360	62.5
Eunice	8,184	56.1	24.[illegible]	5.6	23.4	5.9	2,[illegible]46	7[illegible].1	26.0	5.5	12.4	1,728	58.1
Ferriday	3,847	34.7	29.[illegible]	8.5	60.[illegible]	6.8	[illegible] 326	[illegible]2.5	29.[illegible]	4.1	14.[illegible]	1,245	69.2
Franklin	6 144	43.8	27.6	7.7	30.2	[illegible].9	2,38[illegible]	82.3	29.9	5.4	14.8	2,272	44.9
Golden Meadow (uninc.)	2,820	([1])	22.0	[illegible].0		4.3	890	81.6	12.5	5.7	10.8	2,553	38.0
Goosport (uninc.)	8,318	([1])	22.2	3.9	42.4	6.0	2,574	77.8	1[illegible].8	9.2	24.2	2,083	47.6
Gretna	13,813	2[illegible].0	28.3	6.1	28.8	7.5	5 122	[illegible]9.1	26.3	[illegible].7	26.3	2,284	41.8
Hammond	8 010	32.8	26.7	7.3	[illegible].9	8.9	2,931	65.3	33.6	1.9	12.2	1 276	64.0
Harahan	3 394	213.7	25.7	3.6	0.8	8.9	1,246	86.2	22.4	5.1	17.8	3,189	20.6

[1] 1940 figures not available

Table 11 -- SUMMARY OF POPULATION CHARACTERISTICS, FOR URBAN PLACES 1950

Antenia. ***) denotes this state bases on 20-percent sample. Manus sign (**) denotes .ecrease. Percer, not anown where .ess than 0.1. For complete-count name, seriest and menum not shown where bases in less than 10.0 for sample : one percent and menum not shown where bases in less than 200. For additional states for pares of 10 (9), and over see tables \$3 \to 37 for places or 250 to 10,000 are tables \$3.0 million for sample : one percent and menum not shown where bases in less than 200. For additional states for pares of 10 (9), and over see tables \$3.7 for places or 250 to 10,000 are tables \$3.0 million for sample : one percent and menum not shown where less than 200. For additional states for pares of 10 (9), and over see tables \$3.7 for places or 250 to 10,000 are tables \$3.0 million for sample : one percent and menum not shown where less than 200. For additional states for pares of 10 (9), and over see tables \$3.7 for places or 250 to 10,000 are tables \$3.0 million for sample : one percent and menum not shown where less than 200. For additional states for pares of 10 (9), and over see tables \$3.7 for places or 250 to 10,000 are tables \$3.0 million for sample : one percent and menum not shown where less than 200 is a state for pares of 10 (9), and over see tables \$3.0 million for sample : one percent and menum not shown where less than 200 is a state for pares of 10 (9).

		Tota	population			Persons 25 years old	Persons 14	year old an	d over	Civilan	Employed	Pamilies atod in	and unre
Urban place	Number	Percenting rease 19±0 to 1950	Median age cars)	Purcent So year old and over	Percent non- white	Mequan school year- commeted*	\umber in labor rorce	Male Percent in labor orce	Percent in abor force	Percent unem proyed	Percent eng.gra in ms.u- racturmg	M-diar. income* (dellars)	Percent having mechan less tran \$2 000*
Abbeville ale ardr.a Amite City Bastrop Batron Rouge	9,938 34,913 2,804 -2,769 125 629	40 0 29 0 12 2 92 7 264 8	27 8 29 3 29 7 25 9 26 9	7 2 0 7 9 3 4 4	16 1 44 5 30 7 34 7 28 0	57 87 91 /9	3,110 -3,608 1,025 4,717 49,152	70 8 70 8 70 8 70 8 70 8 70 8 70 8 70 8	25 0 34 0 30 2 27 5 32 2	7 1 5 4 2 5 6 8 4 5	8 8 11 9 14 2 43 9 23 7	1,600 2,012 1 838 2,38/ 2,850	59 49 55 40 38
Bewilk sogalisa bossis Ch., Suncia Church Point	2,619 1° 798 _5,470 4,665 2 897	37 4 21 9 107 4 30 5 53 1	25 0, 26 9 26 0 26 3 23 9	6 3 5 4 3 0 6 /	13 7 32 3 16 1 27 2 13 7	-+ 6 7 7	855 6,350 5,863 -,261 729	81. 7 77. 4 85. 9 76. 9 74. 9	16 9 27 2 26 6 25 0 2/ 7	9 1 5 2 4 1 6 1 4 6	14 6 40 2 10 8 7 2 4 9	2,406 2,112 3,039 -,921 1,519	41 47 28 51 59
Covington Crowley Daig! Wille (_ninc De Quincy De Pidder	5,113 12,784 4,809 3,837 5,799	24 0 34 2 (1) 18 0 54 6	28 3 26 1 21 4 28 4 28 1	9 7 6 7 7 2 5 8 7 3	32 3 26 - 18 8 22 2 29 7	6 9 5 6 8 1	1,658 4,211 -,485 2,425 2,432	70 5 70 5 81. 8 80 6 76 4	25 1 25 9 1" 9 23 0 25 8	2 4 7 5 6 5 2 5 4 7	12 9 13 8 18 2 19 2 26 9	1,500 1 812 1,937 2,523 1,764	53 53 38 54
Donaldsorvalle Eunics Fermiday Franklin Golsen Mendor (unics)	4,150 8,184 3,847 6 144 2,820	6 7 56 1 34 7 43 8 (1)	28 2 24 9 29 1 27 6 22 0	8 7, 5 6, 8 5, 7 7, 3 0	37 8 23 4 60 9 30 2	6.8	2,746 2,746 2,36 2,385	75 1 76 1 72 5 82 3 81 6	25 8 26 0 29 9 29 9 12 5	9 3 5 5 4 1 5 4 5 7	12 1 12 4 14 9 14 8 10 8	1,360 1,728 1,245 2,272 2,553	62 58 69 44 38
Coospo⇒+ (unino) Dretna Havmond Ha∵anax	8,318 13,813 8 010 3 394	(1) 2° 0 32 8 213 7	22 2 28 3 26 7 25 7	3 9 ₁ 6 1 ₁ 7 3	28 8	6 0 7 5 8 9 8 9	2,574 5 122 2,931 1,246	77 8 79 1 65 3 86 2	1º 8 26 3 33 6 22 4	9 2 3 7 1 9 5 1	24 2 26 3 12 2 17 8	2,083 2,284 1 276 3,189	47 41 64 20

^{1 1940} figures not available

Table 11 —SUMMARY OF POPULATION CHARACTERISTICS, FOR URBAN PLACES 1950—Con.

		T **	d population	500 1		Parsons 25 rears old and over	Percus 1-	rears old as	o o er	Cavalina	Employed	Families lated in	and unre- dividuals
i. rban pisce	Names e	1360 1341 to 1341 to 134 fut	Venar age (vena)	Percent for years old and or er	Percent non white	Methan school years rompleted*	\umber in lasor orre	Percent in labor force	Female Percent in labor orce	Pe.cent unem- proyed	Percent engaged in manu- facturing	Median income* (doilars)	Percent having incomes less than \$2,000
Sympat lie Toper Toper Toper Lacksor Lacksor	3 040 4,747 11,5 1,2 4,2	25 7 35 8 27 2 25 8 39 0	20 2 29 4 26 5 44 5 27 9	7 2 8 0 6 5 13 4 8 3	25 7 46 2 46 0 33 4 24 3	9 8 8 0 7 8 6 6 5 9	1,279 1,860 4,187 795 1,647	82 0 78 6 8_ 9 14 5 75.0	30 5 32 1 25 7 10 5 26 0	3 4 2 6 5 5 3 3 40 9	6 2 9 4 10 3 4 7 13 2	3,020 1,750 2,565 1,472	30 54 38 62
os ming- innes.oro Replan Renner uni_vette	- 663 2,097 4,502 5 .30 33,541	3. 0 17 4 60 7 133 1 74 6	2+ 6 29 2 20 7 27 2 25 4	6 7 6 3 5 4 9	20 5 22 1 10 6 34 7 24 8	9 10 2 3 4 7 6 7 0	3,354 1,152 1,347 2,190 42,384	77 5 75 6 68 9 83 4 72 3	28 0 29 6 16 2 30 7 30 9	6 9 2 3 9.3 5 1 4 4	8 1 26 8 16 0 21 9 8 '	2,043 2,572 1,241 2,232 1,d98	49 41 72 42 52
uske Arthur uske Pranies uske Providence useav.lle Kunsteld	2,847 41,272 4 123 4,670 4,440	33 ° 9- 0 1_ 1 55 - 9 2	25 2 27 1 32 1 28 9 29 7	8 7 4 9 1.3 7 2 8 6	12.1 27 0 26 0 29 2 37 4	5 - 9 0 6 2 8 9 9 3	766 16,411 1,432 1,525 1,707	63 7 61 7 66 5 69 3 72 0	14.4 90 7 91 5 26 3 35 3	3 8 5 4 1,0 3 5 2 7	6 9 20 3 4.7 17 0 22 2	1,077 2,825 997 1,441 1,917	78. 35 69 62 51
Maplewood unit , derss-LP Minden Monroe Mongon Cit,	2, 771 3, 635 9, 787 38, 572 9 759	(1) 130 - 46 6 36 3 40 0	26 0 26 0 28 3 29 4 25 0	0 8 7 2 7 5 0 0 5 0	20 8 44 7 43 3 40-4	12 6 7 6 8 7 8 7 6 6	1,182 3,568 10,101 3,373	90 1 70 4 75 7 78 3 80 7	24 9 29 4 37 8 21 4	2 1 8 2 4 1 4 8 5 5	70 3 5 6 11 8 14 6 15 7	5,014 2,014 1,959 1,°36 2,438	49. 51. 51. 39.
Victori roches Yes Then / Ies Chusans Yes Roads Norou-Goodings India	0,914 10,467 570,445 2,818 3,366	45 5 19 8 15 3 25 0 (1)	25.3 27 1 30 9 26 3 25 2	6 1 7 1 7 2 4 0	38 8 20 0 32 0 39 5 18 5	8 7 8 0 8 8 8 8 8 8 8 8 8 8 8 8 8 8 8 8	3,201 5,979 233,979 915 1,146	60 0 77 3 78 3 75 9 79 0	29 3 28 3 32 2 24 7 19 7	4 7 5 - 4 6 2 3	5 6 7 7 14 2 1. 7 41 9	2,449 2,267 1,921 3 474	52 1 26
aknale pelupas ineville laruemne onen-tola	5,598 11,659 6,429 5,747 4,090	42 3 20 K 40 5 13 8 2 2	27 3 26 6 27 0 29 1 28 1	7 1 6 7 5 7 8.0	31 5 41 2 10 4 27 8 35 0	6 0 7 4 10 1 7 6 7 1	1,946 3,705 2,327 1,948 1,407	70.1 69.1 75.0 75.6	24 9) 26 0 31 0 23 6 32 °	6 4 2 5 2 3 4 9 4 6	36 1 10 1 8.6 17 6 12 3	2,003 1,727 2,081 1,983 1,518	49 8 55 2 48 2 50 3 60 5
ort 411-m ayne. ayvalle eserve (unin)	3,097 9,485 3,138 4,465 10,372	30 4 30 1 (1) 42 9	26 5 25 2 30 2 24 8 24 4	5 8 6 7 9 3 6 C	37 0 31 2 48 7 34 3 33 0	78 78 66 1.9	1,185 2,104 -,217 ±,326 3,554	80 6 70 7 74 2 72 1 57 0	30 0 25 4 36.8 15 0 30 0	8 2 6 7 9 3 3 7 1 7	23 5 12 3 4 0 5 4 7 0	2,833 1,507 -,542 2,425 1,395	34.4 61 8 59 0 23.7 61 6
t Martinville meweport lide'l "fapali	4,014 127,206 3,464 3,383 5,990	31 S 29 6 20 9 19.9 7- 1	23 8 29 5 26 9 27 1 25,5	7 3 6 7 6 7 4.3 5 3	43 8 33 2 2° 4 12 9 2.2	5 2 1C 2 8 3 3 6 7.7	1,379 54,396 1 148 1,263 2,537	68 ± 80 8 74 2 83.6 79 7	26.7 3° 1 22 6 23.7 49 2	5 5 3 2 4 6 3.4 6 9	15 1 11 2 18 0 51 C 32 3	1,~05 2,.20 1,953 2,752 2,706	63.6 44.2 50.8 .2.3 28.8
Lillah Locdaux Lie Plat'e tror st Monoe stitego mined mssoro	7,758 7,730 6,631 2,597 10,302 8,328 5,629 3,655	35 8 32 1 78 3 40 3 20 4 6c 6 24 8 29 0	29 6 26 6 25 8 26 5 28 8 24 1 30 2 29 2	8547195002	72.4 18 2 1c 0 18 1 20 4 9 7 36 0 44 7	5 7 7 4 6 5 9 7 9 8 0 8 4	2,790 2,093 1,992 890 4,294 3 013 -,919	75 0 79 9 67 5 77 3 81 6 34 1 73 0 98 8	27 9 23 9 30 4 22 2 24,9 23 6 22 4	3 4 4 1 8 1 3 9 2 6 9	31 6 1 11 7 14 2 21 2 44 4 22 1 4 1	1,135 2,230 1,653 2,482 2,650 2,570 1 433 1,514	75 2 44 7 57 4 37 6 33 8 55 1 59 0

¹⁹⁴⁰ figures not available

GENERAL CHARACTERISTICS

Table 12 —SUMMARY OF POPULATION CHARACTERISTICS FOR PARISHES 1900

Asteriak * terotor un unterhano en 20-arren i unipe. Mei - agri, ri den une destrume. Per un international des international for a superior and median or un or when once is less and 100 for sumpretions prior and median or un or when once is also and on international form. Per a contract of the superior and median or un or when once is also and on the superior and median or un or when once is also and on the superior and median or un or when once is also and on the superior and median or un or when once is also a superior and median or un or when once is also a superior and median or un or when once is also a superior and median or un or when once is a superior and median or un or when once is a superior and median or un or when once is a superior and median or un or when once is a superior and median or un or when once is a superior and median or un or when once is a superior and median or un or when once is a superior and median or un or when once is a superior and median or under the superior and median or underlying the superior and superior and median or underlying the superi

god Cala			7	ota pipi	ILE IUT		-	Lagran A		- The fact the	Petron	- Ambiton	Person .	Person	l - cont	o I and		Fam.	e, and
March 1		4	Perce	n, by res	Sudeus				1	Luner Luner	cla are	Perve.	20. a Soliand	146-011	1 4212	wil and	lov d	flust	inie:
Parish	Number	Percent m crease 1940 to 1950	l ban	Rural non narm	Pursl farm	Acera.	Pchen. 65 cars ocand orer	Pc cent non- white	Persons pe nouse- houd	Pe cont with a community own	Percent as me house 1945 and 1447	Pertent In section	OVER 16: 8: 500 OII car- cum p.e.ed	n n tabut oree	Per es	Pc cen in bor force	Pe cer- engaged in manu- set-ring	Vecan cool lars,	Percent la ing lones less than \$2 000*

Action Assumation Avoyeles	.7,0.0 18 855 22,307 17,278 38,051	55 -02 -31	20.7 .3 5	21 8 40 0 47 0 50 0 26		23 8 2 9 24 4 23 7 41 7	53	19 24 ? 31 + 4	15001	1 1, 278	13 4 2 2 2 2 2 2 2 2 2 2 2 2 2 2 2 2 2 2	1c 8	12	4,° 1 5 907 1 270 1 270	1368874	15.5.4.2	70.25 70.25 70.25	-,55" -,434 -,40 -,165 -,21	01 ± 29 ± 17 72 7
Beaurega.d . Bien"illo Boss.er Camno Celoas.ru	17 706 14, 105 40, 109 176, 247 89, 625	19 7 -20 2 21 0 1 2 58 6	-2 o 4_ E 75 o 72 2	0 5 54 8 34 2 40 0 21 7	24-0 84	26 o 20 9 24 5 28 4 2. 8	83 51 69	27 0 40 2 34.7 77 23 0	3 24 3	45419	82.3	23 1 23 1 25 64.4	C 3 9 7 3	5,359 15,43 73 690 31 782	35 F2 F3	16 2 2 2 2 2 2 2 2 2 2 2 2 2 2 2 2 2 2 2	24 F 22 G 12 2	1,57 1,272 1,744 2,157 2,uco	61 8 70 54 2 47 3 37 9
Chidwell Cumeron Camahausa Chaibonna Concornia	10,2°. 6,244 11,834 25,06, 4,398	-14 6 -13 3 -19 0 -16 .	31 ± 20 7	65 0 -1 0 22 ± 29 \$	44 0 59.0 44 8 41 1	26 ± 25 ± 25 ± 25 ± 25 ± 25 ± 25 ± 25 ±	607	46.5	3 50 3 50 3 50	65	22 c c c c c c c c c c c c c c c c c c	~, °		2,4 91,39 8,290 4,64	70 + 72 6 77 6	1 4 3	6 1	1 355 2,090 - 109 1,458 - 059	12.0
Da Solo sast Biton Rouge East Jarroll East Teliciana Evangeline.	_2,396 18 216 16,302 19,132 21,629	-23.3 /5 0 -14 3 6 1	16 2 65 6 25 3 35 4 21 0	32 1 9 6 7 21 3	49 7 49 0 42 0 45 0	25 8 26 5 22 9 53 1	40.00	36 o 3 . 3 . 38 2 38 2	3."a 3.43 3.77 4.07 3.63	10 9	85 9 76 6 80 7	75 1 85 7 67 2 47 2	00 40 1	7,357 56,72 4,90 5,135	7- 0	20 e 30 - 22 2 19 9	24 4 7.6 -6 -7	2,61 835 -,00	71.5 41 0 81 - 75 8
Cranclin Crant - Theria Thervalle Jorkson	29,376 1-,26- -0 05° 26,-50 15,434	-9 3 -10 5 7 7 -3 3 -12 3	12 4 22 8 21 5 20	1 8 1 4 1 9 5 1 3 5 5 6	74 8 35 6 10 0 14. 3 24 3	21 8 27.0 2 2. 4 20 7	10.66	24 2	- 02 2 52 2 76 3 53 2 72	57 1	188° 2	73 00 73 74 75 9	0 3 3 5 3 0	8,244 2,066 13,40 7 9.0 4,770	06 0 77 - 00 9 72 8	10.0	10 3 10 3 15 7 42 5	- 244 -,147- 1,835 -, 8-	69 8 70 8 53 5
Jefferson Jefferson Davis Lefavette Lafoutne La Saule	103,8°3 2r 298 27,743 42,209	10c 3 8 7 31 4 9 3 -6.0	58 8 77 6 58 1 25 0	10 3 2" 1 1/ 6 54 7 76 6	0 9 25 3 24 4 20 3 21 4	20 5 24 5 23 3 47.0	4 2 5.0 5.0 7.3	15 7 2. 6 	3 6 3 68 3 77 4 00 3.50	5 3 6 6.4 7 3	78 ± 87 : 49 4 46 7 80 2	85 17 8 8 11 8 8 11 8	85045	3,200 20,20 20,20 20,20 20,652	82.3 7: 1 79.3 68.0	23 9	68 50 68 79 6	2 762 1,656 1,680 920	32 0 57 9 57 0 58 7
Lincour Livingston. Manison Morenouse Natch: toones	2,782 20,054 17,451 2,038 8 144	4.0 12 - 5 4 16.2 -7 0	40 2 44 5 39 9 20 0	2, 6 49 8 9 4 -8 6 30 1	34 2 50,2 1 41,5 41 9	24 ± 23 ± 25 2 23 7 23 +	5877	40 2 50 4 48 2 44 9	3 72 3 87 3 82 3 82	37460	78 0 85 2 75.2 70 9 80 0	84 0 5, 0 7, 1	900	6,2°0 5,3°2 10,3°2 10,3°4	61.9 70.0 70.0 70.0 60.0	20 0	2/ 9 10 0 27 5	1,912 1 64 °62 1,533	10 9 16 5 77 7 75 7
Oriens Ouschits Plaguer nes Pounte Coupee Rapiwes	570,445 74,71_ 12,239 21,841 20,648	15 3 2c 3 15 6 25 0 25.0	100 0 65 4 1_ 0 45 6	25 8 82 4 35 6 39 5	0 8 17 6 51 0 10 1	30 ° 28 0 24 1 23 4 27 P	7 1 c.7 2 3 8 11 7 L1	32 U 33 0 28 7 33 7 33 2	3 31 3 42 3 95 3 94 3 54	9 6 6 6 7 7 7	82 4 70 2 85.3 84 0	760	8 3 9 4 5 5	233,979 25,22 4,881 6,919 29,038	78 3 77 0 77 0 77 3 77 3	32 2	14 2 1c 10 4 9 4	2,207 2,052 2,_97 1 124 1,697	49 4 49 0 40 9 73 3
Pen River i'_miand Samme S- Bermard S+ Chailes	12,115 20,672 20,880 11,087 13,365	-2. 7 -7 5 -11 0 2 3 8 5	11 8 23 8 25.2	32 8 24 3 51 9 70 8 65 2	64 0 98 - 54 97	24 2 22 0 25 4 -5 6 24.4	6 4 4 6 6 4 9 6 2 9 6 2 9	50 0 41 0 20 0 14 6 32 6	3 % 3 % 5 80 3 77 3 85	47 68 7)	77 3 74 0 83 1 81 0 86 4	78 1 79 2 86 0 52.4 80 6	5 5 6 5 6 5 7 2 7 6 7 7	2 428 7,959 5,364 3,5°9 4,139	70 0 76 7 67 5 75 0	1° 2 16 1 13 0 19 0 13 3		1 030 22+ 1 2++ 2,020 1,907	75 6 68 6 72 6 49 6 51.7
St Helena St. James St Jorn the Dap 1st St Lanur St Martin.	4,013 15,334 14,861 ,8,4% 26,353	-5 6 6 8 2 -7 0 8 2	30 0 25 3 17 5	24 7 64 2 56 3 27 2 41 4	75 3 35 9 13 0 47 5 41 1	23 2 23 2 21 1 21 8	7 = 2 2 2 2 2 2 2 2 2 2 2 2 2 2 2 2 2 2	53 1 >0 3 -3 0 4-0 37.0	4 12 4 17 4 00 4 20 4 22	3.8 9.0 5.4 6.2	87 5 93 6 91 6 81 8 89 5	36.5 9.0 9.0 9.0 9.0 9.0 9.0 9.0 9.0 9.0 9.0	5 4 5 5 5 5 5 5 5 5 5 5 5 5 5 5 5 5 5 5	2,847 4,20 4,237 22 981 7,9°2	77 5 70 8 72 7 75 2 76 0	15 6 15 b	12 7 22 1 36 9 6 1 5 4	1,058 1,18 1,707 1,242 1,316	73 3 73 0 20 7 69 9 67,4
bt Mary St Tammany Tangipahoa. Icnoss, Terresonne.	35,848 _6,968 ^3,216 13,209 +3,328	14 0 14 2 10 9 -17 1 20 8	51 31 8 28 C	31 0 4~ 7 33 0 36 4 47 7	17 4 20 5 39 0 63 6 14 6	24 7 27 0 -5.2 24 -2 3	7 2 3 0 1 4	36 3 29 4 31.2 54 8 24 6	3 79 3 50 3 68 3 58 4 06	51 57 26	82 3 87 7 79 8 80 8	75.0 \$1.6 76.7 77.7 65.4	5 6 7 5 5 9 5 5 5 5	31 938 8,014 10,889 4,166 13,774	78 7 69 4 74 76 4 80 1	21 8 17.7 20 0 22 1 19.0	17 4 12 4 4 - 7	1,851 1,460 1,204 640 1,901	50 7 64 2 70 7 77 5 52 1
Union. Vermion Vermon. Vashingen	19,141 36,929 18,974 -8,371 >,704	-8.6 -2.2 -0.9 11.4 6.0	37 6 24 0 46 4 36 9	53 J 28 8 33 6 19 3 39 5	40 5 33 5 41 8 34 5 23 7	4- 7 4- 1 47 2 4- 0 4- 7	7 7 0 3 0 3 5 6 7	34 6 12 ~ 11 7 31 5 36 2	3 62 3 60 3 57 3 72 3 75	5 0 5 1 5 1 6 0 6.6	85 1 85 2 97 0 83 8	84 8 79 0 83 1 78 5 %6 5	7 4 4 4 7 7 7 8 9 4	5,530 11,71 5 432 12 749 11,347	72 5 73 0 65 9 7 1 '4 9	1. 0 1' + 10 2 22 5 1) 6	21 1 £ 5 17 0 28 4 25 3	1,473 1,089 1,679 1,920	64 9 68 2 73 6 56 9 51 9
West Baton Rouge. West Carroll West Wellolens Winn,	11,736 ·7,248 10,15 10,15	-10 4 -13 2 -1.8	26 4	38 5 27 7 04 2 29 0	35 ± 72 3 37 8 30 0	20 3 21 " 26 3 48 0	7 4 1 0 7 6 8 8 5	53 2 18 1 71 2 27 4	3 75 4 06 4.07 3 32	6 6 6 5 4 8 5 6	84 8 73 4 80 1 84 2	78 o 71 7 10 9 87 o	5 6 7 0 5 5 7 5	3,817 4,074 2,139 4,057	74 a 72 s 35 ? c9 1	22 5 1, 2 15 0 13.5	14 ? 2 6 18.7 20 -	_,45°. _,064 1,100 _,215	56 9 7° 4 76 4 - 70 5

Table 13 -COLOR BY SEX, FOR THE STATE, URBAN AND RURAL 1930 TO 1950

The fine word is the displaced abuse over time, for the North significant street entering the street with short where less train 0.1 or more base to less than 100 or 100 1-240 1910 ** CA.VS 1.3 0 o 1950 White Norwlite All cations Nonwhi e Na waite All classes What Laber Percent 2,363,880 990,439 3,-67 -,-82 44-533 059 850,782 2,101,5°3 833 532 3,724 1,268 06. 44.,179 826 882 1 324,712 575,244 (1) 747 +68 293,700 453 768 1 5 J. 120 179 ros 385 p 3 -70 39 f -2 32 42 75 3.95 J -1 -1 620 77 75 27,306 -1 55 44 2 27,306 -2 72 75 43 17 Ebo 833 422 91 793 77/8,881 258 288 1 511 739 665,464 er Land for Land for 846,275 376,829 459,446 51 592 -68 -35 463,922 228 921 235,001 100 0 1°3 6 47 ° 52 3 25 8 25 8 100 0 44 0 36 2 2/ 9 31 1 100 0 100 0 43 5 56 5 22 2 34 3 100 0 33 2 66 8 18 9 47 9 5. 4 22 26 100 0 55 9 44 6 49 4 28 3 58 p 22 6 36 C 42 252 250,436 390,314 230,314 21,37 757 379 321,232 (1, 436 147 190,695 245 457 380,750 319,048 11) 261 702 74,229 187,473 89_,414 455,255 1,3.6 436 659 200,743 172 915 1 35" 50 | -27 . 2 201,tu: -77 213 221 96,49 -8 701 172 382 400,19_ 1,04,,843 706 ±91 206,486 439 705 270 044 75,791 194,253 647,794 223,98-386, J92 49 154 236 338 Rural marr Pur farm ... Percent 100 0 21 0 29 0 29 6 100 0 4° 4 5, 6 2> 2 32 4 100 0 42 : 57 9 22 / 3. 4 10 ... 9 4 50 6 200 0 34 0 34 0 27 8 100 C 39 8 60 2 42 7 00 U 31 3 68 ~ 49 4 -12 2 1 100 0 34 9 100 C 38 2 61 8 18 3 40 4 22 1 26,002 1 -20 2 6 127 2 8 127 2 9 70 3.4,35° 1/2,852 1/5 7.4,006 1/7 048 36 5 1 592 1) 652,234 -2-96 7.7 375 873 109 303 41 C 71,378 -134,299 -32 7 904 769 485,52 178 419,146 258 928 160,218 459 582 226 473 794 233 108 116,9-8 116,-63 754,360 34-232 (1) 410,126 183,134 223,994 1 191,4°8 514,248 /1. 2. 7-4 L'emarane 17 8.7 173,73. 10,080 67 J 467 217,196 703,071 258 89. 73 250 18.1,641 52 2 100 0 400 0 400 0 400 3 28 6 17 7 100 0 -9 3 40 7 15 4 25 3 100-0 43-2 56-8 22-4 10C 0 45 6 54 4 24 7 29 7 100 0 38 9 6. 1 18 / 42 7 100 J 47 1 58 9 20 6 38 3 100 0 44 9 55 1 22 0 100 0 35 0 65 0 18 4 46 6 58 2 7 3 24 1

tura. Lura. Lonform Pu al fu ri u Not available

Jercent.

Tible 14 -- RACE BY SEX FOR THE STATE, URBAN AND RURAL 1950, AND FOR THE STATE, 1880 TO 1940

	S .		White	i	- 1		Othe	r races					P	ercent o	f total			
Ina our un your and on	A.1 cla ave	Tota	Native	Foreign nora	Negro	Total	Indian	Japa- nes-	Chi- nese	All other	All olasses	Native whi e	Foreign born wlute	Negro	Indar	Japa nese	Chu- nese	Other
TOTAL								-			l.ma							-11
1950	2,080,510	.,796,683	1 75/ 209	28,384	882 428	4 405	109	_27	526	3,34	200 0	65 9	- 1	32 9			11.75	0:
L pan	-,472,630	1,022 931	437.8/	3 301	26, 491	1,102	9.	79 35	44"	685	700 0	67 9	16	30 4				1 0.
Rural confact	nto 2 dest	3.2 608	330 .59	2,249	24.37	473	243	13	25	× 234	200 0	58 2	0 4	44 3		1	9.3	. 0
040 040 040 520 9.0 900 580	2.36. 880	1,510,739	1,484,467	24,276	8-9 .03	2 8 2	1 601	49	360	631	100 0	50 8	12	12 9	C 1			١ .
940	2 1 4 593	1,322,712	1 28(,721	30,992	776,226	2 5.5	1,500	52	422	>45	100 n	01 2	17	Jr 9	C 1	8		
620	,798,509	1 096,611	1,001, 40	44,871	700 257	1,6 4	1 000	57	38/	-31	400 O	58 5	2 .	s8 9	C 1			0 - 1 6
9.0	7. 300,280	942 386	889 .04	5L 782	723,874	4,448	780	31	507	10	100 0	53 7	11	43 1				
900	1,381,625	729 6.	pon, 750	54,853	650 804	1,207	25.3	±?	599	1	100 0	19 1	3 8	47 ±		8 8	1	10
890	9,9,946	558,395	JO9 555	48 840	559,193	1,000	628	19	333		100 0	45 6	5 6	50 0	01	1		}
	439,976	+34 954	404,177	2	48_ 655	1 337	248		484		130 0	42 8	2.5	3- 3	6.1		01	1
NAU8													1.0					1
3.0	1 319,166	891,9_4 490 249	876, 00 · 483, 970	12,279	424, ~71 208 190	2,481	243	63 40	2-7	1,851	130 0	o6 5	1 17	32 2				C
Rural nensarm	322 508	223,018	221 214	-,80/	98,069	1 421	145	.7	45	.214	100 0	68 b	0.5	30 4				0
Date 1 Covers	201 406	172,647	171,419	4,228	1.8,5 2	249	40		22	,414	700 n	58 8	0.4	10 7				2
40	1,172 382	7-7,379	741,000	5 746	4.3,322	1 68	956	32	258	43*	100 0	63 3	13	35 3	61			1 '
80	1,047 423	667 C a	640,088	20,987	377, 173	1,577	800	33	327	41"	700 C	61 7	2 4	36 2	01			1
920	900,335	557 498	30,6∍C	26,809	344, M4	1,643	550	48	346	99	100 0	28 7	30	38 2	0.			1
10	435,27	480,460	450 A10	29 643	353,824	991	300	25	478	90	1,00 0	54 C	5	42 4	-		01	1
940	694 733	37_,142	342 308	28,834	322,664	927	338	70	5/3		100.0	49 5	4 2	46 +	- 2		01	
		24 ,52	2'4 836	26 ამშ	277: -34	690	336	33	224		10C 0	45 to	4 8	49 5	0.1		01	1
NU	408,754	428,974	200 775	28,199	238,879	901	441		460		100 0	42 8	6.0	51 0	0 +		01	
PEMALE							1 1				36.3		1				1	90
150	_,304,350	907, 69	841,196	د3,97ء	457 607	1,924	166	64	402	1,492	100 0	55 3	- 0	33 5	1		1	0 :
l uan	760,446	526 632	515,627	11,655	239,273	402	37	29	175	239	100 C	57 3	- 4	31 2				
Rural rensurm	22_,857	218,126	21, 629	1,49	102 522	1,209	98	18	13		0 00.	67 3	00	31 9				0
Rural faum	270,347	1,9,961	158,9+0	1,021	115,862	224	31	-	1.3	173	.00 0	5 6	0 4	42 0				0
40	1 191,498	754 360	742 834	4 ,526	43,,981	1,157	845	44	1.32	196	100 0	62 3	1 0	36 6				
30	1,053 770 895 174	6,5 6,9	640,635	15,004	397,153	978	736	_9	05	128	100 0	8 00		37 /			1	
90	895 174	539 1.3	521 050 /38,487	18,003	150,463	598	-16	9	4-	34	100 C	38 2		29 7	01		1	
00	686,802	358,470	335,-21	22,29	360,050	437	795 2,5	2	29	-1	100 0	53 4	2 7	43 8			1	
	-59,237	276,81	25,719	22 .52	282,009	307	292	6	26	2.1	100 0	48 8		47 8				
80	47.,192	225 980	201,402	24, 178	244,776	436	407	6	20	1	_00 0	45 5	5 2	o0 4	01			
MALES PER 100 FEMALES									-	1		76 /		22.9				
āl .	96 7	98 6	°e l	112 8	42 B	129 0	146 4		160 4	124 1			1				1	
Uz' *n	92 0	94 2 1	93 9	144 1	87 0	165 2	240 4		15. 7	-8¢ 6								
Rural nonfarm.	200 2	102 2	102 1	120 5	95 7	14 5	1		400	112 4		1						
Ru al 'arm	103 6	107 9	103 9	15, 3	102 31	112	1			10 4	1	1			1			
40	98 4	_00 4	99 8	36 6	94 8	145 3	1.31		252 4			1 1						
40 30 20	99 4	.0. /	100 9	ا9 °د1	95 5	461 2	108 7			J25 8		i i						
AU	100 9	103 4	10. 9	14E 4	97 C	1-4 4	406 6			2000							1	
06	101 7	104 3	⊥02 R	.33 9	98 _	226 €	07 5					[
	101 1	103 5	(2.3	125 3	98 3	328 7	132 5						100					
90 80	40C 0	101 /	100 C	120 5	2B 3	225 7	115 .											
			14 4	114 /	97 0	206 7	108 4											1

Table 15 -AGE BY COLOR AND CEN, FOR THE STITE, LEBON AND ROBAL AS CAND 1940

the man 1960 and the street of a conduct rest of the conduction of France A. the street of the first inclined cases of the street of the stree

tgr cen us year amis.v		Ine S ate			157:		r	a r court		h	a sim	
	Lita1	7ale	1	le.	1,	'oualst	Tetal	18.4	Nour!	Zeta	ia !	10.00
1950			4									
Total all ages	2,683, 46 (- 20,42	Ser 80 1	-,471,030	- 3 460 3 700	4.76	36.00	forty and minter		67,405	المداءريدد	234 8
der a yes a .	221,460	25-, 429	-2 ,5, 4	73.762	. 2.	2 2/1	77.3	1 5	a3 "/3	75		X,8
der syes s Under tyear Land 2 years	139, 7	40,477	-,8.0	13,108 8	2,24	1,36	16 .06	23,806	6 -3.1	27,47	5,74	7 (
3 277 4 , eura	275, 2"	عددو"ه "ماود"	47,2-2 1 13.,-8.	64, 8 1	A 3.00	-1 De		22.5 7		30, .	1-,322	4.5
o 9 sears	5 . 309	26,045	1J., +8.	30,5	6 30	4. 12	72,2	45,-44	Joens.	7.,822 4	7,507	7,5
	5 .309 37 32	200,927	1,200	30,5	8.2.9	4 12 9,00 9,00	2	47,244 .0, 27 .3, 2.7	5.74	14,75-1	7 794	6,0
	93-ر60ء 1 رزرد2	100,40	38,99	7.,547	9,64 2,54	3-,200	62,45.	28,380	47. Bal	42,428	12, 423	9,
O o 3 ners	-9, 377	1,0,1,0	72 258 6	84 242	-2,302	44.65.	05- 1	32 83C	27 229	36 200	35,472	25,
4 y mrs	-1,962 209,^22	27,22.	2 838	19, 45	-2,-69	- 982	46		: 372	3 483		5,
o and i vears	43 *06	£ ,239	±6 267 [□]	2005	6° 224 -4 908	54,930	12,72 0	4,500	3,24	3797	7,021	20,
o and 1" vears S and 19 years	83,000	52,447 54,348	28,982	128,997	1-,262	2 874		0ر_ر- غقارک	0,7.0	8 - L	14-303	:0,
0 24 vears	212,884	1-4-9-356	F7. 134 4	128,9%	92,22	13,3.2 	.9,	12, "et 2, 12, 12	وو رند 9-رند	2,81	19,495	8, .5,
to 29 /tars	213 003 1	157,955	6,048	L 5. 39	93,0 2 84,6_4	17 097	+9,071 -7,5% 43,96	34,254 32,44m	332	3,308 (48.669	٠٠,
to 39 years	-92, 722	137,814 134,48"	58 435 d	-4,587	84,6	34 083	43 2,0	3.,3%	11,803	3-,585	23,735	ir,
to 44 . cars	1",951	-22,5,	27944	4, 4	73,75_	30,359	2 3420	77,100	10,244	33,683	21,802	24
to 49 y ars	153,95_	104,813 88,946	27,909	75,034	30 مردر 30 مردر	27,27	32,9-	20,417	9 =48	27,009 I	19,243	_C,
o 50 years	100 532	7,023	U,509 [49, 45	42,863	6,282	22,838	18,724	0,94.	2 545	1-,205	8,7
0 64 3 Lars 0 69 - 18.9.	8.,383 78,961	58,253 48,70_	30 200	42,30	33,285 27 290	12,578	8 828 E	-3 222	5,60°	~ ,102	1,746	٥,
o "4 vesrs	46,687	34.399	4.200	24,888	.8, 87	(,7	12,552	3 _^	73	9, 4	9,256	7,
o S. Cars	,6-8	29,848	_3,7\5 ,93	25,09_	10,725	6,-00	14,00°	5,284 1,92	437-27	8,4,18	5 47	2,
ears and over	1,587,245	1, 105,861	481,284	3, 48 940 24	2,62° 570,382	269,860	360,395		07 54	28, 573	.d2.688	104
lian ag.	25 7	28 /	23 9	48 ~	493	4 1	24	222,701	_^7, .C4	21.6	27	10-1
Male au ages	1,3.9,.66	891,914	4.7,252	703,200	496,24	200,001	362,508	22,018	27,490	4 -, +08	1~2,047	.,28,
cru eas.	169,663	207,113 2J,845	12, 84	88,38, 18 C32	13,8,7 11 823	27,248	8,273	29,170	24,402	31,13 C-7	18 799	3,
and 2 cars	33,c22 70 941	44,626 41,639	20 015 20,451	27,4 1	24 761	L2 650	8,499	12,221	12,173 2,577	3,731	3,409 7,644 7 '	7,
and 4 vests 9 veats	65,090	41,639 87,c09	20,451	65, 92	24 761 22,220 -3,650	20,419	30, 74	24,621	10.77	30, 00 1	7 5-10	16,
LATS	138,549 48,798 28 345	18,205	10,593	1_,787	9 3,6	4-64	7,622	5,076	2,577	7,353 1	3,843	-
to 9 years	28 345	18, 253	25,755	37,909	9 267 25,7m	4 579	7,590	5,_58	2,236	7,-09	3,924	3
o 14 years	9, 23	74,504	44,622	51,507	33,480	.8 027	31,702	_4,387 ,129 17,274	7, 364	32, 408	16 892	16.
to 3 vers	96 9,33	13,827	8,357	9,543	27 400 6,080	3,463	25,915	3,850	8 631	29,720	892	13,
o 19 years	102,401	63.718	36,693	40,282	31,309	.A. 993	20,520	17,057	5,468	30, 294	17 352	12,
o years 6 rd 17 year 5 and 19 years	21,810	13,706 26,348	8.104	9.46	*,876 -1,773	14,073 3,270	5,702	3,854	1.8.8	0,902	3.97ć	2,
Sand 17 year	41,357	25,664	15,009	.9,327	_1,773 		10,455 7,368	7 0°1 5,212		10,537	7,484 5 892	3,
0 21 1 2274	100,991	70,243	15,009 -3,570 30,778	28.637	43 290	> 60° 15,*47	24,187	16,782	3,456 7 405	17 907 1	10,471	7,
o 29 years	92,900	70,543 74,347 68,301	28,350	64,784 26,139	43 290 48, 7 42,021	15,607	22,3,2	16,949	5,479	15,061 1 15,061 1	9,2/1	5,
0 39 1 6578	93,639		40,670	74,536	9 444	15,607 _4,118 _12 125	41,000	-0,00	> 620	17 413	10,031	5
to 44 years	86 032	61.590	4 442	49,9-2	30,089	-3,85	19,040	14 141	4,9-8	10,991	11,360	5
o 54 years	63,024	23,041 44,542 35,924	23,184	43,939 3p.58y	31,002 26,2°C	12,937	10,800	12,11	3,752	1,496	9,938	5,
sieny Pt c	-1,438	35,924	15 514	28,416	20,348	10,299 8,0 ₀ 8	11 4.2	8 000	3,427	1,,106 1	7,571	4
0 69 Vests	37,245	28,550	11 489 4.15a	21,197	11,807	5,653	9,206	5,774 5,994	3,929	9,641	3,537 > 201	3,
o 74 years	22,203	15,002	-4,183 ~,201	18,143 10,560	~,_32	3,028	6.347	4,082	2,285	5. 476	3,388	1.
o & vein	3,005	13,201	6,7.2	9,319 1,383	915	Z,835 468	6,084	3,794	2,48° 420	4,510 4	2,922	-
rear- ad o rea	770,580	544,271 20 7	226,309	443, 767	321,6%	122 07	179.347	±2° ,528	4 8 49	142,466	95,47	52,
dur age .	26 4	2- 7	2, 1	28 3	28 9	26 4	24 7	25 7	22 4	21 6 "	25 3	
Female, all ages	1-4 900	904,760	459, "81	760,446	596,682	239,764	321 857	218,126	100,731	2'6,047	109,901	116,
ar > year- nder 1 _ear-	104,833	102,816 20,_22 42,726	61,987 _2,692 2*,*34	85 683 17,403 36,177	26 747 11,369	28,936 6,094	42,8"4 6,585	28,023 5,451 1_,585	3,134 6 042	36,246 6 706 14,446	18,0-C 3 302	18,
nder 1 , ear	68,230	42,726 39,908	21,134	36,177 32,043	25,963 21,415	_2,217	17,607 16 682	-0,287	6 042 5 695	15,034	3 302 7, _ 78 7, _ 66	7
9 years	1.50,55€	85,515	1,041	64,909	42,723	22,_80	25,988	23,873	12,115	35,629 #	18,4-9	16,
YOUTY	28,5,1	17,8/3 17,760	10,668	64,909 13 731 13,540	9,168	4,263	25,988 7,498 7 497	4,971	2 227	7,282	28,4_9	3.
vears	79,600	49,006	29,757	37,638	24,564	13,074	20,093	13 992	2,598	21,032	1,800	9,
o 14 years	94,438	71,839 58,463	35,973	51,063 42,008	33,054	18,609	20,697	20,225	10,772 8,548	3 ,876	. 8 . 580	12
to 13 years.	21,798	13,394	0 404	9,605	6,086	3,519	5,593	3,569	1,924	6,500	3,039	2,
19 year o	107,521	68,366	39,150	53,975	30,015	17, 460	26,443	17,481	8,962	2,100	4,870	. 2
vears and 17 years -	21,696	13,533 36,099	25,580	29,331	5 092 12,489	3.4.17	10 582	3,796 7,01	1,576	6.49"	-,645	2,
	14,210	28,734	15,412	20,115	17,434	7,681	10,159	p. 654	3,551	1,700 8,84a	6,579 4,646 9,024	4
0 24 /ears 0 29 /ears	1.0,306	74,8U7 7a 678	37,085 33,098	70,14	17,434 48,933	20,490	24,801	16,850	6,929	15,747	9,024	H 0;
o 34 years	99,302	n9 97 4	29,784	60,5_6 60,547	49,800	17,922	22,284	10,245 15,326	6,029	15,502	0,674 11,100	5.
o 39 years	99,283 89,019	67, 18	27,692	60,947 54,368	41,08° 37,862	18,955	21,569	15,326	5,330	17,667	11,100	. 0,
o 49 years	77 72e	52,752	24,964	47,006	32 141		16 16		4,859	30,292	10,4-2	5,
o 54 voore	63,863	44,376	19,487	38,497	27 340	14,865	13,263	14,306 9,427	4,,36	12,103	9, Q. 7,209	5,
o 59 vegre	52,094	37,099	14,995	30,749	22,5,5	8,214	100	7.890	3,516	9 959	0.09/	3,
o 64 voars.	41,339	29,698	16,077	23,752	17,741	8,329	9,602	6,748	2,874	7,551	4,355	3.
0 74 years	24,484	17, 3,6	7,088	14,328	_0,655	3,673	n. 185	4,097	2,088	.,971	2,644	1
	23,640	16,647	0,993	2,565	10,301	3,777 851	7,920 4,172	3,789 657	2,.31	0,948 842	2,557	1,
	4.179	2.831										
cars and over	4,579 816,765 27 0	2,832 561,190	1,746 254,975 24 5	496,481 29 0	548,686 29 6	147,795	180,748 25 0	1.25, 203	55,485	137,330	8°,041 25 3	51,

TRIAL 15 -- AGE BY COLOR AND SEX, FOR THE STATE, URBAN AND RURAI 1950 AND 1940-Con.

1		The "tate			Trban		F	tural nontarra			Rural sarm	
A	Fots.	White	Nonatu e	Tota	Wh.te	Vorwhite	i oral	Whic	\onv/hte	Total	White	Norwhie
1950-602	-								i			
Press demouses	1							100 0	100.0	100 0	100 0	100 0
Total all ages	\$ OC.	100 J	10, 0	100 0	1. 1	130 C	100 0	13 0		45.9	1 4	15 6
nder a cura	03	17	1.5	. 8 8 9 7 0	84	9.8	13 5 11 3 9 /	1, 0	14 b	12	140	44 3 43 3
to 9 17875	88	A 7	30	70	6.5	8 2 7 3	81	9 4 7 8	3 b	*0 S	57	10 8
0 24 '48 c 1 23 462 s 1 23 462 s	78	/ 5 b 1	- 6	8 8	90	8.2	7 6	7 6 7 8	7 6	6 1	. 5 9 5 6	6 5
1 29 164.9	791	8 4 7 7 5	72	7 9	9 6 8 3	8 3 7 1 7 6	5.6	7 .	5 2	50 1	6 2	4 0
3 to 39 3 LBT	72	7 5	6 0	7 8	8 3 7 9 7 2	6 8	57	7 1	2 8 2 1	5 9	6 6	5 3
to 44 3tt	50	6 8	24	52	6 2	6 2		4 2	47	> 3	5 8	4 9
to 79 year	19	7 9	3 4	40	4 2	36	41	4 2	3 4	3 8	4 3	,
to the VCST	20	4 1 9 2 2 -	26	3 1	3 3	2 "	3 2	7 D	2 8	29	3 5	2.
to th year-	17	1 7	· 6	28	18	15	1 9	1 0	2 2	1.6	1.8	1
) A Se venra	03	0.3	č.3	16	16,	14	53	0.3	0 5	03	0 3	o.
Miles per 100 females	**									- 1		
Total ail ages	9C 1	98 0	93 0	92 0	94 2	87 2	100 2	102 2	95 9	105 6	107 4	
	10 = 1	.34 2	100 9	02 8	103 7	101 4	103 5 10e 2	105 2	100 3	102 b 101 4	102 4 107 1	707
10 4 11 75	2 -	103 7	99 8 100 6	99 7	01 4	96 9 83 4	103 3	104 J	30. O	176 0	107 1 Li6 7	104
۱۹۲۰ و ۱۹۶۱ و ۱۹۶۱ و ۱۹	95 7	96 L	80 4	85 7 a3 9	88 5	73 3	96 2 97 2	99 6 97 9	92 2	10b 5	97 4	95 85
17:34 todes 0 0 29 vents 1 to 44 vents 1 to 44 vents 1 to 44 vents	93 .	9" 0	84 1	92 1 92 8	88 5 96 7 98 7	1 0 78 d	96 4	99 7	94 5 92 2 92 4 90 7	91 4	34 4	85
) 39 years	9/ 3	100 +	84 0 ed 3	90 8	95 9 95 3	79 8 83 →	104 0	.04 9	90 0	78 m 104 3	200 s	90
1 to 44 ve. 5	Qp. 1	00 6	92 9	93 5	∌o 5 96 2	87.0	10 ,	:07	90.5	106 5	±06 €	136
to 49 teams	02 r	.00 4 96 8		95 2 92 5	96 2	92 3	400 5	105 1	90 4 97 5	116 4	-73 1	10.1
o to 49 (ears	0	90 2	103 5	87 7	87 - 76 9	98 2 88 0	95 7 91 9	95 9 97 3	95 1 84 P	28 0	25 -	132
to 68 tears	8° 3	89 ±	28 2 10. 6 96 0	73 7	70 7	82 4	22 9	99 6 100 2	109 4	2 9	_28 1 _14 3	140
tt 54 years	84 2	79 - o5 2	96 ° 68 3	67 7	53 /	82 7 55 0	8.1	81 4	8. 4	114 2 er 8	92 2	80 .
				3 1 7 4				10.00				
1359—OLD URBAN DEFINITION	2 683 5 6	1 796 683	886,833	1 63,789	940 878	442,911	751,592	542,671	228,921	5o8 135	33 13/	235,00
Total, ad ages	34.46	209,929	-24.5-	-8,020	403.642	54,177	404,932	▲69, .97 ▲17, 345	▲33 74 ₂	73,514	▲ 36,8 3 9	App.61
to 9 rears	275 05 225,359	70 124	101 9AL	94.455	60,030	41 110 34,246	464 632 471,260 459,42	47 8131	A23,447	▲7_ 899 ▲69,843 ▲57,749	438 314 438,517	A33,58
to 19 years	209.922 ₺	_46,360 _34 084 _4, 350	55 638 67,534	94,255 92,746 1.9,756	92.512	34,246 30,734 34 063	459,42	439,809	A19,618	A57,749 A34,895	▲12 263 ▲19,5-4	A25 48 A25,3 A11 6
0 24 10° %	212,824	_50,955 177 814	62,0/8 54,388	124,658	85,773 89,703 77,3.3	34,955	58,72	40, 03 42, 29	A18 120 A1, 463	430 353	A16, 723	A11 6.4
to 44 years	192,922	177 814	54,388	106 227	73,827	32 400	45 ,368 44 1/	A38 032	▲13,25± ▲13,25±	A31,c23	A20 78:1 A22 627	A 2,500
to 41 years	175,05	122,917	52,_3-	97,011	68,002	28,9-9	A44 1/	▲ 33 ^20	A11 694	A33, '26 A30,088	A21,835	ALL 491
0 49 yea 5	_33,951 126 58	100,803 88 928 73,023	48,1/8 37 959	85 363 70,835	38 787 50, 299	20,066	A38,300 A30,780	▲27 7.7 ▲22,029 ▲18,285	A13, 703 A8 7.1 A7,644	▲20,088 ▲20,242	A (500 A (330	Alu,80
	103,532	23.023	30 509	25 018 43,13.	50,299 40,44* 31,329	11,602	42,,920 42,03*	▲18,285 ▲14 959	A : .076	▲23 242 ▲2:,585 ▲17,217		▲7,29 ▲>,4 ⁸
1 to 64 years 5 to 64 years 1 to 74 years	78.961	58,253 48 701	30,260	19,908	25,909	13,939	A22,68	A-3 6x	49,220	A) 6 37%	49 2"-	47 .0 43.24
	-6 567 43,553	29 348	17,289	22,033	25,986	6 04 /	A1, 640 A13 05	48 74	4,63/ 4,63/	A6,469	46,044 45,488 4890	*2,98 68
5 y ars al 0 - 9r	1,310,166	4,709 831 914	427 2:-2	601 693	455,255	96,400	A2,30:	A1 .04	±097	294 .57	12,916	-18,84
Male all ages	169 663	10713	62 350 5	80,007	52,776	27.25	52,430	A: (7)	A16 9.3	37,226	▲ 8 820	A18, 3
to 9 eurs	138,549	87 (-09 7/ oul	50,940	59 578 46,952	39,103	20,415		▲29,1/2 ▲24,479 ▲10,596 ▲.9,705	A13 620	▲36 200 ▲3J 937	A 9 364 A19 914	A) € 93 A16,02
to It s are	1.9,723	65 718	36,68	42.00,	28,745 40 °38	10.954	A3.,234 A29,076	▲10,596	A9,480	▲30,0do	▲ 7 377	A13,24
0 0 24 vers	100,991	70 -43 74 347 65 °31	30,448 20 350 24,590	7 645 19,779	44,211 38 430	14 3.1	48,333	420 897	A8 632	A_8,00, 1	A10,200 A9,239	A7 50
to 3's years	92,69	65,760	26,590	29,779 21,734	38 43C 30,018	15,568 13,304 14,291	42 895	420 897 4.9,773 419,447	4,289 46,44	17 43-	A-1 534	♣5,70 ♣2 \$3
to It ear	86,032	rl 590	24,442	5C,3C9 46 154	33,049	13,145	-24,82	-1 ,-05	A5,661	-1 ', O. 1	A.1 .75	45,63
	63 024	23 0°1 44 552 11,964	23 -84	41,053 34,342 26 847	28 706	12,347	419,601 4.5 500 412,980	A11, 13,	45,273	13,124	A9,97	A5 50
to .0 , cars	54,418	11,944	12,5.4	26 847	24,502 19 106	9 843 7 681	▲12,98°	▲11,3°1 ▲9,171	▲4, ·84 ▲3 809		▲8 679 ▲7,587	44.02
to 69 ye rs	40 044 77 245 2∠,203	28 555 23 062	_L 489 _4, 83 7 20	20,107 17 2 4 10,063	14 674 -1 247	5 431 - 96 < 896	10,841 410,841 46 859	▲7,333 ▲6,6.6 ▲4,443	▲2 95. ▲4,235	▲9, a55 ▲9, 20	45 209	43,10 43,98
10 74 'EFFS	19.9.3	12,000	6 712	10,063	F 10"	2 702	A6 545	A4,443	A, 4-6 A9,491 A440		▲3 392 ▲2 926	884
t at ears to 9 years to 9 years to 9 years to 99 ye rs to 94 cears to 69 ye rs to 94 cears to 89 cears to 89 cears	3,009	. 876	1, 93	1,5/2	8641	448	A1 02>	A7 2/	140	4, 415 4732	A427	A,10
Remaie, all ages	1,164,310	904 769	459,581	712,096 78,013	40,62	220,473	375,876	258,92	-16 148	2.0 3/0	150 2.8	116 16
to C angre	136 556	85 515	>1,041	58 396	21,067 28, '6± 29,922	40 63°	50,50R ▲4,861	▲33,670 ▲28,274 ▲23,134	A16 832 A13,657	36,28c 4,5 694	A18,079 A18,950	6.74
0 to 14 ,care	11a 23a	71,859 65 366	39 155	47 304 53 047	29,922	17 382	▲35 026 ▲30,351	▲23,134 ▲20,21	A1: ,692	A33 906 A., 12.	▲18 60.3 ▲1-, 890	A12,30
10.24 .0.15	111,893	74,807	37,086 73 598	53 047 45,177 64,879	45 362 45 492	16 780 19,7*2 19 387	▲29,886 ▲29,659	86F O₹▼	10 138 10 138 40,488 48,027		A0 04-	▲7 84 ▲0,28
0 2º years 10 3º years 10 99 years	29 302	76,608 69 513	29, 89	55,918 55 918	28,923	16.995	A26.865	\$21,632 \$19,90J	6 964	A15,764	▲9,494 ▲17,087	45,83
to 49 years	99,2 ₀ 3 83,013	67,5.8 61,327	27,692	55 928 50,81"	37 809	_8,±09	±25,672 ±21 887	4.8, 86 415 854	♣/ ∪86 ♣6 0.3	A 7,693	▲11,123 ▲10,460	46,37
	77 716	52,752 44 376	24,964	44 310 36,300	J∩ 081	_4,229!	A_E,839	▲ 3 349	A5 400	A.1., 167	40 221	A5,24
to 10 years					25,757	⊥0,723	▲15 225	A1C,658	A/,507	A 2,148		44,10
to 10 years	63,863	37 799	14.395	29 /-	21 229	7,892	A.2 949	49,1,4		A9 974 1	A6,706	43,200
to 10 years	52,09- 41 359 4716	37 799	14,395	29, . /-	21 229	7,892	ALC 754	A9,114 A7,626		A9 974 1	▲6,706 ▲5,717	A3,20
	63,863 52,09- 41 359 4-,716 54 484 23 640	37 799	14,395 11,641 16 077 7,088 6,99:	29 /-	21,279 16,6 5 14 7,2 10,184 9,8,5	7,892 6 1' 7,972 3,242 3,45	A.2 949	A9,114 A7,626 A6,855 A4,563 A-,250 A719	4,965 4,965 42,218 42,256 4557	A9 974 A1,562 A7,182 A3,977 A3,954 A843	△7,321 △6,706 △5,717 △4,062 △2,649 △1,562 △463	43,20 42,34 43,12 41,34 41,38

Table 15 -AGE BY COLOR AND SEX FOR THE STATE URBAN AND RURAL 1950 AND 1940-LOD

gues of 1950 are presented according to "a and Al Licenter fix torus. I larger A tendes state "pulsor in the rest. Sales see at "Percent and shown when her has the sales as a see at each sold. Make per AS Commandon, scorm where in the reform and beginning.

age census year, and sex		The State			I roun		8	בות וואם יצי	187	1	- a farm	
	iotai	Ar -e	\CDW-L .	Trisl	4>.	Jan.	T , & 1	3 LE	None te	Inta.	147. p	NAW .
1)=0-OLD URBAN DEC'NITION							- 1	i				
Torai, als ages	2,301,380	1,71,739	352,14.	yan,9	655,464	3,4	533,05-	3°0 929	ا ح5,5د	350 382	467 -40	340,93
ner o years	23 ,627 1	138,886	91,741	72 006	-t, 12	27 CoC:	57,20	41, 745	- ,778	-01,03	*4,200	-3 88
to 14 years	243,836 T	28,044 252,95~	89 932 k	83,904	₩. ¥C8	25 814	2,75	-2,801	25 726	-02" 1	52, 35	-8,19
to 19 years	2-0,398	153,221	37,1	3-,428	25,2°2 c1,°60	20,	25 -17	-9 P-3	4 818	-C4, 0	57,50	40,89
to 24 years	2.6,396	138,402	7.934	9 ,822	62 -2	27 300	-3,273	-,770	46,57	71,249		45,6°
to 29 years	2.7,021	.33,,:22	73,050	15,324 \$	64 30"	Japa=7!	-17-1-	3,7		62,209	-, :88	28 12
lo 34 years	_24,45.	22,84_	63,64-	90 113 ,	60,72	27 29	+3, 45	2. 164	_L ~P_	F2,95, E	57 5	22,40
to 39 years to 44 years	-7-7-40	4.349	25 Sc	8-,922	55 4.0	29,008.	9,500 8	21, 771	124,	ا دنـ رباق	48,44.	71.95
	144,381	94,448	47 935 1	40-	40,204	20,.52,	€,323	2 2	2	+2,-22	24,443	-7,-~
o 49 vears	120,685	32,922	43, Th.	61 24	44 99-	14,363	25 -53	-8 r_=1	7 3-6	2,440 \$	22,914	16,54
to o4 , ears	102,269	60,658	-3,61±	48 481	34 A52	10, -2	2. 385	14,100,	6 2501	29,44c \$	24,774	-> F S
0 64 (6an)	8_,324	25,521	20,800 (3" 233 "	27,377	9,-55	1º 705 }	1, 72	4 303	2" 9 4 1	-6,342	1-240
to 10 sears	63,301	44,609	_B 752 [28,942	22,2*-	0,757	12 9_5	,24"	2,500	2.,64	-3,-27	2 93
to 74 years	50,162 31,430	35,352 20,701	20,810 !	24,623	- ,272	,2,1	12 -W 3	7,445	4,522	_9, 1.2 _3 349	20, 125	
to 84 years _	25,417	17,197	8,220	14,323	_U,721 8,588	3,502	1,95	4,463	- 501	_3 349	5,1.07	
years and over	2,788	3 15.	2,637	2,28	467	8,6	ا بددوه ا 40دو	- 928	2,080	2,160	1,001	410
Male all ages	1,172,382	757,379	415,003	400,_11 #	321,232	144,959	260,480	_90,-,5	5,701	-37,705		
der 5 years.	1,0,353	0,305	46,048	36,275	20,710	12,.5	29,120	2.8.	3,713	-0 923	245,452	-9-,25
o 9 years	1,4,345	70,0,4	44,791	36 1.5	20,400	12,750	27,-20	20,023	7,905	57 0 2	26,93	25,1
to 14 years	122,325	ים בלכן די	45,209	41,029	27,804	_3,924	27,910	2., 23,	/ 588	51,002	23,454	22,84
to 9 years	118,480	70,644	41,840 1	43,364	29,884	_3 480	25.4	_8 25o	- o38	49,978	29,504	
to 24 years _	_C3,885 100,294	60,903	32,932	4C 543 }	28,808	1_,655	20,32	_6,758	o 504	40 C.5 \$	2°,504 22,307	17,70
to 29 years .	100,294	66,221	>4,0°-	43,960	30,635	13,323	44,00	≟ 363	8 044	32 24 1	18,22	-4, "4
to 34 years to 39 years	90,968 84,955	01,0,0	5c, c. 7	-2,-39	20,05-	±₽,88°	2,82-	10,58-	5,720	2 2.5	~ 8.00	11,:3
to 44 years	72,289	55,6°2 47,887	24,402	+0,-+2	27,00.	13,141	-9 6	17,42	5,402	2- 920	14 246	,580
to 49 years	14,261	42,125	1	35,132 1	24,0_	11,023	15,927	1_ 372	4 573	21,330	12,498	3,83-
to 14 years	52,61	5,224	22,_36	30,1.4	20,707	9,458	12,556	3,497	4,049	20 243	-4 °21	8, ,10
to 59 years	41,085	22,182	13,503	-7,589	10,-03	6,57	10,658	7,440	3,218	-8,4-4	₹,789	7,392
to 64 years	31,749	24,425	2,524	23,370	13,10+	4,785	6,284	5,824	4,400	15,5.2	.,252	6 25-
to 69 years	27,665	_7,212	10,4-3	10 704	2,448	3 250	5,134	3,790	2, 27	11,020	7,-34 -,9 c 7	-,097
to 74 years	15,61	40,G8b	5,529	6,161	4,574	1,*86	3,149	2,263	1,260	2,925	3,240	2,07
to 84 years _	عددرسد	7,693	3,843	7,3,8	3,255	1,.83	2,899	1,91	443	4,299	2,52	-1772
years and over	2,50	1,293	1,067	. 31	471	200	6_7	335	282	1,000	487	519
Female, all ages	1,191,498	754,300	4,57,1.8	524,248	344,232	170,Clo	266,373	286,234	80,439	420,677	223,994	186 (81
ider o years	114,294	68,581	45,493	J5,731	23,208	12,523	28, 383	19,920	2,-63	20,200	25,453	24,70"
9 years	113,131	07,990	45,141	35,96	22,948	13,059	27,099	10,078	8,021	xC,065	26,004	24,06.
to 14 years	121,01,	75,309	45,642 45,335	42,323	27,698	14,625	27,503	19,455	7,948	,285	28,110	23,009
to 24 years	121 912	70,509	42,002	48,064	31,882	16 182	26,060	_9,030	7,930	46,888	25,065	21 223
to 29 years	106,727	67,111	39,046	50,279	33 539	17,984	25,048	17,979	7,409	36,284	15,00	17,293
to 34 years	95,486	61,324	33,662	48,179	31,068	16,511	25,12.	15,478	6 057	30,250	16,105	14,085
to 39 years	80,_94	55,677	33,527	44,839	28,432	16,400	19,178 2	13,346	2 8.2	25,77~	13,699	1,20
to 44 years	^2,092	46,561	25,532	16,40	24,265	12,129	14,296	10,3-9	4,77	20,702	1_,949	8,845
to 49 years _ to 54 years _	62,424 49 658	40,797	21,627	3189	2 ,284	9,905	12,027	3,520	1.8	-2,908	10,903	7,915
to 39 years		33,434	16 22/	24,409	17,474	6,925	9,727	, 25	3,062	15,522	9,295	0,22
to 61 years	39,629 31,612	27,329	12,300	19,344	14,273	5, m	7,828	=,48_	2,.36	12,477	584	4,893
to 69 years _	28,497	22,384	9 228	15,563	1,930	3,033	0 .76	4,731	. 845	9,473	5 723	3 750
to 74 years.	16,021	10,705	2,316	13,919	6,146	2,010	6,233	3,848	2 385	8,3-5 -,424		3,877
to 84 years	13,881	9 504	4,377	0,974	5,333	1,64_	1,715	2 017	-,098	3,792	2,359	2,065
years and over	3,/28	1,858	1,570	-,546	996	22	723	362	30_1	1,159	200	659

Table 16 -AGE BY COLOR AND SEX, FOR THE STATE 1880 TO 1950

Percent no bran nacro has then 01, percent and median not shown where base is less than 160]

A. TAMAS T. T	STATE OF THE PERSON NAMED IN	Della Control		-	Papala	16.2		-				p	ercent da	stribution	1		
True H. 1979. 1. 1. 1. 1. 1. 1. 1.	the over a diex	250	1,-4	930			1910	1890	1880	950	1940	1930	1920	1910	1900	1890	1880
The figure 1				4.15.400	2 000 500	1 656 388	1 281 625	1, 118, 188	939,9/61	100 0	100 0	100,0	100 0	100 0	100 0	100 0	_00 o
1 1 1 1 1 1 1 1 1 1	I n for a years	. 50,006	210 -71	237,53R	2°9,21 12, 236, 29,22'	224,063	_91,405	163,442 160,462 143,718	15.,083 139,792 1.1,286	10 3	9 8 9 6	10 5	12 4	20 04	13 3	1.4 C 1.7 3 0 Ea	16 1 14 9 14 9
18 us de verson 19 10	Sol to 24 years.	20, 322	21c, 236 21c, 236 207, C21	_78,953	149,668	175,227 164,JL 141,905	_39,081 117,286	106,664	6.54	79	9 2	8 5	9 5 8 3	1C 0	10 1 8 5	95	98
1. On 19 19 19 19 19 19 19 19 19 19 19 19 19	30 to 34 vers	-92,922	17., 49	146,587	96,450 l	105,990 78 452	r4,036	49,141	43,527	6 5	6 1	70	70	6 4 7	5 4 4 5	44	4 6
1. On 19 19 19 19 19 19 19 19 19 19 19 19 19	31. 54 .cars	26,387 23,532	124,685 -2,269 81,324	107,570 85,565 62,463	62,821 (1,78)	38 34-1	54,707 44,690 25,940 25,054	22,812 30,232 23,663 20,986	18 644	3 9		30	35	7 0	1 8	1 2	20
Note years 19.00 19.00 19.00 19.00 19.00 19.00 10.00 1	6. n PO sears	46.087	5C, 162	21,400 21,520	25,600 6,226 47,617	21,068 13,796 14,869	16,545 11,336 12,350	13,277 9,050 10,032	10,199 7,12 7,574	2 9 1 1 9	- 3 - 3		1 -	0.5	0 8	12	0 8
Liefe D. June	Not reprised	20 /	- 1	23 1	21 7	20 4	19 4	18 6		100 3	±00 0	100 0					
11 0 1 1 4 1 1 1 1 1 1 1 1 1 1 1 1 1 1 1	Turder S. N.CF	38,549	115,351	11F, 264 124, 973	105,468	110,154	400,666 97 488		70,249	12 9 10 5	9 9	11 2	12 5		4 5	14 5	16 4
35 to M. S. Lane. 90, 123 100 to 90 to 120 100 to 90 to 90 to 90 to 90 100 to 90 to 90 to 90 100 to 90 to 90 100 to 90 to 90 to 90 100	10 to 14 years 15 to 10 years 20 to 24 years	100,994	103,885			84, 902 79, 383	74,170	39./08	39,92 44,050	78	8 9	9.4	90	95	10 2 9 5	9 _	9 4
48 to 90 Natural 19, 230 64, 261 79, 250 19, 260 19, 2	25 to 23 years 30 to 34 years 35 to 36 years 40 to 44 years	93,639	90,968 84,925 2,285	73,012	60,268 64 057 49,762	41,721	36,32/ 32,844		28,211 25,136 20,936	7 1 6 5	6 2	5 8	71	5 C		4 4	4 5
Types and other (1975) French 114 gets 1, 164, 155 1, 193, 164 1, 187, 187, 187, 187, 187, 187, 187, 1	4o to 49 years -	n3.02	52,01.	56,_00 47, 44 33,117	22,322	28,408 20,509	12,495	18 223	19 350 16,676 10,175	3 9	3 5 4 5 3 6	5 4 2 3 3 2	28	3 4	3/	3.3	3 6
No **Promoted*** **Membrana age*** **See 1 **See 2 ** 4 ** 25 ** 5 ** 2 ** 20 ** 2	70 to 74 years -	22,203	27,665 15,615	24,426 25,664 20,431	8,044	6,671	5,373		9,900 5,420 -,592	28	13	15	. 5	13	12	08	12
5. 6.6 Values 150,500 110,231 110,274	No reported -	26 4	25 5	23 2	2,740	3,425	1,664	18 4	3.8 9			- 1	33	0 4	0.2	02	5-
13 to 19 west = 10,502 11,525 11,525 13,525 10,525	Under p years	164,803	114,274	114 274	10,745	111,492	98,740	80 210		12 1	9 6		11.6	13 6	14 4	.4 3	15 0
30 to 90 years	10 to 14 years	107,520	121.912	111,554	97,587	96, 246 90, 325	74,558	71, 111 64,646 55,539	52,405 44,456 48,393	8 5 7 9 8 2	10.2	10 6	12 3	1. 7	12 2	129	11 8
40 to 44 years	25 to 29 years 35 to 39 years	10,306 99,302 99,283		75,594	61,893	55,558	35, 712	33.072	37,667 28,440 26,299	73	90	8 8 7 2 7 0	8 7 7 9 6 8	8 7	5 2	73 59 55	8 0 6 0 5 6
\$\frac{85 \text{ 60 ft Server}{\text{ 60 ft Server}	40 to 41 years -	89,019 77,716	62,424	51 /26	39,451	36,731	30,456	22 260	17,859 16,058	57	5 2	49	44	36	37		
Not reported 1,500	55 to 59 Years 60 to 64 years	52,094 41,339 41,716	39,639 3,612 26,437	29,346 2,952 15,260	19,26± 17,230	15,150	12,81/	12,376 10,579 6,486	9,048	3 8	2 7	2 8	22	22	19	19	18
Trough, all lights 1, 199, 195 3, 211, 779 4, 252, 712 1, 190, 101 0 10 0 100 100 0	7o years and over No* reported.	28,219		10,969 12,6_7 356	1,580	8,088 1,561	1,542	2,548 5,486 1,775		21	15	- 0	. 1		10	10	0 9
Under Symen 109-929 118 88C 45,289 131,765 131,98 126,511 79,285 6,00 10 17 9 9 11 0 10 0 40 10 16 4 22 115 10 16 14 727 131,770 131,7		27 0	:5 6	23 0		50.7	19 4	18.7	39 1			4		•			
130 to 18 years 124, 360 125, 251 131, 785 131, 785 107, 735 86, 513, 70, 143 144, 147 145 126 117 14 11 0 126	Inder 5 years				131.745			00 004		11 7	92						
30 to 98 years 120, 607	o to 9 years 10 to 14 years	173,,24 146,360 134 084	152.9.5	142,575	136,42/ 131,785 1,2,6/0	107,735		77,059 70,443 62,042	64,243 54,072 43 640	8 1	9 1 10 1 10 1	10 8	12 0	10 4	11 9	12 6	119
30 to 54 years 105, 520 6, 520 12, 520		37 814	_22,841	126,702 109,681 95,870	76,583	78,10/ 95,074 59,750	51,458 47,255 40,240	51,937 40,738 37,704	37,201 29,451 25,454	77	8 -	7 2	70	70	8 4 6 5	68	€ 5
\$8 to \$9 years	40 to 44 years -	122,917	82,9,2	66,149	59,3(1 52,005	45,000 35,650	36,402	20,193	21,000	6 8	C 5	5 7	54	4 8	50	3 9	48
Median alg. — 28 U 26 3 23 2 7 20 2 7 20 5 1 2 7 20 5 1 2 7 20 5 1 2 7 20 5 1 2 7 20 5 1 2 7 20 5 1 2 7 20 5 1 2 7 2 7 2 7 2 7 2 7 2 7 2 7 2 7 2 7 2			55,521	+2 292 31,158	27,118	23,532 18 517	16,969	12,659	9,734 8,436 4,935	3 2	37	3 2 2 4	2.5	20	23	23	19
Median sig. — 28 U 26 3 23 2 7 20 5 19 8 19 2 28 5 19 2 10 0 100 0	70 to 7 vears	32,198 4,557	20,791 20,348	15,289 15 335	10,11.	7,789 7,616 2,758	5,889	4,357 3,848	2,978	18	14	1 2	10	0.8	08	08	0.7
10 10 16 years 70,211 7,485 87,224 86,135 84,342 37,486 33,768 87,887 84,10 21 10 21 10 81 1.0 9 1.4 11 81 10 71 10 10 18 years 70,7131 76,453 11	Median age	891,914	757,379	667,073	2, 7 557,498	20 5 480,460	372,142	281,524	220,974				100 0			100 0	70C 0
30 0.5 , 12	10 to 14 years	107,113 87,609 74,501	70,305	78.419	09,384	22.08_	54,289 50,041 43,866	40,570 39,079 35,708	35,443 32,626 26,995	9.8	10 2	10 8	12 4	12 9	13.5	13 9	14.2
18 to 19 yran. 66,907	20 to 24 years -	70,543	67,953	53,970	49,887	48,664 44,745 19,616	3_,351	25, 211	19.063	79	8 7	10 2 9 2 8 1	8 9	8 2	10 2 9 2 8 3	10 7 9 0 7 2	98
00 to 44 years 25 250 22,227 15,127 2,664 9 674 9,718 5,2766 4,7131 3 2 2 9 2 4 2 3 2 7 1 8 1 6 2 0 1 1 1 1 1 1 1 1 1 1 1 1 1 1 1 1 1 1	40 to 44 years	66,969 61,590	55,672 47,887	38,402	38,613	31,580 24,±39	21,281	17,408	12,913	7 5 6 9	63	- 8	56	50	5 2	6 8	3 6
5 years and ever 15,077 8,986 6,986 4,314 3,382 2,128 1,755 1,080 1.7! 1.2 1.0 0.8 0.7 0.6 0.6 0.5 0.0 reported . 1,080 1.7! 1.2 1.0 0.8 0.7 0.6 0.6 0.5 0.7 0.7 0.6 0.6 0.5 0.7 0.7 0.7 0.7 0.7 0.7 0.7 0.7 0.7 0.7	50 to 5 ₂ years 55 to 59 years	44,552 35,924	28 182 28 225	28,838 21,958	20,948	2,404 9,674	12,880 8,592	9,227 6,293	A. 08	40	3 7	3 :	3.8	3 7	2.3	2 2	2 3
And reported . 248 1,56/ 2,166 504 576 0.3 0.5 0.1 0.2	65 to 69 years 70 to 74 years 75 years and over	23,062	-7,212	6,986	4,514	6,_20 3,669	2,788 2,328	2,169	2,593 .,478	26	13	16	0 9	13	0 8	0 8	
	Not reported Median age			258	1,56	2,166	504						0 3	0 5	0 1	0 2	

GENERAL CHARACTERISTICS

Table 16 -- AGE BY COLOR AND SEX, FOR THE STATE 1980 TO 1950--- Col.

(Percent not seven where see Jun 6 percent and merrian for those in the see Jun 60

Age color and ser	****	***		Pop at .		-					-	in tel. T	etr's 's 01			
	1950	1940	1930	1920	-910	1900	1890	1886	1,75 .	740	13,0	1929	19 0	1901	890	1880
WHITE-Con.	100	1000		1	1	1	1		,					-87.63	Skel	
Female all ages	904,709	754,360	655 639	539,	440,620	348,470	270 27	4_5,760	.x:	ا د سد	_4 .	100 0	- (v3 t)	Jr C	100 0	100
Under 5 vents - 5 to 9 years - 0 to 14 years 0 to 12 years 20 to 24 vents 20 to 24 vents 30 to 34 years 30 to 30 years 10 to 4 vents 10 to 4 vents	102,816 85,515 71 83,4 58,366 74,807 76,608 59,5_3,67,5_8,51,327	68 58. 67,990 75,309 76,577 70,509 67,11 61,824 55,677 46,561	71,339 70,338 70,34 68,338 65,160 55,71 47,890 44,27 36,339	64,700 67,040 68,000 87,31- 52,329 4 998 37,712 38,3821 29,109	64,846 90,1_5 20,193 49,56 45,953 38,488 28,171 20,86	54 344 4, 25 4,647 38, 904 5,072 30 167 42, 534 18 654	39,72,1 27,48 34,73 22,74,2 27,32 28	2 35. 27,27. 22,313. 23,73. 23,73. 2,230. 4,76. 10,825.	1077 8877	2 2 2 2 2 2 2 2 2 2 2 2 2 2 2 2 2 2 2	10 ye	40 F F F F F F F F F F F F F F F F F F F	13 1 1 1 1 1 1 1 1 1 1 1 1 1 1 1 1 1 1	1/ 5	1- 0 13 7 12 5 1 6 9 7 6 5	12 12 10 8 6 9
o to 49 years 0 to 54 3.01 - 5 to 59 years 5 to 69 years 5 to 69 years 5 to 69 years 5 to 72 years 5 years and over	52,712 44,376 37,099 29,698 25,639 17,396 19,480	40,797 33,454 27,339 22,384 -8,140 -0,705 -1,362	20,283 20,234 14,960 10,552 7,841 8,343	24,063 2,790 2,790 -,492 3,305 3,290 3,290 5,307 645	10,002 -5 933 1,038 8,843 6,279 4 20 4,234 592	13,4/9 1,400 8,5°, 6 u.e. 4,73° 3,101 2,783	2,113,	8, 167 7, 199 7, 138 3, -73 2, 232 -, 266 -, 394	33092	54	2 3 1 2 3 1 4 6 1 4 1 3 1	4 33 24 21 -5	35,34	4 8 9 2 3 2 3 2 3 2 3 2 3 2 3 2 3 2 3 2 3 2	3 9 3 3 3 2 2 2 2 8 8 9 9 9	4 3 2 1
Median age	78.2	26 4	23 2	21 4	2C 4	70 -	19 2	19 4					- 1			
NONWHITE	. I	1					-									
Total all ages .	886,833	852,41	778,881	701,898	715 302	652,013	>60,.93	484,~92	100 0	100 0	±00 0	10C 0	100 0	_ar J	_00 0	100
Under 5 vears 5 to 9 years 1 to 19 years 1 to 19 vears 20 to 24 vears 25 to 29 vears 30 to 34 years 30 to 34 years 40 to 44 vears	24,537 101 981 88,999 75,838 67,54 62,048 >4,388 >8,435 >2,435	91,74. 89,932 90,881 87,177 77,934 73,689 63,613 62,800 49,933	85,299 93,430 85,036 84,530 79,794 69,272 52,377 56 532 43,854	77,468; 20,806; 37,442; 7,655; 69,071; 60,085; 40,976; 51,183; 37,149	92,5"8 96,127 86,050 76,976 74,2.7 03,80 47,586 40,240 33,452	92,875 93 527 82,872 99 468 68,806 55,828 58,167 33,796 26,898	8-,-47 83,-03 75,275 62,-72 54,727 39,646 29,060 30,341 22,248	81,289 79,550 37,944 40,737 46,257 38,853 27,200 23,74 2-,874	4 5 10 0 8 6 7 6 7 6 0 9 9	10 8 13 6 11 10 2 10 2 10 5 7 4	1209	12 4 12 8 13 8 14 15 8 15 8 16 5 17 3	12 9 13 4 12 0 10 8 -0 4 8 9 6 7 6 5 4 7	14.2 14.3 12.7 10.6 10.6 5.9 5.2 4.1	15 0 14 9 13 4 11 1 5 8 7 1 5 2 5 4	16 45 14 25 24
15 to 49 years 10 to 54 years 10 to 59 years 10 to 69 years 15 to 69 years 15 to 69 years 15 years and over 15 years and over	48,148 37 959 30,509 23 130 30,260 17,289 16,644	43 763 33,411 25,863 18,752 20,610 10,845 10,857	41,427 0,464 20,171 1,200 9,802 6,111 8,191 351	36,486 24,160 14,405 12,301 3,017 3,752 7,700 2,116	25,6-7 20,767 -4,778 12,696 8,669 0,007 7,253 2,228	22,809 20,320 -2,971 -1,684 7,441 5,449 7,035 2,363	20,789 17,845 1,604 10 285 1,34 4,703 0,484	18,524 17 007 8,510 10 572 5,274 4,143 5,100	34 204 1 9	51 39 30 22 24 13	5 3 9 2 6 P 0 3 8 1 1 1	2 2 4 2 1 1 8 1 2 8 1 3	3 6 2 9 2 1 1 8 2 0 8 1 0	3512081	383201811108	3 3 1 2 0 1
Median age	23 9	24 3	22 3	21 0	20 3	_9 0	18 .	18 4								
Male all ages	427,232	+15,003	380,750	345,831	354 815	323,591	277,827	239 780	100 D	10X O	100 0	200 0	700 D	100 0	200 0	100
Inder 5 years to 9 years to 9 years 5 to 19 years 5 to 19 years 5 to 29 years 0 to 24 years 5 to 29 years 5 to 39 years c to 44 years	62 550 50,940 44 622 36,683 30,448 48,350 24,399 20,670 24,442	40 048 44,791 45,239 4,842 37,932 34,073 29,951 29,283 24,402	42 364 46,484 42 115 38,334 36 698 31,964 24,673 27,130 21,854	38,483 43,525 43 273 35,370 31,274 27,346 21,595 25,444 18 5 70	45,935 48,083 43,003 36,238 34,638 30,956 23,799 23,590 1, 282	46,37, 47,_47 44,707 33,190 32,39° 27,434 19 328 17,043 13,515	42, 753 42 133 33,349 29,347 25 914 19 375 14,089 15,262 10,990	40,806 27,875 24,385 19,194 21,600 19,424 12 903 12 223 10,128	14 6 1 9 0 4 3 6 7 1 6 6 5 8 5 7	11 1 10 9 7 a 40 1 8 7 8 2 7 2 7 1 5 6	1 12 2 1 1 1 2 2 1 1 1 9 6 8 4 6 7 1 1 5 7	12 6 22 5 10 2 9 0 7 9 6 2 7 4 5 4	12 9 10 2 9 8 8 7 6 7 6 6	14 3 14 6 12 9 10 3 10 0 8 5 6 0 5 3 4 2	15 4 15 2 13 8 10 6 9 3 7 0 5 1 5 5	17 12 12 8 9 8 5
5 to 49 years 0 to 54 years 5 to 59 years 0 to 64 years 5 to 69 years - 0 to 74 years 5 to 69 years - 0 to 74 years 6 years and over	22,184 18,472 15,51- 11,489 14,183 7,201 7,905	22,_36 17,387 13,503 9,524 10,453 5,529 4,940	21,457 16,506 11,59 8,23 5,104 2,983 5,703 191	21,005 13,247 7,994 6,623 4,039 2,860 3,500 182	13,180 10,535 8,715 0,59- 4,-24 3,002 3,399 1,259	17,555 10,449 6,973 5,719 3,830 2,585 3,252 1,160	10,174 8,996 5,594 5,131 3,345 2,343 2,8_1	9 627 8 5-8 4,969 5 447 2 827 2 114 2,429	36733719	2 3 3 2 3 5 1 4	540213800101	6 1 3 8 2 3 1 9 1 3 0 8 1 0	3 7 3 1 4 3 1 9 1 3 0 8 1 0	3 6 3 2 2 1 1 8 1 2 0 8 1 0	37 32 2 2 3 2 3 3 3 3 3 3 3 3 3 3 3 3 3	322101
Memar age.	23 1	24 _	22 9	21 9	20 5	19 0	17 o	18 0	1							
Female all ages	455,281	457,138	بور. Sec	356 061	360,487	328,422	282,366	245,212	_00 O	100 0	100 0	100 a	100 0	100 0	100 0	400
nder o years to 9 years 7 to 14 years 5 to 19 years 5 to 19 years 5 to 24 years 5 to 29 years 1 to 24 years 5 to 39 years 1 to 34 years	61,987 51,041 44,377 39,155 37,086 33,698 29,789 31,765 27,692	45,093 45,141 45,642 45,355 42,002 39,640 33,662 33,5-7 25,531	42,935 46,946 42,941 43,216 43,096 37,311 27,704 29,402 22,000	98,985 43,282 44,169 40,276 37,797 32,739 24,181 22,739 18,579	46,643 48,044 43,053 40,738 39,579 32,865 23,789 22,650 15,870	46,498 46,380 41,165 35,978 36,409 28,394 18,829 16,753 13,363	41,394 41,270 36,876 32,665 28,8.3 20,241 14,971 .5,103 11 958	40 48.3 37,675 28 328 21,543 24,597 19,429 14 297 -3,518 -1,760	13 5 13 7 8 5 8 1 7 3 6 5 6 0	10 3 10 4 10 4 9 6 5 1 7 7 7 7 5 8	10 8 10 8 10 8 10 8 9 4 7 0 7 4 5 5	10 9 17 2 12 4 11 3 10 6 9 7 6 8	12 9 3 3 11 9 1 0 9 1 6 6 6 3	14 2 14 : 12 5 11 0 1: 1 8 6 5 7 5 1	14 7 14 6 13 1 11 6 10 2 7 2 5 3 5 3 4 2	10 10 10 7 5 4
5 to 19 years 0 to 54 years 15 to 59 years 0 to 64 years 0 to 64 years 0 to 69 years 0 to 74 years 0 to 74 years vears and over	24,964 19,487 14,995 11 6-1 16,077 7,088 8,739	21,627 16,224 12,300 9,228 10,357 5,316 5,947	19,970 14,158 9,012 6,965 4,699 3,128 ,488 160	15,391 10,913 6,471 5,738 3,978 2,892 3,997 935	12,481 9,832 6,663 6 307 4,145 3,005 3,854 969	11,254 9,871 6,068 5,965 3,611 2,864 3,787 1,203	10,6.5 8,8.9 5,0.0 5,158 3,045 2,360 3,373 695	8,894 8,469 3,941 5 125 2 447 2,029 2,671	54 42 33 25 35	4 9 3 7 2 8 2 1 2 4 1 2	5 0 3 6 2 3 1 7 1 2 0 8 1 1	4 3 3 1 1 8 1 6 1 1 0 8 1 1	3 5 2 7 1 3 1 7 1 1 0 8 1 1	3 4 3 0 1 8 1 8 1 1 0 9 1 2 0 4	3 8 3 1 1 8 1 8 1 1 0 8 1 2 0 2	33112211001
Median age	2+ >	24 4	22 7	21 4	20 2	19 1	18 3	18 7								

Table 1" —CITIZENSHIP AND NATIVITY OF THE POPULATION 21 YEARS OLD AND OVER, FOR THE STATE, URBAN AND RURAL, 1950, AND FOR THE STATE, 1940 AND 1930

(Percent not shown where ess than 0 Lo, where base is 1988 * ran 100)

				Popula	tion 21 ve	ars old and	Ver	-	_	28.7	4.00	Foreign b	orn 21 yea	ars old a	nd over
				Ctan				Alir	_	Catases			Per	cent of t	iotal
Area and eensus vear	Total	All u.u	Pls	Nation 1	e	Valura	dized	140	u	repor		[otal	Va.u	Alen	Citizen-
	10-4	\umber	Percent or total	\us ber	Percent of total	Numbe	Percent of total	Number	Percent of total	Number	Percent of total	1	ralized	- Alien	ship not reported
Form non arm Purel farm	286,-07	2579,244 932,546 355 787 285,330	99 4 39 2 79 0 95 7	1,509,048 917,35, 35, 693 38,,700	98 2 97 6 99 1 99 3	18,196 15,271 17-5 1,130	0.5	5 820 5,251 872 697	0 4 0 6 0 2 0 2	3 081 2,371 435 275	02	28,097 22,893 3,402 2,102	64 8 66 7 97 9 55 8	24 3 22 9 28 1 33 2	10 4 14 3 13 1
1940	, 374,9.7 1,13 852	1,304,933	99 3 98 °	1,147,638	98 1 96 9	17,295 19,5c0	- 3	7,927 14,099	0 6 1 2	2,087 1,910	2 C 2 D	27,309	63 3 55 4	29 C	

Table 18 —SCHOOL AND KINDERGARTEN FAROLLMENT, BY AGE, FOR THE STATE, URBAN AND RURAL 1950 [Resed or 20 percent sample | For totals of ago groups from complete count, so, table 12 | Percent not abown where less than 0.1 or where here is less toam 500]

Raral nonfarm Rural tarm Urban Enrolled Enrolled Enrolled Eng Jed Ace Population Population Populacion Number Perent Population Percent Percent Number Percent Number SCHOOL FAROLLMENT 152,770 265 970 30 735 99,870 26, 22 25 365 19 273 34,602 30,070 Total, 5 to 29 years old 55 355 162,080 38,075 37,800 45,400 48,143 33,220 22,090 155,905 35,475 27,280 10,240 17,140 10,30 3.,020 94,220 22,445 21,350 19,555 49 700 -7,490 37 0 90 0 89 ~ 64 7 25 4 7 4 30 9 93 7 87 4 62 0 26 8 6 3 4 8 116,000 356,170 87 275 84,515 84,221 42, 240 338 990 45, 925 50, 985 26 320 23, 202 14, 370 38 9 95 2 90 4 67 4 31 2 11 3 6 8 40 8 96 2 93 2 72 2 35 8 13 7 1,465 89,465 20,075 13,815 4,915 3,580 2,790 93,620 23,375 15,890 2,465 2,185 1,450 212,450 KINDERGARTEN ENROLLMENT 1,235 11 2 31,020 30,03 135 Total, 5 and 6 years old _

Table 19 -- SCHOOL ENROLLMENT BY AGE, FOR THE STATE 1910 TO 1950

[Asternik (*) denotes statistics based on 20-percent sample For totals or age groups roin compile a rount or 1900 see table 15. Percent not shown where loss shown of 1 or where base as less than 500 for 1900 sample figures 0 100 for series compileto-count figures;

	0.8	*1950			1940		10.00	1930			1920	11		1910	
Age		Enrolled in	school	-	Enrolled u	sebool		En.olled 11	loonse n	D. J. L.	Turolled in	вероој	Population	Enrolled I	n school
	Pupulation	Number	Percent	Population	Number	Percent	Population	Number	Percent	Population	Number	Percent	ropulation	Number	Percent
Total, 5 to 24 years old	941,245	1569,765	160,5	928,506	504,399	43	899,916	472,222	52 5	802,049	(2)		752,670	(2)	al Con-
to 19 years o and 6 years 7 to 13 years 14 and 15 years.	728,795 1,6,610 356,17 87 275	1546,460 145,240 338,990	75.0 -38 8 9> 2 10 4	712,210	492,-68 29,202 307,045 79,603		691 420 99,462 331,101 87 631	460, 792 33,972 295,54 68,275	14 0	630,762 90,910 308, 07 83,86	234,249	77 7 72 9 05 6	74,193	251,050 17,500 165,194 38,502	18 8c
_6 and 17 years 18 and 19 years to 24 years	84,515 84,225 212,450	78,925 56 985 26,320	67.4 5. 2 11 0	96,046	23 020 14,834	55 9	8",624 87,102 206,496	42 364 18,906 11,430	49 5	76,271 73,209 17,,287	28,053 9,849	36 6 23 5	71,0,4	21,343 8 651 (1)	30 12

¹ Excludes kundergarten enrollment 'chown separatel un table 18) largely monded in the earlier enrollment figures

Table 20—YEARS OF SCHOOL COMPLETED BY PFRSONS 25 YEARS OLD AND OVER, BY COLOR AND BY SEX, FOR THE STATE, URBAN AND RURAL, 1950, AND FOR THE STATE, 1940

[Asternak (*) denotes statutes based on 20-secont *arrie. For 'otal' of persons 25 venus old and over from complete count for 1950, see table 15. Persons not shown where less than 0.1 percent and medium no shown where less than 500 or 1950 sample, figures or .00 for 1950 carried for the count farmes]

100	77-4-1			more dis		Years o so	betel, men loor					Median
Area census year color,	Total, 20 years	Lee		Element	ary "chool		High so	loca	Colle	egc	Nut	school
and sex	ord and	Nonc	1 to 4 y ars	5 and 6 years	7 years	3 years	1 to 3 years	4 yea s	1 to 3 years	4 yea 9 or more	reported	pletes
*1950			1									
The State	2,415 145	129,045	276,675	208, 230	116,925	134,650	204,960	260,630	78,423	66 555	38,950	7.6
Ma.o Female	683 815 731,330	65 AGC 6-,380	146,025 130,650	98,205 110,125	55 025 51,900	64,053 17,600	92,330	66,385 94,245	47,320 41,115	36,1°0 30,365	22,630 16,320	74
White Nonwhite	987,255 427 910	28 645 70 400	122,305 154 170	127,755 80,575	82,235 34,640	106,475 28,1%	77,260 27,700	250,380 20 250	72,495	ol,585 4,970	27,900 11,050	88
Urpen	83+,100	10,45	120,825	210,245	65,545	90,550	128,875	26,450	60,285	×3 680	2/,560	8 6
Male Female	390 905 4+3,255	22,435	63 030 62 795	20,325 29 920	30,000 35,475	41,925	57, 47,5 71,300	51,670 74,780	29,705 30,480	30,130 23,550	14,040	8 5 8 7
Wh_te. Nonwhite	595 350 233,810	20,760 27 385	51,060 74,765	62,740	42,535 23,^10	21,405	2_,020	2,535 8,915	5>,860 4,425	49,600 4,080	18,260 6,300	10 4 5.6

Table 20—YEARS OF SCHOOL COMPLETED BY PERSONS 25 YEARS OLD AND OVER, BY CCLOR AND BY SEX FOR THE STATE, URBAN AND RURAL, 1950, AND FOR THE STATE, 1940—Con.

[Asserting of denotes state that has a state of the stat

	Total			The second	11 -14-1	Years of sel	so, ocrapleter	100000	200			Median
Area, census year cole-,	25 years	1		El-nen	arv schoo	- Alexander	High so	ol :	Ceta	50e I		нечосі театя
and our	o.et.	None	I to 4 veam	years	7 years	5 years	1 to a gears	4 year	1 o 3 years	4 years or mo e	reprired	oom
*1950-Con.				i	i					-	- 1 -71	
Aural nonfarm	320,960	43,150	75,3.5	20,6.5	27,460}	24,42	46, 495	2,335	12,575	0,2,0	8,675	6
Kalo	158,755	21 995 21,155	9,9_5 35,400	26,390	13,195 _4,2%	-2,555	24,780	13,090	7,055	4,440	5,250 3,425	6
Thite	96 025	21,205	37,250 38,035	33,76C 16,855	21,235 6,230	3,690	42, 295	22,425 910	1.,580	8,570	5,950	7 3
Rurai farm	260,025	37,750	75,535	47 470	و 19رق	19,675	29,890	40,847	5 365	3,605	5,725	5
fine -	134,155	21,235 36,515	43 080 32,455	23 655 23,815	12,15	9 570	.3,340 .6,550	4,470	2,085	1,620	3,340	5
Vhite	166,950 93,075	21,070	34,165 41,370	31,255 16,215	18,465 5,450	16,595 3,080	27,210 2,680	10,420 425	5,055 510	3,415	3,690	7.
1940												
The State	1,204,647 595,988	79,758	275,222	97,822	108,441	97,561	_44,162	1_7,809	22 وغدو	42,316	10,322	6
Semale	608,659	74,724	127,599	105,385	53,532	46, 938 50, 623	6",#79 76,283	49,996 67 813	22,620 28,505	18,271	5,175 4,547	6.
White	790,171	66,039 88,-43	110,973	122,340 80,867	80,770 27,671	79, .04 18,457	_26,06°	7,262	47,575 3,550	39,792 2,524	6,902 3,360	8.
PERCENT DISTRIBUTION	4 11	Gar.										
*1950												1
The State	100 0 400 0	91	19 6	47	8.3	9 5	14.5	11 4	5.5	47	2.8	
emale	100.0	9.6	17 9	2 1	80	9 4	15 4	9 7 12 9	5.6	23	3 3 2 2	
White	700 O	16.5	12 4 36 0	2 9	8 1	10 8 6 6	18 0 6 5	15 2 2 4	7.3	. 2 . 2	2 8	err.
Urban	100 0		15	13.2	19	10 9	_5 4	15 2	" 2	6.4	2.9	
Male	100 O 100 O	5 7 5 8	16 ± 14 2	12 9	8 0	10 7	14 7 46 1	13 2 16 9	7 6	7.7 5.3	3 6 2 4	
White Nonwate	100 0	13	8 6 31 3	10.5	3 6	11 6	18 1	19 7	9,4	8.3 1.7	2 6	
Rural nonfarm.	100 L	3.1 4	23,5	15 6	8 6	7.6	14.4	73	3 9	2 9	2 7	
Male Cemale	100.0	13 9 13 0	25.1	15 3	8 8	7 9 7 3	13.5	6 5 8 1	4 3	2 8 2 9	3 3	
White.	100.0	9 4 22.9	±6 6 39 6	5 0 17 6	6.5	9 2 3 8	18 8 4 2	10 0	10	3 8 0 7	2 6	
Rural farm.	100 0	2/. 5	29 0	83	9 2	7.6	יו 5	4 2	2.1	14	2,2	
Male	_00 C	15.8	32 1 25 8	18 9	8 8 9 7	7 1 8 0	9 9 13 1	3 3	1 5 2 8	7-5	2 5	
White	100 O	10 0 22 6	20 5 44 4	18 7 17 4	11 1	9 G 3 3	10 3 2 9	6.2 0.5	3.0	2.0	2 2 2	
1940												
The State	100 0	12 6		16 9	9 0	8 1	12.0	9.8	4.2	3.5	0 9	
Maie Female_	100 0 100 0	13 4 12 3	24 8 21 0	10 4	9.0	7 9 8 3	11 4 12 5	8 4 -1 1	3 8 4 7	4 0 3 0	3.7	
White	100 0	8 4 2: 3	14 0 39.6	19 5	10.2	10 0	16 0	14 0	6 0 0 9	5 0	0 2	

Table 21 -- MARITAL STATUS BY COLOR, FOR THE STATE, URBAN AND RURAL, 1950, AND FOR 1HE STATE, 1940 [Percent not shown where 'ess than 0 1 or where base ... less than 100]

				Male							Female			
Area census year and colo-	Total	Sing	.0	Mar :	ed	Widowed or	divorced	Total	que	le	Warm	ed	Widowed or	divorced
	14 years old and over	Number	Percent	Number	Percent	Number	Pe. cont	old and over	Number	Percent	Number	Percent	Number	Percent
1950 White Nonwhite	914,015 636,518 277,497	236,374 160,207 76,157	25 9 25 2 27 4	630,055 440,887 183,168	66 9 70 2 66 0	29,424	5 2 4 6 6 5	968,553 657,973 310,590	185,330 123,716 61,614	1º 1 18 8 19 8	643,519 448,324 495 195	66 4 68 1 62 8	139,704 85,933 53,771	14. 13. 17
White Nonwhite	509,609 366,359 443,250	87,355 35,664	24 ± 23 B 24 9	358,982 261,519 97,463	70 4 71 / 68 0	17,485	5 4 4 8 7 ±	473,796 400,244 173,551	.08,866 77,738 31,128	_9 0 _9 4 17 9	371, 149 263, 355 107, 794	65 8 62 1	93,782 59,251 34,630	16 14 20
Rural nonfarm. White Nonwhite	215,380 151,646 63,734	25,68. 37,870 17,811	25 9 25 0 27 0	147, 713 106, 591 41, _22	68 6 70 3 64 5	11,966 7,185 4,801	5 6 4 7 7 5	217,891 149,674 68,217	37,956 24,706 13,250	19 4	149, 151 107, 004 42, 547	68 6 71 5 62 4	30,384 17,964 12,420	18 12 73

Pural farm	189,026 118,513 70,513	57,67- 34,982 22,792	30 2 29 5 32 2	123, 360 78, 777 44, 583	65 3 66 5 63 2	4,754	4 2 4 6	176,866 108,055 68,811	38 #08 21,272 17 236	21.8 19 25 0	122,8.9 77,965 44,854	69 4 72 2 65 2	15,539 8,818 6,721	8
1940	842,817	283,820	33 7	518, 295	6. 5	40,702	4.8	807,629	224,278	25 a	525,464	60 6	117,887	13

Table 22.—MARRIED COUPLES, FAMILIES, HOUSEHOLDS, AND INSTITUTIONAL POPULATION, FOR THE STATE, URBAN AND RURAL: 1950

[[illegible] * denotes statistics based on 20-percent sample. Percent not shown where less than 0.1 or where base is less than 500]

Area	*Married couples: Total	*Married couples: With own household	*Married couples: Without own household: Number	*Married couples: Without own household: Percent	*Families and unrelated individuals: Families	*Families and unrelated individuals: Unrelated individuals	Households: Number of households	Households: Population in households	Households: Population per household	Institutional population
The State	[illegible]	[illegible]44,272	39,315	6.7	648,413	134,280	724,534	2,616,079	3.61	18,972
Urban	328,595	303,365	25,230	7.7	372,515	112,520	421,022	1,420,436	3.37	10,389
Rural nonfarm	135,360	128,150	7,210	5.3	157,400	31,700	172,568	629,111	3.65	8,583
Rural farm	119,240	112,365	6,875	5.8	[illegible]	10,060	130,944	566,532	4.33	

Table 23.—RESIDENCE IN 1949, BY COLOR, FOR THE STATE, URBAN AND RURAL: 1950

[Based on 20-percent sample. For totals of persons 1 year old and over from complete count, see table 15. Percent not shown where less than 0.1 or where base is less than 500]

Color and residence in 1949	Residence in 1950: The State	Residence in 1950: Urban	Residence in 1950: Rural nonfarm	Residence in 1950: Rural farm	Percent distribution: The State	Percent distribution: Urban	Percent distribution: Rural nonfarm	Percent distribution: Rural farm
ALL CLASSES								
Persons 1 year old and over, 1950	2,625,085	1,440,015	629,950	555,120	100.0	100.0	100.0	100.0
Same house as in 1950	2,114,080	1,132,565	508,450	473,035	80.5	78.7	80.7	85.2
Different house, same county	308,100	182,930	71,110	54,060	11.7	12.7	11.3	9.7
Different county or abroad	148,865	94,370	37,785	16,710	5.7	6.6	6.0	3.0
Residence not reported	54,040	30,220	12,605	11,315	2.1	2.1	2.0	2.0
WHITE								
Persons 1 year old and over, 1950	1,760,890	1,002,550	432,205	326,135	100.0	100.0	100.0	100.0
Same house as in 1950	1,385,480	765,375	340,960	279,145	78.7	76.3	78.9	85.6
Different house, same county	213,915	133,670	51,075	29,170	12.1	13.3	11.8	8.9
Different county or abroad	125,890	81,070	31,445	11,375	7.2	8.1	7.3	3.5
Residence not reported	37,605	22,455	8,725	6,445	2.1	2.2	2.0	2.0
NONWHITE								
Persons 1 year old and over, 1950	864,195	437,465	197,745	228,985	100.0	100.0	100.0	100.0
Same house as in 1950	728,600	367,220	167,490	193,890	84.3	83.9	84.7	84.7
Different house, same county	94,185	49,260	20,035	24,890	10.9	11.3	10.1	10.9
Different county or abroad	24,975	13,300	6,340	5,335	2.9	3.0	3.2	2.3
Residence not reported	16,435	7,685	3,880	4,870	1.9	1.8	2.0	2.1

Table 24.—COUNTRY OF BIRTH OF FOREIGN-BORN POPULATION, FOR THE STATE, URBAN AND RURAL, 1950, AND FOR THE STATE, 1860 TO 1940

[Percent not shown where less than 0.1 or where base is less than 100]

Country of birth	Foreign-born white: 1950 Total	1950 Urban	1950 Rural nonfarm	1950 Rural farm	1940	1930	1920	1910	Percent distribution: 1950	1940	1930	1920	1910	Total foreign born: 1900	1890	1880	1870	1860
All countries	28,884	23,334	3,301	2,249	27,27[illegible]	35,991	44,871	51,782	100.0	100.0	100.0	100.0	100.0	52,903	49,747	54,146	61,827	80,975
England and Wales	1,782	1,442	234	104	1,241	1,578	1,895	2,138	6.2	4.6	4.4	4.2	4.1	2,194	2,556	2,661	2,937	4,087
Scotland	418	331	59	28	327	435	445	455	1.4	1.2	1.2	1.0	0.9	399	465	659	814	1,051
Northern Ireland	16	12	1	3	120	234	2,000	2,753	0.1	0.4	0.7	4.5	[illegible]	6,436	9,236	13,807	17,068	28,153
Ireland (Eire)	709	630	65	14	691	970			2.5	2.5	2.7							
Norway	376	345	21	10	383	487	555	294	1.3	1.4	1.4	1.2	0.6	169	136	78	76	63
Sweden	247	191	35	21	316	433	522	347	0.9	1.2	1.2	1.2	0.7	359	328	270	358	193
Denmark[1]	213	177	25	11	241	315	331	239	0.7	0.9	0.9	0.7	0.5	216	252	285	291	309
Netherlands[2]	263	208	45	10	212	220	250	11[illegible]	0.9	0.8	0.6	0.6	0.2	78	76	170	232	262
Belgium	265	164	64	37	238	307	350	24[illegible]	0.9	0.9	0.9	0.8	[illegible]	315	275	193	230	299
Switzerland	136	113	15	8	191	260	378	420	0.5	0.7	0.7	0.8	0.8	523	521	674	873	878
France	1,521	1,294	157	70	1,840	2,935	4,182	5,302	5.3	6.7	8.2	[illegible]	10.2	6,500	8,437	9,992	14,[illegible]41	14,938
Germany	2,467	1,932	319	216	2,574	3,616	5,147	[3]8,814	8.5	9.4	10.0	11.5	[3]17.0	11,839	14,625	17,475	18,933	24,215
Poland	955	636	154	165	581	655	377	[3]710	3.3	2.1	1.8	0.8	[3]1.4	108	100	164	198	196
Czechoslovakia	234	107	44	83	228	332	302		0.8	0.8	0.9	0.7						
Austria	429	367	37	25	434	467	725	[3]1,417	1.5	1.6	1.3	1.6	[3]2.7	795	585	299	455	399
Hungary	312	135	58	119	393	361	305	397	1.1	1.4	1.0	0.7	0.8	148	56	40	29	
Yugoslavia	42[illegible]	256	102	69	445	397	312		1.5	1.6	1.1	0.7						
U. S. S. R.[4]	1,018	923	56	39	1,193	1,375	1,928	[3]1,369	3.5	4.4	3.8	4.3	[3]2.6	692	345	158	165	84
Lithuania	79	61	5	13	68	31	23		0.3	0.2	0.1	0.1						
Finland	92	76	11	5	74	82	147	117	0.3	0.3	0.2	0.3	0.2	73				
Rumania	116	103	10	3	125	127	93	11[illegible]	0.4	0.5	0.4	0.2	0.2	[illegible]6				
Greece	497	474	18	5	505	574	610	237	1.7	1.9	1.6	1.4	0.5	8[illegible]	44	39	49	18
Italy	7,678	6,191	731	756	9,849	13,526	16,254	20,233	26.6	36.1	37.6	36.2	39.1	17,431	7,767	2,527	1,889	1,279
Spain	388	345	34	9	445	669	1,258	712	1.3	1.6	1.9	2.8	1.4	583	889	987	1,130	1,806
Portugal	47	26	13	8	31	52	100	57	0.2	0.1	0.1	0.2	0.1	94	112	141	125	145
Other Europe[1,4]	232	170	38	24	131	221	137	[5]145	0.8	0.5	0.6	0.3	[5]0.3	40	277	143	23	68
Asia[6]	1,125	954	139	32	1,029	1,146	1,117	1,181	3.9	3.8	3.2	2.5	2.3	1,175	393	499	128	80
Canada—French	[7]175	[7]130	[7]39	[7]4	168	222	157	250	[7]0.6	0.6	0.6	0.3	0.5	[7]2[illegible]	[7]95	[7]726	[7]714	[7]830
Canada—Other[7]	1,029	862	140	27	747	777	1,024	919	3.6	2.7	2.2	2.3	1.8	781	667			
Mexico	1,106	870	133	103	1,030	1,606	2,399	996	3.8	3.8	[illegible]	[illegible]	1.9	488	404	424	409	320
Other America	3,055	2,911	113	31	1,279	1,411	1,359	569	10.6	4.7	3.9	[illegible]	1.1	514	826	1,304	1,7[illegible]	1,205
All other	234	231	42	11	148	170	180	181	1.0	0.5	0.5	0.4	0.3	220	295	431	577	91
Not reported	1,175	667	342	185					4.1									

[1] Iceland included with Denmark prior to 1930, included with other Europe 1930 to 1950.
[2] Listed as Holland prior to 1910.
[3] Persons reported in 1910 as of Polish mother tongue born in Austria, Germany, and U. S. S. R. have been deducted from their respective countries and combined as Poland.
[4] Latvia and Estonia included with U. S. S. R. from 1860 to 1920 and with other Europe from 1930 to 1950.
[5] Includes 15 persons born in Serbia and 1 person born in Montenegro, which became parts of Yugoslavia in 1918.
[6] Includes Turkey in Europe.
[7] Includes Newfoundland.

Table 25 —EMPLOYMENT STATUS BY COLOR AND SEA, FOR THE STATE, URBAN AND RERAL 1550

Employment status and color		The S ate	- 1		. tan	market a freedom		rur = 2-m	1	- F	rei Ann	19 1
	Total	Male	T-erra.	I to	\na.	Temate	7 4	lien	renni.	r ta f	Male	riema.
All Classes	1			1	1	- Carloni				-		
Total population (all ages).	2,003,746	10.66	*	. 41.4×						me al		
Persons 14 years old and over .	1,882,568	9_4,0.5	908,00.	, "81,"	05,250 509,60s	573,79	6-4,312	24,380 j	32 ., 857	260,352	191, mal	27,5
a force	929,626	690,772	278,554	369 79m 1	201,460 l	76,20	184, 26	. Ju pr-	18,76		.46,006	23,
Employed		646./96	232,376	102, 798	386,565 163,4 5 22,6 F	76 2 3	184,72 3	wf		1.269	Sec. 5. 31	. A.
Unumployed Expenses workers	8°5,608 42,19-	646,/96 32,930 32,594	3,254	532,95_ 29,947	22,6 5	105,000	S'mic §	38, 172	30,73. 1,505 1,501	- 36 5	· 200	
New workers	585	3301	249	29,397	22 -46	6,95.	2 710	8,-70	1,530	2,502	1,972	
n ator orce -	953, 9-2 260, 758 115, 934	223,540	729, 43	513,611	23.6	307,27	272	b5 441	-70 -44	المار الد دور ب	42 380	- 53
Jable to work	115,934	67,103 10 984	48,7"1 1		29, 4	203,2321	77.50	25 . 121	:3 ** 81	2 634	42 380 4,036 13,32	.53 .6,
nma es o institutions	17,723 259,527	161.66	118, 365	1-2,35 i 75,522 i	78 C*	63 66.	4-17-3 B	24,94	2,9 9	46 7 0 1		
1 to 19 years old	25e 177 80,222	76 2.0 49 563	79,962	75,422 5 52 5_0 1	2 9731	.9,535	-7,5.5	19,342	0,23	44 89¢	27,3%	27
60 years old and over	23,133	389	118, 365 79, 962 30 659	14,22 }	9, 78	5,_4	1,000	4,5	,487	3,206	2,_54	1
White			1	1		-		1	1			
Total population (all ages)	1,796,683	891,944	904 709	1,022,31	40, 249	526 682		202 1 0	3 0 304	22. 614	103 440	
ersons 14 years old and over	1,294,493	436,5LA	657, 773	756,5C3	x66,329	-00,344	4-1, 44 3 . , 20	223,0_8 _51,646	249,574	332,668 226,268	172,647	
r force	635.786	491,276	144,361	400 035 8	291,022	111.213	128,357	_09,441 _06,02_	22,394	C ,710 10_,63-	90.811	.0,
inan lavor forco	625,707 602,368	481,346 401 958	144,361	390,716	271.70	100,07	128,357			10_,63- 34,910	90 241. 89,238	1,2
nemploved .	2,000	19 388	3,951	16,003	12,908	3,095	5,012	4,000	2.,701	1,724	1,303	-
labor fo.ce _	658 705	145,242	513,463	264 368	75,337	289,031	169,-79	44.203	127,276	174,858	27,702 6_8	9º 76 4
mable o work	05,268	f an poet	2,36	230,797	17, 24	232,293		4,550	7,019	13,399	9,23/	4
ther and not reported	-69,727	95,364	7,663 51,107	6,148 94 763 50,615	3,232 53,51° 25 118	2,916 4_,246 25,497	40,975	2,943	17,2781	33,989	17,870	16
14 to 19 years old _ 20 to 64 years old _	_02 762 51 361	6,175 95,364 51,605 32 951	51,157	34,263	22,069	12,194	4,573 40,975 26,526 10,900	23,09° 13,634 7,36°	12,89 ₄ 3,533	25,62 3,196 2,170	12,853	2
65 years old and over	15,004	_0,508	5,096	9,885	6,330	3,055	3,549	2,696	6.53	2,170	-,482	
Noawhite	1 5		1			- 1	1		1			
Total population (all ages)	886,833	-27,202	459,581	448,765	209, .01	239,764	20.,221	99,490	103,731	234,847	118,76.	116
ersons 14 years old and over	588 077	277,497	310,580	316,802	143,250	173, "52	131,951	63,73	68,217	139,324	70,513	
force	292 8AO 292, 095	198,796	94,044 94,015 88,702	-67,559	102, 4"	65,112	56,585 56,308	40,297	16,071	68,655	55,835 55 802	12
mployed.	273,240 _8,655	198,080 184,_38 13,542	3,702	167,082 133,236 13,84	10.,981 92, 99 9,782	65,101 61,039 4,062	52, 459 4, 199	40,297 37,028 3,269	16,061 15,13,	07,843 812	55,311 491	12
labor force	295,257	78,701	2,6,536	140 243	40,803	108.440	7" :66	23,020		20 628	.4 578	55
Seeping house	>0,666	1,599 2€,⊥95	2,471	71,698 26,561	752 12,838	70 946 13,723	35,428	459	72 146 34, 969 6, 699	40,640 8,035	388 4,586	55 40 4
nmates of institutions.	. 7,002	4,809	43,702	3,392 47,592	2.036		3 610 20,856	8,771 2,773 41,217	835			1
Other and not reported	\$9,800 50,410	4,809 46,098 24,605	28,805	25,007 18,247	25,177 11,523 10,906	22,315 13,484	12,128	5,711	9,6-1 6,417 2,590	2_,350 16,275 3,979	9,704	11 8
20 to 64 years old 65 years old and over	28,861 7 529	16,612	28,805 12,249 2 648	4,338	2,748	2,341 -,790	6,635 2,095	5,711 4,045 1,/61	2,590 634	3,979 1,096	1,661	1
51												
PFRCENT DISTRIBUTION				-								
All Classes	00 0	.00 O	-00 0	100 0	10. 0	100-0	400 O	100.0	100 B	100 0	100.0	,
Persons 14 years old and over .	49 3	75 3	2/ 6	52 6	77.2	30.7	43 5		17 7	46 6 46 5	77.6	
disn labor force	48 8 46 5	7-3	24 6	51 9	75 9	30 7 29 5	42 6	6º 6 67 9 of 1	17 6	46 5 45 8	77.5	1
Jaeusploved	2 2	3 6	10	49 2 2 8	4.5	1 2	2 1	3.8	0 7	0 7	11	1
n labor force	50 2	24 5 0 5 7 3	75 4 57 4	47 4 28 2 2 2	22 8	69 3 52 8	56 5 31 8	30 4 0 7	82 3 62 6	53 4	22.4	5
nable to work.	6 2 0 9	7.3	50	22	7.0	52 8	3.5	0 7 10 8 2 7	6 3	6.2	0.5 7 3	3
nmates of institutions Other and not reported	13 8	15 4	12 2	13 .	15 4	0 7 11 1 6 8	14 3	16 2	12 4	15 1 11 5	1- 6 10 7	5
20 to 64 years old	8 s 4 3	15 4 8 3 5 4	3 2	4.6	7 2 6 5	3 4	4 0	53	8 9 2 8 0 7	28	27	7
60 years old and over	1 2	1 7	0.8	13	1 8	1	1 -	i	1	0.9	. 1	
avilian labor force	100 C	100 0	0000	700 U	00 O	100 0	100 0	100 0		100 0	_00.0	
oyed ploved	95 4	95 2	96 1	94 7 5 3	94 1	95 9	94 7 5 3	94 4 5 6 5 6	95 a 4 1	98 5	98 6 1 4 1 3	4
perprised workers	4 5	4.8	38	5.2	58	3 9	0 1	56	4 1 4 0 0 1	1 5	1.3	3
	100	1				-			10.5			1
White	100	1	1									
Persons 14 years old and over	49.1	100 0	700.0	100 0	100 C	100 0	100 0	100 3	100 0	100 0	100 C	6
r torce.	49 1 48 3	77 2 75 0	22 0 21 9	52 > 51 6	79 ~	27 6 27 8	43 8 42 6	69 9 69 9	15 0 14 9	44 9	76 6	5
Employed	46 5 1 8	72 6	21 3	49 5	74 2 3 5	27 0	40 7	66.0	24 5	08	75 4	3
n labor force	50 9		78,0	A7 5	M 4	72 2 58 0	56 2 34 0	27 8 0 7	85 D	55 1 23 9	23 4	4
	31 9	22 8 0 5 6 4	62 3 3 7 0 7	*O 5	04		7 2	0 7 9 6 1 9	67 7 4 7	23 9	23 4 0 5 7 8	8
Unable to work	5 0 0 8 13 1	14 4	0 7	12.4	0.9	10 2	1.5	1 9 15 6	1 1	15 1	10.	J
Unable to work _		81	7 8	66	14 6 6 9	6 4	. 8 8	90	8 5	15 U	.08	의
Unable to work Impases of institutions Other and not reported	79											
keeping house Unable to wora Inmases of invitutions Other and not reported 14 to 19 years old 20 to 64 years old _ 65 years old and over	7 9 4 0 1 2	5 2	28	1 3	6 0	3 0	3 6	18	2 4	2 7	3 9	3
Unable to work Impases of institutions Other and not reported	79			4 5 1 3 10 0	100 0 95 5 4 5	100 0	100 0	18		2 7 - 0 100 0 96 3 1 7	_000 G	0

Table 25.—EMPLOYMENT STATUS BY COLOR AND SEX, FOR THE STATE, URBAN AND RURAL 1950—Con.
[Remember too shown where less than 01 or waters base at less than 100]

		12.40									_	-
	7	The Sate			Urban		R	ural nonfarm			Rural farm	
Emprovment status and color	Total	Vais	Female	Total	Male	Female	Total	Malı	Famala	Total	Male	Female
PERCENT DISTRIBUTION-Con										1 7		
Persons 14 years old and over	2000	100 0	100 0	2/00 0	100.0	100 0	100 0	0 00 م	100.0		100 0	
Labo. force Civman labor force _ Employed _ Unamplywed	47 S 40 7 46 5 3 2	71 6 71 4 66 4 4 9	30 3 30 3 24 6 1 7	52 9 52 7 48 4 4 4	71.5 7.2 64.4 68	37 5 37 5 35 2 2 2	42 9 42 7 39 5 3.2	63 6 63 4 58 1 5 1	23 6 23 5 22 2 1 4	49 3 49 3 48 7 0 6	79 2 79 1 78 4 C 7	18 7 18 7 18 2 0 5
Not in labo. force Keeping ho ise Unable to work Inmites or institutions Other and not reported 14 to 19 years old	50 2 20 4 1 2 -5 3	2d 4 0 a 9 4 17 16 6	69 7 47 1 7 9 6 7 14 1 9.3	4~.1 22 6 8 4 . 1 15 0	28 5 9 0 4 17 6 8 0	62 5 40 9 7 9 0 8 12 9 7 8	57 1 26 8 11 7 2 7 45 8 9 2	36 4 0 7 13 8 4.4 17 6 9 0	76 4 51 3 9 8 1 2 1/ 1 9.4	50 7 20 2 0 2 15 3 11 7	20 8 0 6 6 5	12 9
20 to 64 years old	13	6 5	39	58	2.6	0 9	16	63	3 8	08	7 0	06
Caviliza labot .orce	100 0	100 0	100 C	100 0	100 0	100 0	100 0	100 0	100 0	100 0	100 0	100.0
Employed_ Unemployed	92 2 8	93 2 6 8	94 3 5 7	41 ° 3 3	90 4 9 6	93 8 6 2	92 5 7 5	9 <u>.</u> 9 8 1	94 2 5 6	98 8	99 1 0 9	97 5

Table 26 —LABOR FORCE, 1950 AND 1940, AND GAINFUL WORKERS, 1930 AND 1920, BY COLOR AND SEX, FOR THE STATE
[Figures for persons and gainful worsers 14 years 3dd and over for 1920 and 1980 include inknown age. Persons not shown where less than 0.1 or where bose is less than 100]

		3	Pota.		1130		М	840				Ter	nale	AZE T	15
	Popu	lation	Perions n or gainful old and o	workers.		Рорг	ilstion	Persons in or gainful old and o	workers	or force 14 years	Popu	lation	Persons in or gainfu old and o	Workers	bor fore
Census year and colo.	Total (all ages)	4 years old and over	Number	Percent of total popu- lation	Percent of population 14 and over	Total (all ages)	-4 years old and over	Number	Percent of total popu- lation	Percent of popu- lation 14 and over	Total (all ages)	14 years old and over	Number	Percent of total popu- lation	Percent of popu- lation 14 and over
ALL CLASSES 1950	2,083,510 2,363,880 2,101,593 1,798,507	1,882,568 1,710 446 1,439 992 1,189,079	884,164	34 6 37 4 38 3 37 2	49 3 51 7 50 9 56 2	1,319,466 1,172,382 1,0-7,823 903,335	914,015 842,817 714,414 596,789	690,072 674,5:8 617,017 519,839	57 5 58 9	75 5 80 0 86 4 87 1	1,364,350 1,491,498 1,053,770 895,174	867,629 725,578	238,554 209,606 187,326 148,308	17 8	24 2 25 8
WHTE 1950	1,796,683 1,511 739 1 322,7.2 2 096,611	1,294,491 1 1°2,753 907,921 722 271	635,786 546,160 465,769 369,463	35 4 36 1 35 2 33 7	49 1 49 1 51 3 51 2	891,914 57,379 667,073 557,498	636,518 555,041 456,360 30°,755	491,276 440,258 386,761 314,802	55 1 58 1 58 0 56 5	77 2 79 3 84 7 85 6	904,769 754,360 655,639 539,113	607,273 557,712 451,561 354,518	144,510 105,902 79,008 54,659	16 0 14 0 12 1 10 1	19 0
NONWHITE 1950	836 833 852,141 778,881 701,898	588,077 597,693 232,077 461,608	292,840 .338,004 338,5% 295,686	33 0 39 7 43 5 42 0	49 8 56 6 63 6 63 9	42", 2.32 41.5,003 380,750 345 837	277,497 287,776 258,054 229,036	198,796 234,300 230,255 205,037	46 5 56 5 60 5 59 3	71 6 81 4 89 2 89 5	459,581 437,138 398,131 356,061	310,580 309,917 274,017 238,572	94,044 103,704 108,318 93,649	23 7	30.3 33 5 39.5 39 3

Table 27 —EMPLOYMENT STATUS BY COLOR AND SEX, FOR THE STATE 1950 AND 1940 [Ongnal 1940 "Employed" figures revised, across excluded to conform to 1970 classification. Percent not shown where less than 0.1 or where base is less than 100]

				19	50							19	40			
	ng desira		p = 0.7	Tabo-	force			1				Labor	force			
	_				Civinan lab	or force			1				Civilian lab	or force		
Sex and color	Penuspon 14 years		Percent of pop-			Unemp	loyed	Not in labor	Population 14 years old and		Percent			Unemp	loyed	Not in
	old and over	Number	ulation 14 and over	Total	Employed	Number	Percent of civilian labor force	force	old and over	Number	of pop- ulation 14 and over	Total	Employed	Number	Percent of uvilian labor force	labor force
Total _	1,882,568	928,626	49 3	917,802	875,638	42,194	4 6	953,942	1,710,446	884,164	51.7	880,964	767,942	113,022	12 8	826.28
Male	908,553	690,072 238,554	75 5 24 6	679,426 238,376	646,494 229,_12	32,930 9,2 ₀ 4	48	223,943 729,999	842,81° 867,529	674,538 209,606	80 0 24 2	07,358 209,606	584,70. 183,241	86,657 26,365	12 9	158,25
White	1,294,491	635,786	49 1	625,707	602,368	23,339	3 ?	636,765	1,112,753	* 546,160	49 .	>42,780	473,603	69,377	12 8	566,593
dale	636,518	49_,276	77 2 22 0	481,346	461,958 140,410	-9,388 3,951	4027	145 242 513 463	555,041 557,712	440,258 105,902	79 3 19 0	+37,078 105,902	383,108 90,495	53,970 15,407	12 3 14 5	114,781
Nonwhite	588,077	292,840	49 8	292,095	273,240	18,855	6.5	290,237	59" 693	338,004	56 6	337,984	294,339	43,645	12 9	259,689
ale	27°,497 310,580	198,796 94,044	71 6	198,080	184,538	13,542	6 8	78 701 216,536	297 776	234,300	81 4 33 5	234,280	201,593 92,746	32,687	14 0	53,476

Table 28—CLASS OF WORKER OF EMPLOYED PERSONS AND MAJOR OCCUPATION GROUP OF THE EXPERIENCED CIVILIAN LABOR FORCE, BY SEX, FOR THE STATE, URBAN AND RUPAL 1930

[For let al. 10/27/10/25 June 1942 at least 10/27/10/25 June 1942 at least 10/27/10/25 June 1942 J

Class of worker and major occupation group		The Stare			1. SAF		P	"a, 1 e"'z'T	n	12. 12.	dun am	1
occupation group	Tetal 3	Maie	Female	7.4	Mair	Female	1 .8	Mai	Tema-r	13,4	Male	"em
Class of Wo ker	1		i	1	Ţ				97.00	1 162		-
Employed	875,008	.40,43cl	223, 2	232 754	363 ***5	+ 2, ME	· 9.4	_35 CT2	35 8,2	'e" 753	+4 5/9	23,
n ate wage and sawary workers	197,325 8 39,209 1	4.6,770 5: 50.	.c- '25	475 B29 B	250,500	.7. 3551	149,153	23 40	45,750	9,_00	4735	
elf-employed workers	39 209 1	151, -50	34 677	55 .00	4,302	20,02	18 mes	22,440	7 19.	8,-00	5,20	2
Inpa.d famuy workers	24 0_2	-4,110	2,302	4 .04	, rae	18.0,	45 CL 2,3	2, 681	3,336	29,395	8-,5_2	3
Мајо Оссиранов эгопр	d			· ·		7000	-,	-,05	2,000	1210	,025	1
Experienced civilian abor to ce, otal.	727,2.7 6	670,00	238 127									1
Professional tachin.cel and aindred workers	74 619			5-2,348	180 342	,32	_4, -14	_46 241	38.760	170,215	140,571	53
farmas and farm managers	9.04	***,053	49,3	25 7.3	12,94	42. 53	816	6 5°0 3 °°4	5 420 208 2,204	3,5.	S. 500 2 550	2,
Yarn's and farm managers Yanagers offi ials, and proprietors "except farm Derical and kind ed workers.	9- 02- 1 8- 44-	87,044	10,73	=,70	-5,7.2	922	4,000 14,009 9,055	1 485	2.23	84,254	2 550	2
Derical and kind ed Workers.	8" 444	الرفر : عد 1 705	20,540	109	.5,5.2 3. 739 24,2.8	3 75 L	7,755	5 97.5 25,423		2 756	1 4 6/3	-
kles workers Jaftsmen foremen and kindred workers.	37 3.3 235 843	104 226	-1474	23 88 4	27,2-8	7 642	3-1(3-	5 926	3,763	2 59"	4 '52	1,
peratives and Lindred workers.	3. 456 6	104 026	2, 15,		73,446	33 363	16 29/	33.43	2.50	11 _79	7,29	
ervice we Acra except private household	40,7_3	38,548	24 /5, 44, -7 = 34 92h	34,454	31 42	33 363	2,852	33, 43 356 5 54	2,6. 8 5.0 6,371	2,612	1 70	2,
Farm isocrets and foremen	57 146	38,348	34 925	3, 3	2,5901	27 428	1,505	4,00	6,57	10 103	20 529	9,
Apprecia except farm and mine	9_,24=	90, 97	2 048	23,991	5. 3.0	547 480	o, 8ed	19.574		7 218	29 529	9,
Decupation not reported	21 523	10,00	6,050	-a, 35-+ 1	25 70	3,-40	6,023	29, 471 2, 192	1 462	3,550	2,396	-,
Employed	a"5 LC8	u46 496	229, 112	534 452	303,375	169 000	4 90º	130,0 1	20مر خ	167 753	144,549	23
bourgement tool morel and bandend worken		4C 709	. 29. 0	54 3°c	12 495	2_891	_1 725	530	5,195	7 78	1 694	2,
farme and farm managers	87,879	8. 818	2,963	1 426 8	1 547	.09	3. 73	u 530	203	34.752	81 50.	2.
lignagers, omdals and propriesors except farm	74,10 PS 530	63,450	10,652	5-,994	49,12	867	13 993	1,790	2.195	3,223	2,533	:
Arme vand form managere Managers, officials and proprisons except farm Bartis and address workers	50,15	63,45 ₀ 35,72 35,79 ₀	20,277	5-,994 1-,9-0 -3,944	1 547 49,127 30 798 26 5 0	47,818 15 434	13 993 2,944 9,565	11,790 4,370 5 85/	3 711	3,23 2,700 2,660	2,533 1,255 1,534	:
	00 922		1 431 20,255	G- 396 E		2 571	24,470	24, 273	197	7,056	4 0,495)
Operatives and kirdred workers Private hous hold workers	43 584	1184	20,255	85,890	69,180	3. 57	34,783	32,038	8,24	10 860	10,036	
Service workers except private household	70.18a II	1,430 36 66u	42 254	32,6_0 5_,380	69,180 -,031 30,1°0	3, 500	2,536	5,337	3,9.6	2,538	- 63-1	2,
Front acts noted workers except private household farmly workers topaid farmly workers farm aboves except unpaid, and farm orementabovers except farm and wine	20 216	36 6(U 13,299	33 519 6 917	164	- 12-0	53 (973	698	2,9.0		14,490	6
Farm aboves except unpaid, and farm uremen	37,302	31, 24	5.681	2,/80	2,775	41	45.084	2 740	2,324	19 13	16 797	z,
Decupation not reported	1,294	8-08	1,890	6 024	3,987	2 04	28,2/7	2 /5	8.5	6 945	6,846	
Experienced usemployed.	44,509	32 594			22 440							
Des consents assents all and bandred and	70		5,010	29,300		0,75_	9 "10	8 7,0	-,534	≥ 502	1,00	
Processional, securical and kindred wo kers Parmers and raim mai.nagers Managers officials and propiets s except farm Regional and kindied workin.	238	54V 224	22.	643	46_	182	91	92	2 5	36 102	22 94	
Managere officials and propueto s except farm	8>8 1 88°	779	-79	733	674	50	9	8	9	20	94	1
Derival and kindsed worken	1 88	1,0,6	853	1,,92	708	751	14.	77	64 58	56	18	
Sales workers	1 338	5.832	528	1,163	/ 419	45"	142	8-	58	1_	1.9	
mentious and kindred workers	6,257	5,955	1,302	4,490	4 278	74	1,161	150	11	26° 319	266 284	
Piivate household workers	2,23/	63	25.	1 844	(2)	7.784	316	نو <i>5</i> 5رہ 21	2051	74	204	1
Service workers except private hou chold	1,530	1,832	-,409 350	-,9:0	1,722	1 248	292 812	137	155	331	232	1
why n re event reem and mure	4.92	6.795	152	4 514	40	1251	812	£ 738	84.	273	232	
Decupation and reporter	9,529	6,796 7,365	2,264	5,300	3,939	1,361	3,294	2,69	29 597	935	20° 729	
PERCENT DISTRIBUTION	i i											
Class of Wo ke	- 1		1				-					l
Employed	_00 D	200	100 0	-00 o	_00 0	20. 0	100 0	100 €	100 0			- 3-
Private wage and aslary workers	6/9	66 0	73.2							100 6	160 0	00
Sovernment workers	10 2	8/	511	11.7	77 -	78 3 14 5	73 8	2 1	o8 b	31 2	29 3	43
Government workers Self employed workers	9 = 1	23 4	51 74 43	11 7 LC 3	12 4	6 0	73 8 10 6 14 3	5 ° 8 1	19 5 9 1 2 9	4 B	3 5 58 5	1
Unpaid family workers	27	2 2	43	0.5	0.1	1 2	12	8.0	29	11 6	87	29
Major Occupation Group	fi.	1	1			1	- 1					
Experienced civilian labor force total	130 0	100 0	100 2	100 0	100 0	100 O	100 0	_ 100 c	100 0	100 0	100 0	100
Professional technical, and kindred workers	7 1			98		12 5		4 2	13 6	2.2		
farmers and farm managers	9 0	14 B	12 3	0.3	8 5	0 1	2 2	46	0.5	2 2 49 5 1 9	35 C 17	71
Farmers and farm managers Managers officials and proprietors, except farm Clerical and kindred storkers	8 2	0 5	4 2	10 3	12 9	4 5	7.6	9.2		19	17	
	2 5	5 4	21 3	23 4	8-0	25 3	53	30	-20	1.6	11	
Craftsmen foremen and kindred weakers Operatives and kindred workers	21 6	اد دي	0.8	-3 1	7.8 71	0.9	13 9	17 4	0 5	4 3	50	
	50	17 3	8 9	16 2	-9 0	10 0	19.7	22 9	22 2	1 5	71	10
Service workers, exoupt private bousehold _	801	5.71	14 7	10 6	8 3	15 6	4 8 6 3 9 1	02	12 8	15	0.8	10
Farm labora's and oremen	6 4	0.8	18 7 14 7 5 4 0.0	10 6	0 7	15 6	91	9 6	15 8 7 2	23 0	20 1	44
abo ers, except farm and mine	2 3	1, 1	2.5	20	13 0	0 8	16 3 3 6	20 2	12	42	49	
	4							-	-			
Employed	100 0	100 0	00.0	130 0	100 0	100 0	_00 0	100 0	100 0	400.0	م بھے	100
Protessional, technical, and kindred workers Farmers and faron managers	10 3	6 3 1	12 7	10 2 C 3	0 4	01	6 "	47	14 +	2 3 50 2	12	
Managers officials, and proprietors, except farm	8 5	9.8	46	10 7	13 5	4 /	80	b 5	60	19	26 4	1
Managers officials, and proprietors, except farm Clerical and kindred workers.	98	5 5	4 6 21 7 8 9	13 0	8 3	2, 9	5 _	32	12 3	7 6	12 56 4 18 09	
inles workers	- 5	15 3	89	10 7	. 8	9 1 1	35	42	10 1	16		
Draftsmen, foremen, and andrea workers Decatives and andrea works a Private household workers	17.0	15 3	88	16 1 6 1	18 6	09	14 0	17 6	0.5	42	48	9
Private household workers	12 0	0.2	_B-4	61	19 0	18 7	19 9 4 9 6 5	23 2	22 3	5 5	70	10
ervice workers except p ivate household	80 1	571	14 6	10 6	8 3	15 5	6.5	3 9	36 4	15	8.0	
revae neutrinos wirkers error private household ram laborers, unpaul amily wo kers ram laborers except unpaul and farm foremen aborers except farm and mune.	23	40	25	0.5	0 6	0.2		39	5 3	15	80	25
aborer except farm and mine.	0 6	12 7	08	9 2	33.1	0.8	8 6 16 2 1 9	20 2	12	41	11 6	1
Occupation not reported	1 4	- 3	08	11	11	12	19	18	23	16	12	
Experienced unemployed	100 0	100 0	100 0	10x 0	100 0	0.00	100,0	۰.00 م	100 0	100 0	TOG 0	100
Protestional technical and kindred workers	7.0		25		2 1	2.6				1 4	11	
armers and farm managers	0 6	1 7 0 7	0.2	0 2	0 5		0.9	0 8	0 3	1 + 4 1 1 2	11	1
Professional technical and kindred workers samers and farm managers. Managers officials and proprietors, except farm Clerical and kindred workers	2 1	2 4	0.9	2.5	30	0.8	±.0	11	0 0	12	09	
Clerica and kindred workers	3 2	2.5	9 5	5 8	3 0 4 2 3 2	10 8	1.5	0 9 1 C	3 8	12	09	
raftsmen foremen and kindred workers	14 2 1	25	101	15 3	19.7	5 6	120	14 1	0.71	40 7	11 5	
De-ratives and kindred workers	16 7	18 3		7.4	19 1	12 2	15.6	14 1	77		14 4	
rivate household workers	5 4	0.3	23 9	400	0 3	25 7	3 0	03	19 2	30	0 4	1
ervice workers except private bousehold	39	3 8	3 9	17	7 7	17 7	30	1 ?	10 1	2 0 13 2	11 8	16
The read and late.rie*	3 7	, ,	3 7		2: 3	18	18 2 33 9	2,3	19	10 9	177 8	14
aborers except farm and mine	16 7	20 9	1 8 24 0	16 7							13 3	

Table 281.—CLASS OF WORKER AND MAJOR OCCUPATION GROUP OF EMPLOYED WHITE AND NONWHITE PERSONS, BY SEX, FOR THE STATE, URBAN AND RURAL 1950

		The State			Urban		P	ual nontar	m		Rural farm	
Clear of worse, me or or tunation group and cour	Tota'	Viale	Female	Fotal	Male	Female	Total	Male	Female	Total	Male	Female
White-Class of Worker							200 044	103 044	2. 703	99,9_0	89,238	10.40
Employed	6Cc 268	461,>36	_40,-10	279,713	271,076	108,037 79,590	127,745	71 234	12,701	29,925	25,385	10 672
Private wage and salary workers	73,063	29° °46 40,413	96,292 2° 250	279,717 57 852	200, <u>27</u> 31 684	. 49 4881	15,815	10,024	5, 791	6 990	4,705	4,30
Government workers. Self-employe workers	123 279 8	114.030	11.639	44,089	39,510	7,479	21 810	14,125	2,691 825	8,787	52,095 c,153	2,63
unpaid family workers	16,420 B	169	5,250	2,155	355	2,800	1,486	061	825	8,78	6,150	2,634
White-Major Occupation Group	- 1											
Employed	602,308	r61 958	147,410	379,713	271,676	_06,037	122,745	10,,044	21,70_	99,910	89,238	-0 672
Description of and builded symbols	ul ,306 5- 952	37 416	23,890	48,043 1,253	^9,938 1,170	18 105 83	10,162	5,043 2,640	4 219	3,101	1,235	1,566
Farmers and farm nanagers	69.74	60.540	9,195	53.388	46, 496	6 u92	2,740		1.959	2,998	2,45/	1 417
Forestonal lettingue and manufers Farmers and Latt' connegers Vanagers, officials, and propuetors, exemplarm. Clerval and hundred workers Sales workers Confirmen foremen, and andred workers	69,741 81,991	60,540 33,368	48 523		46, u96 27 933 27 073	42 726 14, CB	8,548 9 353	4,168	4,480 3,507	2,571	1,20	1,092
Sales workers Craftenen foremen and condred workers	53,205 87,485 91,840	35,48	19,067	41,541 58 970 56,989	J7,689 47 460	1,281	26,025	21,864	14		6,436 7,627	54
	92,840	79,935	1,496		47 460	4,529 1,602	26,557	24,848	1,809	8,194 300 1,773	7,627	567 284
Prin ate bousenole, workers	2,872 36,223	207	2,565	27,06.	15,505	1,496	7,389	3 903	3,486	1,773	873	900
Farm laborers inpaid family workers	9,052	6,~79	2,572	100	66 676	34	4,70	348 4 ,11	10± 348	6,502 6,868	6,065	2,437
Private boulends, workers Service won st excep _private household. Warm laborers impact family workers _earn laborers excep _napad and farm foremen Laborers, excep farm and mine	12,384	32,342	882	757		486	14,413	14.491	222	3,848	3,727	413
Occupation not reported	8,204	5,69*	2,509	4,325	2,871	1,454	2,197	1,667	,30	2 082	1,15"	525
Noowhite-Class of Worker	- 1		1									
Employed .	232/0	_84,538	88,702	153,236	92,_99	6.,039	52,159	37,028	15 -3.	o7,843	5> 311	12 - 532
Pro ate wage and salary workers	20287	29,924	71 999	133,142	80, 273	52,769	45,525	22,666	12,859	22,620	_6,315 419	5,70
Government workers "elf-employed vorkers	44 823	39,525	7,420 5,298	2,636	6,283	5,353	3,201	2,156	1,390	33,51	Ja, 517	1 994
Unpaid family workers	1,484	0,941	4,543	8,111 349	5,452	2,059 258	027	390	237	10 508	6,460	4,148
										100		
Nonwhite Major Occupation Group	27: 240 "	_84,238	88 702	.53,238	92,109	61,033	p2 159	37,028	₄ 5 131	67,8-3	55,311	12,532
Professional technical and kindred workers	8,273	3,293	2,480	6,333		3,786	1,553	287	976	677	150	518
Tarmers and form managers Managers officials and proprietors, excel farm.	34,829	32 821	2,008	403 1	2,347	26	1,233	1,30	_03	33 493	3_ 314	1,879
Managers officials and proprietors, exc., farm	4,369	2 9 2 2 2 3 5 5	1,457	3 606	2 431	1.092	638	402 202	236 64	125	79 48	46
Crattsmen foremen and kindred works s	2,970	1,760	1,184	2,403	1,437	966	472	266	20/	95	25	40
Crartsmen foremen and kindred works s Operate as and kindred workers	13,43"	31,349	135 I	1. 426 28,907	21,720	7, 87	8,120	2,409	36 936	2.6.6	557 2,439	9 227
Private hou apold workers	40,812	1.2.31	39,599	37,896	919	22,277	7 678	236	7,442	2,20	58	2,480
Service varker, except pri ate household	33,562	_6,325 6,820	37 637	29 319	14 615	14,704	3,914	1,48/	2,430	10,577	6,425	503 4 .52
Farm laborers unread namely workers Farm laborers ex ep un and and farm novemen	24,918	20, . 9	4,799	1,729	1,399	330 ·	_C,324	8 336	1.986	.2.865	10,382	2,483
Laborers, except raim and mine Occupation not reported.	3,790	2,4_3	4,345 4,799 1 .21 1,377	34,226	33,352	613	1 122	13,645	≥09 335	3,007	3,059	38 429
	7,	-,	-,-									
PERCENT DISTRIBUTION	1		1		2.1	i						0.9
White-Class of Worker												DATE IN CO.
Employed Private wage and salary workers	65.2	100 0	100 0	_00 0	100 0	100 0	400 0 68 1	100 0	100 0 57 1	1.0 0	100 c	40 4
rovernmen workers	12 2	10 0	68 6	73 7 13 4	73 7	73 7	12 9	70 3	26 7	29 7 7 0	28 4	21 5
(revenuer) workers belf-employed workers Unpaid family workers	12 2 20 # 2 1	24 2	19 ~ 8 3 3 7	13 4	14.7	69	12 9 17 6	18 9	12 /	54.5	5 3 59 4	24 7
Cinpada tamily workers		1 6	37	0 6	0.1	4.7	1 2	67	3 8	8.8	6 9	24 7
Whi.e-Major Occupation Group				i				-				
Employed	100 0	200 0	100 0	100 C	100 0	100 0	.00° 0	100 0	100 0	±00 0	100 0	100 0
Professional technical and kindred workers	10 2	8 1	27 0	27	11 0	16 8	83	5 9 2 6	19 4	51 0	1 7 56 2	14 7
Farmers and jarr managers Managers officials and proprietors except form Clerical and sindred workers	31 6	11 7 13 1 7 2		16 0	17 2 10 3	6 2	10 9	11 3 4 1 5 5	9 0	30	2	
Sales workers Craften.cn forumen and lindred workers	13 6 8 8 14 5	7 2	136	JC 9	10 0	13 4	7 4	5 5	20 6 16 2	2 6	1772	13 3
	14 5	18 6	8 5	15 5	21 2 17 5	1 2	7 4 47 9 21 7	21 6	16 2 0 7	36 6 5 2	7 2	6.5
Operatives and kindred workers	0 3	7,	19	05		13 4 1 2 8 8 1 5	0 7	24 6 0 1	2 6	0 3	8 2	5 3
Operatives and mirred workers Private household workers Serrice workers, everet private household Farm laborers unpaid family workers Fann laborers, except unpaid, and farm foremen Laborers except farm and mine.	60	4 4 1 4 2 5 7 0	11 3	71	5 7	10 6	6 0	3 9	in 1	18	_ 0	8 4
Farm laborers, except unpaid, and farm foremen	2 5	2 5	00	3 9	0 2	01	3 9	03	0 5	6 9	6 E	22 8
Laborers except farm and mine Occupation not reported	5.5	7 0	05	3 9	53	0 4	11 7	14 0	2 4	39	4 2	0 6
	4							- 0	. ~	- 1	- 3	- '
Norwhre-Class of Werker Employed	100 0	300.0	100 0		100 -					100.00		120
Employed - Private wage and salary workers	73 7	100 0 90 4		1.00 0	100 0	100 0	100 0	_00 0	100 0	100 0	100 0	100 0
Coverament workers.	57	4 4 21 4	80 4	86 9	67 2 6 8	86.5	87 3 5 4	88 2	85 0 9 2	33 3	30 6 0 8	45 5 5 5 45 9
Self-employed workers. Unpaid family workers	4 2	21 4	5 2	02	59	86 5 8 8 4 4 0 4	61	5 8 6 9 1 1	9 2 4 3 1 6	1 (49 4 15 6	0 8 57 0 1, 7	45 9 33 1
The second secon		- 0	- 1				**		- 0	77.0	/	23 1
Nonwhite—Major Occapanoa Group												
Emproyed	20.0	-00 O	100 0	100 0	100 0	100 0	200 0	T0C 0	100 0	T00 0	100 0	±00 C
Professional technical, and kindred workers	3 1 12 7	17 8	2 3	41	2 8 0 4 2 6	5 2	3 0	1 6 3 1	6 5 0 7	48 9	0 3 56 6	4 1 15 C
danagers, officials, and proprietors except farm Gerica, and kindred workers	16	16	16	2 4	2 6	± 9	1 2	0.5	1 6	01	01	04
ales workers	111	10	+ 4	2 1	2 3	18	09	0 5	1 6 0 4 1 3	01	01	03
ales workers Infitsmen toremen and kindred workers peratures and kindred workers	4 9	7 1	0 4	6.8	11 0	0 1	47		0 2	8.0	01	0.2
	49	1,0:	46	20 2	25 6 1 0 15 9	11 8 49 1	15 6	19 4	6 2 49 2	39	01	1 8
ervice workers except pri ate household	41	0 7	19 9	19 1	15 9	24 1	75	40	16 I	11(04	40
ervice workers except pri ate household arm laborers unpaid family workers arm laborers, except unraid and farm toremen.	9 -	10 9	4 9	1	1.5	0.5	198	19 4 0 6 4 0 0 9 22 5 36 9	16 I 1 I 13 I	19 6	11 6 18 8	33 ±
sborers except farm and mine	18 7	27 1	1 1 1 1	22 3	36 2 1 2	4	26 6	36 9	1 4	4.6	5 5	0.3
								2 1	2 2	14		3.4

Table 29.—CLASS OF WORKER AND MAJOR OCCUPATION GROUP CF EMPLOYED PERSONS, BY SEX, FOR THE STATE 1950 and 1940

[Img as 1940 fig no recard where necessary to conform to 1900 Casamont. Pe, vin it what where less the ALL * where base is the 100 casamont.

C.ass of worker and najor occupation group	20 04		fan.		7 mal.		Prices cannotter						
							T a'		viate !		Fem	315	
	-950	194	950	1240	1950	240	1959	1940	950	1940	1950	1446	
CLASS OF WORKER	1	i											
Employed	875,608	767,242	0+6,-90	58- 70-1	29	463,241	و بلا۔	130 G		*XC C	₩0 J	1.00	
Pr ate wage and salary workers.	594.325	4,2,450	~26,73°	3 8,208	167,645	_23,882	E . B	5: 9		36 1			
Government workers	89,209	55,3.4	54 53.1	3-,149	34,073	21 41	-2 2	- 3	8 +1	7 81	.3 6	5 1	
Sed-employed workers	468,062	2 2,760	154 155	3-,1d9 _90 776	-6,907	22, 40	-9 Z	12	23 4	32 6	2 1	12 5	
Enpard amay worses	24,2	4:,677	14 1.51	32 4ex	1 902	FOS CT	3 4	16	23	4 41	4.3	2.6	
MAJOR OCCUPATION GROUP				To		-			1		-	-	
Employed	875,608	767,9-2	640,496	584 70,	24 1-2	193,241	200 0	٠. نوټ	اريدا	40C nf	170 0	200 :	
Professional technical, and kindred workers	69 877	6,12"	40 709	2- 600	29.47	258	6.2	9 1	4 3	4 2	12 7	11 '	
l'armers and arm managers	89,781	140,398 1	86.818	134 996	2 963	5,400	-03	-8 3	134	23 1,	1 24	2	
Managers officials, and prophetors except farm	74 21°	48 609	63 458	4" 240	10,652,	363	3 5	63	9 6	- 21	4.5	2	
Clerical and kindred workers	65,530	50 259	32,723,	25,-68	49 8 7	23 791	9.8	15	3 5	4 51	21 7	13	
Sales workers	26 175	40,417	35,894	48 7521	×0 277	1.,665 907 44,355	5 4	23	5.6	4 9	8 9		
Craftamen toromen, and kindred workers	100 922	58,739	99,094	7,852 593 4,5_2 29 93-	. 8.	907	-1.5	7 c	15 3	9 9	0.8	C:	
Ope atives and kindred warkers.	_31,539	85,948	111 284	7,593	20,20	44,350	25 0	1, 2	-7 2 2 2	12 2	8 8	~ 1	
Private household workers	43,684	63 455	1,420	4,0_2	42 264	59.443	4	91	2.2	0.71	A8 +1	32	
Service workers except private household	70,165	48,681	36 666	29 93-	35,519	59,443 18,947 _2,730	80	04	5	5 41	14 6	10	
Farm abovers unpaid amily workers	20,216	42,6.0	13,299	29 88.	€ 917	_2,730	23	5.5	2 -	5 1	3 3	6 5	
	37 302	61,46	31,621	55 738	5,081	5,668	- 3	8 3	4 9	9 3	2 5	3 :	
Iano, ers except arm and mine	84,291	76 745	82 401	75 209	1 290	-, 2	96	-0°	-27	+2 8	OB	. L 5	
Occupation not reported	_1,994	4,373	8,108	2 -97	3 8Bo	-,876	+ 4	06	. 3	0 4	L 7	1 0	

Table 30 —INDUSTRY GROUP OF EMPLOYED PERSONS, BY SEX FOR THE STATE, URBAN AND RURAL 1950

Indus.7, group	The State			- rban			Ru	DOLARD	a	Pural farm			
III.day'y group	Total	Male	Female	Tota_	N-ale	Female	Total	Male	Female	lotal	Male	Female	
Employed.	875,608	646 496	229 112	532,951	363.875	_69_076	174,904	1.8,0.2	36,832	107,753	144 5/9	23,204	
Agriculture, forestry and fishenes	160 595	144,6521	15 943	7 149	6,438	71.	27,9_9	24,968	2,94_	125,527	143 240	12 281	
Agnousture Forestry and fisheries	151,57- 9,021	_35,841 8,811	15,733	5,498	2,8°8 1,960	620 91	21,349 6,570	6,476	2,857	124,72° 800	1 2,471	12,256	
Mining	24 200	23,042	1,16	1. 992	ر99,04ء	1,707	_0,504	_D 774	_30	1,713	1,683	30	
Conatt totion	64,939	03,364	1,575	42,60"	41,340	1,327	16,656	15,469	_87	5,616	5,525	63	
Manufacturing.	132 476	15 381	17,09>	86,426	72,288	14,.38	35,159	32,846	2,3,3	10 891	10 247	644	
Durable goods. Turnsture, and lumber and wood products Frinary metal industries Frinary metal ind (net not specified metal). Machinety except electrical Transportation equipment Transportation equipment, except motor vehiule Other durable goods	49,010 30,553 1,580 3,578 3,224 457 458 4,216 4,924	46,602 29, 04 1,524 3 155 2,98 193 431 4 092 4,505	2,408 1,049 56 423 226 64 27 2,44 7,19	25 705 10,531 1 2,9 3,224 2,591 397 366 3,431 4,006	2, 785 9, 792 1, 71 2,813 2 390 337 3,11 3,298 3,645	1,976 739 48 411 201 58, 25 123 361	17,472 14,907 278 287 506 45 58 555 736	17,149 14 564 271 280 487 41 57 648 701	.23 243 7 19 4 :	-,773 83 67 127 15 34 150 182	5 664 5,048 62 62 13 13 146 159	109 67 1 5 6 2	
Nondrushle goods . Food and knowned products Textus call produces Textus call produces Apps el and other nanneated textile produces Presturg publishung, and aissed indust s.s Chemicals and allied products Other nondrushle goods Nos spondiel manu-facturing undustress.	82 734 25,860 2,011 4 969 6,499 11 177 32,200 732	68,486 21,467 1,413 1,475 5 320 10,389 28,922 493	14,548 4 702 898 3,694 1,179 788 3,287 _39	50 191 28,573 3870 4,684 2,853 7,426 21,815 470	48,149 15,127 979 -,220 4 789 6 775 19 259 350	12,042 3,446 861 2,464 1,064 651 2,556	17 486 5,829 1.5 207 533 2 879 7,903 201	19,508 4 836 107 41 450 2,755 7,319	1,978 993 28 466 83 124 584	5,057 1,467 36 78 113 872 2,491 61	4 529 1,204 27 14 81 829 2,344	528 263 9 64 32 13 147 7	
Transportation, commun and other public util	75,780	66,092	9 688	40,674	52,173	8,501	.2,034	11,107	927	3,072	2,8,2	260	
Transportation Railcods and railway express a nice Trucking service and warehousing Other transportation Telecommunications Utilities and sanitary services	24,081 18,304 6,383 27,394 8,389 13,310	70,810 17,23 7 935 25,342 3,350 11 932	3 271 771 448 2,052 5,039 1,378	43,312 14 345 6,470 22 497 7,339 10,023	-0,407 13,625 6,073 20,679 2,830 8 876	2,905 690 597 1,818 4,-49 1 147	8,5.0 3,362 ,517 3,631 879 2,665	8,24± 3,29± 1,478 3,472 375 2,49±	269 71 39 159 484 174	597 396	2,162 587 384 1,191 85 565		
Wholesaie and recall trade	169,845	113 228	56,617	133,211	88,125	45,086	29 833	20,595	9.238	6,801	4,508	2,293	
Wholevale trade Retail trade Food and darry products stores, and milk retailing Eating and drinking places Other retail trade	31,918 137 927 30,124 29,101 76,705	26,963 86,265 20,968 12,952 52,345	4,955 51,662 9,153 16,149 26,300	27,362 105,849 27,628 22,706 62,515	22,80. 65,324 14,460 10,581 40,^83	4,561 40 525 6,168 12,125 22,232	3,700 26,133 7,363 5 631 13,119	3 391 -/,204 *,148 2,130 9,926	309 8,929 2,235 3,501 3,193	856 5 945 2,1 0 764	771 3,737 1,360 241 2 136	2,206 750 52,	
Finance, insurance, and rual estate	21,969	13,781	884,8	19,729	12,29	7 432	_,800	1,224	5.6	440	260	1.80	
Business and repair services	20,155	18,338	_,820	14 920	13,3,6	1,604	4,215	4,048	167		974		
Businees services	5,071 15 087	3,785 14,553	1,286	4 652 10,268	3,45° 9,861	±,197 407	341	3,778	71 96	78	60 914		
Personal services	77 839	19,460	58,379	60,870	15 523	45 347	13 499	3,371	10 128	3,470	566		
Private households	49,467	5,629	43,838	36 691	3,904	32,787	9 967	1,469	8,498	2,809	256		
Hotels and 'odging places Other personal services	6,703	3,089	3,614	5,956 18 223	2,753 8,866	3,203 9,357	2,808	1,605	1 263	83 578	271		
Entertainment and recreation services	9,071	6,700	2,374	7,648	5,583	2,065	.,248	979	269	175	138	, ,	
Professional and related services	72,028	29,026	43,002	5/,268	21,665	32 603	13,345	3,828	7,517	4,415	1,533		
Medical and other health services Rducational services government Educational services, private Other professional and related previces	23,696 36,400 28,225 8,180 11,927	8,658 12 207 9,098 3 109 8,161	15 38 24,198 19,127 5,071 3 766	20,086 24,551 17,679 6,872 9 631	7,067 8,235 5,614 2,62 6,363	13,019 16,316 12,065 4,251 3,368	2,935 8,469 7,488 981 1,241	2,945 2,945 2,585 360 1,557	7,609 5,524 4,903 621 384	3,385 3,058 3,058 327 3.5	1,027 899 128 241	2,35	
Pubus administration	33,446	24,633	8,83.5	26,036	19,801	6,835	5,046	3,604	1,442	1	1,228		
	13 253	8,799	4,454	6,761	7,341	2,420	3,646	2,659	987	-	+,799	_	
Industry not reported	13 253	8,799	4,424	0,761	4,341	2,420	3,046	2,009	487	1 4,546	41/49	1 400	

Table 50 —INDUSTRY GROUP OF EMPLOYED PERSONS, BY SEX, FOR THE STATE, URBAN AND RURAL 1950—Con.

**Recreet not from where less 1 and 0 for never been it less than 00]

		Th. State			R	aral nonfar	Bural farm					
Industry group	Total	Male	Fernase	Total	Male	Female	Tota	Male	Fema.e	Total	Mae	Femal
PERCENT DISTRIBUTION												
Emproved	700.0	10^ 0	100 0	.00 0	100 0	00 O	100 0	700 O	-	±00 0	¥00 0	100
Agriculture orestry and naheres	18 3	22 4	7.0	4 .	1 8	0/	76 C	18 4	2 8	74 8	78 -	5
pretti ure frestry and fusherses	27 3 C	21 0	69	03	0 4	31	3 8	13 4	0.3	3 =	0.5	
Maning	. 8	3 6	0.5	23	3 0	0.6	6.0	7.5	0/	10	- 2	-
Construction	74	2.8	07	80	11 4	0.8	9.5	19	0.5	3 3	8 د	-
Manufacturing -	3.	17.8	7.5	16 2	19 9	8 4	20 1	23 8	6.3	6.5	3 9	
irake goods Ferniure and lumber and wood products Ferniure and lumber and wood products Fabrua, ed metal ind no no, specified metal) Manniners except electrical	5 6 3 5 0 4 0 4	7 2 4 6 0 2 0 5	0 ± 0 1	4 8 2 0 0 2 3 6 0 5	6 7 2 7 0 3 0 8	0 4	10 0 8 5 0 2 0 7	12 4 30 6 0 4	C 7	30	01	
Machinery except electrical Electrical machinery equipment and supplies Mo.or vehicles and motor vehicle equipment Transportation equipment, except motor vehicle Other cornable goods	0 1 0 1 0 5 0 6	C 1 C 1 O 0	01	0 - 0 - 0 6 0 8	1 2	0 1 C 2 7 1	U 4 C 4	05		31 01 30	0 - 3 1	1
ndurable goods Food and kindred products Foxide mill products Loparel and o her fabricased lextile products vinting publishing and allied industries.	9 4 3 0 3 2 2 6 0 7	10 5 3 3 0 2 0 2 0 8	6 3 2 1 0 4 1 6 0 5	00 00 11	4 2 C 3 O 3 1 3	2 0 0 5 2 0 0 6	3 3 C 1 C 1 C 3	0.3	2 7 0 5 0 2	01	08	
Remicals and allied products Other nondurable goods t sperified manufacturing industries	7 01	1 6	03	1 - 4 1 0 1	1 9	0 4 5 C 1	1645	2 0 9 3 0 1 8 0	16	1 5	1 5	
I ransportation, commun., and other put he und ansportation Radinoids and radway express service. Fruelong service and warenoising - D our transportation leconomium entities.	62:10	7 9 2 7 2 2 3 9 0 2 8	1430090000000000000000000000000000000000	81 27 47 14 19	11 1 3 8 1 7 5 7 0 9 7 4 4	17 04 02 14 26	1 9 0 9 2 1 0 5	0 0 2 / 1 1 2 5 0 3 1 8	0 4	0 7 0 8 0 1 0 4	2 4 0 3 0 8 0 4	
Wholesale and retail trade	19 4	7 5	24 7	25 0	24 2	26 7	17 1	14 9	25 .	4 4	31	
polesale trade taal i nade Food and darry products stores and milk retailing Eating and drinking places Other retail trade.	3 6 15 8 3 4 3 2 9 3	4 2 13 5 2 2 2 0 8 4	2 r 2 p s 4 0 7 0 11 5	51 199 39 43 117	6 3 18 C 4 O 2 d	2 ^ 24 0 7 2 -> 1	2 4 14 9 4 2 3 7	12 7 7 7 1 5 7 8	87	0 5 1 3 0 5 1 8	0 5 2 6 0 9 2 3 1 5	
Finance Permance, and reas estate	2.5	2 1	3 6	37	2 *	4.4	10	0 9	1.6	0.3	0.5	_
Business and repair services	2 3	28	0.8	2.8	ء 7	0.9	: 4	2 9	7.5	0.6	0.7	_
nness ber ices.	17	2 3	0 5	19	2 7	0 2	2 2	2 7	0 4	0.6	0 6	
I erennal services	8 9	3.0	25 *	44	4 3	26 8	77	2 4	27 >	2 1	04	1
vate households tels and 'odging places ter personal semices	5 b 2 p	0 9 0 5 1 7	1º 1 1 6 4 8	11	0 8 4 4	19:	16	0 5	3 4	13	0 2	1
Entertainment and recreation services.	10	0	10	14	1.5	. 2	0.7	0 7	0 7	0.1	0 1	
Professional and related services should not other benith services unstained services Educational services government Educational services unvake professional and related services	8 2 2 7 4 2 3 2 0 9 1 4	4 5 1 9 1 4 0	18 8 6 6 10 6 5 3 2 7 1 6	3 d 4 d 3 d 1 d 1 8	6 G 2 3 1 5 3 7 1 7	19 3 7 7 9 7 2 1 2 5	7 3 1 7 7 8 4 3 0 6 1 1	1021	20 4 4 / 15 C 23 3	26	3 2 0 7 0 6	1
Public seministration	8 د	3 8	3 8	50	j 4	4 01	2 9	2 6	3 9	11	0.8	
Industry not reported	1 2	1 4	19	. 3	. 2	1 4	2 .	19	2 7	4 7	1.2	1

Table 30a —INDUSTRY GROUP OF EMPLOYED WHITE AND NONWHITE PERSONS, FOR THE STATE, URBAN AND RURAL 1950 [Percent not shown where less than 0 to or where boso is less than 109]

	to stable	White		7.72	Nonwhite						
Industry group	T' e State	U1 DER	Pural nonfaru	Rural form	The State	Urban	Rura nonfarm	Rural arm			
Emplored _	602,368	379,713	.22,745	99,316	273,240	150,238	52,153	61,8-3			
Agneulture Greett, and fishenes Unung Omstruction	78, 348 7 8°C 23 385 48,03°	2 66C 1,465 11,681 29 516	5,746 10,-05 13 63	67,0-3 709 1,599 4,960	73 ∠25 1,13 824 10 900	2 538 196 511 15, 11	12,704 854 399 3,043	*7,684 9, 114 656			
Manufacturing Firmthias has humber and wood friedly a Permity metal fire datase. Permity metal fire datase. Machinery, except sace to allow and springles. Machinery, except sace to allow and surpluse. Machinery except sace to allow and surpluse. Machinery to the allow and surpluse. Transportation e-unumare except motor vehicle. Otto divining some	54,38d 1,5,220 1,007 3,126 2,9,3 4,3 4,3 4,3 3,39	63, 962 4, 624 790 2, 847 2, 343 59 331 4, 790 2, 840	22, 799 635 167 225 44 42 51 51,7	7, 27 2 901 60 61 123 12 31 427 415	38,086 15,313 573 459 311 74 45 804 1,527	22, 26/ 7, 907/ 439 384 381 381 35 641	12,360 7,272 1.1 62 59 3 7 7 138	3 1c4 2 156 2 2 6 4 3 23 6 6 6			
Food and kinared products Textile mill products Appard and other fall reased textile products Penting probability and allied industries Chemicals and allied products their conductable goods. Victoria field manufacturing industries	18,082 1 556 3,235 6 021 8,651 26 341	-3 ±46 1,444 2 973 5,705 5,806 1 721	3 727 88 786 506 2,091 511	1, .00 26 74 -10 -54 2 106	7 787 453 1 7:6 478 2,526 5,868	5 327 356 -,711 448 - 620 4 094	2,102 47 21 27 78 ² 1,302	35 1/ 11/ 38/			

Table 30a—INDUSTRY GROUP OF EMPLOYED WHITE AND NONWHITE PERSONS FOR THE STATE, URBAN AND RURAL 1950—Con [Perspected to the phase are seen for 61 of the life has already

Industry group		W ite	50.00	>orw: ite						
Andreet's group	Th. Stave	U-ban	P: as nonfarm	R.J.S. area	Tre S.at.	and a	Pu-al non.arm	Pure		
Radicack and radiracy et. arons service Produng service and warshousing Ottler transnorration. Telecommunications Unities and sanitary services Weisende treds Weisende treds Dating and drainany places Other radiracy and drainany places Other radiracy	11,923 *,256 20,598 #,022 L,419 do 404 21,196 17,429 66,479	9,885. 3 7121 16,21 7,313 6 548. 42,063 10 107 13,02 14 107	1, 77 -,2- -,44 8,5 - 335 3 007 6,54,- 2 66 -,-0-4	317 343 13-7 18- 556 734 1-750 249 2,794	6,38- 3,127 6,770 -6" -1,87- 5,9-4 1,972	4,456 2,754 6,25, 306 -,495 4,699 1,93 9 s87	1,54,7 146 182 24 350 693 836	290 53 125 66 122 154 2.J		
Finance naurance and rul estate	9,108 -,827 -2,646 4,345 -,587 -858 7,234	17,C ₆ 8 4,43_ 8 C ₈ 8 2,U ₈ 8 3,1_4 9 488 6,733	295 296 296 296 296	2, '94 4.5 8.7 4.3 43.	2,861, 2,841, 45,122, 3,44, 1,81, 1,81,	.0, 534 2, 661 2, 180 34, 003 2, 8 2 8, 735 1, 615	615 175 .6 523 8 723 269 928 199	27 25 7 38 2,396 40 1-8		
Medical and other health se vices Ldicational services government Ldicational services private Other processional and related services Public administration Industry no reported	8,985 20,130 0,142 7,804 30,363 8,965	12,085 5,107 7,684 23,9_C 4,73	2,480 ,748 763 4 614 4,7,2 2,413	2,297 2,297 272 306 1,701 1,817	4,710 8,09* 2,038 2,122 3,023 4,288	4, 54 5, 94 1,765 1,767 2,726 2 020	455 ,40 218 327 294 1 233	101 761 55 49 63		
PERCEN: DISTRIBUTION Fmploved	-00 0	2000	_00 o	·m o						
Agriculture Force , and fisheres Mining Construction	13 0 1 - 3 9	0 ? 0 4 3 1 7 8	8 2 11 0	67	26 8 0 4 2 3	130 c 0.2 8 6	100 0 24 4 1 6 0 8	85 0 -00 0		
Ma., fac urug Pumdure, and humber and wood products Pruncy no si industrise Pruncy no si industrise Pruncy no si industrise Pauperator mass, industrise Pauperator mass, industrise Machinery except elec roal Lifectrons massimery equipment and supplies Motor vehicles and motor chiefe equipment	197922551 166	822761178 9-00000000	18 6. 0 7. 0 2. 0 4.	777	13 9 4 7 7 7 7 7 7 7 7 7 7 7 7 7 7 7 7 7 7	4 91 3 9 0 2 0 2	192000	1 0 4 7 3 2		
O har 'standis goods Does end Landed products Settle mill products Possared Lander fabra sied taxale products Prating pubnishing and alled industries Chemicals and alled products Other zondurable goods Not specialer "standishe iring in that ries"	555	35 04 08 15 7	040000000000000000000000000000000000000	0 - 1 1 1 1 1 1 1 1 1 1 1 1 1 1 1 1 1 1	0 0 0 0 0 0 0 0 0 0 0 0 0 0 0 0 0 0 0 0	08	0 6 4 0 0 1 1 5 2 7	0 2 2 3 6		
Ba roads and wilvey, express service Tracking service and surviceousing Other transportation Telecommunia status Telecommunia	209 34 19 44 49	2032266444	2 6 0 7 7 2 4 4 5 3	0010000000	0 3 1 E A 7 U 8 A	0 1 2 9 1 8 4 1 0 2 3 1 2 6 3	01	0412		
Other retail traid. Finance, Insurance, and real *statu. Business services Private households Che sha dio (aging pla ses Oth* y absonal services *retrainment and men eation services	11 0 3 2 8 2 0 7 0 6 0 2 0 2	45 12 21 05 16	9 4 - 3 3 2 7 1 0 3 1 0 9	2 8 0 4 0 1 0 4 0 4	100011100111111111111111111111111111111	6 7 1 2 0 1 1 4 22 2 1 8 5 7	3 - 0 3 1 0 16 7 0 5 1 8	0 2 3 5 0 1 0 2		
Mudius and other bealth segment Accustment services p. 1 a.e. O het professional and related a vices Public adminis is not Industry not epotted	3 2 3 3 1 6 5 0	4 2 3 2 1 3 2 1 6 3	2 0 4 7 0 3 3 9 2 0	0 6 2 . 0 3 0 3 1 7 1 8	1730 070 08	2 7 3 7 1 2 1 1 1 3	0934	0 1 1 1 0 1 0 1 0 1		

Table 31 -INDUSTRY GROUP OF EMPLOYED PERSONS, BY SEX, FOR THE STATE 1950 AND 1940 [Original 1940 figures revised wher, necessary to conform to 1950 classification. Percent not shown where less than 0.1 or where base as less than 100.

Industry group	Total		Male		Female				Percent	distr buts	non	
							Total		Mule		Female	
	1950	1940	1950	1940	1950	1940	1950	1940	1950	1940	1950	1940
Employed	875,608	767,942	616 496	58/,701	229 112	283, 241	100 0	100 0	±00 0	100 0	100 0	100 0
Agriculture crestry and sheres -	160,590	254 465	244,852	232,301	15,943	24,112	18 3	33 4	24 4	39 7	10	13 2
Agneulture Forestry and fisheries	151,574 9,021	249,136 7,32"	135,841	7,275	210	23,960	173	32 2	21 0	38 5	69	13 1
Vining	≥4, 209	14,869	23,042	14,524	1,467	445	28	19	36	2.5	0.5	0 2
Con-truetur	(4,9,19	35,231	03,364	34,777	1,575	454	74	4.5	9.8	5 9	07	0.2
Manuacturing	132 476	98,990	115,38	87,328	1, 009	11,072	15 1	12 9	17 8	14 9	7.5	6 4
Durable goods Turnitur, and lumber and wood n oduets	49,010	4_,892 29 148	46,602 29,>04	40 593 28 539	2,408	1,299	5 6 3 5	5 5 3 8	7 2 4 6	6 9	0.5	0 7
Primary metal inquistries Fauritated metal and (ingl not spec mutal)	5,158	3,375	4,679	3 0031	479	280	0.6	04	0.7	0.5	0.2	0 2
Cleatrical mathinery cay pront and our place	2 224 457	297	2,998	272	226 64 27	124	01	03	05	03	01	0 1
Motor vehicles and motor vehicle equipment Transportation equipment except motor vehicle	4,236	2,000	4,092	2,0-0	144	20	0 1	01	01	01	0.1	
Other du able goods	4 924	4,569	4,505	4 345	419	224	0 6	26	07	0.7	0.5	0 1

Table 31.—INDUSTRY GROUP OF EMPLOYED PERSONS BY SEX FOR THE STATE 1950 AND 1940—Con region. 1946 figures represed and increase and to also clearfectation. Percent not above where less than 0.1 or where been in less than 100;

		1							Percent di	nostudinse		
It distry got _p	Tota	1	\fa	^	Fem	ale	To	tul	M	ale	Fen	ns.e
It was the real shape	950	19-10	1950	1540	1950	1940	1950	1940	1950	1940	1950	1940
Manufarta og Ccu kurdarskå, godd av mand a products Frod er u mand a products Ap are, som a ber faurre ster er ka person cle Parti, y put kelning, an å salen indostrire Chrita, tils an i alled groute. Ar gos hed tils av grandfartarn, utdistarre	82,734 25 869 2,011 7,969 0,449 11,17 32,2.9 732	55,335 20,680 2,931 3,780 4,722 6,301 17 921 763	68,186 21 lu7 1, 13 1,275 5 320 10,389 28,922 593	46, 459 17,772 1 733 1,460 7,049 5 905 25,540	4,548 4,702 898 3,694 -,179 788 3,287 139	10,1°c 2,908 -,198 2,020 -,73 396 2,381	0607	73 27 04 05 06 08 23	10 5 3 3 0 2 0 8 1 6 4 5 0 1	7 9 3 0 0 3 3 2 0 7 1 0 2 7	3146 246 2046 2034 2046	0 0 0
Transportation community of other rathe	7-,780	50,717	60,092	46,479	9,688	4,238	87	6 0	10 2	79	4 2	2
Transporta ior Radrouds and rails av express seriou Trucking service and warevolume Other transporta ion Feler stansmications Trucking as a system of the control of the co	54, Left 10,3,4 8,380 27,394 6,3-9 13,340	38,838 4 476 6 851 17,51 4 747 7,132	50 810 17 533 7,935 25,342 3,350 11 932	37,770 14,169 6 627 16,974 2,126 6,583	3 271 771 448 2,052 5 039 1,378	1,068 307 224 537 2 621 549	62 13 115	19 09 23 06	7 9 2 7 1 2 3 9 0 5 1 8	6 5 2 4 1 1 2 9 0 4 1 1	1432920	2000
Whele ale and retail trace.	149,845	1.2 80.	113,228	83,50	56,617	29,297	19 4	14 7	17 5	14 3	24 7	16
Whoreaste trade Rotal - rade Food and darre wrote, its stores and milk retailing Eating and dran.ng places O her retail trade	31 918 17: 927 33,121 29 _C . 72,705	18,058 9-,1-2 24,00- 8,41. 5-,637	26,963 86,205 20,968 2,952 52,343	10,527 06,976 17,101 10 094 37,721	4,955 51,662 9,153 40,149 25 340	2,231 27,146 4,933 8,317 23,9-0	3 6 15 8 3 4 3 5 0	2 4 12 3 3 4 6 7	4 2 3 3 3 2 2 0 8 1	2 8 11 5 3 3 1 7 6 5	2 2 22 5 4 0 7 0 11 5	1 1/ 2 4:
F.nance ms.rance and real estate	21,969	15,03/	2,781	1.,085	8 188	3,948	2 2	20	21	19	3 6	2
Business and epair services	2º 158	11,538	18,338	10 889	1,820	649	2 3	15	28	19	0.8	0
Business services	5,071 25,087	2 25c 8,962	3,783 14,553	8,772	1,286 534	439 210	0 6	03	2 3	0 4	0 6	00
Personal services	77 839	93,209	19 460	19,682	53, 179	73,526	8 9	-2 1	3.0	3 4	25 5	40
Private households Hotels and longing places Cther pursons services	49 46" a,703 21,669	60,035 b,825 18,_49	5 629 3,089 10,742	7,13, 3 303 9,249	43 838 3,6.4 .0,427	60,904 3,522 9,100	5 6 0 8 2 5	8 9 3 9 2 4	09	1 2 0 6 1 6	19 1 - 6 4 8	33 :
Entertainment and recreation services	9,071	C,23J	6 700	4,894	2,371	۵, ،36	10	0.8	10	٦ 8	. 0	0
Processions, and related vivices	72,028	45,736	29,020	19,084	43,002	26,602	8 2	6.0	4.5	3 3	18 8	24
Medical and whar lealth services Gluca oral services, Educational services, government Educational services private. Liber professional and related services	23,696 35 05 20,22, 8,180 11,927	13,221 24,354 20,052 4,302 8,.61	8,628 12,707 9,098 3 .79 8,161	5,277 7,727 6,347 3,580 5,780	25, 38 24, 198 19, 27 5,071 3,766	7,644 46,627 43,705 2,922 2,381	27 / 2 3 2 0 9 1 4	1 / 3 2 2 6 0 6 1 1	13 19 14 05	1 0 1 3 1 1 0 2 1 0	10 6 8 3 2 2 6 6	9 7 1
Public alministration	33 446	14 784	44,633	14 327	8 81.3	4 457	3 8	2 4	38	2 5	3 8	2
Industry not reported	3,253	8,341	8,799	5,786	1.45/	2,555	15	11	14	10	19	1

Table 32 —INCOME IN 1949 OF FAMILIES AND UNRELATED INDIVIDUALS FOR THE STATE, URBAN AND RURAL 1950
[Based on 26-perfer samile - Pe cent not shown where less than 0.1, median and pr cent not shown where hase 's less shan 500]

	1	amilius and u	inrubted ind	rvaals			F	amilies				Unrela	ted individu	tala	
Income kva	The	Urban a	nd rural nor	farm.	Rural	The	Urbaut a	nd rural nor	rfarm.	Rural	The	Urban	and rural ne	onfarm	Rural
	State	Total	Urban	Rural nontarm	farm	S ate	Tuta	Urban	Rt. al norfarm	farm	S.ate	Total	U∗ban	Rural nonfarm	farm
Total	802 697	668,135	485,035	183,1∿	±34,555	648,440	523,915	372,515	1,1,400	124 495	154 280	14,220	1.2,520	91,700	10 060
Aumber reporting Less than \$500. \$500 to \$999 \$1,000 to \$1,199 \$2,000 to \$1,299 \$2,000 to \$2,499	761,590 110,355 126,403 35,990 77,960 71,635	637 985 83,510 95,495 73,220 64,080 6.,725	458, 955 57, 525 56 450 47, 135 45, 585 45, 425	174 020 25,98* 37,035 26,085 18,495 16,300	28,605 26,545 32,910 22,770 13,880 9,910	619,030 61,450 85,1.0 79,515 67,320 63,690	499, 625 39, 635 55, 705 57, 415 53, 605 53, 900	354,510 24,140 29,7% 34,145 36,610 38,700	145,015 15,495 25,935 23,270 17,085 15,291	119,405 22,315 29,425 22,100 13,625 9,700	142,560 48,.05 41 275 .5,475 .0,640 7,945	33,360 43,871 37,790 15,805 10,385 7,735	104,355 33,385 26,690 2,990 8,975 0 725	10,490	9,200 4,230 3,485 670 255 213
\$2,500 to \$2,999 \$3 000 to \$3 499 \$3,500 to \$3,999 \$4 000 to \$4,999 \$4 500 to \$4,999	52,445 50,435 38,760 31,070 22,535	40,945 45 745 35,360 28,535 21,060	35,790 35,595 27,335 22,635 27,385	1,150 10 150 8,025 5,905 3,675	5 500 4 690 2,900 2,535 1,475	77,420 45,975 35,755 29,430 21,460	42,035 41,345 32,890 26,920 20,005	31,515 31,755 25,185 21,150 16,465	10,520 9,500 7,705 5,770 3,547	5,385 4,630 2,865 2,510	5,025 4,460 2,505 4,640 4,075	4,°10 4,400 2,470 1,615 1,055	4,275 1 840 2,150 1,480 920	635 560 320	11.5 60 35 25 20
\$ 000 to \$ 999 \$6,000 to \$6,999 \$7 000 to \$9,999 \$10 000 and over income not reported	31,745 18,100 19,040 14,065 41,100	29,795 10,795 18,650 13,870 35 150	25 155 14,525 16,130 12,290 26,070	4 540 2,470 2,20 1,580 9,080	1,950 1,105 1,340 1,095 5,950	30,460 17,400 19,325 14,200 29,380	28,540 16,310 18,0.5 13,125 24,290	24,025 13,965 15,560 11,690 17,905	4,515 2,345 2,450 1,505 6,385	1 920 1,090 1 310 1,075 5,090	1,285 700 665 765 11,720	1,255 685 635 745 10,850	1,130 563 565 670 8,165	125 125 70 75 2,695	30 15 30 20 860
Median income.	\$1,810	\$2,018	\$2 251	\$_,460	\$4,406	\$2,-22	\$2,402	\$2,72	\$1,728	\$_,180	\$781	\$802	\$852	\$681	\$553
PERCENT DISTRIBUTION		1													
Number reporting	100 0	100 0	100 0	700 0	٥ ممد	100 0	100 0	100 0	100 0	100 0	100 0	100 0	_ 200 ⊃	100 0	100 3
less than \$000 \$000 to \$999 11,000 tr \$1 499 11,500 to \$1 999 2,000 to \$2 499	14 5 16 6 12 6 10 2 9 4	13 2 14 3 14 6 10 1 9 8	12 5 12 3 10 3	14 9 21 3 15 0 10 6 9 4	20 6 25 6 17 7 10 8	13 8 12 8 10 9 10 3	11 1 11 5 10 7	6 8 8 4 9 6 10 3	10 7 17 9 16 0 11 8	16 7 24 6 18 5 11 4 8 1	33 7 29 0 11 6 7 5	32 9 2 ² 3 41 9 7 8 5 8	32 0 25 6 12 4 8 6 6 4	36 2 38 3 9 7 4 9 3 5	46 0 37 9 7 3 2 8 2 3
2,000 to \$2,999_ 3 000 to \$3 499 3 500 to \$3 999 4 000 to \$4,499	6 9 6 6 5 0 4 1	7 4 7 2 5 6 4 3	7 8 7 8 6 0 4 9 3 8	5 8 4 6 3 4	43 36 23 20	774	8 4 8 3 6 6 5 4	8 9 9 0 7 1 6 0 4 6	7 3 6 6 6 5 3 4 0 0 2 4 1	4 5	3 5 3 1 1 6 1 2 0 8	37 33 39 12 08	3 7 2 1 1 4	22	0704
5 000 to \$5 999 3 000 tr \$8,999 7 000 to \$9 999 10 000 and over	4 2 2 4 2 6 2 0	4 7 2 7 2 9 2 2	3 5 3 2 3 5	2 7 1 4 1 4 0 9	15	4 9 2 8 3 1 2 3	5 7 3 3 3 6 2 6	6 8 3 9 4 4 3 3	3 1 1 6 1 7	1609	09	09	1105	0.4 0.4 0.2	03

Table 32a.—INCOME IN 1949 OF WHITE AND NONWHITE FAMILIES AND UNRELATED INDIVIDUALS FOR THE STATE, URBan and Rural 1950

(Basen on 20-percent sample. Percent not sorwin single uses than 6.1. The last and percent not shown where page a 25 than 2007

			Thate		1			Vocasite.		
Income level	The	liban	and rural nones	יתי	Rurai	- 1	UT542	and rural nonla	m i	
	State	Total	Croan	Rurat Echiarm	Tarre	Siate	Total	Tron	E ral nonfarm	Rura
Total	55C 8LO	446,805	241,710	25,7.	8. 945	251,38	901,270	14,52	57,245	>0,610
Number reporting _ Less than \$500 \$500 to \$999 \$1,000 to \$1,499 \$1,500 to \$1,499 \$2,000 to \$2,499	520,085 58,215 19,490 52,970 45,620 50,352	-09,9% 45,900 43,335 39,295 3c,CsC 42,370	32-,675 32,630 23,935, 23,990 29,800	1.5,25 10,20 15,50 12,00 12,00	20 125 12,325 16 _55 13,-75 9,25 7,985	241, 775 51,840 50,915 43 20 32,46 21,46	193,0.5 27,0.2 50,1.40 33,925 28,150 19,055	.37,29, 24,854 32,525 23,44 2,55 .5620	24,725 12,725 27, 35 2,585 6,455 3,735	48,445 44,23 10,755 9,395 4,290 1,925
\$2,00 to \$2,999 \$3,00 to \$3 499 \$3,500 to \$3,999 \$4,000 to \$4,499 \$4 500 to \$4,999	-2,155 -0,905 -4,905 -29,185 -21,420	37,505 39,780 22,190 20,780 20,035	27 940 20,400 24,600 24,120 46,510	9 625 9,330 7,540 5 660 3,525	4,59° 1 4,125° 1 2,405 1,385	10,29L c.530 3,200 1,875	3,38° 3,965 3,17° -,755	7,850 5,125 2,725 1,520 875	-,530 850 435 245 250	9,1 565 485 130 90
\$5,000 to \$5,998 \$6,000 to \$6,999 \$7,000 to \$6,999 _ \$10,000 and over faccine not reported	20 410 1°,385 19,405 14,665 30,725	28,590 16,340 18,120 12,635 20,895	24,1±0 13,960 .5,670 .2,110 20,335	1,465 2,380 2,450 1,225 0,560	1,815 1,045 1,285 1,030 3,830	-,335 725 585 500	1,200 655 530 235 8,255	1,025 565 460 187 5,735	175 90. 70 55 2,520	135 60 55 65 2,120
Median income	\$2,434	\$2,674	\$2,969	\$1,077	\$1,424	\$1,023	\$.,129	\$1,251	\$915	\$79
PERCENT DISTRIBUTION					1			*	9	
Number reporting	200.0	100.0	130.0	100.0	100 0	100.0	100.0	0.00.0	100.0	200.
Less thun 5500 - 5500 to 8999 - \$1,000+0 \$2,499 \$1,000 to \$2,499 - \$2,000 to \$2,499	11 2 11.4 10.2 8 8 9.7	10.4 9.8 8.9 8.2 9.0	10.2 7.5 7.4 7.5 9.3	11.1 16.3 15.5 16.1 16.5	25.4 20.2 17 1 12.0 10.0	21.5 27 7 17.8 13 4 8 8	.9.5 26 0 17 6 14.5 10 0	18 0 23 5 10.9 12 6 11.3	23.2 32.2 .9.3 18 6 8	29 3 34 5 18.8 8 8 4.0
\$2,500 to \$2,999. \$3,000 to \$3,499 \$3,000 to \$3,999 \$4,000 to \$4,499 \$4,000 to \$4.990	8.2 8 4 6 7 5 6 4.1	8 ; 9.0 7.3 6 1 4.0	8 7 9.0 7 7 6 0 5 1,	8 1 7 8 6 4 4.7 3 0	5.7 5.1 3.4 3.0 1.7	4 3 2.7 4 0.8 C.5	4 9 3 1.6 0.9 0.5	5 7 3 7 2 0 - 1 0.6	2.8 1 6 0.8 0.4 0 3	1.2 0.4 0.3
\$5,000 to \$5 999 \$6,000 to \$6,999 \$7,000 to \$9,999 \$10,000 and over	5 8 3 3 3 7 2.8	6 5 3." 4.1 3	7.5 4.4 4.0 3.8	3 7 2 C 2.1 1.3	2,3 1.3 1.6 1.3	0.6 0.3 0.2 0 1	0.6 0.3 0.3 0.1	0.7 0.4 0.3 0.1	0 3 0.2 0.1 0.1	0.3 C.1 G.1 O 1

Table 33.—AGE BY COLOR AND SEX, FOR STANDARD METROPOLITAN AREAS, URBANIZED AREAS, AND URBAN PLACES OF 10,000 OR MORE 1950

			1950	population				
Area and _ge		Al- classes		Wh	-	Nonw	_	1940 population, total

Table 33.—AGE BY COLOR AND SEX, FOR STANDARD METROPOLITAN AREAS, URBANIZED AREAS, AND URBAN PLACES OF 10,000 OR MORE: 1950

Area and age	1950 population							1940 population, total
	All classes			White		Nonwhite		
	Total	Male	Female	Male	Female	Male	Female	
STANDARD METROPOLITAN AREAS								
Baton Rouge	_58 236	_7 67	80,566	52,832	_3,003	24,838	27,503	88,4_5
Under 5 years	20,402	_0,3_8	10,044	6,792	5,54_	3,56_	3,497	7,449
Under 1 year	4,204	2,1_3	2,101	1,434	_,357	729	744	1 4_4
1 and 2 years	8,76_	4,_57	4 303	2,894	2,7_1	1,5_3	1,512	6,035
3 and 4 years	7,_78	3,7_8	3,_70	2,464	2,399	1,274	1,24_	
5 to 9 years	1_,0_8	7,501	7,_37	4,969	4,875	_,532	2,652	7,_29
5 years	3,2_5	_,578	1,637	_037	_,066	54_	571	_ 42_
6 years	3,25_	_ 625	1,634	1,083	1,069	542	565	_,365
7 to 9 years	8,_64	_,298	4,266	2,849	2,740	1,449	1,52_	4,325
10 to 14 years	_,25_	5 6_3	5,55_	3,484	3,402	2,179	2,_89	8 193
10 to 13 years	9,_66	4,599	4,567	2,8_2	2,790	1,737	1,777	6,49_
14 years	2,08_	1,06_	_,024	622	612	442	4_2	1,698
15 to 19 years	9_6	5,7_0	6,206	3,709	_,931	2,001	2,27_	8,8__
15 years	2,0_8	1,052	966	608	512	444	3_4	1,710
16 and 17 years	_,964	_,922	2,042	1,_81	1,207	74_	835	3,470
18 and 19 years	_,9_4	2,756	3,_98	1,920	2 _2	816	1,_86	3,641
20 to 24 years	_6,493	7,930	8,563	5,780	_,839	2,_50	2,724	3,915
25 to 29 years	_5,99_	7,798	8,176	5,70_	5,71_	2,_9_	2,483	9 028
30 to 34 years	_3,300	6,520	6,780	4,_79	4,717	_,741	_,003	8,_82
35 to 39 years	_2,340	6 096	6,244	4,255	4,138	_,84_	2,106	7,384
40 to 44 years	_0,403	5,123	5 280	3,55_	3,488	1,572	_,792	6,000
45 to 49 years	8,28_	4 107	4,178	2,_14	2,762	1,293	1,416	4,9_3
50 to 54 years	6,691	3 414	3,277	_,433	_,205	98_	1,07_	3,727
55 to 59 years	4 913	2 419	_,494	_ 621	_ 696	798	798	2,668
60 to 64 years	_,720	1,834	1,892	_,23_	_,246	_01	646	2,009
65 to 69 years	3,450	1,521	_,929	_81	1,03_	740	898	_ 8_8
70 to 74 years	1,861	803	1,058	4_3	666	3_0	392	_,061
75 to 84 years	_,80_	747	1,_58	413	671	_34	387	1,092
85 years and over	36_	120	_39	62	_6	64	_0_	
21 years and over	9_,516	47,073	49,_45	3_ 885	33 178	_4,188	1_,2_7	_4,994
New Orleans	_85,405	327 _91	357,4_4	234,284	250,598	93,70_	_06,816	_52,244
Under 5 years	76,_87	38,700	37 _87	25,_13	25,176	_2,787	12,41_	38,313
Under 1 year	15,33_	7,77_	7,559	5,07_	4,922	2,_04	2,6_7	7,793
1 and 2 years	32,_6_	_6 477	15,82_	10,922	10 662	5,55_	_,167	30,520
3 and 4 years	28,647	14,_48	14,199	9,920	9,592	4,528	4,607	
5 to 9 years	57,851	29 _20	28,731	19,608	13,04_	_,512	_,688	39,829
5 years	12,179	6,08_	6,096	4,224	4,147	_,8 9	1,3_9	7,528
6 years	12,074	6 097	5,977	4,_97	_,01_	_,900	1,907	7,_92
7 to 9 years	33,598	16,940	16,6_8	11 _87	10,886	5,7__	_,773	24,709
10 to 14 years	44,_20	2_,207	22,21_	4 _14	_4,320	_ _93	7,893	47,548
10 to 13 years	36,_56	18 09_	18,061	11,871	1_,687	6,224	6 _74	37 645
14 years	8,26_	_ _12	4 15_	2,6_3	2,63_	1,469	1 5_9	9,903
15 to 19 years	43,493	20,_3_	22,_60	1_,990	15,247	5 _43	7,71_	51,798
15 years	8,237	4,0_6	4,141	2,684	2,613	1,412	_,528	9,994
16 and 17 years	16,342	7,957	8,385	5,271	5,457	2,686	2,928	20,710
18 and 19 years	18,914	8,480	10,434	6,035	7,177	2,445	3,257	2_,094
20 to 24 years	57,236	26,461	30 77_	19,444	21,_93	7,0_7	9,_82	47,0_9
25 to 29 years	63,_63	30,437	32,_26	24 _81	23,_96	7,_56	9,430	50,_0
30 to 34 years	5_,629	25,652	27 977	19,152	19,81_	6,500	8,_64	49,099
35 to 39 years	54,447	25,708	28,739	18,7__	19,_50	6,99_	8,789	48,269
40 to 44 years	51,430	24,367	27,063	17,739	19,133	6,628	7,930	42,198
45 to 49 years	45,808	22,13_	23,67_	15,883	16,_4_	6,250	_,13_	36 228
50 to 54 years	38 802	19 028	19 774	14,019	_4,_07	_,009	_,167	28,828
55 to 59 years	30,_10	14,_62	15,548	10,84_	_1 804	3,_19	3,74_	22,496
60 to 64 years	23 089	10,724	12,365	8,_62	9,486	2,56_	2,_79	_7,_94
65 to 69 years	20,093	8,564	11,529	6,101	8,163	2,403	_,_66	_4,525
70 to 74 years	12,257	4,980	7,282	3,786	5,_90	1,19_	1,592	8,888
75 to 84 years	11,4_8	4,280	7,218	3,269	5,818	_,011	1,400	8,00_
85 years and over	1,787	535	1,2_2	40_	914	_28	_78	
21 years and over	453,_37	212,985	2_0 _52	_5 ,054	172,797	_5,93_	67,35_	364,963
Shreveport	176 547	84,062	92,48_	53,114	56,977	30,948	_5,538	150,203
Under 5 years	21 3_4	_0,873	10,471	_ 322	_,012	4,551	4,4_9	12,320
Under 1 year	4,319	2,205	2,1_4	1,285	1,2_0	_20	858	2,5__
1 and 2 years	8,983	4,540	4,443	_,631	2,550	1 969	1,893	9,809
3 and 4 years	8,042	4,128	3,914	_,406	2,260	1,722	1 708	
5 to 9 years	16,263	8,092	8,177	4,439	4,5_7	3,653	3,670	12,022
5 years	3,464	1,713	1,751	959	958	754	793	2,48_
6 years	3,497	1,729	1,768	915	972	81_	796	2,314
7 to 9 years	9,308	4,650	4,658	2,565	2 60_	2,085	2,081	7,222
10 to 14 years	13,515	6,793	6,722	3,702	3 510	_,091	3,1_2	13,298
10 to 13 years	11,066	5,604	5,462	3 097	2 35_	2,507	2,506	10,5_0
14 years	2,449	1,189	1 260	605	654	584	606	2,748
15 to 19 years	11,810	5,472	6,338	_,050	3,65_	2,422	2,69_	14,013
15 years	2 403	1,195	1,208	_60	653	526	555	2,847
16 and 17 years	4,535	2,206	2,329	_,224	1 278	982	_,051	5,355
18 and 19 years	4,872	2,071	2,801	1,157	1,723	914	1,078	5,871
20 to 24 years	14,672	6,_26	8,446	4,102	_,367	2,125	3,079	14,644
25 to 29 years	15,192	7,045	8,_47	5,043	5,4__	2,032	_,690	14,765
30 to 34 years	13,75_	6,447	7,30_	4,663	4 78_	1,784	2,520	1_,817
35 to 39 years	13,295	6,2_3	7,082	4,251	4,522	1,952	2,560	13,400
40 to 44 years	12,046	5,653	6,393	3,841	4 _79	1,812	2,214	10 864
45 to 49 years	11,090	5,302	5,794	3,462	3,687	1,840	2,_07	8,823
50 to 54 years	9 19_	4,476	4,71_	3,026	3 047	1,450	1,66_	6,544
55 to 59 years	_,_20	3 51_	3,603	2,351	2,41_	1,166	1,1_2	4,885
60 to 64 years	5,28_	2,_37	2,744	_,758	1,876	779	868	3,864
65 to 69 years	5,527	2,516	3,011	_,351	1,568	1,105	1,443	3,305
70 to 74 years	3,157	1,438	1,719	879	_,_31	559	588	_,831
75 to 84 years	2,759	1,2_8	_,50_	763	958	495	543	_,688
85 years and over	523	204	319	112	177	92	142	
21 years and over	110,845	51,746	59,099	34,897	38,176	16,849	20,923	95 419

	Tota.	Mase	Fomale	Maie	Fema _e e .	Maie .	Female	
URBAD IZED AREAS			1			3.50	4.00	
Baton Rouge		6",859	·-, Co	47,334	47,729	20 525	23,276	
uder a goars. Under 1 vear and 2 years	17 77" il	A, 236	5, 7c. 1	6 46	5 15:	r,92L	2 9.0	
and 2 yea s	7 164	3.93	3,000 }	2,32	2, 4°7 2, 125	601 44 4	620	
9 vears.	12,652	6,290	6 303	2,482 70-1	2,125 4 24 340	2 0.8	-,2-6 ,92 4 110	
years to 9 years	2 59	3, 24 6, 290 1, 233 1, 380	-1703	620	340 931	43.	44.3	
7 to 9 vears	3.54		3,500 1	2 -41	4,700	4,129	mpatu5	
16 to 13 years	7,454	4,573	3 740 1	2,408	2, 173	1 304	1 c78 -,362 316	
to 19 years	10,268	4,793	8.30 g 8.30 g 9.47.3 g	3 77.1	3 150	1,517	1,919	
5 vers . £ and 17 years . 5 and 19 years . to 24 vears	638 3,2,7 5,364	1,543 2,4_2	300 743 2 954	1.003	525 . 040 . 941	322 540	275 683	
8 and 19 years	15.781 1	2 4_2	2 954	5,46.	5,488	1 8 0	2,273	
	14 705 12,015	7,120	7,436 8	5 "62	5,504	.883	2 438	
to 84 years to 44 years	10 08/ 1	5,20,	5,380	4 365 3,878 2,454	3.7.9	1,344	1 866	
to 49 years	9,224	4 5.3 3,c23	7,711	2 493	3 139	. 357	-,572 1 259	
0 59 3 50 F	4.706	3,005	2,12	2 150	,476 ,984 ,528	855	933	
to let years	3,134 2,636 1 533	2,109 1,552	1 630 \$	357		JP2 -95	669 126	
to 74 years	1 533	1,215 6,0 5,1 100	1,623	65°	99° 39° 364	558 ' 24"	726 324 3_3	
to 84 years year, at d over	31.475	160	2.0 P	333 j	-2-1	428	3_3	
rears and over	36,136	999, ب	44,239	7,700	32 108	-2 -39	-4 -31	
New Or_sanz	.9,742	3.5 O62	*44 ,06	223,78c	244 60.	91 C 6	מב, ש.	
des o years.	"2,638 _4,-99	3, 8, -	3., 67		4,134	12,099 2,69 5,354 4,399		
nde 1 years. nud 2 years. and 4 years. 9 years.	30,737	45,023	. 1 048 3	34,4/2 4,-02 10,704	4. O43 F	3,354	12,02± 2,545 5 0°5	
9 years.	2 ,332 55,UZ	13,792 27 708	27,5 8	9,-73	17,018	9,241	9,430	
years years to 9 years	_1,577 _3 408 31,791	5,770 5,436 15,125 2,,019	5,800 \ 5 662 I 15 856 I	3,968	3,91	- 809	1.90	
to 9 years		14,1251	15 856 21,1.7	10,613	10 2-8	7,406	5 c08 7,c8.	
to 14 years 10 to 13 years	34,331	3,888,	-7,200 3 0-7	1 14	-0,904	5, 18.	6,206	
to 19 years 15 years 16 and 17 years 18 and 19 years	7. 292	19.09 [21.4.1	13 244	2 490	6 362	7 490	
15 veare 16 and 17 vears	7,824 15,636	3,90o 7 587	3, 18 8 0.5 27, 324	4,95. 5 5	2 443 5 182	2,626	1,47	
	_8,162 55,076	8 1.36 25 AC2		5 5	20,024	2, %3	3 178	
to 26 years to 39 years	60.339	29 282	31 527 46 977	2. 73.	22 248 1	7,55,	8,930 9 220	
to 39 years	51,670 52,514	24,703 24 732 23 566	26, 82 26, 277	18 .75	29,179	5,32P 6,842	7 966 8 63	
to 44 years	49 ×53		-3 020	17 777	18 524 C 054	6,084	7 7r_ 4,948	
to 54 years	-4 398 57,657 29,324	21 378 -8 423 1-,125	19,264	13,556	1,215	4 867 3,625	5,019	
to 64 years	22,520	10,41	12,109	7,920	9 202	2 42	2,82"	
to 69 years	11,952	4,826	7,126	3 6 8	3,263	2,304	1,243	
to 74 vers	1,74	4 122 514	1,230	3,154	5,733	970	2,36€	
years and over	438,524	205,560	2,32,962	151,102	±67 16	24,458	05,871	
Shawwepn=t	150 202	70 767	~9 441	48,5°1	52,873	22 296	26,500	
det o years	18,543	2,475	9 168 1,896	6 246 1 2.8	2,961 1,263	3 220	3,207	
and 2 years and 4 years	3 900 7,943 6 830	4 008	3,43,	2 625	2,232	85	1 403	
Queere	12 70 4	b 358	0 34,	3,917	3,926	2,441	2,171	
years. years. to 9 vests to 14 vears	2,770	1,397 1 390 3,5°1	771	831	849	304 559	519 5.2 1,388	
to 14 years	7 2		3,601	2,191	2,213	1 380	2,388	
0 to 12 years	9,834 8,090 1 74	4,017	4,073	2,448	2,938 2,420 518	1,944 1 569 375	1 o5_ 363	
to 10 years	9 .54	3,95	J 158	2,479	3,270	1 527	,8 8 35)	
6 and 17 years	3 395	1,564	1,032	51. 977	525 112	333 287 507	72C	
	4,000	1,588	1,032 2,442 7,969	3,590	1,n53	1 :61	2.5-4	
10 39 years	15 148 13 053	7,088		5, 389 4 92	5,813	1,669	2,24,	
to 39 vegrs	11,79"	5.520	6,754	3,955	4,198	1,565	2,079	
to 44 years	10,248	-,8°0 4 328	4,850	2,495	3, 206	1,375	1,665	
to 54 years	7,208 7,566	3 6.9	3 907	2,56"	2 607	1 094	1,300 897	
to 49 years to 54 years to 59 years to 59 years	5,195 4,236	2,794	2,257	4,458	1.043	847 521	0-4	
	4,300 2,394 2,185	1,865	2,43, 1,36, 1,265	700	965	763 333 324	4,051 39ti	
to 84 years	2,185	920	1,265	596 94	838	324 68	107	
years and over	97,448	45,129	22,499	32,301	35,794	12,020	16,505	

¹ Not avai abue

Tadur 33—AGE BY COLOR AND SEX, FOR STANDARD METROPOLITAN AREAS, URBANIZED AREAS, AND URBAN PLACES OF 10,000 OR MORF 1950—Con.

Charles and a second second second	-	with the second	.930	rpulation		-	10,1	1946	1	1	and the second second	, 950 T	opulat or	1	processing (grys)		1940
Arus and age	-	ALL CLOSSES		W	hite	Von	white	popula-	Area and age		All classes		W	brte .	Non	wlute	popula
	Total	Maie	Female	Mare	Female	Mac	-emale	ro al		Total	Male	Female	Male	Fen.ale	Malc	Female	total
URBAN PLATES	1	-		-					URBAN PIACES	i						1	
e exercinia	14,9~	10,489	-8,024	260	12,70	b 558	1 840	27,006	Bogalues .	17,798	4,629	9,_69	5 886			3,007	14,604
Unger I vest.	4,74	2,0%	2,034	1 - 141	126	863	908	2,061 439	Unger o year	2 361	1,20° 240	1,158. 226	783 1.7	741	420 d9	417 114	288
1 and 2 years	- 450	34- 707	759	456	124	311	360 135	1,022	Unger 1 year 1 and 2 years 3 and 4 years	- 00 859	522 4.5	478	335 291	315 284	187	163 140	1,_8
5 to 0 Teams - o y turn - f y care.	3,1.9	,500 338	1 55.	897	178	69 LJ1	662 235	2,1-t 40o	5 o 3 , cars .	1,76	866 .89 182	495	554	122	112 75 67	298 67 56	1 29" 303
7 to 9 seem -	L 32	320 903	27ر 913	-70 5.2	19-	142	دس1 194	_89 4,32	7 to 9 years	1 010	49*	188 5.5	115 325	132 340	1/0	175	767
10 to 14 ears.	2,5	,043	., 365	A78	745	597 485	5	2,319 1,849 470	10 to 14 years 10 to 13 years	,300	753 621	8±3 679	508 -16	572	405	∡41 202	1,415
1s to 19 years.	2,340	1 027	228	1 558	-28	469	30 6.8	2 6 7	14 years 15 to 19 years	1,205	132 536 -26	134	°2,	9. 44. 1.4	40 167	226	286
15 vesr	443	203 438	345	244	2-8	126	243 243 2 3	. 03.	15 years. 16 and 17 years 18 and 19 years	290 477	232	170 245	8. .71	-05	45 64	36 80	281
18 and 19 years	2,664	- 043	577	4 623	3.4	420	2 3 656	1 .82 2,6.8	20 to 24 years	1,412	178 634	254 176	444	164 528	.90	90 250	594 1,289
25 to 29 years - 30 to 34 years - 35 to 39 years -	2,8_3 2,829	345	1 705	819	1,026	455	656 679 581	2,426	25 to 29 years 30 to 31 years _	1,557	(91 615	866 671	503 4°5	582 470	158	264 198	1,5.2
.0 to 44 veers.	2,50%	1,120	1,511	828	888	463	480	2,342	35 to 39 years	1,394	673 614	721 587	482 435	48. 362	191	236 205	968
45 to 49 vers 50 to 5- years 55 to 59 years	2,214	1,055	1,.60	64. 500	687	410 148	473 387	1 720	45 to 49 years	1,0%	⇒^6 395	52C 449	314 257	341	192	179	819
bu to 64 years	1,427	706. 52.1	7	318	472 3o2	205	269 208	920	55 to 59 years 60 to 64 years	659 569	346 -05	*13 -64	226 224	207	20	106	284
65 to 69 years 70 to 64 years 75 to 64 years	1,107	493 249 25/	614 334 234	252 15/	32. 22	95	292	690 3"4	65 to 60 years 70 to 74 years	463 24_	432	230	135	92	98 40	86 27	292 135
85 years and over .	90	30	66	14	188	-6	106	_07	75 to 84 years 85 years and over	260	124	36 17	06 12	10	38	7	1.5
21 years and over	42 25	۵,194	12,063	6,212	7,195	,982	4,867	17,377	21 years and over	10 6-7	5,155	*,+02	3,598	3,712	1,257	1,780	8 733
Bas ron	.2,769	6,274	6,495	4 19,	4,41	2,08_	2,354	6,526	Bossier C ty	15 470	7 >81	7 889 °	, 404	u,559	1,177	1,320	a, =86
Under 5 years . Under 1 year	1,748 369	928 193	840 174	59e	524 108	3.2	296 68	493 85	Under 5 years Under 1 year	2,623	. 351 234	1,272 257 741 474	1,173	1,112	178	159	539 118
1 and 2 years 3 and 4 years	643 633	39c 343 641	290	250	228 188	162	126	+08	1 and 2 years 3 and 1 years	1,10_	350 497	474	485 438	47-	75	70	421
5 to 9 years 5 rears	27- 200	128	123	432 93 88	406 73	409 58 40	234 50	93	5 tc 9 years 5 years	1 -61	762 _86 181	609 404 450	601	240 130 129	37	159 34 21	473 -04 79
6 venrs 7 to 9 years 10 to 14 years	740	362 484	385	25 L 294	255	1.1	-30	98 326 566	6 years_ 7 to 9 years_	780	394	385	143 309	281	36 86	21 04 92	200
10 to 13 years.	806	382	424	229 67	289	153	30 170 135 27	449	10 to 14 years. 10 to 13 years. 14 years	854 704 150	364 79	-40 71	269	263	1.4 95 19	200	373 113
15 to 19 years	966 18 ²	457 100	512 05	488 60	219	166	.93	127	15 to 19 years	840	ي52د	488	≥71	376	91 22	-42	558
15 years 16 and 17 years 18 and 19 years 1	365 416	1.86	199	39	148	57	81 75	268 245	15 years 15 and 17 years	330 .60	45 142	80 190 218	115 108	138	25	-9 52	108 19 253
20 to 24 years	1,179	548	631	40b	416	.42 .58	215		18 and 19 years 20 to 24 years 20 to 29 years	1,484	554	1,272	441	789	25 34 113 73	4- 118	683 644
30 to 34 years	1 037	5.7 447	518 491	3.7	35.3	-30	164	743 722 638	30 to 34 years -	1,130	940	810	808	72.	72	89	614
40 to 44 years	088 8°a	432 328	330	300 201	277	132	-7	450	40 0 44 years	8e0 643	346	38	396	269	74 81 68	84	378 211
50 to 5- years	491	2/4 2·0 134	247 495	148	158	96. 82	-48 89 70	235	50 to 54 years -	4C2 331	242	220 167	191	157	51 40	63 34 15 52	203 146
65 to 60 years	300 336	153	183	69 89	112	64	67	149	60 to 64 years	26. 235	107	140	74	755	14	52	109
70 to 74 years 75 o 84 years	176	89	97	J9 32	*0	30 30	30 47 7	78 52	70 to 74 vears. 7s to 84 years	103 113	45 46	58 67	35 35	41	40	26 2	57 48
85 vers and over 21 years and over	7 570	3,687	3 883	2 525	2 462	1,162	1.421	4 279	So years and over	9,450	4,974	4,575	3,955	4,119	619	757	-,504
						1	,		#2 // #10 m2			,,,,,,,	,,,,,	*,2	0.27		2,55
Enter o years	125,529	9 100	7,845	5,778	5,-90 1 169	∠.322	8 897 7,325	2,209	Crowley Under 5 years	621	6,162	6 622	4,624	- 828 56°	1 538	1,794	9,24
Under 1 year 1 and 2 years	3,400 6,901	3 497	3 404	2,466	1 169 4 347 1,974	1,031	1,05/1	1,741	1 and 2 year	7 4	144	130	202	91 250	53	29	1.03
3 and 4 years 5 to 9 years 5 years	2,407	2 862 5,557	2,782 5,622	2,063	3.964	1.564	808	2.169	3 and 4 years o to 9 years	1,2,9	6,34	322 623	241 4*6	438	105 10 178	163	704 882
6 YLARS	2,454 6,318 8,029	231	1,241 1 221 3 · e0	836 970 2,287	874 879 2,21	161 8/1	449 949	392 -28	5 years	233	136	147	271	86	39 29 100	31	178
10 to 14 years	6.549	3 . 18 4,034 3 286	3,26	2,745	2,086	1,289	339	2,098	7 to 9 years 10 to 14 years 10 to 13 years	1,140	382 595 483	372 551	282 423 348	3,4 299	172	121	530 97., 768
14 vears	9,0.4	4,213	732	J 102	+83	216	240	579	14 years _	223	112	111	75	/5	35	36	206
16 and 1" years	2,878	738	720	479	492 985	249	226	603 1,25°	15 years 16 and 17 years	209	518 117	534 92	57° 69	392 68	45 28	142 24 64	170
18 and 19 years	4,708	2, .36 6 586	7,350	1,696	1 922	440	050 782	1 475	18 and 17 years	411	191	220 222 585	137	126	63	54 159	.:68 421
20 to 24 years 20 to 29 years 30 to 34 years	13,431	5.394	5,611	5,142	4,089	1,226	1,222	3,836	25 to 29 years .	1 006 898	51° 426 420	550	327	430	106	1201	877
35 to 39 years 40 to 44 years	8 51.		5 176	3 635	3 578	1,297	1 598	3,549	85 to 99 years 40 to 44 years	926 805	446 388	478 480 417	332 352 305	354 354 349	88	26	732 ,17 585
to to 49 years	6,783 5 5.4 3,949	347	3,436	2,076	2,380	974	,056 820	2 150	45 to 49 years	7.9	344	405	281	303	63	-02 -02	523
to to 59 years.	2.935	1,43)	2 035	1 367	0.2	566 426	271	1 209	50 to 54 years 55 to 59 years 60 to 64 years	7.50	97	286	195	170	70 50	6.3	409 330

to 69 years	1 402	152	850	348	801 -71	204	601 279	750 418	65 to 69 years - 70 to 74 years	389	165 177	218 210 139	128	172 137	37 34	46 75 37	230 120
5 to 84 years 5 years and over	1,306	495	186	307 54	542 -15	48 43	7.1	457	75 to 84 years So years and over	188	95	93	66	66	291	27	135
1 years and over	78,956	38,295 4	0 661	28 486	26 847	9,809 1	,814	23,271	21 years and over	7,469	a 506	5,963	2,711	2,954	790	1,0.2	5,649

Table 33—AGE BY COLOR AND SEX, FOR STANDARD METROPOLIT IN AREAS URBANIZED AREAS, AND URBAN PLACES OF 10,000 OR MORE 1550—Cod.

			a 080.	nc. aluqo		- Control of the Cont	ī	134	-	-		1900 :	מכנגמע קט	Deriman Charles	-		1940
Area and age		III classes		W	hite	Year	vinte	puptus	1 rea Little age		All cuasts	-	-	ute	Nort	w'_'e	popula-
120	To-a	Male	Female	Male	Female	Ma.	"TING! 8	total		loai	Mal-	Femal-	Vale	Fema.e	Maie	Female	total
URBAN PLACES					1			out g	JRBAN PLACES								
Gretze	23,813	6,650	763	4,776	5,056	,074	2,-20	Q 379		*- 4 4	20 040	21 ,30	JA 724	15,24	2,523	5,339	24 207
Inder a years	-,047 306	826	821	534	543	292 50	278	8.3	Unger 5 years	2 27	2,08	2,552	. 990	-,787	"3c	705	1.756
1 and 2 years	6%	340 334	15.	213	23	_32	103	£75	Inder 1 ez.	2.2	1,.2	506	737	749	±7¢ 343	300	350
3 and 4 years 5 to 9 years	64.5 379 302	672	707	-65	405	277	442,	840	Sard 4 ears	3 347	3.0	1 932	,25,	66.	273 262	263 5 9	1,6-2
6 years	278	38.	134 4-7	-02	80	20	36.	-64	5 years	900	40	429	200	28-	113	115	231 309
fo 9 years -	4,0,4	506	508	345	349	-40 -46	-21	ا بحاد 294 ر د	7 to 9 streets	2 %	-,592	1,759	700	78"	324	32-	1,803
10 to 13 years	818	41c	406 102	2911	275	14 12	23	878	0 to a tears 10 to 'S tears 14 tears	2 579	1,299	269	89c.	885	409	395	1,435
15 to 19 years	997 ±82	429 05	408	63	729	154	.491	4,'41	5 c 10 mm	2.93	1,332	1 500	9-1	_ 087	39.	5.2	1,642
16 and 17 years 18 and 19 years	35P 357	162	196	103	. 3.	44 59	63	45.	15 /cars 16 a. d 1" years	1 664	503		3.	373	103	90	363 759
20 to 2 x yes =	1.163	5/2	621	139	√5 438	1/2	-83	469 987	18 and 15 years 20 to 2 , ears 25 to 29 years	1,30 3	533	2,096	382	536	45.	633	827 2 1o2
25 to 29 years	1,232	605 507	62°	46c 389	441	139	486 _50	978	30 :0 31 mars	~ 056 f	2,931	2,_25	1,45	1,5%	676	569	2 209
85 to 39 years - 40 to 44 years -	1 022	472	52.	367	384 376	1_5 122	-37 -67	75.	35 to 39 \ ears 40 to 41 \ tears	2 928	1,70.	1,668	1,109	.,08	387	436 470 312	4,687 473
45 to 49 years	854 710	416 363	438 347	292 271	223 247	124	115	674	-U -0 49 rears	2 385	1,2,3	,172	887	887	326	285	-,232
55 to 59 years.	606 395	31_	295	228	239	83	100 56	496 430	55 to 53 years	1 354	90.3 704	866	671 488	48.	232	24L 171 145	772
60 to 64 years 65 to 69 years	386	167	215	121	147	40 46	23	274	65 to 69 .cars	-,C35	70± 477 477	528	32/ 254	213	3	145	571 463
70 to 74 years 75 to 84 years	218 207	87 90	31	25 53	10	32	31	14	65 to 69 - cars 65 to 69 - cars 70 to 7- years 75 to 84 years	566 488	254	3.2	. 486	248	68 63	65	273
85 years and ove 21 years and ove.	8,054	8		1 1	46	5	7	34	80 VLERS and over	89	44	45	41	3.	14	56 14	287
21 years and over	8,004	÷,132	4,522	3 277	3,282	٠,٦55	1,2-0	6,-64	21 years and over	25,447	12,464	12,983	9,240	9 532	3,284	3 451	.3,660
Floura	14,005	5,520	5,985	4,600	4,969	820	1,016	9 .252	Morpha	38 572	18	20,457	au 14"	,435	7,670	9 022	28,309
Under 5 years Under 1 year.	1,482	728 147	754	625	633 123	10	121	90,	Under 5 years	932	2,279	2 -83	1.194	20.	235	- ,u34 239	1 922
1 and 2 years -	594 595	330	294	260	243 267	40	47	71.	Unger 1 year sng 2 /ears 3 and 4 years	± 899	988	911	5e 43	481	464 368	430 -25	1,526
5 to 9 years 5 years	1,228	596 123	632	509 ±06	518 11.	48 87 17	16	8.1	5 to 9 years -	3 306	-,677	1,629	970	846	7981	783	1,809
6 years 7 to 9 years	245 732	12º 346	127 119 380	109 294	95 31.e	18 52	24	177 158 519	6 years 7 to 9 years	074	364	312	.77	201 155	16_	165 157	3 6 356
10 to 14 years	1 000	482	518	395	414	87	104	943		2,773	973	1 374	3e1	138	452 624 500	46. b3u	2,185
14 year	190	84	106	71	79	74.	27	75.5 188	10 to .3 years	2,2.7	2 9	1,137	580 125	134	124	53. 103	1 700
15 to 19 years	857 179	380	477	320 56	404 92	60	73	952 2	5 to 19 years	2 430 4-1	1,095	1,335	601 11_	767 130	494	368 99	2,532
16 and 17 years. 18 and 19 years	351 327	171	111 180 286	115	148 164	22	32	372 36*	16 and 17 years	901	438	443 643	240 249	237	+08 175	226	968
20 to 24 years _ 20 to 29 years _	968 972	475 480	493	426 423	424 410	49	76	9,1	26 to 2x years 25 to 29 years	3 398	7.420	1,973	836	1, 80	584	243 798	2,804
30 to 34 years 35 to 39 years	840	402	438	353	3061	49	72	955	30 to 3y years 30 to 3y years	3,417	1,530	1,887	986	911	544 523	784	2,956 2,914 2,725
40 to 44 years	821 748	418 388	433 360	353 327	359 317	65 61	43	606 504	40 to 4m years.	2,976	-,358 -,232	1 618	820 721	897 829	-38	644	2,725
to to 49 years	UL9 477	277	245	255 196	247	42	65 38	453 339	45 to 10 years -	2,074	1,200	1,390	71.3 60.8	775 649	487	621	1,826
50 to 54 years - 55 to 59 years - 60 to 04 years -	448 262	202	24°0 153	159	207 205 125	43 43	41	270	55 to 59 years	1,567	752	81.5	449	494	303	32.	4,015
65 to 69 years 70 to 74 years	277	112 97	155	85	128	20 27 17	37	186	60 to 64 years 65 to 69 years	1,567	590 563	701	383 286	347	277 1.7	3.39	724 654 315
75 to 84 yea s	208	91,	-17	80	-06 83	21	32	117	70 to 74 years 75 to 34 years	621	ځود 262	340 359	21.8	501	120	134	315
55 years and over	6,762	3,249	20 3,52	2,767	2,917	482	59h	5 203	Se years and over	20,051	11,499	-3,552	17 ε,93	7,764	28	37	
ar years and over	0,702	3,244	٠,٠٠	2,707	2,517	402	390	9 233	2. years am over .	25,051	11,499	ا 352,	6,43	, 764	4,566	2,786	-9 222
Lafayo+te	33,241	-6,330	17 211	12,501	12,718	3,829	4 403	19 210	Ne. Iberia	16,+07	7,991	8,476	6,011	6 176	1,980	2,300	15,7.7
Under 5 years. Under 1 year. 1 and 2 years	4,125	2,056 460	2 073	1,009	324	247 125	579 121	1,616 324	Under 5 years . T'nder 1 year	2,094	1 106	988 210	805 175	714	301 69	274	1,295 296
3 and 4 years _	1,526	843 753	855 773	5°0	62b	239 183	229	1,292	and 2 years	793	440 424	409 369	306 326	288	98	97	999
5 to 9 years	580	1,533	1,501	2,3	219	4.6	426	1,682	5 to 9 years	330	852	780	620	253	232	2.27	1 191
6 years - 7 to 9 years -	65	3.5	339	223 675	252	92	70 87 263	318	6 years	320	173	147	132	341	41	1 :0	22.
10 to 14 years	2,435 2 019	1,233	1,314	840 652	672	258 393	263 430 342	1,033	7 to 9 years 10 to 14 years 10 to 13 years	1,359	079	650 536	500 409	438	179	222	1,226
14 years	476	228	2/8	158	100	323	88	1,588	14 years	249	125	124	97	81	34	40	255
15 to 19 years	2 930 450	1,343	1,58~	1,027	1,165	316	422	2,001	15 to 19 years .	-,713	1.2	649	391	446	173	201. 33	1 320
15 years 16 and 17 years 18 and 19 years	y55 1 525	437	518	300 584	340 668	137	178	768	15 years 16 and -7 years 18 and 19 years	487	24 ₀	24.	170	199	76	88	519 553
20 to 24 years	3,896	910	1,966	1,636	1,537	120 294 322	429	2,0.7	20 to 24 years. 25 to 29 years .	1,342	583	759 779	440	557	340	202	1,478
30 to 34 years	2,670	1,33° 1,2.9	1,337	1,061	1,001 942	280	33×	1,994 1,449	30 to 34 years - 35 to 39 years	1,306 1,203	640	667	54± 500 511	5_1	25 00 189	179 156 171	-,20>
40 to 44 years	2,034	1,2.9 974	1,000	939 765	811	209	249	1,200	40 to 44 years	1,093	341	552	413	407	128	1.45	759
45 to 40 years -	1,747	874 617	873 730	∪79 487	656 521	-95 30	2_7 209	1,027	45 to 40 years 50 to 54 years	913	4p1 336	462 361	35C 242	203	101 54	126	701
05 to 59 years	1,093	500	593	375 288	435	125	158	638	55 to 59 years 30 to 84 years	642 465	282	360 229	2.0 187	283	72	96	470 365
60 to 64 years 60 to 69 years	725	324	401	21.7	392	105	1091	379	65 to 69 years	450 266	190	260	124	80	66	11	313 173
70 to 74 years 70 to 84 years	436 297	184 166	252 231	112	184	57 54	68 49 13	193	70 to 74 years	250	118	.48 14.1	74	_02	33	41	173
85 years and over 21 years and over	20,04	9,796	48 ±0,278	7 680	7,73/	2,116	2 544	11,562	21 years and over _	9,9%	4,687	26 5,267	3,621	3 926	1,066	- 1	8,449
we begus upe page,	20,04	3, 1961	10,276	7 680	1,131	اللنطوة	a, mal	12,002	as /quis and over .	2,724	4,007	, seu!	,	2 1401	2,000	-1	0,

LOUISIANA

 $\begin{array}{l} \text{Table 33-AGE BY COLOR AND SEX, FOR STANDARD METROPOLITAN AREAS, URBANIZED AREAS, AND URBAN PLACES \\ \text{OF } 10,000 \text{ OR MORE } 1950-\text{Con} \end{array}$

			1950	population				940				1950 -	opulation	2		, Ten	1940
Area and age		all classes	-	i W	Lie	You	waite	popula tron	Area and age		All classes		W	hite	Non	white	popula
	Total	Mace	Fettalue	Vals	Female	Jale	Female	total		Total	Мав	Female	Male	Fenale	Male	Female	to-al
URBAN PLACES	l					i			URBAN PLACES								
He crieat	270,445	270.812	299,633	185 858	201,956	B4.954	97.677	494,537	Ruston-Con								
ecer ii vears	60,114	30,298	29,713	JR 979	18,601	21,449	11,2	23,084	20 to 24 years	1,563	906	657	780	462	126	195	,
under year . 1 and 2 years .	12,100	-2,919	.2,481	3,579	2,881	4,985	2,345	6,809	20 to 29 vears. 30 to 34 years.	888	-86 3-2	402 344	366 235	256 198	120	146	7
3 and 4 years - to 9 years	22,5°- 45 56.	22,911	11,2_7	14,384	7,000	4,02. 8,527	8,653	.2,951 34,297	35 to 99 years 10 to 41 years	571	292	359 288	182	221	1.0	138	5
5 cars	9,469	4.705	4. 704	3.045	3.043	1.600		6.434	45 to 49 years	524	441	283	149	18~	92	96	3
6 cars 7 to 9 , ears -	26.667 35.54	3,462	1,205	3,074	2,928 8,926	1,670	1,753	6,484	50 to 54 years 5, to 59 years	409 301 28 ₀	.78 _33 128	231 168	122 83 95	145 126	56 50 33	86 42 37	3
10 10 13 years	28,867	14,288	14.579	10,7_2	8,799	6,881 5,562	7, 60 5,730	12,675	60 to 64 /ears_ 65 to 69 years	28o 292	128	175	95 76	121	37	50	2
14 years	6,675 36,005	50در د	3,370	1,986		1,3.9	1,386	8,660	70 to 74 years 7p to 8a years	202	#7 70	115 96	57 39	83 72	30	32 24	
15 years	0,052	15,981	19,024	2,25	2,998	5,908 1,257	7,026	45,68c 8,788	85 years and over	29	12	17	8	1.	4	6	}
16 and 17 years 18 and 19 years	_3,439 _5,*84 47,753	7,137	8 747	4,932	5,735	2,434	2,645	18,192	21 years and over	6,148	3,045	3,103	2,10	2,041	875	1,002	4,5
to 24 1 cars	4,,895	22,100	25,653	2,778	1°,339 18,229	7,086	8,652	-1,997 45,747	1								
to 39 years.	44.055	20,979	23 056	13,25z 14,731	15,588	5.927	7,468	45.163	Shreveport .	127,206	59,643	67,563	40,406	44,258	19,237	23,005	98,1
to 44 years	45,356 43,450	41,158 43,307	24,198	14,233	15,80~	6,074	~,36	43,704 38,268	Under o years Under 1 year-	-4,757	7,530	7,227	4,792 1,023	4,066	2,738	۷,661	6,73
to of rears	33,742	18,84. 15,346	20,626	1,734	13,992	5,712	4,788	33,194 20,417	I and 2 years	6,261	1,622 3,184		2 07 75	1.943	1,167	1,134	2,7
to 59 years	20,41,			9,287	10,222	3.407	3,495 2,692	2,506	3 and 4 years - 5 to 9 years -	2,335	2,724 5,188 1,121	2,611 5,191 1,105	2,752	1,644 3,215 685	972 2,045 423	967	6.5
to 69 years	17.819	9,412	10,175	5,295	7,272	2.17	3,103	13,359	6 years	2,226	4,225	1,118	557	691	468	1,976 420 427	1,31
to 74 rears	10,072	3,744	6,533	3,331 2,838	5,086	1,074	1,484	6,323	7 to 9 years.	5,910 8,233	4,088	2,968	2,470	1,839	1,154	-, 29	6,5; 1,3; 1,24 2,94 7,45
years and over _	1,514	464	,148	351	837	113	311	1,106	10 to 13 years	6,777	3,356	3,411	2,061	7,042	1,305	, 369	2,8
years and over	384, 162	179,173	205,489	148,082	143,339	1,091	62,153	331,411	14 years. 1o to 19 years.	7,836	3,4.4	4,422	2,114	2,818	1,303	1,604	1,57
Opulusas	12,650	1 501							Io years 16 and 17 years _	2,885	708	760	431 824	449 940	277	324	1,67
uer o years	1,142	748	6,098	3,314	3,539	333	2,559	8,980 860	18 and 19 years	3,480	1.367	2,1.3	856	2.4.0	541	606 684	3,81
Under ' year /	255	129	126	97	78	32	48	179	20 to 24 years. 25 to 29 years.	11,399	2,043	6,455	3,327	4,449	1,420	2,203	10,05
1 and 2 years. 3 and 4 years .	346	348	324	175	176 134	14:	148	s8 1	30 to 34 years 35 to 39 years	10,671	5,0 C 4,713	5,457	3,741	3,831	1,295	1,824	9,93
o 9 vears	1,180	802 131	287	111د	276	291 6L	311	822	40 to 44 jecrs.	8,965	4,193	4,792	2,984	3,296	1,209	1,496	7,71
to 9 years.	245 698	335	359	70	59 55 lo2	62	56 58 197	170 173 512	45 to 49 years 50 to 54 years	8,205 6,852	3,851	3,564	2,620	2,888	1,220	1,466	6,12
to 14 , ears 0 to 13 years	1,071	446 468	525 458	201	257 216	285	268	960	55 to 59 years 60 to 64 years.	3,855	2,528	3,56± 2,74± 2,054	1,783	1,947	480	794	3,27
4 years	1.45	78	67	43	41	12	26	179	65 to 69 years 70 to 74 years	3,886	4,084	2,202	1,007	1,271	677 298	93 ± 358	2,160
to 19 years	158	395	452	218	260 4U	177	192 45	876 173	75 to 84 years	1,985	836	1,149	550	785	286	364	1,7.90
5 vea s 6 and 17 vears _	344	172	172	101	154	27	71.	346	85 years and ove 21 years and over	395 83,907		45,277	21,3:2	30,648 1	59	4,629	185
o 21 voere	975	4_5	560	.82 £77	358	238	202	357 870	an years and ord	۵,۰۰۰	2,000	7,211	7,332	30,047	1,290	4,029	00,733
to 39 years.	920	436	493 480	284 314	318	152	97	875	West Morroe	10.200						2.	
to 39 vears	871	450 378	401 423	283	292	122	169 156	684	Under 5 years	10,302	4,890	384	3,935	4,261	925	,15,	8,560
to 49 years	603	298 213	305	189	274	109	132	426 339	Under year	241	276	148	81 106	93	32	35	157
to 54 years to 59 years	391	178	268	114	177	65	94	262	8 and 4 years	457	241	216	184	±59	5/	72	597
o 64 vears	3-6	133	183 198	89	97	44	86	213	5 to 8 years 5 years	942 201	10.	465 100	3£3 75	305	94 26	100	694 138
o 74 years. o 84 years	20° 196	85 79	121	38	65	48	56 46 1	119	7 to 9 years	-44	93/ 263	84 281	67 221	60 227	26	24	143
ears and over	34	17	17	8	10	9	7	141	10 to 14 years 10 to 13 years	77.2 609	354 295	388	£75	285	70	103	745
rears and over_	6,938	3,2.0	3,728	2,073	2,207	37	432	5,270	14 years	133	59	74	232 43	51	16	23	606
			ļ		1				15 to 19 years 15 years	662 134	278	384 81	220 38	297 60	58	87 21	780 139
theton	10,372	3,148	5,224	3,559	3,394	,589	, 830	7,107	16 and 17 years 18 and 19 years	261	204	140	90 85	110	25	30	300
er 5 years	1,181	133	579 126	350	330 77	252	249	541	20 to 24 years _	91.5	378	537	309	407	1.8 69	130	897
and 2 , ears	520 402	205 204	255	748	148	117	107	105	20 to 29 years 30 to 34 years	938	446	492 50	35-	389 393	72	±10	262 262
9 years	701	367	198 394	194	23.5	173	93 5	537	35 to 39 years	776	428 393	417 383	3321	343	72	74	621 503
years	162 145 454	79 65	83	38 34	47 47 -19	41	36 331	100	45 to 49 years.	660	308	352	243	278	65		416
to 9 years	64~	326	231	122	_19 _78	161 145	112 143	330	50 to 54 years	458 369	226	232	190	185	36	47	348
to 13 years	511 130	259 67	252	147	145	112	143 107 36	508	66 to 64 years_ 65 to 69 years	369 33, 260	179 155 111	190 176 149	143	164 151 20	28	26	166
19 years	1,218	578	640	451	487	127	153	701	70 to 74 years.	154	73	81 /	62 58	20	-2	29	76
years. and 17 years.	122	6°	25	38	32 81	29	23	1.52	7: to 84 years. 8s years and over	18	6	67	58	9	2	3 3	69
and 19 years	871	4.4	457	366	374	48	83	282	21 years and over -	6,613	3,130	3,474	2.575	2,803	564	67	5, an

 $\begin{array}{c} \text{Table 34.--GENERAL CHARACTERISTICS OF THE POPULATION, FOR STANDARD METROPOLITAN AREAS URBANIZED AREAS,} \\ \text{AND URBAN PLACES OF 10,000 OR MORE

Table 34.—GENERAL CHARACTERISTICS OF THE POPULATION, FOR STANDARD METROPOLITAN AREAS URBANIZED AREAS, AND URBAN PLACES OF 10,000 OR MORE 1950

[Asterisk (*) denotes statistics based on 20-percent sample, for totals o age groups from complete count, see table 33. Percent not shown where less than 0.1 percent and median not shown where base is less than 500]

Subject	Standard metropolitan areas			Urbanized areas			Urban places		
	Baton Rouge	New Orleans	Shreveport	Baton Rouge	New Orleans	Shreveport	Alexandria	Bastrop	Baton Rouge
Total population	158 236	685 40[illegible]	[illegible]76,[illegible]47	1[illegible]8,86[illegible]	659,7[illegible]8	[illegible]50,2[illegible]8	34,9[illegible]	12,769	125,629
Urban farm population	345	485	14	354	949	133	[illegible]	62	302
RACE NATIVITY AND CITIZENSHIP									
Male	77 070	327 99[illegible]	84 [illegible]62	6[illegible],854	[illegible]	70,167	16,284	6 274	[illegible] 315
Native white	[illegible] 917	22[illegible],598	[illegible]	40 463	215,5[illegible]8	47,6[illegible]	9 432	4,[illegible]0	44,[illegible]77
Foreign-born white	915	8,086	907	277	[illegible]	84	189	23	853
Negro	24 790	93 089	[illegible] 893	20 487	[illegible]	[illegible]	6 651	2 078	[illegible] 243
Other races	48	638	56	42	614	47	7	1	42
Female	80,566	357 4[illegible]4	92 485	1,00[illegible]	344 [illegible]	[illegible]	[illegible]	6,4[illegible]	6[illegible],3[illegible]
Native white	52,[illegible]	24[illegible] 368	50 349	47 [illegible]16	237 2[illegible]	[illegible],849	[illegible],598	4,120	44,828
Foreign born white	649	7 [illegible]0	948	6[illegible]3	3[illegible]	1 024	210	21	589
Negro	27,472	106 458	[illegible]5 [illegible]	23 2[illegible]	10[illegible]	26 [illegible]	7,815	2,352	8,974
Other races	[illegible]1	348	[illegible]	2[illegible]	348	[illegible]	11	2	23
Persons 21 years old and over	9[illegible] 5[illegible]8	453 [illegible]7	1[illegible]0 845	[illegible]8	438 [illegible]22	[illegible],427	22,257	[illegible],570	78,956
Native	9[illegible] 063	4[illegible]6,946	109 13[illegible]	84 755	[illegible]2 7 8	95 [illegible]	21 86[illegible]	[illegible],532	77,626
Foreign born	[illegible],455	16,19[illegible]	[illegible]	1,383	13,834	1,[illegible]	193	8	1,330
Naturalized	802	11,029	1 194	760	10 [illegible]	1 193	319	19	730
Alien	448	2,786	276	433	[illegible] 676	329	47	14	414
Citizenship not reported	205	1 986	2[illegible]	190	[illegible],35[illegible]	25[illegible]	27	5	186
*SCHOOL ENROLLMENT									
Persons 5 and 6 years old	6,[illegible]93	24 [illegible]95	[illegible] 357	5 550	23 [illegible]55	5 [illegible]05	1,195	505	4,870
Number enrolled in school	2,765	10,52[illegible]	2,825	2,4[illegible]	10,10[illegible]	2,160	477	200	2 050
Percent enrolled in school	[illegible]2 6	43 3	38 4	4[illegible] 2	43 6	39 0	[illegible]	35 4	42 [illegible]
Number enrolled in kindergarten	250	5,0[illegible]	2,0[illegible]	285	5 025	[illegible]60	45	[illegible]	245
Persons 7 to 13 years old	[illegible]7 710	71,[illegible]90	20 520	14,640	37,4[illegible]	[illegible]5,[illegible]	4 [illegible]0	[illegible],735	[illegible]2 935
Number enrolled in school	16 88[illegible]	68,[illegible]	[illegible],760	14,000	35 460	4,[illegible]	3 800	[illegible]25	12 300
Percent enrolled in school	9[illegible]	96 [illegible]	96 3	95 6	9[illegible]	96 2	94.[illegible]	[illegible]	95 [illegible]
Persons 14 and 15 years old	3,995	16,960	4 765	3,200	16 155	3,385	830	400	2,805
Number enrolled in school	3 800	15,870	4,515	3,065	15 140	3 210	745	360	2,670
Percent enrolled in school	95 [illegible]	93 4	94 4	95 2	93 [illegible]	94 8	89.8		93 2
Persons 16 and 17 years old	[illegible],795	16 770	4,[illegible]0	3,190	16,005	3,5[illegible]	1,020	370	[illegible],860
Number enrolled in school	2 870	11,960	[illegible],380	2 [illegible]90	11,565	2 625	760	260	2 [illegible]55
Percent enrolled in school	7[illegible] 6	71 [illegible]	7[illegible] 0	74 9	72 3	[illegible]	74 5		75 3
Persons 18 and 19 years old	6,190	19 3[illegible]0	4 820	5 [illegible]80	18 3[illegible]0	4,[illegible]	965	440	4 900
Number enrolled in school	3,1[illegible]0	6,160	1,[illegible]25	2 9[illegible]	6,050	[illegible],275	205	105	2,475
Percent enrolled in school	50 6	3[illegible] 9	29 6	5[illegible]	[illegible]2.6	30 1	21 2		50 5
Persons 20 to 24 years old	16,[illegible]80	56 940	1[illegible],495	[illegible]4,845	54,[illegible]00	13 275	2 635	1,[illegible]	13,4[illegible]5
Number enrolled in school	4,055	7,285	1,335	3 895	7,1[illegible]	310	220	30	3,330
Percent enrolled in school	2[illegible] 1	12 8	9 2	26 2	13 1	[illegible] 9	8 3	2 6	24 8
Persons 25 to 29 years old	15,330	62 655	14,980	14 585	60 [illegible]	1[illegible] 1[illegible]0	3 700	1 [illegible]85	13,[illegible]
Number enrolled in school	1,710	4,895	935	1 680	4 760	960	205	40	1,[illegible]75
Percent enrolled in school	[illegible]0 7	[illegible] 8	6 2	1[illegible]	7 [illegible]	6	[illegible]	[illegible] 4	11 [illegible]
*YEARS OF SCHOOL COMPLETED									
Male, 25 years old and over	[illegible]0,[illegible]85	188,340	4[illegible],205	36,070	182,[illegible]70	49,925	[illegible],240	370	32 8[illegible]5
No school years completed	2,190	[illegible],36[illegible]	[illegible] 695	[illegible],6[illegible]0	5,675	[illegible],845	500	1[illegible]	1,410
Elementary: 1 to 4 years	[illegible] 930	28 470	7 630	4 91[illegible]	20 95[illegible]	[illegible] 260	1,750	785	4,[illegible]45
5 and 6 years	4,295	27,180	5,040	3 665	26,030	[illegible] 825	1 2[illegible]0	490	[illegible], [illegible]45
7 years	2 515	15,325	[illegible]300	2 [illegible]85	1[illegible]	2 070	665	205	1 965
8 years	3,300	26,480	3,665	2,955	25 890	3,050	695	[illegible]45	2 655
High school: 1 to 3 years	6,345	25,035	7 6[illegible]0	[illegible] 6[illegible]0	2[illegible] 060	6 610	1,450	595	5,190
4 years	5,620	26,630	6,250	[illegible],205	2[illegible]	7,345	1,220	[illegible]40	5 045
College: 1 to 3 years	4 390	12,420	4,[illegible]50	4 100	12,170	4,230	[illegible]90	180	3,920
4 years or more	[illegible],690	14 250	3,[illegible]80	4,475	14 065	3,565	[illegible]30	120	4 245
School years not reported	1 550	4,685	1 645	1 235	6,420	1,325	310	75	1 145
Median school years completed	[illegible] 7	8 [illegible]	9 0	10	8 6	10 2	8 5	[illegible] 7	10 5
Female, 25 years old and over	42 850	[illegible]6,365	52,825	37 950	209,985	46,205	10,9[illegible]0	3 290	34 920
No school years completed	2,[illegible]70	7,[illegible]	2 440	1 [illegible]	6,690	1,880	620	2[illegible]0	1 475
Elementary: 1 to 4 years	[illegible],235	29 110	7,860	[illegible],420	27 8[illegible]	5 750	[illegible]	575	3,890
5 and 6 years	5,005	31,990	5,[illegible]95	4 210	30 900	4,[illegible]70	[illegible],400	500	3 665
7 years	2 855	19 130	4 1[illegible]	2,480	18 455	3,[illegible]65	900	300	2,130
8 years	3 045	31,840	3,985	2,680	31 330	3,44[illegible]	[illegible]	330	2,400
High school: 1 to 3 years	7,405	31,100	9,570	6,695	30,130	[illegible],280	[illegible] 990	675	6 235
4 years	8,145	39,775	9,900	7,550	39,165	10,230	1,[illegible]5	345	7 350
College: 1 to 3 years	4 20[illegible]	[illegible]	4,880	3 340	[illegible]1,340	4,[illegible]40	890	[illegible]	3 7[illegible]5
4 years or more	3,525	[illegible],600	3 220	3 28[illegible]	9 455	3,090	[illegible]	[illegible]35	3 095
School years not reported	1 205	4,81[illegible]	1 020	990	4,695	695	235	65	[illegible]
Median school years completed	10 0	8 [illegible]	9 [illegible]	10 [illegible]	8 6	[illegible]0 3	8 8	8 1	10 7
MARITAL STATUS AND HOUSEHOLDS									
Male, 14 years old and over	55,2[illegible]2	242,076	59,493	48 8[illegible]9	233,352	50 917	11,018	4,[illegible]23	44 [illegible]72
Single	14,[illegible]97	60,723	12 058	12,769	58 627	9,[illegible]2[illegible]	2,295	985	11,345
Married	38,498	167,[illegible]23	43,929	[illegible]4,132	161,[illegible]70	38,510	8 62[illegible]	3 123	31 268
Widowed or divorced	2,21[illegible]	14 030	3 506	1,918	13 [illegible]55	2 882	70[illegible]	215	1,759
Female 14 years old and over	58 418	273,035	[illegible]8 37[illegible]	52,142	264,421	59,85[illegible]	1[illegible]	4,6[illegible]1	47,584
Single	11,1[illegible]	[illegible]4,735	[illegible]0,634	9,967	[illegible]3 [illegible]93	8 [illegible]	2,442	[illegible]3	8,859
Married	39,621	172,228	45,914	35,1[illegible]8	16[illegible],860	40,543	9 01[illegible]	3,1[illegible]	32,292
Widowed or divorced	7,681	46,071	11 827	7 027	45 268	10 397	2,476	701	6,433
Married couples* number	36 005	151,645	40 420	31,8[illegible]	14[illegible],395	35 340	[illegible] 960	3 090	29 205
With own household	33 805	137,885	37,[illegible]35	29,920	131 99[illegible]	32,380	7,380	2 885	27,355
Without own household	2 200	13,760	3 285	1,955	13,400	2,960	580	205	1,850
Families and unrelated individuals*	53 115	226,[illegible]55	58 665	47,925	219,360	51 775	11 655	4,165	43,550
Families	39,490	173 0[illegible]0	4[illegible],315	35,050	166 5[illegible]0	39,630	9 255	3,375	32 100
Unrelated individuals	13,625	53 745	13 350	12,875	52,810	12 145	2 400	790	11 450
Households, number	[illegible]3,118	197,032	50 285	38,301	190,3[illegible]4	43,764	10 427	3,610	35,07[illegible]
Population in households	[illegible]50,645	662 096	1[illegible]7,266	131,745	636,6[illegible]	45 124	34 399	12 5[illegible]3	119 532
Population per household	3 49	3 36	3 41	3 44	[illegible].5	3 32	3 30	3 47	3 41
Institutional population	[illegible]0	3 [illegible]89	561	321	3,289	454	110	39	19[illegible]
*RESIDENCE IN 1949									
Persons 1 year old and over 1950	154 [illegible]90	59[illegible],090	[illegible]72,820	1[illegible]5,415	645 905	146 430	34,290	12,575	122,105
Same house as in 1950	117,840	542 900	[illegible]30,940	102 275	522 540	105,165	26,815	9,340	91,925
Different house same county	22,690	78 875	23,400	20,475	76,985	19 725	4 630	1 930	18 835
Different county or abroad	10,075	36,110	14,[illegible]60	9 465	33 525	17,710	2 125	930	8 705
Residence not reported	3,78[illegible]	13,[illegible]05	4,[illegible]20	3,200	12,855	3,830	720	375	2,640

Table 34.—GENERAL CHARACTERISTICS OF THE POPULATION, FOR STANDARD METROPOLITAN AREAS, URBANIZED AREAS, AND URBAN PLACES OF 10,000 OR MORE: 1950—Con.

[Asterisk (*) denotes statistics based on 20-percent sample; for totals of age groups from complete count, see table 38. Percent not shown where less than 0.1 percent and median not shown where base is less than 500]

Subject	Bogalusa	Bossier City	Crowley	Gretna	Houma	Lafayette	Lake Charles	Monroe	New Iberia	New Orleans	Opelousas	Ruston	Shreveport	West Monroe
	Urban places—Con.													
Total population	17,798	15,470	12,784	13,813	11,505	33,541	41,272	38,572	16,467	570,445	11,659	10,372	127,206	10,302
Rural-farm population	92	15	55	44	3	134	134	119	[illegible]	372	21	35	64	[illegible]
RACE, NATIVITY, AND CITIZENSHIP														
Male	8,629	7,581	6,162	6,656	5,520	16,330	20,242	18,115	7,991	270,812	5,561	5,148	59,643	4,890
Native white	5,815	6,315	4,584	4,695	4,650	12,337	14,543	10,227	5,938	178,227	3,278	3,533	39,614	3,920
Foreign-born white	71	39	45	81	40	44	181	218	73	7,631	36	26	92	15
Negro	2,741	[illegible]	[illegible]	1,874	821	3,829	5,512	7,667	1,976	84,412	2,247	1,588	19,794	953
Other races	2	-	1	20	9		6	3	4	542		1	43	2
Female	9,169	7,889	6,622	7,157	5,985	17,211	21,030	20,457	8,476	299,633	6,098	5,224	67,563	5,412
Native white	6,107	6,539	4,784	4,976	4,719	12,584	14,739	11,225	6,107	195,281	3,497	3,375	43,743	4,24[illegible]
Foreign-born white	55	78	[illegible]	80	50	134	202	210	69	6,675	42	19	815	20
Negro	3,007	1,318	1,793	2,080	1,005	4,489	5,886	9,020	2,299	97,361	2,559	1,828	22,975	1,178
Other races		2		47	11	4	3	2	1	314		2	30	3
Persons 21 years old and over	10,647	9,490	7,469	8,654	6,762	20,074	25,447	25,051	9,954	384,662	6,338	6,148	83,907	6,513
Native	10,513	9,252	7,398	8,486	6,676	19,818	25,073	24,641	9,818	370,333	6,861	6,108	82,389	6,374
Foreign born	[illegible]	218	71	168	86	256	374	410	136	14,329	77	40	1,518	39
Naturalized	74	94	47	110	57	150	252	333	78	9,755	44	29	1,076	23
Alien	31	91	16	43	28	63	74	55	43	3,287	19	10	226	13
Citizenship not reported	25	33	8	15	1	43	48	22	15	1,283	14	1	216	3
***SCHOOL ENROLLMENT**														
Persons 5 and 6 years old	720	645	405	635	450	1,360	1,790	1,290	655	18,870	575	335	4,690	395
Number enrolled in school	285	235	50	250	130	545	655	560	205	8,175	180	140	1,825	155
Percent enrolled in school	39.6	36.4		39.4		40.[illegible]	36.6	43.4	31.3	43.3	31.3		38.9	
Number enrolled in kindergarten	5	10	[illegible]	55	10	100	10	195	20	[illegible],585		15	250	15
Persons 7 to 13 years old	2,250	1,375	1,570	1,590	1,510	3,785	4,645	3,965	2,230	56,5[illegible]	1,625	1,000	19,795	1,155
Number enrolled in school	2,155	1,320	1,465	1,540	1,480	3,58[illegible]	4,430	3,875	2,120	54,770	1,500	980	19,300	1,130
Percent enrolled in school	95.8	96.0	97.7	96.9	98.0	94.7	95.8	97.7	95.1	96.9	92.3	98.0	97.7	97.0
Persons 14 and 15 years old	610	345	350	420	360	1,050	1,250	970	440	13,800	215	225	2,790	195
Number enrolled in school	580	320	355	400	345	915	1,155	900	405	12,890	195	205	2,630	180
Percent enrolled in school	95.8					87.1	92.4	92.8		93.4			94.3	
Persons 16 and 17 years old	520	420	380	285	300	965	1,090	890	555	13,805	355	200	2,975	255
Number enrolled in school	395	[illegible]	250	175	230	640	735	615	355	9,845	255	175	2,195	175
Percent enrolled in school	76.0					66.3	67.4	69.1	64.0	71.3			73.8	
Persons 18 and 19 years old	4[illegible]0	[illegible]	450	370	230	1,585	1,315	1,125	410	16,280	355	875	3,500	295
Number enrolled in school	140	105	125	70	85	820	375	290	110	5,460	1[illegible]	695	1,085	80
Percent enrolled in school						51.7	28.5	25.8		33.5		79.4	31.0	
Persons 20 to 24 years old	1,425	1,430	1,145	1,045	1,020	3,805	2,760	3,425	1,285	47,555	980	1,565	11,275	555
Number enrolled in school	45	110	105	50	35	1,040	190	245	90	6,610	80	855	1,180	50
Percent enrolled in school	3.1	7.7	9.2	4.8	3.4	27.3	6.1	7.2	7.0	13.9	8.2	54.6	10.5	9.2
Persons 25 to 29 years old	1,595	2,395	1,045	1,270	1,035	3,375	4,085	3,490	1,495	51,325	955	860	12,985	945
Number enrolled in school	50	110	35	70	25	450	130	160	75	4,170	45	215	800	35
Percent enrolled in school	3.1	4.6	3.[illegible]	5.5	2.3	13.3	3.2	4.6	5.0	8.1	4.7	25.0	6.[illegible]	3.7
***YEARS OF SCHOOL COMPLETED**														
Male, 25 years old and over	4,440	4,155	3,035	3,590	2,850	7,805	11,170	10,410	4,020	150,250	2,700	2,340	34,230	2,730
No school years completed	170	135	[illegible]	165	205	1,280	915	685	440	4,115	150	90	1,360	85
Elementary: 1 to 4 years	1,005	350	590	775	595	4,210	1,545	1,965	760	23,275	505	290	4,6[illegible]	375
5 and 6 years	625	260	535	720	400	750	1,230	1,215	445	24,185	335	255	3,700	290
7 years	430	205	285	325	220	600	885	710	295	15,015	245	95	2,930	250
8 years	435	300	150	460	230	455	1,115	775	245	23,125	135	135	2,535	235
High school: 1 to 3 years	790	750	500	445	425	1,215	2,060	1,550	775	20,960	450	255	5,825	375
4 years	460	1,220	180	385	345	390	1,340	1,570	425	22,895	215	260	5,890	525
College: 1 to 3 years	255	525	155	105	185	975	920	920	255	10,450	210	495	3,6[illegible]0	185
4 years or more	135	245	5[illegible]	105	135	775	855	685	255	12,550	175	405	3,290	80
School years not reported	155	105	110	145	110	135	305	335	125	5,660	100	90	1,140	[illegible]0
Median school years completed	7.8	11.9	6.9	7.3	7.8	8.0	8.8	8.6	8.0	8.6	7.4	12.1	10.1	9.2
Female, 25 years old and over	5,055	4,000	3,645	4,3[illegible]5	3,160	8,9[illegible]0	11,[illegible]20	11,970	4,800	185,[illegible]15	3,325	2,70[illegible]	40,470	3,305
No school years completed	150	90	725	275	200	1,770	895	675	645	[illegible],425	545	100	1,655	55
Elementary: 1 to 4 years	750	315	640	745	615	1,165	1,320	2,180	865	24,745	555	285	[illegible]	310
5 and 6 years	895	295	435	790	550	1,[illegible]60	1,425	1,505	750	27,470	445	225	4,765	425
7 years	475	260	265	490	240	545	[illegible]70	900	280	16,180	200	120	2,950	205
8 years	555	350	255	585	230	455	865	900	455	28,340	215	220	2,965	385
High school: 1 to 3 years	1,090	835	620	635	510	1,7[illegible]	2,4[illegible]	1,790	805	26,465	580	395	[illegible],145	665
4 years	20	1,215	240	430	455	[illegible]45	1,895	2,125	625	34,475	260	465	8,680	730
College: 1 to 3 years	270	390	240	130	160	820	880	1,130	290	9,805	255	155	4,295	295
4 years or more	160	180	175	130	160	680	600	620	225	8,440	215	430	2,870	160
School years not reported	90	70	60	95	40	185	455	45	30	4,[illegible]70	55	100	690	75
Median school years completed	8.[illegible]	11.4	7.0	[illegible].6	7.8	7.7	[illegible]	8.[illegible]	7.4	8.6	7.5	1[illegible].6	10.[illegible]	10.1
MARITAL STATUS AND HOUSEHOLDS														
Male, 14 years old and over	5,939	5,10[illegible]	4,223	4,740	3,798	11,736	14,345	13,079	5,479	203,215	3,743	3,920	43,550	3,528
Single	1,163	697	1,006	1,112	947	3,41[illegible]	3,10[illegible]	2,623	1,37[illegible]	52,343	917	1,511	8,401	633
Married	4,430	[illegible],254	3,037	3,3[illegible]8	2,6[illegible]3	7,8[illegible]3	10,5[illegible]0	9,631	3,825	138,370	2,660	2,271	32,[illegible]09	2,710
Widowed or divorced	346	148	183	250	198	464	728	825	281	12,502	166	138	2,649	185
Female, 14 years old and over	6,43[illegible]	5,578	4,7[illegible]8	5,229	4,187	12,623	15,26[illegible]	15,505	6,172	232,691	4,358	3,999	51,734	3,049
Single	972	607	882	934	920	2,939	2,670	2,353	1,230	48,235	887	1,049	7,96[illegible]	618
Married	4,488	4,43[illegible]	3,135	3,477	2,700	7,976	10,530	10,[illegible]95	3,967	142,665	2,787	2,375	34,2[illegible]9	2,767
Widowed or divorced	974	540	741	798	567	[illegible],708	2,064	2,[illegible]55	9[illegible]5	41,73[illegible]	684	575	9,524	664
Married couples*, number	3,955	4,130	2,945	3,045	2,495	7,035	10,105	8,800	3,535	124,355	2,495	2,120	29,750	2,520
With own household	3,700	3,970	2,780	2,820	2,360	6,585	9,600	8,195	3,320	112,160	2,330	2,020	27,065	2,360
Without own household	255	160	165	225	135	450	505	605	215	12,195	165	100	2,685	160
Families and unrelated individuals*	6,485	4,750	3,870	4,025	3,295	10,960	14,100	13,570	4,760	194,380	3,480	4,215	45,260	3,450
Families	5,435	4,295	3,275	3,495	2,820	7,875	11,165	10,075	3,975	144,255	2,930	2,380	33,775	2,835
Unrelated individuals	1,050	455	595	530	475	3,085	2,935	3,495	785	50,125	550	1,835	11,485	595
Households, number	5,088	4,670	3,665	3,976	3,153	9,149	11,866	11,566	4,603	168,629	3,271	2,738	37,225	3,063
Population in households	17,559	15,4[illegible]1	12,700	13,753	11,407	31,859	40,198	35,526	16,367	548,247	11,554	9,069	122,241	10,149
Population per household	3.45	3.34	3.47	3.45	3.62	3.48	3.39	3.2[illegible]	3.51	3.31	3.53	3.31	3.28	3.31
Institutional population	18			28	36	158	14[illegible]	20[illegible]	5	3,020	44	11[illegible]	454	14
***RESIDENCE IN 1949**														
Persons 1 year old and over, 1950	17,310	14,810	12,610	13,455	11,210	32,610	40,460	37,575	16,135	558,970	11,365	10,185	124,365	10,210
Same house as in 1950	14,530	7,780	11,040	11,310	9,060	25,[illegible]0	29,845	27,975	13,070	454,970	9,715	7,345	92,230	7,045
Different house, same county	1,715	[illegible]	975	1,205	1,200	4,050	7,115	5,935	2,100	68,870	1,105	1,410	17,350	1,600
Different county or abroad	670	5,360	385	780	780	2,615	2,810	3,495	740	23,615	275	1,145	11,475	775
Residence not reported	395	590	210	160	170	635	695	450	235	11,515	190	285	3,310	190

Table 35.—ECONOMIC CHARACTERISTICS OF THE POPULATION, BY SEX, FOR STANDARD METROPOLITAN AREAS, URBANIZED AREAS, AND URBAN PLACES OF 10,000 OR MORE: 1950

Subject	Standard metropolitan areas						Urbanized areas						Urban places	
	Baton Rouge		New Orleans		Shreveport		Baton Rouge		New Orleans		Shreveport		Alexandria	
	Male	Female	Male	Female	Male	Female	Male	Female	Male	Female	Male	Female	Male	Female
Total population, all ages	77,[illegible]	80,[illegible]	327,[illegible]	357,[illegible]	[illegible]	[illegible]	67,[illegible]	[illegible]	[illegible],062	[illegible]	70,[illegible]	79,441	[illegible]6 289	18,[illegible]
EMPLOYMENT STATUS														
Persons 14 years old and over	[illegible]	58,4[illegible]8	24[illegible],0[illegible]	273,035	[illegible] 493	[illegible],17[illegible]	[illegible]8,3[illegible]9	5[illegible]	[illegible]3 52	[illegible]64,42[illegible]	50,917	[illegible]9,855	[illegible] 6[illegible]8	13,329
Labor force	[illegible],320	17,506	19[illegible],[illegible]60	8[illegible],4[illegible]	47,15[illegible]	22 94[illegible]	6[illegible]	[illegible]	[illegible]	82,6[illegible]	[illegible]	2[illegible],[illegible]89	8,9[illegible]7	4 74[illegible]
Civilian labor force	41,24[illegible]	[illegible]7,5[illegible]2	[illegible]86 [illegible]2	84,[illegible]	[illegible],047	[illegible],928	36,68[illegible]	[illegible]6,[illegible]	1[illegible]9,305	82 5[illegible]3	3[illegible],790	[illegible]	8,905	[illegible],74[illegible]
Employed	[illegible]8,960	16,9[illegible]9	[illegible]74,40[illegible]	8[illegible],435	[illegible] 609	22,293	3[illegible]	[illegible],890	168 004	[illegible]8,768	37,499	[illegible],727	8,[illegible]5[illegible]	4 549
Private wage and salary workers	[illegible]0,542	1[illegible],3[illegible]	[illegible]3[illegible],982	65,140	[illegible]4,293	1[illegible],350	2[illegible]	[illegible],583	[illegible]	63,809	[illegible],[illegible]65	1[illegible],1[illegible]6	6,[illegible]	3,6[illegible]7
Government workers	4,[illegible]5	3,[illegible]2[illegible]	[illegible]0,521	[illegible]0,255	[illegible] 27[illegible]	2 408	3,[illegible]70	3,437	[illegible],054	[illegible]	[illegible],14[illegible]	2,245	1,[illegible]	535
Self-employed workers	4,000	800	20 693	[illegible]	6,[illegible]73	[illegible],608	[illegible]	[illegible]23	[illegible],237	[illegible],[illegible]70	[illegible] 472	[illegible],252	1,1[illegible]	292
Unpaid family workers	[illegible]3	[illegible]77	207	795	2[illegible]3	4[illegible]	28	150	[illegible]40	769	[illegible]	[illegible]	17	[illegible]
Unemployed	2 384	[illegible]93	[illegible]2,219	3,920	1,4[illegible]	635	2,[illegible]40	[illegible]	[illegible],30[illegible]	[illegible],8[illegible]	[illegible],291	642	[illegible]48	191
Experienced workers	2,278	584	[illegible]2 032	[illegible] 774	1 430	[illegible]20	2,031	539	11,72[illegible]	3,670	1,283	627	[illegible]46	189
New workers	6	9	[illegible]87	146	8	[illegible]5	9	[illegible]4	[illegible]80	[illegible]45	8	[illegible]5	4	2
Not in labor force	1[illegible],884	[illegible]0,822	[illegible]	[illegible]88,62[illegible]	12,3[illegible]3	4[illegible],43[illegible]	12 05[illegible]	[illegible]5 [illegible]97	4[illegible] [illegible]28	181,780	9,6[illegible]4	38,46[illegible]	2,691	4,188
Keeping house	200	30,677	1,002	145 [illegible]	[illegible]	[illegible],749	[illegible]77	26,892	975	139,756	200	24,769	48	6,718
Unable to work	2,328	2,[illegible]80	1[illegible],727	[illegible]2,237	4 [illegible]3	[illegible],509	[illegible] 354	[illegible],904	12,[illegible]35	[illegible]1,899	[illegible],03[illegible]	2,891	1,040	1,014
Inmates of institutions	367	16[illegible]	1,522	[illegible],194	325	2[illegible]1	[illegible]	70	1,[illegible]22	1,[illegible]94	248	18[illegible]	65	9
Other and not reported	10,9[illegible]	7 804	36,065	29,946	7,716	6 966	9,832	[illegible],830	34,[illegible]	[illegible]8 [illegible]1	6,[illegible]35	[illegible],625	1,538	1,[illegible]7
14 to 19 years old	4,[illegible]17	4,045	[illegible]5 958	[illegible],025	4,189	[illegible],5[illegible]	[illegible],9[illegible]	[illegible],[illegible]60	[illegible],294	[illegible]6,365	3,084	[illegible] 462	780	982
20 to 64 years old	5 5[illegible]	[illegible],61[illegible]	[illegible]5,428	9,949	2,072	925	5,21[illegible]	2,380	[illegible] 8[illegible]7	9 642	2 3[illegible]	1,762	581	404
65 years old and over	[illegible]27	[illegible]	4,679	2,9[illegible]	875	4[illegible]	700	4[illegible]	4,[illegible]65	2,[illegible]24	[illegible]8[illegible]	401	1[illegible]7	61
MAJOR OCCUPATION GROUP														
Employed	38,[illegible]0	16,999	[illegible]74,403	80,4[illegible]5	4[illegible] 609	22,293	34,[illegible]46	1[illegible],890	[illegible]8,004	78,768	37,499	20,727	8,357	4,549
Professional, technical, and kindred workers	4,454	2,432	14,39[illegible]	9,695	3,911	2,445	4,[illegible]46	2,235	[illegible],587	9,[illegible]85	3,727	2,[illegible]66	666	[illegible]51
Farmers and farm managers	648	42	[illegible]30	28	1,90[illegible]	217	57	1[illegible]	32[illegible]	26	[illegible]08	8	29	5
Managers, officials, and prop'rs, exc. farm	4,[illegible]59	698	23,867	3,774	[illegible],746	928	3,96[illegible]	650	23,243	3,681	5,358	810	[illegible],262	[illegible]31
Clerical and kindred workers	2,400	[illegible],00[illegible]	18 2[illegible]1	23,467	[illegible],33[illegible]	[illegible],182	[illegible],280	857	[illegible],852	2[illegible],[illegible]39	3,255	5,230	546	945
Sales workers	2,450	[illegible],327	13,[illegible]87	[illegible] 26[illegible]	[illegible],620	1,689	2 [illegible]	[illegible],278	[illegible] 026	7,[illegible]15	3,[illegible]	[illegible],653	957	[illegible]68
Craftsmen, foremen, and kindred workers	8,64[illegible]	133	3[illegible],022	942	7,[illegible]4	180	7 779	[illegible]29	29,842	92[illegible]	7,095	[illegible]71	1,404	34
Operatives and kindred workers	7,844	[illegible],[illegible]4[illegible]	29,734	10,[illegible]2	7,874	[illegible] 481	[illegible],387	977	28,442	[illegible]0,[illegible]6	[illegible],637	[illegible],494	1,372	334
Private household workers	88	3,[illegible]98	49[illegible]	11,641	172	5,[illegible]9	7[illegible]	3,095	480	11 3[illegible]4	1[illegible]	4,[illegible]2	19	[illegible],1[illegible]
Service workers, except private household	2 [illegible]2	2,440	[illegible]6,570	1[illegible],[illegible]98	[illegible],061	[illegible],636	[illegible],[illegible]87	2,313	16,20[illegible]	[illegible]1,205	2,985	3 575	790	843
Farm laborers, unpaid family workers	44	2[illegible]	60	31	2[illegible]2	[illegible]12	1	2	27	22	[illegible]0		2	
Farm laborers, exc. unpaid, and farm foremen	494	80	[illegible]4	84	[illegible],[illegible]36	[illegible]98	[illegible]35	38	[illegible]	50	14[illegible]	28	26	5
Laborers, except farm and mine	4,470	[illegible]3	23,[illegible]2	802	4,[illegible]2	103	3,680	[illegible]3	22,183	780	4,316	9[illegible]	1,154	[illegible]8
Occupation not reported	[illegible]22	204	1,608	830	58[illegible]	[illegible]3	353	183	1,5[illegible]9	801	472	346	1[illegible]0	7[illegible]
Experienced unemployed	2,278	584	12 032	[illegible],774	1,430	620	2,031	539	11,72[illegible]	3,670	1,283	627	546	189
Professional, technical, and kindred workers	42	[illegible]9	[illegible]2	1[illegible]4	[illegible]1	9	38	[illegible]7	298	1[illegible]3	3[illegible]	7		3
Farmers and farm managers	10		18		5		9		[illegible]6		2			
Managers, officials, and prop'rs, exc. farm	39	[illegible]0	4[illegible]7	33	29	6	39	8	473	33	29	5	10	
Clerical and kindred workers	37	[illegible]8	717	[illegible]19	3[illegible]	59	40	[illegible]9	7[illegible]0	5[illegible]0	38	59	3	[illegible]3
Sales workers	59	2[illegible]	42[illegible]	285	44	21	[illegible]7	23	[illegible]2[illegible]	281	47	[illegible]	—	[illegible]0
Craftsmen, foremen, and kindred workers	[illegible]2	2	2,592	[illegible]0	218	[illegible]	326	[illegible]	2,[illegible]37	49	18[illegible]	4	55	[illegible]
Operatives and kindred workers	[illegible]	26	2,4[illegible]9	648	258	[illegible]7	3[illegible]	26	2,361	631	[illegible]13	27	68	[illegible]
Private household workers	[illegible]	162	35	771	1	1[illegible]	3	16[illegible]	35	[illegible]53	-	15[illegible]		46
Service workers, except private household	143	107	[illegible] 14[illegible]	7[illegible]4	99	81	14[illegible]	[illegible]08	[illegible],13[illegible]	[illegible]8	9[illegible]	78	28	19
Farm laborers and foremen	31	3	40	15	[illegible]3	13	16	-	[illegible]8	[illegible]	8	6	6	2
Laborers, except farm and mine	4[illegible]3	[illegible]	2,263	78	232	5	478	7	2,194	75	200	5	120	
Occupation not reported	[illegible]47	155	1,[illegible]97	52[illegible]	[illegible]6[illegible]	232	38[illegible]	1[illegible]9	[illegible],500	494	436	257	241	85
INDUSTRY GROUP														
Employed	38,960	16,999	174,403	80 43[illegible]	44 609	2[illegible],293	34,6[illegible]6	[illegible] 890	168 004	78,768	37,[illegible]99	20,727	8,357	4,549
Agriculture	1,262	150	1 342	156	3,915	1,064	243	49	94[illegible]	[illegible]12	489	59	88	10
Forestry and fisheries	20	11	1,154	26	67	[illegible]	15	10	4[illegible]0	[illegible]3	36	4	26	3
Mining	2[illegible]9	[illegible]4	1,895	1[illegible]1	3 201	62[illegible]	21[illegible]	13	1,[illegible]72	165	2 240	624	[illegible]5	1
Construction	[illegible],365	340	17,917	599	5,230	1[illegible]5	[illegible],834	330	1[illegible],104	[illegible]88	4,7[illegible]1	[illegible]27	897	2[illegible]
Manufacturing	12,697	936	30,317	9,578	6,598	940	[illegible],096	901	29,16[illegible]	9,3[illegible]	5,711	9[illegible]2	1,429	[illegible]07
Furniture, and lumber and wood products	3[illegible]2	[illegible]8	2,434	373	[illegible],179	[illegible]1[illegible]	233	[illegible]6	2,074	339	959	[illegible]1[illegible]	638	21
Primary metal industries	372	[illegible]3	[illegible]12	7[illegible]	183	9	311	[illegible]	4[illegible]8	21	1[illegible]8	7	[illegible]9	1
Fabricated metal ind. (incl. not spec. metal)	2[illegible]9	14	2,027	357	3[illegible]7	33	247	1[illegible]	1 978	350	[illegible]6	34	18	
Machinery, except electrical	[illegible]8	15	1,1[illegible]1	114	5 9	43	94	13	1 089	[illegible]3	499	43	31	4
Electrical machinery, equip., and supplies	22	3	223	4[illegible]	[illegible]5	9	24	2	220	42	46	9	[illegible]	
Motor vehicles and motor vehicle equip.	12	2	[illegible]64	[illegible]6	[illegible]8	3	13	2	159	[illegible]5	42	3	[illegible]	[illegible]
Transportation equip., exc. motor vehicle	18	3	2,968	120	16	2	18	3	2,858	[illegible]18	15	1	1	
Other durable goods	221	32	1,973	226	1,105	[illegible]4	203	30	1,[illegible]52	223	923	51	60	7
Food and kindred products	886	[illegible]44	8,079	2,3[illegible]	1,0[illegible]5	161	834	134	7,857	2 304	997	1[illegible]5	393	36
Textile mill products	13	3	907	854	17	5	1[illegible]	2	892	844	[illegible]3	4	4	
Apparel and other fabricated textile prod.	13	5	1,09[illegible]	[illegible],[illegible]23	[illegible]7	177	1[illegible]	5	1,087	3,073	[illegible]4	179	10	6
Printing, publishing, and allied industries	4[illegible]3	118	2,7[illegible]1	520	568	[illegible]33	441	119	2,678	509	578	139	103	23
Chemicals and allied products	3,060	1[illegible]0	[illegible],458	227	375	[illegible]4	2,[illegible]41	161	[illegible],4[illegible]	225	406	33	85	9
Other nondurable goods	6,895	3[illegible]0	4 447	1,104	[illegible]98	[illegible]52	6,094	382	4,23[illegible]	1,087	[illegible]10	144	37	
Not specified manufacturing industries	23	6	198	89	[illegible]6	14	21	6	190	81	6[illegible]	13	10	
Railroads and railway express service	688	30	7,025	424	2,0[illegible]5	90	677	30	[illegible],7[illegible]5	417	1,[illegible]37	91	369	25
Trucking service and warehousing	374	25	[illegible] 5[illegible]5	215	693	66	[illegible]	2[illegible]	3,476	2[illegible]	708	7[illegible]	125	15
Other transportation	[illegible]50	87	[illegible]6,[illegible]78	1,391	1 045	181	629	67	16,086	[illegible],357	[illegible]93	145	1[illegible]5	41
Telecommunications	279	[illegible]01	1,597	2,282	317	407	26[illegible]	289	1,559	2,2[illegible]1	295	400	92	71
Utilities and sanitary services	800	1[illegible]3	3,929	462	1 2[illegible]2	199	741	[illegible]17	3,820	4[illegible]3	1,032	200	[illegible]93	13
Wholesale trade	1,328	183	[illegible]3,092	3,248	2,68[illegible]	465	[illegible],268	180	[illegible]2,888	3,207	2,655	467	512	64
Food and dairy prod. stores, and milk retail	1,245	522	6,640	2,96[illegible]	1 [illegible]	6[illegible]7	1,173	4[illegible]3	6,441	2,864	1,522	552	379	132
Eating and drinking places	819	1,13[illegible]	6,[illegible]44	4,917	759	[illegible],586	803	1,072	5,967	4,742	736	[illegible],[illegible]09	18[illegible]	416
Other retail trade	4,212	2,055	16,646	11,300	4,940	2,666	3,937	1,99[illegible]	[illegible] [illegible]20	11,151	4,723	2,680	1,194	564
Finance, insurance, and real estate	1 011	708	7,090	4,29[illegible]	1,371	872	989	6[illegible]8	7,004	4,247	1,349	866	335	213
Business services	303	92	2,727	758	[illegible]89	166	285	89	2,195	745	[illegible]70	165	69	22
Repair services	834	44	4,06[illegible]	[illegible]63	1,268	77	765	46	3,947	1[illegible]5	1,187	68	182	10
Private households	325	[illegible],634	1,204	12,[illegible]50	7[illegible]9	5,364	288	3,222	1,160	11,8[illegible]9	591	5,091	115	[illegible],169
Hotels and lodging places	[illegible]64	299	1,659	1,579	393	447	160	295	1,623	1,[illegible]61	36[illegible]	434	92	107
Other personal services	795	1,047	3,935	3,784	906	1,293	768	1,01[illegible]	3,880	[illegible],744	894	1,329	267	369
Entertainment and recreation services	352	168	3,424	1,113	442	220	342	167	3,270	1,093	407	217	124	72
Medical and other health services	478	899	4,071	7,255	6[illegible]1	1,554	432	832	[illegible],004	7,093	642	1,563	318	438
Educational services, government	1,675	2,03[illegible]	1,082	[illegible],166	389	1,361	1,59[illegible]	1,908	1,041	3,057	33[illegible]	1,217	108	251
Educational services, private	289	408	1,640	2,374	181	356	262	392	1,623	2,346	178	357	52	96
Other professional and related services	[illegible]23	[illegible]10	2,[illegible]56	1,729	815	414	581	304	2,912	1,716	750	403	[illegible]80	103
Public administration	1,731	1,22[illegible]	11,4[illegible]3	3 381	2,041	637	1,6[illegible]	1,189	11,252	3,[illegible]20	2,051	650	468	118
Industry not reported	387	226	1,766	955	676	465	[illegible]3	196	1,690	9[illegible]4	534	404	[illegible]38	92

Table 35.—ECONOMIC CHARACTERISTICS OF THE POPULATION, BY SEX, FOR STANDARD METROPOLITAN AREAS, URBANIZED AREAS, AND URBAN PLACES OF 10,000 OR MORE: 1950—Con.

Subject	Urban places—Con.															
	Alexandria		Baton Rouge		Bogalusa		Bossier City		Crowley		Gretna		Houma		Lafayette	
	Male	Female	Male	Female	Male	Female	Male	Female	Male	Female	Male	Female	Male	Female	Male	Female
Total population, all ages	6,274	6,435	[illegible]	64,3[illegible]4	8,629	9,149	7,581	7,889	6,162	6,622	6,650	[illegible]	5,500	5,985	16,330	17,211
EMPLOYMENT STATUS																
Persons 14 years old and over	4,323	[illegible]	44,372	47,584	5,939	6,437	5,104	5,578	4,223	4,758	4,740	5,229	3,798	4,187	11,736	12,623
Labor force	3,449	1,268	33,842	15,310	4,599	1,751	3,083	1,482	2,979	1,232	3,748	1,374	3,117	1,075	8,483	3,901
Civilian labor force	3,448	1,268	33,766	15,309	4,597	1,750	3,040	1,473	2,977	1,232	3,734	1,374	3,109	1,074	8,460	3,901
Employed	3,223	1,174	32,027	14,816	4,375	1,642	2,911	1,416	2,704	1,189	3,511	1,305	2,925	1,027	8,069	3,745
Private wage and salary workers	2,696	877	25,232	10,803	3,810	1,332	2,294	1,166	2,033	921	2,897	1,029	2,175	753	6,197	2,827
Government workers	184	180	3,737	3,235	220	166	317	151	266	160	284	194	256	163	867	675
Self-employed workers	340	72	3,029	644	340	140	298	79	399	84	329	67	485	75	995	213
Unpaid family workers	3	39	28	139	5	4	4	20	–	24	1	15	9	36	10	30
Unemployed	225	94	1,739	493	222	108	129	57	273	43	223	69	184	47	391	156
Experienced workers	225	94	1,733	484	222	103	129	57	270	40	222	66	182	45	391	154
New workers	–	–	6	9	–	5	–	–	3	3	–	3	2	2	–	2
Not in labor force	874	3,345	10,530	32,274	1,340	4,686	2,021	4,096	1,244	3,526	992	3,855	686	3,112	3,253	8,722
Keeping house	31	2,610	149	24,627	20	3,572	19	3,442	32	2,669	20	3,062	11	2,474	34	6,497
Unable to work	187	115	1,964	1,645	457	299	192	154	466	302	373	268	247	174	626	471
Inmates of institutions	33	1	137	36	18	–	–	–	–	–	27	1	21	5	75	29
Other and not reported	623	579	8,280	5,966	839	815	510	500	746	555	572	521	407	459	2,518	1,705
14 to 19 years old	349	345	3,431	3,428	466	519	278	280	336	390	344	349	268	352	999	1,099
20 to 64 years old	147	161	572	2,062	264	237	187	154	366	140	191	149	100	76	1,344	543
65 years old and over	127	75	674	476	109	59	45	46	44	25	37	23	39	31	175	63
MAJOR OCCUPATION GROUP																
Employed	3,223	1,174	32,027	14,816	4,375	1,642	2,911	1,416	2,704	1,189	3,511	1,305	2,925	1,027	8,069	3,745
Professional, technical, and kindred workers	230	196	4,066	2,101	221	202	163	77	177	172	146	120	230	192	777	506
Farmers and farm managers	21	4	51	17	12	1	14	–	24	4	10	–	3	–	38	3
Managers, officials, and propr's, exc. farm	304	46	3,802	597	329	85	310	52	423	36	344	71	410	40	1,066	138
Clerical and kindred workers	182	209	2,192	4,774	197	261	236	361	131	227	374	357	167	184	561	897
Sales workers	123	120	2,281	1,198	207	178	252	149	181	111	142	118	216	138	814	356
Craftsmen, foremen, and kindred workers	942	6	7,261	147	826	15	754	9	497	–	702	11	926	3	1,574	21
Operatives and kindred workers	1,069	178	6,417	871	1,405	219	671	125	471	98	786	204	841	104	1,564	269
Private household workers	8	241	72	2,889	7	535	7	273	14	316	3	187	1	194	21	825
Service workers, except private household	193	150	2,488	2,068	248	271	180	260	90	172	282	204	197	149	603	661
Farm laborers, unpaid family workers	2	–	1	2	1	–	–	–	3	–	2	2	–	–	1	–
Farm laborers, exc. unpaid, and farm foremen	23	4	102	31	19	6	25	5	33	2	9	–	22	–	64	6
Laborers, except farm and mine	498	11	2,968	47	765	48	247	11	451	12	618	13	258	7	901	31
Occupation not reported	28	–	326	167	72	21	54	32	43	10	33	23	52	4	85	32
Experienced unemployed	225	94	1,733	484	222	103	129	57	270	40	222	66	182	45	391	154
Professional, technical, and kindred workers	4	2	38	17	4	2	3	–	5	–	4	–	–	1	8	3
Farmers and farm managers	–	–	8	–	–	–	–	–	–	–	–	–	–	–	5	–
Managers, officials, and props., exc. farm	2	1	37	2	2	1	1	1	1	1	3	–	4	2	2	1
Clerical and kindred workers	5	2	36	67	3	3	2	3	9	1	11	3	4	5	1	12
Sales workers	4	11	57	21	2	–	4	1	3	5	4	3	6	4	9	14
Craftsmen, foremen, and kindred workers	48	–	500	–	23	–	16	2	20	–	40	2	41	–	72	3
Operatives and kindred workers	45	6	275	24	21	6	15	2	59	5	32	13	41	8	67	18
Private household workers	1	43	3	149	1	4	–	3	–	9	–	15	1	12	–	56
Service workers, except private household	14	18	135	100	3	8	2	–	–	8	18	11	13	6	30	21
Farm laborers and foremen	8	3	11	–	–	–	–	–	10	–	–	1	4	–	20	–
Laborers, except farm and mine	87	1	421	1	21	4	11	–	93	1	65	3	30	–	109	6
Occupation not reported	14	7	209	90	41	24	74	44	63	10	25	15	18	6	52	18
INDUSTRY GROUP																
Employed	3,223	1,174	32,027	14,816	4,375	1,642	2,911	1,416	2,704	1,189	3,511	1,305	2,925	1,027	8,069	3,745
Agriculture	60	6	199	42	34	7	44	3	76	5	31	2	38	2	14	10
Forestry and fisheries	2	–	15	10	43	35	6	–	–	–	14	–	73	1	3	–
Mining	10	–	206	13	12	3	158	12	36	3	73	4	676	13	526	36
Construction	186	5	4,791	122	500	5	511	8	344	9	328	19	286	1	495	12
Manufacturing	1,743	187	10,217	870	2,185	232	396	73	478	58	1,060	207	342	66	534	199
Furniture, and lumber and wood products	88	2	203	16	325	14	76	15	6	–	39	2	12	2	96	6
Primary metal industries	–	–	226	13	5	1	9	1	3	–	6	–	5	–	4	1
Fabricated metal ind. (incl. not spec. metal)	–	–	201	13	–	1	26	2	1	–	51	15	17	2	14	1
Machinery, except electrical	1	–	93	13	10	–	42	7	7	–	34	1	15	–	46	2
Electrical machinery, equip., and supplies	1	–	22	2	2	–	6	1	–	–	5	–	2	–	2	–
Motor vehicles and motor vehicle equip.	–	–	12	4	–	–	3	–	–	–	1	–	1	–	–	–
Transportation equip., exc. motor vehicle	1	–	17	3	4	–	5	–	–	–	163	5	7	–	10	–
Other durable goods	2	–	168	28	–	1	17	4	2	–	20	1	4	–	62	6
Food and kindred products	21	1	785	130	49	7	53	7	396	36	177	89	236	53	492	78
Textile mill products	2	–	10	2	1	–	1	–	–	–	5	4	–	–	6	–
Apparel and other fabricated textile prod.	–	–	11	4	–	1	1	14	15	20	17	46	3	–	–	–
Printing, publishing, and allied industries	9	7	426	116	38	8	40	13	27	7	28	3	25	7	102	26
Chemicals and allied products	77	9	2,370	159	47	2	57	4	3	–	144	17	7	2	70	73
Other nondurable goods	1,541	174	5,654	373	1,697	198	51	6	13	–	365	29	9	–	19	3
Not specified manufacturing industries	–	–	19	6	–	–	6	1	4	1	5	–	2	–	1	3
Railroads and railway express service	59	3	615	99	42	1	150	6	23	–	332	10	4	–	689	22
Trucking service and warehousing	17	3	320	23	24	2	98	6	74	1	62	4	38	3	123	9
Other transportation	24	2	500	61	7	6	82	2	61	1	229	18	3	1	164	14
Telecommunications	3	28	263	287	14	5	5	28	16	46	9	35	15	27	91	166
Utilities and sanitary services	82	7	689	115	17	4	87	20	64	5	73	20	62	4	230	31
Wholesale trade	64	3	1,226	176	77	1	167	28	135	20	138	54	144	15	374	70
Food and dairy prod. stores, and milk retail	109	54	1,096	424	128	79	139	32	194	30	126	63	145	58	357	157
Eating and drinking places	57	85	761	943	53	148	61	190	73	102	104	140	74	82	255	291
Other retail trade	329	134	3,665	1,911	379	169	328	222	392	137	244	163	312	151	969	410
Finance, insurance, and real estate	37	27	957	632	54	34	65	49	68	32	73	50	63	18	759	145
Business services	5	–	282	85	10	4	13	5	14	10	21	3	16	5	88	23
Repair services	49	2	701	44	100	3	143	4	142	3	63	3	104	2	293	8
Private households	20	345	277	3,009	31	344	22	290	68	330	9	185	17	198	124	847
Hotels and lodging places	14	20	155	261	7	32	17	29	13	12	11	8	13	17	32	49
Other personal services	74	77	720	899	95	111	67	34	78	75	60	50	86	69	204	201
Entertainment and recreation services	37	8	329	164	36	10	25	18	36	10	142	17	50	11	132	28
Medical and other health services	20	5	416	789	39	125	14	77	32	71	32	63	23	41	158	284
Educational services, government	43	134	1,510	1,742	36	121	2	60	56	11	23	97	28	126	287	436
Educational services, private	6	11	157	282	9	24	7	19	4	39	6	[illegible]	5	46	64	104
Other professional and related services	52	23	560	297	58	15	26	22	52	23	37	23	44	22	12	70
Public administration	90	46	1,516	1,156	128	32	210	72	132	37	151	68	137	35	245	77
Industry not reported	37	7	290	179	63	34	50	36	63	20	46	25	57	13	91	36

Table 35.—ECONOMIC CHARACTERISTICS OF THE POPULATION, BY SEX, FOR STANDARD METROPOLITAN AREAS, URBANIZED AREAS, AND URBAN PLACES OF 10,000 OR MORE: 1950—Con.

Subject	Urban places—Con.															
	Lake Charles		Monroe		New Iberia		New Orleans		Opelousas		Ruston		Shreveport		West Monroe	
	Male	Female	Male	Female	Male	Female	Male	Female	Male	Female	Male	Female	Male	Female	Male	Female
Total population (all ages)	20,242	[illegible]	18 115	20,4[illegible]	[illegible],991	8,476	270 8[illegible]2	299,033	[illegible],501	[illegible]	5,[illegible]48	[illegible],224	59,64[illegible]	6[illegible],563	[illegible],690	5,[illegible]2
EMPLOYMENT STATUS																
Persons 14 years old and over	[illegible]4,345	[illegible] 264	[illegible]3,079	15 50[illegible]	5,4[illegible]	[illegible],172	263,21[illegible]	232 64[illegible]	3 [illegible]43	4 352	3,920	3,999	[illegible]	51,734	3,52[illegible]	4,049
Labor force	1[illegible] 727	4,086	10,247	5,860	4,235	1,744	159,029	74,9[illegible]	2,623	1,132	2,23[illegible]	[illegible],320	[illegible]	[illegible]9,20[illegible]	2,88[illegible]	1,[illegible]14
Civilian labor force	[illegible],702	4 684	10,218	[illegible]	4,23[illegible]	[illegible]	[illegible]	[illegible]	2 62[illegible]	1,[illegible]	2,222	[illegible],320	34,[illegible]	1[illegible]	2 880	[illegible],417
Employed	[illegible],027	4,475	9,694	[illegible],6[illegible]7	3,957	[illegible],685	[illegible]	7[illegible],426	2,53[illegible]	[illegible],123	2,179	[illegible] 308	33,057	18,619	2,76[illegible]	[illegible],385
Private wage and salary workers	8,987	3,6[illegible]9	7 477	4,476	[illegible],109	[illegible],238	110 446	[illegible] 850	1,840	[illegible]4	1 4[illegible]	856	26,[illegible]74	[illegible],36[illegible]	[illegible],[illegible]05	1,063
Government workers	650	48[illegible]	980	682	30[illegible]	[illegible]62	17,[illegible]	9,184	2[illegible]3	[illegible]	4[illegible]	333	2 779	2 043	189	[illegible]95
Self-employed workers	1,377	258	1,229	372	629	105	16 0[illegible]	3,[illegible]0	44[illegible]	9	348	[illegible]	4,039	[illegible]	349	112
Unpaid family workers	3	71	14	81	[illegible]1	8[illegible]	[illegible] 7	682	3	[illegible]	[illegible]	13	[illegible]5	[illegible]2	3	15
Unemployed	[illegible]	209	524	243	274	59	10,57[illegible]	3,47[illegible]	85	9	49	[illegible]	1,1[illegible]8	577	11[illegible]	29
Experienced workers	6[illegible]1	206	518	236	273	58	10,40[illegible]	3 34[illegible]	85	9	47	12	[illegible]110	562	114	28
New workers	4	3	6	[illegible]	1	1	164	127			2		[illegible]	[illegible]5		-
Not in labor force	2,618	1[illegible] 578	2 8[illegible]8	9,64[illegible]	1,[illegible]	[illegible] 42[illegible]	44,1[illegible]6	[illegible]	1,120	[illegible],226	1,686	2,679	8,369	32,528	64[illegible]	2,635
Keeping house	[illegible]	8,695	40	7,515	45	[illegible]	80[illegible]	[illegible]	22	2 498	[illegible]	[illegible]	169	[illegible]4,977	[illegible]	1,925
Unable to work	[illegible]83	389	[illegible]	[illegible]	38[illegible]	274	[illegible]	1[illegible],979	42[illegible]	280	21[illegible]	185	2,628	2,529	228	164
Inmates of institutions	12[illegible]	[illegible]	1[illegible]8	[illegible]3	4	[illegible]	1,422	[illegible]	23	1	10	20	[illegible]48	181	14	
Other and not reported	[illegible] 841	1,48[illegible]	1,636	1,253	81[illegible]	682	3[illegible],135	25,85[illegible]	654	44[illegible]	1,[illegible]47	716	5,324	4,850	390	546
14 to 19 years old	[illegible],110	1,065	865	870	437	458	13,2[illegible]	14,297	321	317	51[illegible]	484	[illegible]	2,9[illegible]7	210	264
20 to 64 years old	52[illegible]	342	581	317	295	165	13,[illegible]	8,829	301	110	89[illegible]	219	2,060	1,497	132	24[illegible]
65 years old and over	21[illegible]	73	190	76	32	5[illegible]	[illegible]	2,729	[illegible]	20	4[illegible]	1[illegible]	619	356	48	36
MAJOR OCCUPATION GROUP																
Employed	11,02[illegible]	4,47[illegible]	9 [illegible]	5 61[illegible]	3,95[illegible]	1,685	144,487	7[illegible],426	2,[illegible]	[illegible]	2,179	1,308	33,057	18,[illegible]9	2,766	[illegible],385
Professional, technical, and kindred workers	1 0[illegible]0	608	7[illegible]	640	2[illegible]6	219	[illegible],815	8,672	238	256	242	[illegible]43	3,[illegible]03	2,[illegible]90	[illegible]21	178
Farmers and farm managers	41	2	45	2	2[illegible]		239	17	18		22		84	[illegible]	5	2
Managers, officials, and props., exc. farm	1 575	225	1 [illegible]	355	[illegible]40	[illegible]	19 804	3,2[illegible]9	416	6[illegible]	30[illegible]	43	4,958	728	385	60
Clerical and kindred workers	[illegible]10	1,249	558	1,1[illegible]	22[illegible]	34[illegible]	1[illegible],093	20,724	49	218	[illegible]30	291	2,5[illegible]3	[illegible],291	205	364
Sales workers	[illegible]06	414	8[illegible]	434	333	15[illegible]	11,4[illegible]2	6 363	267	120	190	9[illegible]	3,221	[illegible]	27[illegible]	169
Craftsmen, foremen, and kindred workers	2,343	34	1,511	39	78[illegible]	5	24,8[illegible]5	852	412	6	313	8	6,03[illegible]	[illegible]55	[illegible]09	22
Operatives and kindred workers	2 077	245	1,[illegible]34	509	96[illegible]	9[illegible]	23 810	9,026	463	45	308	76	[illegible],389	1 320	680	178
Private household workers	33	923	38	1,37[illegible]	6	448	45[illegible]	10,[illegible]38	5	25[illegible]	8	338	135	4,38[illegible]	1	190
Service workers, except private household	[illegible]87	714	8[illegible]7	1,012	284	2[illegible]1	14 8[illegible]6	10,334	1[illegible]3	120	182	112	2,494	3,1[illegible]	116	176
Farm laborers, unpaid family workers		1	[illegible]	1	3		19	19	1				8		1	[illegible]
Farm laborers, exc. unpaid, and farm foremen	22	5	[illegible]	37	5[illegible]	3	172	48	7	3	29		104	18	14	[illegible]
Laborers, except farm and mine	1,478	26	1 [illegible]	33	4[illegible]7	[illegible]7	[illegible]	652	308	10	318	5	3,42[illegible]	96	[illegible]69	[illegible]
Occupation not reported	[illegible]35	29	38	22	68	[illegible]	1 325	[illegible]92	37	20	29	19	393	297	[illegible]26	10
Experienced unemployed	[illegible]71	206	518	236	273	58	10 406	3,343	8	[illegible]	[illegible]	[illegible]	1,110	562	114	28
Professional, technical, and kindred workers	11	6	7	7	3	1	272	102	1		1		29	7	3	2
Farmers and farm managers			1		1		15						2			
Managers, officials, and props., exc. farm	16	-	18	2	3		434	30					27	4	3	1
Clerical and kindred workers	23	19	[illegible]3	12	4	4	65[illegible]	[illegible]72	1		3		[illegible]3	55	[illegible]	2
Sales workers	22	1[illegible]	26	1[illegible]	4	1	391	306			2	1	41	19	9	[illegible]
Craftsmen, foremen, and kindred workers	16[illegible]	3	92	2	37		2,252	42	5		[illegible]		1[illegible]	[illegible]	24	
Operatives and kindred workers	[illegible]23	12	[illegible]2	1[illegible]	47	6	2,136	571	3		7		194	25	28	
Private household workers	1	59	1	115	1	12	34	706				5	[illegible]	152		1
Service workers, except private household	56	59	39	48	[illegible]5	4	1,063	673			2		92	[illegible]7		6
Farm laborers and foremen	4		18	9	14	-	32	12					6	6		1
Laborers, except farm and mine	178	3	172	3	52	2	[illegible],9[illegible]1	[illegible]			9		176	5	19	[illegible]
Occupation not reported	[illegible]75	23	19	8	92	26	1,211	404	7[illegible]	9	18	6	349	210	24	9
INDUSTRY GROUP																
Employed	11,027	4,475	9,694	5,6[illegible]7	3,957	[illegible],685	144,487	7[illegible],426	2,53[illegible]	1,123	2,179	1 308	33,057	18,619	2 766	1,385
Agriculture	87	8	146	38	90	[illegible]	733	96	100	2	[illegible]6		400	50	26	5
Forestry and fisheries	27	1	11	1	11		262	1[illegible]			4		29	4	[illegible]	
Mining	363	39	103	17	627	15	780	139	146	3	84	2	2,051	6[illegible]0	63	2
Construction	1,653	41	1,101	40	468	7	14,633	52[illegible]	279	6	270	13	[illegible],962	1[illegible]8	296	9
Manufacturing	2,830	[illegible]	1 514	256	362	71	22,652	[illegible],978	340	28	231	14	4,979	820	749	13[illegible]
Furniture, and lumber and wood products	29[illegible]	16	45[illegible]	27	44	5	1 762	293	71	1	120	2	778	89	93	4
Primary metal industries	1		9		6	1	309	18	5				13[illegible]	[illegible]	[illegible]	
Fabricated metal ind. (incl. not spec. metal)	16	[illegible]	24	3	8		1,510	247	2				322	32	[illegible]	1
Machinery, except electrical	43	2	47	1	26	3	918	98	9		1		436	35	[illegible]	
Electrical machinery, equip., and supplies	4		9		[illegible]	1	187	36	2		1		[illegible]9	8	[illegible]	
Motor vehicles and motor vehicle equip.			3		1		136	12	1				3[illegible]	3		
Transportation equip., exc. motor vehicle	8	1		1	10	1	2,748	100	1				9	1	3	1
Other durable goods	72	5	58	9	3[illegible]	4	1 732	203	17		14	1	817	45	12	[illegible]
Food and kindred products	380	[illegible]2	304	35	151	[illegible]8	6,796	1,726	80	6	32	6	904	141	59	10
Textile mill products	2		5	1	[illegible]		765	735	11	2	1	1	11	4	2	
Apparel and other fabricated textile prod.	3	4	14	43	2		1,008	2,863					52	15[illegible]		12
Printing, publishing, and allied industries	144	39	108	33	37	[illegible]	2,397	475	22	10	25	3	[illegible]32	124	48	18
Chemicals and allied products	525	[illegible]	163	20	12	3	902	189	68	2	11	1	329	28	56	[illegible]
Other nondurable goods	[illegible] 337	138	306	80	28	1	1,726	905	46	6	2[illegible]		[illegible]39	136	458	81
Not specified manufacturing industries	5		7	3	2		171	78	5	1	3		43	13		
Railroads and railway express service	235	9	568	18	[illegible]25	2	5,670	385	40	2	27	1	1,657	82	[illegible]7	2
Trucking service and warehousing	[illegible]47	[illegible]	130	9	48	4	3 096	195	30	3	19	3	581	63	38	2
Other transportation	400	35	18[illegible]	19	74	8	14,39[illegible]	1 223	[illegible]9	1	31	3	879	135	37	3
Telecommunications	68	95	93	220	4[illegible]	[illegible]5	1 34[illegible]	1,977	1[illegible]	[illegible]3	21	50	284	368	27	62
Utilities and sanitary services	292	[illegible]7	384	36	149	30	3,296	378	44	2	[illegible]5	5	964	176	132	25
Wholesale trade	601	75	871	129	314	36	[illegible] 337	2,85[illegible]	144	14	1[illegible]	8	2,395	429	214	42
Food and dairy prod. stores, and milk retail	375	147	401	182	174	76	5,620	2,491	117	57	102	34	[illegible],323	479	138	67
Eating and drinking places	314	384	289	448	11[illegible]	1[illegible]7	5,252	4,251	85	69	54	95	653	1,360	47	103
Other retail trade	1,362	665	1,380	634	472	190	14,406	10,128	415	16[illegible]	289	111	4 278	2 396	407	236
Finance, insurance, and real estate	307	223	341	212	97	40	[illegible],29[illegible]	3,903	68	23	[illegible]	31	1,25[illegible]	806	65	44
Business services	74	26	84	19	20	4	1 962	690	24	4	9	3	353	158	1[illegible]	9
Repair services	2[illegible]	[illegible]3	2[illegible]	13	171	[illegible]	3,413	13	144	5	38	3	1,001	[illegible]9	93	9
Private households	180	962	256	1 427	43	454	1,092	11,221	40	273	42	342	534	4 5[illegible]3	34	194
Hotels and lodging places	[illegible]0	[illegible]3	101	170	19	22	1,521	1,486	1[illegible]	9	10	[illegible]4	331	393	14	24
Other personal services	268	232	302	4[illegible]9	90	73	3,[illegible]42	3,505	80	52	[illegible]6	94	801	1,209	66	108
Entertainment and recreation services	153	58	145	67	69	25	2 62	993	36	7	32	[illegible]3	360	[illegible]95	27	22
Medical and other health services	129	286	1[illegible]9	456	34	59	3,704	6,588	30	52	[illegible]3	64	606	1,452	25	57
Educational services, government	108	325	135	405	52	202	939	2,726	[illegible]2	181	260	299	296	1 131	34	138
Educational services, private	35	85	[illegible]5	[illegible]2	18	28	1,507	2,177	8	46	39	34	163	326	6	24
Other professional and related services	205	[illegible]	210	106	48	27	[illegible],666	1,575	48	18	51	2[illegible]	691	372	37	16
Public administration	385	[illegible]27	437	13[illegible]	160	49	10,286	2,987	122	[illegible]	95	28	1,776	56[illegible]	97	40
Industry not reported	103	38	42	29	6[illegible]	42	1,456	[illegible]97	35	22	37	15	451	349	18	1[illegible]

Table 36.—CHARACTERISTICS OF THE NONWHITE POPULATION, FOR STANDARD METROPOLITAN AREAS, URBANIZED AREAS, AND URBAN PLACES OF 10,000 OR MORE 1950

[Asterisk (*) denotes statistics based on 20-percent sample, for totals of age groups from complete count see table 1 Median not shown where base is less than 500]

Subject	Standard metropolitan areas: Baton Rouge	Standard metropolitan areas: New Orleans	Standard metropolitan areas: Shreveport	Urbanized areas: Baton Rouge	Urbanized areas: New Orleans	Urbanized areas: Shreveport	Urban places: Alexandria	Urban places: Bastrop	Urban places: Baton Rouge	Urban places: Bogalusa	Urban places: Bossier City	Urban places: Crowley
Total nonwhite population	52,341	200 523	66,456	43 801	195,181	48,804	14 484	4,435	35,182	5 750	2,497	3 334
*YEARS OF SCHOOL COMPLETED												
Persons 25 years old and over	27,140	108,805	33,650	23,295	106,120	25 790	8,060	2,295	19,230	2,955	1,135	1 580
No school years completed	3,525	6,930	4 340	2,660	6 505	3,085	835	345	2 265	205	175	600
Elementary 1 to 4 years	8,570	30,245	12,520	7,200	29,220	8 865	2,805	935	6,090	1 120	150	450
5 and 6 years	5 440	22,710	6 455	4,725	22,190	5,010	1 760	455	4 005	710	250	215
7 years	2,310	11,855	3,430	2,025	11,600	2,795	745	215	1 655	275	95	120
8 years	1,655	13,470	2,010	1 580	13,355	1,715	575	120	1,270	250	60	75
High school 1 to 3 years	2,160	11,390	2,345	1,985	11,210	2,070	785	130	1,660	220	40	55
4 years	770	5,685	895	755	5,630	860	205	25	650	75	5	5
College 1 to 3 years	655	2,135	510	615	2 110	440	135	10	375	35	20	5
4 years or more	880	1,670	475	830	1,655	480	65	35	500	15	20	30
School years not reported	1,155	2,715	670	920	2,645	430	150	25	760	50	20	25
Median school years completed	5 3	6 4	4 9	5 6	6 4	5 3	5 4	4 4	5 4	5 4	4 4	2 6
MARITAL STATUS												
Male 14 years old and over	17 003	65,184	20 237	14 291	63 457	14,997	4,641	1,387	11 356	1,806	743	997
Single	4,580	16,671	4,638	3 715	16,251	3,183	981	346	2,641	377	156	268
Married	11,445	44,098	14,062	9,751	42,885	10,612	3,314	949	7,995	1,283	560	661
Widowed or divorced	978	4,415	1 537	821	4,321	1,202	346	92	720	146	27	68
Female, 14 years old and over	19,567	78,343	24,903	16,888	76,473	19,289	5 745	1,689	13,824	2 090	925	1,232
Single	3 876	14,396	3,936	3,309	14,061	2,812	953	360	2,444	328	155	226
Married	12,344	48,560	15,782	10,566	47,296	12,261	3 665	1,024	8,796	1 343	627	729
Widowed or divorced	3 347	15,387	5,185	3,013	15,116	4,216	1,127	305	2,584	419	143	277
Married couples* number	10,120	36,750	12,205	8,555	35 680	8,955	2,810	890	6,980	1,160	540	580
With own household	9,155	31,610	10 525	7 685	30,595	7,430	2,540	805	6,200	1,085	475	540
Without own household	965	5,140	1,680	870	5,085	1,525	270	85	780	75	65	40
EMPLOYMENT STATUS												
Male, 14 years old and over	17,003	65,184	20,237	14,291	63,457	14,997	4,641	1,387	11,356	1 806	743	997
Labor force	12,059	47,888	14,957	10,281	46,655	11,136	3 291	1,019	8,604	1,321	556	589
Civilian labor force	12,052	47,495	14 905	10,275	46,264	11,085	3,285	1 019	8,601	1,321	555	589
Employed	10,749	42 964	14 239	9,109	41,815	10 446	2 912	894	7,654	1 200	498	453
Private wage and salary workers	9,024	37,222	11,505	7,845	36,214	9,316	2,443	803	6,587	1,158	435	388
Government workers	889	3,098	661	775	3,029	657	275	34	665	15	53	29
Self-employed workers	796	2 618	1,854	482	2,550	470	189	56	395	26	10	34
Unpaid family workers	40	26	219	7	22	3	5	1	7	1		2
Unemployed	1,303	4,531	666	166	4,449	639	373	125	947	121	55	136
Not in labor force	4 944	17,296	5,280	4,010	16 802	3,861	1,350	368	2 752	485	187	408
Female, 14 years old and over	19,567	78,343	24,903	16,888	76,473	19,289	5 745	1,689	13,824	2,090	925	1,232
Labor force	7,141	27,920	10,677	6,467	27,317	9 269	2,290	491	5,653	692	463	457
Civilian labor force	7 139	27 914	10 676	6,466	27 311	9,268	2,290	491	5,652	692	463	457
Employed	6,773	25 854	10 255	6,125	25 312	8 847	2 152	424	5,360	620	429	441
Private wage and salary workers	5,730	22,679	8,483	5,195	22,179	7,654	1 886	350	4,612	566	380	406
Government workers	729	2,051	764	668	2,025	719	149	49	533	21	30	24
Self-employed workers	283	1,029	693	246	1,015	463	103	19	199	33	17	9
Unpaid family workers	31	97	315	16	93	11	14	6	16		2	2
Unemployed	366	2,060	421	341	1,999	421	138	67	292	72	34	16
Not in labor force	12,426	50,423	14,226	10,421	49,156	10,020	3,455	1,198	8,171	1,398	462	775
MAJOR OCCUPATION GROUP												
Male employed	10,749	42,964	14 239	9,109	41 815	10,446	2,912	894	7,654	1,200	498	453
Professional technical and kindred workers	355	1 061	281	326	1 048	260	75	26	215	27	4	18
Farmers and farm managers	321	96	1,160	17	82	25	6	8	12		1	4
Managers officials and proprietors, except farm	262	1,268	226	247	1,252	210	80	27	95	10	3	19
Clerical and kindred workers	169	1,516	161	160	1 526	155	31	10	139	14	6	4
Sales workers	128	753	162	120	742	154	59	2	107	7	4	10
Craftsmen, foremen and kindred workers	1,378	4 709	1,161	1,315	7,630	1,093	372	55	1,167	45	46	38
Operatives and kindred workers	2,181	9,396	3,005	2 134	9,147	2,740	726	220	1 764	411	150	108
Private household workers	83	455	161	68	430	137	17	7	67	4	6	12
Service workers, except private household	1,675	7,476	2 043	1,600	7,357	1,993	485	86	1,465	112	70	55
Farm laborers unpaid family workers	33	40	215		6	7	2	1				
Farm laborers except unpaid, and farm foremen	359	186	1,318	84	132	106	18	2	59	15	20	23
Laborers, except farm and mine	3,670	15 593	3,930	3 031	15,035	3,415	1,000	415	2,377	542	178	155
Occupation not reported	135	445	216	107	428	151	43	16	89	16	10	9
Female, employed	6,773	25,854	10,255	6,125	25,312	8,847	2,152	424	5,360	620	429	441
Professional technical, and kindred workers	551	1,303	490	505	1,284	481	105	50	359	26	19	20
Farmers and farm managers	20	7	199	2		2	1		2	1		
Managers officials, and proprietors, except farm	139	512	145	125	503	132	47	13	94	21	3	9
Clerical and kindred workers	46	654	96	139	650	94	35	5	98	4		7
Sales workers	98	444	113	90	433	101	47	8	75	12		5
Craftsmen, foremen, and kindred workers	28	177	39	25	174	32	6		21	2		
Operatives and kindred workers	585	4 372	747	554	4,293	753	201	33	476	45	36	28
Private household workers	3,403	11,022	5,093	3 016	10 783	4,813	1,112	236	2,813	328	259	298
Service workers, except private household	1,576	6 581	2,267	1,514	6,448	2,171	559	69	1,307	137	93	67
Farm laborers, unpaid family workers	15	5	307		4							
Farm laborers, except unpaid and farm foremen	69	64	489	32	36	24	3	2	25	5	4	1
Laborers except farm and mine	54	502	74	44	494	73	15	6	29	37	8	4
Occupation not reported	89	211	196	75	205	151	21	2	61	2	7	4
MAJOR INDUSTRY GROUP												
Employed, total	17,522	68 818	24,494	15,234	67,127	19,293	5 064	1 318	13,014	1,820	927	894
Agriculture, forestry and fisheries	856	643	4,141	153	511	342	57	41	114	85	25	26
Mining	4	70	114	6	53	88	2		4	1	15	
Construction	1 957	6,165	1,785	1,798	6 022	1 601	353	52	1 552	154	87	33
Manufacturing	2,640	9,660	2,275	2 128	9,231	2,020	800	435	1,663	677	115	111
Transportation, commun and other public util.	888	10,224	1,363	854	9,954	1,263	355	66	708	57	57	39
Wholesale and retail trade	3,218	12,954	4,010	3,021	12 770	3 830	976	208	2,627	222	172	136
Finance insurance, and real estate	174	1,589	350	170	1,577	337	86	2	162	12	7	20
Business and repair services	259	982	393	240	966	372	56	8	214	15	16	7
Personal services	5 002	17,467	7,458	4,536	17,156	7,058	1,684	360	4,158	464	347	428
Entertainment and recreation services	134	888	199	127	869	183	77	11	118	13	4	3
Professional and related services	1,921	5,554	1,681	1 800	5,447	1 606	489	98	1,363	87	48	76
Public administration	233	1,863	252	206	1,836	250	68	7	167	7	16	
Industry not reported	236	759	473	195	735	334	61	30	164	29	15	15

Table 36.—CHARACTERISTICS OF THE NONWHITE POPULATION, FOR STANDARD METROPOLITAN AREAS, URBANIZED AREAS, AND URBAN PLACES OF 10,000 OR MORE: 1950—Con.

[Asterisk (*) denotes statistics based on 20-percent sample; or totals of age groups from complete count, see table [illegible]. Median not shown where base is less than 500]

Subject	Urban places—Con. Gretna	Houma	Lafayette	Lake Charles	Monroe	New Iberia	New Orleans	Opelousas	Ruston	Shreveport	West Monroe
Total nonwhite population	3 981	[illegible]	8 [illegible]	[illegible]	[illegible]	[illegible]	[illegible]	4,846	[illegible]	[illegible]	2 [illegible]
YEARS OF SCHOOL COMPLETED											
Persons 25 years old and over	[illegible]	[illegible]	[illegible]	[illegible]	[illegible]	[illegible]	[illegible]	[illegible]	[illegible]	[illegible]	1 795
No school years completed	[illegible]	105	[illegible]	[illegible]	[illegible]	[illegible]	[illegible]	[illegible]	175	[illegible]	[illegible]
Elementary: 1 to 4 years	[illegible]	315	325	[illegible]	[illegible]	[illegible]	[illegible]	[illegible]	[illegible]	2 645	[illegible]
5 and 6 years	[illegible]	[illegible]	[illegible]	[illegible]	[illegible]	[illegible]	[illegible]	[illegible]	[illegible]	[illegible] 930	300
7 years	220	[illegible]	[illegible]	[illegible]	[illegible]	295	20 910	[illegible]	[illegible]	4 520	245
8 years	[illegible]	[illegible]	[illegible]	[illegible]	[illegible]	[illegible]	[illegible]	[illegible]	145	2,530	105
High school: 1 to 3 years	180	[illegible]	[illegible]	[illegible]	[illegible]	[illegible]	[illegible]	[illegible]	180	[illegible]	90
4 years	60	15	5	125	[illegible]	[illegible]	[illegible]	[illegible]	[illegible]	1 940	75
College: 1 to 3 years	[illegible]	5	[illegible]	9	[illegible]	[illegible]	4,[illegible]	[illegible]	30	[illegible]	[illegible]
4 years or more	15	[illegible]	25	[illegible]	[illegible]	3	[illegible]	[illegible]	[illegible]	[illegible]	20
School years not reported	90	35	85	[illegible]	[illegible]	[illegible]	2,4[illegible]	[illegible]	[illegible]	[illegible]	15
Median school years completed	[illegible]	4 9	[illegible]	[illegible]	[illegible]	[illegible]	[illegible]	[illegible]	5 7	5 4	5 6
MARITAL STATUS											
Male, 14 years old and over	[illegible]	566	2 543	[illegible]	5,28[illegible]	[illegible]	[illegible]	[illegible]	[illegible]	[illegible]	[illegible]
Single	[illegible]	140	704	832	[illegible]	[illegible]	[illegible],240	[illegible]	[illegible]	2,769	136
Married	855	[illegible]	[illegible]	[illegible]	[illegible]	[illegible]	[illegible]	[illegible]	[illegible]	9,271	472
Widowed or divorced	89	[illegible]	[illegible]	[illegible]	393	[illegible]	[illegible]	87	[illegible]	1 109	[illegible]
Female, 14 years old and over	1,456	704	3,[illegible]	[illegible]	6,6[illegible]	[illegible]	[illegible]	[illegible]	1,293	[illegible]	807
Single	[illegible]	133	[illegible]	[illegible]	888	[illegible]	[illegible]	355	[illegible]	[illegible]	[illegible]
Married	917	401	[illegible] 842	2,7[illegible]	[illegible]	[illegible]	[illegible]	[illegible]	[illegible]	[illegible]	506
Widowed or divorced	[illegible]	170	520	714	1 466	356	[illegible]	[illegible]	[illegible]	3,833	[illegible]
Married couples,* number	[illegible]	290	[illegible]	[illegible]	[illegible]	[illegible]	[illegible]	785	[illegible]	7,820	430
With own household	[illegible]	260	[illegible]	[illegible]	[illegible]	[illegible]	28,3[illegible]	[illegible]	[illegible]	6 450	380
Without own household	[illegible]	30	[illegible]	[illegible]	[illegible]	75	4,875	75	[illegible]	1 370	50
EMPLOYMENT STATUS											
Male, 14 years old and over	[illegible]	566	2 543	[illegible]	5,285	[illegible]	[illegible]	[illegible]	1,052	[illegible]	[illegible]
Labor force	[illegible]	[illegible]	1,760	[illegible]	3,958	[illegible]	[illegible]	773	[illegible]	9 835	486
Civilian labor force	[illegible]	409	1,759	2,949	[illegible]	[illegible]	43,251	773	674	9 787	486
Employed	[illegible]	349	1 543	2 636	3,646	[illegible]	[illegible]	738	[illegible]	[illegible]	463
Private wage and salary workers	[illegible]	290	[illegible],363	2,419	[illegible]	645	33 809	635	557	8 237	399
Government workers	47	23	84	83	236	37	[illegible]	[illegible]	60	573	26
Self-employed workers	37	35	95	134	[illegible]	45	[illegible]	72	40	418	37
Unpaid family workers		[illegible]	1		6	1	22	1		–	1
Unemployed	95	60	216	[illegible]	[illegible]	126	4,080	[illegible]	[illegible]	558	23
Not in labor force	409	157	783	812	[illegible],327	447	[illegible] 808	[illegible]	378	3 314	163
Female, 14 years old and over	1,456	704	3 [illegible]	[illegible] 180	6 612	1 620	72,[illegible]32	[illegible]	[illegible],293	16 999	807
Labor force	[illegible]82	319	1,331	1,754	2,879	638	25 793	[illegible]	550	8,343	363
Civilian labor force	482	319	1,331	[illegible]	2,879	638	25,787	464	550	8,342	363
Employed	435	301	[illegible]	1 61[illegible]	[illegible]	609	[illegible]929	460	544	7,959	355
Private wage and salary workers	382	260	1 0[illegible]	1,433	2,320	527	20 937	350	444	6,87[illegible]	295
Government workers	33	22	133	[illegible]17	226	53	1 945	84	76	659	[illegible]
Self-employed workers	[illegible]7	19	30	63	[illegible]	26	963	22	22	418	[illegible]
Unpaid family workers	[illegible]		11	6	19	3	84	4	2	8	
Unemployed	47	18	80	[illegible]	183	29	1 858	4	[illegible]	383	8
Not in labor force	974	385	1 [illegible]	2 426	3 733	[illegible]	46 339	[illegible],235	743	8,656	444
MAJOR OCCUPATION GROUP											
Male employed	757	349	1,543	2,636	3 646	748	39,171	738	657	9,229	463
Professional, technical, and kindred workers	10	9	41	55	107	26	1,027	35	21	244	14
Farmers and farm managers	2	1	9	2	15	4	72	1	5	21	2
Managers, officials, and proprietors, except farm	19	6	[illegible]6	79	119	14	1 189	33	9	194	15
Clerical and kindred workers	18	4	9	37	54	4	1,492	2	7	136	7
Sales workers	17	5	19	27	[illegible]	13	712	11	[illegible]	139	4
Craftsmen, foremen, and kindred workers	56	39	[illegible]85	236	372	94	4,464	90	82	994	35
Operatives and kindred workers	[illegible]53	114	287	602	969	179	8 645	171	142	2,428	170
Private household workers	3	[illegible]	20	31	34	7	408	5	8	127	1
Service workers, except private household	97	66	283	437	519	103	7,103	80	75	[illegible],834	34
Farm laborers, unpaid family workers					3	1	6			5	1
Farm laborers, except unpaid, and farm foremen	[illegible]	16	31	5	46	42	[illegible]05	64	23	74	10
Laborers, except farm and mine	370	86	603	1 [illegible]03	[illegible],352	228	[illegible]3 556	231	275	2,909	167
Occupation not reported	7	2	20	22	11	13	392	15	41	124	3
Female, employed	435	[illegible]	[illegible],251	1 619	2,696	609	23,929	460	544	[illegible],959	355
Professional, technical, and kindred workers	12	17	91	95	137	50	1,244	96	28	444	27
Farmers and farm managers							5			2	
Managers, officials, and proprietors, except farm	9	2	15	27	78	6	473	8	7	114	11
Clerical and kindred workers	3	1	15	25	46	5	638	[illegible]	3	91	2
Sales workers	[illegible]	1	16	25	38	13	414	5	5	95	6
Craftsmen, foremen, and kindred workers	–		5	7	9	1	170	2	2	32	
Operatives and kindred workers	110	49	40	122	278	20	3,954	24	50	692	40
Private household workers	173	170	764	872	1 357	405	10 216	247	324	4,290	178
Service workers, except private household	[illegible]	58	293	4[illegible]6	687	84	6,125	55	119	[illegible],982	87
Farm laborers, unpaid family workers					–		4				
Farm laborers, except unpaid, and farm foremen			1	2	36	3	36	3		17	1
Laborers, except farm and mine	8	1	4	21	30	10	459	[illegible]	2	60	2
Occupation not reported	3	2	7	7	3	14	191	8	4	140	1
MAJOR INDUSTRY GROUP											
Employed total	1 192	650	2 794	[illegible],255	6,342	1,337	63,100	1 198	1 201	17,188	818
Agriculture, forestry, and fisheries	15	31	67	[illegible]7	129	56	437	70	32	282	[illegible]7
Mining	2	7	9	6	6	25	34	2	[illegible]	68	12
Construction	84	48	262	416	461	112	5 758	80	110	1,398	23
Manufacturing	317	110	144	672	733	96	7,906	158	137	1 691	173
Transportation, commun., and other public util.	176	24	265	353	486	86	9 461	55	67	1,130	30
Wholesale and retail trade	209	99	543	873	1,354	239	12,102	237	201	3,479	184
Finance, insurance, and real estate	24	9	34	65	101	24	1 530	8	6	319	8
Business and repair services	[illegible]	10	52	65	[illegible]	19	946	48	16	343	19
Personal services	240	257	1,039	1,403	2,252	531	16 376	351	454	6,350	275
Entertainment and recreation services	18	6	21	38	85	11	821	12	3	164	6
Professional and related services	64	44	323	279	539	98	5,270	148	48	[illegible],459	58
Public administration	24	2	2	30	61	11	1 775	7	13	212	8
Industry not reported	16	3	33	38	20	29	684	22	11	293	5

Table 37.—INCOME IN 1949 OF FAMILIES AND UNRELATED INDIVIDUALS, FOR STANDARD METROPOLITAN AREAS, URBANIZED AREAS, AND URBAN PLACES OF 10,000 OR MORE 1950

Statistics pased on 20-percent sample Median not shown where base is less than 500;

	i .	Less	x500	Si,000	81 500	82 noo	\$2,500	\$3,1/0	83,500	\$1,000	84 300	\$5.000	\$6 000	\$7,000	\$10,000 and	Income not re-	Median
2.022	Ali ciarestis	than 8500	te \$999	\$1 499	\$1 999	×2 499	\$2,999	\$3 499	93,999	\$4 499	\$4,999	\$5,999	86,099	59,999	over	portea	(dellars)
STANDARD ME TROPOLITAN AREAS			i i								ein .						
Families and carelated ndiv Pamilies	53,135 39,490	7,180 2 305	5,125 2,490	4,405 2,940	3,810 2,790	3,785	3,025 2,665	3,710	3,205 2,890	3,235 3,720	2,830 2,675	4,055 3,900	2 075 2,010	2,270 2,195	1,325	3,080 2,060	2,618 3,383
Familie: a :1 unrelater indi Families	226,755	2+,470 10 260	24,370 12,230	21,615 14,265	21,655 10 695	29,-25 12,610	18,510 16,145	17,835 10,000	_3,225 _2,295	9,940	7,779	1,250 10,730	6,795 6,470	7,880 7,600	6 305 5,885	12,010	2,330 2,788
Families and carclated indiv Families	.8,665 /5,3.5	6,865	8,185 4,590	5,545 4 190	5,04-J 3,965	4,590 3,840	3,660	4,190 3,685	3 080 2,795	2,715	1,995 1 890	3,050	_,795 _,740	1,850 1,78°	1,555	4,450 3,360	2,137 2,638
URBANIZED AREAS	y s				, r , r					.au	3.5						
PATON RG 122 Families and ur related indiv Families	47,925 35,050	6,425 1,840	7,370 1,950	3,835 2,420	3,400 2,465	3,450 2,735	2 800 2,450	3,455 2,965	2,875 2,580	2,880	2,585 6,435	3,800 3,650	1,980 1,929	2,175	1,215	2,620 1 690	2,699 2,472
Families and _arelated ind : Families	215,360 lon,500	23,615 9,710	23, .32 11,545	20,805 13,6:0	20 825 15,920	24,185	17,955 15,640	17,360 250	12,870 11,945	9,635 9,740	7,265	10,890 10,375	6 605 6,295	7,105 7,435	0 215 5,795	11,67>	2,342 2,814
SPEVEFOR7 Families and unrelated and v Families	39,630	2,060 2,250	6,260 3,085	4,57° 3,270	4,587 3,540	4,390 3,550	3,530 2,965	3,975 3,47u	2,965 2,665	2,585	1,0°C 1,88C	2,820	.,84. ,800	1,800	1,4.5	3,855 2,900	2,396 2,950
URBAN PLACES													.87				
Families and trrelated indiv Families	11,655 9 255	-,410 670	1,385	طور 1,070	1,275	1,450	785 720	710 615	56.5 530	420 410	375 350	510 500	285 285	245 320	370 350	855 645	2,012 2,381
Families and un elated indiv	4, 165 3, 375	455 190	475 280	395 310	295 260	505 435	395 340	34.5 305	280 265	≥70 270	135 _35	205 185	110 105	85 85	65 65	150 145	2,384 2,706
Families and unrelated indiv - Pamilies -	43,550 32,100	5,335 1,540	3,845 . 660	3,425	3,160	3,020	4,570 2,335	3,175 2,720	2,705	2,7.5	2,450 2,315	3,640	1,885 1,830	2 080	1,210	2,325 1,515	2,856 3 5°3
BOGALUSA I amilies and increased indiv	7,4±5 4,435	50o 375	770 465	605 505	490 445	615 >40	44.5 340	345 325	310 295	2.15 225	155 150	262 270	175 _60)10 105	70 70	270 165	2,112 4,319
Familes and unrelated indiv	4,75C 4,295	480 180	2°5 180	340 300	345 305	475 450	455 445	570 53.5	450 420	2e5 2e0	285 280	340 335	200 200	135	35 J:	280 240	3,039 3,157
Families and unrelated indiv	3,67 3,275	515 300	515 3°0	445 395	545 510	445 420	270 250	550 550	140	120 115	95 90	100	30 50	75 70	85 95	2/-0 195	1,812 1,966
Families and unrelated many Families	4,025 2,495	565 360	39° 260	315 310	315 280	560 520	345 340	385 380	2+5 230	145 140	100	200 195	90 90	120	70 n5	140	2,284 2,402
HOUM Families and unrelated mary Families	3,295 2,820	280 155	320 190	350 290	275 22	345 320	255 250	265 240	⊲15 265	170	120 110	200 185	140 140	150 150	60	90 70	2,565 2,890
LAFAYETTE Families and unrelated indiv Families	10,960 7 875	2,080 570	1,275	1,045	1,130	990 850	730 670	655 590	490 430	485 435	300 285	550 520	315 290	275 260	280 265	3e0 230	1,898
Familie and unrelated indiv	14,100 11,165	1,245	1,313	1,055	1,165	1,280	1,130 گيو	-,_80 960	950 840	1,015	695 645	965 925	495 475	cOp 080	0بر5 ر49	520 365	2,825 3,234
N'ROE. Familes and unrels ed indiv Families	13,570	1,820	1,970 990	_,420 _,010	1,505	1,285	9_0 80b	780 675	670 595	560 535	405 395	560 535	285 380	4.5	455 442	525 355	1,936 2,408
NEW IBERIA Families and unrelated non- Families	4,760 3,975	44C 20L	490 255	435 365	505 435	440 +00	365 345	325 320	230 225	3.5	175 165	315 310	200 175	200	95 95	210 190	2,449 2,845
NE- CR. FAMS Families and unrelated indiv Families	194,380 144,255	21 7J0 8 545	21,720 10 445	19,1.0 12,205	19,055	19,320	15,480	14,695	11,055	8,32u 7,750	6,395 6,010	9,35 8,695	5,664 5,380	6,635	5,460 5,060	10,595	≥,267 2,767
CPELOUSAS Families and un.elated indiv 1 armiles	3,480 2,930	490 305	625 435	415 392	315 265	275 250	215 205	195 175	205 185	105 95	65 eO	160	95 90	100	85 85	135 120	1,727
Families and unrelated indiv Fam.hes	4,215 2,380	1,080 .40	580 195	430 270	375 295	250 225	195 170	195 175	180 160	135 100	150 140	100	105	190 100	115 10o	215 110	1,395 2,529
Families and unrelated indiv Families	45,260 33,7°5	4,650	2,720	4,08> 2,835	4,025 3,005	3,750	2 915 2,365	3,280 2,815	2,420 2,150	2,260 2,055	1,600	2,530 2,385	1,605	1,650 1,590	1,360 1,280	3,415 2,515	2,326 2,942
EST MONROE Families and unrelated indiv	3,450 2,955	295 170	315 160	310 250	295 250	3_0 260	320 280	365 325	2:0 240	225 215	140	215 215	115 115	65 65	25 25	215	2,650

GENERAL CHARACTERISTICS

Table 37a.—INCOME IN 1949 OF NONWHITE FAMILIES AND UNRELATED INDIVIDUALS, FOR STANDARD METROPOLITAN AREAS, URBANIZED AREAS, AND URBAN PLACES OF 10,000 OR MORE: 1950

(Statistics based on 20-percent sample. Median not shown where base is sees than 500;

Area	Nonwhite families and unrelated morviduals	Less than \$500	\$500 to \$999	\$1,000 10 \$1,499	\$1,500 to \$1,999	\$2,000 to \$2,499	\$2,500 to \$2,999	\$3,000 to \$3,439	\$3,500 to \$3,999	\$4,000 to \$4,499	\$4,500 to \$4,999	\$5,000 to \$5,999	\$6,000 to \$6,999	\$7,000 to \$9,999	\$*0,000 and over	Income not re- ported	Median income (dollars)
STANDARD METROPOLITAN AREAS																	
Baton Rouge	16,660 64,760 20,950	9,830 4,070	3,085 23,445 5,525	2,430 10,475 3,455	2,000 10,100 2,910	1,680 7,765 1,905	1,025 3,980 895	950 2,680 6.0	475 1,510 245	190 880 135	490		355	205	100	2,505 2,505	1,325 1,375 1,064
URBANIZED AREAS Eston Rouge Mew Onleans Cheemerort.	14,375 63,230 16,515	2,610 9,490 2,670	2,530 _3,120 4,180	2,025 10,180 2,715	1,883 9,835 2,645	1,505	3,935	870 2,655 55.	_,470	175 873 120	490	1 xc	25:	2:	25	2,4-5	
URBAN PLACES Alexandria Bastron Reton Roge.	4,595 1,450 11,310	790 275 1,605	960 260 2,060	865 215 1,705		460 265 1,205	110	x	35	5 45 5 10	3	4		2	10	25	1,424

Rossier City	1,990 790 930	295 125 210	500 190 280	360 165 160	280 145	295 85	120	25	10				5 "		1	8	1,249
Oretna	1,280 560 2,325 3,820	280 230 520 520	250 140 560 760	110	65 375	2.0	25 95	15					月 .: . 月 1			30	1,03
Monroe New Iberia New Jrleans. Opelouses Sweamonort	29,205 1,295 995	1,075 215 8,755 315 .50 2,430	1,515 260 12,365 425 270	9,600 210 170	9,185 225 60	6,973 75	3,675 20 40	2,52	1,43	5 25 5 85.	48	5 1	0 25 0 25	20	5	5 2,5 4	1,160 1,380 860
Smreveport,	760	2,430		2,415					21	0 .2	5	1	5 .		5 ' ''	5 48	

Table 38 —GENERAL CHARACTERISTICS OF THE POPULATION FOR URBAN PLACES OF 2,500 TO 10,000 1950

				111 A P. S. S.	- CONTRACTOR	- Annual Control	No.	-	_	_		-	-	The second name of	- water control	THE REAL PROPERTY.	The state of the s	-
Şub t	1.10	*sute	**ervice	Binkie	or.re.	ton	Sain_e- ville (_nirs)	De De	De Rfuder	Donald- son- ville	Eunice	Ferri-	"ians-	(curum Meadow (coldwn	Coos- port (unime)	dan- nond	Hara- nan	haynes- ville
Total population	9,3.8	2,804	2,619	4,660	2,897	ملارد	7,807	3,837	5,799	4 150	8,184	2,847	6,144	2 820	8 318	8-020	3,394	3,040
Man var white .	- 7-4	9.5	5	4 tais	-,-95	,55.	2,014	L 492	-,917 43	1 .81	052, د 15	753	2,044	1,407	2,403	1 69	1,605	1,126
This born white	71	ي ا	15	979 1	175	788	423	417	709	29.	890	1,040	890	1	1 735	1 207	9	354
Otner races			1			-	19		2,073	1,332	_ 179	749	2,177	1,405	2,369		1,650	1,110
Bum. Ve ware	-,054	1 CIN	.,389	1,740	-,295 3	,834 45	1 875	_,-81 7	45	30	20	5	26	3	13	64	28	
Verry	784	-50	190	€88	120	862	4.9	-33	920	850	1,02-	1,281	904		1,768	1 ×48	-	428
Other races						-												
Male, a., ages	4.47-	. 319	امدد	2,222		2,-67	€ 465	1 916	2 761	1,920	3,963	1. 809	2,966	4,412	4,147	3 952	1,699	1,49
ande 5 years.	542	844	187	325 221	187	283 276	258 299	229	374 285	275 201	609 438	243	36. 300	204 156	5~8 >20	469 350	287	179
5 to 9 years	49-	1 3	,75 3	221	164	204	271	.65	221	128 142 138 146	370	209 157	276	128	436	286 355	±07	14
1o b seems	.53	25 25	110	14-	161	184	204 229	34 1.3	_63	138	281	113	192 40	1-7	320	4.37	73	
20 to 24 years 20 to 25 years 30 to 24 years	325 175	107	9° 90	ໃນ5 199	10	177	229	140	-6.3 426 202	148	341 294	130	251. 224	.19	88c.	232 274 251	2:0	144
90 to 34 years	321	94 92	94	.56 158 120	-10	765	162	-22	⊥93	126	271	115	226 194	97	245	251 251	-52 -25 -00	12
35 to of years	212	لايت 73	32 71	120	00	135	1.03	143	188	109	175	122	.90	76	187	199	.00	90
45 to 49 years of to 54 years	272 199	48	43	102	69 47 47	-28	70 68	.20 .25 96	136	89 74	177		1.02	33	119	170	60	93
55 to 50 years.	474	48 7-	45	6o	32	86 69	68 40	96 70	11.	65	139	63	100	33	112	164 05	31	59 43
55 to 59 years 56 to 69 years 65 to 69 years To to 74 years	1387	.5	23	20	36	104 46	20	→8 32	92 59	23	9.6 60	90 70 63 70 73	96	25	841	21	35	4:
	3 <u>.</u> 87	0,4	26	33	19	25	3.1	31	48	49	2 218	1,072	-,767	±€ 743	.≯8 48 2,197	64 80 2,368	1,027	990
If sears and over	2 0,3	840	73.	1,49	722	1 398	2,340	1,187	3,038	2,21	2 218	2.608	2,1/8	1 408	4, 74	4,058	1 695	1,543
Pemare all ages	4 859 44i	- 465	130	306	21.3	2 746	388	225	361	267	562	e33	/34	175	6*6 515	436	289	
Under 5 years 5 to 9 years 10 to 14 years	-50 -67	.34	.52 -27	246	18,	<74	236	198	282	20.5	441	18.	279 243	160	515 394	31.3 289	153 118	114 92
5 to 19 years	9_	-1	-05	195 496	11.3	231. 205	191 234	145 155	403 278	175	3.1 345	153	222	158	356 432	393	108	96 124
0 to 24 years	4.6	-09	*0°	235	120	188	218	205	278 442 209	_75 _70	/11 352	15.	262 249	144	385	392 341	171 212	150
to 34 years	30.	106	89	186	108	.81	192	139	209	1+1 148	720 -74	153	2×0 219	10-	322 272	289 30/	148	107
to 39 years	63	300	86	183 170	95	154	120	147	198	230	226	1.4	204	80	214	251	108	124
5 to 19 years	30°	94 55	-5	121 93 94	60 74 42	187	104	118	157	13.	430	126	176	70 45	115	207 196	87 63	109
15 to 19 years	215	61	42 37 48	93	42	128	62 53 43	107 72 66	131	110	.8n	95	137	45	-14 85	168	47	72
0 to 64 years	160	56	48	68	37	124	43	56 48	107 98	1.1	120	73	109	1.5	7±	136	40 2	56 55
10 to 74 years -	92	74 45 45	20	73 51 54	20	70	14	38	62	49	69 78	43	/2 82	10	7± 44 39	98	22	31
75 years and over	3,027	903	754	1,460	855	1,704	1,410	4,189	1,888	1,4.6	2,418	4,282	1,933	719	2,174	2,521	1.001	1,049
Nonwhite																		
Male all ages	719	387	170	580	175	789	442	412	801	739	896	1,048	390		1,735	A,208		355
Under 5 years	97	59	23	90 62 73	27	10 ⁴	73	49	101	108 78 62 41 84	159	142 132 104	11/	- 1	305	176 143 116	1	32
5 to 9 years	87 68	20	18 18 17 13 16	73	20 22 17	69	53 62	3. 36 17	77 50 47	78	.00	104	98	- 1	273 130	116	1 2	32 33 27
80 to 24 years 25 to 34 years	-5 73	31	13	77	76	64 5_ 11_0	30 2" 35	29	47	41	7> 46	59 38	66 80	,	148	36 73	4.00	17 64 41
25 to 84 vesss	90	22 31 54 57	21	42 47 66 59	24	97	40	76	108	78,	107	132	100	-1	277 190	102	2	41
16 to of years	-9		11		46	85	41 37			57 50	61. 53	129 87	171	- 1	105	+22	1	54 26
55 to 64 years	43	40 24 10	14 12 7	62 37 42 10	6	48	37	39 15	86 74 32	3"	38	78	56		94 55	86 58	1 3	11
75 years and over	.9 19 366	224	92	307	2	448	220	274	8 461	363	440	37 60b	432	,	24 873	675	م	218
fl years and oser Female all ages -	784	456	190	689	223	864	464	433	920	859	1,022	-, 264	965	1	1,789	1 349	.2	427
Under 5 rears	90	62	12	75	36	1.24	78	55	128	108	142	.43 -11	127		304	169		43
5 to 9 vears	71	13	28	80 53 57	29	87	39 43 30 40	23 24	90	98	98	921	97 95 73		230	124	2	34
15 to 19 years	77 61	35	9	57	20	55 66	30	24 35	69	59	91	8o 87	63		155	1.4		32 32 62
85 to 34 years	119	56 72	241	82	18 29 28	138	70 49	61 84	78 132	121	104	155	158		275 180	208	د	62
50 to 44 years	108	72	27	102	28 14	111		50	117	93	105	193	91	ı	180	193	د	69
5 to 54 years 5 to 64 years 5 to 74 years	31	30	19	61	5	52	37 12	23	62	73	62	122	22		91	86	1	2:
5 years and over	20	32 7	16	43 23	14	40 10	25	18	52 20	76 48	18	39 35	55 24 562		13'	65 23		
I years and over	466	265	124	406	105	512	259	275	540	51.5	543	827	362	1	884	894	مد	276
THARS OF SCHOOL COMPLETED	>,15>	1 665	1,415	2 44*	± J75	2 677	2,160	2 00	3,180	2,170	4 000	2 035	3 420	1,240		4,325	1,755	1,840
Persons 25 years old and over No senool years completed	1,205	80	230	2,455		2,675	2,160	2,480	1,180	2,170	4 090 840	155	3 420	265	3,650			51
Elementary 1 to 4 years.	1,040	222 210	18"	460	380 295 180	475 330	655 425	350 330	510 485	29C	945	585 285	700 415	320	540 920 615	135 710 555	50 175 235	2+0
7 years	590 340	145	125	230	140	245	225 135	295	255	190	315	175	240	130	415	350	195	150
Syears	320 393	140 425	170	175 520	190	300	135 200 145	290 395	280	190 145 425	205	165	240 275 380	80 45 120 35	265 515	350 385 670	220 270	480
d years College 1 to 3 years	300	120	23.5	195	25 55	360	145	20	440	205	405 170 120	55 95	575 245	35 25	160	620 440 305	4.5 110	480 220 240
4 years or more	245	115	15	105	55	245	40 40	10u 8:	230 90	205 125 70 73	120	60	187	.5	75 50	305	40	100
chool years not reported	250 5 7	91	25 6 5	7 7	40	8 2	25 5 6	8 1	85	7 6	85 5 9	50 6 8	7 9	1.85	6 0	155	8 9	9 8
MARITAL STATUS					,			- 1							, ,			
Male 14 years old and over	3,129 728	930 185	862	1,498	906 230	1,648	1,489	1,373	1,920	1,327	2,610	1,224	2,079	949	2,625	2,904	1,144	1,117
farmed	2,236	69	616	1,120	653	416	345 1,093	1,072	38 ₀ 1,431 103	389 870	1,925	239	1,469	249 678	361 1,933	937	905	868
Videwed or divorced	1.60	54	40	63	2.5	85	51	78		68	124	105	94	22	111	1,823	42	- 44
Female 14 years old and over	3 579	173	895 145	1,726	1,014	1,976	1,489 25e	1,387	2,193	1,642	2,915	1,499	2,255	931 171	2,676	3,076	1,163	_,190 148
Married Widowed or dryozced	2,345	173 702 231	622	1,365	678	1,176	1,075	1,004	1,486	9,5	1,967	945	1,491	699	1,992	1,875	909	148 865
Author of divorced	313	231	128	263	120	372	158	208	273	302	448	366	345	61	304	548	106	177

Table 38—GENERAL CHARACTERISTICS OF THE POPULATION, FOR URBAN PLACES OF 2,500 TO 10 000 1950—Con [Asternik (*) denotes statutes based on 20-percent sample, for corresponding complete-count figures on age, we applicate the control of the control o

Suoject	-oner	Ja: kson	Jean- eret's	we	Jores-	day ar	Venner	Lace	ا- مدسرة محر،	-4ez-	17.	1,80 HOUL	Harita-	Minder	'lo ¿*	Vs o'L-	Ne Lade	10-m-
Total populauoo	1,749	0,772	4,692	9,663	3,097	4,502	5,535	2,8-9	4,123	2,670	1,440	רש, כ	1,525	¥,78°	7.7.4	9 ,44	2,818	3,36
dale Na ive white Foreign born white	-,27	2,115	-,47±	3,448	1,130	1,980	1,720	2-3	8-5	-,5-9	-,240	_,:22	1,3.3	2, 142	4,000	2,789	" 2	-,34
Other races	991	1,152	775	1,40	286	227	902	#3	- 5.3	451	24-		305	-, 40	52 '46	-,729	485	32
male Native white Foreign-born white	1,32	2,242	1 582	3,001	.,265	2,082	1,761	.,244	269	4,721	1,503	-, 322	2,474	2,804	3,963	-,212	880	_,37
Negro Other rece-	-,203	-,112	832	1,396	399	259	986	165	10	70	9141	د	36-	2,12,	53 858	2,_15	12	1
Other races	•						1	1	4	-	1		2	-,		4,	020	-
Male all ages	2,214	1,354	2,260	4,583	1,427	2,216	2,720	1,431	_,576	2 240	2,00	1,333	1,76	, ,4	19.79	_+, 53	1,292	1,67
der o vears	281 21.5	80	278	632 529	141	257.	3+5 287	_82	231	30~ 225	242	194	226 182	454 468	e32	55.2 393	-02	21,
to 14 years	-70	129	220	462 340 -74	1.00	223 160	199	120	-28	.83	-68 -43	1_8	102	42/-	-2.	326	44.	12
to 24 years to 29 years	155	229 231	136	307	89 107 104	159	199	121 97	-0"	.83 .37 .127 .47 .179	_31 _54 _40	68	157	37 m	405	5471	84	12
to 34 years	13, 158 149	306 34p	157	348 316	129	171	250	76	22	179	-40	150	1.42 120 132	×2 ×69 347	-28 347	418 279 324	102 97 100	13
to 44 years	149	34a 394	146	273	114	154	⊥76	95 80	129	59 160	158	146		2-1,	.56 .0_	23_	100	10
to 49 years	1.1	391 205	117	218 188	101 74 47	132	162	67	106	13_	106	87 39	96 72	272 225	291 204	200	65	-2
to 59 years	95 71	21.7 221 174	98 77	_57 _21 12/	36	71 65	86 58	60 48 53	87.	123 79 79	72	19	3,	.86 135	1-2	160	35	2
to 69 years -	41	408	78 50	60	28	59 42	62	58 30	78 58	79 46 42	47	4 2	38	152	-07 57 79	1.36	32 23 29	1 1
years and over	46 4,336	124 2,963	-,313	2,570	24 90o	40	29	806	1,164	1,363	44	775	3/ -, 029	2,794	2,757	2,685	7+0	94
Female, ali ages	2,535	3,428	2,432	5,078	_,670	2 346	2,809	1,418	2,247	2 -+2	2 433	1,338	:,87	5,.83	4,880	5,361	1,526	1,68
to 9 years	271 213 186	63 49	213	5.0	140	213 212 237	353 284 199	174 133 138	24R	325 218	272 213	190	193	583 448	53.1	584 424	194	21.
to 19 years	2-1 204	78 151	186	/32 442	120	237	2001	:34	148	169	178	122	145	440	433 380	38 6-29	14-	.6 2
to 24 years	191	276	178	43.3	140	187	268 295	93	1,00	206 177	192	25 157 144	163 147 143	410	426	626 371	128 110 129	12
to 34 years to 39 years to 44 years	200	332 370	169	3A2 349 303	154	171 185 147	255 228	94 74	.40 178	217	184	13*	124	3491	375	333 355	4.2	1.2
to 49 years	.49	366	138	247	87	128	1.25	28	153	178	177	132	10.	368	298	341	20	12
to 54 years	1.40	358	123	2	7/	112	106	621	142 125 108	108	122	52 24 13	74	250	2.~	235	55	12
to 64 years to 69 years to 74 years	81 96	23 258 204	93	140 156	57 52	75 57	52 77	55 49	103	87 78 87	65 95	6	56 75	175	110 157	172	41	1
to 74 years	26 70	151	67	78 95	52 24 35	47	38	39	71 78	43	26 1 75	6	36 28	101	53 87	1.20	32 40	96
years and over	1,620	3,,30	1,479	2,858	1,066	1,373	1,728	8.6	.,481	1,515	1,558	163	1,086	3,212	2, 793	3 _51	902	96
Male, all ages	991	1,152	776	_,147	286	223	93.3	1.81	1,023	052	747		369	2,044	745	1,729	48 5	32
nder 5 years	144 124	21 i	96 78	175 154	51 35	39 34	136 95	25 13	138	94 55	102 97		62 33	251 236	-08 82	246 _70	82 56	
to 9 years	81 96	21 42 97	71	147	25 18	25	83 59 56	21 24 19	32 73 50	50 46 27	66		37 36	225 18C	73 56	157 -46	49	3 2 3 1
5 to 19 years 0 to 24 years 5 to 34 years	62	97 233	27 209	88	21 37	16	56 154	19	50	27	67 49 87		30 53 40	163	103	_30 227	32 56	1
5 to 44 veace	129	270	92	128	38	30 26	133	21	149	72 84	102			286 247	72	195	66	3
5 to 54 years 5 to 54 years 5 to 74 years	1.01 71	224	67	69 63	35 13	18	110 55 47	5	1_?	63	83 42		33 19	195 118	93 57	167 126	41 25	2
	49 23	72 43	16	6J 28	4	112	8	-5	91	63 54 12	36 16	- 1	2.	112	37 19	107 58	25	1
Female all ages	533 1,∉03	1,035	447 852	9دد 96در	399	259	555 987	165	641 1,308	398	404 914		194	2,329	417 858	988	253 628	17 30
nder 5 years	144	24																
to 9 years	114		100	226	58	42	118	21	134	90	112	-	49	26_	_08	269	70	
0 to 14 years	95	9 "	91	159	37	42 40 34	103	13	134 102 89	90 56 58	88	-	35 28	223	_08 88 84	269 183 -65	70 75	
to 19 years	95 103 114	19	91 79 64	159	37 19 32 45	25	103 77 81	13 18 28	134 102 89 75	471	88 7, 80 66	-	35 28 41 46	223 220 208 211	51 51	269 183 -65 -4-	70 75	1
to 19 years to 24 years to 34 years to 44 years	95 103	19 60 487 264	91	159	37	341	103 77 81 92 179 130	13 18 28 14 15 17	134 102 89 75 73 162 207	51 104 123	88 7,3 80 66 127 135	-	35 28 41 46 43 50	223 220 208 211 3 <i>5</i> 7 134	51 51 -09 -18	269 183 -65 -4- -50 273 289	70 751 711 49 40 86 78	1 1 1 1 1 1 1 1 1 1 1 1 1 1 1 1 1 1 1 1
to 19 years to 34 years to 34 years to 44 years to 54 years to 55 years	95 103 114 175 165	19 60 487 264	91 79 64 56 741 93	159 161 140 99 193 158	37 19 32 45 61 55	34 24 17 38 20 24	103 77 81 92 179 130	13 18 28 14 15 17	134 102 89 75 73 162 207 182	27 51 104 123 8-	88 7, 80 66 127 135	-	35 28 41 46 43 50 30	223 220 208 211, 357 134 240 116	51 51 -09 -18	269 183 -65 -4- -56 273 289 234	76 751 711 49 49 86 78	1 1 1 1 1 1 1 1 1 1 1 1 1 1 1 1 1 1 1 1
to 19 years to 24 years to 34 years to 34 years to 44 years to 54 years to 64 years to 74 years to 74 years	95 103 114 175 165 128	19 60 487 264 221 192 95	91 64 56 741 93 86 66	159 161 140 99 193 158 93 81	37 19 32 45 61 55	24 10 5	103 77 81 92 179 130	13 18 28 14 15 17 12 12	134 102 89 75 73 162 207 182 40 1/3	47 51 104 123 8- 39 48	88 72 80 66 127 135 102 51 60	-	35 28 41 46 43 50 35 23 42 4	223 220 206 211, 357, 134, 240, 116,	82 51 -09 -18 87 -9 63	269 183 -65 -4- -256 273 289 234 -48 154 73	76 731 731 49 49 86 78 59 37 30 18	1 1 1 1 1 1 1 1 1 1 1 1 1 1 1 1 1 1 1 1
10. 10 years 10. 24 years 10. 24 years 10. 24 years 10. 34 years 10. 54 years 10. 55 years 10. 55 years 10. 65 years 10. 75 years	95 103 114 175 165	19 60 487 264 221 192	91 79 64 56 741 93	159 161 140 99 193 158 93 81	97 19 32 45 61 55 36 15	34 24 27 38 20 24	103 77 81 92 179 130	13 18 28 14 15 17	134 102 89 75 73 162 207 182	27 51 104 123 8-	88 7, 80 66 127 135	-	35 28 41 46 43 50 30 30 32	223 220 208 211, 357 134 240 116	84 51 -09 -18 87 -9	269 183 -65 -4- -56 273 289 234	76 751 711 49 49 86 78	2 1 2 3 4 3 2
50 19 years 10 24 years 10 24 years 10 34 years 10 34 years 10 44 years 10 54 years 10 54 years 10 64 years 10 74 years 10 75	95 103 114 175 165 128 70 62 30	19 60 487 264 221 192 95	91 79 64 56 741 93 86 67	159 161 140 99 193 158 93 81 66 20	27 19 32 45 61 55 36 15 15 6	34 26 17 38 20 24 10 5	103 77 81 92 179 130 103 42 49	13 18 28 14 15 17 12 12	134 102 89 75 73 162 207 182 40 1/3 61	2,595	88 7, 80 66 127 135 102 51 60 18 548	1,292	35 28 41 46 43 50 35 12 4 224	223 220 206 211, 357, 134, 240, 116, 119, 40, 1,372	84 51 -09 -18 87 -63 20 -16	269 183 -65 -4- -256 273 289 234 -48 154 73	76 75 72 72 49 49 86 78 59 37 30 18 34	2 1 2 3 4 3 2 1 17
16 19 years 16 28 years 16 38 years 16 36 years 16 37 years 16 78 Years 17 Years 17 Years 17 Years 18 18 18 18 18 18 18 18 18 18 18 18 18 1	95 103 114 175 165 128 70 62 30 725 2,740	19 60 487 264 221 192 95 34 1,047	91 79 64 56 741 93 86 56 67 48 488	159 161 140 99 193 158 93 81 66 20 685 4,645	37 19 32 45 61 55 36 15 6 231	34 26 17 38 20 24 10 5	103 77 81 92 179 130 103 42 49 13 592 3,112	13 18 28 14 16 17 12 12 11 3 79 1,390	134 102 89 73 162 207 182 40 1/3 61 947 2,465	2,595	88 7, 80 66 127 135 102 51 60 18 548 2,725	_0 30	35 28 41 46 43 50 30 23 12 4 224 224 255 345	223 220 208 211, 357, 134, 240, 116, 119, 40, 1,372, 2,190, 255, 325,	82 51 -09 -18 87 -9 63 20 -16 4,930	269 123 -65 -4- -269 273 289 234 -48 134 73 -,320 5,180	76 75 71 49 49 86 78 59 37 30 18 34 1 430	2 1 2 3 3 4 3 2 1 17 1,64
150 13 years 150 13 years 150 14 years 150 150 150 years 150 150 150 years 150 150 150 150 150 150 150 150 150 150	95 103 114 175 165 128 70 65 30 725 2,740	19 60 487 264 221 195 34 1,047 5,740	91 99 64 56 741 93 86 66 67 49 488 2,470 432 610 370	159 161 140 99 193 158 93 81 66 20 68 20 68 740 900 605	27 19 32 45 61 55 36 15 6 231 1,730 20 1.85 28	34 26 11 38 20 24 10 5 3 3 11 2,515	103 77 81 92 179 130 103 42 49 13 592 3,113	13 18 28 14 16 17 12 12 11 3 79 1,390 279 365 190	134 102 89 73 162 207 182 40 1/3 61 947 2,465 255 640 510	2,595 150 405 305 405 305	2,725 105 2,725 102 51 60 18 548 2,725	30 30 20	35 28 41 46 43 50 30 32 12 4 224 1,785 255 345 240 70	223 220 206 211, 357, 134, 240, 116, 119, 40, 1,372, 2,190, 255, 320, 320, 453,	84 51 -09 -18 87 -9 -33 20 -16 -4,230 820 975 -765 395	269 127 -659 -4	76 75 72 72 49 49 86 78 59 37 30 18 34	2 2 3 4 4 3 2 2 1 1 1 7 1 ,54 1 5 9 2 0 2 4 1 5 9
10-10 years 10-10	95 103 114 175 165 128 70 65 30 725 2,740 120 505 420 195 200	9 9 9 19 60 487 264 221 1992 95 34 1,047 5,740 280 280 230	91 64 56 71 93 86 67 19 488 2,470 433 610 370 210	159 161 140 99 193 158 93 81 166 20 685 20 685 740 605 330 605	27 19 32 45 61 55 36 12 15 6 231 1,730 20 185 480 185 185	34 24 17 38 20 24 10 5 3 110 2,513 70 565 3,50 140 125	100 77 61 92 179 130 103 42 49 13 592 3,11,2	13 18 28 14 16 17 12 12 11 3 3 79 1,390 275 365 190 75 100	134 102 89 75 73 162 207 182 40 1/3 61 947 2,465 255 640 5100 150 143 280	2,595 1.50 2,595 1.50 4.50 1.50 4.50 1.50 4.50 1.50 1.50 1.50 1.50 1.50 1.50 1.50 1	2,725 115 420 295 127 135 102 51 60 18 548 2,725 115 420 295 195	30 30 20 50	35 28 41 46 43 50 30 32 4 224 1,782 255 345 240 70	223 220 208 211, 357 136 240 116 119 149 2,190 255 920 330 455 455 460	84 51 -09 -18 87 -63 20 116 -4,730 820 975 765 365	269 183 -65 -4- -260 273 289 234 -48 134 73 -,320 5,100 480 1,025 570 290 260 665	700 721 721 86 78 86 78 59 37 30 18 34 1 430 160 26_ 200 700 700 700 700 700 700 700 700 700	1,64
10 19 years 10 19 years 10 18 years	95 103 114 175 165 128 70 65 30 725 2,740 120 505 420 195 220 575 220 575 220	9 9 60 19 60 487 264 221 192 934 1,047 530 280 230 250 270	91, 96, 64, 56, 93, 86, 56, 71, 94, 483, 437, 437, 437, 437, 437, 437, 437, 43	159 140 99 193 158 93 81 66 20 685 740 900 605 330 360 535 570	27 19 32 45 61 55 36 12 15 6 231 1,730 20 185 480 185 185	2,51.5 2,51.5 2,51.5 11.0 2,51.5 11.0 3.67 3.0 140 125 150 80	100 77 61 97 179 130 103 42 49 13 592 3,11,2 90 715 493 230 295 495	13 18 28 14 16 17 12 12 11 3 3 79 1,390 275 365 190 75 100	134 102 89 75 73 162 207 182 40 1/3 61 947 2,465 255 640 5100 150 143 280	2,595 1.50 2,595 1.50 4.50 1.50 4.50 1.50 4.50 1.50 1.50 1.50 1.50 1.50 1.50 1.50 1	88 7,7 80 66 127 135 102 51 60 00 18 548 2,725 115 420 295 195 670 110	105 205 475 200	35 241 46 43 30 30 23 12 4 224 1,785 240 30 30 30 30 30 30 30 4 224 31 325 345 240 35 36 36 36 37 37 38 38 38 38 38 38 38 38 38 38 38 38 38	223 220 208 211, 357, 134, 240 116 119, 40 1,372 2,190 255 325 325 465 465 465 1,485 210	84 51 -09 -16 87 99 63 20 -16 -4,730 820 975 765 305 305 305 305 305 305 305 305 305 30	269 183 -65 -4- -56 273 289 234 -48 154 72 -,320 5,100 460 1,025 570 290 260 665 550	700 751 721 49 49 40 86 78 59 37 30 18 34 1 430 160 26, 200 75 113 125 255	2 2 3 4 4 3 2 2 1 1.77 1,544 19 20 24 19
10. 19 years 10. 19 years 10. 14 years 10. 15 years 10. 15 years 10. 15 years 10. 15 years 10 years and orer 10 years and orer 10 years	95 103 114 175 165 128 70 65 30 725 2,740 120 505 420 195 200 575 265 270	9 9 60 60 687 264 221 192 95 34 1,047 5,740 230 280 230 250 135 135 135	91, 96, 64, 56, 14, 93, 86, 67, 19, 488, 2,470, 210, 220, 225, 225, 220, 200, 200, 200, 20	159 140 99 193 158 93 81 66 20 685 20 685 740 900 605 535 570 240 240	27 19 32 45 61 15 55 6 231 1,730 20 185 185 125 340 146 175	2,51.5 2,51.5 2,51.5 2,51.5 2,51.5 2,51.5 2,51.5 2,51.5 2,51.5 2,51.5	100 777 81 97 179 130 103 422 49 133 592 3,113 .90 280 295 425 195 105	13 18 28 14 16 17 12 12 11 3 3 79 1,390 275 365 190 75 100	134 102 88 9 75 75 162 207 182 400 1/3 61 947 2,465 255 640 190 145 280 185 140 110	2,595 150 48 112 445 2,595 150 405 305 105 225	88 7,7 80 66 127 135 102 51 80 18 548 2,725 115 420 295 195 103 103 103 103 103 103 103 103 103 103	205 205 205 205 275 275 25	35 28 41 46 45 50 30 22 17 22 4 22 4 22 6 70 70 70 70 70 70 70 70 70 70 70 70 70	223 220 208 211, 137, 134, 240, 116 1,372 2,190 255, 925, 30, 455, 400, 1,485, 210, 210, 210, 210, 210, 210, 210, 210,	84 51 -09 -18 87 -9 63 20 116 4,730 820 975 765 395 395 395 395 395 395 395 395 395 39	269 123 .653 .653 .677 .277 .287 .227 .288 .134 .73 .,320 .5,100 .660 .570 .290 .260 .665 .570 .775 .185	76 725 721 49 49 86 86 78 78 37 30 18 34 160 26 200 75 110 155 205 90 100 200 200 200 200 200 200 200 200 20	1,54
50. 19 years 50. 19 years 50. 24 years 15 0. 44 years 15 0. 44 years 15 0. 45 years 16 0. 75 years 16 0. 75 years 16 years 16 0. 75 years 17 years 18 years 18 years 18 years 18 years 18 years 19 years 10 years	95 103 114 175 165 128 70 65 30 725 2,740 120 505 420 195 200 575 220	9 9 60 87 19 60 887 264 221 192 95 34 1,047 530 280 250 270 105	91, 96, 64, 56, 93, 86, 56, 71, 94, 483, 437, 437, 437, 437, 437, 437, 437, 43	159 140 99 193 158 93 81 66 20 685 740 900 605 330 360 535 570	27 19 32 45 61 55 36 12 15 6 231 1,730 20 185 480 185 185	2,51.5 2,51.5 2,51.5 11.0 2,51.5 11.0 3.67 3.0 140 125 150 80	100 777 81 97 179 130 103 429 49 13 592 3,112 .90 715 433 295 425 365 195	13 18 28 14 16 17 12 12 11 3 79 1,390 275 365 190 75	134 102 89 75 73 162 207 182 40 1/3 61 947 2,465 255 640 5100 150 143 280	47 51 123 8- 9 99 48 11 445 2,793 150 403 305 105 223 90 100 105	88 73, 80 66 127 135 102 51 60 18 548 2,725 115 420 295 197 115 670 110 315	105 205 205 475	35 241 46 43 30 30 23 12 4 224 1,785 240 30 30 30 30 30 30 30 4 224 31 325 345 240 35 36 36 36 37 37 38 38 38 38 38 38 38 38 38 38 38 38 38	223 220 208 211, 337, 134, 240, 116 119, 40 1,372 2,190 25,5 32,5 32,45 40,45	84 51 -09 -18 87 -63 20 -16 -4,230 821 97> 765 3°55 3°55 3°55 3°55 3°55 3°55 3°55 3°	269 123 -65 273 289 234 -48 154 73 -,320 5,180 1,025 5,190 260 665 550 280 280 280 280 280 280 280 280 280 28	760 755 771 149 46 86 678 59 37 300 18 34 7 160 26 200 75 1.5 5 90 100 100 100 100 100 100 100 100 100	1,54
50 10 years 50 10 years 50 10 years 50 44 years 50 44 years 50 45 years 50 45 years 50 46 years 60 46 years 7 years 60 40 years 60 40 years 60 years 60 40 years 6	95 103 114 175 165 20 30 725 2,740 120 505 420 195 200 195 250 250 250 250 250 250 250 250 250 25	9 9 9 9 9 9 9 9 9 9 9 9 9 9 9 9 9 9 9	2,470 428 2,470 400 200 200 200 200 200 200 200 200 20	129 140 99 193 158 93 81 66 20 68 20 68 20 68 20 605 330 605 330 340 240 240 240 240 240 240 240 240 240 2	27 19 32 45 66 25 55 6 6 23 1,730 20 1,85 1,85 1,95 1,95 1,95 1,95 1,95 1,95 1,95 1,9	24 17 38 20 24 10 557 3 110 557 3,50 140 125 150 80 50 115 20	100 77 81 99 130 103 42 42 42 42 13 592 3,11,2 90 71,5 220 295 425 195 105 106 7,6	13 12 28 14 16 17 12 12 11 13 3 79 1,390 275 190 100 140 100 90 100 85 5 1	134 102 859 73 152 227 182 40 173 61 11 947 2,465 640,510 120 143 280 0 185 185 185 185 185 185 185 185 185 185	2,795 124 123 8-, 139 488 111 445 145 150 150 150 105 105 105 105 105 105 10	88 7, 75 80 66 8127 135 102 51 80 18 548 2,725 115 420 110 110 110 110 110 110 110 110 110 1	20 30 20 105 205 475 200 275 25 12 6	1,782 255 340 202 4 224 1,782 255 345 240 20 35 36 36 36 36 36 36 36 36 36 36 36 36 36	223 220 208 211, 134, 240 119 40 1,372 2,190 255 320 456 400 1,485 210 236 133 8 7	84 51. -0.9 -18 87 -9- 63 20 -16 -4,230 -4,230 -765 305 305 305 305 102 5 5 5 0 5 0 5 0 5 0 5 0 5 0 5 0 5 0 5 0	269 123 -655 -4260 273 285 224 -48 134 73 -,320 5,100 1,025 570 240 665 570 280 0775 1855 8 5	760 7251 7211 729 49 49 86 78 86 78 86 78 86 78 86 78 86 78 86 78 86 78 86 78 86 90 100 200 8 0 8 59	2 2 2 3 3 4 4 3 3 2 2 1 1 7 7 1 5 4 1 5 1 6 8 8
75 D 3 years 75 D 3 years 75 D 4 years 75 D 5 Years 75 D 5 Years 75 D 5 Years 75 D 75 Years 75 Yea	95 103 114 175 165 20 30 725 2,740 120 505 420 195 220 195 250 175 35 8 6	9 9 9 9 9 9 9 9 9 9 9 9 9 9 9 9 9 9 9	2,470 458 2,470 400 210 225 225 225 220 370 370 370 370 370 370 370 370 370 37	199 161 140 99 193 158 93 81 66 20 685 20 685 20 685 20 60 535 535 530 530 60 60 535 530 60 60 60 60 60 60 60 60 60 60 60 60 60	27 19 32 45 61 55 36 15 6 231 1,730 20 185 185 140 140 140 140 140 140 140 140 140 140	24 17 38 20 24 10 5 3 110 2,513 10 555 3,00 140 129 150 80 10 10 10 10 10 10 10 10 10 10 10 10 10	103 77 81 92 179 130 42 49 13 592 3,113 90 715 433 220 295 445 195 105 140 105 105 105 105 105 105 105 105 105 10	13 18 28 14 16 17 12 11 12 11 3 79 12 13 19 19 10 10 10 10 10 10 10 10 10 10 10 10 10	134 102 89 73 162 207 182 40 40 143 61 947 2,465 280 190 143 280 185 140 10 6 2	2,795 104 129 199 48 111 445 2,795 105 105 105 105 225 930 100 105 8 9	88 7, 75 80 66 127 135 102 51 80 18 548 115 420 115 225 9 3 1 426 322 1 023	20 30 20 105 205 475 200 275 25 12 6	1,785 224 1,785 255 340 20 255 340 20 255 340 20 255 340 20 20 20 20 20 20 20 20 20 20 20 20 20	223 2200 208 211, 357, 134, 2400 116 116 119, 400 255 922, 33C 465 40C 21C 387 120, 130, 8 7	84 51. -0.9 -1.8 87 -9.6 63 20 -1.6 -4.230 820 970 -765 395 395 395 145 105 6 6 3 105 6 3 3 105 105 105 105 105 105 105 105 105 105	269 183 -665 -655 -655 -655 -657 -657 -657 -657	760 7251 7211 729 499 499 866 778 866 778 377 320 18 34" 1 43C 1600 75 1120 1555 255 255 255 255 255 255 255 255 25	2 2 3 3 4 4 3 3 2 2 3 3 2 2 1 1 7 7 1 1 1 6 8 8 4 2 2 3 3 3 2 2 4 4 5 5 7 7 7 5 4 4 5 5 7 7 7 5 4 6 8 8 8 8 8 8 8 8 8 8 8 8 8 8 8 8 8 8
50 19 years 50 19 years 50 24 years 60 24	95 103 114 175 165 128 70 65 30 725 2,740 120 505 420 195 270 265 250 270 270 270 270 270 270 270 270 270 27	9 9 9 19 19 800 187 264 221 192 95 34 1,047 5,740 280 280 280 270 105 2,070 6 6 9 3,147 2,037 300 300 200 105 2,070 6 6 9 3,147 2,037 300 300 300 300 300 300 300 300 300	91, 79, 64, 56, 56, 67, 49, 488, 2,470, 433, 610, 770, 225, 225, 220, 35, 9, 48, 48, 48, 48, 48, 48, 48, 48, 48, 48	199 161 140 99 193 158 93 81 66 20 685 740 900 605 3300 199 199 199 199 24 119 199 199 20 20 21 21 21 21 21 21 21 21 21 21 21 21 21	271 199 322 454 61 61 55 36 61 231 1,730 20 1655 1855 140 140 140 140 140 140 140 140 140 140	2,51.5 2,51.5 2,51.5 2,51.5 2,51.5 2,51.5 2,51.5 2,51.5 2,51.5 3,558 3,40 1,558 3,40 1,558 3,40 1,558	103 77 81 92 179 130 103 42 49 49 13 592 3,11, 90 71,5 433 280 290 425 305 105 105 11,882 303 1,482 66	13 18 28 14 16 17 12 12 12 12 12 13 79 79 279 369 369 190 70 70 70 70 100 100 100 100 100 100 10	134 102 89 73 162 227 182 40 1/3 61 947 2,465 640 510 150 0 145 280 0 145 280 0 16 10 50 110 50 110 50 110 50 110 50 110 50 110 50 110 50 50 50 50 50 50 50 50 50 50 50 50 50	47, 51, 134, 129, 139, 1445, 150, 165, 165, 165, 165, 165, 165, 165, 165	88 7, 80 66 127 135 102 51 60 18 548 155 670 110 315 225 225 23 1 1,426 322 1 023 8	20 30 20 50 105 205 475 205 275 25 12 6	35 35 34 44 45 43 50 50 50 50 50 50 50 50 50 50 50 50 50	223 220 208 211, 357, 134, 240, 116 119, 400 1,372, 255, 320, 455, 400, 1,40, 216, 36, 37, 234, 660, 2,4,3,4,5,4,6,5,4,5,4,5,4,5,4,5,4,5,4,5,4,5,4	84 51. -0.9 -0.3 87 -0.3 20.3 20.3 20.7 20.7 20.7 20.7 20.7 20.7 20.7 20.7	269 143 465 273 229 234 480 1,025 570 260 665 570 260 665 570 260 273 280 280 280 280 280 280 280 280 280 280	76 723 723 723 723 723 723 723 723 723 723	2 1 1 2 2 3 3 4 4 3 3 2 2 1 1 7 7 1 1 1 6 8 8 8 1 2 1 2 2 2 2 2 2 2 2 2 2 2 2 2 2
56 bill years 56 bill years 50 years 60 y	95 103 114 175 165 128 70 65 30 725 2,740 120 505 220 420 195 220 25 25 25 25 25 25 25 25 25 25 25 25 25	9 9 9 9 9 9 9 9 9 9 9 9 9 9 9 9 9 9 9	91, 99 64 56 64 56 67 19 488 2,470 210 225 225 220 20 35 5 9	199 161 140 99 193 158 93 81 66 20 685 20 685 20 685 20 60 535 535 530 530 60 60 535 530 60 60 60 60 60 60 60 60 60 60 60 60 60	27 19 32 45 61 55 36 231 1,730 20 1,85 1,25 340 340 340 340 1,46 1,25 1,25 1,25 1,25 1,25 1,25 1,25 1,25	24 17 38 20 24 10 5 3 110 2,513 10 555 3,00 140 129 150 80 10 10 10 10 10 10 10 10 10 10 10 10 10	103 77 81 92 179 130 42 49 13 592 3,113 90 715 433 220 295 445 195 105 140 105 105 105 105 105 105 105 105 105 10	13 18 28 14 16 17 12 11 12 11 3 79 12 13 19 19 10 10 10 10 10 10 10 10 10 10 10 10 10	134 102 89 73 162 207 182 40 40 143 61 947 2,465 280 190 143 280 185 140 10 6 2	2,795 104 129 199 48 111 445 2,795 105 105 105 105 225 930 100 105 8 9	88 7, 75 80 66 127 135 102 51 80 18 548 115 420 115 225 9 3 1 426 322 1 023	20 30 20 105 205 475 200 275 25 12 6	1,785 224 1,785 255 340 20 255 340 20 255 340 20 255 340 20 20 20 20 20 20 20 20 20 20 20 20 20	223 2200 208 211, 357, 134, 2400 116 116 119, 400 255 922, 33C 465 40C 21C 387 120, 130, 8 7	84 51. -0.9 -1.8 87 -9.6 63 20 -1.6 -4.230 820 970 -765 395 395 395 145 105 6 6 3 105 6 3 3 105 105 105 105 105 105 105 105 105 105	269 183 -665 -655 -655 -655 -657 -657 -657 -657	760 7251 7211 729 499 499 866 778 866 778 377 320 18 34" 1 43C 1600 75 1120 1555 255 255 255 255 255 255 255 255 25	44 32 11 22 33 4. 4. 32 32 32 32 32 32 32 32 32 32

Table 38—GENERAL CHARACTERISTICS OF THE POPULATION, FOR URBAN PLACES OF 2,500 TO 10,000 1950—Con [delvide. (* Secoles addades based on X-percent excepts, fin. on respecting companion-courts figures or age, see age destribution in this table. Median nos shown where case is less than 500]

	and the same of	Augustus de l'augustus de l'au						Agent Programme And					-				_		-
ځی⊅ د	356-810	P.16-	rine	Ponens- tours	A_len	Rayne	72.10	Referve (uninc.)	Martin- ville	Sli- dell	Spring- hill	Sul- prir	Tallu- lah	Thico-	rille Plasto	Vinton	Vent- vego	Winn- fie_d	winzs- boro
Tota population	2,538	6,423	5,747	4,09C	3,097	C 485	3,138	4,465	4,614	3,464	3,383	5 996	,758	7,730	6,633	2 597	8,328	5,629	-,655
Va. t Va. ve waise.	+. Po0	2 772_	١,94٠	50	920	2,20	761	1,-73	1 246	1,162	.,422	2,890	1,029	3,004	2 705	1,051	3,743	1,734	1,001
Forcesp-born white	23 P26	.5 341	30 726	6.78	267	16 991	660	747	959	474	206	69	2,628	687	512	215	37 405 8	972	689
Other waves	_ 035	2,572	2,152	,342	-,00	2,310	840	1 32	1,330	1,247	1 517	2,927	1,089	3,2/8	2 850	1,070	3,709	1,827	± 112
Foreign-born waite Vegro	19	26	27 .72	7.3	578	14	857	783	1,06~	543	231	65	2,975	36 701	13	256	28 398	1,087	8.3 2.8
Otne. races		,						•						3,718	3,223	267	193		
Male allages	2 774	3,07	2 723	1 986	1,,000	3,127	1,424	2,233.	2.21/	.,654	1,631	2 987	3,677	243	434	160	63	2 711	1,701
nder 5 years	3u4 312	346 318	.334 286	255 234 174	.90 .57	415 328	200 133	292 238	331 286	221 67 147	170	36o 331	346 28	412	44.2	131	488	207	228 16. 157
to 9 years	232	243 223	233	109	_27 1.1	326 254	102	230 191	264	1_1	724	265 238	2.1	249	250	124	349 309	7.84	11.
to 19 years to 29 years to 29 years	⊥82	270	184	148	_20 149 1.4	27u	102	133	117	144	128	225 260	261 279	292 322	208 290 259	87 85	389 408	186 180 473	136 140
to 3- years to 39 years	181	20/	2±2 18.	145	120	195	134	147	150	1.8	133	228 264	23u 251	310 273	259 214	91 88	334 309	.73 _99	140
to 39 years	206 182	21.5 182	205	154	84	201	89	18	121	-10	_32	223	255	236	223	83	29_	_497	127
to 49 years.	145 127	157	180	130 97 8_	93 61	1°0 ₄48	9_ 86	113 117	82 69 79	95 84 80	91	148	26. 231	-64 -47	.70 .54	B0 59	200 161	_67 _47	90 78
to 59 years	1_1	110	115	0.2	55 39	122	58 46 47	60	97	44	28 44	92 /3 77	1,66 90 1,59	143 10u	63	66 53 41	105 79 67	442 113	68 49 57
to 54 years to 56 years to 56 years to 64 years to 74 years	82	73	87	88	46	87	47 32	60 63 38	61 37	44 42 31	32 19	77 39	159	84 59	63 35	22	40.	96 62	39
	60	50	56 74	31	22	63	46	25	52	23 970	16	30	2,300	2,:52	37 1 809	31 770	2,36	1 684	43
years and over	1,583	. B93 3,34€	1,601	2,104	897 1, 192	3,358	1,714	2,202	2,400	4,640	1,72	3,009	4,081	3,902	3,410	1,330	4,135	2,918	4,954
CC+ 2 Y*625	33~	36.	341	247	.205	414	198	287	321	229	233	377	450	495	406 320	,35 ,33	565 453	2+3	229 172
to 14 years	207 24c	267 223	303 220	195	164	312 308	128 35	20	242	175	134	255	285	3.3	302	.25	334	185	140
to 19 years	230	326 358	215	183	133	31C	130	200	207	13.	122	246	201	313	289	214	3uc 436	254	157
to 24 years	222	302	2,2.	165	160	257	130 136 168	150	.80 85	76.	190 168	270 255	304 307	330 295	282 262	214 98 98 98	38c	232 189	141
to 34 years	208	25"	205 20J	15.	102	193	105	164	1~3	124	164	260	300	293	254	82	293	2.0	151
to 44 years		208	210	152		228	126	137	1.4	109	103	176	283	245	21.	84 776	254	230	142
to 49 years	_16 _15	182	153	101	87 66	103	128 90 78	120	102	100 79 85	50 48	-28 -21	247	189 208	168	7. 65	140	206 158	114 83 73 87 87
to 49 years to 54 years to 59 years to 69 years	136	140	140	100	52 50	123	78	86 .	14 83	85 46	48	96 63	_76 _26	134	131	65 46	109	139	72
to 69 years - to 74 years -	54	82 52	132	61	28	110	80 48	64 30	8C 45	51 3'	42	73 37	-73 94	ۇنى 76	34	46 50 32	63 43	730	87
vears and over	62	57	84	31	52	67	39	32	60	48	18	35	104	100	52	20	57 2 ×43	70 1 918	1 228
years and over	1,727	2,078	1,913	1,285	950	.,953	T 734	_ 269	1,345	1,105	1 .48	1,721	2 ,97	2,444	2,033	804	2 343	1 918	1 558
Male, sil ages	826	341	726	678	567	991	660	747	959	47"	20o	59	2,634	699	4,2	210	4.3	972	. 6.19
der o vears	110	50	82 89	92	74	168	96 67	-17	171	74	21	2	367 265	109	89 58	33 22	60	118 98	117
to 14 years to 19 years	43 61	42 40 17	64	94 55 40	61 57 45	114	47 60	77 75 58	112 78	35	16	4	204	88	62 58	27 10	28 25 34	331	82 46 47
	33	21	377	40	43 43	63	33	>7	47	35 34 61	15	5 12	1.56 190	65 45	40	121	34	70	28
to 34 years to 44 years	121	44	83	97 86	65	104	79	1.0	143	73	24 40	12	334	27 79	55			124	90
															42	24	68	124	
	101	24	100	70						45	18			11	40	21	63	1.24	
to 64 years	1C1 08	24	100	70	61	91	73	92	51 57	45 27	18	10	352 178	49	40 29	21	63 38 24	124	61 51
years and over	1C1 08 45 26	22	100 58 5/ 33	7° 46 43 8	61 32 30 8	91 52 43 20	73 50 52 25	92 36 45 10	51 57 39 23	45 27 17 9	18 9 14	10	352 178 19'	49 36 17	40 29 1	21 28 14 18	63 24 20 4	124 124 97 56 19	105 61 51 47 23
years and over	1C1 08 45 26 468 9%	22	100	70	61 32 30	91 52 43	73 50 52	92 36 45	51 57	45 27 17 9 255 543	18	10	352 178 19	49 36	40 29	21	38 24 20	124 124 97 56	63 53 47 23 392
years and over years and and Female all ages dor 5 years	08 45 26 468 9%	22 22 9 01 328	100 58 57 33 435 873	7° 46 43 8 290 753	61 32 30 8 322 578	91 52 43 20 476 1,03/	73 50 52 25 382 868	92 36 45 10 708 78°	51 57 39 23 442 1,064	9 255 243 78	18 9 14 2 118 231	10 6 1	352 178 19' 60 1,604 2,979	35 17 355 738	40 29 1 2 229 547	21 28 14 18 6 120 256	38 24 20 4 245 345	124 97 56 19 6(7 1,089	60 50 47 23 392 834
years and over years and assr Female all ages dor 5 vonre 0 9 venre 10 14 venre	08 45 26 468 9% 12+	22 22 9 1°1 328	100 58 5/ 23 435 873 26 78 58	70 46 43 8 290 753	61 32 30 8 322 578 7 58 52	91 52 43 20 476 1,03/	73 50 52 25 382 868	92 36 45 10 408 787	51 57 39 23 442 1,064	9 255 243 78 34	18 9 14 2 118 231 30 27	10 6 1 47	352 178 19' 60 1,604 2,979 342 312 207	49 36 17 355 708 88 67 48	40 29 229 547 77 62 63	21 28 14 18 6 120 256 39 26	38 24 20 245 345 398 56 37	124 124 97 56 19 6(7 1,089 116 97	60 50 47 23 392 834
years and over peers and ease Female all ages dor 5 voure 0 9 vears to 19 vears to 19 vears to 19 vears	08 45 26 468 9% 12- 96 94 79	22 22 9 201 328 32 33 28 23 39	100 58 57 23 435 873 96 78 58 59 45	70 46 43 8 290 733	61 32 30 8 322 578 70 58 52 52 50 41	91 52 43 20 476 1,03/ 160 117 118	73 50 52 25 382 868	92 36 45 10 78 787	51 57 39 23 42 1,064 161 122	9 255 243 78 34	18 9 14 21 118 231 30 27 21	10 6 1 47 65	352 178 19' 60 1,604 2,979 342 312 207 192	49 36 17 355 738 88 67 48	40 29 22 229 547 77 62 63 5*	21 28 14 18 6 120 256 39 26	38 24 20 245 345 398 56 37	124 124 97 56 19 6(7 1,089 118 97 69 97	61 51 47 23 390 834 113 74 74
years and over genera and over female all ages doe 5 voors 9 9 vears to 14 vears to 19 vears to 24 vears to 24 vears	08 45 26 468 9% 12-1 96 94	22 22 9 201 328 32 33 28 23 30 61	100 58 5/ 33 435 873 96 78 58 59 45	77 46 43 8 290 733 123 63 65 65 98	61 32 30 8 322 578 70 58 52 50 41	91 52 43 20 476 1,03/ 160 117 118 102 88 114	73 50 52 25 382 868 404 67 76 51 56	92 36 45 10 78 78 4-6 94 73 72 66	51 57 39 23 42 1,064 161 122	78 54 255 78 54 23 45 49	18 9 14 2 118 231 20 27 21 15 16	10 2 6 1 47 65 6 0 3 1 4	352 178 19' 60 1,604 2,979 342 312 207 192 251	49 36 19 355 708 88 67 48 50 60	40 29 22 229 547 77 62 63 5*	21 28 14 18 6 120 256 39 26 32 25 16 27	38 24 20 245 345 398 56 37	124 124 97 56 19 6(7 1,089 118 97 69 97 104 156	61 51 47 23 390 834 113 74 74
years and over perm and over female all ages doe 5 vones 0 9 years 10 14 vears 10 24 vears 10 24 vears 10 44 vears 10 44 vears 10 44 vears 10 45 vears 10 46 vears 10 47 vears 10 48 vears 10 48 vears 10 48 vears 10 48 vears	08 45 468 9% 12- 96 94 79 48 123 139	22 22 9 1°1, 328 32 33 28 23 30 61, 42	100 58 5/ 23 435 873 96 78 58 59 45 98 1.9	77 46 43 8 590 733 123 63 65 65 98 102	61 32 30 8 322 578 56 52 50 41 97 74	91 52 43 20 476 1,03 160 117 118 102 88 114 136	73 50 52 25 382 868 404 67 76 51 56 40'	92 36 45 10 708 78° 73 72 66 94 97 61	51 57 39 23 422 1,064 164 122 134 85 96 133 69	9 255 543 78 54 53 45 49 81 73	18 9 14 2 118 231 20 27 21 15 16 44 33 26	10 7 6 1 47 65 6 0 3 1 1 1 1 2 1 2	352 178 19 60 1,604 2,979 342 207 192 251 413 426 331	49 36 17 355 708 88 67 48 60 60 405	40 29 27 229 547 77 62 63 5* 42 89	21 28 14 18 6 120 256 39 26 32 25 16 27 33	63 38 24 20 4 245 398 56 37 22 28 47 69 55	124 124 97 56 19 6(7 1,089 118 97 69 97	61 51 47 23 392 834 413 74 74 59 62 11.
years and over Female all ages dee 5 vones 9 5 years 10 14 venas 10 15 venas 10 24 venas 10 24 venas 10 44 venas 10 45 venas 10 45 venas 10 45 venas	08 45 468 9% 12- 96 94 79 48 123 139	22 22 328 328 33 28 23 34 61 42 27	100 58 59 33 435 873 76 78 58 59 45 98 1.9	77 46 43 8 590 733 123 63 65 65 98 102	61 32 30 578 58 52 50 41 97 74 61 33	91 52 43 20 476 1,03/ 160 118 102 88 114 136 80 61	73 50 52 25 382 868 404 67 76 51 56 40'	92 36 45 10 708 78° 73 72 66 94 97 61	51 57 39 23 422 1,064 164 122 134 85 96 133 69	9 255 543 78 54 53 45 49 81 73 42 32	18 9 14 2 118 231 20 27 21 15 16 44 33 26	10 2 6 1 47 65 6 0 3 1 4	352 178 19 60 1,604 2,979 342 207 192 251 413 426 331 213	49 36 17 355 708 88 67 48 60 60 405	40 29 27 222 547 77 62 63 5* 42 89	21 28 14 18 6 120 256 39 26 32 25 16 27 33	63 38 24 20 4 245 398 56 37 22 28 47 69 55	124 124 97 56 19 67 1,089 118 97 69 97 104 156 163	61 51 47 23 392 834 413 74 74 59 62 11.
spears and over- gener need one Femmie all ages for 5 venars 9 years 10 years	12- 468 9% 12- 9% 12- 139 103 12- 12- 139	22 22 22 23 28 23 28 23 61 42 27 21	100 58 52 23 435 873 76 78 55 59 45 1.9 1.2 84 95 29	77 46 43 8 290 733 123 63 65 54 102 81	61 32 30 578 58 52 50 41 97 74 61 33	91. 52. 43. 20. 476. 1,03. 160. 117. 118. 102. 88. 88. 114. 136. 60. 4. 4. 4. 4. 4. 4. 4. 4. 6. 6. 6. 6. 6. 6. 6. 6. 6. 6. 6. 6. 6.	73 50 52 25 382 868 204 (7) 76 51 56 10' 07' 217 76 77 77	92 36 45 10 78 78 4.6 94 66 94 61 34 45 97	51 57 39 23 442 1,064 16. 122 13. 85 66 67 69 69 69 23	78 54 33 45 49 81 73 42 32 24	18 9 14 23 118 231 20 27 21 15 16 44 33 26 9	10 6 14 7 6 6 6 6 7 6 7 7 7 7 7 7 7 7 7 7 7 7	352 178 19 60 1,604 2,979 312 207 192 251 413 426 331 213 216 76	27, 49, 36, 17, 355, 68, 67, 48, 60, 60, 60, 94, 71, 45, 48, 88,	40 29 22 22 547 77 62 63 55 42 89 72 40	21 28 14 18 190 256 39 26 32 25 16 27 33 22 18 13	63 38 24 20 24 345 346 56 37 22 28 47 69 55 40 29	124 97 56 19 67 1,089 118 97 104 156 163 149 97 55 14	61 51 47 23 392 834 413 74 74 59 62 11.
years and over gener need over gener need over gener need over 0 years 0 years 10 years	08 458 9% 124 98 94 123 139 107 123 123 123 123 123 123 123 123 123 123	22 22 9 20 328 22 33 36 61 42 27	100 58 59 33 435 873 76 78 58 59 45 98 1.9	77 46 43 8 290 753 123 63 65 54 98 102 81	61 32 30 8 322 578 56 52 50 41 97 74	91. 52. 43. 20. 476. 1,03. 160. 117. 118. 102. 88. 114. 136. 80. 61.	73 50 52 25 382 868 404 67 76 51 56 40'	92 36 45 100 08 787 73 72 26 66 94 97 61 34	51 57 39 23 442 1,064 16. 122 13. 85 96 65 13 69 69	9 255 543 78 54 53 45 49 81 73 42 32	18 9 14 2 118 231 20 27 21 15 16 44 33 26	10 7 6 1 47 65 6 0 3 1 1 1 1 2 1 2	352 178 19 60 1,604 2,979 342 207 192 251 413 426 331 215	49 36 17 355 708 88 67 48 60 60 405 94 71 48	40 29 27 222 547 77 62 63 5* 42 89	21 28 14 18 6 120 256 39 26 32 25 16 27 33	63 38 24 20 24 245 398 56 37 22 28 847 69 55	124 124 97 56 19 6(7 1,089 116 97 104 156 163 149 97	61 51 47 23 392 834 413 74 74 59 62 11.
yans and over pure need one femnie all ages doe's Youns 0 yeans 10	08 45 468 976 124 48 48 123 139 103 74 23 27 27 27 27 27 27 27 27 27 27 27 27 27	22 22 9 -0, 328 23 33 42 27 21 14 8 207	100 58 59 23 435 873 78 58 59 45 45 1.9 1.29 1.29 572 3,200	70 46 43 8 290 753 123 65 65 65 98 102 81 34 98 102 81 34 98 29 81 82 82 83 83 84 84 85 86 86 86 86 86 86 86 86 86 86 86 86 86	61 32 30 8 322 578 58 52 50 41 97 74 61 53 27 15 336	91 52 476 1,039 165 117 118 102 88 114 126 80 61 42 127 93 93 93 93 93 93 93 93 93 93 93 93 93	73 50 52 28 382 868 404 77 76 51 20 79 27 557	92 36 45 10 708 787 26 94 97 81 34 4-1 2,240	51 57; 39 23; 442 1,064 164, 122 23, 43 66 67 69 69 49 23, 49 23, 40	9 255 243 78 34 45 45 49 81 73 42 32 24 12 37 1,765	18 9 14 22 118 231 20 27 27 15 16 44 33 26 9 10 134	10 7 6 1 47 C5 6 0 3 1 4 12 12 10 3 4 8 4 8	352 178 19 60 1,604 2,979 312 207 192 251 413 215 76 1,869	49 36 16 17 355 708 88 67 48 50 60 405 71 45 48 18 433	40 29 22 229 547 77 62 63 5* 42 89 72 40 47 20 28 3,230	21 28 14 18 6 100 256 32 25 16 27 33 22 18 13 13 132 1,325	63 38 24 20 20 2 2 345 398 56 37 22 28 47 69 55 47 69 55 249	124 124 97 56 19 67 1,089 118 97 104 156 163 149 97 55 14 690	60 50 47 23 392 834 113 7% 59 62 11, 130 81 42 57 21 504
passe and over- pure road out of the pure road out out of the pure road out out out of the pure road out out out of the pure road out	08 458 9% 124 96 94, 123 129 109 103 74 27 27 23 29 20 20 20 20 20 20 20 20 20 20 20 20 20	22 22 29 29 20 328 28 23 33 28 23 36 61 44 8 27 21 14 8 20 7	100 58 33 435 873 76 78 58 59 45 99 1.9 1.2 95 29 572 3,200	77 46 43 8 290 753 123 65 54 98 102 81 61 34 9 432 2,310	61 32 30 8 322 578 58 52 50 41 97 24 61 33 27 15 336 1,710	91 52 476 1,09 160 117 118 102 88 114 126 80 61 42 10 519	73 50 52 22 382 868 404 (77 76 51 56 404 07 79 27 79 27 75 57	92 36 45 10 78 78 2 66 94 77 73 72 66 66 97 81 31 32 4.1	51 57; 39; 23 442 164 122 13, 66 53 113 69 67 49 23 543	9 255 243 78 34 33 49 81 73 42 22 24 12 37 1,765	18 9 14 2 118 231 20 27 21 15 15 44 33 26 9 10 134 1 800 15	10 7 6 1 47 6 6 9 3 1 1 12 10 3 48 48 48 48 48 48 48	352 178 60 1,604 2,979 342 207 192 251 413 426 331 215 76 1,869 4,410	49 36 17 395 708 88 67 48 60 60 60 94 71 48 18 43 33	40 29 22 229 547 77 62 63 55 42 89 72 20 28 3,230	21 28 14 14 18 5 120 256 39 26 32 25 16 27 27 33 22 18 13 13 13 13 13 13 13 13 13 13 13 13 13	63 38 24 24 25 398 56 377 22 28 47 69 55 40 29 27 249 3,095 483	124 124 27 56 19 67 1,089 116 97 104 126 163 149 97 104 155 163 149 690 3 100	61 51 47 23 392 834 130 62 11 130 81 42 59 21 504
years and over pum reed over female all ages 60 Years 60 Years 10 Years	08 475 468 976 979 98 979 48 1239 1037 74 1239 1037 74 239 3,000	22 22 29 29 20 31 28 23 33 61 42 22 21 14 8 20 7 3,495	100 58 23 435 873 76 78 55 9 43 95 95 29 572 3,200	77 46 43 8 290 773 123 65 54 98 102 81 102 9 432 2,310	61 32 30 8 322 578 58 52 50 41 97 74 61 33 27 71 15 336 1,710 140 345 265	91 52 43 20 476 1,03 117 118 102 88 114 126 80 61 142 116 519 3,270 870 905 405	73 50 52 25 382 868 04 77 56 10 76 76 76 77 76 77 76 77 75 77 75 77	92 36 45 5 10 78 78 77 72 66 94 73 65 94 41 2,240 275 515 3353	51 57; 39; 23 442 42, 42, 43, 43, 43, 43, 43, 43, 44, 43, 43	9 255 343 78 34 33 45 49 81 73 42 24 12 24 12 37 37 50 295	18 9 14 2 118 23 118 23 15 15 15 15 15 15 15 15 15 15 15 15 15	10 7 6 1 47 6 6 9 3 1 1 12 10 3 48 48 48 48 48 48 48	352 178 60 1,604 2,979 342 207 192 251 413 426 331 215 76 1,869 4,410	49 36 17 395 708 88 67 48 60 60 60 94 71 48 18 43 33	40 29 22 229 547 77 62 63 55 42 89 72 20 28 3,230	21 28 14 14 18 6 120 256 39 26 32 25 16 27 33 22 18 13 21 13 22 13 25 25 25 26 27 25 25 25 25 25 25 25 25 25 25	63 38 24 24 25 398 56 377 22 28 47 69 55 40 29 27 249 3,095 483	124 124 27 56 19 67 1,089 116 97 104 126 163 149 97 104 155 163 149 690 3 100	61 51 47 23 392 834 113 74 74 75 9 62 11,30 81 42 59 21 504
pages and over gener and deep fees 5 vans 66 5 vans 10 14 vans 10 18 vans	08 458 9% 124 9% 9% 129 139 149 129 129 139 149 129 139 149 149 149 149 149 149 149 149 149 14	22 22 29 -01, 328 33 28 23 39 6 6 23 24 22 21 14 8 8 20,7 3,495 30 390 40 23 40 40 40 40 40 40 40 40 40 40 40 40 40	100 38 33 435 473 76 78 35 59 45 98 12 84 95 772 3,200 285 550 250 250 270	77 46 43 8 790 753 123 63 65 54 98 102 81 61 34 9 432 2,310	61 32 30 8 322 578 50 52 50 41 97 % 61 33 27 15 336 1,710 140 345 115 140	91 52 43 20 476 1,009 117 118 102 88 114 136 80 142 142 142 142 709 705 705 403 237	73 50 52 25 382 868 04 77 56 10 76 76 76 77 76 77 76 77 75 77 75 77	92 36 45 100 08 787 73 72 66 94 97 97 97 97 97 97 97 97 97 97 97 97 97	51, 57, 39, 23, 442, 4,064, 164, 122, 43, 43, 43, 43, 43, 43, 43, 43, 44, 43, 43	9 255 243 78 54 33 45 49 81 73 42 32 24 41 22 37 25 25 25 25 25 25 25 25 25 25 25 25 25	18 9 14 2 118 231 20 27 21 15 16 6 44 33 26 9 10 134 1 800 2 7 5 8 5 2 30	10 7 6 1 47 6 6 7 12 10 3 4 4 13 48 3,030 32 430 430 53 53 53 53 53 53 53 53 53 53	352 178 19 60 1,604 2,979 312 207 192 251 413 426 331 216 76 1,869 4,410 443 1,465 705 223 223	49, 396, 109, 396, 109, 396, 396, 396, 396, 396, 396, 396, 39	40 29 22 22 547 62 63 63 72 40 17 20 28 3,230 780 635 60 185	21 28 14 14 16 100 256 32 25 26 32 27 33 22 13 13 25 13 25 13 27 33 21 13 25 13 25 13 27 33 21 13 25 16 17 18 18 18 18 18 18 18 18 18 18	63 38 22 20 245 398 56 37 722 28 47 69 55 40 29 29 249 3,095 485 -,120 765 420 335	124 124 277 56 19 67 1,089 116 99 104 156 163 149 57 55 14 690 3 105 3 105	613 513 613 3922 834 413 595 622 111 130 211 150 211 122 211 223 122 202
years and over pure rend out of the control of the	08 458 9% 124 9% 9% 129 139 149 129 129 139 149 129 139 149 149 149 149 149 149 149 149 149 14	22 22 22 23 32 33 36 61 42 27 14 8 207 3,495 30 390 40 230 325 8,15	100 38 435 473 473 473 475 478 58 59 45 478 11.2 84 84 84 87 87 87 87 87 87 87 87 87 87	77 46 43 8 290 7733 123 63 65 54 65 102 61 34 122 2,316 17 1 243 425 12 20 130 130 130 130 130 130 130 130 130 13	61 32 30 8 322 578 52 52 50 41 97 24 53 27 71 15 336 1,710	91 52 43 20 476 1,009 117 118 102 88 80 114 126 519 3,270 601 705 705 403 237 237 237 237	73 59 52 225 3858 404 77 76 77 77 75 77 55 77 55 77 52 220 220 220	92 36 45 10 78 73 72 72 72 73 73 73 73 73 74 75 75 75 75 75 75 75 75 75 75	51 57, 39, 23 442 4,064 164 125 85, 86, 62, 49, 49, 23, 54, 54, 64, 65, 66, 67, 68, 69, 69, 69, 69, 69, 69, 69, 69	9 255 243 78 34 33 45 45 45 45 42 22 4 12 22 4 12 29 295 295 295 295 295	18 9 14 2 118 231 20 27 21 15 16 44 33 32 26 9 10 134 15 150 275 85 230 57-235	10 7 6 1 47 6 6 9 3 1 1 1 2 10 3 4 4 8 4 3 4 3 4 3 4 3 4 3 4 5 6 6 9 9 9 9 9 9 9 9 9 9 9 9 9	352 178 60 1,604 2,979 312 207 192 251 413 426 331 215 769 1,869 4,410 445 1,465 225 285 433 330	49 36 12 395 608 88 607 48 60 605 94 71 45 48 18 433 4,025 420 605 605 605 605 605	40 29 22 27 547 77 62 63 63 72 40 28 40 28 3,230 780 635 60 185 193 30 205	21 28 14 18 100 256 32 25 16 32 27 33 22 18 13 132 132 132 132 132 132 132	63 38 22 20 20 21 245 378 56 377 22 28 47 69 39 29 249 3,095 488 -,120 765 420 333 450 450 450 450 450 450 450 450	124 124 277 56 19 67 1,089 116 27 104 125 163 149 27 55 14 690 3 102 45 685 275 385 275 302 400 290 290 200 200 200 200 200 200 200 2	65: 55: 4" 4" 22: 39: 633 41: 13: 65: 65: 65: 65: 65: 65: 65: 65: 65: 65
years and over peer ned one female all ages dee 5 vaurs 5 9 years 10 19 vaurs	25 25 25 25 25 25 25 25 25 25 25 25 25 2	22 22 9 9 9 10 10 10 10 10 10 10 10 10 10 10 10 10	100 38 33 435 873 76 78 55 59 45 45 45 47 97 572 3,200 250 250 250 250 250 250 250 250 250	77 46 43 8 790 753 123 1 65 5 54 65 65 65 102 81 102 102 102 102 102 102 102 102 102 10	61 32 30 8 322 578 52 52 50 41 97 24 61 33 27 15 336 1,710 140 345 140 290 210 290 290 85	91 52 43 20 476 1,03 160 116 102 88 114 126 61 62 10 519 3,270 705 705 705 705 705 705 705 705 705 7	73 59 59 59 59 59 59 59 59 59 59 59 59 59	92 36 45 100 78 78 77 72 26 66 99 4.1 2,740 275 515 285 285 285 285 385 285 385 385 385 385 385 385 385 3	51 57, 39, 23 442 4,064 164 125 85, 86, 62, 49, 49, 23, 54, 54, 64, 65, 66, 67, 68, 69, 69, 69, 69, 69, 69, 69, 69	9 255 243 78 34 33 45 45 45 45 42 22 4 12 22 4 12 29 295 295 295 295 295	18 9 14 2 118 231 20 27 27 15 16 44 33 26 9 10 134 15 190 278 27 27 27 27 27 27 27 27 27 27 27 27 27	10 26 66 6 6 6 6 7 11 12 12 10 10 13 14 13 14 15 16 16 16 17 18 19 19 19 19 19 19 19 19 19 19	352 178 19' 60 1,504 312 207 192 251 113 215 216 76 1,869 4,410 4,42 2,705 2,5	4,025 420 695 405 420 695 405 420 695 405 420 695 405 420 695 405 420 695 405 420 695 405 420 695 405 420 695 405 420 695 405 420 695 405 420 695 405 420 695 405 420 695 405 420 695 405 420 695 405 420 695 405 420 695 405 420 695 695 695 695 695 695 695 695 695 695	40 29 22 22 547 557 62 63 557 28 44 47 28 3,230 780 635 635 635 635 635 635 635 635 635 635	21 28 14 18 10 256 256 32 25 16 12 27 33 32 22 18 13 2 25 15 250 190 110 110 220 90 95 5	63 38 22 20 245 348 56 37 22 28 47 69 59 249 3,095 483 -,120 335 450 253 450 253 450 269 37 37 37 37 37 37 37 37 37 37	124 124 277 56 19 67 1,089 116 27 104 125 163 149 27 55 14 690 3 102 45 685 275 385 275 302 400 290 290 200 200 200 200 200 200 200 2	65: 55: 4/2 22: 39: 63: 42: 42: 42: 42: 42: 42: 42: 42: 42: 42
years and over pure need over female: all ages deed 5 vanas 10 14 vanas 10 18	08 458 9% 124 9% 9% 129 139 149 129 129 139 149 129 139 149 149 149 149 149 149 149 149 149 14	22 22 29	100 58 23 435 673 76 78 78 78 78 78 78 78 78 78 78	77 46 43 8 290 7733 123 63 65 54 65 102 61 34 122 2,316 17 1 243 425 12 20 130 130 130 130 130 130 130 130 130 13	61 32 30 8 322 578 52 50 50 41 97 41 97 15 336 1,710 140 343 285 115 140 290 210 85 95	91 52 43 20 476 1,009 117 118 102 88 114 136 80 142 142 142 142 709 705 705 403 237	73 59 52 225 3858 404 77 76 77 77 75 77 55 77 55 77 52 220 220 220	92 36 45 10 78 78 72 66 94 97 81 34 2,240 275 515 383 290 133 290	51 57; 39; 23; 442 2,064 164. 122 35; 36; 37; 49; 23; 49; 23; 49; 24; 25; 26; 27; 36; 37; 36; 37; 36; 37; 36; 37; 37; 38; 38; 38; 38; 38; 38; 38; 38	9 255 243 78 34 45 45 45 45 42 32 24 12 3C	18 9 14 2 118 231 200 277 22 15 15 44 33 26 6 19 10 134 15 150 275 285 285 285 285 285 285 285 285 285 28	10 76 6 147 C3 147 C3 148 149 149 149 149 149 149 149 149 149 149	352 178 19' 1604 2,979' 342 207 192 251 311 213 213 216 66 1,869 4,410 4,410 445 1,465 225 285 330 330 330 330 330 330 330 330 330 33	4,025 420 420 420 420 420 420 420 420 420 420	40 29 9 1 2 2 2 2 2 2 2 2 2 2 2 2 2 2 2 2	211 288 4 120 256 32 25 16 27 33 22 25 18 13 3 132 25 18 10 110 25 26 27 33 22 18 113 22 18 113 25 25 25 25 25 25 25 25 25 25 25 25 25	63 38 24 20 24 39 56 67 27 22 8 47 69 55 40 29 1,20 24 3,95 420 3,95 420 3,95 420 3,95 420 3,95 420 420 420 420 420 420 420 420 420 420	124 124 97 56 19 67 1,089 97 104 196 163 149 97 55 14 690 3 102 45 685 325 325 325 325 325 325 325 325 325 32	6.55 42 39:63 63 63 63 64 77 77 75 64 65 75 22 2,111 133 142 200 33 33 112 200 33 112 200 33 112 200 34 34 35 36 36 36 36 36 36 36 36 36 36 36 36 36
years and over pure need one feet 5 venue feet 5 venue to 14 venue to 15 venue to 15 venue to 15 venue to 15 venue to 16 venue venue to 16 venue ve	28 468 976 124 129 129 129 129 129 129 129 129 129 129	22 22 9 9 9 9 9 9 9 9 9 9 9 9 9 9 9 9 9	100 38 435 435 46 76 78 58 58 58 58 58 58 58 58 58 5	77 46 49 29 290 733 123 65 74 75 74 75 74 75 74 75 75 75 75 75 75 75 75 75 75 75 75 75	61 32 30 8 322 578 52 52 50 41 97 24 61 33 27 15 336 1,710 140 345 140 290 210 290 290 85	91 52 43 20 476 1,09 116 117 118 88 114 126 80 61 61 61 61 70 70 70 70 70 70 70 70 70 70 70 70 70	73 59 59 59 59 59 59 59 59 59 59 59 59 59	92 36 45 10 08 76 73 73 73 73 73 73 73 73 73 73	51 57, 39, 23 442 4,064 164 125 85, 86, 62, 49, 49, 23, 54, 54, 64, 65, 66, 67, 68, 69, 69, 69, 69, 69, 69, 69, 69	9 255 243 78 34 45 45 45 45 45 45 45 45 45 45 45 45 45	18 9 14 2 118 231 200 27 21 15 15 44 33 26 9 10 134 15 159 159 159 159 159 159 159 159 159	10 26 66 6 6 6 6 7 11 12 12 10 10 13 14 13 14 15 16 16 17 18 19 19 19 19 19 19 19 19 19 19	352 178 19' 60 1,604 2,979 312 207 192 251 11 213 215 66 1,869 4,410 443 1,465 705 228 431 1,465 705 228 431 310 1,609	4,025	40 29 22 22 547 62 63 54 46 17 28 17 28 18 63 63 63 63 63 63 63 63 63 63 63 63 63	21 28 14 18 10 256 256 32 25 16 12 27 33 32 22 18 13 2 25 15 250 190 110 110 220 90 95 5	63 38 22 20 245 348 56 37 22 28 47 69 59 249 3,095 483 -,120 335 450 253 450 253 450 269 37 37 37 37 37 37 37 37 37 37	124 124 97 56 19 67 1,089 116 97 104 156 163 149 67 3 105 45 469 469 47 47 48 48 48 48 48 48 48 48 48 48 48 48 48	6.55 42 39:63 63 63 63 64 77 77 75 64 65 75 22 2,111 133 142 200 33 33 112 200 33 112 200 33 112 200 34 34 35 36 36 36 36 36 36 36 36 36 36 36 36 36
passe and over- pure road over	28 468 976 124 129 129 129 129 129 129 129 129 129 129	22 22 9 9 9 9 9 9 9 9 9 9 9 9 9 9 9 9 9	100 100	77 46 49 29 290 733 123 65 74 75 74 75 74 75 74 75 75 75 75 75 75 75 75 75 75 75 75 75	61 122 36 8 8 22 578 7 9 9 15 15 15 15 15 15 17 10 10 11 14 10 12 12 12 12 13 14 14 14 15 16 16 16 17 17 18 18 18 18 18 18 18 18 18 18 18 18 18	91	73 50 73 82 23 86 88 80 80 77 70 11 557 70 12 11 70 70 12 12 12 12 12 12 12 12 12 12 12 12 12	92 34 45 100 78° 78° 78° 79° 79° 79° 79° 79° 79° 79° 79° 79° 79	51 157 399 23 399 249 249 249 249 259 259 259 259 259 259 259 259 259 25	9 255 243 78 24 24 24 12 3C 24 24 12 3C 255 190 160 175 75 5 5 5 5 5 5 5 5 5 5 5 5 5 5 5 5	18 9 14 12 118 231 231 250 27 12 15 16 44 45 33 26 6 7 10 12 45 15 15 15 15 15 15 15 15 15 15 15 15 15	10 2 6 6 1 4 7 6 5 6 6 0 3 3 1 1 4 1 1 2 1 2 1 2 1 2 1 2 1 2 2 6 0 2 2 5 6 5 5 5 7 7 7 2 0 6 0 6 1 2 1 2 1 2 1 2 1 2 1 2 1 2 1 2 1 2 1	352 178 19 19 19 19 19 2,979 312 207 192 207 192 213 213 213 213 213 213 213 213 213 21	36 177 368 88 877 48 60 00 00 00 00 00 00 00 00 00 00 00 00	40 299 547 77 22 200 547 42 42 42 42 42 42 42 42 42 42 42 42 42	211 288 14 18 6 1200 256 39 26 25 16 39 26 27 33 32 22 18 13 3 22 18 13 3 22 18 13 3 22 18 13 23 25 16 25 16 25 16 25 16 25 16 25 16 25 16 25 16 25 16 25 16 25 16 25 16 25 16 25 16 26 16 26 16 26 16 26 16 16 16 16 16 16 16 16 16 16 16 16 16	63 38'8 24'20'0'4'4'34'8'34'8'34'8'34'8'34'8'34'8'34	124 124 127 56 19 67 1,089 110 126 136 149 97 144 690 3 105 445 683 383 323 323 323 400 400 400 400 400 400 400 400 400 40	61) 51 52 52 634 64 64 65 65 65 66 66 66 66 66 66 66 66 66 66
passes and over- puers and any	08 45 468 976 124 468 976 127 127 127 127 127 127 127 127 127 127	22 22 9 9 21 22 23 33 32 61 42 2 27 11 14 42 2 27 7 30 30 32 5 5 5 5 5 5 5 5 5 5 5 5 5 5 5 5 5 5	100 38 9 5 5 5 5 6 6 7 6 8 5 5 9 9 1.2 6 64 5 78 8 8 5 9 9 1.2 28 28 7 29 7 20 280 20 20 280 20 280 2	774 46 43 3 590 753 123 65 65 4 98 18 11 11 11 11 11 11 11 11 11 11 11 11	61 122 378 322 376 61 32 32 350 41 97 74 15 334 32 32 32 32 32 32 32 32 32 32 32 32 32	91 32 32 32 32 32 32 32 32 32 32 32 32 32	79 5 5 5 7 6 6 6 6 7 7 7 8 6 6 7 7 7 8 6 7 7 7 8 7 7 8 7 7 8 7 8	92 34 5 1 1 1 1 1 1 1 1 1 1 1 1 1 1 1 1 1 1	20 20 20 20 20 20 20 20 20 20 20 20 20 2	9 9 255 243 78 44 24 24 24 24 24 24 25 25 25 25 26 26 26 26 26 26 26 26 26 26 26 26 26	18 9 9 9 14 2 12 12 12 12 12 12 12 12 12 12 12 12 1	10 2 6 6 1 47 47 45 6 6 0 3 3 1 1 4 1 12 12 12 12 12 12 12 12 12 12 12 12 1	352 178 19 60 1,604 2,979 312 207 192 2251 413 216 66 67 61,869 4,410 443 1,465 225 231 170 205 170 207 215 215 215 215 215 215 215 215 215 215	4,025 420,000 400,000	40 299 547 77 62 547 62 59 78 79 79 79 79 79 79 79 79 79 79 79 79 79	211 288 14 16 120 256 39 26 32 25 16 17 37 33 32 21 18 13 21 25 25 25 25 25 25 25 25 25 25 25 25 25	63 38: 22 200 2 2 39: 39: 39: 39: 39: 39: 39: 39: 39: 39:	124 124 97 56 19 67 1,089 118 97 104 136 69 15 69 3 3 109 25 5 5 5 5 5 5 6 7 7 8 6 9 7 7 8 9 7 8 9 7 8 9 7 8 9 8 9 8 9 8 9	600 500 500 600 600 600 600 600 600 600
James and over pears and now pears to 34 years to 34 years to 34 years to 44 years to 44 years to 45 years to 47 years years and over years below to years	08 45 46 46 46 46 46 46 46 46 46 46 46 46 46	22 22 9 9 10 1 28 8 25 2 26 1 28 8 25 2 2 2 2 2 2 2 2 2 2 2 2 2 2 2 2	100 38 38 39 23 34 425 673 76 78 83 59 94 11.2 84 95 77 29 572 225 530 260 270 260 270 270 270 270 270 270 270 270 270 27	77 46 43 3 3 590 753 123 123 123 123 123 123 123 123 123 12	61 122 578 30 32 578 52 52 52 52 52 52 52 52 52 52 52 52 52	91, 43 43 476 476 476 476 476 476 476 476 476 476	79 9 9 9 9 9 9 9 9 9 9 9 9 9 9 9 9 9 9	92 34 45 45 45 45 45 45 45 45 45 45 45 45 45	21 37 39 22 31 32 32 32 32 32 32 32 32 32 32 32 32 32	9 9 255 543 784 53 342 543 9 81 12 22 5 19 9 9 9 9 1 12 25 19 9 9 9 9 1 12 25 19 9 9 9 9 9 9 9 9 9 9 9 9 9 9 9 9 9 9	18 9 9 9 14 14 15 15 15 15 15 15 15 15 15 15 15 15 15	10 2 6 6 1 47 C5 6 6 6 3 1 1 1 4 1 1 1 2 1 1 2 1 1 2 1 1 2 1 2 1	352 178 19 19 19 19 19 2,979 31 12 207 19 22 251 11 21 31 31 31 31 31 31 31 31 31 31 31 31 31	4,025 4,025	40 299 547 77 229 547 762 653 546 789 782 46 77 281 195 195 140 195 195 195 195 195 195 195 195 195 195	21 28 14 16 170 256 29 22 23 22 23 23 22 23 23 24 25 26 27 28 29 29 20 21 21 21 21 21 21 21 21 21 21	63 38:22 20:22 24:34:53 39:83 56:93 72:22 28:84 47:69 69:55 40:29 40	124 124 127 56 10 67 11 116 97 104 115 69 97 107 115 69 97 107 115 69 69 107 115 69 107 115 69 107 115 69 107 115 69 107 107 107 107 107 107 107 107 107 107	613 513 3993 3993 3993 3993 3993 4211 5904 1130 1231 1221 1221 1221 1221 1221 1221
peers and door Female all ages older 5 vouss to 19 veass to 18 veass peers of the completed peers of the veass to 18 veass to 28 veass to 38 veass to 38 veass to 38 veass to 38 veass to 18 veass to 38 veass to 18 veass to 28 veass to 18 veass to 28	08 45 468 976 124 468 976 127 127 127 127 127 127 127 127 127 127	22 22 9 9 21 22 23 33 32 61 42 2 27 11 14 42 2 27 7 30 30 32 5 5 5 5 5 5 5 5 5 5 5 5 5 5 5 5 5 5	100 38 9 5 5 5 5 6 6 7 6 8 5 5 9 9 1.2 6 64 5 78 8 8 5 9 9 1.2 28 28 7 29 7 20 280 20 20 280 20 280 2	774 46 43 3 590 753 123 65 65 4 98 18 11 11 11 11 11 11 11 11 11 11 11 11	61 122 378 322 376 61 32 32 350 41 97 74 15 334 32 32 32 32 32 32 32 32 32 32 32 32 32	91 32 32 32 32 32 32 32 32 32 32 32 32 32	79 5 5 5 7 6 6 6 6 7 7 7 8 6 6 7 7 7 8 6 7 7 7 8 7 7 8 7 7 8 7 8	92 34 5 1 1 1 1 1 1 1 1 1 1 1 1 1 1 1 1 1 1	20 20 20 20 20 20 20 20 20 20 20 20 20 2	9 9 255 243 78 42 432 24 12 2 2 2 2 2 2 2 2 2 2 2 2 2 2 2 2	18 9 9 9 14 2 12 12 12 12 12 12 12 12 12 12 12 12 1	10 2 6 6 1 47 47 45 6 6 0 3 3 1 1 4 1 12 12 12 12 12 12 12 12 12 12 12 12 1	352 178 19 60 1,604 2,979 312 207 192 2251 413 216 66 67 61,869 4,410 443 1,465 225 231 170 205 170 207 215 215 215 215 215 215 215 215 215 215	42, 309 42, 509 42, 509 42, 509 43, 605 420 700 74	40 299 547 77 77 62 63 54 78 72 72 84 19 72 72 84 19 72 72 85 195 56 635 56 635 56 635 56 635 56 635 56 635 64 78 78 78 78 78 78 78 78 78 78 78 78 78	211 288 14 16 120 256 39 26 32 25 16 17 37 33 32 21 18 13 21 25 25 25 25 25 25 25 25 25 25 25 25 25	63 38: 22 200 2 2 39: 39: 39: 39: 39: 39: 39: 39: 39: 39:	134 124 127 56 129 129 129 120 120 120 120 120 120 120 120 120 120	61 51 47 23 392 834 130 62 11 130 81 42 59 21 504

Table 39 —FCONOMIC CHARACTERISTICS OF THE POPULATION BY SEX, FOR LABAN PLACES OF 2.500 TO 10,000 1950

[Asterias *] deno o. *laticus casos on Meperen samp. Manach not bown worse cost is ess fluo 500?

	7	-	-	TOTAL PROPERTY.	-	District on Local	-	-	-	-	Dark below		TOTAL PROPERTY.		-	-	-
Suoject	ville	Am' e Sity	Be	•	Po at	Coving-	10	2. y	PL.	E C	L-1 12	7-r	112	A . 1.79	o war	D. Aft.	
EMPLOYMENT STATUS		100					-	3.5	10	-		i					-
Maie 14 years old and ove	3 400	770	J. 3	- 48	4.	4.54	- 434		. 2:	2251	é	16.4	24	w 21	a 624	29.	
bur force	4,2	691	700	2. 4.	6.9	. 14	2.8	. 30	4140	37	2,90	Raf.	4.742	77,	200	-	_
Employed	824	-91	43	*1 .		4	41-18	Lalue		3"	2.1	198	07	7-2	2,035	10-12	
Private wage and salary workers	7.864	407		7.0	945	- 14	B-3	د قد ١	3.	37	- 38	2 8	- 100	720	- RaC	1,6 0	
Covernment works o	276	6"	-1		2	-6	73	77.	70.	7,1	- 28	70	240		1	78.	
belf-employed workers paid am ly worke s	88	1.53	-11			2.30	301	77.	2.9	. 4	= 1	1.5	2401	5	.5	20.1	
Lremployed	1 _73	22	60	nn.		33	3.1		-		. 75	4.1		46	1,3"	31	
t a laber force	1 4.4	2.39	18	46	227	+86	~7	257	5-	340	044	2301	26		84	- C /	
Ferrale 14 sars old and over	2 500	-,104	89.	1 775	+ 644	- 1 hu	4 11	1 7	4 -, 2	642	2,5 . 1	449	2 1	13.	2 0-1	اوتيو	1
bor for e Civilian labor force.	روم ا	334 3 2		4.2	25.	4+26.1	26		54-		757	4.58	674	0	5	- 44-	
	846	330	7,5	. 4	25"	- 30	26		501	42	70	43 4	6.48.		447	- 4.	
Private wage and salary worker	50	416 '1	1	306	- Free	-94)	£4"	2.81	34	48:1	5'1!	3. 1	423	ãc	-21	722	
Government v.rkers Sed-employed workers	89	42	21	.8	45 29	70	-1	32		621	56°	36	30	2.	25	2 '	
Unpaid amily workers	-2			40	4	44	13	24		401	321	30		1			
Uneraployed	2 584		. 4	.,295	.31			_4	6.1	24	42	14	26	2	34	-3	
	2 384	772	~2	.,295	~6→	. 4.7	- 222	830	,6.7	- 2,8	- 16	Jul	- 50	200	2 -	2 -2.	
MAJOR OCCUPATI IN GROUP			*******						1	- 1		- 1	i	1		r	
Male employed	2 74_	J69	(25)	2,172	5+6	1 0	1 /2	.082	,20	1825	53.,	0'1	1 60	76	<u>. ^36</u>	4,853	_
ressons wechnical and kindred workers	174	-	20	6_	24 5)	4	16	60	1 .	80	* '	28	74 4	22	40	1.5	
mer. s. id farm managers magers, officials and proprietors except fare real and kindred workers	276	2.7 4.4	7C"	82	95	3	د ،	-28	_9.	.0	234	**:31	2.7	91	13	26.	
real and kindred workers	245	4.		7-	29	4 -	54,	43	5-	66	137	3	5.2	- 4	64	9c.	
	3-	49	-02	206	06	-2	231	756	30.1	-63	3.4		25	رنے 83	-46	162,	
atives and kindred worken.	34.5	122	-45	224	-0.	237	3091	3.2	22 1	16:	452-	43	25	260	72	22	
rate household workers	1	4.5	43	70	23		77	20	57	1	6.	-3	7		75 6 123		
n. laboreta a. d foremea	-05	9		2_	2	90	771	2.		2	-35	-3	1.7		123	1 2	
ore.s, except are and nune	57	70	1.76	2± 131	93	152	201	.66	250	70	328 67	202	2	-8-	466	253	
	1000	14	2	30	-0		1	26	24	-	67	4,5	7	2	2-	7.0	
remain employed	B46	3,£C	.42	-13	237	44	20.	30p	5-5		2.3	424,	640	1-1	-7	-0.6	-
fessional technical and kindred workers mers and farm managers	217	344	10	٣.	40 2	09	43	4	86	6.1	4	40	94	d	ت	-5-	
nagers officials, and proprietors except farm . real and kindred workers	-1	12	-2	2.		26		2-	26	51	4.	15	-2		20	26	
rical and kindred workers	-4- 90	42 02 38	25	25 75 43	29 22		30	24 49 50	24	77	7,		36	7	F1	2.5	
es workers	80		1	43	22	42	-	20	7.	23 !	9.	25,	3,	25	5	84	
of workers of the foremen and kindred workers ors wes and undred workers	52	27	1,7	-08	8	ž	43	-2	3.1	261	1	di.	ال	-	- 2	051	
	206	40	17	-08	62	1.2	43	-		51	222	1.1	3	- 4	1 1	134	
me workers excep private nousehod.	1.38		- 32	6.	4."	174	.39	n5	90	51	5,	:	442		.35	*2	
boro.s, except arr and mine		2		2	- 0	4	2	2	9	2 2	-:		4	2	5	36 ±6	
rupauor not reported	-	. 2	+4	÷ .	2	أسه		14	7	8	3 %	4	4	4	4		
MAJOR INDUSTRY GROUP	1 !			100				1		- 1		- 1				3.2	
Male employed	2,041	669	63.	1,072	643	_,125	+1 58	,083	-130	96 -	- 607	6.9	1,600	720	1 8,00	1 006	
niculture, foresity, and nahe.ies	118	30	133 102	52	6	4-	225	9 67 48 25	='	4-1	-	02	4.	-05 -54	1	1.5	
ast uotion	196 265	-2	£8.	460	22	15%	1"-	46	24 1	-26	2:24	. 3	d'a.	22 53 -20	76.3 74	16 -05 2-2	
nufacturing	236	150	TC.	400	40	125	1"-	247	14 i	.0.,	344	-7-	334 39	22		24.9	
anaporta' on commun., and other puole util	246 227 44	49 178	1.1	126	23	55	700	5		2-2	13.	-44 493	334	-20	29- 29- 67- 67-	-77 486	
carce insurance, and real estate	44	1.3	2 '	24	2.50 -4 55 42	28		-4	275	64	45.7		39	3	2:	486 50 -0 97	
sinus and repair services	78 PC -	28	9 20	é	55	39	2	38	23	48 40	95	33	23	11	67	97	
ter summent and recreation services	95				. 5	36	21	38 37 20 29	73		+1	10	15 72	11		2	
ofessional and related services	95 146	-5 40	3	39 33 28	25 %	700	2:	37	55	27	50	.0	72 51	1,	9.0	257	
instry not reported	54	24	3	24	3	27	-1	20	-9	20	07		8	25	27	2.	
Female employed	346	0دد	144		237	404	261	336	545	401		421	644	11.	497		
	P	9		2	2			1	1		-	6	7		1	30	
nung nung netruction	1 1	,	2		1.0	1 -	3	-	ī	31	د	1	5 2		1	-	
netruction	5	3.2 8	25-	3		1.3	82	-	٥.,	11	2	1	2		18	2	
and other public util	300	8	2½ 4	-10	7	10	5	27	41	16	17	1.0 1.0	3.	8 7 34	15	56 7_	
holesale and e-asi tract nance, 'ns mance and real estate _	205	80	53	710	80	130	8.	112	10	-C2-	26	1-0	176	34	157	- 231	1
Biness and reps. " services	13	1:	2	19	2		2	4	29		9	2	14	1	.2	30	l
rsonal services.	275	89	24	1 1 6 21	70	1,16	<i>J</i> 6	69	:55	95	26_	148	412	22			
teriainment and recreation services	12	64	19	21	*	-15	1	6. 5	ئ _ى .	4 81	75	67	107 25	6	52	248	1
ohe administration	38	34	- /	2	57	-9	5 7	5	26	24	4	n	25	3	6	26	1
ust~ no* reported	33	4	12	-0	4	16	7	12	8	-	25		6	7	3	_3	1
*INCOME IN 1949	1							13						-			1
Total families and unrefated individuals	2,900		745	1 525	820	1,70	1,300	.,275	1 *95	~,175	2,640	1,19	4,075	r_0		3 095	
e than \$200	605 395	125	65	172	130	76C 165	105	105	200	230 230	303 390	290	190	45	2.5	20°	1
0 to \$999	33.	90	85	200	1.5	165	.70	1,4	2.5	1951	325	235	2>5	25	E30	397	
000 to \$1,499 500 to \$1 999	243	145	55	170	80	22,	175	145	.80	100	280	35	235	6.	337	230	
000 to \$2 409	243	93 65	60	170 120 130	\$0 ±00 45	90	160	140	.45	95	245 185	65	7.80	70	290	210	al .
500 to \$2 000	دند ا	70	10	130	50 50	70	100	1.5	.80 .95 .30 .15	45 70 45	145	35 63 30 35 40	17-	25 67 70 25 40 50	195	190	
500 to 8\$ 999	125	7^ 40 30	4C 75	90	0	45	85 55 35	1,5 -30	05	40	145	55	110	*0	8:	90	al .
500 to \$8 999 000 to 94,499 500 to \$4 999	85	30	75 20	0.5	20 10	40	44	65 70	80 40	1 5U	80	40	-10 e0	30	1 60	80	5
	1.0	23	45	85	10	55	70 23	95	40 40 30	35 30 5	85	3L 45	15	7.5	60	55	5
,000 to \$6 999 ,000 to \$9 989	80	1 40	45	20	2	55 20	25	35 35	30	5	35	70	65	20	1 45	si sr	,
.000 to \$9.999	75	25	30	2.	10	30	_0	25	40	20	40	15	70	1:		1 30	5
Old and over							1 2		65	9	80	75	70	65		18.	1
,060 and overome not reported	1 20	40	و.	70	35	185	22	25	0.	45	ou	12	70	0.2	7-	160	4
		35	30					ئد ا			2	15	15	1 12	-0	30	1

Table 39—ECONOMIC CHARACTERISTICS OF THE POPULATION, BY SPX, FOR URBAN PLACES OF 2,500 TO 10,000 1950—Con Aniczak (* denoces standous cased on 20-percent sample Medium not above where base is less than 500]

	Anternak (denote 	6

Statusti	a nesed o	n 20-per	cent sam;	ple Mee	iun not s	pown wp	ere base	IS THE TES	in 500)		-	-		
Subject	Haynes- v.lle	-lone-	Jankson	Jess- erettë	Jen- Lugs	Jones- bore	-splan	Kenner	Ake Artsur	Lake Provi- dence	Lees-	Mans- ixeld	Maple- Wood (un.no.)	Marks- v_lle	Minden	Morgan	Natohi-
MPLOYMENT STATUS																	
Male, 14 years and and over	1 417	1,585	3 1-7	1,587	3,005	1,034	1,528	1 882	978	1,351	, 53°	1,420	780	1,211	3 239	3 293	3 344
Caylian augr force	911 315	1,246	450 455	1,191	2,275	782 780	1 073	1,570	523 523	898 898	1,065	1,070	776	850	2,420	2,659	2,006
Emptoved Private v age and salary no kers	875	1,201	150	1,190 1 040 72	1.601	761 533 73 254	958 625	1,5.3	594 452	7°5	1,022	1,039	764 738	765 433	2,301	2 489	1,888
Covernment workers	6.82 44	_20 253	242	72	213 355	73	224	193 139	76	£23 £50	120	75 156	7 18	124 205	306 328	139 459	354 311
angus fam ly wassers	1	5	-7	150	192	15	125	5	29	23	39	30	1	3 85	125	±70	6
Vount short force	40 201	339	2,694	396	690	252	46>	31,2	355	453	472	3.6	86	359	789	634	2,338
Female, 14 years old and over	1 190	1,9:1	3,240	_,752	3,492	1,252	1,688	2,018	990	1,69	1,750	1,804	892 144	± 324	3,796	3,341	4,07
Labor force Civilian labor force	3 s 3 363	614 614	339	456 456	979 978	37C	274	620 619	143 143 143	534 534	450 -60	637	-44	330	1,117	714	1,195
Гтрюмед	350	607 426	3,0 71 2-6	42° 323	941 u59	363 237	254 159	5.9	84	499 323	441 319	521 469	37 99	31.5 20. 85	1803	698 525 70	1,458 C84
Private wage and salary workers. Government workers. belf-employed workers.	51 28	107	2-6	46	151	85 33	26 35	90 24	41	120	88	9± 55	32	85 21	188 93	81	385 76
I npair tamily workers Luemployea	9	1.0	1	2.	94 27 37	8 7	14	83		35	10	1 16	1 7	15	11	22	13
Not in all force	827	1 297	2 901	1,296	2,513	882	1,414	1,398	852	1,102	-,290	1,157	7-8	994	2,679	2 627	2,882
MAJOR OCCUPATION GROUP	8"5	1 201	439	1,040	2~9	701	958	1,513	594	775	1 022	1,039	764	765	2 301	2 489	1,868
Professoral technical and insured workers	n.	1 201	23	49	451	u8	46	2.00	30	87	88	101	-	82	.82	154	223
Professional technical, and incred workers. Farmers and farm managers Manage s, efficials, and proprietors except farm	130	31	.3	15	5 202	150	20	7.52	9	11	7 161	12	5.	35	278	379	24 265
Clercal and kindred workers	47	-5 88	29 1.	32 78	91 175	54	41 72	95 36	25	26 53	60 84	-0	30	44	97 184	108	108
Craftsmen foremen and kindre workers	122 318	20% 3.J	11 8, 91	207	493 495	63 134 154	211	351	133	114	137	.87 21.	170	209 87	477 500	408 702	343 321
Operatives and kindred vorkers Private household workers	318	2	110	2	1		2	288	25	128	90		9	38	9	1 126	6
Service work. s, excep private household - Farm I no ere and foremen	4	207	12 1	49 81	1.1	32	52 51	16	46	29	3	42 20 140		8 109	396	100	28
Laborers except farm and mine Occupation not reported	82 8	-55 11	34 14	143	242	85	201	29£	49	127	204	140	25	139	396	481	210
Female empioyed.	350	607	330	426	941	3(3	264	519	_43	w99	44.	623	1,-	315	1 095	198	1 158
Professional technical and aindred workers Farmers and farm managers	55	7 2	50	45	1.20	62	50	66	25	91	88	94 2 39	41	65 1	15/	84	251
Managers, officials, and propageture except farm	15	26	15 36	10 60	36 208	27 84	25	79	21	44 29 45	78	39 101	4 ∪2 17	9 48	48 177	103	51 189
Sales workers. Craftsmen foremen and kurdred workers	31	64	5	3	-18	84 45 3	-6	51	-8	45	34	101		48 27	₽8 O±	52 6	97
Operatives and kindred workers Private household workers	20	34	0,0	18	239	42 38	25	111	20	16	14	155	2 4 2 4	107	79 35C	108 112	92
Ser ne workers except pr. ate bousehold. Farm laborers and "oremen.	20 31 54	90	200	40	140	56	28	11	2	83	77	731	4	40	146	-3	188
Asborres, except farm and mine Occupation not reported	3	3 7	9	5 24	3	6	2 3	13	2	5		34		1	ر د د	دَد	36
MAJOR INDUSTRY GROUP	1	1	,	24	11		,	9	٥	2	7	34	- 1	5	13	13	,10
Male employed	875	1,901	430	.,040	2,179	761	958	1 513	594	775	1,022	1,039	764	765	2,301	2,489	1,868
Agriculture forestry and fisheries	20	71 173	26 25	112	1_6 304	7	84	29	72	66	21	40 29	31	51	35 156	276 498	72
Construction Manufacturing	82 76	123	35 35	111	249	59	93	238	7. 80 48	128	245	91 313	31. 587	125	260 352	289	243 156 205
Transportation, co.nmun and o he pub s util Whoesale and re all trade.	76 55	261	15	64	2.1	50 215 17 23	65 228	345	62	241	118 245	94 105 32 43 40	18	27 49 217	337	278 463	205
Finance unurance, and salestate .	173	43	25	241 15	51.5 60 98	17	16	234 22 40	3	22- 1, 42	31	32	13	10	60 70	41	498 55 65
Personal services Entertainment and ecreation services	29 47	60 12	19	66 34 17	113	38	32	35	26	61 21	48 13 71	40	8 1 3	42	159	68	127
Professional and rela ed services Public administrat on	6 37	76 43	19 2 214 10 6	33	169	52	36	561	49	26	77	7. 43 43	.1	76	136	51	265
Industry n.st reported	20	11	6	33 25 29	58 20	52 40 9	39	79	40	38 14	73	43	7	51	178	63 15	96 76
Femule, employed	359		3,90	420	241	363	204	559	143	499	41	62_	137	315	, 19:	698	1,158
Agriculture, forestri, and fishenes Mining	7	4	1	5	5		٦	3	3	6	1	3	3	2	3	7	8
Manufacturing	2	13	1	24	11 24	54 9	19	75	3	2 4	1 2	55	1 4b	3	50	95.	14
Transportation, commun. and other public util Wholesale and retail trade	15	33 ;	6 20	12	50 247 30	10.	85	28	48	18	107	55 92 115	46 1 26	3 3	47 223	239	14 36
Finance, insurance and real estate	6	21	. ,		30	10. 10 3	31	-5	4	15	14	22	5	50 3	17	12	221 22 6
Personal se vices. Late tamment and recreation services	. 76	25	40	150	322	72	64	136	34	192	146	209	5	_25	443	157	351
Professional and related services. Public aurumstration	1 66 5	100	2.2	53	191	82	205	120	34	103	168	112	39	79 24	217	17	38"
Industry not reported	5	7	3	25	10	6	7	50	7	30 5	30 6	25	1	24	45	13	55
*INCOME IN 1)49 Total families and unrelated individuals	-,125	1,550	460	1 300	2,905	930	1,405	1, 50	835	1 605		1.500					3 820
Less than \$500	or.	245	40	230		-	240	195	220	280	375		705	1 0/5	2,995	2,925	985
\$500 to \$1 499	95 80 130	255	60	295	2±0 455 365	95 95	280	140	170	290	212	240 175	15	75 170 140	430	230	5/5 320 300
\$1,000 to \$1 499 \$1,5" o to \$1 999_ \$2 000 to \$2 199	130	130	50 40	165	345 290	1.5 85 90 125	175	195	120	120 105 55	170	145	10	120	3 /0 !	215	300
\$2,500 to \$2,999	55 9°	-30 -10	25	80	230	125	75	265	30	55	±05 65	135	15	105 140 70	330	340 295	220 175
\$3 500 to \$3 999 \$4,000 to \$3 999	95	65	25	40	193	85 50	20	130	25 20 20	50 65 45	75	90 90	35 85	40	200	225 140	.50 .50
S=.500 to 31 999	80	35		40 35	155 80	35	20 15	60 50	10	25	65	30	_20 95	40	,15 l	190	65
\$5,000 to \$5,999 \$6,000 to \$6,999	55 75	30	20	40 35	100	90	20	55	. 5	25 30	30 10	75 35	220	40 15	115	170 60 105	113 65 80 105 70
87 030 to \$9 989 \$10,000 and over	30	65	10	10	65	20	15	40	1:	40	10	12	65	30	55 75 45	105	90 45
Income not reported	\$3,020	70 \$1,750	110	10	105	15	25	30 95	35	70	75	180	10	60	125	120	590
and the second s	+5,020	+4,730		\$1,47	\$2,0-3	\$2,572	\$1 241	\$2,200	91 U77	\$99"	\$1,441	#1 917	\$5,014	\$2,314	\$4,959	\$2,438	\$1,286

Table 39.—ECONOMIC CHARACTERISTICS OF THE POPULATION, BY SEX, FOR LYRBAN PLACES OF 2,500 TO 10,000 1950—Con [Asteriak * decodes statuurs consider and the cost warning. Medican not scoped where pine as seen lanc 500.

į.	waterwe .	denotes	RESERVE	s Dassed o	a Al-pa c	en samo	te. Med	an not s	nown whe	are prime in	1 1682 TEST	500		enclas adv			
Subject	New Roads	ocd- ope	DR'zda_e		Pl-q>=-	Tue '28-	T rt	Raym-	Zav.	Referve.	Mar _r-	3	ביין - יו	. 19£-37	"a_l	Thibe-	pla+.e
EMP_OYMENT STATUS Male, 14 years old and over_	859	1,155	.,142	2 228	, 9G.	- 35	4,0	2,103	٠,00٠	,517	1,38	1 252		2 .40	2 36	2,509	2 214
Labor force	652	ero!	1,23	4.40	1 4d	995	850	.,,00		-,004		8 5	972	. 64.	-,962	£, C7	_ 494
Civilian lagor roree Employed	652	912 085	1,356	238	+20	795	23C	- +991	700 1	1, 194	3, 1	27+ 308	972.	. S4C	~,952	4 799	1 495
Private wage and salary workers	/ 09	"00"	1,390	-,01	972	183	5C4	2,000	76c	0,7	2721	587	307	259	629	. 163	- 420
Government workers - Self-employed workers -	.38	4. F.3	264	.7"	165	49	83 (22-	8C	94	172	1.8	9,5	83 -7	250	36	_5C
Unpaid family workers	35		97		-34	- 1		2	5	2	8	5		1		-	8
tot m labor force.	207	242	40	36 688	90 475	356	74 s	1m	82	42	442	403	190	4,0	_33 ²	8c 504	73
Fernale, 14 years old and over	1,004	1 _84	2,00	2, 236	2,210	-,524	1,5	2,3%	-,28-	_ 550	4,6.5	-, 29-	4,226	2,263,	نک ک	4,376	2,438
abor force	263	233	بدة	787	222	502	335	604	4.	232	43.1	293	24.	30€	828	582	498
Civilan labor force Employed	256	232	485	3	522 527 385	501	33-	204	72	222	41	293	291	396	628	688 084	498
Private wage and salary workers	175	61 30	342 84	730 258	385	308	_8	45.	409 84	225	2.9	209	2.4	254	5,8.	463	489 347 85
Private wage and salary workers Government workers Self-employed workers	17	22	51	35	32	14	33	50	28	1.	12	7	200	73 e5	134	51	-6
Unemployed	3	4	28	9	8	3.	25	27	.5	£ 3	12	2	111	12	46	1"	-3
fot m labor force	80,	95.	1 544	1 749	1 668	1 42.	780	- 200	812	1 318	1,199	- 001	975	1 067	2 .37	2,_88	1,940
MA, OR OCCUPATION GROUP		885													1		
Male, employed	247	49	236	1,500	132	72 I	mg se	_,385 ~	662	45	380	80/º	94J 69	90	1,629	1,910	1,420
	00	2	4	6	10	26	55 2	39	S.	8	20	4	1	6	53	4	83 10
fanagers officials, and proprietors except arm lerves and kindred workers	10.	73 2 1	148 5c 8'	107	2.3 62	129 37	49	150	1.09	64 -7	2C 3c	188	34	30	185	97	_80 84 85
ales workers Craftsmen foremen and kindred workers	56 138	7. 206	8"	167	240	14	35 186	-52	51	47	27	149	190	79 387	93	_8S	89
peratives and Lindred workers	105	243	280 378	232	269	.72	186	22:	L03	378	_94	_39	J30	527	461	4.5	397
nvate household workers.	21	56	49	127	84	46		25	52	20	2 54	62	35	· 82	6	125	90
arm laborers and foremen aborers, except farm and mine	11 86	-56	2:1	5 55	22 57	40 211.	17 127	57 230	52 67	: .	54 1 70 116	5 -17	74	14	25 465	13	25
crupation not reported	1	3	30	24	28	TC	127	17	8	479 20	13	2	1.2	A-	25	10	.93
Femrie employed	256	226	485	779	5.	470	309	577	442	229	430	296	280	380	782	682	48
rofessional technical and kindred workers	53	22	70	170	73	46	43	62	86	49	53	43	54	43	1,2	1.7	9.
armers and farm managers lanagers officials and proprie-ors, except farm lerical and kindred workers	6	.4	1.6	41	19	30 54	6	22 66	22	9	31	17	19 59	.9	203	134	2
ules workers	*1 33	74 21	74 79 5	185	143 5a	44	70 38	94	200	39 20	50 39	o5 26	3.1	70	57	82	6
raftamen, foremen and kindred workers peratures and kindred workers	- 40	14	5 21	63	22	58	28	38	24	21	1	26 2 4	49	89 70 3 24	5.	40	19
nvate household workers	71	34	82	42	17	69	-3 60	.90	112	23	112	58	24	36 65	2/9	146 120	19
ervice workers except private household	29 4 5	98	.l.	-04	64	69 68 83	- 4	88	112 72 3	22	F9 2	2	40	60	13	3	
aborers, except farm and mine	5 2		12	4 8	1.0	6	2 4	3	8 4	3	2	2	2	מנ	7 2	- 1	3
MAJOR INDUSTRY GROUP	1			_	-	-									10		
Male employed	61"	885	1,336	1,000	1,336	957	7,8	. 385	n62	1,048	288	808	940	1,016	1 829	. 9.3	1,20
griculture forestry, and fisherses	27	12	12	18	42	+9 3	19	104	7-	83 7	139	18	29	22 160	107	29 145	-33
Construction	8.	83	32 45	206	45 436	82	118 241	1.8.	د8	83	137	89 195	52	189	136	253 264	153
fanufacturing ransportation commun, and other public util	100 32 210	104	623	178 160	303 128	155 70 425	3.0	224	59	662 34	161 59	132	352 23	د56ء 127	100	159	13
holomis and retail trade	16	195	221	321 45	107 27	425	138	407 32	185	90	168	176	171 21	223 33	ە8د 25	521 48	2
Summess and repair services	20 37	9	43 46 13	55	25 54	1.5 34 30	21	9.2 6.3	20 52 9	20	3 41 10	19 42 37	21	3.5	40 83	149	79. 2 6
ersonal services intertainment and recreation services	2	3	13	.4	15	. 6	45	21	59	5 20	8 7	4	38	1. -4 .9 16	71	29 1.3	1 9
rofessional and related services	31 31	11	58° 28	297	62 65	39 19	25	65	39	_0	57	4.3 33	14	-9	55	89	7
ndustry not reported _)	5	28	28	31	-2	1	25	4	6	17	3	1.2		25	1,500,00	
Female employed	256	226	485	779	517	470	309	577	441	229	410	260	280	380	782	<u>082</u>	48
gnultu e forestry, and fisheries	3			3	1	30		, ,		1				1 6	2		i
onstruction fanufacturing	- 2	35	35	12	26	22	1 2	18	3	45	34	2 8	70	29	32	24	1
ransportation, commun., and other public util	5		21 158	25	20 127	1 5	10	16	121	4	110	22 102	10	-34	32 25 187	28 190	1
holesale and retail trade inance, insurance and real estate	61	72	14	167 26	15	154	.0	12	1.3	44	9	9	4		21	23	
	91	42	2 417	3	142	2 94	74	221	49	32	13	64	51	62	328	199	10
ersonal services intertainment and recreation services	-	1 3	2	10	8	1 5		1	100	63	3 76	61	1 2	10	128	175	11
rofessional and related services _	62	30	111	346 30	108	6.3	7.	85	21	8	20	7	4	6	30	26	1 4
adustry not reported -	2	8	16	23	15	8	4	22	4	3	.0		4	10	6	-	
*INCOME IN 1949 Total families and unrelated individuals	785	890	1,690	2 450	1.500	1 335	910	855	1 005	1,090	1,190	925	1,135	1 710	2,820	2 210	1,8
ess than \$500	85	80	245		190	134	30	230	120	75	144	745	65			170	1
500 to \$900	700	50	245	425 275 220	310 125	230	110	340 305 210	210 150 95	110	280 195	180	120	-125 -15 235	525	200	1
1 000 to \$1,499 1 500 to \$1 909	1 95	45 75	.55	205	145	140	70 100	210	95	95	120	75	110	105	285	285	1
2,000 to \$2,409	65	35	180	185	70	135	100	21.5 85 100	95	180 120	115	85	135	120 80 135 140 185	105	20:	
3,000 to \$3,499 3,500 to \$3,499 4,000 to \$4,499	40 30 35	95	100	180	105	o5 25	60 80 70	100	55	180	30	85	90	135	125	130	1
4,000 to \$4.499	30	105	90	80	85	50	50	40	35	30	30 25	35	90	185	65 20	120	ol .
4,500 to \$4 999 5,000 to \$5,999	40	55	55	85	50 90	25 30	50 90	50	25	30	30 5 20	35	65	125	35 65 15	6.5 7.5 6.5	
96,000 to \$6,999	30	30	45	20	35	10	45	10	20 15	35 15	20 45	20	30	55 45	15 35	65	
57,000 to \$9,999	- 25	50 15	25 10	55 45	30	1 40	5	40	25	5	20	20	20	10	10	1 60)
ncome not reported	- 55	40	35	-15	40	55	\$2,833	\$1 507									
fedian moome.	\$_,921	\$3 474	\$2,008	\$2,081	\$_,983	4: , 210	144,000	47 201	1	140,000	400,000	1-1-30	1,7,7	1	1,-,-	1,000	1,70

T_{able} 39—ECONOMIC CHARACTERISTICS OF THE POPULATION, BY SEX, FOR URBAN PLACES OF 2,500 to 10,000 1950—Con.

[Asterisk (*) denotes statistics based on 20-percent sample Median not shown where base is less than 500]

Supject	vinton.	éestvego	Winnfield	vinnsboro	Subject	Virton	Westwego	Wimmfield	Winnsbor
EMPLOYMENT STATUS					MAJOR INDUSTRY GROUP		4.104		
Male, _4 years old and over	874	2,785	480و ل	1,140	Male employed	510		1,384	88
apor veree Civilian labor toree. Employed Private wage and salary workers Government workers	676, 676 6.0 459	2,338	1,381 1,029 163	50_ 120	Agriculture, forestry, and fisheries. Mining Constructuring Transportation, commun., and other punks util	67 155 50 110 39	90 195 999 274	161 399 140	10 5 6
Self-employed workers Unpand family workers Unemployed	111 3 66 -98	265 40 139 442	187 2 41 525	197 3 62 253	Wholesale and retai trade France insurance, and real estate Business and repair services Personal services Entertainment and recreation services	96 5 21 29	334 16 52 44 24	285 32 23 68	
Female, 14 years out and over abor force Civilian labor force Rmployed	96b 214 -:4 -:28	2,843 e70 eo9 602	495	1,443 484 484 448	Entertainment and related services Professional and related services Public administration Industry not reported Fensis, amployed	18 17 2	24 29 45 15 632	7 82 59 27	6 3 1
Private wage and salary workers - Government workers - Ser-employed workers - Unpair family workers	129 39 27 13	526 38 40 28 37	341 100 42 4	296 106 41 5	Agneulture forestry, and fisheries. Mining. Construction Manufacturing	6 1 6:	3	4 2 14	
Unemployed for in Issuer force MAJOR OCCUPATION GROUP M.le, employed	752	2,173	1 719	959	Transportation, commun, and other public util Wholesale and retail trade. Finance, maurance, and real estate Business and repair services Personal services.	67 2 45	15 194 4 4	17 137 4 2	1
rofessional, technical, and kindred workers armers and farm managers fanages, officials, and proprietors, except farm fencal and kindred workes fales workers reftenen, forcinen, and amdred workers	27 35 56 26 48	47 2 160 122 30 48"	23 7 165 100 85 209	29 20 1,57 42 70 123	Personal services Enterlatment and recreative services Professonal and related services Public administration Industry not reported *INCOME IN 1949	3 47 5 11	58 14	156 3 116 19 23	т 1
peratives and kindred workers	190	752	28c	135	Total families and unrelated individuals	620	2,365	-,890	1,15
ernos workers except private household arm isborers and foremen aborers, except fa.m and mine ocupation not reported	45 21 60	139 6 360 171 632	60 4 317 23 487	736 736 66	Less than \$500 \$500 to \$899 \$1,700 to \$1,499 \$1,500 to \$1,999 \$2,000 to \$2,499	75 135 95 45	155 185 195 243 305	290 405 200 235 210	21 21 22 22 22 22 22 22 22 22 22 22 22 2
Fenale, employed. rofessional, and kindred workers. anners and farm vanagers. anagers, offivals and proprietors, except farm. lence, and hardred workers and kindred workers reference foreign and kindred workers persurves and kindred workers reference foreign and kindred workers reference workers, earged private household.	32 1 48 29 22 2 3 58	632 128 119 84 238 36 65	487 80 26 78 40 4 28 101	448 80 28 69 49 2 16	22.00 to 22,999 33,000 to 53,499 54,000 to 54,499 54,000 to 54,499 55,000 to 55,999 85,000 to 55,999 85,000 to 55,999 85,000 to 56,999 10,000 to 39,999 10,000 to 31,0 ver	35 65 75 15 80 25 25	285 260 185 130 60 150 50	55 100 55 40 40 35 25 30	

arm labolers and foremen shorars, except farm and mme coupation not reported	1	8	3	4	Median neome	(2,482	55 -2,570	155 \$1,433	\$1,5

Table 40.-RACE, AGE, AND RURAL-FARM POPULATION, BY SEX FOR PLACES OF 1 NO. TO 2500 1950

Incomprate, cr. maners on test	Tota		1. 1	V-Li	6			-	14/0	100		יובר ייבר	474				Rum
Incorporated crummon, orated place	Tota.	DEC	-B/8/5	`ae	T Substitution .	NE.	C.i	·de-	5 t.	10	35.00	15 to	45 tu	73	and l	21 430	Lette
road_a	2,2-1		2, 79	587		6	remitte i	-25	-70	13	**)	.2	.34		91	-2-	
sal san	30	14	-3575	204	5	34.1	100	91	, SAL	18F	74	-0.1	3- 5- 5- 7-	14	73	3G3 3C3	in.
so.le	-,,">		567	204 201	-	145	1	135	27. -7.	109	7-	99	7-	5.	44)	~41	
ayou Canc (unine)	2,212		28.3	719	*	2000.	i	32,	2.1	138	. 3	-50.	3.	5.3	23	467 530	
emite	.,50-	7	76-	-527	0	393	8	9c 202:	23	170	13	10	53	3000	47	/55	
ream F-1-go	2,472		101	3~	2,	220	1	31	2-1	at .	140	mol	-			718	
roussard	- 47	1 .	612 6	. 1831 4J2	2	272	1.	5	134	-2-4	204	77	-6 59	-30 -37 ,8	-1s	6.3	1
rovnsv.l.e nin-	2,2~	101	635 5	49 1	Éi	201	-1	14	23-	100	.3.	52	59 -1" 80	,8 6.	38 52 64	375 020	1
res Triumph (unin)	1,009	F 4	-,106	83 77-3 24	- 51	291	2.	.~3.	23-	77.1	130	136	5.	6 13 40 18	67 44 35	c22 _C 423	
amp t.1	1,11	2	472	24		.19,	- 2	70	-3	105	130	59	30	63		423	1
arenaro	_,587		76.	24.	*	20-	- 1	9_1	10	1-3	63 +	7- ;	۵۱ ا ۵:		52	1,000	14.8
balmette (uniro ,	7,909	-	25.	540	32	2		92	14	1-3	50 5 5 5 5 5 5 5 5 5 5 5 5 5 5 5 5 5 5	10-1	2-1	71	34	-94	
ark (unin.)	. 345	F	-20 638	9	421		18	90 90 68 92	134 115 128	1-3 . 9 . 7 . 1 . 1 . 1	204	116	72	37	23 30	.10 40;	
anton	1,383	1	655	434 434 28-	21	22	- 1	68	128	1-4	21	96.1	24	50	20	-8- -G8	
DATEX	1 65	1	772	400	81	210	4	100	12	-3	35	1	. s	-3 65		456 447 570	
		1.	42.	25-	-1	*o_		84	Se	33	12-1	730		-13	~7		1
over (unino)	_ 214		530	593 6-1 -77	4		1	.13 AC	_39	91	44	3	30	16		342	
ottonport	1 >34	1	756	076	- 20	90		95 87	175	-22 -C6 95	4.	1.2	3C 77 26 57	2- 48 43	43 45 39	453 336	1 3
otto i Valley	_ 108	7.7	593 595	46. 582	31	-2		-5 -6	95	57	90	93	95 39	38	3/	lang.	
ousharte	2 758	Ľ	839 9-3	587 549 630		250 3.L			171	132	-30	12.	50	577	75 102 19	94 €02 254	1
A. Asbre	1 463	2 4	741	.04	-;	100	- 1	104	142	12:	1.9	99	00	47 03	1	4_9	1
eihi	1,861	ч	871	464	1	274		-29	-39 -42	86	- 0	d	39	53 53 61	61 81	645	
enhan Sp. L.gs	2 053	ü	494	73° 788	٤	207		140	20 ¹⁰	128	1/2	15C 15C	95 96 29	61	23	606	
orline	1 - 13	И	-,35,7 808	474	1 2	700 37		135	109	68	11 30	92	30	27 26	27 25	308 295	
1 .abet. unine)	.,1.3	И	760 193	729 32.	2	259		6n 80 85		92 76 98	'7 '	92 80 90	~	4. 29	322	308	
lton	1,43-	7	70a	518	4	2-8 410	i	85 53	168	122	100	79	76 77	54	6	191 421	1
Ereth	1,514	1	2	658	- 1	72	,	35	1.2	u	1.01	.771	74	55	13	434	1
arme vilia	2,173	1	-100-	03.	1	4.6	-	133 110	181	671	1.9	99 .58 162	115 1.6	30 77 23	71 -04 76 69 98	661	5 2
Frenkl' un	7,542	1	-,122 - 1-3 -,13	947 700	4	-94		173 lob	229	-67 16 203	167	166 168 108	1/8	6 80 84	76	6/9	
METYVile (unima)	1,350	K	924	477	5	-37 400	1	123	201	74-1	17	300	10.	1 84 73 50	98 98)1.s	2
Siteland	1,089	y o	,11 874	337	3	456 230 24_		75	87	60	04 5-	62	10.	50	67	3-8	
Marrora	1 *50	и	7-5	464	1	250	2	88	. 47	**!	74	95	85	28	8	449 22	
Consales	1,642	1 .	3C1 320	699	7,	323 116 -20		129	.51	91 -26 3C 79	14.1	.2C	73 75 45	43	91 42 60 -1	46. 483	
Ci ameroy	1,184	M	822	(9)	3	84		12C 100 82	45 14 1,60 91	79 94	14.1 -37	36 79	45	40	-1	306	5
Grand Toteau	_,173	M	54 5.7 586	497	3	94 206		50	91 1.3	46	7-	54	54 40	1.5	34 50 28	300 300 300 300 384	
Crend Lule (unin)	.,190	М	586 638 557		22	236 8 5		5u 6_ 70 /6	17	109	_17 100	63 99 82	69	25	28	384	5
	2,041		1,000	865	1	101		34	20.		139	136 140	99 87		1	סיכ	2
ighland Park-Splane Place	2,001	P	7,021	850	-	-59		le '	203	175	109			1	1	9:	1
(umine)	1,065	W	8_0 8-5	766 F 0	5 5	39 40 270		98	141 143 157	99 .23	167 180	146	76	. 35	35	509 514 37	-
odge	_, >86	"	56.	363 43	5 5 2 4	250		/3 89	152 152 129	108 108	_33	7.75	68 56	30	33	49:	7
Independance	. ,606	M.	779 827	344	63	160		9° 67	129 136 125	108		124	96	4: 4: 4: 4:	43 20 33 68 75 39	-51	1
Iota	1,162	H	584 578	-69 462	6	109 90		87	125	87	79	82	47	43	1	1	1
Iosa (unin.)	ري. ا	м	553	. 58 184		194		91 90	32	73	89	81	21	3:	32	30.	a l
Jena	1 438	M	772 723	184 104 116 482	1	4	3	8.	125	88 9 10* 131	89 114 128	89 91 92 136	80	31	66	43	8
Jonesville	1,554	M	722 922	16 482	2	468 520	1 1	131	106	131	130	136	91	7 8	66 64 85 90	57 62 66	9
Tentwood	2,4.7	l B	1,0C2 1,129	482	7	415	ا ا	145	440	173	181	1.50	130	8	90	66	8
Kin_or	2,703	8 P	1,129 1,288 9e7 1,036	767 -66 822] 3₹	5_7 192 205	i	_33 137	234 170 206	151	152	120	106	- 61	6.3	75 57 60	6
1 m . a . (m . m .)	2.3.2	1,	1 169	937	l al	541		100	235	163	172	152	104	8	6	0.5	1
Larcae (uninc)	1,260	I F	1,483	6.4 6.50 505	14	257	3	156	235 247 157	182	169 94 8'	144 75 73	12. 59	8 4	81 21	67 32 32	9
		H m	ol.	9 505	1 51	3.	1 3	80	129	_18	8/	73 88 65	70	5	80	39	

LOUISIANA

Table 40.—RACE, AGE AND RURAL-FARM POPULATION, BY SEX, FOR PLACES OF 1,000 TO 2,500 1950—Con

Incorporated (+ unincorporated	Total	1.	All	W.	I,a		Other					Age 'year	(81			-	Ru
place	population	Sea	classes	\u00e4ire	Foreign born	Negs	races	Under	5 to	15 to 24	25 to 34	35 to 44	45 to 54	a5 to 64	60 and over	21 and over	ís
-ookpo=+	1,388	4	679	u~5	3			98	148	97	112	107	57	31	35	382	
wgaraport .	1,27C	M	709 585	705 426		158	1	81	125	103	124	201	64 55	47 59	63	441 364 433	
J'ch',	2,298	*	685 1,074	465 534	6	214 532	,	6_ 21 13/	115 225	129 164	91 122	82 134 135	84 84	104	63 90 109	600	
femot.	2,254	M	1,124	528 -, 027	2	584 95	1	142	225 204	162	131	159	133 122	10. 99	100	662	
findevil.o	1 368	P M	1,130 9-3 725	1,020	20	130 15¢		601	206 i	75	130	149 85 95	155 71 94	24 26 79	89 161 112	718 406	
ansura	ود4,1	ч	684	555	2	228		29 84	152	90 97	78 l	89	54	58	48	495 392	
iany .	_,681	H I	755 826	473 601	9 7	2.6	•	89	134	127	103 126	10"	76 132	66	70 60	525 570	
elale .	1,901	P M	855 940	646 594	7 4 7	200 342	2	93 1.1	122 21a	131	117	152 38	104	65 52	71 85	531	
erryville .	1,383	м	961 660	562 564	1 2	392 11		1.1 104 77 79	201 134	124	130 71 95	.35 108	106 80	52 58 44	85 90 67 58	584 414	
apoleon ile.	1,200	M R	703 590 670	373 : 426	9	208 231		79 80 67	105	97 89 94	95 81 102	102 72 84	60 65 85	74 47 58	58 50 81	427 349 453	
R/e_lton	_,280	М ,	599	240	11	348		73	99	68	82	a.	FB	49	- 1	391	
as Grove	1,796	M	661 623	284 58	8	389 235		62 98	92	95	90	116	7 ₀	65	79 85 84 74	475 50°	
perlin	1,244	N ,	973	6% 550	2 6 5	295 191		120	176	140 116	147	128	107 60	81	74	596 427	
lla .	3,115	F M	797 562	578 547	5	214	i	106	163	125 94 89	107	100	63	66 48	46 50 47	452	
rterson .		M	553 934 1,004	537 432 461	27 24	475 519		128 108	75 194 183	131 162	128 126	72 11. 13.	79 97 98	35 63 86	82 110	342 353 533 623	
ein Desaung	- 1	M	(32	421	3	208		79	119	70	96	88	78	41	ಎ	391	
rt Barre		M	689 533	47_	5	21.4 45	1	88	109	83	76	103	81	56 28	60 27	290	
rt Barrow-Smore Benn (uninc.)	1,619	M F	775	491 375	2	39	:	277	183	129 138	81 78	106	29 62	32 48	15 58	274 401	
tean-Port Supker (unine)	1,255	M	844 620	363 444 467	3	479 173		102 93	167	80,	107	114	64 72	72	80	487 370	
oeland (unine)	2,025	F M P	535 1,317 1,008	880 870	453223658	152 132 130		96 129	139	145	155	102	52 93	23	18	346 575	
sy (unine)	- 1	M	5_6	400	3	113		106	182	152	175	136	102	73	52	632	9
nggolá		F	548 501	423 317	1	125		75 74	109 107 103	±06 87	03 05 50	50 57 61	52 56 54	45 36	53	276 309	2
soland .	1	F	506 496	320 332	1	185		55	103	66 67	74	74:	5C	36 40 40	43	280 304	
Joseph	1	F	542	370 234	2	170	2	82	98 105	94	68	75	63	27	44	309 320	
mesport		4	681	277 470	4	400 270		100	100	111	69 107 98	62 87 90	63	50 71 48	60 104 47	332 474 397	,
set .	1,080		706 499	501 326	1	262		212	156	136	97	83 55	70 "5	48	59	4_0	- 2
nerville (unin.)	1,048	1	581	357 326	1 1	223		85 67	124	106	100	62 56	46	22	32	257 306	4
mas (uninc)	1,004		550	349 492	6	195		85	83	92	78	59	57 55 58 37	33 50 38	42 48	299 329	
acla	1,641 M	,	51.2 760	512 324	2	432		64 98 102	112	91	75	68 74 90	37	36 66	24	280	1
iar	2,426		881 1,177 1,249	318 _,100 1,163	4 2 3 2	261 74 84		102 237 123	135	171	1.4	11.8	103	66	23 58 104 73 96	485 560 744	
angton	_,291 M	- 1	617	290	1	327		82	101	1_0	195	73	143	125	96	321	
erproof .	1,180 M		674 1 546	304 215	3	364 328		93 66	134	10°	74	63	56	64 48	60	381	
s Island (unine)	-,479 M		634 760	227 476		405 284		85 92	100	113	123	93	74	49	69	396 393	1
h.	2,416 M		739 -,192	845	2 4 8	2°7 363		108	106 250	129 16c	121	100 150	59	35 80	21	378 683	14
lake	1,871 4	1	1,224 924 917	840 750 683	8	375 201 233	1	_52 126 104	208 216 205	152	121 172 158 134	139	80	107	107	730 534	1
e Castie	1,839 M		8c2 977	500 550	16	346		101	164	172	142	95	77	69	58 68	506	
ery	1,542 H	1	750	357	2	4141 391	2	120	173 154 157	133	130	426 91	85 68	21 47 53	119	598	73
la	1,555 M		792	366 494	3	421 255	1	104	157	107	127	104	76	53	50 55	459	58

GENERAL CHARACTERISTICS

Table 41.—AGE BY COLOR AND SEX, FOR PARISHES 1950

			1950 p	opulation				1940		-	National Assessment	₁950 p	opulation		NAME OF TAXABLE PARTY.		4940
Pansh and age		Il clames	galle en d	W	tate	hoor	vnite	pepila-	Paneu and age	4-5-65	A.I canses		W	ute	Nunv	rhite ;	popula-

Table 41.—AGE BY COLOR AND SEX, FOR PARISHES: 1950

Parish and age	1950 population: All classes, Total	All classes, Male	All classes, Female	White, Male	White, Female	Nonwhite, Male	Nonwhite, Female	1940 population total
ACADIA								
All ages	47,050	23,374	23,676	19,028	19,025	4,346	4,651	46,260
Under 5 years	5,991	3,049	2,942	2,381	2,245	668	69	5,56[illegible]
Under 1 year	1,073	526	547	403	416	123	131	1,031
1 and 2 years	2,570	1,338	1,232	1,042	939	296	293	4,531
3 and 4 years	2,348	1,185	1,163	936	890	249	273	
5 to 9 years	5,250	2,639	2,611	2,063	2,062	576	549	5,452
5 years	1,014	512	502	403	395	109	107	1,096
6 years	1,102	557	545	438	421	119	124	1,101
7 to 9 years	3,134	1,570	1,564	1,222	1,246	348	318	3,255
10 to 14 years	5,088	2,620	2,468	2,082	1,919	538	549	5,037
10 to 13 years	4,133	2,116	2,017	1,692	1,580	424	437	4,477
14 years	955	504	451	390	339	114	112	1,162
15 to 19 years	4,370	2,166	2,204	1,731	1,742	435	462	4,897
15 years	894	460	434	363	350	97	84	935
16 and 17 years	1,840	922	918	735	734	187	184	1,966
18 and 19 years	1,636	784	852	633	658	151	194	1,996
20 to 24 years	3,710	1,816	1,894	1,511	1,500	305	394	4,229
25 to 29 years	3,308	1,588	1,720	1,309	1,427	279	293	3,925
30 to 34 years	3,121	1,525	1,596	1,307	1,328	218	268	3,220
35 to 39 years	3,222	1,587	1,635	1,330	1,335	257	300	3,041
40 to 44 years	2,867	1,412	1,455	1,185	1,208	227	247	2,997
45 to 49 years	2,524	1,253	1,271	1,081	1,055	172	216	1,981
50 to 54 years	2,025	981	1,044	804	883	177	161	1,611
55 to 59 years	1,564	788	776	663	646	125	130	1,367
60 to 64 years	1,290	589	701	495	592	94	109	1,050
65 to 69 years	1,194	593	601	473	462	120	139	912
70 to 74 years	736	355	381	292	317	63	64	484
75 to 84 years	662	351	311	275	251	76	59	486
85 years and over	128	62	66	45	52	16	14	
21 years and over	25,606	12,556	13,050	10,491	10,740	2,065	2,304	23,791
ALLEN								
All ages	18,835	9,407	9,428	7,176	7,106	2,231	2,322	17,540
Under 5 years	2,447	1,254	1,193	925	841	329	352	1,881
Under 1 year	492	262	230	200	164	62	66	359
1 and 2 years	1,022	499	523	371	360	128	163	1,522
3 and 4 years	933	493	440	354	317	139	123	
5 to 9 years	2,240	1,116	1,124	828	835	288	289	1,834
5 years	468	249	219	172	161	77	58	391
6 years	441	202	239	153	183	49	56	355
7 to 9 years	1,331	665	666	503	491	162	175	1,052
10 to 14 years	1,881	944	937	686	708	258	229	1,930
10 to 13 years	1,510	765	745	557	556	208	189	1,540
14 years	371	179	192	129	152	50	40	390
15 to 19 years	1,564	761	803	571	605	190	198	1,840
15 years	380	194	186	151	139	43	47	365
16 and 17 years	659	312	347	235	257	77	90	726
18 and 19 years	525	255	270	185	209	70	61	749
20 to 24 years	1,304	606	698	489	541	117	157	1,589
25 to 29 years	1,273	625	648	491	494	134	154	1,438
30 to 34 years	1,256	627	629	515	492	112	137	1,266
35 to 39 years	1,271	634	637	483	469	151	168	1,196
40 to 44 years	1,172	603	569	484	441	119	128	992
45 to 49 years	1,040	513	527	391	402	122	125	923
50 to 54 years	815	420	395	325	301	95	94	797
55 to 59 years	758	381	377	289	306	92	71	591
60 to 64 years	610	306	304	237	233	69	71	465
65 to 69 years	518	264	254	197	171	67	83	412
70 to 74 years	346	186	160	144	125	42	35	202
75 to 84 years	287	139	148	104	123	35	25	214
85 years and over	53	28	25	17	19	11	6	
21 years and over	10,443	5,216	5,227	4,078	4,012	1,138	1,215	9,767
ASCENSION								
All ages	22,387	11,234	11,153	7,366	7,102	3,868	4,051	21,215
Under 5 years	3,116	1,683	1,433	1,082	879	601	554	2,290
Under 1 year	611	330	281	204	180	126	101	466
1 and 2 years	1,278	687	591	440	362	247	229	1,824
3 and 4 years	1,227	666	561	438	337	228	224	
5 to 9 years	2,636	1,328	1,308	815	801	513	507	2,185
5 years	513	269	244	161	154	108	90	443
6 years	549	279	270	163	162	116	108	404
7 to 9 years	1,574	780	794	491	485	289	309	1,338
10 to 14 years	2,230	1,158	1,072	711	658	447	414	2,386
10 to 13 years	1,831	961	870	582	533	379	337	1,873
14 years	399	197	202	129	125	68	77	513
15 to 19 years	1,855	919	936	584	605	335	331	2,386
15 years	437	220	217	136	137	84	80	474
16 and 17 years	770	383	387	247	253	136	134	985
18 and 19 years	648	316	332	201	215	115	117	927
20 to 24 years	1,534	763	771	513	498	250	273	1,885
25 to 29 years	1,532	736	796	536	543	200	253	1,565
30 to 34 years	1,462	723	739	542	500	181	239	1,347
35 to 39 years	1,297	663	634	468	419	195	215	1,316
40 to 44 years	1,234	612	622	428	421	184	201	1,110
45 to 49 years	1,165	584	581	391	365	193	216	1,085
50 to 54 years	961	455	506	322	349	133	157	946
55 to 59 years	861	402	459	261	291	141	168	789
60 to 64 years	790	411	379	267	245	144	134	581
65 to 69 years	794	362	432	186	224	176	208	607
70 to 74 years	412	203	209	124	137	79	72	371
75 to 84 years	423	191	232	109	142	82	90	366
85 years and over	85	41	44	27	25	14	19	
21 years and over	12,281	6,017	6,264	4,101	4,071	1,916	2,193	11,520

Parish and age	1950 population: All classes, Total	All classes, Male	All classes, Female	White, Male	White, Female	Nonwhite, Male	Nonwhite, Female	1940 population total
ASSUMPTION								
All ages	17,278	[illegible]	8,73[illegible]	5,007	5,04[illegible]	3,540	3,687	18,541
Under 5 years	2,357	1,185	1,172	616	603	579	569	2,156
Under 1 year	447	227	220	113	112	[illegible]	108	464
1 and 2 years	977	492	485	256	267	236	218	1,692
3 and 4 years	943	476	467	247	224	229	243	
5 to 9 years	2,131	1,056	1,075	541	545	515	530	1,996
5 years	442	231	211	119	97	112	114	392
6 years	432	208	224	108	122	100	102	435
7 to 9 years	1,257	617	640	314	326	303	314	1,169
10 to 14 years	1,835	900	935	513	493	387	442	2,034
10 to 13 years	1,523	749	774	430	408	319	366	1,601
14 years	312	151	161	83	85	68	76	433
15 to 19 years	1,476	756	720	430	432	326	288	2,122
15 years	338	186	152	105	88	81	64	401
16 and 17 years	637	318	319	179	199	139	120	897
18 and 19 years	501	252	249	146	145	106	104	824
20 to 24 years	1,123	547	576	321	334	227	242	1,696
25 to 29 years	1,121	530	587	347	326	192	261	1,418
30 to 34 years	995	503	492	329	324	17	168	1,102
35 to 39 years	1,098	563	535	384	343	179	192	1,058
40 to 44 years	901	464	437	297	275	167	162	931
45 to 49 years	828	398	430	267	271	131	159	883
50 to 54 years	739	351	388	218	253	133	135	816
55 to 59 years	682	359	323	189	185	170	138	658
60 to 64 years	579	287	292	191	202	96	90	555
65 to 69 years	602	263	339	138	170	125	169	517
70 to 74 years	386	175	211	111	144	64	67	295
75 to 84 years	355	165	190	101	128	64	62	304
85 years and over	55	26	29	15	16	11	13	
21 years and over	9,252	4,533	4,699	2,858	2,893	1,675	1,806	9,854
AVOYELLES								
All ages	38,031	19,062	18,969	14,122	13,976	4,940	4,993	39,256
Under 5 years	4,880	2,440	2,440	1,712	1,684	728	756	4,499
Under 1 year	940	460	480	323	311	137	169	832
1 and 2 years	1,927	982	945	680	657	302	288	3,667
3 and 4 years	2,013	998	1,015	709	716	289	299	
5 to 9 years	4,245	2,115	2,130	1,472	1,499	643	631	4,408
5 years	817	394	423	277	291	117	132	892
6 years	889	454	435	291	312	163	123	905
7 to 9 years	2,539	1,267	1,272	904	896	363	376	2,641
10 to 14 years	4,078	2,115	1,963	1,459	1,394	656	569	4,573
10 to 13 years	3,301	1,726	1,575	1,199	1,136	527	439	3,652
14 years	777	389	388	260	258	129	130	921
15 to 19 years	3,372	1,715	1,657	1,177	1,154	538	503	4,197
15 years	782	420	362	287	256	133	106	848
16 and 17 years	1,458	740	718	516	491	224	227	1,687
18 and 19 years	1,132	555	577	374	407	181	170	1,662
20 to 24 years	2,571	1,244	1,327	895	935	349	392	2,599
25 to 29 years	2,511	1,262	1,249	966	980	296	269	3,175
30 to 34 years	2,498	1,209	1,289	995	1,039	214	250	2,708
35 to 39 years	2,497	1,268	1,229	1,034	935	234	294	2,456
40 to 44 years	2,281	1,142	1,139	903	876	239	263	2,142
45 to 49 years	1,992	1,013	979	802	754	211	225	1,857
50 to 54 years	1,686	870	816	693	641	177	175	1,499
55 to 59 years	1,479	747	732	586	584	161	148	1,260
60 to 64 years	1,247	588	659	483	523	105	136	986
65 to 69 years	1,192	567	625	404	451	163	174	893
70 to 74 years	730	388	342	270	262	118	80	466
75 to 84 years	656	324	332	231	230	93	102	538
85 years and over	116	55	61	40	39	15	26	
21 years and over	20,961	10,457	10,504	8,157	8,066	2,300	2,438	20,839
BEAUREGARD								
All ages	17,766	8,819	8,947	7,367	7,372	1,452	1,575	14,847
Under 5 years	2,136	1,067	1,069	897	854	170	215	1,533
Under 1 year	371	192	179	149	138	43	41	267
1 and 2 years	919	440	479	361	377	79	102	1,266
3 and 4 years	846	435	411	387	339	48	72	
5 to 9 years	2,026	1,011	1,015	830	849	181	166	1,601
5 years	391	187	204	148	166	39	38	341
6 years	423	217	206	177	178	40	28	320
7 to 9 years	1,212	607	605	505	505	102	100	940
10 to 14 years	1,795	878	917	746	782	132	135	1,538
10 to 13 years	1,451	708	743	605	632	103	111	1,221
14 years	344	170	174	141	150	29	24	317
15 to 19 years	1,477	751	726	633	594	118	132	1,537
15 years	369	184	185	157	160	27	25	303
16 and 17 years	619	329	290	281	241	48	49	631
18 and 19 years	489	238	251	195	193	43	58	603
20 to 24 years	1,087	472	615	387	489	85	126	1,199
25 to 29 years	1,145	547	598	436	486	111	112	1,191
30 to 34 years	1,151	551	600	482	506	69	94	1,009
35 to 39 years	1,265	606	659	522	563	84	96	922
40 to 44 years	1,161	605	556	527	454	78	102	780
45 to 49 years	955	504	451	428	365	76	86	790
50 to 54 years	802	412	390	337	309	75	81	761
55 to 59 years	714	342	372	273	310	69	62	597
60 to 64 years	671	347	324	276	280	71	44	487
65 to 69 years	635	328	307	247	239	81	68	425
70 to 74 years	374	211	163	184	138	27	25	237
75 to 84 years	324	172	152	148	125	24	27	240
85 years and over	48	15	33	14	29	1	4	
21 years and over	10,136	5,024	5,112	4,188	4,214	836	898	8,400

Table 41.—AGE BY COLOR AND SEX, FOR PARISHES 1950—Con

STORES TO STAND STANDS	1	. HERVINGER	.950 t	continue	9	and the same	-	194C	1	-	-	1950	population	1	-	-	1940
Pe ark age		All clause	e e	F	Thate	'ani	w.ute	popula	Panab are -go		Alı classes		T,	hrte	Non	white	popula-
	Total	Male	Fense	354-	Female	Mag	Female	tota		Total	Viale	Temale	Mal	Femare	Male	Female	total
31.0. 1(15		1		1	i				CA CASTEU								
All ages	9, 05	3 15	مدرد إو	4,860	- 63C	4,590	→, 716	23,733	All ages	87,635	44,772	44,863	34,052	34,400	10,120		56,506
Luder 5 ves re Under 1 year.	2 6.	- 742		/3:		683	(21	2,746	Inde- 5 years.	2,467	6,087	5,784 1,.81 2,376	4,588	4,291 833	1,499	1,493 348	5,760
1 and 2 years.	- 8u2	160	396	-04	163	3.2	233	2,279	and 2 years	4,905	2,527	2,227	1,900	1,792	629 557	⇒64 561	4,634
5 o 9 years	2,398	الله ا	1,072	423	+"2 96	%U3 132	600	2,781	5 tc 9 veers	9,496 2,358	4,735 1,325 1,004	1 033	3,590	803	1, 45	230	5,447 1,132
6 Veers	422	1 .9:	1 223	18 100 184	15:	1.0	125 352 600	548 _,682 2,655	6 years -	1,967	1,004 2,706 4,06	963 2,765 3,814	762 2,051 3,065	2,097	242 6*5 991	217 608	1,.51 3,264 5,795 4,674
7 *0 9 years. 10 to 14 years. 0 to 13 years.	1 1,739	1,25 2,25 1,00 1,00 1,00 1,00 1,00 1,00 1,00 1,0	331	36	355	663 539	4.76	2, 28	10 to 12 years _	7,870 c,380	3,295 761	3,914 3,085 729	2,473	2,852 2,3.2 540	822 169	962 773 189	4,674
14 years.	2,376	123	84	-39	368 368	-24 484	3.7	2 555	15 to 9 years	1,490	3,198	3,580	2,465	2.668	733	912	1,121
10 and 17 years 18 and 9 years	781	409	372	20.	28	208	2101	1,021	15 years 16 and 17 years 18 and 19 years	1,443 2,575 2,760 7,520	734 1,239 1,225	709 1,356	961 900	532 995	180 258 295	341 394	2,128
20 to 24 years -	-,134 94.	570 446	554	138 234 276	11d 72 238	230 220	203 331 257	1,037 2,170 1,845	18 and 19 years 20 to 24 years 25 to 29 years	7,526	1 3 473	1,535	2.624	3.075	789 81.2	1.038	2,183 5,308 5,267
20 to 24 years - 25 to 29 years - 30 to 34 ears - 35 to 39 years	1,220		624	270	33.	2/3	283	1.681	30 to 34 years 35 to 39 years	8,013 7 179 6,942	3,855 3,573 3,531	4,.58 3,606 3 4.1	3,043 2,837 2,855	3,226 2,884 2,637	736 676	932 722 774	4,764
40 to 44 years	-,		61.3	389	328	23.	275	1,522 1,258	40 to 44 years	2,961	3,006	2,895	2,507	2,337	559	774 558	3,432
40 to 48 years	958 802	51.5 492	235 467 403	299 309	323 281	216	-80	970	40 to 54 years - 50 to 54 years 55 to 59 years	4,842 3,679 2,882	2,55° 1,930 1 493	2,285 1,749 1,389	2 003 1,513 1,130	1,787 1,344 1,088	417 363	498 405 301	2,925 2,366 1,917
50 to 54 jears 65 to 59 jears 60 to 64 years 65 to 60 years	. 709	399	346 36	256 25_	259 242 278	.43 :12 .65	24 24 25 25 36	783 663 558	65 to 69 years	2,202	1,119	1,083	678	850 690	272	233	1,479
65 to 69 years. 70 to 74 years - 75 to 84 years -	725 465 429	364 24/ 223	221	156 143	208 155 137	88	66	558 314 332	70 to 74 years 70 to 74 years 70 to 84 years	1 229	6_3 179	616 546	359	5±0 446	134	101	652
85 years and over 21 years and over	58	25	33	6	20	9	3	170.70	85 years and over -	190	95 26,172	95 26,166	20,546	20,384	26 5,626	5.782	33,025
PUTTER	10,601	5,209	5,392	3,033	3,090	2,176	2,302	12,724		32,330	20,172	25,100	20,240	20,304	3,020	3,702	33,025
All ages	40,139	22,044	18,893	14,378	11,850	6,868	7,043	33,162	All ages.	10,291	5,178	5,145	3,722	3,035	1,456	1,480	12,046
Under 5 years	5.813	2,934	2,579	,932	1,862	1,002	,017!	3,380 614	Under 5 years Under 1 year	1,302	670 130	632 120	451 87	435 79	219	197	1,234
Inder 1 year. 1 and 2 years 3 and 4 years.	2,409 2,213	1,208	1,201	727	791 706	405 292	410 388	2,764	1 and 2 years 3 and 4 years	528 524	268 272 542	260 252 577	184	180 376 283	92	76	1,007
5 to 9 years	4,088	2,071	2,017	-,155 277	1,106 252	9,61	97.	3,171 689	5 to 9 years 5 years	1,122 242 210	120,	122	382 85	76	363 35	194	1,306
6 years 7 to 9 years	2,254	1,17	1,137	261 617	256 598	205 500	181	1,878	7 to 9 years	670	326	344	233	222 222	35 93	2C 122	266 782
10 to 14 years 10 to 13 years 14 years	3,113 2,543 -70	-,313 288	1,512 -,230 282	787 643 144	77°0 643 133	670	736 587 249	3,125 2,445 680	10 to 13 years	1,057 846 211	515 415 100	542 431 111	348 279 69	298 72	167 136 31	162 133	1,428
lo to 19 years .	3,194	1.800	1.394	164	750	636	644	3,423	14 vears	888	472	436	379	270	153	1461	2,316
15 vears. 16 and 17 years 18 and 19 years	1,107	265 530	277	131 270	137 286 327	134 258	291	1.200 #	15 years 16 and 17 years	38_	215 142	166	76 153 90	108	36 62 55	58	275 518
20 to 24 years	1,550 4,317 4,220	2,005 2,060 2,176 4,875	1,657	761 d,l o 1.828	4,462	3-4 514 350	218 495	1,623	18 and 19 cars	303 647 593	J07 286	340 313	208	97 233 237	99	107	1,092
30 to 34 years -	3,473	2,875	2,042 1,598 1,298	1,828	+,608 +,215 881	300	404 383 417	3,198 2,717 2,302	25 to 29 years 30 to 34 years 35 to 39 years	601	297	304	239	223	58	70 81	990 790 775
40 to 44 years 45 to 49 years .	2,161	1,169 928	992	804 565	394 499	363	398	1 855	40 to 44 years	620 25e	321	299	240	2.4	72 81 75	90 85	614
56 to 54 years 55 to 59 years	_,798 ±,375	715 553	660 g	422	361	293	299	1,240	45 to 49 years 50 to 54 years 50 to 59 years	518	264	254	198	184	66 59	72 70 52	512 397
50 to 64 years.	917	430 421	454	258	277	272	177	747 680	60 to 64 years	386 350	216	170 108	160	134	56 61 37	36	350 326
85 to 69 years - 70 to 74 years - 75 to 84 years -	503 534	208 209	235	143	179 119 28	14.3	116	401	70 to 74 years	260	154	106	117	86	37	39	-59
35 years and over	78 22,742	39 11,95e	10,786	8,591	16	25	23 3	19,099	85 years and over	3,790	2,922	2,869	2,190	11	24 6 731	720	6,501
CALDEO		-	,,	.,	1,417	,,,,,	-,005	27,029	CAMERON	3,770	2,721	2,007	4,170	2,119	132	790	0,301
All ages	170,547	84 362	92 485	53, 12/	-		5,208	203,203	All ages	6,244	3,200	2,943	2,978	2,683	323	260	7,203
Under 5 years	21,344 4,319 8,983	10,873 2,205 4,40	10,47 2,114 4,443 3,91/	1,285	⊥, 256	920	4,459 858	2,511	Under 5 years. Under 1 year	772 152	431 86	341 66	389 77	30,	42	38	833
1 and 2 years_	8.042	4,.40 4,.28 8,092	3,91/	2,531	2,206	1,722	1,893	9,809	1 and 2 years	325	176	118	157	102	12 21 33	17	672
5 to 9 years	16,259 2,464 3,497	8,392 -,720 -,720 4,5-0	1,751	959	958	754	793	4,486	5 to 9 years	686 1.56	357 75 77	333 81	320 59	301 72	6	32	794
7 to 9 years	9 308	4,50	4 608	2,562	972 2,607 3,610	814 2,085 3,091	2,051	2,314 7,222 3,298 10,550	6 years	388 606	20 320	187	182	168	19	19	137
10 to 14 years 10 to 13 years 14 years	14,066	5,604 1,189	5,462	3,097	2,95c	2,507	2,500	10,550	10 to 14 years. 10 to 13 years 14 years	492 114	320 265 55	286 227 59	286 240 46	252 200 52	34	27	870 704 166
15 to 19 years	11.8.0	-,472	5 338 1,208	3,050		2,422	2,684	14.073	15 to 19 years	527	27/	253	236	233	38	20	711
15 years 16 and 17 years 18 and 19 years	2,403 4,535 4,872	2,206	2,329	1,22/	1,278 1,723 5,367	982 914	555 1,051	2,847 5,355	15 years	213	106	107	93	101	13	6	156 271 284
20 to 24 years. 25 to 29 , ears - 30 to 34 years	-4,672	6,226	8,445	4,101		25	3,079 2,690	5,871 14,644 14,765 13,817	18 and 19 years 20 to 24 years 25 to 29 years	196 515 434	278 278	91 237 21.3	39 244 205	216	16 34 37	21	656
35 to 39 years _ [13,751	6,447 6,213	7,304	4,663	4,784 1	,784 . 2	2,520	13,817	30 to 34 years	406 468	213	20.2 193 226	205 189 224	196 178 206	24	16 15 20	596 490
0 to 44 vears _ 5 to 49 vears	12,046	5,653	6,393	3,462	4,179 4	,812 2	,21	13,460	40 to 44 years	417	212	205	193	494	19	11	419
0 to 54 years	9,190	3,517	4.714	3,026	3,047 1	45n 3	,657 ,657	6,544 4,885	45 to 49 years. 50 to 54 years. 55 to 59 years.	364 326 220	178	163 148 105	186 164 108	39	15	9	330
0 to 64 years 5 to 69 years 0 to 74 years	5,281 5,027 3,157	2,537	3,603 2,744 3,011	2,351 1,758 4,351	1,876	79	868	3,864	60 to 64 years. 65 to 69 years.	131	71	60 70	66 59	94 57 62	10	11 3	196 151 109
to 84 years .	2,759	2,516 1,438 1,258	1,729	763	958	559	588 543 442	1,831	70 to 74 years -	108	50 57	58 43	44	53	6	٥.	59
years and over	523	202	319	112	177	92		95,419	85 years and over	3,540	15	10	12	42 8	3	2	83
			10			, 000 120	1001	12 WIA	21 years and over	3,240	1,863	1,677	1,693	1,545	170	-32	3.871

Table 41 -AGE BY COLOR AND SEX, FOR PAR'SHES 1953-Con.

		115.40	1950 p	op_ation	-	on and the		.946	SEX, FOR PAR	SHES	1952_	Con.	opustion			-	1940
Pansh and age		Ari classes			hile	\one	rate	por	Pa ar and age.		12 cases		43	6	1.09.0	de	potals-
	Total	Male	Fersie	Male	Female	Male	r'ema.e	0.61		Total	Male	A PELBLE	Viale :	I em.h	face	Made 1	Con
AI'M TAL			74									1					
AU sger	1.,834	6,0.7	5,81	3,993	3,693	2 724	2, 24	1-,8	A. ages	1 4- 398	الإورسا	١٤,.35	5,27-	5 450)	٠ إداد ه	. 83	J., PO3
Under 5 years	2,9	8(C)	699	72.	4-1	32C	-20	_ 68_	Under 5 /ears	i Q. 1	1."13	-, 42	530	498	9741 1	.724	3,550 6+8
1 and 2 years	991 609	325	766 680	2.0	164	1.25	1.5	_,399	Under 5 years Under 1 year 1 and 2 ears 3 and 4 years	5-	200	26.	20	27.	3391	187	
K for Q washing	1,41	680	139	44"	40	239	250	,500		1,25	1.423	19	62.	800		42.	3 51"
5 years	306	-2- 151	150	98	102	53	52	,570 ,570	5 years 6 years 7 to 9 /cars	59 . j	,79 29c	247 Z)_	941	ادر-	341	200	716
5 years 6 years 7 to 9 years 10 to 14 years	1,367	41_	663	972 464 375	269	2,39	215	55	7 to 9 /ears 10 .0 ·4 /ears 10 .0 13 years	2.09	8.4	2	3.2 486	497	25.	44.1	e. Ond
10 to 13 years	1,09"	501	23C	375	372	186	.64	- 88 346	10 to 13 years	2,140	272	-,580 -,580	404	207	630	227	3,632 2,86°
o to .9 vears	1.100	559	34_ 130	372	300		4.14	42	16 'o 19 rears	2 4 4.9	2.0	1.14	450	-8"	660	-48 6u	3,500
15 years 16 and 17 years 18 and 19 years	272 444	231	190	100	2° 142	494 41 76	71	557	16 and 1" years - 18 and 19 years	5"	3,5	3	154	5	301	250	3,5UC
to 24 years	364 720 675	186 367	359	22.	714	1.5	145	535 1,237	20 to 24 .ears	7	el K	6 %	21	337	345	472	2,912
0 to 24 years	153	3.5	3e^ 3^	224	248	91	129	2 281	23 to 24 , ears 25 to 29 years 30 to 34 years	1,26	604	737	23	348	343	4.9	2 204
15 to 39 vears 10 to 44 years -	786	404	182 36.	287	246	1.8	341	915	30 to 34 years 35 to 39 years 40 to 44 years	1,434	C57	750	337	369	309	381	-,94
to to 49 years .	645	330 280	31.5	233	190	47	16	610	45 to 49 years - 50 to 54 years		640	627	107	205 27.	330	3!	1 021
0 to 54 years 5 to 59 years	431 3/9	216	233 215	-5± -5± 0	142	94	96 73	584 8 430 8	50 to 54 years 55 to 59 years 60 to 54 years	1 123	536 5:4 (32	593 194	270	342 239	656	252	1.358
to 64 years	404	176 210	173 194	65 67 64	10.	46 97	58	370 360	65 to 63 .ears	1 108 871 -,0-5	51.5	43° 530	248	239	_84 283	200	944
0 to 74 years 5 to 84 years	247	124	274	ారి	39 60	-01 57	37	178	70 to 74 /ears 75 to 84 years	6_3 551	774	25	-to!	46c	3	32	400
5 years and over 21 years and over	42 U,30z	3,180	24	2,176	1 54	~0	54	78,	85 years and over _	_22	53(69	2	30	34	39 1	437
	0,302	2,10-	3,444	2,170	1 94.	1,017	1,-74	~ 595	21 years and over -	.3,403	6,400	7,-103	3,211	3,433	3,189 3	,670	6,948
CLAIBORNE Ad ages	25,063	12,401	±2,002	6,079	6 027	6,382	€ 57±	29,852	All ages .	158,236	77,070	6.,564	54,53	53,003,2	283.	5.33	88,415
Inder 5 years	3,130	1,605	1, 2,	125	60.	971 191	67	3,255	Under 5 years	20,40	1^,258 2,2 4,457, 3,738 7,50 - 278	ا المحاربات	6.792	0.547	3,566	,49"	7 449
Under 1 years 1 and 2 years 3 and 4 years	1,236	683 66a	630	274	243	400	393	2,646	I and 2 years	2,760	4,4571	4 303	2 80	2.75	1,563	512	6,035
to 9 years.	4,640	-,326 259	4.3-4	5.4	J.2	812	81.2	3,,0	3 and 4 years _ 5 to 9 years	-5,03P	7,504	7,37	2,-64		2.532 2	,002	7.119
5 years 6 years 7 to 9 years	517	266 201	276 251	1.5 90	130	1%	166	7	5 years	3,212		1,60,	1,050	- 000	5-21	574	1,30
7 to 9 years 0 to 14 years. 10 to 13 years.	-,588	1,336	78" ,251 993	3_9 536	308	462 800	479	3,5*7	6 years 7 to 9 years 10 to 14 years	8,504	5,663	1,60,	1,263 2,849 3,464 2,842	4,140	2.179	,526	4 325
10 *0 13 venrs. :4 years	2 0o5 524	1,072	993 260	431	381	15	142	2,6-0	10 to 13 years	9,166	1,064	1,02	2,842	2,790	1,737, 1	412	1,698
5 to 15 vea.s	2,325	1,203	1,.22	780	458	71/	064	3 140	a5 to 19 veers	11,910	1 052	0.46	3,709		2 101 2	275	8,821
'5 years .6 and 17 years	984	514 41o	259 270 393	227 227	184	16° 287	286	4.478	16 and 17 years	2,015 3,904 934	1,922	.,042	1,181	1,207	74	354	3.470
0 to 24 years	1.655	786	863	343	59	262 433	237 510	2,723	8 and 19 years 20 to 24 years	16.493	7,930	3,195	5, 80	5 839	2 150 2	,086 ,724	3,64± 8,915
18 and 19 years 0 to 24 years 5 to 29 years 0 to 84 years 5 to 39 years	1,607	754 681 787	873 838	42.5 392	421 473 426	329 289	432 365	1,964	25 to 29 years 30 to 34 years	15,994 _3 300	7,930 7 798 6,520	6,780	5,705	5,713	2,09. 2	,483	9,028 3,182 7,384

	,510	787 £97	*86 \	430 3+9	426	351	367	1,964	35 to 39 years 40 to 44 years	_2,34L 0 403	5,123	5,280	4 2.3	4,138	1,843; 2	,106 ,702	6,070
5 to 49 years 0 to 54 years	,426	705	721	399	353 332	312	323 267	1,441	45 to 49 years	8,28*	4,107	3,27	2,614		1.293 7	40	7. 939
55 to 59 years 50 to 64 years	_,023 67_	-03 474	520 397	319 2F3	330 247	-84	190	920	50 to 54 years 55 to 59 years 60 to 64 years	5,691 4,913	2,4.9	2.494	1.621	1,096	130	798	2 668
35 to 69 years	864	430	434	218	211	212	223	528	65 to 69 years	3,726 3,450	1,834	1,929	ددد. ه	- 331	7-C	646	2,009
D to 84 Ventre	30c	263	2/5	152	142	11	103	379 4C3	70 to 74 years - 70 to 84 years	1 86± 1,80≤	803	1,058	453 413	606	350 334	382	1,061
5 years and over	14,025	44 r,831	7 194	3,844	3,904	2,987	3 290	15,525	85 /ears and over. 21 years and over	96,518	47,077	49,445	62 32,885	33,178 1	P 188 16	267	24,994
	2-,025	.,		3,0.1	5,504	2,50.	220	13,323		10,220	1	45,445	36,003	33,3 10	100 120		74,3-4
Ali ages	14,398	7,046	7,352	3,079	5 848	4 737	4,494	14,562	All ages	16,302	8,455	8,2/7	3,297	3,035	4,758 5	209	19,023
Inder 5 years - Under 1 year-	1,897	964 183	933 172	385 68	354 59	179 115	579	1,448	Under o vears	2.4.1	1,214	1,197	468	445	7461	724	2,056
1 and 2 years 3 and 4 years	786	398	368	15	1.53	243	235	1,182	Under 1 year 1 and 2 years	510 995	495	50U	104 203 161	177	292 297	327 1	_,663
to w years	7,6	363 630	373 810	160 323 74	333	537	477	1.38-	5 to 9 years	2,00	1,017	448 688	432	180	484	268) 6Co	1.937
5 years	336	1d_ 162	155	65	67	107	148	266 278	5 years 6 years 7 to 9 years	442	208	220	86 88	861	136 1<0 329 520	1.50	38
7 to 9 vears	1,4	743	474	184	20u 289	285 453	439	1,450	7 to 9 years	1,149	58 908	562 811	253 388	331	520	341 480	1,151
0 to 14 yea s 10 to 13 years 14 years	1,193 278	298 -45	295	236 54	234	362 91	363	253	10 to 14 years 10 to 13 years. 14 years.	357	20,	125	294 94	265	409	394	1,552
5 to 19 years	247	576 141	637	239 54	237	139 67	-00	1,374	15 to 19 years	1,393	697	098 1.0	293 74	294	40 ₄ 89	404 86	_,850
fo years fo and 1" years 18 and 19 years	505	242 21.5	126 463	93	40	149 123	166	550	16 and 17 years	500	274	295	1_8	-16	126	1.80	387 745
	949	424	248	218	212	206	31.5	1,272	20 to 24 trees.	5.0	260 480	250	101	233	270	345	716 1,733 1,579
to 29 > ears -	883 898	408 401	477	212	246	196	229	1,234	25 to 24 years 30 to 34 years	9,3 876	385	484	226	202	21.96	293 286	2,579
5 to 39 years 0 to 44 , rars	898 868	798 424	500	193	1 '2 '	205	318	1,135	35 to 39 years 40 to 44 years	992	459 463	533	217	216	242	347	-,484 -,402 - 138
to 49 years	820	4.6 343	404	84	167	232	237	82%	45 to 49 years	812 717	_90 336	422	160	135	230	247	968
0 to 54 vears	716 577	300	373	16	137	179 164	175	598 546	56 to 59 years	p29	337	292	127	94	226	270	839 615
to 64 years - to 69 years	455 510	234	2/7	95	57	139	154	418 421	60 to 64 years 65 to 60 years	499 388	267 289	232	88	76	212	232	48,
to 74 years to 84 years	299 281	195	136	42	37	98	10"	225	70 to 74 years. 75 to 84 years.	336 330	170	1/46	4.	4.	120	129	273
vears and ove	41	50	21	7	4	-3	17	210	85 years and over	6.	28	33		3	21	20 3	227
1 rears and over	7,970	3,851	4,119	1,734	1,594	2,116	2,525	8 624 II	21 years and over	P,553	4,123	4,430	1,683	1,540	2 440 2	,890	10,827

LOUISIANA

Table 41 -AGE BY COLOR AND SEX, FOR PARISHES 1950-Con

-	1	THE REAL PROPERTY.	1950 :	opulation	n	CHICAGO TO STATE OF THE PARTY O		1940	T	1		.950 g	opulation	1	-	-	1940
Parish and age	-	All dames		-	Tute	'von'	white	popula-	Parash and agr		All classe	6	W	hite	Non	white	popula- tion

Table 41.—AGE BY COLOR AND SEX, FOR PARISHES: 1950—Con.

Parish and age	1950 population: All classes, Total	All classes, Male	All classes, Female	White, Male	White, Female	Nonwhite, Male	Nonwhite, Female	1940 population total
EAST FELICIANA								
All ages	[illegible]	9,549	9,584	3,946	4,046	5,603	5,536	18,039
Under 5 years	1,835	927	908	200	237	667	671	1,570
Under 1 year	378	194	184	57	57	137	127	280
1 and 2 years	730	375	355	109	99	266	256	1,290
3 and 4 years	727	358	369	94	81	264	288	
5 to 9 years	1,682	809	873	209	220	600	653	1,619
5 years	363	162	201	41	52	121	149	360
6 years	356	179	177	42	51	137	126	316
7 to 9 years	963	468	495	126	117	342	378	933
10 to 14 years	1,580	833	747	206	193	627	554	1,668
10 to 13 years	1,268	670	598	173	156	497	442	1,322
14 years	312	163	149	31	37	132	112	346
15 to 19 years	1,345	705	640	207	172	498	468	1,552
15 years	277	130	147	35	38	95	109	335
16 and 17 years	565	298	267	89	68	209	199	607
18 and 19 years	503	277	226	83	66	194	160	610
20 to 24 years	1,264	687	577	254	211	433	366	1,306
25 to 29 years	1,160	594	566	250	258	344	308	1,321
30 to 34 years	1,173	602	[illegible]	290	258	312	313	1,261
35 to 39 years	1,338	665	673	328	320	337	353	1,349
40 to 44 years	1,416	729	687	373	346	356	341	1,151
45 to 49 years	1,366	678	688	360	356	318	332	1,080
50 to 54 years	1,135	515	620	276	363	239	257	1,015
55 to 59 years	942	424	518	226	288	198	230	881
60 to 64 years	841	408	433	247	247	161	186	756
65 to 69 years	879	414	465	195	230	219	235	671
70 to 74 years	547	260	287	131	158	129	129	409
75 to 84 years	522	254	268	112	159	142	109	430
85 years and over	108	45	63	22	32	23	31	
21 years and over	12,449	6,129	6,320	3,018	3,196	3,111	3,124	11,351
EVANGELINE								
All ages	31,629	15,962	15,667	12,168	11,905	3,794	3,762	30,497
Under 5 years	4,175	2,118	2,057	1,424	1,394	694	663	3,785
Under 1 year	791	399	392	278	261	121	131	678
1 and 2 years	1,717	865	852	591	576	274	276	3,107
3 and 4 years	1,667	854	813	555	557	299	256	
5 to 9 years	3,773	1,916	1,877	1,343	1,291	573	586	3,656
5 years	776	404	372	281	242	123	130	734
6 years	798	415	383	285	249	130	134	719
7 to 9 years	2,219	1,097	1,122	777	800	320	322	2,193
10 to 14 years	3,376	1,672	1,704	1,167	1,167	505	537	3,558
10 to 13 years	2,771	1,373	1,398	939	957	434	441	2,858
14 years	605	299	306	228	210	71	96	700
15 to 19 years	2,844	1,449	1,395	1,005	1,007	444	388	3,100
15 years	657	345	312	241	226	104	86	606
16 and 17 years	1,187	609	578	435	419	174	159	1,238
18 and 19 years	1,000	495	505	329	362	166	143	1,276
20 to 24 years	2,345	1,148	1,197	851	885	297	312	2,958
25 to 29 years	2,183	1,086	1,097	882	835	204	262	2,682
30 to 34 years	2,228	1,115	1,113	923	914	192	199	2,202
35 to 39 years	2,236	1,121	1,115	917	898	204	217	2,076
40 to 44 years	1,891	1,002	889	854	767	148	122	1,509
45 to 49 years	1,736	855	881	722	741	133	140	1,395
50 to 54 years	1,376	710	666	606	571	104	95	982
55 to 59 years	1,130	573	557	484	479	89	78	812
60 to 64 years	804	410	394	349	355	61	39	605
65 to 69 years	702	363	339	291	274	72	65	486
70 to 74 years	385	204	181	171	159	33	22	273
75 to 84 years	356	188	168	159	143	29	25	328
85 years and over	69	32	37	20	25	12	12	
21 years and over	17,010	8,602	8,408	7,081	6,894	1,521	1,517	15,839
FRANKLIN								
All ages	29,376	14,599	14,777	9,367	9,234	5,232	5,543	32,382
Under 5 years	4,110	2,004	2,106	1,109	1,193	895	913	3,905
Under 1 year	818	413	405	224	227	189	178	740
1 and 2 years	1,653	826	827	460	458	366	369	3,165
3 and 4 years	1,639	765	874	425	508	340	366	
5 to 9 years	3,721	1,874	1,847	1,126	1,132	748	715	3,859
5 years	810	407	403	246	226	161	177	842
6 years	783	401	382	234	234	167	148	765
7 to 9 years	2,128	1,066	1,062	646	672	420	390	2,252
10 to 14 years	3,339	1,666	1,673	1,103	1,061	563	612	3,826
10 to 13 years	2,726	1,365	1,361	899	860	466	501	3,129
14 years	613	301	312	204	201	97	111	697
15 to 19 years	2,838	1,415	1,423	878	887	537	536	3,430
15 years	644	312	332	193	224	119	108	698
16 and 17 years	1,239	629	610	406	380	223	230	1,394
18 and 19 years	955	474	481	279	283	195	198	1,338
20 to 24 years	1,937	943	994	618	580	325	414	1,941
25 to 29 years	1,736	784	952	535	606	249	346	2,639
30 to 34 years	1,808	856	952	612	661	244	291	2,378
35 to 39 years	1,922	930	992	651	633	279	359	2,116
40 to 44 years	1,741	892	849	650	564	242	285	1,652
45 to 49 years	1,544	784	760	508	491	276	269	1,416
50 to 54 years	1,149	619	530	412	330	207	200	1,127
55 to 59 years	948	473	475	297	313	176	162	964
60 to 64 years	773	395	378	292	286	103	92	747
65 to 69 years	830	421	409	224	218	197	191	689
70 to 74 years	447	253	194	168	140	85	54	383
75 to 84 years	476	267	209	171	123	96	86	333
85 years and over	57	23	34	13	16	10	18	
21 years and over	14,940	7,452	7,488	5,049	4,821	2,403	2,607	16,748

Parish and age	1950 population: All classes, Total	All classes, Male	All classes, Female	White, Male	White, Female	Nonwhite, Male	Nonwhite, Female	1940 population total
GRANT								
All ages	14,263	7,125	7,138	5,467	5,339	1,658	1,799	15,933
Under 5 years	652	847	805	598	572	249	233	1,690
Under 1 year	302	165	137	112	98	53	39	332
1 and 2 years	713	370	343	260	239	110	104	1,358
3 and 4 years	637	312	325	226	235	86	90	
5 to 9 years	1,649	823	826	612	594	211	232	1,691
5 years	353	173	180	120	131	53	49	359
6 years	338	178	160	138	118	40	42	319
7 to 9 years	958	472	486	354	345	118	141	1,013
10 to 14 years	1,491	759	732	552	544	207	188	1,786
10 to 13 years	1,220	609	611	444	461	165	150	1,417
14 years	271	150	121	108	83	42	38	369
15 to 19 years	1,165	616	549	452	407	164	147	1,744
15 years	234	158	126	117	96	41	30	353
16 and 17 years	500	271	229	207	169	64	60	681
18 and 19 years	381	187	194	128	137	59	57	710
20 to 24 years	853	400	453	287	305	113	148	1,355
25 to 29 years	819	376	443	292	334	84	109	1,208
30 to 34 years	882	430	452	350	357	80	95	1,086
35 to 39 years	903	448	455	378	342	70	113	1,029
40 to 44 years	892	429	463	336	354	93	109	891
45 to 49 years	779	388	391	323	308	65	83	801
50 to 54 years	697	317	380	249	300	68	80	683
55 to 59 years	664	338	326	274	266	64	60	579
60 to 64 years	531	299	232	252	193	47	39	451
65 to 69 years	560	275	285	204	205	71	80	459
70 to 74 years	341	181	160	149	127	32	33	244
75 to 84 years	326	174	152	138	111	36	41	234
85 years and over	59	25	34	21	25	4	9	
21 years and over	8,121	3,997	4,124	3,199	3,165	798	959	8,723
IBERIA								
All ages	40,059	19,913	20,146	13,587	13,499	6,326	6,647	37,183
Under 5 years	5,211	2,721	2,490	1,772	1,605	949	885	4,086
Under 1 year	1,098	593	505	381	324	212	181	790
1 and 2 years	2,072	1,047	1,025	675	658	372	367	3,296
3 and 4 years	2,041	1,081	960	716	623	365	337	
5 to 9 years	4,404	2,219	2,185	1,445	1,361	774	824	3,869
5 years	861	443	418	290	268	153	150	751
6 years	943	500	443	323	274	177	169	772
7 to 9 years	2,600	1,276	1,324	832	819	444	505	2,346
10 to 14 years	3,896	2,001	1,895	1,323	1,182	678	713	3,904
10 to 13 years	3,157	1,627	1,530	1,085	961	542	569	3,112
14 years	739	374	365	238	221	136	144	792
15 to 19 years	3,303	1,623	1,680	1,006	1,043	517	637	3,778
15 years	667	324	343	185	216	139	127	762
16 and 17 years	1,357	695	662	427	392	268	270	1,472
18 and 19 years	1,279	604	675	394	435	210	240	1,544
20 to 24 years	3,024	1,395	1,629	952	1,128	443	501	3,824
25 to 29 years	3,117	1,509	1,608	1,110	1,135	399	473	3,426
30 to 34 years	2,991	1,451	1,540	1,050	1,081	401	459	2,857
35 to 39 years	2,959	1,481	1,478	1,083	1,028	398	450	2,403
40 to 44 years	2,441	1,261	1,180	922	846	339	334	1,935
45 to 49 years	2,060	1,056	1,004	740	709	316	295	1,721
50 to 54 years	1,643	803	840	590	577	213	263	1,300
55 to 59 years	1,446	696	750	475	555	221	195	1,213
60 to 64 years	1,140	579	561	402	403	177	158	904
65 to 69 years	1,096	520	576	322	354	198	222	799
70 to 74 years	663	308	355	212	246	96	109	423
75 to 84 years	551	241	310	150	206	91	104	511
85 years and over	114	49	65	33	40	16	25	
21 years and over	22,657	11,080	11,577	7,861	8,092	3,219	3,485	20,771
IBERVILLE								
All ages	26,750	13,215	13,535	6,777	6,885	6,438	6,650	[illegible]
Under 5 years	3,451	1,705	1,746	785	853	920	893	2,807
Under 1 year	680	340	340	156	162	184	178	592
1 and 2 years	1,414	695	719	332	357	363	362	2,215
3 and 4 years	1,357	670	687	297	334	373	353	
5 to 9 years	2,965	1,466	1,499	651	709	815	790	2,618
5 years	647	306	341	132	161	174	180	556
6 years	639	303	336	153	160	150	176	509
7 to 9 years	1,679	857	822	366	388	491	434	1,553
10 to 14 years	2,558	1,314	1,244	629	630	685	614	2,801
10 to 13 years	2,101	1,087	1,014	520	509	567	505	2,237
14 years	457	227	230	109	121	118	109	564
15 to 19 years	2,088	1,046	1,042	509	547	537	495	2,859
15 years	455	225	230	112	115	113	115	547
16 and 17 years	882	459	423	215	213	244	210	1,177
18 and 19 years	751	362	389	182	219	180	170	1,135
20 to 24 years	1,802	899	903	529	519	370	384	2,521
25 to 29 years	1,786	884	902	528	525	356	377	2,327
30 to 34 years	1,706	819	887	487	496	332	391	1,936
35 to 39 years	1,713	843	870	476	482	367	388	1,842
40 to 44 years	1,529	760	769	436	398	324	371	1,617
45 to 49 years	1,483	742	741	404	379	338	362	1,485
50 to 54 years	1,240	603	637	340	339	263	298	1,296
55 to 59 years	1,196	590	606	301	298	289	308	1,325
60 to 64 years	926	459	467	235	239	224	228	733
65 to 69 years	1,082	493	539	212	154	281	395	851
70 to 74 years	553	262	291	118	135	144	156	477
75 to 84 years	538	275	263	119	107	156	156	504
85 years and over	154	55	79	18	35	37	44	
21 years and over	15,330	7,516	7,814	4,116	4,044	3,400	3,770	16,125

Table 41.—AGE BY COLOR AND SEX, FOR PARISHES 1950—Con.

Parish and age	1950 population: All classes, Total	All classes, Male	All classes, Female	White, Male	White, Female	Nonwhite, Male	Nonwhite, Female	1940 population total
JACKSON								
All ages	15,434	7,566	7,868	5,355	5,486	2,211	2,382	17,807
Under 5 years	1,864	932	932	579	582	353	350	1,682
Under 1 year	305	153	152	92	90	61	62	385
1 and 2 years	788	399	389	243	244	156	145	1,497
3 and 4 years	771	380	391	244	248	136	143	
5 to 9 years	1,685	854	831	563	560	291	271	957
5 years	331	156	175	102	117	54	58	430
6 years	362	198	164	129	114	69	50	390
7 to 9 years	992	500	492	332	329	168	163	1,131
10 to 14 years	1,622	812	810	540	543	272	267	1,947
10 to 13 years	1,303	664	639	439	441	225	198	1,56[illegible]
14 years	319	148	171	101	102	47	69	387
15 to 19 years	1,334	625	709	442	476	183	233	1,786
15 years	350	168	182	130	123	38	59	349
16 and 17 years	558	257	301	176	214	81	87	695
18 and 19 years	426	200	226	136	139	64	87	742
20 to 24 years	1,011	476	535	338	347	138	188	1,685
25 to 29 years	985	432	553	308	369	124	184	1,749
30 to 34 years	1,074	508	566	386	426	122	140	1,479
35 to 39 years	1,165	544	621	407	444	137	177	1,134
40 to 44 years	1,015	513	502	392	361	121	141	875
45 to 49 years	829	455	374	330	265	125	109	819
50 to 54 years	670	329	341	236	259	93	82	675
55 to 59 years	600	286	314	216	264	70	50	565
60 to 64 years	476	244	232	197	183	47	49	470
65 to 69 years	477	234	243	173	161	61	82	392
70 to 74 years	306	161	145	128	115	33	30	196
75 to 84 years	290	146	144	109	123	37	21	202
85 years and over	31	15	16	11	8	4	8	
21 years and over	8,714	4,243	4,471	3,160	3,255	1,083	1,216	9,889
JEFFERSON								
All ages	103,873	51,584	52,289	43,626	43,978	7,958	8,311	50,427
Under 5 years	14,643	7,529	7,114	6,290	5,938	1,239	1,176	4,455
Under 1 year	2,850	1,454	1,396	1,195	1,135	259	261	850
1 and 2 years	6,225	3,221	3,004	2,704	2,488	517	516	3,605
3 and 4 years	5,568	2,854	2,714	2,391	2,315	463	399	
5 to 9 years	11,119	5,622	5,497	4,726	4,561	896	936	4,783
5 years	2,458	1,246	1,212	1,063	1,005	183	207	945
6 years	2,396	1,228	1,168	1,015	977	213	191	942
7 to 9 years	6,265	3,148	3,117	2,648	2,579	500	538	2,896
10 to 14 years	7,916	4,111	3,805	3,396	3,143	715	662	5,390
10 to 13 years	6,491	3,382	3,109	2,804	2,567	578	542	4,325
14 years	1,425	729	696	592	576	137	120	1,065
15 to 19 years	6,699	3,180	3,519	2,607	2,903	573	616	5,328
15 years	1,404	732	672	601	543	131	129	1,058
16 and 17 years	2,591	1,250	1,341	1,023	1,090	227	251	2,192
18 and 19 years	2,704	1,198	1,506	983	1,270	215	236	2,078
20 to 24 years	8,521	3,909	4,612	3,276	3,824	633	788	4,419
25 to 29 years	10,197	4,884	5,313	4,268	4,582	616	731	4,405
30 to 34 years	8,774	4,281	4,493	3,751	3,859	530	634	4,273
35 to 39 years	8,287	4,148	4,139	3,618	3,549	530	590	4,030
40 to 44 years	7,291	3,711	3,580	3,193	3,038	518	542	3,484
45 to 49 years	5,731	2,956	2,775	2,465	2,304	491	471	2,670
50 to 54 years	4,589	2,429	2,160	2,067	1,813	362	347	2,131
55 to 59 years	3,325	1,669	1,656	1,382	1,440	287	216	1,693
60 to 64 years	2,389	1,170	1,219	1,009	1,052	161	167	1,221
65 to 69 years	2,002	957	1,045	756	809	201	236	1,008
70 to 74 years	1,154	505	649	403	551	102	98	587
75 to 84 years	1,083	459	624	369	547	90	77	550
85 years and over	153	64	89	50	65	14	24	
21 years and over	62,023	30,538	31,485	26,106	26,730	4,432	4,755	29,518
JEFFERSON DAVIS								
All ages	26,298	13,039	13,259	10,302	10,307	2,737	2,952	24,191
Under 5 years	3,560	1,763	1,797	1,346	1,333	417	464	2,837
Under 1 year	712	347	365	264	265	83	100	567
1 and 2 years	1,485	739	746	554	560	85	186	2,270
3 and 4 years	1,363	677	686	528	508	149	178	
5 to 9 years	2,925	1,522	1,403	1,161	1,041	361	362	2,718
5 years	632	322	310	242	223	80	87	595
6 years	606	298	308	244	228	54	80	557
7 to 9 years	1,687	902	785	675	590	227	195	1,566
10 to 14 years	2,721	1,361	1,360	1,008	1,011	353	349	2,744
10 to 13 years	2,186	1,090	1,096	800	814	290	282	2,189
14 years	535	271	264	208	197	63	67	555
15 to 19 years	2,320	1,122	1,198	838	882	284	316	2,451
15 years	525	256	269	185	192	71	77	481
16 and 17 years	951	468	483	352	353	116	130	970
18 and 19 years	844	398	446	301	337	97	109	1,000
20 to 24 years	2,046	971	1,075	756	837	215	238	2,142
25 to 29 years	1,819	884	935	745	757	139	178	2,057
30 to 34 years	1,761	845	916	717	728	128	188	1,868
35 to 39 years	1,741	882	859	725	693	157	166	1,569
40 to 44 years	1,602	809	793	683	647	126	146	1,238
45 to 49 years	1,282	641	641	535	539	106	102	1,135
50 to 54 years	1,112	545	567	465	468	80	99	926
55 to 59 years	930	464	466	389	375	75	91	823
60 to 64 years	759	374	385	306	315	68	70	566
65 to 69 years	780	385	395	259	292	126	103	528
70 to 74 years	444	222	222	174	191	48	31	275
75 to 84 years	410	206	204	160	167	46	37	314
85 years and over	86	43	43	35	31	8	12	
21 years and over	14,378	7,099	7,279	5,830	5,875	1,269	1,404	13,017

Parish and age	1950 population: All classes, Total	All classes, Male	All classes, Female	White, Male	White, Female	Nonwhite, Male	Nonwhite, Female	1940 population total
LAFAYETTE								
All ages	57,743	28,478	29,265	20,458	21,053	7,520	8,212	43,941
Under 5 years	7,383	3,679	3,704	2,504	2,469	1,175	1,235	4,567
Under 1 year	1,572	816	756	541	521	275	236	889
1 and 2 years	3,004	1,479	1,525	994	1,034	485	491	3,678
3 and 4 years	2,807	1,384	1,423	969	915	415	508	
5 to 9 years	5,785	2,962	2,823	2,026	1,893	936	930	4,647
5 years	1,143	566	577	[illegible]	382	1[illegible]6	195	891
6 years	1,219	616	603	[illegible]	[illegible]	200	191	956
7 to 9 years	3,423	1,780	1,643	[illegible]	1,299	570	544	2,800
10 to 14 years	5,132	2,569	2,563	1,772	1,614	847	949	5,109
10 to 13 years	4,134	2,056	2,078	1,360	1,324	696	754	4,082
14 years	998	513	485	362	290	151	195	927
15 to 19 years	5,320	2,570	2,750	1,782	1,904	788	846	4,755
15 years	949	470	479	316	298	154	181	926
16 and 17 years	1,963	961	1,002	631	656	330	346	1,907
18 and 19 years	2,408	1,139	1,269	835	950	304	319	1,922
20 to 24 years	5,819	2,880	2,939	2,249	2,158	631	781	4,352
25 to 29 years	4,998	2,502	2,496	1,950	1,879	552	617	3,963
30 to 34 years	4,260	2,106	2,154	1,672	1,635	434	519	3,252
35 to 39 years	4,063	2,028	2,035	1,555	1,538	473	497	2,974
40 to 44 years	3,429	1,668	1,751	1,304	1,319	364	432	2,393
45 to 49 years	3,025	1,539	1,486	1,177	1,142	362	344	2,107
50 to 54 years	2,267	1,056	1,211	833	913	223	298	1,782
55 to 59 years	1,944	939	1,005	725	767	214	238	1,372
60 to 64 years	1,443	771	742	529	579	172	163	1,017
65 to 69 years	1,246	584	662	412	495	172	167	856
70 to 74 years	761	328	433	242	342	86	91	438
75 to 84 years	736	313	423	239	341	74	82	457
85 years and over	142	54	88	37	65	17	23	
21 years and over	32,836	16,118	16,718	12,468	12,635	3,650	4,083	24,018
LAFOURCHE								
All ages	42,209	21,249	20,960	18,385	18,146	2,864	2,814	38,615
Under 5 years	5,765	3,027	2,738	2,580	2,334	447	404	4,620
Under 1 year	1,067	561	506	464	434	97	72	967
1 and 2 years	2,396	1,243	1,153	1,050	988	193	165	3,653
3 and 4 years	2,302	1,223	1,079	1,066	912	157	167	
5 to 9 years	4,934	2,517	2,417	2,118	2,056	399	361	4,379
5 years	1,013	509	504	430	423	79	81	885
6 years	983	485	498	417	416	68	82	826
7 to 9 years	2,938	1,523	1,415	1,271	1,217	252	198	2,668
10 to 14 years	4,342	2,220	2,122	1,895	1,814	325	308	4,492
10 to 13 years	3,583	1,816	1,767	1,549	1,506	267	261	3,540
14 years	759	404	355	346	308	58	47	952
15 to 19 years	3,826	1,885	1,941	1,610	1,688	275	253	4,408
15 years	779	385	394	317	340	68	54	884
16 and 17 years	1,550	772	778	654	670	118	108	1,813
18 and 19 years	1,497	728	769	639	678	89	91	1,711
20 to 24 years	3,423	1,714	1,709	1,526	1,490	188	219	3,862
25 to 29 years	3,291	1,651	1,640	1,460	1,445	191	195	3,309
30 to 34 years	3,075	1,568	1,507	1,417	1,312	151	195	2,713
35 to 39 years	2,810	1,383	1,427	1,227	1,260	156	167	2,269
40 to 44 years	2,332	1,213	1,119	1,079	995	134	124	1,777
45 to 49 years	1,987	978	1,009	870	886	108	123	1,753
50 to 54 years	1,587	754	833	660	708	94	125	1,392
55 to 59 years	1,433	708	725	601	638	107	87	1,111
60 to 64 years	1,115	573	542	476	482	97	60	871
65 to 69 years	1,012	464	548	368	445	96	103	753
70 to 74 years	606	294	312	249	267	45	45	463
75 to 84 years	572	261	311	216	274	45	37	443
85 years and over	99	39	60	33	52	6	8	
21 years and over	22,708	11,311	11,397	9,934	9,954	1,377	1,443	19,879
LA SALLE								
All ages	12,717	6,402	6,315	5,728	5,564	674	751	10,959
Under 5 years	1,440	733	707	665	602	68	105	1,104
Under 1 year	282	135	147	118	123	17	24	203
1 and 2 years	598	302	296	276	253	26	43	901
3 and 4 years	560	296	264	271	226	25	38	
5 to 9 years	1,355	677	678	601	596	76	82	1,125
5 years	272	135	137	118	117	17	20	247
6 years	269	136	133	114	119	22	14	208
7 to 9 years	814	406	408	369	360	37	48	670
10 to 14 years	1,266	669	597	592	528	77	69	1,191
10 to 13 years	1,029	545	484	481	427	64	57	950
14 years	237	124	113	111	101	13	12	241
15 to 19 years	1,091	533	558	480	497	53	61	1,176
15 years	264	112	152	100	138	12	14	240
16 and 17 years	464	247	217	230	195	17	22	478
18 and 19 years	363	174	189	150	164	24	25	458
20 to 24 years	781	388	393	343	354	45	39	997
25 to 29 years	816	386	430	349	378	37	52	834
30 to 34 years	928	447	481	410	439	37	42	823
35 to 39 years	909	454	455	408	397	46	58	812
40 to 44 years	853	424	429	392	395	32	34	667
45 to 49 years	798	425	373	379	320	46	53	563
50 to 54 years	645	314	331	273	292	41	39	466
55 to 59 years	484	249	235	227	199	22	36	395
60 to 64 years	424	212	212	185	191	27	21	309
65 to 69 years	407	222	185	188	156	34	29	258
70 to 74 years	250	125	125	111	112	14	13	128
75 to 84 years	241	128	113	112	97	16	16	111
85 years and over	29	16	13	13	11	3	2	
21 years and over	7,428	3,732	3,696	3,344	3,271	388	425	6,128

Table 41.—AGE BY COLOR AND SEX, FOR PARISHES: 1950—Con.

Parish and age	1950 population: All classes, Total	All classes, Male	All classes, Female	White, Male	White, Female	Nonwhite, Male	Nonwhite, Female	1940 population total
LINCOLN								
All ages	25,782	12,710	13,072	7,771	7,645	4,939	5,427	24,790
Under 5 years	3,031	1,532	1,499	802	785	730	714	2,490
Under 1 year	627	323	304	161	158	162	146	415
1 and 2 years	1,293	659	634	340	338	319	296	2,075
3 and 4 years	1,111	550	561	301	289	249	272	
5 to 9 years	2,358	1,146	1,212	588	621	558	591	2,533
5 years	485	229	256	107	135	122	121	516
6 years	470	235	235	129	117	106	118	492
7 to 9 years	1,403	682	721	352	369	330	352	1,525
10 to 14 years	2,211	1,078	1,133	588	597	490	536	2,751
10 to 13 years	1,738	849	889	470	467	379	422	2,203
14 years	473	229	244	118	130	111	114	548
15 to 19 years	2,835	1,362	1,473	817	848	545	625	2,715
15 years	426	221	205	124	110	97	95	523
16 and 17 years	868	409	459	205	252	204	207	1,129
18 and 19 years	1,541	732	809	488	486	244	323	1,063
20 to 24 years	3,005	1,619	1,386	1,059	697	560	689	2,412
25 to 29 years	1,809	909	900	590	508	319	392	2,106
30 to 34 years	1,548	759	789	497	473	262	316	1,870
35 to 39 years	1,598	750	848	469	528	281	320	1,576
40 to 44 years	1,461	721	750	486	487	245	263	1,324
45 to 49 years	1,300	626	674	401	428	225	246	1,169
50 to 54 years	1,081	509	571	332	363	177	208	1,054
55 to 59 years	878	439	439	298	323	141	116	840
60 to 64 years	758	354	404	255	306	99	98	695
65 to 69 years	818	393	425	242	278	151	147	581
70 to 74 years	523	261	262	189	186	72	76	327
75 to 84 years	460	200	260	130	188	70	72	348
85 years and over	89	42	47	28	29	14	18	
21 years and over	14,539	7,184	7,355	4,699	4,598	2,485	2,757	13,760
LIVINGSTON								
All ages	20,054	10,346	9,708	8,843	8,255	1,503	1,453	17,790
Under 5 years	2,850	1,447	1,403	1,239	1,148	208	255	2,136
Under 1 year	543	292	251	250	210	42	41	426
1 and 2 years	1,132	565	567	482	458	83	109	1,710
3 and 4 years	1,175	590	585	507	480	83	105	
5 to 9 years	2,422	1,231	1,191	1,053	1,027	178	164	2,029
5 years	495	261	234	215	204	46	30	439
6 years	519	268	251	242	224	26	27	368
7 to 9 years	1,408	702	706	596	609	106	97	1,222
10 to 14 years	2,071	1,087	984	929	843	158	141	2,186
10 to 13 years	1,691	887	804	764	689	123	115	1,708
14 years	380	200	180	165	154	35	26	418
15 to 19 years	1,727	901	826	755	676	146	150	2,002
15 years	399	191	208	158	177	33	31	435
16 and 17 years	698	371	327	318	267	53	60	796
18 and 19 years	630	339	291	279	232	60	59	771
20 to 24 years	1,504	728	776	587	640	141	136	1,520
25 to 29 years	1,457	706	751	598	639	108	112	1,397
30 to 34 years	1,289	666	623	581	551	85	72	1,210
35 to 39 years	1,324	682	642	585	537	97	105	1,068
40 to 44 years	1,203	640	563	555	480	85	83	950
45 to 49 years	1,016	521	495	433	423	88	72	804
50 to 54 years	808	445	363	389	326	56	37	687
55 to 59 years	673	327	346	283	314	44	32	558
60 to 64 years	550	318	232	280	208	38	24	427
65 to 69 years	523	306	217	269	175	37	42	367
70 to 74 years	299	154	145	142	136	12	9	218
75 to 84 years	287	162	125	145	108	17	17	231
85 years and over	51	25	26	20	24	5	2	
21 years and over	10,681	5,532	5,149	[illegible]	4,438	785	711	9,127
MADISON								
All ages	17,451	8,608	8,843	2,971	2,920	5,637	5,923	18,443
Under 5 years	2,339	1,178	1,161	375	343	803	818	1,879
Under 1 year	469	240	229	69	61	171	168	385
1 and 2 years	958	485	473	159	143	326	330	1,494
3 and 4 years	912	453	459	147	139	306	320	
5 to 9 years	2,044	982	1,062	319	377	663	685	1,722
5 years	418	209	209	62	69	147	140	345
6 years	437	213	224	68	73	145	151	344
7 to 9 years	1,189	560	629	189	235	371	394	1,033
10 to 14 years	1,776	905	871	304	301	601	570	1,856
10 to 13 years	1,459	728	731	244	255	484	476	1,500
14 years	317	177	140	60	46	117	94	356
15 to 19 years	1,344	672	672	215	215	457	457	1,697
15 years	290	152	138	52	39	100	99	350
16 and 17 years	567	287	280	92	93	195	187	628
18 and 19 years	487	233	254	71	83	162	171	719
20 to 24 years	1,178	550	628	195	183	355	445	1,655
25 to 29 years	1,076	514	562	186	212	328	350	1,712
30 to 34 years	1,028	456	572	201	247	255	325	1,493
35 to 39 years	1,146	516	630	229	225	287	405	1,496
40 to 44 years	1,068	525	543	223	177	302	366	1,198
45 to 49 years	1,074	557	517	188	172	369	345	1,040
50 to 54 years	900	470	430	151	123	319	307	737
55 to 59 years	680	361	319	135	108	226	211	612
60 to 64 years	457	239	218	85	83	154	135	469
65 to 69 years	646	327	319	74	60	253	259	419
70 to 74 years	337	181	156	50	45	131	111	265
75 to 84 years	301	151	150	35	[illegible]	116	109	193
85 years and over	57	24	33	6	8	18	25	
21 years and over	9,704	4,762	4,942	1,726	1,646	3,036	3,296	10,947

Parish and age	1950 population: All classes, Total	All classes, Male	All classes, Female	White, Male	White, Female	Nonwhite, Male	Nonwhite, Female	1940 population total
MOREHOUSE								
All ages	32,038	15,973	16,065	8,438	8,161	7,535	7,904	27,571
Under 5 years	4,563	2,386	2,177	1,133	1,038	1,253	1,139	2,894
Under 1 year	964	493	471	249	212	244	259	480
1 and 2 years	1,872	1,009	863	453	414	556	449	2,344
3 and 4 years	1,727	884	843	431	412	453	431	
5 to 9 years	3,684	1,844	1,840	954	901	890	935	2,834
5 years	812	427	385	202	190	225	195	558
6 years	729	364	365	191	171	173	194	555
7 to 9 years	2,143	1,053	1,090	561	544	492	546	1,721
10 to 14 years	3,188	1,619	1,569	779	776	840	793	2,928
10 to 13 years	2,599	1,311	1,288	629	649	682	639	2,328
14 years	589	308	281	150	127	158	154	600
15 to 19 years	2,750	1,326	1,424	652	667	674	757	2,822
15 years	614	308	306	148	141	160	165	560
16 and 17 years	1,107	531	576	272	250	259	326	1,165
18 and 19 years	1,029	487	542	232	276	255	266	1,097
20 to 24 years	2,508	1,181	1,327	658	710	523	617	2,559
25 to 29 years	2,285	1,103	1,182	697	701	406	481	2,374
30 to 34 years	2,154	1,060	1,094	664	636	396	458	2,188
35 to 39 years	2,104	1,014	1,090	633	582	381	508	2,053
40 to 44 years	1,909	905	1,004	537	515	368	489	1,633
45 to 49 years	1,627	835	792	420	378	415	414	1,360
50 to 54 years	1,297	650	647	300	313	350	334	1,089
55 to 59 years	1,047	538	509	277	252	261	257	847
60 to 64 years	865	443	422	247	226	196	196	701
65 to 69 years	960	497	463	218	211	279	252	657
70 to 74 years	529	293	236	135	123	158	113	351
75 to 84 years	483	233	250	112	116	121	134	357
85 years and over	85	46	39	22	12	24	27	
21 years and over	17,373	8,595	8,778	4,826	4,640	3,769	4,138	15,572
NATCHITOCHES								
All ages	38,144	18,783	19,361	10,511	10,523	8,272	8,838	40,997
Under 5 years	4,969	2,514	2,455	1,273	1,150	1,241	1,305	4,792
Under 1 year	919	463	456	229	223	234	233	884
1 and 2 years	2,055	1,065	990	543	451	522	539	3,908
3 and 4 years	1,995	986	1,009	501	476	485	533	
5 to 9 years	4,357	2,159	2,198	1,112	1,106	1,047	1,092	4,662
5 years	902	437	465	216	226	221	239	968
6 years	890	435	455	222	228	213	227	948
7 to 9 years	2,565	1,287	1,278	674	652	613	626	2,746
10 to 14 years	4,066	2,110	1,956	1,046	957	1,064	999	4,760
10 to 13 years	3,242	1,659	1,583	826	773	833	810	3,831
14 years	824	451	373	220	184	231	189	929
15 to 19 years	3,786	1,772	2,014	954	1,187	818	827	4,365
15 years	767	375	392	193	189	182	203	905
16 and 17 years	1,443	718	725	352	388	366	337	1,734
18 and 19 years	1,576	679	897	409	610	270	287	1,726
20 to 24 years	2,796	1,360	1,436	823	823	537	613	3,652
25 to 29 years	2,334	1,116	1,218	686	682	430	536	3,211
30 to 34 years	2,240	1,055	1,185	662	707	393	478	2,734
35 to 39 years	2,339	1,159	1,180	700	697	459	483	2,514
40 to 44 years	2,113	978	1,135	622	647	356	488	2,082
45 to 49 years	1,883	931	952	560	520	371	432	1,910
50 to 54 years	1,623	783	840	459	485	324	355	1,579
55 to 59 years	1,421	721	700	425	412	296	288	1,386
60 to 64 years	1,146	577	569	354	339	223	230	1,135
65 to 69 years	1,299	645	654	348	331	297	319	1,085
70 to 74 years	850	439	411	245	239	194	172	547
75 to 84 years	767	391	376	208	198	183	178	583
85 years and over	155	73	82	34	39	39	43	
21 years and over	20,273	9,910	10,363	5,926	5,902	3,984	4,461	21,630
ORLEANS								
All ages	570,445	270,812	299,633	185,858	201,956	84,954	97,677	494,537
Under 5 years	60,111	30,398	29,713	18,979	18,601	11,419	11,112	33,084
Under 1 year	12,177	6,162	6,015	3,749	3,660	2,413	2,355	6,809
1 and 2 years	25,400	12,919	12,481	7,934	7,881	4,985	4,600	26,275
3 and 4 years	22,534	11,317	11,217	7,296	7,060	4,021	4,157	
5 to 9 years	45,561	22,911	22,650	14,384	13,997	8,527	8,653	34,297
5 years	9,469	4,705	4,764	3,045	3,043	1,660	1,721	6,434
6 years	9,425	4,744	4,681	3,074	2,928	1,670	1,753	6,484
7 to 9 years	26,667	13,462	13,205	8,265	8,026	5,197	5,179	21,379
10 to 14 years	35,542	17,593	17,949	10,712	10,783	6,881	7,166	41,335
10 to 13 years	28,867	14,288	14,579	8,726	8,799	5,562	5,780	32,675
14 years	6,675	3,305	3,370	1,986	1,984	1,319	1,386	8,660
15 to 19 years	36,005	16,981	19,024	11,073	11,998	5,908	7,026	45,686
15 years	6,682	3,292	3,390	2,025	2,001	1,267	1,389	8,788
16 and 17 years	13,439	6,552	6,887	4,113	4,242	2,439	2,645	18,192
18 and 19 years	15,884	7,137	8,747	4,935	5,755	2,202	2,992	18,706
20 to 24 years	[illegible]	22,100	25,603	15,774	17,339	6,326	8,314	41,997
25 to 29 years	51,895	25,014	26,881	17,928	18,229	7,086	8,652	45,747
30 to 34 years	44,035	20,979	23,056	15,052	15,588	5,927	7,468	45,165
35 to 39 years	45,356	21,158	24,198	14,731	16,050	6,427	8,148	43,704
40 to 44 years	43,450	20,307	23,143	14,233	15,807	6,074	7,336	38,268
45 to 49 years	39,457	18,841	20,616	13,129	13,992	5,712	6,624	32,194
50 to 54 years	33,742	16,346	17,396	11,734	12,608	4,612	4,788	26,417
55 to 59 years	26,411	12,694	13,717	9,287	10,222	3,407	3,495	20,556
60 to 64 years	20,427	9,413	11,014	7,029	8,322	2,384	2,692	16,094
65 to 69 years	17,839	7,464	10,375	5,293	7,272	2,171	3,103	13,359
70 to 74 years	10,972	4,405	6,567	3,331	5,086	1,074	1,481	8,205
75 to 84 years	10,277	3,744	6,533	2,838	5,225	906	1,308	7,429
85 years and over	1,612	464	1,148	351	837	113	311	
21 years and over	384,662	179,173	205,489	128,082	143,339	51,091	62,150	[illegible]

Table 41-AGE BY COLOR AND SEX, FOR PARISHES 1950-Con.

		v (1)	1950 p	pulation	1		1	1940			-	1950 x	opulation	-	-	1	1940
Perish and age		All classes	30	W	hrte	None	brte	popula s	Parah aui age	1	All careers		N.F.	ite	Non	rnite	popula-
10 mm - 10 mm	Total	Mala	Female	Male	Ber.ate	Male	Fernale	totai	150 91	-ota	Male	"emaie	Male	Гепле	Mag	Fema	tetal
3.31								-		-			-			-	-
All ages	74,713	36,38	38,575						RA IDES	1						:	
nder 5 years	8,940	· 552	4,397	24,538		-	13,370	-9, 68	Ail ages.	90,6-8	44 18	46,467	29,79"	30,755		,712	73,370
Under . year 1 and 2 years	3,705	925	836	540	2,698	365,	375	2 214	Under 5 pers.	2 216	5-467	5,340	3,530	3,422	-,887 -08	1 918	6,827
3 and 4 years	3,433	1,917	1.723	- 234	424	603 602	659	4 775	and 2 years and 4 years	. 4,420	2,253	2 _6"	1 464		79.	730	5,506
to 9 years	7,203	3,720	3,-82	2.4 9	2,282	272	-,201	4.965		9 408	2,0971	+ 4.9	3,409	1,344	588 1,366	1,494	6,802
6 vears 7 to 9 years 1 to ¹ 4 years	1,440	767	573	207 201 1,441	514	556	258	9-C 5	6 years 6 years 7 to 9 years 10 to 14 years	- 894	95	925	5.791 b-8	636	326 324	288	1,30
to 14 years	6,128	2,171 3,053	2,038	2,01	2,0.2	730	589	2,985	" to 9 years .	3,302 7,955	2,732	2,500	2,593	2,540	2.6	884	4,122
.0 to 18 years	1 2,003	2,495 558	2,508	7,543	1,639	8121	-,063 869	4,4 2	16 to 14 years	69"	3 980	3 240	2 15	2,50	1,130	4 -20	5 038
to 19 years -	5,376	2,554	2,822	1,714	1,894	8-01	934	5,685	15 to 19 years	6 735	725	3,635	2,0,4	4 373	257 1, 386	263	7,39
15 years. 16 and 17 years	2,095 2,139	593 1,0-8	1,047	715	684	333	179	4,23	-5 , ears 18 and 17 years.	-1-32	-,332	76	442 99J	489 913	2.3	278	3,026
8 and 19 vears to 24 years	6 072	2,621	3,451	605	857	308	363	2 353 8	18 and 19 years	2,5,2	1 _23	3,662	L9~	2,4.3	42a	478	2,92
to 29 years	6,122	2,794	3. 128	2.00	2 2/3	8×8 773	1,0051	5,575	20 to 24 years . 25 to 29 years	6,0-5	2,920	3,662	2,.72	2.54	932	1 239	6,4
to 34 years	5,685 5 635 5 153	2,6.7	3,028	_,907 _ 885	2,011	750	1 027	5,877 5,503 5,148	30 to 3- years	6,7	3,283	3,421	2,7/6	2,344	90"	-,10	5,81
to 44 years. to 49 years.		2,505	2,648	1,787	1,787	J.8	86	3,927	40 to 44 years	1 6,464	2,9%	3,_83	2,012	5,170	904	-,14.	5,36
o 54 veers	3,654	4,250	2,423	1,260	1,795	5971	828 5°2	2,524	45 to 49 years .	3,253	2,528	2,695	1,749	4,481	809 743	909	7,25
o 59 vears. o 64 vears.	4,845	-,428 - 118 1,043	- 103	977	97/	451	44.3	1,990	50 to 54 years -	3,7	919	. 860	1,302	4,310	617	.50	3,43
o 66 vears	2,277	1,043	1.234	612 622 487	940	30C	49-1	1 326	60 to 64 years . 65 to 60 years. 70 to 74 years.	2 810	1,508	. 50	1,040 834	1,000	462	440 582	1,96
0 4 years	2,22 2,277 1,25 1 182	54.7	625 635	487 362	437	233	192	662	70 to 74 years.	,615	809 81o	806	541 525	×3	26-	243	.,00
ears and over	1 2.4	89	125	-49	72	40	53	06.	85 sears and over	274	100	165	64	95	45	24+	*
years and c er	45,913	21,814	24,099	15,2,0	16 152	6 585	7 347	36,643	2. years and over	54,503	28 ≥07	28,396	18,145	19,43	8,262	9,356	43,56
PLAQUIMINES All ages.	14,279	7,~7~	6,~62	4 614	4,177	2,863	2 6-5	ع 312,	And ages	-2,-1,5	5,964	5 146	3,052	3 005	2,912	3.704	45,88
er 5 years	2,00%	_,015	987	573	569	1-2	448	1 -57	mdur 5 vestre	.,572	805	75"	-49	309	456	458	1,81
nd 2 years	412 832	214 433	198	257	215	103	18.	240	I and 2 years	308	-62 323	_46 292	,58	,56	269	458 90 181	28
nd a years 9 years	756	368 85/	390 739	205	237	163 403	-53 324	-,208	8 and 4 years . 5 to 9 years.	6-9	120	320	13	142	123	187	-,52
ears -	328	7.38	150	452 91	41.7 85	87 95	64 74	280	£	293	720 _49 _46	1.5	75. 76	297 55 49	375 77	426 90	-,82
0 9 years	351 91-	.89 487	427	94 266	88 24	221	186	28- 829	6 years	293 863	432	431	76 204	49 493	375 77 70 228	98	06
to 13 years	1,335	665	6,3	359 271	24_ 354 297	306 241	3.9	1.282	10 to 1 = vears 0 to 18 years.	1,365	682 550	683	310	319	372	364	1,85
years	278	1.3	548 125	58	57	65	68	1,048	id years	278	13c1	-46	245 65	246 73	305 67	187 426 90 98 238 364 291	1,49
o 19 vears	1,202	606	596 413 248	320 66	350	280	276	2.2	5 to 19 years	1 082 1	54A 132	53/ 11°	25,	232	292	296 67 _28	7,72
years and 17 years and 19 years	497	249	248	135	, 130	11+1	18	462	16 and 17 'ears	-95	252	243	130	15	122	±28	34 69
24 years _	1 206	433 610	235 596	119	129	212	106	468	18 and 19 years 20 to 24 years	236 200	264 721 640	36*	142	163	10+ 179	2221	1.45
34 vears -	1,012	595 527	5-40 465	332	360 327	187	180	-,161 960	25 to 29 years 30 to 34 years -	652 730	332	362 368	161	17t	120	-So -52 176	1,28
39 years	1,040	544 498	-96 -24	367 349	333	177	163	863	85 to 39 years	7.7	328	38°	199	2_3	129	176	96
	704	44	300	282	194	122	106	592 574	40 to 44 years	73 ₄ 656	329	391	188	220	152	1/1	80 75
49 years - 54 years 59 years	535 43	3_0 225	225 206	228 161	155	80 64	67	467 367	45 to 49 years	532	263 246	269	1.08	156	105	146	66
64 years	37.4	21	163	131	101	90	62	300 1	55 to 59 vears	406	220	186	150 140	123	80	96 63	48
74 1 6678	194	106	88	91 67	79 47	92 39	41 26	266 152	65 to 69 years 70 to 74 years	481 278	240	125	117 64	131	123	140 48 70	36 28
84 years.	186	104	82	67	56	37 10	261	165	7a to 84 years 8a years and over.	248	123	125	65	51	72 58	201	19
sars and over	7,871	4,239	3,652	2,852	2,377	.,387	_ 255	0,780	21 years and over	6,486	3,443	1,343	1,760	1,809	1,363	1,534	8,33
POINTE COUPTE						1			RICHTAND								
All ages	3,018	1,534	1 484	5,101 593	2,013	5,775	5 952 891	24 304	Under 5 years	3,748	17,191	1,905	7,013	1,053	5 278 800	2,654	3,29
or 5 years	558 1,239	269 63s	289 606	96 255	108	173 378	1.81	545	Under 1 year	727	350	377	-46	190	±56	141	65
and 4 years	1,221	6.32	589	242	231.	390	355	2 189	3 and 4 vesus	1,441	799 694	781	462 387	448	7د3 307	332	2,64
9 vears	2,719	1,404	1,315	558 130	523 114	846 166	702 166	2 641	5 to 9 years	1,240	1,630	1,630	920	898	710	732	3,34
rears	587	309	278	112	91	197	187	1,556	6 years. 7 to 8 years. 10 to 14 years. 10 to 13 years.	657	336	319	194	177	159	163 142 427	67
vears to 9 years 14 years to 13 years	2,285	1,133	1.152	462	475	671	439 077	2 662	10 to 14 years	1,902	939	963	532 879	536 852	407 58	6281	1,99
to 13 years years.	1,896	948 185	948	378 84	382 93	671 5°0 101	566	2,115	10 to 13 years	2,360	1,178	1,182	879 707 _72	686 166	58 471 -10	490	3,34 2,68
19 s eare	2,930	966	904	449	440	517	124	2 624	15 to i9 years	2,483	1,266	1,217	713	714	553	503	3,05
and 17 years	436 797	220 403	216 394	90 213	106	130	216	1,061	15 years 16 and 1" years	1 082	278 565 423	266 5⊥7	150 332	.42 306 266	126 233	124 2.1 168	1,25
and 19 years	1,425	343 708	354 720	146 377	. 56 360	197 331	196 360	2,315		1-761	423 804	434 957	229 487	266 579	194	168	2,56
	1,329	61.5	71.4 682	364 340	357	251	357	1,867	20 to 24 years 25 to 29 years 30 to 34 years	1,761	784	896	531	508 546	253	328	2,33
o 34 years o 39 years o 44 years	1,324	642	671	358	366 339	295	332	1,867 1,534 1,501	35 to 49 years	1,599	849	858 872	51.7 550	513 475	224	3_2	1,98
	1,205	605	600	335	31	270	289	1,175	40 to 44 years 45 to 49 years	1,556	755	801	482		273	326	2,52
5 years -	1 _39 895	577 445 365	562 -50	307 240	573 503	2°0 205 1°2	270 231	1,113	50 to 54 years	1,099	708 541	683 558	429 341	391 337	279	292	1,2
	791 680	365	426 31.8	193	226 1.57	172	200 161	675	55 to 59 years	940	498 423	367	284 260	267	214	175 140 201	90
69 years	785	362 402 205	383 229	134	140	268	243	655	65 to 69 years 70 to 74 years	797 457	405	392	186	183	219	211	6
74 years 84 years	434 455	211	244	85	106	126	138	398	75 to 84 years.	331	405 243 21.5	214 166	254 126	125	89 89	89 79	25
ears and over	100	49	51	17	15	32	36		85 years and over	69	26	43	11	14	15	79 29	
ears and over -	11,584	5,694	5,690	2,967	2,906	2,727	2,984	12,824	21 years and over	13,879	6,828	7,051	4,261	4,191	2,567	2,860	15,25

LOUISIANA

Table 41-AGE BY COLOR AND SEX. FOR PARISHES 1950-Con.

talist display on the last	7	and the same	1950 -	opulation	Name of Street, or other Desires, or other Desir	40,	-	1940		1		1950 p	opushor	1		-	1940
Parish and age	-	All classes	2000 1	-	hite	Non	waite	popula-	Parish and ago		All classes		W	hite	Non	white	popula
raman and age	Total	Male	Fenan	Nisle	Female	Male	Persue	total	22	Total	Male	Female	Male	Female	Male	Female	total
	1		-		1				ST HELENA								
eabine	l	10,4.5	10,405	8,3_6	8,203	2 097	2,202	23 586	All ages	9,013	4 556	4 457	2,.5.	2,075	2,403	2,382	9,542
All ages .	20,880	1 273	1,282	961	955	31.2	327	2 647	Under 5 years Under 1 year	1,258	625	633	233 45	263 52	392 79	370 681	1,215
Under 1 year - 1 and 2 years-	529 98	27" 486	252 493	197	_88 373	80 -26	64 120	3.0	1 and 2 years 3 and 4 years	504	238	266 247	89	110	149	156 146	994
3 and 4 years_	2,331	:08 1,292	1,2,9	1,017	394 913	275	246	2,599	5 to 9 years	1,15	605 106	552	244	219	361 63	333 70	267
5 to 9 years 5 years	484	24- 270	240 202	185 218	240	59 52	55 52	528	5 years - 6 years 7 to 9 years -	209 240 009	129 370	120 329	49	1/1	80 218	75	249
7 to 9 years 10 to 4 years	5:5	778	737	614	398 868	164	139 235	2.789	10 to 14 years .	1,048	514	534 429	152 205 158	211	311 258	323 26_	- 49
10 to 13 years_	2 279 1,6-6 43,	1,176 976 200	870 233	797 106	692	-*9 34	178	2,253	10 to 13 vears. 14 years	845 203	416 98	105	45	43	53	02	903 246
14 years	4,779	704	875	7.3	670	191	205	2,679	15 to 19 years.	897 226	452 1.5	445 111	203	169	249 77	276 64	1,038
15 years	782	219 417	193	175 330	154 29-	81	39 74	1,066	15 years 16 and 17 years 18 and 19 years	369 302	180 157	189	85	72	95	17	422
16 and 17 years 18 and 19 years	1.203	268 563	317 640	202 407	225 483	±5€	12 157	1,072 <,092	20 to 24 years.	571	270	292 250	126 148	117 130	153 116	175 120 1_1	786 686
20 to 24 years 25 to 29 years 30 to 34 years 35 to 39 years 35 to 39 years 35	1,203 1 303 1 262	591 602	712	477 496	36+ 350	1.4	.48 .10	1,824	25 to 29 years 30 to 34 years	490 541	264 237 255	253 286	· 33	139 134	104 135	1_1	6.4
35 to 39 years 40 to 44 years	1,310	635 634	675 645	545 530	537 504	9C 104	_38	1,494	35 to 39 years 40 to 44 years	248	296	2*2	154		:42	1.8	540
45 4- 40	1,167	558 480	609 463	456 368	468 378	102	141	4,138	45 to 49 years - 50 to 54 years -	4 ₄ 9 340	224 164 154	197	106 98	107	88 58	90 72	399 347
55 to 59 years	940	468	463 439 342	380 296	3.8	86	85 81 53	946 7-8 6-1	55 to 59 years - 60 to 64 years -	239	1.9	120	68	97 73	50 51	60 47	247
	698 72	396	329	311	257 202	85	72	543	60 to 60 years 70 to 74 years	327	171	156	. 76	73	95 42	83	220 158
65 to 69 \ears 70 to 74 \ears 75 .0 84 \ears	45 416	228	197	184 177 35	167	44	2 30	484	75 to 64 years 80 years and over -	. ⊿6a 24	93	73	51 5	50	42 8	23	153
85 years and over. 21 years and over.	68 1,492	40 5,6-7	28 5 845	4 584	4,688	1,063	157	12,454	21 years and over -	4,525	2,299	2,226	1 250	1,190	1,049	1,036	4,744
S" BERNARD	,	,,							ST JAMES								
All ages.	1 08/	5,595	5,492	4,800	4 664	795	828	7 280	All ager	15,334	7,615	7,719	3,828	3,758	3,787	3,92.	15,596
Under 5 years	1 >33	773 159	"60 _48	644	o37 127	29 32	123	774 134	Under 5 years	2,239	204	1,105	516 100	476 103	618	629 122	1,925
Under 1 year I and 2 years	681 542	3.57 277	34-	284 233	293 217	.3 44	2_ 51 51	640	Under 1 year 1 and 2 years 3 and 4 years	958	44.4	477	218 198	194 179	263	283	1 506
3 and 4 years 5 to 9 years	1,171	587	584 120	498 116	485 99	89	99	749	5 to 9 years	±,857	926 177	931	426 76	390	500	541 129	1,769
5 years	252 253	25	128	108	105	17	23	-66 434	6 years	186	195 554	19.	95 255	68 80 242	.00 299	111	320
7 to 9 years	616 992 798	330 503	3.6 459	774 404	28 394	56 97	55 65	923	7 to 9 years 10 to 14 years.	-,656	871 716	785 662	409 331	366 305	462 38"	30_ 419 357	-,850
10 to 13 years	798 164	425 78	373 86	341 05	32. 73	23 E4	52 43	545 178	10 to 13 years	276	153	123	78	61	75	υ2	369
15 to 10 years	769	372 72	417	31C	346 69	62 14	71	784	15 to 19 years	1,281	656	625	341 75	308 73	315 73	317 80	1,848
16 years	3.2 326	_55 145	157	135 117	125	20	32 29 80	326 310	16 and 17 years 18 and 19 years	301 507 473	269 239	8د2 234	144 122	1,7	125	A20	774 708
'8 and 19 years 20 to 24 years .	902	452 539	510 532	394 485	430 485	58	80 47	503	20 to 24 years	981	504 468	477 452	289 254	254 239	215	223	1,531
20 to 24 years . 25 to 28 years 30 to 34 years	b20	392 402	428 402	3-9	366 35 ₄	54 43 38	52	598 161 535	25 to 29 years 30 to 34 years 35 to 39 years	853 929	411	442	236	229 255	175	213	941 942
35 to 89 vears. 40 to 44 vears	804 689	349	340	313	288	30	52	446	40 to 44 years	~60	391	369	228	513	163	156	824 799
45 to 49 vears	620	336 251	284	289	249 186	47 35	35	364	45 to 49 years - 50 to 54 years -	77o 663	269 296	40° 367	185 172 158	507 555	184 124	185 166	727
50 to 54 years. 55 to 59 years 60 to 64 years	274	253 199 141	170	174 124	142	25 17	20	247 179	55 to 59 years	611 543	326 240	285 303	127	149	168	136 140 181	616 478
55 to 69 years 70 to 74 years	252 136	143	109	212	82 53	31 18	27 13	158	65 to 69 years 70 to 74 years	329	239 160	305 169	89 58	124	150	85	470 264
75 to 84 years 85 years and over	138	77	61	62	46 12	15	15	83	75 to 84 years 85 years and over	321	149 27	1"2	77 12	100 25	72 15	72	266
21 vears and over	6 452	3,274	3 178	2 866	2,726	408	450	4 034	21 years and over .	9,106	3,925	4,184	2,082	2,206	1,843	1,975	8,863
JT CHARLES						9		. 1	ST JOHN THE BAPTIST								
All ages	,3,363	6,660	0,697	4,549	4,453	2 117	2,244	.2,32.	All ages	14,861	7,515	7 346	3,782	3,663	3 733	3,683	14,766
Under 5 years Under 1 year	1,814	902 184	475	565 111	568 124	337 73	72	1,295	Under 5 years Under 1 year 1 and 2 years	2 0+3 429	1,069 206	980 223	475 90	431 96	594 116	549 127	1,722
Under 1 year 1 and 2 years 3 and 4 years	717	36. 357	356 360	222 232	222 222	139	134	1,030	3 and 4 years	845 775	440	405 352	205 180	468	235 243	184	1 350
5 to 9 years	1,493	768 169 171	725 .45 141	101	441 91	272	284	1,4 7	5 to 9 years	1,699	863 180	836	390 78	376 7± 74	473 102	460 88	1,567
6 years	867	428	439	116 279	91 259	49	180	891	5 years .	1,008	_73 510	179 498	66 246	231	207	267	290 944
10 to 14 years	1 254	504	518	41C	398 322	210	236	1,529	10 to 14 years	1,580	668	632	374	342 276	362	435 356	1,685
14 years	232	116	116	. 77	76	39	40	302	19 years	280	135	140	68	66	67	79	354
15 to 19 years	1,223 253 514	134	610	414	440 79	44	170 40	1 393	15 to 19 years	1,268	556 149	612	344 87	309 63	31.2 62	303	1 646 311
	458	256 223	256 234	.73 .51	195	83 72	61 69	5-1		496 480	260 247	236	137	121	-23 -27	112	653 682
20 to 24 years	1,030 1,018 798	512 507	518	. 65 277	359 367	147	159	973 949	20 to 24 years 25 to 29 years	1,123	585 477	538 516	31.4 260	261 262	273 217	277	1,175
30 to 34 years 35 to 39 years _	851	38/ 424	414	287 315	303	97 109	114	842 880	35 to 39 years.	882 918	428 454	454	239 247	2.0 201	289 207	204	962 941
40 to 44 Years 45 to 49 years	770	399 391	409	299 286	ر1ر 280	100	96 99	6.6	40 to 44 years	758	45° 373	40'r	253 195	226	204	181	840 674
50 to 54 years	631 502	314	317 238	238 186	221	76 78	90 81	418 365	50 to A years.	673	3/1	332	180	182	161	1.50	641 457
55 to 50 years	347	1.87	160	112	8	75	79	260	60 to 64 years	5.4	265 255	249 256	138	.43 .51	127	106 105 152	398
36 to 69 years 70 to 74 years	344 219	167 98	177	96 47	63	51	83 58	260 270	65 to 69 years.	477 260	223 136	254	1,04 65	102	71	611	337 193
5 to 64 years	222	101	121	51	56 12	50 10	65	16.	75 to 84 years 85 years and over	242 50	112	130	6.	77 17	51	53	219
21 vears and over	7,393	3,682	3,711	2,608	2,531	▲ 074	1,187	6,430	21 years and over -	8,043	4,011	4,032	2,144		1,867	1,878	7,868

Table 41 -AGE BY COLOR AND SEX, FOR PARISHES 1950-Con

Later year			1980 p	opulation				12+C	A STATE OF THE PARTY OF THE PAR	1		1950 p	opalsuor.			The state of the s	240

Parish and age	-	All classes		W	hite	None	hite	popula-	Paresh and age		All casses		WY	ute	Norw	three	populs-

Table 41.—AGE BY COLOR AND SEX, FOR PARISHES: 1950—Con.

Parish and age	1950 population: All classes, Total	All classes, Male	All classes, Female	White, Male	White, Female	Nonwhite, Male	Nonwhite, Female	1940 population total
ST LANDRY								
All ages	78,476	38,798	39,678	21,726	21,732	[illegible]	[illegible]	71,481
Under 5 years	[illegible]	5,607	5,556	2,798	2,720	2,809	[illegible]	9,550
Under 1 year	2,098	1,013	1,085	520	563	493	522	[illegible]
1 and 2 years	4,599	2,321	2,278	1,174	1,104	[illegible]	[illegible]	[illegible]
3 and 4 years	4,466	2,273	2,193	[illegible]	1,153	1,169	[illegible]	
5 to 9 years	9,889	4,903	4,986	2,392	2,332	[illegible]	2,654	[illegible]
5 years	2,016	1,003	1,013	472	483	531	530	1,778
6 years	1,999	974	1,025	497	484	477	[illegible]	1,931
7 to 9 years	5,874	2,926	2,948	1,423	1,365	1,503	1,583	5,416
10 to 14 years	9,220	4,658	4,562	2,280	2,157	2,378	2,405	8,965
10 to 13 years	7,615	3,868	3,747	1,882	1,766	1,986	1,981	7,258
14 years	1,605	790	815	398	[illegible]	392	424	1,707
15 to 19 years	7,579	3,746	3,833	1,890	1,947	1,856	1,886	[illegible]
15 years	1,662	846	816	398	395	[illegible]	421	1,412
16 and 17 years	3,111	1,546	1,565	783	805	763	760	3,130
18 and 19 years	2,806	1,354	1,452	709	747	645	705	[illegible]
20 to 24 years	6,193	2,925	3,268	1,762	1,873	1,163	1,395	6,550
25 to 29 years	5,330	2,584	2,746	1,654	1,664	930	1,082	5,767
30 to 34 years	5,005	2,447	2,558	1,619	1,597	828	961	4,679
35 to 39 years	5,067	2,529	2,538	1,547	1,531	982	1,007	4,279
40 to 44 years	4,273	2,175	2,098	1,440	1,304	735	794	3,325
45 to 49 years	3,573	1,771	1,802	1,105	[illegible]	666	660	3,036
50 to 54 years	2,943	1,462	1,481	938	939	524	542	2,323
55 to 59 years	2,365	1,184	1,181	752	756	432	425	[illegible]
60 to 64 years	1,844	891	953	553	594	338	359	1,454
65 to 69 years	1,781	834	947	447	482	387	465	1,355
70 to 74 years	1,094	554	540	267	335	287	205	725
75 to 84 years	960	443	517	243	303	200	214	784
85 years and over	197	85	[illegible]	39	56	46	56	
21 years and over	39,256	19,288	19,968	12,052	12,178	7,236	7,790	34,804
ST MARTIN								
All ages	26,353	13,252	13,101	8,409	8,201	4,843	4,900	[illegible]
Under 5 years	3,662	1,856	1,806	1,071	1,029	785	777	3,401
Under 1 year	732	370	362	210	207	160	155	663
1 and 2 years	1,471	740	731	439	420	301	311	2,738
3 and 4 years	1,459	746	713	424	402	324	311	
5 to 9 years	3,232	1,672	1,560	985	851	687	709	3,311
5 years	687	373	314	218	166	155	148	627
6 years	676	341	335	208	195	133	140	663
7 to 9 years	1,869	958	911	559	490	379	421	2,021
10 to 14 years	3,042	1,565	1,477	956	840	609	637	3,275
10 to 13 years	2,497	1,294	1,203	782	691	512	512	2,656
14 years	545	271	274	174	149	97	125	619
15 to 19 years	2,549	1,276	1,273	757	762	519	511	2,869
15 years	505	264	241	150	150	114	91	541
16 and 17 years	1,073	545	528	335	313	210	215	1,144
18 and 19 years	971	467	504	272	299	195	205	1,184
20 to 24 years	1,973	950	1,023	620	632	330	391	[illegible]
25 to 29 years	1,807	904	903	579	593	325	310	2,053
30 to 34 years	1,656	808	848	536	566	272	282	1,688
35 to 39 years	[illegible]	885	832	576	533	309	299	1,581
40 to 44 years	1,406	720	686	522	504	198	182	1,156
45 to 49 years	1,249	622	627	448	[illegible]	174	186	[illegible]
50 to 54 years	978	492	486	369	362	123	124	874
55 to 59 years	876	457	419	330	297	127	122	745
60 to 64 years	710	339	371	218	249	121	122	553
65 to 69 years	666	319	347	192	223	127	124	560
70 to 74 years	353	166	187	119	140	47	47	265
75 to 84 years	400	192	208	120	150	72	58	311
85 years and over	77	29	48	11	29	18	19	
21 years and over	13,444	6,689	6,755	4,523	4,978	2,166	2,177	12,980
ST MARY								
All ages	35,848	17,904	17,944	11,107	10,995	6,797	6,949	31,458
Under 5 years	4,841	2,407	2,434	1,444	1,470	963	964	3,444
Under 1 year	993	468	525	277	325	191	200	704
1 and 2 years	1,932	978	954	591	565	387	389	2,740
3 and 4 years	1,916	961	955	576	580	385	375	
5 to 9 years	4,156	2,169	1,987	1,289	1,157	880	830	3,137
5 years	867	459	408	272	234	187	174	585
6 years	852	447	405	256	234	191	171	612
7 to 9 years	2,437	1,263	1,174	[illegible]	689	502	485	1,940
10 to 14 years	3,571	1,860	1,711	1,064	966	796	745	3,418
10 to 13 years	2,928	1,523	1,405	872	789	651	616	2,739
14 years	643	337	306	192	177	145	129	679
15 to 19 years	[illegible]	1,363	1,451	798	893	565	558	3,308
15 years	567	290	277	177	170	113	107	630
16 and 17 years	1,166	562	604	323	372	239	232	1,343
18 and 19 years	1,081	511	570	298	351	213	219	1,335
20 to 24 years	2,702	1,303	1,399	853	924	450	475	2,947
25 to 29 years	2,578	1,301	1,277	902	857	399	420	2,736
30 to 34 years	2,379	1,130	1,249	777	822	353	427	2,252
35 to 39 years	2,432	1,216	1,216	840	760	376	456	2,058
40 to 44 years	2,114	1,063	1,051	726	692	337	359	1,652
45 to 49 years	1,936	1,024	912	637	573	387	339	1,519
50 to 54 years	1,470	725	745	455	459	270	286	1,265
55 to 59 years	1,230	605	625	361	377	244	248	1,153
60 to 64 years	1,039	508	531	305	309	203	222	866
65 to 69 years	1,167	534	633	285	320	249	313	804
70 to 74 years	630	317	313	170	184	147	129	430
75 to 84 years	669	324	345	180	197	144	148	469
85 years and over	120	55	65	21	35	34	30	
21 years and over	19,940	9,841	10,099	6,348	6,332	3,493	3,767	17,533

Parish and age	1950 population: All classes, Total	All classes, Male	All classes, Female	White, Male	White, Female	Nonwhite, Male	Nonwhite, Female	1940 population total
ST TAMMANY								
All ages	26,988	[illegible]	[illegible]	[illegible]	[illegible]	3,893	[illegible]	23,624
Under 5 years	[illegible]	[illegible]	[illegible]	1,047	[illegible]	574	578	2,364
Under 1 year	590	280	310	173	187	107	123	482
1 and 2 years	[illegible]	674	674	423	434	251	240	1,882
3 and 4 years	1,272	667	605	451	390	216	215	
5 to 9 years	[illegible]	[illegible]	[illegible]	1,025	1,036	487	474	2,380
5 years	628	311	317	223	215	88	102	488
6 years	[illegible]	302	315	200	213	102	102	454
7 to 9 years	1,777	899	878	602	608	297	270	1,438
10 to 14 years	2,620	1,325	1,295	880	875	445	420	2,623
10 to 13 years	2,118	1,064	1,054	707	716	357	338	2,131
14 years	502	261	241	173	159	88	82	492
15 to 19 years	[illegible]	1,106	1,088	769	727	337	361	2,450
15 years	[illegible]	241	[illegible]	175	164	66	67	531
16 and 17 years	925	453	472	307	316	146	156	991
18 and 19 years	797	412	385	287	247	125	138	928
20 to 24 years	1,730	833	[illegible]	590	609	243	294	1,902
25 to 29 years	1,749	835	[illegible]	607	632	248	262	1,834
30 to 34 years	[illegible]	[illegible]	883	583	620	218	263	1,610
35 to 39 years	1,780	832	948	589	657	243	[illegible]	1,508
40 to 44 years	1,631	799	832	587	624	212	208	1,421
45 to 49 years	1,528	737	791	540	585	197	206	1,315
50 to 54 years	1,349	662	687	521	542	141	145	1,115
55 to 59 years	1,202	621	581	477	445	144	136	913
60 to 64 years	991	477	514	366	388	111	126	693
65 to 69 years	1,008	513	495	368	358	145	137	680
70 to 74 years	608	322	286	245	236	77	50	402
75 to 84 years	576	250	326	191	259	59	67	424
85 years and over	100	43	57	[illegible]	40	12	17	
21 years and over	15,610	7,571	8,039	5,567	5,888	2,004	2,151	13,380
TANGIPAHOA								
All ages	53,218	26,628	26,590	18,587	18,032	8,041	8,558	45,519
Under 5 years	6,760	3,422	3,338	2,232	2,067	1,190	1,271	4,517
Under 1 year	1,340	658	682	399	402	259	280	841
1 and 2 years	2,754	1,446	1,308	931	804	515	504	3,676
3 and 4 years	2,666	1,318	1,348	902	861	416	487	
5 to 9 years	5,839	2,998	2,841	1,997	1,806	1,001	1,035	4,695
5 years	1,203	611	592	400	385	211	207	932
6 years	1,254	650	604	446	374	204	230	871
7 to 9 years	3,382	1,737	1,645	1,151	1,047	586	598	2,892
10 to 14 years	5,140	2,607	2,533	1,782	1,690	825	843	5,097
10 to 13 years	4,219	2,156	2,063	1,481	1,377	675	686	4,108
14 years	921	451	470	301	313	150	157	989
15 to 19 years	4,723	2,277	2,446	1,592	1,653	685	793	4,970
15 years	979	462	517	315	334	147	183	932
16 and 17 years	1,861	920	941	641	629	279	312	1,980
18 and 19 years	1,883	895	988	636	690	259	298	2,058
20 to 24 years	3,966	1,989	1,977	1,447	1,324	542	653	4,087
25 to 29 years	3,798	1,840	1,958	1,301	1,318	539	640	3,894
30 to 34 years	3,411	1,607	1,804	1,186	1,282	421	522	3,362
35 to 39 years	3,620	1,720	1,900	1,238	1,332	482	568	3,203
40 to 44 years	3,496	1,786	1,720	1,271	1,215	515	495	2,416
45 to 49 years	2,939	1,518	1,421	1,094	985	424	436	2,274
50 to 54 years	2,308	1,169	1,139	802	792	367	347	1,840
55 to 59 years	1,906	1,022	944	715	679	307	265	1,599
60 to 64 years	1,541	783	758	580	559	203	199	1,259
65 to 69 years	1,689	860	829	570	555	290	274	1,044
70 to 74 years	980	495	485	378	376	117	109	645
75 to 84 years	879	463	416	345	330	118	86	617
85 years and over	163	72	91	57	69	15	22	
21 years and over	29,950	14,943	15,007	10,717	10,537	4,226	4,470	25,361
TENSAS								
All ages	13,209	6,422	6,787	2,316	2,328	4,106	4,459	15,940
Under 5 years	1,851	935	916	299	301	636	615	1,703
Under 1 year	362	174	188	54	64	120	124	328
1 and 2 years	719	366	353	125	108	241	245	1,375
3 and 4 years	770	395	375	120	129	275	246	
5 to 9 years	1,605	807	798	289	288	518	510	1,611
5 years	333	164	169	56	55	108	114	337
6 years	341	166	175	48	49	118	126	318
7 to 9 years	931	477	454	185	184	292	270	956
10 to 14 years	1,353	695	658	237	236	458	422	1,667
10 to 13 years	1,078	542	536	185	188	357	348	1,321
14 years	275	153	122	52	48	101	74	346
15 to 19 years	1,060	534	526	175	187	359	339	1,639
15 years	243	118	125	33	51	85	74	337
16 and 17 years	456	228	228	75	84	153	144	640
18 and 19 years	361	188	173	67	52	121	121	662
20 to 24 years	779	338	441	131	160	207	281	1,390
25 to 29 years	743	321	422	152	178	169	244	1,270
30 to 34 years	740	336	404	156	181	180	223	1,153
35 to 39 years	820	377	443	175	161	202	282	1,095
40 to 44 years	779	356	423	141	132	215	291	883
45 to 49 years	717	358	359	129	110	229	249	831
50 to 54 years	601	283	318	101	101	182	217	606
55 to 59 years	548	275	273	92	87	183	186	632
60 to 64 years	379	196	183	70	67	126	116	466
65 to 69 years	558	271	287	79	65	192	222	474
70 to 74 years	315	157	158	43	36	114	122	270
75 to 84 years	311	160	151	40	34	120	117	250
85 years and over	50	23	27	7	4	16	23	
21 years and over	7,179	3,275	3,804	1,290	1,297	2,085	2,507	8,992

Table 41.—AGE BY COLOR AND SEX, FOR PARISHES 1950—Con.

Parish and age	1950 population: All classes Total	All classes Male	All classes Female	White Male	White Female	Nonwhite Male	Nonwhite Female	1940 population total
TERREBONNE								
All ages	43,328	21,7[illegible]	21,547	16,493	16,164	5,288	5,382	35,880
Under 5 years	6,648	3,37[illegible]	3,297	2,441	2,40[illegible]	910	894	4,5[illegible]3
Under 1 year	1,289	[illegible]	630	485	451	174	179	[illegible]2
1 and 2 years	2,767	1,399	1,368	1,005	993	394	375	3,591
3 and 4 years	2,592	1,293	1,299	951	959	342	340	
5 to 9 years	5,336	2,653	2,683	1,970	1,996	683	697	4,067
5 years	1,133	570	560	419	428	151	132	917
6 years	1,093	554	539	408	[illegible]	146	140	828
7 to 9 years	3,113	1,529	1,584	1,143	1,165	386	419	2,442
10 to 14 years	4,480	2,238	2,242	1,629	1,604	609	638	4,257
10 to 13 years	3,659	1,837	1,822	1,332	1,291	505	531	3,416
14 years	821	401	420	287	313	114	107	841
15 to 19 years	3,594	1,772	1,822	1,326	1,344	446	478	3,951
15 years	771	358	413	264	301	94	112	851
16 and 17 years	1,461	735	72[illegible]	552	529	183	197	1,579
18 and 19 years	1,362	676	686	510	514	166	172	1,521
20 to 24 years	3,510	1,751	1,759	1,400	1,354	351	405	3,349
25 to 29 years	3,368	1,683	1,685	1,326	1,316	357	369	3,120
30 to 34 years	2,950	1,456	1,494	1,189	1,198	267	296	2,468
35 to 39 years	2,896	1,508	1,388	1,165	1,062	343	326	2,173
40 to 44 years	2,344	1,243	1,101	996	854	247	247	1,712
45 to 49 years	1,909	1,005	904	793	734	212	23[illegible]	1,54[illegible]
50 to 54 years	1,544	801	743	631	590	170	153	1,21[illegible]
55 to 59 years	1,357	680	677	496	534	184	143	1,028
60 to 64 years	977	51[illegible]	463	374	337	140	126	880
65 to 69 years	991	47[illegible]	5[illegible]	303	341	17[illegible]	1[illegible]	766
70 to 74 years	648	303	345	219	251	84	94	424
75 to 84 years	614	301	313	216	221	85	92	411
85 years and over	102	46	56	29	35	17	21	
21 years and over	22 010	11,446	11 562	8,890	8,550	2,[illegible]8	2,612	18,365
UNION								
All ages	19,141	9,682	9,459	6,366	6,151	3,316	3,308	20,943
Under 5 years	2,269	1,169	1,100	662	643	507	457	2,261
Under 1 year	442	235	207	129	119	106	88	402
1 and 2 years	953	507	446	287	25[illegible]	220	189	1,879
3 and 4 years	874	427	447	245	267	182	180	
5 to 9 years	2 169	1,104	1,065	655	630	449	435	2,318
5 years	456	230	226	139	128	91	98	487
6 years	402	208	194	117	110	91	84	457
7 to 9 years	1,311	666	645	399	395	267	250	1,374
10 to 14 years	2 002	1,034	968	629	556	405	412	2,376
10 to 13 years	1,614	826	788	497	458	329	330	1,903
14 years	388	208	180	132	98	76	82	473
15 to 19 years	1,747	879	868	539	518	340	350	2,467
15 years	395	195	200	129	118	66	82	502
16 and 17 years	743	375	368	229	236	146	132	996
18 and 19 years	609	309	300	181	164	128	136	969
20 to 24 years	1,210	647	563	379	337	268	226	1,985
25 to 29 years	1,243	579	664	400	418	179	246	1,620
30 to 34 years	1 186	557	629	386	450	171	179	1,344
35 to 39 years	1 248	615	633	429	429	186	204	1,298
40 to 44 years	1,096	579	519	436	377	143	142	1,082
45 to 49 years	1,083	521	562	368	406	153	156	1,346
50 to 54 years	882	442	440	316	304	126	136	873
55 to 59 years	861	452	409	340	299	112	110	668
60 to 64 years	670	350	320	287	255	63	65	577
65 to 69 years	634	354	280	250	196	104	84	524
70 to 74 years	389	188	201	135	129	53	72	274
75 to 84 years	387	192	195	142	147	50	48	462
85 years and over	63	20	43	13	27	7	16	
21 years and over	10 704	5,358	5 346	3 800	3,742	1,558	1,604	11,057
VERMILION								
All ages	36,929	18 47[illegible]	18,456	16 168	16,0[illegible]	2 305	2,397	37,750
Under 5 years	4,285	2,160	2,125	1 822	1,798	338	327	4 126
Under 1 year	858	424	434	350	380	74	54	787
1 and 2 years	1,778	914	864	767	724	147	140	3,339
3 and 4 years	1,649	822	827	705	694	117	133	
5 to 9 years	3,779	1,947	1,832	1,664	1,539	283	293	4,400
5 years	723	394	329	336	276	58	53	889
6 years	825	429	396	374	328	55	68	887
7 to 9 years	2,231	1,124	1,107	954	935	170	172	2,624
10 to 14 years	3,718	1,949	1,769	1 637	1,511	312	258	4,477
10 to 13 years	2 917	1 547	1 370	1 296	1,172	251	198	3,652
14 years	801	402	399	341	339	61	60	825
15 to 19 years	3 391	1 685	1,706	1,461	1,435	224	271	4,063
15 years	727	366	361	324	310	42	51	819
16 and 17 years	1,438	737	701	628	582	109	119	1,648
18 and 19 years	1,226	582	644	509	543	73	101	1 596
20 to 24 years	2,722	1,314	1,408	1,130	1,208	184	200	3,376
25 to 29 years	2,604	1,262	1,342	1,124	1,168	138	174	3,182
30 to 34 years	2,546	1,239	1,307	1,123	1,161	116	146	2,732
35 to 39 years	2 745	1,374	1,371	1,222	1,227	152	144	2,581
40 to 44 years	2,384	1,184	1,200	1,067	1 069	11[illegible]	131	1,913
45 to 49 years	2,145	1,084	1,061	989	944	95	117	1 762
50 to 54 years	1,715	868	847	801	767	67	80	1,417
55 to 59 years	1,434	715	719	639	663	76	56	1,149
60 to 64 years	1,129	556	573	500	524	56	49	861
65 to 69 years	1,017	517	500	446	434	71	66	720
70 to 74 years	609	294	315	267	278	27	37	368
75 to 84 years	587	274	313	239	274	35	39	447
85 years and over	119	51	68	37	59	14	9	
21 years and over	21,215	10 485	10,730	9,377	9,515	1,108	1,215	19,923

Parish and age	1950 population: All classes Total	All classes Male	All classes Female	White Male	White Female	Nonwhite Male	Nonwhite Female	1940 population total
VERNON								
All ages	18,974	9,496	9,478	8,428	8,328	1 068	1,150	19 142
Under 5 years	2 209	1,145	1,064	1,004	915	141	149	2,053
Under 1 year	380	194	186	177	164	17	22	378
1 and 2 years	896	456	440	393	366	63	74	1 675
3 and 4 years	933	495	438	434	385	61	53	
5 to 9 years	2,125	1 062	1,063	975	956	87	107	2,062
5 years	431	213	218	191	201	22	17	432
6 years	463	240	223	217	203	23	20	395
7 to 9 years	1,231	609	622	567	552	42	70	1,235
10 to 14 years	2,007	1,035	972	923	869	112	103	2,136
10 to 13 years	1,656	858	798	765	709	93	89	1,682
14 years	351	177	174	158	160	19	14	454
15 to 19 years	1,571	805	766	710	685	95	81	2,048
15 years	393	200	193	172	174	28	19	378
16 and 17 years	712	365	347	329	314	36	33	847
18 and 19 years	466	240	226	209	197	31	29	823
20 to 24 years	1,078	486	592	434	514	52	78	1,607
25 to 29 years	1,150	514	636	454	545	60	91	1,425
30 to 34 years	1,181	558	623	509	559	49	64	1,257
35 to 39 years	1,289	622	667	561	567	61	100	1,211
40 to 44 years	1,182	570	612	513	542	57	70	1,110
45 to 49 years	1,113	557	556	489	480	68	76	1 013
50 to 54 years	898	447	451	389	393	58	58	880
55 to 59 years	863	447	416	393	376	54	40	787
60 to 64 years	694	365	329	321	298	44	31	548
65 to 69 years	739	400	339	326	280	74	59	481
70 to 74 years	422	242	180	208	158	34	22	25[illegible]
75 to 84 years	387	209	178	190	162	9	16	283
85 years and over	66	32	34	29	29	3	5	
21 years and over	10 848	5 361	5,487	4,739	4,797	622	690	10,505
WASHINGTON								
All ages	38,371	19,167	19,204	13 201	13,162	5 966	6 042	34,443
Under 5 years	5 190	2 662	2,528	1,701	1,618	961	910	3,874
Under 1 year	1,050	526	524	328	304	198	220	747
1 and 2 years	2,141	1,108	1,033	686	672	422	361	3,127
3 and 4 years	1,999	1 028	971	687	642	341	329	
5 to 9 years	4,308	2 162	2,146	1,370	1,440	792	706	3,097
5 years	904	464	440	286	290	178	150	805
6 years	882	442	440	286	310	156	130	726
7 to 9 years	2 522	1 256	1,266	798	840	458	426	2,166
10 to 14 years	3,925	1 987	1,938	1,292	1,301	695	637	3,824
10 to 13 years	3,182	1,606	1,576	1,049	1,057	557	519	3,062
14 years	743	381	362	243	244	138	118	764
15 to 19 years	3,084	1,492	1,592	1,024	1,021	468	571	3,726
15 years	734	352	382	243	251	109	131	767
16 and 17 years	1,284	657	627	460	410	197	217	1,483
18 and 19 years	1,066	483	583	321	360	162	223	1,476
20 to 24 years	2 758	1,295	1 463	908	976	387	487	3,068
25 to 29 years	2 910	1,368	1,542	988	1,040	380	502	3,046
30 to 34 years	2 565	1,240	1,325	950	980	290	345	2,050
35 to 39 years	2,704	1,338	1,366	985	950	353	416	2,391
40 to 44 years	2,409	1 245	1 164	909	819	336	345	1,983
45 to 49 years	2,104	1,028	1,076	699	744	329	332	1,705
50 to 54 years	1,704	861	843	623	608	238	235	1,386
55 to 59 years	1,393	715	678	502	489	213	189	1,025
60 to 64 years	1,159	623	536	469	387	154	149	673
65 to 69 years	1,021	537	484	343	334	194	150	685
70 to 74 years	569	311	258	224	201	87	57	362
75 to 84 years	480	263	217	186	162	77	55	348
85 years and over	88	40	48	28	34	12	14	
21 years and over	21,343	10,613	10,730	7 645	7,543	2,968	3,187	18,622
WEBSTER								
All ages	35,704	17,661	18,043	11,295	11,387	6,366	6,656	33,676
Under 5 years	4,447	2,221	2,206	1,394	1,364	827	842	3,665
Under 1 year	775	380	395	224	232	156	163	712
1 and 2 years	1 925	976	949	607	602	369	347	2 953
3 and 4 years	1 727	865	862	563	530	302	332	
5 to 9 years	4,008	2,067	1,941	1 224	1,144	843	797	3 439
5 years	775	394	381	243	227	151	154	747
6 years	829	436	393	250	225	186	168	646
7 to 9 years	2,404	1,237	1,167	731	692	506	475	2 046
10 to 14 years	3,595	1 831	1,764	1,043	1,005	788	759	3,400
10 to 13 years	2,932	1 492	1,440	861	812	631	628	2,737
14 years	663	339	324	182	193	157	131	663
15 to 19 years	2,926	1 382	1,544	736	860	646	684	3,434
15 years	664	323	341	172	181	151	160	682
16 and 17 years	1,212	600	612	321	338	279	274	1,363
18 and 19 years	1 050	459	591	243	341	216	250	1,189
20 to 24 years	2,575	1 194	1,351	763	847	431	504	3,315
25 to 29 years	2,676	1,250	1 426	851	971	399	455	3 279
30 to 34 years	2,618	1,237	1,381	904	943	333	438	2,728
35 to 39 years	2 630	1,249	1,381	878	893	371	488	2,323
40 to 44 years	2,275	1,166	1,109	775	733	391	376	1,811
45 to 49 years	1,866	947	919	621	580	326	339	1,594
50 to 54 years	1 514	768	746	530	486	238	260	1,268
55 to 59 years	1,268	629	639	442	463	187	176	988
60 to 64 years	973	503	470	360	347	143	123	844
65 to 69 years	1,121	559	562	322	324	237	238	669
70 to 74 years	635	344	291	236	215	108	76	310
75 to 84 years	537	277	260	191	178	86	82	409
85 years and over	90	37	53	25	34	12	19	
21 years and over	20,224	9,933	10,291	6,765	6,841	3,168	3,450	18,966

Table 41.—AGE BY COLOR AND SEX, FOR PARISHES 1950—Con.

post-dramatical and and and		- Total Control	.950 p	opustion	1			1240	I	1		1950	populario	n	-		1940
Paret and ag-	-	Au classos			hite	100	white	popula- tion	Parish and age		Ail classo	,	W	lute	Non	white	DOD JES
	Total	Male	Female	Male	Female	Ma.	Temale	total		Total	Male	Iemale	Male	Female	Maie	Female	total
TURKERLANC		1		2				200	VERNON				1	1			
All ages	~3,328	-1,78_	21 547	af 493	16,164	5,438	1,202	35 880	All ages .	18,974	3,496	9,4"8	8,428	_	1 068	1,150	19 142
Under 5 years _	1,289	3,37	630	2 441	= 40°	9_0	. 179	4 ju3 C_2	Under 5 years. Under 1 year	2 209 380	1,145	-,064 1.8b	177	915	141	149 24 74	2,05,
1 and 2 years 3 and 4 rears	2 767	1,399	-,368 -,299	1,0.5	993	394 342	1 340	3 501	1 and 2 years 3 and 4 years	896 933	456 495	440 438	39.3 434	38.	61	74 53 20°	1 675
	5,336	2,653	. 683 560	1 97.1	-,9% 428	653	697	4,Jo7 3.7	5 tc 9 years	2,125 431 463	1 062 243 240	1,063 238 223	975 491 247	956 201 203	87 22 23	17.	2,062 452 395
7 to 9 years	7,233 2,293 3,123 4,480	1,529	1,584 2,242	1 47	1,165 1,604	38h 6-9	4.0	828 2,442 -,257	5 years 7 to 9 years_ 10 to 4 years	1,231	1,035	622 972	56 923	552 869	12	20 70 103	1,25
5 years. 6 years. 7 to 9 years. 10 to 13 years. 14 years.	3,659	-,827	1 822	-,619 1 332 28°	1 25.	505	531	3,446	10 to _4 years 10 to 13 years	-,656 351	858	798	765 158	709 160	93	89	1,684
5 to 19 years	3,594	779	,,822 413	1,326 264	-,34/ 1C,	445	478	3,952	15 to 19 years .	~,571 393	305 200	7e6 193	7_0 172	68>	95 28	81 19	2.044
15 years 16 and 17 years _ 18 and 19 years	1,461	318 725 976	77 636	257 540	549 51/	180	192	1.529	16 and 17 years 18 and 19 years	712 466	362	347	329 409	314	36	33 29 /8	378 8/7 823
20 to 24 years	2 5 0	1,683	1,7.9	1,326	1,354	351 357	369	1,521 3,349 3,120	20 to 24 years 25 to 29 years	1,778	486 514	592 636	434	514 545	52 60	914	1,607
20 to 24 years	2,990 2,896 2,344	1 -56	1,494	1,189	1,198 ,062 854	2.7 243 2.7	296 32	2,46R 2 173 1 /12	30 to 34 years	1,181	558 622	623 647	509 561	559	61	100	1,257
	1 9-9	4,005	1,101	99b 793	854	2.7	247	1./12	40 to 44 years_ 45 to 49 years_	,182	570 557	512 556	523 489	542 480	57	76	1,110
45 to 49 years 50 to 54 years 55 to 59 years _ 60 to 64 years _	1,544	108	904 743 677 463	531 495	190 534 237	.70	153	21,028	50 to of years	. 898 863	447	451 416	389 393	393 376	58	76 58 40	880 797
60 to 64 , cars _ 65 to 69 years _ 70 to 74 years _	997	54	5	374 103	341	-40 37- 84	143 126 10-	880 766	60 to 64 years	694	365 400	,,29 339	321 326	298 280	44 7 34	31 59	548 481
75 to 84 years _	61.	303	345 323	21.0	251 221 35	85	02	424	70 to 74 years. 75 to 84 years. 85 years and over	422 387	242 209 32	190 178 3/	208 190 29	16r 29	34 9 3	16	25 -
21 years and over	22 010	11,440	11 .62	5,890	8,500	4, 8	2,614	18,365	21 years and over	10 848	5.361	5,487	4,739	4,797	542	J90	40,505
PIZON								- 1	WASTINGTON							200	
All ages	2, 369	1,150	1,100	5,366	6,15.	3.316	3,308	20,943	All sges	38,37L 5 190	19,167	2,528	1,70%	13,162	5 966	910	34,443
Under 5 years _ Under 1 year _ 1 and 2 years _	950	235	207	129	119	106	88	402	Under - years Under 1 year	1.050	52e 1.408	524 1,033	328	304 € 72	-98 t	220	3,874
S and 4 years 5 to 9 years	374 2 169	427 -,104	1,065	4-5 055	630	28.	180 435 97	2,318	1 and 2 years 3 and 4 years 5 to 9 years	1,999 4,308	2 162	2,146	1,370	1,440	792	307 320 706	3,20
	45c 402	230	226 194	139	10	91 91	84	487	5 vears 8 vears	904 882	464	440 440	286 286	310	178	-50 -30	805 726
5 years 5 years 7 to 9 tears 10 to 14 years 10 to 18 years	1,311 2 002 1,014	1,034 826	345 968 788	399 629 447	3°5 556 458	267 - 15 329	250 412 300	2,374	7 to 9 years 10 to 14 years 10 to 13 years	2 522 3,925 3,182	1 987	1,266	1,292	1,301 1,017	458 695	426 63' 519	2,1 ₀ 6 3,824
14 years _	388	208	180	132	98	71	82	-,903	14 years	743	381	362	243	244	138	8س1	3,062 764
15 years - 16 and 17 years -	1,747 395 743	879 -92 375	868 200 Je8	539 1.'9 229	18 236	340 66	350 92 132	2,467	15 to 19 years . 15 years . 16 and 17 years	3,084 734	352 657	1,592 382 627	1,024 243 460	251	109	571 131 2.7	3,726 767
18 and 19 years.	609	339	300	_8_ 379	164	123	- 36	969	16 and 17 years 18 and 19 years 20 to 24 years	1,066	483	563 1 403	321	3tu 976	162	223	1,483 1,476 3,068
25 to 39 years 30 to 34 years 35 to 39 years	1,24,3	557	664 029 033	400	418	170	226 246 179		25 to 29 years 30 to 34 years	2 910	1,295 1,368 1,240	1,542	988	-,540 980	360	202	3,046
35 to 39 years	1 248 1,09k	62.5 579	519	436	379	180	204	,344 1,298 1,082	35 to 39 years 40 to 44 years	2,704	1,338	1,766	985	9.0	353 336	345 416 345	2,391
45 to 49 years 50 to 54 years 55 to 59 years -	1,082	521 442	562 440 409	.68	406 304	153 126	456 -36	1,046	45 to 46 /cars 50 to 54 years	2,104	1,028	1,076	699 023	744 606	329 238	332	1,705 1,386
60 to 64 years	861 670	452 350	°20	340 287	299	63	05	568	55 to 59 years 60 to 64 years	1,391	623	678	.02	469 387 334	213 15. 194	189 149 150	673
65 to 60 vears - 70 to 74 years -	634 389	354 198	290 401	132	196	104 53	12	274	65 to 69 /ears	1,02.	737 31.	484 258	343 224	201	87	150 57 51	685 3c2
75 to 84 years 85 years and over	387 63	20	195 43	142	47	7	48 3	462	75 to 84 years 85 years and over _	480 88	263 40	217	186	162	12	15 }	348
21 /ears and over	10 704	5,328	o 346	3 800	3,742	1,558	1,604	11,057	21 years and over _	21,343	10,613	10,790	7 645	7,543	2,968	3,187	18,622
All ages	.6,929	18 47	18,456	6 168	.6,0.)	2 305	2,397	37,750	AL ages	31,704	17,661	18,043	14,295	14,387	6.366	6.656	33,6%
Under 5 years	4,285 858	°,1£0 424	2,125	1 622	1, 798	338	327	4 126	Under 5 years	4,447	2,222	2,206	1,394	1,104	827	842 153	2,662
1 and 2 years 3 and 4 years 5 to 9 years	1,778	424 14 822	864	767	724	347	140	3,339	Under 1 year	1 925	976 865	949	567	602 530	369 332	347	2 9.3
	723	1,947	1,832	1,60/ 38	270	28. 58	293	4,400	5 to 9 years	4,008	2,367	1,941	+ 22/	1,14.	843	795	3 439 747
6 Jears	2,231 2,718	1,124 1,949	.,107 1,109	954 1 637	925	170	58 172 2 8	2,024 4,477	0 /ears.	2,404	1.237	393	243 250 731	225 602	130 506	168	2 046
10 to 14 years	2 917	1,949 1 547 402	1 370	1 496	1,514	251	198	3,652 825	10 to 14 years 10 to 13 years	3,595	1 831	1,764	861	812	788	759	3,400
15 to 19 years	3 391	1 '85	1,706	1,461	1.435	224	271	4,063	15 to 19 years.	663 2,926	309 1 382	324 1,544 341	736	193 86°	646	131	3,434
15 years 16 and 17 years 18 and 19 years	1,438	727	363 700 644	628	3±0 582 543	109	119 131	81.9 1,648	15 years 16 and 17 years	1,212	323 600	612	322	338	25	274 2 0	682
20 to 24 vears _	4,722	1,314	1,408	1,130	1,208	18/	200	1 596 3,576 3,182	18 and 19 years 20 to 24 years 25 to 29 years	1 050 2,5/5 2,670	1 194 1,250	591 1,35_ 1 426	243 763	347 971	432	504	3, 115
30 to 14 years 35 to 39 years	2,546	1,239	1,37.	1,123	1,161 1,227	116	146 144	2,732	30 to 34 years	2,618	1,237	1,38.	904 878	971 943 893	399 333 371	455 438 488	3 279 2,728 2,323
40 to 44 yea.s 45 to 49 yea.s	2,145	1,184	1,200	1,067	1 009	11 95	117	1,9,3	40 to 44 years 45 to 49 years	2.275	-,.66	1,109	775	733	391	376	,811
50 to 54 years	1,715	868	8/7	601	767	57	80	1,41	50 to 54 years 55 to 59 years	1,366	947 768 629	919	530 442	486 463	326 238	339 260 176	1,268
86 to 69 years	1, 29	517	530	500 446	524	26 74 27	49	1,49 861 720	60 to 64 years	1,268 973 1,121	503 559	6.9 470 562	360	347	187 143 237	176 123 238	986 844 669
70 to 74 years 75 to 54 years 85 years and over	609	294	317	267	278	351	39)	368	65 to 69 years	635	277	291 260	236	2+5	108	76 82	310
21 years and over .	21,215	10 485 1	0,730	9, 277	9,515	14	1,215	19,923	85 years and over	90 20,∠24	9,933	53	6.765	34	12	19 3	409 18,966

Table 41.—ACE BY COLOR AND SEX, FOR PARISHES. 1950—Con

Parish and age	1950 topustion							1940	6.	1950 population							1940
	Ail classes			White		Nonwarte		Sobra-	Pansh and age	Ali casses			White		Nonwhite		popula- tion
	Total	Male	Female	Male	Female	'fale	Ferre.	tous?		Total	Mag	Female	Mue	Female	Male	Famale	
	20.7	7%	1					1		1	-	-	-	-	_		
VEST BATCH POUCE	17 7774				1		- 27		WEST TATIONNA				3	. 1	- 4		
All ages	11,738	5,77	5,96_	∠,699	-		-	,20	All ages	_2,169	6,297	3,872	- 942	.,034	4,382	2,858	1_,72
Under 5 years Under 1 year	1,612	77C 145	842 178	338	372 74	422 85	-0-1	-,1C3 219	Incer 5 years .	1,075	5.8	52"	94		424	424	4,10
1 and 2 years	710 579	360 265	350	150	1 35	201	190.	7	Under 1 year and 2 years	207	88	217	20 39		68 .80		19
3 and 4 years	1,340	654	314 686	119	143 330	146 35_	_7_ J561	_,^95	3 and 4 sars	432	211	251	35	-41	±7o	17	91
5 vears	295 265	_44	151	57	73	87	78	225	5 to 9 years	388	-26 80	462	66	1_0 20	360 66		1,07
6 years	780	378	402	65	197	1,7	73 205	. 2D 66"	6 vents	-75	82	94	2	23	7-	72	21
10 to 14 /ears	1,105	520 440	276	227	507	302	-5	1,1-0	7 to 9 rears	536 858	200	271	#2 81 61	58 74	361	342	1,06
14 years	188	89	99	192 25	30	248	266	903	10 to 13 ters -	108	345	45			28-	282	85
15 to 19 years	913	466	4.0	200	223	26.	2241	1,198	15 to 19 years	920	5.9	351	20	54	430	297	201
15 years 16 and 17 years .	208	109 206	99	53 92	45 84	56 114	78	229	15 /ears	164	74	88	16	8	6C	80	-,032 167
18 and 19 years -	337	151	186	65	94	91	921	483 48c	16 and 17 years 18 and '9 years	344	204	_37 _26	4- 72	20	163	117	391 474
20 to 24 years 25 to 29 years	840 867	399 418	449	200	223	199	224 205	1,018	20 to 24 years	1 083	825	258	272	66	553	192	1,21
30 to 34 years	789	263	426	202	225	10:	201	760	25 to 29 years 30 to 34 years	982 719	7º79 544	203 -75	270	62 54	500 370	141	1,18
40 to 44 /ears	726 687	387 328	339 359	220 160	167	16°	172 195	749 597	35 to 39 years 40 to 44 years	722	456	266	171	8	285	183	904
45 to 49 years	629	317	312	160	126	157	186,	653	45 to 49 years	528	4 ₂ 7	224	150	72	257	153	642
50 to 54 years	499 462	269 228	2:0 234	114	108	155	122	523	50 to 54 years	421	246	175	107	521	139	123	560 480
60 to 64 years	396	208	188	99	76	128	1291	418 330	55 to 59 years 60 to 64 years	347 293	206 167	126	78 57	581 51	170	83	384
85 to 89 years	3 <i>8</i> 7 220	200 106	187	62	63	118	124	372	65 to 69 years	320	272	149	49	40,	-22	109	336 334
75 to 84 years .	225	122	⊥03	4.	46	81 11	57	186	70 to 74 years 75 to 84 years	152	76 89	97	33 22	23	43	54 67	1,85
85 years and over 21 years and over	35 6,598	13	22	4	8	9	14	193	85 years and over	33	10	23	4	6	6	17	173
	0,798	3,277	3,321	1,582	-,576	1,695	2,745	0,487	21 years and over	6,210	4,281	2,029	1,494	· 640	2,087	1,389	7,181
All ages.	±7,248	8,705	8,543	7,175	6,952				# DAN				-0		1		
Under 5 years	2,331	1,164	1,167	925	905	-,530 229	-, 491 262	19,252	Ail ages	16 1_9	8,093	8,026	5,948	5,754	2,145	2,272	16,923
Under I vear	400	193	207	ا 5دے	261	38	40	2,373	Under 5 vears Under 1 vear	1,863	965 174	898 187	673	6.2	292 63	286 76	1,632
1 and 2 years 3 and 4 years	008 -,008 د92	504 467	204 s 456	407 373	386 358	97 94	118	1,907	1 and 2 years.	785	427	358	298	243	129	115	1,293
5 to 9 years	د2,15ء	1,051	1,102	861	912	190	190	2,309	3 and 4 years 5 to 9 years	717 4 752	364 888	353 864	264 629	258; 61.0	100 259	95 S 254	-,766
5 years	439 416	225	214	184	-70 192	41	38 45	49"	5 years	377	198	179	139	126	59	53	375
7 to 9 years	1,298	647	651	526	244	_21	107	1,342	6 years - 7 to 9 years	342	1 ₀₀ 525	177 508	125 365	128 356	160	152	335 1,056
10 to 14 years	2,085	1,379	1,006	891 718	837 l	185	169 128	2,327	10 to 14 years.	1,499	775	724	569	527	206	197	1,866
14 years	414	209	205	173	164	_52 36	41	431	10 to 13 years - 14 years -	1,199	ol8 157	581	122	1.0	171	164	1,5_2
la to 19 years	1,686	873 207	813	7_0	503	163	150	2,109	15 to 19 years _	1,300	657	643	491	440	166	203	1,838
lo vea.s 16 and 17 years.	760	395	365	329	149 304	33 76	32 51	433 800	15 years 16 and 17 years_	308 554	163 277	145 277	126	190	37 68	38	373 718
18 and 19 years _ 20 to 24 years	538	271 526	2e7 565	217 438	210	24 88	57 118	816	18 and 19 vears	438	2.7	221	156	143	OT.	78	747
25 to 29 years	980	455	525	380	40	75	85	1,503	20 to 24 years 25 to 29 years	1,042	485 485	535 F	348 356	367 373	137	190	1,509
30 to 34 years	1 001	473 573	528 569	414	402	59 85	76	1,397	30 to 34 years	1,027	498	529	379	400	119	129	1,216
to 39 years	1,013	2/3	487	453	408	73	93 79	1,174	35 to 39 years - 40 to 44 years	1,105	554 522	551 517	432	394 392	122	157	1,133
5 to 49 years	821	421	400	350	3:3	71	67	844	45 to 49 years	917	443	474	316	321	127	153	905
50 to 54 years	705 595	306 315	339 280	3C2 256	272	64	57 66	7*8 571	50 to 54 years	789 760	382 370	407	278	299 305	104	106	753 600
0 to 64 years	491	248	243	207	204	41	39	417	55 to 59 years 60 to 64 years	ما2 ا	327	305	245	241	82	85 64	505
5 to 69 years _ 0 to 74 years _	523 321	280	243	213	178	39	65 34	344 198	65 to 69 years	al.8 384	331 223	287 161	238	199 128	93	88	436
5 to 84 years .	268	148	220 5	117	97	31	23 }	154	70 to 74 years	332	173	159	133	127	40	32	208
5 years and over	42	23	19	15	n	8	8 3		85 years and over	40	15	25	-0	-9	5	63	1
1 years and over	8,754	4,431	4,323	3,602	3,531	739	792	9,702	21 years and over _	9,501	4,714	4,787	3,513	3,499	1,201	1,288	9,500

Table 42 —GENERAL CHARACTERISTICS OF THE POPULATION, FOR PARISHES 1950

[Patternia - dericts statistics based on 20 review amounts for comin of any groups trong compare count, see table 41 Percent not shown where less than 0.1, percent and middles not shown who a base at less than 500]

The second secon	A STREET, SQUARE, SQUA	The state of the s	-	processor and	_	-		and the latest designation of the latest des	1	_	Total Contract	-	-		1	1	Dast	CHICAGO
iahject	Acedia	Allon	Ascen- sion	Assumo- tion	Avoy- eller	Beau- regard	Bien- vil_e	Bossier	Cadno	Calca- sieu	oald-	Caneron	Dota- houla	borne	Cor- cordia	De Sato	Beton Rouge	Car- roll
Total popula son Lyban farm popula son	47,50	8,230	12,387	17,278	38,C31 239	17,766	19,10	40,139 18	176,547 115	89,623	10,293	6,244	11,634	25,063 44	14,398	24,396 24	158,236 345	16,302
RACE, NATIVITY AND CITIZENSHIP Male Sative white Foreign-born white Negro Other moos	23,374 18,895 _33 4,344	9.407 7,129 /7 2,145	11,234 7,291 75 3,866	8,347 4,971 30 3,539	19,062 14,052 70 4,925	8,819 7,295 72 1,448	9,559 4 855 1° 4,693	21,246 1/,212 166 6,846	84,062 52,206 908 30,896	44,772 34,344 308 10,107	5,178 3,697 25 1,456	3,301 2,966 12 323	6,017 3,367 6 2,023	12,461 6,052 27 6,382	7 046 2,990 9 4,029	11,809 2,150 26 6,631	77,670 51,9_7 915 24,790	8,055 3,269 28 4,739
Other races Female - Astive white Foreign-born white Vegro Othe, races	23,676 18,914 111 4,650	9,428 7,068 38	1,153 7 037 65 4,050	8,731 5 011 33 3,087	18,969	8 947 7 304 68 1,575	9,546 4,813 17 4,714	18,893 11,608 242 7,037 6	92,485 56,049 928 35,402 43	24,863 34,088 312 10,456	5,.15 3,616 19 1,480	2,943 2,673 10 260	5 817 3,6% 7 2,122 2	12,602 6,005 22 6,570	7,352 2,839 19 4,490 4	12,589 5,372 3/ 7,181 2	27,472	8,247 3,010 28 -,197 12
Persons 21 years old and over Natve Foreign born Nat.ratized Ahen. Cibernship not reported	25,606 25,409 197 99 37 61	10,443 10,360 83 53 23	12,281 12,154 127 56 39 32	9,232 9,173 59 32 23 4	20,961 20,834 127 68 51 8	10,136 9,998 138 85 27 26	.0,601 10,770 31 16 12 3	22,742 22,393 349 169 129 51	110,845 109,131 1,714 1,195 276 245	52,338 51,744 594 405 435 74	5,790 4,759 31 21 7	3,540 3,519 21 15 1	6,302 6,290 12 3 3	14,025 13,994 31 16 10	7,970 7,937 33 19 12 2	13,503 13,429 74 27 13	96 518 95,0.3 4,457 602 448 205	8,553 8,488 65 45 17
*SCHOOL ENROLLMENT)							100	on .	l
Persons 5 and 6 years old Number enrolled in school Percent enrolled in school Number enrolled in school	7,135 775 36 3	970 370 38 1	1 965 410 38 5	880 275 21 2 45	1,595 670 42 0 10	880 365 41 5	275 34 4	1 990 710 35 7 20	2,825 38 4 250	4,245 1,305 35 5 35	465 185	340 135	535 220 41 1	1,025 410 40 0 5 3,565	7.295	1 ±25 435 38 7 4,005	6,495 2,765 42 5 250 17 710	40 5
Persons 7 to 13 years old Number enrolled in soncol Persons 14 and 15 years old Number enrolled in school	7,370 6 890 93 5 - 700 1,400	2,825 2,735 96 8 735 705	3,400 3,260 95 9 840 770	2,795 2,620 93 7 700 5°s	5 945 5,690 95 7 1,420 1,295	2,680 2,590 96 6 680 635	3,190 3,110 37 5 805 725	4,400 95 5 1,065 940	20,520 19,760 96.3 4,785 4.515	11,825 11 345 95 9 3 C15 2,755	97 4 420 400	830 95 4 250 230	1,860 94 ~ 505 450 89 1	3,410 35 7 4,125 1,030	2,060 89 8 230 490	3,795 94 8 970 94 3	16,885 95 3 3 995 3,800 95 1	2,605 2,405 92,3 685 600
Percent enrolled a school	85 9 1 770 980 55 4 1,6°5	95 9 720 460 63.9 560	91 7 890 985 65 7 625	82 1 640 365 57 0 490	91 2 1,520 990 65 1 1,235	93 4 585 445 76 1	90 1 800 620 77 5	88 3 - 230 795 64 6	94 4 4 570 3,380 74 0 4,820	2,70 1,60 6> 0	395 250	18.	42, 295	955 755 79 ±	495 275 435	900 095 77 2 755	3,795 2,870 - 6	87 6 645 400 62 0
Persons 18 and 19 years old. Number enrolled in school. Persons 20 to 24 years old Number enrolled in school	430 25 7 3,830 275	75 10 3 1 275 80 6 3	125 20 0 1,6,5 80 4 8	1 18C 85 7 2	285 23 1 2 410 95	1.0 1 095 40 3 7	205 32 8 1,070	270 17 2 4,240 245 5.8	1,425 29 6 14 495 1,315 9 2	805 29 3 7,815 290 3 7	740 65 8 8	35 455 5	720 60 8 3	290 34 9 1 683 72 4 5	910 80 8 8	265 35 1 1,410 95 6 7	3,130 50 6 16,.80 4,065	985 40 4 1
Percent enrolled in a hool Persons 25 to 25 years old Number enrolled in school Percent enrolled in school	3 425	- 260 35 2 8	1,485 90 6 1	1,050 65 6 2	2,635	1,075 30 2 8	865 25 2 9	4 460 250 5 6	14,980 935 6 2	7,910 200 2 5	635 35 5 5	390	790 35 4 4	1,585	950 55 5 8	110 8 0	1,710 1,710 20 7	945 30 3 2
Male, 25 years old and over	10,795	4 660	5,160	3,915	9,725	4,700	4,725	10,4_0	46 20.	22,875	2,690	1,555	2,880	6,480	3,175	6,170	40,781	4,065
No school years completed Elementary 1 to 4 years 5 and 6 years	2,535 2,450 1 685 875	485 1,130 730 395	685 1,450 840 443	905 1,395 650 225	2,745 2,745 1,815 855	260 1,090 835 565	340 1,250 845 530	555 2,050 1,080 605	2,695 7,630 5,040 3,300	2,23C 3,935 2,91C 2,095	105 640 595 265	21.5 44.0 270 165	380 706 535 270	490 ,655 805 510	315 1,060 655 215	535 2,340 860 470	2,190 5,930 4,295 2,015	1,415 760 330
7 years 8 years High school 1 to 3 years 4 years College 1 to 3 years	575 1,285 470 265	590 480 155	355 745 325 100	195 210 -00 60	795 1,985 245 205	460 633 435 180	435 685 280	1,645 1,980 855	3,665 7,650 6,850 4,150	2,09C 3,765 2,520 1,365	300 425 125 50	110 145 110 15	280 370 120 85	,140 375 305	225 450 145 85	350 930 -25 215	3,300 6,345 5,620 4,390	250 330
4 vents or more. School years not reported Median school years completed Female 25 years old and over	355 300 5 3 11,750	115 140 6 8 4,730	5 9 5 9 5 795	200 3 9 4,105	195 190 5 8 9,425	95 125 7 2 4,600	40 70 6 7	425 330 8 8 9,375	3,580 1,645 9 0 52,925	1,335 630 8 0 22,955	70 85 6 9	50 35 5 8 1,450	70 65 6 2 2,875	190 76 7 2 6,550	85 140 5 7 3,870	320 5 6 6,490	4,650 1,550 9 7 42,850	95 95 135 5 2 4,055
No school years completed	3,005	620	725	860	1.375	180	2.0	425	2,440	2,175	95	295	340	330	2,00	460	270	- 445
Elementary 1 to 4 years 5 and 6 years 7 years 8 years	2,370 680 865 680	820 875 490 400	1,385 1,040 545 455	1,320 730 265 495	2,090 1,705 845 670	780 785 470 495	1,060 875 590 545	1,600 1,145 665 795	7,860 5,795 4,135 3,985	3,325 3,235 1,930 1,630	500 490 322 290	315 225 170 120	690 510 2≥0 255	1,230 1,095 540 570	1,070 700 390 280	1,670 1,060 560 390	5,235 5,005 2,855 3,045	1,285 845 355 280
High school 1 to 3 years 4 years Codege 1 to 3 years 4 years 4 years 6 more.	4,420 740 390 360	400 645 *20 160 115 85	770 450 200 130	290 240 90 65	1,660 280 450 485	905 555 235 110	2,150 385 240 195	1,60° 1,915 665 350	9,970 9,900 4,880 3,220	4,365 3,385 1,345 940	160 120	130 120 25 25	400 190 420 90	1,475 525 455 225	675 160 125 95	1,260 175 425 235	7,465 8,145 4,200 3,525	375 175 115 90
School years not reported Median school years completed	240 5 5	7 C	6 4	30 4 6	6 4	8 1	65 7 6	195 8 9	9 5	8 3	7.8	5 9	6 5	.05 8 C	85 6 5	255 6 9	1,205	56
MARITAL STATUS AND HOUSEHOLDS		i																
Male 14 years old and over Single Married Widowed or divorced.	15,570 4,095 10,875 600	6,274 1,509 4,430 340	7,262 2,070 4,794 398	3,547 1,659 3,687 201	12,781 3,376 8,871 534	6 033 -,445 4 246 342	6,504 1,781 4,383 340	14,928 4,714 9,546 668	59,493 12,058 43,929 3,506	30,655 6,786 22,396 1,473	3,548 900 2,429 219	2,252 281 1,576 95	3,970 1,118 2,633 219	8,458 2,487 5,859 412	4,654 1,160 3,159 335	7,813 2,07° 5,249 489	55,212 14,497 38,498 2,217	5,121 1,302 3,529 290
Female 14 years old and over Single	16,106 3,303 11,000 1,863	6,366 1,001 4,510 855	7,542 1,576 4,918 1,048	5,710 1,308 3,704 698	12,824 2,382 8,964 1,478	6,120 4,000 4,290 830	6,603 1,236 4,470 877	12,767 1,840 9,45* 1,472	68,375 10,634 45,914 11,827	31,233 5,133 22,442 3,658	3,475 577 2,397 501	2,042 305 1,540 197	3,867 688 2,716 463	8,770 1,641 5,983 1,146	5,014 867 3,270 877	8,500 1,681 5,463 1,456	58,418 11,116 39,621 7,681	5,403 950 3,585 868
Wirned couples * aumber With own household Without own household	10,385 9,860 525	4,24 3,945 300	4,420 4,145 275	3,370 3,45 225	8,755 8,435 320	4,055 3,890 165	4,125 3,915 210	9,115 8,730 385	40,420 37,135 3,285	21,185 20,145 1,040	2,385 2,285 200	1,460 1,345 115	2,500 2,365 135	5 555 5,195 360	2,750 2,625 125	5,015 4,765 250	36,005 33,805 2,200	3,340 3,140 200
Families and unrelated individuals* . Families Unrelated individuals	12,550 11,180 1,370	5,300 4,570 730	5,780 4,930 850	4,185 3,660 525	10,835 9,540 1,295	5,115 4,425 690	5,120 4,535 585	13,805 9,045 4,160	58,665 45,315 13,350	27,335 22,805 4,500	2,965 2,600 365	1,630 1,460 170	3,270 2,760 510	6,940 6,115 825	4,200 3,285 745	6,820 5,850 970	53,115 39,490 13,625	4,980 3,930 1,050
Households number Population in households Population per household Institutional population	12,422 46,852 3 77 17	3,053 18,674 3 70 2	5,865 22,312 3 80 8	4,286 17,238 4 02 2	10,227 37,894 3 71 52	4,941 17,698 3 58	4,902 19,059 3.84 5	10,264 37,051 3 61 17	50,285 171,266 3 41 >61	24,971 98,249 3 53 178	2,780 10,269 3 69	1,6.6 6,230 3 86 7	3,107 21,804 3 80 6	5,567 24,979 3 60	3,985 14,350 3 60 5	6,420 24,351 3 79	43, 18 150,645 3 49 610	4,282 16,162 3 77 60
*RESIDENCE IN 1949									1.1			1			5			
Persons 1 year old and over 1950 Same 10.18t as in 1950 Different house same county Different county or abroad Residence not reported	46,050 39,765 3,700 1,370 1,2.5	15,080 1,820 1,245 395	21,985 19,245 1,545 845 350	16,700 14,900 1,210 310 280	37,275 31,190 4,210 1,155 720	17,350 13,655 2,230 1,140 325	18,610 15,510 2,195 710	38,985 24,540 3,445 9,610 1,390	172,820 130,940 23,400 14,260 4,220	87,545 66,960 13,035 5,905 1,645	10,225 8,570 940 520 195	5,985 4,940 580 365 100	11,505 9,500 1,315 540 150	24,385 19,480 2,875 1,665 365	14,155 12,0°0 995 720 370	24,080 20,690 2,220 775 395	154,390 117,840 22,690 10,075 3,785	15,935 12,200 2,400 1,200

13-79

GENERAL CHARACTERISTICS

Table 42—GENERAL CHARACTERISTICS OF THE POPULATION, FOR PANISHES 1950—Conlatered (*) Inside places on 20-percent narrols for state of tage percent from our rede counts, see in 4 Percent, in Lorin where feet Land C4.

Subject	Eas*	Fan-	renk-	Gran	Ther's	PT-	-204-	450-1	e' e	La's	, At	A i	b	-1-15-	4ad	Mora-	Natchi-	0
	6.ER	gailu				14	arn	30°	DL. s	Ac	f wret-	9 41	1.72	str.		7-764	insten:	-
rotal population.	4 4	3. 623	29,376	24 203	4 ,559 7c	2. 750	77,424	-03 d7 -	29, 29,	57 74	4-10	2 1"	ارد مان الالمام م	20,054	- 45	2,038	38,	1
LACE NATIVITY AND CIT-ZENSKIP													1		i	ere.	4.	
Male	9,549	15,96£ - ,139	2 329	1,4 7	19 9.0	6,42	. 56e	51 52- -2 434	L 244	28,478	22,249	0,462	7 735	0,30	5,608	3,405	10 424	10,0
reign-born white	, oùz	29 2.793	3,230	. (-6	6,220	- 405	.41	767	2 (35	94	2,027	592	4 93"	- 500	201	7 *2.	~ 24	3-
er akes	3 184		4	4	-	-23	,	Ģ.	4	1	171	est	2	1.	-0.	14	30	
Female	,7.C 98 5 53*	15,667 1 273 12 3,740	34	5 J1C 23 1	1. 378	6,780	472 1-	3, 3	25° 243 74 2.048	29,2 3	5 69	9 223 1	7.21 35	9, 5	2,090	0,50 0,427 37 ,897	27, July 124 124 124 124 124 124 124 124 124 124	299
ier races	12 (49	2			2		.,		4	4		<0	2	-,	. 5	7	32	
Persons 21 years o.d and ove.	1,003	16 952 58	14,940 8_5 -0	8,086	22 433	-5 036 294	8,089	00,-62	14,378	32 A.A.	24 542	7,44	14 2.0	7. 75 7. 75 7. 75	9,704	.7 373 .7 3.4 6.1	20 173 20 144 129	374
egn born a uralised	30	35	-4	17	140	-4C	3,	.,.32	ەر 23	203	26		40	12	42	25	-9	1
litizenanip not reported _	-40		-3	,	ж	29		J.	22	در ا	2.	R1	^!	22	4	6	-4	1
*SCHOOL ENROLLMENT																		
sons 5 and 6 ears old Number enrolled in school Percent enrolled in school Number enrolled in kindergarten	105	785 585 9 3	640 42 6	705 240 39 7	7 oC r n 3 + 7	-,-45 -70 7 8	740 275 37 2	2,-35	305 300 39 0	1,6°,	2 130 730 34 3	15	4.0	-,005 300	-,C3-	1,45. 555 36 1	4,80a 66L 36 G	1 3
None 7 to 13 years old	2,235	5,130	4,900	2,263	6.000	7 540	30	1 43 074	. 000	7,77	6.765	1, +20	3 !	3,20	75v	7, 135	0,175	3
Percent envalled in school	2,110	5,045 34 3	7,775	2,220	95 8	2,7_5 94 g	2,230	-,66°	.59	404	£ 27.1	487	3,140	2,840	2 640	4,735	93.4	
sons 14 and 15 years old Number enrolled in school	5° 5 425	1,005	1,250	540 520	1,300	78U	730 ULT 97 3	2,941	- 140 - 370 93 9	2,.95 -,870 85 2	-,270	487 :	703	660	585	1,305	1,485	
Percent enrolled in school	70 _ 565 325	85 8 1,12 612	87 0 ,_90	89 7 47 335	1 430	860 345	97 3 6-0 475	2,655	93 9 935 595	2, 25	,535	-2°	90 0	78 0 700 411	32 3 545 580	20,7 1,070 660	1 080	-
Percent enroued in school	-65	1,040	3 9	365	1,790	63 4	76 6	1,895	62 0	6. 5	18 4	-36	78 4	% 9 50:	57.3	6. 7	74 5	1
Number enrolled in school Percent enrolled in school	24 8	155	300	82	32	200	,42	60	210	9 5	290	120	1,00	_*0	18-4	275 275	+,560	1
Number enrolled in school	1 425	110	7,_75	c03	3,3/5	1 845	.,020	6,-15	2.19	5,605	2,075	743	3,075	2.4.	18-4 50	2, 40	2.70	4
Percent enrolleg in school	4.1	2,195	1,88*	200	5 9	1,705	1,000	7 3	215	23.8	3 265	44 5	455	25		2 8	22 7	1
Number enrolled in school Percent enrolled in school	_,04L 25 2.4	130	-C	45	3,035 150 4 9	140	5 .	66.	154- 152 6 8	4,965	90	12 L	1,765 265 20 7	- 435 12, 8 7	65	2,°70 75 3 2	2,350 255 15 1	5
*YEARS OF SCHOOL JUMPLETED											1							-
Male 25 years old and over	5 39>	7,240	6,730	3 495	9 710	6,61	3,200	26,600	6,510	23,490	9,600	3,340	5 870	4 990	4 370	7 790	8,765	
school years completed smertary 1 to 1 years 5 and 6 years	1,_80 600	1,650 2,090 1,050	750 2,120 1 170	340 715 605	2,025 2,385 1,245	1,075 2,075 1,045	180 880 e10	4,610 3,860	1,570 1,015	2,790 2,685 1 510	2,270 2,850 1 400	195 680 590	280 1,095 840	260 1,245 955	±,600 60°	2,5e0 1,00	1,240 2 675 1 160	1 2
7 years	460 265 585	490 310	650 505	375 425	67>	50C 43C	565 39 5	3,C45 3,485	550 440	935 690	785 435	425 330	425 ,35	525 570 850	270 305	6.5 665 1 020	540	1 2
gh school 1 to 3 years 4 years	135	585 390 150	840 485 170	570 21 85	1,175 727 385	655 355 180	645 245 120	3.50	620 545 170	1,590	790 470	215 120	930 480 670	180	3°0 2°5 120	965 275	900 440 355	3
allege I to 8 years 4 years or more -	1.080	130	160	90	350	150	130	1,570	150	970	210	80	541	110	130 130	120	330 485	í
hoof years not eported	5 4	195	185	7 :	2,5	30C	130	950 8 3	275 5 7	380 6 4	44	7 3	8 5	0 9	4 9	61	54	4
remale 20 years old and over	5,880	7,440	7,090	3,805	1,895	1,120	1,070	1,725	1,195	3,245	2,085	3,455	0,425	185	4,355	7,665	9,20	
ementary 1 o 4 years 5 and 6 years	1 040	1,605	1,785 1,370 755	710	1,895 2,165 1,700	2,050	623 565	4 005	± 260 880	2 330 -,835 940	1,550	155 450 515	93* 785	870 795	- 400 835	1,995	1,175 2,345 1 435	2
7 years	440	555 510	605	415 375	655 450	475 420	473 493	, 575 3 170 4 115	400 405 655	695	835 485 730	400 345 815	420 580 1,275	440 425 4,060	265 287 465	715	550 1,250	1
gh s-hool 1 to 3 years 4 years dlege 1 to 3 years	735 330	645 370 395	915 405	630 400 135	1,200	8.0 440 275	875 445	5 150	660	2,275 885	77.5	380 215	850	265 225	295 235	1,130 605 310	425	1
4 years or more	230	120	.85 200	120	305	170	215	1,750	285	985 860	350 230	110	645 1:5	90	85	21.5	575 470 470	
hool years not repo ted edian school years completed	7 0	135	165 6 7	7 5	190 6 2	125 5 5	35 8 4	605 8 5	6 1	350 6 6	240 5 1	8 5	9 6	7 "	100 5 8	125 6 9	6 4	
KARITAI STATUS AND HOUSEHOLDS	1				i													18.
ale 14 years old and over	2,877 3,74	10,555 2 534 7,659	9,356 2,448 6,41	4,846 1,252 3 337	13,346 3,641 9,064	8,957 2,605 5,749	5,116 1,209 3,656	35,051 7,482 26 232	8 664 2,168 6,059	19,781 5,819 13,204	3,889 3,878 9,513	4,447 1,080 3,129	9,183	6,78± ±,842 4,620	1,349 4,003	10,432 2,556 7 308	12,451 3,714 8,044	
Married Widowed or divorced	525	162	467	257	641	603	254	1,337	407	758	498	238	375	3.9	4,003	568	69.	3
male 14 years old and over	7,205 -,892 4,086	-,655	9,463 1,76° 6,586 1,110	4,896 779 3,479	13,941 2,836 9,217	9 27c 1,923 5,8.0 1,903	5,466 2,004 3,690 772	36,569 5 795 26,831 3 943	8,963 1,690 6,283 1,090	20 660 4,713 13,538	2 922 9,764	4,4.6 695 3,172 579	9,472 2,405 5,870 1 197	6,3,0 1,024 4,661 625	5,889 879 4,091 9.9	10,760 1,825 7,488 1,447	2,989 8,241 1,895	1 14
Widowed or divorced armed coupler * number W'th own household	2,027 2,027 2,340 285	7,100	6,040 5,725 315	2,985	8.020	5,140	2 /26	24 655	6,060 5,830 230	12. 125	1,352 8,600 8,160	3,010	5,225	4,475	3,725	6,970	7,210	1 1
Witnout own household_ imiles and unrelated individuals* Families	3,570	8,300	7.520	3,800	10.985	7,135	4,165	29 285	7,590	16,950	10,385	3,775 3,285	8 635 5,765	5,410 4 820	4 435	9.220	10.55	1 19
Unrelated individuals	2,900 670	710		3,282	1,485	1,200	430	3,325	6,625			490 3,617	2,870	590	4,_75 1,260 4,801	7,720 1,500 8,309	9,00	6 1
euscholds number Population in households Population per household stitutional population	3,345 13,601 4 07 5,277	31,604	7 278 29,284 4 02 19	3,933 -4,226 3 62 3	10,631 39,938 3 76	7,159 26,170 3 66 488	15,375 3 72 10	28,470 102,804 3 61 267	7,114 26 197 1 68 6	14,855 6,003 3 77 164	10,382 42,123 4 06 2	3,617 12,658 3 50 6	23,653 3 72 234	5,1.6 19 962 3 87	17,234 3 59	31,727 3 82 3 82	37,14	5 3
*RESIDENCE IN 1949					00.3-	26 120	1.0	l.m. m.	25 57-	64 T	4. 436	12 6%	25 414	19,565	17,300	33.,253	37,51	5 5
Same house as m 1950	18,735 16,290 8A; 1,29;	1.025	28,74,2 21,30,2 5,030 1,440	13,890 11,560 1,375 670 285	4,320	26,110 22,425 2,130 995	15,380 12,720 1,640 79X	9,255	1.290	6,830 3,475	2,575	12,575 10,085 1,255 965 270	25,415 19,820 2,94, 2,035 613	19,565 16,660 1,685 865	2,000	23,095 5,520 2,025	30,00 5,09	5 4

Table 42 —GENERAL CHARACTERISTICS OF THE POPULATION, FOR PARISHES 1950—Con.

Latirat *) denotes the "abec pased on 20" arrent sample, or totals of ap, groups your compace count see table 41 Percent not shown where less than 0.1,

October and median to "above where pase is less than 500]

				-		-	-	-	-	_	_	St	-	-		-	-	STATE OF THE PARTY.
Suivec	Cunch-	Plaque- nines	TLL SL	нартия	Red	Proh- land	Eab_ne	St Bernari	St Charles	St nelena	St ,ames	Joan the Baptist	Landry	St Mart_n	94 Mary	St Tasmany	"ang- ipahos	Tersia
Total pop: lattor	74,72	14,239	21 541	9C 48	12,113	26,672	20,646	097, نہ	-3 363 9	9,013	10,134	14,86. 28	78,/76 27	∡6,3¬3 37	35,848 7	26 968 30	53,218 381	500°د۳
RACE NATIVITY AND CITIZENSHIP Male Natise white Foreign born white Negro Other races	36,138 2-233 3/5 11,585	7 477 2,489 125 2,857	.0,87. .,048 	44,181 29,394 403 4,323	5,064 2,04,0 7 2,4,6	13 191 7,687 25 ,275	10,4 8 284 34 2,094	5 595 4,672 128 780	6,566 4,489 60 2,111	4,556 2,152 1 2,403	7,615 3,769 59 3,787	7,515 3,748 34 3,732	38,798 21 603 123 17,068 4	13 252 8,383 26 7,839	17,904 10,946 161 6,7-0 57	13 309 9,246 170 3,891 2	26,628 18,026 56: 8,034	6,422 2,28* 31 4,104
Temale Natire white Foreign-born white. Negro. Other races	38,577 25 225 280 13,062 8	0,°62 4 052 65 2,-23	1J,965 4,95- /9 5,950	46,467 30,355 730 15,644 68	6,149 3 001 4 3,144	23,481 7,805 22 3,050 4	10,465 8,233 30 4,19%	5,492 4,469 75 825	0,097 4,410 43 2,236	4,457 2,072 3 0,382	7 79 3,75, 45 3,919 2	7,346 3,628 35 3 6/9 4	39,678 2.,597 135 17 94.	23 171 8 175 26 4,395 5	17,94/ 10,839 156 6,904 45	13,679 9,465 279 4 031 4	76 590 17,5-2 470 3,555	6 787 2,301 27 4,459
Persons 21 years old and over Native Oreign born Naturalized Alien (linzen hip not reported	45,913 45 3*2 561 -0- -01 50	7,871 1,675 1,675 138 36 22	1-,584 ++,489 95 64 2°	24,803 24 028 7" 529 245 03	6,485 6,475 -3 -3 -3	23,879 13,839 40 15 20 5	11,492 1,-28 54 41 14	0,452 6,251 401 134 55 12	7 373 7,287 106 60 37	4,525 4,520 1	8,106 8,017 89 43 4_ 5	8,043 7,985 28 41 17	39,029 227 124 59 40	35,444 13,390 54 36 7	19,940 296 206 62 28	15,6±0 15 284 326 ±-9 48 -9	29,750 28 930 1,020 576 372 72	7,130 49 26 14
*SCHOOL ENROLLMENT Fersons 5 and 6 years old Number enrolled in school Percent enrolled in school Number enrolled in school Number enrolled in school Aumber enrolled in school Number enrolled in school	2 880 1,200 41 ° 9,050 8 845	065 28 42 9 5 9 005 -,945	990 34 2 15 3,370 3 230	3,0-5 1 370 3' 0 60 -1,835 11,01-	2.5 36 4 1 925 1,775	1,729 520 37 7 5 4,570 4 11	- 110 740 99 6 25 3,195 3,050 95 5	5 1,475 1,430 66 9	7,0 295 40 4 1,940 1,850 95 4	435 205 1,485 1,380	760 3.0 47.4 -5 2,620 2,530 92.3	675 290 /3 0 2,255 2 197 26 3	4,295 1,560 36 3 25 13 4,0 12,595 93 8	1,345 /10 30 3 15 4,335 4,035 93 1	3,600 38 1 56 5 340 5,125 96 1	1,385 560 40 4 55 3 9-5 3 715 94 2	2 430 670 27 6 35 7 600 7,145 93 7	1,99, 1,900
Fer our enrolled, in acnool Person, 14 and 5 years old Number enrolled in school Percont enrolled in school Person 15 and 17 years old Number enrolled in school Person* enrolled in school Person* enrolled in school	2 2.0 2,120 94 2 2 100 1,50 71 7	90 0 2-5 475 87 0 570 380 60 7	86. 770 89 0 87# 235 61 1	2,780 2,40 87 8 895 2,040 70 5	335 430 64 1 430 335	1,125 1,030 91 5 1,115 ? 05 8	950 895 974 970 58, 76 0	295 295 20 220	445 40 560 410 73 2 465	92 9 250 310 40 255	280 20 87 9 525 352 68 9 400	91 > 535 400 74 A	3,045 2,565 84 7 3,250 1,785 54 9 2 950	995 835 33 7 -,160 630 54 3	295 1,105 65 3 1,09- 640 58 4	1 050 930 88 / 990 735 7~ 2 810 255	1,090 88 5 1,925 1 330 69 1 1,755	45 475 87 2 485 325 360 40
Ferons 18 and 18 years old Number enrolled in school Percent enrolled in school Percent enrolled in school Number enrolled in school Percent enrolled in school Percent enrolled in school Percent enrolled in school Number curolled in school Percent enrolled in school Number curolled in school	575 26 4 6, 40 365 8 0 6 155 2.0	1,275 ±05 8 2 1 045 50 4 8	20 9 1,505 80 *1 1,330 75 5 0	635 22 1 6,790 6°D 10 2 7,310 480 3 6	685 35 650 30 4 6	2:0 28 7 1,015 2. 5 3 1,610 70 4	2,4 33 9 1 110 85 7 7 1,100 120 9 2	970 60 62 4,072 6" 6 0	150 100 9 3 -,050	25 25 25 25 25 25 4 6	75 1,700 30 2 8 865 40 2 3	1:00 29 4 - 200 30 2 7 1,125 60 7 2	765 25 9 5,35 432 7 1 5,560 285	160 17 / 1,850 120 6 9 1 810 110 6 -	205 19 1 2,040 1-0 4 9 2,705 80 3 0	3L 5 -,730 20 6 9 1 640 95 5 8	33 0 3,3,0 650 650 3,840 325 3 5	710 22 3 5 715 75 2 1
*YEARS OF SCHOOL COMPLETED Male 25 years old and over	19,600	003رد	5,340	23,96	2,880	L 115	5 372	2,950	3,0201	2,170	3,300	3,555	17,165	6,255	8,800	6 505	13,365	3,055
Yo school years comple vd Discensive I to 4 years o and 6 years years years to 3 years to 3 years	1,_1C 3 760 2,660 620 1,795 3,350 2 565	4°5 910 7_0 385 345 340 250	1 170 1,740 7,5 355 370 310 325	2,1.5 5,125 2,723 1,940 - 990 3,445 1,990	520 865 446 220 215 340 120	1,915 1,045 515 530 745	415 1,385 ,010 ,770 395 d8c 200	295 585 535 2.0 310 500 160	790 450 33_ 175 420 225	157 775 380 -70 410 275	530 1,160 530 235 275 350	525 3,150 535 235 165 473	4,300 5,075 2,270 1,070 760 1,7_5 650	2,070 1,660 865 395 140 480 145	1,785 2,360 1,210 6,5 465 935	3+0 +,585 1 165 675 655 635 480	1,670 3,310 2,190 -,160 1,230 -,620 800	395 1,090 470 155 185 250
College 1 to 3 years - 1 to 4 years - 1 to 5 years	1,405 955 580 8 3 21,520	140 130 1.0 5 4	10 175 120 4 3 5,220	1,395 1,075 1,145 7 2 25,535	5, 35 70 5 1 3,155	235 195 80 6 0	130 9, 45 6 0 5,400	95 30 75 71 2,805	75 125 125 6 6 3,455	30 10 40 1,975	60 90 35 4 8 3,830	50 85 51 3,620	105 365 455 4 2 17,295	215 CO 85 3 3	325 320 165 5 3	255 355 110 7 7,265	540 425 -26 6 4 13,880	145 105 110 5 0 3,280
No achool years romple ed Elementary 1 ro 4 years 5 and 6 years 7 years Figh school 1 to 3 years	1,020 3 470 2,985 1,7.0 1,675 3,960	420 655 270 395 260 295	1,005 ,730 840 210 435	1,995 4 565 3,835 2 405 2,050 4,480	40. 860 510 265 220 485	410 1,230 1,180 575 475	1,150 1,000 1,000 440 460	520 515 375 -30 520	350 705 660 350 2.4	400 410 165 220 365	480 1,095 755 340 275 545	580 740 33° 160 580	4,255 4,505 4,505 140 870 1,760	1 455 775 435 215 560	1,745 2,205 2,390 740 565 860	1 255 785 803 1.155	1,360 2 605 2,375 1,205 -,200 2,115	1,045 385 235 230 380
4 years College 1 to 3 years - 4 Vears or more School years not reported Median school years completed	3,-95 1,745 685 335 8 7	285 90 75 55 6 6	7,345 1-5 135 75 4 C	2,920 1,595 1 090 600	165 105 35 60 6 1	385 265 220 70 9 8	1,465 195 210 190 155 7 3	15.) 60 55 35	320 140 90 40 6 8	216 115 40 35 7 9	120 100 90 30 5 9	100 95 75 60	600. 615 475 340 7	21D 205 125 95 3 8	1,0a5 335 190 120 5 9	820 295 295 65 7 8	1,775 735 475 335 7 4	±50 ±60 90 85 5 8
MARITAL STATUS AND HOUSEMOLDS Maie 14 years old and over Single Married Widowed or divorced	25,171 5,43 18,488 1 452	5,096 1,531 3,320 24,3	6,990 1,995 4,609	30,760 7,625 21,403 1,722	3 883 929 2,744 210	8,540 2,226 5,939 37	6 874 1,823 4,695 356	3,610 898 2,721 191	4,492 1,269 3,031 192	2,9_0 961 1,903 146	4,837 1,542 3,030 205	4,915 ,602 3,076 237	24,42° 7,116 16 388 916	0,430 2,572 5,550 308	11,805 3,176 8,0.6 6,3	9,312 2,492 0,104 51(18 052 4,931 42,145 976	4,138 1,346 2,840 2,2
Fen.sie 14 years old and over Single Married Widowed or divorced	28,18° 4,427 19,145 - 615	4,438 842 3,210 436	7,218 1,516 4,728 974	33,468 6,530 21,953 4,985	4 122 751 2 827 544	8,764 1,*57 6,110 1,097	7,074 -,326 4,807 941	3,775 646 2,772 357	4,542 966 3 034 541	2,843 610 9_2 3_5	5,021 1,181 3,095 745	4,828 1,090 644	25,389 5,779 16,781 2,829	8,532 2,059 5 ball 853	12,118 2,17 8 10 1,697	9,520 -,853 6,237 1,436	18,348 3,52 12,798 2,498	4,53° 778 3,040 719 2,505
Magreed couples,* number With own nonsehold Without own household	17,395 -6,25* 1,140	3,150 2,905 245	4,665 4,335 330	19,325 18 180 1,145	2,565 2,400 160	5,535 5,275 260	4,465 1,270 195	2,455 2,455 8^	2,595 2,400 -95	1,865 1 795 70	2,63° 2 425 205	2 900 2,640 260	15,84, 4,990 655	5,505 5,165 340	7,740 7,265 475	5,380 5,065 315	11 360 10,710 650	2,44C 65
Families and unrelated individuals* Families Unrelated individuals	24,165 19,350 4 83*	3,9.0 3,250 660	5 985 5 170 Pl>	26,475 21,665 4,810	3,180 2,805 375	6,855 5,015 840	5,650 4,965 68,	3,090 2,795 295	3,325 2,890 4,5	2,3,0 2 030 300	3 455 2,965 490	3,665 3,215 50	19 67) 17,285 2,390	6,620 5,985 635	10,015 8,480 1,535	7,765 6,385 . 680	16 160 12,780 3,380	3,665 2,955 710
Households, number Population in households Population per household Institutional population	21,336 72,949 3 42 59*	3,566 1-,073 3 90 8	5,523 21,777 3 94 2	24,071 85,101 3 4 4 404	3,157 11,093 3 83	6,687 26,607 3 98 6	5,479 20 817 3 80 8	2,953 1,065 2 77 2	3,446 13,274 3 85 4	2,_80 8,979 4 12	3,667 15,309 4 17	5,640 4 08ركد 4 08	18,585 77,974 4 20 24	6,235 26,312 4 22 2	9,410 35,673 3 79 33	7,428 26,019 3 58 28	14,178 52,18/ 3 (8 2+	3,680 13 190 3 58 4
RES'DENCE IN 1949 Persons I year old and over, 1950 Same nouse as in 1950 Different nouse same rounts Different counts o. shroad Residence not reported	73,075 25,650 10,890 5 280 1,255	13 950 11 900 875 910 265	21,485 18,170 2,240 795 280	88,695 70,905 _0,900 5,075	11 89 9,195 1,605 530 565	25,875 19,155 /,710 1,650 360	20,330 16,885 2,04* 1,005 395	10,830 8,775 750 1,230 75	13,110 1: 325 864 525 395	8,775 7,675 640 250 230	14,800 13 860 515 363 (5	14,440 1,230 765 295 150	76,575 62,665 9,940 2,395 - 575	25,560 22,875 -,760 545 380	35,040 28,835 4,220 1,505 480	25,270 23,035 1,600 -,325 310	52,3e5 41,805 5,860 3,180 1,520	12,770 10,3.5 1 6.5 6°0 170

Table 42 —GENERAL CHARACTERISTICS OF THE POPULATION, FOR PARISHES 1950—Con.

[Asterak (*) denotes statutus based on 20-person sample, for tokan "radian not shown where twa, in dee, that 50."

DENAS AST TRANSPORTED AST TRAN

Subject	Cerrebonne	Un_an	eraor	74 man	Jashingtor .	hetster !	Ba'c-	carol:	Fe_ic_ans	Wint
Total population. Urban-farm population	43,328	19,14.	3' 929	12 974	38 377	3*,704	11 738	_7,2.8	10,169	.6,11
Mal.	2 001			i		i				
arive white	21,781 16,404 89	6,342	_0,102	8 387 41	13,00	17 a6. 1- 2>7	2,664	8,705 7 -50 1	6,297	8,09
egro her races	4,294	3,320	^,302	± 367	5 204	0,363!	3,57	1 >28	4 381	2,14
Female	10 072	6,:39	18,456	9,-78	19,20	18,043	5,96-	8,543	3,872	8,02
reign born white	93 4 520 864	3,30,	2,394	27	-3 023 79 -,100	62 6,655	31 3 _63	1 589	99- 2.3 2,858	2,27
Persons 21 years old and over	22,610	_0,704	2.45	.0 848	2_,14J	20.22	6,578	8.754	6,2.0	9,50
reign porn	-75 (±03)	1C,679 25	5-,113	10,728	22,157 236 203	20.133	99 1	8 10 4 44	F,168	9,48
Alien Cstigenship no reported	59	12	62	19	44	50 · 23 ;	3.	17	26	2
*SCHOOL ENROLLMENT	13	5	-^	1_ !	39	12	12	8	3	
rsone 5 and 6 years old	2,185	205	1,505	835	1,840	.,BLC	195	91.5	-40	73
Number enrolled in school	725 33 2	350	36	320 _6 2	37 2	675 27 3	210	300 1	80	25 34
Percent enrolled in school Number enrolled in kindergarten rsons 7 to 18 years old	0 730	2,930	20	2.985	5 580	5 = 70	1 695	25	1.200	
Number enrolled in school	6 394 9	2 8.5	4,780	2,625	3,09	5,085	1 6151	2 943 2 705 92 D	1,270 1,130 86 6	2,33
reone 4 and 10 years old Number carolled in school	1,-30	775	1 455	602 570		1,255	375,	795 .	340 (66
Percen enrolled in school isons 16 and 17 years old	86 L	34.2	92.4	94.2	1,355	93 0	355	8- 9 795	280	92
Number enrolled in school	1,590 840	280	1,475 t	285 (1,33	1, _35	270	405	330 195	31
Percent enrolled in school	52 8	75 3 550	55 8	470	66 3	78 9		58 5 1	395	
Number enrolled in school	240	175 31 &	790	180	-,130 300 47 3	1,090 390 34 9	100	110	393	-8
Percent enrolled in school - sous 20 o 24 years old - Number enrolled in school	1 490	1,162	4,590	1,070	2.910	2,195	850	21 6	983	98
Percent enrolled in school.	155	95	5 9	9 3	11.	6 7	9 4	75 7 2	20	8
Number enrolled in school	70	-,170 95	2,500	1,_50	2,925	∠,025 135	530 40	980 70	943	1,01
Percent enrolled in school	20	8 -	8 2	6.	3 9	51	60	" 1	26	10
*YEARS OF SCHOOL COMPLETED	9 895	4 440	0.495							4 1
Male 25 years old and over o school years completed	1.735	4,660	9,435	5,055	9 420	8,735 51.5	690	4,485	3,65, 5x	4, 25
ementary 1 to 4 years	2,970	1 025	2,430	943	2,305	1,895	645	1,140	1,075	1,00
7 years 8 years	730 525	603	650	600	1 277	8.0	210	430 415	250 240	78:
igh school I to 3 vears	1,035	755 190	755 440	1,145	1 500	1,935	370	665	420	49 54 35
d , ears	260	160	270	100	88 430	675 375 180	175	.50 140	240 135	35 16 10
4 years or more	265 31.5	120	27C 295 4 3	150	280 320	210	120	8L 75	80 90	170
edian school ; ears completed _ Female, 25 years old and over	9 837	7 0 5,090	9,380	4,970	7 4	7 9 9,235	3 000	5 3 740	1,770	6 9
n school years completed	1,525	335	2,74	165	392	450	515	190	20.0	4 40
sand byears -	2 525	900	1,390	850 840	1 460	1,404	765 490	655 773	62* 200	690
7 vecr8	725	555 570	275	550	1,015	860 1,035	205	40s	100	46
gh school 1 to 3 years 4 years	1,040	270	940 530	1,390	2,000	2,205 840	405 305	760 ±00	155	74
allege 1 o 3 years - 4 years or more -	325	30° 160	345	170	520 290	415 42C	110	135 160	90	22
hool years no. reported equan school years completed	125	60	235	1.5	170 8 2	125	75 40 6 0	7 6	100 35 5 2	22: 15: 15: 7
MARITAL STATUS AND HOUSEHOLDS	, ,	7 0			6 2	0.31	6.0	7.6	32	7
ate 14 years old and over	13,940	6,582	12,8.9	6,431	12,737	11,881	3,913	5,620	5 008	5,62
Single	3 818	1 708	3,271	1,611	2,989 9,105	2 732 8,590	2,611	3,864	1,952	2,86
Widowad or divorced	6cl	282	546	385	643	259	225	269	402	
male 14 years old and over Sugle Marned	2,814	6,506	13 129 2,565	1,086	12,954 2,189 9,099	2,113	3,956 765	5,473 978	2,508 578	5,68
Married Widowed or divorced	1,474	4,586 779	1,469	4,521 946	9,099	2,113 8,744 1,599	2,635 556	3,881 614	1,542	3,95
writed couples * number With own household	9,055	4,205 3,970	8,545	4,240	8,380 7,875	8 01.5 7,485	2,350 2,195	3,845 3,595 250	1,445	3,57 3,37
Without own 'sousehold	10,850	5,125	1,385	-,515	10,735	9,830	3,095	4,595	2,095	4.84
Families Unrelated individuals	9,785 1	4,540	9,165	4,665	9,140	8,62C	2,570	4,085	1,725	4,04
ouscholds, number	10,620	5,002		5,260	10,257	9 490	2 726	4.242	1.832	4,55
Population in households Population per household estitutional population	43,167 4 06 37	19 11. 3 82	36,866 3 6L	18,872 3 57 34	38,131 3 72 18	35,579 3 75	11,712 3 75 7	17 235 4 06	7,459 4 07 2,609	16,03
*RESIDENCE IN 1949			i							
ersons 1 year old and over, 1950	42,125	18,750	36,215	18,720	37,625	35 100 26,650	11,460	16,930 12,435	9 925	10,63
Same house as in 1950 Different house, same county	35,980	1,8	30,860 3 525	1,540	31,535	5,215 }	11,460 9,715 1,110	12,435 3,225 1,010	7,950	13 00
Different county or abroad	1,595	750	1,110	730	4,405	2,660	345	1 010	1,375	90

Table 43 -- ECONOMIC CHARACTERISTICS OF THE POPULATION, BY SEX, FOR PARISHES 1950

Existing Controlled in Commence Service State State Controlled State Contr		-	1			CONTRACTOR OF THE PARTY OF THE		-	-			-			T	
Stab we		e in	A	62	AJ en	sir	Arun	rtic	N.~?6	lles	r.a.r	brage	Bien	ville	Boss	ter

	ular	I'cma.e	Male	Fer.als	Male	Female	Mae	Female	Male	Female	Maie	Fumale	Male	Female	Male	Female
Total population as ages,	23,-	2,076	1,45	9,-20	11,234	1_,153	8,547	2,751	19,062	18 969	8,819	8,947	9,500	9 546	21,246	18,893
EMPLOYMENT STATUS			4 222	4 1-4	7 262	7 60	5,547	5, /10	12,781	12,824	6,033	6,120	€,504	6,603	-4,928	12 767
Persons 14 years old and over	1,504	2,814	4,784	1,.2-	5 2:0 5,249	1,123	4,C32 4 C30	804 8L4	9 368	1,696 1,696 1,640	4.4.4	994	4,738	_ 121 1,121	12,65	2,962 2,898
C vilian labor force Emproyer Private anguand salary workers	10 8-9	2,814	4,782	1,122 -,075 702	4,859	1,320 1 253 858	2,930	75.3 567	9,364 9,001 3,304	.,640	4,401 202 2,685	964 622 213	4,619 2 316	1,100	7,619	2,804
Seli-employed workers	5,208 659 ,82	245	292	723 110	3ol 1 180	190 125	740	135	50. 4,074 518	306 153 139	1,13.	213 86 43	376 1,673 25-	242 135 189	1,766	382 245
Unpaid jamily Workers Unempt and Experienced Workers	6,1	135 13- 28	2-6	40 49	100 390	20 C7	175	12	363 362	56 56	199	30	1.6	21 20	259	155
Nev workers Nor in Isbar force -	4,0=6	3,292	1,488	5,242	2 0.2	2 219	1,5.5	÷,906	3,413	11,_28	1,629	5,126	1 766	5,482	2,277	9,805
I nable to won Inspace ' mak' thous	125	.0,633 538	50 393	4,308	64 766	4,746 50.	55 590	3,846	1 695	8 654 908	72 473	3,905 239	-12 5	271	656	7,7,2 508
Other and not reported 4 to 19 years old	2, 88,	2,113	. ,043 . ,947	788 609	1 177	971 724	859 487	559 577	39 620 1,246	1,5%	1,124	982 620	,216 7'3	1,062 786	16 1,549 915	1,544
20 .o 64 years old 65 years old and over	o72 378	458	305 141	140	367 12:	195 48	207	138	-27 47	236 27	251 185	273 84	283 220	205 69	429 205	447
MA, OR OCCUPATION GROUP																
Employed Professional tecanical and kindred workers	0,819	2 679	4,542		4 859	1,253	3,354	753	5,061	2,640	4,202	964	2,619	1,100	7,6.9 309	2,804
Farmers and farm managers. Vanagers officials and prope exc fa.m Clenesl and kindred workers	2,893 878	146	354	12 57	682 305	-52 23 53	302 137	19	3,73C 654 190	32 96	743 349 119	51 168	1,301 305 112	51 60 92	1,188	101 98
Cantisoner formers and knowled a culture	311 583 1,291	367 297	165 165	145	252 535	1/6	76 115 414	71 79	304 932	138	162	142	128 456	±02	351 387 1,317	503 250 16
Operatives and kindled workers	1 372	165 726	1,043	5 ₀	816	143 242	600	2 21 234 97	705	47 445	913 2 123	50 27 253	n93	38 260 115	1,363	168 567 391
Service workers except or vate household . Farm laborers unpaid amily workers Farm laborers ex. unpaid, and farm forenen	-96 9_5	403 88 14	.38 55 231	13	180 93 668	242 143 47	126 _3 1,40,	97 1 55,	494 540	208 91 55	43 99	53 9	83 253 194	-59 -23	278 108 716	160
Laborers except arm and mine. Occupanor, not reported	1 139	18	648	10 31	553	1o 31	498 65	33	\$26 118	44	75.	12 23	856 60	27	879 1_34	159 2_ 66
Experienced anemployed	071	128	240	49	38e	65	175	21	3,2	56	198	30	116	20	2,9	94
Professional echnical and kindred workers Farmers and farm managers Managers officials and mone are farm	1	2	4	2	2		3	2	3	+1	1		1	2	3 1 3	,
Managers, officials and prope exe farm Clereal and Lindred workers Seles workers Craftsmen foremen and kindred workers	-0 7	2	1 4 1	2	9	1	2	1	3		4	3	4	2	5	4 3
Oraftsmen foremen and kindred workers Operatives and kindred workers Private household workers	92	10 26	56	1	>8 1	2	13	2	40 31	9	24 29		21	,	23 27	3
Service a orkers, except private household	15 28	3	6	5 2	35	12 5 8	35	2	12	6	4	?	1 4	2	7	2
Laborers, except farm and mine Occupation not reported	138 290	62	61	88	137	34	83	32	161	34	25 115	2/	26 41	5	22 250	1 69
INDUSTRY GROUP	10,819	2,679	4,342	1,075	4, 859	1 253	3,854	753	9,001	1,640	4 202	964	4,619	1,100	7,619	0.04
Agriculture	4,361	122	1 271	31	1,500	139	1,512	58	4,807	_75 1	829	21	1,763	233	2,151	2,804
Forestry and fisheres Mining Construction	457	4	8o 452	3	1/1	1	39 245	1	108	1	157 178 408	1 2	95 384	7	37 310 929	17
Manufacturing Furniture and lumber and wood products Primary metal industries	1,075	87	1,501	52	9C1 237	110	677	83	485	10	1,239	37 10	1,179	22	1 150	108
Farmented metal and (and not mee mo.el)	5 4		5		14		1 1 31	2	9		2	1	2		13	2
Machinery, except electrical. Electrical machinery equip and supplies Motor vehicles and motor vahicle equip	31	-	1		34	-	31	2	1		9	1		1	8 8	1
Motor vehicles and motor valuele squip Transportation equip, exc motor vehicle Other durable goods.	8	1	. 4		فد		2		6	2	2	2	19	1	31	5
Food and kindred products Textule mill products Apparel and other fabricated textule prod	720	*1 21	29	2	183	21	458	50	10	3	50	12	24 3	3	106 2	9 21
Printing, publishing and alked industries	46	8	18	6	21	2	7	1	16	3	26 283	5 2	16	2 4	2 57 80	16
Not apposited manufacturing industries	109	1 2	41.3	28	222 42	1	47	26	21	3	73	4	55 98 1	+	253	20
Railroads and railway express service Trucking service and warehousing Other transportation	237	1	10s 47 47	2	86 13 60	2	25	1	134 38	2	50 30 53	2	97	3 2 5	226	8 9
Telecommunications. Utilities and sanitary services	20 1.87	65	19	26	90 90	24	2u	3	62 13 108	3 24 10	9	22	50 6 77 47	7	146 12 135	35
Wholesale trade Food and dairy prod. stores, and milk retail Eaung and draking places Other well trade	359	131	39 123	65	183	60	34	55	197 305	19	106 131	63	100	4	240	29 33 93
Other retail trade Finance, insurance, and real estate	183 859 129	267 306	302 32	156 118 22	330	133	102	47	103 556	131	26 282	.23	19 251	67 68	529	261 302
Bunness services.	374	26	115	22	54 7 132	26	83		79 6 196	26	40 10 85	36 4 2	29 4 6°	17	106 19 240	71 11 6
Private households. Hotels and lodging places Other personal services	148 18 144	753 1d	43 10	203 14	37	242	24	201	60	456 17	9	182	40	263 8	68 53	587 43
Medical and other health services	55	21 92	63 20 23	39 8 50	36	58 15	32 19 10	27	105 31 46	68 13 60	70	8	51 7	33	101	23
Educational services government Educational services, private Other professional and related services.	153 34 93	278 91 34	1_	169	90	52 113 33	42	98 17 2	145	241	14 88 8	159 12	78	182 6	38 28 79 13	587 43 131 23 113 236 31 28
Other professional and related services. Public administration Industry not reported	93 253 222	34 63 83	90 84	9 37 31	44 90 18 45 -32 -27	57 44	33 49 68	29	10 78 165	18 57	108	12 10 41	41 103	8	51 340	28 112 82
	222	20	~	24	121	44	68 1	37	185	51	67	25	51	25	.55	82

Table 43 -- ECONOMIC CHARACTERISTICS OF THE POPULATION, BY SEX, FOR PARISHES

-950-Con.

Subject	Ged	do	Caros	sie.	202/	-0	Care	חסייו	CA N	021	C.a.c	oor a	Conn	rois	`e :	Scto
	Male	Female	Maie	Female	Maie	Female	Male	Female	Man	Famale	Mais	Patrone	Mase	Tema	Male	Female
Total population (all ages) EMPLOYMENT STATUS Persons 14 years old and over	84 062 59 493	92,445	~~, ~~?	44,863	5,176	5,11.	3,371	2 7-3	6,37	3 82.7	12 -6-	_2,602	-,04-	,3,2	12 809	.2,589
Labor force Civinan labor orce Employed Private wage and salary worzers Government workers Self-employed workers Unpaul family workers Unemployed Experienced workers New workers New workers	47,150 40,047 44,609 34,233 3,275 6,778 263 1,330 3	68,375 22,940 22,928 42,29, 17,850 2,408 1,008 427 635 620 15	30,655 24,453 24 -12 22,946 18,649 ± 514 2 905 78 1 -66 1,-55 11	31,233 7,359 7,327 6,975 5,476 879 485 255 332 227	2,299 2,431 2,377 1,249 2,6 851 61	3,-75 439 438 427 2-2- 34 41 10	2 252 1,725 1,724 1,653 1,933 1,500 7,8	2,0-2 21,1 208 -0° 67 29	2,8-2 2,740 2,8-2 2,740 2 5 22_ 190 102_ 100 2	3, 50° 552 552 -39 26- -43 75 60 13	8,458 0,562 6,559 6,387 3,303 383 2 3.5 3-6 172 -72	8 770 1,730 1,77 1,638 26- 187 222 18	3,-07 3,-04 3,316 1,567 172 1,368 209 88 84	5 0.4 1,20 -,20 1,65 672 117 154 222 41 40	7,813 5,589 5,584 6,468 2,726 274 2,_97 271 16 115	8,600 1,768 1,767 ,698 1,047 279 231 69
Net in labor force Keeping house Unable to work Linnates of institutions Other and not reported 14 to 19 years old 20 to 64 years od 6s years old and over.	12 343 249 4 033 325 7,716 4,189 2 672 875	45,435 34 749 3,509 211 6 966 4,561 1,925 480	6,202 -56 1,520 -56 4,370 2,640 -,167 503	23,904 19,544 809 22 3,529 2,590 767 172	1,049 18 266 665 434 173 58	3,036 2,012 246 478 331 87 10	527 46 159 7 315 190 89	1,831 1,488 85 258 187 57 14	2,.26 28 427 5 668 429 10	3 3.5 2,-84 260 1 770 4.3 98 19	1,098 799 220	7 041 5,427 480 1,134 89 199	1,247 30 331 4 882 430 286 166	3,807 2,755 257 1 794 453 186 155	2 224 44 876 13 1,291 896 279 116	6,832 4 916 612 4 1 300 963 267 70
MAJOR OCCUPATION GROUP											. !		gibbs and			
Implored. Professional trobinesis and kindred workers Farmers and farm managers Managers, officials, and prope out farm Clerical and kindred workers. Clerical and kindred workers. Configuration formers and kindred workers Operatives and kindred workers Private household workers Frivate household workers Farm aborers unpand family workers Farm laborers, our unpand and farm foremen	44,609 3,911 1,905 5,746 3,334 3,620 7,944 7,874 172 3,061 242 1,450	22,293 2,4-5 928 5 .82 -,680 180 -,481 5,219 3,636 498	22,946 1 700 726 2 392 1,30 1,207 4,996 5 567 55 1,305 60 453	6,905 933 1,720 748 57 383 1,404 1,446 6 11	2,377 99 669 143 53 70 205 320 3 66 61 118	92 7 31 50 3 50 3 56 61 52	1,653 46 359 99 32 26 242 400 47 48 97	208 37 18 30 2. 12 27 53	2,740 106 1,254 40 5,69 58 247 5 52 191	539 100 28 48 37 2 14 -09 86 53 20	6,387 257 1 872 402 401 -92 678 1 294 6 128 347 414	1, "L. 222 03 61) 204 .44 .3 75 .471 1866 200	3,316 1,045 205 25 96 388 448 5 81 197	1,30- 96 88 42 91 95 3 50 220 45 213	5,468 2.4 1,824 344 127 174 409 769 11 93 269 409	1,698 233 104 86 .85 140 17 106 393 165
Laborets, except farm and mine Occups ion not reported Experienced unemployed	4,762 582 1,430	403 403	3,14	52 80 327	468 32	1 5	227 30	5 10	1/- 284 12	12	295 62 172	48 9 23	471	16 28 40	6-1	61 12 59
Perfessional technical and kindred workers Perment and farm managers. Managers officials, and stopp one farm Clercol and hundred workers. Sales workers enter the state of the clerk of	31 59 34 44 218 236 1 99 43 232 466	9 6 59 21 27 165 81 13 5	22 5 32 34 44 349 299 299 33 376 277	7 1 28 19 3 16 119 85 1 7	12 10 10 37 38	3	1 3 7 2 19 35	1	20 3 27 24	1 5 2 2	3 3 1 22 44 4 5 50 32	1 1 3 1 3 3	2 2 1 1 1 9 11	1 12 4 4 40 3	2 1 1 2 3 10 20 1	2 1 7 1 3 35
Employed	44,600	22,293	22 946	6,991	2,37	427	1,653	208	2,740	539	6,387	1,71.	3 316	1 ∡65	5,468	1,698
Agundure French and finberne Mannie Mannierunng Furnsture and lumber and wood producis Prumsture and lumber and wood producis Prumsture and lumber and wood producis Prumsture and lumber and wood producis Machinery compt ensektoal. Machinery compt ensektoal. Machinery compt ensektoal. Machinery compt ensektoal. Machinery chiefunder and more valued equip. Transportation equip ere motor vehicle Other durable goods	3,915 67 3,241 5,230 0,598 1 -79 483 337 5/5 55 38 16 1,105	1,064 6 625 135 940 111 9 33 43 9 3	1,296 64 1 291 3,40 9,861 875 12 45 74 5	30 2 64 29 780 36 1 2	820 16 18 217 648 598	33 1 7 4	51.8 153 283 192 122	2522	1,633 120 44 13. 185 154	106	2,661 10 978 4_9 653 465 1 2 4	3°0 8 5 22 7	1,/74 100 159 3.6 376 266	400 3 1 9 39 9	2 530 26 166 385 955 535 89 2 70 148 2 5	3°3 1 2 8 139 15 1 1
Food and kindred products Textile null products Appare, and other fabricated textile prod Printing jubishing and allied indivitres Chemicals and allied products Other nondurable goods No specified manufacturing industries	1,025 17 57 568 374 998 6	141 5 171 133 34 152	188 1,372 3,426	69 1 5 46 91 215	1 26	1	1 47 10	6	3 8 2	2	104	5 1 4 4	5 1 59	25 1	9 12 13 26 18	67 5 1 1 4
Railroads and railway express service Truicking service and warehousing Other transportation Telecommunications Ullitimes and sanitary services Wholesale trade Tood and darry prod stores, and milk retail Eaung and drinking places.	2,025 693 1,045 317 1,262 2,686 1,616 753 4,940	90 66 181 40° 199 465 63° 1,586 2,666	880 340 797 89 468 741 660 501 2,134	36 10 52 24 66 84 33. 205 1,000	38 17 32 3 19 72 53 28 109	1 12 2 3 20 30 4e	19 87 3 21 33 19 33	1 15 42 16	21 39 21 35 72 23 122	1 3 1 2 17 54 34	73 80 97 14 8, 99 122 17 396	5 33 21 4 57 95	72 33 43 4 6. 43 9., 45	19 8 31, 106 60	66 34 59 12 90 67 135 19 297	2 8 32 6 11 68 57 145
Planto, instrunce and real estate Business survices Repair services Retartionment and recreation services Retartionment and recreation services Retartional services, government Retartional services Retartion	1,37 389 1,268 719 393 906 442 671 389 191 8.5 2 041	872 166 77 5,364 447 -,293 220 -,554 -,361 356 414 637 465	431 97 550 269 889 398 233 180 236 45 305 618	288 35 20 1,471 159 346 88 375 638 104 146 191	17 3 38 15 1 25 3 9 44	6 4 89 6 6 1 17 99 6 4 25	2 32 3 6 9 7 5 24 1 1 40 30	2 1 18 2 7 1 3 46 5	2:	7 3 115 2 11 111 4 5 28	58 9 123 57 9 75 30 39 89 3 51 -08	31 3 3 3 3 3 3 4 1 4 1 8 9 1 1 2 3 2 3 3 4 8 1 8 9 1 1 1 1 1 1 1 1 1 1 1 1 1 1 1 1	29 3 41 19 6 37 -8 1 27 12 29 65 20	17 3 229 10 36 3 29 93 1 13 19 34	50 14 80 38 2 52 14 25 58 2 60 115	300 1 6 416 133 55 4 52 206 18 15 61

Trol: 43 -- ECONOMIC CHARACTERISTICS OF THE POPULATION, BY SFX. FOR PARISHES 1950-- Con

Trol: 43—ECON		on Auro	Eso: 1	ar Li	Es	Lotens	f-sr.g	87728	Fren	Alip	Jra	nt	De	ria .	Iber	ville
	Maie	Female	Maie	Female	Male	Fenale	Male	Female	Male	Tescale	Male	Famale	Male	Female	Male	Female
To an population an age.	7,	£ 56	₽,ಟ್*	3,24"	¥,543	9,.84	15 ^62	15,60/	,599	14.77,	7,125	.38	19,9	20 146	13,215	<u> </u>
EMPLOYMENT STATUS		1 ;											13 346	.3.94.		
Persons 14 years old and over	2× 22	52 -19	4 121	5,403	7 143	7 275	10,555	10,335	9,356	7,463	3,221	4,896	10 289	3, .96	6,.69	0,276
C.vu.an lab or force	41 244	17,592	3,799	1,-70	3,724	7.44	7,793	1,360	7 030	1 313	3,082	645	10,281	3,196	0.1of	1,4.
Amployed P va r wagt and salart wo.kers overnment wo.kers	38 961 30 242	2 741	2,6c4	1,.32	_,698 408	1,41° 309 40-	2,747	195	7,701	322	422	623 120 219	7,092	2 281	5,749 3,92 519	1,682 1 244 269
Sel -employed workers	4,975	3,687	192 -,740	-80	⊥ 281	_88	3. 75	160	4 478	209	775	~5	1,947	393 213 107	.,244	132
I npaid amil; workers Unemployed Experienced workers New workers	2,29/. 2 278	293 *64	165 165	118 60 of	53 52	317 15 15	753 235 233 2	255 29 28 1	130 _28 2	48 48 48	137	9 22 22	567 565 2	1115	39u 394	59
Not in labor force	23 986 220 2 34°	40 842 30,6° 2 180	1,_28 26 450	3,0.3 490	3.2	5,774 2, .89 338	2,762 79 1,602	8,946 7 125 61.3	2,126 49 -87	A 150 6,343 502	1 625 32 389	4,25 3 302 304	7,057 92 1,0 2	10 743 8,364 696	2 788 72 1, 95	7,535 5,257 1,05
it mates of institutions.	10 07,	7 804	792	3	2 6.5	2,646	1 124	_ 208	10	1,294	4,002	644. 484	1 889	1,686	1,178	1,076
Other and not reported 14 to 19 years old 20 to 64 years old 60 years old and over	4 617 5 527	9,045 2 (1: 244	482 18. 130	4/ 174 88	315 104 52	42" 12" 47	924 530 170	869 279 60	922 246 -14	1 058 151 55	276 142	484 431 30	589 -73	1,237 358 31	762 370 40	812 230 34
MAJOR OCCUPATION GROUP																
Employed	38,9(1 4.45	2,1999	3,624	1,_32	3,.10	25	7 548	1 360	~ 090 201	1 265	3,082	.3"	9,694	3 084	5,769	1 682
Professional tychnical and undred workers. Farmers and farm managers Managers, officials, and prope, exc. fa.m	648 4,159	2,432 42 F#C	1,561	124	1,.76	_42 _56 _20	3 153	3E 63	4,106 26g	1.31	592 192	45 70	895 836	175	473	7
Managers, omerais, and props, exc is a Clerical and kinerec workers Sales workers	2,-00	5,Xo 1,327	_60 34	50 75 74	6" 57	_20 50	40° 158 246	134	90	51 125 115	27	70	326	518	.74	240 _40
Creftomen foromen and sindred works a	7 844	1,327 _33 1 0+2	34 80 21.2 579	25	3/9	6	697 9851	8	203 397 392	4	10 441 71.5	27	5 48 1 534 2 083	346 10 222	1 066	50
Operatives and kindred workers Private hous hold torkers	88 2,842	3.492	87	228	21	222	120	245	5	179	1 95	.02	19	916	237	388 248
Service workers except private Louseho i Farm laborars unpaid family workers	44	2,443	172 525	103	276 219	J10 50	935 905	197	1.0 5-4 40.	103	197	2	141	-00 49	56 899	
Farm abovers argued and farm foremer. Labore's except farm and mine. Occupation no reported	4 470	73	250	5	569	34	554	7 32	272	4	553	16.	1 017 1 53	49 84	1, 108	250 28 53
Expenenced unemployed.	2,278	584	.65	65	52	15	233	26	_28	48	137	22	593	111	394	59
Processional technical, and amdrea workers. I	42	.9	7	1 2	1		6	2	4	3		1	9	3		2
Farmers and farm managers Managers, officials, and props, exc farm Clerical and kindred vorkers	79	10	2	5	1	-	3		2	1	2	2.	6	9	- 7	-:
Sales workers Craftsmen foremen, and andred workers	552	68 2, 2	2	1	10	٠.	23	ī	5	2	10	1	12	3	3	1
Operatives and kindred workers Private household workers	32.	26 162	27	3	10	1	36	2	16 23	12	_2	2	110	10	76	2
Service workers except private household . !	145	107	3	9	4	¥	*	3	. ,,	12	۰	-	27	7 8	70 3 4 48 62	יוֹ
Farm laborers and foremen Laborers except farm and mube Occupation not reported	31 493 547	150	42	15	7	3	33 43 69	15	17 35 12	8	5 :4 93	-3	69 124 135	35	62	14
ENDUSTRY GROUP		133	-	"	- 10	1				١	~	_	-	. "	-	-
Employed	38,900	10,999	3,624	_ 132	3,60	1 415	7 248	1,300	7 090	1,265	3,082	623	9,694	3,384	5 769	۷,68≥
Acresistance	⊥ 262 20	130	2,426	185	1 603	500	4,005	248	5,175	278	882 62	40	2,413	204	1 250 260	278
Foresty and fisheries Mining Construction	259 5.365	340	12	2	97	1 2	462 424	7 8	41 369	8	26 355	-	274	3	281	6 3 9
Manufacturing	12,69?	926	238	1 5	850	19	643	44	250	9	u59	9	-,142	237	731 971	52
Furniture and lumber and wood products Primary metal industries Fabricated metal and (incl not spec metal)	332	13	162	. 5	655	1	285	5	90	-	586	3	90	1.0	403	16
	279	14	• 1	:	4		2		2		3		15		87	4
Motor "chicles and motor zehade equip	22 _2 _8	3 2			1	1	-	. 1	1	-	1	1	1	1		
Transportation equip., exc. motor veh.cle Other durable good.	221 1	32	25	3	د	1	8	4	1	1	اد		16 47	5	14	1
Food and kindred products Textile mili product	886 13 13	141.	-1	1	2	2	02	1	44	اد	18		425	144	129	7 4
Apparel and other fabricated textile prod Printing, publishing, and allied industries Chemica's and allied products	453	118	2		- 6	. 2	15	1		3	5		2	2	20	-
Other nondurable goods	5 692	170 350	1 6	2	29	1 2	183	1/	.2 5 8	1	31	1	53 353 32	54	84 105	4
Not specined manufacturing inc. 18*rice Roil oads and railway express service	23 68P	30	20	-	55	1	59	1	-9	1	97		197		2	1
Railroads and rails ay express service Trucking service and warehousing. Ober timesportation	37/ 550	25 87	20		16		110	4	33	1	97 27 50		197	6	57 24 48	2
Telecommunications Utilities and sanitary services Wholesale track	279 530	3C1 123	20	17	15	2 3	72	. 18	55	77	21	8	164 52 209	78 40	15 63	20 5 15 105
Wholesale trade Food and dairy prod stores and milk retail La ing and drinking places	1,328 -,2/5	183 522	83	41	20	41	479	7 95	86 137 31	5 40 95	43	44	422 329 136	154	148 15 63 132 244 400	105
Other retail Grade	4,2.2	2 700	173	60	21 90	29 41	477	120	360	95	17 _6C	48	126	329	308	113
Finance insurance and real estate Business services	- 013	708 92	18	-2	-2	10	35	5 2	39	16	23	12	.95	22 5	47	30
Repair services	83/	3 634	52	249	74	232	160	239	96 39	1 84	89	102	329 09	12	1,2	400
Private households Hotels and lodging places Other personal services	755	299	21 21 12	22	23	3 28		131	4		29	1 21	- 15	836	8	14 47 14
Entertainment and recreation services Medica: and other health services	35.1	899	21	6	264	2°3	72 53 61 119	1001	15	5_	7.1		140 97 53	35	28 24	14
Educational services, government	1,673	2 023	34	1.8	9	2	119	199	26 87	202	49	42 48 8	89	299	-74 64 -2	113 141 40
Educational services, proate Other professional and elated services Public administration	623	313	36 51	37	2C 59	37	39	30	47 83	12	27,	43	7-	35 76	65	40 24 57
Industry not reported	38∠	226	30	56	42	30	84	36	71	42	148	16	153	84	159	50

Table 43 —ECONOMIC CHARACTERISTICS OF THE POPULATION, BY SEX, FOR PARISHES 1950—Con.

Subject	Jac.	esur .	·ef	fersor.	Jeffers	- Daris	ruta	m++p	LATOL	rche	LA C	L. P	Lin	E.O.	Liv	gsten
	Male	Female	Male	Female	Male	Fema-e	Male	Female	Male	Femue	Male	Female	Maie	Femare	Male	Female
Total popula ion ali ages,	7 566	7 868	5. >84	52,289	1,,39	13,259	28 -72	29,262	24 240	20,960	0,402	0,335	5,210	13,772	"O 346	3,70
EMPLOYMENT STATLS								1	- 1	i						.,,,,,,
Persons 4 years old and over	5 136	5,466	35 .5.	36, .69	5,664	8,96.1	4,701	20,060	13,989	44 038	4 4.7	4,440	9 132	9,472	6 781	6 M
Labor force Cr Lian layor force	3,742 3 719 3,578	1 047	28,850	8,740	6,49-	1 714	14 86	5,263 5 263 ,C8_	-,085 -,073 -,534	1 95"	3,762 3 000:	59° 589	5,o83 5 673	2 26.	5,.07	1,14
Employed Private wage and suary workers	2,241	729	27,225	8 302 6 /37 96	3,86.	1,05	44 339 8 493	3,544	7,49	1,898	2,136	362 -34	5,528	2,229	4 915	54
Government workers	223 782	185. 89	2,012	96" 504 101	1,74	172	1.837	850	2.503	370	21% 582	-34	E51	629	31.2	211
Unpaid family workers	32 14	89 15 33	FQ	101		5n 57	745	392	12.	37 54 50	.8	21	182	64	20"	20
Unemployed Experienced workers New workers	14_	32	-,445	419	30. 304	57	493	180	474	50	27	14	.43	31	-89 86	3.
Not a labor force	., 394	4 418	e(3)	27,823	2 .73	7 248	4,918	15 397	2,804	_2,081 _C,087	. 385	3 856	3 500	7 21.	3 667	5 16
Keening house Unable to work	21,	306	129	23 045	32 376	5,862	1,233	1 6-6	63 882	-C,^87!	28	3,034	-33 n50	4,750	611	4 05
Inmstes of instrutions Other and ro reported	920	889	4,274 2,452	3 661	1 761	1.259	3, 536	2,631	855	1,450	8.9	200	80	79	1.011	
14 to 19 years old 20 to 64 years old So years old and over	589 21.9	674 161	2,452	2,440	835 509	911	1,693	_,809	420	254 82	445	459	2 727 1,196 1 412	-,971 -,282	621 303	8 55
Bo years old and over	112	54	409	224	417	.21	236	34 351	250	82	62	25	1.9	61	87	23
MAJOR OCCUPATION GROUP		,							1				383			
Employed	3,578	2,014	27 225	8 303	6,486	1,657	1,339	5,082	10,594	-,898	2 933	575	5 528	2 229	4,918	1,11
ermers and form managers	1.56 469	138	1,971	959 _(. 488	267	227 12	2,522	629	354 B20	322	1.51	110	487	399	1 209	21
innagers, officials, and props., exc farm larged and andred workers les workers	298 134 129	53 133	3,828	2.5.7	584 170	79	1,,56	1,072	879 265	82	209	8.1	466 206	24 75	1 209 270 105	15
raftamen, foremen, and knydred worker-	533	134	1,736 5 704	885	287	98	2 24	494	1 452	211	425	74	75R	161	-63 794	12
peratives and kindred workers	, CJ3	229	5,440	1,257	997	79 -30 242	2,117	334 1 C.3 776	2,288	124	1,040	28 87	325	11 122 49,	932	12
ervice workers except private household arm laborers unpaid amily workers arm laborers exc unpaid, and farm foremen	95 30	134	1,774	1,091	194	242	736 736	776 327	40.	291	77 16	11.8	287	340	102	17
arm laborers exc unpaid, and farm foremen	30 55 616	6	136	10	823	3	618	e3 41	1,507	146	37	4	186	32 9	196 247 654	8
accupation not reported	53	14	248	124	102	30	139	35	120	45	103	1.5	64	171	92	25
Experienced unemployed	141	32	1 445	419 12	304	.27	493	160	474	59	-27	14	143	31	186	3
armers and farm managers	5	1	2 41		2		6	3	51	1	2		6		2 6	
fanagers, officials, and props., exc farm	3	2	57	47	1/	5	19	13	3	3	1	1	3	1-1	3 2	1
ales wo kers raftemen foremen, and andred workers	24	5	34 320	19	43	4	1. 88	14	-9	4	12		15	1	6.	
poratives and kindred workers	25	2 5	264	74 64 60	70	3L	83	18	122	8	12	1	26	12	43	1
ervice workers except private bousehold arm laborers and foremen,	2		81	50	13 50	10	32 2~	23	22	5	2	2	4	4	3	
abovers except farm and mine coupation not reported	23 55	2 V	31.4	13 116	82	2	119	6	114	1 2	8	11	26 47	11	24 34	
INDUSTRY GROUP		3 .		-						-	- 1					
Employed	3,578	1 -14	27 225	8,303	6,486	1 657	14 339	5 081	LU, 594	1,898	2,733	57>	5 528	2,229	4,518	4 10
griculture - orestry and fishenes	56,	13	413	28	2 321	45	3 980	431	2,590	171	357	11	4,521	67	1 659	30
Cining	17		554 987	30 97	31 497	~	039	42	936	4 5	103	7	147	2	32 65	
Enufactung	1 680	271	2,987	1.494	516	31	1,079	236	1,304	5	678	1 8	647	28	463	24
Furniture and lumber and wood reoducts	533	11	655 96	1,494 77 3	1.8	1	150	7	219	_42 2 1	633	6	439	4	753	5
Primari metal industries Fabricated metal ind (incl. not spec metal) Machiner, except electrical	4 8	,	498	109	3	- 1	16	1 2	35	1	5		2	1	14	
Electrical machinery equip and supplies	1	1	39	6 4	2	-	2	-	1	- 1	1		î	*	100	
Modern except alcerted and supplies Motor vehicle and motor vehicle equip Transportation equip exc motor chicle Other durable goods			690	10	23	1	14		90	1					1	
	2 _7	1	1,130	612	208	19		100	697	120	8		14	14	2.	
Textile mill products	1		137	236			563		5		78		71	14		
Printing, publishing and alhed udustries	9	2	295 528	40 37	28	7 2	107	26 81	18	7	7	1	28 20	6	16	
Food and sindred products. Textile mill products. Apparel and other faoreased textile prod Printing, publishing and allied uidsizes. Chemicals and allied products. Other nondurable goods. Not specified manufacturing industries.	- 101	256	2,654	187	49	- 4	24	3	29	3	6	,	67	-	416	
ailmade and railway ernress service	60	5	1,277	33	33	2	786	23	67	2	47	-	56	2	33	
racking service and warehousing	29 56	1 3	2 027	160	127	7.	195 226	13	128 542	8	38 51 9	3	:0 87	3 5	36	
elecommunications. thities and sanitary services	50	5	237 599	286	17	52 11	102 278	183 34 107	30 218	44	3	12	28 157	57 7		1
	35 119	3	1,630	359	147	12	752	±07	247 409	21	17	35	179	11 54 141	79 145	7
ood and dairy prod stores and milk retai- ating and dimining places	2	105	807 2 089	632	76 545	147	474 329 1,334	292 352 553	185	111 197 190	202	69 71	156 63 476	141	29 302	10
inance, insurance, and real estate	245	2	740	356	86	45	292	170	92 20	40	28	1.	76	43	26	
UNIDERS SERVICES	90		250 59.3	61.	9	3	104	27	2C 264	9	59	2	10	5 2	90 -7 3	
rivate households oreis and lodging places ther personal services	10	102	94	852	78	4% 10	408 170 56 256 157	1,U88 49	284 54 18	326 17	6	89 7	103	511	±7 3	12
ther personal services	3 52	52	132 362	92 274 104	90 49 32	81.1	256	237	148		3 49 13	26	103	16 127 16	23 28	2
school and other health services	16 16	37	641 346	6371	32	77	1.75	323	42 101	14 77 298	16	26 95	93 418	119	21	3
ducational services, government durational services private ther professional and velated services	63 13	125	124	392 169	213	210	378 100	557 128	19	48	3		46	38	40	
ublic administration	13 35 85	40 14	269	143 348	25 117	17 57	1.44 332 1.51	75 113	171	21. 59	39 62	12 34	169	57	93	3 11 1 7 3
ndustry not reported	34	14!	270	135	113	38	151	62	155	53	118	28	15	173	86	3

Table 43 -- ECONOMIC CHARACTERISTICS OF THE POPULATION, BY SEX, FOR PARISHES 1950-Con

Table 43 —ECON	NCMIC	CHAR	ACTER	LISTICS	OF T	HE PC	OPULA	TION,	BY SE	X, FOR	PARI	SHES	1950-	-Con		
Sub-ect	Mad	isna	4ares	ouse.	Nº.tact	tocher		eens		nhita	Plaque		Pointe			idea .

	Male	Female	Маю	Female	Male	Female	Male	Female	Van	Femalo	Male	Female	Male	Female	Male	Pemale
Total population (all ages)	8,-78	8,84.	15,972	10,065	_8,783	9,361	270,812	299,633	36,138	38,575	7,47"	6,762	10,976	_0,965	44,181	46,467
PMPLOYMENT STATUS																
Persons 4 years old and over	5,770	5,889	10,432	2,147	12,451 d,093	13,125	203,210	232,691	25,371	28,187 8 677	5,096	4,488	6,990	7,218	90 780 20,757	33,468
Lanor force Crynian 'abor force Employed	4,379	1,20° 1,20° 1,1+7 7.4	3,165 8,163 7,832	2,071	0 075	2,498 2 296 2,235	25,057	74,896 71,426 57,850	19,5.6	8,677	4,018	6°5	5,400 5,396 5,161	_ 519 _ 519 1,437	20,715	8,281 8,280 7,955
Private wage and salary workers (severment, we kets	2 .89 2 .4		4,321	279	7,789 7,789 ,398	1,1x6 599 245	25,05° 24,48° 1,0,446 17,302	57 850 9,184	13 987	1.085	2,842	544 -40 75	5,161 2,477 289	874	2,539	
Self-employed workers Unuld amily workers	1,037	70_ 61	4,321 3, 2,947 353 30.	321	3,23,	245 263	15,022	3,710	2,962	606 157	679	75 23	2,082	217	138	1,415 549 203
Lnemploved Experienced wo.kers New workers	164	58 58	30. 329 2	.26 126	286 264 1	63 63	20,406	3,470 43 43 27	90. 894 9	306 295	192 2	23 73 73	235 232 3	82 81	-,1/9 -,1/4	327 319 8
Not in labor force Keeping notice Unable to work	1,34 37	4 682 3,252 366	2,267 59 508	8,013 6,584 356	4,358 85 4,693	10 827 7,627 947	44, 86 863 40,760	147,741 119,734 10,979	5,423 123 2,060	19,510 15,076 1,334	1,070 21 403	3,633 2,886 215	1,590 60 715	5 599 4,174 649	10 023 3_4 2,926	20,187 17,434 2,221
Inmates of institutions Other and not reported	9 800	763	33	1.572	2 565	2 248	3_,422 3_,435 43,247	25 850	317	2,957	6.8	532	81.3	876	4,559	3,700
1. to 19 years on 20 to 64 years old 50 years old and over	509 21/	-97 20:	999 343 125	1 041 356 1,5	1,011	1,583	13,673 13,673 4 215	14,297 8,829 2,729	1,788 1,013 1,013	2,071	459 135	100	53" 179	659 172	2,393	2 709 876 115
	4-7	6	3/25	1.5	100	52	4 215	2,729	3	.36	44	15	97	45	-20	115
MAJOR OCCUPATION GROUP Emp.oved	4,2,4	1 14,	7,832	2,021	7 789	2,233	44,487	7.,426	18,613	8 372	3 804	762	> 161	. 1.37	19,566	7,~53
Professional, technical, and kingred worsers	.391	137	327	275 204	380 4 572 543	397	12,814	8,672	1,173	955	164	103	1.657	1/6	1,237	1 000
Professional, technical, and kingrer' worsers Farmers and farm managers — Managers officials, and props., exc farm Clenical and andered workers	225 82	92 49	2,342	78 26/	543 182	109	19,804	3,259	2,370	517	231	101	254	64 61 85	2 123	53 416
Clencal and condred workers Sales workers Crastamen foremen and kindred workers	14+ 361	1.28 84	205	267 487 8	285 722	152	1.,402	6,393 6,393	466 3.457	1,759	44 591	60	.59 530	89	1,530	660
Operatives and kindred workers	63.	58 304	1,674	245	862	108	23,8.0	3.026	3,975	865	-,041	169	586	273	3,124	1,6%
Service workers, except private household Farm laborers unpaid family workers Farm laborers, exc. unpaid and farm foremen	161	167 6 60	456 343 294	202 78 97	422 55°	290 2- 89	14,866 19 172	C,334	1,387	1,389 26 57	129 37	88 20	87 303 727	143	1,389 111 849	1,511
Labo ers except farm and mine	339 598	7.	764	14	803	8	19,014	-8 352	2,39"	5/	206	6	570	295	2,863	209 34 141
Occupation not reported	35	58	329	126	196 285	63	1 325	3 343	18	42	109	20	3,	34	310	
Professional echn.cal, and andred workers	2	58		120	-		272	3 343	11	495	_92	73	232	84	10,	329
Farmers and farm managers Managers, officials, and proma, exc. farm Clevical and kindred workers	2	21	2 2		4	1	.34	30	26	4	3	1	2		47	5
Ciercal and kindred workers Sales workers Craftemen coronon and kindred workers	. ŝ	1	63	16	1	1	655 371	472 266	23 37	15 25		1		2	23	15 22
Operatives and kindred workers Private household workers	42	2	66	8	23	3	2,202 7,136	571 .06	201	18 126	19	6	36	18	162	15 77
Farm shorers and foremen	6 21	6	171	20	4	6	1 063	673	44 34	57	2	2	2 34	3	36 30	31
Laborers, except farm and mine Occupation no reported	30	14	110 19	10	36 177	43	1,91.	65 404	220	24	37 -05	58	58 40	÷	225 456	.37
INDUSTRY GROUF	4 244	1,147	7,832	2,021	7. 700		144,487									
America Itarrea	2,000	201	3,062	3781	3,600	434	733	1,426	_8,613 ,020	8 37_	3,824	782	2 800	336	19,566 2,859	7,753 348
Forestry and fishenee Mining	11		19	1	64 42	1	∡62 780	19	270	21	1,120	37	67	2	301	5
Costruction Manufacturing	983	37	356 2,492	222	542 827	24	14,033	7 978	3,856	57	399	10-	509	3	2,272	197
Furniture, and 'umber and wood products Pranary meta, industries	866	25	222	3	5~7	7	1,762	203	848	38	23		264	2	2,006	42
Vabricated metal ind. (inc. not spec metal) Machinery except electrica Electrical machinery, equip. and supplies	3	1	1		2 2		1,510	247 98	29 76	4 2	6		1	.	32 49	4
Motor vehicles and moto vehicle equip Transportation equip, exc motor vehicle Other durable goods	1	1	1	i			.36	36 12 170	12	2	22	-	1		23	
	22	2	2	1	32	1	1,732	263	-1.8	13	2		6		.19	45
Textee mil producte	43	5	27	-	79	5	5 796 765	1,726 735	456 16	53	152	1_6	61	7	605	62
Textic mil products Textic mil products Apparel and other fabricated textile prod Printing, publishing, and allied industries Chemicals and allied products	10	4	11	9	18	7	1,008 2,397 902	2,863 475 189	182 492	72 54 34	3 85	3	8		11 104 193	96 1.5
Other nondurable goods Not specified manufacturing industries	8	1,	2,104	205	34 2	2	1,726	905	1,534	265	8	2	154	1 2	201	8
Raircads and railway express service Trucking service and warehousing Other transportation	33 22	3	121	4	115	- 2	5,670	385 195	747	21	29	1	83	4	931 /	31
Pelecommunications	28	5	4.5	34	104	25	3,096 14,397 1 345	1,23	226 269 171	35	235 6	5	22	7 2	243 350	2C 51 115
	42 91 401	8	126	9	14	14 72	3.296	376 2,858 2,491	903	37	38	5	41	4	762	24 81
Unities and sanitary services Wholesale trade Food and dairy prod stores, and milk retail Sating and draining places Other retail rade	36 432	48 97	80	96 115	14. 227 39		11,337 5,620 5,252	2,491	1,314 718 369	32#	80 58	51 58	71 1.52 70	57 97	735 273	292 644 877
inance, insurance, and real estate	∠32 27	85 21.	472	183	478 74 19	158	5,297	10,128	467	1,061	79	35	270	72	1,964	877 286
Cenary sarvines	46	3	100	4	115	26 5 4	3,4,3	135	216	32 25	27	2	4	2	93	286 27 17
rivs s households lotels and lodging places	23 20 32	311 23 65	45 45 86	368	52 14 97 88	4C1	1,092 1,521 3,542	1 486	339 124 408	1,841	19 3 14	116	76 48 2	280	2.3	1,745 163 522
ther personal services intertainment and recreation services fedical and o her health services.	12	5	40	98 8	97 88	1C3	3,542 2,023 3,704	3 105 993	186	648 98	9	10	14	22	238	103
duestronal services enveroment	30	24	31 78	72 197 17	37 296 13	45 486 48	939	2,726	239	584 680	21	26 92 7 9	17 51 5	14C 18	235	1 028
ducational services, private. ther professional and related services ublin administration	37 90	6	74	27	79	48 44 81	2,666	1,575	42 291	108	2 27 119	9	27	18	1.32 360	166 152 228
dustry not reported	43	17	50	15	272	116	1,456	2,987	657 ±10	209	119	23	102	57 38	338	228 184

Tab., 43 --ECONOMIC CHARACTERISTICS OF THE POPULATION, BY SEX, FOR PARISHES 1950-Con.

Subject	Rea -	iver	P_ch.	a.s.	Sa.	den	E. 4	rare	5 (2	20.78	St de	T-613W	34 .	æes	the a	shr spring
	Male	Female	Male	Finale	Male	Female	Maio	Fema.e	Male	Penaie	Man	Fenale	-fale	Fecnase	Male	Female
Total population ali ages).	2,964	0,47	13 -07	13,46.	-045	.2,461	3 -95	5,492	o 66r	4,677	4, 06	4,457	7 6.5	~,719	,14.5	7,34
EMPLOYMENT STATUS						100							0.0			
Persons 14 years old and over	2 717	7-1	8,54	1,412	4,043	7,074	1 000	3,75	4,492	4,546	2,910	2,3,3	4,837	5,621	4,00	4,898
Civilian labor force. Employed.	2,713 2,657 976	737	6,547	1 411	4 640	920	2 681 2,8°5 2 691	728	3,304 5,304 3,084	832	2,255	592 592	3,427	783	3 574	762
Private wage and salary workers	976	367	2,014	1 363	2 4.7	5.1	4,900	53.	4,432	792 535 777	2,240 639	39_ _38	3,256 2,5_ 166	7eq 1	3 375	706 522 127
Governmen* wo*kers Self-employed workers Unpaid family workers	1,3.7	95	3.570	287 -7- -28 48	1,460	265	2.J7 553	31	224 412	68	-,276.	61	548	±51 +0	1∠€ 386	40
Lnemployed	26 25	21 21	299 177 179	48	152 _85 183	30 15	31 184	2 2	222	40	259	282	166	.4	10	20 53
New workers	1		2		2	-	184	-	215	38	-4	^	166	13	197	.~
Legung house	1,166 23 458	2,483	1,993	7,3*2	2,231	6,153	929	2,405	1,486	3,709	نروه اگد	2,251	-,4 0 32	4,238 3,230	1,740	3 17
Inmates of institutions Other and not reported		369	725	5.4	768	479	262	11	377	2,9:9	2+3	-54	472	3,23C 347	456	30
14 to 19 years old	585 424	55° 428	1,233	,169 ,79	774	180	656 259	285	790 -881 214	.46 452	394	458 269	906	661	853	55
20 to 64 years old 65 years old and over	123 38	113	21.8	162	473 163	299	342 55	19	931	7/0	79	84	261	490 -381	238 224 91	52 1
MAJOR OCCUPATION GROUP		1		1							-	-1				i ~
Employed	2 657	688	6 364	1,363	4,455	905	2,601	176	3,082	792	2,240	591	3,256	760	3,375	70
piessonal, technical, and kindred workers	79 1,175	93 49	3,173	210	1,28	21.5 13	120	64	139	91	1,147	74 43	708	102	101	111
mers and farm managers, magers, officials, and props., exc farm ercal and kindred workers	140	37 46	336	90 73 165	263	49	235	27	224	38	661	16	314 192	24 77 77	135	2
es workers L'usmen, foremen and kindred workers	64	40	175	124	150	RRI	206 149	226 80 10	107	157 50	32 -3 127	41 29	96	27	95 110	4
eratives and kindred workers	210 219	25	567	57	506 724 4	39	443 484		565. 775	50 3 97	274	10	386 607	90.	736	7
vice workers except p vate nousehold	33	133 64 95	10 444 488	278 201	94	150	230	75 73 41	152	148	16	321	92 19	112	3 115	12
rvice workers except prvate nousehold rm aborers, unpaid ramlly workers rm laborers, exc unpaid, and farm foremen	139 322	72	346	98 37	167	_? 1!	22 56	26,	1,91	20	254	268 23	945	177	619	10
borers except arm and mine	174	28	252 23	11	158	33	606 35	26 7	231	13	121	10	345 40	21	714	1
Expersenced unemployed	55	21	175	48	.83	14	461	12	21.8	38	14	1	166	13	2.47	5
occessional, technical, and kind ed workers reners and farm managers managers, officials and proms exc farm encal and kindred workers encel and kindred workers es workers aftenien foremen and andred workers	1	1	1,7	1	1		2	1	2	4	•		1	1	1	
magers, officials and props. exc farm	ī	-	1 3	3	1 2	3	2 5		4				2	2	1 2	١.
es workers	٠,		19	6	3	3	1		4	2		- 1		1	1	
vate household workers vate household workers vate workers, except private household, m aborers and foremen.	3	. 1	40	18	27 22		29 19	3	33 39	3			36	1 2	27 35	
vace workers, except private household.	1	1 2	1 3 45	3 8	2	4	2	1	2	7			.3	1	25	
borers, except farm and mine	7 1 35	16	30 24	1 5	47	•	38 90	71	73 20	3	1 2		43 27	6	6.3	2
	33	10	24	. 2	63	5	90	7	201	3	1.	1	2.		38	
INDUSTRY GROUP	2,657	688	6,364	1,363	/ /65	905	2,691	774	2 000	700	2 20	591		740	2 224	_
moulture	1,653	215	4,105	231	1,/49	31	196	706	3,082	792	2,240	333	1,376	769	3,375	10
restry and fishenes	18		234	4	108		338 128	32 1 2	112	3	20		-8		35	
neruction	158	2	372	3	421	6	250	7	377	5	92	1	221	3	293	
anufacturing . Furniture and lumber and wood products.	125 91	3	146	9	1,142	30 14	394 17	106	1,009	102	353 300	6	798 14	90	1,415	9
Primary metal industries	3		2 2	- 1	5	-	17	1	1	2		1	4 3		2 5 4	
Machinery except electrical. Electrical machinery equip and supplies Motor vehicles and motor vehicle equip Transportation equip, exc motor vehicle Other durable goods.	2				2 2	1	19 2 5	1	1	1			3		2	- 1:
Motor vehicles and motor vehicle equip Transportation equip , exc motor vehicle			1				30	1	56	2	1		16		34	١.
Other durable goods Food and kindred products	2	1	22		2	2	153	53	51	28	3	1	644	83	26	7
Pextile mill products			**		-	12	5	-1	6	15		1	14	2	2,002	
Apparel and other fabricated textile prod Printing, publishing, and allied industries Chemicals and allied products	10	i	13	î	13	-	19	24 5 1	1.4	3		1	10 16	. 2	4 9	
Other nondurable goods Not specified manufacturing industries	2 7 2	1	26	4	39	1	67	2	34 7m 1m	30 1	23	1	60	1	174	
alroads and railway express service	56		43	1	50	1	78	6	99	2	2		47	1	49	
ber transportation	13	1	50	12	26 72 3		36 154	8	27 189	5	11	1	32	i	37	
ecommunications alities and sanitary services	30	8	64 64	27 6 8		17	15 34 119	-9	31	3	13	3	32 23 40	10 3 2	18	
	26 60	27	132 50	52 112	122	49	103	31. 57 3/	162 85 86	13 51	10 29	20	123	31	61	2
ating and drinking places.	129	36 46	50 345	112	22	89 79	85 151	3/ 80	86 .42	101 31	29 5 29	10	123 52 40	72 24	49 137	7 4
nance insurance, and real estate	17	7	38	23	25	7	53	377	20	4	7	4	24	6	23	1
spair services.	39	1	.5 88	3	92	?	15 59	81	43	3	24		54 17	2	49	
reals and lodging places	14	137	42	286 7	20 2 45	162	13 6 31	77	22	155		48 3	17 1 35	116	10	12
rrate households orals and lodging places ther personal services atertamment and recreation services edical and other health services.	31 6	28 3	73 30	81	19	41.	150	16	34 20 -2 33	36 6	2	1	5	10	30 12 8	,
edical and other health services.	62	96	30 25 55	218	21 95	209	21 19	30 48	33	30 101	33	81.	97	197	40	1 5
ducational services, government ducational services private.	20 52		11	26 13	4 43 77	23	9 21	8	16	13	1	11 2	33	19	22	1
ther professional and related services.	20	61	60	13	43	51,	21 116	11 46	1.6 65	9	17	27 10	33	32 21	22 44 29	1197

Table 43.—ECONOMIC CHARACTERISTICS OF THE POPULATION, BY SEX, FOR PARISHES 1950—Con

Table 43.—ECON	St L	CHAR.	St M	sr. 'u	8. 1	farv	St 7	many	'angı;	pagoa	~en	863	Terr	equape	IJ	nion

Hubjec	Main	Female	Male	Fernage	Male	Female	Male	Female	Male	Female	Male	Female	Male	Female	Male	Female
	-			-	17 974	-7,-44	.3,309	13 679	26,628	26,590	6.422	6 787	2) 75_	21,547	9,682	9,459
Total population (all ages)	38,798	39,678	2,252 ئا	13,1£1	17 44	_//,	23,309	15 017	20,020	50,7	-,					1,122
Persons 14 years old and over	24 420	25 389	8,430	8 532	11,800	12,116	9,2	9,526	18 052	18,348	4 138	4,537	13,940		6,583	U,506
Labor force Carainan labor rorce Employed	18,356 18,348	4,625 4,624 4,439	o 456 6,453 6,292	1 5.7 1,516 1 466	9,292	2,646	6 328 6,320	1,686	13 393 13,385 15 097	5,496 2,493 5,364	3,161 3,018 3,018	. 005 .,005	1,162	2,608 2,605	4,775	755 755 742
Employed. Provate wage and salary workers	17,715	2 627	2.838	1 466 880 125	8 660 6 655 445	2,490	5,999 4,003 488	1,650 1,174 270	7,_80	1 247	1,253	977 584	0,6-1 630	2,467 1,913 340	2,410	415
Pro ate wage and salary workers Government workers Self employed workers	73 <i>5</i> 7,934 1,763	572 354 882	2,500 514	116	,5.4	30. 267 59	- 433 75	198	4,569	27.3	459	239 226 28	2,221	_47 67	200	70 16
Unpaid smily workers Unemployed Experienced workers New workers	633 630 3	- 85 - 84 1	16.	50 49 1	527 61_ 16	156 150 6	321 317 4	36 24 2	288 286	997) 129 129	143 142 1 977	28 28 3,532	576 576 4 2,774	138 13: 3,	1 806	13
Yot in labor force	6 0o4 232 2 2/2	20,704	1 974 42 776	7,115 5,447 489	·2,513 46 999	9 472 7 432 667	2,784	7 840 6,057 527	4,659 110 1,888	12,852 9,283 1 246	287	2,603	1 .19	8,939 673	35 780	5,751 4,387 470
Inmakes of institutions	3,673	7,455	1,154	1 079	1.444	364	1,823	1,240	2,640 1,352	2.320	672	662	22 4 555	4,520	992	890
Other and not reported 14 to 19 years old	2,302 1,199 172	2,604	700 340	818	900	9º 7 308	957 6.6 250	919 271 50	1,352 1 0e8 220	1,532 658	4.2 106 154	426 151 85	1,095 332 128	235	738 228 26	762 112
20 to 64 years old	172	1,3	114	42	232	79	250	50	220	255	134		- 23	1	20	16
MAJOR OCCUPATION GROUP	17,7.5	4,439	6,/92	1 466	8 660	2,490	5,999	1,650	13 097	o, 364	3,018	977	10,582	2,467	4,622	-42
Professional echnical and kindred workers Farmers and farm managers	586	582	138	132 16	412 273	267	366 665	214	564 3 480 963	466 250	85 ± 283	108	423 394	332	172	178 15
Managers, officials and prope exc. farm Clerical and kindred workers	1,179	197	335	6R	883 253	1.27 309	158	286		_83 539	59	-56 55 74 49	879 219 509	79 334 294	279 108	35 90 69
Sales workers Craftsz en foremen, and kindred workers Operatures and kindred workers	656 1,481 2,068	393 15 134	176 544 721	162	318 1 406 1 866	248	270 1 075 972	11 68	1,411 1 602	382 24 295	7- 213 245	24	1,493	17	127 511 79°	28
	24 459	967 591	162	275	412	550 367	65 295 59	398 288 29	436	602	50	230	486	464 377 31.	85	158 112
Service workers except private household - harm laborers unpad family workers Farm laborers exc unpaid and farm foremen.	693	770	25.2	272 84	1,305	277	289	48	1,601	938	124 510	195	987 2,333	149	274 691	17
Laborers except farm and mine Occupation not reported	376	26 1.67	773 104	37	1,6.9	15	1,341	33	1,485	50 125	219	-7	137	41	60	28
Expenenced unemplored	630	184	160	49	611	1,0	317	34	286	129	142	28	>76 2	135	151	زر
Professional, technical and kindred workers Farmers and farm managers Managers officials, and prope, exc farm	8	1,	2 3		2	1	1		2 2		5		9 7	2	-1	
Clerical and kindred wo.kers Sales workers Oraftemen foremen and kindred workers	5 5 2	4 5	3	4 2	7	3	2	î	9	4	2	2		8	2 8	2
Oraftsmen foremen and kindred workers Operatives and kindred workers Private household vorkers	57 87	1 4 56	22	:	47	41	74		5-	20 13 13	36	2	125	45	28	2
Private household vorkers Service workers except private household Farm leborers and foremen.	8	21	4 20	8 2	19	15	13	1 C 8	9	13	10 23	_2 3 8	26 34	11	8	
Laborers except farm and mine. Occupation not reported	118 318	2 #1	-8	15	185	23	66	11	38	55	1.0		-26 -70	19	1.8 68	8
INDUSTRY GROUP						İ								12.5		
Agriculture_	9,005	918	6 292	1 466 372	1 767	302 19	1,0.9	, 650 99	J3 097	2,204	3 048	977 319	1,653	2,467	-,622 1,797	742
Forestry and fishenes	834 1 142	9	388 478	5	1,092	15	-15 86	4	69 208 899	3 4	25 88	. 1	1,477	21	44 462 329	1 4
Construction Manufacturing	1.2%	16	366	3 54	8.1	216 7	928	55	2 041	248	169	-	1 219	400	1,113	19
	494 22 38	1	62 3		36 2" 21	7	416	7	ر4،4،7 2 13	73	190	?	99 15 57	3	809	9
Machinery except electrical Electrical machinery, courp,, and supplies	19	1	7		44	1	22		144	41			40	1	1	
Furnature and minner and wood producer Primary metal industries Fabricated metal and (incl notapper metal) Marthnery except elevation! Electrical machinery, equip, and supplies Motor vehicles and motor vehicle equip Transportation equip exc motor vehicle	3 2		ور		154	2	4 400	8	29				6 3 40 16	1	-	
Food and kindred products.	59 20-	2	9 422 17	43	716	193	136 77	6	229	93	18	2	816	406	6 17	2
Apparel and other fabricated sextile prod	29 2 57	2 17	17		41	1 9	2	10	1.5 39	45 45	1		6 6 42	12	1 13	1 2
Appaxi and other fabrusted textile torod Printing, publishing, and alised industries Chemicals and allied products Other announce goods Not specified manufacturing industries	1.4	9	30	2	50 21	1	96 100	6	17	-6	1	1	26 38	2 2	-66 93	1 4
Not specified manufacturing industries Railroads and railway express service	7	2 5	7	1	147	,	3	5	50	10	1 17		55	-	36	1
Radroads and railway express service _ Trucking service and warehousing Other *masports*ion	254 155 162	6	116	1	41 330	.3	88 54 196	2	126	13	15	1	411	6	43 64	1.
Telecommunications Uthties and sanitary services	142 565	10 31	27	12	66 151	49 9 19	2± 7 153	53 6 15	49 144 355	70 17	9	17	24 -50 292	35 7 28	149 71	5 4 9
O'anness and santary services Wholessue trade Food and darry prod stores and milk retail Eating and drinking p.aces Ofter retail trade	298	233 369	50 22 116 11 27 -20 -58 92 241	- 04	329	36	153 240 185	15	355 360 182	53 202 292	56 82 14	38 66	413 155	145 178	71 92	29 47
Other retail +rade Fmance, meurance, and real estate	1 093	384	35	43L 416	-48 -48 73	225	437	134	1,020	574	157	84	65. 100	271	232	67 14
Pusiness services	36 430 139	10	-74	1 6	13	4	127	3 8	32	-1	21	1	25	7	83	1 2
Repair ervices Private louseholds. Hotels and 'odging places Other personal services Foresteen personal services	139 33	992 35 138	32	287	89	584 23	200 29 80	416 20 44	96 20 191	622 40	33	239 6	21 139	388 25	23	164
Other personal services Entertainment and recreation services Medical and other health services	195 112 65	33	49 30 21	34 8 37	56 33	83 41 76 218	37	14	78 93 299	1.56	15 13	24 2	139 87	108 14 66 256	44 14	35 6 16
Educational services, government	163	450 138	56	9 <u>1</u> 50 14	69 23 72	218	82 75 87	186	299 48	131 417 80	31	26 91 8	87 38 77 12	256 72	16 86	195
Educational servi es, private . Other professional and related services Public administration	136 711 400	73 101 183	56 14 .3 118	49	_73	40 16 6	1.67	9 <u>.</u> 17 69	48 _18 240	140	29 51	8 7 40	76 262	45 78 40	27 79	7 40
Industry not reported	400	183	124	-L	60	48	68	43	198	140	7	19	155	40	65	. 29

Table 43.—ECONOMIC CHARACTERISTICS OF THE POPULATION, BY SEX. FOR PARISHES 1950—Con

2 8,093 8	93 3, 86 7, 86 7, 62 7, 70 1
88 J 562 1,887 6 1,882 7 3,762 2 3,762 2 3,762 2 1,762 2 1,	85 7 682 7 762 7 762 1 1 1 3 3 3 1 2 1 2 1 2 1 2 1 2 1 2 1
88 J 562 1,887 6 1,882 7 3,762 2 3,762 2 3,762 2 1,762 2 1,	85 7 682 7 762 7 762 1 1 1 3 3 3 1 2 1 2 1 2 1 2 1 2 1 2 1
3,886 1,882 3,762 2,570 410 933 417 41 120 1,736 12 33 1,736 1,736 1,736 1,736 1,736 1,736 1,736 1,736 1,739	8c 7 8c 7 62 7 762 7 76 10 1 33 1 40 18 21
2 3,762 2,376 410 41 123 4 123 4 123 4 123 4 123 739 1 739	62 7776 110 11333 141 151 151 151 151 151 151 151 151 151
2 1,736 2 739 2 1,736 2 739 1 964	76 10 133 43 43 43 18 21 36 44 96 97 98 98 98 98 98 98 98 98 98 98 98 98 98
21 1,736 12 21 21 1,736 22 1,736 23 739 24 739	331 43 181 21 361 4,9
2 1,736 2 1,736 2 739 2 739 2 964	361 4,9
1,736 2 33 2 739 1 964 0 599	361 4,9
5 964 0 599	
5 964 0 599	33 3,8
299	64 3
2 2R1	HI +
	1
2),,62	32 1
32 593 7-8	93
9 127	42 1
1 453 24 768 3- 2	58
33 00	2 1 99 1
.09 L1 824	09
5 709	09
118	
2	2
1 17	
1 ;	
1 2	2
2 33	33
72 2,762	62 7
173	73
35 1,162	62
1,024	1
6	6
i	i
20 15	
-12	
12 19 72 3	12
142	46-
4 12 28 3 59	12
3 59	59
8 25	25
37 37	37
1 68	68
89 22 1 13 4 59 1 10	22 3 13 59
10	24
	78 13 31
01 31	31 .08 .83
3379	2 3379 596 7 1 1 3 35 1.1 1.0 0 20 20 20 20 20 20 20 20 20 20 20 20

Table 44 -- CHARACTERISTICS OF THE NONWHITE POPULATION, FOR PARISHES 1950

[w. 1 ile. "4" 'et... on statutes based on M-perrent sample. for totals of age groups from compute count too table 41. Median not shown where base is less than .00]

	7	-	-	-	-	CONTRACTOR NAME OF TAXABLE PARTY.	-	-	1	A Communication	and the latest of						Zast
nu har	n-ad a	Aus	ASCETT-	OE	1/04-	regard	Bien- vilia	Possier	Caudo	ralca- siou	wol.	Cameron	Cata- houla	Clai- berns	Cra- ocrdia	De Soto	Rouge
F ***u room have population -	8,-9"	4 553	7,919	7,227	9,93	3,027	9,409	13,911	66,456	20,283	2,936	\$83	4,148	2,957	8,531	13,816	52,341
"YEARS OF SCHOOL CON PLETED	1			2 0/0			4 716	4 12	21 450	9,890	1,385	230	2,005	5,695	4,195	6,290	27 140
Persons 25 years old and over	3,655	2,227	3,52	2,040	4,165	240	4 215	6,436	4,340	2,165	90	65	610	735	250	890	3,525
Tier er are 1 to a cars	1,5.0	800	1,425 575	1,380	1.895	575	1,720	2,930	12,520	3,215	530	95 3.	770	2,370	1.820	3,055	8,270
5 and 6 years	190	170	275	575 175	785 205	235	895 470	1,280	3,430	1,835	315	30	265 80	375	930 320	1, 205 385	2,330
8 . 6879	19C 135	30	235 260	120	180	76	175	290	2,010	530	_05	5	100	275 395	202	365	+ 655
High schoo. 1 to 3 years	90	100	145 30	110 10 20	120	225 20 30	335 40 45	295 45 70	895	90	_00 30	1		45	20	20	2, 160
College 1 to 3 years 4 years or more.	10 25 35	10	ۇد 35	20	15	30	50	70 55	510 475	115	10	1	30 30	65 80	40	70 30	655 880
School years not reported	70	45	75	45	85	20	5.0	175	670	225	65		30	65	3.40	270	-,.55
Med.an school years our pleted	2.0	3 3	3 6	3.4	* 6	4 5	4 8	41	4 9	4 3	5 3		3 0	4 5	/ 3	3 8	5.3
MARITAL TATUS											938	223	1,279	3,958	2,589	4,068	17 003
Male 14 years uid and ove Single	2,678	4,40¢	2,375	2,127	3,042 984	998	2,868 875	4,280	4,638	6, 454	266	63	343	1,211	635	2,155	4,580
Married	1 70-	269 123	1,501	1,400	-,90r	684	1,848	2,827	1,537	4,044	598 74	126	837	2,522	226	2,621	11,445
Widowed o divorced	2,968	,492	.,653	2 222	3,167	1,083	3,0.0	4,528	4.903	7,082	956	163	1,452	4,247	3,075	4,602	19,567
Sing'e Married	, 101 101	530	547	1,474	966	163 728	694	2,929	3,936	1,2.1	208 593	24 120 19	274 921	2,680	581	-,024	3,876
Widowed or divorced	460	264	503	303	44	192	398	725	7,185	4,776	155		257	598	67	821	3,344
Married couples * number With own house old	1 4.0	920 835	1,265	1,320	1,805	545 525	1,45	2,770	2,520	3,890	475	100	765 720	2,374	1,510	2,410	9,155
With court nousefuld	700	85	80	1,320	1, 20	20	55	2,620 150	1,680	345	40	25	40	180	80	130	765
EMPLOYMENT STATUS																	
Male 14 years old and over	2 670	1.0-2	2 3 '5	2,12"	2,151	998 682	2,868	4,280	20 23 ? 4 357	0 654	938 652	223	1,279	3,082	2,589	2,857	17,003
Crystan labor force_	1,799	1,043	1,-79	1,/76	2,151	682	2,153	3,230 3,034	4.905	5,107	641	154 154 35	843 842 786	3,080	1,773 1,771 1,715	2,956	12,352
Private wage and salary workers	1 549 9.6	801	1,069	1,405	2,319	506	2,106	1,870	14,239	4,204	109	83	293	1,251	755	1,27,	9,024
Governmen workers Seh-employed workers	35 415	242	59 229	26	15 919	11	656	842	1,854	234	179	47	422	1,360	36	37	889
Unpaid family workers	109	72	32	3	508	2	180	96 103	219	523	15	5	20 27	30L	147	207	1,503
Unemployed Not in abor force	250 878	364	190 796	71 651	89.	3_6	7.5	_,050	5,280	1,547	-0 28a	_9 69	436	876	816	+,211	4,944
remale, 14 years old and over	2,968	1 492	2,653	2,222	3 167	٠,083	3,019	4, "28	24,903	7,082	356	163	_,452	4,227	3,075	4,602	19,267
Labor force	906	347	564	377	70 _e	294	643	1,354	10,67	2,534	164	28 28 27	255 255	-, 233	840	967	7,141
Crylian rebox force	906 8a1	372	518	377	70e 671	294	632	1,349	10,676	2,533	158	27	245	022	8C5	917	7,139 6,773
P-vate wage and salary workers Government workers	765 37	26±	417	31.8	525	234	341	900	8,483	2 085	127	23	271	100	471	567	5,730
belf-employed workers	25 34	20	24	10	29	13	144	128	693 315	85 16	8		24 40 10	288	125 175	24	729 283 3_
Unpaid family workers Unemployed	45	28	- 44	20	31	24	14.	53	421	189	5		10	.71	34	1.9	366
Not in labor force _	2,062	1,121	2,089	1,845	2,400	789	2,376	3, 17-	14,226	4,248	792	135	1,197	-,194	2,2,5	3,63*	12,426
MAJOR OCCUPATION GROUP Male, employed.	1.549	969	1,389	1,405	2,019	628	2,106	2,931	14,239	4.283	609	135	780	3,011	1,715	2 799	10,749
Professional technical, and kindred workers	28	17	33	19	24	131	34	25	28	66	12	-	12	41	19	30	355
Tarmers and farm managers Managers officials and proprietors except farm.	35" 26	115	172	14	892	13	630	792	1,360 220	106	163	45	405	1,306	700	1,239	262
Clerical and kindred workers	9	5	7	. 5	1	;	7	7,	161	-5	2		1	D		11	-60
Sales werkers Oraftemen foremen and kindred workers	97	12 58	88	55	50	21	64	13	1,62	35	23	6	14	108	10.	18	1,376
Operatives and kindred wo.xers Private household workers	776	295	453 11	205	2.41	277	301	409	3,005	4,035	65	27	69	292	278	283	2,181
Service workers except percete he mehold	88	20 15	11 56 32	24	5 64 208	30	33 181	10 11 99	2,043 210	597 8	15 15	4	14 54	56 306	36	36 205	1,675
Farm laborers unpaid fame y workers Farm laborers, except unpaid, and farm foremen	225	77	498	934	≥90	13 311	152	631	1,348	162	61	6	±06	368	146	346 488	359
Laborers except farm and mine Occupation not reported	3°6 23	314	270	27	30°	311	657 26	647 5c	3 930	1,093	239	40	95	462	330	488	3,670
Female employed	861	243	518	357	671	280	632	1,296	10,255	2,344	158	27	245	1,022	8C5	917	6,773
Professional technical and andred workers	31	29	*3	22	50 15	19	69 43	85	490	115	19	1	201	94	35	87	551
Farmers and farm managers Managers, officials and propostors except farm	18	3	5	2	6	7	11	90	145	39	4		6	>2	14		20
Cier cal and knored workers Bales workers	7 7	3	8	• 1	4	11	3 5	11	113	29 36	1		6	3,	1	15 3 15	-46 98
Craftenien forumen and kindred workers Operatives and kindred wo.aers	32	14	2 28	21	9	15	1	47	747	173	2	2	2	11	3	3	28
Private household workers	602	170	217	108	399	154	254	235	2.093	1.257	86	8	105	455	218	381	3.403
Service workers except private household Farm abovers, unusid family workers Term laborers, except unpaid, and farm foremen	33	85	84 30	168 34 1	74 30 46	154 97 1	61 141	176 146	2,267	598	19	1.	39 11 17	107	131	96 125 53	1,576
	3 6	÷	70	48	46	9	22	102	489	38	19		17	44	1.	53	69
Occupation not reported	8	12	15	25	8	6	10	26	196	12	2	5	2	6	19	18	54 89
MAJOR INDUSTRY GROUP												- 1		- 1			
Employed total	2,410	1,312	1,907	1,762	2,690	908	2,738	4,227	24,494	6,927	767	162	1,03.	4 033	2,5,0	3,740	17,522
Agric lture forestry and fisherics Mining	744	223	832	1,388	1,>24	84	1,176	2,036	4,141	251	259	79	625	2,282	1,388	2,079	856
Construction Manuracturing	80 215	25 524	145	2/2	6.1 148	359	751	38L 509	2,785	621	246	11	22	122 412 84	123	110	1,957 2,640 888 3,218
Transportation commun , and other public uti- Wholesale and retail trade	276	50	99	26	100	27	92	126	1,363	1,358	28	1	12	84	80	98	888
Pinance insurance and real care e	26	3	12		4	8	31	276	350	1,219 88	44	14	88	213	229	10	174
Business and repair services Personal *e vices	810	234	12 18 303 11	204	21	214	325	33 715	7,458	2,0.0	108	12	146	622	12 299	480	5,002
Entertailment and recreation services Professional and related services	120	54	117	58	.06	54	141	7	1,681	66 367	42	3	3	169	81	154	5,002 134 1,921
Public administration. Industry no* reported	1 37	1 38	78	6	42	16	9	34 98	252	4-	3	-	8	19	9	12	233
many no reported	37	38	78	58	42	16	32	98	473	69	13	5	4	31	29	82	236

Table 44-CHARACTERISTICS OF THE NONWHITE POPULATION, FOR PARISHES 1950-Con.

[Asternac *) denotes statistics bases on 21-perent sample for totals of age groups from complete count see table . You are not shown where base is see han 600;

Subject	East poll	to_io-	Evan-	Yran	Grant	Ib-r_a	Lien-	Jack- sm	Jeffer- acr	Jeffer- sor De Lo	Jotte	rourch.	la Salle	Lama		Medi-	More- nouse
Tol nonwhite population	9,967	11,739	7,556	10,775	3,457	12,971	23 JES	4,590	16,209	5,689	15 70Z	5,0"8	1,42	10,366	4,250	11 560	25,43
Persons 25 years old and over	5,075	5,540	2,510	4,745	-1,44	5 950	0,500	2,125	7.935	2,30		- 540	765		!		
o achool warm committed	915	_	- 345	9_5	335	1,98	1,235	2,125	950	5,30	2,150	665	765	4,280	1,27	275	7,50
sementary I to 4 years	4,205	1,800 1,800 855	7+5	2,225 735 260	545	480	2.800	ann.	2 7 82	730	1 (35)	1,345	250	-,495	720	2,62L	3,49
7 years .	370	500	65 65 35	260	260 90	290	-,.40	267 140	,r45 P05	3001	235	1257	.40 35	3.5	220 65	1,100	1,39
o years ligh school 1 to 3 years	21C 195	295 105 30	35	175	30	270	240	140	544	35	235	95	3.	327	45 50	2.5	3
4 years	4	30	13	-5	35 14 20	125	601	40	385	15	601	5. 00	3.00	400	1.	215	2
ollege 1 to 3 years 4 years or more	20 20 115	35	20	40	50	75	35	25	50	7:	90		15	170	10	82 43	
nool years not reported		30 740		120	10	35	.45	*O	243	45	2_5	50	24	رند 155	30	185	
edian school years completed	4 0	3 4	0 9	3 5	38	2 9	3 3	1. 3	5 .	2.2	_ 6	3 2	41	5 -	3.7	3 9	3
MARITAL STATUS								1		i							
Ma.e 14 years old and over	3 0_8	3,841	2,093	3,-23	ـ,تـ،3	4,00.	4,130	-,342 324	5,24	1 669	4,713	.,751	-6.	3 272	994	3,687	4,7
ngle acried	739 2,065	2,073	1,371	7, 41	299 655	2,471	2,298	524	-,300 2,e35	1,050	2,928,	.066	108	1,-21	281 652	865	3,2
idowed or divorced.	24	276	75	7, 41	49	285	349	84	310	122	254	118	38	155	64	2,563 259	7,2
Female 14 years o.d and over	3,458	3,770	2,072	3,414	2/2	4,369	4,462	-,563 3-2	5 657	1,8-4	5,203	1,788	50%	3,700	91.9	3,94	5,1
Larmed _	2 152	2,183	1,403	2,288	759	2,605	2,705	971	3,342	1,123	3,162	129	327	2,179	639	2,647	3,3
and here or cars or out	675	602	101	458	1.82		9,33	24 3	900	274	687	253	400 €	446	106	696	-
Marred couples,* number oth own household othout own household	1,795 1,685 1_0	_,u20 _,475 _,45	-,25° 1,225 40	2 005 1,920 85	535 485 50	2,215 -,98 230	2,200	885 860 25	2,970	945 9,0 35	2,540	8≠2 790 102	255 255 10	1,770	500 15	2,350 2,_95 155	2,7
EMPLOYMENT STATUS			1.						,						100		
Male, 14 years o'd and over	010,د	3,841	2,093	3, 23	_ OJ3	4,00.	4,135	,342	5,245	1,569	4,713	-,75	465	3,272	994	3,687	4,7
abor force Civilian labor force	2,115 2,111	2,32.	1,625	2,428	702	2,852	2,570	966	3, 441	1,123	2,61	270	30v	2,024	2748	2,69	3,6
Employed	1,983	2,293	1,568	2,3/8	609	2,809	2,568	930	3,521	1,123	2,012	1,165	3C^ -97	2,020	797 77e	2,496	
Private wage and salar- workers Government workers	932	1,052	436 10	533	454	2,175	1,906	723	3, 168	78	1 877	1,099	277	- 471	022	-,455 60	1,3
Self-employed workers	930	9-7	862	1,,92	-80 15	296	260	172	177	10.	972	55	3 17	_84 577	10	942	1,7
Unpend farmily wollers	77 128	267 28	260	209	15	6.	3^ 256	30	474	134	43.	84	12	_21	21	97	1
ot ir abor force	963	1,580	468	695	33.	1,209	1,566	376	1,304	5-6	1,099	₩8 _	الحا	1,251	190	.42 ∌90	1,0
Female, 14 years old and over	3,458	3,770	2,072	3,414	1,184	4,360	4,462	1,503	5, 057	_ 844	5 203	1,788	507	3,74	91,9	3,944	5,1
abor roree	789	837	406	576	225	1,270	1,004	279	1 967	533	1,539	392	_2	1,021	299	640	1,0
Cryllan labor force Employed	789 733	837	406 397	576 544 289	225	1,276	1,004	278	1,967	532	1,767	392	110	_,020 _,001	299	808 754	1,0
Private wage and salary workers	491 61	341 59	22+	289 83	-0 37	1,753	814	203	1,600	415	1,353	340		699	236	520	5
Self-employed workers	135	1.27	71	ill	22	42 34	48	26	102	53 26	145	34	5	252	13	54 435	5
Unpaid family workers Unemployed	46 56	300 10	121	56 32	5	34 58	11	. 4	11	32	227	12	,	25	32	35 54	
ot in labor force	2,669	2,933	△ 666	2,838	959	3,093	3,408	1,284	3,090	_,311	3,434	1,396	395	2,679	620	3,34	4,4
MAJOR OCCUPATION GROUP				i			1 1		1					Taul			
Male emplored	_,963	2,293	1,568	2,368	609	2 609	2,312	950	3,521	_,009	3,373	_,185	297	1,98/	776	2 554	3,4
re essional terninical and singred vorkers	37	10	13.	23	5	39	44	14	29	10	451	1.5	2	63	2	39	1,6
armers and favon managers (Anagers, officials, and proprietors except falm lerical and kindred workers	o97	940	853	1,569	176	2.6	-17 94	146	19	60	862	20 12	9	529 28	112	864 37	1,6
lenral and kindred workers	15	5	3	2	2	9	13	1.5	40	41	10	2	1	٠2	8	9	2
ales workers raftsmen foremen and kindred workers	60	82	34	30	22		170	63	37 223	127 125	19 214	39	6	140	3 21	24	
peratives and kindred workers	233	280	90	1.8	92	457	391	241	223 705 27	1.5	342 25	129	139	140 313 13	155 6 3	1.20 466	3
rvase noisened workers ervice workurs excep private household arm laiorers unpaud family workers arm laborers except unpaud, and farm foremen aborers, except farm and mine	49	25	15	36	13	_49 62	87	24	352	63	300	03	2.5	124	3	72 91	1
arm laborers unpaid family workers arm laborers except unpaid, and farm foremen	76 402	200	25'1	208	13	62 8 3 0	745	24	53	297	432 324	6 د58	4	133	20 97	91 264	
aborers, except farm and mine	174	.79 475 23	157	163 168 22	215	495 38	521	353	1,913	266	726	287	88	505	328	533	2
Acupation not reported	733	827	4				_02	19	46	24	28	.9	28	-	20	26	
Female, employed _		-	397	544	211	1,218	949	267	1,771	500	_,767	38C	110	٠,001	284	754	9
roresional technical and kindred workers .	111	25 123	28	63 98	18	87	36 6	29 5	53	41	98	22	6	121	9	62. 80	1
fanagers, officials, and proprietors, except farm Zerval and kindred workers	13	4 2	1	11	4	5 7 8	22	7	39	3	18	i	2	.5 14	2	22	
	9		1	7	4	21	15	4	14 26	15	19		4	6	1	22	
raftemen foremen and kindred sorkers	19	20		14		50	38	12	389	29	5	40		3	2	7.	
peratives and kindred workers	221	277	172	14 172 84 54 23	91	751	367	142	738	343	43 949	174	66 17	480	118	298	
ervice works, s except private household arm laborers, unpaid family workers arm laborers except unpaid, and farm foremen	221 76 44	90r	122	84 54	23	32	وجد ا	2 4	440	51.	321	50	17	200	51 32	1 do 32	
arm laborers except unpaid, and farm foremen aborers, except farm and mine	144	48	10	23 5	23	84 13	256	4	43	2	45 12	69	÷	9 4	54	>5	
empation not reported	20	19	4	12	.,	28	33	4	17	2 5	19	17	1 7	57	12	6	
MAJOR INDUSTRY GROUP								1									
Employed, total	2,716	3, 120	_,965	2,9.2	088	3,827	3,264	1,197	5,292	1 509	2,140	1,565	407	2,985	م60ر	3,308	4,1
gnoulture, forestry, and nahenes	1,802	1,868	⊥,392	2,158	36	1,318	1,271	196	241	361	1,930	797	25	81.5	325	1,459	2,
imng onstruction	67	38 89	33	57	40	14	289	28	35 371	80	91	5	6	193	33	84	
	155	567	1.07	52 30	155	354	450 79	558	1,670	102	29. 174	185	160	369 114	353	761 82	6
ransportation, commun. and other public util Vb.lesale and retail trade	29 140	56 67	43 74 1	30 151	46	162 374	79 250	80	713	169	290 549	47 89	23 37	294	140	285	3
mance, insurance, and real estate	3	3	1	7	4	31	250 15	11	790 55	10	35	9	2		. 1	13	,
ensonal services	20 324 18	271	224	264	113	31 54 964 17	35 475	12	1,010	448	1,258	231	13	29 65_ 5	139	423	
intertainment and recreation services .	18	2	. 9	-	100	17	15	2	59	6	1,258	31	1 1	5	11	423	
rofessional and related services	10	78	59	12.7	51.	100	222	58	265 84	158	355	61 5	1	440	11	107	
idustry not reported	47		22	41	27	73	138	22	64	34	63	46	95	70		44	

Table 44.—CHARACTERISTICS OF THE NONWHITE POPULATION, FOR PARISHES 1950.—Con
Asterick (*) denotes a*sunties based on 20-person sumps. for souls of age, groups f om complete count see table 41 Median no. shown where base is less than 000]

Asternik (*) denotes s'alletics	political and	no perco			-		the same of the same of	-	-	-		-	-	O+			
Subjec	Vatoni-	Orleans	-dosc0	P_sque- mines	Pointe Coupee	Repides	Red River	Rico- land	Sabine	St Bernard	St Charles	St Kelens	St James	John the Beptist	8+ Landry	St Martin	St Mary
Total nowhite population	-7,1-0	_82,63_	24 670	5,508	11,720	30,096	6,056	10,932	4,299	.,623	4,361	4,785	7,708	7,416	35,018	9,743	13,746
*YEARS OF SCHOOL COMPLETED	7,760	100,070	12,980	2,320	5 255	15,990	2 6"5	4 /35	1 950	800	2 075	4,915	3,450	3,320	13,010	3,750	6,585
Pe.sons 25 years old and over	1,790		.675	,000	1.630	2.595	810	755	280	140	425	125	760	825	4,995	1.860	
No school years completed	3 315	27,130	4,780	857	2,390	5,855 3,340	1,185	2,360	865	135	8.0	960	1,600 575	1,390	4,775 1,685	1 380	1,735 2,635 1 065
5 and 6 years	410	20,910	2,470	450 -70	225	1,275	125	950 255	400	155 75 25	395 185	435 100	230	2.0	490	1.80	395
7 years -	260	2,800	860	1 40	60	845	80 75	140	08	25	90	125	105	80 90	25 <i>2</i> 305	70 65	220 220
High school 1 to 3 years 4 years	50	10 765	930 480	10	5	285	3	25 30	15 20	5 5	75 35	70	20	20	40	1 2	105
College 1 to 3 years	90	2,080	270 165	4000	75 5 10 5	185	15	40	20 25	10	5	35 15	20		95 110	10	90
4 years or more Schoo years not reported	-40	1,605 2,470	180	90	•0	450	45	55	60		5 25	30	30	30	260	60	85
Veguan school years completed	3 3	6.5	50	3 4	2 6	4.5	2 7	3 8	4 -	4 1	, 9	4-4	3 4	3 3	2 2	1.0	3 3
MARITAL STATUS										- 1				8777			
Male 14 rears old and over-	7,151	59,446	7,777	-,777	3,418	9,801	1,776	3,297	1,331	493	371	1,392	2,282	2,304	9,766	2,859	4,303
bingle		40 13.	1,755	62.	9e9 2,224	6,590	1.212	2.251	902	131	880	879	1,470	1.439	5,952	1,764	2,726
Widowed or divorced	317	4,275	502	116	225	7.4	101	2,251	85	20	86	77	454	_39	469	124	330
Female, 14 years old and over	5,634	72,132	9,301	1 652	2,773	1 130	1 969	3,57/	1,451	454	1,420	1,418	2,19/ 458	2,3.8	2 25-	2,902	4,539
Single	1 205	13 356 44,368	1,4-1 6,013 1,887	1,038	2,306	2,045 7,130	1 268	2 378	270 944	350	910	880	1 517	-,460	6.25_	1,8 2	2,808
Widowed or divorced	960	14,408		199	592	- 957	293	531	237	79	268	154	410	33.	1,273	265	867
Married couples * number With own household	2,680	33 220 28,345	4 760	9773 86.5	2,175	5,185 410	1,025 70	1,890	855 ,95 60	320 295	760 685	870 835	1,260	1,370	5,595 5,180 415	1,605	2,475 2,275 200-
Witcout own household	2.0	4,875	440	202	130	410	70	80	60	25	75	35	100	100	415	95	200
EMPLOYMENT STATUS														7.0	10.00	ani.	
Mue 14 years old and over	×,151		1,7%	1,777	3,418	9,801	1,776	3,297	-,33-	493	1,337	1,392	2,282	2,304	9 766	2 859	4,303
Labor force	3,432	43,251	5,72	,29°	2,581	6,352	1,2,5	2,488	885	309 309	872	1,102	1,56.	- 653 - ,652 1,544	7 1 52	2,209	3,182
Employed . Private wage and salary we kers	1,370	39 171 33,809	5 344 4,393	1,160	2 / 56	5 748	1,275 1,252 444	2,487 2,387 733	849 647	272	87. 748 638	284	.,459	1,544	6,766	1 028	2 871 2 580
Private wage and salary we kers	130	2,910	283	5.	20	386	26 683	351	36	11	34	7	33	22	80	6	66
Governmen, workers Self-employed workers	1,470	2,430	60-	287	917	786	683	1,368	148	13	70	650 157	118	71	3,242	8 ₄ 1 286	198
Unpard family works.s Unemployed	125	4,080	362	.33	125	593	23	400	36	3"	124	4	29	103	282	68	,-11
Not in labor force	-,719	808, كد	2,0,0	484	837	2,449	501	809	446	184	465	290	721	651	2,714	650	1,121
Female 14 years old and over	5,631	72,132	9,301	1 652	3,703	1_,130	1,569	3,574	1,451	354	1,420	1,-18	2 39/	2,318	_0,475	2,902	4,539
Labor force Caritan labor force	1,214	25,793	3,623	430	956 056	3,468	408	705	258 258	160	324	338	432	384	2,326	681	1,343
Emp. cyed Private wage and salary workers	1,169	23 929 20 917	3,623 3,422 2,906	37L 328	898 654	2,821	293	673	256 198	42	303 242	337	363	342 286	2,36	625	1,0%
Covernment workers	182	1.945		€0	-1 57	21.6	3.	57	35	8	37	75 30	37	.36	1581	15	94
Capaid family workers	103 238	963	1.80	8	.36	150	43 84	89 77	21	4	24	26 206	78	17	612	184	57 13
Unemployed.	44	1,800	201	60	68	211	17	32	2	6	21	2	8	42	120	26	127
Not in labor force	4,417	46,339	5 078	1,222	2,747	7,662	1,560	2,869	1,193	394	1,096	1,080	1,967	1,934	8,149	2,220	3,196
MAJOR OCCUPATION GROUP	3,295	39,_71	5,344	1 460	2.454	5,748	1,252	2,387	849	272	748	1,098	1.459	1 544	6.766	2.14.	2 871
Male, employed	45	1,027	133	2 100	74	94	1,454		15	5	16	14	-7	13	72	9	38
Professional technical, and kindred workers Farmers and farm managers	1,396	72	36.8	118	867	551	674	1,344	131	5.	32 13	644	67	34	3,092	777	86
Managers officials and proprietors except farm Ciercal and hindred workers	29	1 189 1,492	148	9	11	103	- :	13	8	3	13	6	14	6	63	-1	20
bales workers	12	712 4 464	53	- 7	101	77	3	81	47	22	11.	10	8	11	29	100	184
Craftsmen foremen, and undred workers Operatives and kindred workers	326	8.645	-,313	72	205	1,113	49	174	165	46	1,5	124	196	324	525	144	553
Private household workers	124	7,103	38	2	33	606	12	10	23	21	37	31	30	59	128	4,	125
Service workers except private household Farm laborers, unpaid analy workers	317	6	60	221	163	34	10.	242	-6	3	7	156	8	2	1.091	278	20
	392 428	105	296	-72 200	762 372	1,910	240	250	373	28	109	64	762	514	438	551	-,114
Laborers excep farm and mine Occupation not reported	68	392	29	60	14	90	22	10	21	124	3	17	21	461	244	28	27
Female employed	-,169	23,929	2,422	:70	588	3,257	39.	673	256	154	303	337	424	342	2,206	655	1,216
Professional terrinical, and kindred workers	102 75	+,244	177	16	37	146	25	60	22	6	16	27 26	29	31	162	9	81
Farmers and farm managers. Managers, officials and proprietors except farm Clerical and kindred workers	18	473	93	3	6	63	4-1	16	8	4	5	26	11	1 2	25	7	4
Clerical and kindred workers Sales workers	2 5	638	53 50	1 5	3 6	42	2	4	2	2	7		10		8 20	12	2
Craftemen foremen, and kindred workers Operatives and kindled workers	1	170	3	1	3	6	-		1		il		-	1	2		5
Private household workers	66 364 175	3 954	1,734	110	257	1,615	124	34 259	126	29 68	134	43 7	23	21	55 879	248	51_
Service workers, except private household Farm laborers, unpaid famil; workers Farm laborers, except unpaid and farm foremen	1°5 233	6,125	838	21	74 132 285	741	21 85	109 74 75	66	16	64	7	50	55	258	74	149
Farm laborers, every unpaid and farm foremen	84 7	36	52	43	285	183	69	75	- 1	25	19	203	175	96	601	71.1	11 274
Laborers, except farm and mine Occupation not reported	7	459 191	38	43 43 15	7 21	24	2	6	6 5	3	7	8	1.6	5	22	17	14
MAJOR INDUSTRY GROUP			٦	-		-		-				٩		1	, ,		
Employed total	4,464	63,.00	8,760	1,530	3,344	9.005	1.643	3,060	4.405	426	1,051	1,435	1 883	1,886	8,972	2,796	4,087
Agnoulture forestry and fishenes	2,552	437	855	5"6	2,166	1, 85	1,221	2,088	109	65	189	1,1.7	1,099	700	5,374	1,884	1.689
	120	5,758	32 536	18	132	25 534	21	59	41	36	2	2		117	121	93	31 164
Mining Construction			1,162	328	299	1,499	48	101	419	84	219	169	268	648	61d	145	746
Manufacturing	328	7,906															119
Cons ruction Manufacturing Fransportation, commun and other public util		9,461	591	83	192	1.309	75	170	481	50	85	12	101	52	222	126	368
Cons rution Manufacturing Fransportation, commun and other public util Wholssale and retail trade Thance, insurance and real estate	328 141 220	9,461 12,102 1,530	591 1,660	831	192	1,309	36	171	-16	56	164	13	101	52 115 2	645 18	176	368 15
Cons rutton Manufacturing Fransportation, commun and other public util Wholesale and retail trade Finance, meurane and real estate Rusness and repair services	328 141 220 42 30	9,461 12,102 1,530 946	591 1,660 -14 1/7	83 74 6	192 5	1,309	36	171 8 19	1 1 12	56	164	1	101	12	222 645 18 109	176	368 15 23 708
Come ru mon Manufacturing Pransportation, commoun and other public util Wholesale and retail trade Pransport months and retail trade Pransport months and recreation services Personal services Personal services Personal services	328 141 220 12 30 543 33	9,461 12,102 1,530 946 16,376 821	2,87 2,87 2,87	6 126	192 15 347	1,309 110 93 2,387 107	36 3 11 159	171 8 19 384 9	16 1 12 181	56 4 7 81 8	164 3 9 194 3	1 6 48	101 5 8 142	12 160	222 645 18 109 1,166 26	176 4 44 308 7	368 15 23 708
Cons rutton Manufacturing Fransportation, commun and other public util Wholesale and retail trade Finance, meurane and real estate Rusness and repair services	328 141 220 42 30	9,461 12,102 1,530 946 16,376	591 1,660 14 1/7 2,80	83 74 6	192 5	1,309 110 93 2,387	36 3	171 8 19	1 1 12	56 4 7 81	164	1	101	12	222 645 18 109 1,166	176 4 44 308	368 15 23 708 10 468 13

Table 44—CHARACTERISTICS OF THE NONWHITE POPU".ATION FOR PARISHES 1950—Con [Assemble **] denotes sta article based on 20-percent sample for tota s of age groups from complete orders, see .ab.= 11 Median not moven wares base a less than 500,

Subject	St Tammann	Tang- ipahos	Tensas	Terre- bonne	Jaic	ermi-	/ern~ı	angton	We ster	Baton Rouge	Carroll	Felio- iana	Hom
Total nonwhite population *YEARS OF SCHOOL COMPLETED	7,928	16,599	8,505	_6 e70	6,624	4,702	2,2_8	12,068	14,422	6,241	3,121	7,240	4,4.5
Persons 25 years old and over	2,795	7,865	4 055	4 HOC	2,795	≥ 075	- 400	5,465	5,970	,050	1 415	3 305	2 22
vo school years completed.	1,055	3,435	€75	1,190	420	230	-20	455	740	955	275	645	31
Jementary 1 to 4 years 5 and 6 years	795	1,365	760	1,945	4,043	260	525	1,975	2,365	1,120	520 26*	1,510	870
7 years	305	550	760 210 110	220	230	1.0	250 75 65	540; 415	500	165	_05	₂ 70	1.6
gh school 1 to 3 years	215	455	165	145	190	75	-05	400	420 360	105	.00	1.0	13:
d years	35	120	30	25 40	15	20.	5	70	55	30	251	3.	
4 vears or more	32	2C I	51	-0'	20	01		35	F5	±0	25	2	20
hool years not reported	25	240	130	_05		1.05	35	-00	85	46	15		145
edian school years completed _	4.4	41	9.7	2 2	4 7	2 4	- 4	5 /	4	3 C	4 3	3 6	- 1
MARITAI STATUS				1			1		1	1	1		
Male, 14 years old and over _	2,475	5,175	2 595 C73	3,190	2,03_	470	747	3,656	÷,065	2,047	959	3,324	1,42
igle. arried. adowed or divorced.	1.60-	5,532	-,709 183	2 01_	59_ 4,355	803 j	218 473	2,47	2,695	568 1 333	253 430	1,354	33°
	152	392		250	85	100	Sr	646	227	140	70	2.8	12
female, 14 years old and over	2,643	5,560	2,986	3,260	2,086	1,579	80,5	3 967	4,389	2,071	-,017	1,790	1,56
ogiearried	1,668	3,576	518	2,052	1 35_	907	136	796 4,509	2.807	258	202 64.7	1,041	1,02
idowed or disorced	436	849	5.8	542	252	2_8	174	642	2,807	344	162	287	27
Married couples,* number	1,300	3 020	1,485	1,895	1 150	20u	4±5 380	2,315	2 425	1,085	>65	1,040	78
thou own household.	95	190	30,	2.	55	95	35	2,170	2,255	1,010	510	1,005	70
EMPLOYMENT STATUS	İ				- 1		-			- 1			u
Male 14 years old and over	2,475	2,-75	2 >95	3 490	2,00	24	8/-	2 46-	1.00				
Male 14 years old and over	1 694	3,359	1,935		1,492	1,400,	747	2,765	4,060	2 047	959	3,314	1,42
Civilian labor force.	4,694	3 8.81	1,905	2,357	1,492	+Q4 !	448	2.765	2,913	1,442	663 663	1,170	91
Employed. Private wage and salary workers	1,615 1,357	3,773	1,793 77L	2 124 -,707	1,470	866	366	2,634	2,75€	1 304	652	1,162	914 89
Government workers		86	25	73	٥د	2.	19	57	158	1,084	202	503	720
Self-employed workers Unpaid family workers	170	836	780 88	330	507	220	44	691	667	-37	389	276	125
Unemployed	79	8"	4.2	433	22	128	4	133	151	138	-1	70	30
of in labor force.	781	-,310	090	833	509	439	299	891	1 152	-005	246	2,138	508
Female 14 years old and over-	2,645	5 566	2,986	3,460	2,084	1 ,579	805	3,961	4,389	2, 772	1,000	1,790	1,568
bor force	6'-	2,156	71 ₄ 712	97_	308	509 509	221 221	1,.01	1, 27	494	150 150	242	299
Kennlox ad	6L	4, 1.00 1,592	680	890	303	482	221	1,024	1,090	-46	148	2-4	29
Private ware and colery morkers	*43	1,592	441	738	223	391	-89	768	833	400	qg.	1.60	244
Government workers Self-employed workers	12	129	176	64 3±	17	28	121	60 90	71	22	20	22	25
Unpaid family workers Unemployed	10	∡78 50	20	74	5	47 27	5	106	69	11	14	3.	3
ot in labor force.	2,014	3,440	2,274	2,289	1,778	1,00	84	2,866	264	1,572	b6.	1,548	1,269
MAJOR OCCUPATION GROUP								i					-,
	1,615		~ 1	0.10/	3 .50	2.4		2 632					
Male, employed ofessional technical and kindred workers	32	3,773 4c	4,793	2,124	1,470	806	444	2 432	2,756	2,304	602	1,162	884
rmers and farm managers	.DL	778	826	Ju l	40L	192	76	648	622	ນດ໌ເ	280	560	78
lanagers officials and proprietors, except farm	1 2	21	23 :	23	11	-11	8	18	17	10	4	4	
des vorkers	1.1	22	141	-3!		اور	5	13	16	31	2	6	9
raftsmen foremen, and kindred workers peratives and kindred workers	325	153 97	80	8º 370	254	82	21	92 608	148 530	142	44	30	2.1
	43	24	9	4	6	20	5	n	16 134	1'	- 7	1	
revice work, s, except payate household arm laborers, unpaid family workers arm laborers except farm and anim. aborers except farm and anim.	97	145	30, 83	1 2	20	31	51	127	134	60 49	54	15	
arm laborers except urpaid and farm foremen	135	861	4.1	577	102	c13	- 6	143 114	121 207	562	62 78	68 1.0°	39
borers except farm and .nin.	640	960	161	748	-17	15	193	763 31	833.	275	78	204	39
cubanda not reported				-	1		1				,	1	
Female employed	6L	2,100	689	696	303	452	212	1,024	1,090	448	148	239	29
ofessional, 'echnical and singred workers .	361	72 9/	140	-5	48	23	13	57 78	87 23		17	8	2
anagers officials, and proprietors except sarr	2	0	19	5	3	3	2	25	21	3	2	-	
erick, and kindred workers	2 1	2	8	5	1	6	3		22.	3		1	
aftymen, foremen, and kindred workers		2	11	242	1	10	3,	3	5	2		í	
eratives and kindred workers	307	57C	227	322	2461	312	108,	52 450	51 -51	123	70	24 84	12
vice workers except private household .	150	267	72	دند	95	47	30	171	165	111	70 15	24 36	7
vice workers except private household im laborers unpaid family workers im laborers except unpaid and farm foremer	24	644	130	-37	اد ا	24	2	32	67 36	15	8	36	
loorers except farm and mine	10	30 44	8	14	1	51	2	41 19	27	10	41	3¢ 10	
coupation not reported	4	42	12	9	11	,	2	19	21	10			1
MAJOR INDUSTRY GROUP	1				- 1								
Employed total	2,230	5, 27.	2,482	_,020	△ 773	1,348	656	3,656	3 840	1 702	P00	1,401	1,17
griculture, forestry and fishenes.	324	2,77,	1,666	2,335	731	541	P_	-,179	1,389	920	537	822	15
onstruction	2.9	اود	83	14,	38	50	2.	178	163	_58	36	23	5
anufac uring ansportation commun. and other public util	556	965	99	5791	532	an.	_85 25	262 102	805	126	31	280	42
ansportation commun. and other public util	246	577	181	18"	87	49	85	309	320	±40	44	46	
nance, insurance, and real estate	R	21	3	20	13	9	4	31	_8 27	4	1		
usiness and repair services	2 2 2 3 3 s	790	292	452	196	424	176	619	7^5	78,	92	11	Z
ntertainment and recreation services	6	71	5	117	3	51	4 38	15	_8 209	64	25	1 29	4
intertainment and recreation services - rofessional and related services - ublic administration -	148	224	82	16	30	4 25	-0	11	84 90	7	1		3

LOUISIANA

Table 45—INCOME IN 1949 OF FAMILIES AND UNRELATED INDIVIDUALS, FOR PARISHES 1950 (Bastating bases on 20-percent sample Media: not shown where case a fees Jana 200)

	per contract contract		-	-	-	_	-		-	-	-	-				_	-
Parush	4·1 classes	Less tnan \$500	\$500 to \$999	\$1,000 to \$ 499	\$1,500 to \$1,999	\$2,000 to \$2,499	\$2,500 to \$2,999	\$8,000 to \$3,499	\$3,500 to \$3,999	\$4,000 to \$4,499	\$4,500 to \$4 999	95,000 to \$0,999	\$6,000 \$6,098	\$7,000 to \$9,999	\$10,000 and over	Income not re- ported	Median income (dollars)
Families and unrelated indiv	12,750	1 7.	2,455	1,870	1,500	1,46	67> 650	680 63	405 38,5	30» 300	220 P15	270 251	450 40	205 190	240 230	690 /70	1,563 1,697
Familes and unrasted indiv	3,300 4,570	70° 430	935 700	750	635 290	960 52"	4e0 400	310 300	205	150 150	105 95	115 1 o	95 95	65 65	60 60	110 155	-,634 1,820
ASCACION Families and unrelated radiv Families ASSAMPTION	4,930	875 570	1,245	73u 675	5C5 490	440 41 9	322 315	344 3.0	210	235 235	140	165 155	95 95	95 95	20 40	345 285	1,410
Families and unrelated indiv.	4 185 3,660	98° 950	1,_50	765 745	535 545	285 270	190 165	140 140	90	55 55	55	45 42	30 30	45 45	40	130 95	1,169
Families and unrelated indiv Families	10 835	1,655	2,690	1,960	1,150	780 760	650	420	300	235	9C 9O	200	85	85	49 40	385 320	-, 211
Families ATENTILLE	2,-15 4 425	110 325	1,065	67, 645	671 635	5^0 555	29,2 40,2	277 240	225 220	160 153	90	95 95	65 6:	75	₹C SC	220 290	1,573
Families and unrelated must Families	5,120 7.55	9,5 650	1,080	850 805	6±0 585	470	220 201	295 280	1*5 150	105	62	65 65	40	30 30	30 30	155 150	1,272
Families and unrelated indiv Families	1.,805 9 645	1,295	2,.75	2,125	1,070	\$75 830	975 6 5	960 870	720 680	400	395 385	490 475	290 290	265 255	135	1 570 505 4,450	2 364
Families and unrelated indiv Families CALCASINU	58,665 45 3.5	6,865 3,525	4,590	5,545 4,190	3,985	4 69u 3,840	3,660	4,190 3 685	3,080 2 795 1 925	2,7.5	1,995	3,050 2,895	1,795	1,850	1,460	3,360	2,157 2,638 2,668
Familes and unrels ed indiv Familes	27,305 22,805	2,530 1,390	2,705	2,305	2,350	2 550 2,2.5	1,750	2,225	1,790	1 960	1,272	1,785	860	880	610	7:0	2,6.2
Families and unrelated indiv Families	2,965 2,600	470 355	560 455	535 475	390 365	310	165	08 08	90	50 50	30 30	30 30	5° 25	30 30	25 45	145 85	1,355
Families and unrelated adda Families CATAROULA	1 (30 1 460	195 155	240 270	170 135	140 140	210 210 212	30 30	120 110	175	100 100	40 15	70 70 40	50 05 30	25 25	25 25	5. 55	2,090
Families and unrelated indiv Families CARBOPNE Families and unrelated indiv	3,2°0 2,700 6,940	440	61	530	345	210	1 0	1,5	43	35	150	40	غر قمد	180	15	75 275	1,276
families concernia Families and unrelated indiv	4,010	1,040 %0	-,460 - 190	85.5 5LO	6U3	380	357	31C	4-0	235	160	120	120	175	85 +5	24C 190	1,008
Families	3 285 6.840	1,800	0.5	505	344 605	230	130 325	305	130	-65	45	150	45	10	40	130	1,26
Families and unrelated indiv lamilies. MAST E/ZON ROUGE Framilies and unrelated indiv	2,80	8 ₀ 0	1,225	1,030	970	3,78	295	3,710	3,20	3.2.5	75 2,830	4,05>	75 75 2,0,*	65 2,270 2,195	60 60 1,325	530 /**0 3 (80	1,294 2,618
Pandies BASI CAPROLL Families and un elated indiv	39 490	2 305	1,115	2,943 560	2,790	260	2,665	3 240	2,890	3,020	2,675	3 900	2,020	50	1,270	2,	83درد 3ه
L-ST FFLICIANA Famues and un_elazed indiv	3,570	1,2.5	720	590 590	2/5	220	140	90	85 55	75 60	50 50	60	45 30 30	50 45	35	245 130	1,007
Tamiles EVANORLINE Famu s and unrelated mon Famules.	8,300 7,590	995 -,370 - 120	490 1,940	,375 ,335	245 8 40 905	210 680 679	350 345	75 365 3.0	345 340	240 230	95 95	120	80	45 75	1.0	325	1,247
FRANKLIN Families and unrelated mon	7,630	1.440	ا ا اے5' رے	.125	845	700	3.5	325	295	1.35	24	140	95	120	65	230	1.224
Families GRANT Families and unrels ed indiv	3 80.	1,.10	1,405	1,005	335	665 345	300 230	310 140	190	95	85 45	140 75	90 25	25	15	185	-,309 -,194 -,334
Families and unielated indiv	3,285 -0 985 9,500	385 -,444 945	1,775 1,280	1,305 1,185	1,150	1,110 1,055	820 790	135 690 675	420 4.0	480 460	253 235	445 440	290 465	26 > 26 >	140	100 420 3>>	1,835
Faralles DERVILE Families and unrelated indiv Families	7 135	81.	1,283	P70 535	755	620	335 325	300	265 255	23 235	150 140	180	85 65	.35 .30	85	385 300	1,381
JACKSON Families and unrelated many Families	4 165	440 3.0	643 543	640 595	425 395	480 445	415 40*	300 265	180 165	180	95 90	170	30 30	70 70	20	72 65	1,994
Partiles and unrelated indiv Pamilies	29,285 2,960	2,375	2,195	2,162	2,275	3,487	2 790	2,930	1,905	1,460	7 260	1,960	1 .6:	1,150	805	1,340	2,764
Families and unrelated indix Families	7,590	910	- 300 935	1,480	735	6±0 570	545 540	370 365	335	330	-50 -45	19-	35	220	180	290	1,636
Families and unrelated indiv Families	16,950	2,900	2,520	2,103	1,820	1,505	1,000	940 875	7:0 680	595 545	375 360	69° 665	355 330	38 : 370	340 325	589 425	1,6du 2,C18
LAFOUR.HR Famules and unrelated indiv Famules LA SALLE	10 385 9,480	8°0 6'00	1,50	1,485 1,390	1,255	1,160	8°0 863	645 630	530 525	435.	290 280	3Q5 305	20s 20J	210 200	_2> _25	410 365	1 9≥0 2,057
Famues and unrelated indiv Famues	3,775	400	70* 560	180 35	400 365	350 331	270 260	190 180	275 265	405 405	96 85	35 35	65 60	30 25	35 35	222 280	1,613
Families and unrelated indiv	8,635 5,765	2,275	1,375 790	1,484	725 62	600 565	415 385	570 330	3u5. 280	240 205	200	180	140 130	145	150	330 200	1,2.2
Families and unrelated indiv Families	5 410 4,820	840 55*	920 730	710 665	475 460	475 450	2°0 270	ے 20 315	29 ° 1 29 5	270 270	220 220	125	85 85	135 125	45 40	25. 2.5	1,645

GENERAL CHARACTERISTICS

Table 45 —INCOME IN 1949 OF FAMILIES AND UNRELATED INDIVIDUALS, FOR PARISHES 1950—Cor Statistics used on 20-percent, water or Montage 10, th. JT. Horry base at the than 2001

Parish	A.I classes	han 850	\$500 8009	3 (a)(31,+99	\$1,500 \$1,000	\$2,000 to \$2,197	\$2,500 \$0 \$2.990	\$3,000 \$3,090	\$3,560 \$3,560	\$4,609 &- \$- 429		\$2,000 to	\$6, 400 \$0,999	-7,60°C to \$0,909	000,015 pag 970	Increase not re- ported	Vecum in ome dolars
Families and incelated india.	5,435	1,160	-,295	>20	-75	345	_255	_85	دف	45	55	as		-0	30	221	9/do
Farmes Families and unrelated must	9,224	820 1,235	913	775	735	320	175	575	153	35 255	25	80	42	145	105	265	-,167 -,533 1,347
Families Families and unrelated and the Families and the	10,555	2,525	2,395	9.5 -,380	675 890	735 535	365	525 3x0	410	230	255	265	150	_35	105	1,05	9-5
Families and unrelated main	194 380	2,700	4,720	-,255 -9,0	19,055	-85	350 15,-80	4,695	23.	8,320	.05	9,.55	5,065	6,65	5,460	10,495	2,267
Families and unrelated indiv	24, .85 19,350	8,545 2,805 1,445	3 470	2,585 2,585 2,035	4,370 2, 10	2,220	1,940	-,78J -,635	10, 22 -,305 -,260	1,050	9,313 775 765	1,030	53C 52C	6,405 590 575	5,060 560	1.025	2,767
P.AQU'MINES ramilies and unrelated indiv	3.9.0	445	590	400	265	390	25^	3-0	_80	195	2.5	170	235	"Cs	30	2.0	2,434
Families CINTE COUPEE Families and unrelated indiv	3,250 2,985	960	450	1,025	235	330	195	300	65 LaG	175	130	160	125	105	25	180	1,124
Families APIDES Families and unrelated indir	5,170 26,475	3,470	4,315	960	2,775	2,410	235 4,875	195	1,130	165	110	±00	425	475	75 75 495	1,770	-, 263
Families EED RIVEE Families and unrelated indiv	21,665	1,870 5e0	925	3,060	2,490	2,195	1,760	-,510 -,360 1.5	1,090	725	615	860	440	465 35	475	1,360	1,964
Pamihos RICHAND Families and unrelated indiv	2,805 6 850	1,255	770	520 950	345 690	190	125	285	65 255	70 1-0	35	55	25	35	20	120	1,147
Fan.iles	6,015	940	1,335	867	670	505	240	260	230	190	205	135	40	\$0	70	285	1,336
Families Families Families Families	5,650 4,965	885 -60	1,340	1,065	616 590	400 375	255 240	225 210	150 140	120 115	35 35	ے 125	5. 55	-0 40	50 50	290 220	1,214
Families and unrelated indiv	3,090 2,795	3-95 285	455 360	3 ₂ 0 310	325 295	325 305	240 235	190 190	175	360 0	110 110	13o 125	65 60	75 70	40 40	72	2,020
ST CHARLES Families and unrelated indiv Families	3,325	475 310	540 415	340 310	295 280	26.5 250	190 160	240 230	.~0 .62	180 175	105 105		110	105 95	25 25	135 140	2,-50
Families and unrelated indiv Families	2,330	560 425	525 455	325 310	23.5 22.5	_90 165	85 55	75 75	ບ ວ 60	o5 65	45 45	25 25	20	15 15	15	85 70	1,056
Families and unrelated indiv Families	3,455 2,965	600 370	940 765	530 510	360 340	260 245	310 310	150 1.0	25 52	85 80	30 30	50 50	20	20	20	125	1,118
ST. JOHN THE BAPTIST Families and unrelated indiv Families	3,465 3,215	400 250	735 605	475 455	405 380	485 445	315 295	280 265	125 110	80 75	85 85	75	50 50	35	10	310 85	-,707 -,836
Families and unrelated many - Families -	19,675	3,675 2,595	4,230 3,450	3,155	2,1.5	1,495	905 880	720 685	610	485 475	285 275	460 455	210	290 250	190 290	815 705	1,242
Families and unrelated indiv	6 620 5,985	975 740	1,575	990 965	740 720	665 630	345 330	335 330	180	_70 _65	55 55	08 08	60	85 85	95 85	270	1,314
ST Mar.: Families and unrelated mary Famuer	10,015	1,290 765	1,095 1,205	1,165	1,055	1,000 925	650 630	630	415 380	48> 475	285 255	400 390	170 160	295 270	120 -20	320 230	1,833
Families and unrelated indic Families	6,765 6,085	1,430 750	1,355	995 905	935 850	695 630	480 445	380 355	265 250	195 480	145 140	720 210	85 85	95 90	70 60	420 220	1,44
Families and unrels ed indiv Families	16,160 12,780	3 380 1,955	3,315	2,260 1,952	1,810	1,265	755 685	745 675	440	380 370	20C 195	215 205	125 125	215 210	.30 125	925 685	1 204
Families and unrelated indiv Families	3 665	1,240 930	810 550	490 450	235 195	250 175	150 145	90 85	75 60	50 50	30 30	90 85	40	50	30	85 75	844 964
Families and unrelated indiv Families	10,850	985 715	1,895	-,495 1,405	1,120	1,130	770	770 735	595 270	415 410	300 290	420 405	280		125	305 240	2,06
Families and unrelated indiv. Families	5,125 4,540	715 495	1,070	750 720		510 490	375 365	250 250	.95 .90	110	55 55	12C	35 35	5.	35	135 100	1,47
Families and unrelated indiv Families	10,385	1,990	2,195 1,710	1 5.5 1,465	1,080	830 780	470 450	470 455	ئيد 295	275 270	ىد 115	255 245	145	145	165 155	365 340	1,26
VINON Families and unrelated indiv Families	5 J15 4 065	-,275 800	1,245	845 805	565 550	445 420	205 205	210 210	160 150	-00 30	95 90	75 70	50	35 35	35 35	175 140	1,283
Families and unrelated indiv Families	10,735	1,425	1,890	1,375	1,095 1,005	1,055	760 620	570 535	500	30o 295	230 220	395 375	260 245	195	1.0	570 440	1,67
Families and un-elated indiv l'amilies	9,830 8,620	1,045 660	1,405	1,315	1,05	1,130	690 665	680 600	6.C 580	385 370	270 260	285 285	165 160	140	1.0	445 37>	1,92
EST BATON ROUGE Tamilies and unrelated indiv Families	3,095	365	775 55.0	435	245 215	230 215	150 160		_45 _45	102	110	130 120	60 60	65	30	55 35	-,43 -,78
WEST CARROLL Families and unrelated indiv Families	4,59 ⁴ 4,085	955 797	1,165 940	815	510 505	32C 305	160 150	150	95 90	400	40	75 75		35	25 25	±45 ±20	
WEST FELI(IANA. Families and unrelated indiv.	2,795	345 2°0	570 425	350 305	240 220	125	60 55	80 70	50 45	32 35	رد 15	45 40		30	3	125	1,10
Families and unrelated indiv Families	4,840	680 445	1,130	710	665 615	540 500	155 145	105	130 135	100	65 65	50 45	30	50	35	325 275	1,3

Table 45a.—INCOME IN 1949 CF NONWHITE FAMILIES AND UNRELATED INDIVIDUALS, FOR PARISHES 1950 [Statistics based on 20-person. source. Median .os source where once a 'ess text 500]

Planting the Party of the State	Contract Con	a continuo	location.	d Doged Or	av-he ner	· senzie.	Mentan	- CO CLIONA	71000000		ST 2001	_				_	
Paneh	Vonwarte families and un reland undividual	6 perce	\$500 to \$366	\$1,46µ	\$1,500 to \$1 999	\$2 (%) to \$2 499	\$2,500 to \$2,999	\$3,000 to \$3,499	\$3,500 50 \$3,939	\$4 000 to \$4,499	\$4,500 .0 \$4,399	\$5,000 to \$5,999	86,000 to \$6,999	\$7,000 to \$9,999	810,000 and over	Income not re- ported	Med.an moome (do.lars)
A.edia A.en Assensina Assensina Assensina	2 (85 1,325 2,64 1,735 7,546	29. 463 3.5	280	400 245 340 85 470	200 175 105 155 305	125 .70 .50 85 .10	6C 65 67 35 65	_0 35 20 15 25	25 5 5 15 20	20 10 10	5 5 5	5 3 20	5 5	12	5	100 65 130 40 65	935 4,128 844 891 889
Beauregard Simmiliae Boosier Jaadu Calcapte_	2,.65 -,035 20,05 6,245	-50 >50 8.5 4 370 820	6.5 1,725 2,525	235 470 880 3,455 900	C 280 42u/ 2,9_0 _,040′	75 190 230 1,905 903	25 80 80 895 445		5 20 245 140	15 5 1.5 50	5 5 5 65 55	10 115 70	5 10 05 5	5 35 25	5 10 20	55 45 200 885 250	978 952 942 1,364 1,499
Caidwell lameron Cataboule Claboune Conportis	3,175 2,470	186 360 770 695	. 50	275 20 275 580 470	130 320 220	40 10 20 140 145	35 85 40	5 25 50 15	5 10 5	5 10	5	5	5	5 10 15	2	25 110 85	764 855 813
De Soto Zes+ Ba*en Ruige East Ca. volu Zes+ Frliciana Evangeline	3,515 16,660 3,155 2 130 1,480	3,110 1,400 660 370	1,065 3,085 835 650 450	765 2,430 425 415 335	335 2,050 385 155 150	95 2,680 85 75 40	85 -,025 25 50 40	35 950 10 10 25	15 475 20 5	150 15 5	5 115 20 5	10 190 20 5 10	1.0	5 110 5	5 30 5 5	190 1,110 105 90 80	856 1,325 575 777 867
Franklin Oren Ibe-'a Lorville Jackson	2,845 780 3,240 3,665 1,240	780 140 790 570 _90	840 900 925 1,400 245	490 130 540 600 280	335 55 340 425 465	170 55 235 250 285	65 40 130 105 80	50 30 65 45 25	15 25 30 15	25 45 20 15	_0 2 15 10 10	10 15 15	5	5	5 5	55 20 105 190 10	856 900 921 917 1,321
Lefferson Lefferson Devis Lafayette Lafc_rone La Saule	5,070 4,495 3,645 1,38* 48>	920 250 800 265 95	70 465 1,010 510 135	310 325 540 220 110	890 215 510 195 65	755 90 245 55 20	290 55 130 40 20	150 25 70 35	55 25 10	45 15 20	10 10 10 5	5	5 10 15	5 10		30 160 40	1,355 1,028 967 900
Linco_n _ivingston Maoi=on Morehouse Natchitoches	3,085 865 3,705 4,290 4,080	965 245 -,140 990 1,230	700 175 1,090 1,355 1,290	500 2°5 725 665 525	290 120 345 410 320	150 35 155 430 160	95 25 55 170 55	45 10 55 60 55	45 20 60 20	20 10 10	5 30 10	15 5 10 20 5	10 5	5 10 15	5	140 55 150 70 340	863 957 806 91,3 748
Orleans Ouaonita Plaguemines Pointe Coupee Rapides	59,200 8,035 1,205 3,030 8,470	8,755 -,460 275 070 -,540	12,365 2,075 360 1,160 2,195	9,600 1,420 230 570 1,570	9,185 1,265 140 270 1,240	5,970 780 75 100 e90	3,675 400 35 30 360	2,520 175 20 25 150	1,435 105 10 5	835 30 5 20 60	480 20 10 15 45	490 45 5 5	250 25	200	95 5	2,350 2±5 35 160 400	1,381 1,132 931 830 1,096
Ped River Plobland Sebine St Bernard St Charles	1,505 2,665 1,270 485 1,190	390 770 220 155 270	575 925 360 110 335	270 410 295 65 185	110 190 125 55 165	60 140 70 40 95	25 50 30 -5 35	5 35 20 10 30	20 5 10	15	10	10	5		5	65 80 35 15 45	787 783 983
St Helena St James St John the Baptist St Landry St Martin	1,430 1,885 1,815 7,370 2,110	405 430 265 1,910 415	330 710 325 2,490 740	185 310 295 1,295 390	95 200 235 715 220	35 80 250 355 140	25 40 105 1_5 45	15 45 55 45	5 10 35 10	15 20 20 5	5 5 20	5 15 10	5	15	10	30 70 60 310 85	720 837 1,149 825 904
St Mary St fammany Tangipuboa Jensas Terrebonne	3,700 2,200 5,610 2,410 2,670	785 460 1,475 1,035 450	1,140 580 1,500 680 1,000	965 390 790 340 545	540 305 570 135 290	300 155 220 85 440	90 85 95 25	65 45 55 40 45	10 25 40	5 25 15	15 5 10	15	10 5 5 5	5	5	75 100 230 45	951 4,013 805 609
Unior vermilior Vermon Vashington Veneter	1,560 1,±50 720 3,460 3,500	260 355 340 650 640	4±0 350 ±70 930 845	330 .90 65 620 760	280 75 70 485 530	120 95 15 380 350	45 20 150 90	35 20 5 40	5 10 40 35	15	5	20 5 15		5	10	55 30 30 50 130	1,144 793 493 1.069
West Bato Rouge West Carroll West Feliciana	1 645 860 1,490 1,435	305 260 270 295	610 345 525 440	280 115 325 230	145 85 4°0 225	110 10 65 95	75 10 45 10	45 10 15 5	10 5	5	10	5		5	5	40 20 65	908 734 926 915

Table 46.—INCOME IN 1949 OF URBAN AND RURAL-NONFARM FAMILIES AND UNRELATED INDIVIDUALS, FOR PARISHES 1950

[Statistics pased on 20-percent sample Median ac shown where base _ see than a00'

	Urban and rura			44.4		Familie	and inre	latea mar	duals h	ring spe	ufied ne	mes		-	a the color of		Med.an	mone !	dollars
Pareh	nonfarm families and unrelated individuals	Less Jhan \$500	\$500 to \$999	\$1,000 to \$1 499	\$1,500 to \$1,999	\$2,000 to \$2,499	\$2 500° to \$2 999	\$3,300 \$3,499	\$3,500 to \$3,999	\$4,000 to \$4,499	\$4 500 to \$4 999	\$5,000 35,999	\$6,300 to \$6,999	\$7 000 to \$6 999	\$10,0.0 and over	Ireome not reported	Lrbur and rure. non arm	7 rha	Rura
Acedia Allen Ascension Assumption Aconstitut	9 310 2,955 3 950 2,420 6,55	1,33. 495 600 380 99,	1 475 685 856 5°0 1 445	1 305 485 485 430 1,170	-,090 440 360 3-0 640	065. 425 295. _75. 4401	525 360 245 1.5 485	250 230 35 3-0	360 160 _50 60 215	240 135 145 45 200	190 30 40 45 75	4-5 95 4-5 35	110: 85: 45: 15: 65:	70	19C 50 45 45	140 140 230 90 2-5	1,63 1,76 - 4.2 1,250	2,008 ,360	1,43 1,43 1,23 1,00
Bosuregard Rien ille Bossier Caddo Ce casieu	3 365 3,025 1. 260 54,985 25,970	370 540 910 5 835 2,285	30 545 1,510 7,285 2 625	445 1 -20 4 945 2,165	415 400 830 ,823 2,270	345 295 820 4 50 4,430	210 1_5 785 3,285 4 925	4,760 2,140	160 1.0 675 3,040 1 840	125 80 390 2,645 1 990	70 35 385 1,950 1 305	>5	255 -,750 870	25 25 25 20 20	20 20 20 2,2 5 6,5	25. ند	2,0/5 2,0/5 2,7% 2,7%	-,764 3,0/4 2,504 2,789	1 27
Candwell Cemeron Catahonla Claiborne Concordia	1,860 1,045 1,600 4,195 2,495	220 110 335 520 495	270 125 415 690 -30	300 100 260 480 350	295 70 1,0 390 225	245 165 -15 200 -65	20 65 65 285 200	65 85 -05 240 -00	80 90 30 365	35 20 283 73	30 42 54 54	30 30 -80 90	43 25 15 120 25	25 27 30 140 20	25 15 15 63 30	95 40 40 16° 125	1,658 2 297 -,058 1 917 -,222	2 332	1,650 2 29 1 05 1,46 1,18
De Soto East Baton Rouge East Carroll East Felician: Evangeline	3,935 -,330 2,425 - 755 -,955	6,910 6,910 675 240 735	715 4,920 255 380 1,145	625 4,245 3,0 270 680	360 3,700 225 135 515	215 3 715 145 -65 400	230 2 960 65 105 235	7,600 65 50 280	130 2,100 75 40 275	3,070 43 45 180	2,705 30 30 85	3,900 25 45	2,035 4- 20 50	2 215 -0 45	30 -,275 -5 20	315 2 950 85 145 180	-,320 2 616 94- 1,343 1,374	1,9.7 2,696 997	1,96 89 1,26
Tranclin Gran: Theria Thervile Jackson	2 460 2,555 9,40* 6,365 3,375	420 3°5 1 140 /40 310	595 695 -,364 -,625 460	305 455 1,065 895 470	205 225 1,020 670 _55	215 230 975 530 420	14.5 72.5 30.2 360	147 6 4 27. 25:	65 375 243 163	50 73 -70 -95	25 240 45 90	60 420 170 105	20 20 80 20	60 15 260 1.5 65	30 15 120	65 75 345 340 55	1,300 -,187 1 cm3 1,362 2 U77	2,193 1 983 2,572	1,79 1,18 1 60 1 24 1,97
Cefferson Dav.s Leferson Dav.s Leferson Dav.s Leferson Dav.s Leferson Dav.s	29 020 5,875 23,920 8,350 2,985	2 3.0 675 2,420 730 280	2,170 1,040 1,810 1,065	2 .65 915 1,460 1,005 4:0	2,250 685 1 495 1,050 335	3 465 .00 1,300 980 295	2,760 455 945 755 190	4,930 295 805 535 160	-,980 280 675 485 260	1 455 255 540 375 75	1 255 135 355 250 %	1 950 140 650 275 55	1,025 _00 350 285 65	1,130 120 545 175 30	790 80 310 115	205 460 330 150	2 763 1,653 1,848 2,061 1,428	2,841 1,780 1,898 2,313	2,19 1,43 1,69 1,95
limoln Livingston Madison Morehouse Matenitoches	6,-20 2 920 3 450 5,990 7,240	1,795 410 685 715 1 200	915 435 790 875 1,403	760 330 603 570 890	505 300 350 445 630	395 250 245 690 415	305 145 140 550 270	280 135 135 497 265	275 200 11,0 355 21,5	25 315	1,60 1,5 45 205 100	145 90 75 250 125	125 55 25 -30 130	125 1 0 35 115	140 20 25 80 72	140	1,236 1,638 1,149 2 203 1 111	1,395 1,38- 2,38- 1,286	1,02 1,83 1,30 1,64 1 01
Orleans Ocaohite Plaquemines Fointe Coupee Repides	194,380 22,,15 3,345 3,200 23,150	21 700 2,540 395 450 3,015	21,720 3,195 495 730 3,570	2,235 325 300 2,920	19,055 2,295 200 370 2,400	19,32 2,100 320 190 2 135	15,480 1,775 230 ±23 1,695	14,69 1,095 285 	11,053 1 310 150 85 1,750	8,320 1 010 -60 145 720	6,395 735 195 85 605	9,155 1,005 100 45 810	5,665 565 130 50 420	6,655 570 95 40 420	545 30	930	2 267 2,11/ 2 766 1,345 2 769	2 267 2,0.6 1,92, 2,026	2,20 2,26 1,20 1,40
Bed Biver Eichlen_ Tebine St Bernard St Charles	2 930 3,880 2,945 3,030	440 605 375 420	260 570 910 430 495	195 340 715 310 270	80 250 395 310 250	75 300 275 305 250	205 230 180	80 135 270 290	40 .75 115 105	35 135 70 150 180	240	90	55 30 65	35 35 35 75 100	40	190 190	1,226 ± 570 -,231 2 021 ±,982	1 542 3 153 3,474	1,59 1,59 1,64 1,55
St Helphe St James St John the Baptist Ct Landry St Kartin	675 2,335 3,450 12,0,5 4,275	415 385 1 780 260	110 -60 70 2 -15 965	100 330 410 1,780 615	370 370 1,3_5 480	190 445 1,050 435	50 290 675 200	40 -25 2°5 570 260	15 35 110 560 145	35 65 80 705 125		45 70 400 40	10 20 45 -90 60	35 240 75	155	400	1,795	2,425 1 727 1,405	1,26 1,21 1,45 1,32 1,42
St Mary St lemmany Tangupahoa Tenses Terrebonne	8 640 6,4_5 10,885 1 605 9,420	1,210 1,210 2,160 340 870	1 260 1,125 2 280 380 1,440	260	9,5 770 1 45 45 930	54 790 100 102	615 400 540 93 705	605 305 555 65	395 245 300 55 555	475 145 305 30 395	15	390 19: 180 50 395	260 90 85 35 260	275 75 170 30 230	115	380 630		2,383 1 613 1,448 2,338	1,35 1,35 1,03 1,13 -,73
dn_or Termilion Vermon vasmingtor .cboter	3,090 7,185 3,400 7,675 7,905	1,270 775 880 730	595 1,415 725 1,490 1 045	410 1,C50 495 845 945	420 780 370 775 870	285 620 255 815 990	270 360 115 620 e15	165 365 105 465 590	1:0 250 115 415 550	75 180 70 280 335	100 75 200	€.5	30 135 40 215 150	50 1.0 25 135 137	140 30 90	140 140	1,131 1,966 2,093	1,435 1,441 2,112 2,175	1,30 1,30 98 1,66 2,02
Vest Bator Pouge Vest Carroll Vest Felicians Vinn	2,070 1,695 1,175 3 160	2±0 29° 115 435	380 395 335 715	275 270 185 440	185 130 365	190 107 80 365	135 65 40 90	125 80 65 145	-25 45 40 100	65 25 55	_0	45	60 25 -0 25	25 15 40	20	75	1,270	2,833	1,25

Table 47.—INDIANS, JAPANESE, AND CHINESE, BY SEX, FOR SFLECTED PARISHES AND CITIES 1950
[Pagures shown for parabel and for cities o 10,000 inhabitants or more with 10 or nore Indiana, Japanese or Chinese in 1950]

-		Indians			Japanese			Ch.nese		Parish or city		Indians	100		Japanese			Chinese	
Pansh or city	Total	Male	Female	Total	Male	Femalo	Tota.	Male	Female	Parish or elev	Total	Male	Female	Total	Male	Female	Total	Male	Fema
PARISHES									ł,	PARISEES-Con								1	5
Boss or Caddo Consordia	12 25	13	12	3	2	1 2	6 48	± 28 28	20	Orleans Ouachita Flagueminso	79 13 15	40 9 10	4	35 6	21 4	14 2	36~	182 1	11
East Beton Rouge East Carroul	12	16 8	8 4	14	8	6	28 9	16	12	Rapiles St Mary	89	2	35	10	3	7	4	.2	
Thorville Jefferson	2 3	1 3	1	4 26	3	21	30	16	1 8	CITIES					١.				
La Salle Madison Norehouse	49	29	20	2	1	1	0	6	4 2	Baton Rouge New Orleans Shreveport	79 21	15 40 -3	39 8	35	21	14	300 40	82 22	11

T-ble 48 —Characteristics of the Bural-Monfary Population, for Parishes 1950

hattrail. * concless anaetics have on 20-percent sampes or corresponding compete-court figures on age, see age distribution in this table. Median not shown where base is less than 500]

	-	and the last of th		_	MANAGE THE	-	Married World	-						Clai-	Con-		Enst
Bult est	A. dia	~1-6-	-18° IA I	Ar. Jap-	\$40) - 680	Bes - regard		Bossier	Oaico	Ca_sa_ a_at	Cald-	Cameron	Cata- nol_a	borne	cordia	De Soto	Baton Rouge
	-			902	-		9 888	3 74	28,23/	-9,473	5,901	4 050	4 852	5-550	4,207	7,82/	. 2, 284
Tota, ran-nontarm population	13,24	6.0	10 502	_	4, 122	6.10.	2 -95	5,728	9,8-4	2,110	∠,058	924	1,576	1,705	1,_40	1.807	4,072
Male Native write	4,500	2,87	3 339	4,5-	2			_0	72	00	12 863	11	787	1,02	903	1,93	3 -58
Negro	547	£**,	1 930	355	- 1622	5.7	2 339	2,3 -	4,.38	1,04	863						6
Other was	- 2m2	2,370	3,	2 074	4 737	2,.21	c 6.2	3,096	9,684	7.763	2,100	1,750	⊥ 293	a 677	1,070	1,829	4,045
Female Native was e	18	-/		2.	2_	11	2,423	38 2,452	*,472	43 723	8 860	167	892	1,1.9	1 084	2,240	3,530
Negro Other acea	20.5	1.	2 039	-,	72	552	2,423	2,402	4,472	- 72	000	201	4,-	2	1		4
Other aces	1 .				1		- 1										
Marc all ages	5	a 80%	- 296		6 G47	2 .30	4,34	8,,50	.3,998	9,944	2,933	2,126	2,365	2 744	2,048	3,743	7,273
Lnoer 5 mars .	7.0	*0J	P 9	F-5	~	40	o06	833	1,870	_,468	403	31.3 25.5	324 241	392 3_8	259 208	-70	1 .18
o to 9 years	615	372	237 527	570 4 '2	601 601	245	527	524	- 528	1,003	430	2_+	220 174	271	.00	380	809
15 to 19 years.	5 40	202	362	3.6	404	245 213	316	9:2	1,045	723	251 94	149	174	271 213 179	1/2	269 206	632 536
20 to 24 years.	1Jc	257	300	3_6	404	152	- 26 204	1,808	351	798	386	158	160	202	15	21.6	553 514
25 tr 29 /ears	340	295	358	304 276 303	40_ 290	402 482	,2,	650	9-2	731.	17 /	165	136 170	167	139 ±27	202 217	514 560
30 to 34 years	374	2.7	3_2	1,05	. 94 x09	785	302	4e5 368	950 gon	709 627	182	140	144	153	1.28	202 202	445 358
40 to 44 years	278 265	240 _92	29.	25-	294	446 446	31º 254	290	873	533	160	122	121	-40	131	202	358
55 to 54 years 45 to 99 years 55 to 5- years 55 to 59 years	ele.	158	202 170 169	_87	294 254	-09	252	215	725	290		.06 58	219	153 -40 132 98	95 86	_43 178	264
55 to 59 years	7	145	1./	203	248	85 85 _70	18.	_27	436	226	128	58 25 29	71.1	79	70	-19	-74
65 to 63 years 70 to 74 years	1321	102	1:55	_50 164	_89 24u	_70	12	.36	428	222	95 82	29	99	80 25	83 56	161	132
70 to 74 years	-86 -06	52	104	118	-70	C2	1.34	118	298	136	87	34	83	619	63	125	-46
75 years and over								1,590	14,236	9,532	2,908	1,930	2,487	2,806	2,159	4,684	7,611
Female zil ages	5 072	3,0%	5,226	*,556	6.34	2 784	5,047	872	- 772	1,300	365		281	371	272	/69	1,137
nder o years	57/	4/3	009	5401	641	327	516	646 489	1,576	1,300	303	232	260	297	21.4	478	896
5 to 9 years 10 to 1 a years 15 to 19 years	560	3.4	473	.C7 394	501	278 266	462 429	489	984	9.3 790	281 249	186	243 195	263 245	_66	324	75 , 548
15 to 19 years	560 461 38.	358	396 407	320	440	210	350	392 469	1 065	838	204)	162 178	17-	217	156	296	651
20 to 24 years	350	2-2	4.C 352	3-0	4.8	19.	330	469	1,054	725	135	170	165	21.1	164	560	712
30 to 34 years	3,0	2-2	352 287	281	368	_80 197	348 36+	445 379	97-	69.	2.3	-39 142	154	177	48	270 242	498
35 to 39 years	202	244	296	300 246 25	337 294	144	321	305 250	943	577	179	132	150	173	1.2	233	123
50 to 59 years 55 to 59 years	259	20_	296 245 207	205	294 273	92	283 250	194	675	427 298	165	101	135	108	122	194	258
50 to 54 years	1,5	125	200	208	272	96 109	1.94	122	534	265	135	-6	95	AO1	86	190	200
60 to 64 years 65 to 69 years	147	121	2.0	88 238	279 J15	100	172	144	431	178	205	25	±00 133	73	62	131	227
65 to 69 years 70 to 74 years	122	10.	2:0	248 148	752	-02	200	172 85	473 304	196	96 7-	33 24	53	94 54	47	1.9	107
75 years and over	92	65	120	148	204	41 58	142	123	256	132	9_	24	82	54	52	109	148
*YEARS OF SCHOOL COMPLETED		- 1		1			- 1	- 1		1	- 1			300	4.1		
Persons 25 years old and over	4,845	3,725	500	4 650	0 525	2 710	5,240	4,215	15 055	9,700	3,120	±,845	2,580	2,~15	2,400	3 945	7 440
No school years comple.ed	1,405	-35	020	96C	1,215	190	325	320	820 2,745	1,055	\$2 615	300 375	380 550	21.0 485	180 625	1,115	- 35 - 450
Elementary 1 to 4 years	1 030	675 670	1,420 855	790	1,000	440	840	810	1,755	1 375	590 310	30o	/35	390	355	585	1.140
7 years	300	330	405	310	535	345	565	470	1,330	875	310	190	200	240	270	300	5.5
H.gn school 1 to 2 years	275 520	36C 460	380 640	330	435 965	255 375	360 995	1,050	1,520 3 240	7.5	335 670	135	_85 4.1	3.5	450	230	1.150
	270	385	370	250	145	300	43.5	365 440	1,735	1,330	J951	225 170	145	220	450 135	733 125	8.5
Coilege I to 3 years	150	60	70	95	280	70 65	270 250	2.5	865 535	360 280	115	35	_20	190	65	160	370 270
Sepool years not reported	1.0	1	10 5 9	SC	21.5	45 7 2	1.00	2.0	5,0	224	90	50	95 55	70	70	1,60	395
Median schoo years completed	4 "	68	59	40	2 0	7 2	7 5	8 3	8 4	- 3	7 7	0.5	6 5	c 8	70	6 2	74
EMPLOYMENT STATUS AND MAJOR OCCUPATION GROUP		i			-	1		- 1	- 1		. 1				-		
Male, 14 years old and over	3,357	2 518	3,342	3 101	4 078	7,774	3.299	6.25	9.434	6,500	2.42	1.38.	1.62	1,808	1 426	2,424	4,863
Lapor roree Civilian labor 'oree	2.334	1,837	2,283	3 101 2,089	4 078 2,577 2,477 2,405	1,203	2,35	5,452 2 171	9,434 7,009		2,042	1,38.	1,030	1,34/	913	1.6.4	3,463
Employea-	2,331	1,835	2,283	2,089	2,404	1,203	2,354	2,091	6,939	4,931	1,423	1,087	950	1,292	9_3 8"5	1,612	3,404
\nemployed \ Not in labor force	201	97	2.21	143	172	84	82	801	244	309	93	55	-8	50	36	59	25"
	1 025	681	±,□o8	± C12	1,501	571	942	823	2 425	1,562	619	293	901	464	513	810	1 400
Female 14 years old and over . Labor force	3,354	2,525	3,50	3,356	4,402	-,359	3,992	787	3 827	6,212	2,069	± 200	1,750	273	1,509	2,829	4,976
Civilian iabor force	410	469 469	590	558 558	549 549	257 257	720	7-	1,950	903	328	171	353 353	275	587 587	605	1,076
Employed	281 12	454	595 559 36	537	532	252	708	75	1,920	868	319	168	343	209:	264	568	1,019
Not in abor force	2,04-	2.056	2,911	2 828	3,854	1,602	2,866	2,882	7,867	5 309	1.741	1.129	1,39%	1.648	1,228	2,424	3,900
Mair employed	2,130	1,738	2,071	- 946	2,405	1,119	2 272	2,091	6,698	4,622	_,330	1 032	940	1,292	872	4,553	3,204
Professional technical and cindred workers	102	8	96	82	124		56 56	89	336 134	237	76	38 34	9	68	47	77	_85
Farmers and farm managers Managers, officials, and proprietors except farm	178	46 172	143	26	145 290	43 95	58 243	73 177	625	333	28	87	118	0.3	84	62 118	80 181
Clencal and kindren workers	57	60	43	54	78	21	82	66	303	149	46	20	35	20	18	39	1.4
Sales workers	57 68	287	119	93	433	43 489	105	76	325	1.31	201	2 <u>.</u> 196	35 55 139	56 32 230	28	39 74 210	9.5
Craftamen, foremer, and kindred workers.	320 422	287 509	428	390	31.2	298	3±6 484	361 407	1,528	1,069	240 244	196 323	157	427	192	334	689 678
	1.1	1	7	2	2	1		81	29	14	21		21		31	6	14
Private household workers Service workers except private household Farm laborers, unpaid family workers Tarm laborers except untaid, and farm foremen. Laborers except turn and mini.	74 36	70	95	100	75 21	33	70	66	232	200	56 16	4.	43	20	30	34 26	153
Carm inhorers excep unpaid, and farm foremen.	421	105	274	334	282	28	123	368	453 925	174	38	68	220	143 176	48	202 336	242
Cocupation not reported	321 45	292	325	424	-√73 36	288	588 33	3*6	925 108	72.	401	24	220	±76	203	336 35	72E 41
Female, employed	381	454	559	537	532	252	708	714	1 920	868	313	168	243	209	264	518	1,019
Professiona' technical, and kindred workers		68	61	90	105	46	-32	-17	_90	107	69	31	68	/1	39	83	116
Farmers and farm r.anagers	01 1 4'	2	2		4		1	01	14	2	2				6	2	4
Managers officials, and proprietors except farm.	4/	36	26	16	43	15	47	35	150	58 152	27	18	23	12	19	-0	47 138
alse workers	28	40	04	52	39 50	32 40	75 84	66	313 477	102	39	24	32	33	35	50 47 7	60
raftemen foremen and andred workers.		31	5	1	2		1	21	19	5	3/		11		1.1	7	- 4
Prerawves and kinured workers	9.	30 94	133	57	15	12	20	230	104	49	2	8	11	11	19	782	78
er ice workers except private 'icusehold	23	99	74	239	-05 73	41	90	94	434 286	201	46	41	-2	21	24	71	355 460
ram isomers except private busehold and service except unit blade except unit blade except unit blade and arm foremen.	4	2		11	37		15	-6	15.	1			30	3	5	182 71 5	20
Aborers, except 'arm and mine		. 5	40	12	2	2	4	7	17	10	6	4	70	23	8	6	12
ecusation not reported	10	14	1_	22	-0	2	18	12	24	19	2	\$	3	=	2	6	13

Table 48—CHARACTERISTICS OF THE RURAL-NONFARM POPULATION FOR PARISHES 1950—Con.

(Asteroik (*) denotes statutum based on 20-percent sample, for corresponding compute-count figures or age, see ugo distribution in disc table. Means not above where case is see than a00

			East				1		No. of Concession,	Discourage residence	_	-	- entrantement	-				_
	Subject	Carron	Pa .c-	gel_ne	Trank-	Grant	Therie	ville	e.skaur	erter-	Jeffer- Dav.s	A-		.a.	Lin ou	in 'ng-	Marison	40 .7
	al raral-nonfarm population	2,240	4 163	10,485	-,762	9 187	12,234	17 723	9,052	20,707	7,134	л ,138	43,08A	9,347	6,604	v,99r	-,640	1 5
ale	Native white.	489	965	1,416	1,346	3,406	3,890	3 652	3, .82	4,44	2,553	4 121	10,220	4,369	-,*02	3,005		
	Foreign-born white Negro Other races	626	_,042	704	396	34 86-	2,210	3,050		581	10	25 842	→ D	580		1,738		3
male	Other races	3		41	7	2	1		4,386	893	2746		222	580	-,398		355	1
CLANE .	Foreign born white.	415	983	4,388	1,491	3,66+	3 824	3,608	3,152	4,239	2,538	1,226	9,984	4,32	1,416	3,962	443	1
	Negro	697	1,159	8 9	5.2		2,208	1,40	1,41	903	1,016	892	1,202		1,474	20	340	
		4				-,	1	6	2	6	3	032	1,202	6e0 20	1,000	973	1	
	AGE	1 122	2 010						- 1									1
per 5	all ages		320	5,228	4,753	4.506	6,9	8,840	4,473	5,431	3 502	4,969	1_,683	→ , 989	3,10-	5,042	842	2
9 yes	LTS	172	219	587	2_5 201	587 519	889	1,195	579 526	2031	509	7c5	1,750	612	577	730	108	
0 14:	PRAPE	97	165	507	253 129	443 356	658	923	500	520 404 425	372	526	1,437	557	324	273 484	88	1
0 24 3	Vears	8c 78	-31	434	129	355 256	523	~02	372	404	261	39"	1,009	392	325	274	43	1
29	PERITR	72 49 68	.68	340	-20 98	250	424 438	590	279	483	254	298	93b	327 318	413 252	4.6		1
34		49	_44	358	- 4	297	428	578 541 552	294 327	325	223	3£3	393 753	355 371 318	200 204 187	349 340	52	
0 44 3	TOATS	56	_20	308 317	9 86	316 273	446 384 309	499	288	405	238 208	351 295	753 627	371	204	340 296	75 54 56	1
0 49	PORTS	48	94 78	268	130	232	309	499 46c	361	34.	186	203	524	334 233	147	271	54 5b	1
0 09	MAIS	56 48 20 47	54	222	130 56 72 54	_90 207	242	368 385 311	185 155	235	ي36	lu" 173	379 340	233	97	94 138	56 31	1
0 64	rears	36	64	160	54	.70	158	311	129	1:0	124	1.4	201	179	97 89 59 89 48 57	138	31	
0 69	Pears	25 38	64	93	80 53	164	155	343	127	103	154	-23	22- 108	155	89	138	30	
ests	and over	49	36 57	125	75	127	93	214	78	51,	75 62	73 96	129	92	48	70 94	33 30	
	ie, ail ages	2,118	2,155	5,257	2,009	4,681	6,2,5	8, 983	4,578	5,276	3,572	5,149	11,408	5,008	3,500	4,954	8C4	1
er 5	rears	154 113	294 251	309 578	237	524	836	+ 195	368	836	497	693	1,50	590	429	786	116	-
9 year	ATS	113	251	578	184	537	766	1,007	-84	6.5	CR21	492	1 397	54.8	310	562	90	1
19	rears	70	161	440	1.4	329	628 539	849 670	471	4-7	359	430 420	1,002	469 440	309	436	90 76 97	1
		90 70 82 78 66 62	194	367 382	136	307	500	590	329	423 483	321	/701	970	324 371	309 369 473 272	393 486 418	63	1
29	766275	66	118	362	152	323	45%	564 590	330	4% 392	2351	445	921	371	272	41.8	54	1
39	rears	62	130	290	136	321	442	563	330 344 363	403	21 81	389 344 289 247 207	844 784	406 363 317	202 233 196 50 23 99 97	325	53 54 52 55 35, 48	1
49	COATS	54	104	200	92 115	305 228	332	472	283 216	30 ₀	202	289	564 514	317	196	21.9	35	
54	rears	01 54 53	114	513 378	90	234	253 224	403	178	207	139	2471		290 251 172 1.77 1.78	-50 23	227	48	1
59	/eazs	47 37 54	65	SOO	90 99	2001	164	392		43	130	201	330	172	99	162	32	i
a 69 :	rears	54	66 97	193	87 113	1.56 1.98	167	309	150	-43 94 65	114	142	33° 255 283	1.7	97	109	27	
0 74	rears .	36 47	57	161	40	102	94	392 309 -04 182	90	63	60	991	283 28 28	89	60	91	14	1
	and over	47	83	88	64	128	101	233	87	59	797	110	728	91	69	84	4.	1
	ns 25 years old and over	1,340	2,080	5,145	2 155	4 625	5,775	8,865	4,482	5,155	3,385	5,050	10 370	5 185	3 030	4 750	990	١.
	vesrs complexed	185	_90		90	400	7 (40	7 660	180	660	752		2 630	325	3 030	210	90	1
nen.	ry 1 to 4 years	510	505	1,525	345 235	830	1,460	1 660 3,110 ,480 530	900	995	F85	1,130 995 680	3,005	81.5	575 350	985	200	1
	7 years	210	300 140	700	345	780 490	945 385	*,480	63.5	910	235	680	1 545	870	350	780	2°0 135	
	8 years	95 85	160	160	133	605	255		2101	465	230	320	835 430	555	190	48C	55 70 130	ł
u acu	ool. 1 to 3 years	85 55	310	470 320	400 1_D	76C 440	4.35 52.5	730	930	535	350 240	520	430 645	475 1,1_5 5_5	220 710 315	1,030	130	1
ege	1 to 8 years	25 30	110	_35 _00	140	270	140	170	300 140	2.5	100	520 490 285	450 240 155	285	33.5 285	235	75 20 20	1
	4 years or more	30	160	100	1.0	180	80	110	75	145	400	270	155	160	230	140	20	
lian s	ars not reported	30 4 7	50 7.1	4 3	7 3	7 5	95 4 8	205	75 120 7 6	6 9	55	6 3	135	8.0	70 9 3	77	5 9	l
EM	PLOYMENT STATUS AND MAJOR OCCUPATION GROUP			,,	, ,	, ,	10		, ,	6 9	-	6.3	•	8 4	,,	77	5.9	1
	14 years old and over	753	1,336	3,501	1,201	3,046	3,992	5,882	2,965	3,640	2,327	1 184	7 454	3,409	2 231	3 374	504	١,
	labor force	476	1,041	2,240 2,237 2,091	1,211 758 757	984	3,017	3,851	2 129	2,797 2,786 2,667	1 688	3,384 2,494 2,490	5,923 5,919 5,633	2,380	1 220	3,314	596 429	1 1 1
Emp	loved.	475 450 25	1,024	2 091	725	.,876	3,015 2,867		2,128	2,786	1,687	2,40	5,919	2 385	1,217	2 452	429 404 25	1 3
Unet	aployed	25	17	1,321	32		148 975	2,031	113	1,9	55	85	285	105	43	120	25	1
	ber force	277	290		453	1,062		2,031	836	813	639	890	1 534	-, 023	991	858	167	1
or for	e 14 years old and over	779	1 474	3,626	1,453	3,220	3,994	1,083	3,347	3,482	2,394 408	3,608	7,483 860	3,490 534	2,503	3,236	533	2
ivilia	oe a labor force	141 150	409 409	468 468	307	490	708	1,083	589	613	408 394	The	860	533	467	676	94 94 91	1
Lore	loyed	250	405	458	303	476	690	1,039	564 25	57°	394	685	821 39	5.9	456 11	655	91	1
m la	bor force	658	1 065	3,158	1,146	2,730	18 3 286	4,9.1	2,557	2,869	1,980	2,907	F,623	2 956	2 035	2 560	437	1
Male	amploved	450	1,024	2,091	725	1,876	2,867	3,557	2,018	2,667	1 022	2,404	5,633	2,280	1,174	2,332	404	1
08800	nal, technical, and kindred workers and farm managers , officials, and proprietors, except farm and kindred workers.	24	52	125		105	78	113	70	139	74	130	140	133	104	102	15	-
ners	and farm managers	20 42	26	92 1.89	48	37 158	39 150	226	35	17	188	76	84	31	43	60	21	1
ical s	nd kindred workers	42	91 38	1.89	72 48 64 25	158	150	22.C	35 -27 68	293 125	250	242 89	84 472 119	194 66	43 106 47	208	20 13	1
s wo	kers	6 :4 54 1:0	33	128	72	891	67 100	92	58	98 480	77	149 561	195	97	60 245	107	12	1
		1:0	156 242	353 513	72 146 124	335 385	512 793	458 695	742	480 586	289 273	561. 45>	812	384 899	245 28b	509	73 81	1
ate h	s and kindred workersousehold workers	1	1	5	1.1	1	8	5		5	1	5	6	2	266	568	2	1
n lak	orkers except private household orers, unpaid family workers	11	39	92	26	72	89	137	13	124	54	117	188	68	60	62	11	1
n lab	overs except unpaid and farm foremen.	91	71	24 143	69	83	544	742	30	37	265	22	712	3	12	11.		
gle10	except farm and mine	81	257	334	62	445	344 440 44	804	437	735	258	255 271	712 1 488	22 304	49 148	_23 442	91	1
	on not reported.	3.30	405	29 458	303	93 476	650	1,039	39	25 577	394	2a 685	/8 821	78 51.9	13 456	51	3	1
	e, employed.	2.30	51	458 85	303	101	650	91	61	97	394 56	685 89	250	519 91	115	655 78	14	+
Ders.	and farm managers	3	5	3	1	2	41			1	4	1		2	3	4	1	1
nagen	and farm managers officials and proprietors, except farm.	9	24	27	19	40	25	30	24	20	22	32	33	42	19	57	1 2	
	nd kindred workers	9 4	55	41 65	32	50 58	25 90 68	27 77 74 3	22	89	49 44 4	119 96	102	73	56 31	111 94 1	12	
ical i	n loremer and kindred workers		55 27 2	3 1	32 39 1 9	1 21		3	4	42	4	/	91	71	2	1	12 13	
acal s s wou tisme		7	17	12	9	21 85	104	33 266	267 105	69	113	47 157	79 109 119	24 84	26 89	108		
rical in second in the second	e and kindred workers		207															11
rical in second in the second		37	121	98	29	98	171	166	89	120	59	92	119	-02	84	118	26	
rical in second in the second	e and kindred workers ousehold workers orkers except private bousehold orers, unpaid family workers	37 16	67	12 98 97 7	29	98	82	166	89	120	59	92	119	⊿0 7	84	118	22 16	
rical in second in the second	is and kindred workers outseloid workers orkers except private bousehold overs, scoept unpaid, and farm foremen except farm and mine	37	121 67 6 20 2	98 97 7 7	9	98	82	166	89	120	59	92 7 19	119 2 90 14	3 3 34	84 1 5 1 24	118 7 43 1		

Table 48 —CHARACTERISTICS OF THE RURAL-NONFARM POPULATION FOR PARISHES 1950—Con

MOTE -- Crueuns Parish, endirely urban, not showr " this bable

GENERAL CHARACTERISTICS

18-101

Table 48 —CHARACTERISTICS OF THE RURAL-NONFARM POPULATION, FOR PARISHES 1950—Con.

[Asteralk (*) cenotes statistics based on 20-percent sample, for corresponding complete-count figures on aga, are age distribution in this tacle. Medium not access where case is less than 500°

- 1	Subject	Canga shoa	7ensam	"етиерияле	union	~~E1ca	(r=-0=	*385-	de.s.er	wes B on	de t	Feld_ana	/um
	rural nonferm population.	17,264	4,800	20,069	10,237	12,652	_ € 367	7,-18	1_050	- 14	4,782	6,328	~, 6P
For	reign-born white	5,341 152	1,020	7,730	3,410	4 -6	2 838	≥,£47 16	5 24 J	349	813	1,5-0	-,73
Ne	gro	2 132	1,200	1,845	1,6	764	283		- 8:1	1 245	454	2,717	580
male Na	steve white	5,575	1 086	7,470	3,40	4 489	2 933	2 587	5,342	995	-,964	693	1,08
Ne	reign-born white	3,426	-,467	1,979	±,°20	~28 ~79	294	13	1 275	121	5	**	
Ott	her races			/62	-,		2500	-,007	7 =/5	-,3G-2	5.5-	1,504	6.5
Male all	1 sges	8,029	2.24	13,466	5,000	1,050	3,,321	3,730	7 30	2,213	2,278	4,324	2,380
der 5 years	un	1,230	28.2 238	1,708	682	694	392	573	-,5-2	529	250	25.	325
to 14 year to 19 /ear	Mi	813	207	1,092	532	577 609	387 240	435 370 265	718	23- 192	24.	179	289
to 24 year	Ars	605 605	147	905	347	377	2+0 170	265 288	527 469	185 153	181	29	.9'
to 34 year to 34 year to 39 year	Ars	643 506	130	790 697	359 368 344	379	193	290 253	538	169	1.79	690	16
to 39 year to 44 year	urs	530	145	744	358	413	-95	263	529 58	14/	131	460. 373	.5 16
to 49 year	urs	532 487	125	528	323	335 280	179	250	468	131	200	307	-3
to o4 year to u9 year	N79	39,1 29,5	103	356	2.5	225	108	104	265	108	106	166	8
to 64 year	LT8	7.39	7	28/	145	205 140	108	91	229	77	99	131	8
to 69 year to 74 year	MT8	307 189	68	206	170	144	122	107	185	81. 73	-C2	88	8
YEARS ADO	dover	195	92	155	123	103	07	74 59	124	58 58	81	46 64	5
	sil ages	8,935	2,568	10 203	5,158	5 297	2,235	3,088	6,948	2,308	2,504	2,004	2,30
der 5 years		1,277 1,505 782	291 226	1 728	652 533	6.38 258	349 40/	551	93a 798	378 2e5	299 265	275 22-	33
to 14 year to 19 year	in	782 796	196 165	1,154	444	527	327	412 315	652	2,3	224	172	21
to 19 yea to 24 yea	in	708	160	829	368	429	2051	328	572	163	164	153	18
to 29 year to 34 year	ATS	683 57.	180	785	410	386 390	204	296 268	5-4 620 590	169	196 154 -55	132	
to 39 year to 44 year	urs.	570	480	632	375	345	20/	250	520	126	.68	137	13
to 49 year to o4 year	NT	435	-75 -53	470	282	327	189	213 185	368 317	128	135 136 103 101	121	17.
to of year	MT	238 284	ر35	3C3 273	223	284 219 186	150	128	259	91	136	71	25
to 64 year to 69 year	urs	253	75	1.98	200	128	11.	117 92 102	197 155	88 67	,C3	65	90 80
to 74 year	urs	226	125	225	162	149	_34 62	102	202 105	76 40	122	52	81
years and	ARS OF SCHOOL COMPLETED	189	99	144	140	117	20	69	113	50	71	78	40
	25 years old and over	8,935	2,600	005 8	5,460	5,310	3,250	605,د	ь 845	2 220	2 725	3,835	2,340
school y	ears completed	1,175	265	2,000	355	1,425	11.5	260	390	390	.90	465	760
ementer y	1 to 4 years	1.460	7-∕1 350	2 540	1,025	1,365	765 595	610 550	910	595 415	530 465	980 675	470
	7 years 8 years	655 775	160	585	835 523	6n5 3.0	435	345	690	170	240 305	275	205
gh school	1 to 3 years	1,100	170 -85	425 780	265 1,125 335	2-5 400 370	365 680	325 620	905	110 250	305 465	275 405	270 330
llege	1 to 3 years	71.5	220	160	335 350	370 185	_00 60	320	84J 21J	250 175 30	155	265	230
	4 years or more	2/0	125	125	225	140	70	250	140	50	180	125	90
edian scho	ool years completed	6 4	6 7	4 6	7 9	4 4	73	8 C	8 2	35 5.5	7 0	6 3	1.35
EMPL	OCCUPATION GROUP				i . i		1						
bot force.	years old and over	5,711	1 261	5,194	2,467	3,594 2,529 2,529 2,375	2,004	4,424	4,608	1,49,	1,564	3 756 826	1,037
Civilian a	abor force	4, 12 4, 106 3,978	144	2 104 4,916	2,466	2,529	-,110	4,772	3,235	1,020	957	826	1,035
Employ Unempl	loyed	3,978	1,022	278	117	1541	,073 37	1,720	193	123	923 34	802	993
e m labor	r force	+ 59□	417	1 254	358	4,060	946	649	1,234	473	604	2,9.50	349
bor force	14 years old and over	6 012	1,893	6,174	3 60p 560	3 G95 661	2,205	2,467	4,677 706	.,490	1,755	2, -07	1,539
	abor force.	1 650	*62	-88	550	66C	244	530	733	269	394	219	171
Unempl	loved.	+,631 49	539	830	549 11	23	234	52°	67> 28	267	385 8	3	16
t in labor	n force	3,978	1,331	5,291 4,910	2,249	3,036 2,375	1,961	1,971	3,5 12	:,201	1,361	1 448	_,36
	uptoyed	3,978					1.073	1,720	2,047	897 21	923	802 46	993
ferronal	technical, and kindred workers	176		138									3/
fessional	technical, and kindred workers	176 146	72 38	138	-22 03	105	77	133	13/	17	62	25	,
rmers and	officials, and proprietors, except farm	345 101	72 38 143	138 50 337 130	235	9, 105 227 61	77 74 73 32	133 39 154 27	257 257	17 5⁄ 34	38	72	0.
rmers and	officials, and proprietors, except farm	146 345 101 183	72 38 143 29 64	136 50 337 130 200	235 80 97	9, 105 227 61	77 73 32	133 39 144 57	257 257	17 5⁄ 34	38	72	0.
ressional rmers and magers of grical and se worker aftemen in	d farm managers officials, and proposetors, except farm kindred workers foreman and kindred workers and kindred workers	345 101	72 38 143 29 64 174	138 50 337 100 200 651	235 80 97 343	9, 105 227 61	77 74 73 32	133 39 154 27	257 -25 06 290 9-0	17	36 63 172 126	25 76 23 43 449 4361	2 2 2 1 3
ofessional rimers and singers of grical and les worker aftsmen if eratives a syste hour	I farm managers. fificals, and proprietors, except farm kindred workers forcemen and kindred workers and kindred workers which workers which workers are truyers becausehold.	146 345 101 173 571 695 4	72 39 143 29 64 174 15.	138 50 337 100 200 651 1,134	235 80 97 343 604	9, 105 227 61 111 395 437 7	77 73 32 54 193 237	133 39 154 57 11_ 294 434	257 -25 -06 -290 9-0 6	1.7 5/ 34 26 50	38	72 23 43 49 4361 7	24 26 13 27:
ofessional rimers and singers of grical and les worker aftsmen if eratives a syste hour	I farm managers. fificals, and proprietors, except farm kindred workers forcemen and kindred workers and kindred workers which workers which workers are truyers becausehold.	146 345 101 183 571 695 4 139 30	72 38 143 29 64 174 15. 7	138 50 337 100 200 651 4,134 2 20_ _2	235 80 97 343 604 6	9, 105 227 61 111 395 43° 7 105 24	77 73 32 54 193 237 237	133 39 154 57 11_ 294 434 1 46 13	297 -25 -26 -590 9-9 6	17 % 24 25 50 177 48	15/ 38 63 172 126 3 30 7	72 23 43 449 4361 7 49 3	20 20 137 27:
ofessional rmers and maggers of rical and les worker aftsmen i eratives a rvate hous vote work rm lapore	if farm managers. fiftings, and propuretors, except farm kindred workers foremen and kindred workers- and kindred workers- such old workers such old workers are, unpead farmly workers are, unpead farmly workers are, except unpead and farm foremen	146 345 101 173 571 695 4 139 30 825 668	72 39 143 29 64 174 15.	136 50 337 130 200 651 1,134 2 21 _2 23_ 339 1,727	22 03 235 80 97 343 704 6 74 6	9, 105 227 61 111 395 43° 7 105 24 460 318	77 73 32 54 193 237 239 8 48	133 39 144 27 11_ 294 434 1 46 132 261	257 -25 -25 -26 -290 9-0 6 6 97 -389	17 54 26 50 177 48 1	15/ 36 63 172 126 3 30 7 52	72 23 43 49 4361 7 49 3 61	24 26 137 27:
ofessional rimers and singers of grical and se worker aftsmen is eratives a crutives a rivate house vivate house vivate house vivate house rivate br>rivate house rivate br>rivate house rivate	i farm managers. findinals, and propurators, except farm funded workers foreman and kindred workers and kindred workers such convictors workers and kindred workers such cold workers eas, except private household, suppad family workers , except ungad, and farm foremen copt farm and mine my reported	146 345 101 183 571 695 4 139 30 825 668 63	72 36 143 29 64 174 15 7 45 5 147 44	136 50 337 100 200 651 4,134 2 201 2 339 1,717	235 80 97 343 704 6 74 6 48 524 37	9, 105 227 61 111 395 43° 7 105 24 450 318 34	77 73 73 73 73 73 73 73 73 73 73 73 73 7	133 39 144 57 11_ 294 434 434 132 132 261_ 45	5% 297 -25 56 590 9-5 6 6 97 589 67	17 54 26 50 177 48 1 480 184	15/ 38 63 172 126 3 30 7 52 12/ 23	72 23 43 49 43 49 49 49 49 49 61 208	2/2 2/1 2/7 2/7: 2/2 3/2 2/4
ofessional rimers and magers o rical and ses workers aftsmen i eratives a tvate house rical and magers rical and restives a tvate house rical and restives rical and restives rical and restives rical and restives rical and restives rical and restives rical and restives rical and restives rical and restives rical and	i farm managers. finals, and proposetors, except farm kindred workers with the control of the c	146 345 101 183 571 6°5 4 139 30 825 668 63	72 39 143 29 64 174 15, 15, 17 45 12 45 17 45 17 17 17 18	136 50 337 130 200 651 1,134 2 21 _2 23_ 339 1,727	22 235 235 40 97 343 704 6 46 48 524 37	9, 105 227 61 111 395 43° 7 105 24 460 318	77 73 32 54 193 37 39 48 48 48 19 234	133 39 144 27 11_ 294 434 1 132 261 261	257 -25 -25 -26 -290 9-0 6 6 97 -389	17 54 26 50 177 48 1	15/ 38 53 172 126 3 30 7 52 12/ 23 38	72 23 43 449 4361 7 49 3 61 208	24 24 26 137 272 24 25 25 47
ofessional rimers and magers o rical and ses workers aftsmen i eratives a tvate house rical and magers rical and restives a tvate house rical and restives rical and restives rical and restives rical and restives rical and restives rical and restives rical and restives rical and restives rical and restives rical and	i farm managers. finals, and proposetors, except farm kindred workers with the control of the c	146 345 101 173 571 605 4 137 30 825 608 53 1,631	72 3e 143 29 64 174 15, 7 45 5 147 4 539 78	138 50 337 100 200 651 1134 2 21 22 21 22 39 1,717 35 830	235 80 97 343 604 6 6 74 6 48 524 37	9, 105 227 61 111 395 437 7 105 24 450 318 34 637	77 73 73 73 73 73 73 73 73 73 73 73 73 7	133 39 144 27 11_ 294 434 1 46 13 132 261 45 526	54, 257, -25 56 590 9-0 6 5 97 589 67 675	17 94 25 50 17 48 1 180 184 5	15/ 38 63 172 126 3 30 7 52 12/ 23 38/ 101	72 23 43 449 436 7 7 49 3 61 208 0 216 23	24 26 137 27: 24 30 256 47
ofessional rimers and magers o rical and ses workers aftsmen i eratives a tvate house rical and magers rical and restives a tvate house rical and restives rical and restives rical and restives rical and restives rical and restives rical and restives rical and restives rical and restives rical and restives rical and	i farm managers. finals, and proposetors, except farm kindred workers with the control of the c	146 346 101 173 571 695 4 139 30 835 658 65 1,631 124 25 51	72 38 143 29 64 174 15, 7 176 45 177 45 7 7 7 8 7 7 8 8	138 50 337 100 200 651 1.34 2 21 2 39 1,717 30 830 101 1 32 90	235 80 97 343 60 6 6 48 524 37 549	9, 105 227 61 111 395 43° 7 105 24 450 318 34 637 86	77 73 32 54 193 237 19 8 48 22 19 234 52 2 18	133 39 144 27 11_ 294 434 13 132 261 45 526	94- 297- 25- 56- 590 9-5- 6- -6- -9- 589- 67- 575- 87- 5- 5- 5- 5- 5- 87- 87- 87- 87- 88- 88- 88- 88- 88- 88	17 94 25 50 17 48 1 1 80 184 5 7 17	15/ 38 63 172 126 3 3 3 7 52 12/ 23 38 101	72. 23. 49. 49. 49. 49. 3. 61. 200. 200. 216. 23.	20 21 27 27: 20 20 20 40 40 20 41 20 20 41 20 41 20 41 20 41 41 41 41 41 41 41 41 41 41 41 41 41
ofessional rimers and magers o rical and ses workers aftsmen i eratives a tvate house rical and magers rical and restives a tvate house rical and restives rical and restives rical and restives rical and restives rical and restives rical and restives rical and restives rical and restives rical and restives rical and	i farm managers. finals, and proposetors, except farm kindred workers with the control of the c	146 346 101 143 571 695 4 139 30 835 698 53 1,601 124 25 51 115	72 3e 143 29 64 174 15, 7 45 5 147 4 539 78	138 50 337 100 601 200 6.1 34 21 -2 239 1,717 30 830 101 1 32 90 88	235 80 97 343 704 6 6 46 48 524 37 549 121	9, 105 227 61 111 395 437 7 105 24 450 318 34 637	77 73 32 54 193 237 19 8 48 22 19 234 52 2 18	133 39 144 27 11_ 294 434 1 46 132 261 45 526	94, 297, 25 oc 590, 9-0 6 6, 9, 97, 589, 67, 67, 55, 85, 55,	17 94 255 27 48 1 480 184 5 7 27	15/ 38 63 172 126 3 30 7 52 12/ 23 38/ 101	72 23 43 449 436 7 7 49 3 61 208 0 216 23	2/2 2/2 1.37 2/7: 2 30 25/4 16/2
ofessional mere and amagers of articles and several and several and several and several and several and several and several and several and several and several and article and es worker afterne, several article and es worker afterne, several articles.	i farm managers, indicate workers compt farm landied workers landied workers and kindred workers and kindred workers sheld workers sheld workers sheld workers and kindred workers and kindred workers and kindred workers and training to the sheld workers are seen's ungad, and farm foremen copt farm and mine by reported seen forest sheld workers technical, and kindred workers and kindred workers and kindred workers and kindred workers.	146 345 101 173 571 695 695 695 698 63 1,631 124 25 51 117 144 8	72 38 143 29 64 174 17, 45 2, 45 2, 46 539 78 64 20 20	138 50 377 120 200 651 1-134 2 20_ -2 399 1,717 30 830 101 11 32 90 88 3	235 80 97 343 604 6 6 48 524 37 549 121	9, 103, 227, 61, 1,1, 1,395, 43°, 7, 105, 24, 450, 318, 34, 637, 86, 97, 61, 62, 61, 61, 61, 61, 61, 61, 61, 61, 61, 61	77 73 32 54 193 237 39; 8 48 22, 19 234 52 24 18 24 41 27	133 39 144 57 11	3	17 24 25 27 48 180 184 5 207 1 14 18 18 18 18 18 18 18 18 18 18	15/ 38 53 172 126 13 3 3 3 7 52 12/ 23 38- 101	72.1 23.1 49.1 36.1 7.49.3 61.200 .0.216.23 10.34.15.1	20 22 22 23 27: 20: 20: 4: 20: 20: 20: 20: 20: 20: 20: 20: 20: 20
ofessional immers and anagers of serical and se worker afternatives a treatment for the series of th	i farm managers. I farm managers. I fard managers. I farm and cindred workers. And kindred workers. I farm and mine. In reported. I farm managers. I farm formers. I fa	146 346 101 173 571 695 4 137 30 835 608 53 1,601 124 25 51 117 144 8 96	72 329 64 174 174 17 18 18 18 18 18 18 18 18 18 18 18 18 18	138 50 377 100 200 651 134 21 22 399 1,717 32 830 101 1 32 90 88 3 3 223	235 235 80 97 343 704 6 48 524 37 549 121 33 76 28 2 24	9, 103, 227, 61, 1,1, 1,395, 43°, 7, 105, 24, 450, 318, 34, 637, 86, 97, 61, 62, 61, 61, 61, 61, 61, 61, 61, 61, 61, 61	77 24 73 32 54 193 32 54 193 35 8 48 48 48 48 48 48 48 48 48 48 48 48 4	133 39 144 57 11_ 294 43 1, 45 261 45 265 30 88 55 51 24	3	17 26 50 77 48 1 80 184 5 707 14 38 82 16 50	15/ 38 53 172 126 13 3 3 3 7 52 12/ 23 38- 101	72. 23 49 49 49 49 49 49 49 49 49 49 49 49 49	24 22 137 27: 24 44 166 24
ofessional immers and anagers of serical and se worker afternatives a treatment for the series of th	i farm managers. I farm managers. I fard managers. I farm and cindred workers. And kindred workers. I farm and mine. In reported. I farm managers. I farm formers. I fa	146 346 101 173 571 695 4 137 30 835 698 63 1,601 124 25 51 112 144 8 96 148 96	72 32 32 34 34 35 34 35 36 36 36 36 36 36 36 36 36 36 36 36 36	138 50 337 200 651 	22 33 215 80 97 343 704 6 8 8 24 37 7 549 121 33 766 28 22 24 130 76	9, 103 227 61, 11, 139, 24, 24, 24, 24, 24, 24, 24, 24, 24, 27, 176, 24, 27, 176, 24, 27, 176, 24, 27, 176, 24, 27, 176, 24, 22, 24, 27, 176, 24, 27, 22, 24, 27, 27, 27, 27, 27, 27, 27, 27, 27, 27	777 273 324 354 397 88 48 22.1 19 9 234 52 22.1 18 22.1 19 234	133 39 194 27 11_ 244 1 445 455 526 455 526 92 117 52 52 52 54 117 59 4	24, 297, -25, 66, 56, 56, 56, 56, 56, 56, 56, 56, 5	17 24 26 50 17 48 1 48 184 5 7 1. 14 38 18 18 18 18 18 18 18 18 18 1	19/ 38/ 63/ 172/ 126/ 3/ 30/ 7/ 52/ 12/ 23/ 80/ 101/ 24/ 62/ 44/ 105/ 59/ 3/ 3/ 3/ 3/ 3/ 3/ 3/ 3/ 3/ 3/ 3/ 3/ 3/	72. 23 449 4361 7 7 8 8 61 20 216 23 1 20 34 32 34 33 34 34 34 34 34 34 34 34 34 34 34	24 22 137 27: 26 26 4' 16' 21 22 23 24 33 33
ofessional immers and anagers of erical and less worker affirmen in creatives a rivate house voice, arm langue and less worker and anagers of erical and less worker affirmen, in the creatives a vivate house voices affirmen, it is a vivate house vivate house vivate house vivate house and vivate house vivate	i farm managers, in distance of the managers, and indicate workers of foreman and cindred workers and kindred workers and kindred workers are foreman and histories workers, and conduct workers are, succept puryate heasthold, are, unput and farmly workers foreman, and kindred workers in the managers of	146 345 101 173 571 695 695 695 698 53 1,631 124 25 51 112 48 86 838 144 86 838 848 848 848 848 848 848 848 848 848	72 329 64 174 174 17 18 18 18 18 18 18 18 18 18 18 18 18 18	138 50 377 100 200 651 134 21 22 399 1,717 32 830 101 1 32 90 88 3 3 223	235 235 80 97 343 704 6 48 524 37 549 121 33 76 28 2 24	9, 105 227 61 111 395 437 7 105 24 4500 31.6 31.6 31.6 31.6 31.6 31.6 31.6 31.6	77 24 73 32 54 193 32 54 193 35 8 48 48 48 48 48 48 48 48 48 48 48 48 4	133 39 144 57 11_ 294 43 1, 45 261 45 265 30 88 55 51 24	25-7 2-25-5-6 5-90 9-2-6 6-6 6-75-89-6 67-5-5-5-5-5-5-5-5-5-5-5-5-5-5-5-5-5-5-5	17 26 50 77 48 1 80 184 5 707 14 38 82 16 50	15/ 38 53 172 126 13 3 3 3 7 52 12/ 23 38- 101	72. 23 49 49 49 49 49 49 49 49 49 49 49 49 49	20 21 27 27: 20 20 20 40 40 20 41 20 20 41 20 41 20 41 20 41 41 41 41 41 41 41 41 41 41 41 41 41

Tadis. 482.—CHARACTERISTICS OF THE RURAL-NONFARM NONWHITE POPULATION, FOR PARISHES 1950
[Asternac ** ostocies statistics rassed an As-person's sumple. For corresponding or incontenous figures on any, see age distribution in this table. Violan not shown where base as less than 500]

(Automix " actiones statutus resea on A-	percert s	numple fo	s. cousselb	neding c	monste-c	oun ngu	Los OG ST	z, see age	disease.	1022 882 1122		-		-	manuscript of	-	-
Subject	Acm'is	m,La	yasea-	Assump-	1 TOT- elies	Beau- regard	Biso- v_lle	Bossier	Caddr	Calca- sieu	cald- vell	Cameron	Cata-	Clea- borne	Con- cord_a	Da Soto	Bastor Rouge
Total rural nonfalir nonwhile popula ion	1,051	1 902	3,969	3,815	3,074	1,071	4,^63	4,828	8 595	3,497	1,725	358	±,67°	2,148	1,988	4,172	6,998
allow and account	549	937	- 940	1 655	1,497	519	2,339	2,372	4,112	1,771	863	191	787	1,027	903	1,931	3,464
Male, all ages	72	150	2%	269 25"	227	55	369	353	632	2o8 227	131	26 18	75	201.	14 91 86	31.5 269	525
to 9 years	69	_C_	255	257	241 472	6+ 47	305	275 258	520 467	218		20 19	8C	139	86	20h	429
to 19 years 15 to 19 years	51 52 45	79	150	177		48	490	23	34.5 250.	123	75	19	58 29	76 93 80	60 55 75	140	-1.6 429 364 258 208
20 to 24 vesrs 25 to 29 years 60 to 34 years	45	nR!	134	1.77 1.9 107 65	_00 _00 72	30	1 188	159	202	-27 t	75 60 40 37	24 _0 _7	80 58 48 52 44	80	15	123	208
00 to 34 years	33	57 59	94 92 36	85 86	72 63	39 25	150	106	182 215	_06 97	37 47	9	52 33	55 51 37	56 48	85 90	185 226 174
5 to 39 years -U to 44 years	25	-4	9.	85	61	32	117	1_9	233		54	14			47	82	174
the to 40 mans	24	52	87 73	64 68 86 57	54	29 27	104	114	233 170 133	91 84	47 38	1 8	38 36	39 22 24 24 38	56 61	96 58	105 85 67
to 54 years.	181	52 34 38 24 25	73 73 83	86	54 53 50 30	26	63	80 75	133	49	41 39 35	1	29 18	24	41 47 33 54 34	58 89 52 92 52	85
30 to 64 years	19	24	83	57 78	30 49	26 20 21	53 85	63	104	57	35	6	42 33	38	54	92	:23
70 o 74 years	6	13	52	53	92	12	38 50	61.	127	29	19	2 5	33	21 33	34 36	52 65	-23 73 95
5 years and over-	19	-4	-	- 1		100		2,456	4 483	1,726	b60	167	892	1,121	1,095	2,241	3,524
Female, ail ages.	62 62	9e5	2,029	260	241	552	338	-	627	282	115		92	1.80	139	299	505
nder 5 years 5 to 9 years 0 to 14 years	54	126 96	233	245	183	63 50 59 41	274	384 307	537 446 343	222 193	99	24 19	77 72 58 64 54 54	-37 -00	86 98	266 210	432 405 291
5 to 19 years	.5	70	174	221	_66 _31	59	252 241 211	232	343	152	88	24 16	58	107	83	189	291
5 to 19 years 20 to 24 years	40	68	112	147 12 135		43	211	165 179	328	132	52 53 54	16 13	54	89	83 77 62	163 156	323 277
25 to 29 years 80 to 84 years 85 to 39 years	30	52	117	83	93 78 85	32 35	129 153 124	128	274 270	128 118 121	54	10 13	54	65	61 79	141	217
35 to 30 years 10 to 44 years	28	51	105	93	71	39	143	134	247	98	61. 57	6	63 64	40 51	57	110	486
t5 to 49 years	23	-cl	_07	90 85	57	12	115	1_6	233 173	77 57	45	7	27 31	43 30	48	99 108 91	116 89 86
50 to 5- vears	10	39	87		62 42	2-	70	63	167 122	44	40 30 22	3 3 5		30 30	48	91	89
50 to 54 years 35 to 69 years	24	32	64	168	51 85	13 27	52 88	70 122	243 123	48	22 26	5	41 69	28 44 21	38 67	62 108 60	1,2
70 to 74 years	12 7 16	1.	45 60	49	3-	5	32	20	123	18	26 13 24	î	23 41	21 36	30 4_	60	132 57 71
75 /ears and over	10	-4	00	0Z	90	۰	-	~		- 1							-
Persons 25 years old and over	433	845	2,835	1,810	1,420	500	2,235	2 300	4,240	1,580	870	130	950	945	1,140	2,000	3,160
No school years completed	225	245	450	325	345	120	280	260	665	432	45	45	330	.70 355	155	385	1,085
Elementary 1 to 4 years 5 and 6 years	115	245 170 80	755 283	365	650 220	185	845 480	1,030	1,895	61.5 21.5	350	55 20	29C 14C	245	e15	384	60-
7 years	25	80 30	283 105 95	365 125 75	95	65	240	455 -85 70	×25	15	65	5	40	65 15	115	90 50 65	265 110
High suboul 1 to 3 years -	5	30 10	65	85	40	15 25 25	100 165	145	195	60	50 65	5	45 70	45	60	65	170
College 1 to 3 years	- 1	10	156	10	5		25	20	40 50	50	20		1.5	15	10	10 35 10	25 30
4 years or more Schoo, years not reported	10	30	20 35	40	20	5	40 45	85	130	65	40		15	10	15	100	40 215
Median school years completed		3 7	3 +	0	3 2	3 8	4.4	4 3	3 9	31	5 2		3 (4 3	2	30	4 2
EMPLOYMENT STATUS															- Tito	MAN I	-
Male, 14 years old and over	346	587	1,209	1,257	920	365	1,425	1,502	2,570	1,100	566	132	538	609	633	1,_74	2,189
Labor orce Civilian labor force Employed Chemployed	236 236	43o 435	719 719	668	583 583	224 224	1,039	1 111	-,707 -,705	PO8 BO8	394	60 80	287 287	439 438	313 313	766 766	1,392
Employed	191	396	6_8 101	606	523 60	200	999	887 31	4,642	743	361 33	74 16	236 51	423	289 24	735	1,233
Nof in labor force	110	151	490	489	337	141	386	421	863	291	_72	42	577	170	3.00	406	.58 797
Female 14 years old and over_	31.8	597	0/در1	1,279	1,0.5	270	1,012	1,580	2,959	000ر ـ	574	105	ഔ	27	777	1,496	2,263
Labor force Cryshan labor force	69	154 154 140	277	244	2.5	70	383 383	398	854 854	271 271	116	22 22	375	145 14*	15/	343 343	6.3 6.3
Employed .	69 64 5	140	276 253	235	200	7C 68	372	394 384	836	260	114	21	175 165	143	142	31.4	576
Employed	249	443	1 093	1,035	800	306	1,229	1,182	2,105	789	456	83	495	572	12 623	1,29	37 4,650
MAJOR OCCUPATION GROUP																di e	
Male employed	171	396	518	60a	523	200	999	887	1,642	743	364	74	236	423	249	735	1,233
Professional technical and kindred workers		6	17	18	5	3	31	13 29	49		17	13	+0	15 48	8	8 3C	23 40
Farmers and farm managers Managers officials, and proprietors, except farm	3	5	6	2 5	2	3	10		15	20	3	13	-8	1	3	4	16
Clencal and kindred workers	2	7	2	1	-		2	1 6	9	2	2		5	2	7	7	6 7
Sales workers Craftsmen foremen, and kindred workers	6	23	52 68	39 26	72 61	6 49	234 234	42 142	29 348	62 186	51	13	12	17	40	30	78
Operatives and kindred workers. Private household workers			6	23	1		2	1 71	348 26 106	1.0	2		57 2 13	49 3	40 48 2 11 4	6	137 14 77 5
		13	29	1	-5 0	3	27 27	28	6	>5	5	3		17	1 4	6 14 22 178	5
Farm laborers, unpaid family workers	4			261	176	- 6	108 467	327 2.46 18	796 552 29	59 338	21.8	33	21 90	126 130	34 115	178 258 22	201 609 20
Service workers excep pn ate household Farm laborers, unpaid family workers Farm laborers except unpaid, and farm forwhen Laborers except farm and mine	93 58	37 129	221	.00	177	128											20
Farm laborers, unpaid family wurkers farm laborers except unpaid, and farm foremen Lacorers except farm and mine Jecupa son not reported	93 58 3	129 9	29	23	177	126	17	18	29	8	6	2		7	2	22	20
Pecupa son not reported	58	129 9	253 253	23 23 235	177 8 206	128	372	384	836	260	114	21	165	143	142	30.4	576
Labores except tarm and mine Decups and not reported Femile employed Professional tachnicas, and kindred workers Formers and farm managers	58 3 64	129	29	235 235	177 8 206		372	384	836	1	114	_	165	143 21	142		576
Labores except tarm and mine lecups and not reported Female employed. Professional tachnics, and kindred workers armers and farm managers American difficults. and proprietors except farm	58	129 9 140 3	253 253	23 23 235	177		372	384 30 5 4	836	260	3	21	16		142	30.4 33 4	576 32 3 12
Laborers except farm and mine lecups and not reported Female employed. Female employed, and kindred workers Farmers and farm managers farmers and farm managers fanguers officials, and proprietors except farm fanguers	58 3 64	129 9 140 3 2	253 253	235 235	177 8 206		372	384 30 5 4 3 8	836	260 6 6	3	21	16		142 15 6 4	30.4 33 4 4	576 32 3 12
Aboyees except tarm and man becapes and not reported. Female employed. Professional tackmen, and kindred workers stremen and farm managers damagers officials, and proprietors except farm literal and landed workers because of the control of th	58 3 64 1 2	129 9 140 3 2 9 1 3	253 26 253 16 1 19	235 19 1	206 8 1	68 4	372 55 1 11 3 4	384 30 5 4 3 8	836 -1 8 -4 2 1.2 6	260 6 6	3	21	16		142 15 6 4	31.4 33 4 4 4	576 32 3 12 6 6 0
According energy internation name feeting and not international control of the feeting and feeting and feeting and feeting and feeting and proprietors except farm feeting and landered workers feeting and landered workers feeting and the feeting and the feeting and the feeting and feeting and feeting and feeting and feeting and feeting and feeting and feeting and feeting and feeting	58 3 64 1 2	129 9 140 3 2 3 1 3	253 26 253 16 1 19	235 19 1	206 8 1	68 4	372 55 1 11 3 4	384 30 5 4 3 8	836 -1 8 -4 2 1.2 6	260 6 6 3 3 15	_4 3 2 1 65	21	16 6 1 5 7	21. 1. 4. 80	142 15 6 4	314 33 4 4 5 1 1 6 175	576 32 3 12 6 6 0
According energy internation name feeting and not international control of the feeting and feeting and feeting and feeting and feeting and proprietors except farm feeting and landered workers feeting and landered workers feeting and the feeting and the feeting and the feeting and feeting and feeting and feeting and feeting and feeting and feeting and feeting and feeting and feeting	58 3 64	129 9 140 3 2 9 1 3	253 26 253 16 4 19 121 43	235 19 1	206 8 1 • • 140 15	68	372 55 1 11 3 4 7 212 51	384 30 5 4 3 8 1 4 217 61 7	836 -4 -2 -2 -2 -6 29 415 162	260 6 6 3 3 15 143 73	2 1 69	21	16 6 1 5 7 81 36	21 1 4 80 8	142 15 6 4 1 1 3 65 13	314 4 4 5 1 1 275 39	576 32 3 12 6 6 0 2 35 3,9 94
Labores except tarm and man because and not troported Female employed. "Ordensonal takbones, and kindred workers written and fartu managara "Admangara officiasa, and proprietors except farm lierced and kindred workers label workers. "Inflament forement, and kindred workers"	58 3 64 2 2 52 6	129 9 140 3 2 9 1 3 6 81 93	253 26 253 16 1 19	235 19 1	206 8 1	68 4	372 55 1 11 3 4	384 30 5 4 3 8	836 -1 8 -4 2 1.2 6	260 6 6 3 3 15	_4 3 2 1 65	21	16 6 1 5 7	21. 1. 4. 80. 8	142 15 6 4 1 1 3 65 13	314 33 4 4 5 1 1 6 175 39	576 32 3 12 6 6 9 35 3,9 94

Table 48a.—CHARACTERISTICS OF THE RURAL-NONFARM NONWHITE POPULATION FOR PARISHES 1950.—Con [Areask **) denotes statute; based on 20-percent sar-pue to corresponding complete-sount names on age are determined in a relater. Various and shown where case a less man 361.

rubjers	East Carc.1	Zast FeC- iana	gar-De g-au-	Frank-	Grant	Iberia	_ber- v_lle	Jaces 12	-etter-	erfer- cor Deris	La- raveute	'CE M	La Sae	Lagos.	Living-	Aud_seon.	Mone- XXX8e
Total rural nonfarm nonwhite population	1,330	2,201	1,654	920	_ 887	+,480	10,434	2,804	1 4.8	2,8	1,750	2,8,0	. 28,	3,075	2 0-1	607	-,9%
Male, all ages	629	.,042	795	397	985	2,21_	5,083	4,386 م	909	999	842	,440	639	. 199	_,039	356	020
Under 5 years	25	17"	1,29	50,	141	303	745	227	120	149	وز	224	51	174	1-5	-0	899
10 to 14 years	52 40	120	-01 97	57	107 97	279 240	6,38 5-0	-85	20"	135	37	3.5	-72 68	140	154	34	95
15 to 19 year 20 to 24 years	5. 48	71	87	26	50	221 146	5-0 -22 297	-9 92	63	90 78	94	133	43	.83	45	.9	67
25 to 29 years 30 to 34 years	39	31 Ot	6. 45	15	51 47	132	290	58	65	A_1	57	92 86 76	42 37	284	20°	19	-06 67 8-
35 to dy years	27 33	66	36 34	21	49	-40,	262 294	77· 85	62	49	29	76	37	78	64 75	24	4"
40 to 44 years	25	52		-2	49	_09	260	72	45	/1	42	79 50	69	48	53	72	32
45 to 49 years 50 to 54 years 55 to 59 years 65 to 69 years	29	45 22 25	31 18	.7	30	72	248	74	54 49	13	4-1	5e 47 51	36 39	46	63	24 30	46 31
55 to 50 years	28	25 24	20,	20	38 41 20	72 72 60 58	183	47	3,	20	22	51	22	32	34 24		25
65 to 69 years	25 36	36	32	32 16	37	58	228	27	33	50	28	47	23	34	27	20	33
70 to 71 years	30 40	36	19	16	22 24	36	102	16	22	22	10	42 19 26	22	13	13	.7	36 31
Female all ages	701	1,129	859	2,رد	,001	2,269	5, 151	1,4_8	909	1,019	892	1,390	680				
Under 5 years -	82	173	125	61	114	32.1	698	217	146	163	142	204	680 71	1,676	972	34 <u>-</u> 56	1 031
5 to 9 years	52 52 55	97	110	32	961	324 252	019	148	90 25 72	1.3	101	192 172	71	147	108	29 28	102
15 to 19 years	45	-06	89	41	70	229	489 385	132	72	94	63	124	62 58 36	238	102	32	92
25 to 29 years	49	104 86	70	41 37 38	83	160	301 295 311	118 118 87	81. 67 44	103	96 58 42	207	36 5.	344	99	30 18	70
30 to 34 years	37	67	48	23 34 25	58 75 64	159	311	107	44	61	42 53	84 96	51 39 53	82	102 99 76 57 20	11	46
40 to 44 years	35	64 39	43 28			140 113	301 275	78	70 54	50	48	22	30	82 83 68	59	12	57 60
45 to 49 years	38	50	45 27	25	47	8_ 93	266	51	62 48	33	44	62 57	47		45	25	46
50 to 54 years_ p5 to 59 years_	39 32	34	25	18 27 17	43	55	224 245	24	32	34	38	3".	38 29	60 47 29	23	21	61
60 to 64 years	28	27	15 28	17	21 49	54	293	26 49	32 .2 33	19	17 27	27	29	25	13 27	23	39 46
70 to 74 years 75 years and over	31	64 27 42	15	56 9 3.	18	34	1,8	21	20	2.3	T-	24	7	40 17	8	6	5u 29
*YEARS OF SCHOOL COMPLETED	~	~	20	~	-25	34	159	-5	13	20	18	21	15	20	-2	13	41
Persons 25 years old and over	860	1,050	670	>20	822	1,940	5.030	1,260	880	830	710	4,170	690	1,140	8501	370	1,000
No school years completed	150	170	38,	1.35	230	750	-,230	105	190	375	460	380	. 70	65		75	140
Elementary 1 to 4 years - 5 and 6 years - 7 years	395	435 230	.80 55	210	305	600 300	2 245 845	245	255	230	-45 45	485 120	210	39a 175	90 460 13,	175	485
7 years	50	65	20	45	50	100	-90	155	100	50	40	55	35		30	20	33 60
High school 1 to 3 years.	35	35	10	20	65 40 15	45 70 15	_80 1.25	90	35 55	20	151	25	20 60	45 90 35	35	5	15
College 1 to 3 years	10	13	5		15	20	40 10	25	20	15	12	40 45 15 10	60 20 13	35	5	5	- 5
4 years or more	15	50		10	20	40	15	٦٠,	9	5	5	5		95		-1	12
School years not reported Median school years completed	3 8	4 2	10	3 3	3 6	2 4	120	5 1	25 4.7	10	8 0	2 6	4 1	40	30	45	25
	1 0		4	,,	3 6	- 1		3.1	7.7	1.0		2.0	4.1		3 6		29
Male, 14 years old and over	4.0	671	480	250	560	1,380	2 2/11	846	8e¢		500	***			-		
Labor force	245	520	291	251	362	970	1,991	604	41	3+8	369	616	282	±,009	556	268	372
Cavilian labor force	244	510	291	133 128	362	959 913	_ 989	604 573	444	378	369	€le	2.82	431	555	190	394
Employed	13	502	253	5	334	56	- 989 1,770 210	31	384	367	348	57 43	270	417	537 18	-72	374
No in labor force	205	_61	_89	118	198	410	1,249	242	±87	216	133	219	134	577	1.31	78	178
Female, 14 years old and over.	522	753	526	387	693	1,418	3,436	930	619	630	579	854	458	1,213	621	233	769
Labor force	90	220	121	95 95	158 158	292	763	173	178	150	184	-59	107	267	208	41	177
Livilian labor force Employed	8,	218	-17	94	1.50	285	720	162	-63	150	177 7	152	105	257		39	103
Unamployed Not in labor force	432	543	405	292	535	1,14	2,673	757	441	480	395	695	35.	946	12 413	192	552
MAJOR OCCUPATION GROUP							1						E 175	180	1	top:	
Male employed	231	502	253	128	334	913	4, 170	573	384	367	3-8	573	270	41.7	537	192	374
Professional technical, and kindred workers	-0	16	22	8	3	10	29	3	4 2	4	2 8	4	- 2	41	11	7	33
Farmers and farm managers Managers officials, and proprietors except farm		2	22	3	8	4	28	25	4	7	5	7	3	8	6	2	33
Clercu and kindred workers Sales works s.	2 2	3	1	1	5	5	11		5	. 2	1	2		4	2	1	2
Craftsmen foremen and andred wo. sers .	15	50	اقد	-î	14	70	129	55 -8.	18	34	22	9	3	35	17	8	26
Operatives and kindred workers Private household workers	1	-26	21	1	49	2-0	29 3 65	-8.	80 2 30	34 41 1	46 3 19	4.	132	1,2	130	34	87
Service workers except private household	9	11	5	3	11	24	65	16	30	13	19	16	د	33	3	1 5	17
Farm laborers urpaid family workers Farm laborers, except unpaid, and farm foremer	57	61	73	24	39	390	05-	L7	1.6	127	117	269	. 3	33	63	40	72
Laborers except farm and mine Occupation not reported	49	206	104	34	187	171	407 90	255	205	129	.14	202	82 24	122	276	69	1.4
Female employed	8.	2.8	417	94	±50	285	720)	_62	.63	139	177	152	105	257	196	. 39	169
P ofessional, technical, and kindred workers	3	13	9	20	20	17	22	10	3	12	1	10	4	72	1	4	5
P ofessional, technical, and kindred workers - Farmers and farm managers Managers, officials, and provinctors except farm.	2	4 2	3	2	1	1	18	. 5	1	,	3		. 1	3	2	1	3
Clerical and kindled workers	î	1			1	2	2	- 1	2	1	- 1	1		8	-		. 1
Sales workers	-		1	4	4	- 1	11	3	. 3	2	2	. 1	4	1	:1	1	2
Operatives and kindred workers Private household workers	7	11	2	6	4	2)	257	5	33 68	2	,,,	27	. 5	10	3	1	4
Service, workers except private souschold .	37	118	76	36 21	76	159 29	119	93 36	46	94 23	124 2- 2	37	65 17	88 53	102	2.	90 12
Farm laborers unpaid amily workers Farm laborers except unpaid, and farm foremen	1,8	18	6			44	222	- 1	3		2	45	0.59	. 5	29		6
		7.8	6	21	- 4	766	224	2	3		1>	40	1 7	,	29	2	44
Laborers except farm and mine Occupation not reported		2		11	a	2	3,	4		1	8	2		1	1 6		

Tance \$82 — CHARACTERISTICS OF THE RURAL-NONFARM NONWHITE POPULATION, FOR PARISHES 1950—Con.

NAME OF TAXABLE PARTY.	- PRODUCTION	CONTRACTOR OF THE PERSON NAMED IN	punnou PC	-	1	-	-				C+	St	St John	St	S+	St	St
¥1. se	hetona- nuber	.ta1-	min-	Tr p	Rap de	Pen Fivez	ara.	San ne	St Bemiara	St Charles	welens	Tomas	t_e Baptier	Linery	Martin	Mary	Tumany
Tina me-poulare purveix populaine	4,-54	2 .8-	+ 484	- P25	15,04	,52-	-,942	3,429	1 499	3,300	855	4,651	• ,7 17	8,174	2,996	5 671	4 110
Maa ah 2ges	2 -27		2 335	-,777	3,-28	590	870	2,67-	730	1,.68	399	2,26#	2 395	_ 812	1 448	2 796	2,011
Upor o years	232	237	3**5	294	054	1.09	.28 97	252	116	252 22	65 47	30°7 286	377 306	635 513	225 189	365 357	306 250
5 of years	241	212	315 236	459	48	81 77	6.	22. 164	83 94 53	8گد	49	280 177	271 201	440 345	178 128	342 249	228 167
0 to w Vea. s	-4.7	10	200	-25 146	349	45	53	143	53	107	29 38	1.24	172	256	93	183	129
20 to 24 ve 25 o 20 vear	, IOC	38	173 59	pg	335	26 40 27	30 34	90 90	23 42	97	3º 20	128	158	233 209	72 84	165	138
30 to 34 years	1_2	3C	145	-04	357	27	57	72	33	83 62	24 22	126 99	125	220	95 65	129	_25 99
4c to 44 years	94	7	9 99	69 85	337	36 32	48	82	47	69	8	106	110	131	63	152	
45 to 45 years 50 to o4 years	67	477	6	6/4	305	16 23	37 37	92 92	30 24	56 51	13	120	97	113	40 41 32 54	108	73
.5 to 99 ₃ •acs 69 to 84 year≈	19	28°	49 60	50 50	191	19	65	42	16 3L	51 52	10 13	72	88	94 137	32	80 123	60
65 to 69 years	1.4 30 91	~6 48	70 34 4.	-2 35		37 35	-10	-1	1/	39	19	67	76 49 43	131	24 35	65	92 73 75 60 74 -7 37
75 , ears and over	1		1	86	164	28	٥ر	30	15	50	8 -	2 383	2,322	4.362	1,578	2,875	2,099
Femase all ages	2,332	1,624	2,20,	1,748	5,650	817	1,072	269	764	1 732	456	347	34.	b68	222	36,	
Under years	329 267	234	359 2~4 169	3_7 244	662 519	80	142	182	91	221	57 50	299	266	566 470	24_ 190	252 311	3,35 260 23°
0 to 14 years	6	151	214 177	_88	519 423	75 70 54 56 51	102 80 65	171	66	134	45 49	187	175	407	465	257	201
20 to 24 years	1.5	125 10t	177	_39 119	403 420	54	69	130	43	112	29	140	183	300	404 98	167	140
30 .0 34 years	126	25° 235 79	134 137 99	109	379	51	621	87 113	60 66 77 43 27 47	8> 94	29 20 25	126 141	128 123	239 270	91	168	1.5
40 to 44 years	122		99	93 79	371	49	79 7-	122	45	65	18	92	409	179	73	1,39	95
45 to 49 years	108	ŋ. 8	g.,	89	354	40 33	55	ئيد 69	34 29 20	70	11	130	108	_42 148	59 39	142	84 82
	89	57 39	66 54 64	90 73 61	225	18	48 33 48	61	20 19	65 56	10	90 104	78	121	3.5	103	65 77 79 24
60 to 69 years	126	74	64	127	271	62 15 32	58 32 34	44 56	26 12	72	20	126	136 45	204 73	23	146	79
70 to 74 years 75 years and over	77 78	34	3" 26	70 35	73	32	34	_8 28	-7	52	9	64	53	30.	30	91	47
*YEARS OF SCHOOL COMPLETED							955	1 595			340	2,245	2 150	ه,430	1,225	2,805	2,000
Persons 25 years old and over	2,195	1,515	1,965	1,800	1,480	740 215	190	220	740	1,500	35	325	535	1,450	505	680	2,000
No sensol years completed Kiementary 1 to 4 years o and 6 years	8/5	595	710	775	2,470	330	390 180	685	326	60 ₂ 31 ₅	460 80	1 015	905 395	1,185	395 170	465	925 445
7 years	320 95	255 25- 90 63	395 155	85	1,210	90 95	55	335 120	130	-50	101	190	125	130	45	170	105
High school 1 to 3 years	60 65 10	6.5	55 35	35 30	235 250 /5	25 5	35 55	55 80	20 45	70 45	25 5	85 75	65 50	60 80	2	110	100
College 1 to 8 years		30 45	10		45		5	15 15 20	5	30	10	15	10 2.5	15 35	5	45 30	15 20
4 years or more School years not reported	10	40	10 55	ة دد	215	10	25 25	40	10	40	10	25 25	4	85	40	15 50	.0
Median school years completed	3 7	+ 2	3 4	2 6	37	2 9	3 8	/ 3	40	4 0		3 9	3 3	_ 8	19	3 4	12
EMPLOYMENT STATUS						9			1					Canco			100000
Mass, 14 years old and over	1,328	290	1,438	1,117	3,782	Adam	193	-10e4	458	958	245	906	1,480	2,293	847	1,794	859
Labor force	742	649 649	1,041	736 736	2,016	239	382 382 354	687 687	284 284	61.2	167	904	-,045 -,044 962	1,369	594 594	1,247 1 247 1,071	859
Employed. Unemployed	74. 701 40	607	118	653	195	221	54	655	248 36	105	106	822	82	1,173	568 2a	176	81.6 43
Not in labor force	286	347	397	381	1 766		211	378	174	356	78	508	435	924	253	547	402
Female, 14 years old and over	±,557	1,103	1,359	1,320	4 008	566 172	768	241	513	1,08"	279 61	259	263	2,752	961	1,902	274
Labor force	276	279	346 346	328	680	-71	225	241 229	1.39	238	64	2*9	263	689	232	459	274
Employed	260	273 6	299 47	284	877	-60 -1	219		1.33	222	90	253	222 41	609 80	225	388 71	265
Not in labor force	1,280	824	1,013	1 001	3,128	_94	543	935	374	84.e	218	⊥,272	-,231	2,043	729	1,443	1,008
MAJOR OCCUPATION GROUP Male, employed	701	607	92	650	1,818	221	354	626	248	507	160	813	962	1,173	568	_ 07_	815
Professional technical, and kindred workers	8 46	7	3	5	-7	10	2.0	14	5	_4	8	16	10	21	2	16	8
Farmers and farm managers	46	12	27	18	22	15	17	20	3	12	16	24	9	46 23	30	25	10 11
Managers officials, and proprietors, except farm. Clerical and kindred workers Sales workers	1	6	1	2	1	,	1	1 3	3	3	4	12	3	8	3 3	9	4 5
Cra.tsmen. foremen, and kundred workers Operatives and kindred workers	42	33 144	59 155	6.5	122	26	30 85	43	22	39	53	58 139	72	79	42	51 218	99 128
Private household workers Service workers, except private household.	1 34	2	3	_16 7	5	2	61	3	20	5	-	1	258	1	2	5	29
Farm aborers unpaid family workers Farm laborers except unpaid, and farm foremen	25	12	19	23	103	7	20	23	25	20	1	29	44	52 26 151	19	26 5	28
Faim laborers except unpaid, and farm foremen Laborers, except farm and mine	274 195	105	4.33 50	19C 216	808	37 71 9	104	2° 37	25 113	55 253	3/ 35	276 228	302 259	151 440	29C 114	331	82 404
Occupation net reported	21	۵۵.		5	30		1	21	- 1	3	2	10		43	8	18	8
Female employed	260	273	299	284	811 32	160	219	239	133	122	60	253	222	609	22€	388	265
Profe somal sechnical, and kindred workers Fermers and farm managers	13	1	1	6	3	14	4	16 2 8	4	13	1"	21 1	14	4? 1	11	37	15
Managers, officials, and proprietors, except farm Clerical and kindred workers	1	2	-	3	15 3		6	2	2				2	9 2	± ±	1	2
Sales workers Craftsmen foremen and amdred workers	7	20	3	3	13	2	1	6	4	6		9	5	7	4	5	1
Operatives and kindred workers	_05	16	125	-10	428	93	16	121	28	39 96	21	14	17	19 341	218	40 183	175
Semula washers event preveta household	39	56	19	42	428 150 3	93 -5 5	41	121 63	57 15	50	21	45	78 42	103	27	45	34
Farm laborers unpaid amily workers Farm laborers, except unpaid and farm foremen	69	9	40 2	8.	102	16	9	1	22	€ 7	14	74	50	22 29	7 37	63	18
Lacorurs except farm and mine Occupation not reported	6	2	7	8	13	2	3	6 5	1	7		12	5 2	13	3 7	3	. 5
														1			

WOIE --Orleans Parish, entirely urban not shown in this table

Table 48a.—CHARACTERISTICS OF THE RURAL-NONFARM NONWHITE POPLLATION, FOR PARISHES 1950.—Con-Assertak **) denotes statistics based on 20-per-ent sample or corresponding completa-on ** games in age, see age data diction in this while Meron not above more "see at seen than 500

Subject	ا سنرټون	*naes	Te Tooonne	u	·e=1=0	16 -	aftitue Light	debate .	e_1 7p+ -	ses" Carrala	N.S.	N-DC
lota, rural nonfarm nonwhite repulstion.	6,502	2,669	5 %	3,378	,541	578	٠.٦	3,758	2 348	982	4, 21	1 .497
AGE	1		i					1		97		
Naie all ages	3, . 36	- 2C2	2,70	-, . 57	70	48-	A,06"	1,884	1,746	454	2,737	58C
nder 3 vears	372	-53 -27	492 300	2.0	44	49	190	257	-3	72 50	-85	98
0 to 14 years	3.72	-08	323	240	12	41	146	21-	-15	42 22	17	4.0
10 to 1 years 10 to 1 years 10 to 1 years 10 to 1 years 10 to 12 years 10 to 24 years 10 to 24 years 10 to 34 years 10 to 34 years	2,5	6.4	254	14	75	30	36.		25	22	2.6 45o	50 35
to to 29 years	233	55	-84	1_6	42	75	7	2	52	25	4.33	39
to 39 years	190	62 54	177	-16,	-5	-41	22	95 143	6.	28	3/3	39 31
14.0 (0.0000	39	66 85	107	72 80	4.	34	04		8.	22	176	28
17 to 4 y cours 30 to 54 years 35 to 59 years 30 to 64 y cors.	148	60 71	2	04	3C	43	25 27	63	5. 63	20 27 10 27	-40	27 17 21
30 to 64 3 ears.	107	71 4 ₄ 68	77	48 26	2:	-0.	33	47	4	27	69 56	19
55 to 69 years	10,	68 48	82	50 22	18 18 14	26	33	80	57	27 16	55	23
75 years and over	26	62	52	40	-4	8	_9	36	44	24	27 48	12
Female, all ages	3,426	1,467	2,70.	1,72	780	294	., 88	1,875	1,302	530	1 304	6.7
inder 5 years	525	156	493 27±	224	108	34	185 132	247 216	224	75	179	04
to 9 years	325	03	351	178	82	26	105	_93	_41 _25	65 40	140	04 77 52 44 49
5 to 19 years	338	86 83	243	1671	83 74	_9 1"	103	132	ಕ್ಕ 95	40 25 41	מנו	44
15 to 29 years	267	84	174	135	28 47	2/	82	146	82	30	86	42
35 to 24 years	229 197	110	130	100	49	13	65 65	.29 .26	90	30 25 25	73	42 42 32
i0 to 44 years	181	121	_29	74	40	16	60	-0	73	37	72	24
45 to 49 years 90 to 54 years 55 to 59 years	450 -18	90	17	75	32	20	46 27	96	73 47	22	50 58 36	22
55 to 59 years	91	83	40	58 30 47	25 25 16	13	29 24	64 49	53 47	24	38	31 23 22
50 to 64 years	80 15	45 92	59 89	47	12	3.7	26	77	25 16	15 37	64	26
70 to 74 years	48 46	65 75	40 48	26 42	12	8	10	24	19 28	20 17	.8 57	13
*YEARS OF SCHOOL COMPLETED									-	Mari		-
Persons 25 years old and over	3,080	520	2,170	1,245	695	.45	885	1 805	1,220	390	2,015	565
No school years non-pleted	1,220	250 670	755 840	220 570	2.5 255	20 180	135 310	295 /20	305 490	100	410	70
5 and 6 years.	460	285	330	330	75	70	145	360	255	115	4.5	115
7 vears	165	80 90	40	1.50	15	20	75 65	135	70	25	125	30
High school 1 to 3 years	145	105	10	90	20	20	60 20 35	75	40 15	45	90	35
College 1 to 3 years	60		-5	50	10	5	35	-5	15	2	35 25	10
4 vears or more	140	20	35	50 15 25	.0	20	15 25		15	2C 10	35	80
Median school years completed	3 7	4 0	2 4	48	2.4		4.8	4 3	3 5	4.4	3 0	48
EMPLOYMENT STATUS											2 7/1/ 1	
Male, 14 years old and over.	2,042	8-2	1,586	∠ 023	457	206	533	1,179	834	303	2 307	368
Lebor force	1,531	563 563	1,144	728 728	292 292	106 10e	400	788 787	525 545	187	427	224
Employed.	1.489	46I	1,144	70"	256	106	441	733	448	176	11/	209
Not in labor force	43	102 279	442	21 295	3e 165	100	426 447 9 177	391	448 77 309	11	1,380	144
Female, 14 years old and over	2,192	1.1.4	1,543	1,141	5,1	204	584	1,252	834	361	883	39-
Labor force	823	340	296	216	175	43	:91	278	3.69	.11	125	52
Civilian labor force	823 796	340	297 273	216	167	42	191	276	169	111	125	52 50
Unemployed	796 27 1,363	19 774	1,245	925	3.36	264	493	974	22 662	2 250	7:8	342
MAJOR OCCUPATION GROUP	1,505	//-	2,240	~	220	-04	4,,,	7,7	00,	•~	120	-
Male, employed.	1,488	464	1,015	707	256	106	4-7	733	449	76	414	209
Professional technical, and kindred workers	17	73	R	10	4	3	2	-2.	2	3	6	6 5
Farmers and arm managers	56	1~	9 5	14	?	4	16	26	10	13	16	
Managers officials and proprietors, except farm Olympia and kindred workers	7	4	3	2	-		3	7	- 4		2	1
Bales workers Craftemen, foremen and hindred workers .	9 67	14 69	30	2 32	25	9	5 35	36		14	28	3
Operatives and kindred workers Private household workers	245	69	138	195	47	34	-32	106	6.	43	100	68
Service workers except private household Farm laborers unpaid family works.s	17	25	32	16	2	8	12	37	24	6	-2	2
Farm laborers, except unpaid and farm to emen .	528	. 80	228 542	61.	97	3 5	8 >4	c7	161	2 19	54	17
	435	137	542	13	63	35	146	342	143	56	177	86 15
Labovers, except farm and mine Occupation not reported	603		2/3	2-2	167	42	-		14"		123	_
Occupation not reported	Mos		2/3		167	1	186	266	3	109	3	50
Occupation not reported	794	32.	10	25								
Professional technical and andred workers.		29	1	-			2	3			100	
Decupation not reported temale employed Foressonal technical and andred workers. Formers and farm managers Managers officials and proprie ors, except farm Cleroal and kindred workers.	33 11 2	29 3 19	1 2	د			2 2	11	2	2		
Occupation not reported remale employed Permile employed Permile and and andred workers. Farmers and farm managers Minagers officials and proprie ors, eccept farm Gleroal and kindred workers	33	29	1	-	4	3	2 1 1 1		2 4	2	3	
Occupation not reported benale employed Professional teshinical and audired workers. Farmers and farm managers Managers officials and proprie ors, except farm Clemels and kindred workers Carlament foremen and kindred workers	33 11 2 3 2	29 3 19 7	1 2 2	1	1	3	1 1 7	2 2 10	11	1 6	3 1	5
Occupation not reported. Jensile employed. Professional technical and anidred workers Professional technical and anidred workers Jensile and farm managers on, except farm. Cleration and Indred workers Jensiles workers Jensiles and Endred workers Jensiles and E	33 11 2 3 2 45 426 73	29 3 19 7	1 2	1	119	3	1 1 1 7 106 25	11 2 2 17 147 48		1	3	5 26
Decupation not reported remain employed Professional technical and andred workers. Farmers and farm managers Clernoal and kindred workers on, except farm Clernoal and kindred workers also workers Darlamm foremen and kindred workers Darlamm foremen and kindred workers Darlamm foremen and kindred workers Darlamm foremen and kindred workers	33 11 2 3 2	29 3 19 7 9	1 2 4 98 82	1 6 121	119	3	1 1 7 106	11 2 2 10 142	11 48	1 6 61	3 1 22 63 19	26

Table 49 -- CHARACTERISTICS OF THE RURAL-FARM POPULATION, FOR PARISHES _1950

Phylerics (*, remotes statuture bases or 20-percent sample or xerresp.ming complete-count figures on age, see age distribution or this table. Median not shown where base is less than 500]

					-	-	-	- Automore	-	-	-	-	-	-		-	-
Broke,	Acadia	Austr	ascen-	Assump- t.or	A '0y-	Beau- regard	Bien- ve	Boss er	Caddo	"alca- sicu	Cald- vell	Cameron	Cata- houls	Clai- borne	Con- cordie	De Soto	Bast Baton Rouge
Tou rura-fare popula oc.	4,003	. 56.	7 715	1 606	.7,035	0,553	9,2:1	9,620	14,884	5,47-	4,392	2,.88	6 982	1.,724	6,344	12,134	7,28
Mare Sauve white -		2 399	2 27	1 2 12	6 *2	3,27	2,360	-,53	_ 704	2,533	1,639		2,41	± 994	1,097	2,097	2 31
Foreign-norm white -	1.092	432	,2,8	1,58	2,49	1.32	2 354	3 313	5,779	395	593	132	1,236	4,009	2,086	3,953	1,44
Pemak Pat "e whate	5 983	2,263	2,524	1 -		-,010	2.20	475	1 553	2,214	1,516	918	2,093	_,893	1	2,040	1
Foreign-bur wille	12	5	19	3	1.4	4 12	1 5	13	5, 783	13	620	93	1,230	3 822	2 125	7	14
Other races	- 795	379	62	-,727	2,338	_03	2,25	3,260	3,783	20	620	73	2,230	3 024	2 125	4 027	1,269
AGE										100					100		1
Mare al ages	7,*35	330	4, 109	3,831	9,028	3,428	4,718 515	4,872	1,007	2 939	2 245	175	3,052	6,006	3,_89	6,059	3 743
Under 5 years 5 years 1.5 to 14 years 1.5 to 14 years 1.5 to 19 years 20 to 34 years 20 to 34 years 30 to 34 years 30 to 35 years 30 to 35 years	Cal	355	470	.84	1,110 1,014 1,116 965 555 505	نته	490	628	1,0%	329	252	100	445	684	4.3	757	394 435 408 396 194
15 to 14 years	-42 85 454	340	73 392	428 152	965	412 412 345	549 244 171	606 475	307	347 309	279 221	125	476 385	684 783 78	318	724 637	408 396
20 to 24 vesm	442	467	253	231 235	555	156	171	255	240	133	113	98 64	230 155	352 252	183	278	194
30 to 34 years	-26 506 479	16.	211	227	505 541 596	187	1º3 256	290 230	311	166	1.22	64	179	242 300	1.52	260 267	143 211 257
35 to 39 years 4C to 44 years 45 to 49 years	479	181	199	258	581.	201 248	305	274	413	178	123	64 77 72 79	235	29/	156 173	291 322 336	257
45 to 49 years 50 to 54 years	20.	173	2.3	.83 169	480 443 349	194	26	290 245	416 347 325	189 164	112	79 72 57	209 lol 128	*12 289	163 158 135	338	249 219 206 164 147
55 to 64 years 60 to 64 years	251	125	.59	137	349 300	.46 .51	21.8 202	222 170	325 255	122	109	57 36	129	260 241	135	290 241	164
65 to 69 years	151	80 60	64	99	219	156	⊾85	205	303 154	89	87	40	1,1	238	113	290	155
65 to 69 years 7C to 74 years 75 years and over	112	55	79	63	141	88 77	29	115	250	72	72	26 38	23	127	56 60	158	77 88
fema.e all ages	7 _03	2 689	3,706	3,775	8,307	3 125	4 499	4,748	7,313	2,532	2,147	1 013	3 330	5 718	3,155	o 075	3,542
Under 5 years	919	303 354	444	562 535	1,087	342 400	471 550	625	932	261	267	97	43.0	71.7 690	428	781	300
5 to 9 years	919	327	466 363 189	428	1 011	388	579	576	302	275	261	101	455 422	7.2	413 377	730 739 247	386 300
20 to 24 years	786 492	152	189	326 256	793 519	257 127	456 198	446 256	711 421 374	244 141 147		91 59 42	345	580 324	318 218	321	300 -84
25 to 29 years	443	151	216	247 211	491	165	185 268	232 262	374 373	147	122	54	195	2 ₇ 7	218 168 174	300 320	90
35 .0 39 Years	5.1	185	256 199 193	Z35 191	5.4 510	228	295	302 274	448	164	128	8- 73	203	302	186	340	263
40 to 40 years	423 374 293	164 190 134	204	175	443	167	292 248	2,3	428	1.5	120	62	190	341 306	166	338	228
20 to 28 years	205	134	243	1o3 115	376 299	_45 1,08	23.7	+72	3-8 239	147	119	66 49	143	273	149	277	168
AS to 60 sears	120	73	111	104	254	108	161	163	203	81	65	35	73	187	78	274 223	140 117
70 to 74 years 75 years and over	82 81	39 33 46	58 78	63	75	60	93	86	238 117	64. 38	35	37 34	64 43 56	203	87 42 62	254	54
*YEARS OF SCHOOL COMPLETED	01	40	70	0.3	107	62	91	105	113	47	51	29	56	136	62	162	94
Persons 25 years old and over.	6,375	2,637	3,735	3,370	8,395	3 415	4,600	4 725	6,700	2,670	2,235	1,160	3,170	5,435	2,810	5,990	3,885
No school years completed Elementary 1 to 4 years	1,560	365 620	520 - 025	1,225	1 005	635	225 1,200	1,725	2,405	215 640	11.5 525	210	340 845	1 655	270 920	460	395
5 and 6 years.	1 115	620 590 270	680 395	590	1 875	695	890	820	1,250	455	435	190	610	925	715	2,275	730 550 285 270 645 405
8 years	320	2451	285	200 175	720	435 420	325 420	330 420 4*5	425	195	280	95	290 350	465 515	160	535 355 785	285
4 Sears	5°0 240	245	490 200	170 80 30	1 005	592 270	840 250	200	530 190	405	390	50 }	355 165	9551	265	785	645
College to 3 years - 4 years or more	60	15	55	30 45	150	50 85	75 35	70 105	175	30	90 55 30	60 5	85	140	5C	1e5	265
School years not reported Median school years completed	150	61	5 8	50	70 170 5 8	85	35	105	145	75 6 5	60	10	65 65	60	100	290	100
EMPLOYMENT STATUS AND MAJOR OCCUPATION GROUP			,		2 0	13	70	2 4	21	0.5	70	, 8	6 2	6 3	5 5	5 3	7 8
Male 14 years old and over	4,059	1,514	2,593	2 446	5 994	2,330	3,205	3,129	4,606	2,012	1,506	87_	2 349	3,948	2 004	3 963	4,585
Civilian labor force.	4.010	1 514	1 996	1,941	4,786 4,786 4,755	1,735	2,38_	2 427 2,422	3,610	1,542	1.076	637	1.814	3,948 3,057 3,056	1,606	2,905	1,948
Cavilian labor force. Employed Unemployed	58	1 468	71	1,908	4,755	1 (93	2,347	2,377	3,563	1,488	2,068	621	1,730	3,0_9	1,593	2,876	1 888
Not in labor force	947	398	397	>03	1,207	604	824	305	1,056	470	430	234	535	891	398	1 0.8	59 637
Female, 14 years old and over labor force Civilian labor force	31.5	142	2,393 303 302	2,314	386	2 068	3,011	3,068	4,723	1,773	1,406	742	2,117	3,748	2,006	3,367	2,4.5
Civilian labor force. Employed	31.5	142	202	236	386	172	395	612	1 137	136	111	40	. 99	479	488	525 509	410
Lnemploved	20	1 042	2,090	20	6	4	3	15	16	124	108	40	190	476	477	-6	399
Male, employed _	3,952	1,468	1,925	1,908	4,75%	1,693	2,016	2,455	3 570	1 637	⊾ 295		1,918	3,269	1,5_8	3,441	2,005
moleonana) tachunat ana malaut (anamalaut	23	37	27	23	37	40	2 347	2,377	3,563	1,488	23	621	1,790	3,719	1,593	2,876	78
armers and farth managers fanagers officials, and proprietors except farm lencal and kindred workers	2,697	725	624	276	3,523	699 56	1 243	1,170	1,678	36	641	325	1 191	1,766	1,011	1 750	114
dencal and kindred workers	19	36 14 13	52 38	22	18	3.	30	52 23	38	26	20	12	22	49	18	66	. 84 55 32
	go	124	238	142	135	177 265	23 140 209	13.	146	29 206	2± 55 76	46	14 39 90	16 20 122	18	35	32
peratives and kindred workers rivate household workers	11.5	1	232	210	138	265	209	245	19C	246	76	46	90	236	53 74	102 220	3.0
rivate household workers graves workers, except private household arm laborers, unpaid family workers arm laborers except unpaid and farm foremen aborers, except farm and mine.	1C 452	19	29	20	470	3.5	236	25	31	23	10 45	6 46	3	10	8	17	55
arm laborers except unpaid and farm foremen	380	1.22	30"	1 067	232	40 71	71 268	96 320	885	192	45 80	46	-83 -27	324 242	193	239 189	37
ocupation not reported	48 70	27	150	74	83 48	194	268	273 46	171	92	67 42	49	64	182	66	165	363 1.0 1 55 37 134 489 29
Female, employed.	295	_36	293	216	380	167	392	597	1,137	124	108	40	198	476	477	28	
ofessional technical and kindred workers	28	10	25	-3	49 25	33	35 50	49	37	15	23	6	32 34	49	19	509	399 64
amers and farm managers anagers officials and proprietors except farm . erical and kindred workers	10	5	12	3	20	-01	13	9	195	5	4	2	34	49 61 8	19 82 1	59 97 17	28
	24	15	31	19	18	28	17	32 23 1	28	28	8	6	11	22	1	25	81
sitamen, foremen and kindred workers eratives and kindred workers wate household workers	6	5	27	20 2		- 1	1	1	20	18	1.	3	1	22 17 2 10	11	33	28 17 81 27 1
runce work are except permets household	63 25 84	16	25 40 24 45	55 18	75	16	1 44 25 154	19	109	20	17	4	3	10	5	18	15
rm labovers, unnaid family workers	84	21	42	1.0	30 I	22	25	32	42 300	20	17	12	14	21	42 6	56 21	91 27 20
borers except fa-m and mme.	1	5	35	40	18	1	8	143	324	2	16	İ	27 14 50 10	64 21 196 23 1	210 64 2	1.32 33	20
rupation nos reported	22	4	12	1.	19	8	9	2	42	3	3	1	1 3	1	24	1.3	7
				-	<u> </u>					-1	-1	-1	- 31	- 31	241	1.3	7

Table 49 —CHARACTERISTICS OF THE RURAL-FARM POPULATION, FOR PARISHES 1950-Con.

rak (*) denotes statistics based on 20-percent sample for corresponding complete-count figures on age, see age distribution in this those. Median not shown where been is less than 5001

Subject	Bas. Carroll	East Felic- iana	Bvar- ge_ine	-17	Grant	The=*s	Yber- vilue	- 80 ABOD	Jeffer-	effer- son Da s	Ia-	10.m'e	IA Salar	necln	F-A-DE-	Madas 75	More
Total ural-farm population	9,939	8,196	~+ 511	22,959	j Jan	4,606	3 280	3 286	95.	6,472	-4.14	p 572.	2,720	8,506	35C 25	8 047	
Native white	- 935	769	5,018	6,982	1,841	2,_72	1,716	1 20	433	3 329	- 286	3 667	1 348	2 '00	-,-2	1,431	2 2
Negro Other races	3 100	3,400	2,447	4 145	772	1,359	029	539	22	*_0	2,848	74-	65	-,951	68 462	2,646	4 5
male Native white	1,726	735	4.635	5,.99	1,652	.,865	980	1,055	-52	2,800		3.432	1,236		2	1,340	20
Foreign born wh.te	3,30	3,26	2,355	4,195	797	12	14	565	9,	371	4,0.5	4		2,-19	ης.		
Negro. Other races	4	1	1	4,195	1	1 240	620	262	201	371	2,82~	723	71	1 92	480	2,603	4.5
AGE	2,057	4,185	2							!							
Male all ages	811	527	7,511	1,.61	2,619	3, 243	1,460	-83	175	3,461	7,159	524	- 413	4 458	5.304	4,049	6,7
n 9 years	7.7 o55	536	1,02C 987		304	-42	208	_87	50 5	415	92.0	52.7	121	5.3 -65 -96	652	548	1,
to 14 years	-81	58_ 445	881 765	1,370	31	-42 444 351	168	273	79 71 27 27	365	420	5C.3	164	469	527	757 408	1
to 29 /ears	295 257	279 195	540 429	726	142	252 23s	122	90	71	222	552	319	14± 61 68	469 300	3	240	
to 34 years	21/	152	498	602	133	227	95	56 85	21	_83 198	425 391	266 24£	42 83	17.	2°3	_65 _64	
to 39 years	261	27.5	539 462	671 677	132	229 1°0	83	136	22 30 35	232	458	272	83 10e	254	342 344	21/	
to 49 years	234 196	193	392	594 775	156	140	83 96 87	90	35	248	399 402 272	27'3 214	10r 91 81 70	261 238 234	250	21.6 238 183	
to 50 years	203	155	240	222	127	130-	\$0 \$0	70 84 74	34 22 1" 1"	16.	260	.92 .5n	30	217	179	204	
to 64 years	157	176	107	282 278	130	108	80	Dead	17	104	-93 -37	.5n	20	_67	148	137	
to 74 years years and over	74	116	58	161	6/ 72	97 47	35 42	55 39	- 4	57 6C	71	85 /2	33	126	84	67	
Female all ages.	7,882	4,01	7 0.0	10,814	4 407	3,123	1,620	1,62	481	3,191	p,9U5	4,152	1,30	1.348	4 734	3 958	٨.
oder a vesre	795	525	4.342	64C	281 289	393 40-	2_0	179		424	938	499	.1"	45	547	593	-
to 14 years to 14 years to 19 years	696 571 478	5:'9 223 401	9/3 875	1,361	289 259 220	380	_89 _75	207	52 55 381 30	369	83J 871 743	480	_30 _28	499 503	54B	558	
to 19 years	478 338	232	566 509	1,118	220		50	17.	54	3_0	743	377	_18	46 256 226	433	354	
to 29 years	338 261	.93	4.2	56	146	191	"Con l	57 74	30	-97	503 25	2751	9 59	226	433 257 333	228 204	
to 34 years	295 293	21_	470 51"	-02	1.34 1.58 1.63	22/	_07	106	201	554	448	264	7.4	2.4 250	3,7	21.3	
to 44 years	266 226	213	38 ₆ 375	615	.63		27	98	35	2,4	402	230	112) DEC	225	
to of years	202	178	240	355	.4C _26		Pl	94	20	7ند 14ء	306 274	302 200	93	217	100	222	
to 64 years.	7ريد 92	109		305 276	76	6 92	94 P1 72 36	25	15	72	49	_88 _43		1 149	268 -07 -23 -05	111 71 1_9	
to 69 years	114	16+ 79	12 84 31	2.76 2.3	37 58	81	53	41 31	14	45	119 82	ائد ا	47	50 87	405	1_9 45	
vests and over.	72	99	66	139	5R	46 45	23 25	36	اد		-16	양	35 35	125	54 67	58	-
*YLARS OF SCHOOL COMPLETED Persons 25 years old and over	4,315	3,455	6,305	r 560	2 075	2,9.5	1,630	4,655	405	3,145	6 Cop	4 194	161	4,220	4,720	3,380	3
segoo, wars completed	49_	305		945	14	940	2,0	85	43	υ00	1 855	1 2.0	25	.75	235	-22	7
ementary 1 to 4 years 5 and 6 years	1, 0	د1,16ء 000	1,70° 1,845 1,09°	2,900	590 46,	850 435	4u5 200	415	95 85	780 565	1 2.5	435	3.5	880	1,130	1 245	2,
7 years	420	295	466	1,050	300	166	183	235	30	315	4.0	300	270	1 4.0	485	255	
8 years	290 340	295	30° 400	1 025	31* 440	85 165	120	240 250	30 30 65	160 250	365	245	280 280	845	510	230 270	
d years	100	100	70 70	205	175	100	130	5C	25	295 65	205	245 13°	90	290	210	165	
4 years or more	45	50	50	707	50 30	55 25	55	20	20 25	32	120	80 50	90 30 30 65	120	1.0	85 25	
edian school years completed	145	50	165	225 5 7	7-0	100 3 2	2~ 5 ¥	25	20	5 >	3.4	80 3 8	15	- 4	6 9	4 9	A.
EMPLOYMENT STATUS AND MAJOR OCCUPATION GROUP										2			4.1.	1	100	7	
Male 1a years old and over	3,017	2,000	4,780	6,949	٨,800	2,288	1,174	1, 17	337	2 294	4,661 3,886	2,977	1,038	3 352	3,407	2,508	4.
Soc force C-vilian lapor force.	2,419	2,227	4,056 4,053 4,037	6,949 5,527 5,520	1 237	2,288 1,846 845	392 892	811	269 269	1,808	3,886 3,883	2,383	676 675	2,229	2,655	1,985	3,
Employed	2,416	2,207	4,037	2 484	1,206	+,830	87€	81_ 799	257	1,7,1	3 866	2,322	653	2,275	2,586	1,981	3,
Unemployed	17 598	433	724	36 -,422	31 563	442	282	306	12	180	775	594	22 362	823	809	520	1
Female 14 years old and over	2,928 523	2,491	4,271	6 567 522	1,070	2,023 288	. 072	1,06/	328 5*	2,382	4,429	2,748	956 56	2,473	3,54	2,393 285	4
sbor force Crvilian labor fo.ce	-23	683 682	423	522	155	288	135 1°6	88	35 54	185	061	293 293 284	>6	473	466	283	
Employed	503	68h	413	514	147	283	126	87	54	179	921	284	56	465	455	2,4	1
ot m labor force.	2,405	± 808	3,848	6,045	1,421	4,735	236	979	273	-,847	3,768	2 455	900		2,608	2,108	3,
Male employed	99د 2	2,207	4,037	5,484	1,206	1,830	876	"59 18	257	1,792	3,866	2,322	653	2,175	2,586	1,981	3,
ofessional technical, and kindred workers	1,530	137	3 051	4,038	255	814	382	430	7	989	2,408	738	207	1.082	- 40	1,317	2,
orescent terminate, and annuel workers rimers and farm managers anagers, officials and proprietors, except farm encal and kindred workers	9	32	40 20	47	34	29	38 10	12	29 11 4	30 11	48	3-	15	51 29	62 42	21	
les workers	13	별	29	23 61	21	27	10	8	4	10	31	57	14	1 40	56	19	
aftsmen, foremen and kindred workers	- 14 ₄	85 178	20 75	128 133	106	48 83	102	5C _07	43 49	84	313	165 247	143	231	344	94	
rvate bousehold workers rvace workers, except prayate household.	2	1 22	15	1.8	23	1 7	10	10	2 8	81 445 43	3	26	9	39	40 185	2 8	
em laborers unpaid family workers em laborers except unpaid and farm foremen	167 406	22 269 136	15 504 141	26 206 318	23 39	635	135	25		81	713	26 06 782	13 15	159 108	185	152	1
borers except farm and mine	42	278	67	74	108	1.7	4	24 94	10	43	33	88	83	168	212	42	1
rupation not reported	21 503	23 685	23 413	→0 514	147	21.	126	87	34	16	651	22 284	25 56		43	274	1
femule employed	24	24	34	84	32	13	15	15		20		37	19				
ofessional, technical, and kindred workers rmers and farm managers anagers, officials and proprietors, except farm.	121	J36	34	130	21	11	0	6		8	34 26 0	9	3	21	40	88	
	37	17 29	20	2/	20	22	2C	2	14	18	56 42	12 34 23	8	13 34 37	32 40 18 44 27	13	
les workers raftsmen foremen, and kindred workers	15	18	23	27	9	25	10	8	3				3		1	12	
	2	12	3	5	6	9	12	20	9	8 57	18 71	26	4	20	12	33	
rvate household workers rvace workers, except private household tru aborers unpaid family workers um laborers, except unpaid and farm foremen	4C 15	20 22 304	56 13	33 35	_7 _8	63	12	14	6	6	23	40 28	- 41	70	33	0	
arm abovers unpaid family workers	±01	30%	190	133	25	82 44	26	2	3	17	320 38	54	1	3.	169	43	

Table 49 -- CHARACTERISTICS OF THE RURAL-FARM POPULATION, FOR PARISHES 1950--- Con

[Axtersit. *) dense as statutes named on 20-percent sample for corresponding complete-rount figures on age, see age distribution in this table. Median not shown where base is less than 500]

	Surgest	mat_hi-	Outc's-	P_10710-	Pointe Coupes	Remides	Ged River	Rich- isad	Sab (ne	St Bernard	St. Charles	St Helens	St James	St Johr the Baptist	9- Landry	St Martin	S ⁺ Mary	St
		1 000	1595	2,500	239	3,67_	8, 44	17,097	7.957	594	1,290	6,786	5, 90	2,022	37,257	10,828	6,231	>,53
ا جلما	Strve white	2,72	2,033	773	2,292	5,013	1,823	4,933	3,675	277	451	1,488	1,202	447	6,785	3,197	963	2,24
2	Foreign-born wa.ie	7,413	1 25	27 523	20 1.3 1.3	1,961	2,215	3,748	422	32	227	2,004	29	591	10,112	2,452	2,187	6.
	Vatrye white	3,.83	_,851	710	2,119	-,621 +7	1,754	4,647	3,393	227	390	1,364	_,185	39	8,271	2,888	985	2,09
F	foreign-born white	4 382	282,1	15 436	19	1,86/	1	3,723	446	31	212	1,926	1 538	576	9,909	2,255	2,058	52
0	Agen Laces -	6	1	6	4	35	•		-		1				1	,	,	
Male.	AGE	8,192	3,453	378	5,825	7,081	A_041	8,090	4,109	322	685	3,493	2,750	1,044	18,938	2,671	3,176	2,89
der 5 v	ANTE .	1,109	278 42.	128	788 781	811 912	551 494	1,198	42.	30 33	84 70	476 468	443 336	153 145	2,754	783 746	463 430	31 33
byeau to 14 w	oard -	1 03	438 363	143	673 597	964	484	1,204 MD	522 395	26	70 71 70 48 38	370	316 267	127	2,640	707 675	375 252	36 31 13
to 24 w	mare	37/	202	89	350 282	43_ 303	21.0 180	529	135	26 27 17 27	48	195	176	76 48	1,458	425 375 318	187 173 175	1.5
0 29 v 0 3- y	P079	392	452	72	302 3-3	341 480	204	436 532	233 239	15	32	189	137	99 76 48 55 49	990	318 353	218	14
0 39 y	68.09	4-6	210 220	88	322	452	232	484 464	258 204	24	19	228 174	143	63	990	283 266	164	17
10 44 yr 10 49 vr 10 5- yr	9878	435 142	_97 _8°	88 09	304 229	354 366	232 229 176 179	333	204	15 22 24 30 22 20	28 27 28	126	141	56 38 37	70? 552	198	1.21	13
0 5 _m yr 0 m9 yr 0 64 yr 0 69 yr	ests	,40 240	_62 _41	6	221 21.4 208	294 257	179 142 163	323 270	209	9	33	100	72	30	380 285	140	125 100 92	11
59 yr	ears	255 150	72	.6 51 34	88	219	84	237 119	168	8	31 15	17	76 55	27	174	48	62	-
ears at	ng over	_6,	56	27	103	6 590	7,103	8,367	3,848	8	505	3,293	2,740	20	_76 18,319	5,157	3,055	2,0
Female or 5 v	e, all ages	7,789	387	1,1,2	5,414	795	549	1,279	403		88	449	436	129	2,761	772 693	483 379	30
0 year	D	1,056	372	2.04	704 633	794	530	1,172	498	27 26 20 16 20 20 16	70	416	JO8	130	2.609	543	336	33
19 y	ears	833 428	3_3 158	1_0 122 98	520 307	614 372	503 365 258	844 556	343	16	40	348	224	93	1,373	558 387	246 225	21
		439 428	162	61	315	354 428	226 215	789 5.77	219	20	50 31 50	151	171	65	1,026	3 19	172	15
34 yr 39 yr	nars -	451	237	70 80 97	334 305 296	438	259	527	239	21 28	39	220	152	57 16 48	1,070	3.4	194 195 161 127 135 104	18
	PATS	44£ 398	200 174	69 60	296	460 315	252 203	470 392	236 230	23	26 37	_581	116	54 34 35	205	238	127	1.4
04 yr	PRIFE	324 251	157	55 35	228 222 154	226 233	155	32_ 255	197 _83	12 10 13	30 20	115	124	35	600 434 341 254	167	104	-1
69 y	ears	.80 188	90 85	35 28 19	155	22R 174	108	168	136	8	18	104	77	23	254	108	94	
74 ye	ears	107	60	19	121	148	69	94	97 86	6	20	45 52	53 72	9	191	38	45 55	4
*1	TEARS ON SCHOOL COMPLETED													875	13,960	4,420	2,785	2.69
Person rhool	years completed.	6,915	3,125	1,240	1,270	495	3 845	7 125	3,805	33.5	635 85	3,1,20	2,365 460	400 400	4,280	1,825	920	9
entar	v 1 to 4 years 5 and 6 years	2 285	7.0	32J 265	1,985	1,710	1,175	2,380	860 845	75 65 25	155	955	625	170	4, 755	1,145	89 ₄ 390	66 59
	7 vears	64L 385	625 280 320	.05	290	785 635	31.5	750 655	390 400	25	60	275	125	65	790 465 775	300	155	35
schoo	al 1 to 3 years	755 130	500 265	-50 94 80	240 295 365	905	305 930 55	832	710	40 40 25	65 65	485 235	210	80	775	830 95	185	40
ge ·	4 years	130	1.5	20	85	240	60	110	60	10	35	80	70	45 25 10	135	40	50	. 9
ol yes		345	50 60	50	140	220	90	25	1201	10	2.5	45	15	30	290	45	25 35	3
EMF	JOYMENT STATUS AND MAJOR OCCUPATION GROUP	4 9	7 0	6 1	3 7	6 6	5 2	5 8	5 9	- 1	0 8	6 5	4.5	/ 8	3 1	2 2	3 3	6
	OCCUPATION GROUP	5 178	2 29+	959	3,702	4,667	2,601	5 452	2,76	240	477	2,220	1,702	642	11,418	3,505	1,97	1,90
r fore	Inpor force	3,760	1,753	727	3,009	3,355	1,900	4,321	1,981	189	345	1,774	1,270	495	9,180	2,965	1,183	1,42
Exaplo	ryed	3,703	1,728	694	2,971	3,240	1,877	4,298	1,920	187	323	1,764	1,240	48~	9,105	2 945	2,549	4,38
	ployed	1,418	543	432	690	1,112	701	1,231	783	21	735 55	446	432	147	2,236	500	32	53
-	14 years old and over	4,826 549	2,0c8 208	835 162	719	4, 117 562 562	3,629	5,095	2,>98	109	396	2,092	250	596 84	10,755	3,165	1,923	1,77
inan Cmplo	labor force	548	208	148	719 696	544	333	40	170	24 34	77	454	250	84	1,347	450	408 385	50
nemy	ployed	+, 277	4,960	573	23	3,755	2,29	4,684	2,428	145	319	1 6.8	1,434	572	9 428	2,704	1 515	1,56
falc, e	mployed.	3,705	_ 728	694	2,971	3 240	1,877	4,298	1,420	18"	322	1,7.4	1,2+0	487	9,135	2,942	1,549	1,38
PER BE	d, seconsoal, and kindred workers.	2,451	847	243	31 -,607	1,268	20 1,138	3,096	1,047	85	9	50	261	6	6,318	.,078	16	57
gers,	officials, and propnetors, except farm	49 18	44 20	243 35 1/	53	92	30 16	39	39	12	17	23	33	12	8C	281	23	- 5
works	foremen, and kindred workers.	24 82	29 155	9 20	35	57	14	20 3/	24	6	8	-4	18	10	43 42 109	12	14	27
tives	and kindred workers	144	191	121	1.87	264 343	92	142	21.4	16	28	144	218	36 5b	147	49	84 162	4.2
e wor	ers, unpaid family workers ers, unpaid family workers ers, except unpaid, and farm foremen	38.	17	23	17	52	3	2	12	6	10		16	c	18	71 7	24	2
labor	ers, except unpaid, and farm foremen	2361	37.0 87	27 51 90	455	98 367	128 ∠68	200	95	10	76	47	538	212	354	465 326	899	2 5 12
ers, e	xcept farm and mine not reported	1./9	36 12	17	135	40	32	10	158 51	5	24	56 22	36	33	122	53 28	1	14
	employed	5-2	ZC.	148	696	544	324	404	167	54	73	454	248	82	۵,302	4>2	395	20
mons	technical and kindred workers	55 98	28 15	20	5± 56	74 41	32 48	-4 82	43	11	7	²⁶ 43	23	14	80 63	10	15	1
ers an	officials and proprietors except farm.	1 9	10	20	26	53	6	8	15	3	11	141	10	2 5	23	15	19	1
u and			21	7	30	33	3		15	4	6	23 40	-7	3	42	30	0	4
worke men.	foremen, and kindred workers	1	1	2	1		21	3!	-				2.1	-	7	1	- 1	
worke smen, tives	foremen, and kindred workers and kindred workers	7	13	27	14	19	7	2 3 10	9	4	15	8	50	6	12	23	14	10
worke men, tryes	foremen, and kindred workers and kindred workers	36 33	13	27 23 11	1 14 83 27	19 48 63	2 7 30 19	39	9	4 4 3	13	8 22 20	1.1	6 23 7	1 104 59	21 24 21	14 74 20	2
worker men, tryes a te house work labore	foremen, and kindred workers	7	13 72 20 24 7	27	14 83	19 48	2 7 36 19 89 55	43	9		13	8	38 38	6	1 104 59 747 45 4	21	14 74 20 11 206 2	1 2 1

NOTE -- Orleans Parish ertirely urban, not shown in this table

Table 49 —CHARACTERISTICS OF THE RURAL-FARM POPULATION, FOR PARISHES 1950—Con.

(Arterial. (*) denotes statutes based on 20-percent sample, for corresponding complete-count figures on age, see age custrib. 1-on it. 1-but table - ided as not above where base is on than 500-

Subject	TREETIDELY 9	Tengas.	פ מנלמיים	**AGN	vers. or	*******	dub at tu	Webste	yough	egut	re_'c'an_	¥22.
Total rural-ferm population	AD 7°C	3,/00	6 345	c 974	2 3~-	7 917	_1 _55	440	4 .20	2,450	.,64.	5,80
le Native white Foreign-porn white	7,792 318	. 2.5	2,6_0	3 247	5,2.7	1,94,1	4, 20	2,003	"86	10-27	300	2,00
Negro Other races	2 030	2 904	_ 2C2	1 -59	59	3	S - 40	6,4.	2.0	1 37.	1 604	59
Other races	2		-06		2			11. 1		21		
Foreign born whi e	7,189	1,215	- 53	2 "111	2,304	2,047	4 29	4,934	708	4 465	13	2,27
Other races	2,572	2,0,2	- 13-	1 %	5.4	244	≥ 00	-,400	1,73	المركب	- 15	54
AGE Male all ages	LC, 142	4 182	3 _30	4 00_	6,423	410	9 8,3	4.483	2 359	6,42	1,9%	٤, ١
or 5 years	27. 27. .,2.,	623	45	487	6.2	440	âân l	427	2-	So*	24	3
9 vears 14 ears 10 years 24 vears 29 vears	. 27.1	488	422	522 55-	742	1-5	64	1.2 2.5	2-3	3.6	266	3
10 years	644		30,	232 280	5-12	428	09-1	46"	570	634	1.7	2
24 vears	644	2.3	230	280	400	183		2.3	.26	394	1_7	1
	588	199	.84	2_6	30"	192	. 9-	204	_UC	345	241	1
39 years	29	232	.54	257	439	2.08	402	220	34	4.26	63	
49 years	746	23_	149	≥50 238	400	2 -	281	26#	100	197 321	1_C	:
of years	462	.80	143	22"	334	2021	222	21.		230	80	
.9 years	-11	164	126	241	256	2.6	200	120	04	210	75	
64 years	326 316	_67	_09	205	212	1%	197	190	3.	7a_ 6°_	75 E3	
60 years	851	89	2.	95	88	1.2	1-8	-06	52	دو <u>د</u> هو	30	
Lis and over	700	91	59		94	102	TO	78	50	8.	25	
emale, all ages	10 308	4 -19	3,015	- 201	294	- 21	6,34	+ 1.0	4,06.	0,029	- h-16	2,
5 years	1 134	625 5 /2	427 296	5.32	Co^	390	8.9	04 51.3	254	8.2	382	
14 years	1,154	402	360	224	נפר	4-6	AJ9	233	233	782	244	
19 vears	954	304	265	454	285	323	. 2	449	-67	649	198	
24 years	61.5 6:0	242	203	254	-04	2.6	357 3.30 3.00 89	20¢	133	179 3 _	109	
3- years	70_	22.	_ 70	231 258	395 458	2421	- 10	2-	122	.73	70	
89 years	743	257	1%	258	458	240	189	.90	1 2	40_	129	
-4 years	670	204	151	230	.8.	245	264	270	-32	32 2nh	103	
o4 years	4.9	18,	146	417	3€.	1931		كرك 18^	2.	203	84	100
00 years	322	141	10,	309	2:5	195	249	191	94	1.02	61	
69 years	232	-62	83	100	13	16	152	124	7	121	65	
74 years	13"	71 79	54	82		.91	c3 83	62	75	~o	25	
sars and over	.44	79	54	98	.0,	75.	83	ER		60	44	
*YEARS OF SCHOOL COMPLEYED	1		1	10.00		1.1						
Persons 25 years old and over	10 010	3,600	2,755	1,290	b 315	4,180	6 125	4,.25	1,995	5,210	∠ 5°C	, ,
school years completed	1 495	450	575	390	1,630	1.5	1,300	30» 990	470	295 1 265	24.5 720	;
5 and 6 years	2,3.1	x 395	1,090	900	1,030	8001	1.2.0	62.5	26C	125	250	
7 years	1,040	230	163	640	4.5	>30	763	440	_30	295	75	
8 years	1,220	245	145	450	325	530 925	1,005	500 610	80 165	632 960	5Q i	-
4 years	260	85	75	175	250	45	555	230	9,	130	45	
ege 1 to 3 vears.	190	. 75		415	St	05	175	70	25	106	55	
d rears or more ol vears not reported	250	70	.5 65	55 60	15	10	105	90 75	50 20	60 4.i	25	
an school years completed	6 +	4.3	3 9	7 0	4 3	7 6	7 3	6 8	3 5	5.8	40	
EMPLOYMENT STATUS AND MAJOR OCCUPATION GROUP											1	
OCCUPATION GROUP	1			1 40		2 220		2 000	2 4-1	4.056	1.252	2.
Male 14 years old and over .	7,126	2,017	2,131	3 -58	4 538 3,617 3,615	2 830	3 444	2,872	1,303	4,056	937	1
or force	2.096	2,117	1,641	2,308	3,615	£,034	3.44	2,099	-,055	-,_co	937	1
Employed	> 337	,998	1, 13	2 273	3,596	2 034	3 423	2,051		3 052	933	1
Unemployed	.,458	250	28 489	34 850	19 921	776	3± 532	770	32 306	915	315	
temale 14 years old and over	0,623	2 644	1,850	2,90-	4 405	2 598	4 050	2,757	1,35	3,718	1 14.	1.
or torce	1 976	443	363	-95	454	291	646	330	206	219	157	
vilian labor force	1,974	438	363 349	-93	454 450	291	644	330	26o 253	218	156	
Employed.	2,947	5	34	2	4	12	2	7	L	3	1	
Unemployed	1,624	2,201	1,512	2,700	رد, 11	4,307	J 404	2 427	1 085	3 499	984	1
Male employed	2 037	1,990	: 023	2,275	3,796	2 034	3 4.2	2,051	1,023	3,092	9.3	
essional, technical and kindred workers -	53	_3	17	40	∠3	4-	69	26	7	2	4	
ners and farm managers	3 26C	1,245	133	1,347	2,/67	,099	1,906	C06	184	2 313	13	
agers officials and prop setors, except farm	- 1 40	16		<8	20	_5	39	23	- 5	_1	5	
s workers	66	7	30	30	26	32	51	25	8	18	8 21	
ftamen foremen and kindred workers -	273	39 92	118	118	8>	2-0	19°	153	90 90	80		
atuves and kindred workers	333		247		3	1	1	1			1	
nos workers except private household m laborers unpaid family workers m laborers, except unpaid, and farm foremen	36	2	3.	11	13	28	29	28	73 442	320	4	
m laborers unpaid family workers	483 663	119	609	94	260 421	124	297	120	73	370 126		
m laborers, except unpaid, and farm foremen orers except farm and mine	206	396	10	1/6 167	6b	190	175	172	25	4.5	32	
upation not reported	63	_0	13	23	-9	19	-0	49				
Female employed	1,94"	438	149	193	420	279	644	323		2.5		
fermional, technical, and kindred workers	91	.~	26	57	44	51.	72	25	6	26	1	To the
mere and farm managers	220	149	6	15	22	22	75	18		32	25	
mer and farm managers magers, officials and proprietors except farm mal and kindred workers	24	1 .3	3	14	25	10	16 51	18	3 22	!	3	
	75	12	30	.1	17	20	34	1 7	1	15	-3	
ftsmen foremen, and kindred workers	14			2	1	1			1			
itsmen foremen, and kindred workers eratives and kindred workers	1,5		96		11	12	36	44		1 15		
	45	63	38	26 36	37 16	12	16 33	1 4		11	8	
vice workers, except private household m laborers unpaid family workers m laborers except unpaid and farm foremen	879	16		5	220	83	235	of	13	32	36 31	
	360	123	121	6	1.5	2	62	1.4	119		31	
rm laborers except unpsud and farm foremen borers, except farm and mine	360	****	3		1		5	1.0	1 8			

lable 492.—CHARACTER STICS OF THE RUR L-FARM NONWHITE POPULATION, FOR PARISHES 1950

14500 992---CHARACTERASTICS OF THE REACTEMENT INCOME THE VOICE AND THE V

· 3- fr.,	- 64 -	1	A5 e7:-	nd	-/ 12	Bra	B'	Boscie-	Gadio	Calca-	Calq-	Cupurar	Jata- houls	Clai- torne	Con- cordia	De Solo	East Ba*co Ro_ge
Total rural-carr is southite populative	2,.91	E 2	2,.82	3,4.2	4 c 7.5	235	4,60	6,574	11,>65	700	_,213	225	2,/69	7,833	4 211	7,983	2,687
Male Linges Uncer 5 years 5 to 7 con-	2:2	46P	197 186 153	6/J	2,494 349 337 374	_32 _4 15	2,354 3,4 298 372	3 342 409 460 42	5,781 870 853 794	195 40 63 50	293 88 17 08	132 16 15 14	200 264 .58	4,009 582 51 597 518	32,086 234 243	5°5 5°5	1,4.6 195 169 177
0 to 1 m reach 5 to 9 to 24 mars 20 to 24 mars 25 to 24 mars 30 to 24 mars 33 to 39 years 40 to 44 mars	100 M	75 70 25 44 44	58.020	143 178 65 89	332 74 149 CO	8 20 8	148 83 73 209	182 1.8 1.8 1.4 1.5 16-	643 326 474 206 256 286	24 12 15 15 21	78 29 20 21 25 27	19 10 7 7	68 39 48 65 85	256 259 249 202 283	22. 113 93 87 99 100	181 172 127 170 170	76 50 50 11 69
45 to 49 years 50 y 14 years ou to 3d years (2 or 64 years to 1: 69 years 70 to 74 years - 8 years and over-	1 24 7 6	1	25.54 75	67 65 8- 39 -7	32 73 57 80 40	12	95 85 85 9	181 162 -43 -65 -20 54 82	286 239 227 _68 240 109 104	18 13 13 13 17 8 6	28 18 17 26 16 11	4664447	30 28 50 13 29	-56 12- 109 -57 72	98 87 87 67 81 44 38	196 170 167 118 164 85	49 61 51 82 37 37
Female all ages Loder 5 care : 10 % years : 10 % years : 10 10 % rears : 27 to 24; Years	1,398 -79 167 -76 -44 29	66 67 49 49 20 26	170 176 1-76 1-78 98 73 70	1 727 30° 26 221 2-1 2-0 26	2 3+ 385 33- 322 274 458 13	12	2,292 283 326 348 475 420 98	3 260 4/3 -42 4_2 714 488 1/7	5,784 785 846 742 585 349 287	42 29 47 43 21 10	82 95 74 65 55 23	92 14 43 40 7	1,232 166 173 144 120 81 75	3 824 557 527 525 422 247 214	2,125 297 280 249 231 49	4, J28 613 524 537 395 743 202	1 271 152 272 276 415 69
45 to 25 vests 35 to 35 vests 35 to 35 vests 45 to 35 vests 45 to 45 vests 45 to 45 vests 55 to 35 vests 55 to 57 vests 55 to 57 vests 55 to 57 vests	29 .7 20 68 40 40 20	22 26 15	5 48 48 7 31	85 99 % 6° 50 42	110 132 117 108 77 5-	34 0	130 130 132 98 88 7/ 52	_65 _85 _80 _7; _47 _10 92	324 352 302 257 273 47	17 16 16 20 14 13	27 29 28 27 30 22 1	5 7 5 6 8	69 73 70 59 59 59 41 27	196 201 279 46	97 15 -30 -40 102 97 64 56	189 207 2.6 205 156 128 123	59 77 72 50 40 34 53
60 to 64 years 62 to 60 years 70 to 74 years 77 years and ove **YEARS OF SCHOOL COMPLETED Persons 5.5 "exts old and over	625	360	42	45 45 .8 .3	40 20 35	110	62 3- 48	2,982	.91 82 89	6 6 300	7 4-	3 2 100	133 14 26	8J -14 -31 -64	68 29 40	148 57 88	60 18 32
No school years competed Elementary 1 to 4 years 5 ann 6 years 7 years 8 years H.gt school 1 to 3 years	31.5 31.0 80 1.5 1.5	45 -5 -5	240 4-50 -4-5 55 20	34, 510 157, 50 45	32.5 900 -62 80 55 32	15 45 20 1,	1-5 875 4-5 230 75 170	38./ 575 575 185 _60 _05	765 2,210 115 405 195	130 80 20 30 7 10	180 90 65 55 35	20 40 15 25	280 480 125 40 55 20	400 -,475 680 460 450 229	260 762 500 82 60 42	4.5 1 835 640 235 9,	33. 34.5 230 80 20 3.5 5
4 years College 1 to 3 vears 4 years or more. School years not reported Median school years computed. EMPLOYMENT STATUS	3 1 4	,	10 20 3 0	2 8	30 30 3 5	5	25 20 10 5 4 8	50 25 65 4 0	30 15 105 3 8	20	25		15 25 2 0	20 25 20 30 4 3	65	20 5 90 3 7	25 15 35 3 3
Male 14 years old and over Labor force. Cyriuan labor force. Employed Unsemployed Not in labor force	527 526 524 2 91	2 ₆₃ 2 ₄₀ 2 ₁₀ 2 ₀₂	720 578 578 56 14 142	970 808 808 799 9 162	1 *03 1,1°, 1 .95 1,190	96 72 72 71 1 24	1,144 1,144 1,07 329	2 003 1 561 1,561 1 544 17	3 4.5 2 672 2,670 2,651 19 743	248 184 284 176 8	258 255 248 7	54 54 61 3 27	741 336 336 356 350 6	2,437 1,905 1,946 9	1,714 1,312 1,007	2 30m 1 768 1,767 -,759 8	665 \$0. 640 25
Female _4 years old and over Labor force Cruitar labor force. Employed Unemployed	91 91 92 82	2+6 29 29 26 3 217	687 133 133 149 4 254	940	176 176 176 172	65 5 3	260 260 260 260	2,020 492 491 482 9	3,583 1,018 1,018 1,02 16	203 25 25 20 20	1_4 382 46 45 44 1	,8 6 6	782 80 80 80 80	2,316 354 35 352 2	2.6 367 386 376 10	352 352 352 343 8	242 820 187 186 181
Not in lacer force. MAJOR OCCUPATION GROUP Male, employed Profesional technical and kindred wo.kers Farmers and term inamagers	524 336	205	564 564	799	1,-90 3 622	7_	1,147	1 526 1,544 8 762	2 565 2,651 1 296	178	336 248 1 157	61	250 250 287	1,962	1,007	2 101 -,759 5 1,203	640
Manager officials, and proprietors, except farm Clerical and kindred workers - Sales workers - Craftzmen foremen and kindred workers Operatives and kindred workers Private bousened workers	1 5	18	7 45 1	1 16 79	8 22	10	2 2 12 6°	3 20 126 3	3 1 22 68	19	2 15	1 7	1 2 12 3	2 12 57	3 7 31	16 19	206 3 4 1 20 54
Service workers, except private household Farm laborers, unpaid family workers Farm laborers except unpaid, and farm feremen Laborers except farm and mine. Occupation i.o. raported. Female employed	107 67 6 2	14 38 23 1	24 257 51 19	673 15 4	96 25 10	7 22 3	6 .67 44 190 9	25 88 264 212 28 462	202 835 142 45	72 72 75 2	10 40 41 4	3	51 85 5	298 2.7 2.9.	140 97 33	183 260 109	27 28 87 131 9
Professional technical, and kindred workers. Farmers and "arm managers" Managers officials and propietors except farm. Clemenal and kindred workers Sales workers. Craftamen, toremen and kindred workers.	2	3 2	3 4	3	11 3 1	1	14 42	36 85 2 3	17 189 2	20	5 2 1 1	Б	80 4 26	352 24 50	376 4 76 1 2	34. 27 84 2	161 13 15 3 1

Cratesian, includes and solution of vocation. Private household workers Private household workers Private household workers Parm laborers unpaid family workers Farm laborers except unpaid and fam foremen. Laborers except man and mine Cocupation in "sported"	-2 -2 -2 1	14 1 1 1 1 2	35 8 29 34 2	21 49 3 35	9 50 11 1	1	42 10 136 8	56 22 139 113 2 14	1 105 27 297 322 3 38	13 4	1 17 3 1 13	3 2	24 3 10 9 1	184 20 1	1 42 5 169 59	2 52 14 120 28	7 89 12 15 18

GENERAL CHARACTERISTICS

18-111

Table 49a.—CHARACTERISTICS OF THE RURAL-FARM NONWHITE POPULATION, FOR PARISHES 1950.—Con.
Aster 46.49 (**oscion datas "exclusive Land on Al-percent sample, or corresponding complete sums fig. 46.70 mag, as age for things in the land. Modern and down we are been as 90g

displect	Ea.	Telle- inth	ior ha	hmar.k- uxb	Gran	Toeri-	Tier-	8º escr	-0.20-	T. TE -	farotto	Le-	64 0	_tr o	AVL#-	_91 _0	Yorr-
To ai rura-farm nonwhite popular on	F,2=6	٠,6 ٠,٠	-,8-3	2,342	-, 770	2,-1.5	,255		D.	702	401	2,40	2.0	", 72	94"	5,25.	٥,٥
Mule ali ages	3,106	3 40=	2.480	4,146	772		1 29							(:			
	323	464	4/0		CIP	24	-	-3	22	41°	2,349	****		7.1	-64	2,677	4.5
to 1) vents	323 4.3	465	346	290	14	-#5 go	¥.	5			7731		4	30/	6-1	396	51
	363	514 385	346	13.	1.70	.50	5-1	36	2,	62 !	367 .	77	4	2 .	54	347	5
to 24 years	13-	2"2	436	464	5° 3° 3°	-20	2.1	40.	21	7		771	-	215	4-1	222	x
to 29 years	1 136	47.		-93	3.	83	0	4.	*	5	206	47.1	-	74.	52	15.	- 3
to 39 years	14.	-47	142	103	43	81	30	2-	÷ .	= +	: 234	37		73 (57 .	20	3
1 1 44 years	1 14.	404	88	13.	4	25	2	31	1	20	10-1	30	5	2.65	-2 32	- vul	2
tt. 49 years -	9	135	84	£2*	35	20	Jr	32	41	-51	200	20					2
to 34 years	123	1,3	2	161	35 30 23		251	271	4	1-		3	0.5	~0;	22	-62	
to 64 veara	106	83	36	-74	27	37	\$21	-5	21	-21	- 2	3.		03	50	931	î
to 39 Years	121	136	36 29	. 14	34	32	20	50	- :	271	39	not .	9	761		130	
to 74 years years and over	34	80	10	51	1 16	-0	ī	13	!	71	25	15	2	29	-7	50 1	
	1						1	7	-1	5	- 1			1 4		26	
temate all ages		3,46.	2,346	7 .96	~98	1,2-6	62c	ا بنانہ	20	372	2.82	16	7.	1 92_	-82	2,601	4,5
der o vears	236 45.	497	4dl 412	739 609	119	192	90	96	1	52	51 412	1.2	6	100	34	344	
o 9 years	236	4-8	364 2-4	499	92		92	82	3	33	412	99	1, 1,	202	9	332	
to 19 /ears	282	343 202	2-4	4.6 315 253	92 77	43 70 85	*1	6.3	-	37	34.	.9 54 58	1	234 150	.8 48	23 1	
o 24 years	221	145	200	253	65	7"	, p	22		14	256	54	,	1 250		16.	
0 34 3 tare 0 39 years	16	16	1.1	20b	5	78	28	92 26 35	- 1				3 5	9.	15	115	
0 44 years	178	16/	124	253	33	80 42	5	35	3	15	144	40	5	9-	15	+68	
o 49 years	_49	- 63	76	196	45		20	32	-	23	رتد	30	4	96	24	146	
o 54 years	149	127	76	1-2	36	42	22	25		12	E3	33	6	°01	27	246	
0 54 VCAPS	r3	PR .	44	17.0	36 36 19	45 34	الله	18	2	-5	12	25	=	45	27 16 -3 -1	120	- 1
o 64 years	61	12	16 20	38	10	26	3	22		5	29	9	4	76	-1	41	
o 69 years	80 41	123	20	32 9:	3.	10		22	1	í	12	19	-	27	-2	41 90 35	4
car and over	.0	14	13	52	15	21	12	8	1	5	25	6	3	40	1 5	45	
*YEARS OF SCHOOL COMPLETED						-				- 1				1			
Persons 25 years old and over	2,690	2 505	4.477	3,300	585	ء 100	235	520	20	2005	4.75°	טייט.	75	1,400	425	21	
school years (ompleted	4.0	295	780	670	105	490				150	845	בים	12	170	40	365	3,
mintary 1 to 4 years . 5 and 6 years	1,250	1.09	450	1.650	240	365	125	40 205	30	120	505	32	-5	590	260	1,0.5	2.
	560 27,5	540 240	±30	555 165	140	170	72	1.00	5	_5	145	1.00	~5 5	59C 32C 95	85	1	2,
& years	70	19*	30	110	40	15	-01	64	- 1	5	30	25 10 15	10	95	15	-30	
r school 1 to 3 years	75	90	-	40	2,	10	1º.	30	1	21	5	15	1 20	25	15	55	
d yearsllege 1 to 3 years	10	2.	5	22	15	1.5	51	1.	5				_	25 25 20 15	5	10	
4 vears or more	10	۷.	5	25	1.	1.5		70						15		10	
cool years not reported	90	30	40	62	-	20	5	20	1		110	.00	1	20	6	70	
cian school vears completed	38	15	0.9	3 3	4 .	1.5	. 3	51	- 1	- 1	09	29		47		3 6	
EMPLOYMENT STATUS	1							- 1	- 1		1			1 1			
Male 14 years old and over _	1,822	2,070	1,3.2	2,42_	4"3	833	395	3,4	17	235	1.668	~6"	50	- 24	307	1,576	2,
por force	1,449	1,707	1,15/	1,963		675	282	236	14	188	1,425	CBC	2	915	242	1,220	2,
Civilian labor force	1,442	1,757	1,152		340 340	675	282	238	14	T88	4,484	.18L 375	27	9_5	2/2	1,219	2,
Employed Unstroloyed	1,428	1,741	1,150	1,95	131	672	272	236	14	187	1,/82	375	27	910	239	1,216	2,
et in labor force	377	3.3	158	458	133	158	10	76	4	47	_83	87	23	296	65	356	
Female, 14 years old and over	1,877	4.931	1,,87	2 448	491	7:3	375	354	12	211	1,568	425	49	1,194	298		2,
or force	175	566	190	259		146		33		40	344		49		91	1, 59	
avilyan labor orce	375	566	_90	259	6"	140	76	13 [0	40	34/	58 58		204	91	207	
Employed	34^ 15	764	_87	252	61	144	67	33	0	39	339	**	5	200	91 88	137	
Unem, loyed	1,502	1,3€5	997	2,179	424	607	299	321	5	171	1,224	367	14	990	207	1,302	2,
	1 -,	-,		.,,	127		/	744	1		2344	201	-	750	20"	1,352	4,
MAJOR OCCUPATION GROUP	1,428	1 741	1,.50	1 954	333	672	272	256	14	187	1,482	***	-	1			
Male employed	1,420	1 41	1,100	4 924	-	6/2	-		14	15"		375	2"	-	239	1 20	2,
russ.na., technical and kindred workers mers and farm managers	684	y23	829	1 500	172	198	118	. 4	, ,	53	842	16	,	499	101	830	1
nagers, officials, and propuetors except farm	1	2	049	2 300	1	470	2	ب 1	1	21	941	TP	,	1	101	690	1,
a workers	1 1	2		-	î		i		-				1	l i	0	- 1	
sa workers fismen foremen and kindred workers		28	-	1	,	2	+	4	1	1	7	,	:	23	1	7	
ratives and kindred workers	96	131	2	16	43	15	29	2_	1	1 3	9	34	1 - 5	59	25	53	
	2 2	8	2	2	2	1	3			1	2	4		4		2	
ne workers except private household in laborers, unpaid analy workers in laborers except unpaid and farm foremen	2	25	2/8	30 5 5	13	59	15	12		8	424		, ,	106	16	85	
m laborers except unpaid and farm foremen	323	U8	50	125	62	377	52.	12	6	113	+76	304	1	106 76	34	202	
oreis except farm and mine	24	253	11	±8 ±6	28	4	27	46	2	-	٥	13	5	108	52	50	
	1 :							- 1			- 1		,				
Female employed	360	564	187	2.5	61		67	33	6	39	339	54	5	200	88	197	-
fersional technical and kindred workers	9	15	5	22	27	6	3	8	- 1	1	6 7		2	21 1	1	. 4	
mers and farm managers - nagers officials and proprietors except farm steal and kindred workers	109	119	15	98	1"	3	6	3	1		7			1 1	1	76 2	
real and kingred workers	1	1					2	- 1					٠.	3		1	
's work rs_ 'tsmen fortmen, and kindrid workers	2	1		2	i 1	1	1	- 1	1		1					1	
Station forumen, and kindred workers	1	6			1		1	, ,	- 1		3	,		اب ا			
	43	70	43	32	25	58	10	12	4	29 3	63	21	1	68	.,6	32	
misborers unpaid family workers	1 5	12	3	32 26	6	2	13	3	2		7			26 20	3	5	
m saborers unpaid family workers _	12.	296	116	19	12	30 35	24	2 2		ĩ	21.4	23		50	29	29 43	
m laborers except unpaid and farm foremen		29						~	1		-	-	1	1			
supation not reported	. 24	12	3	ـ2	1	2	2		99	-	11	3		39	- 6	4	
Mupation not reported	24	12	3	ـ2	1	2	2		150	-	п	3		39	5	4	9

Table 49a —CHARACTERISTICS OF THE RURAL-FARM NONWHITE POPULATION, FOR PARISHES 1930—Con.

Arten v. **: decident as state from harder of them are supported to community in page of the page age of the side in this solds. Merban not above vibere base in less than 530]

Arters s. *: det o es statution hased on 20	- In	CO The .	-	anches sur	date and the	-	-	-	and the same of the same			-	St				- Distance of the last of the
tions t	.a	725 - 26	1 BES	F dura	Pq+ .i=z	9.0		Sautre	Tomar.	S. CUMPTOS	St ne_ena	St Jane	John the	St Tandry	St Martir	Mars E+	St TATESC:
Total rura-tarm nonwhite topuls of n	1 776	. 40	en.	700	3.0%	- 40	7, 2	_~	-	439	3,930	7,057	1,100	20 120	- 724	4,2%	-11.7
Ma e all ages	1 4.20		9	3 5	1 997	2,45	3, 4	me 3	32	427	2,00→	1,5.9	*91	٠٥,117	2,/66	2 195	618
unier 5 vere	63		40	16.	5	1 347	577	0	3	28	327 31.4	281	_00 50	1,682	389 3.48	353 321	go
5 to 9 wary	1 2	95	100	544	5.7	294 295	3.0	5	41	25	262	187	83	255	37 9	265	97 77 29
Is to a Vente 15 to 13 years	1 65	-3		354	142	23/	430 23.	48	5	23	220	138	23	,259 /23	71.3	177	7 29
20 to 3, vuars 25 to 29 mars	1 13	5	33	1-3	142 74	7,74	1 .82	21	-	23 -2	86	38	24	-09 /39	178	12.	.8
30 to 34 /tars	4.5		.0	108	-15	_na	#04	-D	,		84	6'	3* 28	533	↓50	146	2) 22 29
85 to 39 years 40 o 11 /mrs	230	6-	5	28	90	-1-	-2-	2.	2	:2	120	64	32	407	99	96	
45 .c 40 tars	1	27	2,	_0.	2	417	_79 _28	20	3	43	80 45	78	20 14	3 19 31.2	88 55	73	30 13
ab of years	1	72 54	2.	-42	20	99 76	1-0	-2	-	40	51	48	17	250 1 6	5a 52	77	23 22
till to 64 years	110	100	-0	137	*3	20	119	18	1	8 7	87 3'	38 46	1 9	1.50	45	63	25
65 to 66 years 77 to 74 years	67	67		48	ران 13	3"	40	13	1	7 4	3'	35	9	9/	12 32	40 50	13
"5 years and over		18		57		1			- 1				J-78		2 258	2,061	-
Female all ages	~ ×88	. 283	-4	2,276	1 902	∠,327	3 ***4	447 58	52	212	_,1º6 294	282	92	10,003	394	356	529
Under 5 years.	- v42	15° 15°	59 50 50	428 428	11.6 240	246	563	64	3	29 17	276	244	98 97	1,569	3/6	270 235	71 73 60
10 .0 14 years	6_8	-73 3C	50	428 326	708	499 276	531 53	64	5	17	276 273 23.	130	56 28	1,1°€	1_1 261	168	6.
5 to 19 years 2t to 24 years	272	78	39 23	172	1-1	*8	257	25	1	20	±26	83 90	28	740 527	491	1.48 124	30
20 to 29 years	229	62	23	194	45	1°2	20. 20.	18	3 2	6	91	87	32	452	30	12"	7_ 3.
30 to 3- years 35 to 39 years	212	38 74	26 20	193	757	172	238 190	23 29	1 2	12	121	85 64	26 29	505 23	7 72	170	36 27
40 o 11 years. 45 to 49 years .	1 94	52	2	150	PA PA	106	160	26	. 1	٠	79	50	20	345	92	85	23
50 to 5- vears 55 to 59 vears	1.3	3c	L	107	₹ 42	80 69	123 99	16	3	6	63	-2 46	14	250	ন 56	^8 65	22
60 to 64 years	79	39 17	19	111	43	45	50 89 32	5	- 1	6 9 5 3	50 37 57	36 53	13 9 1	_84 -29 _38	56 49 29	65 49 69	18
60 to 69 years 70 to 74 years	79 87	32	8	97	-8	78	32	10	1	3	78	50	5	69	13	25	5
75 years and over	~	25	;	61	53	50	47	10			19	27	6	91	24	31	9
*YEARS OF SCHOOL CLMPLETED																400	
Persons 25 years old and over	3,380		3-4	2,945	1, 90	بر_ 935	2,^60	35 5	20	190	1,575 90	1,205	435	2,530	960	A,800	475
No school years completed	845 ± 580	150 410	70 45	935 1,400	265	59.5 25.5	1,542	1.80	20	95	800	385 285	170	2,500	410	732	25 22.*
Elementary 1 to 4 years 5 and 8 years	125	20.5	.45 55	-15	286	5-0	170	15	5	10	3,5°2 90	150	9; 1;	825 215	110 80	235 55	80 45
7 years 8 years	1.5	80	2.	_5	25	75	80		- [15	100	20	1.5	90	10	15	20 25
High school 1 to 3 years 4 years College 1 to 3 years	85 45 10	95	10	35	10	50	13)		3	5	10	2			10	5	45
College 1 to 3 years	10	50		ś	٥	5	,	5	- 1		25	5	,	5		1	5
School years not reported	105	25	2*	35	75	40	25	200	- 1	5	20	-	,	⊥25 2.0	.5	30	15
Median school years composted	2 9	4 8	1	2 5	3 5	2 %	27	0.00			4 4	2 5		20	0.8	21	
EMPLOYMENT STATUS		1										863				1 200	24.0
Male 14 years old and over-	2,626	63-	339	1,997	918	1,332	2 247	26b	18	13-	937	453	335	4,701	1 457	1,302	363 253
Labo force.	1,980	634	252	1,439	916	1,036	1,844	7.68	-	12/	932	654	264 248	6.519	1,258	1 003	253
Employed	1,367	528	237	1,620	89.s 23	7 037	1,800	193	1-	13		637 17		/ 506 13	1,255	1,636 -7	249
Not in labor force	6.06	21.3	87	159	243	296	435	68	- 1	27	212	213	7	±,034	199	249	110
Fernale, 14 years old and over	4,738	700	29 ·	⊥ 960	1,135	1,403	2,168	275		132	1,139	863	306	2,349	1 266	1,244	34.
Labor rovce	390 390	102	84	497 494	218	237 237	248	17	1	36 36	277	173 173	46	819 859	250 249	343 343	47
Employed	387	98	71	477	218	434	245	17	11	32	277	171	46 45	850	246	321	46
Vot m 'abor force	2 148	877	209	.,466	927	4,366	1,420	238	8	4	862	690	360	4,490	- 416	90_	507
MAJOR OCCUPATION GROUP													i				
Male employed	1 9/	648	237	1 620	593	_,031	1,806	193	11	211	032	637	228	4,>06	1,255	1,030	249
Professional mechanical and kindred workers	3,342	336	91	848	492	629	1,20	11	2	20	628	1	25	7	2 738	1 59	95
Farmers and farm 'namagers. Managers officials and proprietors, except farm Clerical and kindred workers.	3	5	1	3			عادون					43	,	3,044	738		95
Clerical and landred workers	2	1	,	1 2	2	1 2		1	1	1	2	2	,	2	1	2	
Sales workers	9	30	18	28	10	9	12 48	10	,	20	6	5	29	14	8	25	25
Operatives and aindred workers. Private household workers	4	31	4	2	51 8	-8	98	-01	1		71	57	29	23	10	_03 2 7	25
Service workers, except private household. Farm laborers uni aid famili, workers. Farm laborers except unpaid and farm foremen.	290	44	15	176	27	96	230	1>	1	5	151	4	1	1,064	260	22	19
Farm laborers except unpaid and farm foremen Laborers except farm and nunc	157	135	18 47	357 93	224 57	203	-62	14	3	8	27 24	206	175	215	202	763 45 6	37
Occupation not reported	20	3	70	9	1'	13	5	,61	3	°	:5	2	3	03	-2	5	2
Female employed	387	98	71	47"	21	231	24,	27	31	32	277	↓71	45	850	246	321	40
Professional technica and andred workers .	22	_0	5	41	7	P	. 0	7 2	1,		10	8	2	19	1 7	4	1
Farmers and farm managers Managers officials, and proprietors except farm	68	2	2	35	22	40	62	2	1	1	26	2		34	7	3	2
Ciencal and kindred workers.	1	î	3	,	3		1					1		100		- 7	17.75
Chaftsmen foremen and kindred workers			4				1						1	3	- 1		7
Operatives and amdred workers Private howehold workers	.4 13	40	25	77	40	31	39	2 5	4	10	22	9 34	20	3 29	22	72	2
Service workers except private household Farm laborers unpaid family workers Farm laborers, except unpaid and farm foremen	210	16	5	1.9	12	6 \$0	23 72	3	1		199	5	2	29	-20	12	2
Farm laborers, except unpaid and farm foremen Laborers except farm and mine	12	6	3	200	73	50	23	- 1	د	13	6	101	⊥9	579 77	32	207	+
Occupation not reported	20	2.	5	1.2	٥	14	1	1	1		7	6		41	4	2	1
				-											-	~	

NO.E --Orleans Parish entirely urben, not show in this table

Table 49a — CHARACTERISTICS OF THE RURAL-FARM NONWHITE POPULATION FOR PARISHES 1950—Con [Astensis 7] deed as statistics based to 20-percent sample for corresponding compartes over legal is not go one apr use. Inc. in this was a Meana and share where base is less than with

Subject	Tangitatoe .	"es: as	'er-come	Jr. or	-12	ermor	ad h- -ngtor	ecor".	der tar.	We t Carry, 1	o cuena	A-DF
Total rural farm conwhite population	5,206	390, د	2,514	3 244	2	2-8	- 1t3	4,454	2 2-9	2 132	-,21	1,_5
Male all ages	2,632	2 9.4	1 3-1	-,05	5'8	13.	2 .56	2 232	المحرا	+ 276	. ~65	5.0
nder o years	394	-83 391	242	24.	-3	4"	324	268	₄ 65	257	237	
to 9 years	327	350	47	234	66	-1		32 / 3 0	150	14.	230	76 83 7- 51 33 21 22
to 19 years to 24 years	269	2/8	120	222	041	-17	221	280	109	3.	220	ź
to 29 years to 34 years	136	.14	34	63	36 26	. 2	1.5	_29 _:3 89	5B	50	7	2
to 39 years	153	148	70	94 32 71	26 36		99	89 104	£3,	57	65	2
to 44 years	155	1_9	61		3_{	-	73	182	58	5	9_ i	5
to 49 years	104	122	42 38	73 62	25	2	120	-17 83	64	37	71	2
to 64 years -	106	112	42	62 64 -7	27	2	54	54	67	32	59	3
to 69 years	67 98 +2	124 60	38 42 35 54 26	54 11	-81	-2	ol.	2.5	56 58	31 40	52	
years and over	-3	74	15	.7	-11	-2 6	33 2°	30	37 38	23	25	1
Female, all ages	2 .74	2,992	1,201	. 587	574	A-4	2,077	2,22_	1 283	1,056	1,55-	56
ager 5 years	392 363	459	202	20_	87	45 17	308	304	176	_87	255	
to 14 years	302 249	-19	173	248 234 183	82 7_ 85	17	2°6 291	325 325	1.38	125	206	8
0 to 24 years	100	253	123	183 91	85	15	242 127	269	91 88	125	_82	
to 34 years	137	2.60	88	96	48 33	6	136	118	72	15	55	
-0 39 vears	72	140	55 77 5-	761	25 30 28		81	109	7C 55	51	108	1
to 44 years	. 44	1.80		68		4	80	129	A5 (42	a1	- 1
to 40 years	147	159 102	44 38	81 6#	23 15	9 4 7 7	107	102 71 60	53	45	C2	
to 59 years	79 37	103	2 ₀	52 35	12	4	54 41	60	62	42	34	
to 69 years	63 26	_30 57	33	37	9	ź	38	65	40	28 1/	45	
years and over	23	64	14	22	2	3	20	19	31 28	1-	27	
*YEARS OF SCHOOL COMPLETED					1					May to get to	0	
Persons 25 years old and over	2,275	2,535	_,005	-,250	400	105	1,625	1,855	_,_90	825	1,290	53
o school years completed lementary 1 to 4 years	470 875	1 255	275 540	470	105	15	1.5 545	235	565 360	175 295	235 710	.1 21
lementary 1 to 4 years 5 and 6 years 7 years	435	477	130	270	uO)	20	500 1,00	425	125	150	235	4
8 years	100	20	51	145 40	20	5	1.0	150	10	85 40	40 25	2
(gh school 1 to 3 years. 4 years. follage 1 to 3 years.	105	20	3	65	5	ر	120 25	20	30	55 20	20	1
ollege 1 to 3 years	. 20	10		35 10	5		5	5	5	5	100	•
shoot vears not reported	40	±=0	_5	10	5		25	10	20	5	20	2
fedian school years completed	7 9	3.5	26	4 6			50	4 6	1 7	4 2	3 3	3
EMPLOYMENT STATUS	1				1		1.1					
Male, 14 years old and over	1,317	1,342	765	1,008	382	90	1,217	1,369	829	656	1 007	30
Civilian labor force	1,319	1,342	67.8	764 764	306 306	71	988 988	1,063	638 638	476	749	2:
Employed . Unemployed .	1 302	1,332	FC.	763	3.6	71	995	1,044	638 693 15	476	749 748	22
let in labor force	316	411	177	244	76	19	229	306	191	.80	258	13
Female 14 years old and over.	1,57	1,872	705	945	352	88	1 193	1,320	833	650	907	16
sbor torce	623 523	372 372	243 243	92	81	10 10	218 218	⊥94 ⊥94	204	30	127	-
Employed _	610	368	213	92 91	81 81	10	218	_02	204 172	39	117	
ot in labor force	053	1,500	30 4 0 2	8:3	271	78	975	1,_20	12 629	oll	790	3:
MAJOR OCCUPATION GROUP						-		-,		3/50	100	
Male employed	1 303	1,352	501	763	306	71	98.	44.04	623	476	7+8	22
rofessional technical and kindred workers	687	811	25	6	1		6	593		-		-
armers and farm manage-s	2	2	25	472	195	32	632	2	87	367	1	
anagere officials, and properetors except farm ancal and kindred workers les workers	2	1		1			1	2	1		3	
raftsmen foremen and kindred workers	22	11	9	8	:	1 5	14	13 57	13		2	

penatives and kindred workers ate household workers	- 98 4 7	2	89	39		,	65 1	_	1	1	16	
rvice workers, except private nousehold	90	80	3	49	52	5	خوق	.03	49	50	66	
workers, everet private nousehold arm aboters unput family workers arm laborers, except mpaid, and farm forumen.	9C 254 123	331 24	421 41	101	52 57	11 7	45	129 113	368 31	43	83 25	1
cupation not reported.	123	-2	3	6	4		75 7	19	3	1	5	
Female employed	010	368	213	್ನ	81	-0	218	192	192	30	116	
ofesional technical and kindred workers.	.4	18	2	23			11	17.		2 11	17	
arrages and farm managers	76	135	1	10	4	1	4+	20 3		11	17	
anagere officials, and proprietors except rarm erical and kindred workers	1	1	1		2		2	1	1			
les workers aftsmen, foremen and kindred workers cerative and kindred workers				+	2			-	1			
avate household workers	44	60	42 34	25	24	5	16	40 13	34	9	21	
ervice workers except private household	25 245	6	9	25 -5	1 43	4		13	18	14	36	
arm laborers except unpaid, and ta m foremen	480	18	120	2	5		±04 20	15	116	1	29	
borers except farm and mine	2.	5	3				10	8			1	

Table 50—URBAN AND RERAL POPULATION ACCORDING TO OLD DEFINITION, BY AGE, COLOR, AND SEX, FOR SELECTED PARISHES 1950

"Note: es usted are 16 be where 195, urban any tural rigures offer under new and old urban definitions]

	Bouis		/addu	1	(a., *4s*	Leu	Esst Bato	n Rouge	Jef.er	son
Lamoclar arising.	198au	Fema.e	Maie j	Fena_c	Male	Female	Male	Penale	Male	7cmale
r han (it possil.bra ARIA Bi COLOR	2 2007	2 9- 2	84 (62	97,48-	272	44 803 101	7",670 167	80 56n	51, 584, 103	>2 289 63
n ben n lite Norwhad Real roof ma	C, 40+ 1 Z, 40- 1	7 389 4, 8-9 -, 327 4 206	59,6+3 40 406 -0 237 45 874	67,503 -4,558 23,005 -7 532	26,4_2, 26,_93 6,219 15 309	27,290 20,647 €,643 44 935	61 3.5 45,030 16,285 12,592	64,3.4 45,4.7 18,897 12,687	15,268 -2 03/ 3,234 35,701 3,003	15,802 17 298 2,504 35,884
While Yearning Rara favra What	4. J	3 75 2 463 4 750 1,490	5,921 7,25	-0,825 6 707 7 390	3,458 3,05: 2 608;	11 455 3 480 2, 38 2 298	5,471 7 121 3 763 2 331	7,315 3,565 2,274	4 698 615 589	31 097 4,787 603 583
AREA BY COLOR AND ALER Leben, 1982.	3 314,	7 889	5,788	5,776 67 5e3	4-3) 27 412	27 290	51 315	2,291 64 314 j	13,268	20 15 802
cader 5 vears 5 to 14 vears 15 to 19 years	1,20° 702 443	1,2.2	7 530 5,_88 4 De8	7 227	3,-60	2,289	8 100 5,557 4,034	,845 5 n22 3,995	2,139	2,028 1,597 1,59
25 to 29 years 30 to 3a years	258	930 427 8.0 177	3 4.4 4 747 2 643 5,036 4,71 4,20°	4,422 6 692 6, 55 5, 65 5, 65	2,52 1,76 2,125 2,416 2,24 2,185 - 877	2,603 2,603 2,638 2,232 2,149 1,787	4 213 6,586 6 610 5 394 4,932 4 157	4,821 7 050 6,823 5,61 5,176 4 354	3243 1,446 1,243 1,51 1,046	1,_42 1,496 1,520 1,289 1 1.50
40 to 4 years 45 to 45 years 50 to 45 years 55 to 69 years 65 to 65 years 65 to 65 years	32- 2-2 -6- 123	31.7 220 167 140 128	3 851 3,291 2 128 1 601	2 74 2,754 2,754 2,002	1,561 -,189 950 679	1 494 1 165 885 733 642 4_9	3,3/7 2,800 1,933 1 433	3,436 2,734 2,036 1,302	964 735 551 348 331	878 665 531 408 382
70 to 7-s years 75 vears and over	43 51 -,177 179 -6-	72 1,320 159 159	950 986 19,237 2,738 2,045	1,394 2,005 2,56 2,76	346 6,219 880 621	4_9 4_9 6 643 865 634 5/7	552 592 -0,285 2,322 364	850 997 18,897 2 355 1,658	3,234 486 392	234 252 3,504
20 to 24 years	1.4 81 113 73 72 74 61	92 112 41 418 89	1,610 -,103 -,20 1,491 1,295	2 403 1,985	421; 497 517 404 445	5/7 562 688 635 471 533	1,289 1,108 1 298 1,468 1 2,6	1 309 1,421 1,782 1,796 1,292 1 508	258 240 232 260 219 204	382 260 248 322 309 278 233
40 to 44 years	61. 68 51 40	90 84 72 62 34 15	1 209 1,225 968 745 480	1,850 1,496 1,466 1,157 794 560	364 384 271 243 184	378 334 279 194 166	974 24 566 426	1,339 1 C56 820	421 204 161 136 67	233 259 200 158 91 92
65 to 64 years 65 to 69 years 70 to 74 years 75 years and over Rural total	33 _D _14	52 13 27 11,004	677 248 345 2/,419	93_ 358 462	176 84 88	20. 71 85	451 204 23_	601 279 140	90 58 44	5_ 57
Under o years 5 to 9 years 10 to 14 years	1,583 1,309 1,158 1,448	1,607 1 3.8 -,101 900 727	3,343 2,904 2,705 2,058	3,244 2,986 2,597 1,916	18,360 2,627 2,180 1,904 1,422 1,288	2,-95 2,140 1,724 1,476	16 355 2 258 2 944 2,629 497	16,252 2 199 1 912 1,996 1,385	36,316 5,390 3,994 2,950 2,226	36,487 5 086 3,900 2,6-6 2,377 3 116
20 to 24 years 25 to 29 years 30 to 54 years 35 to 39 years 40 to 44 years	2,106 1,092 935 747 692 602	726 609 543	1,479 1 40? 1,411 1,500 1,460	1,794 1,697 1,649 1,625 1,60	1,352 1,346 1,189	1,510 1,500 1,374 1,262 1,108	1,188 1,125 1,164 966 760	.513 1,373 1,169 2,068	2,628 3,388 3,038 2,997 2,665	3,793 3,204 2,989 2,309
50 to 54 years on to 59 years 60 to 64 years 65 to 69 years 70 to 74 years	473 389 307 344 223	358 374 328 177	1,45. 1,185 989 736 832 488	1,4/0 -,153 862 690 809 458	996 741 543 440 399 266	701 584 504 350 336 197 222	614 486 401 446	742 543 458 390 467	2,092 1 094 1,1.8 822 626	1,897 1,425 1,125 811
Rural,nonwhite	5,69.1 824 755	232 5 723 858 752 644	476	426 42,503 4 798 1,56	228 3,901 619 524 444	3,820 628 481	251 28. 6,553 1,244 968	208 300 8,606 1,142 1,004	325 363 4 724 751	415 401 4,807 724
10 to 14 years 10 to 14 years 15 to 19 years 20 to 24 years 25 to 29 years 30 ω 34 years	700 555 401 277 228	532 354	1,608 1,473 1119 705 511 489	1,-43 1,080 876 705 596	3.2 292	415 350 350 297 251	890 893 852 625	880 854 942 687	324 457 333 401 356	4,807 724 554 402 368 466 422 356 357 283 277 189 125
35 .o 39 years 40 to 44 years 45 to 49 years	228 245 284 295 242 219	294 327 314 289 236	582 603 615	701 718 641 510 398	242 231 175 170 146 120	241 180 164 126	546 435 319 257	308 453 360 252	326 297 287	357 283 27- 189
50 to 54 years 50 to 54 years 60 to 64 years 55 to 69 years 70 to 74 years 78 years and over	158 239 115	162 235 103 133	421 299 488 261 242	308 512 230 223	98 118 50 58	107 67 87 30 46	232 175 289 146 167	22_ 202 297 113 150	151 94 111 44 60	125 75 124 47 44
Rural gonfarm	8,792 967 1,233 2,814	6,254 1,000 1,427 931	16,874 2,333 3,559 2,318	17,532 2,307 3,638 2,578 2 592	15,309 2,302 3,379 2,207	2,222 2,282 2,585	12 592 -, 962 2,727 2,249	2,687 L 826 2 077 2,412	35,701 3,329 6,830	35, 884 5,030 6,421 5,381 6,925 5,412 3,318
S to A years 25 to A years 25 to A years 45 to A vears 55 to 64 vears 65 years and over	934 537 304 366	1,1.3 759 490 337 397	2,261 2,202 -,872 1,143 -,180	2 592 2,290 1,794 1,110 1,221	2,477 2,163 1,374 724 683	2 533 2,005 1,058 648 602	1,953 1,623 947 572 657	2,102 1,500 909 557 709	4 736 6,352 5,590 3,693 -,891	6,925 5 412 3,318 1 904
Roral faron Under 5 years 5 to 14 years 15 to 24 years	4,873 616 1 234 740	4,750 607 -,192	7 545 1,010 2 050 1,219	7,390 937	3,051 325 705 503	2,638 273 582	3 763 396 846	3,565 373 839 486	615 61 114 118	603 76
20 to 34 years 35 to 44 years 55 to 54 years 35 years and over	390 505 538 392 458	495 576 493 335 350	552 758 764 582 610	1,132 749 936 797 442 472	314 372 363 259 210	401 341 365 317 206 153	592 359 507 427 31.5	440 494 376 291 266	74 72 93 49	112 72 86 74 32 26

Table 50—URBAN AND RURAL POPULATION ACCORDING TO CLD DEFINITION, BY AGE COLOR, AND SEX, FOR SELECTED PARISHES 1950—Con Franks used are how where the order than and "the trade mere are ad trade definition."

Area, color, and age	_efou		5. 3d	raard	St Ib	Ur.46	S* ohn h	Bap .st	"erreba	proe
	Ma_s	lemale	Ma_o	Fest.e	160.0		40	Fecal	4. 0	Female
Total population Urban-farm population AREA BY COLOR	21 244 2	20,960	5,198	5,4-21	0,060	0,627	7 225	7,346	2_,701	2.,5
Leben h.te pawhite contains Rarel contains hite control rare hite and contains hite and contains hite and contains and contains hite and contains hite	3,738 3,009 699 13,671 1,491 7,419 3,675	3,992 3,284 708 12,8.5 11,-25 4,153 3,437 724	5,27 4,507 7A3 32- 293	5,223 4,426 7,47 269 2,3	5 975 4,025 -,890 ovil	6,089 4,057 2,032 608 394 2.12	5,~56 2,3.5 3 3.1 3,089 467 5×2	6,353 3,252 3,273 992 4.1	2,120 4,620 3371 -2,9051 -,762 3,343 2,041 -,545	5,94 4,94 - C; -2,5; -9,3; -3,16 -3,0; -1,26
AREA BY COLOR AND AGE	2 000		-		471		276	~	1	
Lebas 10sal dec years 10 87 years 10 18 years 10 18 years 10 18 years 10 24 years 10 24 years 10 24 years 10 24 years 10 24 years 10 24 years 10 24 years 10 24 years 10 24 years 10 24 years 10 24 years 10 24 years 10 25 years 10 26 years 10 27 years 10 27 years 10 27 years	3 738 412 311, 249 292 320, 273 234 167 43 106 84 59 57	1,992 -30 -34 -31 -3 -3 -3 -3 -3 -3 -3 -3 -3 -3	•		::				5,520 728 996 482 390 497 402 4.3 388 297 202 202 122, 1.2 97	5,9 6 5,4 4,4 4,4 4,4 4,4 4,4 4,4 4,4 4,4 4,4
Urbas conwhite 66 5 years 9 1 cars 10 1 cars 10 1 cars 10 1 years 10 1 years 10 1 years 10 2 years 10 2 years 10 3 years 10 4 years 10 4 years 10 4 years 10 4 years 10 4 years 10 4 years 10 6 4 years	1099 1091 841 700 655 455 660 377 388 411 221 263 233 231 17, 27, 521	708 88 67 48 60 60 53 52 22 42 22 23 17 18 4,968		5 492	6,666	6,597	7,5.5	740	830 37 87 60 49 55, 49 65 61 42 20 20 27 77 20 21 22, 24	-,
uder y verifs 0 1 years 0 1 years 10 14 verifs 10 14 verifs 10 14 verifs 10 15 verifs 10 16 verifs 10 26 years 10 26 years 10 26 years 10 26 years 10 26 years 10 40 years 10 40 years 10 50 39 years 10 50 49 years 10 50 49 years 10 50 74 verifs 10 60 years 10 60 years 10 74 verifs 10 60 years 10 74 verifs 10 60 years 10 70 years	2,484 2,.05 . 889 .,536 -,422 .,329 .,229 1,110 604 607 505 467 380 235 233 2,465	2, 243 2, 053 1, 80- 1, 632 1, 34- 1, 34- 1, 34- 1, 34- 1, 34- 820 623 57- 408 413 236 27- 27- 27- 20- 20- 21- 21- 21- 21- 21- 21- 21- 21- 21- 21	773 587 -03 572 452 339 372 442 349 336 273 173 441 -43 70 84	760 584 499 417 510 532 482 402 540 284 218 175 175 175 176 66 676	902 768 620 611 J12 507 J84 /2 J99 J91 264 187 167 98 116 2,17	912 725 634 613 511 4.4 427 409 379 3.17 236 100 177 121 143	1,069 86.1 803 656 983 47" 428 454 457 370 341 265 223 136 130 5,713 594	980) 856 777 612 :38 546 454 467 335; 132 49 256 254 127 128 128 128 128 128 128 128 128 128 128	2,622 2,037 1,755 1,375 2,031 1,095 1,095 708 953 708 355 355 364 206 4,458 4,458	2, 2, 1, 1, 1, 1, 1, 1, 1, 1, 1, 1, 1, 1, 1,
0 9 years 10 19 years 10 19 years 10 19 years 10 19 years 10 24 years 10 25 years 10 26 years 10 38 years 10 38 years 10 38 years 10 38 years 10 54 years 10 56 years 10 56 years 10 56 years 10 56 years 10 56 years 10 56 years 10 74 years 10 74 years	311/ 255 210 143 113 114 18 90 83 77 81 73 32 44	31.5 294, 280 199 142 143 115 82 95 62 35 62 27	897 97 92 98 94 43 96 47 35 25 27 31 18	99 62 71 80 47 62 51 32 33 20 13 18	272 210, 199 147. 130 97 100 100 105 76 78 75 71 51 60 60	2,844 344 284 296 170 159 144 114 126 99 96 61 79 83 55	473 425 31,2 273 217 185 207 204 1,76 151 127 119 71	460 435 303 277 254 204 200 181 175 150 105 105 105 61	986 932 386 302 300 218 278 185 170 134 141 120 246 67	4,
Rusal nonfarm dater 5 years to 16 years to 26 years to 36 years to 54 years to 54 years to 54 years to 54 years to 64 years to 64 years to 64 years Rusal faren does 5 years	13,092 1,960 2,981 2,269 2,075 1,542 1,031 682 552 4,419	12,845 2,745 2,364 1,992 1,511 1,008 647 662 4,153 4,98	5,270 743 1 031. 780 889 705 537 311 274 325	5, 223 733 997 891 924 697 467 794 234	5,975 814 4,246 1,006 822 731 639 391 324 691	5,089 824 1,229 1 028 844 770 629 360 405 608	e,456 914 -,393 1,060 800 797 618 446 426 1,059	6,355 849 1,341 1,000 847 766 627 442 473 991	.2,905 2,165 2,985 2,113 1,885 1,570 962 626 569 3,356 428	12, 2, 3, 2, 1, 1,
ader 5 years to 14 years to 24 years to 34 years to 34 years to 54 years to 54 years to 54 years years and over	1, CI3 789 512 545 390 390 296	4, 153 498 982 625 530 491 437 332 258	325 30 59 44 42 46 52 29	27 46 36 36 49 35 23	86 142 119 69 92 66 60 57	85 130 100 81 66 67 38 38	273 181 105 114 96 74 63	131 272 240 123 105 90 63 67	818 555 372 375 295 237 246	

그는 그렇게 된 하는 하는 사람들이 어떻게 되었다.

11 11 11 11 11 11

A46

DETAILED CHARACTERISTICS

Louisiana

LIST OF TABLES

[Page numbers listed here omit the State prefix number which appears as part of the page number for each page The prefix for this State is 18]

Fable	GENERAL POPULATION	Page	Table	OCCUPATION AND INDUSTRY	Page
color, natuvity, sor more, 1985. 52 — Single years of ago of the State 19 53 — Age by race, nature urban and rural and cutes of 100 54 — Age, by color, nate 55 — Clazenshup, by age 100,000 or more	, by sex, for the State 1950 and 1940, and band sex, for the State and for cities of 250,00, by color and sex, for urban and rural are 50. "tv, and sex, for the State, 1950 and 1940, for areas, and nor standard retropolitan area (000 or more, 1950. "vity, and sex, for the State 1950. "color and sex, for the State and for cities 1950.	0 . 119 s . 121 or s . 122 125 of . 125	of em metro; 74 — Detailed 1950 2 75 — Occupat ployed 76 — Age of e State: 1950 77 — Race an	occuration of the experienced civilian labor force and ployed persons, by sex, for the State, and for standard politan areas and cities of 100,000 or more 1950	174 186 189
57 —Marital status and for the State, ur	age and sex, for the State 1890 to 1950 I presence of spouse, by age, color, and se ban and rural, and for standard metropolits	t, n	78 —Income 1	x for the State and for standard metropolitan areas of 0 or more 1950	204
58 —Persons in househ- sex for the State	of 100,000 or more 1950 olds by relationship to head, age, color, an te urban and rural, and for standard metro 100,000 or more 1950	đ -	t.on ar of 250 79 —Detailed	no. sex, for the State and for standard metropolitan areas 000 or more 1950	210
59 —Persons in househ and persons in	olds by relationship to head color and sequest households, by color and sex, for the 1940, for urban and rural areas, and for	e e	80 —Detailed	obltan areas and cities of 100,000 or more 1950	216
standard metro	politan areas and cities of 100 000 or mor		81 —Industry	of employed persons, by sex, for cities or 50,000 to	LLO
60 —Persons in quasi ho urban and rural, or more 1950	ouseholds, by age, color and sex, for the Stat and for standard metropolitan areas of 100 00	138	82 —Age of en for sta	0 1950 mployed persons, by industry and sex, for the State and indard metropolitan areas of 250,000 or more 1950	221
and sex, for the sor more 1950	llment of children 5 and 6 years old, by cole State, urban and rural, and for cities of 100,00	139	100,00 84 — Major o	or the State and for standard metropolitan areas of 0 or more 1950	225
State, 1950 and of 100,000 or mo	by single years of age, color, and sex, for the 1940, for urban and rural areas and for citic ore, 1950.	8 . 139	250,00	or the State and for standard metropolitan areas of 0 or more 1950	229
and sex, for th 100 000 or more	which enrolled by single years of age, colo e State, urban and rural, and for cities of 1950	f _ 142	86 —Income	lustry and sex, for the State and for standard metro- n areas of 250,000 or more 1950	233
years of age, col urban and rural and cities of 250 65 — Years of school co	npleted by persons 5 to 24 years old by sing or, and sex, for the State, 1950 and 1940, fit areas, and for standard metropolitan area, 1,000 or more, 1970	r s _ J47	dustry areas	and sex, for the State and for standard metropolitan f 250,000 or more 1950	235
and rural areas	and for standard metopolitan areas an		and no	n 1949 of persons, by race and sex, for the State, farm onfarm, and for standard metropolitan areas and cities ,000 or more 1950	239
1	EMPLOYMENT STATUS		88 —Income 1	n 1949 of persons, by color and sex, for the State, urban	240
and rural and : 100,000 or more	is, by age, color, and sex for the State, urbs for standard metropolitan areas and cities of 1950	f _ · 159	89 —Income and no	m 1949 of persons, by age and sex for the State, farm onfarm, and for standard metropolitan areas of 250,000 re 1950	241
and rural, and r 100,000 or more 68—Status of persons	l persons, by age and sex, for the State, urba for standard metropolitan areas and cities of 1950	f _ 165	the St	in 1949 of persons, by family status, age, and sex for ate, farm and nonlarm, and for standard metropolitan of 250,000 or more 1950	242
for the State, un areas and cities 69—Labor force status,	ban and lural, and for standard metropolita of 100,000 or more 1950 by age and sex, for the State 1950 and 1940 by marital status, age, color, and sax, for the	166 167	for the politar 92 – Income	e State, farm and nonfarm, and for standard metro- n areas of 250,000 or more 1950	243
State, urban an of 100 000 or m	d rural, and for standard metropolitan area ore 1950	9 _ 158	of 250	farm and nonfarm, and for standard metropolitan areas ,000 or more 1950	245
persons 14 to 25 and sex for th	ns and hours worked during census week h θ years old, by school enrollment, age, colo e State, urban and rural, and for standar as of 250,000 or more 1950 as of 250,000 or more 1950	i	State, of 250	farm and nonfarm, and for standard metropolitan areas 000 or more 1950	246
72 —Weeks worked in State, and for st	1949, by labor force status and sex, for the andard metropolitan areas of 100 000 or more	е	by sex	t, for the State (with comparative data for 1940), for rid metropolitan areas of 250 000 or more, and for ottes 000 or more.	248

Table 51.—SINGLE YEARS OF AGE, BY SEX, FOR THE STATE, 1950 AND 1940, AND BY COLOR, NATIVITY, AND SEX, FOR THE STATE AND FOR CITIES OF 250,000 OR MORE, 1950

[Statistics for 1950 based on 20-percent sample available complete-count data in tables 14, 15 and 33. Medians computed on basis of 5-year intervals. Median not shown where base is less than 500 for 1950 or 100 for 1940]

Area and age	Total						White, 1950							Nonwhite, 1950		
	1950			1940			Total			Native		Foreign born				
	Both sexes	Male	Female	Both sexes	Male	Female	Both sexes	Male	Female	Male	Female	Male	Female	Both sexes	Male	Female
The State	2,677,370	1,310,620	1,366,750	2,363,880	1,172,382	1,191,498	1,792,305	885,315	906,990	870,400	893,[illegible]	14,915	13,2[illegible]	885,065	425,305	459,760
Under 1 year	67,005	33,985	33,020	44,672	22,548	22,124	40,720	20,685	20,035	20,675	20,015	10	20	26,285	13,300	12,985
1 year	67,900	34,105	33,795	44,250	22,223	22,027	42,210	21,255	20,955	21,205	20,915	50	40	25,690	12,850	12,840
2 years	71,915	36,620	35,295	48,260	24,384	23,876	45,385	23,085	22,300	23,015	22,250	70	50	26,530	13,535	12,995
3 years	73,820	37,635	36,185	46,962	23,620	23,342	47,955	24,825	23,130	24,765	23,100	60	30	25,865	12,810	13,055
4 years	56,185	28,505	27,680	46,483	23,578	22,905	34,835	17,770	17,065	17,675	16,985	95	80	21,350	10,735	10,615
5 years	57,705	29,395	28,310	46,136	23,324	22,782	36,250	18,535	17,715	18,450	17,640	85	75	21,455	10,860	10,595
6 years	57,905	29,410	28,495	44,575	22,330	22,245	36,755	18,725	18,030	18,645	17,970	80	60	21,150	10,685	10,465
7 years	56,185	27,945	28,240	44,430	22,361	22,069	36,160	18,140	18,020	18,085	18,005	55	15	20,025	9,805	10,220
8 years	54,085	27,525	26,560	47,490	23,969	23,521	33,490	17,140	16,350	17,115	16,320	25	30	20,395	10,385	10,210
9 years	50,510	25,825	24,685	45,375	22,861	22,514	31,660	16,365	15,295	16,350	15,260	15	35	18,850	9,460	9,390
10 years	50,060	25,275	24,785	48,503	24,546	23,957	31,000	15,860	15,140	15,850	15,100	10	40	19,060	9,415	9,645
11 years	46,550	23,645	22,905	45,020	22,663	22,357	29,620	14,975	14,645	14,945	14,605	30	40	16,930	8,670	8,260
12 years	49,630	25,485	24,145	50,342	25,562	24,780	30,545	15,675	14,870	15,650	14,830	25	40	19,085	9,810	9,275
13 years	46,325	23,235	23,090	50,966	25,596	25,370	28,560	14,565	13,995	14,520	13,975	45	20	17,765	8,670	9,095
14 years	43,655	22,030	21,625	49,005	24,458	24,547	27,215	13,755	13,460	13,715	13,410	40	50	16,440	8,275	8,165
15 years	43,320	21,495	21,825	47,526	23,599	23,927	26,980	13,445	13,535	13,385	13,485	60	50	16,340	8,050	8,290
16 years	41,960	20,955	21,005	48,945	23,946	24,999	26,275	13,360	12,915	13,285	12,885	75	30	15,685	7,595	8,090
17 years	42,265	20,580	21,685	47,101	23,766	23,335	27,180	13,295	13,885	13,235	13,815	60	70	15,085	7,285	7,800
18 years	43,105	20,690	22,415	50,969	25,013	25,956	27,405	13,220	14,185	13,190	14,130	30	55	15,700	7,470	8,230
19 years	40,700	18,695	22,005	45,857	22,162	23,695	27,055	12,525	14,530	12,445	14,470	80	60	13,645	6,170	7,475
20 years	41,145	18,410	22,735	46,096	21,371	24,725	26,840	12,440	14,400	12,365	14,285	75	115	14,305	5,970	8,335
21 years	41,580	20,080	21,500	44,033	21,959	22,074	28,785	14,145	14,640	14,060	14,510	85	130	12,795	5,935	6,860
22 years	41,895	19,765	22,130	42,648	20,436	22,212	28,480	13,680	14,800	13,535	14,620	145	180	13,415	6,085	7,330
23 years	43,670	21,110	22,560	42,011	20,083	21,928	30,290	14,875	15,415	14,785	15,260	90	155	13,380	6,235	7,145
24 years	42,790	20,430	22,360	41,608	20,036	21,572	29,830	14,545	15,285	14,460	15,000	85	285	12,960	5,885	7,075
25 years	43,730	20,430	23,300	42,952	20,592	22,360	30,585	14,775	15,810	14,650	15,530	125	280	13,145	5,655	7,490
26 years	41,640	19,910	21,730	41,303	19,830	21,473	29,450	14,350	15,100	14,135	14,860	215	240	12,190	5,560	6,630
27 years	42,850	20,740	22,110	40,765	19,968	20,797	30,210	14,785	15,425	14,630	15,180	155	245	12,640	5,955	6,685
28 years	43,195	20,465	22,730	42,592	20,538	22,054	30,720	14,855	15,865	14,705	15,650	150	215	12,475	5,610	6,865
29 years	40,145	19,185	20,960	39,409	19,366	20,043	29,125	14,345	14,780	14,205	14,545	140	235	11,020	4,840	6,180
30 years	43,625	20,640	22,985	45,868	22,193	23,675	30,305	14,750	15,555	14,635	15,355	115	200	13,320	5,890	7,430
31 years	35,440	17,230	18,210	31,580	15,634	15,946	26,290	13,110	13,180	13,010	13,020	100	160	9,150	4,120	5,030
32 years	38,565	18,065	20,500	39,723	19,088	20,635	27,600	13,190	14,410	13,095	14,280	95	130	10,965	4,875	6,090
33 years	35,445	17,100	18,345	34,607	17,041	17,566	25,625	12,665	12,960	12,565	12,865	100	95	9,820	4,435	5,385
34 years	37,105	18,145	18,960	34,676	17,012	17,664	26,815	13,620	13,195	13,505	13,090	115	105	10,290	4,525	5,765
35 years	38,965	18,575	20,390	38,999	19,226	19,773	27,920	13,560	14,360	13,405	14,250	155	110	11,045	5,015	6,030
36 years	36,320	17,295	19,025	33,747	16,440	17,307	25,875	12,550	13,325	12,455	13,200	95	125	10,445	4,745	5,700
37 years	37,600	18,055	19,545	30,999	15,152	15,847	26,155	12,995	13,160	12,855	13,020	140	140	11,445	5,060	6,385
38 years	41,080	19,875	21,205	35,503	16,917	18,586	27,545	13,760	13,785	13,605	13,585	155	200	13,535	6,115	7,420
39 years	37,940	18,250	19,690	34,901	17,220	17,681	25,505	12,505	13,000	12,395	12,825	110	175	12,435	5,745	6,690
40 years	41,480	20,120	21,360	39,869	19,623	20,246	27,530	13,750	13,780	13,595	13,605	155	175	13,950	6,370	7,580
41 years	30,075	15,030	15,045	22,113	11,195	10,918	22,155	11,060	11,095	10,915	10,975	145	120	7,920	3,970	3,950
42 years	37,055	17,905	19,150	31,832	15,983	15,849	26,315	12,845	13,470	12,645	13,340	200	130	10,740	5,060	5,680
43 years	33,065	15,925	17,140	25,324	12,836	12,488	23,335	11,465	11,870	11,265	11,735	200	135	9,730	4,460	5,270
44 years	30,855	15,075	15,780	25,243	12,652	12,591	21,850	10,850	11,000	10,580	10,860	270	140	9,005	4,225	4,780
45 years	33,255	16,595	16,660	29,975	15,347	14,628	22,870	11,445	11,425	11,220	11,240	225	185	10,385	5,150	5,235
46 years	28,130	13,925	14,205	23,304	11,725	11,579	20,245	10,015	10,230	9,815	10,045	200	185	7,885	3,910	3,975
47 years	28,190	13,770	14,420	23,640	12,067	11,573	19,875	9,980	9,895	9,755	9,680	225	215	8,315	3,790	4,525
48 years	29,815	14,310	15,505	26,404	13,190	13,214	20,400	9,880	10,520	9,600	10,270	280	250	9,415	4,430	4,985
49 years	32,405	16,125	16,280	23,362	11,932	11,430	21,165	10,910	10,255	10,570	10,015	340	240	11,240	5,215	6,025
50 years	33,125	16,370	16,755	28,141	13,980	14,161	21,365	10,745	10,620	10,305	10,335	440	285	11,760	5,625	6,135
51 years	20,485	9,980	10,505	16,901	8,962	7,939	15,255	7,500	7,755	7,295	7,600	205	155	5,230	2,480	2,750
52 years	26,075	12,840	13,235	21,572	11,176	10,396	18,680	9,185	9,495	8,875	9,240	310	255	7,395	3,655	3,740
53 years	22,745	11,045	11,700	17,380	8,957	8,423	16,195	7,850	8,345	7,535	8,120	315	225	6,550	3,195	3,355
54 years	23,760	11,615	12,145	18,275	9,536	8,739	16,765	8,280	8,485	7,930	8,275	350	210	6,995	3,335	3,660
55 years	22,560	11,400	11,160	19,166	9,842	9,324	15,500	7,745	7,755	7,450	7,500	295	255	7,060	3,655	3,405
56 years	20,855	10,305	10,550	16,776	8,696	8,080	14,825	7,250	7,575	6,915	7,330	335	245	6,030	3,055	2,975
57 years	19,740	9,575	10,165	14,393	7,414	6,979	14,340	6,840	7,500	6,555	7,295	285	205	5,400	2,735	2,665
58 years	20,845	10,015	10,830	16,563	8,389	8,174	14,480	6,670	7,810	6,350	7,570	320	240	6,365	3,345	3,020
59 years	18,820	9,265	9,555	14,426	7,344	7,082	13,395	6,495	6,900	6,100	6,635	395	265	5,425	2,770	2,655
60 years	18,520	9,030	9,490	18,283	9,068	9,215	12,820	6,225	6,595	5,820	6,295	405	300	5,700	2,805	2,895
61 years	14,055	6,765	7,290	10,117	5,168	4,949	10,760	5,175	5,585	4,910	5,395	265	190	3,295	1,590	1,705
62 years	15,560	7,715	7,845	11,985	6,022	5,963	11,380	5,630	5,750	5,325	5,485	305	265	4,180	2,085	2,095
63 years	16,120	7,900	8,220	11,634	5,817	5,817	11,560	5,645	5,915	5,235	5,710	410	205	4,560	2,255	2,305
64 years	15,760	7,940	7,820	11,342	5,674	5,668	10,845	5,425	5,420	5,060	5,110	365	310	4,915	2,515	2,400
65 years	20,150	9,420	10,730	16,330	7,848	8,482	12,060	5,765	6,295	5,345	5,920	420	375	8,090	3,655	4,435
66 years	15,705	7,435	8,270	10,737	5,427	5,310	9,895	4,740	5,155	4,470	4,875	270	280	5,810	2,695	3,115
67 years	16,270	7,650	8,620	10,367	5,230	5,137	9,555	4,345	5,210	4,005	4,995	340	215	6,715	3,305	3,410
68 years	14,910	6,975	7,935	10,167	4,957	5,210	9,220	4,175	5,045	3,890	4,765	285	280	5,690	2,800	2,890
69 years	11,645	5,640	6,005	8,561	4,203	4,358	7,905	3,860	4,045	3,545	3,815	315	230	3,740	1,780	1,960
70 years	12,925	6,105	6,820	9,848	4,779	5,069	8,495	3,950	4,545	3,625	4,270	325	275	4,430	2,155	2,275
71 years	7,940	3,845	4,095	5,225	2,647	2,588	5,965	2,865	3,100	2,675	2,975	190	125	1,975	980	995
72 years	10,120	4,855	5,265	6,468	3,213	3,255	7,060	3,215	3,845	2,915	3,660	300	185	3,060	1,640	1,420
73 years	8,565	4,020	4,545	5,416	2,636	2,780	6,040	2,810	3,230	2,610	3,070	200	160	2,525	1,210	1,315
74 years	7,810	3,720	4,090	4,669	2,340	2,329	5,520	2,535	2,985	2,330	2,855	205	130	2,290	1,185	1,105
75 years	7,995	3,710	4,285	4,986	2,316	2,670	5,340	2,420	2,920	2,175	2,740	245	180	2,655	1,290	1,365
76 years	6,730	3,055	3,675	3,282	1,558	1,724	4,545	1,955	2,590	1,820	2,445	135	145	2,185	1,100	1,085
77 years	5,355	2,650	2,705	2,713	1,238	1,475	3,910	1,865	2,045	1,750	1,970	115	75	1,445	785	660
78 years	5,520	2,660	2,860	3,218	1,488	1,730	3,785	1,765	2,020	1,610	1,860	155	160	1,735	895	840
79 years	4,390	2,030	2,360	2,437	1,129	1,308	3,130	1,375	1,755	1,250	1,655	125	100	1,260	655	605
80 years	4,795	1,980	2,815	3,025	1,317	1,708	3,030	1,200	1,830	1,045	1,770	155	60	1,765	780	985
81 years	2,665	1,235	1,430	1,522	689	833	1,940	895	1,045	805	980	90	65	725	340	385
82 years	2,895	1,260	1,635	1,651	725	926	1,980	825	1,155	760	1,095	65	60	915	435	480
83 years	2,290	1,085	1,205	1,362	569	793	1,670	715	955	645	895	70	60	620	370	250
84 years	2,120	1,005	1,115	1,221	507	714	1,435	620	815	540	780	80	35	685	385	300
85 to 89 years	5,150	2,080	3,070	3,935	1,648	2,287	3,350	1,340	2,010	1,150	1,810	190	200	1,800	740	1,060
90 to 94 years	1,765	610	1,155	1,201	470	731	1,095	400	695	365	620	35	75	670	210	460
95 to 99 years	555	195	360	426	162	264	230	90	140	75	130	15	10	325	105	220
100 years and over	245	70	175	226	80	146	40	30	10	25	10	5		205	40	165
Median age	26.6	26.1	27.0	25.5	25.5	25.6	27.8	27.4	28.2	27.1	27.9	55.8	52.0	23.[illegible]	22.8	24.4

Table 51.—SINGLE YEARS OF AGE, BY SEX, FOR THE STATE 1950 AND 1940, AND BY COLOR, NATIVITY, AND SEX, FOR THE STATE AND FOR CITIES OF 250,000 OR MORE, 1950—Con

Statistics for 1940 massal on 20 percent sample available complete-sount data on abres 14, 14, and 33 Medians commuted on bass or 5-year intervals. Median not shown a here base in res han 560 to 1950 or 1940;

Management of the Control of the Con		-	To	in.			Г			White, 1950				Non	white, 15	150
Aren and age		1950			1940			Total		Na	tive		n born	Both sexes	Male	Female
	Both sexes	Vale	Female	Both sexes	Maie	Female	Both sexes	Male	Female	Male	Female	Male	Геmale		-	T on the
TEN CRUEANS	568, 90	147,235	300, 144				386 760	183,475	203,285	175,650	96,035	7,825	5,650	181,920	8-,460	
l nor i year .	12 205	5 440	6,2a, 4,120				7,170	3 425 3 835	3,745	3,420 3,825	3,740 3,750	10	15	5,035 5,0.5	2,515	2,5%
2 years 3 years	1,745 1,280	6, 90 4,900	6,275 6,5%			1	8,670	4,480	3,950 4,170	4,765	4,185	25	20 5	4,71C	2,425	2,32
5 Venrs	9,370	4,900	4,7 0				3,945 3,940	3,070	2,879 2,895 2,990	3,040 3,010 3 100	2,850 2,670 2,580	35 30	15 35 10	3,590 3,430 1,280	1 530 1,615 1,630	- 81.5
6 years 7 /ears 8) ears	9,-30 _C,185	3 1.0 4,95	4,546 5,075 4 4:0				6,255 5,335	3,130 3,155 2 6.0	3,300 2,72	3,235	3,095	20	10	3,930	1,955	1,650
9 vears	7,955	3,495	3,900				4,894	2,430	2,455	2,430	2,435	20	20	3,070	,,,65	1,505
11 years	7,675	3,4701	3,765 3,765 3,725				4,400 4,400 4,380	2,020	2,285	2,315	2,270	10	20	3,070 2,835	1,480 1,450	1 208
13 years	6,725	3 5.0 3,.05 3 .60 3 415	7 410				4,380 4,260 4,065 4,000	2,105	2,275 2,000 2,065	2,095 2,235 1,970	2,245	10 25 30	30 5 5	2,855 2,655 2,780	1,405 1,245 1,360	1,450
15 years	6,905	3 415	3,485 3,490 3 -50				4,000	2,000 1,980 2,205	2,020	2,170	1,995	15 35	25	2,905	-,435 1,285	1 420
16 years 17 years 18 years	5,910	3,795	3,73.5 4 3.5	- 1			4.345	2,001	2,322	1,980	2,065 2,310 2,815	25	25 45 25	2,550	1,190	1,360
19 years.	8,_50	3,665	4 485				5,470	2,395	2,870	2,37C 2,56C	2,825	40	45	2,680	1,3.0	1,615
20 years	8,435 9,235	3,642 -,205 4,230	5,030				6,575	3,030	3,255 3,545 1,350 3,710	2,490 3,015 2,8_0	3,195 3,505 3,260	25	60 40 90	2,66° 2,660 3,020	1,175	1,485
	9,195 _^,174 10,190	-,705 4,790	4,965 5,470 3,400				6,_/5 7 045 7,105	2,825 3, 334 3,49	3,710	3,305	3,600	30 45	102	3,085	1,370	1,6,5 -,760 -,785
23 years 24 years 25 years 26 years	10,135	-, 603 l	5,550 5,350				7,030 7,150	3, 325	3,705	3,2,5	3,550 3,540 3,755	125	150	3,125	1,250 1,350 1,425	-,845
28 years	10,240 _0,55 _10,375	4,890 - 875 5,000	5.375				7,250	3,530 3,450 3,530	3,630 3,875 3,730	3,405 3,380 2,450 3,325	3,665	70 8 75	110	3,225 3,115 2,82	1,470	1,045
29 years	9,670	4,64	5,285				6,850	3,400	3,450	3,325	3,3,5	7>	75	2,945	1,150	1,670
31 years .	8,715 8,715 8,263	4,005 4,1,0 3,980	4,170 4,500 4 285				5,845 6,050	2,885	3,460	2,825	2.905	50 70 65	55 85	2,665 2,390	1,265 1,120 1,220	1,680 1,210 1,445 1,370
33 years	8,840	4.195	4,645	1	195		3,875	2,960	2,915	3,015	3,075 2,865 3,070	65 60	50 62	2 630	1,026	1,370 ,510 1,580
35 years 36 years 37 years	9,245 8,570 8,810	4,085 4,085 4 205	5,165			-	6,400 5,945 6,705 6,115	2, 67, 2, 945 2, 960	3,585 3,000 3 045	2,805 2,890 2,875	3,520 2,955	60 70 55 85	65 42	2,785	1,205 1,140	1,580
38 years 39 years	9,355	4,673	4,605 4,945 - 880	- 1	463		6,115	2,960	3,1-5	2,865	2,965 3,010 3,030	85 60	80 135 75	2 805 3,240 3,180	1,245 ,440 1,405	1,560 1,800 1,775
	9,900 7,655	7,435 3 6 ₄ 0	5 465		14		6,765	3,070	3,695	2.995	3,600	75 9°	95	3,135	4,365	1,770
40 years 41 years 42 years 43 years	7,525 7,465 8,400	4,405	2,045 3,060 4,525	.			6,590 5,770	2,515 3 050 2,575	2,880 3,540 3,095	2,420 2,955 2,590	2,810 3,480 2,995	95 85	70 60 100	2,250 2,875 2,630	1,355 200	1,520
44 years	8,420	3,505 4,205	4,020				5,255	2,475	2,780	2,340	2,740	135	80 95	2,270	1,290	1,520 1,430 1,240 1,295
46 years.	7, 10	3,450	3,6cm 3,805	- 1			2,925 2,097 4,970	2,915 2,400 2 375	3,016 2,695 2,595	2,285	2,595	110	100	2,015	1,050	965
47 viars 48 years 49 years	7, 10 1,065 7,770 1,775	3,660	4 1_0 4,130				5,380	2 545 2,730	2,79>	2,430	2,655	125	140 115	2,390	1,075	4,31 4,460
50 years 51 years	8,720	4,070	4,650	- 1		8	5,945	2,790	3,255	2,530	2,985	200 95	170	2,775	1,280 550	1,495
o2 years o3 years 54 years	5,480 6,920 6,085	2,500 3 430 2,920	2,980 3,490 3,165				5,015 4,555	2,450	2,565 2,390 2,215	2,265	2,435	185	130	1 9.5	980 755	925 775
so years	5,965 5,820 5,350	2,800	3,105 3,335 2 745				4,275	2,060	2,280	-,940 -,865 -,775 -,620	2,130	220 155	85 135	1,690	800 765	890 755
of years	5,182	2,605	2.840	- 1			3,967	1,925	2,035	1,775 1,620	2,100	150 150	135	1,3-0	680 572	710 615
58 vers -	2,265 4,925	2,420	2,845	1			3,880	1,655	2,155	1,405	2,010	152 250	145	1,385	695 7°0	690 680
60 years	4,775 3,645	2,330 1,650 1,775	1 995	-			3,225 2,825 3,035	1,690 1,3.0 1,345	1,835	1,165 1,160	1,425	240 140	40 90	1,250 830 920	640 340 430	610 48L 500
62 years 63 years	3,645 3,965 1,845 3,740	1,790	2,055 2,065				2,990	1 320	1,610	1,150	1,550 1,470 1,350	185 230 185	_40 _40 1.70	930 855 770	410 410	445 540 940
64 veurs 65 veurs 65 veurs	4,935	2,000	2,890				3,400	1,245	1,950	1,240	1,770	21.0	180	1,535	295 430	940 550
67 years	3, -90 3,433 2,7_0	1,350	2,050 1,600				2,430	1,340	1,390	880	1,290	160	100	1,260	510 415	750 550
69 Jenis	2,740	1 050	1,600		1	- 1	2,355	855	1,260	69°	1,120	185	140	185	230	330
70 3 tals - 71 years 72 5 tars -	2,095	870 875	1,225		1		1,615	6/5	1,500 940 1,075	550 500	1,370 160 980,	165 25 155	#50 95	/80 573	195	2F 3.0 315
74 years	2,040	790 640	1 050		: 1	. 1	1,555	620 495 545	935	525	855	91	601	345	170	200
70 years 76 tears	2,030	820 65	925	- 1	i		1,535	415	990 765	385 365	885 692	160	40 40 73	195 340	275 150	220 190
77 56'rs 78 5'ears 19 Years	-,200 -,365 1,005	50 555 375	750 810 630				-,065 940	360 435 310	585 63C 53C	295 345 270	545 560 473	65 90 40	40 70 50	300 165	90 120 65	165 180 100
90 3 4475	1,100	36C	740 440				885	310	575	295	242	75	30	2,5	5.	165
SI Vears	660	240	445 405 3_5	1			970 2_0 970	205 1,25 205	365 345 365	135	330 345	45 3L	35 30 40	145 150	70 50 35	100
Vears 4 years 5 to 59 years	1,415	230 345	~7D	A 100 P	-		445 850	200	365 245 375	165 450 475	325 230 425	40 50 100	40 25 80	75 100 265	30.	40 70 195
to 94 years to to 99 years	365	40	290		-		2>> 60	40 20	215	30	165	10	50	110	70 35 20	75
00 years and over	30.8	3	10		1		10	2	5		5	2		5	1	•
fedian age.	30.8	30 0	31. 6		- :		32 3	31 4	J3 1	30 4	12 5	55 7!	13 5	27 7	25 8	28 4

DETAILED CHARACTERISTICS

18-121

Table 52.—SINGLE YEARS OF AGE, BY COLOR AND SEX, FOR CRBAN AND RURAL AREAS OF THE STATE 1950
[Based on 20-percent sample available complete-rount data in table 5. focuses of record on home of the stat

			Urban				Par	nonfarm	-			R,	ral farm	**********	NAME OF STREET
Age		Total	-2	None	rò te		Total		Non	watte		Tota	- term	Non	wate
	Botn sexes	Male	Female	Male	Female	Both sexes	Male	Female	Mass	Pemale	Boto sexes	Male	Fernane		Гетаю
Ad ages nder i vest year, years vests vests years years years years	1,467,090 35,540 36,480 37,610 38,185 27,240 27,430 27,440 27,400 27,400 27,000 22,080 22,930	698,613 -8,070 18,255 19,175 19,475 14,210 14,085 13,960 13,465 12,75 11,600	768,475 7,470 12,225 18,710 13,050 3,325 13,680 13,45 12,355 11,330	207,5 80 6,390 6,795 6,795 4,755 4,660 4,905 4,470 4,475 3,925	239 60° 0,18, 6,2,5 6 20% 6,14, 4,480 4,555 4,575 4,575 3,970	643 57, 27,324 -7,375 18,900 17,425 14,09 15,44 15,200 1,505 -4,340 -7,025	72 715 8,670 7,579 9,559 9,80 7,-85 7,871 7,920 7,920 7,930 7,030	312,960 2,655 8,550 9,345 4,020 7,625 7,280 7,105 6,590	98 895 2,100 3,260 2,955 2,640 2,750 2,750 2,440 2,530 2,260	2 220 3,005 2,985 3,125 2,405 2,400 2,705 2,360 2,360 2,275	66,6 % 4,-0 14,04% 15,40% 16,217 47,800 47,900 17,800 17,800 17,800 17,800 17,800 17,800 17,900	29. 290 7 7-5 7 890 8 J55 6, 810 7, 530 6, -80 7, 505 7 95	275,315 (,876 ,022 7,515 7,625 7,020 7,535 7,300 7,287 0,760	118,830 3,914 3,445 3,830 3,40 3,550 3,550 3,540 3,540 3,750 3,750 3,750 3,750	3,525 3,525 3,626 3,825 3,490 3,490 3,495 3,285 3,285 3,285 3,145
0 years 1 years 2 years 3 years 4 years 5 years 5 years 7 years 7 years 9 years 9 years	22,170 20,785 21,630 20,285 .9,145 18 \$30 .6,435 19,705 22,255 22,940	11,085 10,315 10,640 13,050 9,575 2,240 8,820 8,885 9,950 9,770	11,485 10,470 10,960 1,235 9,570 9,570 9,61* 10,320 12,305 13,170	2,705 3,605 3,450 3,450 3,420 3,420 3,780 2,960 3,125 2,730	4,065 3,685 4,025 3,840 3,020 3,485 3,495 4,0-0 3,990	10, -95 -2,435 10,375 -1,800 11,270 -1,050 10,765 10,500 10,100 9,335	6,805 7,065 7,065 5,830 5,260 5,265 5,265 2,205 4,775 4,530	6,690 6,700 6,3.0 5,470 5,795 5,487 5,325 4,805	2,453 2,453 2,255 1,955 1,975 1,775 1,776 1,630 1,545 2,545	1,705	14,395 1,730 34,075 4,240 13,240 13,435 12,760 12,530 10,750 8 425	7,385 9,89, 1,780 2,355 6,835 6,995 5,550 0,496 2,966 4,395	7 010	3,255 2,905 3,690 3,305 2,930 2,855 4,775 2,695 2,800 1,935	3,295 2,930 3,415 2,855 2,750 2,866 2,955 2,270 1,875
U years 1 years 2 years 3 years 3 years 4 years 5 years 5 years 5 years 7 years 5 years 8 years 9 year	23,320 24,515 25,210 26,965 27,180 27,765 24,640 27 185 27,415 25,090	9,430 11,170 11,345 12,625 12,625 12,790 12,825 2,870 23,010 -,875	3,890 3,865 4,340 4,320 14,975 13,825 -4,345 -4,405 -2,5-5	2,000 2,920 3,50 3,340 3,275 3,15 2,210 3,475 3,430 2,785	4,350 3,725 4,260 4,175 4 320 4,455 3,970 4 140 3,885	10,130 9,850 9,750 9,730 9,915 9,115 9,770 9,685 8,770	5,079 -,285 4,925 4,760 4,680 4,795 4,225 4,965 4,495 4,495	5 0-0 4,865 5,025 4,970 5,050 5,120 5,120 6,805 4,805 5,490	1,795 1,375 1,510 1,505 1,505 1,405 1,405 1,240 1,370 1,106	1,940 1,565 1,535 1 490 -,40, 1,550 1,400 1,450 1,450 1,185	7,695 7,415 6,735 6,975 5,880 6,050 5,883 6,950 6,095 5,485	3,910 3,925 3,495 3,725 5,890 7,8-5 2,905 2,905 2,906 2,905	3,785 3,190 3,240 3,290 2,990 3,208 3,00,5 2,960 3,_15 2,990	1,775 1 640 1,415 1,515 1,095 1,110 1,110 1,100	2,64: 1,53: -,48: 1,35: 1,48: 1,27: 1,09: -,27:
O years 1 years 2 years 3 years 4 years 5 years 7 years 7 years 9 years 9 years	26,635 21,880 23,240 21,485 22,410 23,395 21,373 22,370 24,440 21,995	12,360 10,755 10,810 1J 395 10,910 10,995 10,095 10,510 11,435 10,140	14,275 71 125 12,430 11,090 12,500 12,600 11,860 13,005 14,855	3,130 2,490 2,885 2,345 2,060 2,860 2,750 2,925 3,315 3,125	4,505 2,900 3,640 3,110 3,580 3,390 3,710 4,53, 3,950	9,925 8,000 9,155 6,140 5,025 8,886 8,525 8,425 8,425 8,425 8,435	4,800 3,830 4,390 3,985 4,420 4,155 4,420 4,155 4,425	5,125 4,170 4,765 4,155 4,040 4,465 4,370 4,255 4,300 4,410	1,385 830 1,080 875 1,115 1,045 1,065 1,255 1,350	1,615 1,180 1,345 1,070 1,185 1,140 1,40 1,370	7,005 5,560 0,170 5,520 6,670 6,685 0,440 6,805 7,905 7,100	2,480 2,645 2,866 2,720 3,250 3,.60 3,045 3,375 4,005 3,685	3,585 2,713 3,000 3,100 3,420 3,527 3,399 3,430 2,900 3,475	1,175 800 910 4 000 990 ,040 990 4,070 4,070	-,316 956 1,102 1,205 1,245 -,265 1,435 1,512 1,512
O Years 1 Years 2 Years 3 Years 3 Years 4 Years 5 Years 5 Years 7 Years 7 Years	24,485 8,260 22,195 19,875 18,235 19,950 16,475 16,440 17,655 18,785	11,490 8,535 10,475 9,350 8,760 9,885 7,930 7,890 8,325 9,010	12, 995 9,325 11,720 10,525 9,475 10,065 8,545 8,550 9,330 9,775	3,370 2,270 3,015 2,595 2,390 3,000 2,142 2,045 2,305 2,790	4,380 2,4.5 3,365 3,185 2,690 3,080 2,370 2,985 3,640	9,050 6,300 7,970 6,775 6,625 7,205 6,015 6,185 6,220 7,0	4,580 3,230 4,045 3,360 3,570 3,185 3,060 2,995 3,640	4,470 3,000 3,925 3,415 3,635 2,830 3,125 3,225 3,520	1,455 775 1,025 86' 900 1,000 745 835 855	-,575 720 -,-15 970 -,135 750 920 960 1,196	7,945 6,890 6,415 5,995 6,-00 5 6-0 5 565 5,40 6,-60	4,050 2,865 3,385 3,215 3 005 3,140 2,810 2,820 2,990 3,475	3,899 2,650 3,505 2,500 2,960 2,830 2,745 2,950 2,985	-,545 925 1,020 1 000 935 1,150 1,000 910 1,070 1,343	1,62 8: 1 20 1,12 1,12 1,02 85: 1,00 1,04
O yours 1 rouns 2 years 2 years 4 years 5 years years 5 years 5 years 5 years 5 years	19,480 12,190 15,420 13,543 13,040 12,010 11,110 11,940 10,645	9,295 5,740 7,480 6,600 6,610 6,765 5,720 5,145 5,525 4,980	-0 185 C,450 7,940 7 040 6 930 5,675 5,290 6,165 5,415 5,660	2,960 2,335 2,135 1,690 1,915 1,870 1,620 1,335 1,710 1,465	3,490 1,680 2,-25 1,870 1,815 1,655 1,505 1,700 1,495	6,785 4,425 5,415 4,605 5,160 4,835 7,790 4,210 4,485 4,215	3,380 2,70 2,695 2,190 2,465 2,465 2,275 2,175 2,175 2,065	3 405 2,255 2,720 2,415 2,685 2,570 2 260 2,935 2,310 2,150	1,080 505 685 660 620 81.0 685 655 720 605	1,280 505 710 765 780 800 700 513 710 655	6,860 3,877 5,240 4,500 5,060 4,685 4,355 4,220 4,420 3,960	3,695 2,070 2,565 2,255 2,530 4,570 2,355 2,135 2,135 2,20	3, _65 1, 800 2,575 2,245 2,530 2, _15 2,000 2,060 2,105 1,740	1, 85 640 855 875 875 750 745 915 700	1,36 56 90 72 90 79 62 60 60 50
years years years years years years years years years years years	10,815 7,795 8,665 6,870 8,525 1 370 7,945 8,680 7,785 6,085	5 155 3,530 3,980 4,163 3,980 4,815 3,380 3,725 3,340 2,640	5,660 4,265 4,685 4,705 4,545 6,555 4,565 4,955 4,445 3,465	1,420 965 1,090 1,140 1,805 1,13,- 1,440 1,210 675	1,200 1,200 1,270 2,565 1,595 1,430 980	4,1.0 3,225 3,740 2,795 3,875 4,890 4,225 4,145 2,980	1,965 1,530 1,890 1,910 1,885 2,290 1,960 2,005 1,950 1,485	2,145 1,695 1,850 1,885 1,990 2,600 2,265 2,160 2,195 1,495	955 430 610 595 620 860 700 945 80.5	755 410 575 580 700 1,190 935 870 885 570	3,595 3,035 3,155 3,455 3,360 3,890 3,535 3,425 2,980 2,580	1,910 1,845 1,845 2,075 2,315 2,395 -,920 -,685 1,535	1,685 1,330 1,310 1,630 -,285 2,575 1 440 1,505 1,295 1,045	730 450 5_0 570 755 990 860 920 775 605	54 34 41 52 43 68 56 68 57,
vears vears years	6, 795 4,260 5,230 4,400 4,090 4,335 3,490 2,735 3,020 2,220	2,880 1,845 2,160 1,760 1,740 1,320 1,320 1,200 1,255 900	1,9.5 2,415 3,070 2,640 2,345 2,555 2,1 m 1,535 1,765 -,320	845 415 600 445 450 630 405 515 585 715	1,030 560 765 645 615 690 970 370 430 235	3,510 2,100 2,815 2,415 2,145 2,165 1,855 1,645 1 705 1 260	1,750 1,055 1,525 1,305 1,025 1,095 925 855 810 660	1,760 1,045 1,290 1,110 1,085 1,070 930 790 695 595	290 545 410 355 370 430 265 300 255	760 300 370 370 325 390 330 195 260 260	2,620 1,580 2,075 1,750 1,610 1,495 -,385 975 995 910	1,475 945 1,170 955 950 835 810 595 595 468	1,145 905 795 660 660 475 380 400 445	620 275 445 355 380 290 265 208 21.0 1.85	46 13: 28: 30 16: 28: 18: 9: 15:
years years years years years years to 89 years to 94 years to 99 years O years and over	2,510 1,490 1,505 1,270 1770 2,685 915 275 95	925 640 550 510 530 950 285 85	1,585 850 915 760 640 1,735 630 190 65	295 195 210 125 185 300 140 45	460 175 230 135 165 510 200 125 55	1,340 770 810 650 515 1,460 460 200 90	400 400 330 275 630 160 90 25	690 370 405 320 240 830 300 110 65	290 105 150 155 115 245 30 50	295 120 160 95 80 585 480 70 65	945 405 580 370 435 1,005 390 80 60	405 195 245 245 200 200 165 20	5/0 210 315 125 205 505 225 60 45	295 400 75 900 85 295 55 100 15	23K 9K 9X 20 53 163 8K 25
edian age	28 5	28 0	29 0	26 0	27 5	2- 7	24 4	25 0	22 3	23 7	21.4	21 >	21.3	18 1	16.

Table 13—AGE, BY RACE, NATIVITY, AND SEX, FOR THE STATE, 1950 AND 1940, FOR URBAN AND RURAL AREAS, AND FOR STANDARD METROPOLITAN AREAS AND CITIES OF 100,000 OR MORE, 1950

Statustion for 1969 homeo on 33-percent name of seventile complete-seemt data in tables 4, 15, and 33 Median not shown where been in less than 500 for 1960 or 100 for 1940]

		Ал сізаня	A Seminar on		hative waste	1	Fore	gn-oom who	te		Negro		0	ther races	
Arro consess vest and same	Total	Maie	Female	T.Aal	Maie	Penale	Total	Male	Female	Total	Male	Female	Total	Male	Female
										1					
THE STATE 1950	2 277 370	, 31°,620	_,366,75C	وسدرجات م	870 400	893,715	28 490	24,9.5	.3,275	880 690	422,885	457,805	4,375	2,420	1,95
All ager	136,825	170,650	465,975	2.2 600	1 7 235	-03,265 85,195	505 475	285 260	220	125 025	62,905 50,895	62,120	695 590	325 300	371 291
5 to 9 years 10 to 4 years 15 to 49 years	27, J90 236 220	140,100	1.6,550 1.6,550 1.38.335	173,840 .46 600 134,325	88 645 74,680	71,920	340	_50 305	190 265	88,780 76,110	44,590 36,390 29,885	44 190 39 720	500 345	250 180	25 16
20 to 24 years.	24, 350 21,080	1025 99 795	1.1,200	142.980	65,540 69,305 72,325	73 675	1,245	380 785	865 1,215	66.450	29,885	36 565 33,690	405 335	225 175	18
25 to 39 years 30 to 34 years 35 to 39 years	2,560 190,_80 191,905	12,30 42,050	0,830 99,000 99,855	.48,090 .35,420 131 595	66,810 64 715	68,61C 66,380	1,215	525 655	690 750	61,135 23 330 58,590	27,445 23,710 26,475	29,620 32,115 27 160	215 315	135 205	8
40 to 44 year	72,530	84 75"	88 47.	-13,5-5	59 000	00,0151	1,670	970 1,270	1,075	51,080	23,920	27 160 24,650	265	165	10
45 to 49 'ears. 50 to 54 years	151 795 126 193	74 725 6_ 850	77 070 6~,340 72 260	102,210 85,510	50.96C 41,940	51 250, 43,570	2,345 2 750 2 840	1,62C 1,630	1,130	37,760 30,175 22,545	18,155 15,480	19,605 14,695 11,365	170	135	3
55 to 59 years	20 82° 80 015 78,680	50.560 39.330 37,125	40 665 41,560	85,510 69,700 54,345 45 625	41,940 33,370 26,330 21,255	43,570 36,330 27,995 24,370	3,020	750	1,20	22,545	11,180 14,210 7,150	11,365 15,790 7,090	105	70 25	1
70 to 74 years	47,260	22 545	24.8.5	30 985 19,275	8,605	15,830	2,095	1,6°0 1,220 775	875 660	9,260	4,720	2 54D	20	20	1
80 to 84 years	14,765	6,565	8,200	2 315 / 185	3 795 4 615	5,520 2,570	1,435 740 530	460 245	280 285	4,690 2,990	1,085	1,905	20	15	
Mechan age	24 0	26 1		27 5	27 .	27 9	54.2	55 8	52 O	23 7	22 8	24 4	20 7	23.4	17
THE STATE 1940	242 890	1 .72 382	1	1.484 467	74. 633	7/2 82/	27,272	15,746	11,526	849,303	413,322	435,981	2,838	1,681	1,15
Afiages	2,363,880 230 n27	1 4 845	114.274	138 865	741,633	742,834 68 569	21	9	_2	91,305	45 813	45.492	436	235	20
5 to 9 years 10 to 14 years	227,976 2-3,836	122,825	2,01	137 981 152 809	77,508	67 960 75 301	146	33 78	30 68	89,580 90 586	44,603 45 082	45,504	352 295 296	188 157 146	16 13 15
15 to 19 years	240,398 210,396	1_8,486 103,885	121,912 12,511 196,727	152,904 138,005	76,486 67,747	76,418	317 45° 754	1.58 206 359	159 251 395	90 586 86,881 77,737 73,471	41,696 35,844 33,937	45,185 41,893 39,534	197	88 136	10
35 to 39 years	207,02 .86,-5- 174,.49	101,885 106,294 90,968 84,955	95,48 ₀ 89,194	132,578 121,654 109,280	67,747 65,862 60,382 54,560	66,716 61,272 54,720	1,187	635	552 957	63 387 62,592	29,8JL 29,129	33,586 33,463	225 208	720 727	2
10 to 44 years	14,38,	72,289	72,092	91,743	46,234	45,509	2,705	1,653	1,052	49,775	24,290	25 486 21 598	157	112	
55 to 49 years 50 to 54 years 55 to 59 years	102 209 81 324	52,611	49,658	79,744 65,077 52 078	40,229 33,038	39,515 32,039 25,925	3,178 3,581 3,443	1,896 2,186 2,029	1,282	43 646 33,519 25,732	22,048 17,330 13,455	16,189	92	57 48	
to 64 years	63,361	47,685 31 749 27,665	39,639 3.,612 28 497	-1,780 32 852	26,153 20,596 15,744	21,184	2,829	1,629	1,4.4 1,200 1,032	18 697	Q ASN.	9,2.1	55 52	38	8.7
70 to 74 years	31,636	15,615	16,021 17,30°	18,925 18,192	8,970	9,955	1,866	1,116	750	10,809	10,417 5,502 4,889	5,307 5 938	36	38 36 27 21	
Viednan age	25 5	25 5	25 6	25 8	25 7	26 0	53 8	54.0	53 6	24 3	24 1	24.4	21 0	26 0	17
URBAN: 1950					1										
All ages	1,467,090 -75 075	698 6.5 89 185	768,475 85,890	996,725	478,905 59,020	517,820	23,120 355	12,130	10,990	445,965 59,020	29,890	234,120	1,280	795	54
to 9 years	130,880	66,335 51,665	64,545	86,540	44.175	42,365	335	1.85	150	43.900	21,930	21,970	105	45 45	6
15 to 19 years	101,665	46,665 57,430	69,860	67,265 90,105	33,425 3 ,120 41,810	36,_45 48,295	1,050	230 315	225 735	36,955 33,875 35,980	18,080 15,285 15,210	18 590 20,770	140 70 155	30 95	
25 to 29 years 90 to 34 years 15 to 39 years	134,395 115,650	63, ×0 55,230 53,175	71,055 60 420	96,115 83 120	46,670	49,445	1,625	655 440	970 580	36,555	15,950	20,605	100 75 130	50	
10 to 44 years	103,050	49,010	50,740	78,220 71,955	37,650 34,570	37,385	1,195	550 800	645 620	34,010 29,575	4,890 13,570	19,120	130	85 70	1
65 to 49 years 50 to 54 years	99 305 74,270	43 040 35,725 27,735	46,265 38,545	60,165 50,705 40,405	29,475 24,265 18,385	30,690 26,440	1,980 2,385 2 370	1,080	900	27,095	9,980	12,650 11,130	65 70	40 55	
55 to 59 years 60 to 64 years	58,945	20 810	23 860	30.710	14 045	22 020 16,665	2,500	-,350	1,020	16,130	7,965	6,165	40	35	
70 to 74 years	41,865 24,775 15,800	17,830 10,390	23,985	24,810 16,670 10,390	10,390 6,630	10,040	2,360	955	710	6,430	5,250 2,800	8,430 3,630	20 15 10	15	
75 to 79 years 80 to 84 years 85 years and over	7.945	6 455 3,195	9,345 4,750	10,390 >,195 2 170	1,820	6,490 3,375	1,165	505 365	560 210	2,165	1,945	2,290	10	10	
Median age	3 970 28 5	1,350 28 0	2,620	2 170	675 28 2	29 3	425 54 0	190 55 2	235 52 1	26 3	25 9	890 27 5	25 5	31.8	17
BURAL NONFARM: 1950								1.00						16	
All ages	643,675 56,120	320,7.5	322,960 43,780	438,005	220,220	217,785	2 915	_,600	1,315	200,135	97,445	102,690	۷,520	1,450	٠,١
5 to 9 years 10 to 4 years	73,145	44,3 0 97,515 31,755	35,630 30,620	56,125 48,755	25,165	28,765 23,590 20 410	70 70 60	35 40	35 30	29,475 23,910	14,740	14,735 11,830 10,045	450 410	205 230	24
15 to 19 years . 20 to 24 years .	51,785 49,390	25,355 24,420	26,430 24 970	41,515 34,620 33 940	21,105 17,115 17,005	17 505	65 150	20 45 50	40 20	20 490 16,875	10,445 8,075 7,245	8,800	310 225	185 120	1
25 to 29 vears 30 to 34 years	47,255	22 795	24,460	33,850 31,790	16 520 15 875	17,330	250 110	95 55	1.00 155 55	15,080 12,960 11,230	7,245 5,085 5,000	7,835 6 875	220 195 115	120 95	19
35 to 39 years 40 to 44 years	43,405 36 720	21,605 18,525	21,800	31,085 26,190	15,705	15,380	145	70	75 35	12,005	5,720 4,930	6,230 6,285 5,290	170 150	110	-
45 to 49 years 50 to 54 years	32,785 26,390	16,450 12,910	16,335 13 480	23 105 18 570	11,825	1, 280	205	110	95	9,360	4 460	4 900	55	52	
55 to 50 years	22,235	11,210	11 025 9 565	15,085 12,565	9,230 7,565 6,135	9,340 7,*20 6,430	255 250	100 170 135	85 15	6.850	3,520 3,435	4,035 3,4-5	125	60 40	
60 to 64 years - 65 to 69 years - 70 to 74 years -	20,405	9,690 6,660	10 715	11,790 8,285	5,655	6,135	345 250	215 145	130 105	2,660 8,240 4 395	2,865 3,810 2,280	2,995 4,430	70 30	45 10 10	
75 to 78 years	8,430 4,085	4,350 2 0 ₀ 0	6,290 4,080 2,025	5,205 2,435	2 635	1,250	170	95	75	3,050	1,620	2,115 -,430 745	20 5 10	10	
So years and over	2,210	905	1,305	1 095	530	565	80	40	40	1,025	325	700	10	10	
Median age	24 7	24 4	25 0	25 3	25 1	25 0	54 4	56 8	50 9	23 1	22 3	23 8	18 1	19 4	1.6

Table 55—AGE, BY RACE, NATIVITY, AND SEX, FOR THE STATE, 1950 AND 1940, FOR URBAN AND RURAL AREAS, AND FOR STANDARD METROPOLITAN AREAS AND CITIES OF 100,000 OR MORE, 1950—Cor.

[Statistics for 1940 based on 20-nerosco sample available complete-count data in tables 14-15, and 25 Median not allows where case is seen than 500 for 960 or 100 for 1940]

Area, census year		Alı classes			auve write		Fore	gn-born who	te		/ ogn		0:	ther races	
and age	Total	Male	Female	Total	Male	Female	Total	Male	Female	Total	Male	Female	Total	Male	Fem

RURAL FARM: 1950									i						
All ages	560,605	291,290	275,315	J29 385	171,275	56 30		2 100		*** ***					
der 5 vests	73,630	37, 325	36,305	36.940	18,955	17 985	2,155	1 185	970	234,590 36 530	La 595	115,795	4°5	235 50	_
9 years.	72,365	36 250	36 115	38,435	19,305	19,240	79	30,	35	33,675	_4,385	16,790	75	25	
o 19 years.	57,900	30,250 30,395	27,505	32,440	17,305	_8,245 _5,135	50	15	25	31,33» 25,360	₩,065 ₩ 030	15,270	50 50	20 30 10	
to 24 years	34,400 29 910	_7,945 4,595	15,315	18,935	10 490	8,440	45 1	36 15	20	12,390	1,430	7.960	30	10	
to 34 years	31,285	14,960	16,325	20,510	10,022	10,455	125	35	90	10,620	4,80	5,815	40 25	25	
to 39 years	34,945 32,760	17,270	17,675	22,290	11,360	8,445 8,940 10,455 10,930 -0,325	6*	30 35	90 95 30 45	12,575	2,365	5,716	15	10	
40 Mare	29,705	16,520	4 470	21,370	11,045	-0,325	95 160	50 80		11,285	5,490	5,805	10		
10 02 years	25,530	-5,235 -3,215 -1,615	24,479 12 3.5 10,025		9 660 8 445	9,280	165	95 110	90 70	9 295	4 655	4,440 3,115	35	20 5	
to 64 Vears	16,600	9,360	7,240	14,210	6,170	4,900	215	110	305 95	7,195 5,245	4,080	2,240	20	5	
o 69 years	9,635	9,360 9 550 5,495	6 860 4 140	9,025	3,300	3,815,	305	190	115	7,080	4,150	2,930			
to 79 years	5,760	3,300	2 460	6,030 3,680	2,070	1,610	180	120	50	1,975	2,070	1,34"	10	5	
to 84 years	2,735	1,3_0	1 425 835	1,685	790	895	80	35	25 45	970	1,.55 485	485	- 1		
years and over	1,235			920	410	510	25	15	n	590	275	31.5			
distr sgr	21 4	21. 5	21.3	24 8	24 7	25 0	57 3	60.5	52 9	18 1	18 1	_8 -			
TANDARD METROPOL- ITAN AREAS 1950	10000					. !									
BATON ROUGE	157,740	77 335	80,405	103,862	51,595	52 270	1 500	780	720	52,290	24,910	27,30	95	50	
der 5 years	20,800	10,440 7,340 5,730	7,410	_3,380 9,730	6,610	6,770 4,770	30 40	15	15 35	7,390	3 815 2 380	3,575	5	20	
to 14 years	14 755 11,200 1,905	5,750	5,470	6,835	3,510	3,345	_5 1	- 5	10	4.305	2 210	2,095	25	5	
to 19 years	-6,065	5,680 7,725	8,340	1,285	3,705 5,570 5,745	3,345 3,940 5,725	55 190	45 113 75	10 80	4,200	1,930	2,270	10		
to 29 years	15,855	7,840 6,355	8,015 6,835	9,210	5,745 4,560	5,380 4,650	1/0	75 20	80 95 50 45	3,895	2 00s 1 760	2.5401	15	15	1
to 39 years	12,545	2,975	6,570	8,415 7,005	4,095	~ 320	75	30	45	4,045	1.845	2,135	_0	12 5	
6 44 years		5,175	5,375		3 535	3,470	75	45	30	3,465	.,590	1 875	5	5	
to 49 years	8,045 6,695	4,070	3,475	5,230	2,720	2,520	_05 _90	55 120	70	2,705	1,030	7,400 975	5	100	
0 59 years	5.040	3,475 2,590	2,450	4,500 3,200	1,595	1,605	115	55	60	-,725		785		45.	0
to 64 years	3,480	1,805	1,675 2,005	2,330	1,200	9,5	85 135	55 60 75	60 25 60	1,700	545 730	520 970			
to 69 years to 74 years to 79 years	3,440	840	1,120	1 100	437	670	60	35	25	800	375	425		100	
to 84 years	1,180	470 270	710 395	705 390	255 125	450 265	45 20	10 10	35 10	430 255	205 135	225 120	0.00		
years and over	370	270 11.5	255	155	35	120	20 25	10	10 15	190	70	120			
dian age	26 3	26 1	26 5	26 4	26 3	26 5	46 4	48 6	43.3	25 8	202	26 2			
NEV ORLEANS .	683,330	324,885	358 445	467,535	222,830	244 700	16,250	8,820	7 440	198,590	92,680	105 910	945	555	
der o years	76,915 58,520	39,170 29,475	37,745 29,045	50,950 38,985	25,935 19 765	25,015	175	100 140	75	25,655	13,075	12,580	135	60 35	
to 14 years	44,630	22,335	22,295	28,765	14,465	19,220	170	85	851	15 595	9,535	9,695 7,850 7,995	100	40	
o 19 years	44 460	20,985	23,45	29,315	24,040	15,275	340 550	160	180	14 760	6,765	7,995	45	20	
to 24 years	56,520	25,935 29,175 25,575	30,085	39,946 44,460 38,515	18,690 21,375	2_,250	1,055	475	410	15,940	7,050	8,890 9,350	90 50	55 30 25	
to 34 years	53,435	25,575	27,860 28,700	38,515 37,185	⊾8,920 ⊾7,825	19,595	760 855	355 400	405 455	14,1.5	7 295 6,275 7,020	7 840 8,850	110	25	
to 39 years	62,210 53,435 54,020 50,750	23,710	27,040	35,390	15,480	18,910	1,015	560	455	14,260	6,620	7,640	85	75	
to 49 venzs	44.465	21,445	23,020	30,425	14,715	15,710	1,445	840	60.	12,540	5,8:C	6,690	55	. 40	
to 54 years.	37,915	18,290 14,350	19,625	26,190 21,125	12,525	13,665	1,690	7,050	640 750	9 970 7,365	4,665 3,690	5,305 3,675	65	35	
to 64 years.	22.690	10,600	12,090	15.695	7,100	8,595	1.820	1,065	755	5 155	2.400	2,735	. 20	50 35 15 10	1
to 69 years	20,265 12,4.0 7,965	8,495 4,885	7,525	12,750 8,>15	5 185	8,595 7,565 5,425	1,685	925 700	760 490	2,700	2,375	1,610	10	5	
to 79 years	7,965	3,115	4,850 2,605	5,380 2,905	1,860	3,520 1,950	850 425	455 265	395	1,730 765	800	930 495	5		
to 84 years	4,100 1,790	525	1,265	1,045	265	7/10	265	115	150	475	140	335	5	5.	
dian age	29 9	29.2	30 5	₩ 2	29 3	31.1	54 5	55 5	53 0	27 4	26 5	28 2	27 8	25.8	
SEREVEPORT	175,900	83,800	92,100	108,010	52,085	55,925	1,825	905	920	65,965	30,750	35 215	100	60	
der 5 years	21.305	10,940 8,570 6,810	10,365	12,230	6,355	5,875	60	25 20	5	8,995 7,305	4,520 3,665	3,640	20	10	
9 years to 14 years	16,540 13,495	6,810	7,970 6,685	9,210 7,150	4,885	4,325 3,440	15	10	**5	6,320	3,080	3,2401	10	10	
to 19 years	11.725	5 445 6,180	6,280 8,250	6,760 9,315	3,065	3,675	30 80	15	15 63 125	4,920	2,340	2,580	15	15 5	
	14,430	6,180 6,590 6,230	8,285	10,090	4,695	5,395 4,550	160 70	35	125	4,520	1.855		5	73	
to 24 years	13,265		7,035	8,990 8,885	4,695 4,440 4,200	4,550	110	25	45 55	4,195 4,290	1,755	2,440	10	10	
to 29 years		5,700	6,530	8,135	3,825	4,310	125	25 70	55 55	3,970	1 805	2,165			
to 29 years	13,285	2,700			3,245	3,43.0	185	90 85	95 85	3,900	1,775	2,125	5		
to 34 years	12,230	5,330	5,635	6,655											
to 29 years to 34 years to 54 years to 44 years to 54 years to 54 years	12,230 10,745 9,115	5,110	4,775	5,840	2,635	3,025	205	115	90	2,310	1,435	1,155	ıc	5	1
to 29 years	12,230 10,745 9,115 7,165 5,335	5,110 4,340 3 450	4,775 3,715	5,840 4,650 3,420	2,815 2,180 1.670	2,470 1.750	170 205 185	11.5 90	90 95	2,310	1,155 825	1,155	10		
to 29 years to 34 years to 39 years to 49 years to 49 years to 54 years to 54 years to 59 years to 50 years	12,230 10,745 9,115 7,165 5,335 5,575	5,110 4,340 3 450 2,585 2,585	4,775 3,715 2,750 2,990	5,840 4,650 3,420 2,735	2,815 2,180 1,670 1,910	2,470 1,750 1,425	205 185 185 100	115	90 95 100	2,310 1,730 2,655 1,265	1,155 825 1,190 650	1,155 905 1,465 415	10		
20 29 years 20 34 years 20 34 years 20 49 years 20 49 years 20 56 years 20 56 years 20 59 years 20 59 years 20 59 years 20 79 years 20 79 years	12,230 10,745 9,115 7,165 5,335 5,575 3,295 2,015	5,110 4,340 3,450 2,585 2,585 1,560 900	4,775 3,715 2,750 2,990 1,735	5,840 4,650 3,420 2,735 1,930 2,180	2,815 2,180 1,670 1,910 655 470	2,470 1,750 1,425 1,075	185 185 100 70	11.5 90 85 55 55	90 95	2,310 1,730 2,655 1,265 765	1,155 825 1,190 650 375	1,155 905 1,465 415 390	10		
to 29 years	12,230 10,745 9,115 7,165 5,335 5,775 3,295	5,110 4,340 3,450 2,585 2,585 1,560	4,775 3,715 2,750 2,990 1,735	5,840 4,650 3,420 2,735 1,930	2,615 2,180 1,670 1,910 655	2,470 1,750 1,425 1,075	185 185 100	11.5 90 85 55	90 95 100	2,310 1,730 2,655 1,265	1,155 825 1,190 650	1,155 905 1,465 415	10		

Table 53.—AGE, BY RACE, NATIVITY, AND SEX, FOR THE STATE, 1950 AND 1940, FOR URBAN AND RURAL AREAS, AND FOR STANDARD METROPOLITAN AREAS AND CITIES OF 100,000 OR MORE, 1950

[Statistics for 1950 based on 20-percent sample; available complete-count data in tables 4, 15, and 33. Median not shown where base is less than 500 for 1950 or 100 for 1940]

Area, census year, and age	All classes			Native white			Foreign-born white			Negro			Other races		
	Total	Male	Female	Total	Male	Female	Total	Male	Female	Total	Male	Female	Total	Male	Female
THE STATE: 1950															
All ages	[illegible]	1,310,620	1,366,750	[illegible]	870,400	893,715	28,190	14,915	13,275	880,690	422,885	457,805	4,375	2,420	1,955
Under 5 years	336,825	170,850	165,975	[illegible]	[illegible]	103,265	505	285	220	125,025	62,905	62,120	695	325	370
5 to 9 years	[illegible]	140,100	136,290	173,840	88,645	85,195	475	260	215	101,485	50,895	50,590	590	300	290
10 to 14 years	236,220	[illegible]	116,550	146,600	74,680	71,920	340	150	190	88,780	44,590	44,190	500	250	250
15 to 19 years	[illegible]	[illegible]	[illegible]	134,325	65,540	68,785	570	305	265	76,110	36,390	39,720	345	180	165
20 to 24 years	[illegible]	99,795	[illegible]	142,980	69,305	73,675	1,245	380	865	66,450	29,885	36,565	405	225	180
25 to 29 years	[illegible]	[illegible]	[illegible]	148,090	72,325	[illegible]	2,000	785	1,215	61,135	27,445	33,690	335	175	160
30 to 34 years	190,180	[illegible]	[illegible]	135,420	66,810	68,610	1,215	525	690	53,330	23,710	29,620	215	135	80
35 to 39 years	191,905	92,050	99,855	131,595	64,715	66,880	1,405	655	750	58,590	26,475	32,115	315	205	110
40 to 44 years	172,530	[illegible]	[illegible]	[illegible]	59,000	60,515	1,670	970	700	51,080	23,920	27,160	265	165	100
45 to 49 years	151,795	74,725	77,070	102,210	50,960	51,250	2,345	1,270	1,075	47,045	22,395	24,650	195	100	95
50 to 54 years	126,190	[illegible]	[illegible]	85,510	[illegible]	43,570	2,750	1,620	1,130	37,760	18,155	19,605	170	135	35
55 to 59 years	[illegible]	50,560	72,260	69,700	33,370	36,330	2,840	1,630	1,210	30,175	15,480	14,695	105	80	25
60 to 64 years	80,015	39,350	40,665	54,345	26,350	27,995	3,020	1,750	1,270	22,545	11,180	11,365	105	70	35
65 to 69 years	78,680	37,120	41,560	45,625	21,255	24,370	3,010	1,630	1,380	30,000	14,210	15,790	45	25	20
70 to 74 years	47,360	22,545	24,815	30,985	[illegible]	16,830	2,095	1,220	875	14,240	7,150	7,090	70	20	20
75 to 79 years	29,990	14,105	15,885	19,275	8,605	10,670	1,435	775	660	9,260	4,720	4,540	20	5	15
80 to 84 years	14,765	6,565	8,200	9,315	3,795	5,520	740	460	280	4,690	2,295	[illegible]	20	15	5
85 years and over	[illegible]	2,955	[illegible]	[illegible]	[illegible]	2,570	530	245	285	2,990	1,085	1,905	10	10	
Median age	[illegible]	26.1	27.0	27.5	[illegible]	27.9	54.2	55.8	52.0	23.7	22.8	24.4	20.7	23.4	17.0
THE STATE: 1940															
All ages	2,363,880	1,172,382	1,191,498	1,484,467	741,633	742,834	27,272	15,746	11,526	849,303	413,322	435,981	2,838	1,681	1,157
Under 5 years	230,627	116,353	114,274	138,865	70,296	68,569	21	9	12	91,305	45,813	45,492	436	235	201
5 to 9 years	227,976	114,845	113,131	137,981	[illegible]	67,960	63	33	30	89,580	44,603	44,977	352	188	164
10 to 14 years	243,836	122,825	121,011	152,809	77,508	75,301	146	78	68	90,586	45,082	45,504	295	157	138
15 to 19 years	240,398	118,486	121,912	152,904	76,486	76,418	317	158	159	86,881	41,696	45,185	296	146	150
20 to 24 years	216,396	103,885	112,511	138,005	67,747	70,258	457	206	251	77,737	35,844	41,893	197	88	109
25 to 29 years	[illegible]	100,294	106,727	132,578	65,862	66,716	754	359	395	73,471	33,937	39,534	218	136	82
30 to 34 years	186,454	90,968	95,486	121,654	60,382	61,272	1,187	635	552	63,387	29,801	33,586	226	150	76
35 to 39 years	174,149	84,955	89,194	109,280	54,560	54,720	2,069	1,112	957	62,592	29,129	33,463	208	154	54
40 to 44 years	144,381	72,289	72,092	91,743	46,234	45,509	2,705	1,653	1,052	49,776	24,290	25,486	157	112	45
45 to 49 years	126,685	64,261	62,424	79,744	40,229	39,515	3,178	1,896	1,282	43,646	22,048	21,598	117	88	29
50 to 54 years	102,269	52,611	49,658	65,077	33,038	32,039	3,581	2,186	1,395	33,519	17,330	16,189	92	57	35
55 to 59 years	81,324	41,685	39,639	52,078	26,153	25,925	3,443	2,029	1,414	25,732	13,455	12,277	71	48	23
60 to 64 years	63,361	31,749	31,612	41,780	20,596	21,184	2,829	1,629	1,200	18,697	9,486	9,211	55	38	17
65 to 69 years	56,162	27,665	28,497	32,852	15,744	17,108	2,500	1,468	1,032	20,758	10,417	10,341	52	36	16
70 to 74 years	31,636	15,615	16,021	18,925	8,970	9,955	1,866	1,116	750	10,809	5,502	5,307	36	27	9
75 years and over	31,205	13,896	17,309	18,192	7,807	10,385	2,156	1,179	977	10,827	4,889	5,938	30	21	9
Median age	25.5	25.5	25.6	25.8	25.7	26.0	53.8	54.0	53.6	24.3	24.1	24.4	21.0	26.0	17.5
URBAN: 1950															
All ages	1,467,090	698,615	768,475	996,725	478,905	517,820	23,120	12,130	10,990	445,965	206,845	239,120	1,280	735	545
Under 5 years	175,075	89,185	85,890	115,535	59,020	56,515	355	205	150	59,020	29,890	[illegible]	165	70	95
5 to 9 years	130,880	66,335	64,545	86,540	44,175	42,365	335	185	150	43,900	21,930	21,970	105	45	60
10 to 14 years	103,985	51,665	52,320	66,650	33,425	33,225	240	115	125	36,955	18,080	18,875	140	45	95
15 to 19 years	101,665	46,665	55,000	67,265	[illegible]	[illegible]	455	230	225	33,875	15,285	18,590	70	30	40
20 to 24 years	127,290	57,430	69,860	90,105	41,810	48,295	1,050	315	735	35,980	15,210	20,770	155	95	60
25 to 29 years	134,395	63,340	71,055	96,115	46,670	49,445	1,625	655	970	36,555	15,950	20,605	100	65	35
30 to 34 years	115,650	55,230	60,420	83,120	40,880	42,240	1,020	440	580	31,435	13,860	17,575	75	50	25
35 to 39 years	113,555	53,175	60,380	78,220	37,650	40,570	1,195	550	645	34,010	14,890	19,120	130	85	45
40 to 44 years	103,050	49,010	54,040	71,955	34,570	37,385	1,420	800	620	29,575	13,570	16,005	100	70	30
45 to 49 years	89,305	43,040	46,265	60,165	29,475	30,690	1,980	1,080	900	27,095	12,445	14,650	65	40	25
50 to 54 years	74,270	35,725	38,545	50,705	24,265	26,440	2,385	1,425	960	21,110	9,980	11,130	70	55	15
55 to 59 years	58,945	27,735	31,210	40,405	18,385	22,020	2,370	1,350	1,020	16,130	7,965	8,165	40	35	5
60 to 64 years	44,670	20,810	23,860	30,710	14,045	16,665	2,500	1,440	1,060	11,740	5,310	6,130	20	15	5
65 to 69 years	41,865	17,880	23,985	24,810	10,390	14,420	2,360	1,225	1,135	14,580	6,250	8,430	15	15	
70 to 74 years	24,775	10,390	14,385	16,670	6,630	10,040	1,665	955	710	6,430	2,800	3,630	10	5	5
75 to 79 years	15,800	6,455	9,345	10,390	3,900	6,490	1,165	605	560	4,235	1,945	2,290	10	5	5
80 to 84 years	7,945	3,195	4,750	5,195	1,820	3,375	575	365	210	2,165	1,000	1,165	10	10	
85 years and over	3,970	1,350	2,620	2,170	675	1,495	425	190	235	1,375	485	890			
Median age	28.5	28.0	29.0	28.8	28.2	29.3	54.0	55.2	52.1	26.8	25.9	27.5	25.3	31.8	17.8
RURAL NONFARM: 1950															
All ages	643,675	320,715	322,960	438,005	220,220	217,785	2,915	1,600	1,315	200,135	97,445	102,690	2,620	1,450	1,170
Under 5 years	88,120	[illegible]	43,780	58,125	29,360	28,765	70	35	35	29,475	14,740	14,735	450	205	245
5 to 9 years	73,145	37,515	35,630	48,755	25,165	23,590	70	40	30	23,910	12,080	11,830	410	230	180
10 to 14 years	62,375	31,755	30,620	41,515	21,105	20,410	60	20	40	20,490	10,445	10,045	310	185	125
15 to 19 years	51,785	25,355	26,430	34,620	17,115	17,505	65	45	20	16,875	8,075	8,800	225	120	105
20 to 24 years	49,390	24,420	24,970	33,940	17,005	16,935	150	50	100	15,080	7,245	7,835	220	120	100
25 to 29 years	47,255	22,795	24,460	33,850	16,520	17,330	250	95	155	12,960	6,085	6,875	195	95	100
30 to 34 years	43,245	20,990	22,255	31,790	15,875	15,915	110	55	55	11,230	5,000	6,230	115	60	55
35 to 39 years	43,405	21,605	21,800	31,085	15,705	15,380	145	70	75	12,005	5,720	6,285	170	110	60
40 to 44 years	36,720	18,525	18,195	26,190	13,385	12,805	155	120	35	10,220	4,930	5,290	155	90	65
45 to 49 years	32,785	16,450	16,335	23,105	11,825	11,280	205	110	95	9,360	4,460	4,900	55	55	60
50 to 54 years	26,390	12,910	13,480	18,570	9,230	9,340	200	100	100	7,555	3,520	4,035	125	60	5
55 to 59 years	22,235	11,210	11,025	15,085	7,565	7,520	255	170	85	6,850	3,435	[illegible]	45	40	5
60 to 64 years	18,745	9,180	9,565	12,565	6,135	6,430	250	135	115	5,860	2,865	2,995	70	45	25
65 to 69 years	20,405	9,690	10,715	11,790	5,655	6,135	345	215	130	8,240	3,810	4,430	30	10	20
70 to 74 years	12,950	6,660	6,290	8,285	4,225	4,060	250	145	105	4,395	2,280	2,115	20	10	10
75 to 79 years	8,430	4,350	4,080	5,205	2,635	2,570	170	95	75	3,050	1,620	1,430	5		5
80 to 84 years	4,085	2,060	2,025	2,435	1,185	1,250	85	60	25	1,555	810	745	10	5	
85 years and over	2,210	905	1,305	1,095	530	565	80	40	40	1,025	325	700	10	10	
Median age	24.7	24.4	25.0	25.3	25.1	25.5	54.4	56.8	50.9	23.1	22.3	23.8	18.1	19.4	16.7

Table 53.—AGE, BY RACE, NATIVITY, AND SEX, FOR THE STATE, 1950 AND 1940, FOR URBAN AND RURAL AREAS, AND FOR STANDARD METROPOLITAN AREAS AND CITIES OF 100,000 OR MORE, 1950—Con.

[Statistics for 1950 based on 20-percent sample; available complete-count data in tables 14, 15, and 33. Median not shown where base is less than 500 for 1950 or 100 for 1940]

Area, census year and age	All classes			Native white			Foreign-born white			Negro			Other races		
	Total	Male	Female	Total	Male	Female	Total	Male	Female	Total	Male	Female	Total	Male	Female
RURAL FARM: 1950															
All ages	566,605	291,290	275,315	329,385	171,275	158,110	2,155	1,185	970	234,590	118,595	115,995	475	235	240
Under 5 years	73,630	37,325	36,305	36,940	18,955	17,985	80	45	35	36,530	18,275	18,255	80	50	30
5 to 9 years	72,365	36,250	36,115	38,545	19,305	19,240	70	35	35	33,675	16,885	16,790	75	25	50
10 to 14 years	69,860	36,250	33,610	38,435	20,150	18,285	40	15	25	31,335	16,065	15,270	50	20	30
15 to 19 years	57,900	30,395	27,505	32,440	17,305	15,135	50	30	20	25,360	13,030	12,330	50	30	20
20 to 24 years	34,400	17,945	16,455	18,935	10,490	8,445	45	15	30	15,390	7,430	7,960	30	10	20
25 to 29 years	29,910	14,595	15,315	18,125	9,135	8,990	125	35	90	11,620	5,410	6,210	40	15	25
30 to 34 years	31,285	14,960	16,325	20,510	10,055	10,455	85	30	55	10,605	4,870	5,815	25	25	-
35 to 39 years	34,945	17,270	17,675	22,290	11,360	10,930	65	35	30	12,575	5,865	6,710	15	10	5
40 to 44 years	32,760	16,520	16,240	21,370	11,045	10,325	95	50	45	11,285	5,420	5,865	10	5	5
45 to 49 years	29,705	15,235	14,470	18,940	9,660	9,280	160	80	80	10,590	5,490	5,100	15	5	10
50 to 54 years	25,530	13,215	12,315	16,235	8,445	7,790	165	95	70	9,095	4,655	4,440	35	20	15
55 to 59 years	21,640	11,615	10,025	14,210	7,420	6,790	215	110	105	7,195	4,080	3,115	20	5	15
60 to 64 years	16,600	9,360	7,240	11,070	6,170	4,900	270	175	95	5,245	3,005	2,240	15	10	5
65 to 69 years	16,410	9,550	6,860	9,025	5,210	3,815	305	190	115	7,080	4,150	2,930			-
70 to 74 years	9,635	5,495	4,140	6,030	3,300	2,730	180	120	60	3,415	2,070	1,345	10	5	5
75 to 79 years	5,760	3,300	2,460	3,680	2,070	1,610	100	75	25	1,975	1,155	820	5		5
80 to 84 years	2,735	1,310	1,425	1,685	790	895	80	35	45	970	485	485			--
85 years and over	1,335	700	635	920	410	510	25	15	10	590	275	315		-	-
Median age	21.4	21.5	21.3	24.8	24.7	25.0	57.3	60.5	52.9	18.1	18.1	18.1			-
STANDARD METROPOLITAN AREAS 1950															
BATON ROUGE	157,740	77,335	80,405	103,865	51,595	52,270	1,500	780	720	52,280	24,910	27,370	95	50	45
Under 5 years	20,800	10,440	10,360	13,380	6,610	6,770	30	15	15	7,390	3,815	3,575			-
5 to 9 years	14,755	7,345	7,410	9,730	4,960	4,770	40	5	35	4,980	2,380	2,600	5	-	5
10 to 14 years	11,200	5,730	5,470	6,855	3,510	3,345	15	5	10	4,305	2,210	2,095	25	5	20
15 to 19 years	11,905	5,680	6,225	7,645	3,705	3,940	55	45	10	4,200	1,930	2,270	5		5
20 to 24 years	16,065	7,725	8,340	11,285	5,570	5,715	190	110	80	4,580	2,040	2,540	10	5	5
25 to 29 years	15,855	7,840	8,015	11,125	5,745	5,380	170	75	95	4,545	2,005	2,540	15	15	-
30 to 34 years	13,190	6,355	6,835	9,210	4,560	4,650	70	20	50	3,895	1,760	2,135	15	15	
35 to 39 years	12,545	5,975	6,570	8,415	4,095	4,320	75	30	45	4,045	1,845	2,200	10	5	5
40 to 44 years	10,550	5,175	5,375	7,005	3,535	3,470	75	45	30	3,465	1,590	1,875	5	5	-
45 to 49 years	8,045	4,070	3,975	5,230	2,710	2,520	105	55	50	2,705	1,305	1,400	5		5
50 to 54 years	6,695	3,475	3,220	4,500	2,325	2,175	190	120	70	2,005	1,030	975		-	
55 to 59 years	5,040	2,590	2,450	3,200	1,595	1,605	115	55	60	1,725	940	785		-	-
60 to 64 years	3,480	1,805	1,675	2,330	1,200	1,130	85	60	25	1,065	545	520			-
65 to 69 years	3,440	1,435	2,005	1,605	630	975	135	75	60	1,700	730	970	-	-	
70 to 74 years	1,960	840	1,120	1,100	430	670	60	35	25	800	375	425			-
75 to 79 years	1,180	470	710	705	255	450	45	10	35	430	205	225			-
80 to 84 years	665	270	395	390	125	265	20	10	10	255	135	120			-
85 years and over	370	115	255	155	35	120	25	10	15	190	70	120		-	-
Median age	26.3	26.1	26.5	26.4	26.3	26.5	46.4	48.6	43.3	25.8	25.2	26.2			-
NEW ORLEANS	683,330	324,885	358,445	467,535	222,830	244,705	16,260	8,820	7,440	198,590	92,680	105,910	945	555	390
Under 5 years	76,915	39,170	37,745	50,950	25,935	25,015	175	100	75	25,655	13,075	12,580	135	60	75
5 to 9 years	58,520	29,475	29,045	38,985	19,765	19,220	230	140	90	19,230	9,535	9,695	75	35	40
10 to 14 years	44,630	22,335	22,295	28,765	14,465	14,300	170	85	85	15,595	7,745	7,850	100	40	60
15 to 19 years	44,460	20,985	23,475	29,315	14,040	15,275	340	160	180	14,760	6,765	7,995	45	20	25
20 to 24 years	56,520	25,935	30,585	39,940	18,690	21,250	550	140	410	15,940	7,050	8,890	90	55	35
25 to 29 years	62,210	29,175	33,035	44,460	21,375	23,085	1,055	475	580	16,645	7,295	9,350	50	30	20
30 to 34 years	53,435	25,575	27,860	38,515	18,920	19,595	760	355	405	14,115	6,275	7,840	45	25	20
35 to 39 years	54,020	25,320	28,700	37,185	17,825	19,360	835	400	435	15,870	7,020	8,850	110	75	35
40 to 44 years	50,750	23,710	27,040	35,390	16,480	18,910	1,015	560	455	14,260	6,620	7,640	85	50	35
45 to 49 years	44,465	21,445	23,020	30,425	14,715	15,710	1,445	840	605	12,540	5,850	6,690	55	40	15
50 to 54 years	37,915	18,290	19,625	26,190	12,525	13,665	1,690	1,050	640	9,970	4,665	5,305	65	50	15
55 to 59 years	30,270	14,355	15,915	21,125	9,640	11,485	1,740	990	750	7,365	3,690	3,675	40	35	5
60 to 64 years	22,690	10,600	12,090	15,695	7,100	8,595	1,820	1,065	755	5,155	2,420	2,735	20	15	5
65 to 69 years	20,265	8,495	11,770	12,750	5,185	7,565	1,685	925	760	5,820	2,375	3,445	10	10	
70 to 74 years	12,410	4,885	7,525	8,515	3,090	5,425	1,190	700	490	2,700	1,090	1,610	5	5	
75 to 79 years	7,965	3,115	4,850	5,380	1,860	3,520	850	455	395	1,730	800	930	5		5
80 to 84 years	4,100	1,495	2,605	2,905	955	1,950	425	265	160	765	270	495	5	5	
85 years and over	1,790	525	1,265	1,045	265	780	265	115	150	475	140	335	5	5	
Median age	29.9	29.2	30.5	30.2	29.3	31.1	54.5	55.5	53.0	27.4	26.5	28.2	27.8	25.8	-
SHREVEPORT	175,900	83,800	92,100	108,010	52,085	55,925	1,825	905	920	65,965	30,750	35,215	100	60	40
Under 5 years	21,305	10,940	10,365	12,230	6,355	5,875	60	55	5	8,995	4,520	4,475	20	10	10
5 to 9 years	16,540	8,570	7,970	9,210	4,885	4,325	20	20	--	7,305	3,665	3,640	5		5
10 to 14 years	13,495	6,810	6,685	7,150	3,710	3,440	15	10	5	6,320	3,080	3,240	10	10	
15 to 19 years	11,725	5,445	6,280	6,760	3,085	3,675	30	15	15	4,920	2,340	2,580	15	5	10
20 to 24 years	14,430	6,180	8,250	9,315	4,040	5,275	80	15	65	5,015	2,110	2,905	20	15	5
25 to 29 years	14,875	6,590	8,285	10,090	4,695	5,395	160	35	125	4,620	1,855	2,765	5	5	
30 to 34 years	13,265	6,230	7,035	8,990	4,440	4,550	70	25	45	4,195	1,755	2,440	10	10	
35 to 39 years	13,285	6,220	7,065	8,885	4,200	4,685	110	55	55	4,290	1,965	2,325	-		
40 to 44 years	12,230	5,700	6,530	8,135	3,825	4,310	125	70	55	3,970	1,805	2,165			
45 to 49 years	10,745	5,110	5,635	6,655	3,245	3,410	185	90	95	3,900	1,775	2,125	5		5
50 to 54 years	9,115	4,340	4,775	5,840	2,815	3,025	170	85	85	3,095	1,435	1,660	10	5	5
55 to 59 years	7,165	3,450	3,715	4,650	2,180	2,470	205	115	90	2,310	1,155	1,155			
60 to 64 years	5,335	2,585	2,750	3,420	1,670	1,750	185	90	95	1,730	825	905		-	
65 to 69 years	5,575	2,585	2,990	2,735	1,310	1,425	185	85	100	2,655	1,190	1,465	-	-	-
70 to 74 years	3,295	1,560	1,735	1,930	855	1,075	100	55	45	1,265	650	615	-		-
75 to 79 years	2,015	900	1,115	1,180	470	710	70	55	5	765	375	390	-		-
80 to 84 years	1,005	395	610	575	210	365	20	15	5	410	170	240	-		
85 years and over	500	190	310	260	95	165	35	15	20	205	80	125	-	-	--
Median age	28.5	28.0	28.9	29.6	29.2	30.0	51.7	53.7	47.7	25.5	24.2	26.4			

Table 53.—AGE, BY RACE, NATIVITY, AND SEX, FOR THE STATE, 1950 AND 1940, FOR URBAN AND RURAL AREAS, AND FOR STANDARD METROPOLITAN AREAS AND CITIES OF 100,000 OR MORE, 1950—Con.

[Statistics for 1950 based on 20-percent sample available complete-count data in tables 4 5, and 33 Median not shown where base is less than 500 for 1950 or 100 for 1940]

Area, census year, and age	All classes			Native white			Foreign-born white			Negro			Other races		
	Total	Male	Female	Total	Male	Female	Total	Male	Female	Total	Male	Female	Total	Male	Female
CITIES: 1950															
BATON ROUGE	125,150	61,045	64,105	88,620	43,945	44,675	1,380	735	645	35,070	16,320	18,750	80	45	35
Under 5 years	16,230	8,180	8,050	11,300	5,655	5,645	30	15	15	4,900	2,510	2,390		-	
5 to 9 years	11,050	5,475	5,575	7,925	3,985	3,940	35	5	30	3,085	1,485	1,600	5	-	5
10 to 14 years	8,110	4,155	3,955	5,445	2,780	2,665	10	5	5	2,635	1,370	1,265	20		20
15 to 19 years	9,080	4,270	4,810	6,520	3,160	3,360	50	40	10	2,510	1,070	1,440		-	
20 to 24 years	13,350	6,350	7,000	10,220	5,055	5,165	190	110	80	2,930	1,180	1,750	10	5	5
25 to 29 years	13,285	6,665	6,620	9,900	5,185	4,715	150	75	75	3,220	1,390	1,830	15	15	
30 to 34 years	10,845	5,215	5,630	7,985	3,925	4,060	65	20	45	2,780	1,255	1,525	15	15	-
35 to 39 years	10,195	4,815	5,380	7,195	3,505	3,690	70	30	40	2,925	1,275	1,650	5	5	
40 to 44 years	8,620	4,200	4,420	6,035	3,010	3,025	60	35	25	2,520	1,150	1,370	5	5	
45 to 49 years	6,540	3,310	3,230	4,435	2,290	2,145	95	50	45	2,005	970	1,035	5		5
50 to 54 years	5,430	2,805	2,625	3,760	1,920	1,840	190	120	70	1,480	765	715		-	
55 to 59 years	4,020	2,040	1,980	2,710	1,350	1,360	110	50	60	1,200	640	560	-		-
60 to 64 years	2,800	1,425	1,375	1,985	1,010	975	80	55	25	735	360	375	-		
65 to 69 years	2,485	985	1,500	1,270	460	810	110	65	45	1,105	460	645			-
70 to 74 years	1,450	565	885	920	340	580	55	35	20	475	190	285	-	-	
75 to 79 years	835	300	535	555	195	360	40	10	30	240	95	145	-		
80 to 84 years	530	195	335	320	90	230	20	10	10	190	95	95			
85 years and over	295	95	200	140	30	110	20	5	15	135	60	75	-		
Median age	26.8	26.6	27.0	26.5	26.3	26.7	46.[illegible]	48.3	44.5	27.3	27.0	27.5			-
NEW ORLEANS	568,680	267,935	300,745	372,285	175,650	196,635	14,475	7,825	6,650	181,120	84,005	97,115	800	455	345
Under 5 years	60,480	30,600	29,880	37,240	18,775	18,465	145	85	60	22,975	11,685	11,290	120	55	65
5 to 9 years	45,860	23,010	22,850	28,360	14,265	14,095	175	105	70	17,270	8,615	8,655	55	25	30
10 to 14 years	35,905	17,645	18,260	21,555	10,625	10,930	155	80	75	14,125	6,920	7,205	70	20	50
15 to 19 years	36,825	17,370	19,455	23,055	11,045	12,010	305	140	165	13,430	6,170	7,260	35	15	20
20 to 24 years	47,230	21,570	25,660	32,185	15,065	17,120	485	130	355	14,470	6,320	8,150	90	55	35
25 to 29 years	50,990	23,920	27,070	34,725	16,825	17,900	900	410	490	15,315	6,655	8,660	50	30	20
30 to 34 years	43,885	20,895	22,990	30,260	14,835	15,425	665	315	350	12,930	5,730	7,200	30	15	15
35 to 39 years	44,930	20,850	24,080	29,540	14,060	15,480	755	355	400	14,535	6,370	8,165	100	65	35
40 to 44 years	42,945	19,830	23,115	28,885	13,300	15,585	890	485	405	13,100	6,005	7,095	70	40	30
45 to 49 years	38,430	18,420	20,010	25,490	12,270	13,220	1,280	735	545	11,620	5,390	6,230	40	25	15
50 to 54 years	33,170	15,780	17,390	22,330	10,455	11,875	1,545	960	585	9,230	4,315	4,915	65	50	15
55 to 59 years	26,545	12,510	14,035	18,120	8,235	9,885	1,560	860	700	6,830	3,385	3,445	35	30	5
60 to 64 years	19,970	9,220	10,750	13,475	5,985	7,490	1,670	985	685	4,805	2,235	2,570	20	15	5
65 to 69 years	18,060	7,480	10,580	11,200	4,505	6,695	1,490	795	695	5,365	2,175	3,190	5	5	
70 to 74 years	11,065	4,285	6,780	7,530	2,675	4,855	1,070	625	445	2,460	980	1,480	5	5	-
75 to 79 years	7,120	2,765	4,355	4,820	1,660	3,160	745	405	340	1,550	700	850	5	-	5
80 to 84 years	3,665	1,320	2,345	2,590	845	1,745	390	240	150	680	230	450	5	5	
85 years and over	1,405	465	1,140	925	225	700	250	115	135	430	125	305			-
Median age	30.8	30.0	31.6	31.5	30.4	32.5	54.8	55.7	53.[illegible]	27.7	26.7	28.5	28.0		
SHREVEPORT	126,575	59,185	67,390	82,980	39,535	43,445	1,590	750	840	41,920	18,845	23,075	85	55	30
Under 5 years	14,640	7,645	6,995	9,220	4,855	4,365	50	45	5	5,360	2,740	2,620	10	5	5
5 to 9 years	10,410	5,375	5,035	6,445	3,425	3,020	10	10		3,950	1,940	2,010	5		5
10 to 14 years	8,135	3,925	4,210	4,890	2,410	2,480	10	5	5	3,225	1,500	1,725	10	10	
15 to 19 years	7,865	3,520	4,345	5,000	2,230	2,770	20	5	15	2,830	1,280	1,550	15	5	10
20 to 24 years	11,225	4,715	6,510	7,555	3,250	4,305	70	10	60	3,580	1,440	2,140	20	15	-
25 to 29 years	11,945	5,335	6,610	8,345	3,905	4,440	130	30	100	3,465	1,395	2,070	5	5	
30 to 34 years	10,355	4,890	5,465	7,145	3,535	3,610	70	25	45	3,130	1,320	1,810	10	10	
35 to 39 years	10,115	4,680	5,435	6,895	3,250	3,645	100	45	55	3,120	1,385	1,735			
40 to 44 years	9,150	4,190	4,960	6,365	2,980	3,385	105	55	50	2,680	1,155	1,525			
45 to 49 years	8,050	3,765	4,285	5,200	2,515	2,685	165	75	90	2,680	1,175	1,505	5		5
50 to 54 years	6,730	3,175	3,555	4,515	2,170	2,345	155	75	80	2,055	925	1,130	5	5	
55 to 59 years	5,240	2,440	2,800	3,580	1,620	1,960	175	95	80	1,485	725	760			
60 to 64 years	3,890	1,820	2,070	2,650	1,245	1,405	170	85	85	1,070	490	580			
65 to 69 years	4,010	1,725	2,285	2,165	985	1,180	150	60	90	1,695	680	1,015			
70 to 74 years	2,285	1,015	1,270	1,490	630	860	95	50	45	700	335	365			
75 to 79 years	1,465	565	900	885	310	575	65	50	15	515	205	310			
80 to 84 years	725	275	450	445	155	290	20	15	5	260	105	155			
85 years and over	340	130	210	190	65	125	30	15	15	120	50	70			
Median age	29.6	29.1	30.0	30.0	29.6	30.5	52.1	54.7	49.7	27.9	26.9	28.6			

Table 54.—AGE, BY COLOR, NATIVITY, AND SEX, FOR THE STATE 1950 [Based on 20 percent sample avalable complete-coun. cata in table 15 Merican not shown where base a see than 500]

The State of State of		and the same	and to prove	D- 157 Park	Total						Labor	Nonwh			
Age		All classes			Nauve		20	reign born			Native		£0°	renga born	9
196	Total	Male	Female	Total	Male	Fecua e	Total	Male	Femare	Total	Male	Female	Toa	Mae	Female
All ages	2,677,370	1,340 620	1,364,770	2,647,695	-,294 835	1,352,860	29,675	15,785	_3,890	883,580	424,435	450,145	. 482	870	51
Under 5 years to 60 years 10 to 14 years 15 to 16 years 25 to 28 years 25 to 28 years 25 to 29 years 25 to 39 years 45 to 39 years 46 to 44 years 45 to 49 years	336, 825 276 390 236, 220 211 350 211, 560 190, 180 191, 905 172, 530 151, 795	1°0,850 1/0,100 119 √70 102,415 99 795 100 730 91,280 92,050 84,055 74,725	136,290 116 550 108,915 111,285 110,850 99,000 99,855 88 475	334,295 275,980 235,840 210,750 209,745 209,440 198,860 190,325 170,720 249,280	170 5-3 -39,633 1.9,503 -32,100 99 380 90,585 91,280 82,970 73,340	87,750	530 510 380 600 1,335 2,20 1,320 1,500 1,810 2,515	305 263 165 315 415 845 595 770 208 1,385	2.5 245 2 5 285 920 1,27, 25 820 725 -,.30	125,695 102 040 89,240 76 425 66,765 61,350 53 440 58,720 51,205 47,070	63,210 5-,.90 4-,825 30,360 80 075 27,560 23,775 26,565 23,970 22,380	62,485 50,850 44,415 39,865 36,690 33,790 29,665 32,155 27,235 24,690	25 35 40 30 90 120 -05 185 140	20 1,7 1,0 35 60 70 2,1,5 11,5	3
50 to 64 vears 55 to 59 vears 55 to 59 vears 70 to 74 years 70 to 74 years 90 to 84 vears 55 years and over	126,190 102,820 80,015 78,680 47,360 29,90 14,765 7 725	61,850 50 560 39,350 37,120 22,345 14,105 6,565 2,955	57 260 40,665 41,560 24,815 15,885 8,200 4 760	123,280 99,855 76,925 75,615 45,250 28,905 14,015 7,125	60,114 48,825 37,560 35,460 21 325 13,115 6,095 2,695	39,365 40,155 23,925	2,910 2,965 3,065 2,110 1,489 750 590	1,735 1,735 1,790 1,6-0 1,220 790 4'0 260	1 _7_ _,250 1 300 1,405 690 695 280 330	37 770 30,155 22 580 29,990 14,255 9,230 4,700 2,940	18,175 15,475 1, 210 14,205 7,170 4,710 2,300 7,080	19,595 14,680 11,370 15,785 7,095 4,520 2,400 1,860	160 125 70 55 15 50 40	115 85 40 30 15	1 2
Median agu.	26 6	26 1	27 0	25 3	25 8	26 8	53 7	55 O	11 6	23 6	22 7	24.4	44 0	46	4-

Table 55 —CITIZENSHIP, BY AGE, COLOR, AND SEX, FOR THE STATE AND FOR CITIES OF 100,000 OR MORE 1950
[Based on 20-person. eample available complete-occurt data in tables 15, 17, and 38 Percent not shown where set than 0.1 or weere been as less than 500

	580	380			Te	tal				777		White		,	Nonwitte	4
Area e-tizenship and sea	All	Und	er 21 years	old		. / .	21 years old	and over		1 .					Louer	
and sex	ages	Total	Under 18 Vears	18 to 20 years	Total	21 to 34 years	35 to 44 years	45 to 04 3 ears	55 to 64 years	55 and over	All ages	Under 21 years	21 and over	ages	21 years	OVER
THE STATE							1	E	1.33	6 1					1	
Total	2,577,370	1,101,930	970,980	124,950	1,575 44	972,675	364,435	277 985	182,835	178,516	1,792,305	694,095	1,098,210	885,065	407 835	47 ,23
tuseo	2,560,290	1,100,370			1,565,920	568,665	363,245	276 635	181,375	176 000	1 782,_00	692,650	1 089 450	884,190	407 720	476 47
Native	18,595	1,099,595	975,195	124,500	17 920	567 115 1,550	361,035	272,560 4,075	176,780	170,510	17 985	692 CL5	17,390	61.0	407,680	475,9
Naturalized.	11,080	-,260	1,235	125	9,520	3 010	1,190	1 350	. 460	2,510	10 205	1,445	8,760	875	210	
Percent	0 4	0 1	01	0.3	0.6	0.5	0 3	0 5	0.8	. 4	0.6	0 2	0.8	01		1
Alien Citizenship not rptd	7,905	1,07,	830 405	245 80	6 830	2,385 625	850 340	820	955 905	1,820	7,200	985 460	6 215	705 170	90	
Male .	1,310,620	551,445	493,650	57,795	759,175	273,295	176,105	136,575	89 930	83,290	885,315	349,140		425,305	201,805	
men	1,305,560	120,690	493,035	57,655	754 870	272,250	170,105	135 890	89,200	81,965	880,6*5	3-8 930	531,725	424,975	201,750	
varive	1 294,835	550,320	492,710	57,600	744,525	271 525	_74,250	133,455	86 405	78,890	870,400	348,565	عد 154, العد	424,435	201, 745	222,4
aturalized	5,060	380 755	325 615	140	10,345	1,045	4 33.5 540	2 435 685	2,795	1,325	4,660	365 710		470	15	
en and cit not rptd _ Percent	3,000	0 -	0.1	0.2	0.6	0 4	0.3	7.5	0.8	1 6	0.5	C 2	0.7	0 1	-	1 6
Lhen	3,480	575	455	120	2,905	855	390	380	410	870	3 180	540	2.640	300	35	
htsenship not rptd .	1.580	180	160	20	1 400	190	150	305	300	455	1 480	170	1,310	100	-0	1
Female -	1,366 750	550 485	483 330		816,265	798,380	188 330	141,410		-	906,990	344,450	562,535	459 760	206 030	
nen	1,360,730	549,680	482,710		811,050	296,415	187,680	240,745	92,175	94 035	901,445	343,720		459,285	205,960	253,
ative	-,352,860 ^,870	549,385	482,485	66 900	7,500	295,590	±86 785 895	1 640	90 375	91,620	893,715 7,730	343 450	7 400	459,145	205,935	
and cit. not rptd	6 020	805	620	185	5,210	1,965	650	665	750	1,185	5 240	735	4,810	475	70	
Percent	4,425	0.1	01		0 6	0.7	0 3	0.5	0.8	1 2	0.6	0 2	3,575	605	1 -	
Ottigenship not rptd	1 995	500 305	-75 245	-25 60	3 925 1,290	435	-60 190	225	205		1 525	290	1,235		1	
							1,2									
CITIES	1. 1	1									1					1
BATON ROUGE		1	1			1					1					
Total _	125,150	46,980	39 600	7,380	78,170	34,970	18 813	11,970	-	> 595	90,000	33 245	56,755	35 150	13,733	
Native	124 410	46,835	19 520 39 495	7,315	77,275	34,570	18 755	11 890	6,775	5,325	89,355	33,080	55,540	35 050	3,725	
Na uralized	740	30	25	5	710	95	90	21.5	145	165	735	30	755			
en and at not rptd.	740	145	80	65	595	305	0 3	30		105	645	135		95	0.7	
Lien	505	95	45	50	410	230	45	30	30	75	410	85	325	95	10	,
attrenship not rptd	235	50	35	15	185	75	15	50	.5	30	235	50	185		1	
Mule	61,045	23,155	19,780		37,890	17,155	9 02.5	6,115			44,680	16,010		16,365	6 645	-
vative	60,690 60 265	23,080	19,755	3 325	37,610	17,000	8,985 8,945	5,080		2,095	44,365	16,435	27 990 27,530	16,325	6,645	
aturalized	425	20	15	5	37,205 405	50	40	140	90	85	-20	20	400	5	1	1
en and cit not rptd	355	75	25	50	280	155	30	35		45 2 1	31.5	0 5		40	1	1
Percent	250	0 3	0 1	1 5	190	0 9 125	20	0 0	10	30	20	60	150	40	1	1
Misen-hip not rptd	105	15	3	10	90	30	20	30	5	15	105	15	90		1	1
Femzle	64 105	23 825	19,820	4 005	40,260	17 815	9,800	5,855	-		45,320	16,735		18,785	7 090	
izen.	63,720	23 755	19,765	3,990	39,965 39 660	17,665	9,770	5,810	3,325		44,990	16,675 16 665	28,315	18,730	7,080	
ative	63,405	23,745	19 755	3,990	37 660	17,520	9,720	75		3,313	315	10 000	305			1
en and cit. not rptd _	385	70	55	15	31.5	1.50	30	45	30	60	330	60	270	25	0.7	
Percent	0.6	35	0 3		0 8	08	0 3				200	25	175	0 3	20	
Alien Citizenship not rptd _	130	1 75	25			45	25				130	35	95		1 -	1

Table 55 —CITIZENSHIP, BY AGE COLOR, AND SEX, FOR THE STATE AND FOR CITIES OF 100,000 OR MORE 1950—Col.

[Sametric on XC-persons, maniph], available composite-count catal, at tables 4, 17 and 20 Percent not above where less than 01 or where base is less than 500]

	1		ALL THE STREET, CO.		Te	ta	A Designation of the last	ANTIQUES PARTIES	Section 1	-		White		1	Nonwhite	
trea, citasenship	100000	Und	er 2: vears	0.4			2 years of	and over			All	Under 21	21 and	All	Under	21 at
and sex	Aul agos	Tota.	Under 8		Tota	21 to 24 years	35 to 44 years	45 to 54 veals	55 to 64 years	65 and over	ages	years	over	ages	21 years	ove
CITIES—C:m.			200					0.00								
NEW CREENIS			1						law.					3		
Total .	5.8,680	197,505	162,900	24,605	361,175	133,670	87,875	71,500	46,515	41,515	386,760	116,760	270,000	181,920	70,745	
Staten	563 730	180,80	1:2,420	24,455	376,855	132,405	87,250	70,960	45,790	40,450	382,240 372,285	116,190	266,050 256,390	181,490	70,685	
Native Naturaniad	553,335	186,560	_62,200 220	24,360	366,775 IL 080	±31,560 845	86,340 1,210	68,560	43, 25	2,960	9,955	295	9,660	440	20	1
ber and est, not rotd	+,950	630	480	15C	4,320	_,265	625	640	725	2,005	4,520	570 0.5	3,950	430 0.2	60 0 1	
Parcent	3,705	2-3	0 3 350	120	3,235	1,0:0	480	0 9	1 6	795	3,375	41.5	2,960	330	55	
Citizenship not rpiq.	1,245	160	130	30	1,065	215		215	240	270	1,145	155	990	100	,	
M.Je	267,935	92,265	81,255	11,010	175,600	62,745	40,680	34,200	21,730	16,315	183,475	57,635	عد, 840	84,460	34,630	49,8
tusen	265,550	91,950	81,000	40,950	_73,600	62,250	40,405	33,840	21,365	15,740	181,320	57,350	123,970	84,230	34,600	49,
hative	259,535	91,795	80,885	10,910	167,743	61,830	39,695	1,500	19,775	1,640	175,650 5,670	57,200 150	5,520	345	34,595	49,
Naturaised see and of not rote	6,015 2,385	315	255	60	5,860 2,070	495	275	360	365	570	2,155	265	1,870	230	30	
Percent -	0.9	0.3	03	0.5	1 2	0.8	220	240	1.7	3 5 375	1,2	0 5 225	1,325	0 3	0 1	
Alsen Categoronip not uptd.	1,720	255 50	200 55	55	1,465	42.0 85	35	120	145	200	-,05	60	545	60		
Female	300,745	95 240	81,645	13,590	205,505	70,925	47,195	37,400	24,785	25,200	203,285	59,125	144,160	97,460	36,115	61,
tasen	298,180	94,925	81,420	_3,500	203,255	70,155	46,845	37,120	24,425	24,710	200,920 196,635	58,840 58,695	.37,940	97,260 97,165	36,085	61,
Nature Naturalized_	293,800 4,380	94,765	81,315 .05	.3,450 55	199,035	69,730 425	46,345	36,220	23,350	23,390	4,285	145	4,140	95	15	1
en and sat not rptd	2,565	31.5	225	90	2,250	770	350	280	360	490	2,365	285	2,080	200	01	
Percent.	1,965	215	0.3 _50	0 7	1,770	1.1	260	0 7	265	1 9	1,825	0.5 190	1,635	0 2 160	25	
Citasenship not rptd	580	100	75	25	480	130	90	95	95	20	540	95	445	#	5	
SHREVEPORC					ž.											
Total	126,575	43,150	37,565	5,585	83,425	31,425	19,265	14,780	9,130	8,825	84,570	27,035	57,535	42,005	16,115	25,
tusen	126,090	43,070	37,495	5,575	83,020	31,250	19,230	14,720	4,080	8,735	84,095	26,960	57,135 56,050	41,995	16,110	25,
Native Natoralised	1,135	43 035	37,475	5,560	1,100	31,165	19,060	14,450 270	8,780	8 465	1,115	20,930	1,085	47,412	10,105	40,
en and on not rptd	485	80	70	10	405	175	35	60	45	90	475	75	400	10	5	
Percent	0 4 260	0 2. 35	0.2 25	0 2	0 5 225	0 6	0 2	0 4	20	10	0 6 255	0 3	220	. 5		
Ctmenship not rptd.	225	45	45		180	60	30	40	25	25	220	40	180	5	5	
Male -	59,185	22,250	19,045	2,205	37,935	24,255	8,870	6,940	4,260	3,720	40,285	13,560	26,725	18,900	7,690	Ľ,
hative .	58,985 58,425	21,200	18,995	2,205	37,785 37,240	14,110	8,860	6,905	4,080	3,660	40,090 39,535	13,510	26,590	18,895	7,690	11,
Vaturalised	560	15	15	2,207	545	25	90	120	170	140	555	1.5	540	5	,000	,
en and est not rptd	200	0.2	0.3	- 1	150	0.3	0 1	0 5	10	50	0,5	50 0 4	145	5	4000	
Percent	105	20	20	: 1	85	35	0.1	10	0 2	1 3	100	20	90	5	-	
Citisenahip not rptd.	95	30	30		65	10	10	25	10	10	95	30	65			
Female	07,390	21,900	18,520	3,380	45,490	17,270	10,395	7,840	+,870	5,115	44,285	13,475	30,810	23,105	8,425	14,6
native	67,105 66,530	21,870	18,495	3,370	45,235	17,140	10,370	7,815	4,835	5,075 4,945	44,005	13,450	30,555	23,100	8,420	14,6
Naturalised -	975	20	5	15	555	60	80	150	4,700	130	560	15,435	545	23,085	5,40	14)
en and at not rptd	285	30	20	20	255	130	25	25	35	40	280	25	255	5	5	
Percent	155	01	31	0.3	0 6	0 8	0 2	0 3	0 7	0 8	0 6	0 2	0.8		0 7	
Citizenship not rptd	130	15	-5	-	115	50	20	15	15	15	125	10	11.5	5	5	

DETAILED CHARACTERISTICS

18-127

Table 56.—MARITAL STATUS, BY AGE AND SEX, FOR THE STATE 1890 TO 1950

[Statistics for 1950 based on 20-percent sample available complete-count data in tables 15 and 21 Percent not shown where less than 0.1 or where base is less than 500 for 1950 or 100 for earlier census years]

Male 14 years old and over

Census year and age	Total	Single Number	Single Percent	Married Number	Married Percent	Widowed Number	Widowed Percent	Divorced Number	Divorced Percent	Marital status not reported
1950	902,030	234,065	25.9	620,935	68.8	35,020	3.9	12,000	1.3	
14 years	22,030	21,805	99.0	185	0.8	10		30	0.1	
15 to 19 years	102,415	98,000	95.7	4,270	4.2	105	0.1	40		
20 to 24 years	99,795	51,605	51.7	47,265	47.4	220	0.2	705	0.7	
25 to 29 years	100,730	19,945	19.8	79,105	78.5	290	0.3	1,390	1.4	
30 to 34 years	91,180	9,685	10.6	79,525	87.2	450	0.5	1,520	1.7	
35 to 39 years	92,050	7,600	8.3	82,145	89.2	780	0.8	1,525	1.7	
40 to 44 years	84,055	6,405	7.6	74,845	89.0	1,270	1.5	1,535	1.8	
45 to 49 years	74,725	5,150	6.9	66,120	88.5	1,975	2.6	1,480	2.0	
50 to 54 years	61,850	3,305	5.3	54,770	88.6	2,640	4.3	1,135	1.8	
55 to 59 years	50,560	2,945	5.8	43,495	86.0	3,200	6.3	920	1.8	
60 to 64 years	39,350	2,505	6.4	32,360	82.2	3,845	9.8	640	1.6	
65 to 69 years	37,120	2,395	6.5	28,135	75.8	6,025	16.2	565	1.5	
70 to 74 years	22,545	1,380	6.1	15,620	69.3	5,245	23.3	300	1.3	..
75 to 79 years	14,105	790	5.6	8,670	61.5	4,475	31.7	170	1.2	
80 to 84 years	6,565	345	5.3	3,250	49.5	2,930	44.6	40	0.6	.
85 and over	2,955	205	6.9	1,175	39.8	1,560	52.8	15	0.5	.
1940	842,817	283,820	33.7	518,295	61.5	33,893	4.0	6,809	0.8	...
14 years	24,458	24,420	99.8	38	0.2	.				
15 to 19 years	118,486	114,970	97.0	3,456	2.9	38		22		
20 to 24 years	103,885	64,380	62.0	38,919	37.5	300	0.3	286	0.3	
25 to 29 years	100,294	28,541	28.5	70,423	70.2	606	0.6	724	0.7	
30 to 34 years	90,968	15,181	16.7	73,962	81.3	921	1.0	904	1.0	
35 to 39 years	84,955	10,297	12.1	72,152	84.9	1,421	1.7	1,085	1.3	
40 to 44 years	72,289	6,910	9.6	62,518	86.5	1,921	2.7	940	1.3	.
45 to 49 years	64,261	5,386	8.4	55,436	86.3	2,590	4.0	849	1.3	.
50 to 54 years	52,611	4,190	8.0	44,491	84.6	3,245	6.2	685	1.3	.
55 to 59 years	41,685	3,241	7.8	34,248	82.2	3,688	8.8	508	1.2	.
60 to 64 years	31,749	2,417	7.6	24,981	78.7	4,009	12.6	342	1.1	.
65 to 69 years	27,665	1,865	6.7	20,420	73.8	5,119	18.5	261	0.9	
70 to 74 years	15,615	1,105	7.1	10,207	65.4	4,183	26.8	120	0.8	
75 to 79 years	7,729	558	7.2	4,425	57.3	2,690	34.8	56	0.7	.
80 to 84 years	3,807	230	6.0	1,800	47.3	1,756	46.1	21	0.6	
85 and over	2,360	129	5.5	819	34.7	1,406	59.6	6	0.3	
1930	714,414	252,494	35.3	422,524	59.1	32,461	4.5	6,121	0.9	814
14 years	22,254	22,232	99.9	21	0.1	1				.
15 to 19 years	106,048	102,930	97.1	2,972	2.8	49		38		59
20 to 24 years	98,240	60,236	61.3	36,648	37.3	658	0.7	569	0.6	129
25 to 29 years	85,931	24,938	29.0	58,770	68.4	1,208	1.4	938	1.1	77
30 to 34 years	72,653	12,170	16.8	58,054	79.9	1,502	2.1	848	1.2	79
35 to 44 years	133,268	14,894	11.2	112,044	84.1	4,580	3.4	1,629	1.2	121
45 to 54 years	101,244	8,346	8.2	84,760	83.7	6,859	6.8	1,156	1.1	123
55 to 64 years	57,543	4,172	7.3	45,679	79.4	6,978	12.1	638	1.1	76
65 and over	36,784	2,441	6.6	23,396	63.6	10,593	28.8	295	0.8	59
Not reported	449	135	30.1	180	40.1	33	7.3	10	2.2	91
1920	596,789	222,482	37.3	342,114	57.3	27,173	4.6	2,519	0.4	2,501
14 years	21,289	21,234	99.7	52	0.2	3		.	.	
15 to 19 years	90,718	87,913	96.9	2,531	2.8	43		12		219
20 to 24 years	81,161	50,214	61.9	29,781	36.7	580	0.7	185	0.2	401
25 to 29 years	71,931	23,244	32.3	47,001	65.3	1,136	1.6	340	0.5	210
30 to 34 years	60,268	12,106	20.1	46,290	76.8	1,380	2.3	340	0.6	152
35 to 44 years	113,819	14,563	12.8	94,111	82.7	4,188	3.7	693	0.6	264
45 to 54 years	83,835	7,500	8.9	69,634	83.1	5,932	7.1	543	0.6	226
55 to 64 years	41,639	3,138	7.5	32,454	77.9	5,702	13.7	240	0.6	105
65 and over	29,384	1,851	6.3	19,195	65.3	8,116	27.6	122	0.4	100
Not reported	2,745	719	26.2	1,065	38.8	93	3.4	44	1.6	824
1910	534,659	214,984	40.2	288,824	54.0	25,500	4.8	1,677	0.3	3,674
14 years	19,670	19,643	99.9	27	0.1					
15 to 19 years	84,902	83,026	97.8	1,334	1.6	33	.	12		497
20 to 24 years	79,383	52,494	66.1	25,604	32.3	646	0.8	141	0.2	438
25 to 29 years	70,552	23,860	33.8	44,875	63.6	1,332	1.9	259	0.4	226
30 to 34 years	58,104	12,143	20.9	44,006	75.7	1,536	2.6	251	0.4	168
35 to 44 years	96,891	13,180	13.6	78,760	81.3	4,331	4.5	426	0.4	194
45 to 54 years	60,762	5,984	9.8	49,159	80.9	5,211	8.6	314	0.5	94
55 to 64 years	36,874	2,689	7.3	28,565	77.5	5,389	14.6	159	0.4	72
65 and over	24,096	1,413	5.9	15,606	64.8	6,900	28.6	108	0.4	69
Not reported	3,425	552	16.1	828	24.2	122	3.6	7	0.2	1,916
1900	427,204	179,305	42.0	224,719	52.6	20,989	4.9	1,194	0.3	987
14 years	15,898	15,879	99.9	15	0.1					4
15 to 19 years	71,176	69,975	98.3	1,143	1.6	35		7	.	46
20 to 24 years	66,600	44,535	66.9	21,280	32.0	537	0.8	121	0.2	127
25 to 29 years	58,785	20,378	34.7	36,943	62.8	1,168	2.0	213	0.4	83
30 to 34 years	44,228	9,822	22.2	32,903	74.4	1,297	2.9	140	0.3	66
35 to 44 years	71,168	10,207	14.3	56,885	79.9	3,655	5.1	306	0.4	115
45 to 54 years	50,813	4,792	9.4	41,109	80.9	4,606	9.1	213	0.4	93
55 to 64 years	27,732	2,072	7.5	21,258	76.7	4,196	15.1	138	0.5	68
65 and over	19,140	1,262	6.6	12,454	65.1	5,326	27.8	53	0.3	45
Not reported	1,664	473	28.4	759	45.6	89	5.3	3	0.2	340
1890	334,970	141,484	42.2	178,220	53.2	13,372	4.0	632	0.2	1,262
14 years	14,261	14,254	100.0	.		.			.	6
15 to 19 years	59,408	58,835	99.0	544	0.9	6		2		21
20 to 24 years	51,125	34,269	67.0	16,410	32.1	264	0.5	54	0.1	128
25 to 29 years	39,755	12,854	32.3	26,081	65.6	590	1.5	72	0.2	158
30 to 34 years	33,692	7,033	20.9	25,619	76.0	782	2.3	83	0.2	175
35 to 44 years	57,159	7,545	13.2	46,827	81.9	2,365	4.1	172	0.3	250
45 to 54 years	39,680	3,499	8.8	32,966	83.1	2,951	7.4	115	0.3	149
55 to 64 years	22,694	1,652	7.3	18,156	80.0	2,739	12.1	80	0.4	67
65 and over	15,849	1,105	7.0	11,066	69.8	3,584	22.6	48	0.3	46
Not reported	1,347	438	32.5	550	40.8	91	6.8	6	0.4	262

Female 14 years old and over

Census year and age	Total	Single Number	Single Percent	Married Number	Married Percent	Widowed Number	Widowed Percent	Divorced Number	Divorced Percent	Marital status not reported
1950	969,560	183,700	18.9	645,780	66.6	120,865	12.5	19,215	2.0	
14 years	21,625	21,355	98.8	260	1.2		.	10		
15 to 19 years	108,935	82,320	75.6	26,140	24.0	170	0.2	305	0.3	.
20 to 24 years	111,285	26,515	23.8	82,325	74.0	815	0.7	1,630	1.5	.
25 to 29 years	110,830	10,840	9.8	95,815	86.5	1,480	1.3	2,695	2.4	
30 to 34 years	99,000	7,160	7.2	87,130	88.0	2,155	2.2	2,555	2.6	
35 to 39 years	99,855	6,525	6.5	86,820	86.9	3,770	3.8	2,740	2.7	
40 to 44 years	88,475	5,815	6.6	73,520	83.1	6,320	7.1	2,820	3.2	.
45 to 49 years	77,070	4,905	6.4	61,135	79.3	8,980	11.7	2,050	2.7	.
50 to 54 years	64,340	4,345	6.8	46,270	71.9	11,910	18.5	1,815	2.8	
55 to 59 years	52,260	3,620	6.9	33,700	64.5	13,815	26.4	1,125	2.2	
60 to 64 years	40,665	2,815	6.9	22,300	54.8	14,860	36.5	690	1.7	
65 to 69 years	41,560	2,905	7.0	17,850	42.9	20,370	49.0	435	1.0	..
70 to 74 years	24,815	1,935	7.8	7,795	31.4	14,870	59.9	220	0.9	.
75 to 79 years	15,885	1,470	9.3	3,240	20.4	11,110	69.9	65	0.4	..
80 to 84 years	8,200	765	9.3	1,135	13.8	6,270	76.5	30	0.4	
85 and over	4,760	410	8.6	350	7.4	3,970	83.4	30	0.6	.
1940	867,629	224,278	25.8	525,464	60.6	106,652	12.3	11,235	1.3	
14 years	24,577	24,373	99.3	169	0.7	3		2		
15 to 19 years	121,912	97,495	80.0	23,874	19.6	303	0.2	240	0.2	
20 to 24 years	112,511	39,841	35.4	70,351	62.5	1,157	1.0	1,162	1.0	
25 to 29 years	106,727	18,400	17.2	84,248	78.9	2,327	2.2	1,752	1.6	
30 to 34 years	95,486	11,462	12.0	78,228	81.9	3,848	4.0	1,948	2.0	
35 to 39 years	89,194	8,094	9.1	72,799	81.6	6,418	7.2	1,883	2.1	
40 to 44 years	72,092	5,773	8.0	56,636	78.6	8,248	11.4	1,435	2.0	
45 to 49 years	62,424	4,571	7.3	46,674	74.8	10,066	16.1	1,113	1.8	
50 to 54 years	49,658	3,642	7.3	34,068	68.6	11,276	22.7	672	1.4	
55 to 59 years	39,639	2,883	7.3	24,395	61.5	11,871	29.9	490	1.2	
60 to 64 years	31,612	2,534	8.0	16,355	51.7	12,449	39.4	274	0.9	
65 to 69 years	28,497	2,341	8.2	11,103	39.0	14,880	52.2	173	0.6	.
70 to 74 years	16,021	1,426	8.9	4,265	26.6	10,280	64.2	50	0.3	.
75 to 79 years	8,907	778	8.7	1,568	17.6	6,531	73.3	30	0.3	.
80 to 84 years	4,974	436	8.8	503	10.1	4,026	80.9	9	0.2	
85 and over	3,428	229	6.7	228	6.7	2,969	86.6	2	0.1	
1930	725,578	200,487	27.6	424,977	58.6	89,149	12.3	10,148	1.4	817
14 years	22,501	22,284	99.0	203	0.9	8		6		
15 to 19 years	111,554	89,165	79.9	21,273	19.1	600	0.5	489	0.4	27
20 to 24 years	108,256	39,997	36.9	64,097	59.2	2,366	2.2	1,731	1.6	65
25 to 29 years	93,022	15,937	17.1	71,138	76.5	3,910	4.2	1,958	2.1	79
30 to 34 years	75,594	8,266	10.9	61,076	80.8	4,602	6.1	1,557	2.1	93
35 to 44 years	132,034	10,927	8.3	103,852	78.7	14,603	11.1	2,475	1.9	177
45 to 54 years	91,917	6,651	7.2	64,473	70.1	19,362	21.1	1,283	1.4	148
55 to 64 years	51,278	4,163	8.1	27,796	54.2	18,728	36.5	498	1.0	93
65 and over	39,066	3,015	7.7	10,937	28.0	24,887	63.7	144	0.4	83
Not reported	356	82	23.0	132	37.1	83	23.3	7	2.0	52
1920	593,090	176,849	29.8	339,067	57.2	71,284	12.0	4,418	0.7	1,472
14 years	21,751	21,573	99.2	170	0.8	6		2		.
15 to 19 years	97,587	79,671	81.6	17,045	17.5	493	0.5	191	0.2	187
20 to 24 years	90,126	33,168	36.8	53,738	59.6	2,236	2.5	671	0.7	313
25 to 29 years	77,737	14,378	18.5	58,859	75.7	3,486	4.5	863	1.1	151
30 to 34 years	61,893	7,471	12.1	49,698	80.3	3,973	6.4	648	1.0	103
35 to 44 years	107,779	9,784	9.1	84,282	78.2	12,350	11.5	1,178	1.1	185
45 to 54 years	68,087	5,494	8.1	46,817	68.8	15,084	22.2	552	0.8	140
55 to 64 years	36,491	2,816	7.7	19,142	52.5	14,205	38.9	215	0.6	113
65 and over	30,059	2,082	6.9	8,625	28.7	19,127	63.6	74	0.2	151
Not reported	1,580	417	26.1	691	43.7	324	20.5	24	1.5	129
1910	524,173	162,095	30.9	290,630	55.4	66,808	12.7	2,989	0.6	1,651
14 years	19,377	19,276	99.5	94	0.5	7			.	.
15 to 19 years	90,325	74,426	82.4	14,660	16.2	530	0.6	134	0.1	575
20 to 24 years	85,532	32,427	37.9	49,597	58.0	2,664	3.1	562	0.7	282
25 to 29 years	71,353	13,288	18.6	53,353	74.8	4,006	5.6	560	0.8	146
30 to 34 years	55,558	6,899	12.4	43,844	78.9	4,266	7.7	469	0.8	80
35 to 44 years	87,551	8,115	9.3	67,044	76.6	11,565	13.2	728	0.8	99
45 to 54 years	54,428	3,875	7.1	36,817	67.6	13,317	24.5	338	0.6	81
55 to 64 years	32,851	2,075	6.3	17,470	53.2	13,105	39.9	135	0.4	66
65 and over	25,637	1,372	5.4	7,073	27.6	17,022	66.4	50	0.2	120
Not reported	1,561	342	21.9	678	43.4	326	20.9	13	0.8	202
1900	425,666	136,989	32.2	225,525	53.0	60,224	14.1	2,313	0.5	615
14 years	15,993	15,862	99.2	119	0.7	10	0.1		.	2
15 to 19 years	74,558	61,762	82.8	12,180	16.3	467	0.6	111	0.1	38
20 to 24 years	72,481	28,997	40.0	40,535	55.9	2,439	3.4	439	0.6	71
25 to 29 years	58,501	12,254	20.9	42,185	72.1	3,510	6.0	506	0.9	46
30 to 34 years	41,494	5,838	14.1	31,483	75.9	3,788	9.1	355	0.9	30
35 to 44 years	66,168	6,253	9.5	49,403	74.7	9,971	15.1	475	0.7	66
45 to 54 years	46,584	3,074	6.6	30,621	65.7	12,551	26.9	263	0.6	75
55 to 64 years	27,262	1,530	5.6	13,091	48.0	12,496	45.8	103	0.4	48
65 and over	21,083	1,054	5.0	5,175	24.5	14,749	70.0	54	0.3	51
Not reported	1,542	365	23.7	733	47.5	249	16.1	7	0.5	188
1890	342,110	110,559	32.3	179,458	52.5	50,270	14.7	1,193	0.3	630
14 years	13,853	13,802	99.6	44	0.3	1		4	.	2
15 to 19 years	64,646	54,328	84.0	9,970	15.4	264	0.4	61	0.1	23
20 to 24 years	55,539	21,804	39.3	31,842	57.3	1,619	2.9	214	0.4	60
25 to 29 years	40,599	7,634	18.8	30,287	74.6	2,390	5.9	219	0.5	69
30 to 34 years	33,072	4,178	12.6	25,812	78.0	2,832	8.6	177	0.5	73
35 to 44 years	55,487	4,583	8.3	42,074	75.8	8,428	15.2	285	0.5	116
45 to 54 years	39,364	2,180	5.5	24,914	63.3	12,027	30.6	144	0.4	99
55 to 64 years	21,955	1,024	4.7	10,050	45.8	10,758	49.0	65	0.3	58
65 and over	16,520	709	4.3	4,011	24.3	11,723	71.0	22	0.1	55
Not reported	1,075	317	29.5	454	42.2	228	21.2	1	0.1	75

Table 57.—MARITAL STATUS AND PRESENCE OF SPOUSE, BY AGE, COLOR, AND SEX, FOR THE STATE, URBAN AND RURAL, AND FOR STANDARD METROPOLITAN AREAS AND CITIES OF 100,000 OR MORE: 1950

[Based on 20-percent sample adjusted to complete-count data in tables 15, 21, 33, 34, and 36. Percent not shown where less than 0.1 or where base is less than 500]

Area, color, and age	Male, 14 years old and over: Total	Male: Single	Male: Married: Total married	Male: Married: Wife present: Total	Male: Wife present: Head of household	Male: Wife present: Not head of household	Male: Wife absent: Separated	Male: Wife absent: Other	Male: Widowed	Male: Divorced	Female, 14 years old and over: Total	Female: Single	Female: Married: Total married	Female: Married: Husband present	Female: Husband absent: Separated	Female: Husband absent: Other	Female: Widowed	Female: Divorced
THE STATE—TOTAL																		
Total	[illegible]	[illegible]	620,[illegible]35	581,14[illegible]	542,[illegible]	38,[illegible]	22 8[illegible]5	16,94[illegible]	35,020	12 010	969,560	183,700	645,780	590,940	37,740	17,100	120,865	19 215
14 years	22,330	21,805	185	85	20	65	10	70	10	30	21,625	21,355	260	190	20	50		10
15 to 19 years	102,[illegible]	98,300	4,270	3 445	1,840	1,605	130	495	105	40	108,935	82,320	24,140	22,805	2,010	1,325	170	305
15 years	21 495	21 310	145	50	15	35	40	55	35	5	21 825	20,895	900	670	95	135	20	10
16 years	20 95[illegible]	20 730	120	85	10	75	35	100		5	21,005	18,855	2,110	1,790	180	140	20	20
17 years	20,480	20 000	480	340	145	195	15	95	35	5	21,685	17,070	4,565	3,720	360	285	20	30
18 years	20,640	19,5[illegible]	1,135	[illegible]	5[illegible]	455	90	75	10	10	22,415	14,425	7,865	6,895	620	350	35	90
19 years	18,695	16,36[illegible]	[illegible],290	[illegible],300	1,455	845	120	170	25	5	22,005	11,075	10,700	9,530	755	415	75	155
20 to 24 years	99,795	51 6[illegible]	47,265	42,925	34,415	8,510	2 530	1,840	220	705	111,285	26,515	82,325	74,145	5,420	2,760	815	1,630
20 years	18,410	13 935	4,420	3,850	2 765	1,085	320	250	25	10	22,735	8,580	13,785	12,205	965	615	135	235
21 years	20,380	12 415	7,525	6,830	5,085	1 745	360	335	25	115	21,500	6,105	15,005	13,605	930	470	115	275
22 years	19,765	10,035	9,490	8,590	6 700	1,890	565	335	80	140	22 130	4,820	16,820	15,045	1,235	540	170	320
23 years	21,110	8 495	12 415	11 360	9,350	2,000	630	425	30	170	22 560	3 955	18,035	16,390	1,135	510	165	410
24 years	20,430	7,705	13,415	12,295	10,505	1,790	625	495	60	250	22,360	3,055	18,680	16,900	1,155	625	235	390
25 to 29 years	100,730	19,945	79,105	73,655	65,410	8 245	3,065	2,385	290	1 390	110,830	10,840	95,815	87,445	6,015	2 355	1,480	2,695
25 years	20,430	5,[illegible]95	14,685	13,570	11,700	1,870	685	430	55	195	23,300	2 780	19 785	17,910	1,320	555	270	465
26 years	19,910	4,445	15,125	13,930	12,200	1,730	735	460	70	270	21,730	2,485	18,405	16,795	1,180	430	255	585
27 years	20,740	4,030	16,305	15,170	13,475	1,795	505	530	35	370	21,110	2,145	19,160	17,550	1,150	460	330	475
28 years	20,465	3,330	16,775	15,615	13,985	1,630	655	505	70	490	22,730	1,835	19,975	18,300	1,240	435	300	620
29 years	19,185	2 645	1[illegible],215	15,270	14,050	1,220	485	460	60	265	20,960	1,595	18,490	16,890	1,125	475	325	550
30 to 34 years	94,190	7,685	79,525	74,880	69,635	5,245	2,530	2 115	450	1,520	99,000	7,160	87,130	80,190	4,960	1,980	2,155	2,555
35 to 39 years	92,050	7,600	82 145	77,290	73,450	3,840	2,585	2,270	780	1,525	99 855	6,525	86,820	79,920	5,135	1,765	3,770	2,740
40 to 44 years	84,055	6,405	74,845	70,570	67,815	2 755	2 455	1 820	1,270	1,535	88,475	5,815	73,520	67,820	4,115	1,585	6,320	2,820
45 to 49 years	74,725	5,150	66,120	62,175	60 100	2,075	2,455	1,490	1,975	1,480	77,070	4,905	61,135	56,350	3,590	1,195	8,980	2,050
50 to 54 years	61,850	3,305	54,770	51,640	50,095	1,545	1,730	1,400	2 640	1,135	64 340	4 345	46,270	42,785	2,265	1,220	11,910	1,815
55 to 59 years	50,560	2 945	43 495	41,055	40,000	1,055	1,545	895	3 200	920	52,260	3,620	33 700	31,295	1,695	710	13,815	1,125
60 to 64 years	39,350	2,505	32,360	30,595	29,605	990	1,130	635	3,845	640	40,665	2,815	22,300	20,720	975	605	14,860	690
65 to 69 years	37,120	2,395	28,135	26,200	25,020	1,180	1,260	675	6,025	565	41,560	2,905	17 850	16,185	990	675	20,370	435
70 to 74 years	22,545	1,380	15,020	14,605	13 850	755	615	400	5,245	300	24,815	1,975	7,790	7,080	320	390	14,870	220
75 to 79 years	14,105	790	8,670	8,060	7,435	625	325	285	4,475	170	[illegible]5 885	1,470	3,240	2,805	180	255	11,1[illegible]0	65
80 to 84 years	6,565	345	3,250	2 975	2,670	305	150	125	2,930	40	8 200	765	1,135	965	25	145	6,270	30
85 years and over	2,455	205	1 175	1,090	935	155	40	45	1,560	15	4,760	410	350	240	25	85	3,970	30
Percent Distribution																		
Total	100.0	25.[illegible]	68.8	64.4	60.1	4.3	2.5	1.9	3.9	1.3	100.0	18.9	66.6	60.9	3.9	1.8	12.5	2.0
14 years	100.0	99.0	0.8	0.4	0.1	0.3	0.1	0.3	*	0.1	100.0	98.8	1.2	0.9	0.1	0.2		
15 to 19 years	100.0	95.7	4.2	3.4	1.8	1.6	0.3	0.5	0.1	*	100.0	75.6	24.0	21.0	1.8	1.2	0.2	0.3
15 years	100.0	99.0	0.7	0.2	0.1	0.2	0.2	0.3	0.2		100.0	95.7	4.1	3.1	0.4	0.6	0.1	
16 years	100.0	98.9	1.0	0.4		0.4	0.2	0.5			100.0	89.8	10.0	8.5	0.9	0.7	0.1	0.1
17 years	100.0	97.[illegible]	2.3	1.7	0.7	0.9	0.2	0.[illegible]	0.2		100.0	78.7	21.1	18.1	1.7	1.3	0.1	0.1
18 years	100.0	94.4	5.5	4.7	2.5	2.2	0.4	0.4			100.0	64.4	35.1	30.8	2.8	1.6	0.2	0.4
19 years	100.0	87.5	12.2	10.7	6.2	4.5	0.6	0.9	0.1	0.1	100.0	50.3	48.6	43.3	3.4	1.9	0.3	0.7
20 to 24 years	100.0	51.7	47.4	43.0	34.5	8.5	2.5	1.8	0.2	0.7	100.0	23.8	74.0	66.6	4.9	2.5	0.7	1.5
20 years	100.0	75.7	24.0	20.9	15.0	5.9	1.7	1.4	0.1	0.2	100.0	37.7	60.6	53.7	4.2	2.7	0.6	1.0
21 years	100.0	61.8	37.5	34.0	25.3	8.7	1.8	1.7	0.1	0.6	100.0	28.4	69.8	63.3	4.3	2.2	0.5	1.3
22 years	100.0	50.9	48.0	43.5	33.9	9.6	2.9	1.7	0.4	0.7	100.0	21.8	76.0	68.0	5.6	2.4	0.8	1.4
23 years	100.0	40.2	58.8	53.8	44.3	9.5	3.0	2.0	0.1	0.8	100.0	17.5	79.9	72.7	5.0	2.3	0.7	1.8
24 years	100.0	32.8	65.7	60.2	51.4	8.8	3.1	2.4	0.3	1.2	100.0	13.7	83.5	75.6	5.2	2.8	1.1	1.7
25 to 29 years	100.0	19.8	78.5	73.1	64.9	8.2	3.0	2.4	0.3	1.4	100.0	9.8	86.5	78.9	5.4	2.1	1.3	2.4
25 years	100.0	26.9	71.9	66.4	57.3	9.2	3.4	2.1	0.3	1.0	100.0	11.9	84.9	76.9	5.7	2.4	1.2	2.0
26 years	100.0	22.3	76.0	70.0	61.3	8.7	3.7	2.3	0.4	1.4	100.0	11.4	84.7	77.3	5.4	2.0	1.2	2.7
27 years	100.0	19.4	78.6	73.6	65.0	8.7	2.4	2.6	0.2	1.8	100.0	9.[illegible]	86.7	79.4	5.2	2.1	1.5	2.1
28 years	100.0	16.3	82.0	76.3	68.3	8.0	3.2	2.5	0.3	1.4	100.0	8.1	87.9	80.5	5.5	1.9	1.3	2.7
29 years	100.0	13.8	84.5	79.6	73.2	6.4	2.5	2.4	0.3	1.4	100.0	7.6	88.2	80.6	5.4	2.3	1.6	2.6
30 to 34 years	100.0	10.6	87.2	82.1	76.4	5.8	2.8	2.3	0.5	1.7	100.0	7.2	88.0	81.0	5.0	2.0	2.2	2.6
35 to 39 years	100.0	8.3	89.2	83.9	79.7	4.2	2.9	2.5	0.8	1.7	100.0	6.5	86.9	80.0	5.1	1.8	3.8	2.7
40 to 44 years	100.0	7.6	89.0	84.0	80.7	3.3	2.9	2.2	1.5	1.8	100.0	6.6	83.1	76.7	4.7	1.8	7.1	3.2
45 to 49 years	100.0	6.9	88.5	83.2	80.4	2.8	3.3	2.0	2.6	2.0	100.0	6.4	79.3	73.1	4.7	1.6	11.7	2.7
50 to 54 years	100.0	5.3	88.6	83.5	81.0	2.5	2.8	2.3	4.3	1.8	100.0	6.8	71.9	66.5	3.5	1.9	18.5	2.8
55 to 59 years	100.0	5.8	86.0	81.2	79.1	2.1	3.1	1.9	6.3	1.8	100.0	6.9	64.5	59.9	3.2	1.4	26.4	2.2
60 to 64 years	100.0	6.4	82.2	77.8	75.2	2.5	2.9	1.6	9.8	1.6	100.0	6.9	54.8	51.0	2.4	1.5	36.5	1.7
65 to 69 years	100.0	6.5	75.8	70.6	67.4	3.2	3.4	1.8	16.2	1.5	100.0	7.0	42.9	38.9	2.4	1.6	49.0	1.0
70 to 74 years	100.0	6.1	69.3	64.8	61.4	3.3	2.7	1.8	23.3	1.3	100.0	7.8	31.4	28.5	1.3	1.6	59.9	0.9
75 to 79 years	100.0	5.6	61.5	57.1	52.7	4.4	2.3	2.0	31.7	1.2	100.0	9.3	20.4	17.7	1.1	1.6	69.9	0.[illegible]
80 to 84 years	100.0	5.3	49.5	45.3	40.7	4.6	2.5	1.9	44.6	0.6	100.0	9.3	13.8	11.8	0.3	1.8	76.5	0.4
85 years and over	100.0	6.9	39.8	36.9	31.6	5.2	1.4	1.5	52.8	0.5	100.0	8.6	7.4	5.0	0.5	1.8	83.4	0.6
THE STATE—NONWHITE																		
Total	274,315	75,265	181,000	159,865	145 415	14,450	14,610	6,525	15,170	2,880	310,115	61,115	195,485	161,095	27,275	7,115	47 090	6,425
Percent	100.0	27.4	66.0	58.3	53.0	5.3	5.3	2.4	5.5	1.0	100.0	19.7	63.0	51.9	8.8	2.3	15.2	2.1
14 years	8,275	8 215	50	25		25	5	20		10	8,165	8,080	85	70	5	10		
15 to 19 years	36 570	34,955	1,545	1,205	545	660	190	150	45	15	39,885	30,075	9,610	7,535	1,405	670	90	110
15 years	8 050	8,025	20	10	5	5	5	5	5		8,290	7,865	415	305	70	40	5	5
16 years	7 595	7,530	65	40	5	35	5	20			8,090	7,180	890	665	140	85	5	15
17 years	7 285	7,065	205	140	60	80	35	30	10		7,800	6 040	1,745	1 340	265	140	5	10
18 years	7,470	7,005	435	355	150	205	65	35	10	5	8,230	5,190	3,000	2,330	470	200	20	20
19 years	6,170	5,340	800	660	325	335	80	60	20	10	7 475	3 800	3,560	2,895	460	205	55	60
20 to 24 years	30,110	15,045	14,775	12 395	8,895	3,500	1,575	805	115	175	36 745	9,605	26,210	20,770	4,100	1,340	445	485
20 years	5 970	4,330	1,615	1 295	865	430	210	110	15	10	8,335	3,330	4,875	3,785	740	350	70	60
21 years	5,935	3,465	2,430	2 040	1,345	695	230	160	5	35	6,860	2,055	4,670	3,760	695	185	80	85
22 years	6,085	2,950	3,040	2,495	1,640	855	385	160	50	45	7,330	1,795	5,330	4,115	940	275	105	100
23 years	6 235	2,365	3,830	3,270	2 455	815	3[illegible]5	185	15	25	7,145	1,305	5,600	4,510	865	275	100	140
24 years	5,885	1,935	3,860	3,295	2,590	705	375	190	30	60	7,075	1,120	5,765	4,600	860	305	90	100

Table 57.—MARITAL STATUS AND PRESENCE OF SPOUSE, BY AGE, COLOR, AND SEX, FOR THE STATE, URBAN AND RURAL, AND FOR STANDARD METROPOLITAN AREAS AND CITIES OF 100 000 OR MORE 1950—Con

[Based on 20-percent sample, available complete-count data in tables 15, 21, 33, 34, and 36 Percent not shown where less than 0.1 or where base is less than 500]

Area color and age	Male, 14 years old and over: Total	Single	Married: Total married	Wife present: Total	Wife present: Head of household	Wife present: Not head of household	Wife absent: Separated	Wife absent: Other	Widowed	Divorced	Female, 14 years old and over: Total	Single	Married: Total married	Husband present	Husband absent: Separated	Husband absent: Other	Widowed	Divorced
THE STATE—NONWHITE—Con																		
25 to 29 years	27,620	5,505	21,535	18 690	15,374	3 31[illegible]	920	845	13[illegible]	[illegible]	33 8[illegible]0	3,340	28,[illegible]15	[illegible]	4,705	1,175	740	975
25 years	5,655	1 620	3,970	3,365	2,59[illegible]	773	433	170	30	[illegible]	7,490	885	6,295	5,060	1,015	220	140	190
26 years	5,560	1,165	4,290	3,645	2,945	700	475	170	40	65	6,630	870	5 4[illegible]5	4,295	930	190	140	205
27 years	5,958	1,140	4,695	4,175	3 405	770	295	215	[illegible]	[illegible]	6,685	635	5,730	4,570	930	230	160	160
28 years	5,610	970	4,535	3,875	3,250	625	500	160	50	55	6,865	585	5,920	4,765	965	190	130	240
29 years	4,840	670	4,045	3 630	3,140	490	375	140	35	90	6,180	565	5 255	4,145	865	245	170	190
30 to 34 years	23,845	2,620	20,040	18,010	15,975	2,035	1,200	830	220	365	29,700	2 235	25,290	20,745	3 715	830	1,195	980
35 to 39 years	26,680	2,220	23,670	20,980	19,635	1,345	1,840	850	470	360	32,225	1,845	27 395	22,810	3,765	820	2,000	985
40 to 44 years	24,085	1,800	21,305	19 110	18,230	880	1,495	700	615	365	27,260	1,365	21,665	18,195	2 825	645	3,290	940
45 to 49 years	22,405	1,390	19,825	17 625	16,870	755	1,615	585	920	360	24,745	1,195	18,570	15,600	2,510	460	4 240	740
50 to 54 years	18,290	940	15,730	14,115	13,595	520	1 107	515	1,335	285	19 640	850	13,245	11,280	1 540	425	5,030	[illegible]
55 to 59 years	15 560	705	13,165	11 815	11,500	315	955	395	1,500	190	14,720	615	8 740	7,440	1,125	175	5,080	285
60 to 64 years	11,250	510	9,085	8,200	7,945	255	645	240	1,500	155	11 400	470	5,955	5,125	645	185	4 790	185
65 to 69 years	14,235	710	10 320	9,275	9,005	270	765	280	3,060	145	15,810	595	6,445	5,605	600	240	8,625	145
70 to 74 years	7 170	265	4,845	4,365	4,170	115	330	150	1 995	65	7 110	245	2 195	1 920	205	70	4,605	65
75 to 79 years	4 725	180	2,845	2,585	2,390	195	175	85	1,670	30	4,555	245	955	760	95	100	3,340	5
80 to 84 years	2,310	80	1,225	1 055	960	95	115	45	1 010	5	2,400	75	335	285	20	30	1,980	10
85 years and over	1 095	55	450	415	375	50	25	10	585	5	1 905	80	175	120	15	40	1 640	10
URBAN—TOTAL																		
Total	501,005	121,850	352, 40	327,035	302,240	24,795	14,830	10,275	18,395	8,620	575,290	107,805	373,845	335,960	27,420	10,465	78,365	15,275
Percent	100 0	24 3	70 3	65 3	60 3	5 0	3 0	2 1	3 7	1 7	100 0	18 7	65 0	58 4	4 8	1 8	13 6	2 7
14 years	9,575	9,445	105	50	15	35	20	35		25	9,570	9,460	110	75	5	30		
15 to 19 years	46 605	44 530	2,065	1,670	920	750	155	240	50	20	55,000	41,685	13,015	11,020	1,240	755	80	220
15 to 17 years	26,945	26 490	410	225	75	150	50	135	40	5	29,525	26,130	3,330	2 635	395	300	20	45
18 and 19 years	19,720	18,040	1,655	1,445	845	600	105	105	10	15	25 475	15,555	9,685	8 385	845	455	60	175
20 to 24 years	57,430	29,635	27,220	24 690	19 640	5,050	1,615	915	100	475	69,860	18,085	50,170	44,790	3,895	1,485	455	1,150
20 and 21 years	20,600	14,120	6 385	5,665	4,145	1,520	450	270	15	80	27 335	9,970	16 920	14 935	1,305	680	120	325
22 to 24 years	36,830	15 515	20,835	19 025	15,495	3,530	1,165	645	85	395	42,525	8,115	33,250	29,655	2,590	1,005	335	825
25 to 29 years	63,340	12,805	49,480	45,780	40,455	5,325	2,090	1,610	140	915	71,055	7,755	60 250	54 245	4 425	1 580	925	2,125
30 to 34 years	55,230	5,775	48,235	45,085	41,545	3,540	1 765	1 385	210	1 010	60,420	5,085	51,835	46,795	3,770	1,270	1,475	2 025
35 to 39 years	53,175	4,330	47,205	43,800	41,210	2,590	1,940	1,465	460	1,180	60,380	4,665	50,935	45,965	3 900	1,070	2,465	2,315
40 to 44 years	49 010	3 935	43 200	40 335	38,405	1,930	1 660	1,205	675	1,200	54 040	4 215	43,025	38,870	3,125	1,030	4,460	2 340
45 to 54 years	78,765	5,130	69 070	64,470	61,925	2,545	2,700	1,900	2,545	2,020	84,810	6,505	60,605	54,795	4,265	1 545	14 485	3,215
55 to 64 years	48,545	3,110	40,475	37,995	36,555	1 440	1 655	825	3,855	1 105	55,070	4,720	29,635	27,145	1,770	720	19,370	1,345
65 to 74 years	28 270	2,155	19,740	18,300	17,100	1,200	945	495	5,845	530	38,370	3 670	12,140	10,695	885	560	22,085	475
75 years and over	11,000	800	5 545	5 060	4,470	590	285	200	4 515	140	16 715	1 960	2 135	1 765	140	220	12 565	65
URBAN—NONWHITE																		
Total	141,010	35,720	95 325	82 090	72 395	9 695	9,605	3,630	7,900	2,065	174 855	30,725	107 760	83,765	19,735	4,260	29,410	4 960
Percent	100 0	25 3	67 6	58 2	51 3	6 9	6 8	2 6	5 6	1 5	100 0	17 8	62.3	48 5	11 4	2 5	17 0	2 9
14 years	3,490	3,455	25	10		10	5	10		10	3,415	3 380	35	25		10		
15 to 19 years	15,315	14,990	700	535	210	325	95	70	20	5	18,630	13,770	4,745	3,440	910	395	50	65
15 to 17 years	9,460	9,305	145	85	30	55	25	35	10		10,600	9,185	1 380	955	315	150	10	25
18 and 19 years	5,855	5,285	555	450	180	270	70	35	10	5	8,030	4,585	3,365	2,525	595	245	40	40
20 to 24 years	15,305	7 535	7,575	6,145	3,955	2,190	1 045	385	55	140	20,830	5,160	15 150	11,430	2,905	815	240	280
20 and 21 years	5 520	3,595	1 890	1,465	855	610	315	110		35	8,075	2 745	5 200	3,885	975	340	70	50
22 to 24 years	9 785	3,940	5,685	4 680	3,100	1,580	730	275	55	105	12,755	2 405	9 950	7 545	1,930	475	170	230
25 to 29 years	16 015	3 335	12,445	10,540	8,300	2,240	1 330	535	65	210	20,640	2,220	17,215	13,040	3 445	730	440	765
30 to 34 years	13,930	1,690	11,830	10,030	8,525	1,505	1,300	500	330	260	17 600	1 410	14,570	11 275	2,785	510	830	790
35 to 39 years	14,975	1 290	13,110	11,265	10,230	1,035	1,330	515	265	310	19,165	1,175	15 850	12,435	2,885	530	320	820
40 to 44 years	13 640	1,130	11,880	10,415	9,750	665	1,025	440	300	300	16 035	885	12,075	9 500	2,150	425	2,300	775
45 to 54 years	22,520	1,450	19 335	16 915	16,010	905	1,770	650	1,275	460	25,820	1,295	17,070	13,625	2,915	530	6 475	980
55 to 64 years	13 325	620	10 870	9,615	9,205	410	960	295	1,600	235	14,305	560	7 025	5,725	1,150	150	6 305	315
65 to 74 years	9,070	490	5 880	5,115	4 870	245	580	185	2,590	110	12 065	540	3,535	2 900	510	125	7,840	150
75 years and over	3,445	135	1,715	1 505	1,340	165	165	45	1,575	25	4,350	250	490	370	80	40	3,610	20
RURAL NONFARM—TOTAL																		
Total	212,725	55,165	145 515	135,300	128 205	7,095	4,955	5,260	9,780	2,265	218,580	37,745	149,770	138,125	6,705	4,540	28,225	2,840
Percent	100 0	25 9	68 4	63 6	60 3	3 3	2 3	2 5	4 6	1 1	100 0	17 3	68 5	63 4	3 1	2 1	12 9	1 3
14 years	5,620	5 560	50	20	5	15	10	20	5	5	5,650	5 550	90	70		20		10
15 to 19 years	25,355	24,145	1,155	910	550	360	95	150	45	10	26,430	18,945	7,390	6 715	375	300	55	40
15 to 17 years	16,050	15,800	220	115	45	70	50	55	25	5	16,300	14,000	2,275	2,045	115	115	15	10
18 and 19 years	9,305	8,345	935	795	505	290	45	95	20	5	10,130	4 945	5,115	4,670	260	185	40	30
20 to 24 years	24,420	11,900	12 285	11,120	9,275	1,845	490	675	85	150	24,970	4,440	19 995	18,470	860	665	220	315
20 and 21 years	10,055	6 565	3 415	3 055	2,365	690	125	235	30	45	9,925	2,370	7,335	6 810	280	245	90	130
22 to 24 years	14,365	5,335	8,870	8,065	6,910	1,155	365	440	55	105	15,045	2,070	12,660	11,660	580	420	130	185
25 to 29 years	22,795	3 905	18,430	17 145	15 585	1,560	605	680	85	375	24,460	1 730	21,900	20,305	1,010	585	405	425
30 to 34 years	20,990	2 080	18 430	17,375	16,520	855	445	610	140	340	22,255	1,270	20,160	18 895	790	475	410	375
35 to 39 years	21,605	860	19 300	18 135	17,430	705	495	670	205	240	21,800	1,115	19,470	18,055	875	540	900	315
40 to 44 years	18,525	1,360	16,610	15,535	15,125	410	540	535	340	215	18 195	890	15,730	14,630	680	420	1,230	345
45 to 54 years	29,360	1,865	25,945	24,250	23,685	565	920	775	1,190	360	29,815	1,695	23,215	21,430	1 120	665	4,405	500
55 to 64 years	20,390	1,270	16,935	15 740	1,5445	295	640	555	1905	280	20 590	1,025	12,965	11,880	650	435	6,260	340
65 to 74 years	16 350	910	12 010	11,040	10 765	275	560	410	3,185	245	17,005	660	7,415	6,840	280	295	8 795	135
75 years and over	7,315	310	4 365	4,030	3,820	210	155	180	2,595	45	7,410	425	1 440	1,235	65	140	5,505	40
RURAL NONFARM—NONWHITE																		
Total	62 865	17,315	40,700	35,545	33 115	2,430	2,945	2,210	4,345	505	68 595	13 280	42 570	35,940	4,720	1,910	11 680	1,065
Percent	100 0	27 5	64 7	56 5	52 7	3 9	4 7	3 5	6 9	0 8	100 0	19 4	62 1	52 4	6 9	2 8	17 0	1 6
14 years	1,855	1,855									1,895	1,870	25	25				
15 to 19 years	8,195	7,805	365	275	130	145	40	50	20	5	8,905	6,525	2,345	2,010	215	120	25	10
15 to 17 years	5,145	5,085	55	40	10	30	10	5	5		5,375	4,580	795	680	70	45		
18 and 19 years	3,050	2,720	310	235	120	115	30	45	15	5	3,530	1,945	1,550	1,330	145	75	25	10
20 to 24 years	7 365	3 645	3,650	3,075	2,415	660	275	300	40	30	7 935	2,030	5,660	4,730	630	300	110	135
20 and 21 years	2,970	1 920	1,025	835	615	220	60	110	15	10	3,505	1,190	2,195	1,890	200	105	60	60
22 to 24 years	4,395	1 725	2,625	2,220	1 780	440	215	190	25	20	4,430	840	3,465	2,840	430	195	50	75

Table 57.—MARITAL STATUS AND PRESENCE OF SPOUSE, BY AGE, COLOR, AND SEX, FOR THE STATE, URBAN AND RURAL, AND FOR STANDARD METROPOLITAN AREAS AND CITIES OF 100,000 OR MORE: 1950—Con.

[Based on 20 percent sample; available complete-count data in tables 15, 20, 33, 34, and 36. Percent not shown where less than 0.1 or where base is less than 100]

Area, color, and age	Male 14 years old and over: Total	Single	Married: Total married	Wife present: Total	Wife present: Head of household	Wife present: Not head of household	Wife absent: Separated	Wife absent: Other	Widowed	Divorced	Female 14 years old and over: Total	Single	Married: Total married	Husband present	Husband absent: Separated	Husband absent: Other	Widowed	Divorced
RURAL NONFARM—NONWHITE—Con.																		
25 to 29 years	[illegible]80	1 230	[illegible]	4,110	3,545	565	400	285	60	9	6,975	680	5,900	4,890	775	265	290	145
30 to 34 years	5,760	355	4,390	3 835	3,555	280	295	260	50	45	6,285	545	5,380	4,525	630	225	240	120
35 to 39 years	5 830	555	5 125	4 520	4,285	275	345	260	110	40	6,345	395	5,370	4,575	580	215	460	120
40 to 44 years	4,025	395	4,495	3,900	3,760	140	300	225	100	40	5,335	235	4,330	3,680	470	180	665	125
45 to 54 years	8,095	535	6,930	6,050	5 830	220	545	335	540	90	9,000	460	6,470	5,420	775	275	1,845	225
55 to 64 years	6,385	400	5,075	4,420	4,340	80	385	270	840	70	6,440	270	3,690	3,115	425	150	2,360	120
65 to 74 years	[illegible]110	230	4,310	3,890	3,830	60	265	155	1,500	70	6,575	180	2,825	2,515	190	120	3,520	50
75 years and over	2,770	115	1 615	1,470	1 415	55	95	70	1,025		2,885	90	545	455	30	60	2 235	15
RURAL FARM—TOTAL																		
Total	185,300	57,250	123,080	118,610	111 750	6,860	3,060	1 410	6,845	1,125	175,690	38,150	122 165	116,455	3,615	2,095	14,275	1,100
Percent	100 0	30 4	65 4	63 0	59 3	3 6	1 6	0 7	3 6	0 6	100 0	21 7	69 5	66 3	2 1	1 2	8 1	0 6
14 years	6,835	6,800	30	15		15		15	5		6,405	6,345	60	45	15			
15 to 19 years	30,395	29,325	1 050	865	370	495	80	105	10	10	27,505	21,690	5,735	5,070	395	270	35	45
15 to 17 years	20 035	19 810	215	135	50	85	20	60	5	5	18,690	16,690	1,970	1,700	125	145	25	5
18 and 19 years	10 360	9,515	835	730	320	410	60	45	5		8,815	5,000	3,765	3,370	270	125	10	40
20 to 24 years	17,945	10,070	7,760	7,115	5,500	1,615	395	250	35	80	16,455	3,990	12,160	11,085	665	410	140	165
20 and 21 years	7 8 5	[illegible]	2,145	1 960	1,340	620	105	80	5	20	6,975	2 345	4,535	4,065	310	160	40	55
22 to 24 years	10,1[illegible]0	4,405	5 615	5,155	4,160	995	290	170	30	60	9,480	1,645	7,625	7,020	335	250	100	110
25 to 29 years	14,595	3,235	11,195	10,730	9 370	1,360	370	95	65	100	15,315	1,355	13,665	12,895	580	190	150	145
30 to 34 years	14,960	1,830	12,860	12 420	11 570	850	320	120	100	70	16,325	805	15,135	14,500	400	235	230	155
35 to 39 years	17,270	1 410	15,640	15,255	14,710	545	250	135	115	105	17 675	745	16,415	15,900	360	155	405	110
40 to 44 years	16,520	1,210	15,035	14 700	14,285	415	255	80	255	120	16,240	710	14,765	14,320	310	135	630	135
45 to 54 years	28,450	1,460	25,875	25,095	24 585	510	565	215	880	235	26,785	1,050	23,585	22,910	470	205	2,000	150
55 to 64 years	20 975	670	18,445	17 915	17,605	310	380	150	1 285	175	17,265	690	13,400	12,990	250	160	3,045	130
65 to 74 years	15,045	710	12,005	11,465	11 005	460	370	170	2,240	90	11,000	510	6,085	5 730	145	210	4,360	45
75 years and over	5,310	230	3,185	3,035	2,750	285	75	75	1,855	40	4,720	260	1,160	1,010	25	125	3 280	20
RURAL FARM—NONWHITE																		
Total	70,440	22 230	44,975	42,230	39 905	2,325	2 060	685	2,925	310	68,665	17,110	45,155	41,390	2,820	945	6,000	400
Percent	100 0	31 6	63 8	60 0	56 7	3 3	2 9	1 0	4 2	0 4	100 0	24 9	65 8	60 3	4 1	1 4	8 7	0 6
14 years	2,930	2,905	25	15		15		10			2,855	2,830	25	20	5			
15 to 19 years	13,060	12,570	480	395	205	190	55	30	5	5	12 350	9,780	2,520	2,085	280	155	15	35
15 to 17 years	8,325	8,230	90	65	30	35	10	15		5	8 205	7,320	875	715	90	70	5	5
18 and 19 years	4,735	4,340	390	330	175	155	45	15	5		4,145	2,450	1,645	1,370	190	85	10	30
20 to 24 years	7,440	3,865	3,550	3,175	2,525	650	255	120	20	5	7,980	2,415	5,400	4,610	565	225	25	70
20 and 21 years	3,415	2,280	1,130	1 015	720	295	65	50	5		3 615	1,440	2,120	1,770	260	90	20	35
22 to 24 years	4,025	1,585	2,420	2,160	1,805	355	190	70	15	5	4,365	975	3,280	2,840	305	135	75	35
25 to 29 years	5 425	1,000	4,335	4 040	3,490	550	250	45	45	45	6,235	640	5,470	4,905	485	80	90	45
30 to 34 years	4,875	375	4,420	4,145	3 895	250	205	70	40	40	5,815	280	5,340	4,945	300	95	125	70
35 to 39 years	5,875	375	5 435	5 195	5,120	75	165	75	55	10	6,715	275	6,175	5,800	300	75	220	45
40 to 44 years	5,425	275	5,000	4,795	4,720	75	170	35	125	25	5,870	245	5,260	5,015	205	40	325	40
45 to 54 years	10,170	345	9,290	8,775	8,625	150	400	115	440	95	9,565	290	8,275	7 835	360	80	950	50
55 to 64 years	7,100	195	6 305	5,980	5 890	90	255	70	560	40	5 375	155	3,980	3,725	195	60	1,205	35
65 to 74 years	6,225	255	4,975	4,635	4,475	160	250	90	965	30	4,280	120	2,280	2,110	105	65	1,870	10
75 years and over	1,915	70	1 160	1,080	960	120	55	25	670	15	1,525	80	430	340	20	70	1,115	
STANDARD METROPOLITAN AREAS																		
BATON ROUGE	54,915	14,420	38,285	36,045	33,845	2,200	1,390	850	1,530	680	58,095	11,[illegible]	39,460	36,450	2,375	635	6,240	1,385
Percent	100 0	26 3	69 7	65 6	61 6	4 0	2 5	1 5	2 8	1 2	100 0	19 0	67 9	62 7	4 1	1 1	10 7	2 4
14 years	1,095	1,085	10	10		10					930	920	10	10				
15 to 19 years	5,680	5 410	250	180	115	65	10	40	10	10	6,225	4,890	1,280	1 135	100	45	5	50
15 to 17 years	2,795	2,735	45	15	15		15	15	10	5	2,965	2,630	330	290	20	20		5
18 and 19 years	2,885	2,675	205	165	100	65	15	25		5	3,260	2,260	950	845	80	25	5	45
20 to 24 years	7,725	4,465	3,200	2,915	2,525	390	195	90	20	40	8,340	2,280	5,920	5,435	375	110	35	105
20 and 21 years	2,925	2,120	800	700	545	155	60	40	5		3,295	1,325	1,925	1,755	140	30	15	30
22 to 24 years	4,800	2,345	2,400	2,215	1,980	235	135	50	15	40	5 045	955	3 995	3,680	235	80	20	75
25 to 29 years	7,840	1,600	6,120	5,755	5 210	545	210	145	30	90	8,015	840	6,950	6,350	460	140	90	135
30 to 34 years	6 355	490	5,770	5,520	5,200	320	150	100	20	7[illegible]	6,835	485	6,035	5 600	375	60	135	180
35 to 39 years	5,975	395	5,440	5,100	4,885	215	215	125	40	100	6,570	350	5,740	5,335	340	65	245	235
40 to 44 years	5 1 5	270	4,755	4,490	4,320	170	100	165	55	95	5,375	105	4,395	4,100	220	75	405	270
45 to 54 years	7,545	375	6,765	6 485	6,295	190	185	85	255	150	7,190	405	5,385	5,055	270	60	1,145	260
55 to 64 years	4,395	155	3,875	3,635	3,510	125	180	60	285	80	4,125	255	2 415	2,240	125	50	1 370	85
65 to 74 years	2 275	120	1,595	1 460	1,360	100	105	30	535	25	3,125	180	1,090	970	100	20	1 790	65
75 years and over	855	55	505	485	425	60	20	15	280	15	1,360	100	240	220	10	10	1,020	
Nonwhite	17,045	4,350	11,470	10,135	9,160	975	990	345	820	205	19,420	3,695	12,465	10,275	1,880	310	2,755	505
Percent	100 0	26 [illegible]	67 3	59 5	53 7	5 7	5 8	2 0	4 8	1 2	100 0	19 0	64 2	52 9	9 7	1 6	14 2	2 6
14 years	495	490	5	5		5					300	300						
15 to 19 years	1,930	1,830	95	55	20	35	20	20		5	2,275	1,730	530	420	85	25		15
15 to 17 years	1,150	1,125	20	5	5		5	10		5	1,105	935	165	130	20	15		5
18 and 19 years	780	705	75	50	15	35	15	10			1,170	795	365	290	65	10		10
20 to 24 years	2 045	1 110	920	715	540	175	160	45	10	5	2,545	740	1,755	1,370	315	70	15	35
20 and 21 years	800	540	260	195	140	55	45	20			1 105	430	660	520	125	15	5	10
22 to 24 years	1,245	570	660	520	400	120	115	25	10	5	1,440	310	1,095	850	190	55	10	25
25 to 29 years	2,020	475	1,510	1,310	1,050	260	145	55	15	20	2,540	280	2,170	1,740	355	75	35	55
30 to 34 years	1,775	150	1,585	1,410	1,260	150	115	60	15	25	2,135	150	1,810	1,485	305	20	55	120
35 to 39 years	1 850	160	1,630	1,425	1,335	90	150	55	15	45	2,205	155	1,795	1,495	265	35	165	90
40 to 44 years	1,595	80	1,465	1 330	1,230	100	80	55	30	20	1,875	115	1,455	1,240	175	40	230	75
45 to 54 years	2,335	130	2,040	1,890	1,825	65	140	10	120	45	2 380	105	1,670	1,420	225	25	530	75
55 to 64 years	1 485	55	1,275	1,135	1,100	35	110	30	130	25	1,305	45	715	615	100		525	20
65 to 74 years	1,105	50	710	630	600	30	65	15	325	10	1,395	45	475	415	50	10	855	20
75 years and over	410	20	235	230	200	30	5		150	5	465	30	90	75	5	10	345	

Table 57—MARITAL STATUS AND PRESENCE OF SPOUSE, BY AGE COLOR AND SEX FOR THE STATE, URBAN AND RURAL AND FOR STANDARD METROPOLITAN AREAS AND CITIES OF 100,000 OR MORE 1950—Con

[Based on 20-percent sample available complete-count data in tables 15-21, 33, 24, and 36 Percent not shown where less than 0° or where beat than 0° or where beat than 0° or where beat the or where the sample available complete-count data in tables 15-21, 33, 24, and 36 Percent not shown where less than 0° or where beat than 0° or where beat than 0° or where the sample available complete-count data in tables 15-21, 33, 24, and 36 Percent not shown where less than 0° or where the sample available complete-count data in tables 15-21, 33, 24, and 36 Percent not shown where less than 0° or where the sample available complete-count data in tables 15-21, 33, 24, and 36 Percent not shown where the sample available complete-count data in tables 15-21, 33, 34, and 36 Percent not shown where the sample available complete-count data in tables 15-21, 33, 34, and 36 Percent not shown where the sample available complete-count data in tables 15-21, 33, 34, and 36 Percent not shown where the sample available complete-count data in tables 15-21, 33, 34, and 36 Percent not shown where the sample count data is a sample count of the sample count of

	14 2 90	-	7-	Maie, 4	vesre ald an	nd over			-			-	Female, 1	4 years old	and over			-
	11.56				Магнес									Marne	Xu .			
Area polor and age	To al	Single		P	ne present		Wide a	beent	V.d	Di-					Husoand	ansen	War	D _F
	16 81	Single	To al marned	Total	Hena of house- need	Not head of house- no.d	Sepa- ra-ed	Other	Owed	vorceu	Tous	Sungle	Total marne.	In_ebenu presen	Sepa- rated	Other	owed	varced
STANDARD METRO- POLITAN AREAS—Con.													To .					
Percent	238 050 100 0	60,315 25 3	_b3,975 68 9	151,160	13° 50./	≥ 655 5 ml	7,505 3 2	2 4	9,25	4,605	273,555 100 0	94 _90 1, 8	-/3,205 6° 3	.54 885 56 6	11 420	. 8	38,415	7,755
4 years 5 to 19 years 15 to 19 years 18 and 19 years 18 and 20 years 20 and 2. years 22 to 24 years 22 to 24 years 22 to 24 years 22 to 24 years 22 to 24 years 24 years 25 years 25 years 26 years 26 years 27 years	20 985 12,270 8,725 25,935 9,210 16,745 29 1 5	2,073 20,245 12,0-5 8 100 14,480 6,690 7 790 6,780	810 210 600 11,170 2 470 8,700	35 515 25 4°0 10,050 2 175 7 8°5 19 985	305 35 270 7 4-0 1,420 6 020	313 90 220 2-510 755 -,955	65 40 45 645 165 -80	130 65 65 475 133 345	30 15 15 45 4	740 45 -95	,195 2,475 2,475 10,470 30,585 1,650 18,93	4,150 -8,525 11 700 9 825 8,670 4,515 4,155	4,800 1,285 3 575 21,260 6,950	3,925 940 2,385 48,505 5,995 12 640		325 170 185 805 350 455	30 5 22 50 40 1_0	57: 14: 36:
25 to 29 years S0 to 34 years S0 to 34 years 40 to 44 years 40 to 44 years 55 to 64 years 55 to 64 years 75 years and over	25,57, 25,320 23,710 35,7.5 24,955 13,380 5,235	2,520 2,210 3,030 2,030 2,030 -,340 470	21,755 22,015 20,515 34,255 20,125 8,955 2,-10	20,170 20,170 18 895 31,805 18,945 8,920 2,215	27,035 1d 120 18,735 17,813 30,340 8,090 7,725 7,895	2,950 2 005 1,432 1,085 -,475 855 585 585 320	1 035 865 1,030 970 1,000 820 (45	893 763 81,2 650 840 360 200 80	50 95 215 315 1,280 2,180 4,795 2 180	430 540 570 670 1,150 620 290 75	27,950 27,950 28,700 27,040 42,045 28,005 13,295 8,720	4,200 2,730 2,502 2,635 3,855 3 021 4,415 1 445	27,430 23,620 23,870 21,025 30,030 14,425 5,740 900	24,515 21 14, 21 400 18,950 27,215 13,31: 5 060 725	2,145 1,850 1,955 1,615 2,135 830 430 63	70 5.5 460 (80 286, 270 116	380 340 1,070 2,120 7,045 9 800 -0,930 6,350	1,62: 970 1,19: 1,260 1,72: 760 210
Percent	64,275 100 0	16,925 26 3	42 965 66 9	36 650 57 J	31,540 79 1	5,110 8 0	4,605	-,690 2 6	3,340 5.2	1,025	77,570 100 0	_4,190 18.3	48,_40	37 155 47 9	9,0%	.,895 2 4	12,940	2,300
ld vears lo to 19 years lo to 19 years lo to 17 vears l8 and 19 vears 20 to 24 years 20 and 21 years 22 to 24 vears	1,510 6,785 4 170 2,615 7,105 2 555 4,550	1 495 6,485 4,095 2,300 3,745 1 750 1,995	280 70 210 3,245 775 2 470	210 45 165 2 695 610 2,085	76 10 60 1540 170 1,245	140 35 105 1 150 370 840	35 10 25 385 120 265	35 15 30 165 45 120	20 5 15 30	10 80 95	3,570 8 020 7,645 3,375 8,945 3 350 5,575	1 544 6,380 + 125 1,0,5 2,265 1 165 1 100	25 1,8°5 510 1,385 6 4°5 2 1°0 4,325	1,295 295 1,000 4,750 1,500 3 250	400 125 275 1,305 432 870	5 200 90 110 420 215 205	25 75 20 55	120
to to 29 years 10 to 34 years 10 to 34 years 10 to 44 years 10 to 44 years 10 to 44 years 10 to 54 years 15 to 64 years 15 to 64 years 15 to 64 years	7,325 4,300 7,09 6,070 .0,60* 6,160 3,480 1,220	1,69.0 880 675 605 780 300 205 65	5,547 5 255 6,175 5,710 9,010 4 920 2,220 600	4,650 4,470 5,250 4,870 7,715 4 370 1,910 525	1 435 3 685 4,695 4,500 7,220 4 _05 1,825 480	1 215 785 535 570 405 265 85 65	650 580 670 560 2,015 435 440 65	245 205 275 280 280 115 70	20 40 .05 .55 590 832 1 000 545	205 140 205 225 105 55 10	9 370 7,860 8,885 7,675 1.1,025 6,420 5,055 1,765	- 207 720 580 5-0 670 350 320 145	7 855 6,540 7,325 5,745 7 875 2 945 1 355 105	5,920 5,000 5,745 4,500 6,305 2,445 1,110 65	1 790	305 275 215 185 190 50 40	170 280 560 1,040 3,010 2,950 3,325 1 500	349 429 429 479 123 5
SEREVEFOP7 Percent	58,6.5 100 0	11 835 20 2	43,215 73 7	40,160 68 5	30,920 53 0	3,240	1,835	- 2 T	۷,60, ۷ ۷	980 1 7	68,345 100 C	10,295	45 875 67 1	41 090 60 1	3 660 5 4	1,125	10,290	1 88:
4 Years 15 to 17 Years 15 to 17 Years 15 to 17 Years 10 to 28 Years 20 to 28 Years 20 to 28 Years 22 to 28 Years 20 to 28 Years 20 to 29 Years 20 to 29 Years 20 to 29 Years 20 to 29 Years 20 to 29 Years 20 to 29 Years 20 to 29 Years 20 to 29 Years 20 to 39 Years 20 to 39 Years 20 to 39 Years 20 to 39 Years 20 to 39 Years 20 to 39 Years 20 to 39 Years 20 Years	5,125 5,445 2,060 6,180 2,325 3,835 6,990 6,230 5,220 5,700 9,40 6,03,414 2,485	1,150 5,150 3,345 1,805 2,645 2,95 1,350 1,000 475 290 225 440 185 210 65	3 285 40 245 3,460 1,005 2,455 5,245 5,740 5,740 5,740 5,740 740	240 25 214 3,105 895 2,210 4,960 5,225 5,320 4,965 7,870 4,965 2,820 690	135 120 2,315 660 4,780 4,780 4,780 4,790 7,530 4,80b 2,620 605	105 10 95 790 235 555 560 445 325 340 160 85	35 15 20 20 60 160 275 255 260 185 270 165 25	10 10 135 50 85 200 -35 160 115 280 105 55 25	50 20 10 10 40 30 69 85 380 850	5 55 55 15 40 115 125 200 110 65 30	1,265 6,280 3,365 2,740 8 250 3,365 4,885 8 285 7,035 7,065 6,530 6,530 4,725 4,035	1,250 4,325 3,055 -,460 4,805 1,020 785 405 1450 240 450 210 195	15 1,775 46C 1 265 6,185 2 260 3,925 7,035 6 165 5,390 7,750 3,805 1,515 230	1 4e0 370 -,090 5,325 920 3,405 6,300 5,615 9,365 4,490 7,045 3,525 1,350 210	75 110 520 200 320 605 435 970 405 540	80 15 65 340	10 10 125 30 95 225 170 670 1,850 2,930 1,675	1
Percent	20,095	4,405 21 9	13 965 69 5	12,140 60 4	10,490 52 2	±,650 8 2	1,355 6 7	470 2 3	7 3	260 2 3	24,500 100 C	3,795 15 5	15,365 62 7	11,790 48 1	3,060 12 5	515 2 1	4,770	57X 2 :
14 years 1c to 19 years 1c to 17 years 18 and 19 years 20 to 24 years 22 to 24 years	2,245 1,425 890 2,125 780 -,345	570 2,185 1,420 765 900 395 4-5	150 3- 115 1,300 385 915	25 90 1,050 300 750	40 13 25 640 175 465	75 10 65 410 125 285	30 10 20 160 40 120	5 90 45 45	10	5 15	a15 2,590 1,540 1,050 2,940 1,635	61.0 1,845 1,320 525 620 380 270	5 215 520 2,170 865 1,305	540 155 385 1,535 615 920	5 -45 95 90 470 180 290	50 5 45 165 70 95	5 5 80 25 55	3 20 3 3 140
25 to 29 years 30 to 34 years 55 to 39 years 40 to 44 years 45 to 54 years 55 to 64 years 55 to 74 years 75 years and over	-,860 1,765 1,965 1,905 3,215 1,980 4,640 625	255 125 120 1.0 1.0 1.0 45 50	1,525 1,585 1,745 1,615 2,795 1,475 1,260	1,240 - 350 -,480 -,470 2 535 1,490 -,120 290	925 1,085 1,325 1,375 2,375 1,445 1,030 250	315 265 155 95 160 45 90 40	200 210 210 210 200 140 110	85 55 55 35 60 45 30	35 55 60 215 245 513 300	45 30 45 30 50 15 15	2,765 2,440 2,325 2,165 3,795 2,060 2,080 755	270 120 90 40 75 30 50	2,2×0 2 085 1,990 1,635 2,660 1,130 630 75	1,640 1,645 1,445 1,295 2,170 935 515 70	400 485 295	40 60 10	100 135 190 405 945 875 1,370 665	14/ 100 5: 8: 11: 2: 30
BATON BOUCE Percent.	44,020 100 D	11 365 25 0	30,250 70 3	29,250 66 4	27,395 62 2	1,855	2,100	600	1,105	600 1 4	47,190 100 0	8,780 18 6	32,13, 68 1	29,690 62 9	1,990	455	>,090 10 8	1,18
14 years 15 to 19 years 15 to 17 years 18 and 19 years 20 to 24 years 20 and 21 years 22 to 24 years	785 4,270 1,970 2,300 6,350 2,330 4,020	775 4,055 1,900 2,125 3,660 4,671 1,985	10 200 30 376 2,645 650 1,994	10 160 15 145 2,455 585 4,870	100 15 85 2,165 475 1,690	290 110	15 5 10 145 50 95	25 10 15 45 15 30	10 10 15 5	5 30	66* 4 810 2,240 2,570 7 000 2,705 4,295	655 3,690 1,960 1,730 1,865 1,045	10 1,065 275 790 5,015 1 625 3,390	10 935 240 695 4 645 1,515 3,130	300 95	70	5 25 10 15	45

 $\begin{tabular}{ll} Table 57.-MARITAL STATUS AND PRESENCE OF SPOUSE, BY AGE, COLOR, AND SEX, FOR THE STATE, URBAN AND RURAL, AND FOR STANDARD METROPOLITAN AREAS AND CITIES OF 100,000 OR MORE 1950—Con recognition of the control o$

deem on Al-prive it sample, available in pro-count tata I tables 5 2 38 34 and 36 Percent not shown a are less than 0.1 or where base is less than 500]

				Val 14	rears old at	d ove							Female 1	4 years old				
		1	1		Married	3			1			- 22		Marrie	d			
A and	1	1	,	l v	ife present		Nufe a	Deent		_					Husband	absent	Wid-	-
Area moior and age	Tota.	-single	Total marreo	lota	Feau of house- noid	head of house- bold	Repa rated	O her	Wid	Di- vorced	[otal	Single	Total ma_nea	Husband present	Sepa- rated	Other	owed	D ₁ - vereed
CTTIES—Com.	-													-				
PAT N TUOTCL: 20 to AP years 25 to 39 years 40 to 44 years 41 to 44 years 56 to 64 years 56 to 74 years 75 years and over	6,665 5 .25 4,615 - 200 6,.14 3 465 1,.50	3 31.0 720 305 .20 85 40		4,90 4,40 4,40 3,67 5,270 2,890 970 320	4,460 4,225 3,925 2,525 5,085 2 70 270	185	1.00 1.00 1.00 70 1.65 1.50 75	100 100 100 100 100 100 100 100 100 100	20 30 25 190 200 390 200	80 70 95 85 130 80 14 10	6,620 5,630 5,40 4,420 5,855 3,355 2,385 1,070	730 725 300 260 360 270 170 75	5,700 4,950 4,685 3,580 4,3.5 1,885 75 179	5,210 4,605 4,40 3,340 4,055 1,750 640 160	400 290 305 190 21.3 90 100 _0	90 55 40 50 45 42 15	175 345 965	11 14 22 23 21 77
VEL CR.EACT Perren.	.00 n_0	*2 005 20 0		-24,145 62 C	2,0.5 56 7	13 100 6 C	r 855	2,735 24	8,465	4,165	233,240 100 0	47,900 20 5	143,6_0 61 5	1/7,140	12,175 5 2	4,295 1 8	14,690 14 0	7,06
4 years 5 to 19 years '5 to 17 years 15 and 19 years 10 to 24 years 20 and 21 years 22 to 24 years 5 to 29 years	7,570 10,000 1,370 -,570 7 845 1,725	1 700 10,08° 9,815 £,870 12,57° 2 79° 0,780 6,035	40 663 490 8,725 2,000 6.725	29 485 105 380 7, '63 -, 730 6,030	20 20 10 5,500 1,090 4,410	82 190	5 65 20 5 5 5 380 940	10 1.5 50 65 435 40 215	20 10 10 45 45 40	225 .45 .80	3,485 19 455 10,6.5 8,800 25,660 9 825 15,835	3,445 2,630 9,712 2,912 7,870 4,090 3,775	40 3,740 920 2,820 17,205 5,575 11,630 22 095	2,92, 005 2,260 14,875 4,740 40,135	5 535 145 390 1 645 535 1 10	280 1_0 1_0 685 300 387	30 5 25 135 30 105	5 1 4 45 12 32 86
to 54 years to to 44 years to to 54 years to to 64 years to to 64 years to to 64 years to to 64 years to to 64 years to to 64 years to to 64 years	20,895 20,895 19,890 34,200 21,790 11,765 4,550	2,250 2,000 2,000 2, 15 1,220 420	17,505 -7,880 -6,-15 29,270 -7,305 -7,743 3,195	16,010 16,260 15 465 27,040 10,200 7,150 2 020	14,215 14,920 14 495 25,730 15,440 6,650 1,7.0	1,795 1,340 970 1,340 60 500	905 920 865 1,450 765 405 105	090 700 585 780 340 -85	60 195 205 1,130 1,965 2,545 1 875	425 525 620 1,065 770 250 60	22,390 24,080 23,115 37 400 24,765 17 3-0 7 840	2,420 2,355 2,425 3,550 2,81.5 2,27 -,353	19,210 19,680 17,590 25,799 14,460 5 019 780	16,975 17,445 15,690 23,245 11,470 4,385 625	1,660 1,775 ,48* - 940 745 375 65	375 460 4.5 610 245 255 90	495 965 1,910 6,430 8,810 9,880 5,600	86 4,08 1,19 -,62 70 19
Norwh *e Percent.	58,500 100 0	15 540 26 6	38,940 66 6	33,140 56 6	28,290 48 4	4 850 8 3	4,250 7 3	1,550	3,^8 5 3	935 1 6	71,585 120 0	13,155	44,145 61.7	33,975 47 5	8,420	1,750	12,110 16 9	2 .7
4 years 5 to 19 years	1,3c0 6 185 ,,810 , 375 6,375 2,300 4,073 6,685 5,745	3,745 2,100 3,445 1,584 1,860 4,585 610	5 270 65 275 2,820 685 2,235 5,020 4,800	205 45 160 2,340 575 1,805 4,95 4,075	65 10 55 :,255 245 :,010 3,040 3,330	-40 3, -05 ,C85 290 795 1,15° 745	10 25 325 105 220 605 540	30 10 20 1=5 45 110 220 185	10 10 30 30	80 30 50 65	1,420 7,280 4,190 ,,090 8,185 3,025 5,160 8,680 7,215	1,400 2,575 1,760 1,815 2,1-0 4,050 4,050	20 1,665 420 1,245 5,870 1,915 3,955 7,200 5,980	1,125 255 8°0 4 305 1,330 2 975 5,455 4,5°5	370 _05 265 1,185 395 790 1,5.5	5 100 60 110 380 190 190 290 260	30 5 25 75 20 55 160 255	100 100 100 300 300 320
0 to 39 years 0 to 39 years 0 to 44 years 5 to 34 years - 5 to 64 years - 5 to 64 years - 5 to 74 years 5 years and over	6,435 6,045 9,780 5,665 3,465 1,060	630 570 735 275 190 50	5,575 5,140 8,285 4,500 1,975	4,720 4,355 7,075 3,995 1,695 430	4,205 4,005 6,6.0 3,750 1,615	515 350 464 245 80 65	610 520 940 400 217 60	245 265 270 1.5 65 10	40 150 545 790 950 455	120	8,200 7,125 11,175 6,025 4,670 1,610	545 465 620 343 300 40	6,730 5,323 7,250 2,710 1,240 95	5,265 4,145 5,765 2,265 1,000	1,270 1,000 1,305 400 200 30	180 180 45 40	525 975 2,840 2,805 3,080 1 365	40 36 46 16
SHEEVZFORT Percent	42,6°5 100 0	*,260 19 3	32,010 74 7	29,610 09 1	26,935 62 9	2,605 6 2	1,420	980	1,735 4 0	870 2 0	31,890 100 0	7,530 14 7	34,430 66 4	30,415 78 6	3,085 5 9	730 1 8	E 100	1,73
4 years o to 19 years 18 to 17 years 18 and 19 years 18 and 19 years 20 and 21 years 22 to 24 years 5 to 29 years 0 to 24 years	635 3 520 2,100 1,420 4,715 1,685 3,030 5,335	630 3,305 2,080 1,225 2,025 920 1,10	210 20 290 2 625 745 1,880 4,405	180 170 2,380 680 1,700 4,01°	145 40 105 725 490 1,735	65 655 1°0 465 490	25 20 20 20 20	5 85 70 170	10 5 5 25	5 55 40 90	740 4,345 2,280 2,065 6,510 2,600 3 910 6,610	730 3,080 1,955 1,125 1 515 835 680 560	1 235 310 925 4,795 1,700 3,095	5,045 2,50 795 4,090 1,410 2,680 4,975	130 55 75 435 165 270 475	55 55 270 -20 -45 -40	10 10 75 15 60 40	2 12 57 7:

0 to 24 years to to 39 years to to 44 years to to 54 years 5 to 64 years 5 to 74 years 75 years and over	4,890 4,680 4 190 6,940 4,260 2,740 970	410 230 150 320 145 171 45	4,335 4 285 3,855 6 160 1,080 1,970 480	4,040 3,945 3,60 5,720 3,465 1,805 445	3,685, 3,680, 3,415, 5,430, 3,335, 1,655,	275 275 290 290 130 150 55	185 190 165 205 125 120 20	110 140 81 235 90 45	25 45 75 265 335 550 415	120 120 110 195 100 45	5,465 5,435 4,760 7,840 4,870 3,555 1,260	340 355 210 390, 170, 480 200	4,720 4,545 4 030 7,630 2,695 _,040	4,250 3 965 3,590 5,020 2,450 900 125	395 490 345 4°5 215 110	75 90 95 125 30 30	200 290 525 1 460 1,825 2,255 1,320	20: 24: 19: 36: 18:

Table 58.—PERSONS IN HOUSEHOLDS, BY RELATIONSHIP TO HEAD, AGE, COLOR, AND SEX, FOR THE STATE, URBAN AND RURAL, AND FOR STANDARD METROPOLITAN AREAS OF 100,000 OR MORE: 1950

Based on 20 percent sample; available complete-count data in tables 22 and 34. Number of heads same as number of households. Percent not shown where less than 0.1 or where base is less than 500

Male

Area, color, and age	Total	Head	Child	Grandchild	Parent	Other relative	Lodger	Resident employee
THE STATE—TOTAL								
All ages	1 269,230	594,420	[illegible]	[illegible]	10 7[illegible]5	57 505	28,[illegible]	550
Under 5 years	169,985		127 275	17,405		4,100	4,090	5
5 to 9 years	139,410		124,660	10,815		3,[illegible]	725	20
10 to 14 years	118,060	85	106,605	7,265		3,915	780	10
15 to 19 years	97,190	2,300	83,305	4 170		5,450	1,700	55
15 years	21,225	105	19,065	1,140		785	[illegible]	
16 years	20,690	95	18,595	935		870	190	5
17 years	20 145	250	17,680	855		1,365	280	15
18 years	19,220	665	15,980	720		1,375	475	[illegible]
19 years	15,910	385	12,985	520		1,365	655	10
20 to 24 years	89,400	36,715	[illegible]	4,605		8,440	4,305	65
20 years	15,635	3 050	10,100	485		1 305	180	15
21 years	17 795	5,455	9,055	760		1,2[illegible]	905	25
22 years	17,820	7 300	7,660	265		1 380	705	10
23 years	19,430	9,870	6 555	245	.	1,700	1,045	15
24 years	18 720	11 070	4,900	170		1,640	970	.
25 to 29 years	95,510	68,640	15,835	480		6,945	3,570	40
25 years	19,075	12,260	4,285	185		1,515	825	
26 years	18,855	12 810	3 635	105		1,500	780	25
27 years	19,075	14,255	3,265	85		1,365	705	
28 years	19,505	14,070	2,335	60		1 490	725	5
29 years	18,400	14,645	2,095	45		1,375	575	5
30 to 34 years	87,985	72 645	7,825		30	[illegible]	2,530	50
35 to 39 years	89,100	77,220	5,030	.	50	4,500	2,240	65
40 to 44 years	81,495	72,310	3,740		70	4,420	2,015	50
45 to 49 years	72 465	65,125	1,965		240	2 960	2,135	[illegible]
50 to 54 years	60,100	54,690	890		610	2,225	1,640	45
55 to 59 years	49,005	44,615	395		690	1,9[illegible]	1,370	30
60 to 64 years	38,175	34 105	165		1,110	1,705	1,070	20
65 to 69 years	36,170	31,180	100		1,955	1,515	1,385	35
70 to 74 years	21 800	18 365			1 745	915	765	10
75 to 79 years	13,035	10,425			2,015	725	455	15
80 to 84 years	6 315	4,210			1 425	375	265	
85 years and over	2,830	1,650			805	245	130	
14 years	21,755	85	9,335	1,225		930	180	
Under 18 years	490 115	535	433,880	38,465		13,985	3,195	55
Percent Distribution								
All ages	100 0	100 0	100.0	100 0	100 0	100 0	100 0	100 0
Under 5 years	13 4		27 5	41 8		7 2	3 9	0 9
5 to 9 years	11 0		23 3	25 9		5 5	2 6	3 [illegible]
10 to 14 years	9 3		9.9	17 4		6 8	2 8	1 8
15 to 19 years	7 7	0 4	15 5	10 0		9 5	6 0	10 0
20 to 24 years	7 0	6 2	7 1	3 8		14 7	15 3	[illegible] 8
25 to 29 years	7 5	11 5	3 0	1 1		12 1	12 7	7 3
30 to 34 years	6 9	12 2	1 5		0 3	8 5	9 0	9 1
35 to 39 years	7 0	13 0	0 9		0 5	7 8	8 0	10 9
40 to 44 years	6 4	12 1	0 7		0 8	5 9	7 2	9 1
45 to 49 years	5 7	11 0	0 4		2 2	5 1	7 6	7 3
50 to 54 years	4 7	9 2	0 2		5 7	3 9	5 8	8 2
55 to 59 years	3 9	7 5	0 1		6 4	3 3	4 9	5 5
60 to 64 years	3 0	5 7			10 3	3 0	3 8	3 6
65 to 69 years	2 8	5 2			18 2	2 6	4 9	6 4
70 to 74 years	1 7	3 1			16 2	1 6	2 7	1 8
75 to 79 years	1 1	1 8			18 7	1 3	1 6	2 7
80 to 84 years	0 5	0 7			13 2	0 7	0 9	
85 years and over	0 2	0 3			7 5	0 4	0 5	.
THE STATE—NONWHITE								
All ages	414,270	168,430	178,205	25,505	2,640	25,885	13,345	260
Percent	100 0	40 7	43 0	6 2	0 6	6 2	3 2	0 1
Under 5 years	62,690		48,790	10,205		3,000	695	
5 to 9 years	50,890		41,530	6,725		2 230	395	10
10 to 14 years	44,465	10	37,100	4,655		2,265	430	5
15 to 19 years	35 505	860	28,440	2,735		2,695	745	30
15 years	7,530	30	6,665	770		410	55	
16 years	7 505	10	6,315	620		465	95	.
17 years	7,125	20	5,750	535		530	180	10
18 years	7 195	235	5,640	460		675	185	
19 years	5,750	465	4,070	350		615	230	20
20 to 24 years	27,965	9,885	12,020	890		3,660	1,490	20
20 years	5,570	1,025	3 400	295		645	205	
21 years	5,515	1 500	2,605	250		835	310	15
22 years	5 660	1,850	2,495	145		870	240	
23 years	5,865	2,085	2,015	130		560	370	5
24 years	5,445	2,825	1 505	70		650	365	
25 to 29 years	26,260	16,685	4,895	295		2,920	1,445	20
25 years	5,275	2,880	1 390	95		630	280	.
26 years	5,325	3,250	1,030	70		640	320	15
27 years	5,655	3 640	1,095	65		585	270	
28 years	5,340	3,545	780	30		630	350	5
29 years	4,665	3,370	600	35		435	225	
30 to 34 years	22,705	17,285	2,170		15	[illegible]	1 280	45
35 to 39 years	25,715	21,425	1,735		35	1,595	1,205	20
40 to 44 years	23,295	20,155	870		15	1,125	1,090	20
45 to 49 years	21,890	19,170	540		70	965	1,125	20
50 to 54 years	17,775	15,705	215		195	785	850	25
55 to 59 years	15,135	13,510	135		125	715	635	15
60 to 64 years	10,955	9,770	45		200	500	435	5
65 to 69 years	14,030	12,150	20		475	615	775	15
70 to 74 years	7,025	5 915			410	310	390	
75 to 79 years	4,605	3,660			480	270	185	10
80 to 84 years	2,260	1,595			375	180	110	
85 years and over	1,085	650			225	145	65	
14 years	8,170	10	6,735	810		530	115	
Under 18 years	180,605	170	146,150	[illegible]		8 900	1 850	25

Female

Area, color, and age	Total	Head	Wife	Child	Grandchild	Parent	Other relative	Lodger	Resident employee
THE STATE—TOTAL									
All ages	1 340,66[illegible]	[illegible]	[illegible]	[illegible]	39,83[illegible]	[illegible]	65 [illegible]	23,6[illegible]5	[illegible]
Under 5 years	[illegible]			[illegible]	[illegible] 345		4 [illegible]45	1 1[illegible]0	5
5 to 9 years	[illegible]5,455			120,9[illegible]0	10 845		3 475	725	20
10 to 14 years	115,645	20	9[illegible]	103,555	[illegible]		4,290	725	20
15 to 19 years	104 [illegible]	690	16,620	72,240	3 73[illegible]		8,625	2 375	140
15 years	21,615	50	375	18,790	1,630		1,220	165	5
16 years	20,780	3[illegible]	[illegible]	17 12[illegible]	395		1,285	315	20
17 years	20,145	135	2,070	15,445	6[illegible]0		1,815	390	10
18 years	20 985	195	5 180	14,180	640		2,155	625	30
19 years	19 955	295	7,365	8,705	5[illegible]		[illegible]	860	45
20 to 24 years	106 995	3 [illegible]35	61 740	25,[illegible]0	1,090		8 690	4,505	135
20 years	2[illegible],395	425	9 825	7,390	30[illegible]		2,160	890	30
21 years	2[illegible] 420	[illegible]	1[illegible] 540	5,390	195		1 760	970	15
22 years	2[illegible],475	[illegible]	[illegible]	4,9[illegible]	[illegible]		1,800	900	30
23 years	2[illegible],955	885	14,440	[illegible]	220		1 495	845	25
24 years	2[illegible],990	905	14 960	2,5[illegible]	140		1,775	900	35
25 to 29 years	108 72[illegible]	5,830	80,565	13 [illegible]95	345		5 690	2,720	125
25 years	22,760	1,[illegible]40	16,160	3 310	115		1,370	635	30
26 years	21 270	1,[illegible]00	15,21[illegible]	2 940	75		1,285	540	20
27 years	21 690	1,095	16 17[illegible]	2,680	65		1 100	550	20
28 years	22 375	1 225	17,795	[illegible]	75		1,225	500	40
29 years	20,635	1,270	15 800	2,050	60		910	495	15
30 to 34 years	9[illegible],465	5,940	73,865	8 370		45	4 045	1 885	115
35 to 39 years	98,11[illegible]	[illegible],080	76,780	6 200		240	3,770	1,835	155
40 to 44 years	87,045	11,120	65 805	4,475		145	3 365	1,360	125
45 to 49 years	7[illegible] 765	12 2[illegible]	54,805	2 865		1,4[illegible]	3,125	1,200	125
50 to 54 years	62,925	12,770	41,660	1,555		2,500	3,035	1,190	175
55 to 59 years	5[illegible],030	12,620	30,200	785		3 480	2,835	840	170
60 to 64 years	39,660	1[illegible] 540	19,865	255		4 555	2 510	750	185
65 to 69 years	40,635	14,220	13,3[illegible]	165		6,770	3,075	1 010	60
70 to 74 years	24,[illegible]80	9,285	6,535			5 055	1,985	570	50
75 to 79 years	15 240	5,895	2,515			4,755	1,580	45[illegible]	4[illegible]
80 to 84 years	7,780	2,770	830			2 995	985	190	10
85 years and over	4,520	1,365	195			2 365	685	205	5
14 years	21,400	20	90	19,205	985		840	160	10
Under 18 years	479 755	220	4,225	418 31[illegible]	37,200		16,230	3,460	110
Percent Distribution									
All ages	100 0	100 0	100 0	100 0	100 0	100 0	100 0	100 0	100 0
Under 5 years	12 3	.		28 4	42 3		6 3	[illegible] 7	0 3
5 to 9 years	10 1			23 9	27 2		5 3	3 1	1 2
10 to 14 years	8 6			20 6	17 4		6 5	3 1	1 2
15 to 19 years	7 8	0 6	3 0	14 4	9 4		13 1	10 0	8 4
20 to 24 years	8 0	2 9	[illegible]	5 0	2 7		13 2	19 0	8 1
25 to 29 years	8 1	4 9	14 6	2 7	1 0		8 6	11 5	7 5
30 to 34 years	7 3	5 8	13 8	1 7		0 1	6 1	8 0	6 9
35 to 39 years	7 3	7 6	13 9	1 2		0 8	5 7	7 8	9 3
40 to 44 years	6 5	9 3	11 9	0 9		2 2	5 1	5 7	7 5
45 to 49 years	5 7	10 2	9 9	0 6		4 [illegible]	4 7	5 1	7 5
50 to 54 years	4 7	10 6	7 6	0 3		7 1	4 6	5 0	10 5
55 to 59 years	3 8	10 5	5 5	0 2		10 1	4 3	3 6	10 2
60 to 64 years	3 0	9 6	3 6	0 1		12 9	3 8	3 2	11 1
65 to 69 years	3 0	11 9	2 8			19 1	4 7	4 3	3 6
70 to 74 years	1 8	7	1 2			16 0	3 0	2 4	3 0
75 to 79 years	1 1	4 9	0 5			13 4	2 4	9	2 7
80 to 84 years	0 6	2 3	0 2			8 5	1 5	0 8	0 6
85 years and over	0 3	1 1				5 8	1 0	0 9	0 3
THE STATE—NONWHITE									
All ages	451,995	54,035	145,965	174,000	24,730	10 265	30 955	11,360	685
Percent	100 0	12 0	32 3	38 5	5 5	2 3	6 8	2 5	0 2
Under 5 years	61,925	.		48,125	10,165		2,900	730	5
5 to 9 years	50,470	.		41,060	6,695		2,280	430	5
10 to 14 years	44,070	.	15	36,360	4,505		2,775	410	5
15 to 19 years	38 915	330	4,905	25 805	2,395		4,345	1,075	60
15 years	8,205	5	130	6,590	640		755	85	
16 years	8,015	5	320	6,190	625		695	180	10
17 years	7,640	75	870	5,225	385	.	895	175	15
18 years	7 975	105	1,575	4,580	390		1,030	285	10
19 years	7,080	140	2,010	3,220	365		970	350	25
20 to 24 years	35,570	1,840	16,275	10,310	680		4,350	2,045	70
20 years	7,985	230	2,690	3,255	235	.	1,130	425	20
21 years	6,615	270	2,855	2,090	115	.	890	390	5
22 years	7,100	430	3,270	2,000	100		875	420	5
23 years	6 925	425	3 705	1,530	155		730	360	20
24 years	6,945	485	3,755	1,435	75		725	450	20
25 to 29 years	33 060	3,435	20,065	4,965	290		2,880	1,360	65
25 years	7,280	685	4,320	1,230	80		690	260	15
26 years	6,465	615	3 675	1,170	55		665	280	5
27 years	6,470	650	4,100	930	45		535	300	10
28 years	6,695	700	4,220	915	60		530	245	25
29 years	6,050	785	3,750	720	50		460	275	10
30 to 34 years	29,100	3,990	19,085	3,015		25	1,955	945	85
35 to 39 years	31,070	5,255	21,700	1,750		185	1,745	940	95
40 to 44 years	26,780	5,730	17,535	1,190		360	1,225	685	55
45 to 49 years	24,280	6,150	15,075	675		565	1,230	555	30
50 to 54 years	19,285	5,505	10,975	415		815	1,005	515	55
55 to 59 years	14,430	4,895	7,170	200		935	820	360	50
60 to 64 years	11,190	4,145	4,930	50		1,130	615	275	45
65 to 69 years	15,645	6,290	5,355	80		2,205	1,227	475	15
70 to 74 years	6,980	2,990	1,830			1 380	545	220	15
75 to 79 years	4,445	1,965	710			1,105	460	185	20
80 to 84 years	2,305	915	240			825	255	65	5
85 years and over	1,875	600	100			735	345	90	5
14 years	8,070		15	6,725	565	.	570	95	
Under 18 years	180,325	85	1,335	143 550	23,005	.	10,300	2,010	40

Table 58.—PERSONS IN HOUSEHOLDS BY RELATIONSHIP TO HEAD, AGE, COLOR, AND SEX, FOR THE STATE, URBAN AND RURAL, AND FOR STANDARD METROPOLITAN AREAS OF 100 000 OR MORE 1950—Con.

[Based on 29-perce. v sample, available complete-ec.m. data in labes 22 and 34. \under of heads on 1. as number of households. Percent not known where less than 0 1 or where base is less than 500]

	-			Viac				,				Fer	male		100		r
Area court and age	Tn _	Head	Chan	fb/	Parer)taut rela 10	Locge_	Resident employee	Total	Head	Wife	Child	Grand- child	Parent	Other rela- tive	Lodger	Residen employe
URBAN-TOTAL				§ [ī.									X ¹	
Ali ages Percen	- 3.0 - 3.0	-35 E4 49 4	37.7	1 3 -	2,9.0	25 245	21 -95	100	747,065 100 0	82,990	310 100 +1 5	248,260 33 2		22,565 3 0	42,595	19 2.0	1,12
der 5 years	80,00		7.,7	9,320		2 4-0	-te	. 5	a5,,20			73,170	8,670 > 420 3,395		2,565	770 +80	
to 14 years c 19 years 5 to 17 years	7, 180	. 204	3,,645	- 1050		2 23	4.0	20	51,685	525	7, 8,5	45 325 33,980	3,395 805 2,25		2 440 4,975 2 435	1 860 630	
Rand 19 years	6,015	2.,475	23,155 4,490	1.100		1,740	830	10	28,808	10	6,210	22,780 11,400	6.0		2,540	1,230	
to 24 years 20 and 21 years 22 to 24 years	32 7 6	2,,275 -, 90 2,25	7,890 0 .60	830		1,780	3 485 -,200 2,285	20 10 5	24,940 41,200	2,90 835 2,065	37,700 12 095 25,605	15,1 5 7,500 7,645	3,0		2,485	2,480	
to 29 years.	59,623 53,055	42,7 5	السيه	255	_0	4,63,		25	69 305	4.455	49,420	8,920	245	30	2,765	2.405	
to 39 years. to 39 years	5 ,260	43,630	4,1_0 2,795 2,14	-	3*	2,925	1,600	20	58,995	5 355 0,720 8,525	43,815 43,665 37,525	4,085		165 525	2,750 2,280 4,250	1,640	2
to 64 years to 64 years	755	41,095 (7,79) 41,280	1,49		175	3, 15	2,940	30	82,800 53,315	18,080 16,195 14,585	52,935	2,660 585		2,740 5,570	3,725	1,120	2
to 74 years.	26,900 10,280	22,065 6,640	45		2,100	2,255	590	20	36,985	14,585	9,855	75		7,725 5,820	1,995	61,260	
years	4,375	5.5	8,200	535		52.0	75		9,420		35	8,330	470		/65	120	
URBAN-NONWHITE																-	2
Ail ages Percent	300, 150	84,165	75,865	12,200	1,350	₁° 925 8 0	10,095 5 0	120	233,600 100 0	36,780 15 7	73,450 31 4	76,355 32 7	12,095	5,890	19,305	9,195	67
der 5 vears	29,-75 21,715 -7,865		21,815 17,_35 14,465	3,100		1,195	505 240 250	5	20,750			21,360	5,035 3,225 2,115		1,800 1,305 1,575	550 330 280	4
o 14 years o 19 years 5 to 17 years 8 and 19 years	-4 655 0,235	31.5 25	1,,180	1,905 1,240 800		1,450	455 1.85	10	17,900 10,370	250 60	2,0≥5 480	14,700	1,130		2,600	840 315	5 2
ls and 19 years to 24 years on and 21 years	5,420	,5.4	3,755 5,4J0	410		7.5	270	10	12 935	1,425	1,545 8,275 2,560	7,410 2,590 5,200 2,560	425		2,800	1.785	
2 .o 24 vears	4,905 3,870	3,500	2,465	25.		2,320	335	,	7,640	385	2,560	2,560	190 21:2		1,195	735	3
to 20 years to 34 years	15,195	9,120	2,720	1-0	5	-,950	1,2/5	10 25	-9,990 -7 120	2,550	10,010	3,005	85	25	1,975	1 225	
to 44 years	14,340 1,1,1 2,,745	11,330	855		25 25 1°0	1 110	905	10	28. /15	3,885 4,370 8,340	9,075	.,070 640		90	1,250	765 545	9
to 64 years	12,380	18,450	42* 35	1.5	180	765	1 535	25	25,665 25,259 13,945	5,705	13,055	105		1,3,5	1,485	635 465	5
o 74 yea.s years and over _	8 905 3,295	2,280	10		475 470	425 33.5	770	-3	11,640	5,585 ± 075	2,7_0	35		1,475	985 510	530 220	2
уеаля	3 410	5	2, 40	345		275	15		3,340		5	2,630	325		305	~5	
'RAL NONFARM—TOTAL	*04,690	.42 705	139.165	10,195	2,325	11,335	4,195	80	318,745						1,20	4	
All ages Percent	100 0	42,395 46 O	4/ 9 39 125	3 3	0.8	7 7 920	1 4	80	100 0	47,590 8 7	131,350 41 2	128,510 40 3	9,465	6,525	איר ,850 3 7	3,140	0 1
o 9 years	44,255 *7,380 3_,*45	20	34,010	2.555		630	125		45,695 35,520 30,395		30	38,923 31,933 27,765	3,81.0 2,695 1,655	3 - 1	755 765 785	210 125 145	4
to 19 years 5 to 17 years 18 and 19 years	25,665	740	20,675	1,990 1,070 775		1,245	240 110	15	45,985	115	5 162	17,375	1,005		1,725	370 165	30
8 and 19 years - to 24 years 0 and 21 years	8,320 21,615	9,745	9,105	295		1,750 685	130	5	-6,100 9,889 2/,/50	65 540	16,655	4,595	300		1,450	205 4601	31
2 to 24 years	8,460 4,.55	7,275	4,790	245 175		1,065	265 325	. 5	9,695	183	5,995	2,525	125		705 745	305	-
to 29 years to 34 years to 39 years	21,330 9,980 20,585	17,10	3,265	130	٠٠.	1,280	430 315	10	24, ±20 21 950 21,460	1,275	10 100	2,415	85	.5	980	270	
to 44 Years -	17.760	18,290 16,20 26,090	790		15 20	845 530	280 300	10	17,910	1,825	18 145 17,550 14 280	1,56		65	530 545	270	3
to 54 vears	28,400 19,695 16,050	18,040	71.5 155 30		145 390 735	875 645	560 460	10	29,125 20,145	5,020	21,015	1,050		.,320	985 835	3/5 280	40
rears and over	7,200	14,285 5,745	-		1,0.0	565 265	175	2	16,770	3,275	1,160	60		2 375	675	570	
PURAL VONTARN	, 20	20	5,015	3.0		175	25		5,580	15	30	5,115	270		1.30	15	
RURAL NONFARM— NONWHITE	95 -40	39 570	42,.50	6,180	555	-,960	1,985	40			i				i		
All ages Percent	95,-40 00 0	41 5	12,055	2,420	0.6	5 2	2 1		102,350	12,875 12 6	33,,60 32 8	40,955	5,020 5 7	1,995	5,550	1,460	0 1
to 14 years	10,530	5	8,750	1,625		440	70	5	10,115	i	5	12,100 9,775 8,525	1,695		465	55	1 1000
to 19 years 5 to 17 years 8 and 19 years	5,005	210 35	4,115 2,090	7/5 540		540 270 270	95 40	10	8 70° 5,315	65 25	-,420 405	5,605 3,890	640	4.	820 470	150	
S and 19 years. to 24 years 0 and 21 years.	2,800 6,675	175 2 655	2,820	205 255		700	245	5	7,660	335	1,015	2,185	150		350 685	75 75 205	10
2 to 24 years	2,685 3,990	1,940	1,450	100		430	95 150		4,3.0	105 20	2,505	-, 115 -, 070	95		300	60	5
to 36 years to 34 years	5, c55 4,680	3,900	4,025	80		51.5 345	130	20	6,845	730 785	4,290	995 660	70	ĺ	415	110	25 25
to 34 years to 44 years to 54 years to 54 years	5,500 /,735	4,700	345 220		10	305 170	140	5	6,240	1,015	3,540	360		35 90	230	150	5 5
to 64 years	7,765 6,110 6,050	6,59° 5,490 5,435	180 40 5		50 85 165	230	300 265	5	6,310	2,335 2,415 2,785	2,285	310		255	380 285	160	25
years and over	2,740	2,300	. 1	1	240	220	85 85		6,515	1,420	435	30		695	425 310	105	10
years .	1,830	5	1,530	200	- 1	85	10	- 1	1,875	1	5			200	80		

Table 58—PERSONS IN HOUSEHOLDS, BY RELATIONSHIP TO HEAD, AGE, COLOR, AND SEX, FOR THE STATE, URBAN AND RURAL, AND FOR STANDARD METROPOLITAN AREAS OF 103,000 CR MORE 1950—Col.

[Based on 20-percent sample available complete-count data in tables 22 and 34 \ more of heads mine as number of .completed. Percent in t shows when, see than 0.1 or where base in less than 5.

Area color, and age				Ma'e	_	0		-				Fen	nale				
Area color, and age	Total	Head	Child	Grand- child	Parent	Otner rela- tre	Loage.	Rendent sm, soyee	Total	Hee.	W-4e	Chila	could	Pa.eo	Other rela- uve	Lodger	Remaeut employee
RIJRAL FARM—TOTAL											i			i	e 7	7	
All ages	290,890 100 0	121, 435 41 6	142,930	10,885	2 9	10 645	2 480	285 0 1	274 855 100 C	+,330 3 4	110,015	126,040 45 °	10,20	6 325	17,465	1 305	205
Under 5 years 10 10 18 years 10 10 18 years 10 10 18 years 10 10 18 years 10 10 18 years 18 and 19 years 18 and 10 years 18 and 10 years 22 10 24 years 22 10 24 years 25 10 29 years 26 10 29 years 27 10 29 years 27 10 29 years 28 10 29 years 28 10 29 years 28 10 29 years 28 10 29 years 28 10 29 years 28 10 29 years 29 10 29 years 29 10 29 years 20 1	37,290 3,225 36,205 30,325 20,030 10,295 7,895 14,950 14,950 17,255 16,500 28,410 20,955 15,020 5,300 6,835	10 555 120 439 5,795 1,445 4 350 9 705 11,995 12,300 26,455 19,400 13,195 3,740	32, 215 32, 360 32, 925 26, 985 18, 165 8, 820 10, 115 5,475 4,640 3,960 2,960 1,080 795 6,900 1,35 2, 25	4,105 2,990 2,-95 1,145 855 290 355 215 140 95	10 100 360 865 -,155	800 720 850 1 305 715 300 355 855 81 030 730 730 545 880 790 4.0	165 -3., 225 305 -55 -40 230 -20 110 -65 113 123 230 -20 230 -20 230 -20 230 -20 230 -20 230 -20 230 -20 230 -20 230 -20 230 -20 230 -20 -20 -20 -20 -20 -20 -20 -20 -20 -2	20 40 20 20 20 10 30 30 40	36, 2-0 35, 080 33, %65 27, 400 48, 635 5, 765 16, 405 16, 305 17, 655 16, 235 26, 765 17, 260 10, 260 4, 727 6, 400	75 220 310 533 680 1,900 2,200 2,275 -,105	25) 3,667 1,085 3,975 9,385 3,285 6,100 11,965 11,965 11,965 12,655 22,650 5,435 900	30, 920, 22 495 30,461 20,885 12,795 5,990 5,080 2,755 2,225 2,350 1,463 925 780 780 780 780 780 780 780 780 780 780	4,365 2,730 1,885 910 713 195 .85 105 90 65	500 1300 5235 1,255 2,335 2,020	825 725 1,065 -725 900 825 1 540 010 9490 540 540 240	110	20 20 20 20 20 20 20 20 20 20 20 20 20 2
RURAL FARM— NONWHITE																	
All ages Percen	1 8,710	44,295 37 3	60,190 50.7	7,125 6 G	735 0 6	5,000	1,265	100	116,045 100 n	4,380	38,955 33 6	56,690 48 9	6,8.5		6,035 5 2	0 6	
Under 5 wears 10 % class 10 % class 10 % class 10 % class 10 % class 15 % class 15 % class 15 % class 16 % cla	15,289 13,900 15,900 15,900 15,900 15,900 15,900 15,900 15,900 15,800 15	335 70 265 2,715 7795 1,920 3,669 4,090 3,395 5,070 9,530 6,655 5,515 1,325	14,910 14,305 13,883 12,050 7,885 3,865 3,860 2,090 1,710 1,160 500 2333 145 45 5 5	2 630 2 000 1,495 750 455 195 -80 136 45	10 5 45 60 645 370	540 545 585 702 400 305 510 300 310 455 180 145 775 220 280 165	110 45 105 195 105 90 120 85 35 50 66 60 140 105 170 60	10 3 3 20 20 20 20 21 21 21 23 23 25 25 25 25 25 25 25 25 25 25 25 25 25	18,23: 16 823 -5,280 12,310 8,173 4,136 4,361 4,361 6,703 5,802 6,703 5,802 6,703 1,623 2,656	.5 80 .0 70 133 370 920 920 933 9410 383	5 1,460 4,35 1,025 3,910 1,400 2,510 4,535 4,735 5,675 4,925 7,710 3,620 2,000 305 5	14, 665 12, 497 13, 135 9, 200 6, 7.5 2, 485 2, 925 1, 677 1, 250 965 530 240 160 45 15	65 60 33	60 60 260 450 915 635	22.5 370 240 360	45 66 66 66 66 66 66 66 66 66 66 66 66 66	15 5 10 3 3 3 3 10
STANDARD METRO- POLITAN AREAS						.03				~						12:00	
Percent	72,340 100 0	36,260 50 1	28,015	2,050	0.6	3,175	2 360	10	77,690 100 0	6,535 8 4	34 350 44 2	2,370 35 2	1,885		3 650	2 4	
Under 5 years 10 to 16 years 10 to 16 years 10 to 16 years 10 to 16 years 11 to 17 years. 15 to 17 years. 15 to 18 years 15 to 18 years 22 to 16 years 22 to 16 years 25 to 19 years 30 to 84 years 30 to 84 years 45 to 56 years 45 to 57 years 45 to 58 years 45 to 58 years 45 to 56 years 56 to 79 years 45 to 56 years 56 to 79 years 56 to 79 years 57 years 57 years 58 to 79 years	10,385 7,300 9,630 4,550 2,600 1,350 5,545 1,840 3,09 7,195 6,195 5,830 2,070 2,070 2,070 2,070 1,265 8,235 8,235	10 .65 45 120 2,655 2,655 2,060 5,435 5,385 5,140 4,585 6,670 3,815 1,815	9,205 6,605 4,993 3,735 2,310 1,445 1,840 830 31,15 205 1,000 1,00	890 485 350 150 95 55 115 65 50 60	5 20 95 180 40	220 155 225 330 120 210 200 320 485 225 265 160 115 50	73 557 500 145 301 125 290 385 270 220 170 255 166 120	5	10, 315 7, 350 5, 325 2, 885 2, 440 7, 620 2, 790 7, 790 6, 710 6, 480 5, 260 6, 045 1, 130 915	40 10 260 105 125 450 640 755 1,310 1,115 1,115 450	10 845 1955 650 4 7955 7 335 6,035 5,335 5,320 2 130 890 1°55	9 155 6,695 4,830 3,429 1,230 1,230 1,230 745 695 477 265 190 170 35	412 335 155 100 75 75 33 44 22	5 20 55 195 46,5 730 513	19: 18: 31: 31: 39: 59: 30: 36:	550 243 6 243 6 263 6 263 203 263 250 250 250 250 250 250 250 250 250 250	14 20
Nonwhi **	23,855	10,365	8,965	1 500	125	1,695	1,160	,	26 545 100 0	3,360	9,290	8 890 33 a	1 38	610	2,130	83	
Percent Lnder 5 years \$ 10 0 years \$ 10 0 years \$ 10 0 years \$ 10 0 years \$ 10 0 10 14 years \$ 10 0 10 14 years \$ 10 0 10 14 years \$ 10 0 14 years \$ 10 0 14 years \$ 10 0 14 years \$ 10 0 15 y	100 0 1,770 2,340 2,127 1,665 1,030 1,650 393 1,095 1,733 1,733 1,735 1,735 1,735 1,735 1,735 1,740 2,305 1,540 2,305 1,660 400 400 400	43 2 20 2* 585 1,55 1,255 1,450 1,995 1,995 1,975 883 305	37 7 7 2,940 1,839 1,622 1,265 653 265 1202 80 20 333 320 320 320 320 320 320 320 320		5 25 60 35	7 1 185 1160 170 55 512 233 105 105 115 70 115 83 60 40	459 459 459 459 459 459 459 145 145 145 170 70 77 72 20	5	3,540 2,770 2,060 1,995 1,080 950 2,320 1,360 2,470 2,185 1,825 1,825 1,335 1,395 1,395 460	15 5 10 140 100 100 100 1250 1440 1435 6600 6000 6000 6000 6000 6000 6000 60	250 70 .80 1,025 3-2 680 1,585 1,170 1,450 1,185 1,360 595	2,660 2,147 1,660 1,065 1,065 555 555 250 305 305 243 100 75 75 75 75	64: 27: 25: 13: 5: 5: 5: 5: 5: 5: 5: 5: 5: 5: 5: 5: 5:	20 20 20 20 20 20 20 20 20 20 20 20 20 2	200 120 131 390 191 191 192 181 183 183 184 150 160 160 160 160 160 160 160 160 160 16	33 33 100 133	

Table 58.—PERSONS IN HOUSEHOLDS, BY RELATIONSHIP TO HEAD, AGE, COLOR, AND SEX, FOR THE STATE, URBAN AND RURAL, AND FOR STANDARD METROPOLITAN AREAS OF 100,000 OR MORE 1950—Con.

Based on 20-person sample, available complete-count data is table 22 and 24 Number of heads same as number of households. Percent not shown where less than 0.1 or where base is less than 200 percent not shown where less than 0.1 or where base is less than 200 percent not shown where less than 0.1 or where base is less than 200 percent not shown where less than 0.1 or where base is less than 200 percent not shown where less than 0.1 or where base is less than 200 percent not shown where less than 0.1 or where base is less than 200 percent not shown where less than 200 percent not shown where less than 0.1 or where base is less than 200 percent not shown where less than 2

	1 11 11 1			Valo			70.100					Fee	male				
trea rolor and age	Total	Head	Child	ema-	Parent	O-her rela tree	Louger	Resident employee	Total	Hend	Wife	Child	Grand- child	Parent	Other rela- tive	Lodger	Renden
STANDARD METROPOL																	
NEW ORLEADS Percent	17. KAO	113,78,	4,800 26 9	9,640	3,105 1 C	20,445 6 5	9,45	700	349,015 100 0	40,075	140,660 40 3	112,795 02 l	9,835	12,710 3 6	24,765 7 1	8,240	63:
Lndr x vene 5 to 9 vener. 10 to 14 years 10 to 14 years 10 to 19 years 15 to 17 years 15 to 17 years 15 to 17 years 20 and at years 20 and at years 20 and at years 25 to 29 vener 25 to 29 vener 25 to 29 vener 26 to 24 vener 26 to 25 vener 26 of evener 26 of evener 26 of evener 26 of evener 27 ovener 28 of 6 years 28 of 64 years 28 of 64 years 28 of 64 years 29 ovener 20 ovener 20 ovener 21 ovener 22 ovener 23 of 64 years 25 of 64 years 26 of 74 years 26 years 26 of 74 years 26 years 26 of 74 years 26 years 26 years 26 of 74 years 26 years 26 years 26 years 26 years 26 years 26 years 26 years 26 years 26 years 27 year	38 "U 39, "S 11, "CS 39, 61u 12, 015 ", 599 27, 265 7, 964 27, 265 7, 964 27, 265 24, 315 24, 325 24, 325 26, 325	30 4-7 85 8,385 6,387 6 435 8,397 19 190 20,155 19,278 27,875 10,220 2,984	32,422 25,555 2,455 16,775 0,20 2,00 10,32 4,605 5,35 4,900 2,210 1,485 1100 20	2,580 2,410 -355 8.0 -305 305 305 200 165 -20	10 20 32 313 4,045 1,045	375 390 -, -00 720 680 -, 925 1, 930 -, 835 -, 835 -, 835 2, 570 -, 835 2, 170 1, 755 2, 170 1, 79, 71, 71, 71, 71, 71, 71, 71, 71, 71, 71	385 2-0 195 455 340 1,170 4,250 690 835 1,515 980 500 1,515 980 600 315	20 10 20 5 20 5 20 20	37, 35, 28, 640 24, 28, 640 22, -75 -2, 640 9, 53, 29, 050 10, 750 18, 300 32, 16, 27, 35, 28, 603 28, 603 41, 810 27, 270 48, 630 7, 990 4, 110	255 50 205 1,370 320 1,050 2,135 2,550 3,265 4,445 8,900 7,670 6,523 2,720	2,480 485 995 15,30 4,590 4,590 4,645 19,475 19,475 18,210 26,100 2,555 4,54c 10	31,755 2,740 19,720 15,642 10,45 5,680 3,880 3,870 5,075 2,955 2,955 2,340 1,615 2,66 2,66 2,66 2,66 2,66 2,66 2,66 2,6	4,340 2,715 1,53: 815 540 295 296 155 135 120	20 80 280 1,630 3,233 /,435 3,030	1,325 1,060 1,230 2,430 -,195 -,235 3,025 1,280 1,745 2,220 1,540 1,465 2,705 2,510 1,255	335 225 185 525 220 305 -,340 520 945 710 67 535 980 67 755 355	3 44 5 44 5 7 2 2 3 4 3
homehate .	89,620 1.30 C	37,495 41 8	33,210 37 1	5,140 5 7	ы⊙ 0 7	8,42U 9 4	4,0/5	60 0 L	103,660 110 0	lo,185 15 6	31,760 30 6	32,05 32 0	5,265	2,685 2 8	10 045	4,065 3 9	300 0 2
Under 5 years 0 to 9 3 cars 10 to 11 years 10 to 11 years 10 to 17 years 10 to 17 years 10 to 17 years 10 to 17 years 90 and 21 years 20 to 24 years 25 to 26 years 25 to 26 years 26 to 26 years 26 to 26 years 26 to 26 years 26 to 26 years 26 to 26 years 26 to 26 years 26 to 26 years 26 to 26 years 26 to 26 years 26 to 26 years 26 to 26 years 26 to 26 years 26 to 26 years 26 to 26 years 26 to 26 years 26 to 26 years 27 to 27 years 28 to 26 years 28 to 26 years 28 to 26 years 28 to 26 years 28 to 26 years 28 to 26 years 28 to 26 years 28 to 26 years 28 to 26 years	12,875 9,460 7,550 6,445 4,050 2,415 6,396 2,310 4,040 6,865 5,445 6,775 6,425 0,270 -,9-5 3,790 1,470	2.0 20 105 1,840 3800 1,460 4,135 5,900 7 1400 7 525 5,070 760	9 165 7,757 6,180 7,925 7,925 7,929 2,685 7,207 4,480 1,305 831 431 431 431 431 431 431 431 431 431 4	2,440 1,290 780 420 265 155 165 95 70 55	5 15 15 15 205 190	985 570 600 705 370 335 1,255 505 705 1,035 800 600 550 603 591 1,00	275 145 100 190 120 440 125 325 570 465 472 485 479 295 295 100 10	10 10 5 5 20 5	12,415 9,5=0 7,790 4,523 8,230 1,-73 5,37 5,37 5,650 8,650 7,565 8,650 7,565 8,650 7,565 4,57 1,805	115 20 115 63* .60 475 .,129 .,780 2,045 2,045 2,455 2,455 2,455	5 670 140 3 235 660 2,375 7,763 4,330 5,210 4,302 5,20 4,302 4,002	9,0/0 7,280 6,060 4,920 3,300 1,625 2,435 1,235	2,2_5 1,495 675 470 290 160 165 75 90	15 40 110 475 720 940 985	920 640 71.5 1,240 665 575 1,425 605 820 1,115 730 675 443 815 249 265 270	240 133 95 265 106 100 530 235 395 495 396 272 310 440 270 220	30 25 25 25 26 30 30 30 20
SEREVIPORT Percent	80,955	39,910	29,980 27 0	3,170	790	3,910	3,170	45	89,600 100 0	9,815	37, <i>5</i> 35 41 9	28,61 21.9	2,685	2,625	4,720	3,485	120
Index 5 years (10 to 16 years (10 to 16 years (10 to 16 years (10 to 16 years (15 to 17 years (15 to 17 years (15 to 18 years	10, 750 8, 480 1, 735 5, 770 7, 180 3, 525 6, 260 6, 003 5, 530 5, 800 1, 400 1,	50 -80 -35 -145 -2,545 -2,795 -4,940 -1,190 -2,190 -2,190 -3,100	8, 8a5 7, 325 5, 850 4 215 2, 850 1, 455 910 940 760 420 275 165 185 185 970	1,390 840 490 315 235 80 125 60 10	10 75 10 200 3.0	335 265 335 245 166 180 570 220 350 50* 315 260 190 35 125 100 80	160 50 45 110 20 80 80 82 220 385 410 350 225 417 245 225 65 20	10 55 55 55 55 55 55 55 55 55 55 55 55 55	10,100 7,235 6,587 2,965 2,500 7,790 3,120 6,670 8,000 6,490 6,490 6,490 6,270 4,570 1,240	55 15 40 275 80 19 585 1,000 7,050 1,820 1,845 703	5 932 200 755 4,285 1,495 2,790 5,630 5,140 4,730 6,820 3,345 1,240 200	8,555 6,750 5,750 1,780 2,720 1,060 1,555 815 740 840,480 2265 2265 225 13	1,100 715 440; 290 190 60 160 69 20	15 45 280 595 935 705	3 3 3 3 3 3 3 3 3 3 3 3 3 3 3 3 3 3 3	2 9 150, 95 90 365, 80 285, 835, 370, 465, 485, 300, 265, 170, 340, 120, 265, 175, 95	10 5 5 5 5 10 10 13 13 15 5 5
Non-thine Fercent	29 A05 100 0	12,135 40 7	1,295 37 9	2,220	259 0 9	2,15,	1,71	30 C 1	34,225 100 0	5,230	10,015	1.,515	1,935	925 2 7	2,745	, ens	45 0 1

Index 5 years 0 to 19 years 0 to 19 years 0 to 19 years 0 to 19 years 10 to 10 years 10 years	4,395 3,595 3,060 2,260 2,260 4,40 8,57 1,970 723 1,215 1,765 1,673 1,760 3,130 4,982 1,785 600 525	230 230 530 530 590 1,160 1,460 2,670 1,695 1,475	3,120 2,730 2,405 -,690 1,090 650 332 275 4-0 -20 70 5	920 595 390 435 170 60 75 45 30 5	10 30 40 85	245 225 221 40 90 120 260 90 170 260 140 145 150 160 85 65 45	110 25 40 65 30 35 20 60 160 239 225 160 150 230 239 225 79	10 5	4,350 3,530 3,195 2,500 1,500 1,500 1,500 1,200 1,540 2,625 2,370 2,085 2,270 2,085 3,730 2,045 7,30 610	30 10 20 20 30 110 375 415 525 525 1,1.5 620 935 270	275 70 205 975 395 395 1,415 1,435 1,235 2,070 880 475 70	3,170 2,695 2,582 1,535 -,095 440 648 975 110 375 100 77 77 5 40 40 40 40 40 40 40 40 40 40 40 40 40	785 545 305 485 230 55 97 45 50 20	10 20 125 135 370 265	265 225 245 300 166 137 400 185 215 280 185 170 220 135 165	25 60 65 24 440 440 170 270 295 150 105 55 90 40 20	10 5 5 5 5 5 5 5 5 5 5 5 5 5 5 5 5 5 5 5

Table 59.—PERSONS IN HOUSEHOLDS, BY RELATIONSHIP TO HEAD, COLOR AND SEX AND PERSONS IN QUASI HOUSE-HOLDS, BY COLOR AND SEX FOR THE STATE. 1950 AND 1940, FOR URBAN AND RURAL AREAS AND FOR STANDARD METROPOLITAN AREAS AND CITIES OF 100,000 OR MORE, 1950

Planutes for 1950 hased on 20-percent sample available complex-count data in tables 22 and day Percent in a share winere less than 0 meters have in less than 500 for \$50 or 100 or 1940,

Anna annatus Passa asla-				In	nok deenor			- 7-30		in quan c	ousehouds
Area, census year, color, and sex	Total	Head (number of bouseholds	W ife	(hild	Granden ld	Pare t	Other relave	Lodger	Resident employer	Total	Head number of quasi households)
THE STATE			1		1						
Total 1950 Percent	2 609 8° ₂ 100 J	.~ 335 27 4	*5. 400 2. 1	يمة,عد م ع ود	82,+2	46 -80	437-1	~ 2°5	3 9.7	6725	2 930
Male	1,269,2.0	594 420 11°,°_5	55, 465	*J2,51^	4-,79C 39,83	5 4 .	57 205	25,470	120	41, % 46,085	1 601
Nonwhre Percent	866 265 100 0	222,4A5 25 7	45,5¢	22,2°2 40 7	50,235	12,90,	5+- 840	-4,70e 29	24	L8,900	977
Viale Pemale	414 270 451,995	168,43u ,G3	45,968	178,200	25, 505	2,640	2= 885 3= 955	1. 3.00	263	7 705	×.
Total, 1940	2,325,689 100 C	297,574	449,2.8	970,804	6',402	.9 94C	4 526	74 9.5	4,647	38,191	1,110
Percent Male	1,149,243	499,099 94,-75	449,218	904,336 406 528	34,690	9,442	49 424 65 1C2	34,34	1,656	23, 139	656 454
Urbsa, 1950 Percen*	1 41.1,715	413,880 29 2	310,.00	502, .95	40, 435		78, 20 5 5	43 705	1 305	51,375	2,560
Percen*	100 0 68,650 747,065	29 2 0 89C 82,99C	2. 9 4_0,_00	35 4 253 935 2-8,26	2C 7.0 20,237	28,477	325	2 . 495 2 . 495	185	29,965 21 415	1 360
Nonwhite	423 720	24. ميل 28 C	73,450 16 9	_52,220	24,293	7 24	35 290	_0,290	-90	_3,525	835
Percent	200,120 233 600	84 363 30, 180	73,450	35 1 75,865 6,305	12 095	3.0	5 925 19 365	9 195	140	7 -60 6 065	1 390
Rural nonfarm 1950 .	628 435	169,994) 27 0	131,35	26" 675	.9,coO	8,850	23, 185	,335	390 C 1	15,240	300
Percent Male Female	100 0 309 590 318,745	27 0 -42,395 27 595	20 9	42 6 39 _65 128,510	10,_94	2 725 6 525	1.,335	4,135	8C 310	11,65	4C*
Norwhite	197 790		33,560	83, _0,	2,000	2 5>0	10, 4_5	2,45	. ~	4,900	100
Percent Male Female	100 0 95,440 _02,350	52,442 26 : 39,570 12,675	17 0 I	42.0 42.150 40.955	6 1 6,_\$0 5,820	555	4 9eO 5 555	,985 . 460	40	3,455	70
Rural farm 1950	565 745	1 1	110,0.0	268 970	21,025	8,855	22,.10	3,785	520	860	7
Percent Male Female	100 0 290,890 274,855	130,465 22 1 121,135 9,330	19 4	142 930 126,040	10,885 0 140	2,530 6,325	10,645 11,-62	3,785 0 7 2,480 1,305	0 1 285 275	400 460	31
Nonwhite		48,67	38 94	116 080	13 940	11.4	11 035	2,970	_85	31.0	3:
Male Female	23/,755 _00 0 118,710 116,045	20 7 44,295 4 380	16 ← 38,955	49 8 60 190 56,690	, 125 6,815	1 3 735 2,380	5,000 6,035	0 8 1,265 705	0 1 100 85	120 190	×
STANDARD METROPOLITAN AREAS: 1950											
Percent	150,030 100 0	42 79.5 28 5	34,350 22 9	55,385 3€ 9	3,9.5	2,440	6,825	4 220	&C 0 1	7,710	32:
Vale	22 340 77,690	36,260 6,735	×,350	28 C15 27,1%	2,6 2,050 3,885	1,970	3,1.5 3,650	2 8 2,360 1,860	10	4,995 2,715	18
Housenate	50,380	745, ئىـ 27 3	9,290	17,875 3: 1	2 865	725	s 67*	1,995	30	1,990	110
Percent	23,855 26,525	27 3 -0,382 3,060	9 290	8 985 8,890	5 7 500 1,385	1 5	7 6 1 695 2,_30	4 0 .,160 835	01	1,105	5
Female					A lots		45 240	17 685	73"	23,265	1,13
VEW ORLEANS Percent Male	560,065 200 C	193,360 29 3 153 285	21 3	226, 895 34 4 114 800	12,475 3 0 9,640	15,845 2 / 3 13>	6 8 20,4-5 24 765	9 645	100	13,835	
Fercale	349,015	40,075	140,660	112,095	9,835	12,710	24 765	8 240	634	9,430	46
eonwhite Percent	193,280 100 0	53,680 27 8	34,760	66,365 34 -	10 405	3,535	18,+65 9 6	8,710 4.5	360 0 2	6,255	1
Male Female	\$9,620 103,660	37 492 15,182	3., 760	33,210 33 150	5 140 5,260	650 2,885	8,420 10,045	4,645	300	2,640	
CHREVEPORT	176 .05	49 725	37,535 22 0	58, 95 34 /	2,825	3,39>	8,630	6,655	162	5,34	4.
Male Fernale	80,955 89,600	29 2 39,910 9,815	37, 53:	29,980 28,015	3 4 3,170 2,685	2 0 770 2,625	3,9±0 4,720	3,9 3,170 3,485	45	2,845	20 20
		1			1	1 180		3,530	75	2,035	3
Nonvini te Percent	64,030 200 0 29,805	27,365 27 1 2,135 5,230	10,015	22,810 35 6 11 295	4,155 6 2 2 220	1 8 255	4,900 7 / 2,155 2 745	1 712	30	1.00	12
Female	29,805 34,225	5,230	10,015	11,515	1,032	925	2 745	1,830	45	1,030	
CPTOES: 1950		3			11			1			1
Percent	118,955 100 0 56,905	34,665 29 1 29,200	27,945 23 5	42 275 35 5 21,320	2 855 2 4 1,435	2,020 1.7 365	5,370 4 5 2 490	3,775 3 2 2,085	30	6 195	
Male Fernale	56,905 62 J50	29,200 5,465	27 945	20 955	1,420	1,655	2,375	1,690	45	2,055	3 26
NEW CRILEANS	546,500 100 0	162,610 29 8	.14 565	181,140	16,865	13,527	40,290	16,875	635 0 1	22,18	1
Male -	130 0 254,855 291,645	26,050 36,560	21 0	90,745	8,335 8 530	2,520	18,115 22,175	9 0_	75	13,080	

Table 59—PERSONS IN HOUSEHOLDS, BY RELATIONSHIP TO HEAD, COLOR AND SEX AND PERSONS IN QUASI HOUSEHOLDS, BY COLOR AND SEX FOR THE STATE 1950 AND 19-0, FOR URBAN AND RURAL AREAS, AND FOR STANDARD METRO-POLITAN AREAS AND CITIES OF 100,000 OR MORE, 1950—Con

"Stata" is jet 10.00 based on 20-purper) sample at an access on please-on in data in lables 22 and 34. Percent not shown where less than 0.1 or where once is less than 500 or 1900 or 100 for 1940.

		and the second s	THE REAL PROPERTY.	n,	bousenolds				11	In quan l	aplonesuo
Area census , ear color and sex	Total	head (number of houseboars	Wife	Chir	Grandchad	Paren*	Otoer relative	Lodger	Readent employee	Total	Head (number of quasi households)
CITIES 950Con.											
NEW OFLEAMS-COR		,	1		1						
Notivia e	_7s 790	48,572	28,793	59,560	9,505	3,305	17,275 9 B	8,410	315	6,130	370
Male Percent	_00 · 80,935	27 6 33,6c0	16 4	33 9 29,690	4,565	1 9 595	7,865		45 270	3,525	210
Pemale	9 ,655	,91.	28 790	29,675	4,840	2,700	9,410	3,995	270	2,605	160
SHRETEROTT	12, 520	26,950	27,450	38,400	3,520	2,615	0,620	6,055	.10	5,055	400
Yale	200 €	30 -	22 6	31 4	1,890	525	2,975	2,830	0 1	2,645	185
Female	56,5+C 64,98.	3,000	27,450	28,879	1,090	2,090	3,645	3,222	25 85	2,4_0	21.5

Table 60—PERSONS IN QUASI HOUSEHOLDS, BY AGE, COLOR, AND SEX, FOR THE STATE, URBAN AND RURAL, AND FOR STANDARD METROPOLITAN AREAS OF 100,000 OR MORE. 1950

Based on 20-percent sample]

Area color and sex	All ages	Under 14 years	14 years	15 to 19 vears	20 to 24 years	20 to 29 years	30 to 34 years	35 .o 39 years	40 to 44 years	45 to 49 years	50 to 54 years	55 to 59 years	60 to 64 years	65 to 69 years	70 to 74 years	75 to 79 years	80 to 84 years	85 and over
THE STATE					,	177	1 6	7.0		35	11.00	5 6						100
Total	67,475	4,665	500	9,680	4,585 م	7,330	4,730	4,695	3,990	3,565	3,155	2,785	2, 20	1,875	1,480	1,115	670	365
Male	41,390 26,085	2 290 2,375	275 225	5,225	10,395 4,290	5,220	3,95	2,950	2,560	2,260	1,700	1,555	1,175	950 925	740 735	470 645	250 420	25 240
Nonwhite Maje Female	18,800 11,035 7,765	2,365 1,1.5 1,250	200 105 95	2,035 1,065 970	3,320 2,45 1,45	2,150 1,360 790	1 140 600	1,520 965 935	1,270 790 480	1,070 605 465	870 515 355	72.5 425 290	505 295 210	350 185 162	275 145 130	230 120 110	145 50 95	40 10 30
Urban - Male - Female -	5.,375 29,96, 21,410	3,625 1,740 1,685	350 200 150	7 690 3, 785 3, 905	11,260 7,540 3,720	5,470 3,720 1,750	3,385 2,175 1,2.0	3,300 1,915 1,385	2,915 1,775 1,140	2,715 1,71, 1,005	2,305 1,300 1,005	2,140 1,165 975	*,630 850 780	1,560 78. 780	-,_95 590 605	955 415 540	365 200 365	315 105 21.0
Nonwhite Male. Female	13,525 7 460 6,065	1,995 925 1,070	155 80 75	1,390 600 730	2,345 1,450 895	1,470 820 650	1,235 755 480	1,085 635 450	870 500 370	750 4±0 340	590 365 225	520 280 240	265 165 120	280 45 -35	210 120 90	180 100 80	130 45 85	35 30
Rural nonfarm. Visie. Female	12,240 11,025 4,215	795 445 350	145 75 70	1 815 1,370 445	2,325 2,805 520	1,805 4,465 340	1,315 1,010 305	1 360 1,020 340	1,050 %5 285	520 290	840 440 400	625 390 235	515 303 210	28.° 160 125	250 _40 110	160 55 105	95 40 55	50 20 30
Nonwhite Male Female	4,965 3,405 1 5±0	230 135 95	45 25 20	590 390 200	965 690 275	655 525 130	490 380 110	425 330 95	390 285 105	310 185 125	2°0 145 125	185 145 40	220 130 90	50 30 20	65 25 40	50 20 30	15 5 10	5
Rural farm. Male	860 400 460	245 105 140	5	175 70 105	100 50 50	55 35 20	20 20	35 15 20	25 20 5	40 30 10	20 10 10	20	35 20 15	30 20	35 35 20		10	
Nonwhite Viale Female	310 120 190	140 55 65	•	22 15 40	±0 5 5	25 15 10	اد 10	10	10 5 5	10	10 5 5	10 10		15 5 10				
STANDARD METROPOLITAN AREAS															İ			
Male Female	7,710 4,995 2,715	335 155 180	60 45 15	2,030 1,_30 300	2,900 2,180 720	870 645 225	285 160 125	235 145 90	260 145 115	150 110 45	140 70 70	-55 65 90	95 63 30	70 35 35	20 5 45	35 20 15	20 15 5	15 5 10
Male	1,995 1,105 890	245 130 115	55 45 10	545 265 260	580 355 225	165 95 70	85 40 45	65 45 20	105 55 50	40 20 20	35 10 25	10 10 5	-5 10 5	15 15	15	10	5	
NEW ORIEANS . Male Female	23,265 13,835 5,430	2,020 995 1,025	205 120 85	2,675 1,375 1,300	4,385 2,850 1,535	2,7*0 1,910 8*0	1,260 50b	1,670 1,000 670	1,250 815 435	1,210	1,055 655 400	1,000 990 410	755 430 325	750 415 335	6±0 280 330	590 210 380	370 11.0 260	75 45 430
Nonwhite	6,255 3,615 2,640	1,015 485 530	95 40 55	640 320 320	1,085 710 3°5	755 4oC 295	255 312 200	530 300 230	355 245 110	325 170 150	230 165 65	210 130 80	135 85 50	110	60 30 25	35 35 30	75 25 50	15
SHREVEPORT Male Female	2,345 2,845 2,500	730 340 390	35 15 20	490 175 315	935 471 460	330 255	365 215 150	370 2.5 155	300 170 130	3.5 225 90	295 185 110	225 125 100	100 95	18* 85 100	140 105 35	75 55 201	75 10 65	30 20 10
Norwhite Male	2,035 1,005 1,030	210 220 290	20	175 85 90	325 155 170	235 95 140	160 90 70	135 80 55	110 45 70	65 35 30	85 50 35	50 35 15	20	40	50. 40	25	20	5

 $\begin{array}{c}

Table 61.—KINDERGARTEN ENROLLMENT OF CHILDREN 5 AND 6 YEARS OLD, BY COLOR AND SEX, FOR THE STATE, URBAN AND RURAL, AND FOR CITIES OF 100,000 OR MORE 1950

[Based on 20-percent sample, available complete-count data in tables 15 and 33. Percent not shown where less than 0.1 or where base is less than 500]

Area color and age	Both sexes Total	Both sexes Enrolled in kindergarten Number	Both sexes Enrolled in kindergarten Percent	Male Total	Male Enrolled in kindergarten Number	Male Enrolled in kindergarten Percent	Female Total	Female Enrolled in kindergarten Number	Female Enrolled in kindergarten Percent
THE STATE									
Total	115,610	7,820	6.8	58,805	3,925	6.7	56,805	3,895	6.9
5 years old	57,705	5,880	10.2	29,395	2,925	10.0	28,310	2,955	10.4
6 years old	57,905	1,940	3.4	29,410	1,000	3.4	28,495	940	3.3
Nonwhite	42,605	1,965	4.6	21,545	995	4.6	21,060	970	4.6
5 years old	21,455	1,405	6.5	10,860	695	6.4	10,595	710	6.7
6 years old	21,150	560	2.6	10,685	300	2.8	10,465	260	2.5
Urban	55,070	7,195	13.1	28,045	3,610	12.9	27,025	3,585	13.3
5 years old	27,430	5,545	20.2	14,085	2,780	19.7	13,345	2,765	20.7
6 years old	27,640	1,650	6.0	13,960	830	5.9	13,680	820	6.0
Nonwhite	18,395	1,805	9.8	9,265	905	9.8	9,130	900	9.9
5 years old	9,215	1,325	14.4	4,660	665	14.3	4,555	660	14.5
6 years old	9,180	480	5.2	4,605	240	5.2	4,575	240	5.2
Rural nonfarm	30,695	425	1.4	15,790	215	1.4	14,905	210	1.4
5 years old	15,495	240	1.5	7,870	105	1.3	7,625	135	1.8
6 years old	15,200	185	1.2	7,920	110	1.4	7,280	75	1.0
Nonwhite	10,095	95	0.9	5,100	55	1.1	4,995	40	0.8
5 years old	5,150	50	1.0	2,550	20	0.8	2,600	30	1.2
6 years old	4,945	45	0.9	2,550	35	1.4	2,395	10	0.4

Area color and age	Both sexes Total	Both sexes Enrolled in kindergarten Number	Both sexes Enrolled in kindergarten Percent	Male Total	Male Enrolled in kindergarten Number	Male Enrolled in kindergarten Percent	Female Total	Female Enrolled in kindergarten Number	Female Enrolled in kindergarten Percent
THE STATE—Con.									
Rural farm	29,845	200	0.7	14,970	100	0.7	14,875	100	0.7
5 years old	14,780	95	0.6	7,440	40	0.5	7,340	55	0.7
6 years old	15,065	105	0.7	7,530	60	0.8	7,535	45	0.6
Nonwhite	14,115	65	0.5	7,180	35	0.5	6,935	30	0.4
5 years old	7,090	30	0.4	3,650	10	0.3	3,440	20	0.6
6 years old	7,025	35	0.5	3,530	25	0.7	3,495	10	0.3
CITIES									
BATON ROUGE	4,845	295	6.1	2,375	150	6.3	2,470	145	5.9
5 years old	2,385	225	9.4	1,190	110	9.2	1,195	115	9.6
6 years old	2,460	70	2.8	1,185	40	3.4	1,275	30	2.4
NEW ORLEANS	18,770	5,120	27.3	9,420	2,540	27.0	9,350	2,580	27.6
5 years old	9,370	3,980	42.5	4,660	1,980	42.5	4,710	2,000	42.5
6 years old	9,400	1,140	12.1	4,760	560	11.8	4,640	580	12.5
Nonwhite	6,710	1,345	20.0	3,245	660	20.3	3,465	685	19.8
5 years old	3,430	1,025	29.9	1,615	505	31.3	1,815	520	28.7
6 years old	3,280	320	9.8	1,630	155	9.5	1,650	165	10.0
SHREVEPORT	4,605	365	7.9	2,345	180	7.7	2,260	185	8.2
5 years old	2,395	290	12.1	1,260	150	11.9	1,135	140	12.3
6 years old	2,210	75	3.4	1,085	30	2.8	1,125	45	4.0

Table 62.—SCHOOL ENROLLMENT, BY SINGLE YEARS OF AGE, COLOR, AND SEX, FOR THE STATE, 1950 AND 1940, FOR URBAN AND RURAL AREAS, AND FOR CITIES OF 100,000 OR MORE, 1950

[Statistics for 1950 based on 20-percent sample available complete-count data in tables 15 and 33. Percent not shown where less than 0.1, or where base is less than 500 for 1950 or 100 for 1940]

Age	1950 Both sexes Total	1950 Both sexes Enrolled in school Number	1950 Both sexes Enrolled in school Percent	1950 Male Total	1950 Male Enrolled in school Number	1950 Male Enrolled in school Percent	1950 Female Total	1950 Female Enrolled in school Number	1950 Female Enrolled in school Percent	1940 Both sexes Total	1940 Both sexes Enrolled in school Number	1940 Both sexes Enrolled in school Percent	1940 Male Total	1940 Male Enrolled in school Number	1940 Male Enrolled in school Percent	1940 Female Total	1940 Female Enrolled in school Number	1940 Female Enrolled in school Percent
	The State 1950—Total									The State 1940								
Total, 5 to 29	1,146,600	580,580	50.6	562,710	300,845	53.5	583,890	279,735	47.9	(1)			(1)			(1)		
Total, 5 to 24	935,040	566,215	60.6	461,980	289,495	62.7	473,060	276,720	58.5	928,606	504,399	54.3	460,041	252,854	55.0	468,565	251,545	53.7
5 years [2]	57,705	4,960	8.6	29,395	2,450	8.3	28,310	2,510	8.9	46,106	4,505	9.8	23,324	2,206	9.5	22,782	2,299	10.1
6 years [2]	57,905	39,845	68.8	29,410	19,980	67.9	28,495	19,865	69.7	44,575	24,697	55.4	22,330	11,934	53.4	22,245	12,763	57.4
7 years	56,185	52,540	93.5	27,945	26,040	93.2	28,240	26,500	93.8	44,430	39,059	87.9	22,361	19,444	87.0	22,069	19,615	88.9
8 years	54,085	51,175	94.6	27,525	26,035	94.6	26,560	25,140	94.7	47,490	43,724	92.1	23,969	21,913	91.4	23,521	21,811	92.7
9 years	50,510	48,130	95.3	25,825	24,515	94.9	24,685	23,615	95.7	45,375	42,564	93.8	22,861	21,372	93.5	22,514	21,192	94.1
10 years	50,060	47,925	95.7	25,275	24,140	95.5	24,785	23,785	96.0	48,503	45,553	93.9	24,546	22,954	93.5	23,957	22,599	94.3
11 years	46,550	44,865	96.4	23,645	22,780	96.3	22,905	22,085	96.4	45,020	42,481	94.4	22,663	21,320	94.1	22,357	21,161	94.7
12 years	49,630	47,590	95.9	25,485	24,305	95.4	24,145	23,285	96.4	50,342	47,029	93.4	25,562	23,697	92.7	24,780	23,332	94.2
13 years	46,325	44,105	95.2	23,235	22,080	95.0	23,090	22,025	95.4	50,966	46,635	91.5	25,596	23,269	90.9	25,370	23,366	92.1
14 years	43,655	40,805	93.5	22,030	20,575	93.4	21,625	20,230	93.5	49,005	42,532	86.8	24,458	21,063	86.1	24,547	21,469	87.5
15 years	43,320	37,850	87.4	21,495	18,805	87.5	21,825	19,045	87.3	47,526	37,071	78.0	23,599	18,212	77.2	23,927	18,859	78.8
16 years	41,960	31,215	74.4	20,955	15,540	74.2	21,005	15,675	74.6	48,945	31,807	65.0	23,946	15,249	63.7	24,999	16,558	66.2
17 years	42,265	25,610	60.6	20,580	12,520	60.8	21,685	13,090	60.4	47,101	21,891	46.5	23,766	10,875	45.8	23,335	11,016	47.2
18 years	43,105	16,435	38.1	20,690	8,340	40.3	22,415	8,095	36.1	50,969	14,633	28.7	25,013	7,465	29.8	25,956	7,168	27.6
19 years	40,700	9,875	24.3	18,695	5,200	27.8	22,005	4,675	21.2	45,857	8,387	18.3	22,162	4,597	20.7	23,695	3,790	16.0
20 years	41,145	6,435	15.6	18,410	3,535	19.2	22,735	2,900	12.8	46,096	4,997	10.8	21,371	2,834	13.3	24,725	2,163	8.7
21 years	41,580	4,775	11.5	20,080	3,220	16.0	21,500	1,555	7.2	44,033	3,086	7.0	21,959	1,970	9.0	22,074	1,116	5.1
22 years	41,895	4,190	10.0	19,765	3,160	16.0	22,130	1,030	4.7	42,648	1,796	4.2	20,436	1,155	5.7	22,212	641	2.9
23 years	43,670	4,235	9.7	21,110	3,370	16.0	22,560	865	3.8	42,011	1,152	2.7	20,083	763	3.8	21,928	389	1.8
24 years	42,790	3,655	8.5	20,430	2,905	14.2	22,360	750	3.4	41,608	800	1.9	20,036	562	2.8	21,572	238	1.1
25 years	43,730	3,315	7.6	20,430	2,635	12.9	23,300	680	2.9	(1)			(1)			(1)		
26 years	41,640	3,265	7.8	19,910	2,625	13.2	21,730	640	2.9	(1)			(1)			(1)		
27 years	42,850	2,780	6.5	20,740	2,120	10.2	22,110	660	3.0	(1)			(1)			(1)		
28 years	43,195	2,545	5.9	20,465	2,015	9.8	22,730	530	2.3	(1)			(1)			(1)		
29 years	40,145	2,460	6.1	19,185	1,955	10.2	20,960	505	2.4	(1)			(1)			(1)		

[1] School enrollment not available for persons 25 to 29 years old.

[2] Enrollment figures for 1940 include some kindergarten enrollment, which was excluded in 1950 (shown separately in table 61).

						7				SHREVEPORT s cars old 6 years old	4,305 2,395 2,2_0	365 290 75	44 4	2 345 1,260 1 08.	180 250 30	7 7	2,260 -,135 1,-25	485 140 45	12 3

Table 62—SCHOOL ENROLLMENT, BY SINGLE YEARS OF AGE, COLOR, AND SEX, FOR THE STATE, 1950 AND 1940, FOR URBAN AND RURAL AREAS, AND FOR CITIES OF 100,000 OR MORE, 1950

[Stausucs for 1950 based on 20-percent sample available complete-count data in tables 15 and 33. Percent not shown where less tonn 0.1, or where base is less than 500 for 1304 or 100 for 1540]

	В	oth sexes		_	Male			Female		В	oth sexes			Male			Female	
Age	Total	Enrolled school		Total	Enrolled		Total	Envolled		Total	Enrobed		Total	Enrolled	i m	m !	Enrolle schoo	d m ol
91	Total	Number	Per	Total	Number	Per cent	Total	Number	Per-	Total	Number	Per- cent	Lotal	Number	Per- cent	Total	Number	Per-
				The State	1950 To	ra1			1				The S	State 1940			1.2	
Total, 5 to 29	1,146,600	580,580	50 6	562,730	300,845	53 5	583,890	279,735	47 3	(2)	4		(2)			(1)		
Total, 5 to 24	932,00	566,225	60 6	+62,980	289,495	62 7	473_060	276,720	28 5	928,606	504,399	54 3	460,041	252,854	55 0	408,565	251,545	53 7
5 years 2 6 years 4 7 years 8 8 years 10 9 years 10 10 years 11 years 12 years 13 years 13 years 13	57,705 57,905 56,185 54,085 50,510 50,060 46,550 49,630 4c,325	4,960 59,845 52,540 51,175 48,130 47,025 44,865 47,590 44,105	58 B	29,395 29,410 27,945 27,525 25,825 25,275 23,645 23,235 22,030	2,450 19,980 26,040 26,035 24,515 24,140 22,780 24,305 22,080 20,575	8 3 67 9 93 2 94 6 94 9 95 5 96 3 95 4 95 4	28,310 28,495 28,240 26,560 24,685 24,785 22,905 24,145 23,090 21,625	2,510 19,865 26,500 25,140 23,615 23,785 22,085 23,285 22,025 20,230	8 9 69 7 93 8 94 7 95 7 96 0 96 4 95.4	45,106 44,575 44,430 47,490 45,375 48,503 45,020 50,342 50,966 49,005	4,505 24,697 39,059 43,724 42,564 45,553 42,481 47,029 46,635 42,532	9 8 55 4 87 9 92 ± 93 8 93 9 94 4 91 5 86 8	23,324 22,330 22,361 23,969 22,861 24,546 22,663 25,562 25,596 24,458	2,206 1,934 19,444 21,913 2-,772 22,954 21,320 23,697 23,269 21,063	9 5 53 4 87 0 91 4 93 5 93 5 94 1 92 7 90 9	22,782 22,245 22,069 23,521 22,514 23,957 22,357 24,780 25,370 24,547	2,299 12,763 19,645 21,811 21,192 22,599 21,161 23,332 2,356 21,469	38 9 92 7 94 1 94 3 94 7 94 2 92 1
14 years 15 years 16 years 17 years 18 years 19 years 19 years 20 years 22 years 22 years 22 years 24 years 24 years	43,320 41,960 42,265 43,105 40,700 41,145 41,550 41,895 43,670 42,790	31,850 31,215 25,010 16,435 9,875 6,435 4,775 4,190 4,235 3,655	87 4 4 74 4 4 60 6 38 1 24 3 15 6 11 0 0 9 7 8 5	21,495 20,955 20,580 20,690 18,695 48,410 20,080 19,765 21,110 20,430	20,5% 15,540 2,520 8,340 5,200 3,535 3,220 3,160 3,370 2,905	87 5 74 2 60 8 40 3 27 8 19 2 16 0 16 0 16 0 14 2	21,825 21,825 21,005 21,685 22,415 22,005 22,735 21,500 22,130 22,360 22,360	29,045 15,675 13,090 8,095 4,675 2,900 1,555 1,030 865 750	87 3 74 6 60 4 36 1 21 2 12 8 7 2 4 7 3 8 3 4	47,526 48,945 47,101 50,969 45,857 46,096 44,033 42,648 42,011 41,608	37,071 31,807 21,831 14,633 8,387 4,997 3,086 1,796 +,-52 800	78 0 65 0 46 5 28 7 8 3 10 8 7 0 4 2 2 7 1 9	23,599 23,946 23,766 25,013 22,,62 2,,37, 21,959 20,436 20,083	13,212 15,249 10,875 7,465 4,997 2,834 4,970 1,155 763	77 2 63 7 45 8 29 8 20 7 13 9 9 0 5 7 2 8	23,927 24,999 23,335 25,956 23,695 24,725 22,074 22,212 21,928 2_,5~2	18,859 _6,558 _1,016 7,168 3,790 2,163 1 _16 64_ 389 236	78 8 66 2 47 2 27 c 16 0 8 7 5 1 2 9
25 years	43,730 41,640 42,850 43,195 40,145	3,3,5 3,265 2,780 2,545 2,460	76 78 05 59 61	20,430 19,910 20,740 20,465 19,185	2,635 2,625 2,120 2,015 1,955	12 9 10 2 9 5 10 2	23,300 21,730 22,110 22,730 20,960	680 640 660 530 505	29 30 32 4	(1) (1) (1) (1) (1)			(1) (1) (1) (1) (1)			(1) (1) (1) (1) (1)		M. A.

¹ School enrollment not available for persons 25 to 29 years old.

⁸ Eurollment figures for 1940 include some kindergarten enrollme soh was excluded in 1950 (shown separately in table 61)

Tabe 62—SCHOOL ENROLLMENT, EY SINGLE YEARS OF AGE, COLOR, AND SEX, FOR THE STATE, 1950 AND 1940, FOR URBAN AND RURAL AREAS, AND FOR CITIES OF 100,000 OR MORE, 1950—Con

[Statistics for 90] based to 31-percent sample. 2 malls complete-ours cata to takes 15 and 33. For east not shown where less than 0.1 or where base is eas from 500 for 1850 or 100 to 1940]

(Statistics for 92) base	-	reat sample. 1	1	Vale		remule	-	В	our sexes			Male			Female	Winds of
1		ar follod in	1	I are led an	l	Enrolle			Enrolled		74	Darollec schoo			En oller	d m
Age	T tal	mber Per		achoos Per-	Total	/most	Per-	Total	Number	Pur-	Total	Numper	Pe-	Total	\umber	Per-
		*_mooi rec	Tr S . c	- 12-New hile	_		cent			- Control	Jrban	_950Tota	al			-
		1	1								204 (25	2/8 200	51 Q	=_2,780	135,480	1
Total, 4 to 29	3×35 21,45 21 -53	200,735 54 5,-55 0	5 - 860 71 -0.685	2 55 0 7	205, 300 _C *9*	1,200	11 3	598,2.5 27 430	283,680	9 4	285,435	1,250	89	13,345 3,680	1,32-	9 9
C years	20,12.	18. 344 2	91 9,875	6,950 65 0 8,945 30 9 9,575 32 2	220 20,210	7 105	58 5	27 540 27,800	19,87; 26,340 24,115 22,020	94 71 9 94 7 96 2	13,960 13,965 2,725	1,250 9 965 13 190 12,225	94 5	23,832	بازاردا بازاردا 1. 890	95 0
o years.	18, 350		10 365	8.9051 94 -	0,390	8,340	92 8 94 - 92 5 95 8	25,080 22,930 22 170	22,020	96 0 95 8 97 5 96 8 96 5	1,600 11,08- 10,315 10,640	10,750 10,750 10,050 10,230	94 5 96 1 95 8 97 0	11 330	10,905	
10 years 11 years 12 years	19 075 1 19 075	.87 9: - ,287 9:	8 9,415 6 8,473 4,823	8,850 9- 0 8,260 90 J	9,645 8 260 9,275	8,805	75 8 35 b	20,785	20 260	97 5	10,315	10,050	97 4 96 1 96 6	10,490	U) 685	97 5
3 years			6,670	81062 e3 3	A,00,	8,575	24.5	21,600 20,795	19,575	96 5 96 1	9,575	9,"13	ac p	9,570	9 865	96 4
14 years.	16,4-0 16,2-0 15,48€	.5,044 22 13 525 62 20 940 69	5 F 275 8 0,050 1,595 7 285	6,710 83 4 9,240 69 0	8,290 8 090	6 825	99.2	d dan	14,580	90 4	9,240 8,820 8,885	9 220 0,420 7,135	96 3 91 1 80 9	9,570 9,590 9,615	8,605 7,445 9 590	96 0 90 7 77 4 63 9
16 years		,790 J	7 - 282	3,655 50.2	7,800 9,200 7,475 8,335	2,700 4,2-0 2,745 1,620	33 1	18,435 19,205 22,255 22,940 23,320	12,665 9,480 6,755	79 1 66 0 42 f	9,950	6,075 4,775 3,545 2,640 2,300	68 4 48 0 36 3 28 0 22 3 21 1 20 7	9,515 10,320 12,335 13,-70 13,890 13,445 13,865	4,735	63 9
19 years	13 645 4,305 22,79	4, 760 37 2 850 20 1,755 _2 1,135 R	3 7,-70 9 6,170 5,970 9 5,935	1,230 19 9	8,335		12 5	22,940	6,755	29.4	9,770	2,640	36 3 28 0	13,_70 13,890	3,210 2,215 1,250	24 4 15 0
27 Years - 22 Years 23 Years		2 850 20 1,755 _2 1,135 R 1 070 8	5,970 9 5 935 0 6,385	714 11 8	7,330 7,330 7,345 7,075	-,65 355 -05	6 8	24 61.5 25 210 26,905	4,555 3,670 3,080 3 .95	29.4 20.8 14.9 12.2 11.8	11,170 11 345 12,625	2,300	21 1	13,865	690	38 2 24 4 16 0 8 6 5 0 4 1 3 3
23 years 24 'ears	12,380	1 070 8 1 100 8 1 040 8	7 6,235 0 5 885	8.60 12 A 8.5 13 9	7,075	25	3,2	27,480	2,720	10 0	12 860	2,245	113	14 36.	470	100
25 years 27 years	13,140	950 ,	2 5,655 7 5 560	750 ;3 4 680 4 2	7,490)95 140	26	27,765 26,040 27,105	2,450	8 8	12,790	2,000	15 6 15 1 11 9	14,975	425 420 440	30
	12,170 14,640 12,475	750 6	0 5 6.0	680 4 2 65 11 2 65 11 0 550 11 4	6,630 6,685 6,865 6 180	185 135 175	28	27,105 27,415 25,390	1,965 1,695 1 645	8 9 7 2 6 2 6 5	12 840 13,010 1_,875	1,940 1,350 1,350	11 9	14,975 13,8.5 14,345 14,405 13,515	345 310	24
29 years	11,020	725 0	6 4,8-0 Urban	550 1 4 1950—Norwitate	6 180	1/3	40	25,390	1 043	-	turel nonfe			3,323		-
Total, 5 to 29	187,835	92,485 49	2 26 772	46 305 _3 4	101,100	46,130	42.0	283,950	145,35	51 1	141,840	75,795	52 9	142,110	77,040	49 3
о уевля	9 180	1,080 11	2 86,735 7 4,660 7 4,601	620 10 1	4,575	610	40 o 23 4 70.3	15,495	1,250	81	7,870	655 5 180	8 3 65 4	7,625 7,280 7,105 7,025	600	7 9
6 years	3,925 5 790	8 395 94 8,305 94	4.370	4.065 93 0	4.555	4,230	95 1		13,475	92 9	7 400	6,865		7,105	6,610	67 7 93 0 94 0
8 years 10 years	7,695 7,70 7,240		3,925 1 3,925 0 3,615	4,135 93 7 3,725 94 9 3 550 95 8	4,375 3,970 4,065	4,030 4,170 3,785 3,980	95 3 96 4	13,925	13,475 13,485 12,945 12,885	92 0	7,030	6,620	94 2 95 4	6,690		95 9
12 years	7,890	7,025 96	0 3,615	3,500 96 8	3.625	3, 525 3, 885 3, 685	95 3 95 3 96 4 97 2 96 5	14,305 13,625 -3,495 12,435 10,375 11,800	12,885 12,815 11,275	66 5 92 9 94 2 93 0 95 5 95 6 95 8	6,435	6,162 6,780 5,545	95 8 95 8 96 0	6,310 5,970	6,4.5 5 720 6,035	95 ° 95 3 95 6 96 0
18 years	7,290 6 905						30 C	11,800		95 6	5,620		92 /		5,730	96 0
Lo years 16 years 17 years	7,040	6,195 88		3,290 94 3 3,790 90 4 2,400 77 9	3,415 3,620 3,465 3,495 4,040 3,990	3,225 3,105 2,605	9' 4 85 8 74 7	11,270 11,055 10 765	10,435 9,535 7,775	26 3	5,260	4,090	87 6 3 2	5,650 5,795 5,325 5,325 4,405	4,925 3,685 2,985	85 0
18 years	6,455	3,725 p7 2,475 p4	2,960 5 3,125 4 2,730 3 2,600	2,400 77 9 1,7_5 97 1 050 33 6 645 23 6	3,495	4,010	37	10,100	5,980	72 2 56 8 33 2 16 7 9 7	2,205 4,775	2,995	57 5 35 5 17 8	5,325 5,325	2,660	56 ± 31 2
19 years 20 years	6 950	1,505 22 925 13 665 10	2,730	385 14 8	4,300	660 540	264	9,35	1,555	9 7	5,070 5,985	809 545 450	10 21	5,060 4,865	750 435 205	86
21) ears. 22 years 23 years.	6,045 7,420	665 10 660: 3 785 10 710 9	0 2,920 9 3,-60 4 3,340	385 14 8 430 14 7 470 14 9 495 17 8	4,350 3,725 4,260	190 190	45	9,850 9,950 9,730	625 745 625		4,925	5°5 460	90	2,025	220	8644
24 vears	7, 15			575 17 3	4,275	135	3 +	9,730	575	5 9	4,680	420	00	5,050	155	3 +
25 vears	7,570 7,180 7,665	585 7 500 7 570 7	7 3,1.5 0 3,2.0 4 3,4.5 1 3,430	485 15 o 425 13 2 465 13 4	4 455 3,970 4,190	100 75 305	2 2 2 2 2 2 2 2 2 2 2 2 2 2 2 2 2 2 2 2	9,915 9,115 9,770	590 595 540	6 0 6 5 5 5	4,705	~35 455 385	91 108 78 99	5, ±20 4,890 4,805 5,190	155 140 155	
26 years	7,570 6,670	460 6 490 7	3,430	465 13 4 375 10 9 370 13 3	4,140 3,885	250	2 1	9,685	545 520	5 6	4,965 4,795 4,315	445 410	99	5,190 4,455	100	25
			Eurel nonfe	rm 1950Nouwh	7.0				7		Rura_ for	n 19501	otal			
Total, 5 to 29 _	90,675	47,360 52	2 44,580	23,900 53 7	45,995	23,370	50 8	264,435	151,765	57 4	13>,435	77 330	57 3	129,000	74,215	57 5
5 years	5,150 4,942	525 ±0 3,220 65	2 550	260 10 2 1,550 00 8	2,600 2,395	265	10 2 69 7	15,065	1,130 9,800	7 6 65 4	7,530	545 4,835	7 1 64 2	7,340 7,35 7,300 7,180 6,760	595 5,025	8 0 66 7
7 years	4,800 4,890 4,535	4,405 91 4,525 92	8 2,420 5 2,530 4 2,260	2,205 91 1 2,345 92 7 2 110 93 4	2,380	2,260	92 4 92 4 93 4	13,880	12,725	92 4	8,580	6,930	92 3	7,300 7,180	6,740 €,645	92 3 92 5
9 years 10 years 11 years	4,740	4,525 92 4,235 93 4,490 94 3,645 94 4,345 94		2.483 92 0	2,275	2,125	95 A	14,682 13,955 _4,395 _3,330	13,165 13,585 12,720	94 9 94 4 95 /	7,385	6,780 6,920	93 7	6,760 7,010 6,435	6 385	92 5 94 5 95 1 95 6 95 5
12 years 13 years	3,855 4,400 4,055	3,642 94 4,245 94 3,850 95	6 2,150 2 2,255 2 1,915	2,035 94 7 2,115 93 8 1,850 35 6	1,705 2,144 2,140	1,410 2,730 2,630	94 6	14,655	13,860	94 0	7,335 7,503 7,503 7,383 6,893 7,780 7,351	6,565 7,295 6,825	93 8	6,875	6,665 6,155 6,565 6,430	95 5
14 years	3,750	3,430 91	.,850			100000			11.965	90.4	6 835	6,145	89 9		5,820	00.0
15 years 16 years - 17 years -	3,695 3,485 3,340	2 955 80 2,30 66 1,575 47	0 1,775 1,740 1,630 1,545 7 -,505	,710 92 2 1 420 80 0 1,165 67 0 730 44 8	1,895 1,920 1,745 1,710 1,920	1,720 1,535 1,165 845	80 0 66 8	13,435 12,760 -2,530 -0,750 8,425 7,695 7,1-35	11,290 8,860 6,965	84 0 69 4 55 6	6,995	4,315	82 6 65 9	6,405 6,440 6,210	5,515 4 545	85 6 7, 2 58 2 36 2
18 years	3,465 3,115 3,535	935 27 615 19	1,545	355 23 0	1,920	580 385 340 120	30.2	8,425	6,965 3,600 1,565	33 5	6,490 5,965 4,395	3 450 1,870 450	31 3	6,040 4,785 4,030	1,515 1 730 7_5	36 2 17 7
20 years -	3,535 2,940 3,045	51 14 250 8	0 1,545 -,505 6 1,595 5 1,375	21 . 12 4	1,610 1,940 1,560 1,530	3C0 120	23 9 -5 5 7 7	7,695	600	78	3,91^	350 260	9.0	3,785	250 190	8 6
22 years 23 years 24 years	3,045 2,870 2,910	615 19 51 14 250 8 270 8 245 8 230 7	9 1,510 5 1,380 9 1,303	130 9 5 160 10 6 140 13 0 175 11 6	1,535 1,490 1,405	110 65 55	12		365 415	33 5 48 6 7 6 3 5 4 5 9	3,495	300	6 6 7 0 8 1	3,240	120 115	3 5
95 70470	2 955	230 7	8 1 405		1,550 1,550			5 880	360 270	0.4	2,890	24U 200	8 3	2,990	120	40
26 years.	2,630	230 7 225 6 185 6 180 7 160 7	6 1,240 7 1,370	185 14 9	1 390	50	3 6	5,885	3 ₂ 0 275 305	4 5 5 3 4 7 5 0	2,860	230	7 C 8 D	3,025	80 65	26
28 years 20 years	2,550	180 7 180 7	1 1,005	155 14 1 135 12 7	_,400 1,450 1,185	25 25	27	6,095 5,985	305 295	5 0	2,960	220	74	3,135 2,990	85 85	2 2 7 2 8
							-									

Tab'e 62—SCHOOL ENROLLMENT BY SINGLE YEARS OF AGE, COLCR, AND SEX, FOR THE STATE, 1950 AND 1940 FOR URBAN AND RURAL AREAS, AND FOR CITIES OF 100,000 OR MORE 1950—Con

Statustics for 1900 based on 20-review sample available complete-count data in labels 19 and 32 Pt. mer. to some notice than (1 ... where case is less mer of 1 1940 on 1941).

	Be	oth sexes			Male			er.c.e		B	th sexes-	1		alale	-	-	emale	-
Age	Total	Enrole	d in	To-al	Enrolee school	a. i		Enrolle	m		En-mea	m		Enreller	ın		Enrie	
	100	Number	Per-	1041	\umber	Per-	Total	Number	Per cen*	Total	Number i	Per-	Total	Namine.	Par-	Total	Number	Per
				Rural fare	- 195J k	mwni te							Baton	Rouge 195	-		-	Cac
Toral, 5 to 29	117,625	65,890	46 D	58,920	32,920	25 9	58,70	32,9%	26.2	54,875	26,3.5	4.	26,4.5	14,680	4 1	27.9nt	4, 635	41
years	7 090	650 4,495 5,5°> 6,220	9 2 64 0	3 650 3, 30	325 2,215 2,6-1	8 9 62 7 87 7	9 //*	325	9 4	2,385	22,	724	.,.30	10		-, ir:	1	69
vears	6,300 6,915 6,420 0 550	5,220	88954401	3,50 3,40 3,40 3,25 2,90 3,690 3,305	3,095	90 0	3,475 3,475 3,475 3,47 3,293 2,930 3,445	2,950 3,-2, 2,930 3,-30	89 8 89 93 2 93 2 93 93 95 95 95 95 8	2,385 2,467 4,310 ,960	2,5	72 4 92 4 93 4 75 9 77 8 95 9 95 9	. 200	1,520	8 50 MG 148	255 775 865	290 290 920	90 95 95 95
0 vears	5 835 6,795	5 700 6,120 5 510 6 300 5,825	38788	2,905	3,095 3,070 3,020 2,730	90 0 93 7 92 8 94 0 93 2 89 7	2,930	2,780 2,950 2,860	94 1	1,830 1,580 1,665	1,5-5	3. 8	9-5 975 800,	890 92 - 790 755	29	255 775	920 965 831 751	37
3 years 4 years	5,78	5,825		3,305	3,440 2 %	1				1,58,			800 800 800	765		. 195	840 755	95
o vears	5,60 5,635 5,200	4,385 1,60° 2,495	88 4 78 2 6/ 0 4/ 2 86 6 1 2 8 6 9 4 7 4 5	2 851 2,775 2 695 2,830	2,550 2,200 1,675	87 0 77 1 60 4	2,835	2,550 2,485 1,430	85 3 79 -	1 355 1 355	- 4-C	97 2 93 3	655 610 705 2,010 1,240 2,070	620 535	94 71	960 760	640 640 550	96 91 76 99 51 36 25
7 years	5 200 5 070 3 840	1,350	47 2 26 6	2,830	1.210	44 9 21 8 18 3	2,751 2,860 2 795 2,270	2,185 1,-30 1,285 740 375	79 . 67 5 . 9 5 32 6	1 5,0	-,08. -,065 240	8. 9 69 6 56 1 46 4 36 1 23 8 2 9	7,000	495 650	7 18 6 4 6	825	570 590	54
0 years 1 years 2 years	3,210	3.5 220 140	8 2 6 9	1,935 1,775 1,640	3>5	6 2	1,675 2 045 1,570	500	20 0 9 8 7 0 3 6 3 4	2,000 2,000 2,525 2,525	9,5 685 625	36 -	1,240	650 (80 335	49 8	1,420	570 590 5.5 370 150 100	25
23 vears	2,992	135	47	1,640 1,445 1,545 1,095	85 85 65	6 C 5 6 5 9	1 575	35 25 25 26 26	3 6 3 4 2 6	2,622 2,895 2,795	625 615 400	23 8	1,4.0	535 525 533 395	37 6 27 2	-,484 1 440	1:00 105 70	1 7 4
25 years	2,620 4,380 2,205	735 92 95	5 2 4 0 4 3 4 7	1,110 1,110	90	79	1 49.	45 25	3.0	a phi.			1 440	35C			50	١,
26 years 2" years 28 years 29 years	2,205 2,355 2,100	95 1_0 75	4 3 4 7 3 6	1,110	70 65 80	63	1,09	 25	200	2 653 2,655 2,665	245 260	3 5 t t 6	-,395 ,260 -,340	220	24 3 22 6 15 5 16 4	1,435 1 260 4,375 1,325	35 50 60	1
an years		- "	3 6	New Orlea	ns 1920-	4 5	- 1+0	3.0	41	2,-55	195	-	ev Orlean	175	14 2	1,245	20	-
Total 5 to 29	215 810	102,200	47 .	_03, >15	52,855	21 al	.13,295	40,345	43 6	74.910	37,040	40 4	34 825	18,595	53 4,	-n on-	18 445	Γ.,
5 years	9,370 9,400 10,185	1,235 7,135 9,785		4.660	1.612	.2.6	4 710	1.00		3 430 3 263	F0#		. p' 5	200		1 815	305	16
years		9,785 8,685	96 1 97 0 97 2 97 1 97 3 97 3 97 2	4,760 2,110 4,485 3 995	4,900 4,360 3,860	95 9 97 2 96 6 97 0 97 0	9,075 4 465 3,960	3,520 4,885 4,325 3 87* 3 69 3,655 3,340	96 9 96 9 97 3	3 030	2,375 3,750 3,475 2,950 2,975 2,755 2,755 2,345	14 7 72 4 95 4 96 1 96 9 96 5 95 9	1,630 1,955 1,875	1,845 1,805 1,505	72 4 94 4 96 2 96 2 96 2 96 7 96 7	1,975 1,975 -,740	1,905	96
9 years 10 years 11 years	7,955 7,675 7 235	8,685 7,735 7,450 7,040 7,040	97 1	3,800 3,470 3,510 3,510	3,685 3 a6a 3 38a	97 0 97 0	3 875 3 765 3,725 3,410	3 762	97 4	3 615 3 070 3 070 2 835	2 950 2 975 2 740	96 9 96 6	1,565 1,480 1,405 1,405	1 425	96 2 96 3	2,743 2,50* 2,590 1,385 1,470	1 343	16 72 96 96 96 96 97
12 years	7,230 6,913	6,723			3,410	97 3		3,655	98 L 97 1	2,855				1,345		1,410	,4 0 -,255	1 30
14 years 15 years 16 years	6,845 5 905 6,840	6,63± 6,345 2,610	96 9 91 9 82 0	3 415 1 190	3,245 3,140 2,735	96 6 91 9 80 7 64 6 43 9 29 9 23 9 21 0	3,485 3,490 3 450 3 7_5	3 390 3,205 2,875 2,495 1,635 1 105	97 3 91 8	2,905	2,670 2,540 2,040	96 0 90 4 80 4 60 4 33 9 22 8 13 1	1 360 1 495 1, -95 1, -90 1, 310 1 (X.5)	1,340 930	93 4 78 5 56 7 33 2 22 5	1,/20 1,470 1,350 1 360 1 475	1,385 2,300 1,25	97 88 82 63 34 22 13 7 4 3
17 years	8,020 8,150 8,35	4,560 3,260 2,200 1,685	66 0 40 6	3,195	3,140 2,735 2,065 1,625 1,055	64 6	4.575	2,495	67 2 37 9	2,905 2,545 2,550 2,785 2,680	-,540	60 4 33 9	1,200	675 435 340	56 7 33 2	1 360	865 5. 0 370	63
19 vears 20 years 2 vears	9 235	1,685	91 9 82 0 66 0 40 0 20 0 30 0 40 0 20 0 30 0 40 0 40 0 40 0 40 0 40 0 40 0 4	3,415 3,390 3,495 3,705 3,665 3,665 4,205 4,205 4,205	885	23 9	4,485 4,795 5 030	815 545	91 8 83 3 67 2 37 9 24 6 17 0	2,66. 2,66. 2,660 3,020	610 360 295	13 5	1,125 1,175 1,405	150	13 3 15 7 14 6	1,615 1,540 1,485	370 2.0 2.0	13
22 vears. 23 years 24 years	9,195 10,175 10 190	1,210 1,220	11 0	4,230 4,705 4,790	830 970 940	19 6	7,960 5 470 5 400	330 240	66	3,020 3,130 3 085	28.J 29.5 250	94	1,405 1,370 ,300	20h 230 200	14 6 16 8 15 4	1 615 1 760 1,785	75 55 50	3
2) vears	10,155	90:	8.9	4.005	725		5.550	180	3.2	3 12:	24.0	- 1	1,280	.95	1, 2	1,845	42	
26 years 27 years 28 years	0,375	865	8 2	4,890 4 875 5 000	845 640 55>	11 1	,350 ,675 5,375	225 145	27	3,080 3,225 3,145	230 209	77	1,3eC 1 429 1 470	150 185 165	11 0 13 0 11 2 11 3	1 720 _,800 1,640	35 45 40	3 3 3 3
29 vears	a 070	655	6.8	4 550 Shres	525 report 19	77. 2	2,120	. 20	5 5	2 920	190	6 4	1,.50	_30	41 3	1,970	50	3
			140		Te.					-				22			Γ	T
Total, 5 to 29 5 years 6 years	4,395	21,8.5		1,200 1 082	11 263 85 740	6 7	26,720 النمرة 1,125	10,555 75 890	6 0			\neg			-			+ -
7 years	1 975 1 970	160 1,630 1,600 910	94 4 97 0	1 045 1 060 985	985	94 3	930		79 1 94 6 96 9			- 1						
9 years 10 years	1,860	1,785	96 3 97 5	985 950 750	940 915 735	CR 0	875 955 857	940 845 970 830	94 6 96 9 96 6 96 3 97 1									
11 years 12 years 13 years	1 690 2 560	1,655 1,530	97 9	740 850	730 835	98 6 98 2	950	925 695	97 4			-		-				
14 years 10 years	1,375	1,345	97 S	635 685	62 630	98 4 92 0	730	720 633	97 3 89 7									
16 years 17 years 18 years	1,410 1,515 1,730 1,755	1 195 1 030 675	58 0 34 0	720 695 695	630 595 525 370	92 0 82 6 75 5 53 2 28 3	730 730 820 1 C35	560 505 395	97 3 89 7 76 7 61 6 29 5 19 9 11 8 7 0 2 5		İ							. "
19 years 20 vears 21 vears	2,100	410	23 4	725 ,85	205 140 480	28 3	1,030 1,315 1,285		19 9									1
22 year 23 year 24 years	2,185 2,455 2,455 2,455	270 145 265	10 8	1.062	190	12 0	1,265	30 30 77 45	25									
2o years	2 - 20	205	1 81	1 160	45	1 15 4	1.370	00 35	44			ı			1			
26 years 27 years 28 years	2,315 2 3C5 2.440	165 140	7 01	1,020 1 0¢0 1,070	_00 130 100	12 3	1,295 1,305 1,370 1,270	35 35 40	27									
29 years	2,440 2,295	160	70	1,025	-20	U 7	1,270	40	31									L

Table 63—YEAR OF SCHOOL IN WHICH ENROLLED BY SINGLE YEARS OF AGE, COLOR, AND SEX, FOR THE STATE, LEBAN AND RURAL, AND FOR CITIES OF 100,000 OR MORE 1950

n tah as . 5 snn 32 Median school year in which ext rolled Persons enro. ed m schou. High secool Not re-THE STATE Tota., 5 to 29 -3 535 Tota, 5 to:
Male 5 to 29
5 to 24 years
5 years
7 years
8 years
10 years
11 years
12 years
12 years
13 years 52 (C) 12 (A) 12 49 940 19,005 14 230 1 780 11,815 9,935 8,475 272 510 483 675 270 17, 200 17, 200 33 987 765-6 53 765-6 54 765-6 54 765-6 54 765-6 55 765-6 56 77 765-6 70 97 6 0 7 785 8,40 4 62* 3 43. 2 010 50 50 50 50 40 40 40 40 50 60 65 425 3U 1.5 550 6,840 7 -60 4 945 3,355 7,045 1 255 575 215 65 225 45 45 77 72 90 450 20,660 20,560 20,550 90 450 5 88L 7,285 4 350 2,865 870 300 85 70 90 90 1.55 1.05 1.05 24,240 24,240 24,155 80 4,935 5 900 3 940 2 680 1 40,580 120 120 175 145 1_0 650 60 415 3,410 4,590 1,380 470 170 85 110 125 105 550 11,390 80 3 140 3 725 2 165 910 295 100 100 125 490 13 275 13 100 65 315 605 560 565 505 185 130 115 475 480 500 16 June 14 June 14 June 15 Jun 70 360 2,399 2,700 1,150 555 385 245 280 210 1 075 170 970 760 385 305 310 485 175 520 40 635 020 635 460 420 340 195 725 575 780 580 495 500 400 985 130 45, 585 615 660 595 730 165 125 285 270 065 20 34,260 765 10,825 10,695 2,665 505 245 115 115 130 60 60 21 40 2,855 2 345 670 9,330 9,330 3,60 2,235 1,290 300 160 110 20 35 15 15 65 113 733 8 305 7,485 4,725 2 24 1 330 525 300 95 20 25 15 10 35 30 140 105 650 7,315 7 825 3 865 2 410 1,125 55 50 35 30 42 10 5 85 100 470 6,515 6,845 3,700 1,895 950 360 45 20 25 35 35 30 270 590 5,685 6,010 3,540 1,630 633 415 80 32 25 10 32 32 32 33 35 25,000 5,630 2,370 9:25 345 140 15 35 40 10 170 95 590 4,890 1,875 680 280 90 60 175 4,010 1,230 510 275 85 50 75 60 125 695 920 205 070 505 205 215 140 540 330 950 545 205 ,5 60 45 55 155 100 750 915 445 195 105 105 165 755 670 235 110 80 55 255 220 565 450 230 135 95 365 30 20 8 8 8 4 4 5 30 60 25 80 5 910 5 445 205,733 103,265 100 005 6,950 6,950 8,965 8,965 9,265 7,550 6,710 5,265 1,230 715 670 715 670 715 860 815 3,265 6544559:28518 745244.21289 886597429703414/17 34,920 16,690 16 650 430 6,235 4,950 1,_C5 575 325 215 115 535 20 10 27,775 14,575 14,510 20 20 3 250 4,400 2,635 1,685 920 125 100 45 35 100 585 270 13,470 L 270 15 4.0 2 1°5 3,145 2 710 1,610 1,410 20° 1/5 50 25 · : Main, 5 to 29 for Advance A years A years A years R years R years I dy years 2,550 2,525 390 285 240 230 185 135 140 110 75 125 85 5 270 1 575 2 475 2 120 1, 345 2 120 1, 345 250 110 255 30 10 30 40 3 305 45 145 1,625 1,670 -,485 1,060 625 225 65 60 60 50 80 80 395 5,690 8,632 45 155 690 1,195 1 265 763 420 115 45 60 70 50 377 7 470 7,375 3, 20 165 580 115 ,095 62* 26, 400 35 35 60 75 90 469 500 915 840 260 1.5 35 40 35 55 55 225 4 675 4,620 405 595 495 395 145 45 60 65 75 85 277 505 315 -90 80 35 80 75 150 20 70 215 295 255 140 95 60 95 90 445 40 40 40 40 40 50 85 1,0 70 60 50 25 60 55 15 27 6 7 4 8 25 35 70 200 200 10 200 200 2,220 60 2,480 2,480 2,480 2,480 1205 535 210 1205 30 40 200 2,48 13 40 10 20 6* 5 25 A yearLoranke, 5 or
5 of 20 years

Loranke, 5 or
5 of 20 years

O years

O years

O years

10 years

11 years

12 years

14 years

15 years

16 years

17 years

16 years

17 years

18 years

20 years

21 years

22 years

23 years

24 years

25 years

26 years

27 years

28 years

29 years

20 years

20 years

21 years

22 years

23 years

25 years

26 years

27 years

28 years

29 years 9,910 6,360 102,470
10a 640
200
10a 640
200
7 165
9,480
9,475
8,840
9,210
7,915
8,865
8,75
7,499
6,825
5,700
4,140
2,745
1,520
4,520
2,55
3,15
2,25
830 ,210 502 310 ,905 ,810 790 55 30 35 5 5 15 2 870 2,160 50 ,585 360 315 17 12,12 107 145 105 105 105 105 55 50 320 1 640 2 340 2 ,225 440 65 20 10 10 -0 25 75 300 1,195 2,240 1,880 1,375 780 420 45 20 25 15 10 55 55 205 1,215 1 885 1 750 1,075 69* 27' 1.5 20 15 15 20 95 40 270 1 060 1 480 1,595 1 110 440 30 15 5 25 40 325 750 380 760 295 270 80 35 15 10 24 245 770 1,090 430 430 130 65 15 10 235 560 865 565 355 130 45 20 10 17L 4°5 675 360 245 30 60 25 20 25 25 25 25 15 20 20 35 135 175 175 45 45 45 25 70 55 125 110 55 40 20 25 45 105 80 80 50 20 65 5 15

Table 63.—YEAR OF SCHOOL IN WHICH ENROLLED, BY SINGLE YEARS OF AGE, COLOR, AND SEX, FOR THE STATE, URBAN AND RURAL, AND FOR CITIES OF 100,000 OR MORE 1950—Con

Persons enrolled in school Not year in which re-1 2 8 2 3 3 4 283 680 140,020 140,020 9,965 12,190 12,225 11,15 10,050 10,230 9,710 2,220 8,420 7,135 6 07-8,230 12,39 8,170 27/72 la, las 27/2 la, las 27/2 la, las 27/2 la, las 27/2 la, las 27/2 las 6,625 3 385 3 3,3-5 38,3-5 235 235 235 240 180 180 180 150 245 25 45 25 45 :5,315 15,275 25,275 25 25 7,255 7,915 1 /95 565 285 115 25 45 40 50 16,465 10,450 4.0 9,075 5 145 1,075 350 90 65 30 651123334567 89012244 55 122444567 890688907 35 35 340 4 380 3,865 ,930 1,-70 600 130 130 80 85 25 100 235 30 310 3,860 3,285 2 020 760 4.0 115 55 25 16* 220 40 55 295 3,290 1,480 1,130 285 70 30 230 3,35 2,645 2,645 2,845 2,840 1,715 1,090 5°C 195 115 300 355 10,035 9 970 25 205 2,400 2,400 2,595 1,575 930 425 240 405 535 9,040 8,965 20 270 2,990 2,180 1,480 515 240 311 330 7,590 7,510 250 1,800 1,800 1,850 955 34, 32, 6,750 6,750 50 190 1,5.0 1 870 1,040 460 230 20 20 25,7 30 1,5.5 1,460 1,...5 ...703 420 50 2 ...33 2,303 790 2,...95 35 70 240 1,440 2 170 1,075 845 40 15 15 740 2 505 910 150 40 9 605 850 -,515 1,000 25 to 29 years female, 5 5 to 24 years 5 years 6 years 7 years 8 years 9 years 10 years 11 years 12 years 18 years 35,480 133,510 1 32,59,910 3,1,0 11,890 10,90 10,705 10 210 10,68,9,865 14,145 14 110 40 505 7,640 4,125 1,060 400 35 80 20 225 10 835 5,765 6,605 2,005 217 740 495 320 190 200 200 165 120 165 130 145 69 1 525 -10 270 15 70 445 5,250 3,565 1 4.0 695 405 125 -0 50 45 15 15 30 355 4 460 3,730 1,770 700 41-170 85 30 10 25 20 35 260 3,845 2,545 -,60^ 770 390 105 62 40 2:5 3,750 3,005 1,585 690 325 140 55 85 65 40 360 3,315 2,750 1 395 6,5 260 120 70 50 425 81,510 ,510 ,395 345 180 80 2 685 2 685 2 185 790 375 135 35 395 2,225 1 9_0 835 215 140 14 years 15 years 16 years 17 years 18 and 19 years 20 to 24 years 5 to 29 years 9,185 8,605 7,445 6,590 7 915 5,125 1 970 40 85 520 2,405 2,370 810 375 20 25 10 10 35 305 1,275 395 145 20 80 445 650 2₂0 1 305 320 Nonwhite, 5

Male, 5 to 29
5 o 24 years
5 years
6 years
9 years
8 years
10 years
11 years
12 years
13 years
14 years
15 years
16 years
16 years
16 years
17 years
18 years
18 years
19 years
19 years
19 years
10 years 92,485 4c,15, 470 3,185 4,065 4,135 3,725 3,550 3,500 1,690 3,270 _0 210 4,175 5,085 5 3J 21,, 1 175 1 430 1,015 440 380 170 95 45 35 10 5 90 6,17) 6,60 200 2,815 1 975 680 245 75 40 2,25 5,670 5 640 10 205 1,725 2,013 860 415 200 100 30 20 20 3 255 3,520 2,220 365 325 5 1 5 0 15 145 980 1,185 960 20,395 205 50 15 15 180 4 ~40 4,~35 50752164 2190554 4466197541 - 998000 25 15 145 664 1 090 1,080 655 485 310 75 35 20 105 165 15 25 10 595 835 805 580 400 205 50 10 175 235 25 100 400 725 755 580 320 145 70 170 225 15 110 3-0 570 5-0 265 -45 210 3,130 3,105 325 480 315 14.1 180 155 4 years
10 years
10 years
17 years
18 and 19 years
25 to 29 years 3,250 3,090 2,400 1,695 2,455 2,455 55 280 380 265 285 190 120 75 175 360 305 185 105 10 60 175 390 260 120 30 145 155 35 370 360 15 5 10 30 20 90 225 70 490 760 35 2-3 160 315 290 20 235 70 10 25 55 50 25 to 29 years.
5 to 34 years.
5 years.
5 years.
5 years.
6 years.
1 years.
1 years.
1 years.
1 years.
1 years.
1 years.
12 years.
13 years.
14 years.
15 years.
16 years.
17 years.
18 and 19 years.
18 and 19 years.
25 to 29 years. 2,125 330 282 46,130 45,645 6,0 3,215 4,330 /,170 0,765 3,920 3,525 3,885 3,105 2,010 2,285 1,225 2,010 2,285 1,260 485 5,700 5,605 28,755 2,755 4,870 105 405 30 5 115 15 5 205 5 250 30 240 2,015 1,700 295 100 55 10 15 1,035 5,015 50 240 1,600 1,435 885 360 217 120 40 10 10 10 20 20 4,425 3,780 3,575 2,4:2 1,395 10 55 24:2 1,225 1,790 700 700 75 40 30 40 5 25 1,0°5 1,0 10 25 170 720 720 84J 440 275 65 45 25 15 10 30 160 735 960 870 375 235 100 20 35 45 15 30 1°5 660 780 730 400 1°0 95 50 25 35 250 4e5 780 350 190 120 45 25 25 190 505 640 710 265 45 20 190 360 543 450 110 40 130 357 630 215 45 20 240 185 30 60 193 100 10 15 145 45 40 220 45 RURAL NONPARI TOTAL, 5 to 29. Male 5 to 29. 5 to 24 years 5 voats 6 years 7 voats 8 voats 9 years 10 years 12 years 12 years 12 years 100 80 35 143,135 75,055 72,965 53,180 6,860 6,860 6,470 6,160 6,760 2,965 2,500 2,960 2,130 10,270 10,270 10,255 1,797 3,310 1,065 195 115 65 .5 60 25 25 395 225 16,525 8,900 8,785 15 175 2,480 2,430 1,460 790 6.0 280 135 67 150 85 35, 35, 890 2 315 1,255 935 330 165 85 85 80 80 .0 1,585 1,915 1,405 885 545 345 130 69 45 20 85 395 2,055 1,120 850 535 210 60 120 30 30 .00 1,265 1,485 4 055 425 160 60 175 225 25 880 335 875 555 280 140 180 285 20 25 90 725 765 360 465 30 55 50 640 9.5 300 175 14 years 15 years 16 years 17 years 17 years 18 and 19 years 20 to 24 years 5 to 29 years 30 620 830 495 175 15 13 235 225 10 215 150 25 145 60

LOUISLANA

Table 63—YEAR OF SCHOOL IN WHICH ENROLLED, BY SINGLE YEARS OF AGE, COLOR, AND SEX, FOR THE STATE, URBAN AND RURAL, AND FOR CITIES OF 100,000 OR MORE 1950—Con.

	Persons								Jest or 8	ennel in						G-11		-	
es noto , age and sex	Persons enrolled ar school				-	ery school	T			-		Icodes	_			College		5 or	Not re-
	school	1	2	3	4	5	6	7	8		2	8	4	I	2	3	4	more	ported
RAL NONFARM-Con.		C.	1		1				1		1						-		
Tota 5 to 49—Con. emale, 5 to 29	0,210	8,775	0,.75	7 425	6,973	6 980	6,650	1,460	4 530	3,955	3,125	2 610 2,560	2 210	2.5	365 345	225	175	20	1,945
24 /cars ears	60. 4,9 €	104	1 -	7 193 5	0, 130	0,+50	6 620	1 3,40	4.475	-,073	3,180	2,200	1 250	-				-	46C 280
ears suas	6 000	7,8:0	2,770	2,800	25	40	15										- 1		160
Seria cera	6 415 5,720	290	9.0	2 433 1,150 420 275	2,50	2,25° -,915	1.25	7.0	2								- 1		14,5 85 110
years	5,720 6,034 3,73	90 20	95 95 90	275 145	500 310	-,915 -,18° -,85	2,190 1,100	1,475	1,_95	15	.5	. ,			l		1		105
reary	5 225	11111	35	_0 55	1-5	305	655	96	. 45	1 200	1,132	25 105	20			-	.		90 50
rears rears rears and 19 years	3,685	15	1	25	25 20	-50 20 20	-65 75 -5 6* 30	56° 545 22, 80	92 425 150 55 35	1,510 595 260 105 30	1,135 1,065 460 255	1 005	105 75c	15	15				79 95 15 10
to 24 vesrs	2 4,0 1,180	10 20	. 30	2-	20 25 40	20 40	64	60 30 55	55 35	105 30	255 c0 45	395 140 50	1,000 215 80	45	182	125 45	105 45	10	10
29 vears Nonwhee, 5 to 29	66L		6,890	6,365	5 350	4,620	4,040	3, 25	2 380	80 675	1,150	8.0,	583	260	425	175	195		1 330
ale 5 to 29 years.	20,990	4 125 4 120	3,645	3,425	2,980	2 280 2,160	1,905	1 540	1 182	725 670	480	320 280	175 153	±50 ±35	150 130	45 35	100		760 750
828	260	10.	45	105											1				140
828 828 827	2,205 2,345 2,-1	1,285 69, 345	1,060	455 /35 705	325	ود د د	10 10 20								- 1				60 40 75 ≥0
ears	2, _l 2, 280 2,035	_55 80	525 275	495	635 5o5	190 355	150	30	2.5								1	- 1	85 30
CATS	1 830 1,7.0	45 35 15	135	42.5 200 .00	205 300 225	460 4±0	330 370	150 235 340	30 _35 200	5	5 20	14	1			- 1			53
nars	1,420	1.5	35 20	401	120	240 240 80	395 255 130	270	200	15	42	55		1		1	- 1		20 50 42 32
od 19 same	,30 -85	10	15 5	5 5	.5	80	57 45	105	_20 80 55	165 125 80	120 100 55 25	60 85 70 40	35	65	30 90 40				- 1
9 years	860 750	10	15	80	60	50 120	60 80	70 10.	85	80 35 55			25	15		35 10	70 30		10
years .	23,370 23,180 205	3 650 3,645 100	3,245 3 245 20	2,940 2,950	2,410	2,340	2 135	1,585	1 395	950 930	670	490 490	405 402	105	275 250	130 105	95 75		540 540 145
nts -	1.u70	100 100 100	110	.DS	.2	10								- 1	- 1		- 1		55
MS -	2,200 2,180 2,125 2,190	210	970 620 310 ±50 75	635	45	20	10	5					- 1				- 1		65 25 20
Pane Sars	2 190	100 50	310 150	80.5 660 250	700 430 355 225	125 460 525	50 2±5	15 25	5 35	10									20 _5 J, 30
nars	2,010	10	65	21C 115 50	120	90و	575 400	200 440 365	182	45	10		5						10
8878 E	1 720 1,535 1 155	5 5	0	45	80 20 10	270 135 52	205 285 220	265	375 280	250 215	20 12- 10	20 65	25		5	- 1			30
ears	965 65C	5	20 20	20 20 5	10	52 15 10 30	65 13 30	35 30 5	_5 20	155 75	165 130 20	200 73	2.5	15	10 70 165	30	40		25
24 vears	196	-10	-	10	. 15	20	10	2.5	5	20	20	~		5	25	75 25	20		
Cotal 5 to 29	151, 765	21,085	18 420	17 930	16,200	.4,865	±3,810	11 650	9 905	7,530	6,305	4 955	3 825	210	200	270	230	25	4 100
vears	76,480	10,890	9 5.0	0,150	8,680	8,065	6,900	5,665	4,885	3,015 3,050	2 840	2,215	_,785 _,685	110	120	140	90	23	2,0,5 2 030 400
urs .	5,985	135 7,410 3,19* 1 370	150 2,415	15	10	10			. 1		-						i	1	250 170 225
RTS	6 937 6,78 6,920	725	2,415 3,050 1 370	2,670	35 1,5_0 2 225	30 11C	25 70	.0 1#	20					1			-		140
BATS	6 565 7,295	210	49± 495 300	1,705	2 225 1,440 1,330	1,960	1 250	_,325	10	10	15						1		150
55/5 55/5 55/5	6,145	°0 85	195	240	895 J10	746	1,350 880,	1,170	1 570	695	15	5				1			70
bars	5,775 4 3,5 3 450	55 35 15	55 30 22	115 85 35	265 150 _05	470 260 95	540 375	915 4_0 225	1,065 680 335	695	700 460 173	95 475	80	1					105
nd 19 , ears	2,720	10	20	40 35 50	35 50 75	70	-70 70 125	125	183	405 235 50	+30 430	860 535 150	5±0 875 220	70 40	60 60	30 105	90		70 10 15
9°years	1,070	20, 6,	8 890		7 54	e 800	0.755	5,91	135 2 090	4,015 4,005	65	2,740	2,040	15 80	165	415	65	2^	25
years ars	73,830 585 5,025	4 155	8,863	8,3°0 6,270 1.0 25	7,530	0,770	6 740	1,865	5,040	4 005	3,400	2,710	,955	80	150	25	75 75		2,045 2 04* 425
ars -	6,645	3,280	2,980	20C	15	15	10								-	-	- 1		295 250 255
ears	6,385	450 275 1 0	1,220 710 385	2,345 2,605 1,345	2,305	194 -,ol0 -,940	34	2.5	15			.			!			i	255
ears ears	6,565	90 40	385 215	780 445 325	890	1,270	165 1 575 2,000 -,160	90 1,965	1.5 130 1 175	25 405	25			- 1		1			90
ears	5,820	50	45	1.35	260 140	520 1	79C 445	1 50	1,095	985	95 1 070	110	20	i	1				90
ears ears nd 19 _ears	3,515	25 25 15	35 25 20	85 30 5	62 45 42 20	205 145 46 15	25C 115	560 400 140	225	080	1,243	905	70	n	3				82
nd 19 jears o 24 years	2,445	15	13	20	20	15 35 30	35 15	30 50	35	40 10	230	1,095 510 90	703 930 -70 85	1(50 20	80 60	35 60 20	65		10

Table 63—YEAR OF SCHOOL IN WHICH ENROLLED, BY SINGLE YEARS OF AGE, COLOR, AND SEX, FOR THE STATE, URBAN AND RURAL, AND FOR CITIES OF 100 000 OR MORE 1950—Con

Area, color, age, and sex Hage school College Vot vean sehool BURAL LARM-Con Nonwhite, 5
Male 5 to 29
5 to 24 years
6 years
6 years
7 years
10 years
11 years
12 years
13 years
14 years
15 years
16 years
16 years
16 years
26 years
27 years
28 years
29 years
20 years
20 years
20 years
20 years
5 years
5 years
6 years
7 years
7 years
7 years
7 years
8 and 9 years
8 and 9 years
8 years
8 and 9 years
9 years
7 years
9 years
9 years
9 years
9 years
9 years
9 years
9 years
9 years
9 years
9 years
9 years
9 years
9 years
9 years
9 years
9 years
9 years
9 years
9 years
9 years
9 years
9 years
9 years
9 years
9 years
9 years
9 years
9 years
9 years
9 years
9 years
9 years
9 years
9 years
9 years
9 years
9 years
9 years
9 years
9 years Nonwhite, 5 to 29 9,950 65,890 32,920 32,555 3,255 2,645 3,095 3,095 3,095 3,095 3,095 3,095 2,750 2,950 1,675 1,210 965 2,530 9,1.5 4.840 4.840 6,395 6,370 122 1,975 1, 115 775 1,330 1,090 745 350 180 50 25 20 20 15 20 4,690 4 675 1 12N34 15 661 60 40 495 480 40 775 470 330 203 95 50 45 15 3,08 3,090 2 775 2,765 25 280 295 320 240 1/0 30 40 5 5 5 116 155 47 1,5 9,5 92,5 8° 195 -90 -50 5 15 1,260 125 45 50 45 Female, 5 to 25 years _ 32 y70 22,8.5 325 2,280 2,950 3,125 2,930 3,100 2,787 2,030 2,860 4,245 4,235 5 10 -05 590 - 070 935 585 385 300 120 70 25 20 10 10 2,310 355 1,835 Female 5 to 24 veu 5 years 6 years 7 years 8 years 9 years 10 years 11 years 12 years 13 years 640 545 677 610 340 180 105 45 25 20 10 55 650 650 650 245 120 50 45 120 10 20 70 260 550 550 320 235 200 55 30 300 615 690 605 -70 -13 30 15 20 -85 435 435 435 150 85 15 25 60 215 375 450 450 170 95 20 20 350 350 250 250 250 250 13 years
14 years
15 years
16 years
17 years
17 years
18 and 19 years
20 to 24 years
5 to 29 years 2,550 2,400 1,265 1,115 450 155 5 6 7 6 4 6 5 9 5 250 250 250 250 15 290 20 40 200 to 20 CITTES 1,035 BATON ROUGE 25,315 14,680 13,425 105,890 9,089 990 995 790 705 760 620 5,55 495 1,370 1,250 1,250 1,250 2,270 -,155 1,15: 2 050 1,045 1,045 830 755 705 490 760 1,.30 Male, 5 to 29
sto 24 years
vears
6 wears
7 vears
9 vears
1 years
1 years
1 years
2 years 1,315 1,315 30 835 370 55 533 325 85 40 10 5 74489746974 470 5 5 50 7 5 5 45 430 340 95 65 40 20 363 245 200 65 25 255 255 25 25 20 290 40 55 30 10 10 290 80 60 25 25 15 180 65 20 20 10 20 135 165 140 50 175 70 35 30 140 65 60 255 175 40 40 285 720 185 870 33.7 5 to 29 years

kenale 5 to 29
to 24 years
5 years
6 years
7 years
8 years
10 years
11 years
12 years
3 years 1,225 1,200 35 785 315 50, 20, 11,535 11,420 890 1,750 920 965 830 /55 840 940 865 755 800 575 520 355 285 360 80 70 30 15 25 30 15 15 15 15 10 70 10 1,410 1 5 2 3 3 2 4 1 5 1 5 9 7 0 7 8 8 7 9 9 10 7 11.7 13.9 15 7 650 315 83 15 335 80 10 470 270 110 30 25 405 260 120 20 355 260 45 323 200 105 25 215 185 85 20 20 275 175 55 35 25 295 240 65 20 40 5 14 years 15 years 15 years 16 years 17 years 18 and 19 eavs 20 to 24 years 5 to 29 years... 640 5,0 570 1 105 7°5 215 175 2_0 80 45 210 85 30 265 80 5 45 220 155 35 8,800 4,780 4,445 2 250 1 090 1,070 279 -40 1335 90 55 35 42 25 55 45 55 45 55 45 202,200 52,855 49,565 585 5,410 3,860 5,340 3,340 3,140 2,720 2,720 2,720 2,720 3,220 8,385 4,385 4,330 9,505 4,837 4,840 5 15 2300 2,045 1,395 620 220 150 20 15 31 10 N.N. ORL TAI Maile, 5 to 29 5 to 24 vears 5 vears 6 years 7 years 8 yea.s 10 years 11 vears 12 vears 13 vears 2,8"5 1,675 2,8"5 1,675 375 180 90 3,740 5,680 5,675 285 ,90 1,640 20 20 25 5 15 160 1,390 1 115 730 390 1/0 29 1/0 25 20 5 30 17C 1 117 1,045 705 44C 28G 125 20 90 10 130 980 980 605 450 220 90 55 450 95 940 875 655 325 165 95 140 230 135 695 745 500 2-0 80 110 160 605 700 3.0 180 1.35 14 years 15 years 16 years 17 years 18 and 16 years 20 to 24 years to 29 years 105 605 545 310 -85 80 50 95 490 830 565 790 500 500 390 195 ±0 20

Table 63—YEAR OF SCHOOL IN WHICH ENROLLED, BY SINCLE YEARS OF AGE, COLOR, AND SEX, FOR THE STATE, URBAN AND RURAL, AND FOR CITIES OF 100,000 OR MORE

Table 63.—YEAR OF SCHOOL IN WHICH ENROLLED, BY SINGLE YEARS OF AGE, COLOR, AND SEX, FOR THE STATE, URBAN AND RURAL, AND FOR CITIES OF 100,000 OR MORE: 1950—Con.

[Based on 20-percent sample available complete-count data in tables 15 and 33. In general, persons were enrolled in grade above one they had completed. Median not shown where base is less than 500]

Area, color, age, and sex	Persons enrolled in school	Year of school in which enrolled: Elementary school: 1	2	3	4	5	6	7	8	High school: 1	2	3	4	College: 1	2	3	4	5 or more	Not reported	Median school year in which enrolled
CITIES—Con.																				
NEW ORLEANS—Con.																				
Female, 5 to 29	49,345	5,300	5,_60	_,720	4 320	4,195	3,825	3 620	3,320	2,750	2,565	2 235	2,780	860	8_0	810	625	220	_,_60	6 1
5 to 24 years	48,475	5,295	5 _50	4 710	_,_0	4,165	3 810	3,600	3,285	2,725	2,510	2 180	2 595	825	825	695	500	_50	_,145	6 0
5 years	650	330	25	15															280	1 6
6 years	3,520	3,005	335	25															155	1 6
7 years	4 885	,490	2 980	2_5	50	15													135	2 3
8 years	4,325	260	1,275	2 440	455	15	10												70	3 2
9 years	3,875	70	345	_,190	2,005	205	10	5											45	4 2
10 years	3,765	20	55	505	,225	_,655	_70	20	20										65	5 0
11 years	3 675	10	30	150	_15	_,32_	_,490	155	35	5									60	5 9
12 years	3,655		30	70	_5	595	1,125	1 420	170	10	5								65	6 8
13 years	3 210	20	5	25	55	195	535	1,0_0	1,160	190	25	5							45	7 8
14 years	3 390	35	5	15	30	115	290	610	965	1 020	205	20	35						_5	8 6
15 years	3,205	10	10	5	0	2_	125	210	570	890	970	240	75						70	9 7
16 years	_,875	20	20	25	10	10	30	90	205	420	805	895	285		10				50	10 7
17 years	2,495	5		5	5	10	10	40	85	115	335	665	990	150	25	10			35	11 9
18 and 19 years	2 740	15		10	5		5	15	35	40	135	285	875	525	495	235	25	20	20	12 9
20 to 24 years	2,110	5	5	5	40	5	10	25	40	35	30	70	335	150	295	430	475	130	5	15 0
25 to 29 years	870	5	10	10	10	30	5	20	35	25	55	55	185	35	55	115	125	70	15	12 9
Nonwhite	37,040	4,275	4,325	3 860	3 555	3,705	2,980	2,945	2,735	2,_20	_,725	1,440	1,105	380	340	250	340	55	785	5 5
Male, 5 to 29	18 595	2,185	2 280	2,030	1,895	1,960	1,560	1,475	1,390	1,060	705	525	465	215	170	130	190	20	340	5 4
5 to 24 years	17,770	2 180	2,275	2,020	1,870	1,915	1,515	1,380	1,235	970	655	480	390	180	150	95	110	10	340	5 2
5 years	200	115	10																75	
6 years	1,180	985	115	10	15														55	1 6
7 years	1,945	745	880	145	5	10													60	2 2
8 years	1,805	240	320	605	95	10													35	2 8
9 years	1,505	55	255	58_	525	55	15												15	3 7
10 years	1,425	5	115	365	5_0	350	60	10	5										15	4 4
11 years	1,40_	10	60	145	350	480	295	40	10	5									5	5 3
12 years	1,345	10	15	100	170	450	350	220	45										5	5 9
13 years	1 190	5		45	90	220	295	300	190	30	10	5								6 8
14 years	1,285	5		5	65	195	230	290	280	170	20	5	5						15	7 5
15 years	1,540			5	25	105	165	240	310	305	125	40	10						10	8 4
16 years	930		5	10	10	25	70	110	160	190	205	80	30	5					30	9 3
17 years	675	5			5	5	10	70	100	145	95	145	75	5		5			10	9 9
18 and 19 years	675				5	5		35	60	50	120	100	160	95	25	10	10			11 6
20 to 24 years	970				10	25	25	65	75	75	80	105	110	75	125	80	100	10	10	12 2
25 to 29 years	825	5	5	10	25	45	45	95	155	90	50	45	7_	35	20	35	80	10		9 _
Female, 5 to 29	18,445	2 090	2,045	1,830	1,760	1,745	1,420	1,470	1,365	1,060	1,020	9_5	640	165	170	120	150	35	445	5 7
5 to 24 years	18,230	2,090	2,040	1 820	1,755	1,720	1 405	1,455	1,350	1,050	1,000	895	620	165	150	115	130	30	440	5 7
5 years	305	165	15	15															110	
6 years	1,195	990	130	20															55	1 6
7 years	1 905	685	1,015	85	40	5													75	2 2
8 years	1,670	150	570	760	155	10	5												20	3 1
9 years	1 445	60	220	485	565	80	5	5											25	3 9
10 years	1,550	10	35	285	560	530	75	15	10										30	4 8
11 years	1,340	5	20	80	205	560	320	100	30										20	5 6
12 years	1,410		15	35	100	305	495	340	90	5									25	6 5
13 years	1 355	15		20	75	125	250	410	310	115	20								15	7 5
14 years	1 385			15	15	70	145	370	360	260	110	15	5						20	8 2
15 years	1,300	5	5		10	20	75	115	290	325	275	155	15						10	9 4
16 years	1,115	5	10	10	5		20	50	140	230	330	215	80		5				15	10 2
17 years	865					10	5	35	60	65	160	285	165	45	10	5			20	11 3
18 and 19 years	880			10	5		5	5	30	35	80	185	265	100	75	60	15	10		12 3
20 to 24 years	510		5		20	5	5	10	30	15	25	40	90	20	60	50	115	70		13 5
25 to 29 years	215		5	10	5	25	15	15	15	0	20	20	20		20	5	20	5	5	
SHREVEPORT	2_,815	2,430	2,300	2,125	1,865	1,865	1,705	1,610	1,475	1,195	1,125	930	1,4_0	340	295	205	400	100	440	6._
Male, 5 to 29	1_,260	1,190	1,200	1,150	945	880	905	780	765	580	560	500	650	185	200	150	285	90	245	6 2
5 to 24 years	10 665	1,190	1,195	1,140	905	875	860	760	735	560	535	455	565	145	_65	125	165	45	245	5 9
5 years	85	15																	70	
6 years	740	665	20	10	5														40	1 5
7 years	985	390	550	25		5													15	2 2
8 years	970	70	435	44_	5		5												10	2 9
9 years	940	30	115	400	365	10	5	5											10	3 8
10 years	915	10	40	145	310	335	30	15											30	4 8
11 years	735		15	45	85	260	300	10	5										15	5 8
12 years	730	5	15	25	70	75	200	240	30										10	6 7
13 years	835			25	30	95	115	255	240	40	15								20	7 6
14 years	635			5	15	45	80	70	205	150	40	5	5						5	8 5
15 years	630				5	25	40	55	115	170	195	20	5							9 4
16 years	595		5		5	10	10	50	45	170	155	170	95						10	10 4
17 years	525						5	10	30	45	45	185	185	10					5	11 6
18 and 19 years	575			5				10	25	20	35	65	225	75	55	55			5	12 6
20 to 24 years	780	5		10	5	15	10	40	40	35	50	10	110	65	110	70	165	45		14 0
25 to 29 years	595		5	10	40	5	45	20	30	20	25	45	85	40	35	25	120	45		12 6
Female, 5 to 29	10,555	1,240	1,100	975	920	985	800	830	710	615	565	430	760	155	95	55	115	10	195	6 0
5 to 24 years	10,345	1,240	1,095	970	920	980	800	805	700	605	550	415	695	135	75	55	105	5	195	5 9
5 years	75	25																	50	
6 years	890	825	20	20															2_	1 5
7 years	880	305	540	10															25	2 2
8 years	940	55	400	455	20	5													5	3 0
9 years	845	15	80	325	380	15	10												20	4 0
10 years	920	5	30	75	300	440	4_	5	5										1_	5 1
11 years	830		5	55	125	315	310	15											5	5 7
12 years	925		15	5	55	125	305	370	30	15	5									6 9
13 years	695		5	15	20	15	70	225	285	45	10								5	8 0
14 years	720	5		5		50	25	115	225	260	30								5	8 7
15 years	655				5		30	35	85	185	275	25	5						10	9.9
16 years	560				10	5	5	30	65	60	140	195	35	5					10	10 7
17 years	505			5	5					25	40	135	270	10					15	12.1
18 and 19 years	510	5				5				15	30	50	250	70	50	15	20		5	12 6
20 to 24 years	395					5		10	5	5	20	10	135	50	25	40	65	5		
25 to 29 years	210		5	5		5		25	10	10	15	15	65	20	20		10	5		

Table 64.—YEARS OF SCHOOL COMPLETED BY PERSONS 5 TO 24 YEARS OLD, BY SINGLE YEARS OF AGE, COLOR, AND SEX, FOR THE STATE, 1950 AND 1940, FOR URBAN AND RURAL AREAS AND FOR STANDARD METROPOLITAN AREAS AND CITIES OF 250,000 OR MORE, 1950

[Statistics for 1950 based on 20 percent sample, available complete-count data in tables 5 and 33. Median not shown where less than 1.0, or where base is less than [illegible] for 1950 or [illegible] for 1940]

Area, census year, color, age, and sex	All persons	Years of school completed: None	Elementary school: 1	2	3	4	5	6	7	8	High school: 1	2	3	4	College: 1	2	3	4 or more	Not reported	Median school years completed
THE STATE, 1950																				
Total																				
Total, 5 to 24	935,040	47,995	70,775	69,[illegible]	8[illegible]50	68,[illegible]	67,760	47,740	96,2[illegible]5	58,51[illegible]	47,470	4[illegible],[illegible]25	38,[illegible]2	6[illegible]	[illegible]2 900	10,[illegible]	7,080	9,[illegible]	2[illegible],340	5 5
Male, 5 to 24	461,98[illegible]	77 085	37,150	37,345	3[illegible] 920	36,[illegible]05	34,950	34 235	3[illegible],795	27,2[illegible]5	2[illegible] [illegible]8[illegible]	[illegible]7 [illegible]85	[illegible]5,[illegible]5	[illegible]3,400	6,2[illegible]	5,725	4,[illegible]15	4,400	1,225	5 0
5 years	23,395	2[illegible],[illegible]95	120	45		.													1,035	
6 years	29,41[illegible]	25 915	2,160	110	75	.	.												1,150	.
7 years	27,945	11,565	13,960	1 830	135	45													770	1
8 years	27,525	3,695	10,378	11,045	1 [illegible]50	1[illegible]9	65												740	1 9
9 years	25,825	1,715	4,195	9,285	8,590	[illegible]95	50	[illegible]00											595	2 7
10 years	25,275	975	2,085	4 825	3,220	7,535	980	[illegible]30	70										455	3 [illegible]
11 years	23 [illegible]45	[illegible]05	1,015	2,[illegible]55	[illegible] [illegible]80	7,000	6,430	900	120	75	.	.				.			605	4 4
12 years	25 485	[illegible]15	700	1,755	3,425	4,760	7,285	3 550	825	130	30								520	5 2
13 years	23,23[illegible]	390	380	1,0[illegible]5	2 020	3 330	4,360	5,290	4,[illegible]95	735	130	35							435	6 0
14 years	22 030	375	245	380	1 235	2 115	2,950	3,980	5,540	3,920	580	[illegible]0	50				.		400	6 8
15 years	2[illegible] 495	365	210	395	760	1,570	2,12[illegible]	3 055	3,680	4 795	3,480	630	100	40			.		295	7 6
16 years	20 955	350	285	310	740	915	1,460	2 260	2 935	3 430	4 050	2 975	635	85	10				2[illegible]5	8 3
17 years	20 580	340	165	390	735	900	1 205	1 820	2,110	2 515	2 820	3 840	2 785	570	55	20			260	9 0
18 years	20,690	380	220	455	710	900	1 255	1,680	1,835	2,040	2,010	2,195	3,200	2 380	880	185	10		325	9.4
19 years	18,695	355	200	420	755	795	1,030	1,205	1 555	1,500	1,220	1,430	1,870	3,320	1,275	860	280	60	345	9 9
20 years	18,410	395	205	440	670	920	1 185	1 435	1,470	1,345	1,140	1 115	1 270	3 3[illegible]	995	975	570	205	425	9 8
21 years	20,080	320	280	380	765	970	1 160	1,575	1 795	1,565	1 280	1,195	1,245	3,840	840	890	785	645	350	9 7
22 years	19,765	495	265	430	605	975	1 135	1 420	1,865	1,770	1,390	1 210	1,315	3,130	800	940	755	800	405	9 5
23 years	21,110	455	260	500	705	1,[illegible]0	1,[illegible]5	1,550	1,850	1,660	1,465	1,350	1,420	3 200	745	955	855	1,303	465	9 7
24 years	20,430	465	225	560	765	985	1 025	1 565	1 640	1 635	1 385	1 450	1,495	3,185	585	900	750	1 39[illegible]	445	9 8
Female, 5 to 24	473 080	70 910	33 625	32,205	31 630	31,965	32,810	33 505	34 420	31 295	26 490	25 040	23,220	38,355	6,655	5 100	3 0[illegible]	4,955	10,115	5 9
5 years	28,310	26 075	125	60															2 350	
6 years	28,495	24 640	2 310	185	50										.			.	1,340	
7 years	28,240	13 400	14,585	2,160	180	45		.											870	1 2
8 years	28,540	2 985	9 155	11 825	1 7[illegible]5	190	45												615	2 1
9 years	24,685	1,190	3,000	8,220	10,090	1 460	170	70							.		.		435	3 0
10 years	24 785	730	1 455	3,775	7,885	8,885	1,285	185	80										5[illegible]5	3 8
11 years	22,905	420	690	1 650	3,400	7,300	7,725	1,150	100	40									430	4 7
12 years	24,145	305	385	970	2,000	3,915	7 715	7 000	1 245	145	45			.					420	5 0
13 years	23,090	325	230	600	1,265	2,100	3,755	7,005	6,065	1 150	140	50							405	6 4
14 years	21,625	300	130	295	605	1,390	2 260	3 550	6,080	5,180	1 010	105	40	.					285	7 4
15 years	21,825	265	125	200	450	770	1,345	2,165	3,705	5,890	5,425	1,340	185	50					210	8 3
16 years	21,005	265	130	145	335	580	1 095	1 670	2,345	3,275	5,365	4 550	1,095	175	40				240	9.1
17 years	21,685	275	125	255	305	495	830	1 320	1,765	2,455	3,035	4 515	4,495	1 150	180	20	.		265	10 0
18 years	22,115	265	145	235	385	495	565	1 300	1,84[illegible]	2,375	2,245	2 570	4 020	4,130	1,085	315	50		280	10 4
19 years	22,005	275	140	185	490	80[illegible]	900	1,235	1,620	1 750	1,600	2 010	2,465	5,505	1,380	1,090	365	100	375	11 0
20 years	22 735	285	210	280	440	745	925	1 375	1,940	1 665	1,635	1,900	2 140	5 730	985	1,130	780	315	255	10 8
21 years	21,500	325	170	290	340	640	880	1,335	1,785	1,620	1,500	1,455	2 225	5,400	845	740	705	875	270	11 1
22 years	22,130	450	175	220	455	800	950	1,400	1,885	1 680	1,575	1 600	2 190	5 385	800	630	460	1 220	285	10 8
23 years	22,560	570	130	355	570	765	1,105	1,475	1 940	1,735	1 535	1,005	2,170	5 210	640	670	360	1,310	315	10 6
24 years	22 500	465	210	370	640	810	1,160	1,270	2 020	1,865	1,580	1 440	2,195	5 220	700	635	330	1,275	31[illegible]	10 4
Nonwhite																				
Total, 5 to 24	334,665	62,860	31,280	30,870	30,765	29,595	27,425	27,070	25 660	19,815	13 390	10,010	6,545	7 465	1 755	1,295	910	855	7 100	4 3
Male, 5 to 24	162,715	32 905	16,660	16,720	16,565	15,630	13 855	12,765	11,330	8 015	5,000	3,500	2,080	2,380	635	470	385	210	3,630	3.8
5 years	10,860	10,355	65	20				.		.				.	.	.			720	.
6 years	10 685	9,310	925	45	45			.					.			.		.	360	
7 years	9,805	5,145	3 615	675	70	45						.	.						275	
8 years	10 385	2,580	4,330	2,580	510	75	35			.		.							275	1 6
9 years	9,460	1,230	2,570	3,205	1,800	340	70	35		.									210	2 3
10 years	9 415	780	1,580	2,740	2,500	1,345	225	70	25							.			150	2 8
11 years	8,670	490	850	1,580	2 195	2,035	1,085	250	40	25		.	.						160	3 6
12 years	9,810	360	615	1,350	2,180	2 230	1,810	835	235	35	10	.							150	4 1
13 years	8,670	225	325	790	1 400	1,800	1,770	1,335	740	105	35	15			.				130	4 9
14 years	8,275	180	175	465	865	1 350	1,540	1,620	1,295	530	145	10	10			.			90	5 7
15 years	8,050	220	145	315	590	1,075	1 230	1 400	1,330	1 015	465	145	25					.	95	6 3
16 years	7,595	220	190	330	550	640	900	1,110	1,135	1,065	395	350	95	30					85	6 8
17 years	7,285	205	120	285	525	660	585	970	1,030	1,015	745	590	290	65	20	10			70	7 2
18 years	7,170	260	165	350	520	570	770	900	965	880	735	500	420	250	65	10	10	.	100	7 2
19 years	6,170	230	140	330	500	500	635	680	740	675	395	410	360	315	100	20	20		120	7 0
20 years	5,970	235	140	330	450	565	635	740	640	565	350	320	235	365	125	80	25	15	140	6 8
21 years	5,935	290	200	260	500	520	585	760	720	525	390	260	180	385	95	75	75	25	90	6 7
22 years	6,085	320	180	295	400	615	665	655	765	605	405	255	130	350	90	95	75	65	140	6 8
23 years	6,235	305	190	375	495	705	610	725	775	475	305	335	165	330	105	95	85	65	145	6 5
24 years	5,885	305	140	400	470	580	590	680	745	500	325	310	170	290	35	85	95	40	125	6 6
Female, 5 to 24	171,950	29,955	14,620	14,150	14,200	13,965	13,590	14,305	14,330	11,800	8,390	6,510	4 465	5,085	1,120	825	525	645	3 470	4 8
5 years	10,595	9,720	80	30							.				.				765	
6 years	10,465	8 865	1,015	115	20							..						.	450	
7 years	10 220	4,905	4 070	760	115	15						..				.			355	1 0
8 years	10,210	2 015	4,005	3,235	640	85	15				.						.		195	1 7
9 years	9,390	940	2 070	3,295	2 310	500	80	40						.				.	[illegible]	2 5
10 years	9,645	535	1,135	2,385	2,990	1,935	395	75	40										165	3.2
11 years	8 260	285	570	1,130	2,015	2,375	1,380	335	45	10			.						125	4 0
12 years	9,275	200	305	765	1,450	2,165	2 310	1,430	380	75	25			.				.	180	4 9
13 years	9,095	207	185	515	1 010	1 365	1,955	2,095	1,160	415	70	20							110	5 6
14 years	8,165	150	115	210	490	995	1,425	1,705	1 665	975	290	40	15						85	6.4
15 years	8,290	170	90	170	300	600	875	1,280	1 785	1 635	935	320	45	10	.		.		65	7 4
16 years	8,090	155	100	80	245	430	700	1,580	1,395	1,465	1,355	670	225	60	30		.		100	7 9
17 years	7,800	160	80	160	235	325	555	840	980	1,165	1,22[illegible]	1,105	650	185	35	15			85	8 4
18 years	8,230	155	95	165	280	320	420	825	1,035	1,185	930	1,040	865	550	155	70	20		120	8 6
19 years	7,475	145	85	135	360	420	480	700	810	880	695	815	670	755	200	150	55	30	90	8 6
20 years	8,335	275	155	200	345	550	625	795	1 055	855	770	645	540	905	225	180	130	25	60	8.2
21 years	6,800	190	125	165	260	420	480	725	960	795	535	465	440	733	15[illegible]	105	95	100	115	8.1
22 years	7,330	280	100	125	315	525	515	795	970	765	655	525	400	825	130	90	90	160	65	8.0
23 years	7,145	340	105	230	405	440	645	835	1,030	775	475	450	325	585	105	120	55	140	85	9.5
24 years	7 075	250	135	280	435	500	755	750	1,320	805	430	415	290	480	85	95	80	190	1[illegible]0	7 4

Table 64.—YEARS OF SCHOOL COMPLETED BY PERSONS 5 TO 24 YEARS OLD, BY SINGLE YEARS OF AGE, COLOR, AND SEX, FOR THE STATE, 1950 AND 1940, FOR URBAN AND RURAL AREAS, AND FOR STANDARD METROPOLITAN AREAS AND CITIES OF 250,000 OR MORE, 1950—Con.

[[illegible] 1940 based on 20 percent sample; [illegible] complete-count data in tables 15 and 33. Median not shown where less than 1.0, or where base is less than 500 for 1950 or 100 for 1940]

Area, census year, color, age, and sex	All persons	Years of school completed																	Median school years completed
		None	Elementary school								High school				College			Not reported	
			1	2	3	4	5	6	7	8	1	2	3	4	1	2	3	4 or more		
THE STATE, 1940																				
Total, 5 to 24	[illegible]	[illegible]	78,0[illegible]	75,2[illegible]9	80,158	9[illegible]	7[illegible]	76,08[illegible]	7[illegible],846	[illegible]1,[illegible]18	48,[illegible]60	42,383	36 255	65,798	9,663	7,966	4,951	6,971	5,167	5.3
Male, 5 to 24	460,[illegible]	64,[illegible]	42,[illegible]	40,675	42 885	43,[illegible]89	39,745	36 789	34 648	14,365	22,261	19,[illegible]44	16 204	25,687	4,709	3 745	2,471	3,329	2,767	4.9
5 years	23,324	22,776	515	22	9														10	
6 years	22,330	16,[illegible]	5,082	432	33	10													620	
7 years	22,5[illegible]	[illegible]	[illegible]	1,898	237	24	5	14											259	1.3
8 years	21,969	3 [illegible]	9 060	4,120	2 [illegible]	279	37	13	7										167	1.9
9 years	22,[illegible]6	1,647	4,582	7,4[illegible]	6,64[illegible]	2,[illegible]31	230	32	14	2									120	2.7
10 years	24 [illegible]	1,258	3 040	5 [illegible]37	7,000	5,844	1,852	230	44	10	7								123	3.4
11 years	22 60[illegible]	749	[illegible]9	3,085	4,443	5 848	4 9[illegible]0	1 577	197	22	18	11							118	4.2
12 years	25 5[illegible]	717	1 272	2,484	3,256	4,919	5,679	4,717	1 506	133	133	23	-						137	4.9
13 years	25,536	624	603	1,764	2,80[illegible]	3,792	4,41[illegible]	3 0[illegible]6	3,893	890	1,246	145	20						159	5.7
14 years	24,456	447	627	1,2[illegible]2	2 089	2 809	3,503	3 884	3 929	1,420	3,152	1,012	126	35	5				98	6.4
15 years	23,599	549	471	959	1,777	2,212	2,615	3,167	3,2[illegible]8	1 446	3,482	2,821	897	87	9	8			77	7.1
16 years	23,956	612	573	795	1,460	1 938	2,276	2 62[illegible]	2,884	1,358	2,985	3 135	2 751	572	64	6	12	1	79	7.6
17 years	23,766	748	427	801	1,077	1,762	2,076	2,276	2 916	1 220	2 1[illegible]	2,514	1,079	2,056	407	52	18	5	92	7.9
18 years	25,012	829	444	851	1,394	1,950	2,06[illegible]	2 337	2,749	1,217	1,836	2 046	2,503	3,415	914	291	38	16	100	8.5
19 years	[illegible]	776	377	758	1 261	1 606	1,792	1,982	2,335	1,110	1 359	1,494	1,701	3,629	936	674	235	37	93	8.1
20 years	[illegible] 371	921	367	790	1 199	1 661	1,719	1 897	2,238	1 008	1,235	1,237	1 283	3 639	555	689	511	210	112	7.9
21 years	21,[illegible]	[illegible]	407	757	1,220	1,770	1,750	1 872	2,368	1 153	1,276	1,215	1,005	3,627	562	578	580	481	[illegible]	7.9
22 years	20,4[illegible]	1,726	378	799	1 291	1,62[illegible]	1,582	1,803	2,436	1,012	1,103	1,178	990	3,313	439	505	395	686	104	7.7
23 years	[illegible]	[illegible]	401	68	1,177	1 604	1,606	1,661	2,[illegible]8[illegible]	1 114	1,[illegible]34	1,169	925	3,210	363	428	347	859	100	[illegible]8
24 years	20 036	1 053	379	787	1 215	1,534	1 604	1,696	2,079	1,150	1,145	1,092	900	3,064	355	414	315	1,041	119	7.8
Female, 5 to 24	468,565	57,853	36 038	37 574	37 473	40,022	39,489	39,293	40 198	16,7[illegible]	25,999	23,259	20,051	40,110	4,954	4,221	2 480	3 642	2,400	5.7
5 years	22,782	22,208	539	21	9														5	
6 years	22,245	15 561	5,705	308	38	5													608	
7 years	22,069	5 6[illegible]6	11,260	3,429	352	42	15	6											180	1.4
8 years	23,5[illegible]	2 699	7 871	9 102	3,240	388	54	11	14										142	2.1
9 years	22,[illegible]4	1,310	5,5[illegible]0	6,615	7,595	2,762	347	38	20	3									108	2.9
10 years	23,957	857	2,083	4,096	6 835	7,047	2 514	322	59	12	18								120	3.7
11 years	22,757	5[illegible]5	1 037	2 344	3,723	5,966	6,021	2,250	299	44	20	4							99	4.6
12 years	24,780	500	728	1,678	2,960	4,212	6,015	5,847	4,198	228	211	22	8						133	5.4
13 years	25 570	418	524	1,156	1 097	3,163	4,074	5,373	5,341	1,247	1,643	217	22						85	6.2
14 years	24,5[illegible]7	193	318	713	1,[illegible]8	2,263	3,064	3,849	4,635	1,807	4,222	1,503	227	35	9				91	7.0
15 years	23,927	14[illegible]	2[illegible]2	50[illegible]	935	1 687	2,213	2 966	3,605	1,647	4,164	3,846	1,726	163	14	8			69	7.8
16 years	24,999	98	239	485	907	1 387	1 926	2,171	3,[illegible]92	1,475	3,160	3,894	4,061	983	92	13	24	5	86	8.8
17 years	23,235	[illegible]4	175	390	770	1 321	1,644	2,075	2,719	1,210	2,179	2,672	3,546	3,346	573	92	26	[illegible]	69	9.4
18 years	23,956	643	249	49[illegible]	915	1,442	1,700	2,174	2,915	1,375	1,980	3 159	2,695	4,430	1,112	460	100	23	93	9.5
19 years	23,695	58[illegible]	241	468	829	1,298	1,600	1,902	2,597	1,195	1,539	1,772	1,857	5,593	860	796	382	54	66	9.7
20 years	24 725	829	218	508	998	1,514	1 813	2,164	2 842	1 367	1,509	1,563	1,437	5 515	583	685	456	735	78	9.0
21 years	22,074	712	254	461	859	1,286	1,576	1,861	2,468	1 219	1 362	1,410	1,219	5,160	479	585	[illegible]62	644	78	9.2
22 years	22,2[illegible]	794	275	521	928	1 [illegible]	1 634	2,019	2,458	1,216	1,340	1,432	1,161	4 801	444	540	[illegible]2	8[illegible]	96	8.9
23 years	21,928	814	231	31[illegible]	[illegible]07	1 479	1,643	1,957	2 463	1,308	1,292	1,368	1,167	4,590	427	513	307	853	94	8.7
24 years	21 [illegible]	850	245	479	958	1,330	1,616	1,900	2,373	1,400	1 360	1,377	1,125	4,479	361	549	271	859	90	8.7
URBAN, 1950																				
Total																				
Total, 5 to 24	463,820	65,720	31,205	29,520	29,010	29,215	29,320	30,410	31,795	30,210	24,930	22,900	22,410	44,275	10,175	9,265	6,175	7,930	10,055	6.4
Male, 5 to 24	222,095	34,035	16,31[illegible]	15,185	15 090	15,150	15,010	15,190	14,560	13,870	10 985	9,825	8,445	15 915	4,995	4,995	3,515	3,785	5 230	5.8
5 years	14,085	13 930	35	30															890	
6 years	13 960	12,475	91[illegible]	6[illegible]	45														460	
7 years	13,96[illegible]	5,175	7 565	760	75	35													355	1.2
8 years	12,725	1,105	4,805	770	530	65	30												270	2.0
9 years	11,600	470	1,430	4,140	4,645	555	70	25											265	2.9
10 years	11,025	180	500	1,760	3,855	4,055	435	70	20										190	3.8
11 years	10,315	135	285	680	1,825	3,27[illegible]	3,540	465	55	35									220	4.6
12 years	10,640	110	130	515	1,145	1,585	4 365	2,800	340	55	10								185	5.4
13 years	10,030	85	40	240	595	1,195	1,860	2,780	2,540	415	80	15							205	6.3
14 years	9,575	65	50	20	340	755	1,150	1,760	2,570	2,155	310	45	30						215	7.2
15 years	9,240	70	70	85	140	515	835	1,205	1,540	2,330	1 890	320	85	30					125	8.0
16 years	8,820	55	55	100	140	195	455	855	1,435	1,605	2,025	1,650	755	65					130	8.8
17 years	8 885	80	20	70	185	270	350	600	780	1,005	1,310	2,025	1,[illegible]8[illegible]	360	40	15			130	9.7
18 years	9,930	100	50	85	160	180	385	655	730	885	925	1,180	1,755	1,705	715	170	[illegible]5		175	10.6
19 years	9,770	115	30	115	180	260	300	530	635	860	550	785	960	2,070	1,065	805	235	[illegible]0	165	11.4
20 years	9,430	120	50	95	150	265	380	515	600	725	560	550	615	2,220	765	880	520	155	25[illegible]	11.9
21 years	11,170	125	[illegible]0	65	225	365	[illegible]75	675	925	810	795	690	630	2,405	655	745	590	550	215	11.3
22 years	11,945	120	95	145	175	395	475	635	925	975	805	670	[illegible]5	2,210	660	810	600	675	210	11.2
23 years	12,625	140	45	140	270	400	510	815	910	915	865	895	825	2,295	615	815	765	1 155	250	11.3
24 years	12,860	130	55	205	310	385	51[illegible]	805	835	1,[illegible]00	8[illegible]5	1,000	885	2,[illegible]95	480	755	620	1,200	310	11.2
Female, 5 to 24	241,725	31,685	14,890	14,335	13,920	14,065	14,310	15,220	16,[illegible]3[illegible]	16,340	13,945	13,075	13,965	28,360	5,180	4,270	2,660	4,145	4,825	7.0
5 years	1[illegible],345	12,355	85	30															875	
6 years	13,680	11,965	1,020	95	15														585	
7 years	13,835	4,560	820	955	9[illegible]	30													375	1.3
8 years	12,355	960	1,935	6,260	855	85	25												235	2.2
9 years	11 350	305	1,000	3,670	5 44[illegible]	645	35	35											230	3.1
10 years	11 085	180	395	1,470	3,525	4,640	500	80	35										230	4.0
11 years	10,470	120	125	135	1,310	3,605	4,050	495	45	15									170	4.8
12 years	10,960	30	75	275	670	1 645	3,520	3,905	590	75	20								155	5.8
13 years	10 2[illegible]5	70	25	150	395	645	1,775	3,050	3,400	635	65	35							190	6.[illegible]
14 years	9,570	100	30	65	135	410	800	1,5[illegible]5	2,760	2,975	525	60	30						135	7.6
15 years	9,590	75	30	40	95	205	470	815	1,480	2,090	2 930	570	130	40					120	8.6
16 years	9,6[illegible]5	65	50	40	95	150	33[illegible]	580	885	1,[illegible]05	2,505	2,480	655	135	20				130	9.4
17 years	10 320	65	15	75	65	150	230	520	695	1,020	1,340	2,380	2,670	780	160	20			135	10.4
18 years	12,305	65	35	85	110	130	190	490	755	1,170	1,190	1,450	2,215	3,055	890	280	[illegible]0		145	11.2
19 years	13 170	70	50	40	205	200	345	515	840	1,015	850	1,080	1,430	3,870	1,120	960	330	85	195	11.9
20 years	13,890	125	25	20	160	235	405	565	970	905	915	1,170	1 310	4,215	730	895	695	270	180	12.0
21 years	13,4[illegible]	95	50	60	110	240	400	610	875	1 035	835	885	1,440	4,065	610	600	640	725	170	12.0
22 years	13,865	125	55	65	185	375	390	640	1,020	1,020	950	1,025	1 310	4,055	620	465	380	1,005	180	11.8
23 years	14,340	180	35	195	20[illegible]	335	515	75[illegible]	1,030	1,110	930	990	1,380	4,080	475	525	300	1,125	175	11.6
24 years	14,320	175	35	140	250	370	510	650	1,155	1 170	960	950	1,395	4,065	555	525	265	935	215	11.5

Table 64.—YEARS OF SCHOOL COMPLETED BY PERSONS 5 TO 24 YEARS OLD BY SINGLE YEARS OF AGE COLOR AND SEX, FOR THE STATE, 1950 AND 1940, FOR URBAN AND RURAL AREAS, AND FOR STANDARD METROPOLITAN AREAS AND CITIES OF 250,000 OR MORE 1950—Con

[Statistics for 1950 based on 20-percent sample available complete-count data in tables 15 and 33. Median not shown where less than 1.0 or where base is less than [illegible] for 1950 or [illegible] for 1940]

Area, census year, color, age, and sex	All persons	None	Elementary school: 1	2	3	4	5	6	7	8	High school: 1	2	3	4	College: 1	2	3	4 or more	Not reported	Median school years completed
URBAN 1950—Con																				
Nonwhite																				
Total, 5 to 24	[illegible]91,180	[illegible]3,990	[illegible],705	[illegible],520	11 [illegible]	12 [illegible]70	[illegible]	[illegible],7[illegible]	[illegible],770	11 3[illegible]5	[illegible]08[illegible]	6 [illegible]5	[illegible] 460	5,78[illegible]	[illegible]170	[illegible]	645	680	[illegible],990	5.[illegible]
Male, 5 to 24	[illegible]0,720	12,425	6,230	5,450	[illegible]130	[illegible],585	[illegible],040	[illegible],085	[illegible],335	4 7[illegible]0	[illegible],060	2,30[illegible]	1 445	[illegible],730	[illegible]	[illegible]30	740	[illegible]65	1,425	4.6
5 years	[illegible] 660	4,350	10	[illegible]															290	
6 years	4,005	4,050	365	30	20														70	
7 years	4,370	2,045	[illegible]	26[illegible]	[illegible]	20													[illegible]	1.0
8 years	4,415	770	[illegible]	1,240	2[illegible]5	[illegible]0	[illegible]												[illegible]15	[illegible].7
9 years	3,925	310	630	1,450	[illegible],040	185	40	10											80	2.[illegible]
10 years	3,705	13[illegible]	365	1,000	[illegible]	745	[illegible]	45	5										65	3.3
11 years	3,6[illegible]	90	20[illegible]	430	[illegible]10	[illegible]	[illegible]45	[illegible]	[illegible]5	[illegible]0									40	4.[illegible]
12 years	3,865	[illegible]5	120	370	710	[illegible],055	93[illegible]	420	[illegible]	20	5								40	4.[illegible]
13 years	3,450	40	30	[illegible]60	420	670	81[illegible]	[illegible]5	415	[illegible]0	30	5							40	5.5
14 years	3,490	[illegible]0	[illegible]0	95	230	520	59[illegible]	[illegible]0	[illegible]80	340	90		5						50	[illegible].3
15 years	[illegible] 420	[illegible]0	[illegible]5	55	120	[illegible]45	480	630	[illegible]15	[illegible]20	[illegible]05	[illegible]0	25						30	7.0
16 years	[illegible],080	[illegible]0	25	[illegible]	90	140	[illegible]00	425	[illegible]0	580	[illegible]	200	90	20					45	7.7
17 years	2,960	25	5	[illegible]	1[illegible]0	155	275	335	41[illegible]	530	[illegible]05	3[illegible]	[illegible]20	50	[illegible]0	5			20	8.3
18 years	3,[illegible]25	50	40	75	120	[illegible]	255	[illegible]75	40[illegible]	[illegible]05	405	5	290	[illegible]00	50	[illegible]	40		30	8.3
19 years	2,7[illegible]0	[illegible]0	[illegible]5	8[illegible]	125	[illegible]00	240	105	3[illegible]0	380	[illegible]	2[illegible]0	2[illegible]5	[illegible]8[illegible]	90	40	70		55	8.0
20 years	2,[illegible]00	70	35	75	110	[illegible]50	205	[illegible]	[illegible]	[illegible]55	[illegible]80	[illegible]0	120	280	65	65	[illegible]	[illegible]0	90	8.1
21 years	2,920	40	65	45	170	200	260	4[illegible]	330	320	[illegible]65	[illegible]65	[illegible]5	[illegible]60	75	40	55	20	50	7.8
22 years	3,160	70	55	95	[illegible]05	2[illegible]5	265	[illegible]	[illegible]45	[illegible]40	275	1[illegible]0	95	245	55	90	50	60	55	7.8
23 years	3,3[illegible]0	80	[illegible]0	[illegible]0	[illegible]85	205	[illegible]5	[illegible]	405	315	[illegible]	255	100	250	90	90	60	50	75	7.6
24 years	3,285	[illegible]0	[illegible]0	[illegible]0	2[illegible]0	235	285	39[illegible]	440	355	[illegible]0	245	40	230	95	85	80	25	80	7.[illegible]
Female, 5 to 24	8[illegible],4[illegible]0	1[illegible],[illegible]65	[illegible]565	5,670	[illegible],775	5,885	5,735	5,[illegible]5	7,2[illegible]5	6,655	[illegible],0[illegible]	4,1[illegible]0	2,95[illegible]	3,85[illegible]	7[illegible]	595	355	315	[illegible]565	5.9
5 years	4,55[illegible]	4,[illegible]75	[illegible]5	15															220	
6 years	4,575	3,900	410	[illegible]5	[illegible]0														90	
7 years	4,555	[illegible],[illegible]35	2,060	3[illegible]0	70	[illegible]0													[illegible]30	1.1
8 years	4,375	560	[illegible]	1,725	340	40	[illegible]0												60	2.0
9 years	[illegible],970	2[illegible]0	670	480	[illegible],265	2[illegible]5	30	20											80	2.7
10 years	4,065	[illegible]0	[illegible]75	625	[illegible]	1,095	20[illegible]	[illegible]	[illegible]										80	3.6
11 years	3,625	65	9[illegible]	345	7[illegible]	1,235	785	2[illegible]5	5	5									70	4.4
12 years	4,025	[illegible]	55	200	48[illegible]	990	1,115	[illegible]20	[illegible]25	45	10								65	5.2
13 years	3,840	40	1[illegible]	130	295	41[illegible]	85[illegible]	1,000	6[illegible]	[illegible]0	40	[illegible]5							50	6.1
14 years	3,415	[illegible]0	2[illegible]	35	[illegible]5	255	475	[illegible]30	3[illegible]0	[illegible]0	[illegible]5	[illegible]5	10						40	6.9
15 years	3,520	35	[illegible]	25	55	150	305	475	8[illegible]0	85[illegible]	[illegible]60	[illegible]30	40	[illegible]0					35	7.9
16 years	3,785	30	[illegible]0	[illegible]0	70	[illegible]	1[illegible]	360	530	[illegible]	795	[illegible]	[illegible]45	45	15				50	8.6
17 years	3,495	3[illegible]	[illegible]	25	45	10[illegible]	140	[illegible]45	[illegible]20	[illegible]0	57[illegible]	695	430	[illegible]45	20	[illegible]			25	9.3
18 years	[illegible],040	2[illegible]	25	50	70	95	1[illegible]0	[illegible]25	4[illegible]5	[illegible]70	[illegible]	[illegible]40	490	4[illegible]	30	60	[illegible]5		55	9.5
19 years	3,990	[illegible]0	40	30	1[illegible]	135	150	290	4[illegible]0	555	40[illegible]	4[illegible]5	39[illegible]	520	[illegible]35	1[illegible]0	35	30	[illegible]0	9.3
20 years	4,350	80	20	70	110	[illegible]65	275	3[illegible]0	540	480	44[illegible]	4[illegible]0	[illegible]50	65[illegible]	[illegible]05	135	80	[illegible]0	40	[illegible].1
21 years	3,725	3[illegible]	45	[illegible]0	75	[illegible]5	230	[illegible]25	450	500	[illegible]40	280	32[illegible]	5[illegible]0	75	[illegible]0	70	85	60	8.9
22 years	4,260	[illegible]0	[illegible]	[illegible]5	135	255	2[illegible]0	375	540	5[illegible]	4[illegible]5	3[illegible]	280	6[illegible]5	95	[illegible]5	60	125	30	8.9
23 years	4,175	[illegible]	25	120	155	220	3[illegible]	[illegible]0	600	530	[illegible]0	3[illegible]5	235	4[illegible]	[illegible]5	[illegible]5	45	1[illegible]5	35	8.2
24 years	4,320	75	25	105	[illegible]70	245	345	42[illegible]	[illegible]	[illegible]	325	310	260	3[illegible]5	[illegible]0	85	50	140	80	8.1
RURAL NONFARM 1950																				
Total																				
Total, 5 to 24	236,6[illegible]	40,175	18,785	19,080	[illegible]8,435	[illegible]8,950	18 820	18 [illegible]	17,170	1[illegible],5[illegible]0	11 [illegible]55	9,[illegible]	9,[illegible]35	10,935	1 9[illegible]5	[illegible],130	635	[illegible],050	5,855	5.0
Male, 5 to 24	119,045	21,145	9,[illegible]35	10,6[illegible]	10,0[illegible]5	10 005	9,[illegible]85	9 495	8,220	6 755	5 070	4 160	3,88[illegible]	4 725	905	520	340	465	3,190	4.6
5 years	7 870	7,[illegible]20	[illegible]	15															595	
6 years	7 920	7,010	530	15	15														550	
7 years	7,40[illegible]	3,230	3,365	5[illegible]5	[illegible]0														220	1.1
8 years	7,295	1,070	2,800	2,800	350	65	20												190	1.9
9 years	[illegible],330	510	1,[illegible]35	2,630	[illegible],120	290	30	[illegible]5											170	2.6
10 years	6 805	295	650	1,405	2 205	1,025	240	30	40										1[illegible]5	3.5
11 years	6,4[illegible]	[illegible]0	305	[illegible]55	1,210	1,865	1,570	[illegible]50	35	15									250	[illegible]3
12 years	7,065	110	1[illegible]5	[illegible]80	955	1,3[illegible]	1 980	1,490	200	45	5								1[illegible]5	5.1
13 years	5,830	110	85	270	555	845	1 1[illegible]0	1,495	975	170	25	20							1[illegible]0	5.9
14 years	5,620	[illegible]15	[illegible]0	155	330	580	8[illegible]	1,070	1,380	845	135	[illegible]	10						90	6.6
15 years	[illegible]26[illegible]	95	45	[illegible]	240	395	535	[illegible]	940	[illegible]	685	120	5						95	7.3
16 years	5,585	[illegible]10	60	165	205	26[illegible]	450	[illegible]10	820	900	985	580	145		10				85	8.0
17 years	[illegible] 205	10[illegible]	60	150	180	245	33[illegible]	[illegible]30	550	705	790	335	590	[illegible]	15	5			65	8.6
18 years	4,775	75	[illegible]0	[illegible]05	210	285	365	[illegible]40	49[illegible]	470	[illegible]95	535	74[illegible]	3[illegible]0	90	5			80	[illegible].7
19 years	4,530	[illegible]20	65	[illegible]35	[illegible]60	33[illegible]	31[illegible]	32[illegible]	41[illegible]	380	320	410	[illegible]65	720	140	35	20	[illegible]	75	8.7
20 years	[illegible],0[illegible]	[illegible]50	75	[illegible]50	260	300	420	440	4[illegible]5	35[illegible]	360	[illegible]35	3[illegible]0	1,005	1[illegible]0	60	40	45	90	8.6
21 years	4,985	130	75	[illegible]65	[illegible]5	310	340	490	440	420	[illegible]	3[illegible]0	390	940	140	85	50	75	[illegible]0	8.5
22 years	4,925	130	85	[illegible]35	215	295	380	410	[illegible]25	4[illegible]0	340	3[illegible]	395	6[illegible]5	145	105	75	70	125	8.4
23 years	4 76[illegible]	[illegible]15	75	[illegible]60	275	395	290	420	45[illegible]	41[illegible]	335	31[illegible]	365	63[illegible]	95	110	[illegible]5	105	130	8.3
24 years	4,68[illegible]	145	90	210	2[illegible]5	350	280	50[illegible]	490	41[illegible]	325	275	425	390	100	115	7[illegible]	165	90	8.0
Female, 5 to 24	[illegible]7,650	19,030	8,850	8,4[illegible]	8,350	8 945	9,335	9,040	8,950	7,82[illegible]	6 455	[illegible],445	5,5[illegible]5	6,210	[illegible],060	610	295	585	2,66[illegible]	5.4
5 years	7 [illegible]25	7,000	1	25															585	
6 years	7,280	6,300	61[illegible]	[illegible]0	20														335	
7 years	7 [illegible]05	2 795	3,530	525	50	5													200	1.2
8 years	7,025	800	2,53[illegible]	3 060	415	70	5												200	2.0
9 years	6,595	370	860	2,705	2,490	44[illegible]	[illegible]	10											160	2.9
10 years	6,6[illegible]	205	[illegible]65	1,075	2,160	2,400	335	30	25										100	3.8
11 years	6,000	145	18[illegible]	4[illegible]0	91[illegible]	1 845	2,010	320	25	15									130	[illegible]
12 years	6,310	115	100	270	535	1,050	2,205	1,630	250	30	10								115	5.[illegible]
13 years	[illegible],070	105	90	140	290	655	[illegible] 030	1,970	1 280	260	40	5							105	6.[illegible]
14 years	5,650	[illegible]	30	85	175	410	670	955	1,620	1,325	[illegible]20	25	10						55	7.2
15 years	5,795	65	35	60	155	240	390	620	1,040	1 [illegible]10	1 310	205	30	[illegible]					30	8.2
16 years	5,180	9[illegible]	10	25	110	170	315	45[illegible]	640	830	1,165	1,[illegible]5	235	25	15				[illegible]0	8.9
17 years	[illegible],325	100	20	90	95	155	245	33[illegible]	490	635	825	1,[illegible]0	925	155	15				90	9.5
18 years	5 325	90	55	50	95	185	220	345	570	680	585	590	960	660	[illegible]30	25	5		80	9.6
19 years	4,805	[illegible]10	45	65	115	[illegible]55	28[illegible]	[illegible]00	405	385	365	505	[illegible]75	[illegible],005	180	85	[illegible]5	[illegible]5	85	10.1
20 years	5 060	10	100	85	115	245	[illegible]05	425	480	435	405	490	530	9[illegible]5	185	95	55	35	50	9.[illegible]
21 years	4,865	80	65	85	135	175	230	43[illegible]	525	370	425	340	560	905	190	105	40	105	65	9.7
22 years	5,225	130	75	75	140	250	325	390	500	[illegible]00	400	390	[illegible]70	860	140	1[illegible]	65	140	65	9.5
23 years	4,970	170	25	75	150	250	320	395	595	410	325	375	585	790	115	100	[illegible]	140	95	9.1
24 years	5,050	180	95	60	190	240	390	32[illegible]	510	440	380	335	575	890	90	90	50	150	60	9.2

Table 64.—YEARS OF SCHOOL COMPLETED BY PERSONS 5 TO 24 YEARS OLD, BY SINGLE YEARS OF AGE, COLOR, AND SEX, FOR THE STATE 1950 AND 1940 FOR URBAN AND RURAL AREAS, AND FOR STANDARD METROPOLITAN AREAS AND CITIES OF 250,000 OR MORE, 1950—Con.

[Statistics for 1950 based on 20-percent sample; available complete-count data in tables 16 and 33. Median not shown where less than 1.0 or where base is less than 500 for 1950 or 100 for 1940]

Area, census year, color, age, and sex	All persons	None	Elementary school: 1	2	3	4	5	6	7	8	High school: 1	2	3	4	College: 1	2	3	4 or more	Not reported	Median school years completed
RURAL NONFARM, 1950—Con.																				
Nonwhite																				
Total, 5 to 24	77,520	15,415	7,855	7,770	7,460	7,255	6,655	6,350	5,755	3,890	2,530	1,765	1,090	1,155	460	220	190	135	1,770	3.9
Male, 5 to 24	38,500	8,150	4,230	4,375	4,210	3,875	3,190	2,915	2,540	1,570	985	635	255	460	150	60	70	40	990	3.5
5 years	2,590	2,390	25	10															165	
6 years	2,550	2,250	190		10														100	
7 years	2,420	1,330	825	190	10														65	
8 years	2,530	500	1,270	555	120	30	5												50	1.5
9 years	2,260	330	635	725	425	60	5	5											75	2.2
10 years	2,465	225	505	735	650	270	40	5	15										20	2.7
11 years	2,380	30	270	775	570	420	165	55	10										85	3.3
12 years	2,255	70	130	400	560	465	355	180	55	10									30	3.9
13 years	1,915	60	70	180	325	375	380	255	175	15		10							70	4.8
14 years	1,855	20	55	115	215	305	400	350	255	90	30	5							15	5.5
15 years	1,775	55	40	85	160	275	285	330	270	160	60	15							40	5.9
16 years	1,740	55	30	75	125	160	210	120	320	210	120	75	5						35	6.6
17 years	1,630	50	45	110	115	140	150	270	205	230	170	75	20	5	10	5			30	6.7
18 years	1,545	40	35	50	135	145	185	155	245	200	160	80	35	30	15	5			30	7.1
19 years	1,505	75	45	100	150	145	180	130	170	140	75	125	25	105	10				30	6.3
20 years	1,575	90	40	95	150	160	135	200	175	125	95	45	60	70	55	15	5	5	15	6.3
21 years	1,375	110	45	95	105	140	140	130	160	110	70	55	20	75	15	5	15	5	20	6.2
22 years	1,510	115	65	85	135	180	230	125	170	90	75	50	15	70	30	5	20		50	5.7
23 years	1,380	80	50	95	155	210	105	170	130	95	35	50	55	60	15	5	15	15	40	5.8
24 years	1,505	85	60	150	135	195	150	165	185	95	95	50	20	45		20	15	15	25	5.8
Female, 5 to 24	39,020	7,265	3,625	3,395	3,250	3,380	3,465	3,435	3,215	2,320	1,545	1,130	835	695	310	160	120	95	780	4.2
5 years	2,600	2,395	15	10															180	
6 years	2,395	2,040	260	5															90	
7 years	2,380	1,160	945	180	20	5													70	
8 years	2,360	465	935	745	120	25													70	1.7
9 years	2,275	270	570	760	480	130	20	10											35	2.4
10 years	2,285	130	275	655	720	385	80	10	10										20	3.1
11 years	1,705	80	135	250	430	470	280	35		5									20	3.9
12 years	2,145	65	75	200	350	465	630	265	30	15	5								45	4.8
13 years	2,140	65	65	105	200	375	500	520	200	50	10								30	5.5
14 years	1,895	20	25	50	145	265	385	375	370	205	35	5	5							6.1
15 years	1,920	40	30	55	100	180	235	315	430	320	160	45							10	7.0
16 years	1,7[illegible]	55	10	15	60	120	160	260	335	295	220	105	50	10	10				30	7.5
17 years	1,710	40	10	55	55	85	140	215	230	260	280	160	135	10	10				25	8.0
18 years	1,920	50	30	30	50	115	110	195	290	295	220	190	180	90	25	10	55		35	8.2
19 years	1,610	35	20	35	65	110	130	215	170	105	115	165	165	155	55	30	20		20	8.1
20 years	1,940	70	[illegible]	65	80	165	180	220	210	180	155	170	100	130	85	30	35	5	15	7.5
21 years	1,565	40	50	5	95	100	70	235	280	150	100	90	75	85	65	25	15	5	30	7.4
22 years	1,535	70	35	45	75	135	150	190	200	140	115	90	60	120	30	20	20	25	15	7.3
23 years	1,490	75	15	40	90	110	175	210	270	140	70	70	55	50	15	40	5	45	35	7.0
24 years	1,405	80	50	40	100	135	220	165	190	160	60	70	10	40	15	5	20	35	5	6.5
RURAL FARM: 1950																				
Total																				
Total, 5 to 24	234,525	42,100	20,785	20,950	21,105	20,205	19,620	18,795	17,950	13,720	10,985	8,020	6,780	6,245	760	430	270	375	5,430	4.5
Male, 5 to 24	120,840	21,905	10,900	11,495	11,745	11,250	10,455	9,550	9,015	6,590	4,925	3,500	3,080	2,760	345	210	160	150	2,805	4.3
5 years	7,440	6,845	45																550	
6 years	7,530	6,430	715	30	15														340	
7 years	6,580	3,180	2,630	515	50	10													195	1.0
8 years	7,505	1,470	2,770	2,475	470	55	15												250	1.8
9 years	7,195	735	1,530	2,515	1,825	350	50	30											160	2.5
10 years	7,385	500	935	1,660	2,160	1,655	285	30	10										150	3.2
11 years	6,895	290	425	920	1,445	1,860	1,520	245	30	25									135	4.2
12 years	7,780	295	395	660	1,325	1,405	1,940	1,260	275	30	15								180	4.8
13 years	7,355	195	255	525	870	1,290	1,370	1,615	980	150	25								80	5.4
14 years	6,835	195	125	305	565	780	965	1,150	1,590	920	130	10	5						95	6.4
15 years	6,995	200	95	200	380	660	750	1,005	1,200	1,315	905	190	10	10					75	7.1
16 years	6,550	185	170	245	395	460	555	695	1,000	925	1,040	645	155	20					60	7.5
17 years	6,490	155	85	170	370	435	550	690	780	745	720	980	610	135					65	8.0
18 years	5,965	205	120	265	340	435	505	585	610	685	590	480	705	285	75	10			70	7.8
19 years	4,395	120	105	170	315	305	355	410	540	360	350	235	445	530	70	20	25	5	65	7.8
20 years	3,910	125	80	195	260	355	385	480	405	265	220	230	305	425	60	35	10	5	70	7.1
21 years	3,925	205	115	150	305	295	345	410	430	295	215	205	225	495	45	60	45	20	65	7.2
22 years	3,495	185	85	150	215	285	280	375	415	325	245	210	205	285	55	25	30	55	70	7.3
23 years	3,725	200	140	200	220	365	355	315	485	330	265	140	250	275	35	30	15	40	85	7.4
24 years	2,890	190	80	145	220	250	230	255	295	220	205	175	185	300	5	30	35	25	45	7.2
Female, 5 to 24	113,685	20,195	9,885	9,455	9,360	8,955	9,165	9,245	8,935	7,130	6,060	4,520	3,700	3,485	415	220	110	225	2,625	4.7
5 years	7,340	6,720	25	5															590	
6 years	7,535	6,375	675	80	15														390	
7 years	7,300	3,045	3,235	680	35	10													295	1.1
8 years	7,180	1,225	2,685	2,565	475	35	15												180	1.8
9 years	6,760	515	1,140	2,345	2,160	400	80	25											95	2.7
10 years	7,010	345	685	1,260	2,200	1,845	390	75	25										175	3.5
11 years	6,435	155	380	705	1,175	1,830	1,665	335	30	10									130	4.4
12 years	6,875	160	210	425	795	1,220	1,990	1,465	405	40	15								150	5.3
13 years	6,885	150	115	310	580	800	1,150	1,985	1,385	255	55	10							110	6.1
14 years	6,405	130	70	145	295	570	790	1,080	1,700	1,280	235	20							90	7.0
15 years	6,440	125	60	100	200	325	485	730	1,185	1,590	1,285	265	25	5					60	8.0
16 years	6,210	110	70	80	130	260	460	635	820	940	1,395	1,035	205	15	5				50	8.5
17 years	6,040	110	90	90	145	190	355	465	580	800	870	1,185	900	215	5				40	9.2
18 years	4,785	110	55	100	180	180	255	465	520	525	470	530	845	415	65	10	5		55	9.0
19 years	4,030	95	45	80	170	225	300	320	375	350	385	425	460	630	80	45	10		35	9.1
20 years	3,785	150	85	75	165	265	215	385	490	325	315	240	300	600	70	40	30	10	25	8.2
21 years	3,190	150	55	75	95	225	250	290	385	285	310	230	225	430	45	35	25	45	95	8.2
22 years	3,240	195	45	80	130	175	235	370	365	260	425	185	310	470	40	25	15	75	40	8.0
23 years	3,250	220	70	85	215	180	270	325	315	215	280	240	205	440	50	45	5	45	45	7.8
24 years	2,990	110	80	170	200	200	260	295	355	255	240	155	225	265	55	20	20	50	35	7.5

Table 64.—YEARS OF SCHOOL COMPLETED BY PERSONS 5 TO 24 YEARS OLD, BY SINGLE YEARS OF AGE, COLOR, AND SEX, FOR THE STATE, 1950 AND 1940, FOR URBAN AND RURAL AREAS, AND FOR STANDARD METROPOLITAN AREAS AND CITIES OF 250,000 OR MORE, 1950—Con

[Statistics for 1950 based on 20-percent sample; available complete-count data in tables 5 and 33. Median not shown where less than 1.0 or where base is less than 500 for 1950 or 100 for 1940]

Area, census year, color, age, and sex	All persons	Years of school completed: None	Elementary school: 1	2	3	4	5	6	7	8	High school: 1	2	3	4	College: 1	2	3	4 or more	Not reported	Median school years completed
RURAL FARM: 1950—Con																				
Nonwhite																				
Total, 5 to 24	105,965	23,455	11 660	11 580	12,400	10,270	9,015	7,980	7,115	4 560	2,780	1,790	1,055	725	125	80	75	40	2,240	3 5
Male, 5 to 24	53,495	12,330	6 230	6 495	7,225	5,570	4,625	3,765	3,235	1,735	955	560	380	190	25	10	25	5	1 115	3 2
5 years	3,650	3,355	30																265	
6 years	3,330	3,010	370	15	15														120	
7 years	3,015	1,770	910	220	25	5													85	
8 years	3,440	1,120	1,230	785	165	25	5												110	1 4
9 years	3,275	420	1,105	980	375	95	25	20											55	1 9
10 years	3,255	425	710	1 065	655	350	50	10	5										65	2 5
11 years	2,905	260	375	675	715	495	275	55	15	15									25	3 2
12 years	3,690	235	365	580	910	710	520	235	45	5	5								80	3 7
13 years	3,305	125	225	450	655	755	575	315	150	30	5								20	4 2
14 years	2,930	120	90	255	720	525	545	460	360	100	45		5						35	5 1
15 years	2,855	135	70	175	310	455	465	440	425	230	170	20							25	5 6
16 years	2,775	135	135	190	335	340	390	355	405	275	125	10		10					5	5 6
17 years	2,695	130	70	130	300	365	300	365	[illegible]	255	170	120	50	15					20	6 1
18 years	2,800	170	90	225	265	320	330	370	315	275	[illegible]	135	95	30					40	5 9
19 years	1,935	95	80	[illegible]	225	165	215	245	270	155	125	55	30	25	10				35	6 1
20 years	1,775	75	65	160	190	255	230	235	205	85	75	[illegible]	50	35	5		5		35	5 5
21 years	1 640	140	90	120	225	180	185	225	170	95	55	40	40	30	5	10	5		20	5 3
22 years	1,415	135	60	115	160	170	170	165	170	35	55	35	20	15	5		5	5	35	5 3
23 years	1,515	145	110	160	135	230	190	145	190	65	25	30	10	20			10		30	4 8
24 years	1,095	130	50	110	125	150	135	125	120	50	20	15	10						20	4 8
Female, 5 to 24	52,470	11,125	5,430	5,085	5,175	4 700	4 390	4 215	3,880	2,825	1,825	1,230	675	535	100	70	50	35	1,125	3 8
5 years	3,440	3,150	20	5															265	
6 years	3,495	2,925	545	45	10														170	
7 years	3,280	1,810	1,065	250	25														135	
8 years	3,475	1 010	1,430	765	180	20	5												65	1 5
9 years	3,145	460	830	1,055	565	155	30	10											40	2 2
10 years	3,295	295	585	905	860	455	100	25	5										65	2 8
11 years	2,930	140	340	515	810	670	505	85	10										35	3 5
12 years	3 105	120	175	365	595	710	575	345	125	15	10								70	4 4
13 years	3,115	75	105	280	515	575	595	575	285	55	20	5							30	5 0
14 years	2,855	90	65	125	250	475	570	500	465	220	40	10							45	5 7
15 years	2 750	95	45	90	145	270	345	490	545	460	195	45	5						20	6 8
16 years	2,860	70	50	55	110	210	345	460	530	475	340	155	30	5	5				20	7 2
17 years	2,595	85	65	80	135	135	275	280	330	435	370	250	85	30	5				35	7 7
18 years	2,270	85	40	85	160	110	200	305	100	320	195	210	195	35					30	7 5
19 years	1,875	70	25	70	140	115	200	195	180	220	175	195	110	80	10	10			20	7 3
20 years	2,045	125	60	65	155	220	170	215	305	195	170	95	90	110	35	15	15		5	7 0
21 years	1,570	115	50	60	90	155	180	165	250	145	95	95	45	85	15	20	10	10	25	6 9
22 years	1,535	140	50	45	105	135	155	230	230	110	85	70	60	90	5	5	10	10	20	6 6
23 years	1,450	170	65	70	160	110	170	175	160	105	35	65	35	60	15	15	5		15	5 9
24 years	1 350	95	60	135	165	120	170	160	180	70	45	35	20	40	10	5	10	15	15	5 5
STANDARD METROPOLITAN AREAS, 1950																				
NEW ORLEANS—TOTAL																				
Total, 5 to 24	204,070	27,935	14 250	12 985	12,285	12,435	12 605	13,765	13,950	14,670	11 155	10,600	9 200	21,410	3 815	3,420	1,895	3 405	4,290	6 [illegible]
Male, 5 to 24	98,730	14,350	7,545	6,555	6,350	6,765	6,655	7,045	6 760	7,080	5,080	4,605	3 455	7 925	1,845	1 805	1 020	1 620	2,270	6 0
5 years	6,015	5,595	35	15															370	
6 years	6,155	5,380	510	40	30														195	
7 years	6,515	2,180	3,670	430	10	15													210	1 3
8 years	5,670	455	2,155	2,550	325	30	15												140	2 1
9 years	5,120	160	575	1,750	2,195	305	35	10											90	3 0
10 years	4 655	85	235	770	1,620	1,815	240	35	15										50	3.8
11 years	4,515	70	120	295	775	1,480	1,425	220	10	20									100	4 6
12 years	4,505	45	35	220	435	850	1,320	1 330	160	35	5								70	5 5
13 years	4 515	35	5	80	205	490	915	1,095	1,140	185	40	5							100	6 3
14 years	4 145	45	20	30	120	350	570	760	1,015	960	125	25	20						105	7 1
15 years	4,280	30	20	25	55	205	395	630	765	1,035	830	160	55	25					50	8 0
16 years	4,155	20	25	60	55	65	245	455	490	750	950	775	175	40					50	8 9
17 years	4,835	30	5	15	45	135	165	280	380	580	800	730	630	185	10	10			55	9 4
18 years	4 380	25	15	20	60	95	175	340	380	490	380	480	730	850	200	40	15		80	10 3
19 years	4,335	35	20	35	65	90	150	270	360	475	280	415	390	1,010	375	250	50	25	60	10 9
20 years	4,270	35		10	60	135	160	295	290	440	290	280	270	1 135	260	305	110	70	125	11 3
21 years	4,940	30	20	35	85	195	230	270	435	530	560	325	210	1,160	270	260	225	195	105	10 7
22 years	5,070	20	45	40	30	175	225	275	485	605	385	345	255	1,125	300	250	175	270	65	10 6
23 years	5 810	30	25	40	85	180	195	375	445	455	480	510	310	1,220	245	145	245	510	115	11 1
24 years	5,875	45	10	95	90	155	195	415	570	520	575	555	410	1,175	205	145	200	550	135	11 1
Female, 5 to 24	105,340	13,585	6,705	6 430	5,935	5,670	5,950	6,720	7,190	7,590	6 075	5,995	5,745	13,485	1 970	1,615	875	1,785	2,020	7 [illegible]
5 years	5,990	5,525	75	10															380	
6 years	5,995	5 415	575	50	10														245	
7 years	6,435	1,890	3,760	505	75	15													190	1 3
8 years	5,680	445	1,535	3 015	510	35	15												125	2 3
9 years	4 945	120	440	1,530	2 470	285	15	15											70	3 1
10 years	4,700	55	120	610	1,470	2,050	305	40	20										110	4 0
11 years	4,520	30	35	230	520	1 490	1,825	275	40										75	4 9
12 years	4,655	10	45	85	215	705	1,375	1,815	260	45	10								90	5 9
13 years	4,140	40	5	40	105	235	645	1 225	1 420	290	25	15							95	6 8
14 years	4 195	45	5	20	50	135	155	690	1,160	1,300	300	40	25						65	7 7
15 years	4,280	10	15	5	35	40	195	365	680	1,130	1,260	350	85	30					80	8 [illegible]
16 years	4,180	30	30	25	30	40	130	215	350	535	1 015	1,165	360	90	10				55	9 6
17 years	4,545	30		40	10	70	75	170	285	495	535	1,025	1,260	415	85	10			40	10 5
18 years	5,180	20	5	30	35	40	75	210	335	490	460	590	890	1,560	270	105	10		55	11 3
19 years	5,290	15	15	15	65	60	120	245	375	480	455	460	505	1,710	445	270	55	40	60	11 8
20 years	5,715	15	5	55	70	65	130	210	440	375	410	540	530	1,930	295	310	195	85	55	12 0
21 years	5,935	25	15	20	40	85	190	275	355	580	385	360	570	1,880	260	255	265	320	55	12 0
22 years	5,920	45	15	25	75	130	90	300	500	475	435	520	505	1 885	225	205	105	375	10	11 7
23 years	6,500	60	5	65	60	105	270	355	470	630	420	460	530	1,990	175	235	130	525	65	11 7
24 years	6,455	60	5	55	80	85	190	315	500	660	465	470	485	1,995	205	225	115	440	105	11 6

Table 64.—YEARS OF SCHOOL COMPLETED BY PERSONS 5 TO 24 YEARS OLD, BY SINGLE YEARS OF AGE, COLOR, AND SEX, FOR THE STATE, 1950 AND 1940, FOR URBAN AND RURAL AREAS, AND FOR STANDARD METROPOLITAN AREAS AND CITIES OF 250 000 OR MORE, 1950—Con

[Statistics for 1950 based on 20-percent sample; arabic complete-count data in tables 16 and 33. Median not shown where less than 1.0, or where base is less than 500 for 1950 or 100 for 1940]

Area, census year, color, age, and sex	All persons	None	Elementary school: 1	2	3	4	5	6	7	8	High school: 1	2	3	4	College: 1	2	3	4 or more	Not reported	Median school years completed
STANDARD METROPOLITAN AREAS 1950—Con.																				
NEW ORLEANS—NONWHITE																				
Total, 5 to 24	65 735	[illegible]	5,125	4,750	4,750	4,985	4,780	5 550	5 550	5,760	3,965	3,370	1,895	2,980	500	440	265	305	1,235	5 7
Male, 5 to 24	31,245	[illegible]	2,715	2,470	2,460	2,750	2 585	2,660	2,535	2 620	1,595	1 205	675	950	215	190	115	85	555	5 0
5 years	1,875	1,730	5	10															95	
6 years	1,905	1,620	150	15	15														75	
7 years	2,100	800	975	175	10	5													75	1 2
8 years	2,000	270	980	630	130	10	5												45	1 8
9 years	1,755	95	515	530	565	105	20												25	2 7
10 years	1 675	50	130	435	550	405	60	20											25	3 4
11 years	1 625	[illegible]	85	190	365	530	320	70	5	10									20	4 3
12 years	1,620	25	35	130	290	470	405	235	55	5	5								5	4 8
13 years	1 555	15	5	40	125	230	330	345	230	25	20								5	5 7
14 years	1 510	15	5	20	60	240	295	320	300	180	35	5	5						30	6 3
15 years	1,565	10		5	50	130	205	285	295	335	175	50	15						10	7 4
16 years	1,310	[illegible]		20	[illegible]	55	135	185	230	220	255	70	50	20					20	8 0
17 years	1,345			5	30	75	90	140	170	275	180	200	95	15		5			10	8 5
18 years	1 435	5	10	15	35	30	100	175	190	240	190	125	115	135	30		5		5	8 6
19 years	1 240	20	5	20	45	60	95	175	140	190	85	115	85	100	30	15			25	8 [illegible]
20 years	1,240	10		5	35	35	75	190	105	215	95	130	65	150	25	30	5	10	40	8 6
21 years	1,315	5	15	15	25	95	105	120	185	230	115	80	45	130	40	35	20	10	15	8 2
22 years	1 330	10	25	25	15	95	110	160	205	295	40	100	55	150	35	40	15	30	25	8 4
23 years	1,500	15	10	30	30	105	120	155	200	160	170	165	50	155	40	40	30	25	40	8 5
24 years	1,460	30	10	65	65	70	95	135	205	220	130	145	95	100	15	25	40	10	[illegible]	8 2
Female, 5 to 24	34 490	4,700	2 415	2 280	2 290	2 235	2,295	2 890	3 015	3 140	2,370	2 105	1 220	2,085	285	250	150	220	650	6 3
5 years	2,020	1,830	35	10															145	
6 years	1,885	1,570	205	35															75	
7 years	2 195	785	1,120	145	35	5													85	1 2
8 years	1,965	225	725	855	240	20	10												30	2 1
9 years	1 670	90	255	560	625	90	10	10											30	2 8
10 years	1,745	35	55	305	615	560	110	25	10										30	3 8
11 years	1,545	10	30	110	260	595	375	130	35										20	4 6
12 years	1,575	10	25	40	115	350	505	390	90	20									30	5 5
13 years	1,495	20		25	75	120	260	460	330	155	20	5							15	6 5
14 years	1,570			15	35	80	180	380	400	295	135	20	10						20	7 2
15 years	1,640	5	5	5	15	30	95	210	345	385	315	175	30	10					15	8 3
16 years	1 505	10	20	5	15	20	55	115	190	295	405	235	85	30	5				15	9 0
17 years	1 505	10		5	[illegible]	40	25	100	170	210	430	395	185	100	10				15	9 8
18 years	1,605	5	5	15	25	20	35	125	160	200	210	280	210	245	40	3	5		20	10 0
19 years	1,740	15	5	10	30	40	55	140	180	270	175	205	165	270	35	25	15	20	15	9 [illegible]
20 years	1,625			20	30	35	85	140	230	200	130	205	35	325	45	40	30		15	9 3
21 years	1,625	10	15	20	20	55	90	110	140	265	180	140	145	245	45	40	45	55	25	9 5
22 years	1,790	20	5	15	40	85	45	170	240	220	205	185	135	295	40	40	15	20	15	9 2
23 years	1,850	25	5	45	35	55	15	200	265	300	170	150	115	230	10	30	15	50	5	8 5
24 years	1,935	35		40	35	65	125	205	230	325	155	170	85	275	25	35	25	65	30	8 6
CITIES: 1950																				
NEW ORLEANS—TOTAL																				
Total, 5 to 24	165 820	21 295	11,135	10,250	9,750	9,765	9,840	10,990	11 210	12,390	9,360	8,945	7,580	18,460	3,415	3 095	1,775	3,125	3,440	6 8
Male, 5 to 24	79,595	10,885	5,825	5,180	4,920	5,180	5 130	5,595	5 485	5,985	4,230	3,940	2 900	6,875	1,690	1 600	955	1,500	1,790	6 3
5 years	4 660	4,315	30	10															305	
6 years	4,760	4,070	455	40	10														165	
7 years	5 110	1,610	2 945	385	10	10													150	1 3
8 years	4 485	355	1 630	2,070	290	25	10												105	2 1
9 years	3,995	125	375	1 455	1,780	250	3	10											65	3 1
10 years	3 800	45	140	615	1,255	1 455	215	25	10										40	3 9
11 years	3,470	35	85	215	595	1,125	1,140	175	10	15									35	4 7
12 years	3 510	35	15	150	30	695	1 055	1,045	145	30	5								35	5 5
13 years	3,505	25	5	35	155	395	715	915	985	165	40	5							65	6 4
14 years	3,300	25	10	20	95	285	455	630	845	770	120	25	20						80	7 2
15 years	3 415	20	10	20	25	135	285	505	635	845	655	145	50	20					45	8 0
16 years	3 390	15	25	40	25	30	200	340	405	615	805	655	150	40					45	9 0
17 years	3,195	25	5	15	35	85	130	200	305	530	480	610	540	165	10	10			50	9 5
18 years	3,705	20	10	20	40	60	130	255	315	430	550	425	600	745	190	35	10		60	10 5
19 years	3 665	15	10	25	50	60	95	215	270	410	235	350	340	910	305	225	50	20	60	11 1
20 years	3,640	25		10	40	85	110	260	195	390	240	260	260	980	230	285	110	65	95	11 6
21 years	4 205	20	20	20	80	145	160	215	335	460	320	280	155	1,0[illegible]	245	245	215	185	90	11 0
22 years	4,230	10	[illegible]	30	15	115	145	235	380	500	725	300	210	965	365	225	170	250	65	11 0
23 years	4,795	20	20	20	50	110	125	285	360	375	380	425	235	1,035	185	280	220	470	110	11 5
24 years	4,750	35	10	85	50	95	145	285	290	450	275	460	340	990	190	795	180	520	105	11 5
Female, 5 to 24	86 225	10,410	5 310	5,070	4,830	4 585	4,710	5,395	5,725	6 405	5,130	5,005	4,680	11,585	1,705	1,495	820	1,625	1 650	7 3
5 years	4 710	4,305	70	10															325	
6 years	4 640	3 905	500	45	5														185	
7 years	5 075	1,430	2,995	415	65	15													155	1 3
8 years	4,465	280	1 170	2,430	450	30	10												95	2 3
9 years	3,960	100	335	1 150	2,025	270	15	15											50	3 2
10 years	3,875	40	90	490	1,195	1,685	255	30	15										75	4 1
11 years	3 765	30	25	145	405	1,240	1 560	255	40	5									60	5 0
12 years	3,725	10	30	65	160	550	1,100	1,470	230	35	10								65	5 9
13 years	3 410	35	5	30	85	185	510	1,010	1 180	275	20	15							60	6 8
14 years	3 485	35	5	20	25	115	270	595	975	1 050	275	30	25						65	7 7
15 years	3,490	10	15	5	25	35	120	255	545	960	1,015	370	85	30					70	8 7
16 years	3,450	30	25	25	30	10	100	140	280	515	865	970	340	70	10				50	9 6
17 years	3 7[illegible]	15		25	5	40	25	115	225	425	435	865	1,045	395	70	10			30	10 6
18 years	4,315	20	5	15	30	25	40	150	250	405	410	470	725	1 355	245	100	5		55	11 4
19 years	4,485	15	10	15	55	40	100	200	265	430	320	395	365	1,460	425	245	55	40	50	12 0
20 years	4 755	[illegible]		35	75	35	90	110	325	290	340	425	435	1,775	270	285	185	75	45	12 1
21 years	5,030	20	10	20	25	50	120	230	265	505	295	325	435	1,640	240	245	255	305	45	12 1
22 years	4,965	35	15	25	60	115	80	210	360	470	355	415	390	1,605	200	190	105	330	55	11 9
23 years	5,470	45	5	60	55	70	165	300	390	525	380	350	430	1,625	100	220	110	470	55	11 8
24 years	5 400	40		45	35	65	150	263	390	565	410	425	405	1,650	175	200	100	405	60	11 7

Table 64—YEARS OF SCHOOL COMPLETED BY PERSONS 5 TO 24 YEARS OLD, BY SINGLE YEARS OF AGE, COLOR AND SEX, FOR THE STATE, 1950 AND 1940 FOR URBAN AND RURAL AREAS, AND FOR STANDARD METROPOLITAN AREAS AND CITIES OF 250,000 OR MORE, 1950—Con

Statistics for 1950 based on 20 percent exemple available complete-count data in tables to and 33. Mention not shown where ten than 1.0 or where take in eas can 600 or 1560 or 0° for 1960

									Jean o	school o	mapleter									Mena
Area, census year, color age, and sex	All				1	Elementa	ry seboor			-		Eghs	chool			Colo	ege		Not	school veara
color age, and acc	pulsus	None	1	2	3	4	5	В	7	8 1	1	2	3	4	1	2	3	4 or more	re porten	pleteo
CITIES, 1950—Con.				i					ė.		!	1	i	1					70	
KC. ORLEANSNONVEITE						1			1	,	1			- 1		- 1				
Total, 5 to 24	59,545	8,350	4,465	4,290	4,210	4,460	4,_85,	5,060	5,035	5,40	أكارد	1,130	1,090	2,790	482	احويه	26,	300	بكدو	5
Male, 5 to 24 oyears years years 9 years 8 years 10 years 11 years 12 years 12 years 14 years 15 years 16 years 17 years 18 years 19 years 22 years 22 years 22 years	28,140 1,613 1,613 1,953 1,973 1,560 1,405 1,405 1,405 1,245 1,190 1,310 1,065 1,125 1,175 1,175	4,205 -,315 -,360 780 270 75 25 25 20 10 -,0 5 5 5 5	2,375 10 170 920 813 230 \$C 23 5 5 5	2,240 275 5175 510 290 375 125 200 30 10 51 15 20 20 20 21 25 20 25 25 20 25 25 25 25 25 25 25 25 25 25 25 25 25	2,165 15 16 125 525 500 335 19 110 50 20 40 30	2,430 100 1390 485 410 200 200 110 20 55 30 55 75	2, 215 20 300 305 205 205 205 205 205 205 205 2	2,440 20,05 235-29-310 260 155;125 155-260 180 100-155	2 220	10 5 25 180 335 205 260 222 175 195 215 225	5 25 16C 255 16C 190 75 125 125 120	-,1.33 -,1.33 -,1.33 -,2.33 -,3.33 -,	55 10 50 95 110 85 85 85	20 15 30 95 95 121 143	 30 30 25 35 35 35	196 	5 5 20 .5 30			11 23 4. 45. 078 8888888888888888888888888888888888
23 years	31,405 1,815 1,815 1,815 1,815 1,815 1,815 1,925 1,925 1,410 1,420	10 30 4,145 1,640 1,365 170 20 10 10 20 5 10 10 10 20	2,000 (10 10 10 10 10 10 10 10 10 10 10 10 10 1	20 50 10 30 30 135 805 435 275 75 5 10 10 10 10 15 15 15 15 15 15 15 15 15 15 15 15 15	25 50 2,045 21,0	75 45 2,030 5 5 520 300 120 70 30 5 5 5 5 20 30 20 30 4 7 5 20 5 5 5 5 20 5 5 5 5 5 5 2 6 5 6 7 6 7 7 7 8 7 8 7 8 7 8 7 8 7 8 7 8 7	90, 90 1, 970 10, 970 360, 480, 240 150 77, 45, 20 30, 55, 65, 70 70, 40	2,600 2,600 10,25 130 385 420 350 160 85 80 100 130 100	2,715 2,715 2,715 30 90 925 270 290 150 150 150 150 210	2,5-2 2,5-2 255 280 375 265 205 175 255 250 255 250 250 255 250 250 250 25	155 11C 2 _c5 20 125 285 395 285 395 165 175 175 185	2,030 2,030 15 15 17 22 37C 24 19, 185 145 165	50 95 225	140 95 1,905	286 · · · · · · · · · · · · · · · · · · ·	40 25 240 	150 150 150 150 150 150 150 150 150 150	200	585 1355 655 200 200 200 200 200 200 200 200 200 2	1 2. 2 3 4. 5 5 6. 7 8. 9 9 9 9 9 9 9 9 9 9 9 9 9 9 9 9 9 9

Tadie 65 —YEARS OF SCHOOL COMPLETED BY PERSONS 25 YEARS OLD AND OVER, BY AGE, COLOR, AND SEX, FOR THE STATE, 1950 AND 1940, FOR URBAN AND RURAL AREAS, AND FOR STANDARD METROPOLITAN AREAS AND CITIES OF 200,000 OR MORE, 1950

Stat. 10- for 17.0 hased on 30-percen sample available complete count data t anles 15 and 33 % edian not shown where sess han 1.0 or where has us less than 500 for 1980 or 100 for 1960

	1		-	CAME PERSONS	-			l cars .	f school o	mple-ed							Median
Area, census year, color age and sex	persons	hone			lementary	803004			High	schoo.			Col	lege		Not re-	years
		None	I and	3 and	5 and	7	8	1	2	3	4	1	2	3	4 or more	ported	pleted
THE STATE 1950 Food Total 25 years and over.		127,700	90,33	AB- 9-6	207,413	116,050	136,0.5	71,475	65.870	65,015	162,680	25,970	34,930	17,08	68,890	30,435	77
Male 25 years and over 25 to 29 years	6 460	6-,850	49 140	30,180 2,285	97 850	34,565	64 °32 8,030	32,810			6",200 36 68	12.400	un. 264	8.44	3 .620	17,095	74
30 to 34 years 30 to 39 v. ars 40 to 44 years 55 to 64 years 55 to 64 years 75 years and over	2,180 2,180 2,055 36,575 36,575 20,47	355 - ,85 - ,85 12,88 13,38 - ,70	4,34.0 5,9.0 5,9.0 -,32 8,45	11,725	750	8,0.0 9,70 7,005 1,455 0,645 1,295	8,160 9 135 6,725 15,120 9,010 4,885 4,370	5,405 5,320 4,205 6,42 3,600 7,490 540	4,917	5,725 4,850 3,685 3,960 2,045	13,440 10,705 7,885 9,895 5,235 2,510	1 505	2,615 2,715 2,330 2,055 2 850 -,675 755	1,750 8b: 1,750 630 40:	6,983 5 835 4,533 5,983 3,820 1,760	2,020	88 7 6 6 6 6 6 6 6 6 6 6 6 6 6 6 6 6 6 6
Female, 25 years and over 25 to 29 years 30 to 34 year. 30 to 39 years 4) to 44 years to to 54 years 65 to 74 years 65 to 74 years 75 year and over	727,7.5 117,837 90,000 94 ? 9 88,4 5 141 4 0 02,325 66,375 26,445	62,-40 2,515 3,723 / 390 5 285 -3, 30 12,-5, 1,-5,-7,375	41,443	88,510 8,710 8,865 10,740 10,850 27,640 4,370	109 960 14,303 14,430 15,330 13,925 22,400 15,3.3 10,-85 3,790	6.,465 9,760 9,795 0,625 7 820	71,280 8,865 8,470 10 245 9,490 15,420 9,65 6,640 2,587	38,603 6,775 6,300 5,915 5,050 7,775 4,213 2,110	2 735 2,640 6 470	7,630 6,270 4,090 4,965 2,942	95,480 24,845 28,055 15,345 10,915 13,265 7,015 4,105, 1,935	13,570 3,200 2,280 1,730 ,700 2,430 1,325 510 275	18,682 3,010 2,545 2,635 2,580 2,972 2,350 2,175 4,175	1,505 1,620 1,100	6,2.5 5,3.5 4,865 4 445 5,450 2 865	2,670	10 1 9 1 8 5
Nonwhite							,										- "
Total, 25 years and over	124 686	£9,795	5°, 625	90 BBC	80,±70	34,625	28,510	12,910	9,245	5,350	10,420	1,920	2,555	1,445	5,220	8 630	4.7
Male 25 years and over 20 to 29 years 30 to 3- years 35 to 39 years 40 to 44 years 45 to 14 years 55 .0 64 years 65 to 74 years 75 years and over	29,360 47,620 43,845 46,080 24,085 40,747 26,810 21,405 8,130	36, 970 1,880 4 93L 3,-30 3,-35 7 785 6,860 7 755 3 995	30,730 2,720 2,635 3,25 3,25 7,50 5,00 4,315 1,475	5,310 5,310 6,515 6,435 0,820 6,640 4,579 1,255	3,465 5,25 5,25 4,50 6,855 3,755 4,10 560	2,140 3,175 2,530 2,285 1,830 2,290 1,255 600 175	11 993 2,475 1,985 -,910 1,4-0 2 285 1,030 635 163	5,220 1,381 975 790 620 705 410 265 70	3,675 985 625 603 425 560 285 225	2, 70, 725 425 365 340 90 70	4,190 1,115 800 683 485 575 345 140 85	695 225 125 90 45 75 70 40 25	980 280 135 210 120 145 55 25	545 24 85 50 50 50 35	1,920 375 4_0 460 180 275 150 85	4,875 610 610 620 585 935 763 563 190	43 57 50 45 39 33 22
Female, 25 years and over 25 to 29 years 30 to 34 years 35 to 39 years	-25,-20 33,850 39,700	33,425	26,875 0.060 2,230	48,510 5,430 5,500	46,085 7,620 7,040	20,485 4,700 3,98,	16 5_5 3,0_0 2,d61 2,900	7,690 2,210 1,435	1 600 1,155	3,380 1 155 235	6,230 2,035 1 175	345 215	1,575 345 33,	900 235 160	3,300 745 730	3,755 395 4.5	5 1 7 1 6 5
40 to 44 years 40 to 54 years 55 to 64 years 65 to 64 years 75 years and over	39,700 52,225 27,260 44,385 26,120 22,420 8,000	-, 10, 2,485 2,734 7 065 -,955 7 850 4,065	2,930 3,140 3,290 4,495 4,245 1,505	6,410 6,410 11,695 6,820 4,20 1,560	8,0.5 6,260 9,0-0 4,575 2,810 615	3,910 2,600 2,995 1,275 770 220	2,900 2,245 2,790 1,160 730 190	1,400 880 1,055 385 245 20	1,010 29° 585 27* 180 70	575 305 335 130 80 15	1,140 685 713 290 150 70	210 140 102 50 40 20	270 160 295 80 65 25	180 95 145 55 30	500 505 470 165 85 10	650 435 805 410 390 235	6 - 5 4 4 4 3 7 2 6 1 3
THE STATE 1940																e l	
Total 25 years and over Male, 25 years and over	1,204,647	79,728	40,628	191,_m 100,995	≠03 20° 97,822	23,-32	97,J€1 46,958	57,094	52,779	34,289	117,809	15,520	25,149	10 456	42,316	10,322	6.6
25 to 29 years 30 to 34 years 35 to 39 years 40 to 44 years 45 to 34 years 55 to 64 years 65 to 74 years 75 years and over	100,294 90,968 64,955 72,289 116,872 73,/34 43,280 13 896	6,117 6,90_ 8,779	6,069 6,163 6,478 3,623 10,112 6,494 4,389 1,201	14,50° 14,156 ->,500 12,719 21,380 13,779 7 7 4 2,389	16,340 1,263 4,495 12,22 19,663 12,108 9,085 1,645	25, 52 20,394 8,980 8,235 6,577 10,034 5,660 2,323	7,416 7,716 7,008 6,1-3 9,505 5,765 2,883	5 667 4,884 4,355 3,703 4,873 2,416 926 262	24,983 5,501 4,973 4,087 3,288 4,240 1,860 755 170	15,790 4,138 3,477 2,450 1,906 2,303 1,031 189	9,996 13,475 9,646 6,9-2 5,424 7,581 4,224 1 937 *32	7,449 1,535 1,192 1,040 922 1,350 787 363 84	1,940 1,946 1,785 1,582 1,353 1,382 -,450 474	4,73_ 1,_4_ 8e5 665 500 840 436, 221	2/,0/5 ,257 ,222 3,492 2,753 4,270 7,04 1,196	5,775 654 690 777 615 1,211 929 622 287	677 66 25 42
Female 25 years and over 25 to 29 years 35 to 34 years 55 to 39 years 40 to 44 years 40 to 54 years 55 to 64 years 67 to 74 years	608,659 100,727 93,486 8°,194 72 092 112,082 7, 251 44,218	74 724 -,862 5,522 7,73 7,5_5 16,155 13,774 12,700	37,493 4,253 4,461 5,331 4,771 8,203 5,317 3,8e4	90,106 12,265 12,687 13,816 11,695 18,706 11,714 6,914	105, 385 17, 922 16, 866 16, 133 13, 2.0 20, 173 12, 373	54,909 	50 623 8,451 8,143 7,333 6 1.03 9,252 6,183	29,988 6,591 5,622 4,932 7,737 5,127 2,203 1,098	27 796 6,557 5,509 4,603 3,459 4,705 2,179	18 499 4,769 3,847 1 035 2,162 2,622 1,113	67,810 19 168 19,352 9,568 6,856 9,055 5,773	8,07. 1,775 1,499 1,496 997 1,391	14,709 2,804 2,8,7 2,395 -,836 2,688 1,286	2,725 1,362 1,279 949 600 854 443	18 271 4,090 3,721 2 871 4,118 2 932 1,548 771	4,547 509 474 540 436 950 715	69 78 72 68 62
75 years and over	17 309	0,483	1,288	2,309	6,600 2,008	1,622 1,017	1,424	303	907 7دخ	589 162	1,099	312 92	200	181	217	538 323	3 6
Total											- 1						
Total, 2-3 years and over Male, 25 years and over 25 to 29 years 30 to 36 years 30 to 36 years 40 to 44 years 40 to 44 years 50 to 39 years 65 to 64 years 65 to 74 years 75 years and over	828,195 387 335 63 340 55,230 53,475 49,010 78,765 48,545 28 270 11,000	22,135	37,990 19,435 1,550 1,645 2,090 4,580 4,795 3,210 2,520 1,005	87,115 43,435 3,905 4,010 4,930 5,630 10,555 7,590 5 02, 1,660	109,930 49,997 6,330 6,145 6,530 6,535 11,380 7,610 4,085 1,585	29,710 7,760 4,305 4,395 4,125 6,225 3,620 63*	91,615 42,375 5,135 5,230 5,960 5,935 10 320 5,705 3,030 1,030	43,010 19,54. 3,770 3,333 3,255 2,512 3,810 1,843 725 290	42,892 19,620 3,870 3,445 3,170 2,875 3,850 1,690 6,4	41,255 17,670 4,170 3,390 3,095 2,430 2,545 1,340 510	128 255 52 430 12,565 10,400 8,20 C,285 8,20 4 24C 1,99C 67C	9,705 2 5.35 1,815 1,40 1,220 1,585 865 370	26, 93.5 12, 930 2, 985 2, 230 1, 840 1, 690 2, 255 1 240 525 165	12,975 0,875 2,320 1,255 850 700 925 440 295	50,375 31,18* 7,020 5,685 4,635 3 690 5,0.5 3,165 1 325 450	18,875 10,495 1 410 1,315 1,325 1,195 2,240 4,530 995 485	8 C 2 2 2 2 2 2 2 2 2 2 2 2 2 2 2 2 2 2
Penale, 25 years and ower 23 to 29 years 23 to 29 years 23 to 28 years 25 to 28 years 24 to 26 years 25 to 25 years 25 to 25 years 25 to 27 years 25 to 74 years 25 to 75 years and over	240,860 71 055 60,420 60,380 54,040 84 810 55,070 38,370 10,715	330 1,075 1,635 2,150 5,673 5,200 5,405	18,555 1,310 1,295 1,855 2,20 4,330 3,290 3,130 1,135	43,880 5,390 3,950 4,655 5,230 10,710 7,695 6,000 7,250	59,940 7 185 7,255 7,875 7,49* 12,265 8,950 6 295 2,320	35,030 5,575; 5,330 3,340; /,385 6,735 4,215 2,380 4,070;	49,240 *,870 5,505 6,910 6,750 10,670 6,980 4,533 2,020	23,465 4,380 3,920 3,665 3,125 4,230 2,780 4,260 505	23,275 4,680 3,890 3,720 3 005 4,14° 2,245 1,135 -60	23,585 6,030 4,660 3,835 2,660 3,305 -,725 990 380	75,825 19,505 13,655 11,800 8,670 11,145 5,880 3,490 1,680	0,330 2,595 1,750 1,775 1,347 1,815 1,000 36,185	183 2,435 1,955 2,000 1,870 2,865 1,630 890 330	6,.00 1,265 1,070 .,115 820 920 560 245	24,190 4,975 4,150 3,725 3,370 4,1.5 2,170 1,240 4*5	8,380 1,030 960 985 945 1,295 1,150 1,020 695	8734 1074 8814 63

Table 65.—YEARS OF SCHOOL COMPLETED BY PERSONS 25 YEARS OLD AND OVER, BY AGE, COLOR, AND SEX, FOR THE STATE, 1950 AND 1940, FOR URBAN AND RURAL AREAS, AND FOR STANDARD METROPOLITAN AREAS AND CITIES OF 100,000 OR MORE, 1950

[Statistics for 1950 based on 20-percent sample available complete count data in tables 15 and 33. Median not shown where less than 1.0 or where base is less than 500 for 1950 or 100 for 1940]

Area, census year, color, age, and sex	All persons	None	Elementary school: 1 and 2	Elementary school: 3 and 4	Elementary school: 5 and 6	Elementary school: 7	Elementary school: 8	High school: 1	High school: 2	High school: 3	High school: 4	College: 1	College: 2	College: 3	College: 4 or more	Not reported	Median school years completed
THE STATE 1950																	
Total																	
Total, 25 years and over	[illegible]	127,770	90,380	184,940	207,210	116,050	136,015	71,475	65,870	65,515	162,680	25,970	34,930	17,085	68,890	30,455	7.7
Male, 25 years and over	677,790	64,850	49,140	96,180	97,850	54,565	64,735	32,810	30,390	28,270	67,200	12,400	16,245	8,430	37,630	17,095	7.4
25 to 29 years	100,730	2,090	4,170	7,285	12,770	8,375	8,050	5,935	5,735	6,870	16,685	3,140	4,615	2,710	8,095	2,155	9.6
30 to 34 years	84,180	2,440	4,340	7,170	14,760	8,010	8,160	5,205	4,915	5,725	13,440	2,755	2,715	1,540	6,985	2,020	8.8
35 to 39 years	[illegible]	3,355	7,590	11,125	14,460	8,170	9,135	5,320	4,950	4,855	10,705	1,505	2,330	1,020	5,835	2,095	8.[illegible]
40 to 44 years	87,055	[illegible]	5,910	12,420	12,485	7,505	8,725	4,205	4,525	3,685	7,885	1,550	2,005	865	4,535	1,980	7.6
45 to 54 years	136,575	14,375	11,320	21,705	20,595	11,455	15,720	6,445	6,060	3,965	9,895	1,965	2,850	1,150	5,985	3,495	6.9
55 to 64 years	[illegible]	12,880	8,145	15,780	15,920	6,645	9,010	3,600	2,770	2,015	5,235	1,170	1,675	620	3,810	2,635	6.0
65 to 74 years	59,485	13,335	7,100	11,205	8,500	3,295	4,885	1,490	1,140	845	2,510	545	555	405	1,760	1,835	4.5
75 years and over	23,615	6,730	2,670	4,160	3,290	1,310	1,370	510	295	310	845	270	240	120	625	880	3.9
Female, 25 years and over	727,715	62,440	41,240	88,810	109,960	61,485	71,280	38,605	35,480	37,345	95,480	13,570	18,685	8,655	31,260	13,360	7.9
25 to 29 years	110,830	2,515	3,280	8,010	14,305	9,960	8,865	6,775	6,870	9,810	24,845	3,200	3,010	1,600	6,215	1,510	10.1
30 to 34 years	99,000	3,020	3,360	8,865	14,430	9,795	8,470	6,300	5,900	7,630	18,055	2,280	2,545	1,505	5,315	1,530	9.1
35 to 39 years	99,[illegible]5	7,390	4,235	10,090	15,330	9,625	10,245	5,915	5,735	6,270	15,345	1,730	2,635	1,620	4,865	1,765	8.5
40 to 44 years	88,4[illegible]5	5,285	4,840	10,850	13,925	7,820	9,090	5,050	4,640	4,090	10,915	1,760	2,580	1,160	4,445	1,[illegible]23	8.1
45 to 54 years	141,4[illegible]0	13,[illegible]30	9,485	20,620	22,400	11,010	15,420	7,775	6,470	4,965	13,265	2,430	2,975	1,445	5,450	2,670	7.3
55 to 64 years	92,325	12,45[illegible]	7,070	14,665	15,115	6,985	9,965	4,215	3,470	2,615	7,015	1,325	2,350	815	2,865	1,780	6.3
65 to 74 years	64,375	13,670	6,305	11,340	10,485	4,030	6,040	2,110	1,710	1,450	4,105	510	1,175	340	1,520	1,585	5.2
75 years and over	28,[illegible]45	7,375	2,665	4,3[illegible]	3,790	1,660	2,587	825	685	515	1,935	275	415	170	535	995	4.8
Nonwhite																	
Total, 25 years and over	424,680	69,795	57,625	95,860	80,570	34,625	28,510	12,910	9,145	5,550	10,420	1,820	2,555	1,445	5,220	8,630	4.7
Male, 25 years and over	199,360	36,370	30,750	47,350	34,485	14,140	11,995	5,220	3,675	2,170	4,190	695	980	545	1,920	4,875	4.3
25 to 29 years	27,620	1,880	2,720	5,600	5,875	3,175	2,475	1,385	985	725	1,115	225	280	24	375	610	6.[illegible]
30 to 34 years	23,845	1,930	2,635	5,310	5,265	2,530	1,985	975	625	425	800	125	135	85	410	610	5.7
35 to 39 years	26,080	3,130	3,525	6,515	5,415	2,285	1,910	790	605	365	685	90	210	55	460	620	5.0
40 to 44 years	24,085	3,135	3,765	6,635	4,560	1,830	1,440	620	425	250	485	45	120	40	180	585	4.5
45 to 54 years	40,765	7,785	7,150	10,820	6,855	2,290	2,285	705	560	240	575	75	145	50	275	935	3.9
55 to 64 years	26,810	6,860	5,005	6,640	3,755	1,255	1,030	410	285	90	345	70	55	35	150	765	3.3
65 to 74 years	21,405	7,755	4,315	4,575	1,150	600	635	265	105	70	140	40	25	25	85	560	2.2
75 years and over	8,130	3,995	1,475	1,255	580	175	105	70	25	15	85	25	10	10	35	190	
Female, 25 years and over	225,320	33,425	26,875	48,510	46,085	20,485	16,515	7,690	5,470	3,380	6,230	1,125	1,575	900	3,300	3,755	5.1
25 to 29 years	33,850	1,535	3,060	5,430	7,620	4,720	3,610	2,210	1,600	1,155	2,035	345	345	235	745	395	7.1
30 to 34 years	29,700	1,70[illegible]	2,230	5,505	7,040	3,98[illegible]	2,86[illegible]	1,435	1,135	735	1,175	215	33[illegible]	160	730	435	6.5
35 to 39 years	32,225	2,485	2,930	6,040	8,015	3,910	2,900	1,400	1,010	575	1,110	210	270	180	590	650	6.[illegible]
40 to 44 years	27,260	2,735	3,140	6,410	6,280	2,600	2,245	880	59[illegible]	395	685	140	160	95	505	435	5.4
45 to 54 years	44,385	7,065	5,290	11,695	9,040	2,995	2,790	1,055	585	335	715	105	295	145	470	805	4.4
55 to 64 years	26,120	1,055	4,495	6,820	4,575	1,275	1,160	385	275	130	290	50	80	55	165	410	3.7
65 to 74 years	22,920	7,850	4,245	4,250	2,810	770	730	245	180	80	150	40	65	30	85	390	2.6
75 years and over	8,000	4,065	1,575	1,560	645	220	190	30	70	15	70	20	25		10	235	1.3
THE STATE 1940																	
Total, 25 years and over	1,204,647	154,182	87,121	191,101	203,207	108,441	97,161	57,094	52,779	34,289	117,809	15,520	25,149	10,456	42,316	10,322	6.6
Male, 25 years and over	595,988	79,758	40,628	100,995	97,822	53,532	46,958	27,106	24,983	15,790	9,996	7,449	10,440	4,731	24,045	5,775	6.4
25 to 29 years	100,294	6,117	6,069	14,507	16,340	10,391	7,416	5,687	5,601	4,138	13,475	1,505	1,956	1,14[illegible]	5,257	654	7.7
30 to 34 years	90,968	6,901	6,165	14,156	15,263	8,980	7,379	4,884	4,973	3,477	9,846	1,392	1,785	865	4,224	690	7.3
35 to 39 years	84,955	8,779	6,478	14,600	14,495	8,235	7,008	4,355	4,087	2,450	6,947	1,040	1,582	665	3,492	777	6.7
40 to 44 years	72,289	8,444	5,629	12,719	12,221	6,577	6,183	3,703	3,288	1,906	5,494	922	1,353	500	2,753	615	6.5
45 to 54 years	116,872	17,471	10,112	21,380	19,663	10,054	9,505	4,873	4,240	2,303	7,581	1,350	1,982	840	4,270	1,211	5.9
55 to 64 years	73,434	14,288	6,495	13,779	12,108	5,660	5,765	2,416	1,865	1,057	4,224	787	1,150	436	2,[illegible]04	929	5.3
65 to 74 years	43,280	12,448	4,389	7,774	6,085	2,823	2,883	926	755	389	1,932	363	474	221	1,196	622	4.2
75 years and over	13,896	5,290	1,291	2,389	1,645	812	819	262	170	92	432	84	118	63	51	287	3.2
Female, 25 years and over	608,659	74,724	37,495	90,106	105,385	54,909	50,623	29,988	27,796	18,499	67,813	8,071	14,709	5,725	18,271	4,547	6.9
25 to 29 years	105,72[illegible]	4,862	4,253	12,265	17,922	11,319	8,451	6,591	6,557	4,769	19,168	1,775	2,824	1,362	4,090	509	8.3
30 to 34 years	95,486	5,522	4,461	12,687	16,866	9,625	8,143	5,644	5,509	3,847	15,352	1,499	2,817	1,279	3,721	474	7.8
35 to 39 years	89,194	7,713	5,331	13,816	16,133	8,679	7,333	4,934	4,603	3,035	9,568	1,296	2,395	949	2,871	540	7.2
40 to 44 years	72,092	7,515	4,771	11,695	13,210	6,540	6,103	3,730	3,459	2,162	6,858	997	1,836	600	2,118	438	6.8
45 to 54 years	112,082	16,155	8,203	18,706	20,173	9,566	9,252	5,127	4,705	2,622	9,055	1,391	2,688	854	2,935	950	6.2
55 to 64 years	71,251	13,774	5,317	11,714	12,373	5,341	6,189	2,503	2,179	1,413	5,773	709	1,286	443	1,548	715	5.7
65 to 74 years	44,518	12,700	3,864	6,914	6,650	3,822	3,654	1,098	907	589	2,940	312	615	181	771	538	4.6
75 years and over	17,309	6,483	1,288	2,309	2,078	1,017	1,424	303	237	162	1,099	92	200	57	217	323	3.6
URBAN 1950																	
Total																	
Total, 25 years and over	828,195	47,225	37,990	87,115	109,930	64,740	91,615	43,010	42,895	41,255	128,255	20,035	26,905	12,975	55,375	18,875	8.0
Male, 25 years and over	387,335	22,135	19,435	43,435	49,997	29,710	42,375	19,545	19,620	17,670	52,430	9,705	12,930	6,875	31,185	10,495	8.6
25 to 29 years	63,340	1,035	1,550	3,905	6,330	4,760	5,135	3,770	3,850	4,170	12,565	2,535	2,985	2,320	7,020	1,410	11.[illegible]
30 to 34 years	55,230	1,005	1,685	4,010	6,145	4,305	5,230	3,330	3,445	3,390	10,400	1,815	2,230	1,235	5,685	1,315	10.4
35 to 39 years	53,175	1,590	2,090	4,930	6,580	4,395	5,960	3,255	3,170	3,095	8,120	1,140	1,840	850	4,835	1,325	9.[illegible]
40 to 44 years	49,010	1,835	2,580	5,630	6,305	4,125	5,935	2,515	2,875	2,430	6,285	1,220	1,690	700	3,690	1,195	8.6
45 to 54 years	78,765	5,125	4,795	10,555	11,380	6,225	10,320	3,810	3,850	2,545	8,160	1,585	2,255	925	5,015	2,240	8.0
55 to 64 years	48,545	4,490	3,210	7,520	7,610	3,625	5,725	1,845	1,690	1,340	4,240	865	1,240	440	3,165	1,530	7.2
65 to 74 years	28,270	4,020	2,520	5,025	4,085	1,640	3,030	725	615	510	1,990	370	525	295	1,325	995	5.7
75 years and over	11,000	2,435	1,005	1,660	1,555	634	1,030	290	145	190	670	75	165	110	450	485	5.[illegible]
Female, 25 years and over	440,860	25,090	18,555	43,880	59,940	35,030	49,240	23,465	23,275	23,585	75,825	10,330	13,975	6,100	24,190	8,380	8.7
25 to 29 years	71,055	830	1,310	3,390	7,185	5,575	5,870	4,380	4,680	6,030	19,505	2,595	2,435	1,265	4,975	1,030	11.3
30 to 34 years	60,420	1,075	1,295	3,950	7,255	5,330	5,505	3,920	3,890	4,660	15,655	1,750	1,955	1,070	4,150	960	10.4
35 to 39 years	60,380	1,635	1,855	4,655	7,875	5,340	6,910	3,665	3,720	3,835	11,800	1,275	2,000	1,115	3,715	985	9.4
40 to 44 years	54,040	2,150	2,230	5,230	7,495	7,385	6,750	3,125	3,005	2,660	8,670	1,345	1,870	820	3,370	945	8.8
45 to 54 years	84,810	5,675	4,330	10,710	12,565	6,735	10,670	4,230	4,140	3,305	11,145	1,815	2,865	920	4,115	1,595	8.1
55 to 64 years	55,070	5,200	3,290	7,695	8,950	4,215	6,980	2,780	2,245	1,725	5,880	1,000	1,630	560	2,170	1,150	7.4
65 to 74 years	38,370	5,405	3,120	6,000	6,295	2,380	4,535	1,260	1,135	990	3,490	365	890	245	1,240	1,020	6.3
75 years and over	16,715	3,125	1,135	2,250	2,320	1,070	2,020	505	460	380	1,680	185	330	105	455	695	6.3

Table 65.—YEARS OF SCHOOL COMPLETED BY PERSONS 25 YEARS OLD AND OVER, BY AGE, COLOR, AND SEX, FOR THE STATE, 1950 AND 1940, FOR URBAN AND RURAL AREAS, AND FOR STANDARD METROPOLITAN AREAS AND CITIES OF 100,000 OR MORE, 1950—Con.

[Statistics for 1950 based on 20-percent sample; available complete-count data in tables [illegible] and 33. Median not shown where less than [illegible] or where base is less than [illegible] for 1950 or [illegible] for 1940]

Area, census year, color, age, and sex	All persons	Years of school completed: None	Elementary school: 1 and 2	Elementary school: 3 and 4	Elementary school: 5 and 6	Elementary school: 7	Elementary school: 8	High school: 1	High school: 2	High school: 3	High school: 4	College: 1	College: 2	College: 3	College: 4 or more	Not reported	Median school years completed
URBAN 1950—Con.																	
Nonwhite																	
Total, 25 years and over	276 580	27 095	25,620	48,735	47,520	22 895	[illegible]	9 980	[illegible]60	4,200	9,055	[illegible]55	[illegible],920	1,060	4,270	4,730	5 6
Male, 25 years and over	106,900	13,035	12,085	23,370	20,365	9 565	9,350	[illegible]	2,900	1 735	3,565	560	805	[illegible]	1 620	2 665	5 3
25 to 29 years	16,015	595	1,095	2,435	3,275	2,390	[illegible],890	[illegible]	[illegible]	5 0	950	180	250	195	280	360	7 2
30 to 34 years	13,710	480	1,150	2,510	3,065	1,680	[illegible],535	775	515	[illegible]	695	95	120	70	125	390	6 6
35 to 39 years	14,975	480	1,410	2,160	3,230	1 575	1 500	660	475	[illegible]	625	80	170	50	380	355	6 [illegible]
40 to 44 years	13,640	1,065	1,825	2,230	2 640	1,285	[illegible]	400	350	200	420	35	95	[illegible]	155	330	5 3
45 to 54 years	27,520	3,030	3,330	5 805	4,295	1 [illegible]	1,825	515	430	185	460	65	110	45	245	570	4 6
55 to 64 years	13,325	2,560	2,125	3 370	1 255	515	760	155	190	55	260	80	45	20	135	380	4 1
65 to 74 years	9,070	2,750	1,535	2 215	1,105	345	415	135	105	65	105	25	10	10	60	190	3 1
75 years and over	3 445	1,475	605	545	300	125	130	40	15	5	50	20	5	10	30	90	1 7
Female, 25 years and over	129,980	14,060	12,535	25,365	27,155	13,330	12 385	5,680	4 260	2,465	5 490	745	1,115	640	2 650	2,065	5 9
25 to 29 years	20,640	125	835	2,410	4 175	2,930	2,710	1 725	1,260	855	1,790	225	235	175	540	270	7 8
30 to 34 years	17,600	630	880	2,750	3 825	2 455	2 105	1 345	935	555	1,335	185	245	120	375	265	7 2
35 to 39 years	19,105	950	1 325	3,995	4 665	2,595	2,110	1,015	780	455	960	155	200	120	500	340	6 8
40 to 44 years	16,035	1,175	1,530	3,385	3,745	1,670	1,730	625	430	250	605	90	100	60	405	215	6.0
45 to 54 years	25,820	3,120	3,005	6,490	5,040	2 075	2,175	760	455	345	655	70	95	100	410	425	5.0
55 to 64 years	14,305	2,660	2,115	3,620	2,880	910	825	270	400	80	255	35	70	35	140	210	4 3
65 to 74 years	12,065	3,205	2,125	1,925	1,780	550	590	190	130	35	130	20	45	20	75	245	3.4
75 years and over	4,350	1,795	720	790	445	145	140	50	55	1[illegible]	60	15	25		5	95	1 9
RURAL NONFARM 1950																	
Total																	
Total, 25 years and over	318 860	42,685	25 975	49 100	50,625	27,380	24,520	16,345	14,065	15,625	23,570	4,060	5,530	2 915	9 690	6,775	6 5
Male, 25 years and over	157,330	21,740	13 980	25,710	24,265	13 100	12,610	7,820	6,575	6,925	10,365	1,945	2,395	1,145	4 740	4,015	6 3
25 to 29 years	22,795	985	1,275	2 895	3 025	2,060	1,930	1,375	1 270	1,851	2,910	505	530	510	835	475	8 2
30 to 34 years	20,990	1,240	1,250	2,970	3,485	2,175	1 695	1,180	955	1,590	2,030	205	360	225	1,015	515	7 6
35 to 39 years	21,605	1,845	1,630	3,275	2,610	1,995	1,800	1,295	1 100	1,080	1,910	295	370	150	770	480	7 1
40 to 44 years	18,525	1,995	1,450	3,160	2 920	1,690	1,570	965	1,070	840	1 160	210	245	110	605	535	6 6
45 to 54 years	29,360	4,270	2,865	5,135	4,565	2,605	2,630	1,605	1,350	905	1,190	265	425	160	675	715	5 9
55 to 64 years	20,390	4 125	2,260	3,860	2 925	1,455	1 660	925	495	385	700	180	270	115	420	615	4 8
65 to 74 years	16,350	4,620	2,340	3,035	2,145	875	1,005	370	270	225	260	105	145	75	300	480	3 6
75 years and over	7,315	2,660	910	1 380	990	245	320	105	65	85	155	80	50		120	200	3 0
Female, 25 years and over	161,530	20,945	11,995	23,390	26,360	14,280	11 910	8 525	7,490	8,700	13,205	2,115	3,135	1,770	4,950	2,760	6 7
25 to 29 years	24 460	860	1 015	2,455	4,075	2,580	1,740	1,515	1,515	2,550	3,720	470	450	265	935	315	8 6
30 to 34 years	22,255	1,050	1,005	2,455	3 860	2 660	1,545	1,405	1,245	1,850	2,910	390	400	290	845	345	8 0
35 to 39 years	21 800	1 480	990	2,545	3,950	2 235	1,785	1,270	1 215	1 530	2 330	315	500	355	825	395	7 7
40 to 44 years	18,195	1,520	1,255	2,750	3,135	1,715	1,605	970	905	840	1 575	200	440	230	740	275	7 2
45 to 54 years	29,815	4,170	2 825	4,810	4,820	2,375	2,455	1,705	1,385	1,645	1,410	165	670	355	905	520	6 2
55 to 64 years	20,590	4,205	1,950	3,805	3,275	1,385	1,595	850	730	495	705	230	430	150	410	370	5.2
65 to 74 years	17,005	5 090	2 005	3,200	2,390	1,040	860	520	345	280	370	85	185	75	210	350	3 8
75 years and over	7,410	2,670	850	1 330	875	290	325	185	150	110	185	60	60	50	80	190	3.1
Nonwhite																	
Total, 25 years and over	95 310	21,770	15,105	22 780	16,880	6,265	3,715	1,920	1,230	835	945	285	405	285	680	2,210	3 8
Male, 25 years and over	45,450	11,260	7,900	11,180	7,305	2,485	1,525	785	470	265	445	100	125	100	225	1,280	3 5
25 to 29 years	6,180	520	660	1,595	1,510	595	410	230	90	125	135	40	25	45	40	160	5 3
30 to 34 years	5,060	600	700	1 385	1,085	520	225	115	80	45	60	15	15	10	45	160	4 7
35 to 39 years	5,850	1,035	945	1,580	1,125	390	250	80	95	20	60	10	25	5	80	130	4 1
40 to 44 years	5,020	985	825	1,505	885	260	165	80	40	25	40	5	10	10	20	165	3 8
45 to 54 years	8,095	2 320	1,605	2,185	1,220	310	225	120	75	15	50	5	30	5	20	210	3 3
55 to 64 years	6,385	2,015	1,300	1,540	750	245	120	75	50	25	45	10		10	10	190	2 7
65 to 74 years	6,110	2,530	1,370	2,040	545	140	95	15	35	5	25	10	15	15	10	210	1 6
75 years and over	2,770	1,555	495	350	185	25	35	20	5	5	30	5	5			55	
Female, 25 years and over	49,860	10,510	7,205	11,600	9,575	3,780	2,190	1,135	760	570	500	185	280	185	455	930	4 2
25 to 29 years	6,975	460	515	1,300	1 875	1,020	495	310	260	210	180	70	75	45	160	60	6 3
30 to 34 years	6,285	500	575	1 315	1,710	880	410	265	115	115	95	25	55	15	100	110	5 8
35 to 39 years	6 34[illegible]	745	630	1,345	1 675	630	440	215	130	65	105	35	40	50	70	170	5 4
40 to 44 years	5,255	690	725	1,475	1,210	445	290	100	80	80	50	20	30	20	70	70	4 7
45 to 54 years	9 000	1,945	1,735	2,480	1,510	450	280	140	65	35	25	15	60	30	35	195	3 6
55 to 64 years	6,440	1,845	1,240	1,790	875	160	170	70	50	30	25	10	5	15	10	145	3 1
65 to 74 years	6,575	2,800	1,315	1,360	620	170	70	15	45	30	10	10	15	10	10	95	[illegible] 7
75 years and over	2,885	1,525	470	535	160	25	35	20	15	5	10					85	
RURAL FARM 1950																	
Total																	
Total, 25 years and over	258,450	37,380	26,415	48 775	47,255	23,930	19,880	12,120	8,910	8 735	10,855	1,875	2 495	1,195	3,825	4,805	5 6
Male, 25 years and over	133,125	20,975	15,725	27,235	23,595	11,755	9,750	5,445	4,195	3,675	4,405	750	920	410	1 705	2 585	5 1
25 to 29 years	14,595	1,070	1,335	2,585	2,825	1 525	965	790	615	885	1,210	100	100	80	240	270	6 5
30 to 34 years	14,960	1,195	1,305	2,790	3,130	1,530	1,235	690	515	745	1,010	135	125	80	285	190	6 3
35 to 39 years	17,270	1,920	1,870	3,520	3 270	1,780	1,375	770	680	680	675	90	120	20	230	290	5 7
40 to 44 years	16,520	1,855	1,880	3,630	3,260	1,790	1,220	725	580	415	440	120	150	55	240	250	5 5
45 to 54 years	28,450	4,940	3 665	6,045	4,050	2,625	2 270	1,130	880	515	545	115	170	65	295	540	4 8
55 to 64 years	20,975	4,265	2,675	4 400	3,385	1,565	1,615	830	585	290	295	125	165	65	225	490	4 5
65 to 74 years	15 045	4,095	2,240	3,145	2,330	780	850	395	255	110	160	70	85	35	135	360	3 6
75 years and over	5,310	1,635	755	1,120	745	230	220	115	85	35	70	15	25	10	55	195	3 3
Female, 25 years and over	125,325	16,405	10,690	21 540	23,660	12,175	10,130	6,675	4,715	5,060	6,450	1,125	1,575	785	2 120	2 220	6 1
25 to 29 years	15,315	825	955	2,165	3,045	1,805	1,255	880	675	1,230	1,620	195	125	70	305	165	7 3
30 to 34 years	15,325	895	1,060	2,460	3,315	1,805	1,420	975	765	1,120	1,490	140	190	145	320	225	7 2
35 to 39 years	17 475	1 275	1,290	2,890	3,585	2 050	1,550	980	800	905	1,215	140	135	150	325	385	6 8
40 to 44 years	16,240	1 615	1,365	2 830	3,195	1,720	1,335	955	730	590	670	215	270	110	335	305	6 4
45 to 54 years	26,785	3,690	2,330	5,100	5,015	2,500	2 295	1,540	945	615	710	250	440	170	430	555	5 7
55 to 64 years	17,265	3,150	1,830	3,165	3,110	1,385	1 390	880	495	395	430	95	290	105	285	260	5 2
65 to 74 years	11,000	3,175	1 180	2,140	1 800	610	645	330	230	180	245	60	100	20	70	215	4 0
75 years and over	4,720	1,580	680	790	595	300	240	135	75	25	70	30	25	15	50	110	3 1

Table 65.—YEARS OF SCHOOL COMPLETED BY PERSONS 25 YEARS OLD AND OVER BY AGE, COLOR, AND SEX, FOR THE STATE, 1950 AND 1940 FOR URBAN AND RURAL AREAS, AND FOR STANDARD METROPOLITAN AREAS AND CITIES OF 100,000 OR MORE, 1950—Con.

[Statistics for 1940 based on 20 percent sample available complete-count data in tables 16 and 33. Median not shown where less than 1.0 or where base is less than 500 for 1950 or 100 for 1940]

Area, census year, color, age, and sex	All persons	Years of school completed: None	Elementary school: 1 and 2	Elementary school: 3 and 4	Elementary school: 5 and 6	Elementary school: 7	Elementary school: 8	High school: 1	High school: 2	High school: 3	High school: 4	College: 1	College: 2	College: 3	College: 4 or more	Not reported	Median school years completed
RURAL FARM 1950—Con.																	
Nonwhite																	
Total, 25 years and over	[illegible] 490	20,930	[illegible]	[illegible]	[illegible]	5,465	[illegible]	[illegible]	755	515	420	180	230	100	270	1,690	3 6
Male, 25 years and over	[illegible]	[illegible],075	[illegible]	[illegible],870	6,815	[illegible]	[illegible]	535	305	170	180	35	50	15	75	930	3 2
25 to 29 years	5 [illegible]25	[illegible]	[illegible]	1 570	1 [illegible]	491	[illegible]	120	70	40	30	5	5	5	5	90	4 2
30 to 34 years	4,875	75	785	[illegible]	[illegible]15	30	475	85	30	35	45	15		5	30	60	4 2
35 to 39 years	5,675	1,[illegible]	[illegible]	[illegible]	1,080	320	[illegible]	50	40	25	.		15			135	3 7
40 to 44 years	5,425	485	[illegible]	[illegible]	915	265	130	55	35	15	25	5	15		5	90	316
45 to 54 years	10,[illegible]	2 775	[illegible]	[illegible],330	1 320	370	230	70	55	40	25	5	5		10	155	3 0
55 to 64 years	7 100	2,285	[illegible],40	[illegible],730	[illegible]	155	150	80	45	10	40		10	5	5	195	2 4
65 to 74 years	6,[illegible]	2,47[illegible]	1,410	1 320	500	115	125	5	25	.	10	5			15	60	1 8
75 years and over	1,9[illegible]5	965	175	[illegible]	35	25	20	10	5	5	5	.				40	
Female, 25 years and over	45,720	6 815	7,135	[illegible]54[illegible]	9,345	3,375	[illegible],940	875	450	345	240	145	180	85	195	760	4 [illegible]
25 to 29 years	6,2[illegible]	350	10	1 520	1 630	780	405	175	85	110	65	50	35	1[illegible]	4[illegible]	65	5 4
30 to 34 years	5,8[illegible]	5[illegible]	775	1,440	1,505	650	345	125	1 0	65	45	5	35	25	55	60	4 [illegible]
35 to 39 years	6 [illegible]5	790	875	700	1,995	585	180	175	100	55	45	20	30	10	20	140	4 9
40 to 44 years	7,870	870	865	[illegible],550	1,325	480	225	155	65	25	30	30	30	15	30	150	4 4
45 to 54 years	9,[illegible]	2,[illegible]	1,520	2,72[illegible]	[illegible],690	470	330	155	65	55	35	20	40	15	25	185	3 8
55 to 64 years	7,3[illegible]5	1 450	[illegible]	1 410	820	205	165	45	25	20	10	5	5	5	15	55	1 1
65 to 74 years	4,280	[illegible],84[illegible]	505	76[illegible]	410	50	70	40	5	15	10	10	5			50	1 7
75 years and over	[illegible],625	[illegible]	395	235	60	50	15	10		-		5			5	55	1 1
STANDARD METROPOLITAN AREAS: 1950																	
BATON ROUGE—TOTAL																	
Total, 25 years and over	83 015	4 [illegible]0	[illegible]515	7 605	[illegible]	[illegible],405	6 395	[illegible],885	4 540	4,250	13,905	2 [illegible]95	3 745	2 205	8,465	2 045	9 8
Male, 25 years and over	40,4[illegible]5	2 150	1 955	2 9[illegible]	[illegible],215	[illegible]	3,[illegible]	2,350	2 130	[illegible],795	5,090	1,185	1,800	[illegible],385	4 820	1,140	9 6
25 to 29 years	7,840	100	17[illegible]	365	550	420	15	400	375	430	1,520	315	495	650	[illegible] 340	270	12 3
30 to 34 years	6 355	30	145	460	575	[illegible]70	465	[illegible]35	370	400	1,095	250	325	23[illegible]	965	125	11 5
35 to 39 years	[illegible],975	180	705	509	700	390	[illegible]	460	385	320	860	145	285	140	830	475	10 1
40 to 44 years	5 175	155	250	560	605	415	435	330	320	235	690	145	200	90	620	125	9 3
45 to 54 years	7 545	550	410	905	875	515	815	400	435	285	935	195	280	110	590	235	8 5
55 to 64 years	[illegible],395	450	[illegible]5	5[illegible]	[illegible]8	27[illegible]	385	240	170	90	400	75	160	55	465	115	7 [illegible]
65 to 74 years	2,275	435	300	405	250	105	205	65	30	25	145	45	35	25	80	105	[illegible] 7
75 years and over	855	200	115	150	[illegible]	4[illegible]	50	20	25	10	45	15	20	0	30	40	[illegible]
Female, 25 years and over	42 600	2,[illegible]0	[illegible]560	[illegible] 690	[illegible] 985	2,875	3,080	2,535	2,410	2,45[illegible]	8,215	1,410	1,945	820	3,645	905	10 0
25 to 29 years	8 [illegible]	[illegible]	140	495	685	[illegible]	405	480	455	650	2,015	380	435	200	800	1[illegible]	[illegible]9
30 to 34 years	6 835	70	125	400	770	470	400	420	450	57[illegible]	1,610	245	285	150	765	100	[illegible]5
35 to 39 years	6,5[illegible]	120	1[illegible]	760	750	495	465	380	395	590	1 505	135	300	120	700	165	10 9
40 to 44 years	5 375	200	200	480	485	380	375	320	315	265	1,075	195	225	110	450	120	10 0
45 to 54 years	7 [illegible]5	39	310	805	985	490	575	480	44[illegible]	400	1 [illegible]10	250	335	120	525	80	9 0
55 to 64 years	4,125	340	230	425	540	285	435	240	165	135	515	125	190	65	315	130	8 4
65 to 74 years	3,125	9[illegible]	285	400	430	140	275	145	9[illegible]	4[illegible]	245	45	135	45	95	100	6 1
75 years and over	1,360	200	80	185	140	45	50	70	50	45	140	35	40	20	15	45	6 3
BATON ROUGE—NONWHITE																	
Total, 25 years and over	26,875	3,480	2,810	[illegible]080	5 4[illegible]	2,3[illegible]	1,670	995	700	465	770	180	245	210	950	900	5 [illegible]
Male, 25 years and over	12,575	1,775	1 550	2 840	2 265	905	760	485	265	165	360	60	115	125	370	495	[illegible] 9
25 to 29 years	2 020	85	140	340	370	220	140	160	80	45	115	10	50	70	80	115	7 1
30 to 34 years	1,775	45	125	3[illegible]0	395	180	160	95	45	60	105	15	10	30	105	55	6 7
35 to 39 years	1,850	175	195	400	430	145	110	60	65	25	65	10	30	20	70	50	5 6
40 to 44 years	1,495	140	210	38[illegible]	[illegible]55	125	105	70	[illegible]	20	20		5		50	75	5 1
45 to 54 years	2 [illegible]35	435	335	[illegible]	[illegible]45	125	160	50	25	40	30	15	20	5	45	100	4 1
55 to 64 years	1,[illegible]85	265	265	405	240	65	45	40	[illegible]		15				15	[illegible]	3 5
65 to 74 years	1,105	470	225	25[illegible]	100	40	30	5	4	5	10					60	2 4
75 years and over	410	160	95	70	30	5	10	5	5			10			5	15	
Female, 25 years and over	14 300	[illegible] 705	1,270	2,840	3,[illegible]40	1,460	910	510	435	300	410	120	130	9[illegible]	580	405	5 7
25 to 29 years	2,540	80	110	430	5[illegible]0	380	205	115	120	80	150	55	55	45	135	70	7 [illegible]
30 to 34 years	2,[illegible]35	60	[illegible]0	[illegible]40	595	285	145	145	115	90	50		[illegible]0	10	130	[illegible]0	6 8
35 to 39 years	2 205	10	[illegible]	345	53[illegible]	285	60	110	85	55	110	20	15	[illegible]0	1[illegible]0	[illegible]5	6 6
40 to 44 years	1,875	[illegible]70	170	410	470	180	150	45	35	25	60	5	[illegible]	10	100	[illegible]	5 7
45 to 54 years	2,780	3[illegible]0	2[illegible]	50	560	205	150	50	30	30	15	15	20	5	65	20	4 9
55 to 64 years	[illegible] 305	255	180	285	[illegible]75	80	55	5	25	20	25	[illegible]0	5		35	50	4 4
65 to 74 years	[illegible] 395	490	225	305	175	[illegible]	45	35	10			10	1[illegible]	5	5	45	2 6
75 years and over	465	23[illegible]	55		20	10	20	5	[illegible]			5				23	
NEW ORLEANS—TOTAL																	
Total, 25 years and over	402,[illegible]85	13 340	15 555	41,640	38,92[illegible]	34,050	58 900	19,150	21,005	15,225	67,235	8,115	11,[illegible]35	[illegible],690	24,375	8,945	8 6
Male, 25 years and over	186,985	6,24[illegible]	7,630	20,630	26,900	15 150	26,730	8,545	9,590	6,645	26 920	4,205	[illegible],520	2,510	1[illegible],580	5 090	8 5
25 to 29 years	29,175	305	410	1 405	3,21[illegible]	2,390	2 890	1,815	2,065	1,675	6 330	1,090	1 195	750	3,305	655	10 9
30 to 34 years	25,575	245	480	1,560	2,795	2 100	3,055	1 675	1,810	1,315	5,175	745	930	440	2,600	650	10 3
35 to 39 years	25,320	450	775	2,095	3,150	2 240	3 965	1,465	1 600	1 145	3 890	465	920	360	2 120	670	8 9
40 to 44 years	23,710	530	970	2 5[illegible]	[illegible]	2 120	3 835	[illegible]70	1,320	945	[illegible],265	540	760	240	1,550	590	[illegible] 5
45 to 54 years	39,735	1,425	2,010	5,365	6,560	3 350	6,705	1 620	1,795	930	4 415	695	1,060	375	2 420	990	8 1
55 to 64 years	24,955	1,245	1,555	4,200	4 655	1,900	3,730	635	705	410	2 490	415	480	155	1 580	800	7 2
65 to 74 years	13,380	1,335	1 055	2 [illegible]05	2 [illegible]40	750	1,900	255	220	145	1 230	170	220	135	705	515	6 4
75 years and over	[illegible],135	725	385	925	790	400	650	110	45	60	425	85	60	55	390	220	6 1
Female, 25 years and over	215,300	7,[illegible]	7,925	21 0[illegible]0	32,0[illegible]5	18,900	32,170	10,605	11 415	8,580	40,31[illegible]	3 910	5,515	2,180	9,795	3,855	8 6
25 to 29 years	33 035	180	405	1,045	3,060	2,855	3,340	2,205	2,445	2 295	10,120	1 010	955	560	2,080	480	11 3
30 to 34 years	27 860	245	505	1,[illegible]80	3,210	2,775	3 320	1,975	2,050	1,750	6 865	645	775	280	1,665	420	10 2
35 to 39 years	28,700	415	705	1,840	3 760	2 685	4,640	1 725	1 945	1,330	5,950	550	860	420	1,400	425	9 0
40 to 44 years	27,0[illegible]0	610	915	2,31[illegible]	4 135	2,555	4,740	1 440	[illegible],520	990	4,630	495	755	265	1,265	420	8 6
45 to 54 years	42,645	1 550	1,830	5,335	7 170	3 905	7,225	1,765	1 870	1 175	6,320	720	1 005	290	1,665	725	8 1
55 to 64 years	28,005	[illegible],350	1 495	4,385	5,650	2,310	7,470	845	880	585	3,340	350	730	205	9[illegible]5	495	7 4
65 to 74 years	9 295	1 545	1 500	3,3[illegible]5	3,[illegible]00	1 180	3,080	415	505	320	2,010	95	315	120	625	465	6 6
75 years and over	8,720	1,[illegible]5	510	1 385	1 340	625	1,355	235	210	140	1 080	65	120	40	180	430	[illegible] 9

Table 65.—YEARS OF SCHOOL COMPLETED BY PERSONS 25 YEARS OLD AND OVER, BY AGE, COLOR, AND SEX, FOR THE STATE, 1950 AND 1940, FOR URBAN AND RURAL AREAS, AND FOR STANDARD METROPOLITAN AREAS AND CITIES OF 100,000 OR MORE, 1950—Con.

[Statistics for 1950 based on 20-percent sample, available complete-count data in tables 15 and 33. Median not shown where less than 1.0 or where base is less than 200 for 1950 or 100 for 1940]

Area, census year, color, age, and sex	All persons	None	Elementary school: 1 and 2	Elementary school: 3 and 4	Elementary school: 5 and 6	Elementary school: 7	Elementary school: 8	High school: 1	High school: 2	High school: 3	High school: 4	College: 1	College: 2	College: 3	College: 4 or more	Not reported	Median school years completed
STANDARD METROPOLITAN AREAS 1950—Con.																	
NEW ORLEANS—NONWHITE																	
Total, 25 years and over	107,910	6,860	9,545	20,500	22,875	1[illegible],825	13,560	5,055	4,065	2,625	5 775	6[illegible]5	[illegible]45	410	1 745	1 970	[illegible].4
Male, 25 years and over	48,855	3,245	4,050	10,070	10 195	5,060	5,935	1 955	1,735	935	2 220	520	455	180	715	1 135	6.2
25 to 29 years	7,325	125	245	865	1 485	1 590	1,450	810	455	580	540	125	125	80	125	125	7.8
30 to 34 years	6 300	115	305	950	1 290	810	945	435	335	165	450	65	75	45	155	180	7.5
35 to 39 years	7,095	235	470	1,355	1 515	830	995	315	315	215	370	35	100	20	160	165	[illegible].9
40 to 44 years	6 670	320	640	1 495	1,485	700	845	265	200	100	315	25	70	10	70	160	6.1
45 to 54 years	10,605	830	1 120	2,620	2 365	930	1,185	265	270	130	275	20	70	20	95	240	5.5
55 to 64 years	6,160	650	930	1,540	1 330	475	545	95	105	40	185	30	15	10	65	145	4.9
65 to 74 years	3,480	620	550	990	545	165	255	60	50	75	50	15		10	45	90	4.1
75 years and over	1 220	350	190	255	180	60	75	10	3	-	30	5		5	20	30	3.4
Female, 25 years and over	59,055	3,615	4,895	10,430	12,480	6,765	7,575	3 100	2,330	1,290	3,555	335	390	230	1,030	835	6.6
25 to 29 years	9,370	85	420	665	1 525	1,365	1,555	1 025	705	430	1,095	110	125	75	205	85	8.4
30 to 34 years	7,860	145	300	935	1,535	1,155	1,220	550	775	255	680	70	150	45	250	125	7.9
35 to 39 years	8,885	205	510	1,180	2 125	1,215	1 325	535	420	245	590	30	105	40	185	125	7.3
40 to 44 years	7 675	325	600	1,375	1,850	920	1,095	310	280	170	410	20	45	15	160	80	6.8
45 to 54 years	12,025	920	1,185	2 855	2 745	1,205	1 395	305	255	130	475	35	80	30	140	200	5.7
55 to 64 years	6,420	645	870	1,755	1,435	520	505	165	100	35	70	15	35	15	45	90	4.9
65 to 74 years	5,055	865	925	1,285	880	300	395	70	65	20	80		25	10	40	95	4.1
75 years and over	1,765	45[illegible]	285	400	265	85	85	30	30	5	55	5	25		5	35	3.6
SHREVEPORT—TOTAL																	
Total, 25 years and over	98,435	5,0[illegible]5	5,475	9 965	10 800	7,410	7 685	5 615	5 385	5 945	17,035	4,960	3 955	1 995	7,110	2,025	9.3
Male, 25 years and over	45,855	2,680	2,730	4,825	5,035	3,280	3,670	2,545	2,500	2,475	6,985	1,345	1 770	975	3 780	1 200	9.0
25 to 29 years	6,590	95	135	485	565	380	320	410	415	460	1,530	295	365	225	745	170	11.9
30 to 34 years	6,230	95	220	420	540	500	400	410	355	370	1,335	225	300	170	745	160	11.3
35 to 39 years	6,220	100	345	565	660	570	415	370	365	455	1,230	175	210	120	600	150	10.2
40 to 44 years	5 700	160	315	575	620	460	500	320	405	300	875	190	165	135	540	140	9.5
45 to 54 years	9 420	525	725	1,255	1 080	640	840	590	575	425	1,065	290	390	170	650	260	8.5
55 to 64 years	6 035	565	435	785	705	505	675	290	245	325	655	125	225	80	265	155	7.9
65 to 74 years	4,145	785	500	555	625	225	325	185	110	60	460	50	75	65	185	110	5.6
75 years and over	1,485	355	145	185	240	80	130	50	30	50	65	15	20	15	50	55	5.3
Female, 25 years and over	52 550	2,365	2 685	5,140	5,765	4,130	4,015	3,070	2,885	3,470	10,050	1,615	2,185	1 020	3 330	825	9.6
25 to 29 years	8,285	90	140	435	725	675	560	500	495	730	2,420	270	305	200	530	110	11.6
30 to 34 years	7 015	60	135	475	680	735	500	430	360	600	1,745	340	240	150	485	125	11.1
35 to 39 years	7 065	120	215	475	770	610	445	410	500	585	1,605	170	280	245	575	90	10.9
40 to 44 years	6,530	150	250	675	730	465	490	380	400	470	1,340	210	285	155	590	110	10.4
45 to 54 years	10,410	390	705	1 365	1,295	685	855	600	560	645	1,560	205	535	105	630	125	8.8
55 to 64 years	5,465	435	495	805	760	435	635	465	375	275	845	130	305	105	285	115	8.4
65 to 74 years	4,725	740	535	660	560	390	415	210	110	150	490	70	170	15	135	75	6.4
75 years and over	2,035	380	210	220	245	135	185	75	35	45	145	50	65	20	100	75	6.4
SHREVEPORT—NONWHITE																	
Total, 25 years and over	33,440	4,310	4 750	7,735	6,440	3,470	2,025	1 215	780	450	905	140	160	185	505	470	4.9
Male, 25 years and over	15,055	2 285	2,455	3,620	2 690	1,345	765	440	275	180	355	60	55	70	165	295	4.5
25 to 29 years	1,860	75	140	415	430	250	130	115	75	35	95	10	15	15	15	35	6.[illegible]
30 to 34 years	1,765	75	205	380	415	250	135	85	30	35	90	10	15	10	40	30	6.0
35 to 39 years	1 965	85	285	470	435	270	135	60	40	25	75	5	5	5	55	15	5.6
40 to 44 years	1,805	145	280	910	365	200	80	40	40	25	40		5	10	20	45	[illegible].8
45 to 54 years	3,215	485	640	925	530	180	150	70	55	35	55	25	5	15	10	55	4.0
55 to 64 years	1,980	460	980	515	255	130	85	30	25	5	20	5	5	10	10	45	3.5
65 to 74 years	1,840	675	425	310	230	40	35	35	10		20	5	5		10	40	2.1
75 years and over	625	305	110	95	30	25	15	5	5					5	5	30	
Female, 25 years and over	18,385	2,025	2 295	4 115	3,750	2,125	1,260	675	505	270	550	80	105	115	340	1[illegible]5	5.4
25 to 29 years	2,765	[illegible]	125	410	605	505	320	190	125	110	185	15	10	20	45	25	7.[illegible]
30 to 34 years	2,440	60	100	445	540	485	255	155	110	65	95	40	15	35	45	25	7.2
35 to 39 years	2,325	95	180	410	605	420	180	100	100	40	70	5	10	15	60	35	6.5
40 to 44 years	2,165	130	210	565	550	225	135	50	75	16	75		10	20	90	20	5.6
45 to 54 years	3,793	100	610	1,160	835	270	200	120	60	20	70	10	35	15	95	15	4.7
55 to 64 years	2,060	340	420	585	325	120	95	30	25	10	50	5	15	10	25	25	3.9
65 to 74 years	2 080	180	455	410	245	90	65	30	5	10	25		10			15	2.5
75 years and over	755	345	195	120	45	10	10		5	5		5				15	1.3
CITIES 1950																	
BATON ROUGE																	
Total, 25 years and over	67 330	2,800	2,460	5,495	6,730	4,105	5,105	4,000	3 745	3,560	12,515	2,340	3,335	1,975	7,580	1,585	10.6
Male, 25 years and over	32,615	1,375	1,335	2 795	3 080	1 965	2 665	1 915	1,750	1 460	5 110	1 065	1,585	1,260	4,380	875	10.4
25 to 29 years	6,665	45	150	240	395	320	420	345	315	360	1,380	285	435	595	1,150	230	12.5
30 to 34 years	5 215	50	105	335	445	260	325	340	315	305	980	225	290	270	870	100	12.1
35 to 39 years	4,815	115	150	330	505	315	370	360	320	240	765	120	240	125	760	100	10.7
40 to 44 years	4 200	120	175	420	445	300	360	250	260	200	615	135	195	90	550	85	10.0
45 to 54 years	6,115	410	250	675	660	435	665	355	330	245	850	180	245	105	550	175	8.8
55 to 64 years	3,465	280	260	420	420	215	315	200	140	90	345	70	135	45	430	100	8.3
65 to 74 years	1,550	240	160	275	155	80	175	55	40	10	130	40	30	20	70	70	5.8
75 years and over	590	115	85	100	55	40	35	10	25	10	45	10	15	10	90	15	4.8
Female, 25 years and over	34 715	1 425	1,125	2,700	3,650	2 140	2 440	2 085	1,995	2,100	7,405	1,275	1,750	715	3,200	710	10.7
25 to 29 years	6 620	70	115	350	500	415	285	405	400	370	1,800	340	400	165	660	140	12.1
30 to 34 years	5,630	50	75	290	580	335	320	335	350	475	1,440	235	265	135	670	75	11.9
35 to 39 years	5,380	80	135	320	565	370	365	300	325	390	1,315	115	265	120	675	130	12.5
40 to 44 years	4,420	115	140	375	510	270	295	265	285	225	960	185	205	100	390	100	10.7
45 to 54 years	5,855	260	215	650	690	395	450	385	370	250	1,050	230	295	90	460	65	9.6
55 to 64 years	3,155	245	190	300	420	195	360	155	135	120	480	110	170	60	490	85	8.8
65 to 74 years	2,385	405	190	280	290	115	235	135	85	75	225	35	115	35	90	75	6.9
75 years and over	1,070	200	65	135	95	45	130	65	45	35	135	20	35	10	15	40	7.4

Table 65 — YEARS OF SCHOOL COMPLETED BY PERSONS 25 YEARS OLD AND OVER, BY AGE, COLOR, AND SEX, FOR THE STATE, 1950 AND 1941 FOR URBAN AND RURAL AREAS, AND FOR STANDARD METROPOLITAN AREAS AND CITIES OF 100,000 OR MORE. 1950—Con

Statistics for 1905 bases in Morrorio margine associate reconstitution in tables 5 and 33. Median not shown where few than 1.0 or where base is less than 500 for 1930 o 100 ion 1940]

	!							lears o	schoo' cor	mpieted							Medu
Area. census year,	All			-	ementar,	esus.			High	school			Çall	ege		Nou	school year
color, age, and sex	ben are	None	1 and 2	3 ard 4	5 and o	7	8	1	2	3	4	1	2	8	4 or more	ported	plete
CITIES: 1950—Con		T. Aller				1					1 10						
NEW CHLEANS-TOTAL																	1
Total 25 years and over	3/2,380	- 590			+9,795	28,830	51,990	16,060	48,010	⊥2 555	58,155	0,775	9,420	3 980	21,425	7,810	
Mase, 25 years and over	23,740	4,-15	240	16,885 - 400	22,500	2,855	23,345	7 _00	8,000 1,705	5,550	23,180 5,100	3,510	4,725	2,140	2,835	4,440	
25 to 29 years	1 20,835	55	375	1.:55	2,-75	,78C	2,505	1,375	1.470	1,090	4,275	eO5	760 740	360 295	2,250	565 570	10
5 to 39 years 0 to 44 years	20,850	285 350	560 735	2,340	2,575	1,810	3,495	1,150	1,335	925 785	3,335 2,815	350 445	625	185	1,360	5.0	8
5 to 1 ear	34,200	1,025	_,660	4,385	5,700	2, 20,	2,892	± 3°5	4,560	815	3,920	600 335	930 425	345 145	2,135 1,455	885	8
5 to 74 vears	21,730	850	355	3,6_5 2,190	2,040	1,680	3,305	555 225	625	360 140	2,220	150	190	-25	645	455	6
5 years and over	+,550	25.	345	800	695	285	585	105	45	60	405	85	50	50	290	200	0
Female, 25 years and over	184,640	5,.75	6,555	18,045	27,495	975, د	28,645	8,960	9,950	7,105	34,975	3,265	4,695 825	1,840	8,290	3,370	
25 to 29 years.	27,070	135	3,0	785	2,420	2,255	2,805	1,860	2,085	1,815 _,355	8,290 5.790	495	530	200	⊥.405	375	10
5 to 39 years	24,000	26C	560	1,500	3,090	2,310	4,070	1,440	1.680	1,145	5,095	445 390	675 635	335 235	1,130	345 365	
0 to 44 'e.rs - to 54 years	23,15	1,205	1,520	1,-25	3,490 6,270	2.1551	6,475	1,210	1,310	1,010	4,060 5,770	630	900	255	1,505	650	8
5 to 74 years	24,785	2 01G	1.265	3,860	5,045	2,015	6,475 4,035	735	795	520	3,060	325	640 280	190	865 595	420	
5 years and over	17,3c0 7,940	1,210	1,3,5	3,010	3,275 1,220	575	2,880	385	465 205	285	1,900	85 55	110	40	170	420	6
4				,	,		1		- (al 5
NEW OFLIANSNAWWITE																	
Total 25 years and over	99,280	5,785	8,380	18,580	20,870	10,960	_2,870	4,765	3,855	2,095	5,585	645	1,000	405	⊥,675	1,805	6
Male, 25 years and ove.	44,580	2,690	4,070	8,970	9,265	4,710	5,680	1,855	1,655	880	2,135	315	450	180	680	1 040	6
to 29 years to 34 years	5,742	_10 90	250	70C 805	1,340	770	4,105	485	445 320	265 160	520 430	125	125 75	80 25	130	115 -75	8 7
o to 39 years -	6,435	190	385	1,220	1,375	745	950	285	290	190	360	35	100	20	155	135 155	?
to 44 years 5 to 54 years	9,780	250 720	1,195	2,365	2,175	655 870	1,170	255	190 255	200	310 252	25	70	7C	90	225	5
5 to 64 years	5,665	500 540	855 465	1,425	1,240	460 150	510 240	95 55	105	35 35	180	30	15	10	65 40	140	3
5 years and over	1,060	290	105	220	160	55	70	10	5	33	30	5		5	20	25	3
Femzle, 25 years and over	54,700	3,095	4,310	9,610	11,605	0,250	7,185	2,010	2,200	1,215	3,450	330	555	225	995	765	6
to 29 years	7,215	85	_90 255	590 820	1,425	1,235	1,440	965 520	665 450	400 245	1,070	105	11.5	75	195 240	±20	8
to 39 years.	8,200	175	430	⊥,005	1,940	1,135	1.255	520	390	240	575	30	95	4C	180	110	7
to 44 years.	7 125	2°5	540	2,665	2,580	1,120	1,040	290 375	260	160 115	3°0. 460	35	40 80	<u>ئد</u> 30	150	70 195	6
to 64 years	6,025	590	770	_,605	1,415	500	490	100	100	35	170	15	35	15	45	80	5
to 74 vears.	4,670	725	830	1,230	825 255	285	395 80	70	30	15	80 55	5	25	_0	40	75 35	4 3
, june and ord 1 to 5 1	,		100			. ~	-	-	~i	1		1	-				
SHECT/EFORT	1										1		100				0.09
Total, 25 years and over	74,300	3,135	3,400	6,380	7,440	5,245	5,500	4,135	3,975	4,605	14,820	2,595	3,460	1,745	6,445	1,420	10
Male, 25 years and over to 29 years	34,005 5,335	1,050	1,590 92	2,955	3,390	2,315	2,525	1,940	1,815	-,955	5,995 1,320	1,165	1,535	870 200	3,470 715	830 125	10
to 34 years	4,890	25	1.0	310	385	390	30C	255	255	370 270	1,123	190	240	150	655	110	12
to 39 years.	4,680	_D0	205 190	365 310	390 390)	350 325	3.D 360	295	320	365 230	1 015	155	185	115	555 495	±10	11
to o4 years	6,940	310	440	770	745	415	605	415	430	345	925	240	335	150	620	±95	9
to 64 years	4,260	35. 415	245	440 350	455	385 150	435	220	175	270	560 220	115	485 t 65 j	70	240 155	115	8
5 years and over	970	e05	85	700	180	25	80	40	20	35	60	50 10	15	33	35	35	5
Female, 25 years and over to 29 years	40,295	1,585	1,710	3,425	4,045	2,930	2,975	2,195	2 160	2,650	8,825	1,430	1,925	875 185	2,975	590 90	10:
to 34 years	5,465	35	70	305	482	500	375	285	265	450	1.5.0	280	210	135	425	80	11
to 89 years	5 435 4,960	20	255	335	525	420	31.5 295	300 265	345 270	405 370	1.395	150	260	160	5.0	70	11
to 54 years.	7,840	270	480	875	875	490	560	470	440	485	1,040	190 275	260	130	505 575	95 105	11
to 64 years	4,870	285	290 345	510 455	440	315	505	360	28>	230	765	115	200	85	265	60	8
o vears and over	1,560	280	250	155	165	115	335	135	95 75	130	460	60	145	15	125	45	7.

Table 66.—EMPLOYMENT STATUS, BY AGE, COLOR, AND SEX, FOR THE STATE, URBAN AND RURAL, AND FOR STANDARD METROPOLITAN AREAS AND CITIES OF 100,000 OR MORE: 1950—Con.

[Based on 20-percent sample; available complete-count data in tables 15, 25, 33, 35, 36, and 76. Percent not shown where less than 0.1 or where base is less than 500]

Area, color, and age	Male 14 years old and over: Total	Male: Labor force: Number	Male: Labor force: Percent of total	Male: Civilian labor force: Total	Male: Civilian labor force: Employed	Male: Unemployed: Number	Male: Unemployed: Percent of civilian labor force	Male: Not in labor force	Female 14 years old and over: Total	Female: Labor force: Number	Female: Labor force: Percent of total	Female: Civilian labor force: Total	Female: Civilian labor force: Employed	Female: Unemployed: Number	Female: Unemployed: Percent of civilian labor force	Female: Not in labor force
RURAL FARM—TOTAL																
Total	188,300	146,615	77.9	146,305	144,255	2,050	1.4	41,685	175,690	24,245	13.8	24,195	23,640	555	2.3	151,445
14 to 19 years	37,290	16,830	45.2	16,790	16,445	345	2.1	20,460	35,910	4,155	12.[illegible]	4,150	3,960	190	4.6	29,755
14 years	6,835	1,335	19.5	1,335	1,335			5,500	6,475	415	6.5	415	405	10		5,990
15 years	6,995	1,770	25.3	1,770	1,770			5,225	6,440	515	8.0	515	495	20	3.9	5,925
16 years	6,550	2,675	40.8	2,675	2,620	55	2.1	3,875	6,210	640	10.3	640	595	45	7.0	5,570
17 years	6,490	3,540	54.5	3,530	3,445	85	2.4	2,950	6,040	860	14.2	860	805	55	6.4	5,180
18 years	5,965	4,020	67.4	4,000	3,905	95	2.4	1,945	4,785	840	17.6	835	800	35	4.2	3,945
19 years	4,395	3,490	79.4	3,480	3,370	110	3.2	905	4,030	885	22.0	885	860	25	2.8	3,145
20 to 24 years	17,945	16,190	90.2	16,140	15,585	555	3.4	1,755	15,455	3,280	19.9	3,275	3,140	135	4.1	3,175
20 years	3,910	3,380	86.4	3,380	3,275	105	3.1	530	3,785	855	22.6	855	805	50	5.8	2,930
21 years	3,925	3,610	92.0	3,600	3,450	150	4.2	315	3,190	725	22.7	725	705	20	2.8	2,465
22 years	3,495	3,175	90.8	3,160	3,060	100	3.2	320	3,240	645	19.9	645	615	30	4.7	2,595
23 years	3,725	3,385	90.9	3,375	3,235	140	4.1	340	3,250	545	16.8	545	535	10	1.8	2,705
24 years	2,890	2,640	91.3	2,625	2,565	60	2.3	250	2,990	510	17.1	505	480	25	5.0	2,480
25 to 29 years	14,595	13,570	93.0	13,510	13,275	235	1.7	1,025	15,315	2,375	15.5	2,370	2,305	65	2.7	12,940
30 to 34 years	14,960	14,195	94.9	14,165	14,010	55	1.1	765	16,325	2,460	15.1	2,455	2,435	20	0.8	13,865
35 to 39 years	17,270	16,540	95.8	16,530	16,330	200	1.2	730	17,675	2,805	15.9	2,805	2,770	35	1.2	14,870
40 to 44 years	16,520	15,795	95.6	15,765	15,620	145	0.9	725	16,240	2,795	17.2	2,775	2,750	25	0.9	13,445
45 to 49 years	15,235	14,440	94.8	14,415	14,305	110	0.8	795	14,470	2,175	15.0	2,175	2,140	35	1.6	12,295
50 to 54 years	13,215	12,125	91.8	12,115	12,005	110	0.9	1,090	12,315	1,705	13.8	1,695	1,670	25	1.5	10,610
55 to 59 years	11,615	10,130	87.2	10,115	10,000	115	1.1	1,485	10,025	1,170	11.7	1,170	1,155	5	0.3	8,855
60 to 64 years	9,360	7,555	80.7	7,540	7,495	45	0.6	1,805	7,240	690	9.5	690	685	5	0.7	6,550
65 to 69 years	9,550	5,740	60.1	5,720	5,700	20	0.3	3,810	6,860	465	6.8	465	460	5		6,395
70 to 74 years	5,495	2,380	43.3	2,375	2,375			3,115	4,140	110	2.7	110	110	...		4,030
75 years and over	5,310	1,125	21.2	1,115	1,110	5	0.4	4,185	4,720	60	1.3	60	60	...		4,660
RURAL FARM—NONWHITE																
Total	70,440	56,240	79.8	56,095	55,560	535	1.0	14,200	68,665	13,030	19.0	12,995	12,675	320	2.5	55,635
14 to 19 years	15,990	8,790	55.0	8,760	8,645	115	1.3	7,200	15,205	2,430	16.0	2,430	2,360	70	2.9	12,775
14 years	2,930	810	27.6	810	810			2,120	2,855	285	10.0	285	280	5		2,570
15 years	2,855	995	34.9	995	995			1,860	2,750	320	11.6	320	310	10		2,430
16 years	2,775	1,375	49.5	1,375	1,360	15	1.1	1,400	2,860	440	15.4	440	425	15		2,420
17 years	2,695	1,840	68.3	1,835	1,800	35	1.9	855	2,595	535	20.6	535	515	20	3.7	2,060
18 years	2,800	2,135	76.3	2,115	2,090	25	1.2	665	2,270	420	18.5	420	410	10		1,850
19 years	1,935	1,635	84.5	1,630	1,590	40	2.5	300	1,875	430	22.9	430	420	10		1,445
20 to 24 years	7,440	6,785	91.2	6,760	6,615	145	2.1	655	7,980	1,810	22.7	1,805	1,735	70	3.9	6,170
20 years	1,775	1,585	89.3	1,585	1,555	30	1.9	190	2,045	505	24.7	505	485	20	4.0	1,540
21 years	1,640	1,510	92.1	1,505	1,485	20	1.3	130	1,570	395	25.2	395	390	5		1,175
22 years	1,415	1,305	92.2	1,300	1,260	40	3.1	110	1,535	360	23.5	360	335	25		1,175
23 years	1,515	1,390	91.7	1,380	1,340	40	2.9	125	1,480	295	19.9	295	290	5		1,185
24 years	1,095	995	90.9	990	975	15	1.5	100	1,350	255	18.9	250	235	15		1,095
25 to 29 years	5,425	5,050	93.1	5,030	4,970	60	1.2	375	6,235	1,310	21.0	1,305	1,250	55	4.2	4,925
30 to 34 years	4,875	4,625	94.9	4,615	4,595	20	0.4	250	5,815	1,270	21.8	1,270	1,260	10	0.8	4,545
35 to 39 years	5,875	5,660	96.3	5,660	5,625	35	0.6	215	6,715	1,505	22.4	1,505	1,470	35	2.3	5,210
40 to 44 years	5,425	5,210	96.0	5,195	5,180	15	0.3	215	5,870	1,300	22.1	1,285	1,260	25	1.9	4,570
45 to 49 years	5,495	5,220	95.0	5,200	5,155	45	0.9	275	5,110	1,140	22.3	1,140	1,125	15	1.3	3,970
50 to 54 years	4,675	4,355	93.2	4,350	4,315	35	0.8	320	4,455	920	20.7	910	885	25	2.7	3,535
55 to 59 years	4,085	3,705	90.7	3,700	3,675	25	0.7	380	3,130	630	20.1	630	615	15	2.4	2,500
60 to 64 years	3,015	2,650	87.9	2,645	2,630	15	0.6	365	2,245	410	18.3	410	410			1,835
65 to 69 years	4,150	2,690	64.8	2,685	2,660	25	0.9	1,460	2,930	255	8.7	255	255			2,675
70 to 74 years	2,075	1,070	51.6	1,070	1,070			1,005	1,350	35	2.6	35	35			1,315
75 years and over	1,915	430	22.5	425	425			1,485	1,625	15	0.9	15	15			1,610
STANDARD METROPOLITAN AREAS																
BATON ROUGE—TOTAL																
Total	54,915	41,410	75.4	41,335	39,015	2,320	5.6	13,505	58,095	17,460	30.1	17,450	16,860	590	3.4	40,635
14 to 19 years	6,775	2,120	31.3	2,110	1,865	245	11.6	4,655	7,155	1,315	18.4	1,310	1,220	90	6.9	5,840
14 years	1,095	175	16.0	175	155	20		920	930	30	3.2	30	30			900
15 years	1,005	155	15.4	155	145	10		850	965	65	6.7	65	60	5		900
16 years	850	185	21.8	185	160	25		665	950	135	14.2	135	115	20		815
17 years	940	385	41.0	380	320	60		555	1,010	135	12.9	130	105	25		925
18 years	1,345	570	42.4	565	490	75	13.3	775	1,485	390	26.3	390	365	25		1,095
19 years	1,540	650	42.2	650	595	55	8.5	890	1,775	560	31.5	560	545	15	2.7	1,215
20 to 24 years	7,725	4,845	62.7	4,845	4,415	430	8.9	2,880	8,340	3,230	38.7	3,230	3,080	150	4.6	5,110
20 years	1,290	695	53.9	695	605	90	12.9	595	1,760	660	37.5	660	630	30	4.5	1,100
21 years	1,635	955	58.4	955	870	85	8.9	680	1,535	610	39.7	610	585	25	4.1	925
22 years	1,520	915	60.2	915	860	55	6.0	605	1,580	620	39.2	620	590	30	4.8	960
23 years	1,635	1,105	67.6	1,105	985	120	10.9	530	1,760	670	38.1	670	645	25	3.7	1,090
24 years	1,645	1,175	71.4	1,175	1,095	80	6.8	470	1,705	670	39.3	670	630	40	6.0	1,035
25 to 29 years	7,840	6,590	84.1	6,570	6,250	320	4.9	1,250	8,015	2,725	34.0	2,725	2,640	85	3.1	5,290
30 to 34 years	6,355	5,865	92.3	5,850	5,635	215	3.7	490	6,835	2,130	31.2	2,130	2,060	70	3.3	4,705
35 to 39 years	5,975	5,670	94.9	5,660	5,395	265	4.7	305	6,570	2,290	34.9	2,290	2,240	50	2.2	4,280
40 to 44 years	5,175	4,915	95.0	4,910	4,710	200	4.1	260	5,375	2,120	39.4	2,120	2,070	50	2.4	3,255
45 to 49 years	4,070	3,825	94.0	3,815	3,610	205	5.4	245	3,975	1,490	37.5	1,490	1,450	40	2.7	2,485
50 to 54 years	3,475	3,165	91.1	3,165	3,005	160	5.1	310	3,220	1,010	31.4	1,005	990	15	1.5	2,210
55 to 59 years	2,590	2,230	86.1	2,225	2,070	155	7.0	360	2,450	550	22.4	550	520	30	5.5	1,900
60 to 64 years	1,805	1,230	68.1	1,230	1,160	70	5.7	575	1,675	330	19.7	330	330			1,345
65 to 69 years	1,435	645	44.9	645	600	45	7.0	790	2,005	185	9.2	185	175	10		1,820
70 to 74 years	840	215	25.6	215	210	5		625	1,120	65	5.8	65	65			1,055
75 years and over	855	95	11.1	95	90	5		760	1,360	20	1.5	20	20			1,340

to 64 years to 69 years	20,F,0 17,580	15,340 8,070 2,850	73 7 45 1 27 4		7,620	44	5 25	9,8,0	23,985	2,390	10 0	2,39	2.31	5 73	3 1	21.,
to 74 years years and over	10,390	2, 850	27 4	2,850	2,765	8 8	3 0	9,425	14,385	395	2 4	395	38	0 2	1	16,

Table 66.—EMPLOYMENT STATUS, BY AGE, COLOR, AND SEX, FOR THE STATE, URBAN AND RURAL, AND FOR STANDARD METROPOLITAN AREAS AND CITIES OF 100,000 OR MORE: 1950—Con.

[Based on 20-percent sample; available complete-count data in tables 25, 33, 35, 36, and 76. Percent not shown where less than 0.1 or where base is less than 500]

Area, color, and age	Male, 14 years old and over: Total	Labor force: Number	Labor force: Percent of total	Civilian labor force: Total	Civilian labor force: Employed	Unemployed: Number	Unemployed: Percent of civilian labor force	Not in labor force	Female, 14 years old and over: Total	Labor force: Number	Labor force: Percent of total	Civilian labor force: Total	Civilian labor force: Employed	Unemployed: Number	Unemployed: Percent of civilian labor force	Not in labor force
STANDARD METROPOLITAN AREAS—Con.																
SHREVEPORT—TOTAL																
Total	58,635	46,200	78.8	45,050	43,675	1,375	3.0	12,435	68,345	22,050	33.1	22,045	21,395	650	2.9	45,695
14 to 19 years	6,620	2,455	37.2	2,440	2,310	130	5.3	4,145	7,545	1,615	21.4	1,615	1,510	105	6.5	5,930
14 years	1,155	185	16.0	185	180	5		970	1,265	70	5.5	70	55	15		1,195
15 years	1,155	240	20.8	240	235	5		915	1,205	55	4.6	55	50	5		1,150
16 years	1,100	270	24.5	270	260	10		830	1,145	155	13.5	155	140	15		990
17 years	1,130	460	40.7	460	430	30		670	1,190	230	19.3	230	225	5		960
18 years	1,070	585	54.7	585	540	45	7.7	485	1,455	545	37.5	545	530	15	2.8	910
19 years	930	715	72.2	700	665	35	5.0	275	1,285	560	43.6	560	520	40	7.1	725
20 to 24 years	6,180	5,265	85.2	5,010	4,775	235	4.7	915	8,250	3,640	44.1	3,640	3,475	165	4.5	4,610
20 years	1,150	905	78.7	835	765	70	8.4	245	1,725	790	45.8	790	740	50	6.3	935
21 years	1,175	995	84.7	955	900	55	5.8	180	1,640	720	43.9	720	695	25	3.5	920
22 years	1,250	1,105	88.4	1,070	1,015	55	5.1	145	1,425	660	46.3	660	635	25	3.8	765
23 years	1,350	1,190	88.1	1,130	1,105	25	2.2	160	1,800	710	39.4	710	690	20	2.8	1,090
24 years	1,255	1,070	85.3	1,020	990	30	2.9	185	1,660	760	45.8	760	715	45	5.9	900
25 to 29 years	6,590	5,955	90.4	5,600	5,425	175	3.1	635	8,285	3,070	37.1	3,065	2,995	70	2.3	5,215
30 to 34 years	6,230	5,775	92.7	5,450	5,300	150	2.8	455	7,035	2,680	38.1	2,680	2,615	65	2.4	4,355
35 to 39 years	6,220	5,825	93.6	5,700	5,555	145	2.5	395	7,065	2,945	41.7	2,945	2,860	85	2.9	4,120
40 to 44 years	5,700	5,360	94.0	5,315	5,190	125	2.4	340	6,530	2,765	42.3	2,765	2,710	55	2.0	3,765
45 to 49 years	5,110	4,725	92.5	4,710	4,600	110	2.3	385	5,635	2,255	40.0	2,255	2,205	50	2.2	3,380
50 to 54 years	4,340	3,955	91.1	3,950	3,820	130	3.3	385	4,775	1,655	34.7	1,655	1,630	25	1.5	3,120
55 to 59 years	3,450	3,025	87.7	3,025	2,935	90	3.0	425	3,715	1,010	27.2	1,010	995	15	1.5	2,705
60 to 64 years	2,585	2,035	78.7	2,030	1,975	55	2.7	550	2,750	560	20.4	560	550	10	1.8	2,190
65 to 69 years	2,585	1,235	47.8	1,235	1,205	30	2.4	1,350	2,990	365	12.2	365	365			2,625
70 to 74 years	1,560	395	25.3	395	395			1,165	1,735	55	3.2	55	50	5		1,680
75 years and over	1,485	195	13.1	190	190			1,290	2,035	35	1.7	35	35			2,000
SHREVEPORT—NONWHITE																
Total	20,095	14,785	73.6	14,720	14,085	635	4.3	5,310	24,500	10,545	43.0	10,540	10,135	405	3.8	13,955
14 to 19 years	2,915	1,360	46.7	1,360	1,290	70	5.1	1,555	3,205	720	22.5	720	655	65	9.0	2,485
14 years	570	125	21.9	125	125			445	615	60	9.8	60	55	5		555
15 years	495	160		160	155	5		335	525	35	6.7	35	30	5		490
16 years	485	185		185	180	5		300	540	120	22.2	120	110	10		420
17 years	475	295		295	270	25		180	475	115		115	115			360
18 years	485	310		310	295	15		175	610	215	35.2	215	200	15		395
19 years	405	285		285	265	20		120	440	175		175	145	30		265
20 to 24 years	2,125	1,755	82.6	1,740	1,645	95	5.5	370	2,910	1,490	51.2	1,490	1,365	125	8.4	1,420
20 years	390	310		310	290	20		80	745	370	49.7	370	330	40		375
21 years	390	320		320	305	15		70	530	265	50.0	265	245	20		265
22 years	475	420		410	390	20		55	535	285	53.3	285	270	15		250
23 years	430	385		385	375	10		45	520	250	48.1	250	240	10		270
24 years	440	320		315	285	30		120	580	320	55.2	320	280	40		260
25 to 29 years	1,860	1,560	83.9	1,540	1,460	80	5.2	300	2,765	1,415	51.2	1,410	1,370	40	2.8	1,350
30 to 34 years	1,765	1,530	86.7	1,520	1,440	80	5.3	235	2,440	1,410	57.8	1,410	1,360	50	3.5	1,030
35 to 39 years	1,965	1,755	89.3	1,750	1,675	75	4.3	210	2,325	1,345	57.8	1,345	1,290	55	4.1	980
40 to 44 years	1,805	1,630	90.3	1,630	1,565	65	4.0	175	2,165	1,250	57.7	1,250	1,225	25	2.0	915
45 to 49 years	1,775	1,610	90.7	1,605	1,555	50	3.1	165	2,130	1,195	56.1	1,195	1,180	15	1.3	935
50 to 54 years	1,440	1,295	89.9	1,295	1,245	50	3.9	145	1,665	735	44.1	735	715	20	2.7	930
55 to 59 years	1,155	955	82.7	955	920	35	3.7	200	1,155	505	43.7	505	495	10	2.0	650
60 to 64 years	825	635	77.0	630	615	15	2.4	190	905	265	29.3	265	265			640
65 to 69 years	1,190	490	41.2	490	470	20		700	1,465	195	13.3	195	195			1,270
70 to 74 years	650	145	22.3	145	145			505	615	15	2.4	15	15			600
75 years and over	625	65	10.4	60	60			560	755	5	0.7	5	5			750
CITIES																
BATON ROUGE																
Total	44,020	33,780	76.7	33,710	32,040	1,670	5.0	10,240	47,190	15,115	32.0	15,115	14,625	490	3.2	32,075
14 to 19 years	5,055	1,680	33.2	1,675	1,510	165	9.9	3,375	5,475	1,150	21.0	1,150	1,080	70	6.1	4,325
14 years	785	145	18.5	145	125	20		640	665	30	4.5	30	30			635
15 years	655	135	20.6	135	130	5		520	700	55	7.9	55	50	5		645
16 years	610	150	24.6	150	135	15		460	715	120	16.8	120	100	20		595
17 years	705	300	42.6	300	260	40		405	825	110	13.3	110	95	15		715
18 years	1,060	435	41.0	430	370	60		625	1,150	325	28.3	325	305	20		825
19 years	1,240	515	41.5	515	490	25	4.9	725	1,420	510	35.9	510	500	10	2.0	910
20 to 24 years	6,350	3,945	62.1	3,945	3,665	280	7.1	2,405	7,000	2,885	41.2	2,885	2,765	120	4.2	4,115
20 years	1,075	590	54.9	590	525	65	11.0	485	1,435	565	39.4	565	540	25	4.4	870
21 years	1,255	750	59.8	750	695	55	7.3	505	1,270	540	42.5	540	520	20	3.7	730
22 years	1,255	720	57.4	720	695	25	3.5	535	1,370	575	42.0	575	545	30	5.2	795
23 years	1,410	920	65.2	920	835	85	9.2	490	1,485	620	41.9	620	595	25	4.0	865
24 years	1,355	965	71.2	965	915	50	5.2	390	1,440	585	40.6	585	565	20	3.4	855
25 to 29 years	6,665	5,625	84.4	5,605	5,380	225	4.0	1,040	6,620	2,395	36.2	2,395	2,325	70	2.9	4,225
30 to 34 years	5,215	4,850	93.0	4,835	4,675	160	3.3	365	5,630	1,810	32.1	1,810	1,755	55	3.0	3,820
35 to 39 years	4,815	4,585	95.2	4,575	4,370	205	4.5	230	5,380	1,980	36.8	1,980	1,930	50	2.5	3,400
40 to 44 years	4,200	4,000	95.2	3,995	3,835	160	4.0	200	4,420	1,805	40.8	1,805	1,770	35	1.9	2,615
45 to 49 years	3,310	3,105	93.8	3,095	2,950	145	4.7	205	3,230	1,275	39.5	1,275	1,240	35	2.7	1,955
50 to 54 years	2,805	2,585	92.2	2,585	2,470	115	4.4	220	2,625	845	32.2	845	830	15	1.8	1,780
55 to 59 years	2,040	1,765	86.5	1,760	1,650	110	6.3	275	1,980	490	24.7	490	460	30		1,490
60 to 64 years	1,425	1,015	71.2	1,015	955	60	5.9	410	1,375	270	19.6	270	270			1,105
65 to 69 years	985	435	44.2	435	400	35		550	1,500	135	9.0	135	125	10		1,365
70 to 74 years	565	135	23.9	135	130	5		430	885	60	6.8	60	60			825
75 years and over	590	55	9.3	55	50	5		535	1,070	15	1.4	15	15			1,055

Table 66—EMPLOYMENT STATUS, BY AGE, COLOR. AND SEX, FOR THE STATE, URBAN AND RURAL, AND FOR STANDARD METROPOLITAN AREAS AND CITIES OF 100,000 OR MORE 1950—Con

[Based or All-percent sample available complete-count data in ables 15 25 35, % 38, and 70 Percer not sown where seen can 0 1 0 where been is seen han 500

	Water Street		113	le 14 years	old and over	1	-	- 41/2		11	Γem	a.e 14 'ear	ok and eve	r	- A Department	
landari i	1		-	Lace	force	-	·		-			Lahor	0.06			
	***				(ivi.an ,abo	L totce		411					C-viber lace	r force	-	
Area color and agu	Total		Dercent			Unemp	ploved	na tov	"ota.		Per-			1. nemp	k yea	Not in
	-54	Number	of total	Total	Employed	\umber	Percent of ca- villan abor force	foru.	OLE.	\umbir	cent of	Total	Employed	Numbe.	Percent of c vilian labor icros	force
RJEAL FARM—TOTAL									ing sa					1		
Total	187,300	140,61,	77 9	146,305	144 255	r v50	- 4	14,68	.75 €90	2 245	13 8	2-, 5	's and	155	2 3	151 44
14 to 19 years 15 years 15 years 16 years 17 years 18 years 19 years 20 years 21 years 22 years 23 years	31, 290 6 835 6, 995 6, 550 6, 490 1 965 4, 395 1, 945 3, 910 3, 925 3, 925 3, 725 2, 890	1(,330 1,33, 1,700 2,075 3,440 4,020 3,490 1w,190 9,380 3,710 3,380 3,175 3,335 2,640	49 5 25 3 40 8 24 7 67 7 90 2 86 4 92 8 90 9	16,790 1,335 1,770 4 675 3 330 4,000 -,480 16 740 3,380 3,160 3,160 3,375 2,625	1 33* 1,770 2,620 3,445 3,905 3 77. 15 585 3,005 3,005 2,275 3,006 2,275 2,567	555 555 555 150 100 40	21 24 32 34 2 3 2 3 2 3 2 3 2 3 2 3 2 3 2	20,4.0 5 5.0 1,225 3,879 2 950 1,942 955 3,755 320 340 250	3.945 6 475 6 2.49 6 4,75 3,25 3,25 3,25 3,25 3,25 3,25 3,25 3,2	3 280 325 325 3 280 3 280 3 280 3 290 6.5	12 · 6 5 6 7 14 22 0 9 6 7 9 9 6 8 4 7 1	2 5 2 5 3 14 64C 64C 64C 64C 7 7 7 7 7 7 7 7 7 7 7 7 7 7 7 7 7 7 7	3,960 405 4 505 3,20 3,20 805 70- 115 735 440	19C 20 20 35 35 50 20 30 30	4 9 6 4 2 5 1 5 8 7 8 0	29 75 5,95 5 77 5,18 3,17 2,95 2,44 2,57 2,45
25 to 29 years 30 to 34 years 40 to 34 years 40 to 54 years 40 to 54 years 50 to 59 years 50 to 59 years 50 to 59 years 50 to 59 years 50 to 59 years 70 to 64 years 71 to 64 years 72 years 73 years 75 years 76 years 77	14, 395 14, 960 17, 270 16, 320 12, 213 11, 213 11, 613 9, 360 0 350 5 495 5, 310	3 570 -(,195 16 540 -5,795 1/,440 14,125 10 130 7,555 5,740 2,380 1,121	94 8 92 6 94 8 91 8	13,5.C 14,05 16,530 15,705 4415 10,115 10,115 7,740 5,7.0 2,37,5 1,15	1,275 14,0.0 16,33 14,620 14,335 12,00 10 000 7,495 5,75 2,775 1 11.	255 555 200 445 1100 1100 1113 45 20	7 12 10 9 8 0 0 1 1 6 6 7 6 7 6 7 6 7 6 7 6 7 6 7 6 7 6	1,025 765 730 72 795 1 090 1 483 1,80 3,810 3,115 4 185	15 315 16 325 17 675 10,240 24 47, 10 025 7,240 6 860 4 140 4,720	2,-75 2,-75 2,-75 2,-75 2,-75 - 170 690 465 110	155 1720 67 186 21	2 270 2 305 2 305 2,77; 2,175 1,693 	2, 505 2, 770 4, 750 2 140 - 600 - 155 685 46C 1.0	655 22D 357 2035 35 85 55	782 296537	14,85 14,85 14,25 10,01 8 85 6,75 4,05
RURAL FARM—NONWHITE	j.						1									
I oral	70 440	56,240		56,097	55,560	535	10	1-,200	68,660	_3 0:0	19 0	12 995	2,675	520	2 3	\$5,63
4 to 13 vectors 14 years 15 vectors 15 vectors 15 vectors 15 vectors 15 vectors 15 vectors 9 years 9 years 20 years 20 years 22 years 22 years 23 years 23 years 24 years 24 years 25 years 2	15,990 4,930 4,835 4,775 2,695 2,800 1,935 7,440 1,75 1,640 1,415 1,515 1,95	8,790 810 922 1,375 840 2,135 4,635 6,785 1,510 1,510 1,205 1,205	27 6 34 9 49 5 68 1 76 3 84 5 91 2 80 3 92 2 92 7	8,760 810 907 1,375 2,115 1,630 6,764 1,585 1,505 1,300 1,380 990	8,645 810 995 1,360 1,800 2,490 6,615 1,255 1,485 1,250 1,340	15 3, 25 40 145 30 20 40 40 40	19222123	7 230 2 120 1,860 1,860 1,40, 855 665 300 653 190 110 110 110	10,200 2 8"5 2 700 2,450 2,595 2,270 1,875 7,980 2,045 1,570 1,535 1,480 1,350	2,430 28r 320 440 435 430 430 -,810 -,05 360 295 457	16 0 0 1 6 4 6 5 9 22 7 7 22 5 5 19 9 9 10 9	2,430 265 320 4-0 534 420 430 1,805 505 197 360 295 250	2 260 280 310 423 512 410 420 1,005 390 390 290 275	70 5 10 10 10 10 10 20 5 25 25	37	2,7 2,5 2,4 2,0 1,8 1,4 6,1 1,1 1,1 1,1 1,0
25 to 25 years 30 to 34 years 30 to 34 years 30 to 34 years 30 to 35 years 30 to 35 years 30 to 35 years 30 to 35 years 30 to 36 years 30 to 36 years 30 to 36 years 30 to 36 years 30 to 36 years 30 to 36 years 30 to 36 years 37 to 47 years 37 to 48 years 37 to 48 years 37 to 48 years 38 to 36 years 37 to 48 years 38 to 36 years 38 to 36 years 37 to 48 years 38 to 36 years 38 to	5,425 7,875 8,875 5,425 4 675 4 085 3 10 4,150 2,075 1 915	5,050 7,625 5,660 5,210 5,220 4,355 3,705 2,650 2,650 4,30	94 9 96 3 90 0 95 0 93 2 90 7 87 9 64 8 51 6	5 030 4,615 5,660 5,195 5,200 4,320 3 700 2,642 2,685 1,070 425	4,970 4,595 5 625 5,180 5,155 4 315 2 630 2,660 1 070 425	60 20 35 45 35 25 25 10 25	12 04 03 04 07 07 08 09	375 250 215 215 275 32C 38C 365 1,460 1 003 1,485	6,23° 5,8-5 6,715 5,870 5,110 4,455 3,110 2,245 2,930 1,625	1,310 1,505 1,505 1,300 1,140 1,140 2,30 4,00 2,35 3,5	21 0 21 8 22 4 22 1 22 3 20 7 20 3 20 7 20 3 20 9	,305 1,270 1,505 1 28, 1,1/0 630 410 255 37 15	1,250 1,260 1,470 1,260 1,125 885 615 410 255 15	55 10 32 25 13 25 25 15	4 2 8 3 3 1 9 3 7 2 4	4 95 5 2 5 3 95 3 5 5 2 6 1 3 3 1 6
BATCH ROUGE TOTAL Total	915,4د	4 ,413	75 /	41,375	39,015	2 320	26	13 205	>6,091	17 460	30 1	17,450	16,860	>90		40,63
Total 14 years 14 years 14 years 15 years 15 years 15 years 19 years 19 years 20 to 24 years 20 years 21 years 22 years 23 years 24 years	54,915 6,775 1,095 1,005 35C 94C 1 345 1,500 1,725 1,290 1,645	4,413 2,200 175 355 385 370 6°0 4 845 9°15 9°15 105 2 175	31 0 5 4 21 8 41 0 40 4 42 2 53 9 50 67 6	2,110 175 155 185 380 500 600 4,840 605 955 945 1 105 1 175	1,805 155 145 160 320 490 595 4,415 605 870 860 985 1,095	245 20 20 25 60 75 75 430 90 85 85 80	1. 6 .3 3 8 5 8 9 12 9 6 0 10 9 6 8	- 655 920 850 665 255 775 850 2,880 995 680 605 5.70	7,155 963 960 1,0.0 1,455 1 775 6,440 1 760 1 555 1,380 1,380 1,760	1 3.5 30 05 135 13.7 790 550 3 220 600 610 620 670	1° 4 2 6 7 14 2 12 9 26 3 31 5 7 39 7 39 2 38 1 39 3	1,310 30 69 1,35 130 390 560 3,730 660 60 60 670	220 30 50 115 105 555 545 3,980 585 590 645 645	96 20 25 15 150 30 25 30 25 40	2 6 9 2 6 6 7 4 6 7 6 0	5,84 90 81 9,1,00 5 11 1,10 72 76 1 09
20 to 29 years 30 to 24 years 30 to 24 years 35 to 39 years 40 to 44 years 50 to 54 years 50 to 54 years 60 to 64 years 60 to 65 years 77 to 74 years 77 to 74 years 77 years and over	7 84U 6 355 5,975 5,175 4 070 3,475 2 190 1,605 1,435 840 855	6 590 5,865 7,670 4,9.5 3,825 3,165 7,230 1,230 645 215	92 3 94 9 95 0 94 0 91 : 86 1 68 1 25 6	5,570 5,650 5,660 4 910 3 810 3,165 2 225 1,230 645 215	6,250 7 63* 5,395 4,710 3,610 3,005 2 0*0 1,160 600 210	320 21.5 265 200 203 .60 .5, /0 45	4 9 7 4 1 1 5 4 1 7 7 0 5 7 7 0	1,250 490 305 260 2/5 310 360 574 790 62.	8 CL5 c,875 6,370 5,375 3,975 3 200 2 45C 1 675 2 005 -,12C 1 360	2 72÷ 2 ±30 2,250 2 ±20 4,490 550 130 185 655	34 0 31 2 34 9 39 4 37 2 31 4 22 4 19 7 9 2 5 8	2,725 2,.30 2 296 2 120 1,490 1,005 550 3,50 185 65	2,640 2 060 2 240 2,770 1,430 990 520 330 175 65	50 50 50 40 40 15 30	3 1 3 2 2 2 4 2 7 5 5 5	5,29 4,28 3,25 2,48 2,41 1,90 1,34 1,82 1,05

Table 66.—EMPLOYMENT STATUS. BY AGE COLOR, AND SEX. FOR THE STATE, URBAN AND RURAL, AND FOR STANDARD METROPOLITAN AREAS AND CITIES OF .00,000 OR MORE 1950—Con Based on Supercert issups a statistic complete-event data r tables 1°. 25 33, 35, 98 and 76 Percent act shrwn where less than 0., or where base is less than 0.001

		-	VI	ale 14, man	יחור אמר מיים	-					F(m	ale 14 vear	s old and ove	r		
					force							Labor	force		7	
	1				C vihan lex	r fore.		- 1					Cavilian labo	or force		
Area color and age						U emp	doved	Not ma					T	Unemp	loyed	Not in labor
	Total	\umber	Percent % otal	Tous	Employed	\unider	Perren of ci van iabor force	labor force	Total	·\umbor	Per- cen. of total	Total	Employed	Number	Percent of co vilian labor force	force
STANDARD METROPOL- ITAN AREAS—Con																
BATON ROUGE -NONL', I'E												7.075		370	5.2	
Total	2,425	2ر1,2,5 935	3€ 6	12,200	17,814	1,320	14 5	4,910	2,112	7,080	17 9	7,075	6,7C5 4C5	55	2 %	22,34
14 years 5 years 16 years 17 years 18 years 19 years 10 years 20 years 20 years 22 years 22 years 24 years	2,423 430 330 390 430 390 2 045 363 432 390 333 420	95 60 30 245 245 2,5 1,270 250 285 285 315 290	6 7 0	95 60 2.5 2.5 265 21,370 230 250 250 250 250 250	95 25 25 230 185 230 250 240 250 250	5 50 50 35 34 45 45 45	17 5	-,490 470 370 25C 1,0 165 1,5 675 135 185 105 120	2,5"0 300 340 410 355 .80 590 2,545 610 495 525 480	15 40 40 45 115 145 945 215 175 170 175 210	19 8 24 6 37 1 30 2	400 1000 45 115 145 945 215 175 170 175 210	40 85 30 100 39 860 195 165 150 168	15 15 10 85 20 10 20 20 20 20 20 20 20 20 20 20 20 20 20	9 0	28 30 31 31 44 1,00 39 34 26 35
to 29 years to 34 years to 49 years to 49 years to 49 years to 56 years to 56 years to 56 years to 69 years to 69 years to 69 years to 74 years years and over	2,020 1 "75 1 850 1,505 1,305 -,030 940 545 730 375 410	3,530 -,525 -,700 -,445 -,180 -,360 -,35 -,360 -,35	85 9 90 6 90 6 90 6 90 6 90 6 90 6 90 6 90	1,53C 1,725 1,700 1,444 1,186 980 750 345 26C 80 35	1,455 _,-00 1,535 1,335 1 055 820 655 325 215 75	1 '5 .25 163 -100 .25 8c 8c 8c 8c 8c 8c 8c 8c 8c 8c 8c 8c 8c	10 7 8 4 9 7 7 6 .0 9 12 7	350 250 250 250 124 250 290 470 295 375	2 540 2,135 2,205 1,87, 1,405 975 785 520 970 425 465	1,130 1,045 1,160 890 645 425 175 100 85 15	44 5 48 9 52 6 47 5 43 6 22 3 19 2 8 8	1,130 1,045 1,160 890 645 420 175 100 85 5	1,065 1,005 1,125 850 615 410 175 100 75 15	65 40 35 40 30 30 30	383047	1,41 1,09 1,04 98 76 55 61 42 88 44
NEW OFLEANS-TOTAL								50.346	001.444	en ene		en 105	77. 255	4,100	4 9	190 1e
Total Le voice Le voi	238,050 25,130 4,14* 4,280 4,.55 3,835 4,380 4,335 25,935 25,935 25,935 3,70 4,940 5,070 5,840	167,890 8,090 245 485 1,035 1,475 2,480 2,970 20,680 3,140 3,920 4,045 4,715 4,860	5 9 11 3 24 9 36 5 56 6 68 5 79 7	183,655 8,110 245 485 1.035 1,450 2,330 2,550 19,455 2,760 3,680 3,845 4,530 4,640	271,500 6,730 225 425 855 1,190 1,884 2,155 17 560 2,410 3,335 3 505 4,032 4,775	1, 360, 20, 60, 1,80, 270, 475, 395, 3,895, 3,50, 345, 340, 495, 365,	6 6 17 0 27 4 18 2 19 5 15 5 9 7 12 7 9 4 8 8 10 9 7 9	50 160 25,440 3 970 3,795 9,120 9,360 1,960 1,965 1,130 1,025 1,025 985	273 555 27 670 4,195 4,280 4,345 5,380 5,290 30 585 5,715 5,935 5,980 6,500 6,455	83,275 b 020 300 160 415 985 1,960 2,470 12,500 2,615 2,560 2,515 2,260	21 8 9 9 7 8 46 7 9 45 8 45 1 42 3 32 7	83,195 6,010 30 160 415 985 1,950 2,460 12,500 2,615 2,960 2,330 2,515 2,280	79 095 5,500 305 135 355 870 1,785 2,325 11,695 2,430 2,430 2,430 2,325 2,430 2,325 2,430 2,325	510 510 25 60 115 175 135 805 188 140 165 165	8 5 11 79 5 5 6 6 6 6 6 6 6 6 6 6 6 6 6 6 6 6 6	190,280 21,550 4,165 4,120 3,765 3,560 3,220 2,820 18,085 3,200 3,275 3,450 3,965 4,175
to 29 venrs to 34 venrs to 39 venrs to 49 years to 49 years to 49 years to 54 years to 54 years to 69 years to 69 years to 69 years to 69 years to 74 years years and over	29 175 25,575 25,720 23,710 21,445 18 290 14,355 10,600 8,495 4,885 5,135	25,750 23,840 23,840 22,100 19,885 .6,320 12,250 7,945 4,920 1,050 835	88 3 93 1 94 2 93 2 92 7 89 2 8° 3 70 0 40 7 31 7 15 3	24, 95 23,130 23,515 21,900 19,77, 16,215 12,220 7,940 4,215 1,550 835	23,215 22,000 22,760 20,685 18,640 15,315 11,510 7,425 5,990 1,495	1, 580 1, 330 1, 255 1, 215 1, 165 900 "10 51.5 225 >5 40	645555555555	3,425 1,735 1,475 1,610 1,560 1,970 2,105 2,655 4,275 3,335 4,300	33,035 27,860 28,700 2°,040 25,020 16,625 15,915 12,090 11,770 7,525 8,720	1_,175 9,100 10,735 -0,855 7,915 6,3_0 4,240 2,355 1,259 400 235	33 87 44 14 2 6 0 7 3 7 4 4 1 4 2 6 0 7 3 7 4 1 1 5 7 8 7 7 8 7 7 8 7 7 8 7 7 8 7 8 7 8 7	11,145 9,09, 10,720 10,855 7,900 6 310 6,235 2,535 1,255 400 235	10,535 8,670 10,250 10,510 7,575 6,035 4,090 2,440 1,190 385 220	610 425 470 345 325 275 125 95 65 13	57 442 144 335 2	21,800 28,760 17 96; 16,18; 15,10; 13,31; 11,67; 9,55; 10,51; 7,12; 6,48;
NEW ORLEANS-NOWHETZ																
Total 4 to 19 years 14 wars 15 years 15 years 15 years 17 years 17 years 20 years 21 years 21 years 22 years 23 years	64,255 8,295 1,510 1,065 1,310 1,295 1,400 1,210 7,105 1,240 1,315 1,590 1,560 1,460	47 245 2 720 65 180 32, 520 835 795 5,445 915 1 015 1,145 1,220 1,150	73 5 32 8 4 3 11 5 24 8 40 2 59 4 65 7 76 6 73 8 77 2 8 78 2 78 8	46,825 2,685 55 180 525 515 835 765 5,280 885 995 -,110 1 175 -,1_5	42 440 2,052 25 145 270 400 595 600 4,500 240 840 950 980 590	4 385 620 10 30 53 115 240 65 780 45 45 45 45	9 4 23 1 29 3 26 7 2 0 14 8 16 4 19 6 14 4 46 6 11 2	17,010 5 575 1,4/5 1 385 985 775 570 415 1,660 325 330 385 340 3.10	9,5°0 2,5°0 2,5°0 3,640 3,500 1,635 1,740 8,925 1,725 1,625 1,725 1,625 1,730 1,630 1,930	27,185 1 330 70 125 240 375 520 3,040 5-00 580 625 620 675	35 0 13 9 4 3 8 3 25 0 22 9 49 9 34 1 31 3 35 7 34 9	27,170 1,325 90 125 2/0 375 515 3 04c 540 580 625 620 675	25,075 1,085 105 205 285 440 2,600 465 510 510 605	2 095 240 20 20 35 90 75 440 70 115 110	7 7 18 1 14 6 14 5 13 9 12 1 16 4 10 4	*0,385 8,260 1,570 1,375 1,265 1,260 5,885 1,185 1,045 1,165 1,230 4,260
5 to 29 years 0 to 34 years 5 to 39 years 0 to 44 years 5 to 39 years 0 to 44 years 5 to 49 years 5 to 49 years 5 to 59 years 5 to 59 years 5 to 69 years 5 to 69 years 5 to 79 years 5 to 79 years 5 to 60 years 5 to 60 years	7,325 0,300 7,095 6,070 5,990 4,715 3,725 2,435 2,385 1,095 1,220	0,150 5,530 6,480 5,990 5,305 4,000 2,905 1,635 790 215	84 0 87 8 91 3 89 8 90 1 8-8 78 0 67 1 33 1 19 6 5 6	0 020 5,500 6 440 5,975 5,300 4,000 2,905 1 635 790 2,5	5,400 5,100 9,000 5,545 4,935 3,673 2,700 1,505 745 205	020 400 440 430 365 33C 205 130 45 10	10 3 3 8 2 9 3 1 5 7 6 8 3 7 6 8 5 7	1,175 770 615 680 585 7.15 820 800 1,595 880 1,140	9,370 7,860 8,885 7,675 6,705 5,320 3,680 2,740 3,445 1,610	3,625 3,520 4,220 3,850 3,035 2,080 1,235 695 380 65	38 7 44 8 48 3 40 2 45 3 39 1 33 6 25 4 11 0 2 3	3,620 3,520 4 290 3,850 3 035 2 080 1,220 695 380 65	3,275 3,275 4 010 3,670 2,875 1,995 1,175 670 345 65	345 245 280 160 160 25 35 35	9505 473 445 36	5,745 4,340 4,595 3,825 3,670 3,240 2,445 2,445 3,065 1,545 1,725

Table 66—EMPLOYMENT STATUS, BY AGE, COLOR, AND SEX, FOR THE STATE, URBAN AND RURAL, AND FOR STANDARD METROPOLITAN AREAS AND CITIES OF 100,000 OR MORE 1950—Con. [Based on 20-percent escape is alianle complete-count data in Tables 10 25, 35 35 36, and 76. Perce 7 not anown where last than 0.1 or when base is less than 50 1

	10		Ma	_	ug and over				we fast	- N. W	Fema	sie .4 year	s oad and ove	r		-
				Labor	force	- 4.0						Labor	force	Trans.	1	
					Cruhan abo	r force			-0.5				Civilan ish	or force	1	
Area, color, and age	Total		Percent			Unemp	noeq	labor force	Total		Per			Lnemp	loyed	labur force
	a page	Number	of total	Total	Employed	y mper	Percent of ca- ultar abo. roroe	force	1012	\amber	cens or otal	Tota.	Employed	Number	Pe con of ca vulcan labor force	force
STANDARD METROPOLITAN AREAS—Con SEPEVEPORT—TOTAL											i		Marchinelle ville	i de la compania del compania del compania de la compania del compania del compania de la compania de la compania de la compania de la compania del compania		
Total	58,62	46,200	78 8	45,050	43 675	1,,275	3.1	_£ ~35	68 345	22,050	1	225	21,995	650		-5,693
4 to 19 years 14 years 10 years 10 years 10 years 10 years 18 years 18 years 20 years 21 years 22 years 23 years 23 years 24 years	6 600 1,155 1,155 2,100 1 130 1,070 930 6,480 1 120 1,175 1,250 1,350 1,350	2,455 185 440 77n 450 585 71r 5,265 99: 1,105 1,100	37 2 16 0 20 5 24 5 40 7 54 7 72 2 85 7 84 7 88 4 88 1 85 3	2,440 28- 24- 270 460 585 700 5 C10 835 955 1 070 1,130 1 020	2 31.0 280 275 200 430 40 665 4,775 900 -,005 -,005	13.0 55 100 30 35 235 70 55 55 55	5 75748129	47.4 970 913 8 0 670 482 245 180 145	7,54 -,205 -,205 -,149 -,90 -,955 -,255 -,	3,540 3,540 3,540 3,540 790 720 760	37 43 4 47 37 43 4 47 43 4 47 43 4 47 43 4 47 47 48	27,527 700 55 155 230 545 560 3 643 790 720 663 710	1,912 50 50 140 2,5 540 3,475 740 695 690 715	15 15 15 15 15 15 15 15 15 15 15 15 15 1	5 2746 2525	2,930 2,199 2,156 990 900 901 720 4,610 933 960 900
5 to 29 vears 0 to 54 vears 0 to 54 vears 0 to 54 vears 0 to 54 vears 0 to 54 vears 0 to 54 vears 0 to 55 vears 0 to 56 vears 0 to 56 vears 0 to 56 vears 0 to 56 vears 5 to 59 vears 0 to 64 vears 5 to 69 vears 1 to 74 vears 5 vears and over	6 590 6,220 5,700 5 110 4,340 3,450 2,585 2,585 1,564 1,445	5,955 5,775 5 825 5,360 4 725 3,955 3,025 2,035 -,235 395	90 4 92 5 93 6 94 0 92 5 91 1 87 7 47 8 25 3 13 1	5,600 5,450 5,700 5,315 4,710 3,950 3,02° 4,030 1,235 345	5,425 5,300 5,555 5,40 4,600 3,82 2,935 -,975 1,205 395	175 140 145 125 1. C 134 90 95 35	32222333074	635 395 340 385 385 425 450 1,350 1,465 1,290	8,285 7,065 6,35 6,635 4,7,5 3,725 2,750 2,950 -,735 2,035	2,550 2,765 2,765 2,765 2,255 1,005 -,000 560 385 55	37 ± 7 42 3 43 43 43 43 43 43 43 43 43 43 43 43 4	3,065 2,680 2,94, 2,765 2,255 1,655 1,010 560 365 55	2,995 2,615 2,860 2,720 2,205 -,630 995 550 365 50	65 85 55 50 25 45 40	9 14 CHUNCH	5,213 4,353 4 _20 3,763 3,380 3,120 2,700 2,680 2,680 2,000
SEEEVEPOPT-NONVHITE														1		
Total 14 to 19 years 14 years	20,095 2,915 570	14,785 2,560 125	73 6 46 7 21 9	1,360	14,085	635	4 3 5 1	5,3±0 1 555 445	24,500 3,205 615	10 5-5 720 60	43 0 22 5 9 8	13,540 720 60	10, 35 650 55	6.5	38	2,489 500
14 years 15 years 16 years 17 years 17 years 18 years 19 years 20 vears 20 vears 22 years 22 years 23 years 24 years	495 485 475 485 405 2,125 3°0 3°0 475 433 740	160 185 295 310 285 1,755 510 320 420 388 320	82 6	160 18* 295 310 285 1,740 310 320 410 385 3.5	255 270 270 255 265 1,645 290 305 390 375 285	5 5 25 25 20 20 20 20 30	5 .	235 300 280 175 -20 370 80 70 55	25 540 475 6.0 440 2,9.0 745 53 535 520 580	35 120 1:5 2:5 175 1,490 370 265 245 250 320	30 2 30 2 49 7 50 0 53 3 48 1 55 2	255 120 113 215 179 1 490 265 285 250 32v	110 113 200 14, 1,363 245 270 240 250	10 15 30 25 40 20 15		490 420 360 390 260 1,420 260 270 260
25 to 29 years 30 to 34 vears 30 to 34 vears 15 to 39 vear 10 to 44 vears 15 to 49 vear 15 to 49 vear 15 to 49 vear 15 to 59 vear 15 to 59 vear 15 to 59 vear 15 to 59 year 15 to 59 year 15 to 69 year 17 to 74 vears 15 to 69 year 17 to 67 vears 18	1 860 1 765 1,965 1,805 1 775 1 440 1,455 815 1,190 #30 625	1,560 1,755 1,755 2,630 2,630 2,295 955 635 490 1,45	867 337 99 99 97 422 3 +	1,540 1,520 1,630 1,635 1,605 1,295 637 490 145	1,400 1,440 1,675 1,565 1,565 1,245 920 615 470 145 60	80 90 72 95 50 50 35 15 20	5544337 Q	300 235 210 175 165 145 20° 190 700 505 560	2,765 2,440 2,320 2,105 2 130 1,605 50 905 1,405 613 755	1,415 1,4-0 1,345 1,250 1,195 735 505 265 195 15	51 2 57 6 57 8 57 7 56 1 43 7 29 3 13 2 0 7	1 4.0 1,410 1 345 1,250 1,195 735 505 265 195 10	1,370 1,360 1,280 1,220 1 180 715 493 265 295	50 52 25 15 20 10	13	1,35 1,03 98 91 93 93 65 64 1 27 60
CTYCES BATON ROUGE																e a
Total .	44,020	33,780	76.7	33,710	32,040	1,670	5.0	10,240	47,190	15,115	32 0	15,115	14,62	490	3 2	32,07
14 to 19 vents 14 vents 14 vents 15 years 16 years 17 years 18 vents 18 vents 20 to 24 years 20 years 21 vents 22 years 22 years 24 vents 25 years 24 vents	5,055 765 950 910 70; 1,060 1,240 6,350 1,075 1,255 1,255 1,255	1,680 142 130 300 433 213 3,945 590 750 720 920	20 6 6 4 4 4 4 5 5 1 6 2 4 9 8 5 9 8	1,672 145 135 150 300 430 515 ,945 590 750 720 965	1, 31, 125 125 130 135 260 370 490 3,663 693 693 823 823 823 823	20 5 1.5 40 60 25 280 65 55 25	9 9 10 5 5 8 8 8 9 5 8 9 5 8 8 9 5 8 8 9 5 8 8 9 5 8 8 9 5 8 8 9 5 8 8 9 5 8 9 5 8 8 9 5 9 5	3,375 640 520 460 405 625 725 2,40* 485 505 535 490 390	5,475 665 700 715 925 1,150 1 420 7,300 1,435 1,270 1 370 1,485 1,440	1,150 30 30 120 110 325 510 2 885 564 540 575 620 585	7 9 8 3 3 9 4 4 5 9 6 6 4 6 6	1,150 30 55 120 120 325 510 2,885 565 540 575 6&4 585	1,080 30 100 90 300 90 2 765 540 580 540 540 540 540	20 20 15 20 10 10 10 10 10 10 10 10 10 10 10 10 10	20244725414	4 32: 63: 59: 71: 82: 91: 4,11: 87: 79: 86: 85:
25 to 29 years 30 to 34 years 30 to 35 years 45 to 39 years 45 to 49 years 45 to 49 years 55 to 69 years 56 to 69 years 66 to 64 years 70 to 74 years 77 to 74 years 77 years and over	6,665 5,215 4,815 4,200 3,310 2,805 2,040 1,425 985 565 565	5,4.29 4,985 4,000 3,105 2,985 1,765 1,015 135	84 4 93 0 95 2 95 8 92 8 5 71 2 2 3 9	5,605 4,835 4,575 3,995 3,095 2,585 1,760 1,015 135	9,380 4,675 4,370 3,833 2,950 2,470 1,650 955 400 130	225 160 205 45 115 110 60 35	33	-, 340 365 230 205 220 275 410 450 430 535	6,420 5,630 5,080 4,420 3,237 2,625 1,980 1,375 1,500 885 1,070	2,395 1,810 1,980 1,005 1,275 845 490 270 115	36 2 32 1 36 8 40 8 39 5 32 2 24 7 19 6 6 8	2,39* 1,810 1,980 1,865 1,275 845 490 270 135 60	1 930 1,770 1 240 830 460 270 125	55 50 36 36 15 30 30	25	4, 22: 3,82: 3,40: 2 61: 1,95: 1,78: 1,49: 4,10: 82: 1,05:

Table 66.—EMPLOYMENT STATUS, BY AGE, COLOR, AND SEX, FOR THE STATE, URBAN AND RURAL, AND FOR STANDARD METROPOLITAN AREAS AND CITIES OF 100,000 OR MORE 1950.—Cor

[Based on 20-percent status available complete-or-rat fats in its less 15 28, 33 35, 36, and 78. Percent not shown where less than 0.1 or while base is less than 500]

	-	-	71	an 14 year	s old and one						Fem	nie, 14 vea	rs old and ov	er		-
	1		_		r force			74. S				Lebo	r force			
			1		Cirilian isb	or force							Civilian Iso	or force		
Ares ocsor and age	ł	1	1			Unem	p.oyed	ot in			Per-			Unemy	ploved	Vo m
Č, se	Total	\un.ber	Percent	Trtal	l-mpioved	\muser	Percent 0 es- olian labor force	labor force	Total	∖₃mber	ent of total	Tota:	Employed	Number	Percent of er vilun labor force	labor force
C'TIES-Cor																
NEW ORLEANS-TOTAL													1			
Total	24-2-	ره8 صد		152 845	142 3-0	10 505	£ 7	43,255	2:3,240	" 040	34 7	73 905	70 334	3,635	4.9	1.59,200
14 to 19 years 4 years 15 years 16 years 17 years 18 years 19 years	3,445 3,445 3,334 3,175 3,175	7,0/5 _05 370 0ec _,195 2,070	3 8 23 0	194 3mc 780 1,185 1,925	5 36' 175 340 445 955 1,343 4,730	125 20 50 135 2,4 385	17 3 19 4 20 0 15 0	13,605 3,165 3,045 2,610 2,000 1,035	2 940 3 485 3 490 2,40 3,7.5 4,3.5 4 485	2,050 75 110 300 825 -,u50 2,140	22 0 0 7 3 2 8 7 22 2 38 2 47 7	5,040 25 110 300 825 1,600 2,130	4,605 25 100 255 725 1,490 2,010	10 45 100 460 120	12 ± 9 7	17,890 3,460 3,380 3,140 2,890 2,665 2,455
20 to 24 years 20 years 21 years 22 years 23 years 24 years	3,065 1,170 3,6,0 4,203 4 2,0 ,702 -,790	2,070 2,4,7 6,885 2,720 3,455 3,31 3,730 3,730	7, 01	15,6/2 4,245 2,45 3,15 3,70 3,720	14,110 - 960 2,760 2,820 3,140 3,420	1,565 285 265 285 -30	10 0 1, / 8 6 9 1 12 C 8 1	4,685 -,020 940 940 953 855	25 660 4,795 5,030 4 969 5,470 5 400	2,280 2,280 2,275 2,245 2,235 1,985	43 0 47 5 45 2 45 2 41 2 36 8	2,280 2,280 2,27 2,24 2,255 1,982	3 1,325 2,120 2 160 2,090 2,160 -,850	71.5 16. 1.5 155 150 135	50 50 67 0 8	2 3,5 14,620 2,715 2,755 2,720 3,21 3,415
25 to 29 vessire 30 to 3+ cours 30 to 3+ cours 40 to 44 vessire 40 to 44 vessire 50 to 59 vessir 50 to 59 years 90 to 64 years 90 to 64 years 77 to 77 years 77 to 77 years 5 vessir and over	23 9±0 20,855 20,850 19,830 18,440 15,780 ±2 510 0,440 1,480 4,285 4,285	20,°4c 19 375 19 570 15,425 17,075 14,005 10,670 6,900 3,7 C 1,390	87 7 92 7 93 9 92 9 92 7 88 8 85 3 74 8 9 9 32 4 17 9	40,08 1d,740 14,255 4 200 1,970 13,905 6 895 3,725 1 390 8.5	18,705 -7,77- 18,440 17,850 19,905 13,090 10,020 6,425 3,510 -,335 775	1,375 970 1,115 ,080 -,065 815 025 440 215	62893941809	2,940 1,520 1,680 1,405 1,775 840 2,20 3,750 2,835 3,735	27,070 22,990 24,080 25,415 20,010 17,390 14,035 10,750 11,280 9,780 7,840	9,805 7,960 9,345 9,700 7,355 5,845 3,860 2,285 -,17,385 235	36 2 39 6 42 0 5 6 33 6 27 5 21 7 0	9,779 7,955 9,530 9,700 2,145 5,845 3,855 2,285 1,175 385 235	9,240 7,580 7,120 9,400 6,840 5,53 3,730 2,125 1 115 370 220	335 375 410 300 305 255 125 90 50 15	173 13429 1	17,465 15,030 14,235 13,415 12,855 11,245 10,175 8,465 9,405 0,395 7,605
NEW ORLEANS—MONWHITE			i								200					
14 to 10 years 14 years 5 years 6 years 16 vears 17 years 18 years 19 years 20 years 20 years 21 years 22 years 22 years 23 years	7 45 1,360 1,435 1,185 -,190 1,310 1,065 6,375 1,125 1,175 -,405	4,955 2,425 50 175 480 475 775 4 855 830 899 1,050 1,070	73 4 32 1 3 7 12 2 43 0 30 0 59 2 62 0 76 2 76 7 76 7 78 1	2,515 2,393 50 175 280 470 77- 640 4 690 830 873 1 315 1 025	40 -40 -25 -35 -370 -555 -515 -4,040 -675 -720 -885	3, 80 235 10 25 45 100 220 125 670 125 130	22 4 28 4 49 5 14 3 6 12 8 17 1	1,545 5,120 1,10 1,260 9C5 /15 535 395 1,720 295 280 355	71 .83 8,700 1 /20 1,-70 1,360 1,475 1,5.5 8,350 1,445 1,615	20,165 1,260 45 90 215 330 480 2,833 470 573 593	30 2 13 3 3 1 6 6 15 8 22 4 29 7 34 5 30 2 37 4 5 7	25,150 4,155 45 90 215 330 475 2 83,7 470 555	2, 255 45 75 76 245 410 2, 435 405 500 480	210 1C 20 30 85 65 400 65 55	7 5 18 2 14 1 9 9 18 6 17 4 10 6	46,420 7 540 1,420 1 425 -,770 1,145 1,-45 1,-35 5,350 1,070 930 1,025
24 Years 25 to 29 years 30 to 54 years 35 to 59 years 35 to 59 years 45 to 49 years 45 to 49 years 45 to 49 years 50 to 50 years 50 to 50 years 50 to 50 years 70 to 65 years 70 to 74 years 70 to 74 years 77 years and over	1,370 2,000 6,605 3,745 6,623 5,415 4,335 4,335 3,417 2,250 2,180 985 4,060	5,000 5,060 5,060 5,060 5,865 3,580 2,665 3,580 2,665 3,580 2,670 195	77 7 8.3 8 88 1 9.4 4 89 8 80 8 84 3 78 6 67 3 33 3 19 8 6 5	975 9,470 5,030 5,355 4 850 2,680 2,680 2,685 1 215 725 195	550 860 4,905 4,000 5,450 5,00, 4,%0 3,305 2,495 4,985 60 185	175 115 267 370 390 380 315 490 130	17 1 11 8 10 3 4 7 7 7 7 7 7 7 7 7 8 6 4 6 2	30° 290 - 085 685 252 645 500 685 730 735 1,425 790	1,760 1,7%, 8,680 7,215 8,200 7,125 6 245 4,930 3,450 2,575 3,450 1,610	005 615 5,370 3,370 2,830 1,965 1,160 625 50 60	34 4 54 5 38 8 44 8 2 70 1 45 3 9 9 32 7 11 C 2 5	605 615 3,365 3,950 3,570 2,830 1,965 1,155 635 350 65 40	3,045 3,045 3,015 3,095 3,410 2,680 -,895 4,410 615 300 -55 35	105 65 320 220 255 160 50 70 45 20 30	27 46 58555369 L	3,980 4 250 3,980 4 250 3 55, 3,415 2,965 2 290 1,940 1,415 1,570
SEREVEPORT	.0 006	34 540			** .**									1		
Total 14 to 10 veazy 14 years 14 years 16 years 16 years 18 years 18 years 20 years 20 years 22 years 22 vears 24 years 24 years	42,8% 4,133 63 685 720 615 695 743 4,75 785 900 900 1,065 1,005	- 635 115 160 175 285 370 \$30 3,945 575 740 840 915 865	*0 6 19 4 18 1 2 4 2 4 3 1 5 3 2 7 3 1 7 3 7 8 3 7 8 5 9 8 6 1 9 0 9	35,480 1,520 160 175 285 70 518 3 720 575 725 803 860 825 4,510	1,515 110 155 164 265 340 430 2,60 2,60 690 760 850 805	20 30 30 35 160 50 32 40 40	65 6 8 3 4 8 6 2 2 4 5 1	8,335 2,520 520 525 545 410 325 770 210 130 120 120	51,890 5 085 240 250 6 20 1,335 1 030 6 5 0 1,485 1,180 1,97 1,340	1,305 30 35 115 195 450 450 450 5125 555 540 580 564	36 6 26 1 2 7 4 8 15 8 15 8 23 8 43 5 49 0 49 8 49 8 40	19,005 20 20 115 195 450 510 3,125 555 565 580 605 645	1,435 100 35 100 435 47 2,980 610 655 85 605	90 10 15 15 35 45 45 20 15	3 2 6 8 0 6 9 0 6 3 2 3 2 6 3 2	3,760 720 691 615 625 58,520 1,385 660 645 600 785
27 to 29 years 33 to 29 years 33 to 29 years 44 to 49 years 45 to 49 years 55 to 20 years 55 to 20 years 55 to 20 years 55 to 20 years 75 years 75 years 75 years 75 years 75 years 76 years	0,335 4,890 4,680 4,190 3,"65 3 175 2,440 1,420 1,720 1,015 970	4,830 4,725 4,400 3,985 3,500 2,880 2,465 1,460 810 265 120	92 9 92 5 94 0 95 0 90 7 82 7 83 4 47 0 26 1 12 /	4,510 4,220 4,280 1,945 3,490 2,87* 2,165 1,462 810 265 120	4,370 4,160 4,165 3,835 3,425 2,780 2 105 1,415 780 26* 120	48 119 18 88 48 48 48 48 48 48 48 48 48 48 48 48	1878938 17	485 365 280 205 265 295 275 360 915 750 850	6,610 5,465 7,475 4,960 4,285 3,755 2,800 2,070 2,293 1,270 1,560	2,050 2,225 2,510 2,220 1,880 1,300 460 300 450 305 55	40 1 41 1 46 2 43 4 43 4 43 4 13 4 14 6	2,645 2,245 2,510 2,240 1,880 1,390 800 460 305 5" 25	2,580 2,180 2,430 2,185 1,850 1,365 7d5 450 305 50	65 65 80 55 50 25 15 10	2925789	3,960 3,220 2,925 2,720 2,405 2,465 2,160 1,610 1,980 1,215 1,535

Table 67.—STATUS OF EMPLOYED PERSONS, BY AGE AND SEX, FOR THE STATE, URBAN AND RURAL, AND FOR STANDARD METROPOLITAN AREAS AND CITIES OF 100,000 OR MORE 1950

Based on 20-percent sample, available complete-count data in table 76.

Area and status of employed persons	Male 14 years old and over: Total	14 to 19 years	20 to 24 years	25 to 34 years	35 to 44 years	45 to 54 years	55 to 64 years	65 to 74 years	75 and over	Female 14 years old and over: Total	14 to 19 years	20 to 24 years	25 to 34 years	35 to 44 years	45 to 54 years	55 to 64 years	65 to 74 years	75 and over
THE STATE																		
Employed, total	638,650	[illegible]	[illegible]	159,650	155,935	[illegible]	[illegible]	22,365	[illegible]	[illegible]	[illegible]	[illegible]	[illegible]	[illegible]	[illegible]	17,340	[illegible]	[illegible]
At work	622,465	40,210	[illegible]	156,435	[illegible]	113,950	64,430	[illegible]	[illegible]	[illegible]	[illegible]	[illegible]	[illegible]	[illegible]	[illegible]	[illegible]	[illegible]	485
With a job but not at work	16,185	[illegible]	1,580	3,215	3,515	3,220	2,335	[illegible]	275	[illegible]	775	985	[illegible]	[illegible]	525	935	430	50
URBAN																		
Employed, total	358,280	[illegible]	[illegible]	97,365	[illegible]	67,245	[illegible]	[illegible]	[illegible]	[illegible]	[illegible]	[illegible]	[illegible]	[illegible]	[illegible]	[illegible]	2,955	380
At work	348,755	[illegible]	36,480	95,365	87,670	65,360	[illegible]	[illegible]	[illegible]	[illegible]	[illegible]	[illegible]	[illegible]	[illegible]	27,240	[illegible]	2,775	350
With a job but not at work	9,525	490	880	2,000	2,245	1,885	[illegible]	[illegible]	150	5,040	320	630	[illegible]	1,350	[illegible]	575	180	30
RURAL NONFARM																		
Employed, total	136,115	9,040	17,345	34,800	34,070	23,615	12,875	3,905	465	[illegible]	[illegible]	[illegible]	8,645	[illegible]	[illegible]	2,955	740	105
At work	132,305	8,750	16,910	33,965	33,225	22,825	12,435	3,760	435	[illegible]	[illegible]	4,900	[illegible]	9,285	[illegible]	2,780	675	90
With a job but not at work	3,810	290	435	835	845	790	440	145	30	[illegible]	185	135	325	390	[illegible]	175	65	15
RURAL FARM																		
Employed, total	144,255	16,445	15,585	27,285	[illegible]	26,310	17,495	[illegible]	[illegible]	[illegible]	[illegible]	[illegible]	[illegible]	5,520	3,810	[illegible]	[illegible]	60
At work	141,405	16,120	15,320	26,905	[illegible]	[illegible]	17,045	[illegible]	[illegible]	[illegible]	[illegible]	2,920	[illegible]	5,145	3,495	[illegible]	485	45
With a job but not at work	2,850	325	265	380	475	545	450	365	95	[illegible]	[illegible]	220	315	375	[illegible]	185	85	15
STANDARD METROPOLITAN AREAS																		
BATON ROUGE																		
Employed, total	39,315	1,865	4,415	11,885	10,105	6,605	3,230	810	90	16,860	1,220	3,080	4,700	4,310	2,440	850	240	20
At work	38,415	1,805	4,345	11,660	9,930	6,425	3,100	760	80	16,295	1,205	3,035	4,535	4,125	2,360	785	230	20
With a job but not at work	900	60	70	225	175	180	130	50	10	565	15	45	165	185	80	65	10	--
NEW ORLEANS																		
Employed, total	171,590	6,730	17,560	45,215	42,945	33,925	18,935	5,485	795	79,095	5,500	11,695	19,205	20,760	13,610	6,530	1,575	220
At work	166,585	6,540	17,095	44,180	41,695	32,965	18,185	5,200	725	76,725	5,350	11,400	18,705	20,140	13,155	6,285	1,490	200
With a job but not at work	5,005	190	465	1,035	1,250	960	750	285	70	2,370	150	295	500	620	455	245	85	20
SHREVEPORT																		
Employed, total	43,675	2,310	4,775	10,725	10,745	8,420	4,910	1,600	190	21,995	1,510	3,475	5,610	5,570	3,835	1,545	415	35
At work	42,600	2,205	4,715	10,560	10,505	8,190	4,745	1,505	175	21,215	1,475	3,400	5,460	5,375	3,670	1,435	370	30
With a job but not at work	1,075	105	60	165	240	230	165	95	15	780	35	75	150	195	165	110	45	5
CITIES																		
BATON ROUGE																		
Employed, total	32,040	1,510	3,665	10,055	8,205	5,420	2,605	530	50	14,625	1,080	2,765	4,080	3,700	2,070	730	185	15
At work	31,255	1,455	3,600	9,855	8,070	5,255	2,495	485	40	14,145	1,065	2,720	3,945	3,535	2,005	680	180	15
With a job but not at work	785	55	65	200	135	165	110	45	10	480	15	45	135	165	65	50	5	-
NEW ORLEANS																		
Employed, total	142,340	5,365	17,110	36,475	35,320	28,995	16,455	4,845	775	70,300	4,605	10,325	16,820	18,520	12,430	5,925	1,485	220
At work	138,210	5,220	16,760	35,670	34,265	28,165	15,840	4,585	705	68,295	4,485	10,085	16,390	18,005	12,015	5,705	1,410	200
With a job but not at work	4,130	145	350	805	1,055	830	615	260	70	2,005	120	240	430	515	415	220	75	20
SHREVEPORT																		
Employed, total	32,435	1,515	3,560	8,470	8,000	6,205	3,520	1,045	120	18,400	1,235	2,980	4,760	4,615	3,195	1,235	355	25
At work	31,715	1,470	3,510	8,335	7,830	6,065	3,415	985	105	17,830	1,220	2,910	4,645	4,485	3,060	1,160	330	20
With a job but not at work	720	45	50	135	170	140	105	60	15	570	15	70	115	130	135	75	25	5

Table 68.—STATUS OF PERSONS NOT IN THE LABOR FORCE BY AGE, COLOR, AND SEX, FOR THE STATE, URBAN AND RURAL, AND FOR STANDARD METROPOLITAN AREAS AND CITIES OF 100,000 OR MORE: 1950

[Based on 20-percent sample; available complete-count data in tables 25 and 3[illegible]]

Area, color, and status of persons not in labor force	Male 14 years old and over: Total	14 to 19 years	20 to 24 years	25 to 34 years	35 to 44 years	45 to 54 years	55 to 64 years	65 to 74 years	75 and over	Female 14 years old and over: Total	14 to 19 years	20 to 24 years	25 to 34 years	35 to 44 years	45 to 54 years	55 to 64 years	65 to 74 years	75 and over
THE STATE—TOTAL																		
Not in labor force, total	219,625	77,5[illegible]	18,485	19,905	12,030	14,030	19,925	36,570	20,455	731,245	108,765	74,755	152,325	128,325	101,710	75,080	62,000	28,285
Keeping house	4,365	42[illegible]	[illegible]	715	6[illegible]0	6[illegible]	620	720	270	559,880	26,925	65,1[illegible]0	142,825	119,875	92,370	63,395	39,2[illegible]0	10,170
Unable to work	68,090	945	1,[illegible]	3,[illegible]75	4,000	7,040	11,925	24,365	15,360	50,070	795	820	2,110	2,895	4,215	7,170	17,270	14,775
Inmates of institutions	10,860	[illegible]105	1,[illegible]	2,460	2,400	1,535	1,045	705	460	6,305	545	2[illegible]5	850	1,115	1,160	9[illegible]	785	780
Other and not reported	136,320	75,040	15,470	10,755	5,610	4,845	6,23[illegible]	10,800	4,365	114,950	80,500	8,610	6,540	4,440	3,965	3,600	4,735	2,560
THE STATE—NONWHITE																		
Not in labor force, total	76,570	25,190	5,780	7,985	5,055	4,965	6,485	13,805	7,305	215,915	40,095	24,545	39,825	34,200	27,810	19,440	21,270	8,730
Keeping house	[illegible]	1[illegible]	195	235	165	215	140	270	105	45,905	10,625	20,100	35,540	30,205	23,190	14,080	10,090	2,105
Unable to work	26,650	395	505	1,165	1,740	2,715	4,245	10,065	5,820	25,355	415	495	1,235	1,770	2,655	3,875	9,140	5,770
Inmates of institutions	4,420	325	685	1,115	880	540	400	160	115	2,005	175	90	335	410	410	295	145	145
Other and not reported	44,025	24,120	4,395	5,470	2,270	1,495	1,700	3,310	1,265	42,620	28,880	3,860	2,715	1,815	1,535	1,190	1,895	710
URBAN—TOTAL																		
Not in labor force, total	113,260	47,135	12,855	12,075	6,830	7,690	9,900	17,350	9,425	399,790	50,655	42,040	87,6[illegible]5	69,950	55,565	42,125	35,320	16,320
Keeping house	1,980	135	100	360	300	230	385	380	100	307,180	10,690	35,845	81,900	64,685	49,930	35,100	22,605	6,425
Unable to work	30,215	355	630	1,565	1,905	3,740	5,495	10,205	6,300	27,005	385	460	1,2[illegible]	1,800	2,540	4,075	9,010	7,520
Inmates of institutions	5,155	550	550	805	1,070	790	515	500	375	3,960	285	90	505	645	640	555	600	640
Other and not reported	75,920	36,095	11,515	9,345	3,495	2,930	3,6[illegible]5	6,265	2,650	61,645	39,295	5,545	4,195	2,820	2,455	2,395	3,105	1,735
URBAN—NONWHITE																		
Not in labor force, total	40,015	12,065	3,560	4,97	3,010	2,990	3,635	6,600	3,180	108,070	18,010	12,620	21,055	16,895	14,065	10,055	11,090	4,280
Keeping house	690	55	85	3	90	75	80	125	45	70,790	4,120	10,200	18,395	14,400	11,135	6,6[illegible]5	4,835	1,050
Unable to work	12,995	210	285	715	955	1,660	2,340	4,475	2,355	14,305	215	290	755	1,170	1,730	2,4[illegible]	4,980	2,710
Inmates of institutions	2,080	270	130	435	395	280	165	115	90	1,225	125	55	220	240	195	180	90	120
Other and not reported	24,250	11,530	2,860	3,690	1,570	975	1,050	1,885	690	21,750	13,550	2,075	1,685	1,085	1,005	745	1,185	420
RURAL NONFARM—TOTAL																		
Not in labor force, total	64,690	10,280	3,775	6,140	4,345	4,455	6,735	12,315	6,845	180,010	28,355	19,540	37,70[illegible]	30,060	23,240	17,550	15,255	7,305
Keeping house	1,335	150	155	185	95	225	220	240	125	137,140	8,310	17,725	35,650	27,985	20,785	14,475	9,915	2,345
Unable to work	23,955	290	385	1,040	1,415	2,245	4,125	8,905	5,550	14,250	245	195	475	690	1,085	2,070	5,105	4,385
Inmates of institutions	5,705	555	600	1,405	1,330	745	530	205	85	2,405	260	125	345	470	520	360	185	140
Other and not reported	23,635	18,985	2,635	3,360	1,505	1,240	1,850	2,965	1,085	26,215	19,540	1,505	1,235	915	850	685	1,050	435
RURAL NONFARM—NONWHITE																		
Not in labor force, total	22,355	5,925	1,565	2,385	1,615	1,380	2,105	4,740	2,640	52,210	9,310	5,755	9,300	7,325	6,240	5,050	6,190	2,840
Keeping house	395	50	60	35	25	80	50	80	15	34,875	2,680	4,765	8,405	6,530	5,100	3,645	3,045	705
Unable to work	9,005	80	125	280	600	775	1,370	3,635	2,200	7,060	120	95	260	390	615	1,040	2,610	1,930
Inmates of institutions	2,340	255	355	680	485	260	235	45	25	780	50	35	135	170	215	115	55	25
Other and not reported	10,615	5,540	1,025	1,390	505	325	470	980	380	9,495	6,460	860	520	435	310	250	480	180
RURAL FARM—TOTAL																		
Not in labor force, total	41,685	20,400	1,755	1,730	1,455	1,885	3,290	6,9[illegible]	4,185	151,445	29,755	13,175	26,805	28,315	22,905	15,405	10,425	4,660
Keeping house	990	140	80	170	185	155	115	100	45	115,560	7,925	11,550	25,275	27,205	21,655	13,860	6,690	1,400
Unable to work	13,920	300	255	570	660	1,055	2,315	5,255	3,510	8,795	165	165	420	405	590	1,025	3,155	2,870
Inmates of institutions																		
Other and not reported	26,775	19,960	1,420	1,050	610	675	860	1,570	630	27,090	21,665	1,460	1,110	705	660	520	580	390
RURAL FARM—NONWHITE																		
Not in labor force, total	14,200	7,200	655	625	430	495	745	2,465	1,485	55,635	17,775	6,170	9,470	9,780	7,505	4,335	3,990	1,610
Keeping house	390	45	50	65	50	60	30	65	25	40,270	3,825	5,135	8,740	9,275	6,955	3,760	2,210	370
Unable to work	4,650	105	95	170	185	340	535	1,955	1,205	3,990	80	110	220	210	310	380	1,550	1,130
Inmates of institutions																		
Other and not reported	9,160	7,050	510	390	195	195	180	445	195	11,375	8,870	925	510	295	240	195	230	110
STANDARD METROPOLITAN AREAS																		
BATON ROUGE—TOTAL																		
Not in labor force, total	13,505	4,655	2,880	1,740	565	555	935	1,415	700	40,635	5,840	5,110	9,995	7,535	4,695	3,445	2,875	1,340
Keeping house	205		35	40	35	15	50	45	5	30,940	1,140	4,010	9,340	7,055	4,370	2,690	1,810	525
Unable to work	2,320	20	20	100	125	290	510	795	460	4,195	55	50	115	150	150	325	740	630
Inmates of institutions	350	155	50	45	35	30	25	5	5	125	30	35	40	20				
Other and not reported	10,630	4,480	2,775	1,555	370	220	370	570	290	5,375	4,635	1,015	500	310	175	230	325	185
BATON ROUGE—NONWHITE																		
Not in labor force, total	4,910	1,490	675	640	300	275	390	765	375	12,340	2,115	1,600	2,500	2,030	1,310	1,030	1,295	460
Keeping house	105		20	15	15	10	10	30	5	8,290	515	1,155	2,210	1,760	1,140	765	625	120
Unable to work	1,360	20	15	70	75	165	250	510	255	1,400	25	45	85	105	105	210	530	295
Inmates of institutions	245	155	35	25	15		15			70	20	15	25	10				
Other and not reported	3,200	1,315	605	530	195	100	115	22	115	2,580	1,555	385	180	155	65	55	140	45
NEW ORLEANS—TOTAL																		
Not in labor force, total	50,160	16,440	5,455	5,180	3,085	3,530	4,760	7,610	4,300	190,280	21,650	18,085	40,620	34,150	28,420	21,230	17,640	8,485
Keeping house	950	80	60	200	145	120	130	180	35	147,125	3,930	15,375	37,745	31,620	25,675	18,010	11,460	3,310
Unable to work	12,820	160	325	655	915	1,635	2,410	4,035	2,685	12,700	135	245	550	965	1,305	1,730	4,075	3,715
Inmates of institutions	1,370	280	135	195	225	75	135	175	170	1,110	170	20	55	55	75	90	230	415
Other and not reported	35,000	15,920	4,735	4,130	1,800	1,700	2,085	3,220	1,410	29,345	17,415	2,445	2,290	1,510	1,365	1,400	1,875	1,045
NEW ORLEANS—NONWHITE																		
Not in labor force, total	17,010	5,575	1,660	1,945	1,295	1,300	1,620	2,475	1,140	50,385	8,260	5,885	10,085	8,420	6,950	4,490	4,610	1,725
Keeping house	325	40	30	90	45	30	35	40	15	34,930	1,665	4,705	8,755	7,110	5,395	2,975	1,930	395
Unable to work	5,065	70	165	225	485	755	1,025	1,545	795	6,110	90	145	300	670	885	1,030	1,960	1,030
Inmates of institutions	455	150	75	90	50	15	20	25	30	175	85	10	10		5		15	50
Other and not reported	11,165	5,315	1,390	1,540	715	500	540	865	300	11,170	6,420	1,025	1,020	640	625	485	705	250

Table 68 —STATUS OF PERSONS NOT IN THE LABOR FORCE, BY AGE, COLOR AND SEX, FOR THE STATE, URBAN AND RURAL, AND FOR STANDARD METROPOL'TAN AREAS AND CITIES OF 100,000 OR MORE .950—Con

Based on 20-percent sample available complete-count data in tal les 25 and 351

Area, color, and status			V	fale 14 J	ears old a	nd over						F	emsle 1 _x	Y8875 410	and ove	r		
of pursons not in labor force	Total	14 to 19 years	20 to 24 years	25 to 34 Vears	35 to 44 years	40 .0 54 vears	55 to 64 years	65 .0 "4] JP878	75 and	Total	14 to 19 years	20 to 24 years	25 to 34 years	35 10 v4		50 to 64 years	85 to 74	75 and
STANDARD METROPOLITAN AREAS—Coo	大型				1					- 1	1		1 .	2 1 H	1.00	e de la	1975	
SHREVEPORT-TOTAL	200						100					1 54	. 4	2	i	- 12		
Not in labor force, total. Inable to work Inmates of institutions Other and not reported.	12,435 250 4,470 295 7,420	4,145 15 80 30 4,020	915 50 95 40 730	1,090 25 210 20 835	735 50 200 80 405	420 35 285	975 30 495 22 330	2,5_5 45 1,795 25 6~0	1,290	45,635 35,_05 3,360 185 6,745	1,930 1,237 80 15	4,50 3,-80 50 10	9,570 9,0.5 225 414	7,884 ,385 17* 15	6,005 5	4,895 4,200 -70 25 200	4,335 2,47, 1,485 40 305	2,00 76 1,04 6
SHREVEPORT-NONITE			6.		2.				1		1				1	1		
Not in labor force, total Keeping house Unable to work Inmates of institutions Other and not reported	5,3_0 105 2,310 160 2,735	1,555 10 50 30 1,465	370 30 60 25 255	10 10 10 15 400	385 125 55 200	310 15 140 3	2°0 2°0 2°0	-,202 25 977 210	560 515 10 35	13,955 8,740 2,495 45 2,675	2,~85 590 70	1,420 - 160 25 5	2,390 2,075 95 5	1,854 1,620 -43 10	1,865 1,505 175 5 100	1,290 900 350 40	1,080 1,080 1,080	751 144 566
CITTLES								- 3										
BATON FOUGL		1						596	esta (1							- 6		
Not in labor force, total Keeping house Unable to work Inmates of institutions Other and not reported	10,240 155 1515 110 8,460	3,375 25 5 3,355	20	25	4,0 25 100 47 290	425 15 215 20 172	685 30 350 5 300	980 20 465 485	535 5 290 5 235	32,075 24,785 1,634 25 5,630	7,325 890 30 5 3,400	4, 15 3,285 30 5 795	8,045 7,035 80 _5 41	6,015 5,670 95	3,480	2,595 2,120 26° 210	2,190 1,400 510	1,05 40 50
N'W ORLEANS-TOTAL							i				1			İ			in do	
Not in labor force total Keeping house	43,155 795 10,910 1,315 30,135	13,665 60 120 230 13,255	4,685 30 265 130 4,260	533 180	130	3,120 95 4,455 75 1,495	2,160 110 2,055 135 1,820	6,645 105 3,410 175 2,895	3,735 30 2,250 170 1,305	1.9,200 121,180 1.,300 1.,10 2,*50	17,890 2,925 115 170 14,580	_2,135 220 20	32,29. 29,720 460 55 2,060	27,950 25,665 865 55 1,365	24,875	_3,640 _5,730 1,560 90 _,260	15,800 10,190 3,665 230 1,715	7,50 2,94 3,30 41 94
NEW ORLEANS-ACHITE	1200											PG.				10.00	1	5
Not in labor force, total. Keeping house. Unable to work. Immates of institutions Other and not reported	15,545 280 4,560 445 ±0,260	35 65 150 4,870	150	85 215	45 445 30	15	. 20	2,245 40 1,375 20 805	990 10 680 30 270	30,240 30,240 3,690 175 10,315	7,540 1,470 85 85 5,900	4,250	280		4,950 630	4,230 2,830 960 470	1 770	1,57 34 95 5 22
SHREVEFORT										10						3		76
Nor in labor force, total. Keeping house Unable to work Institutions. Other and not reported	8,335 155 2,915 215 5,050	2,520 10 30 25 2,405	80 30	130	105 105 45	30: 20:	415 10	1,665 25 1,165 20 455	850 685 45	25,515 2,650	3 760 830 44 2,880	2,895 45	80	5,270 10	4,180	3,080	1,905 1,030 35	59 79 6

Table 69 —LABOR FORCE STATUS, BY AGE AND SEX, FOR THE STATE 1950 AND 1940

[Statistics for 1900 based on 20-percent sample, available complete-count data in table 10. Percent not shown where less than 0 1, or where base is less than 500 for 1950 or 100 for 1940]

		Male	e 14 years	old and over				Fema	le, 14 year	s old and ove	a .		Pero	ent distri	outton of	the
n (1950	1 (4)		1940			1950	1/4-1	1 1 16	1940	4.7	1	abor fore	e by age	
\ge		Labor	force		Labor	orce		Labor f	force		Labor	orce	Ma	le	Fem	nale
	Total	Number	Percent of total	Total	Number	Percent of total	Total	Number	Percent of total	Total	Number	Percent of total	1950	1940	1950	1940
Total	902,050	o82,395	75 7	842,817	C74,558	80 0	969,560	238,315	24 6	867,629	209,606	24 2	-00 o	100 C	100 0	200
4 and 15 years	43,525 41,535 39,385 99,795 100,730 91,_80	6,430 15,475 25,025 81,210 88,400 83,605	37 3 63 5 81 4 87 8	48,0°7 47,712 47,175 103,885 100,294 90,968	7,374 19,599 32,859 9_,703 95,045 86,531	15 3 41 7 69 7 88 3 94 8 95 1	43,450 42,690 44,420 11,285 110,830 99,000	2,145 6,110 13,540 36,530 30,655 26,850	32 8	48,474 48,334 49,651 112,511 106,727 95,486	2,573 7,232 15,390 37,875 32,095 27,680	31 0 33 7 30 1	0 9 2 3 3 7 11 9 13 0 12 3	1 1 2 9 4 9 13 6 14 1 12 8	26 5.7 15 3 26 3	3 7 18 15
0 to 44 years	176, 05 136, 575 89, 910 37, 120 22, 545 23, 625	122,545 69,985 16,785 6,290	89 7 77 8 45 2 27 9	157,244 1.6,872 73,434 27,665 15,615 13,896	148,083 106,753 60,889 10,592 6,363 2,767	60 0	188,330 141,410 92,925 41,560 24,815 28,845	50,005 39,700 17,845 3,475 900 560	28 1 19 2 8 4	161,286 112,082 7_,251 28,497 16,02_ 17,309	44,305 26,173 11,881 2,951 977 474	23 4 16 7 10 4 6 1	24.0 18 0 10 3 2 5 0 9 0 5	22 0 15 8 9 U 2 5 0 9	25775542	21 12 5 1 0

Table 19—LABOR PCRCE STATUS, BY MARITAL STATUS, AGE, COLOR, AND SEX, FOR THE STATE, URBAN AND RURAL AND FOR STANDARD METROPOLITAN AREAS OF 100,000 OR MORE 1950

**Basec on 21-person suntrile annuable competencent gais in tables 15 and 33 Persons not about where one than 31 or where base is one than 500:

,	Total	1. years of	a an. ave	7		braje	-		м	arned spou	se preser			Oth	r	
i		Labor				Labor	forme			Labor	force			Labor	force	
Arre, color age and sex	Trasi	\umber	Percent of otal	Abo orce	Total	Nunse.	Percent of total	labo force	Total	Numorr	Percent o. total	Not in labor force	Total	Number	Percent of total	labor force
TAR STATE—TOTAL	972 ಬಳ	587,295	75.7	219,034	27~ Seó	124, 705	53 3	109,36C	581 2-5	.07,225	87 3	73,920	60,820	10,465	58 1	36, 755
1- to 1.5 years 20 o 24 years 25 o 29 years 30 to 34 years 85 o 44 years 45 years and over	14-,-45 99,795 .30,730 7_ 180 -75	40,930 41,210 35 400 8,,005 10,,005	37 9 9 9 9 9 9 9 9 9 9 9 9 9 9 9 9 9 9 9	77 5.4	5-,609 19 945 9 945 ,005 19,020	38,3.0 38,3.0 25,235 7,270 0,430 10,787	73 6 70 4 78 2 74 5 54 6	76,7_5 _3,605 4,710 2,115 3,575 8,640	3,530 -2,925 -3,655 74,880 -27,760 238,395	3,155 39,305 67,775 7_,105 141,750 184,135	99 4 92 0 95 0 95 9 77 2	375 3,620 3,775 6,010 54,200	1,110 5,265 7,130 6,615 4,340 52,360	685 3,905 5,390 4 930 1,29* 24 260	ol 7 74 2 75 6 74 5 76 8 46 3	1,360 1,740 -,685 3,045 28 100
Female 4 to 19 years 20 to 24 years. 25 to 29 'east. 30 to 34 years. 35 to 45 years 45 years and over	96°,>60 15°,540 111,28, 110°50 9°,000 188 330 129,555	23\$,5 21,795 3n,530 ,1,655 26,85 80,005 ,2,480	10 ° 32 8 21 7	7,2-5 -08,705 74 75* 80,- 5 72,100 128,325 247,075	183,700 103,675 20,525 10,840 7 160 12,540 2, 170	64,045 17,997 17,040 7,480 4,770 8,040 9,320	16 8 64 3 64 0 66 6 65 2 40 2	1.9,655 e4,280 9,475 3,360 2,390 7,300 13,850	22,995 74,145 87,445 80,190 147,740 178,425	2,135 14,475 -6,500 15,780 26,170 25,170 25 410	13 6 19 5 18 9 19 6 23 0 14 2	480,530 19,860 59,670 70,945 64,470 112,570 153,015	3 090 10,625 12,545 11,640 23,250 127,960	63,860 1,265 5 0,5 6 67, 6,360 16 795 27,750	32 5 47 2 5_ 2 54 6 59 5	131,060 7,625 5,610 5,870 5 290 11,455 100,210
THE STATE—NONWEITE	274 315	.97,745	72	7. 570	75 26	40,220	73 5	34 985	159 865	.34, 195	8/ 1	20,470	39 1.85	23 070	58 9	و ارس
14 to 19 years 20 to 24 years 20 to 29 years 30 to 34 years 35 to 44 years 45 years and over	44,95 50,1 ° 27,920 23,6-5 50,765 97,430	1º,655 2-,330 22,905 70,575 45,710 64,570	43 8 80 8 82 9 86 3 90 0 66 5	27,190 5,780 7,715 3,276 5,955 32,560	4.3 leQ .5 045 5,5.5 2,420 4,020 4,835	.8,270 1.,150 3,862 .,240 .,760 2,395	42 3 74 ± 69 5 10 ± 68 7 49 5	24,910 3,895 1,700 180 1 260 2 440	1,230 12,395 18,690 18,010 40,090 69,450	1,100 11,255 10,535 10,225 37,685 51,395	89 4 90 8 88 5 9_ 2 94 0 74 0	130 1,,40 2,,35 1,585 2,405 18,035	435 2,370 3,365 3,215 6,655 22,845	285 1,925 2,505 2,310 5,265 10,780	77 1 74 4 71 9 79 1 47 2	150 745 860 905 1,390 -2,065
Female 14 to 19 years 20 to 24 years 20 to 25 years 30 to 34 years 30 to 44 years 45 years and over	210,5 48,.50 36,745 35,850 29,700 59,485 102,285	94 200 12,200 2,070 11,630 25,285 25,035	30 4 16 6 33 2 35 7 39 2 42 5 24 5	215,915 40,095 24,5-5 21,780 18,045 34,200 77,250	38,155 9 605 9,540 2,235 3,210 4,770	6,195 4,8.0 2,040 1 300 1,795 1,465	28 3 16 2 50 3 57 6 58 2 50 9 53 5	43,490 31,960 4,775 1 500 935 1 415 2,905	7,605 20 774 22,835 20,745 41,005 48 175	43,030 1 095 4 510 6,195 6,565 14,160 10,05	26 7 2-7 27 - 31 0 34 - 21 8	118,065 0,5-1 16,200 16,640 14,_80 26,845 37,630	87,905 2 290 6 370 4 475 6,720 15,270 49,780	33,545 665 2,860 3,635 3,790 9,300 13,065	29 0 44 9 51 3 56 4 6. 1 26 4	1,625 3,510 3,640 2,930 2,940 36,715
URBAN- TOTAL																
Male 14 to 19 years 20 to 24 years 25 to 29 years 30 o 34 years 35 to 44 years 45 years and over	501,005 50,2-0 57,430 63,3-0 55,2-0 -02,165 166,580	387,74 9,102 44,575 55,505 50,990 95,250 22,215	77 4 34 0 7, 6 87 0 92 3 93 3 73 4	37,135 10,855 7,835 4,240 6,830 44,365	121,650 53,975 29 635 12,80: 5,775 8,265 ,195	64,350 17,210 19,960 9,740 4,700 6,370 b,370	52 9 31 9 67 4 76 1 81 4 77 1 56 9	57,300 36,765 9,675 3,065 1,075 1,895 4,825	327,235 1,720 24,690 45,780 45,085 84,137 125 825	290 645 2565 22 310 42,035 42,900 80,995 101,040	91 8 91 8 95 2 96 3 80 3	36,390 155 2,380 3,745 2,185 3,140 24,785	52,_20 545 ^,_05 4,755 4,370 9,785 29,560	32,550 330 2,305 3,730 3,390 7,990 14,805	50 6 74 2 78 4 71 6 81 7 50 1	19,570 215 800 -,025 980 1,795 14 755
Female	575 290 64,570 69 860 71,055 60 ~30 14,420 94,965	175,500 23 915 27,827 23 825 19,835 44 470 45,635	30 5 24 6 39 8 33 5 34 8 38 9 23 4	50 655 42,040 47,230 40 585 69,050	107, 905 51,145 18,095 7,755 5,085 8 890 16,855	47,970 10,770 12 855 3,055 3,895 6,580 7 815	21 1 71 1 78 1 76 6 74 1 46 4	59,835 40,375 5,230 1,700 1,190 2,300 9,040	335,960 11,095 -4,590 -4,245 46 795 84,835 94,400	77,550 2 225 11 175 12 410 14,655 24,505 16,380	23 1 27 ± 25 1 22 9 23 2 28 9	258 410 8,870 35,415 41,835 35,940 60,350 78,020	131,525 2,550 7 185 9,65, 8,540 20,705 83,710	920 920 9790 5,360 5,085 13 385 21,440	38 0 39 3 52 7 59 2 59 5 64.6 25 6	81,545 1,410 3,395 3,695 3,455 7,320 62,270
URBAN-NONWHITE																
Male 14 to 10 vesre. 20 to 24 years 20 to 29 years 30 to 34 years 45 vesrs and over	141,010 18,905 15,305 16,015 17,910 28 6.5 48,360	0,740 11,745 13,090 11,860 25,605 31,955	76 7 81 7 85 3 89 5	40,015 12,065 3,560 2,925 2,050 3,010 16,405	35,720 -8,045 7 535 -3,335 1 690 2,420 2,695	17,770 6,140 5,187 2,315 1,240 4,710 1,410	50 3 33 9 68 8 69 4 73 4 70 7 52 3	17 750 11,935 2,350 1,020 450 710 1,285	545 6,445 10,540 10,030 21,680 33,150	68, 775 490 5,330 9,155 9,005 20,215 24,520	8, P 89 9 67 7 P6 9 89 8 93.2 74 3	13,315 755 385 1 025 4,465 8,630	23,200 2.5 2,140 2,190 4,513 12,515	140 1,170 1,620 1,645 -,680 6,025	72 C 75 7 73 7 81 0 48 1	2,950 75 40^ 520 575 835 6,490
Female 14 to 19 years 20 to 24 years 25 to 29 years 30 to 34 years 30 to 44 years 45 years and over	22,045 20,830 20,640 17,000 35,200 56,540	64,785 4,035 8,210 8,750 8,435 15,305 47,050	18 3 39 4 42 4 47 9 52 0	08,070 18,010 12,420 1 890 9,165 16,895 30,490	30,725 17,_50 5_60 2,220 1,4_C 2,000 2,725	2,935 2,985 1,405 955 -,300 1,140	17 1 57 8 03 3 07 7 03 1 41 8	20,005 14,215 2 -75 815 425 760 1,585	83,765 3,465 11,430 15,040 11,275 21,935 22,020	28,980 630 3,165 4,390 4 580 9,745 6,470	34 6 18 2 77 7 3° 7 40 6 44 4 28 6	2,8°5 8,650 6,4°5 12,190 16,130	58,365 1,430 4,240 ,380 4,915 11,205 31 195	25,085 470 2,060 2,955 2,900 7,250 9,440	43 0 32 9 48 6 54 9 59 0 64 8 30 3	960 2,180 2,425 2,015 3,945 21,755
RURAL NONFARM—TOTAL	212 725		60.4	4 400	55.145		19 4	27 925		110 595						201
Maio 14 to 19 years 20 to 24 years 25 to 29 years 30 to 34 years 35 to 44 years 45 years and over	30,975 24,420 22,795 20,990 40 130 75 ~15	10,995 20,445 19,325 18,420 35,785 4,065	83 7 84 8 87 8 89 2	64,590 19,980 3,975 3,470 4,570 4,345 30,350	55,165 29,705 44,900 3,905 2,080 3,220 4,355	9 990 9,360 2,795 1,370 1,795	3: 6 78 7 7. 6 65 9 59 9	27,925 19,715 2,540 1,1.0 710 1,290 2,560	930 11,120 17 145 17,375 33,670 55,060	800 10,165 15,425 16,110 31,740 36,355	81 7 86 0 91 / 90 0 92 7 94 3 66 0	24, 705 255 1,720 1,265 1,930 48,705	32,260 340 1,400 1,745 1,535 3,240 4,000	205 420 1,105 940 2,115 7,915	65 7 63 3 64 2 65 3 35 1	12 060 135 480 640 590 1,120 9,085
Female 14 to 19 years 20 to 24 years 25 to 29 years 30 to 34 years 35 to 44 years 45 years and over	218,580 32,08L 24,970 24,460 72,245 39,995 74,820	35,770 3,725 5,430 4,455 4,255 9,935 10,470	17 6 3 11 6 21 7 18 2 20 5 24 8	80,0.0 28, %5 19,540 20,005 17,700 30,060 64,350	37,740 24,495 4,440 1,730 1,270 2,005 3,805	8,965 3,020 2,515 890 570 970 4,000	23 8 14 3 56 6 51 4 44 9 48 4 26 3	28,780 2_,475 1,925 840 700 1,035 2,805	138,525 6,785 18,470 40,305 18,495 .2,683 41,385	20,145 500 2,43, 2,635 3,090 6,570 2,245	7 4 11 6 19 0 10 4 20 1 12 0	118,380 0,285 16,337 17,670 15,875 26,115 36,170	42,310 500 2,060 2,425 2,0°C 5 305 29,630	9,460 205 780 930 895 2,395 4,255	22 4 25 6 37 9 38 4 42 8 45 1 14 4	32 850 595 1,280 1,495 1,195 2,910 25,375

Table 79.—LABOR FORCE STATUS, BY MARITAL STATUS, AGE, COLOR, AND SEX, FOR THE STATE, URBAN AND RURAL, AND FOR STANDARD METROPOLITAN AREAS OF 100,000 OR MORE: 1950

[Based on 20-percent sample; available complete-count data in tables 15 and 33. Percent not shown where less than 0.1 or where base is less than 500]

Area, color, age, and sex	Total 14 years old and over: Total	Labor force: Number	Labor force: Percent of total	Not in labor force	Single: Total	Labor force: Number	Labor force: Percent of total	Not in labor force	Married, spouse present: Total	Labor force: Number	Labor force: Percent of total	Not in labor force	Other: Total	Labor force: Number	Labor force: Percent of total	Not in labor force
THE STATE—TOTAL																
Male	[illegible]	[illegible]	75.7	[illegible]	[illegible]	124,705	53.3	109,360	[illegible]	507,225	87.3	73,920	86,820	40,465	58.1	36,355
14 to 19 years	[illegible]	46,930	[illegible]	[illegible]	[illegible]	[illegible]	[illegible]	[illegible]	3,530	3,155	89.4	375	1,110	685	61.7	425
20 to 24 years	99,795	81,210	[illegible]	[illegible]	51,605	[illegible]	73.6	13,605	42,925	39,305	91.6	3,620	5,265	3,905	74.2	1,360
25 to 29 years	100,750	[illegible]	87.8	12,330	19,945	15,235	76.4	4,710	73,655	67,775	92.0	5,880	7,130	5,390	75.6	1,740
30 to 34 years	[illegible]	[illegible]	91.7	[illegible]	[illegible]	7,770	78.2	2,115	74,880	71,105	95.0	3,775	6,615	4,930	74.5	1,685
35 to 44 years	[illegible]	[illegible]	[illegible]	12,630	14,005	10,430	74.5	3,575	147,760	141,750	95.9	6,010	14,340	11,295	78.8	3,045
45 years and over	[illegible]	[illegible]	[illegible]	[illegible]	19,020	10,380	54.6	8,640	238,395	184,135	77.2	54,260	52,360	24,260	46.3	28,100
Female	969,560	[illegible]	[illegible]	[illegible]	183,700	64,045	34.9	119,655	590,940	110,410	18.7	480,530	194,920	63,860	32.8	131,060
14 to 19 years	[illegible]	21,795	[illegible]	108,765	103,675	17,395	16.8	86,280	22,995	3,135	13.6	19,860	3,890	1,265	32.5	2,625
20 to 24 years	[illegible]	36,530	32.8	[illegible]	26,515	17,040	64.3	9,475	74,145	14,475	19.5	59,670	10,625	5,015	47.2	5,610
25 to 29 years	[illegible]	31,455	27.7	[illegible]	10,840	7,480	69.0	3,360	87,445	16,500	18.9	70,945	12,545	[illegible]	[illegible]	5,870
30 to 34 years	99,000	[illegible]	[illegible]	72,150	7,180	4,770	66.6	2,390	80,190	15,720	19.6	64,470	11,650	6,360	54.6	5,290
35 to 44 years	188,330	60,005	31.9	128,325	12,340	8,040	65.2	4,300	147,740	35,170	23.8	112,570	28,250	16,795	59.5	11,455
45 years and over	329,555	82,480	25.0	247,075	[illegible]	9,320	40.2	13,850	178,425	25,410	14.2	153,015	127,960	27,750	21.7	100,210
THE STATE—NONWHITE																
Male	274,315	197,745	[illegible]	76,570	[illegible]	[illegible]	53.5	34,985	159,865	134,395	84.1	25,470	39,185	23,070	58.9	[illegible]
14 to 19 years	44,845	19,655	43.8	25,190	43,160	18,270	42.3	24,910	1,230	1,100	89.4	130	435	285		150
20 to 24 years	[illegible]	24,330	80.8	5,780	15,045	11,150	74.1	3,895	12,395	11,255	90.8	1,140	2,370	1,925	77.1	745
25 to 29 years	27,620	22,905	82.9	4,715	5,555	3,865	69.5	1,700	18,690	16,535	88.5	2,155	3,365	2,505	74.4	860
30 to 34 years	[illegible]	20,575	86.3	3,270	2,620	1,840	[illegible]	780	18,010	16,425	91.2	1,585	3,215	2,310	71.9	905
35 to 44 years	50,765	45,710	90.0	5,055	4,020	2,760	68.7	1,260	40,090	37,685	94.0	2,405	6,655	5,265	79.1	1,390
45 years and over	[illegible]	64,570	66.5	32,560	4,835	2,395	49.5	2,440	69,450	51,395	74.0	18,055	22,845	10,780	47.2	12,065
Female	[illegible]	94,200	30.4	215,915	61,115	17,625	28.8	43,490	161,095	43,030	26.7	118,065	87,905	33,545	38.2	54,360
14 to 19 years	48,050	[illegible]	16.6	40,095	38,155	6,195	16.2	31,960	7,605	1,095	14.4	[illegible]	2,290	665	29.0	1,625
20 to 24 years	36,745	12,200	33.2	24,545	9,605	4,830	50.3	4,775	20,770	4,510	21.7	16,260	6,370	2,860	44.9	3,510
25 to 29 years	33,850	12,070	35.7	21,780	3,540	2,040	57.6	1,500	22,835	6,195	27.1	16,640	7,475	3,835	51.3	3,640
30 to 34 years	29,700	11,655	39.2	18,045	2,235	1,300	58.2	935	20,745	6,565	31.6	14,180	6,720	3,790	56.4	2,930
35 to 44 years	59,485	25,285	42.5	34,200	3,210	1,795	55.9	1,415	41,005	14,160	34.5	26,845	15,270	9,330	61.1	5,940
45 years and over	102,285	25,035	24.5	77,250	4,370	1,465	33.5	2,905	48,135	10,505	21.8	37,630	49,780	13,065	26.2	36,715
URBAN—TOTAL																
Male	501,005	[illegible]	77.4	113,260	121,650	64,350	52.9	57,300	327,235	290,845	88.9	36,390	52,120	32,550	62.5	19,570
14 to 19 years	56,240	9,105	34.0	37,135	53,975	17,210	31.9	36,765	1,720	1,565	91.0	155	545	330	60.6	215
20 to 24 years	57,430	44,575	77.6	12,855	29,635	19,960	67.4	9,675	24,690	22,310	90.4	2,380	3,105	2,305	74.2	800
25 to 29 years	63,340	55,505	87.6	7,835	12,805	9,740	76.1	3,065	45,780	42,035	91.8	3,745	4,755	3,730	78.4	1,025
30 to 34 years	55,230	50,990	92.3	4,240	5,775	4,700	81.4	1,075	45,085	42,900	95.2	2,185	4,370	3,390	77.6	980
35 to 44 years	102,185	95,355	93.3	6,830	8,265	6,370	77.1	1,895	84,135	80,995	96.3	3,140	9,785	7,990	81.7	1,795
45 years and over	166,580	122,215	73.4	44,365	11,195	6,370	56.9	4,825	125,825	101,040	80.3	24,785	29,560	14,805	50.1	14,755
Female	575,290	175,500	30.5	399,790	107,805	47,970	44.5	59,835	335,960	77,550	23.1	258,410	131,525	49,980	38.0	81,545
14 to 19 years	64,570	13,915	21.6	50,655	51,145	10,770	21.1	40,375	11,095	2,225	20.1	8,870	2,330	920	39.5	1,410
20 to 24 years	69,860	27,820	39.8	42,040	18,085	12,855	71.1	5,230	44,590	11,175	25.1	33,415	7,185	3,790	52.7	3,395
25 to 29 years	71,055	23,825	33.5	47,230	7,755	6,055	78.1	1,700	54,245	12,410	22.9	41,835	9,055	5,360	59.2	3,695
30 to 34 years	60,420	19,835	32.8	40,585	5,085	3,895	76.6	1,190	46,795	10,855	23.2	35,940	8,540	5,085	59.5	3,455
35 to 44 years	114,420	44,470	38.9	69,950	8,880	6,580	74.1	2,300	84,835	24,505	28.9	60,330	20,705	13,385	64.6	7,320
45 years and over	194,965	45,635	23.4	149,330	16,855	7,815	46.4	9,040	94,400	16,380	17.4	78,020	83,710	21,440	25.6	62,270
URBAN—NONWHITE																
Male	141,010	100,995	71.6	40,015	35,720	17,770	50.3	17,750	82,090	68,775	83.8	13,315	23,200	14,250	61.4	8,950
14 to 19 years	18,805	6,740	35.8	12,065	18,045	6,110	33.9	11,935	545	490	89.9	55	215	140		75
20 to 24 years	15,305	11,745	76.7	3,560	7,535	5,185	68.8	2,350	6,145	5,390	87.7	755	1,625	1,170	72.0	455
25 to 29 years	16,015	13,090	81.7	2,925	3,335	2,315	69.4	1,020	10,540	9,155	86.9	1,385	2,140	1,620	75.7	520
30 to 34 years	13,910	11,860	85.3	2,050	1,690	1,240	73.4	450	10,030	9,005	89.8	1,025	2,190	1,615	73.7	575
35 to 44 years	28,615	25,605	89.5	3,010	2,420	1,710	70.7	710	21,680	20,215	93.2	1,465	4,515	3,680	81.5	835
45 years and over	48,360	31,955	66.1	16,405	2,695	1,410	52.3	1,285	33,150	24,520	74.0	8,630	12,515	6,025	48.1	6,490
Female	172,855	64,785	37.5	108,070	30,725	10,720	34.9	20,005	83,765	28,980	34.6	54,785	58,365	25,085	43.0	33,280
14 to 19 years	22,045	4,035	18.3	18,010	17,150	2,935	17.1	14,215	3,465	630	18.2	2,835	1,430	470	32.9	960
20 to 24 years	20,830	8,210	39.4	12,620	5,160	2,985	57.8	2,175	11,430	3,165	27.7	8,265	4,240	2,060	48.6	2,180
25 to 29 years	20,640	8,750	42.4	11,890	2,220	1,405	63.3	815	13,040	4,390	33.7	8,650	5,380	2,955	54.9	2,425
30 to 34 years	17,600	8,435	47.9	9,165	1,420	955	67.7	465	11,275	4,580	40.6	6,695	4,915	2,900	59.0	2,015
35 to 44 years	35,200	18,305	52.0	16,895	2,060	1,300	63.1	760	21,935	9,745	44.4	12,190	11,205	7,260	64.8	3,945
45 years and over	56,540	17,050	30.2	39,490	2,725	1,140	41.8	1,585	22,620	6,470	28.6	16,150	31,195	9,440	30.3	21,755
RURAL NONFARM—TOTAL																
Male	212,725	148,035	69.6	64,690	55,165	27,240	49.4	27,925	135,300	110,595	81.7	24,705	22,260	10,200	45.8	12,060
14 to 19 years	30,975	10,995	35.5	19,980	29,705	9,990	33.6	19,715	930	800	86.0	130	340	205		135
20 to 24 years	24,420	20,445	83.7	3,975	11,900	9,360	78.7	2,540	11,120	10,165	91.4	955	1,400	920	65.7	480
25 to 29 years	22,795	19,325	84.8	3,470	3,905	2,795	71.6	1,110	17,145	15,425	90.0	1,720	1,745	1,105	63.3	640
30 to 34 years	20,990	18,420	87.8	2,570	2,080	1,370	65.9	710	17,375	16,110	92.7	1,265	1,535	940	61.2	595
35 to 44 years	40,130	35,785	89.2	4,345	3,220	1,930	59.9	1,290	33,670	31,740	94.3	1,930	3,240	2,115	65.3	1,125
45 years and over	[illegible]	43,065	58.7	30,350	4,355	1,795	41.2	2,560	55,060	36,355	66.0	18,705	14,000	[illegible]	35.1	9,085
Female	218,580	38,570	17.6	180,010	37,745	8,965	23.8	28,780	138,525	20,145	14.5	118,380	42,310	9,460	22.4	32,850
14 to 19 years	32,080	3,725	11.6	28,355	24,495	3,020	12.3	21,475	6,785	500	7.4	6,285	800	205	25.6	595
20 to 24 years	24,970	5,430	21.7	19,540	4,440	2,515	56.6	1,925	18,470	2,135	11.6	16,335	2,060	780	37.9	1,280
25 to 29 years	24,460	4,455	18.2	20,005	1,730	890	51.4	840	20,305	2,635	13.0	17,670	2,425	930	38.4	1,495
30 to 34 years	22,255	4,555	20.5	17,700	1,270	570	44.9	700	18,895	3,090	16.4	15,805	2,090	895	42.8	1,195
35 to 44 years	39,995	9,935	24.8	30,060	2,005	970	48.4	1,035	32,685	6,570	20.1	26,115	5,305	2,395	45.1	2,910
45 years and over	74,820	10,470	14.0	64,350	3,805	1,000	26.3	2,805	41,385	5,215	12.6	36,170	29,630	4,255	14.4	25,375

Table 70.—LABOR FORCE STATUS, BY MARITAL STATUS, AGE, COLOR, AND SEX, FOR THE STATE, URBAN AND RURAL, AND FOR STANDARD METROPOLITAN AREAS OF 100,000 OR MORE: 1950—Con.

[Based on 20-percent sample; available complete count data in tables [illegible] and 33. Percent not shown where less than 0.1 or where base is less than 500]

Area, color, age, and sex	Total 14 years old and over: Total	Labor force: Number	Labor force: Percent of total	Not in labor force	Single: Total	Labor force: Number	Labor force: Percent of total	Not in labor force	Married, spouse present: Total	Labor force: Number	Labor force: Percent of total	Not in labor force	Other: Total	Labor force: Number	Labor force: Percent of total	Not in labor force
RURAL NONFARM—NONWHITE																
Male	[illegible]2,865	[illegible]	6[illegible].4	22,[illegible]	1[illegible]	3,5[illegible]	[illegible]9.2	[illegible]	35,[illegible]	2[illegible]	[illegible]6.[illegible]	[illegible]	1[illegible],005	4,71[illegible]	47.[illegible]	5,27[illegible]
14 to 19 years	10,050	4,125	[illegible]	5,92[illegible]	9,6[illegible]	3,825	[illegible].6	5,[illegible]	275	250		[illegible]51	[illegible]	70		45
20 to 24 years	7,[illegible]	5,200	79.[illegible]	[illegible],565	3,6[illegible]	4,620	73.9	[illegible]	[illegible]	2,775	9[illegible]	790	[illegible]5	305	[illegible]1.2	4[illegible]
25 to 29 years	6,180	4,765	77.1	1,415	[illegible]	725	58.9	[illegible]5	4,[illegible]	[illegible],500	95.[illegible]	[illegible]0	[illegible]40	[illegible]	64.3	[illegible]00
30 to 34 years	5,060	4,090	80.8	970	555	320	57.[illegible]	235	3,835	3,375	88.0	460	670	395	59.0	275
35 to 44 years	10,850	9,235	85.1	1,615	450	425	55.3	425	8,420	7,735	91.9	685	1,[illegible]40	775	65.9	505
45 years and over	23,360	12,495	53.[illegible]	10,865	1,275	500	3[illegible]	775	[illegible],835	9,[illegible]	[illegible]	[illegible]	6,255	2,360	37.7	3,89[illegible]
Female	68,595	16,385	23.9	52,210	13,280	3,190	24.0	10,090	35,9[illegible]	7,[illegible]5	2[illegible]	28,285	19,775	5,540	28.6	13,835
14 to 19 years	10,800	1,490	13.8	9,310	8,395	1,160	[illegible].8	7,235	2,0[illegible]	220	10.[illegible]	1,[illegible]315	370	1[illegible]0		260
20 to 24 years	7,935	2,180	27.5	5,755	4,030	930	2[illegible].8	3,100	4,730	765	16.2	3,965	[illegible],175	485	[illegible].3	690
25 to 29 years	6,975	2,010	28.8	4,965	680	[illegible]65	53.7	315	4,890	1,035	2[illegible]	3,855	1,405	610	43.4	795
30 to 34 years	6,285	1,950	31.0	4,335	545	225	4[illegible]	320	4,525	1,105	24.4	3,420	1,215	620	5[illegible].0	595
35 to 44 years	11,700	4,175	35.7	7,525	6[illegible]0	310	49.2	320	[illegible],255	2,460	2[illegible].8	5,795	2,81[illegible]	1,405	49.9	1,410
45 years and over	24,900	4,580	18.4	20,320	1,000	200	20.0	800	11,505	2,070	18.[illegible]	9,435	12,395	2,[illegible]10	[illegible]8.6	10,085
RURAL FARM—TOTAL																
Male	[illegible]8,300	146,61[illegible]	77.9	41,685	57,250	3[illegible],115	[illegible]	24,135	1[illegible]3,610	105,785	89.[illegible]	12,825	[illegible]	7,[illegible]	62.0	4,725
14 to 19 years	37,230	16,830	45.2	20,400	36,125	15,890	44.0	20,235	880	790	89.[illegible]	90	225	[illegible]		75
20 to 24 years	17,945	16,190	90.2	1,755	10,070	8,680	86.2	1,390	7,115	6,830	96.0	285	760	680	89.[illegible]	80
25 to 29 years	14,595	13,570	93.0	1,025	3,235	2,700	83.5	535	10,730	10,1[illegible]	96.1	4[illegible]	630	555	88.1	75
30 to 34 years	14,960	14,195	94.9	765	1,[illegible]30	1,500	82.0	330	12,[illegible]	12,095	97.[illegible]	325	710	600	84.[illegible]	110
35 to 44 years	3[illegible],790	[illegible]2,335	95.7	1,455	2,520	2,130	84.5	[illegible]	29,955	29,015	96.9	940	2,3[illegible]	1,190	90.[illegible]	25
45 years and over	69,780	53,495	76.[illegible]	16,285	3,470	2,215	63.8	1,255	57,510	46,740	81.3	10,770	8,800	4,540	51.6	4,260
Female	175,690	24,245	13.8	151,445	38,150	7,110	18.6	31,040	116,455	12,715	10.9	103,740	21,085	4,420	21.0	16,665
14 to 19 years	33,910	4,155	12.3	29,755	26,035	3,605	[illegible]2.9	22,430	5,115	410	8.0	4,705	760	140	18.4	620
20 to 24 years	16,455	3,280	19.9	13,175	3,390	1,070	41.9	2,320	11,085	1,165	10.5	9,920	1,300	445	32.2	935
25 to 29 years	15,315	2,375	15.5	12,940	1,355	535	39.5	820	12,895	1,455	11.3	11,440	1,065	385	36.2	680
30 to 34 years	16,325	2,460	15.[illegible]	13,865	805	305	37.9	500	14,500	1,775	12.2	12,725	1,020	380	37.3	640
35 to 44 years	33,915	5,600	16.5	28,315	1,455	490	33.7	965	30,220	4,095	13.6	26,125	2,240	1,015	45.[illegible]	1,225
45 years and over	59,770	6,375	10.[illegible]	53,395	2,510	505	20.1	2,005	42,640	3,615	8.9	38,025	14,620	2,055	14.1	12,565
RURAL FARM—NONWHITE																
Male	70,440	56,240	79.8	14,200	22,230	13,795	62.1	8,435	42,230	38,360	90.8	3,870	5,980	4,085	68.3	1,895
14 to 19 years	[illegible]5,990	8,790	[illegible].0	7,200	15,475	8,335	53.9	7,1[illegible]	410	380		30	105	75		30
20 to 24 years	7,440	6,785	91.2	655	3,865	3,345	86.5	520	3,175	3,080	97.0	95	400	360		40
25 to 29 years	5,425	5,050	93.1	375	1,000	825	82.5	175	4,040	3,880	96.0	160	385	345		40
30 to 34 years	4,875	4,625	94.[illegible]	250	375	280		95	4,145	4,045	97.6	100	355	300		55
35 to 44 years	11,300	10,870	96.2	430	650	525	80.8	125	9,990	9,735	97.4	255	660	610	92.4	50
45 years and over	25,410	20,120	79.2	5,290	865	485	56.[illegible]	380	20,470	17,240	84.2	3,230	4,075	2,395	58.8	1,680
Female	68,665	13,030	19.0	55,635	17,110	3,715	21.7	13,395	41,390	6,395	15.5	34,995	10,165	2,920	28.7	7,245
14 to 19 years	15,205	2,430	16.0	12,775	12,610	2,100	16.7	10,510	2,105	245	11.6	1,860	490	85		405
20 to 24 years	7,980	1,810	22.7	6,170	2,415	915	3[illegible].9	1,500	4,610	580	12.6	4,030	955	315	33.0	640
25 to 29 years	6,235	1,310	[illegible].0	4,925	640	270	42.2	370	4,905	770	15.7	4,135	690	270	39.1	420
30 to 34 years	5,815	1,270	21.8	4,545	280	120	•	160	4,945	880	17.8	4,065	590	270	45.8	320
35 to 44 years	12,585	2,805	22.3	9,780	520	185	35.6	335	10,815	1,955	18.1	8,860	1,250	665	53.2	585
45 years and over	20,845	3,405	16.[illegible]	17,440	645	125	19.4	520	14,010	1,965	14.0	12,045	6,190	1,315	21.2	4,875
STANDARD METROPOLITAN AREAS																
BATON ROUGE—TOTAL																
Male	54,915	41,410	75.4	13,505	14,420	6,370	44.2	8,050	36,045	32,195	89.3	3,850	4,450	2,845	63.9	1,605
14 to 19 years	6,775	2,120	31.3	4,655	6,495	1,900	29.3	4,595	190	170		20	90	50		40
20 to 24 years	7,725	4,845	62.7	2,880	4,465	2,065	46.2	2,400	2,915	2,515	86.3	400	345	265		80
25 to 29 years	7,840	6,590	84.1	1,250	1,600	1,045	65.3	555	5,765	5,190	90.0	575	475	355		120
30 to 34 years	6,[illegible]35	5,865	92.3	490	490	355		135	5,520	5,250	95.1	270	345	260		85
35 to 44 years	11,150	10,585	94.9	565	665	535	80.5	130	9,590	9,305	97.0	285	895	745	83.2	150
45 years and over	15,070	11,405	75.7	3,665	705	470	66.7	235	12,065	9,765	80.9	2,300	2,300	1,170	50.9	1,130
Female	58,095	17,460	30.1	40,635	11,010	4,320	39.2	6,690	36,400	8,840	24.3	27,610	10,6[illegible]	4,300	40.4	6,335
14 to 19 years	7,155	1,315	18.4	5,840	5,810	1,030	17.7	4,780	1,145	195	17.0	950	200	90		110
20 to 24 years	8,340	3,230	38.7	5,110	2,280	1,335	58.6	945	5,435	1,570	28.9	3,865	625	325	52.0	300
25 to 29 years	8,015	2,725	34.0	5,290	840	625	74.4	215	6,350	1,590	25.0	4,760	825	510	61.8	315
30 to 34 years	6,835	2,130	31.2	4,705	485	380		105	5,600	1,260	22.5	4,340	750	490	65.3	260
35 to 44 years	11,945	4,410	36.9	7,535	655	490	74.8	165	9,435	2,665	28.2	6,770	1,855	1,255	67.7	600
45 years and over	15,805	3,650	23.1	12,155	940	460	48.9	480	8,485	1,560	18.4	6,925	6,380	1,630	25.5	4,750
BATON ROUGE—NONWHITE																
Male	17,045	12,135	71.2	4,910	4,550	2,180	47.9	2,370	10,135	8,525	84.1	1,610	2,360	1,430	60.6	930
14 to 19 years	2,425	935	38.6	1,490	2,320	855	36.9	1,465	60	55		5	45	25		20
20 to 24 years	2,045	1,370	67.0	675	1,110	570	51.4	540	715	635	88.8	80	220	165		55
25 to 29 years	2,020	1,630	80.7	390	475	320		155	1,310	1,130	86.3	180	235	180		55
30 to 34 years	1,775	1,525	85.[illegible]	250	150	100		50	1,410	1,260	89.4	150	215	165	•	50
35 to 44 years	3,445	3,145	91.3	300	240	185		55	2,755	2,595	94.2	160	450	365		85
45 years and over	5,335	3,530	66.2	1,805	255	150		105	3,885	2,850	73.4	1,035	1,195	530	44.4	665
Female	19,420	7,080	36.5	12,340	3,695	1,230	33.3	2,465	10,275	3,570	34.7	6,705	5,450	2,280	41.8	3,170
14 to 19 years	2,575	460	17.9	2,115	2,030	360	17.7	1,670	420	50		370	125	50		75
20 to 24 years	2,545	945	37.1	1,600	740	340	45.9	400	1,370	405	29.6	965	435	200		235
25 to 29 years	2,540	1,130	44.5	1,410	280	185		95	1,740	645	37.1	1,095	520	300	57.7	220
30 to 34 years	2,135	1,045	48.9	1,090	150	100		50	1,485	605	40.7	880	500	340	68.0	160
35 to 44 years	4,080	2,050	50.2	2,030	270	180		90	2,735	1,205	44.1	1,530	1,075	665	61.9	410
45 years and over	5,545	1,450	26.1	4,095	225	65		160	2,525	660	26.1	1,865	2,795	725	25.9	2,070

Table 70—LABOR FORCE STATUS, BY MARITAL STATUS, AGE, COLOR, AND SEX, FOR THE STATE, URBAN AND RURAL AND FOR STANDARD METROPOLITAN AREAS OF 100,000 OR MORE 1950—Con

[Based on 20-pe and sample avails, is complete even, do a in tables 15 and 35 Perces (not snown where low than 0 1 or who e base is less than 800]

i	Total	1+ years	a sna r	6-	-2 - 7	Single		031	\.\ \\ \\ \\ \\ \\ \\ \\ \\ \\ \\ \\ \\	arned, spou	y present			Oth		
		Labo*	fo ce			Labor	fo cu			Labor	orce	Not a		Labor	force	500
4r s, co. r, ags, and sex	Total	Nambe	Percent or lotar	labor force	Total	\umb*r	Percent of total	lapor oree	Total	\umber	Percent of total	labor	To al	Number	Percent o total	labor force
TANDARD METROPOLITAN ABEAS—Con																
TCT-SMABLES TOT-								05 500	_51,160	395,395 دي	89 6	15,760	26,575	17,630	66 5	8,8
Male	£32,05√	187,890	-8 g		30,3.4	34,815	57 7 32 8	25,500	650	282	90 0	65	260	170	00)	۰,
to 19 years to 24 years to 24 years to 34 years to 44 years years and over	25, 29 21, 935 29, 1,5 25, 57, 49, 10 83, 205	2,690 20,63 25,750 23 840 45,944 63,002	34 6 75 7 88 3 9 9 7	255,425 ,425 ,755 3,035 20,200	24,22J 24,48° 0,73L -,2-3 4,730 6,390	7,935 10,545 5,410 2,780 3,895 7,250	72 8	3,9_5 1,370 435 835 2,040	10,050 19,985 20,125 19,0€5 61,285	9,105 28 235 19,200 37,660 50,510	90 e 91 7 95 4 96 4 82 4	945 1,650 925 1,405 10,7 5	1 405 2,410 2,2:5 2,2:5 2,2:5	1,090 2,005 1 840 4,390 8 245	82 3 83 9 24 9	6,
Female _	273,,55	83,275	30 4	190,290	54,_80	25,630	47 3	28 550	154,585	33,850	219	121,035	64,490	23,795	J6 9	40,
to 19 years. to 24 years to 29 years to 29 years to 34 years to 44 years.	27 470 20,585 23,635 27,860 55,740 93,465	6,020 12,500 1-,175 9,100 24,290 22,240	24 8 40 9 33 8 32 7 38 7 2, 2	21,650 1~,035 21,860 _8 760 _4,150 75,775	22,977 8,070 4,200 2,730 5,200 _C,705	4,855 6,390 2,155 2,165 3,975 4,920	21 5 73 7 78 9 79 3 70 4 40 0	17,810 2,280 885 065 1,225 5,785	1,955 18,605 24,225 2, 145 40,350 46,225	4,570 5,4.0 4,635 1.,135 7,260	20 7 24 6 22 1 21 9 27 6 10 7	3,135 14,035 19,085 16,510 29,215 39,055	1,040 3,510 4,320 3,985 10,190 4_,645	1,540 2,430 2,300 6,480 20,710	32 2 46 5 56 3 57 7 63 6 25 7	1, 1, 1, 3, 30,
EN OR EAST-JOHNSTTE															Editor	ust ;
Male	64,255	47,240	73 5	17,010	16,925	8,830	ɔ2.2	8,095	36,650	31,320	85 5	20,330	10,680	7,095	60 4	3,
to 19 years to 24 years to 24 years to 39 years to 34 years vears and over	8,295 7,100 7,025 6,300 13,765 21,465	2,720 5,445 6,150 5,430 12,470 14,930	32 8 76 6 84 0 87 8 90 6 99 6	5,275 1 660 1,175 770 1,295 6,535	7,980 3,745 1,690 880 1,280 1,350	2,455 2,635 1,255 720 965 800	30 8 70 4 74 3 81 8 75 4 59 3	5,,25 2,,10 435 160 ,15 550	2,695 4,650 4,470 10,100 14,520	2,345 4,100 4,085 9,480 11,115	8° 0 88 2 91 4 93 7 76 5	350 556 365 680 3,405	665 985 920 2,385 5,592	465 79, 725 2,025 3,015	69 9 60 7 76 3 84,9 93 9	2,
Female	77 570	27,185	35 0	50,381	14,190	4,760 955	رد 12.5	9,430	37,155	⊥, n70 230	31 4 17 5	25,485	26,225	10,755	41 0 22 3	15,
to 19 years. to 24 years to 24 years. to 34 years. to 34 years. to 44 years. years and over.	9,590 8,925 9 370 7,860 16,560 25,265	1 3,040 3,040 3,625 3,520 8,140 7,530	1.9 .41 78 7 44 8 49 2 29 8	8,260 ,885 5,745 4,340 8,-20 11,735	7,625 2,265 1,005 720 1,090 1,485	1,265 635 520 710 675	55 8 63 2 72 2 65 1 45 5	6,670 1,000 370 270 380 810	4,750 5,920 5,000 10,245 9,925	1,025 1,750 1,835 4,225 2,595	21 C 29 7 36 7 41 2 26 1	3,725 4,160 3,165 6,020 7,330	1,910 2,445 2,40 5,225 13,855	7>0 1,230 1,165 3,205 4,260	30 3 50 3 54 4 61 3 30 7	1,
SHREVEPORTTOTAL																
Male	53,035	46,200	78 9	12,435	1.,835	6,320	53 4:	5,510	40,_60	35 745	89 0	4,415	6,640	4,135	62 3	2,
to 19 years . 10 24 years . 10 24 years . 10 29 years . 10 34 years . 10 44 years . 10 years and over .	6,000 6,180 6,590 6,230 11,920 21,115	2,455 5,265 5,955 2,775 21,185 12,565	27 2 85 2 90 4 97 7 93 8 73 F	4,145 91.5 4.5 4.5 73.5 5,550	6,300 2 645 1,000 475 215 900	2 190 2,045 820 385 390 490	34 8 77 3 82 0 73 7 54 4	4,110 600 .80 90 125 410	3,105 4,960 5,22, 10,265 16,345	215 2,850 4,650 4,955 9,835 13,270	92 1 94 0 94 8 96 1 80 6	25 245 300 270 400 3,175	60 430 630 530 -,_20 3,870	50 360 475 435 910 1,905	75 4 82 1 81 3 79 2	1,
Female .	68,345	22,650	ـ م ـ م	45,695	_0,295	4,260	41 4	6,035	41,090	.0,885	26,5	₹0,205	16,960	1,500	44 3	9,
to 19 vears to 24 vears to 24 vears to 24 years to 34 years to 44 years 5 years and over	7,545 8,250 8,285 7,035 13,595 23,639	1,615 3 640 3,970 2,680 5,730 5 935	21 4 37 - 38 - 42 0 20 1	5,930 4,610 5,25 4,355 7,885 17,700	2,775 1,805 705 405 625 987	1,320 560 310 493 470	19 2 73 1 79 4 78 4 48 0	4,665 485 145 95 135 510	1,460 5,325 0,300 5,610 10 255 12,130	340 1,620 1,655 1,655 3,220 2,385	23 2 30 4 26 3 49 7 21 4 19 7	1,125 3,705 4,645 3,90 7,0°2 9,745	-,120 -,280 -,015 2,715 10,525	700 855 705 2,000 3,080	62 5 66 8 69 5 73 7 29 3	7,
SHREVIPORTMONUPPLE		- 1								10		i		1 9 10		
Male -	20, 190	14,785	6 د7	5,.10	4,400	2,390	54 3	2,015	12,140	10,220	84 2	1,920	3,550	2,175	61 2	-,
to 19 years to 24 years to 25 years to 34 years years years and over	2 915 2 125 2 360 1 765 2,770 7,060	1,360 1,755 1,560 1,530 3 385 5,195	46 7 82 0 82 9 86 7 89 8 67 8	1,555 370 300 235 385 2,465	2,755 800 255 425 420 250	230 630 165 100 145 120	44 6 78 8	1,525 170 90 25 75 130	1.5 1 C50 1,240 1,350 2,950 5,432	95 910 1,200 1,200 2 735 4,160	96 7 90 3 88 9 92 7 76 2	20 140 120 150 215 1,275	275 365 290 600 1,975	215 275 230 20> 915	84 2 46 3	1,1
Female	24,,0	10,545	43 0	13,955	3,795	1,285	33 9	2 510	11,790	4,790	40 6	7,000	8,9.5	4,470	50 .	4,
to 19 years to 24 years to 29 years to 29 years to 34 years to 44 years years and over	3,205 2,910 2,765 2,440 4,490 8,690	720 -,490 1 41 ⁴ 1 410 2,595 2,915	22 5 51 2 57 8 57 8 33 5	2,485 1,420 1,350 1 0,0 1,895 5,775	2,455 650 2°0 120 130 1°0	485 405 175 70 90 60	19 8 62 3	1,970 245 95 90 40 1_0	1,535 1,640 1,645 2,740 3,690	125 620 690 855 1,295 1,205	23 40 4 42 1 52 0 47 3 32 7	415 915 950 790 1,445 2,485	210 725 855 675 1,620 4,830	110 405 550 485 1 210 1 650	64 3 7- 9 74 7 34 2	3,:

Table 71—EMPLOYMENT STATUS AND HOURS WORKED DURING CENSUS WELK BY PERSONS 14 TO 29 YEARS OLD BY SCHOOL ENROLLMENT, AGE COLOR, AND SEX FOR THE STATE URBAN AND RURAL AND FOR STANDARD METROPOLITAN AREAS OF 250,000 OR MORE 1950

Based on 20-percent sample Percent no shown where less han , 1 or where case is eas han \$40

Area color employment status,	- m	,	knroll	er in seboo		1				Ye. 01-	uled in sele	NA .		
hou s worked and sex	Total 14 to 29 years old	14 and 13 _/es_s	6 and 7 years	18 and 19 years	20 ears	21 to 2,	25 to 29	Ti to 29 yea∼ old	in mad 15 vents	6 and 7 years	-8 and 9 reary	2C years	21 -0 24 years	25 to 29
THE STATE						_						1-		
Male, total	108,520	39,380	£3,060	13,540	3 53*	2,655	350	216,450	45	75,د	2,,845	_4 875	(8 73.	89,390
Abor force Percent in labor force or in labor force	24,355 22.4 84, 60	4,340 _1 C 35,646	5,040 18 C 23,020	2,2.5 20 3 .0,725	8#0 44 9 2,455	,145 38 6 7,770	57 °	-72,_85 83 3 2,265	2,.90 51.4 2.55	3 140	22 /8. 26 2 3 365	,300 8# 575	90 -	81,935 31 7,445
Employed With a ob but not at work At work 1 to 14 hours 15 to 34 hours 35 tours or more	22,320 370 2,450 2,675 6,050 31,475	4,140 135 4,035 66, 1,720 1,025	4,720 230 -,490 885 -,813	2,470 2,300 395 395	720 73 73 225	4 325 4,270 27C 845	755	3,44 3,45 64,45 2,355 5,565	- 395 3 - ,955 70 370	770	18,610 345 18,405 385 2 +10	-1,_50 175 -0 985 200 - 170	6, 40 -,20; 4,-35 650 4,475	75 515 1,5 73 97 74 1,23
Hours nor reported Noowhite total	1,250	400	37.	.00	400	2,495	-,24	24, 1080	1,253	6,870	480	9 330	-8,604 ,_05	1,5
Labor force Percent in labor force Not in labor force	7,931 23 - 25,585	13 7 12,300	1,970 22 1 6,925	3,245 865 26.7 2 350	کد، 2008 8 کا 1 کا	3,0.0 1,1,1,1,1,1,1,1,1,1,1,1,1,1,1,1,1,1,1,	3,265 1,070 21 1 1,595	30,100 49 035 69,34	2,065 1,255 60 3 8_0	5 985 4,82° 80 6 -,150	6,395 8,780 84 3 1,015	5,255 4 550 50 6 705	24,080 .8,390 87.2 2 p90	24,35: 24,23: 87: 3,42:
Female, total	90,925	29 275	<8,765	12,770	2,900	4,200	3,0,5	261,75.	4,175	_3,925	37, 650	19,835	84,350	107,81
Labor fo ce Percent in labor force Not in labor for e	8,340 9 2 82,25	4,750 3 7 37,825	2,090 7 2 26,685	-3.9 -3.9 -1,000	665 22 2 2,235	34.3 2,°00	782 32 7 2 050	30,5% 30 B	695 26-6 3,480	4 000 24 0 9,895	37 2 49,890	7,210 36 3 12,625	27,2.5 32 3 57,.33	29,67 27 78,44
Employed With a job but not at work	7,840 420	1,385	1,900	1,645	605 30	5	35	74,120 2,137	59u 40	3,580	. 290	6 755	28,795	28,42
At work 1 to 14 hours 15 to 34 hours 35 hours or more Hours not reported	7,420 1,350 2,075 3,630 355	1,30° 290 580 31.0 125	1,775 490 590 *55 40	400 475 475 35	5°Y) 75 75 195 25	220	135	73,940 2,265 ,385 58,425 1,865	550 15 145 375 15	3,435 140 77 2 390 435	10,640 290 .,200 8,880	6,620 160 890 5 440 130	3,565	27,6 94 4,81 2- 2- 02
Nonwhite total Labor force Percent in labor force Not in labor force	31 7-5 2,8:0 8 9 28,9:5	-4,320 760 5 3 ひっ60	9.840 840 8.5 9,000	4 36° 530 42 1 1,835	1,0X1 80 7.7 960	340	23.7	% 100 29 335 33 8 57 505	2,135 435 20 4 1,700	4 ±80	11,340 3,520 31 0 7 820	7,295 2,520 34 5 4,775	27,060 9,260 34 2 17,800	35,02 1,79 35 21,23
TIRBAN														
Male rotal Labor force Percent in labor force Not in labor force	59,7·5 23,690 22 9 46,025	17 040 1,740 9 6 15,940	2,250 17 0 10,960	8,320 1,570 16 9 6,750	2,640 340 20 5 2,100	3,300	4,330	_05,495 89 9 _1,800	1 .º5 455 38 7 720	4,495 3,365 74 9 -,130	9,765		34,700	
Employed -	12,345	1,535	2,070		500	1		93,395	385	2,733	7,305	4,895	3.,0-0	46,54
With a job but not at work At work 1 to 14 hours 1s to 34 hours 85 nours or more Hours not reported	11,825 2,045 2,785 6,210 785	200 239	3,943 683 400 205	1,340 335 47(530 65	48: 66 160 240	2,810	3,770 -65 480	1,855 -1,540 -,715 6,75 82,160 -,875	375 50 65 235 25	2,635 430 417 2,005	7,690 -55 73.	4,810 95 350	30,375	48,67
Nonwhite total Labor force Percent in labor force Not in labor force	10,765 3,480 20 F _3,285	,380 605 9 5 5,775	4,115 735 47 9 3,360	1,690 355 20 9	365	2,070	2,120 1,005 47 4	33,360 28,095 84 2 2,265	530 255 48 1 275	1 925 1,425 7/ 0 500	4,160 3,365 80 9	2,2 7 1,850 94.0	10,635	12,08
Female total	46 835	17,790	14,055	-,910	2,215	2,9.0	1,970	150 650	1,370	5,900	±º 560	11,675	>3,060	69,08
Labor force Percen in labor force Not in labor force	2,700 ± 7 41 3°5	515 2 9 17,275	-,195 8 5 12,840	1,285	580 26 3 4,635	129	800	60 060 .7 9 98,590	255 18 6 1,415	2,280 38 6	8,385	5,260 45 1 6,415	20,855	23 02
Employed With a job but Lot at work 1 to 14 hours 15 to 34 hours 35 hours or more Hours not reported	5,165 230 4 935 1,05c 985 4 690 210	483 25 425 215 20 70	1,09: 6! - 030 330 265 360 75	1,155 340 290 490	3	30 1,040 60 150 820	25 740 35 105 565	56,735 1,230 35,505 1,345 6,865 46,010 1,285	215 210 3 3 3 3 3 3 3 3 3 3 3 3 3 3 3 3 3 3 3	1,955 35 1,920 50 350 1,475	7,710	4,875 80 495 4,215	39,260 460 2,465 16,190	21,53 59 3,22
Nonwhite total Labor torce Percent in labor force Not in labor force	15,005 1,370 9 13,635	6,350 205 3 2 6,125	1	2 285 305 13 2	5-4 3; 6 : 50;	235	485	48,5±0 10,625 4C 5 26,885	705 165 23 4 540		37 0	3,810 1,560 40 9 2,250	6,380	20,15 8,55 42 11,60
RURAL NONFARM		1	1	1		100 M 100 M								
Male, total Labor force Percent in labor force	23,935 4,375 10 3	9,82C 665 6.8 9,455	7,08 88: 42 : 6,20	8 2	19:	90:	1,277	54,255 46,390 85 5 7,855	1,060 505 47 6 555	2,760	5,725	4,030	15,315	18,05
Not in labor force Employed With a job but not at work At work I to 14 hours 1 to 14 hours 35 hours or more Hours not reported.	19,560 3,815 160 3,655 415 960 1,950	630 +0 590 440 221 135		365 350 45 70 215	111111111111111111111111111111111111111	777 21 25 25 25 26	1,150 40 -,'10 20 190 840	40,250	470 3 463 25 460 275	2,370 85 2,285 100 495	4,430 4,315 138 679 3,340	3,130 75 3 055 50 380 2,540	13,320 325 12,995 180 1,475 11,125	16,54 44 16 10 19
Now hite, total Labor force Percent in labor force Not in labor force	7,250 1,305 18 0 5,955	1,130 255 8 1 2,875	1,89	58:	4.	5 64 24 38	5 790 775 47.5	13,385		78	2,030	1,170	5,125 4,340 84 7 785	5,39 4,39 81 1,00

LOUISLANA

Table 71.—EMPLOYMENT STATUS AND HOURS WORKED DURING CENSUS WEEK BY PERSONS 14 TO 29 YEARS OLD BY SCHOOL ENROLLMENT, AGE, COLOR, AND SEX, FOR THE STATE, URBAN AND RURAL, AND FOR STANDARD METROPOLITAN AREAS OF 250,000 OR MORE: 1950

Based on 20-percent sample. Percent not shown where less than 0.1 or where base is less than 500

Area, color, employment status, hours worked, and sex	Enrolled in school: Total 14 to 29 years old	Enrolled: 14 and 15 years	Enrolled: 16 and 17 years	Enrolled: 18 and 19 years	Enrolled: 20 years	Enrolled: 21 to 24 years	Enrolled: 25 to 29 years	Not enrolled in school: Total 14 to 29 years old	Not enrolled: 14 and 15 years	Not enrolled: 16 and 17 years	Not enrolled: 18 and 19 years	Not enrolled: 20 years	Not enrolled: 21 to 24 years	Not enrolled: 25 to 29 years
THE STATE														
Male, total	108,520	39,380	23,060	13,540	3 535	12,655	14,350	216,450	4,045	15,475	22,845	14 875	68 730	89,390
Labor force	24,355	4,340	5,040	2,745	880	4,985	6,065	192,085	2,090	10,[illegible]	22,780	13,300	62,140	81,935
Percent in labor force	22.4	11.0	18.0	20.3	24.9	38.6	57.0	88.8	50.4	77.4	76.2	89.4	90.4	91.7
Not in labor force	84,165	35,040	23,020	10,795	2,655	7,770	4,885	24,265	2 055	3 040	5 365	1,575	6,580	7,445
Employed	22,320	4,140	4,720	2,470	745	4 325	5,900	172,800	1 985	9,290	18,810	11,160	6[illegible],[illegible]40	79 515
With a job but not at work	370	135	230	110	45	155	195	3 545	3	255	345	175	1,205	1,545
At work	21,950	4,005	4,490	2,360	720	4,170	5,705	169,255	1,955	9,035	18,465	10 985	54,135	73 970
1 to 14 hours	2,675	860	885	395	75	270	190	2,385	30	270	385	200	650	850
15 to 34 hours	6,050	1,720	1,810	395	225	845	755	15,505	370	1,730	2 410	1 170	4,475	5,235
35 hours or more	11,475	1,025	1 420	1,170	400	2,895	4,585	146,080	1,255	6,870	15 190	9 330	48,605	66 430
Hours not reported	1,250	400	375	400	20	160	175	5,285	40	130	480	285	1,405	1,535
Nonwhite total	33,440	14,260	8 895	3,245	715	3,060	3,265	69,135	2,065	5 985	10,395	5,255	21,080	24,355
Labor force	7,855	1,960	1,970	865	200	1,190	1,670	59 035	1,255	4,825	8,780	4 550	18,390	21 235
Percent in labor force	23.5	13.7	22.1	26.7	28.0	38.9	51.1	85.4	60.8	80.6	84.5	86.6	87.2	87.2
Not in labor force	25,585	12,300	6,925	2 380	515	1,870	1,595	10,100	810	1,160	1,615	705	2 690	3,120
Female, total	90,925	39 275	28,765	12,770	2,900	4,200	3,015	261,755	4,175	13,925	37 650	19,835	84,350	107,815
Labor force	8,390	1,450	2,080	1,770	665	1,440	985	80,595	695	4 030	14,770	7,210	27,215	29,670
Percent in labor force	9.2	3.7	7.2	13.9	22.9	34.3	32.7	30.8	16.6	28.9	37.2	36.3	32.3	27.5
Not in labor force	82,535	37,825	26,685	11,000	2,235	2,760	2 030	181 160	3,480	9,895	19,880	12,625	57,135	78,145
Employed	7,840	1,385	1,905	1,645	605	1,360	940	76,120	590	3,580	10,980	6 755	25,795	28,420
With a job but not at work	420	80	130	90	35	50	35	2,180	40	145	290	135	765	805
At work	7,420	1,305	1,775	1,555	570	1,310	905	73,940	550	3,435	10,640	6,620	25,030	27,615
1 to 14 hours	1,360	290	490	400	75	60	45	2,265	15	140	290	160	720	940
15 to 34 hours	2,075	580	590	475	75	220	135	11,385	145	775	1,200	890	3,565	4,815
35 hours or more	3,630	310	555	645	395	1,015	710	58,425	375	2 390	8,880	5 440	20,100	21 240
Hours not reported	355	125	140	35	25	15	15	1,865	15	135	320	130	645	620
Nonwhite total	31 745	14,320	9 840	4 365	1,040	1,350	830	86 900	2,135	6,050	11,340	7,295	27,060	33,020
Labor force	2,850	760	840	530	80	340	280	29 395	435	1,870	3,520	2,520	9,260	11,790
Percent in labor force	8.9	5.3	8.5	12.1	7.7	25.2	33.7	33.8	20.4	30.9	31.0	34.5	34.2	35.7
Not in labor force	28,915	13,560	9,000	3,835	960	1,010	550	57 505	1,700	4 180	7 820	4,775	17,800	21,230
URBAN														
Male total	59,715	17 640	13 210	8,320	2,640	9,755	8,150	117,295	1 175	4,495	11,400	6,790	38,245	55 190
Labor force	13,690	1,700	2,250	1,570	540	3,300	4,330	105,495	455	3,365	9,765	6,035	34,700	51,175
Percent in labor force	22.9	9.6	17.0	18.9	20.5	33.8	53.1	89.9	38.7	74.9	85.7	88.9	90.7	92.7
Not in labor force	46,025	15,940	10,960	6,750	2,100	6,455	3,820	11,800	720	1,130	1 635	755	3,545	4 015
Employed	12,345	1,535	2,070	1,405	500	2,925	3,910	93,395	385	2,730	7,805	4,895	31,040	46,540
With a job but not at work	520	55	130	65	15	115	140	1,855	10	115	115	85	665	865
At work	11,825	1,480	1,940	1,340	485	2,810	3,770	91,540	375	2,615	7,690	4,810	30,375	45,675
1 to 14 hours	2,045	605	625	335	65	250	165	1,215	50	130	155	95	300	485
15 to 34 hours	2,785	440	680	470	160	615	480	6,290	65	410	735	350	1,915	1,795
35 hours or more	6,210	200	400	530	240	1,835	3,005	82,160	235	2,005	6,610	4,235	27,545	41,530
Hours not reported	785	235	295	65	20	110	120	1,895	25	70	190	130	615	865
Nonwhite total	16,765	6,380	4,115	1,695	385	2,070	2,120	33,360	530	1 925	4,160	2,2[illegible]	10,635	13,895
Labor force	3,480	605	735	355	90	690	1,005	28,095	255	1,425	3,365	1,850	9,105	12,085
Percent in labor force	20.8	9.5	17.9	20.9		33.3	47.4	84.2	48.1	74.0	80.9	84.0	85.6	87.0
Not in labor force	13,285	5,775	3,380	1,340	295	1,380	1,115	5,265	275	500	795	355	1,530	1,810
Female total	46 835	17,790	14,055	7,915	2,215	2,910	1,970	150 650	1,370	5,900	17 560	11,675	53,060	69,085
Labor force	5,300	515	1,195	1,285	580	1 125	800	60 060	255	2,280	8,385	5,260	20,855	23 025
Percent in labor force	11.7	2.9	8.5	16.2	26.2	38.7	40.6	37.9	18.6	38.6	47.8	45.1	39.3	33.3
Not in labor force	41 375	17,275	12,840	6,630	1,635	1 785	1 170	98,590	1,115	3,620	9,175	6,415	32,205	46,060
Employed	5,165	480	1,095	1,210	545	1,070	765	56,735	215	1,955	7,845	4,935	19,770	22,015
With a job but not at work	230	25	65	55	30	30	25	1,230	5	35	135	60	510	485
At work	4 935	455	1 030	1,155	515	1,040	740	55,505	210	1,920	7,710	4,875	19,260	21,530
1 to 14 hours	1,050	215	330	340	70	60	35	1,345	5	50	155	80	460	595
15 to 34 hours	985	20	265	290	55	150	105	6,865	55	350	580	495	2,165	3,220
35 hours or more	2 690	70	360	490	365	820	585	46,010	145	1,475	6,725	4,215	16,190	17,260
Hours not reported	210	90	75	35	25	10	15	1,285	5	45	250	85	445	455
Nonwhite total	15,005	6,350	4,615	2 285	540	750	485	48,540	705	2,365	5,745	3,810	15,730	20,155
Labor force	1,370	205	390	305	35	235	200	19,625	165	845	2,125	1,560	6,380	8,550
Percent in labor force	9.[illegible]	3.2	8.5	13.3	6.5	31.3		40.5	23.4	35.7	37.0	40.9	40.6	42.4
Not in labor force	13,635	6,125	4,225	1,980	505	515	285	28,885	540	1,520	3,620	2,250	9,350	11,605
RURAL NONFARM														
Male, total	23,935	9,820	7,08[illegible]	2,500	545	1,855	2,130	54,255	1,060	3,705	6,805	4,525	17,495	20 665
Labor force	4,375	665	885	455	195	905	1,270	46,390	505	2,760	5,725	4,030	15,315	18,055
Percent in labor force	18.3	6.8	12.5	18.2	35.8	48.8	59.6	85.5	47.6	74.5	84.1	89.1	87.5	87.4
Not in labor force	19,560	9,155	6,200	2,045	350	950	860	7,865	555	945	1,080	495	2,180	2,610
Employed	3,815	630	775	365	125	770	1,150	40,260	470	2,370	4,430	3,130	13,320	16,540
With a job but not at work	160	40	30	15	15	20	40	1,045	5	85	115	75	325	440
At work	3,655	590	745	350	110	750	1,110	39,215	465	2,285	4,315	3 055	12,995	16 100
1 to 14 hours	415	140	180	45	10	20	20	680	25	100	135	50	180	190
15 to 34 hours	960	225	315	70	30	130	190	4,450	160	495	675	380	1,415	1,325
35 hours or more	1,995	135	170	215	70	565	840	33,175	275	1,635	3,345	2,540	11,125	14,255
Hours not reported	285	90	80	20		35	60	910	5	55	160	85	275	330
Nonwhite, total	7,260	3,130	1,895	585	215	645	790	16,135	500	1,475	2,465	1,380	5,125	5,390
Labor force	1,305	255	260	125	45	245	375	13,385	295	1,160	2,030	1,170	4,340	4,390
Percent in labor force	18.0	8.1	13.7	21.4		38.0	47.5	81.9	59.0	78.6	82.4	84.8	84.7	81.4
Not in labor force	5,955	2,875	1,635	460	170	400	415	2,950	205	315	435	210	785	1,000

Hours not reported	6,715	20	20	905	220	21.5	215	675	5 265	25 890	3,030	55	7,280	210
Nonwhite rotal Labor force Percent in labor force	390	2,945	2 113 90 4 3	903 90 9 9	5	100	90	21,170 7,505 35 9	265 55	89C 275 30 9	8,5	1 505 535 35 5	6,885 2,400 34 9	9,155 3,535 38 6
Not in labor force	6,325	2,930	2,045	815	215	215	125	13,565	210	615	32 6 1,665	970	4,485	5,620

Table 72 —WEEKS WORKED IN 1949, BY LABOR FORCE STATUS AND SEX, FOR THE STATE AND FOR STANDARD METROPOLITAN AREAS OF 100,000 OR MORE 1950

[Based on 20-percent sample available comprehending data in tables 2, and 35 Proceed as, sl. win where less man 91 or where less is less than 20,

	Total, 14	years old a	nd over	Lab	or force, 9	50	Not in	apor force.	1950	1			Pe.ner	t distri	etio			
Area and weeks worked in 1949	Both seres	Male	Female	Both sexes	Male	Female	Both sexes	Mair	Female	Total	, 14 yes: and over	rs old	Laby	r ir tep	1950	Noti	r labor 4950	force,
						1 country	DOM BEAGS	van.	remate	Both sexes	Mae	Fe-	Both sexes	Viale	Fe- male	Both sexes	Male	Fe- male
THE STATE																		
Total.	1,871,590	904,030	969 563	920,710	682,345	238,.15	950,823	219,625	73_,2-5	_00 o	a.	12.0	1000	100 0	100 0	.00 0	-00 0	130 0
Did not work in 1949 Worked in 1949 1 to 13 weeks 1 to 25 weeks 27 to 39 weeks 40 to 49 weeks 50 to 52 weeks Work in 1949 not reported	825,155 930,820 89,565 97,855 90,420 106,385 952,995 11.,615	185,885 628,650 40,015 54,815 50,505 81,330 424,985 57,495	637,270 273,170 49,850 49,040 32,915 24,755 1co,610 54,20	7u,055 80y,095 98,665 67,155 75,670 97,195 530,420 41,562	38,840 011,911 22,400 44,285 50,800 77,010 417,411 31,045	31,2.5 197,185 -6,0.5 22,870 24,870 20,175 -13,005 9,915	753,100 ,27,725 52,200 30,700 ,4,750 8,900 22,75 70,055	-47,045 40,740 17,613 10,530 5,705 4,320 8,570 25,850	60c, 055 80, 985 33, 585 27, 170 9, 45 4, 500 4, 200	44 C 48 52 5.7 29 5	2.66736 4 2 3 4 2 4 2 4	65 7 28 7 5 4 4 4 3 7 2 0 13 1 5 0	7 6 87 9 4 2 12 6 12 6 5 4 5	57 597 33 55 74 4.6	10 0 0 0 0 0 0 0 0 0 0 0 0 0 0 0 0 0 0	79 2 13 4 5 4 3 2 1 0 0.9 2 3 7 4	66 9 2 3 8.0 4 8 2 6 2 0 3 9	82
STANDARD METROPOL ITAN AREAS																		
BATON ROUGE Total	11,010	E/ 014	-0.000	50.000								1						
Dad not work in 1949 Worked in 1949 1 to 13 weeks 14 to 25 weeks 27 to 39 weeks 40 to 49 weeks 50 to .2 weeks Work in 1949 not reported	45,020 61,735 0,005 6,110 5 140 5,965 38,5 5 6,255	54,915 10,035 42,080 3,065 3,325 3,040 4,110 28,540 2,600	28,095 34,985 19,652 2,940 2,785 2,100 1,855 9,975 3,452	58,670 5,685 52,780 2,205 3,980 4,270 5,255 5,700 2,405	1,725 37,995 1,130 2,455 2,640 3,840 27,925 4,630	17,460 1,30° 4,78; 1,07. 1,07. 1,600 1,600 1,600 7,14; 7,500	54, 40 41, 335 8, 955 3, 800 2, 30 80 710 1, 445 3, 85c	10,505 8,250 4,085 1,930 870 400 270 e.5 -,170	40,637 33,085 4,870 1,873 1 260 470 440 830 2,680	54 6 5.3 5 4 4 5 2 3 34 1	18 3 76 6 5 5 5 5 5 5 5 5 5 5 5 5 5 5 5 5 5		6.3 7 6 8 7 7 9 6 6 6 6 6 6 6 6 6 6 6 6 6 6 6 6 6	100 0 4 3 9_ 8 2 7 5 9 6 4 9 3 67 4 3 9	150 0 84 7 6 1 8 7 9 3 8 1 52 4 4 4	16 2 7 3.9 1 0 1 3 2 7	6. 1 30 2 14 3 6 4 3 0 2 0 4 6 8 7	3.
NEW CRLCANS														1		i	- 3	
Total Dist not work in 1949 Norked in 1949 1 to 13 weeks 14 to 26 weeks 27 to 39 weeks 40 to 49 weeks 50 to 52 weeks Work in 1949 not reported	214,605 272,555 272,555 29,795 25,345 23,190 20,00 178,905 24,445	238,C50 42,975 182,900 8,580 14,115 14,250 17,550 128,405 12,175	273 555 171,630 8°,055 11 215 11,2.0 8,940 7,760 50,510 12,270	2°-,165 -0,580 244,125 9,590 1° 920 19,430 27,265 1°3,220 10,460	187,890 7,760 172,785 5,210 11,045 12,720 16,655 126,545 7,345	83,275 8,620 71,.40 4,38° 6,975 6,70. 0,010 40,075 3,115	2,045 5,695	5,160 -5,2.5 10,1.5 3,70 2,470 1,020 895 1,860 4,830	190,280 -02,810 -0,010 -6,8-5 -,25- 2,240 1 150 3,83> 9,157	53 3 3 9 5 0 4 5 4 9	100 0 18 1 76 8 3 6 6 0 7 4 5 9	28	6005 6005 6005 6005 6005 6005 6005 6005	28 6 2 6 8 8 0 07 4 3 0	10 6 85 7 9 3 8 4 8 0	21 8 2 8 1 6 0 9 2 4	200 0 20 2 20 2 6 7 4 9 3 0 1 8 3 7 9 6	85 g 3 g 2 1 1 2 1 2 1 2 1 2 1 2 1 2 1 2 1 2 1 2
SKREVIPORT	120,980	58,635	68,345	58,850	46 200	22.6-2						100.0						

Total Dia not work in 1949 Worked in 1949 1 to 13 vicess 14 to 26 weeks 27 to 39 weeks 40 to 49 weeks 50 to 52 weeks Work in 1949 not reported	48,415 70,295 2,550 32C 6,52C 8,550 42,335 8,270	9 700 44,480 2,045 3,090 422 5,682 30,235 4 455	.8,715 25,815 3,505 4,230 3,095 2,965	4,000 00,960 2 470 4,900 5,385 7 825 40,380 3,890	1,645 41,775 1,165 2,500 5,400 5,400 29,596 2,780	22,650 2,255 19,185 1,205 2,40 2,325 2,365 10,790 1,110	44, 415 9,335 3,380 2,420 1,135 725 -,975	2,405 8,055 2,705 880 590 565 225 645 1,675	45,000 36,300 0,630 2,200 1,820 770 200 1,530 2,135	38 : 50 4 4 4 5 8 5 1 6 7 33 4	100 0 16 5 5 0 5 5 5 8 9 7 5 1 0 7 6	56 6 37 8 5 1 6 2 4 5 4 2 17 7	28 5 3 5 11 4 58 6 5 6	3 6 90 4 2 5 5 4 0 6 0 6 0	10.4 84 7 5 8 10 6 10 3 10 4	lo 1 5 3 4 2 2 0 1 2 3.4	10G 0 64 8 21 8 7 1 4 7 2 9 1 8 3 2 3 5	79

Table 75—DETAILED OCCUPATION OF THE EXPERIENCED CIVILIAN LABOR FORCE AND OF EMPLOYED PERSONS, BY SEX, FOR THE STATE, AND FOR STANDARD METROPOLITAN AREAS AND CITIES OF 100,000 OR MORE 1950

	1	Tes	27.0			alla :		tandard met	tropolitan a			
	·	14.5	416	1		Baton	Louge .			hes 0	_cens	
Detailed o cupation	atrer.	ar .	Emp.	be\c	c1v_	enced lian force	Explo	uea .	Experi	ian	Empl	oyed
	Male .	Female	4a_r	Female	Male	Fomee	Male	Female	Male	Female	Male	Penale
Total, a vests old and over	77,-02	270 .44	6-6,782	22, 145	-1 2-3	.7,598	38,961	±7 003	186, >29	84,225	174,498	80,452
Professional, technical, and kindred workers	-1 8_P	29, 9.	,262	29,_69	4,494	2,451	4 454	2,432	15 210	9,872	.4,908	9,698
coun ants and auditors ctors and actresses. splane pilots and navigators	249	538	3,54	222 lo 3 1	4-° 3 3	112	441	110	2,108 17 150 164	281	2,074 15 154 163	279
rists and art teachers	30.	23_	3.0	22.	37 20	23	37 20	23	218	147	209	141
thetes	244 1	3-	23n 58	35	18 3 2-0	ā	18	8	39	13	39	13
emats iropractors	828	130	343 38	120	174	24	238	1 5	283	79	279 15	79
ergymen illege presidents, professors, and instructors (n.e.c.)	3,_78	100	3 .82	504	174	_46	449	_45	717 479	23 152	713 475	23 148
ancers and dancing teachers	51. 884	-53	~3	-40	. 1	11	1	10	33	92	32 349	82
entists entipers etitians and nutritionists	53	25 39	880 53	24 38	6++ B	4	64	4	351 31	14	31	82 13 27
raftemen .	97	274 139	1. 883	272 135	94	30 21	93	30 21	453	73	445	120
Lors and reporters	534	267	527	26_	70	39	70	38	267	114	202	109
gineers, technical Aeroosutacsi	_0 _091	45	6,469	1	96**	7	954	7	2,417	16	2,361	14
Chemical .	2,014	23	688 1,091	22	309 258	4	308 254	4	713	7	701	6
Electrical Industrial Mechanical	249	6	24.	6	109	2	103	1	425 124	-	415	1
Metallureness and metallureness	1,318	١	-,288	5	171	1	170	-	577	3	558	2
Mming . Not elsewhere classified .	571 754	2	567 746	3	16		18 55	-	124 315	1 2	124 310 i	1 2
tertainers (n.e.c)		63	153	58	4	u	4	6	101	39	89	34
rm and home management advisors resters and conservationists	271 770	169	201	169	15	101	15	15	29	25	8 29	25
neral durectors and embalmers wyers and judges orarans	2,204	27 57	2,198	27 57	3L 287	2	29 187	1 2	973	301	±03	5
essensa and music teachers	73 -,155 975	662 925	4.076	638 908	19	104	.9 98	104	33 558	⊥92 292	33 504	190 281
stural sesentists (n.e.e.)	975	4,937	969	4,894	105	375	105	373	272	2, 235	269	2,213
rsee student professional .	22	1,029	22	1,027	1	20	1	26	14	828	14	828
tometrists teopaths	171	12	170	12	-1	1	-1	1	52	6	34	6
remnel and labor relations workers.	284	140	1,:11	144	50	26 12	50	26	185	84	184	1 63
otographers yancians and surgeons	457 2,5-2	120 163	2,838	119	86 38 175	1. 7	96 35	12 11 7	438 220	55	433 210	96 54 121
dio operators creation and group workers	408	23	396	23	18		175		1,533	±21 8	246	8
digious workers	117	200	117	59 266	16	11	1.6	11	44	35 145	42	35 143
etal and weliare work*rs except group	230 178	±,0°0 72	229	-,064 71	28	58	28	58	63	402	82	400
orts instructors and officials	514 785	159	50o	159	62 24	16	52	.6	_02 _51	36 51	102 145 136	36 51
achers (n.e.c.)	5,4/0	10,514	5, 192 536	15,451	306 47	1,078	302	1,072	139 932	3,350	915	3.425
chnicians testing.	9o5 397	139	955	132	312	35	342	41	297 129	30	286 127	344
serapusts and healers 'n.e c.)	109	73	106	72	2	8	12	6	153 56	33	150	26 33 32
ofessional technical, and kindred workers (n e.c.).	992	235	965	232	141	43	141	43	28 394	1_7	28 379	32
Farmers and farm managers	86,60.	2 077	86,380	2,043	657	42	647	42	548	26	530	28
urmers (owners and tenants)	85,87° 728	2,94_	85,656 724	2,927 36	644 23	40 2	634 13	40 2	529	27	521	27
Managers, officials, and proprietors, exc farm	64,234	10,725	w3,507	10,045	4,196	710	4,157	700	24,363	3,805	23,884	3,773
ivers and department heads store	1,252	360	1,238	139	1.5	44	114	37	647	197	639	194
yers and shippers farm products nductors railroad	411	90	410	3	33		33	S II " 15	25 88	2 47	88	2
ormen and floor management store	934	81	427	90 80	46	16	46	3	255 48	61	255	47 60
spectors, public administration. Federal public administration and postal cervice State public administration	469	23	923 465	21	161	2	10	2	515 318	9	506 31.5	8
local public administration	293	13	269 289	18	14 27	i	14	1	43 154	4	152	4 3
nagers and superintendents, building. cers, pilots pursers, and engineers, ship _ ceals & administrators (n e.c.), public administr n_	246 2,65/ 2,104	140 26	244	139	19	4	49	3	135	99	1.4	96 15
icals & administrators (n e.c.), public administr n. Federal public administration and postal service	718	298 39	2 C87	297	_86	31	182	31	756	_6 79	4,390 698	15 79 31
Federal public administration and postal service State public administration Local public administration	468 918	42 197	46 ₋ 913	297 58 42 197	44 89 53 96 7	14	87	14	130	31	369	31.
Schale lodge society union, etc	261	25	25.	25	28	12	52 28	2	130	15	230 126	44 15 14
rchasing agents and buyers (n e c.)	684	52	671	347	7	7 7	52	2 7	28 311	14 32	27	14

Table 73—DETAILFD OCCUPATION OF THE EXPERIENCED CIVILIAN LABOR FORCE AND OF EMPLOYED PERSONS, BY SEX, FOR THE STATE, AND FOR STANDARD METROPOLITAN AREAS AND CITIES OF 100,000 OR MORE 1950—Con.

		7 . 5	3°C			deter		out metro	C. *40 6744	Nat Jr.		
Detailed occupation	Exre-	ian	Es-Lo	ved	Exper- d_Vi- labo.	er.oed	Repla	700	Expert oi'i.	er_ed	Parp.o.	yed
	Ma_e	Female	Male	Pena.o	Ma	FETTALE	Ma_e	Ferale	Mele	"eng."	Maue	Pen.Le
Managers, officials & proprietors, ecc. farm—Con. Managers officials, & proprietors (n.e.)—salaried. Constitucion. Manufacturing.— Transportation Telecommunications, & utilities & sanitary services Wholessel intel®	2_ 455 1,778 4 147 1,604 925 2 475	3,10, 21 183 4° 7d 10'	23,216 1,429 4,48 498 923 4,455	-,067 182 6 .8	75 17 317 54 66 120	266	1,73/ 183 313 54 66	267 9 5 5	9, 220 481 ,538 740 292 265	1,227 35: 23: 4- 64	8,902 /02 1 522 905 299 248	1 210 7 84 22 41 64
Retail stade Food and daary products stores, and malk retailing General merchanicles and five and ten cent stores. Furniture home furnaling and equipment stores Motor valueles and accessories retailing Gescoims serves stations. Hardware, farm implements, & bidg material retail Other retail stade	7 191 1 390 789 346 446 955 703 969 913	1,438 3.2 18° 2°3 15 12 407 41 203	1,373 8/ 34, 4/3 46, 688 930 610	425 360 184 203 50 15 .2 404 4_ 207	29 29 83 66 61 99	22 22 25 7 2 2 36 4 18	5081 3 65 3 29 82 63 64 49	22 22 25 6 2 36 4	2,339 4/3 22, 62 152 278 150 443 166 342	5°2 1°0° 73 6 25 6 3 128 14	2,339 454 284 162 -52 2°6 7 42/ 163 335	494 106 72 66 23 6 3 126 14
Banking and other finance Insurance and real estate Business survivos. Automobile replan services and garages Hissoliancour repar services Fersonia services All other mulutines (incl out reported)	1,459 220 220 290 85 527 2,137	202 556	7, 455 948 202 297 85 521 2 107	233 139 13 9 28 646	88 .4 15 40 51 126	1.0 2 21 -5	88 2- 15 50 50	1 1 19 45	507 5 -00 33 213 637	42 65 20 2 137 2	305 134 19 33 209	135 239
Managers officials & propre ("n.e.o")—self-employed Construction, Manufacturing - Transportation - Transportation - Treicommunications, & utilities & sanitary services Wholesale trade	31 C=0 2,400 2,21 738 38 2 172	131 36 2 89	30,810 2,356 2 204 722 37 2,4-3	361	1 8 8 266 8 40 5 99	325 1	1,839 264 63 39 5	325 1 7	10,781 982 7/6 348 2 1,099	2 005 20 14	742 742 730 2 1,078	. 998 64 43
Retail trade Food and dary products stores and milk rotating General merchanding and five and true out stores Furnature forms furnishing and equipment stores Motor vehicles and accessores retailing. Gasoline service stations. Bardware farm implement & bidg material retail Other retail trade	-8 636 6,776 987 530 795 905 1,627 3,456 1,073 2,498	20 55 1,56	28 511 6,729 978 29 794 908 1,627 3,399 1,069 2,488	5,046 1,048 284 67 20 56 1,564 57	1,007 34,3 34 22 59 59 -22 -97 74,	271 97, 10 10 4 10-	1,362 940 34 82 59 102 190 74	271 97 20 .0 /. 1 1 7 10-	5 778 2,014 133 206 25_ 212 369 1,468 301 824	654 38 86 29 5 465 20 20	5,712 1,987 132 205 250 212 366 1 439 302 619	1,577 651 86 19 463 25 193
Bankung and other finance Insurance and real ostate Business services. Austomobile reports environs and garages. Austomobile reports services Personal Services Austomobile reports services All other midstrates (mel not reported)	348 547 287 640 472 1,233 -,326	24 492	346 547 284 647 471 1,225 1,317	8	20 44 32 37 23 71 56	20 8	20 24 3. 3.7 28 71 56	3 ,4 2 1 1 20 6	163 242 155 225 237 507 301	7 34 24 199 56	163 242 153 22/ 237 503 298	32 26 14 195 56
Clencal and kundred workers Agenth (i.e. of Attendants and assistants, library Attendants and dentaris office. Beat Stalies Booklespers Contains, Manual and account Deptholers and destrees white Express messengers and railway, and clerks.	36,397 1 513 56 27 44 42 3 737 8 9 51 237 128	207 133 409 3 256 6,134 3,505	35,37/ 1,880 55 26 43 423 3,7-4 795 -94 23/ 12c	400	2,442 135 13 1 26 245 55 48 9	5, 375 21 33 27 63 326 11 9	2 -05 1:2 -2 1 26 241 24 46 9	5,007 10 21 33 27 62- 3.7 11 9	18,558 401 24 12 174 1,349 486 270 142 94	2 937 1.2 32 177 3 69 1 890 1 674 39 6	17,855 782 23 12 3 173 1,29- 48 260 140	23,419 113 172 173 65 1,850 1,590
Mail carness Massengers and office boys Other mashine operators Shipping and recovering elect some contracts. The contract of the contracts. The contracts of the contracts. The contracts are contracts. The contracts operators. The contract of the contracts of the contract of t	1,901 58: 31. 2,55: 1,36: 13: 38: 26: 91: -9,96:	7 1 299 146 18 670 1 138 4 148 5 135	1,872 310 2,473 1,313 117 376 264 910 19,370	1,27° 143 18 40° 7 136 4,473	145 39 30 151 96 5 16 48 34	2 116 2,090 5 296 10 1 467	145 38 32 151 94 5 16 68 33 1 298	2 6 11? 14 2,762 5 292 9	223 1,387 808 72 -15 81 -74 1.,017	9,250 2 66 1,900	663 388 219 1,335 770 60 110 70 373 10,605	1,000 81 9,090 61 1,856 7,333
Sales workers Advartung agents and salesmen Auericoners Demonstrators Hutsaters and opedilers Lauracie agents and brokers. Lauracie agents and brokers. Soule and bond salesmen Soule and bond salesmen Manufocturing Whoseast trade.	36,72 6 3 58 4 19 1,22 1,33 7 99,17 2,98 6 09 18,80	5 122 57 55 77 55 547 55 44 56 245 9 8 9 19,743	6,00	1 55 7 7 3 109 5 52 6 539 5 43 1 241 1 6 8 9 19 237 1 188 9 19 237	2 508 29 20 20 329 108 4,924 1.83 367 1,307	77 39 4 16 1,275 27 1,229	1,874 81 359 1,270	1,254 10 14 2,206	13 720 1 N 23 7 409 1 83e 422 526 43 10,21/ 1,459 2,709 5,488	23 4 68 20 249 18 130 4 7,041 91 1221	13 234 160 22 6 384 1 797 467 517, 41 9,900 1,430 2,656 5,285 525	7 27 2 6 1 24 1 1 22 6,77 8 11 6,36

Table 73.—DETAILED OCCUPATION OF THE EXPERIENCED CIVILIAN LABOR FORCE AND OF EMPLOYED PERSONS, BY SEX, FOR THE STATE, AND FOR STANDARD METROPOLITAN AREAS AND CITIES OF 100,000 OR MORE 1950—Con.

Detailed occupation	The State				Standard metropolitan areas: Baton Rouge				Standard metropolitan areas: New Orleans			
	Experienced civilian labor force		Employed		Experienced civilian labor force		Employed		Experienced civilian labor force		Employed	
	Male	Female	Male	Female	Male	Female	Male	Female	Male	Female	Male	Female
Operatives and kindred workers	1[illegible]	2[illegible],273	1[illegible]	20,2[illegible]	8,[illegible]73	[illegible]	[illegible]	[illegible],042	32,2[illegible]4	[illegible]	29,792	10,[illegible]
Apprentices	1,131	29	1 055	29	[illegible]58	3	14	3	[illegible]	[illegible]	49[illegible]	[illegible]
Auto mechanics	49	[illegible]	40	1	[illegible]	1	[illegible]		23		23	
Bricklayers and masons	78		[illegible]		18		[illegible]		29		2[illegible]	
Carpenters	[illegible]43		[illegible]		[illegible]5		[illegible]2		[illegible]		4[illegible]	
Electricians	12[illegible]		[illegible]15		24		21		60		54	
Machinists and toolmakers	84	[illegible]	[illegible]2	[illegible]	4		[illegible]		73	[illegible]	52	1
Mechanics, except auto	67	6	[illegible]2	[illegible]	4	1	4		32	2	29	2
Plumbers and pipe fitters	1[illegible]	4	[illegible]02	4	22		20		5[illegible]	[illegible]	48	2
Building trades (n.e.c.)	81		[illegible]		[illegible]2		[illegible]		42		36	
Metalworking trades (n.e.c.)	85		79		1		[illegible]		53		50	
Printing trades	106	4	103	4	[illegible]9		19		[illegible]		48	
Other specified trades	92	9	88	9	[illegible]		7		44		41	
Trade not specified	109	4	10[illegible]	4	16	1	1[illegible]	1	46		[illegible]5	[illegible]
Asbestos and insulation workers	340	6	321	[illegible]	88		80		[illegible]4	1	96	1
Attendants, auto service and parking	4,075	81	[illegible],88[illegible]	[illegible]	35[illegible]	1[illegible]	326	10	[illegible]	[illegible]	938	8
Blasters and powdermen	[illegible]		4[illegible]0		2		2		[illegible]0		9	
Boatmen, canalmen, and lock keepers	[illegible]83	4	752	4	8		8		[illegible]31		12[illegible]	
Brakemen, railroad	918	1	8[illegible]	1	[illegible]		[illegible]		189		[illegible]79	
Bus drivers	3,238	[illegible]8[illegible]	[illegible],212	188	[illegible]72	42	1[illegible]0	42	[illegible],0[illegible]	9	99[illegible]	9
Chainmen, rodmen, and axmen, surveying	373	[illegible]	3[illegible]2	3	2[illegible]		23		[illegible]	1	60	1
Conductors, bus and street railway	206	[illegible]	206	1					20[illegible]		202	
Deliverymen and routemen	5,[illegible]48	11[illegible]	5 419	[illegible]09	[illegible]	[illegible]3	[illegible]	12	[illegible]	[illegible]2	[illegible],830	[illegible]
Dressmakers and seamstresses, except factory	[illegible]4	2,572	52	2,504	9	[illegible]0	8	149	2[illegible]	1 242	23	1,1[illegible]
Dyers	22	[illegible]	21	9	[illegible]		1		[illegible]	[illegible]	[illegible]4	7
Filers, grinders, and polishers, metal	48[illegible]	3	[illegible]37	3	[illegible]7		17		93	2	88	2
Fruit, nut, & vegetable graders & packers, exc factory	243	[illegible]5	229	50	[illegible]		[illegible]		95	24	84	21
Furnacemen, smeltermen, and pourers	94	3	90	3	11		[illegible]0		56	2	53	2
Heaters, metal	1[illegible]	2	[illegible]4	2					5		5	
Laundry and dry cleaning operatives	2,[illegible]62	5,[illegible]39	2,627	[illegible],3[illegible]3	192	603	183	589	[illegible]	1 814	950	1,724
Meat cutters, except slaughter and packing house	2,1[illegible]5	3[illegible]	2,07[illegible]	39	115	1	[illegible]5	1	705	[illegible]	[illegible]78	21
Milliners	4	[illegible]3	4	73		1		1	1	[illegible]	1	43
Mine operatives and laborers (n.e.c.)	12,[illegible]17	[illegible]	11,9[illegible]	89	135	6	129	5	739	10	702	7
Coal mining	28	1	24	1					[illegible]3		10	
Crude petroleum and natural gas extraction	[illegible]1,315	[illegible]3	10 814	41	111	3	[illegible]0[illegible]	2	[illegible]9	2	[illegible]37	1
Mining and quarrying, except fuel	1,[illegible]74	51	[illegible],[illegible]39	47	24	3	23	3	5[illegible]	8	55	6
Motormen, mine, factory, logging camp, etc	[illegible]25		121		1		1		20		19	
Motormen, street, subway, and elevated railway	389	1	387						[illegible]	1	223	
Oilers and greasers, except auto	1,557	[illegible]1	1,45[illegible]	8	44		42		434	4	390	[illegible]
Painters, except construction and maintenance	854	35	818	33	[illegible]8	2	[illegible]	2	32[illegible]	[illegible]7	298	1[illegible]
Photographic process workers	14[illegible]	[illegible]79	[illegible]42	174	[illegible]	6	1[illegible]	[illegible]	8[illegible]	130	[illegible]9	127
Power station operators	239	9	237	9	22	1	22		56	4	56	[illegible]
Sailors and deck hands	3 058	22	2,356	20	41	3	36	3	1 946	14	[illegible],346	12
Sawyers	[illegible],918	29	1,832	29	37		34		135	[illegible]0	127	10
Spinners, textile	34	76	32	73	2		2		18	6	16	73
Stationary firemen	1,994	17	1 918	15	84	1	82	[illegible]	489	8	460	8
Switchmen, railroad	946	4	934	4	48		[illegible]		532	3	524	3
Taxicab drivers and chauffeurs	4,[illegible]33	51	4,163	51	[illegible]72	1	160	1	2 [illegible]78	2[illegible]	2,374	21
Truck and tractor drivers	24,9[illegible]1	16[illegible]	23,7[illegible]5	[illegible]5[illegible]	[illegible],342	14	[illegible],267	14	6,285	40	5,870	36
Weavers, textile	42	152	40	14[illegible]		1		1	29	143	29	[illegible]37
Welders and flame-cutters	4,032	22	3,72[illegible]	20	384	4	357	3	[illegible],044	9	720	8
Operatives and kindred workers (n.e.c.)	[illegible]7,576	11 660	35,812	10,968	3 965	205	3 877	199	[illegible]0,143	7,317	9,529	6,841
Manufacturing	27,975	9,967	26,79[illegible]	9,309	3 430	117	3,378	1[illegible]3	[illegible],61[illegible]	6,366	[illegible],215	5,948
Durable goods	8,306	[illegible]31	7,905	693	243	13	230	11	2,316	[illegible]58	2,149	430
Sawmills, planing mills, & misc. wood products	4,220	226	4,037	210	54	2	48	1	361	102	330	93
Sawmills, planing mills, and mill work	3,652	83	3,512	[illegible]8	51	2	[illegible]6	1	217	28	206	26
Miscellaneous wood products	568	143	525	132	3		2		144	74	124	67
Furniture and fixtures	496	168	462	160	13	4	11	[illegible]	258	81	235	74
Stone, clay, and glass products	1,203	24	1,172	23	43	[illegible]	42	2	417	16	399	1[illegible]
Glass and glass products	519	6	513	5	9	1	8	1	40	3	35	2
Cement, & concrete, gypsum, & plaster products	275		262		20		26		87		82	
Structural clay products	103	7	[illegible]00	7	8		8		2[illegible]	5	2[illegible]	6
Pottery and related products	42	3	41	3		1		1	38		37	
Misc. nonmetallic mineral & stone products	264	8	256	8					228	7	221	
Metal industries	1,0[illegible]7	179	971	[illegible]76	102		[illegible]00		60[illegible]	171	573	168
Primary metal industries	322	5	302	5	59		58		124	2	1[illegible]4	2
Blast furnaces, steel works, & rolling mills	33	[illegible]	31	1	3		2		13	1	[illegible]3	1
Other primary iron and steel industries	208	3	[illegible]94	3	8		8		103	1	95	1
Primary nonferrous industries	81	1	77	1	48		48		8		6	
Fabricated metal ind. (incl. not spec. metal)	695	174	609	171	[illegible]3		42		[illegible]6	169	459	[illegible]66
Fabricated steel products	6[illegible]8	167	596	[illegible]64	31		31		[illegible]42	163	428	160
Fabricated nonferrous metal products	59	7	56	7	8		7		26	6	24	6
Not specified metal industries	18		17		4		4		8		7	
Machinery, except electrical	430	1[illegible]	401	14	6		6		[illegible]33	9	11[illegible]	9
Agricultural machinery and tractors	44	[illegible]	44	[illegible]	1		[illegible]		5	[illegible]	5	1
Office and store machines and devices	[illegible]		4		[illegible]		1		[illegible]		1	
Miscellaneous machinery	382	13	3[illegible]3	1[illegible]	4		4		127	8	111	8
Electrical machinery, equipment, and supplies	[illegible]2	5	39	3	6		6		20	5	18	3
Transportation equipment	[illegible]1[illegible]	17	456	[illegible]	2		2		3[illegible]	14	289	12
Motor vehicles and motor vehicle equipment	72	5	67	5	[illegible]		[illegible]		24	3	21	3
Aircraft and parts	[illegible]	1	4	1					2		1	
Ship and boat building and repairing	427	11	3[illegible]4	9					299	[illegible]1	2[illegible]1	[illegible]
Railroad & misc. transportation equipment	[illegible]1		11		1		[illegible]		[illegible]		6	
Professional & photographic equip., & watches	51	19	49	17	5	[illegible]	[illegible]	1	29	1[illegible]	27	15
Professional equipment and supplies	36	1[illegible]	35	16	3		3		24	15	23	15
Photographic equipment and supplies	4	[illegible]	[illegible]	[illegible]	1	1	1	1	1		1	
Watches, clocks, & clockwork-operated devices	11	2	[illegible]0		1		1		[illegible]	[illegible]	3	
Miscellaneous manufacturing industries	331	79	318	75	10	4	10	3	167	44	161	41

Table 73.—DETAILED OCCUPATION OF THE EXPERIENCED CIVILIAN LABOR FORCE AND OF EMPLOYED PERSONS, BY SEX, FOR THE STATE, AND FOR STANDARD METROPOLITAN AREAS AND CITIES OF 100,000 OR MORE 1950—Con

Detailed occupation	The State				Standard metropolitan areas: Baton Rouge				Standard metropolitan areas: New Orleans			
	Experienced civilian labor force		Employed		Experienced civilian labor force		Employed		Experienced civilian labor force		Employed	
	Male	Female	Male	Female	Male	Female	Male	Female	Male	Female	Male	Female
Operatives and kindred workers—Con												
Operatives and kindred workers (n.e.c.)—Con												
Manufacturing—Con												
Nondurable goods	19,524	9,472	18,750	8,818	3,180	102	3,141	100	4,261	5,859	[illegible]	5,474
Food and kindred products	[illegible]	3,323	5,324	3,024	182	79	171	77	2,059	4,679	1,913	1,515
Meat products	643	184	6[illegible]	175	15	2	15	2	259	121	246	113
Dairy products	360	86	344	74	25	3	25	3	115	55	111	49
Canning & preserving fruits veget & sea foods	[illegible]	[illegible]	640	1,[illegible]7	2	7	2	6	164	706	135	619
Grain mill products	544	94	457	83	17	5	13	5	52	11	45	9
Bakery products	482	252	458	242	67	35	64	35	189	158	177	151
Confectionery and related products	83	242	79	224	2	5	2	5	60	205	58	189
Beverage industries	927	83	877	73	36	11	33	11	665	38	627	30
Misc food preparations and kindred products	2,025	499	1,825	466	18	10	17	9	523	329	484	303
Not specified food industries	37	63	35	59		1		1	32	56	30	52
Tobacco manufactures	47	652	45	610	1	.	1		41	557	39	515
Textile mill products	564	579	340	486	4	1	4	1	298	496	282	475
Knitting mills	28	227	25	220					21	224	19	217
Dyeing and finishing textiles, exc. knit goods	6	4	5	4	.				4	7	3	4
Carpets, rugs, and other floor coverings	2	3	2	3	1		1			3		3
Yarn, thread and fabric mills	274	245	257	232	3	1	3	1	246	239	235	228
Miscellaneous textile mill products	57	30	51	27					27	26	25	23
Apparel and other fabricated textile products	[illegible]	3,334	486	3,184	3	3	3	3	446	2,836	419	2,698
Apparel and accessories	289	2,772	274	2,655		1		1	252	2,316	238	2,211
Miscellaneous fabricated textile products	225	564	212	529	3	2	3	2	194	520	181	487
Paper and allied products	5,102	1,075	5,028	1,054	3	.	2		795	192	779	181
Pulp, paper and paperboard mills	4,135	384	4,080	378	2		1		669	42	662	41
Paperboard containers and boxes	46[illegible]	239	456	231	.		1		114	119	105	113
Miscellaneous paper and pulp products	500	452	492	445			.		12	31	12	27
Printing publishing and allied industries	176	74	165	69	13	8	11	8	100	36	93	32
Chemicals and allied products	3,243	143	3,173	133	1,070	4	1,067	4	255	33	247	29
Synthetic fibers	7		7								.	
Drugs and medicines	28	54	27	49	1		1		5	10	5	8
Paints varnishes and related products	66	9	65	9	2		2		54	5	54	5
Miscellaneous chemicals and allied products	3,142	80	3,074	75	1,067	4	1,064	4	196	18	188	16
Petroleum and coal products	4,010	30	3,945	29	1,860	6	1,839	6	231	7	224	7
Petroleum refining	3,829	28	3,768	27	1,860	6	1,839	6	100	5	97	5
Miscellaneous petroleum and coal products	181	2	177	2					131	2	127	2
Rubber products	218	11	214	11	45		42		11	9	10	9
Leather and leather products	32	19	30	18	1	1	1	1	25	14	24	13
Leather tanned curried, and finished	8		7		1		1		6		6	
Footwear, except rubber	8	11	8	11		1		1	6	7	6	7
Leather products, except footwear	16	8	15	7		.	.		13	7	12	6
Not specified manufacturing industries	147	64	139	58	7	2	7	2	39	49	35	44
Nonmanufacturing industries (incl not reported)	9,601	1,693	9,018	1,599	535	88	499	86	3,527	951	3,314	893
Construction	1,562	18	1,405	16	125	2	112	1	371	10	335	9
Railroads and railway express service	1,143	14	1,115	14	40	1	40	1	422	7	407	7
Transportation, except railroad	814	75	779	70	29	1	27	1	401	42	382	40
Telecommunications, & utilities & sanitary services	974	18	936	16	55	1	49	1	303	7	298	5
Wholesale and retail trade	2,645	1,064	2,517	1,000	140	44	135	44	1,271	709	1,194	661
Business and repair services	904	53	871	52	74	4	70	4	284	19	273	19
Personal services	126	183	119	177	8	15	8	14	50	72	45	70
Public administration	418	33	405	31	11	9	11	9	165	10	159	9
All other industries (incl not reported)	1,015	235	871	223	53	11	47	11	262	75	221	73
Private household workers	1,496	44,406	1,416	42,257	92	3,662	88	3,500	521	12,402	488	11,634
Housekeepers private household	115	2,160	99	2,083	4	41	3	41	30	463	27	437
Living in	1	223	-	225	1	8	1	8		70	.	70
Living out	114	1,937	98	1,860	3	33	2	33	30	393	27	367
Laundresses private household	82	4,087	77	3,956	7	232	7	223	16	1,095	15	1,033
Living in		9		9	.					4		4
Living out	82	4,078	77	3,947	7	222	7	223	16	1,091	15	1,029
Private household workers (n.e.c.)	1,299	38,159	1,240	36,218	81	3,389	78	3,236	475	10,844	446	10,164
Living in	66	855	66	855	3	30	3	30	34	454	34	454
Living out	1,233	37,304	1,174	35,363	78	3,359	75	3,206	441	10,390	412	9,710
Service workers, except private household	38,580	34,931	36,694	33,523	2,985	2,547	2,838	2,440	17,743	12,239	16,538	11,505
Attendants hospital and other institution	1,047	1,470	1,009	1,443	39	70	38	70	480	689	461	672
Attendants, professional and personal service (n e c.)	289	937	282	898	30	105	30	103	100	476	96	451
Attendants recreation and amusement	1,039	135	977	135	40	9	38	9	597	28	557	28
Barbers beauticians, and manicurists	2,987	2,872	2,962	2,832	203	224	202	222	1,061	1,082	1,046	1,056
Bartenders	3,353	269	3,154	260	148	17	135	15	1,516	77	1,384	73
Boarding and lodging house keepers	94	310	94	308	5	14	5	14	48	146	48	145
Bootblacks	371	9	341	9	31	1	25	1	111	3	98	3
Charwomen and cleaners	359	781	341	64	29	47	27	47	150	375	140	362
Cooks except private household	2,758	6,483	2,531	6,243	211	383	194	364	1,182	1,233	1,091	1,138
Counter and fountain workers	269	374	249	361	37	23	36	23	125	201	114	192
Elevator operators	547	402	519	375	19	38	19	38	408	241	386	225
Firemen fire protection	1,655	5	1,644	5	175	1	173	1	887	7	878	4
Guards watchmen and doorkeepers	3,774	53	3,567	51	234	7	223	7	1,752	29	1,625	27
Housekeepers and stewards except private household	370	1,015	323	1,303	9	104	9	104	305	472	263	462
Janitors and sextons	4,294	754	4,170	738	584	66	559	64	835	340	807	332
Marshals and constables	207	7	204	4	2		2		23	2	23	2
Midwives	7	75	3	70		3		7	2	7	2	7
Policemen and detectives	2,374	14	2,349	13	171		169		1,245	11	1,230	10
Government	2,075	10	2,061	10	153	.	152		998	7	993	7
Private	299	4	288	3	18		17		247	4	237	3
Porters	7,123	131	6,683	121	609	9	572	9	4,253	83	3,942	75
Practical nurses	93	2,620	90	2,474	12	195	11	179	19	801	18	726
Sheriffs and bailiffs	579	10	571	10	38		38		181	5	173	5
Ushers, recreation and amusement	116	61	104	59	12	8	12	8	52	8	42	7
Waiters and waitresses	2,113	8,367	1,959	7,888	165	614	157	580	1,253	2,946	1,154	2,693
Watchmen (crossing) and bridge tenders	327	14	325	14	2	2	2	2	103	2	102	2
Service workers, except private household (n e c)	2,438	7,766	2,243	7,445	82	601	162	573	1,057	2,980	958	2,808
Farm laborers and foremen	46,203	12,955	44,924	12,604	569	107	538	104	464	130	424	115
Farm foremen	556	20	549	20	9		9		8	7	5	3
Farm laborers, wage workers	32,200	5,963	31,024	5,649	511	82	481	79	385	88	353	79
Farm laborers, unpaid family workers	13,393	6,951	13,299	6,922	45	24	44	24	65	32	60	31
Farm service laborers, self-employed	54	21	52	17	4	1	4	1	5	3	6	2

Table 73.—DETAILED OCCUPATION OF THE EXPERIENCED CIVILIAN LABOR FORCE AND OF EMPLOYED PERSONS, BY SEX, FOR THE STATE, AND FOR STANDARD METROPOLITAN AREAS AND CITIES OF 100,000 OR MORE: 1950—Con.

Detailed occupation	The State				Standard metropolitan areas							
					Baton Rouge				New Orleans			
	Experienced civilian labor force		Employed		Experienced civilian labor force		Employed		Experienced civilian labor force		Employed	
	Male	Female	Male	Female	Male	Female	Male	Female	Male	Female	Male	Female
Laborers, except farm and mine	89,071	2,039	82,273	1,86[illegible]	4 954	[illegible]	4,[illegible]1	[illegible]	26 [illegible]	78	24 [illegible]	800
Fishermen and oystermen	7,56[illegible]	82	358	9	4	.	4	.	1 3[illegible]	9	1,[illegible]92	9
Garage laborers and car washers and greasers	1,648	64	1,540	60	130	.	126	4	364	35	327	28
Gardeners, except farm, and groundskeepers	2,412	60	2,283	58	152	3	143	3	785	19	758	17
Longshoremen and stevedores	5,351	63	4,870	58	17[illegible]	.	161		4 954	59	4,31[illegible]	54
Lumbermen, raftsmen, and wood choppers	6,[illegible]	50	5,800	6	34		29		37	3	34	3
Teamsters	994	3	948	3	101		101		65	-	73	1
Laborers (n.e.c.)	65,060	1,71[illegible]	59 472	1,577	4,287	7	4 123	7	19 016	757	17,296	688
Manufacturing	22,025	729	21 004	640	1 72[illegible]	4	1 647	14	[illegible]	325	5,099	319
Durable goods	10,772	198	10,079	177	3[illegible]4	2	250	2	1,937	94	1,745	83
Sawmills, planing mills, & misc. wood products	7,902	114	7,460	91	1	1	53	1	446	19	427	16
Sawmills, planing mills, and mill work	7 299	65	6,896	58	58	1	50	1	318	8	295	6
Miscellaneous wood products	603	39	564	33	3		3		128	11	[illegible]	10
Furniture and fixtures	213	20	199	24	1		1		123	21	122	19
Stone, clay, and glass products	869	8	821	6	56		50		345	5	329	3
Glass and glass products	130	1	128	1	.				3	-	3	
Cement, & concrete, gypsum, & plaster prod	257	4	238	4	45		40		131	3	123	3
Structural clay products	201	1	241	1	13		1		13	.	12	
Pottery and related products	4	.	4		-			-	4		4	.
Misc. nonmetallic mineral & stone products	217	2	207		..		.		194	2	187	.
Metal industries	76[illegible]	42	714	42	189	.	179	.	367	39	345	39
Primary metal industries	371	3	35[illegible]	3	135	.	122		113	1	109	1
Blast furnaces, steel works, & rolling mills	35	-	37		-		1		18	-	18	.
Other primary iron and steel industries	17[illegible]	3	164	3	8		8	.	87	1	84	1
Primary nonferrous industries	165	.	156		126		123		8	.	7	.
Fabricated metal ind. (incl. not spec. metal)	395	39	360	39	54		47		254	38	236	38
Fabricated steel products	313	38	287	38	27		22		217	37	205	37
Fabricated nonferrous metal products	78	1	70	-	27		25	.	34	1	29	1
Not specified metal industries	4	.	3		.				3	.	2	
Machinery, except electrical	129	2	117	1	1	.	1	1	41	1	33	
Agricultural machinery and tractors	16		16						4		2	
Office and store machines and devices			.		..			.		.		
Miscellaneous machinery	113	2	101	1	1		1	1	39	1	31	
Electrical machinery, equipment, and supplies	31	7	25	6	2		2		15	2	14	1
Transportation equipment	764	4	653	3	.				556	4	470	3
Motor vehicles and motor vehicle equipment	18	.	18		.				5		5	
Aircraft and parts	3		2		.				2		1	
Ship and boat building and repairing	735	4	627	3	-				548	4	463	3
Railroad & misc. transportation equipment	8		6		.			.	1		1	
Professional & photographic equip. & watches	5		5		2		2		1		1	.
Professional equipment and supplies	3	.	3		2		2					-
Photographic equipment and supplies	1	..	-						.	.	.	
Watches, clocks & clockwork-operated devices	1		1		.	.			-		1	
Miscellaneous manufacturing industries	93	5	85	4	2		2		33	3	29	2
Nondurable goods	11 760	525	10,848	479	1,402	15	1 35[illegible]	12	3 529	257	3 322	234
Food and kindred products	4,622	253	4 075	229	132	7	128	6	1,559	98	1,451	87
Meat products	207	18	192	17	7		6		103	10	97	9
Dairy products	154	8	147	7	17	3	17	2	73	2	67	2
Canning & preserving fruits, veget. & sea foods	356	108	316	98	1		1		119	40	105	35
Grain-mill products	906	8	704	7	16	.	12	.	72	.	64	
Bakery products	153	18	143	15	19	4	17	4	62	10	60	8
Confectionery and related products	15	5	14	4					12	4	11	3
Beverage industries	732	17	692	15	43		40		476	7	451	6
Misc. food preparations and kindred products	2,065	61	1 835	56	27	.	23		617	15	572	14
Not specified food industries	34	10	32	10	2		2		25	0	24	10
Tobacco manufactures	11	18	11	17					10	18	10	17
Textile mill products	237	75	218	73	2	1	2	1	186	61	170	59
Knitting mills	8	2	7	2				.	5	2	4	2
Dyeing and finishing textiles, exc. knit goods				.								
Carpets, rugs, and other floor coverings	-	1	1	1	1	1	1	1			-	.
Yarn, thread, and fabric mills	173	57	158	55		.			161	57	148	55
Miscellaneous textile mill products	55	15	52	15	1	.	1		20	2	18	2
Apparel and other fabricated textile products	97	48	90	44	1	.	1		87	40	80	36
Apparel and accessories	15	21	14	21	.			.	13	17	12	17
Miscellaneous fabricated textile products	82	27	76	23	1		1	.	74	23	68	19
Paper and allied products	2 633	60	2,523	56	2		2	.	921	15	896	13
Pulp, paper, and paperboard mills	2,342	28	2,241	26	2		2		838	7	824	6
Paperboard containers and boxes	166	20	151	18					70	8	59	7
Miscellaneous paper and pulp products	125	12	121	12	.		.		13		13	
Printing, publishing, and allied industries	52	1	49	1	2		2		29		27	
Chemicals and allied products	1,814	49	1,709	39	323	3	314	2	324	14	299	11
Synthetic fibers	3	.	2	.			.		.			..
Drugs and medicines	26	11	23	8	1	.	1		2		2	.
Paints, varnishes, and related products	37	3	37	3	2	.	2		25	1	25	1
Miscellaneous chemicals and allied products	1 748	35	1 647	28	320	3	311	2	297	13	272	10
Petroleum and coal products	2 168	15	2 063	14	901	4	876	3	406	6	382	6
Petroleum refining	1 836	12	1 742	11	901	4	876	3	113	3	100	5
Miscellaneous petroleum and coal products	332	3	321	3			-		293	3	282	[illegible]
Rubber products	114	2	111	2	37	.	37		5	1	5	1
Leather and leather products	12	4	9	4	2		2	.	2	4	2	4
Leather: tanned, curried, and finished	6	4	3	4	1		1		.	4		4
Footwear, except rubber	3	.	3		-		1		1		1	
Leather products, except footwear	3		3				.		1	.	1	
Not specified manufacturing industries	93	6	77	4	5		3		25	4	19	2
Nonmanufacturing industries (incl. not reported)	42 435	988	38,468	917	2,866	54	2,475	49	13,525	402	12,207	369
Construction	16 841	111	14 785	99	1,442	12	1,160	11	4,300	26	3 710	22
Railroads and railway express service	5,255	138	5,047	134	112	1	105	1	2,007	115	1,926	113
Transportation, except railroad	2,741	41	2,482	37	121	1	114	1	1,683	30	1,512	26
Telecommunications, & utilities & sanitary services	2,904	28	2 760	27	188	2	179	2	1,003	8	960	8
Wholesale and retail trade	6,629	265	6 201	251	541	8	508	8	2,593	113	2 439	102
Business and repair services	306	8	288	8	14		14		94	2	92	2
Personal services	2,775	163	2,536	156	156	16	150	16	246	42	227	40
Public administration	1 815	27	1 696	21	92	2	87	1	819	15	750	13
All other industries (incl. not reported)	3 171	207	2,613	184	200	12	169	9	780	51	601	43
Occupation not reported	15 650	6 052	8 280	3,889	973	359	426	204	3 272	1,361	1,674	835

Table 73.—DETAILED OCCUPATION OF THE EXPERIENCED CIVILIAN LABOR FORCE AND OF EMPLOYED PERSONS, BY SEX, FOR THE STATE, AND FOR STANDARD METROPOLITAN AREAS AND CITIES OF 100,000 OR MORE: 1950—Con.

Detailed occupation	Standard metropolitan areas—Con. Shreveport: Experienced civilian labor force		Employed		Cities: Baton Rouge: Experienced civilian labor force		Employed		New Orleans: Experienced civilian labor force		Employed		Shreveport: Experienced civilian labor force		Employed	
	Male	Female	Male	Female	Male	Female	Male	Female	Male	Female	Male	Female	Male	Female	Male	Female
Total, 14 years old and over	46,[illegible]	[illegible]	[illegible]	[illegible]	33,768	5,304	32,03[illegible]	14,819	154,986	74,786	144,[illegible]81	71,444	34,188	19,180	33,077	18,623
Professional, technical, and kindred workers	3,9[illegible]	[illegible]	3,9[illegible]	2,446	4,104	2,[illegible]	4,066	2,131	15,099	9,777	12,827	8,675	3,533	2,198	3,504	2,160
Accountants and auditors	687	57	686	57	434	[illegible]	428	104	1,826	256	1,793	254	644	57	643	57
Actors and actresses	3	-	5	-	2		2		17	8	15	7	3	1	3	1
Airplane pilots and navigators	23		[illegible]		-			•	94	1	92	1	21		21	•
Architects	48	2	46	-	32		-		149	6	148	6	45	2	45	2
Artists and art teachers	39	23	39	23	19	20	18	20	95	140	89	137	24	21	24	21
Athletes	[illegible]		25	•	6		10		78	3	73	3	26		24	
Authors	4	4	4	4	4	9	4	8	35	12	35	12	4	4	4	4
Chemists	48	4	47	4	219	23	217	23	232	67	228	67	45	4	44	4
Chiropractors	4		4		1	1	-	1	14	3	14	2	4		4	
Clergymen	195	9	193	9	141	4	141	4	654	20	650	20	195	7	194	7
College presidents, professors, and instructors (n.e.c.)	36	21	35	21	390	106	390	106	446	142	443	140	35	21	35	21
Dancers and dancing teachers	3	9	3	8		1	-	10	32	86	31	76	3	9	3	8
Dentists	80	2	80	[illegible]	61	•	61		315	14	313	13	76	2	76	2
Designers	6	5	6	6	8	4	8	4	29	25	29	24	6	6	6	6
Dietitians and nutritionists	1	23	-	23	-	24	1	24	5	109	5	108	1	23	1	23
Draftsmen	154	22	146	21	92	2	91	2	370	68	366	67	143	22	143	21
Editors and reporters	56	[illegible]	56	21	68	39	68	38	242	105	238	100	55	20	55	20
Engineers, technical	7[illegible]	4	7[illegible]	4	917	5	906	5	1,956	14	1,906	12	641	2	636	2
Aeronautical	1		1						5	1	4	1	1		1	
Chemical	20	-	20	1	294	•	293	•	110	1	108	1	16	1	16	-
Civil	180	2	179	2	244	3	241	3	578	5	567	4	165	1	164	1
Electrical	103	-	101	1	105	1	99	1	352	1	343	1	85		83	•
Industrial	30		30	•	30		30		94		88		29		29	
Mechanical	125	•	124		162	1	161	1	478	3	462	2	115		114	•
Metallurgical, and metallurgists	3		3	•	6		6		6		4		3		3	•
Mining	105	•	105		18	•	18		76	1	76	1	89		89	
Not elsewhere classified	144	•	143	• •	93		92		259	2	254	2	138		137	•
Entertainers (n.e.c.)	9	4	7	4	4	6	4	6	83	36	77	31	9	4	7	4
Farm and home management advisors	4	6	4	6	10	4	10	14	4	19	4	19	3	5	3	5
Foresters and conservationists	26	2	26	2	16	1	16	1	26	2	26	2	15	-	15	1
Funeral directors and embalmers	29	2	28	2	26	2	26	2	95	5	94	5	25	-	24	1
Lawyers and judges	271	5	267	5	178	4	178	4	892	28	888	28	258	5	256	5
Librarians	1	51	1	51	19	89	19	89	31	175	31	173	1	43	1	43
Musicians and music teachers	78	105	76	105	99	77	94	76	309	276	257	256	65	94	64	94
Natural scientists (n.e.c.)	240	7	239	7	99	11	99	11	186	28	183	27	227	7	226	7
Nurses, professional	11	534	11	530	11	355	11	353	31	1,954	29	1,933	10	494	10	493
Nurses, student professional	2	109	2	108	1	24	1	24	12	826	12	826	2	108	2	107
Optometrists	26	1	25	1	10	1	10	1	43	4	42	4	24	1	24	1
Osteopaths	3		3		2		2	•	2	1	2	1	3		3	
Personnel and labor relations workers	30	10	30	9	46	26	46	26	149	72	148	[illegible]	28	8	28	7
Pharmacists	82	4	82	4	79	12	79	12	379	83	374	82	74	4	74	4
Photographers	40	10	40	10	37	11	34	11	203	52	194	51	36	10	36	10
Physicians and surgeons	250	9	249	9	167	7	167	7	1,417	113	1,415	113	232	9	231	9
Radio operators	34	1	34	1	15		15		172	6	166	6	29	1	29	1
Recreation and group workers	5	6	5	6	11	8	11	8	43	38	41	35	5	6	5	6
Religious workers	9	34	9	34	15	9	15	9	44	137	44	136	6	33	6	33
Social and welfare workers, except group	11	71	11	71	25	36	25	36	74	368	73	366	11	68	11	68
Social scientists	20	4	20	4	27	16	27	16	91	34	91	34	18	4	18	4
Sports instructors and officials	35	18	34	18	31	12	31	12	133	45	128	45	27	17	26	17
Surveyors	63	1	63	1	24	4	22	4	106	2	103	2	54		54	
Teachers (n.e.c.)	274	1,137	269	1,134	240	874	236	868	810	2,892	794	2,870	217	965	212	963
Technicians, medical and dental	58	77	58	77	41	33	40	32	264	313	254	312	52	74	52	74
Technicians, testing	35	4	33	4	278	41	276	39	76	21	74	19	29	4	27	4
Technicians (n.e.c.)	21	4	20	4	14	2	14	2	129	32	126	32	18	4	17	4
Therapists and healers (n.e.c.)	10	13	10	13	11	8	11	8	50	29	48	28	9	13	9	13
Veterinarians	12	3	12	3	14		14		23	2	23	2	9	2	9	2
Professional, technical, and kindred workers (n.e.c.)	72	14	69	13	132	42	132	42	327	108	316	107	66	12	64	11
Farmers and farm managers	1,909	217	1,904	217	59	10	51	10	254	17	239	17	86	7	84	7
Farmers (owners and tenants)	1,884	214	1,879	214	57	8	49	8	247	16	232	16	82	6	80	6
Farm managers	25	3	25	3	2	2	2	2	7	1	7	1	4	1	4	1
Managers, officials, and proprietors, exc. farm	5,779	936	5,7[illegible]0	929	3,837	607	3,806	599	20,[illegible]34	3,287	19,821	3,258	4,989	734	4,962	729
Buyers and department heads, store	118	24	117	22	113	42	112	37	564	178	557	175	112	24	111	22
Buyers and shippers, farm products	15	3	15	1	3		3		27	1	26	1	7		7	
Conductors, railroad	85	1	84	1	32		32	•	67	2	67	2	77	1	76	1
Credit men	46	5	46	5	45	16	45	16	215	41	212	41	45	5	45	5
Floormen and floor managers, store	16	3	16	3	1	3	1	3	42	55	41	54	14	3	14	3
Inspectors, public administration	54	1	54	1	43	2	43	2	442	9	435	8	50	1	50	1
Federal public administration and postal service	26		26		15		15		273	1	270	1	24		24	
State public administration	7		7		13	1	13	1	35	4	33	4	5		5	
Local public administration	21	1	21	1	15	1	15	1	134	4	132	3	21	1	21	1
Managers and superintendents, building	28	10	28	10	13	4	13	4	121	95	120	95	25	10	25	10
Officers, pilots, pursers, and engineers, ship	9		8		40	3	39	3	1,257	12	1,100	1	6	•	5	
Officials & administrators (n.e.c.), public administration	148	17	148	17	172	30	168	30	588	62	581	62	134	16	134	16
Federal public administration and postal service	77	5	77	5	40	5	39	5	317	27	313	27	71	5	71	5
State public administration	20	2	20	2	84	13	82	13	85	4	84	4	19	2	19	2
Local public administration	51	10	51	10	48	12	47	12	186	31	184	31	44	9	44	9
Officials, lodge, society, union, etc.	28	2	28	2	27	2	27	2	110	14	106	14	26	2	26	2
Postmasters	12	10	12	10	5	1	5	1	19	5	18	5	5	1	5	1
Purchasing agents and buyers (n.e.c.)	71	3	70	3	48	6	47	6	255	29	249	29	64	3	63	3

Table 73.—DETAILED OCCUPATION OF THE EXPERIENCED CIVILIAN LABOR FORCE AND OF EMPLOYED PERSONS, BY SEX, FOR THE STATE, AND FOR STANDARD METROPOLITAN AREAS AND CITIES OF 100,000 OR MORE: 1950—Con.

Detailed occupation	Standard metropolitan areas—Con.				Cities											
	Shreveport				Baton Rouge				New Orleans				Shreveport			
	Experienced civilian labor force		Employed		Experienced civilian labor force		Employed		Experienced civilian labor force		Employed		Experienced civilian labor force		Employed	
	Male	Female	Male	Female	Male	Female	Male	Female	Male	Female	Male	Female	Male	Female	Male	Female
Managers, officials, & proprietors, exc. farm—Con.																
Managers, officials, & proprietors (n.e.c.)—salaried	2,459	339	2,445	336	1,620	241	1,599	238	7,581	1,383	7,464	[illegible]	2,180	275	2,168	292
Construction	142	1	138	1	178	9	170	9	374	5	365	5	119	1	116	1
Manufacturing	372	20	369	20	280	8	276	8	1,232	72	1,219	71	309	18	306	18
Transportation	190	4	190	4	52	5	[illegible]	5	745	[illegible]	741	20	[illegible]	4	174	4
Telecommunications, & utilities & sanitary services	105	6	105	6	62	5	62	5	246	37	246	37	88	5	88	5
Wholesale trade	275	12	275	12	112	9	111	9	1,073	59	1,058	58	255	11	255	11
Retail trade	677	149	672	147	545	117	529	116	1,994	421	1,948	418	609	129	604	127
Food and dairy products stores, and milk retailing	116	20	116	20	97	13	96	13	375	86	369	85	102	14	102	14
General merchandise and five and ten cent stores	51	19	51	18	58	19	58	19	177	65	174	64	47	17	47	16
Apparel and accessories stores	41	35	41	35	32	24	32	24	149	58	149	58	39	34	39	34
Furniture, home furnishings, and equipment stores	72	7	71	7	28	7	28	6	126	21	126	19	66	7	65	7
Motor vehicles and accessories retailing	106	.	106		78	2	77	2	215	6	213	6	96	.	96	.
Gasoline service stations	57	1	55	1	58	2	55	2	121	3	118	3	44	.	42	.
Eating and drinking places	65	34	64	33	58	31	58	[illegible]	378	104	354	102	61	27	60	26
Hardware, farm implement, & bldg. material retail	56	3	56	3	46	3	46	3	142	11	141	11	51	3	51	3
Other retail trade	113	30	112	30	90	16	89	16	291	71	284	70	103	27	102	27
Banking and other finance	134	11	134	11	108	10	108	10	554	36	551	36	125	10	125	10
Insurance and real estate	96	6	96	6	85	9	85	9	430	59	428	59	90	6	90	6
Business services	19	7	19	7	13	[illegible]	13	4	116	19	115	18	15	7	15	7
Automobile repair services and garages	36	2	36	2	15	.	15	.	86	1	85	1	30	1	30	1
Miscellaneous repair services	13		13	.	9	1	9	1	28	.	28	.	13	.	13	.
Personal services	56	28	55	28	47	20	46	18	188	118	184	116	49	23	48	23
All other industries (incl. not reported)	344	93	343	92	114	44	113	44	515	231	496	228	304	80	304	79
Managers, officials, & propr's (n.e.c.)—self-employed	2,690	518	2,679	518	1,675	257	1,666	257	8,966	1,702	8,842	1,694	2,244	373	2,233	373
Construction	277	3	277	3	247	1	245	1	772	7	746	7	240	3	240	3
Manufacturing	184	15	183	15	73	6	72	6	621	54	617	54	151	13	150	13
Transportation	49	7	49	7	38		37	.	292	13	281	13	38	2	38	2
Telecommunications, & utilities & sanitary services	6	1	6	1	4		4	.	[illegible]		[illegible]		4	.	4	.
Wholesale trade	208	7	208	7	96	6	96	6	924	32	908	32	184	6	184	6
Retail trade	1,264	394	1,256	394	940	207	935	207	4,802	1,298	4,743	1,291	1,024	273	1,016	273
Food and dairy products stores and milk retailing	360	169	358	169	289	68	286	68	1,669	530	1,646	527	259	102	257	102
General merchandise and five and ten cent stores	44	16	44	16	25	8	25	8	119	78	118	78	27	9	27	9
Apparel and accessories stores	55	35	55	35	22	8	22	8	193	75	192	75	54	35	54	35
Furniture, home furnishings, and equipment stores	92	5	92	5	59	4	59	4	211	19	210	19	81	4	81	4
Motor vehicles and accessories retailing	76	1	75	1	52	1	52	1	170	4	170	4	66	1	65	1
Gasoline service stations	128	6	128	6	107	7	107	7	272	6	269	6	103	4	103	4
Eating and drinking places	198	104	193	104	181	79	179	79	1,212	396	1,186	394	159	73	154	73
Hardware, farm implement, & bldg. material retail	89	3	89	3	65	.	65	.	228	19	229	19	79	1	79	-
Other retail trade	222	55	222	55	140	32	140	32	728	171	723	169	196	44	196	44
Banking and other finance	49		49	.	19	2	19	2	145	3	145	3	46	.	46	.
Insurance and real estate	80	4	80	4	44	4	44	4	203	30	203	30	75	3	75	3
Business services	38	8	38	8	31	2	31	2	131	22	129	22	36	8	36	8
Automobile repair services and garages	63		63		33	1	33	1	186	2	185	2	51		51	.
Miscellaneous repair services	41	4	41	4	28	1	28	1	207	13	207	13	38	4	38	4
Personal services	100	52	99	52	68	19	68	19	452	181	449	181	83	42	82	42
All other industries (incl. not reported)	336	23	335	23	54	8	54	8	231	46	228	46	274	19	273	19
Clerical and kindred workers	3,368	5,242	3,334	5,183	2,233	4,783	2,197	4,715	15,978	21,148	15,337	20,677	2,947	4,847	2,914	4,792
Agents (n.e.c.)	286	22	286	22	127	10	124	10	665	102	648	101	264	18	264	18
Attendants and assistants, library	1	4	-	4	13	15	13	15	24	28	23	28	1	4	1	4
Attendants, physician's and dentist's office	3	54	3	54	3	29	2	29	11	149	11	144	3	51	3	51
Baggagemen, transportation	5		5		1		1		27	3	26	3	5	.	5	.
Bank tellers	44	38	44	38	26	25	26	25	158	55	157	55	37	35	37	35
Bookkeepers	365	670	363	662	227	591	223	584	[illegible]	[illegible]	1,122	1,582	309	594	307	586
Cashiers	91	369	90	360	51	306	49	297	403	1,479	367	1,412	86	340	85	333
Collectors, bill and account	33	15	32	14	42	9	40	9	243	35	233	34	31	13	30	12
Dispatchers and starters, vehicle	19	3	19	3	9	9	9	9	123	3	123	3	18	2	18	2
Express messengers and railway mail clerks	14		14	.	1		1	.	80	1	78	1	11	.	11	.
Mail carriers	181	6	179	6	126	1	124	1	628	7	608	7	147	2	146	2
Messengers and office boys	36	11	34	11	31	5	30	5	389	38	366	37	27	10	25	10
Office machine operators	24	112	24	109	32	114	32	113	194	887	190	871	23	108	23	105
Shipping and receiving clerks	231	21	226	21	134	13	134	13	1,213	79	1,165	76	202	20	197	20
Stenographers, typists, and secretaries	94	2,256	91	2,238	89	1,988	87	1,961	732	8,293	695	8,148	90	2,117	87	2,101
Telegraph messengers	11		11		4		4	.	68	1	56	1	11		11	.
Telegraph operators	42	10	42	9	16	5	16	5	100	57	96	56	31	9	31	8
Telephone operators	13	413	13	409	[illegible]	281	59	277	72	[illegible]	67	1,637	13	375	13	371
Ticket, station, and express agents	74	10	73	10	33	10	32	9	310	48	309	48	59	8	58	8
Clerical and kindred workers (n.e.c.)	1,801	1,228	1,784	1,213	1,209	1,372	1,191	1,353	9,357	6,589	8,997	6,433	1,579	1,141	1,562	1,126
Sales workers	3,664	1,710	3,620	1,689	2,337	1,220	2,280	1,199	11,800	6,570	11,409	6,404	3,262	1,480	3,221	1,461
Advertising agents and salesmen	44	9	44	9	27	5	25	4	153	20	145	20	42	9	42	9
Auctioneers	1	2	1	2	2	1	2	-	19	4	8	4	1	2	1	2
Demonstrators	4	8	4	7	1	6	1	6	6	62	5	59	4	8	4	7
Hucksters and peddlers	31	5	31	5	20	3	18	2	365	16	340	14	28	4	28	4
Insurance agents and brokers	405	53	399	53	311	37	308	37	1,565	227	1,530	221	375	44	369	44
Newsboys	137	2	132	2	87	4	86	4	424	16	401	16	131	2	126	2
Real estate agents and brokers	121	49	120	49	99	13	98	13	460	121	452	118	106	49	105	49
Stock and bond salesmen	17	1	17	1	4		4		41	4	39	4	16	1	16	1
Salesmen and sales clerks (n.e.c.)	2,904	1,581	2,872	1,561	1,786	1,151	1,738	1,132	8,767	6,200	8,478	5,948	2,559	1,361	2,530	1,343
Manufacturing	378	21	376	21	174	9	173	9	1,240	81	1,212	78	342	19	341	19
Wholesale trade	748	30	741	30	357	12	349	12	2,308	110	2,263	108	690	28	684	28
Retail trade	1,625	1,489	1,606	1,469	1,190	1,108	1,155	1,089	4,741	5,815	4,551	5,581	1,390	1,277	1,372	1,259
Other industries (incl. not reported)	153	41	149	41	65	22	61	22	478	194	452	181	137	37	133	37

Table 73.—DETAILED OCCUPATION OF THE EXPERIENCED CIVILIAN LABOR FORCE AND OF EMPLOYED PERSONS, BY SEX, FOR THE STATE, AND FOR STANDARD METROPOLITAN AREAS AND CITIES OF 100,000 OR MORE: 1950—Con.

Detailed occupation	Standard metropolitan areas—Con.				Cities											
	Shreveport				Baton Rouge				New Orleans				Shreveport			
	Experienced civilian labor force		Employed		Experienced civilian labor force		Employed		Experienced civilian labor force		Employed		Experienced civilian labor force		Employed	
	Male	Female	Male	Female	Male	Female	Male	Female	Male	Female	Male	Female	Male	Female	Male	Female
Craftsmen, foremen, and kindred workers	8,104	[illegible]	7,887	81	7,762	124	7,262	124	27,086	938	24,834	893	6,146	158	5,983	156
Bakers	[illegible]	14	[illegible]	4	[illegible]	10	[illegible]	10	668	66	632	59	111	11	111	11
Blacksmiths	28		[illegible]		14		[illegible]	.	87		82	.	18		16	.
Boilermakers	27	.	[illegible]		133	[illegible]	[illegible]	1	284	1	237	1	24		21	
Bookbinders	[illegible]	5	7	5	[illegible]	7	9	7	43	44	43	42	5	4	5	4
Brickmasons, stonemasons, and tile setters	[illegible]	.	[illegible]	1	243	1	226	1	551	2	510	2	125	1	122	1
Cabinetmakers	[illegible]	[illegible]	62	2	52	.	49	1	410	12	387	11	54	1	50	.
Carpenters	1,24[illegible]	7	[illegible]	7	[illegible]	2	9[illegible]2	2	3,884	21	3,409	21	888	2	856	2
Cement and concrete finishers	93	.	90		[illegible]	1	51	1	187	1	172	1	71	.	68	
Compositors and typesetters	[illegible]	10	113	10	120	[illegible]	115	10	544	36	534	35	104	9	103	9
Cranemen, derrickmen, and hoistmen	48	.	46		48	.	41	1	360	3	341	3	35	.	33	
Decorators and window dressers	[illegible]	[illegible]	39	[illegible]	43	[illegible]	40	21	138	108	133	101	38	33	37	33
Electricians	242	2	236	2	465	1	437	1	1,208	3	1,045	3	192	2	190	2
Electrotypers and stereotypers	[illegible]	1	[illegible]	1			.	.	31	1	31	1	10	1	10	1
Engravers, except photoengravers	6	1	6	1	2		2	.	30	2	28	2	6	1	6	1
Excavating, grading, and road machinery operators	9[illegible]	2	9	2	85	2	75	2	252		234		57	2	55	2
Foremen (n.e.c.)	743	22	738	[illegible]	889	19	882	19	1,923	241	1,881	240	545	20	542	19
Construction	109	.	105		85	.	82	.	228	1	217	1	74	.	71	
Manufacturing	205	12	205	11	605	7	603	7	726	134	712	133	144	11	144	10
Metal industries	18	2	18	2	25		25	.	80	2	80	2	14	2	14	2
Machinery, including electrical	20	.	20	.	3	1	3	1	24	3	23	3	15	.	15	
Transportation equipment	2	.	2	.		.	.		89	1	84	1	2	.	2	
Other durable goods	65	2	65	2	19	1	18	1	131	7	125	7	44	2	44	2
Textiles, textile products, and apparel	3	6	3	6	1		.		100	72	100	71	3	5	3	5
Other nondurable goods (incl. not specified mfg.)	97	2	97	1	557	5	557	5	302	49	300	49	66	2	66	1
Railroads and railway express service	68	1	68	1	36	.	36	.	168	1	68	1	50	1	50	1
Transportation, except railroad	40	1	40	1	17	.	17	.	149	4	144	4	33	1	33	1
Telecommunications, & utilities & sanitary services	56	2	56	2	[illegible]	.	40	.	161	1	161	1	44	2	44	2
Other industries (incl. not reported)	265	6	264	6	106	12	104	12	491	100	479	100	200	5	200	5
Forgemen and hammermen					1	.	.		10	1	8	1	.		.	
Furriers	3	2	3	2	2	1	2	1	17	8	16	6	3	2	3	2
Glaziers	21	1	21	1	8	.	8		62	1	58	1	18		18	.
Heat treaters, annealers, and temperers	.		.		.		.	.	1		1				.	.
Inspectors, scalers, and graders, log and lumber	38	2	38	2	13		11	.	59	4	52	4	34	2	34	2
Inspectors (n.e.c.)	127	2	126	2	63		60	.	460	43	450	43	97	2	96	2
Construction	11	.	10		15	.	15	.	42	.	42		10	.	9	
Railroads and railway express service	70	.	70		19		19	.	149	2	146	2	52		52	
Transport. exc. r. r., communic'n, & other public util.	22	.	22		4		4	.	96	4	93	4	16		16	
Other industries (incl. not reported)	24	2	24	2	25		22	.	173	37	169	37	19	2	19	2
Jewelers, watchmakers, goldsmiths, and silversmiths	57	1	56	1	30		29		194	8	184	5	56	1	55	1
Job setters, metal	1	.	.				.		2	.	1		1		1	
Linemen & servicemen, telegraph, telephone, & power	274	4	274	4	242	10	240	10	791	30	774	30	234	3	234	3
Locomotive engineers	122		121	.	65	2	64	2	198		195	.	95		94	
Locomotive firemen	104	1	102	1	52		47		155		150		89	1	87	1
Loom fixers	1		1	.				.	44	.	43		1	.	1	
Machinists	313	3	311	3	380	3	377	3	1,110	10	1,030	10	2[illegible]2	1	250	1
Mechanics and repairmen	1,771	22	1,743	22	1,3[illegible]9	10	1,275	10	5,591	60	5,310	55	[illegible],370	19	1,347	19
Airplane	58		58	.	5	1	5	1	79	1	75	1	46		46	
Automobile	810	5	799	5	508	3	487	3	2,197	27	2,062	24	603	4	595	4
Office machine	34		34	.	17		17		117	1	113	1	30		30	.
Radio and television	60	4	58	4	48	1	43	1	297	3	275	3	49	3	47	3
Railroad and car shop	49		49		23		23		131	2	130	2	37		37	.
Not elsewhere classified	760	13	745	13	718	5	700	5	2,770	26	2,655	24	605	12	592	12
Millers, grain, flour, feed, etc.	3	.	3	.	1	.	1		8		8	.	3	.	3	.
Millwrights	14		14	.	45	.	36		49		46		9	.	9	.
Molders, metal	31		29		4	.	4		44	1	41	1	26	.	25	.
Motion picture projectionists	31	1	31	1	22	.	22	.	75		73		23	1	23	1
Opticians, and lens grinders and polishers	20	2	20	2	11	1	11	1	83	2	80	2	20	1	20	1
Painters, construction and maintenance	663	3	636	3	474	1	429	1	2,353	21	2,015	17	538	3	517	3
Paperhangers	50	2	48	2	43	.	40		76	3	64	3	43	2	42	2
Pattern and model makers, except paper	11	2	11	2	11	.	10	.	64	2	63	2	7	2	7	2
Photoengravers and lithographers	15	1	15	1	5	.	5	.	76	2	75	2	13	1	13	.
Piano and organ tuners and repairmen	11	.	11	.	9		9		24	2	24	2	11		11	.
Plasterers	43	.	42	.	120	1	99	1	449	5	378	4	37	.	37	.
Plumbers and pipe fitters	368	3	332	3	752	4	678	4	1,124	3	1,033	3	255	3	243	3
Pressmen and plate printers, printing	41	3	40	3	38		38		155	2	152	2	38	3	37	3
Rollers and roll hands, metal	2	.	2	.	1		1	.	4		4	.	2		2	
Roofers and slaters	95	.	92	.	61	1	51	1	400	3	35[illegible]	3	78	.	76	
Shoemakers and repairers, except factory	66	4	64	4	53	1	52	1	240	6	230	5	56	4	54	4
Stationary engineers	394	1	390	1	264	1	258	1	700	2	678	2	149	1	145	1
Stone cutters and stone carvers	11	.	11	.	5		4	.	19	1	19	1	10	.	10	
Structural metal workers	60	.	58	.	98		73		296	1	258	1	38	.	36	
Tailors and tailoresses	34	10	33	10	24	9	22	9	183	139	170	133	30	8	29	8
Tinsmiths, coppersmiths, and sheet metal workers	127	1	123	1	95		90		558	3	499	3	103	1	99	1
Toolmakers, and die makers and setters	8		8		1	.	1	.	32	.	29	.	6		6	
Upholsterers	58	12	57	11	26	2	25	2	274	25	258	25	52	10	51	9
Craftsmen and kindred workers (n.e.c.)	53	.	52		107	.	105	.	328	5	311	5	44		43	
Members of the armed forces	25	.			9		.		178	2			24			

ents (n.e.o) sendants and assentants, library sendants and assentants, library sendants physicians and declint's office aggregation sendants transportation objections shares absent spectators but and account spectators and sateriers, volusie spectators and sateriers, volusie	286 2 3 5 44 365 90 33 19	22 4 54 18 670 369 -5 3	286 3 5 44 363 90 32 49	38	127 3 3 1 26 227 51 42 9	10 15 29 25 591 306 9	124 13 2 1 26 223 49 40 9	10 15 29 25 584 297 9	665 24 11 27 158 1,17- 403 243 123 80	26 149 3 55 1,6.4 1,479 35 3	648 23 11 26 157 1,122 367 233 123 78	201 28 44 3 55 1,562 1,412 34	264 1 3 3 37 309 86 31 18	35 344 340 13	264 1 3 5 37 307 65 30 18	
Il carmers. mengers and office boys mengers and office boys or machine operators organization mengerships, typust and secretaries megraph mesengers, megraph operators megraph operators het station and express agents het senten and express agents het senten and express agents het senten and meterships he	181 36 24 231 94 11 42 13 74 1,801	6 11 112 21 2,256 413 10 1,228	179 34 24 226 91 11 73 1,784	11 109 21 2,238 9 409 10	126 11 32 134 89 4 16 79 33 1,209	114 13 1,988 281 10 1,377	24 30 32 24 87 4 16 59 32 1,191	113 13 1 981 277 9	628 389 194 1,213 732 68 100 72 310 9,357	7 38 887 79 8,293 1 57 1,68 48 6,589	608 366 190 1,165 695 56 96 67 309 8,997	37 671 76 6,148 1,637 48 6,433	1 13	108 20 2,117 9 375	146 25 29 197 87 11 31 13 13 13 13	2
Sales workers	3,664	4,710	3,620	1,689	2,357	1,220	2,280		11,600		11,409	6,404	3 262		3,221	_
verusing agents and salesmes ctionness	11 405 137 12 17 2,904 378 748 1,625 153	1,581 21 30 1,489	120	2 7 5 53 2 49 1 1,561 2,30	1,786 1,786	5 1 6 3 37 4 13 1,151 9 1,108	25 2 18 308 86 98 4 173 349 -,155	1,132 9	153 19 6 365 1 565 424 460 /1 8,767 1,240 2,308 4,741	6,200 81 110	145 8 5 347 -,530 452 39 8,478 1,212 2,263 4,551	116	133 106 16 2,559	2 8 4 44 2 49 1 1,361 29 28	28 369 126 105 16 2,530 341 684 1,372	1

Table 73 —DETAILED OCCUPATION OF THE EXPERIENCED CIVILIAN LABOR FORCE AND OF EMPLOYED PERSONS, BY SEX, FOR THE STATE, AND FOR STANDARD METROPOLITAN AREAS AND CITIES OF 100,000 OR MORE 1950—Cod

	1		atan area			Da co	Dauma			hea Or	leans			Shrev	report	
Data led	Pur	S'rvi	repor.		Frace	Es-on lenced	made		Experi				Exper	Lenced		
Detailed occupation	civi	lian force	Emp. c	yed .	_ivi	iar force	Emp?	loyed	labor	ian	Emple	oyed	_abor	force	Emp!	Loyed
	Мале	₹eme_e	Ma.e	7esa_4	чь_е	Femle	Ma_e	Penale	Male	venale	Male	Female	Male	Female	Male	Fenal
Craftsmen, foremen, and kindred workers	8,104	.02	7,68~	81	^,752	1.4	7,262	.24	27,0%	938	24,834	893	6,146	128	5,983	1
akers	12,	14	£51	4	14	_0	-12	70	668 87	66	6.37 82	59 1	111	11	111	
or ermakers	27	. 5	20	5	133	+	200	1 7	43	4	237 43	42	24 5	4	21 5	
nexmasons, stonemasons and tile setters	,6C	-	50	2	240	-	22c	1	551 410	12	510 387	11	125 54	1 2	122 50	
rpenters	2,24"	. 7	- 207 Su	7	, 2	2	9_2	2	1,884 ⊥87	21 1	3,409 172	1	888 71		856 68	
mpoutors and typesetters	- 4	, 10	40	13	_20 48	12	1.5	10	544 360	36	534 34.	35	104 35	9	103	
corators and window dressers	242	3-	39	2.2 2	43	2.	40 437	21	1,238	108	133	101	38 192	33	37 190	
etrotypers and stereovypers	1-	4		1		1	2		34	1 2	3_ 28	1 2	10	1	-0	
gravers, except photoengravers	9	1	9	2	85 85	2	75	2	252	1	234		57	2	55	
remen (n.e c)	743	22	738	4-	889	.9	882 82	19	1,923	24_	1,881	240	545 74	20	542 T	
(anufacturing	205	12	405 18	1.	605 25	7	o03	7	726 80	114	71.2 80	23	144	2	144	
Machinery including electrical - Transportation equipment	20	•	20		3		3		24 89	3	23 84	3	15	:	15	
Other durable goods	65	2 6	65	2	19	1	18	1	131	7 72	122	7 71	44	2 5	3	
Textiles, textile products and apparel Other nondurable goods (incl. not spenfied m.g.) illroads and railway express service	97	2	97	1	557 36		557 36	5	302 168	19	300 68	49	66 50	2	66 50	
ansportation, except railroad	40	î	40	1	17		17	:	149	4	144 161	4	33 44	1 2	33	
decommunications & utuities & sanitary services ther industries (incl. not reported)	205	6	264	b	106	12	104	12	491	100	479	00	200	5	200	
emen and hammermen	3	2	3		2		. 2	1	10	1 8	8 16	1 6	3	2	. 3	0
treaters annealers and temperers	87	-	21	1	8	•	8		62	1	58	3	18		18	
ectors, scalers, and graders, log and umber _	38 127	2	36 126	2	13 63		11		59 460	43	52 450	43	34 97	2	34 96	
ectors (n.e.c.) onstruction allroads and railway express service	70		10	1	15		15		42	. 2	42 146	2	10 52		9 52	1
sinsport exc r r, communic'n, & other public uti	22	2	22	2	25		4 22	÷	96 173	37	93 169	37	16 19	2	16 19	
lers, watchmakers, goldsmiths, and silversmiths.	57		56	1	30		29		194	8	184	5	56	1	55	-
setters, metal men å serv:cemen, telegraph, telephone, å power	274	4	274	4	24	≟ 0	240	10	791	x	774	30	234	3	234	
motive engineers	122	1	12.	. 1	52	2	47	2	198		195 150		95 89	. 1	94 87	
m fixers	313	3	5_1	. 3	380	3	377	• 3	1,110	10	1,030	10	2-2	.:	250	
hance and repairmen.	1,771	22	1,743	22	.,37.9	10	1,275	10	5,59.	60	\$,310	55	.,370	19	1,347	
rolane	010	5	799 34	5	508	3	487	3	2,197	27 1	2,062	24	603	4	595	
dio and televimon	- 60	4	58	. 4	48	1	43	-	297	3	275	3	49	3	47 37	
ulroad and car shop ot elsewhere classified.	760	13	745	13	7.8	5	700	5	2,770	20	2,650	24	605	12	592	
ers, gram, four, feed etc	3 14		3	:	45		1 36		8		8 46		3 9	:.	3	
iers, metal	31		31	1	22	:	22		44	1	41	1	26 23		25 23	
mans, and lens granders and pohshers	663	2	20 638	2	474	1	11	4	83 2,353	2 21	2.0.5	2 17	20	3	20 517	
changers	50 11	2	48	3 2 2 1	43	:.	40		76 64	3 2	64	3 2	43	2 2	42	
oengravers and lithographers	15	ī	15	1	5	:	5		76 24	2	75 24	2	13	1	13	
berers and pape fitters	43	: 3	332	:	120 752	1	678	1 4	449	5	378 _,033		37	3	37	
smen and plate printers, printing	41	3	40	3	38	*	38	4	1,124	2	152	3 2	38	3	37	
ers and roll hands, metal.	95	•	92	:	1 61	1	51	• 1	400	3	4 35*	. 3	2 78		2 76	
makers and repairers, except factory	- 66 394	1	64 390	4	.73 264	1	52 258	1	240 700	6 2	230 678	5 2	>6 149	4	145	
e cutters and stone carvers	- 60		11 58 33	:	5 98		73	•	19 296	1	258	1	16 38	:	10	
ors and tailoresses smiths, coppersunting, and sheet metal workers imakers, and die makers and setters	34 127	10	123	10	24 95	9	22 90	9	183 558	139	170 499	133	30 103	8	36 29 99	
nolsterers	58	12!	8	11	26	. 2	25	. 2	32 274	25	29 258	25	6 52	10	6	
Itemen and kindred workers (n.e c.)	5.º 25	:	52	-1	107		105		328 178	5	311	5	44		43	

Table 73—DETAILED OCCUPATION OF THE EXPERIENCED CIVILIAN LABOR FORCE AND OF EMPLOYED PERSONS BY SEX, FOR THE STATE, AND FOR STANDARD METROPOLITAN AREAS AND CITIES OF 100,000 OR MORE 1950—Con.

(Italiard			.S				-		111						
4 2000		Sare	ep~m		-		~U**	-		1.4. 2.	- TS			E-In-	-pc	
Detailed occupation	Exp***	COPOC .	Ing.	DAL-T	2 Mill	ad V	Ls.	ge*	1.7-1. 11.	R.;	Estage	- !	A TAT	P.	Emp.	_v=i
	40	Fema.	Male	"ensie	Male	ena e	Mg (- mole	MCLC	.c.de. 6	hate F	em. o	4.0	Frms_e	Ma .e	7emale
Operatives and kindred workers	6 180	34	^ 92	447	6,75	29-	£1.	g	4. 40	300 €	23 8.0	7, 35	5 02	- 45	642	_ 32
prentices	98	9	96	9		3	1-1	3	454	-1	4.5	5	2:	9	83	-
Auto mechanics Brickiayers and masons.	_0		_0	:	2	1	, 5	-	201		يت	• .	4			
Corpenters	7				او	í	53	1	50	-1	47		9		3	rt-
Machanes and toolmakers Mechanes, except auto	4		-2		4	- 13	1		-3	1,	4-		2		. 3	
Plumbers and pipe ritters .	11	-	1.			-1	5	1	40	21	21	1	p		8	A 42.5
Building trades (n.e.c.) Metalworking trades (n.e.c.) Printing crades	10		9 9		-0	.	-01	• '	3"	• !	34			:	8	
Other spenned trades	8		5	1		1	-5		4		40		0 ~	6	9	- W
Prade not specified			1		1	+	-		40	-		-	-	•	7	
hestes and insulation workers tendants, auto service and parking	30	9	25	1	7.50	ıċ.	260	4	8.4	2	795	7	2_0	1 7		
atters and powdermen atmen, canalmen and look keepers	14				6				6	- 1	3	**	2,		10	
akemen, railroad	25	42	3,	-	67	40	2.7	.5	.47	-	202	-7	120	6	72	
sammen rodmen and axmen, surveying.	19		70		-29 ?1	20	50		521	-	54		1		1,	
nductors, bus and street ranway.	595	8	569	8	723	ń	497	٠,	800,	4-	- 73	33	528	77	012	
essmaker, and seamstresses, except factors	3 2	240		23-	8	36	7	351	15	-, *?	20	- 3¢	21	بادج	3 2	52
ers granders and poleners, metal uni, nut. & vegetable graders & packers, exc. fac-ory	27		21		.6	i	1.6		00	2	5.	2	43 3		42	
rnacemen smeltermen and pourers	3 6		1		9	i	8		43	.31	38	20	6		, 6	
aters metal	1.78	67-	169	. 6		5.13	.54	4.89	953	200	3 14	1,6_~	154	628	4	61
ent cuitere except sistighter and packing house	105	3	17	J€	109	1	-01	7.07	640	1	296	41	-8	3	48	
iliners ine operatives and aborers (n e.c.)	1,032	7	'n	, ,		5	125	4	-5.5	74	_56	41	264	7	24	
Coal mining -	1,010		45	-	98	3	931		25		6 120		254	7	235	
Mining and quarrying, except feel otormen, mine factory logging camp etc otormen, street, subway and elevated raiway	20		1	2)	3	2	-4	2	3.	5	33	3	10		9	72.
	.5.	١.	-				1		176	1	-95		140		29	
ers and greasers, excep suto	76	2			33	,	30	2	339	14	2-3	10	83	1	33	100
otographic process workers	11	5	2.		23	6	20	1	280 72	4.6	7.	172	23	3	43	1
wer station operators dors and deck hands	1 7	-1	1.	1	27	2	22	2	1,75	13	.,_37	41	6	1	3	1
awvers	85	3	8.	3	1	,			16	63	71	60	25	2		
ationary firemen	88 404	-	10:		6,	-	61	,	3.5	7	327	2	23 85	1	20	1
exican drivers and chauffeurs	209	3	20	3	1#3	13	:4-	,*	2,230	10	2,.90	1.9	238	2	1,372	
ruck and tractor drivers	1	2		. 2	1 ' 1	10000	1,C·2	1 2	5,333 26	35 95	2b	92	1 .	2		
alders and flame ou ters	288		27		3,1	2	290		683	8	892	,	1-3	1	-87	4
peratives and kindred workers (n.e c) Manufacturing	2,389	3,7	1.49	33:	3 98 2,758	177 100	2,1-3	172 97	4,954	5,352	7,368	5,776	1,781	412 293	1,726	1 2
Durable goods. Sawmils planing mills & mae wood products. Sawmils, planing mills and mill work	956	78	94		37	8	1c"	_ ^	241	35.2 65 10	1 (86	61	688	62 14		
Sawmula, planing mills and mill work Miscellancous wood products.	.42	.1			35		31		99	48	123 82	47	36	8	77	
Francisco and technique	40	41))	44	1	3	.D	3	357	~9	22-	~3 13	1 .6	34	33:	
Stone clay, and glass products. Grass and glass products	-65 2		44	2 .	18	î	5	i	36	3	331	2	318		318	
Structural clay products	1 2			9	18		25 3		74 24	>	241	5	3	- 4	1	
Pottery and related products Miss nonmetallic mineral & store products	1	2		2					36 187	6	180 180	6	1		1 2	
	10	3	9	9 3	75		~3		437	113	410	-1-2	87	3	82	1.11
Metal industries Pennary metal industries Biast furnaces steel works, & rolling mills	39		. 3	5 1	*1 3 2	:	40	٠.	96 é	1	86	1	32 7	-	25	
Other primary iron and steel industries	2			2 4	2		2 36		82	1	74	1	21	1	1 4	
	5	1 2	. 6	4 2	36 34 28 2		.3 .3 28		3_2	141	320	209		2 2	1 54	. (
Fabrusated metal ind (inc. not spec metal). labrusated steel products. Fabrusated nonferrous metal products.	59		1 3	8 2	28		28		22	106	20	24	3		4	
	66			4 .	6	٠	6		- 7	7	6	7		ĺ	44	
Machinery except electrical - (gricultural machiners and tractors Office and store machines and devices	3		1	3	1 1		1		1.5	1	4	1	1		1 2	1
Missellaneous macounary	6		6	0 2	4 6		4		103	C	80 I	6	45		4	1
Elec -cal machinery equipment, and supplies	1	1	1	7 2	0		9		242	1	200	10	1	2		
Transportation oquipment Motor vehicles and motor vehicle equipment	1	7 2		6	1		1		19	2	_6 1	2		2		
Account and marks	1 .	1	1	1 .	1		l		20.6		184	8		1	1	1
Ship and boat building and repairing Railroad & miss transportation equipment Professional & photographic equip , & watches Professional southment and supplies	1	1			i 6	,	1 1	1	24	16	24	15	**3		1	1
Professional & photographic ecuip , & watches Professional ecuipment and supplies				6	3		3	1	20	15	10	15	3		1	3
Professional eculpment and supplies Photographic equipment and supplies Watches, clock, & clockwork-operated devices Miscellaneous manufacturing industries.	1	2 .1		2 11	1	:	î	1	161		156	38	55	9		

Table 73 —DETAILED OCCUPATION OF THE EXPERIENCED CIVILIAN LABOR FORCE AND OF EMPLOYED PERSONS, BY SEX FOR THE STATE, AND FOR STANDARD METROPOLITAN AREAS AND CITIES OF 100,000 OR MORE 1950—Cop

	2 ar '2r	EC 7 70	-	· famon m						C**	148.16			Saret	POTOT	
			ep			F . ~r	7 .ge			_	14878		źxper		ejor	-
Detailed occupation	Erper	.s.	Earp 1	o "ea	Tab. L	-1a-	TID.	_oved	nodx3	Liar	Emp_c	gred	labor	1.85	Smp?	loyed
	Man .	Fema.	14 c	Ve.31.0	Mana.	Teu e	-taue	Fetr e	Ma_e	Fenale	hale	Female.	Ma_e	Fена.е	Male	Гена
Operatives and audred workers—Con		1														
ratives and kindred workers rea ;—Oso lanufarturing—Cor Nondurable goods Food and kindred products	1	1				i										
Yondurable goods	1 105		5%	2-9 72 37	2,573	10	2,538	88 67	3,089 1,769	-,961	2,89A 1,642	1,629	407 198	.126 65	390 195	
	22.		5v	רנ	_4	4	4	2	235	1 44	22 83	98 43	198 57 32	27 2	56 31	
Dairi products Canning & preserving fruits veget , & sea foods Grain mili products	, ,	21	دد	• 2	2	5	1	5	106	293	87	242	2		2 5	;
Grain mili products Bastery products	300	-3	48	*0	.3 57	5	2,	30	45 165	9 .45	38 ±53	7.08	39 4 31	13 10	39	1
Our fectionery and related products	3+ 30	n ni	- 4		43	2	20	2	57 594	178 35	48 558	-52 27	31	3	39 31 27	
Basery profu is Confectionery and related products Borneage industries Just food preparations and kinered products to spenfied nod industries	30	3	37	3	7	14	20 10	9	463 46	278 54	425 25	250	27	8	27	
Tobacco martiactures							. 2		38	ر21	36	-82 433	:		2	
Texule mill produces	2		-	:.	. 2	-	2		246 17	220	233 16	214	-			
During and finishing textules eac crist goods Carpets rugs and other floor roverings. Yarr thread and factor mills		1		٠.	:	:.			3	3 198	2	3		:	**	
Yarr thread and faorie mills	2		2		-	-	2	1	232	198	.93 38 391	-94	2		-	
hiscolaneous textule mill products Appares and societalemill products Appares and socessories Appares and socessories Appares and socessories Appares fabricated extule products	24	54	24	.43	3	1	1	2	ر_4 246	24 2 6.2 2,151	391 232	2,478	22	135 123	22	
	-	1	 1.	3.	• 3	2	3	2	167	451	259 236	43.	13 9 10	12	13	
Paper and alled products Pulp paper and paperboard mills Paperboard containers and boxes A secilar outs pape and only products Printing, publishing and allied industries	.8	4 9	1.6	7 9	2		-		244 438 94	153 27 105	_35	26 99	10	12 14 4 9	12	
Paperboard containers and boxes I receils ents pape and built products		1		9	13				.2 90	21 33	89 12	17		6		
Printing, pullisning and allied industries	12	0		6	823	8	11 820	9 4	149	27	84 43	29	10	4	82	
Chem. sals and allied products. by unlette fibers. Louis and menuines.	_,4	. 1	"	300		. "	020	. "				7	09	• 1		
Pain's varnishes and related products.	4	1	1	1	* 2	.	2		39	9 3 15 2	39	3	2		1	
Miscellaneous chemicals and allied products Pet oleum and coal products	.02 .70 .37	4	65	2 2	821 1 5.8	4	318	4	135	15	99 105	10 2	87 70 45	3 1 1	81 65	19
Pe roleun rehning Miscellaneous pitroleum and coal products	.37	- 4	3.	2	1 538	ь	1,527	6	44	1	42	1	45 25	1	- 0 25	
	.3. 1	. 1	3-	1	34		33		8	1 8 12	63 7 41	11		1		
Leather and eather products Leather tanned curried and smaked	-	1	1	-	1		1		6		6					
Foo wear, except rabber Leather products except footwear Not specified manufacturing industries	1	1 5	2	1					-1	6 4 30	5	6 5				
	20 351	-31	,9 832		440	2	410	75	2,933	30 832	2,753	35 781	13	1_9	.2 650	
commanufacturing inclistnes inclinut reported. Construction. Railroads and ailway express service	138	2	114	128 2 3	97 35	77 2 1	87 35	1	29 ₀ 300	7	262 290	6 5	√73 79 ⊥19		69	
Hailroads and allway express service Transportation except railroad Telecommunics ions, & unities & sanitary services	78	ī	136 77 76	3	20 43	1	20	1	376	57		35	5-	1 2 1 2	50 45	8
Wholesale and retail trade	\$3 253	1 3	251	65.	129	42	43 124	42	1,126	617	243 1 057	575	219	61,	218	
Business and repair services	90 8	6 26	82	26	56	42 3	52	10	245	68	236	66	72	23	72	
Public administration All other industries (incl not reported)	36 56	21	35 50	20	6 6 42	8	377	8	142	62	179	8	33 45	2	32 40	
Pravate household workers	1/3	3 3aL	172	5 217	'5	3,332	2	2,890	481	11,434	449	10 731	1.46	4 5/2	135	4,
sekeepers pr vine household	10	78 20	0	75 20	2	35 7	1	35 7	26	422	23	398	병	43 14	7	
ving in	70	8*	9	56	1 7	28	-	174	26	303	23	339	8	- 29	,	
tareses private household	lo	564			7	183	7		-2	992	11	935		486	14	
ving out . a.e household workers ,n e c]	147	7 740	147	556 4,58	65	183	64	2,68	12 -43	988	415	931	14	486 4,013	114	3
ving out	.36	4 700	11	40	62	4 794	6.	2,654	416	9,61	27 388	8,992	104	33,980	104	3
Service worke a except private household.	3 _52	3 717	3 065	3,636	2 623	2,16=	2,484	2,0.5	5,9:7	1 ,314	14,895	10,341	2,789	3,265	-,697	3,
ndants hospital and other institution	29	-24	25	123	20	54 98	32 28	54 96	442 93	625	424	609 415	29	115	25	
ndants professional and personal service (n.e.e.)	11 52 246	322	50	12	35 -83 -44	205	32	9	321	2.	295	21	49	8	46	
ere, beauticians and manicurists.	119	.7	244 117	16	_44	13	131	203 14	1,305	975 64 143	905	952 60	577	302 12	209 100	
ding and lodging house keepers blicks women and cleaners	41	29	40	29	2	14	24		106		45 93	142	37	29	12 36 23	
rwomen and cleaners	24	670	22	657	191	39 312	27	39 294	1,078	1.075	116	989	241	195 572 29	23	
eter enerators	10	32	9	32	37	312	36 36	21	377	184	355	175	9	29 54	۶ 51	
nen fire protection rds, watcamen and doo keepers	-31	-1	151		150	38 1 4 94	150		357	4	848	4	123	4	143	
	-86	73	15.	3 7L	191	94	181	4	293	28 434 299	1 377	26 425	-31	68	122	
ore and sextons	36s 7	48	3_6	43	491	41	467	40	746	299 2 7	721	292	293	35	28o	
ermen and detect vos	195	2	194	2	159	5	157	3	1,180	7	2,166	7 9	179	1	178	
overnment	189	1	194 188	i	143		142	:	963	7 3	958 208	2	173	ı	-72	
ors .	1,0.4	11	1,01/	10		9	4.89	9	4,050	74	3,759	58	972	10	934	
treal nurses	8 32	287	32	28T	2.4 10 32	170	32	155	10	74.8	14	679	6 22	256	6	
ers, "erreasion and amovemen	108	742	304	716.	11	530	142	497	1,173	2 7	22	6	3	642	22 3 93	
chmen crossing and bridge tenders noe workels, except private bousehold (n.e.)	3 239	1,009	3 226	984	2	2	2	21	721	2,561	4,781 1	2,332	96		3	
Farm Isborers and foremen	239	1,0091	1.696	984	166	497	146	472	955 223	2 "34	863	2,575	138	875	184	
r foremen	32		32	64.4	3		3		223	7	2	3	6	241	6	_
n saborers, wage workers	4,43.	507	1 /2	494 312		31	98	30							96	

Table 73—DETAILED OCCUPATION OF THE EXPERIENCED CIVILIAN LABOR FORCE AND OF EMPLOYED PERSONS, BY SEX, FOR THE STATE, AND FOR STANDARD METROPOLITAN AREAS AND CITIES OF 100,000 OR MORE .950—Con.

	utander	metr.p.	ica- aresa	C_m ·						C1 .	1			_		-
		Shre	*p. *1			56-5-	Po are			vew " .	rana .	-		Chry	repower	
Detailed occupation	_ebo=	en^ed . Jn .orwe i	Erp.ov	w.e	1 p = 0	· · ·	Em ¹	o.ed	Exter e	a-	Eng.03	red	Caperi civi. accr	ian orce	Emp	oyei
THE PERSON NAMED IN COLUMN TWO	Mene	rem_c	Male V	*28.0	Ma e	cma_e	Mais	PEALS.	Maun 1	9140	1670	800 B	42.0	FORM-R	Male	Foss .e
Laborers except farm and mine	4 200	6	4 73.	L23	- 58.	22.	الدوري	+5	1	7.	9 50	540	1,57	41	1,395	70
Pahermen and oystermen Jarage laborers and car washers and greasers Jardeners expert farm and groundskeepers Longshoremen and stevedores Lumberman raf.amen, and wood ohoppers Pannstern	48 .39 251	2 2 2 2	-3.1	5 2 2	73	2	991	4	*.35 4 673	1 6 16	23- 288 266 -,252	48.07	195 4	40400	.1 197 488 4 3.	105
Laborers (n.e.o.) Masufactorung Durable goods Sawmills planing mils, & maes wood products Sawmills planing mils, and mill work Mascellaneous sood products. Furnature and hittere	4 395 939 552 309 266 43	91 25 1- 6 5	975 575 195 256	45	943 -4- 27	in vin	- 74: 44* 20 3	36	54 3 562 5 63 467 6 63 467	3	3,8%	×4 4 14 14 16	3,.9° 653 385 200 172 26	604	91 .65 -7	6
rumoute and actures from the control of the control	1 3		-5- -19 9 3*	ī	4.	:	36 33 3		3.9 .23 .3 2 1 3	3	304	3	10z 8. 1"		.01 81 10	
Metal industries Primary metal industries Blass furnaces steel works, & rolling rails Other primary iron and steel industries Primary nonferrous industries. Fabricated metal ind. (ind. not spec metal)	1))	31	2	6' 48' 1 6 41	:	46		458 83 3 63 7	15	13! 01! 6;	1	7	:	33 9 2 6	
Faories ad stee: products Faories ad stee: products Faories and indications metal products Not rescaled metal indistries Machinery except electrical Agricultural machinery and tractors Office and store machines and devices	23 2 32 1		32	·	1.	11	. 1		175 43 29 3	1	20 20	13	20 1		20 4	
Electrical mach nerv equipment and supplies Transportation equipment	31		2 2	-	1	: 1	2	1	32 10	1	25 9 383	2	19 1		1	
Motor vehicles and motor vehicle equipment Autoral, and nexts. Ship and borse building and repairing Railroad & mise transportation equipment Professional & photographie equip, & watcher Professional equipment and supplies Photographie equipment and supplies	1 .		1		1		•		4-2	.5	4 1 277 1	. 2			-	4
Professional equipment and supplies Photographie equipment and supplies Watenes clorks, & clockwork-operated devices Miscellangors manufacturing undstrics	1,		-71	:	1		-			:	1 29			:	12	are.
Nondurable goods Food and kindred products Meat products Darry products Canning & preserving ruits reget & sea foods Grain mill products	335 114 1e		318 106 7 2	_1 2	854 100 5 1	11 5	817 88 4	1	2 071 1,-82 74 oC 38	186 61 5 2	-,933 - 2,1 71 - 55 - 33 - 62	166 51 4 20	267 103 16 6 2		253	
Baker, products Contextoners and related products Beverage industries Mise 'nod preparations and kindred products Vot spe_ried food_industries			9 2 41 24	1	35 25 1	. 3	30 20 1	5	68 11 432 527 19	7 8	10 411 489 19	12000	44 20	1	40 20	
Tobacco manufactures Textule mill products Kintting mills Dyeing and finishing textules exc kint goods Carpets, rugs and other floor coverings Yarn, thread and fabric mills	1	1	3		2		1	•	63	51 2 47	148	49	. 1	in-	1	
Carpen, rugs and Outer not covering. Yare, threat and fabre mile.— Apparel and other fabreasted tecture products. Apparel and other fabreasted tecture products. Aspecilaneous fabroasted tectile products. Paper and aired products. Paper and paper and papertoard mills.		1 2	3 1 2 7 3	1 2 2			1	•	80 1" 98 227 15*	40 -7 23 6 2	15 14 14 63 210 149 49	26 27 17 19	5		5	1
Pulp paper and paperoard mills Pulp paper and paperoard mills Paperboard containers and boxes Miscellaneous paper and pulp products Printing publishing and allied industries	1			,	2	٠.	2		28)	- 10	12 26 121		.4		4	
Chemicals and allied products Synthetic fibers Drigs and medicines Paints variables, and related products. Miscellarcous chamicae, and allied products.	11.	1	7 72		166	3	160 1 2 157		.06	م	1 2 99	8	1		98	
Petroleum and coal products Petroleum refining Mmcellaneous petroleum and coal products Rubber products Leather and leather products	8	1	80 51 29	1	566 566	3 3	47 47	3	48 40 408 4	1 4	138 35 103 4	1	23 24	Page 1	20	1
Footwear except rubber Leather products, except footwear Not specified manufa turing industries	1		112		3		1 2	٠.	1 1 21	. 4	1 10	2	;		3	
Nonnanufacturing industries (incl. not reported) Construction Radroads and radiway express service Pransportation except radroad Telecommunications, & utilities & sanitary service Wholesals and retail trade Busness and repair services Personal services	1,43 40 40 44 27 50 2 38	20 26	1 341 382 139 215 486	62 8 1 2 25 1	1,138 1,081 67 67 126 396 13	31 9 1 1 2 6	1,798 8,2 04 80 140 369 13	27 8 1 1 2	3,665 1,711 1 :08 894	260 24 109 28 7 101 2 41	10 %5: 3, 61 1,638 1,360 855 2,46	333 27 107 25 92 39	276 132 177 405 22 263		262 106 172 369 22 254	
Public administration All other industries (incl. not reported)	23	9 40	208	14	63 145	1_	56 127 330	167	724 6.51	1,099	660 483 ,378	36 694	147		9 129	
Occupation not reported	1,10	6 533	637	402	539	257	330	167	2,590	1,099	1,378	696	/96	30	1 443	1

Table 74 -- DETAILED OCCUPATION OF EMPLOYED PERSONS, BY SEX, FOR THE STATE 1950 AND 1940

"Criginal" 1943 Egares worked where necessary is inclined to 1950 classification. "No. " means not elsewhere classified]

	11	AL	Per	1.20	D. co les constants	Ma	k	Гen	na¹e
DA. CC MAN	940	1940	950	1940	Detailed occupation	1950	1940	1950	1940
		1 1	2 2	-85 -42	Managers, officials, and proprietors excitate—Con.				
Total, 14 ve.rs old and over			2,16		Officials odge society mion etc	255	499 311	34	32 350
Professions seconical, and sind was workers	-, 3-		-32	143	Purcasang agents and buyers nec)	0 1	357	25	15
artors and social serves	2,0		- 1	-2	Managers official, via propine on (nee f	2,794	34,568	9,213	4,540
kebitati.	371	2 4	7	c	Construction Marufacturing	0.2721	4,288	31°	144
Artists and arr Address	23		3-1	د	Telecommunications & utilities & minitary services -	2,32L 960	+84	80 192	144 14 52 94
Account and see Auditors Actions no nee need Aughter pure same navalues Aughters' Aughter pure Aughters' Aughters' Aughters' Aughters' Aughters' Aughters' Aughters' Aughters' Aughters' Aughters' Aughters' Aughters' Aughters	843		35	-2	Whokeale trade	4,608	2,803		
hiropiteters	3 _ "2	1-	= '.'	pe.	Read trade	25 60° 8 102	18,720	2,357	3,457
Le gymen Lollege presidents professors and an ruetors nucl Dancers and dancing teachers	2	#	24	414	Food and dairy products stores and milk retailing General merchanduse and live and on cen stores	1,742	718	407	2
Dancers and dancing teachers	882- 53		44	. 2	Apparel and accessories stores Furniture, home furnitures and equipment stores.	1,237	606	117	37
Denuis s. Descripts Dettinans and nutritions: s. Draft.men DL: tors and reporters		4	. ,	,2,	Furniture, home furnitungs and equipment stores. Viotor vehicles and accessories retailing Gasclini service stations	2,305	1.945	968	46 49 1 348
Omft.men 2d tors and reporters	527	354	261	13	Hardware, farm implement, & bldg material retail		2,791	98	36
Engineers teconical	4, /9	2,746	(2)	اد (م	Other retail trade	3,4-7	2,624	861	447
Seronsationi Chemical	682	22-	4	- 1	Banking and other finance Invariance and run, estate	1,901	1,729	146 183	26
Fleetrui	1, whi	1 213	24	2	But mess services	485 974	240 a36	80 17 25	32 10
Fleetruil Industrial Mechanical	2-3	92	(2)	, 2 ·	Miscelaneous repair services and garages Miscelaneous repair services	225 1 745	149	25 77	385
Mc'all great, and metal-argests	1 140	2.2	2		L other odustnes (incl not reported)	3,484	2 228	6-2	290
Aeronau r.al	2,743	701	9					1	
of elsewhere elassified	1				Cler cal and kindred workers	35,374	26,27.	49,702	23 808
Milmig Aeronau r.al Met anica Ge class here classified Enertanica (n.e.t.) Furm. in home management advisors	201	23 (1.	16,	24 (1)	Attenuants and assistants, library	, 880 55	145 45	137	70
Foresters and conservations	701	45	د7 د7	32	Attendants physician's and deptate's office	26 43 (*)	27	400	337
ANYPER AND JUGGES	2 . 20	1,82	G*8	37	Bank tellers. Bookkeepers			(,)	15)
	1,000	24	9.2	644	Cashiers Collec ors bill and account.	4,555	4,.04	9 452	4 379
Nuscians and music teachers	1_9	26	5,918	4,214	Distatchers and starters vehicle	494	917	-08	(°)
Aurer student professional Optometrists	. 70	-	12		Dispatchers and starters vehicle Express mea-engers and rack av mail clerks.	⊾2 5		1	1
Personne any labo elations workers	(7	(1)	,1	(4)	Mail carriers Messengers and office boys	-,872 251	1 171	68	36 18
harmacais .	1 1-1	1 010	119	84	Messengers and office boys Office ma him operators Shipping and receiving cierks	2,475	120	- 272 143	388 51
hotographers hymeians and surgeons Radu operators	2,355	2.30	140	84		1 312	2,183	18,408	10,846
	396 (3) 11"	(3)	(3)	(3)	Telegraph pera ors. Telegraph operators	376	449	4,473	2,328
Religious workers		4	2.6	425	Tieget station and express agents	910	6:6	132	38
local and welfare workers except group	323	230	(-)	(1)	Bune tellers Dispatche s and starters wehill Clorical and kindred worke (n c v)	20 02-	13,419	14,74.	4,854
tocial wantists.	50.5	21.	4 30	27	Ciorical and Rindred Worke. (R * ()	1		3.5	
urvevors	7,1	3 %	10,451	:2 910	Sales workers	3> 90-1	29,002	20,231	11,576
Penchers n.e.c) Perhusers suctival and cental Pechnicians towing Pechnicians (n.e.c)	1,401	44	30	180	A.I so tome a country and solutions	311	356	55	9>
Therapists and healers (n.e.c.)	38° 106	212	55 72	24	Auctioneers Demonserston	33	12	100	26
etennatiuns	135	735	13	1	Hucksters and pendlers	4 126	3 327	539	84 271
Dietitians and nutritionists Foresters and conservationists			- 1	- 1	Newsboys Pea, estate agents and broi ers Look and bend salesmen Salesmer and sales Lerks (n.e.c.)	4,_83	834	241	33
vature sciennists (n e c.)	7,273	1,-42	796	J28	Selegener and sales units (n.e.c.)	26 539	2,701	17,237	10,799
cetal screptists Professional se hincan and kindred workers (c.e.e.)		1		1	Manufacouring Wholesale trade	20 12.			
Facutors and fa m transpors	Ao, 320	134,99	2,263	5,402	Retail trace	28,539	35 JJ	19 237	10,999
formers (owners and terants)	85,6 6	_34 18±!	2,927	5,393	Other industries (incl. not reported) .	1		l	
erm manegers	-24	87.	2'	9	Craftsmen, toremen, and kindred workers	98 973	57,583	1,872	814
Managers, officials and proprietors exc farm	3,507	571	339	5,223	Bakers	-,399	1,470	138	(6)
Suvers and shippers arm products .	370	581	12	3	Baskemi ha. Boilermaker. Bookbindere	701	1011	2	2
ondurtor, rairoud redit men loomen and loor mar gers store	410 427 74	357 348	9	41		1 72	423 (1)	76	(7)
Toomen and foor mar gers store - repertors public administration and postal service	923	4c 905	17	30 42	Cabinetmakere	891	094	20	34
State public administration	463 463	246	2	8	Cement and concrete unshers Compositors and typesetters Cranearen dirrickmen and noistmen	585	217	4	1
Local mulder administ motion	269	251	1.	3	Craner on derrokmen and noistmen	1,263	-,013	100	(8)
Local public administration									
faragers and superintendents, building ficers piloto, nursers, and sugmeens, ship	2 442	,002	20	3 1	Lecorators and window diessers	2,922	279	203	61 5
form point summer and specimens, building infects pilot, sursers, and sugments amplificate & administrators (ner.), public administration and postal service State public administration	2 442 2,087 711 463		25 297 58 42 197		Decorators and window dissers Pleatrotypers Pleatrotypers and stereorypers Eng area, except photoengravers C anemen derrickmen and oustmen Petas stung grading and road maconne, ope alors	2,920 55 45	-,279 38 6	203	5 2 3

⁽Combined with 'Profes ional teranical and aindred workers (n e c.) ' below

^{*}Combined with "Social and weare wower, except group below

Appears it two parts—salared and sel-employed—in the 1950 occupational classification comparable separation not shown in the 1940 system

Combined with Clerical at a kindred workers to et a below

¹ Data not available for adequate 1940 estimate for surposes of major group consparability, however, a rough allowance for his occupation has been in ludes in the major group total Control of the construction of the constructi

Table 74-DETAILED OCCUPATION OF EMPLOYED PERSONS, BY SEX, FOR THE STATE 1953 AND 1940-Con Ongma 1940 Lgures revised who ary to conform to 1940 _aestication "N c.c" means not elsewhere c.assified,

1950 1940 1950 1940 Traditioner foremen and kinderd workers—Com Foremen (the *)
Countriction
Manufacturing
Metal andustretin
Metal andustretin
Transportation equipment
Textile retrieval
Thansportation equipment
Textile retrieval
Other conduste product, and appaid
Other conduste product, and appaid
Other conduste product, and appaid
The commission of the condustretin
Transportation, assign a lived
Transportation, assign a lived
Theorems makens, a stuffatte as sanitary services
Other industries (ind. not reported.) Bus drives.

Bus drives.
Chammer roders and samers surveying.
Coccurrors out and samers rainway.
Deutserment and rotemen.
Deutserment and rotemen.
Deutserment and rotemen. , 151 -,295 3,448 5,+2 236 1, 12, 3.3 415 182 . . . 2 2 2 _22 _05 91 . Five graders and possible metal.

First and & vegetable graders & packers our factory.

Furnesseems such owner and postures

Laundry and day newing operatives

Matter utters excent singupter and pocking bouse

Min were

attive into abovers n.d.c.)

Coar manue;

Cytic petroleum and sturid gas currection

Kaming sind (agenying except folion etc.

Monomers (agenying except folion etc.

Monomers (agenying except folion etc.) 3 324 1 873 737 327 2.9 1,090 4 3 146 d ... 27.1 813 33° 53~ . 43. Other notations unto air reported,
Blackmuth's
Forguma and hammermen.
Furires
Glasses
Glasses
Heat twaters, annoulers, and temperes
Impecor sealers and graders, log ann humoer
Impecors (no et al., pages 1997),
Railrodd, and railway grapess service.
Transport or, r. communion of other unbiac unil
Other industries (incl. not reported). 1,40 -2 34 1,759 - 82 7 42 82 1, 19 172 442 195 51 708 1,032 122 322 155 433 12 12,07 52 2 79 Olers and greaters, except auto
Panters ex ejr rock-recon and ran intenance
Parter stator opera.ors
Fewer stator opera.ors
Sources and etc. tande
Sources and etc.
Sources and etc.
Sources and etc.
Sources and etc.
Sources and etc.
Tande and recommended the etc.
Tande and recommended the etc.
Tande and recommended the etc.
Tande and recommended the etc.
Tande and recommended the etc.
Tande and recommended the etc.
Tande and recommended the etc.
Tande and recommended the etc.
Tande and recommended the etc. 1-2 23" 2,1 1 804 32 - 912 evanantes (mid noi reportes and nivermucha levelen, watchmakers, goldsmuthe and nivermucha clouds as metal consenter supposes telegraph, telenhous is power. Leomenters supposes Leomenters from Leomenters and Leomenters from Leomenters of the Leomenters of the Leomenters of the Leomenters of the Leomenters of the Leomenters of the Leomenters of the Leomenters of the Leomenters of the Leomenters of the Leomenters of the Leomenters of the Leomenters of the Leomenters of the Leomenters of the Leon 523 (1) 3,027 846 672 64 297 (1) -,197 660 -°1 11. 1 (1) 3 2 2 1 2 2 2 1 31, 2" 21, 12 3 230 34 24 2 226 24 Mechanis and repairmén
inplain
inplain
displain
displain
displain
displain
displain
displain
displain
displain
displain
displain
displain
displain
displain
displain
displain
displain
displain
displain
displain
displain
displain
displain
displain
displain
displain
displain
displain
displain
displain
displain
displain
displain
displain
displain
displain
displain
displain
displain
displain
displain
displain
displain
displain
displain
displain
displain
displain
displain
displain
displain
displain
displain
displain
displain
displain
displain
displain
displain
displain
displain
displain
displain
displain
displain
displain
displain
displain
displain
displain
displain
displain
displain
displain
displain
displain
displain
displain
displain
displain
displain
displain
displain
displain
displain
displain
displain
displain
displain
displain
displain
displain
displain
displain
displain
displain
displain
displain
displain
displain
displain
displain
displain
displain
displain
displain
displain
displain
displain
displain
displain
displain
displain
displain
displain
displain
displain
displain
displain
displain
displain
displain
displain
displain
displain
displain
displain
displain
displain
displain
displain
displain
displain
displain
displain
displain
displain
displain
displain
displain
displain
displain
displain
displain
displain
displain
displain
displain
displain
displain
displain
displain
displain
displain
displain
displain
displain
displain
displain
displain
displain
displain
displain
displain
displain
displain
displain
displain
displain
displain
displain
displain
displain
displain
displain
displain
displain
displain
displain
displain
displain
displain
displain
displain
displain
displain
displain
displain
displain
displain
displain
displain
displain
displain
displain
displain
displain
displain
displain
displain
displain
displain
displain
displain
displain
displain
displain
displain
displain
displain
displain
displain
displain
displain
displain
displain
displain
displain
displain
displain
displain
displain
displain
displain 1,335 21, 19, 383 9,901 (~ (2, 420 158 4.9°U (2') (2') 3,° 27 2 15 43 2000 Operatives and kindred voraris (n.a.c.)

Manufact.rang.

Durathe gradient rathe & mac wood groducts.

hav-malls planning mills and mill work

Macellanace, wood products.

Furniture and instance shood products.

Furniture and instance shood products.

Game and gloss products

Center 1, deconcret to puum & caster products

Frince and day products

Frince and dashed conducts

Like noon stalls, minera & stone products

Like noon stalls, minera & stone products 15,812 27,797 7,03 7,12 50 462 1 713 201 256 -7,674 -2,674 -2,52 -1,52 -1,52 -2,50 -2,5 (2) 2^ Millers, gram, flour feed etc Millwaghts Moders, metal 13.3 7.8 130 290 638 423 423 105 6,287 301 19 -13 80 (13 4,903 10 -1 8 8 4,_24 2 18 9 When home sense, meres a source proposes.

Head Immusters and resident resident sense when the following realist Coher primary norm and stees indivities.
Fairnased re-el products.
Fairnased re-el products.
Fairnased re-el products.
Vot repeated management of the resident sense when the resident resident sense when the resident resident sense when the resident resident sense realised and devoted for the and dress machines and devoted for the sense when the resident re 97: 255 -2 170 1 104 443 101 2 277 nbers and pipe fitters . . . smen and plate printers prin 2 401 Presume and paste promote proming Rollies and roll hands, metal Rodger and sisters Shoumaker and repuress except actors Santonary segment Shoumaker and aton-carver Structural roads worker Tumanital, coppermentes, and short metal workers Tumanital, coppermentes, and short metal workers Tumanital, coppermentes, and short metal workers Tumanital or promote and section Tumanital coppermentes and section Tumanital coppermentes Tumanital coppermente 22 594 720 3,793 59 851 2 473 .05 3,196 .9 .40 .62 652 23 257 2 5 345 97 1 239 401 374 374 31 367 330 1,185 64 484 75° Mo or vehicles and motor vehicle equip Arrents and parts.
Slup ann boat building and repairing Railroad is max transportation equipm All other cumble goods.
Professional equipment and supplies. Photographie coupment and supplies. Photographie coupment and supplies was the coupment and supplies of the coupment and supplies was the coupment and supplies of the cou 3) 219 men and kurdred workers 's e.c.) _ 92 63 39 22 9 Operatives and kindred workers 328 297 16 - 025 (4) (4) -25 11, (2) 102 (4) 103 Minocitaneous muniferturns industries

Nordurn-lie good,
Food and fundres, produce.
Meet produced
Meet produced
Conning & preserving fruits vaget. & see foods
Conning & preserving fruits vaget. & see foods
Conning all preserving fruits
Bakery produces
Bakery produces
Bakery produces
Meet food products
Meet food preparations and fundred products
Notes procedure flood industries
Meet food preparations and fundred products
Not specified flood industries 28,750 5 32' £16 3-4 640 4.0 458 8,6_8 3 (24 1/5 19 1 617 83 242 224 8,536 2,73-390 118 254 148 201 108 418 741 741 115 19 730 28 203 201 77 (4) (') (2) 977 1 800 Training trades (if ec.)
Training trades
Auto mechanics
Brickiayers and missons
Mechanics, except auto
Building trades (n e.c.)
Metalworking trades (n e.c.)
Other specified trades
Trade not specified 525 1,002 308 Tobsoo nanufacture
Textic mil products
Kattung mills
Diweng and insalung textiles see kmit goods
Diweng and insalung textiles see kmit goods
Varn thread and falune mills
Macellassews textile, mill products.
Apparal and other chromated textile products
Apparal and areasseries
Miscellasseus faluntaide textile products 422 9 10. 360 124 3 170 59 415 237 620 49-220 4 3 232 27 3 184 2 655 529 1 Asbestos and insulation workers
Attendar is, auto service and parking
Blasters and powdermen
Boattome ensumen, and lock keepers
Buskemen railroad 321 3,886 420 752 898 201 33

Combund with Machanits" below

Combund with Mechanics and repairmen—Not elsewhere classified below

Data not available for adequate 1040 ceimate, in: purposes of mayor group comparability, however

Combund with Apprentices—Other specified itseles, "below

Combund with "Tomosa duries and charificants and "Truck and unsetter drivers," below a rough allowance for this occupation has been included in the major group total

Table 74-DETAILED OCCUPATION OF EMPLOYED PERSONS, BY SEX, FOR THE STATE 1950 AND 1940-Col Original 946 figures review where necessary to conform to 1950 classification. Nec. means not elsewhere classified

Defaueu оог аркыст	у	is'e	Fe	nale	Detailed occupation	М	als	Fen	nale
эльна он аркион	1950	940	1950	.940	Desard occupation	1950	1940	1950	194
Operatives and kindred workers—Con perative and kindred workers ("i.e.e./—Con Manufac uring—Con			1		Laborers, except farm and mine—Con Laborers (n e c.) Manufacturing	59,472 21,004 10,079 7,460	57,205 27,632	1, 377	٠,
Nos durable goods—Con Paper and allied products Pulp, paper and paper sourd mills Paper and consumers and comes	, 20	-, 431	1	49	Duranie goods	7,460	27,632 15,439 11,745	177	
Pulp, paper and paper seard mills	7,030	4, "	3.8	202	Sawmills, plan ng milis & mise wood products Sawmills, planing mills, and mill work	6,896	10.796	91 58 30	
liscella, ecus paser and rule products	1 15	16.7	23.	12 ⁴ 238		564 199	949 337	30	
Pri C. g. Jubust and albed industries	1 15	125	.9	t-	Furniture and fixtures Stone clay and glass products	521	1,960	F	
Chemicals and allied products	1,13	- '6	1,3	0_	Giaes and glass products - Coment, & concrete, gy psum, & plaster products.	12d 238	1 359	1 4	
Synthe to more	1 05		9	29	Structural elay products	44	297	1	
D are and need often	h	-, 29	-24	5.	Po ten and related products _ Visc nonmetallic nuneral & stone products _	207	143	90 100	
Macrianeous chemials and alleg products Petroleun and roal products	.45	-, -	29		Vietal inous÷nes	714	620		
Petroseum "suning Misseameous petroleum and eusl products	-, 763	الا درما	27	-	Blas fi maces steel works and rolling mills	34	43	42	
Rubber products	30	43	2		Other primary iron and steel industries Fabrica ed steel products	451	455	41	
	30	2^	4.	- 7	Primary nonferrous industries	226	92	1	
Less her tanned curried and imaged Footwear except ober	1 0	1 5		41	Pabnes ed nonferrous metal products ot specified metal industries.		30	-	
Leather products ex eps contrear Not specified manufa furni, industrice	10	4	- 7	5		117	134	1	
	1		38		Agr custural machinery and *ractors Office and store machines and devices	16	27		
Construction	2,45	4,80	1,035	59	viscellaneous maclunery_	101	100	-	
Railro.ds and railway express service	-,1_0	124	14	7	Electrical machiner, equipment and supplies	25	-5	5	
Transportation except rairoad Felecomount at one deutilities desaltare services	936	300	70	6 2	Transportation equipment. Motor vehicles and motor vehicle equipment	053	552 50	3	
Whitesale and retail trace	2,51"	398	-,-0	365		.8 2	30		
Personal services	110	**0	170	23	Ship and bost building and repairing Railroad & mase transportation equipment.	627	492	3	
Public norman: atton All other industries (incl. not reported)	4C2	- 08	3 ₁	112	All other durable goods	90	76	4	
		1			Professional equipment and supplies	4	1	400	
Private household workers.	1 416	2 8001	42,207	59,471	Photographic equipment and supplies. Watches clocks, & clockwork-operated devices	86	701	4	
skeepers p avate household	99	42	2 %	5,311	Viscellaneous manufacturing industries.			1	
lying out	99	→2	2, 23	5,311	Nondurable goods.	10,848	.212	470	
nd.esees private household	777	1.3	3,350	1,383	Food and kindred products Meat products.	4,075	5 275	229	
a ing out	240	2, 00	3,9.6	1,383	Dairy products	192 147	136	1,	
rving in	1		3c, 218	42 777	Canning & preserving fruits veget & sea foods. Grain-mill products	326	414	98	
4Ving out	1,2+0	2, 103	36 218	42,77	Bakery products	143	971	15	
Service workers, except private household	36,694	29,97	33 >23	18,511	Confectioner, and related products Beverage industries	1	16	4	
endarts hospital and other institution	1,005	~3 ₇	- 443	426	Misc foud p eparations and kindred products Not specified food industries	1,867	548		
endants professional and personal revice (n.e ^)	282	20y 625	898	155	Not specified food industries	1,86"	2,652	90	
bers beauticians, and manicurass	2,902	2,554	2,832	2,86.	Tobacco manufactures Textile mill products	11	14	17	
rding and indging nouse keepers	3,134	2,115	250 308	85 936	battime mills	218	647	70	
t blacks	341	322	2	3	Dreing and finishing textiles, ear kint goods Carpets rugs and other foor coverings. Nam thread and fabric mills	- 1	2	-	
arwomen and cleaners oks, except private household	2,531	2,607	6 243	_60	harn thread and abric mills	J58	467	55	
inter and 'ountain wo.xers	(1)	77.	6,243	2,101	Macellaneous textile mill products Apparel and other fabricated textile products	52	171	15	
sator operacors.	5.49	*24	375	143	Appare and accessories	90	167	44	
men, fire protection rds was limen and doc-keepers.	3 507	3,149	5	47	Miscellaneous fabricated textile products.	76	1:0	23	
sekerpers and stewards, except private household	323	244	1 003	045	Paper and allied products Pulp paper and papercoard mills	2,513	1,837	26	1
tors and extens	204	2,329	738	462		251	40	48	1
WIV-5		222 (2)	(2)	12	Miscellanerus paper and pulp products - Printing publishing and alled industries	49	35	12	
emen and detectives _	2,349	1,679	13	6	Chemicals and allied products	1,709	2 126	39	
rvate	288	248	د	2	Synthetic fibers	2	2,126	34	
ers	6,683	5,847	12.	99	Oruge and meucines	37	42	3	
tical nurses	93	46	2,544	1,444	M. scellaneou, chemicals and allied products Petroleum and onal products	2,060	2,08/	36	
offs and broudfy	572	~39	10	1"	Petroleum refining	1,742	1,737	14	
ter and form an workers	101	114	50	28	Misoal aneous petroleum and coal products Rubber products	121	212	3	
ters and waitrespes	2,208	2,469	8,249	5 71.5	Leather and leather products	9	4	2.	
rhmen (crossing) and undge tenders see workers except private bousehold (n e.c.)	2,243	1,783	7,-45	3,626	Leather tanned curred and finished Footwear excep rubber	3	1	4	
			100		Leather products. except notwear No. specified manufacturing industries	3	3		
Farm laborers and foremen	J,924	85,880	12,004	28, ا	The specified manufacturing industries .	77	174	4	
n foremen _ n laborers wage wu-kers	549 31,024	22 094	2,649	5,655	Nonmanufacturing industries (incl. not reported)	38,468	25,573	917	4
a laborers unpaid family workers	13,299	29,895	6,922	12,730	Construction	14,785	9,228	99	
service laborers self-employed	22	(*)	-7	(2	Transpor ation, except railroad lelecommunications & utilities & sanitary services	2,482	2,738	134	
Laborers excep farm and mun	52,273	75,914	1,881	1,563	1 eleccommunications of utilities & sanitary services Wholesale and re-all trade	2,700		27	
ge laborers, and car washers and greasers	7,358	2 913	73	60	Business and wears servens	6,261	4,335	25 ₁	
ge laborers, and car washers and greasers	2,285	1 790	60 58	19	Personal services Public administration	2,336	2 457	156	
				47	- court - constitutions	1.696	520	22	
shoremen and stevedo es bermen, rafumen and wood choppers.	4,87C	3,709 5,076	£8 46	19	All other industries (incl. act reported)	2,613	4,155	184	1.5

Combined with Watters and wattrouges, below Combined with "Practical Durses, below Combined with "Practical Durses, below to the proposes of major group comparability however a rough allowance for this occurration has been included in the major group total "Data not available for adequate 1940 estimate for purposes of major group comparability however a rough allowance for this occurration has been included in the major group total "Data not available for adequate 1940 estimate for purposes of major group comparability however a rough allowance for this occurration has been included in the major group total "Data not available for adequate 1940 estimate for purposes of major group comparability however a rough allowance for this occurration has been included in the major group total "Data".

Table 75—OCCUPATION OF THE EXPERIENCED CIVILIAN LABOR FORCE AND OF EMPLOYED PERSONS, BY SEX, FOR THE STATE, URBAN AND RURAL 1950
["N ac mease now energing classified]

Conception, and sex Regenerated Registrate Regist		The S	tate	Urba	An.	Rum no	on farm	Bural	ium
Professional industries, and filtered wickers	Occupation and sex	Experienced civilian labor force	Employed	cryilian	Emp.oyed	Experienced		Expeneueed	
Problements, sentences, and factored worker security of the control of the contro	Male, 14 years old and over	579,402	n4C,782	J86 "73	30-19	146 -41	.537	14. 188	4- 21:
April Apri	Professional, technical, and kindred workers	41,817	4_ 262	33,17,		- 240			
1	coountants and a ditors.	4,0-5	3,99,		2.76.				3.77.
### Services Service	rtuts and ar teachers		300 i	482	200			4	3
Semilar and decisions. 100	hemists		58-	552	24	5'	27	-0	15
Semilar and decisions. 100	Rergymen	3 198	2, 8	2,024	2.04	.240	642	33	.2
Segment surroutined Segment surroutined	Dentists	884	1,4,2	741	4,453 }	7	91	C	6
Suppose service	Designers and draftsmen	948	930	des	85.	77	7-	0	
Part	ingineers civil	2.014	2 991	1 6,6		29	400	.2	
Part	agineers mechanical .	1,338	4.288	17		9.		-3	
## agree on the properties of		2,286	2 263	1 945	-, 125	282	28	53	
started recordinate (C.A.C.) 772 782 783 784 785 785 785 786 786 787 787 788 788	Awyers and purges	1 155	2,198		2,005	-53		40	
Section Sect	stural scientists (h.e.c.)	975	960	334	153	1_R	.18	23	
Section Sect	hysicians and surgeons.	2.842	2 838	4,514					
Program Prog	ocial scientists	178		16~	136	7	7	- 1	
Note Part		765	76.	504	482	205	400	2	
Percents and form managers 60,600 1,000 1,207 1,807 3,709 21,300 21,000 3,709 21,300 21,000 3,709 21,600 3,709 21,600 3,709 3,660 3,709 3,709 3,660 3,709 3,709 3,660 3,709	Sechnicians medical and dental	548 1	23c (48o 1			6	9
Managers officials, a propressure, sec fam 64,20- 69,07 9860 40 208 — 694 11,67 2,500 2,07 166 3 3,400 40 208 787 166 3 3,400 40 208 787 166 3 3,400 40 208 40 208 40 208 787 166 3 3,400 40 208				4 .50	2,232	1,277	رور د	496	4
			B6,38C	1,000	1,55"	J,803	3,725	81,192	81,0
***State of real trade of real trade of the state of the	Managers officials, & proprietors, exc farm								2,5
***State of real trade of real trade of the state of the	Officials & inspectors, State & local administration	1,851	7.65		6 000		376	166	1.
Des reduxines fund non-reported,, ***, ***, ***, ***, ***, ***, **	Managers, officials, & propr s (n.e.c., -salaried	23,455	23,2.0	-2,-75	18,904	1 5.0	3,=00	750	7
Other inclusioner timel non-reported, 1, 1, 1, 1, 2, 2, 2, 2, 2, 2, 2, 2, 2, 2, 2, 2, 2,	Woolesale and retail trade	9,066	9,451	7,904	7,802	1.48_	+.470	281	2
Cartispee foremen and knodred workers 2,10	O her indusines (incl no reported	2,379	2 373	2,396	2 091	4.323	234	48	
2.12	dgre. officials & propr's (n e.c -self-employed,	31,050	30 8.0	29,043	22,635	6 690	6.662	1,317	1,3
The device and universe in the passes. 1, 102		2 214	<,204	1, 12	1,500	504	203	198	1
## 16664 *** 439- 680 Lating and crimicing places. 5,007 7,508 7,005	Eating and drinking paces	2,173	2 153 3,299	2,650	2.604	200	259	51	
Clinical and knadred workers	Retail "ade exe cating and drmking places	15,104	1, 112	10.39	10.334	3,380	3,37-	637	8
Bookbergers Mail claraters J, 507 J, 67 J, 68 J, 60 J,			35 274					1	1
This detects and numer orders	Bookkeepers	3,857	1,14	3 945	2,860	UP7		21.5	2
Sales workers	Mail carners	1.901	1 872	26,344	. 365		345 3 353	163 894	81
Real estate agents and brokers	Sales workers	36,771			28 526	2,9.3	5,847	2,554	1,5
Other pumbed save workers	insurance agents and brokers	4,_90	4,_26		3,564		470		
Manufacturing 7,961 2.75 2,669 3.5.6 38.1 72 4.1	Other spended sales workers	2,310	2,223	4,952	1 803	298	294	66	
Retail table 18,800 18,300 19,3	Manufacturing	29,170	28,500	22,728	22,183	5,077	5,000	1,374	1,3
Confisione forement and kindred workers 1.04, 81.4 88,971 72, 49 67,700 2,407 24,231 7,258 6,9 Blackmeths torganism and hammerman 1.05 1.050 1.050 1.050 1.050 Blackmeths torganism and hammerman 20,000 20,000 20,000 20,000 20,000 Calmientakers and patterminishers 1.128 1.062 880 851 1.06 1.050 Calmientakers and patterminishers 1.128 1.062 880 851 1.068 1.06 1.050 Calmientakers and patterminishers 1.000 1.000 1.000 Calmientakers and patterminishers 1.000 1.000 Calmientakers and patterminishers 1.000 1.000 Calmientakers and patterminishers 1.000 1.000 Calmientakers and patterminishers 1.000 1.000 Calmientakers and patterminishers 1.000 1.000 Calmientakers and patterminishers 1.000 1.000 Calmientakers and scontinus maconicity operators 1.000 Calmientakers and scontinus maconicity operators 1.000 Calmientakers and scontinus maconicity operators 1.000 Calmientakers and scontinus maconicity operators 1.000 Calmientakers and scontinus maconicity operators 1.000 Calmientakers and scontinus 1.000 Calmientakers and scontinus maconicity operators 1.000 Calmientakers and scontinus 1.000 Calmientakers and scontinus maconicity operators 1.000 Calmientakers and scontinus 1.000 Calmientakers and scontinus 1.000 Calmientakers and scontinus 1.000 Calmientakers and scontinus 1.000 Calmientakers and scontinus 1.000 Calmientakers and scontinus 1.000 Calmientakers and scontinus 1.000 Calmientakers 1.000 Calmientakers 1.000 Calmientakers 1.000 Calmientakers 1.000 Calmientakers 1.000 Calmientakers 1.000 Calmientakers 1.000 Calmientakers 1.000 Calmientakers 1.000 Calmientakers 1.000 Calmientakers 1.000 Calmientakers 1.000 Calmientakers 1.000 Calmientakers 1.000 Calmientakers 1.000 Calmientakers 1.000 Calmientakers 1.000 Calmientakers 1.000 Calm	Wholesale cade	6,096	o 000	4 414	5,327	570	>64	. 0	1
Confisione forement and kindred workers 1.04, 81.4 88,971 72, 49 67,700 2,407 24,231 7,258 6,9 Blackmeths torganism and hammerman 1.05 1.050 1.050 1.050 1.050 Blackmeths torganism and hammerman 20,000 20,000 20,000 20,000 20,000 Calmientakers and patterminishers 1.128 1.062 880 851 1.06 1.050 Calmientakers and patterminishers 1.128 1.062 880 851 1.068 1.06 1.050 Calmientakers and patterminishers 1.000 1.000 1.000 Calmientakers and patterminishers 1.000 1.000 Calmientakers and patterminishers 1.000 1.000 Calmientakers and patterminishers 1.000 1.000 Calmientakers and patterminishers 1.000 1.000 Calmientakers and patterminishers 1.000 1.000 Calmientakers and patterminishers 1.000 1.000 Calmientakers and scontinus maconicity operators 1.000 Calmientakers and scontinus maconicity operators 1.000 Calmientakers and scontinus maconicity operators 1.000 Calmientakers and scontinus maconicity operators 1.000 Calmientakers and scontinus maconicity operators 1.000 Calmientakers and scontinus 1.000 Calmientakers and scontinus maconicity operators 1.000 Calmientakers and scontinus 1.000 Calmientakers and scontinus maconicity operators 1.000 Calmientakers and scontinus 1.000 Calmientakers and scontinus 1.000 Calmientakers and scontinus 1.000 Calmientakers and scontinus 1.000 Calmientakers and scontinus 1.000 Calmientakers and scontinus 1.000 Calmientakers and scontinus 1.000 Calmientakers 1.000 Calmientakers 1.000 Calmientakers 1.000 Calmientakers 1.000 Calmientakers 1.000 Calmientakers 1.000 Calmientakers 1.000 Calmientakers 1.000 Calmientakers 1.000 Calmientakers 1.000 Calmientakers 1.000 Calmientakers 1.000 Calmientakers 1.000 Calmientakers 1.000 Calmientakers 1.000 Calmientakers 1.000 Calmientakers 1.000 Calmientakers 1.000 Calm	O her industries inel not reported)	18,805	18,363	1 098	1,003	152	249	1,179	1,1
Salester 1,6-3 1,999 1,899 1,234 1/4 356 350 Solider values 798 772 294 296 296 313 311 326 1,11 Solider values 798 779 296 296 296 313 311 326 1,11 Solider values 798 799 296 296 313 314 315 Solider values 798 799 296 296 318 318 Solider values 798 799 296 296 318 318 Solider values 798 799 296 296 296 296 Solider values 798 296 296 296 296 Solider values 798 296 296 296 296 Solider values 798 296 296 296 296 Solider values 798 296 296 296 Solider values 798 296 296 296 Solider values 798 296 296 296 Solider values 798 296 296 Solider values 798 296 296 Solider values 798 296 296 Solider values 798 296 296 Solider values 798 296 296 Solider values 798 296 296 Solider values 798 296 296 Solider values 798 296 296 Solider values 798 296 296 Solider values 798 296 296 Solider values 798 Solider values 798 296 Solider values 798 296 Solider values 798 Solider values 798 296 Solider values 798 Solider values 798 Solider values 798 Solider values 798 Solider values 798 Solider val	Craftsmen foremen and kindred workers					2,407	24,251	7,258	6,9
## 3rde **Lulosa* State **Lulosa* \$70 797 6681 986 .32 116 97 Chamstenakors and pattermankers .1,128 1,092 899 815 1,888 146 .51 Lapesters 20,124 12,022 899 815 1,888 146 .51 Lapesters .2,24 .2,24 .2,24 .2,24 .2,24 Lapesters .2,24 .2,24 .2,24 .2,24 .2,24 Lapesters .2,24 .2,24 .2,24 .2,24 .2,24 .2,24 Lapesters .2,24 .2,24 .2,24 .2,24 .2,24 .2,24 Lapesters .2,24 .2,24 .2,24 .2,24 .2,24 .2,24 Early and the special goods and capee mfg. .2,24 .2,2	Bakers	1,403	1,399	1 289	1.234	1//	136	30	
Appendix Appendix		870	757	681	58b	- 32	116	5-	,
Toleran Table Table Table Table Tabl	Cabon et a al a a de a de a de a de a de a de a	1,128	18 643			188	181		2.1
100 100	Compositors and typesetters	301	1,283		1,136	126	225	22	
100 100	Cratemen houstmen, & const macoinery operators.	4,024	3,799	3.2.4	2.948	82°	782	202	1 3
Mg. noutlarshie goods that not spec mfg.) 1, 996 2, 902 3,474 3,400 1,100 300 100 100 100 100 100 100 100 100	Manufacture of mahla made	9.271	9,151	6,178	6 0%	2 50%	2,477	102	1 2
American description American description	Mig. nondurable goods incl not spec mig.)		2,502	1.913	1 905		510	168	1
Decomposity Company	Nonmanufacturing industries (incl. not rptd.)				2.333	546	-35	161	
Administration of the control of the	Locomotive Chilingurs	85+	846	736	~28	93	93	25	
##ement telestrien and stoon, outstare - 9-12 1.764 1.492 1.393 1.20 2.20 2.20 2.20 2.20 2.20 2.20 2.20		3,681	3,535	2 678	2.764	615	590	3.88	
	Masons tile setters and stone outlers	~,912	1 784	248	1 399	32	32	9	
L'exameles and replarment ration and blott upon 97 000 7.369 2.268 2.201 605 100 metals and replarment and born fixers 10 77 10,185 7.00 7.369 2.268 2.201 605 100 metals and replarment and born fixers 10 77 0.000 7.369 2.26 1.20 100 100 100 100 100 100 100 100 100 1	Meelcanes and repairmen automobile .	10.259	0,904	6.047	6,382	2,899	2,827	713	
21 22 7 7 7 7 7 7 7 7	ther mechanics and repairmen radio and television	10 473	10,185	7 (00	7,369	2,268	2,221	605	
Parters (construction parentangers & glassers. 7,447 6,775 5 00 5,118 1,426 1,322 11.5 11.6 1,426 1,323 1.5 11.6 1,426 1,323 1.5 11.6 1,426 1,427 1.5 11.6 1,427 1.5 11.6 1,427 1.5 11.6 1,427 1.5 11.6 1,427 1.5 11.6 1.6 11.6 1	Mulwrights Moliers metal	674	638	358 115		23	22	7	
Flaster vs. and census financer		7,447	6,739	5 00	5,:18	1.426	1,325		
Purifug traffsmen axe dompositors & typesetiers . 131 522 7.0 587 118 1.66 17 720 0.05 587 118 1.66 286.		1,442	4,250	3,751	3,489	1,168	1,067	371	
Shoemakers and renames except factory 740 722 02 500 521 1,999 286 540-032 109 53 5,007 2,016 222 109 53	Flumbe s and pipe fitters Printing craftsmen axe compositors & typesetiers	231	222	476	468	39	38	17	
ORMODAY SIGNATURE - 199 51	Shoemakers and repaire s except factory		3, 793	2,057	2,016	+,521	1,-99	286	
8*nictural motal workers. 35 11 32 38 35 11	Structural metal workers_	971	851	688	597 322	38	35	11	
		1,276	1,185	1,083	1,001		147	38	
276 1,083 1,003	Poolmakers, and die makers and setters		64			1,170			

Table 75—OCCUPATION OF THE EXPERIENCED CIVILIAN LABOR FORCE AND OF EMPLOYED PERSONS, BY SEX, FOR THE STATE, URBAN AND RURAL 1950—Con.

	The 8	ia.	Urbe	AG.	Rural n	onfarm	Rural	farm
For ups. or. and sex	cavilian labor tome	Em.,sloyed	Experiment evilian labor force	Amployed	Experienced ervilian lapor force	Employed	Experienced avilian labor force	Employed
Maso-Cor. Operances and condred workers	. (n	نة-7رىد	יסר, נד	ا دامهرات	33,660	ون يو	_0,404	10 11
Annestices	- +	A 055	961	899	1 38	1,030	32 227	2
Attendan e auti service and parking - Brakenien and switchmen railroad	7"	1,232	- 627	2,633 538	1 075 214 755	209	25	20
Street, ser or of switchigh land and	414	∦ تصديرو ۱	628	2.8	200	745	8>5 50	9,4
us or vers. Ters garders, and poinhers metal	110	2,00	_00	95	8	7 4u3	2 59	
aundry and dry clear ag operatives. feat culters cheept slaughter and packing house Lips operatives and laborers (n.e.c.)	4, 125	2 000	2 2 4	2, _6	4.54	446	59 135	1.
Loe operatives and laborers (n.e.c.)			4,70	4 u55	6,/61	2,232 10	-,144	4,0
lotomen street subway and elevated railway	Rus	31.0	6.0	622		14:	44	
arture *xeep construction and maintenance. over station operators. uton and deck ands	237 1	47	:40	627	1-7 3° 605	88 605	101	3
alors and deck ands	3 C- S	- 232	4,092 502	523	999	9.14	367	3
	4,744	72	54	.55 097	688	666 405	160	1
ationary fremen aucao devers and chaufeurs	37,039	29, 74	3 830	3 080	7 875	405 7 560	3,399	3,2
e.ders and flames atters	4,022	29, 74	2 3/4	2,273	1,103 (7 560 1 087 1 497	3C5 3^8	2
ther specifier operatives and kindred workers	4 483	4,074	2,34.	7,236	1,563			3
peratives and kindred workers (n e c.)	31,47	45 14.	24,20_	23 047 16,647	10 277 8 169	9,803 7,837	3,005	2,9
peratives and kindred workers (n e c.) Manufa turing Durable goods Rewritis planing rails & mass, wood prod	27, 375 -,2 0	76 794 7,905 -,037	-7,435 4,774 1,486	4 500	8 169 2,732 2 088	7,837 2,32/ 2,002	800 646	
	-,20	-,037	399	305 1	78	~7	20	
Stone . as and glass products	4.603	4C2	956 253	920	214	209 47	33 20	
Primari metal industries . Fabric d metal ind (incl not spec metal) Machinery except electrical.	322	o49 4	1.5	282	95	63 93	.6 26	
Machinery except electrical.	437 42 73	401	30 ⁴ 35	23	5 1	4	2	
The real escalary, equipment, & supplies Motor veloces and instor velock equipment Transportation equip. ex motor vehicle.	444	·7*	49 340	46	78	12	9 20	
Other du alle grods	382	307	34a 32,	31~	4	46	8	
vonduracie guocs	9,522	18 -6	2,5 9 3 643	12,067	5 39: 1 63m	5,484	1,551 362	1,5
Yood and landred products.	5,8.4	257	2.4	23.	ın.	10	362 10	
Kintting and other seviale mill provides Anner & other fabricated textile products Paper and, allied products Chemical's and amed products	9C	42	490	53 463	29	26 16	7,	
Paper and ailed products	5,102	5,00° 3,113 20	2,57	2 787	1,742	1, 13	532 293	
Leaner and leather products Other nondurable goods	3,2-3	20	29 .	3	3	او		
Other nondurable goods Not spenfer manuscturing industries	4,451	4 269	د . رد ع ا	3 09u	923	932	343 20	. 3
Normanufactume industria (ne) not mid)	r 601	9.718	6,859	6 450	2,108	1 906	634	6
Nonmanufacturing industries (.nel. not rptd.) Fransport, commun, a other public utilities Wholesau and retail trade Other industries (incl. not reported).	2 331 2 64:	a 530 2,517	2 109	2,041	656 368	1 906 629 353	166	
Other 'ndustries find not reported).	4,025	3,0~_	2,176	2,0 0 5 2 344	1,084	984	367	
Prava.e household workers	-,4 c	± 4±0	⊥ 084	1 027	336	315	76	
Service wo kers except private bousehold -	JB,580	2 902	2,200	30,214	5,51.8	5 791 587	1,122 cli	1,0
arbers benuticians and manicinets harwomen janitors and porters books, except in ate household	2 987 ,776	14.134	10 2-2	9 700	1 262 1	1,238	262	ž
ooks, except an ate household	2,758	2 531 519	2,280	2,053	402 32	3"2		
eva-or operators	4.650	3 892	1 551	.542	73 949 457	73	2 31	
uards and watchmen. observes siems, and marchais arters, bartenders, and counte workers	3,130 5 73.	3,124 5 362	2,886	2,578	457	32 73 525 4_4	26+	
ther service workers except private nousehold	5 73.	5 362	4,042	4,783	886 838	804 830	1.3	11 1
Farm laborers and fo.emea	/6 23	44 924	2,569	2,18-	14,095	13,45	29,519	20,2
arm laborers unpaid family workers arm laborers, except unpaid, and farm foremen	L: 393	13 2 79	1,1	2,075	724	598	12,538	1°,4 16,7
	32,820	32,625			13,371	12,753	16,581	
Laborers, except farm and mane	89 071	02,473	1 411	4, 901	29,328	27,589	7,049	6 *
indermen and oystrimen ongsho emen and stevedores um >= ren raftsmen and wood choppers.	7,565 5,351 6,06.	356	2,270	1,324	5,819	5,703	355 18	
im >= ren raftsmen and wood choppers.	6,06. 5,03/	5,300	%67 1:2	2,940	3,540	3 373 1 _9_	-, 354 456	1,0
aboret in e.c	r5,060	59 474	42,1.4	38 -21	18,360	lu 968	4,586	
Manufacturing	22 625 10 772	24,004	13,205	12 152	7,075	7,170	4.745	4.4
Duranic good. Furnitus saw & plan g mills, mise wood pr.	8,145	7 059	3,0">	4,736 2 862	4,028	4,268 3,814 170	112 1014	-,1
Stone, clay and glass products	869	821 354	545 279	611 I	52 92	170	42 10	
Frimery meta in testries Fahra d metal ind (inc) not spec meta.)	371 395 160	30L 142	33° 122	209	51	47	8 7	
Machinery including electrical.	764	653	616	200 1	.1:	96	52	
Other durable goods - Nondurable goods Food and kindred produces	98 1 760	±0 848 II	6,021	7 178	1,_11	30 2 667	628	
Food and kindred products Textile mill products and a sparel	2,622	4 072	3,134	2,748	-,3_1	1,164	628	
Chemicals and allied products	1,814	1 709	-,150	1 13.	241	27 5' 0	113	
Chemicals and allied products Other none unable goods. Not specified manufac uring industries	7,990	4 /16	2 430 48	3,266	1 2-1	1,169	329	:
Normanusaet aring industries unel not rotd.)	-		21 909	21 969	10,685	9.75	2 841	4
Construence	42,435 16,841 5 253	36,465 14,785 0 047	10,C92 3 372	0 103	4,642 1,590	4 134	1,537	1.
Railroads and railway express service Transportation except railroad	2.741	2,782	2,457	2,227 2 034 2,118	1,393 /1A *53	1,"48 380 515	28b	ĺ.
Telecommunications & Lithines & sanitary se v W polessle and retail made	4 904	2,760	2 21	2,118	1 217	1,172	130	
O ner industries inel no reported)	8,067	7,133	5 182	4,518	2,204	2,05	#98	
Occupation not reported	L5 650	8,260	8,084	4 140	5,_69	2,472	2,307	1,0

Table 75 —OCCUPATION OF THE EXPERIENCED CIVILIAN LABOR FORCE AND OF EMPLOYED PERSONS, BY SEX, FOR THE STATE, URBAN AND RURAL 1950—Con.

	The S	state	Urp	LD.	Rural n	onfarn.	Rural	farm
Occupation and sex	Expenenced civilian labor force	Employed	Experienced cryman labor force	Employed	Experienced civilian tabor force	Employed	Experienced civ han abor force	Employed
Female, 14 years old and over	208 144	22,125	176,043	1,0,001	38 304	30,927	20,73/	23,20
Professional, technical, and kindred workers	29,391	29, 459	22,07*	21,992	5,2_8	- 1/3	2,099	2,084
Accountants and auditors Actresses dancers and en ertainers (n e c	243	532	508 219	502	24	2-7	14	
Artists and art teachers Authors edi on, and reporters	231 303	225	279	210	12 17	1	14	1
	198	195	7.60	210 272 178	1.	- 11	7 13	
College preadents pro "ra & inst uctors (n.e.c Designers and draftsmer	770	173	450	443	4	43	13	1
Dietirans and nutritionists	27/	272	235 54	272 234 54	28	27	11	1
Labrarians . Musicians and music teachers	Cu2 925	653	-30 765	52 A	105	104	27	20
	4,937	4,891	4.207	4.129	127 580	-20 -72	33 150	3.
Nurses, professional Nurses student professional Physicians and surgeons		1 027	1,01,4	1,012	12	12	4	_5
onal stientists Sonal, webere, and recreation workers	-c3 72	1,135	66	6L	4	4	. 2	
Teachers (nec	15,014	15,451	10 010	933 9,963	3 415	139	1,689	1,68
Teachers (n e.c.) Technicians medical and dental Therapia and healer (n e.c.)	6C1 73	598 72	5u3 62	560	ن 10	10	.3	
Other professional technical and kindred workers	.,748	1 72/	1,450	1 4.	225	234	43	6.
Formers and form managers	2 900	2,103	110	-09	200	203	2,659	2,65
Managers officials & proprietors exc farm	10,725	۵, 45	7-91	7,453	2,2^>	2,193	100	581
Specified manager and officials Managers officials & propr's (nec.)—salaried Wholesale and regail trade	1,469 3,101	1,733 3,0c7 1,528	2,546	2,520	320 444	31o 438	_36	_21
	1,542	1,528	,244 1,302 4 362	1,231	247 197	24o 192	51	51
Mgrs officials & propr s n.e.c)—self-employed	6,105	6 145	4 362	4 352	-,439 439	1 439	60 344 38	354 35
More officials & proof s n.e.c)—self-employed Eating and drinking places Wholesale & retraited, exc eating & drinking pl Other industries (incl not reported)	3,578	3,571	2,444	2,437	8.9	839	295	20
Clencal and kindred workers	50,015	49 762	628 44, 522	928 +3 771	4,609	16	1,484	1,44
Bookserpers	6,15 3,505	6,058	4 995	4,910 3 072	858	4,545	228	20'
Cathers Straggaphe s, typiste and scoretanes -	3,505 18,670	3,39/	3.182	3 072	2n5 1,288	1,22	58 437	43
Telephone operators Other denos' and kundred workers	4,548 17, 41	18,-08 4,473 -7,423	3 964 15 43e	16,705 3 599 12,172	478 1,720	470 1 994	106 585	10
Sales workers	20,819	20,291	15,904	10,447	3,708	3,7.0	1 127	1,13
	722	'80	703	69.	75	75 34	14 6	1
Insurance and real estalle agents and brokers Other specified sales workers Salesmen and sales clerks (ne.c.), retail trade Salesmen and sales clerks (re.c.), exo retail trade	18,348	274 18 381	14,197	13.786	3,554	3,50±	,107	1,09
Salesmen and sales clause (r e.c.), exe retail track	885	820	761	13,780	-04	100	20	21
Craftsmen, foremen and kindred workers_	1,961	⊥ 872 372	1,689	2,012	208	197 27	64	6.
Other craftsmen and cdred workers	1,583	-,500	346 1 343	1,271	280	170	co	5
Operatives and kindred workers	21,273	20,269	17,578	16 727	2,863	2,743	832	79
Dreamakers and seamstresses, except factory Laundry and dry elemning operatives	2 372 5,5*9	2 504 5 373	2,2 4 4,75	2, <u>.51</u> 4,630	252 618	248	106 146	_0: 14:
Spinne s and weave s textile Other specified operatives and kindred workers. Operatives and kindred workers (n e c.)	228 1,254	2_8	224 862	21.4 82.3	27 ₀	3 268	116	-1
Ope stives and kindred workers (n e c.) Manufacturing	11,660	10,968	6,483	8 909 7 550	1,714	1 624	463 400	43
Durable goods Meta_industries	731	693	631	507 _73	80	79	18	37
Machine y, including electrical Ofter durable goods	19	17	16	410	3	3	1.0	1
Ventrum ale mode	972	8,618	7 3.9	6.308	. 434	73 1 357	_6 379	15
Nondurante goods Food and kindred products	3,323	3 024	2,291 225	2,082	818	754	2_4	_81
	282	266	270	218 257	10	7	2	
lexine mill products, except knitting Apparel & other fabricated textile products. Leatner and leather products	3 3.6	3,184	3,129	2,987	140	244	58	26
	4,982	_,90o	1 427	± 35∃ 51	403	445	ر٥۔	10
Not specified man ifacturing industries. Nonmanufacturing industries (incl. not rptd.).	1,693	۵,599	1,42	1,150	د19	184	63	62
Private household workers	14,+06	42,257	35,352	31,570	8,519	8 22/	2,035	2 46:
Private household worker—hving in Private household worker—hving out	43,319	4,173	12,520	30,738	8,339	8,044	2,460	2,38
Service workers, except private household	34 931	32,523	27,436	20,235	4,068	^,913	1 427	1,40
Attendar is hospital and other institution Baroers beauticians and manicurists	2,470	1 /43 2 832	1,178	1,157 2,413 1,374	22o 356	2 ₄ 3 35°	56 57	6:
Charwomen, anitors and ports	1,650	6,243	4,091	1,374	225 1,837	1,804	28 555	66 28 55
Charwomes, anitors and ports a Cooks except private hor schold Housekeepers & s ewards exe private household	1,014	1,003	844	832 2,000	137	40.	34 146	34
Waitreves burienders and counter workers	2,695	8 509	2,125 7,054	6,627	1,660	1,595	226	28
Other service workers, ex-est private household _	9,700	9 326	8,282	7,018	1,203	1, 175	235	233
Farm laborers and foremen	12,955	6,922	546 58	53	2 761.	2 612	9,n28 5,613	9,525
Farm laborers unpaid amily workers Farm laborers except unpaid, and farm foremen	6,004	5,682	488	410	2,501	2 33"	3,01	6,094 2,935
Laborers, except farm and mine .	2,039	1,881	1,479	1,756	457	428	103	9'

Occupation not reported	6,052	3,880	3,431	2,072	1,462	864	1,159	953

Table 76.—AGE OF EMPLOYED PERSONS BY OCCUPATION, COLOR, AND SEX, FOR THE STATE AND FOR STANDARD METROPOLITAN AREAS OF 250,000 OR MORE: 1950

Area, occupation, color, and sex	Total 14 years old and over	14 and 15 years	16 and 17 years	18 and 19 years	20 to 24 years	25 to 29 years	30 to 34 years	35 to 44 years	45 to 54 years	55 to 59 years	60 to 64 years	65 and over
THE STATE—TOTAL												
Male, employed	[illegible]46,782	79[illegible]	13,518	[illegible],301	[illegible]2,[illegible]2	82,838	79,674	158,[illegible]11	1[illegible]9,397	[illegible]0,348	27,627	25,313
Professional, technical, and kindred workers	[illegible],262	16	[illegible]	350	3 988	7,577	6,525	10,799	6,[illegible]78	2,1[illegible]8	[illegible],442	[illegible],710
Accountants and auditors	[illegible]99[illegible]			15	281	682	332	1,054	79[illegible]	240	162	136
Architects	300			1	24	44	36	76	47	22	18	30
Artists and art teachers	[illegible]01		-	3	34	67	[illegible]	[illegible]9	45	[illegible]7	10	15
Authors, editors, and reporters	[illegible]8[illegible]		[illegible]	7	83	25	62	[illegible]58	78	32	16	22
Chemists	823			7	89	172	180	2[illegible]3	105	36	30	1[illegible]
Clergymen	[illegible] 182			[illegible]	1[illegible]3	276	390	871	757	283	18[illegible]	33[illegible]
College presidents, prof'rs, & instructors (n.e.c.)	1 [illegible]			1	84	237	225	422	273	[illegible]	[illegible]	49
Dentists	[illegible]			1	[illegible]	106	[illegible]16	222	19[illegible]	65	7[illegible]	89
Designers and draftsmen	[illegible]36		2	15	2[illegible]3	259	53	180	70	22	1[illegible]	1[illegible]
Engineers, aeronautical	[illegible]				2	2	[illegible]	1				
Engineers, civil	1 99[illegible]			8	174	305	228	627	412	103	65	69
Engineers, electrical	918			2	108	[illegible]86	152	230	156	45	23	16
Engineers, mechanical	[illegible] 288			1	1[illegible]0	289	188	309	235	69	50	37
Other technical engineers	2 263			2	224	563	491	558	275	79	30	35
Lawyers and judges	2 198			1	54	298	3[illegible]3	[illegible]35	448	15[illegible]	11[illegible]	162
Musicians and music teachers	1,0[illegible]6	4	22	[illegible]9	188	19[illegible]	165	248	123	29	2[illegible]	33
Natural scientists (n.e.c.)	969			3	92	2[illegible]3	204	286	1[illegible]0	36	12	13
Pharmacists	[illegible]11[illegible]			1	[illegible]6	83	90	312	310	128	77	89
Physicians and surgeons	2 838			1	15[illegible]	[illegible]9	48[illegible]	708	302	136	122	25[illegible]
Social scientists	177			1	8	37	32	44	31	14	5	5
Social welfare, and recreation workers	323		1	4	29	51	58	95	50	11	8	16
Surveyors	76[illegible]			22	207	134	68	17[illegible]	81	15	13	15
Teachers (n.e.c.)	5,392		1	12	560	1,[illegible]23	991	1,535	735	201	142	92
Technicians, medical and dental	[illegible]36	1	2	21	125	1[illegible]5	95	100	60	8	[illegible]	3
Other professional, technical, and kindred workers	6,976	11	28	148	990	1 397	1,[illegible]28	[illegible] 668	925	310	191	180
Farmers and farm managers	86 380	181	[illegible]	1,145	5,773	8,038	9 229	21,573	18,[illegible]1	7,576	6,045	7,705
Managers, officials & proprietors exc. farm	6[illegible],[illegible]07	[illegible]8	53	232	2,536	[illegible],581	7,430	19,088	16,087	5,[illegible]29	3,525	3 418
Officials & inspectors, State & local administration	1,834			4	59	14[illegible]	157	[illegible]45	[illegible]60	212	157	195
Other specified managers and officials	7,653	7	8	40	413	817	95[illegible]	2,172	[illegible],843	691	403	302
Managers, officials & propr's (n.e.c.)—salaried	23,210	16	30	123	1 2[illegible]7	2,443	2,967	7,083	5,540	1,76[illegible]	1,089	945
Manufacturing	4,068	4	6	17	157	[illegible]39	[illegible]9	1,339	1,007	366	212	162
Wholesale and retail trade	[illegible],551	[illegible]	12	82	684	1,2[illegible]4	1,[illegible]98	2 [illegible]89	[illegible],909	620	354	329
Finance, insurance, and real estate	2 373	1	[illegible]	3	83	246	2[illegible]1	671	627	[illegible]81	12[illegible]	163
Other industries (incl. not reported)	7,218	6	1[illegible]	21	283	[illegible]94	839	2,[illegible]79	[illegible],997	600	397	291
Mgrs., officials & propr's (n.e.c.)—self-employed	30,810	25	15	65	657	2 176	3,349	9,388	8,22[illegible]	2,859	1 876	1,97[illegible]
Construction	2 [illegible]56	3		4	[illegible]5	198	324	744	578	[illegible]87	143	110
Manufacturing	2 204		1	4	54	144	224	657	573	219	163	165
Wholesale trade	2,153	3		5	45	137	212	[illegible]56	619	20[illegible]	127	[illegible]42
Eating and drinking places	[illegible] 399	2	1	[illegible]	116	278	415	1,026	922	304	195	134
Retail trade, exc. eating and drinking places	15 112	14	13	38	4[illegible]7	1,078	1 [illegible]07	4 593	3 905	1 388	94[illegible]	1 090
Other industries (incl. not reported)	[illegible],[illegible]80	3		10	138	341	567	1,712	1,627	554	299	335
Clerical and kindred workers	35,37[illegible]	5[illegible]	417	1 462	5,94[illegible]	5,86[illegible]	4,459	7,130	5,45[illegible]	2,074	1,39[illegible]	1,115
Bookkeepers	3 741		9	140	746	705	[illegible]21	[illegible]8[illegible]	490	169	[illegible]42	136
Mail carriers	1,872	1	7	13	181	339	2[illegible]1	[illegible]22	[illegible]30	169	[illegible]9	40
Other clerical and kindred workers	29,761	50	401	1,30[illegible]	[illegible]	4 822	[illegible],647	6,[illegible]25	4,635	1,736	1,[illegible]76	939
Sales workers	35 909	665	932	1,[illegible]36	4 338	[illegible],667	4,871	8,096	5,630	1,856	1,36[illegible]	[illegible],338
Insurance agents and brokers	[illegible],126	3	3	2[illegible]	[illegible]	690	57[illegible]	944	797	[illegible]06	[illegible]01	185
Real estate agents and brokers	1,021		1	4	27	85	9[illegible]	206	248	118	99	137
Other specified sales workers	2,223	[illegible]23	359	90	155	146	130	279	269	1[illegible]5	73	84
Salesmen and sales clerks (n.e.c.)	28,539	139	569	1,037	3,761	4,74[illegible]	4,0[illegible]	6,667	[illegible],[illegible]16	1,[illegible]7	987	932
Manufacturing	2,931	12	13	[illegible]	258	530	468	[illegible]85	[illegible]19	136	99	74
Wholesale trade	6 000	1	1[illegible]	63	[illegible]39	1,060	1,005	1,666	980	293	191	189
Retail trade	18,36[illegible]	110	526	920	2,835	2 [illegible]54	2 428	3,885	2 599	828	[illegible]55	623
Other industries (incl. not reported)	1,245	16	17	17	129	202	167	331	2[illegible]8	60	42	46
Craftsmen, foremen, and kindred workers	[illegible]8,973	76	308	[illegible],432	9,528	13,[illegible]50	13,81[illegible]	27,872	20,311	6,101	3,9[illegible]0	2,331
Bakers	1,399	3	[illegible]3	59	17[illegible]	[illegible]82	188	379	7[illegible]	72	36	17
Blacksmiths, forgemen, and hammermen	727		2	2	17	24	43	[illegible]34	197	1[illegible]9	86	103
Boilermakers	757	-	1	3	35	[illegible]6	109	222	206	64	39	11
Cabinetmakers and patternmakers	1,082	3	5	13	100	[illegible]72	[illegible]	243	183	87	63	69
Carpenters	18,643	9	[illegible]7	252	1 432	2 271	2,361	5,1[illegible]4	[illegible] 082	1,480	1,0[illegible]	574
Compositors and typesetters	1,283	1	8	34	168	172	1[illegible]3	343	230	74	60	30
Cranemen, hoistmen, & const. machinery operators	3 799		9	40	[illegible]16	496	617	[illegible],225	780	[illegible]73	102	31
Electricians	3,922	1	1	35	436	600	680	[illegible],189	664	14[illegible]	83	31
Foremen (n.e.c.)	9,151	[illegible]	[illegible]	15	288	609	1,059	[illegible],052	2,586	[illegible]89	478	267
Manufacturing, durable goods	1,276	2		2	[illegible]5	101	1[illegible]6	396	[illegible]24	113	[illegible]	62
Mfg., nondurable goods (incl. not spec. mfg.)	2,582	2	1	6	62	146	3[illegible]7	947	736	209	104	42
Nonmanufacturing industries (incl. not rptd.)	[illegible],293	[illegible]		7	181	362	586	1,709	[illegible] 526	467	289	[illegible]63
Linemen & servicemen, t'graph, t'phone, & power	3,027		4	[illegible]33	896	775	417	42[illegible]	282	46	40	13
Locomotive engineers	846				9	2[illegible]	54	[illegible]18	281	[illegible]6	144	67
Locomotive firemen	672			3	65	175	129	[illegible]66	110	35	28	11
Machinists and job setters	3,535	2	[illegible]	17	262	4[illegible]3	[illegible]30	1,035	768	237	149	8[illegible]
Masons, tile setters, and stone cutters	1,784	2	7	33	259	296	211	403	326	98	85	64
Mechanics and repairmen, airplane	283			3	31	92	74	50	28	2	[illegible]	
Mechanics and repairmen, automobile	9,901	9	32	184	[illegible],217	1,81[illegible]	1,8[illegible]5	2,996	1,474	223	101	34
Mechanics and repairmen, radio and television	885	1	[illegible]	1[illegible]	134	217	164	245	88	9	8	4
Other mechanics and repairmen, and loom fixers	10,185	[illegible]	2[illegible]	136	1,090	1,532	1 529	2,[illegible]73	[illegible],910	500	292	[illegible]87
Millwrights	638	1		1	24	61	76	23[illegible]	156	39	3[illegible]	17
Molders, metal	138			6	16	1[illegible]	22	30	29	9	[illegible]0	2
Painters (construction), paperhangers, & glaziers	6 739	12	40	146	564	794	901	[illegible],940	[illegible],463	444	287	168
Plasterers and cement finishers	[illegible],250		6	16	95	144	133	367	318	93	50	28
Plumbers and pipe fitters	4 [illegible]03	2	9	44	[illegible]90	635	7[illegible]2	[illegible],567	[illegible],092	28[illegible]	147	64
Printing craftsmen, exc. compositors & typesetters	[illegible]22		[illegible]	12	53	81	64	136	112	35	20	8
Shoemakers and repairers, except factory	[illegible]20	[illegible]	3	23	59	76	[illegible]	174	156	57	41	62
Stationary engineers	3,793	1	2	11	212	409	409	[illegible],078	[illegible],013	310	208	140
Structural metal workers	851			13	82	141	185	257	1[illegible]	25	14	3
Tailors and furriers	368	1	2	2	26	32	42	76	8[illegible]	30	34	37
Tinsmiths, coppersmiths, and sheet metal workers	1,185	[illegible]	4	37	174	246	178	260	17[illegible]	55	35	22
Toolmakers, and die makers and setters	64				8	8	5	13	15	8	4	3
Other craftsmen and kindred workers	5,921	7	70	145	697	824	734	[illegible],425	[illegible],137	419	280	183

Table 76.—AGE OF EMPLOYED PERSONS, BY OCCUPATION, COLOR, AND SEX, FOR THE STATE AND FOR STANDARD METROPOLITAN AREAS OF 250,000 OR MORE 1950—Con

Area occupation, color and sex	Total, 14 years old and over	14 and 15 years	16 and 17 years	18 and 19 years	20 to 24 years	25 to 29 years	30 to 34 years	35 to 44 years	45 to 54 years	55 to 59 years	60 to 64 years	65 and over
THE STATE--TOTAL												
Male—Con												
Operatives and kindred workers	111,790	537	2,165	[illegible]	[illegible]	7,[illegible]	16 103	28,712	16 777	4,434	2 550	1 317
Apprentices	1,055	[illegible]	4[illegible]	15[illegible]	379	256	[illegible]	8[illegible]	21	3	5	4
Attendants auto service and parking	3,886	42	224	386	907	657	402	680	313	83	53	37
Brakemen and switchmen railroad	1,832	-	-	12	153	241	274	4[illegible]	356	172	112	51
Bus drivers	2 212	1	3	24	160	360	436	1,068	724	246	143	47
Filers, grinders and polishers metal	457	1	3	5	2[illegible]	26	43	89	129	50	51	47
Furnacemen smeltermen, and heaters	10[illegible]		•		19	33	13	17	14	[illegible]	2	1
Laundry and dry cleaning operatives	2,627	1[illegible]	27	138	4[illegible]3	395	34[illegible]	673	408	91	50	21
Meat cutters except slaughter and packing house	2,070	3	20	73	2[illegible]	296	26[illegible]	522	363	128	87	56
Mine operatives and laborers (n.e.c.)	11,977	5	63	288	1,998	2,259	2,022	3 295	1 588	377	115	97
Motormen, street, subway, and elevated railway	387				19	77	57	80	96	34	18	6
Painters, except construction and maintenance	818		8	28	107	[illegible]	1[illegible]1	225	140	34	19	9
Power station operators	237		-	[illegible]	[illegible]9	4[illegible]	36	62	30	17	7	4
Sailors and deck hands	2 356	2	3[illegible]	133	357	411	[illegible]	498	324	66	[illegible]8	18
Sawyers	1,832	7	30	77	2[illegible]0	203	184	728	375	168	86	34
Spinners and weavers textile	72				6	7	11	19	17	8	•	2
Stationary firemen	1,918	2	2	11	109	178	16[illegible]	763	532	212	154	90
Taxicab drivers and chauffeurs	4 163	2	2	90	489	626	601	1,234	797	194	75	34
Truck drivers and deliverymen	29,[illegible]	354	1 041	1,473	4,823	4,909	[illegible],396	7 400	3,587	592	383	156
Welders and flame cutters	3,727		2	32	311	651	864	1,304	452	73	22	[illegible]6
Other specified operatives and kindred workers	4,074	8	64	179	693	622	513	990	648	184	122	51
Operatives and kindred workers (n.e.c.)	35,812	9[illegible]	546	1,394	5,229	5,37[illegible]	4 929	9,125	[illegible],851	1,667	1 011	596
Manufacturing	26,794	[illegible]4	308	978	3 918	[illegible],21[illegible]	3,861	7,065	4 2[illegible]7	1,130	679	357
Durable goods	7,905	1[illegible]	10[illegible]	373	1 223	1,[illegible]60	1 001	1 840	1,33[illegible]	351	268	158
Sawmills planing mills, & misc wood prod.	4 037	6	74	208	653	533	439	930	747	211	158	78
Furniture and fixtures	462	2	6	30	70	59	-	[illegible]	67	23	17	[illegible]6
Stone, clay and glass products	1,172	4		78	180	183	175	466	206	51	3[illegible]	28
Primary metal industries	302		3	5	44	44	42	98	43	15	2	2
Fabric'd metal ind (incl not spec metal)	669	1	2	34	107	146	107	175	85	22	13	7
Machinery except electrical	401	1	1	17	54	73	64	97	52	22	15	5
Electrical machinery equipment, & supplies	39		2	3	5	7	8	6		2	1	
Motor vehicles and motor vehicle equipment	67			1	8	14	1[illegible]	15	9	4	2	
Transportation equip exc motor vehicle	389	3	2	9	4[illegible]	[illegible]	5[illegible]	9[illegible]	79	23	15	6
Other durable goods	367		[illegible]	24	58	5[illegible]	43	76	61	18	11	16
Nondurable goods	18,750	18	204	603	2 680	3,01[illegible]	2,835	5,186	2,870	734	408	198
Food and kindred products	5,324	11	137	293	880	7[illegible]1	640	1,227	856	250	176	113
Yarn, thread, and fabric mills	257		1	8	40	40	19	73	51	14	8	3
Knitting and other textile mill products	83	•	3	6	21	9	1[illegible]	16	8	3	2	1
Apparel & other fabricated textile products	486		6	39	94	73	47	117	80	13	10	7
Paper and allied products	5,028	1	24	159	814	808	803	1,418	688	142	68	43
Chemicals and allied products	3,473	1	10	47	481	694	578	885	433	89	38	17
Leather and leather products	30		2	6	1	3	2	3	8	4		1
Other nondurable goods	4 369	5	21	45	345	586	732	1,447	846	219	106	13
Not specified manufacturing industries	139		3	2	15	23	25	39	23	5	3	1
Nonmanufacturing industries (incl not rptd)	9,018	59	238	416	1 311	1,15[illegible]	1,068	2 06[illegible]	1,604	537	332	239
Transport., commun & other public utilities	2 830	1	8	66	322	339	317	738	603	218	126	82
Wholesale and retail trade	2 517	39	128	182	391	329	292	488	[illegible]	122	79	85
Other industries (incl not reported)	3,671	19	92	168	598	486	459	834	619	197	127	72
Private household workers	1,416	21	36	35	155	118	136	337	313	104	75	102
Service workers except private household	36,697	351	930	1,284	3 704	5,829	3,673	7,806	7,647	3,076	2,308	2,029
Barbers beauticians, and manicurists	2 962		1	12	181	256	249	733	858	289	210	173
Charwomen, janitors and porters	11 194	91	297	437	1,181	1,080	1 035	2,432	2,444	982	683	51[illegible]
Cooks, except private household	2,531	7	31	73	222	348	387	670	526	137	84	46
Elevator operators	519		13	13	44	32	32	78	112	65	62	68
Firemen, fire protection	1,644			23	245	247	217	424	339	91	44	17
Guards and watchmen	3 892		6	15	98	128	165	555	995	631	632	667
Policemen, sheriffs, and marshals	3 124			2	167	415	436	747	716	280	174	195
Waiters bartenders, and counter workers	5,362	44	172	258	757	700	684	1,263	866	265	193	140
Other service workers except private household	5 466	209	410	451	815	623	471	944	788	336	226	193
Farm laborers and foremen	44,924	3,137	5,821	5,615	7,453	3,997	3,106	5,990	4,682	1,937	1 467	1,719
Farm laborers, unpaid family workers	13,299	2,163	3,398	2,848	2,625	728	343	448	269	132	117	228
Farm laborers except unpaid, and farm foremen	31,625	974	2,423	2 767	4,828	3 269	2 763	5,542	4,413	1,805	1,350	1,491
Laborers, except farm and mine	82,273	510	[illegible] 904	3,742	10 801	9,826	9,440	19,806	16 016	5,047	3 [illegible]73	2 038
Fishermen and oystermen	7 378	170	384	440	1,043	855	810	1,729	1,256	368	232	113
Longshoremen and stevedores	7,870	2	7	51	258	524	615	1,665	1,298	263	155	52
Lumbermen raftsmen, and wood choppers	5 800	41	167	324	900	624	583	1 336	1 200	353	213	79
Other specified laborers	4,723	56	169	254	599	535	491	964	812	326	210	317
Laborers (n.e.c.)	59,472	271	1,179	2,663	8 001	7,288	6,041	14 122	11,450	3,757	2,323	1,477
Manufacturing	21,004	33	263	929	3,253	2,840	2,646	5 173	3,763	1,159	660	331
Durable goods	10,0[illegible]9	1[illegible]	132	492	1,580	1,2[illegible]2	1 147	2,359	[illegible],915	657	362	168
Furniture, saw & planing mills, misc wood pr	7,059	14	113	387	1,262	886	797	1,736	1,485	576	304	14[illegible]
Stone, clay, and glass products	821		8	50	162	147	110	211	138	30	14	1[illegible]
Primary metal industries	357			7	48	58	63	89	71	12	4	2
Fabric'd metal ind (incl not spec metal)	360		5	20	60	53	30	89	57	16	11	2
Machinery, including electrical	142	-		5	23	15	27	30	28	7	4	2
Transportation equipment	653	1	2	13	69	85	9[illegible]	84	128	48	22	10
Other durable goods	90		3	12	16	8	9	20	11	8	3	
Nondurable goods	10,848	18	129	427	1,6[illegible]7	1,578	1,468	2,800	3,834	500	297	160
Food and kindred products	4,075	13	99	231	686	534	473	937	666	210	142	84
Textile mill products and apparel	308		[illegible]	12	40	3[illegible]	25	78	61	26	15	12
Chemicals and allied products	1,709	2	11	51	268	278	271	447	278	56	38	9
Other nondurable goods	4,7[illegible]6	3	14	133	643	732	699	1,336	829	208	102	59
Not specified manufacturing industries	77		2	4	10	10	11	14	14	2	1	3
Nonmanufacturing industries (incl not rptd.)	38,468	238	916	1 740	4,768	4,448	4,315	8,949	7,687	2,598	1,663	1,146
Construction	14,785	28	287	755	2,124	1,897	1,751	3,507	2,772	901	537	225
Railroads and railway express service	5,047	1	7	48	316	457	544	1,518	1,424	368	251	113
Transportation except railroad	2 482	8	53	105	334	335	318	575	493	174	78	39
Telecommunications & utilities & sanitary serv	2,790	2	25	81	303	274	330	674	583	231	143	114
Wholesale and retail trade	6,261	107	307	450	1,024	829	705	1,465	983	246	178	117
Other industries (incl not reported)	7 133	92	237	301	667	656	667	1,410	1,432	658	476	357
Occupation not reported	8,280	200	329	376	1,107	1,143	888	1,642	1,273	496	335	491

Table 76.—AGE OF EMPLOYED PERSONS, BY OCCUPATION, COLOR, AND SEX, FOR THE STATE AND FOR STANDARD METROPOLITAN AREAS OF 250 000 OR MORE 1950—Con

Area occupation rolor and sex	Total 14 years old and over	14 and 15 years	16 and 17 years	18 and 10 years	20 to 24 years	25 to 29 years	30 to 34 vears	35 to 44 vears	4o to 54 years	55 to 59 years	60 to 64 years	60 and over
THE STATENOW-HITE		7			1						7	
Male, employed	18,5 069	۷,88.	6,374	. 8,184	2_,524	2_ 229	19,865	43 280	34 -00	42,624	7,579	7,91
Professional, sechnical, and kindred workers	1,428	2										
Accountance and auditors	17		-	23	237	426	405	947	654	251	139	24
	12		2		1	2	1 3			-		
artists and art teachers	20				1 4	1 3	3	4	3 4			
Chemists -	1,00				2 2	12		125	37.4	147	3 93	16
College presidents, prof rs, & instructors (ne.c.) Dentists	118	1			1,	FI	, 4	36	:4	4	2	10
Designe s and draftsmen	4				- 2	í	2	2	-4	6	3	
Engineers aeronautical	14				2			7	3	2		
Engineers electrical _ Engineers mechanical _	3	1					1		í	_	1 3	
other technical engineers	6	1			-	1	1	5	2	1	3	
Awyers and judges Musicians and music teachers	6	1					_	2	2		1 7	
Musicians and music teachers	213		2	7	22	26	34	***	35	6	7	
Pharmacusts Physicians and surgeons	43 X0	1			4	10	7	8	1_	- 5	3 2	,
core ementada	20	1		1 1	1 4	2	±0 2	3		2		
Sousi, welfare, and recreation workers	9	1	1		;	3	2	-2	2 2	1	1	
Caschers (n.e.o.:	1,238			1	-23	2-1.	245	409	12/	36	30	:
Technicians medical and dental. Other p ofessions technical and kindred workers	28 497	2			43	9	7	_45	85	32	7	
Fa mers and turm managers	32 888	99	27"	560	2,_75	2 807				2,924		
					-	_	J, 169	7,910	7,236		2,156	3,35
Managers officials, & proprietors exc farm Officials & inspectors State & loss, administration	5,912		- 6	.8	95	191	26.	886	806	287	174	
Other specified managers and officials Managers, official & propris in equi-salaried	14-	,	3	1 4	9	15	3	33	37	5	9	
Managers, off.cial- & propris in e c \—salaried	52	,		8	3 [≥]	58	6A	187	162	.6	32	
Manufacturing Who,esale and retail trade	285			. 5	18	29	27	88	56	32	16	:
Finance, ms trailes, and real cs ate Other advatues (mel not reported)	555 89	1 2		,	15	19	10	62	30	13	7	:
Agre officials, & propr's (n.e.c.)—self-employed Cons ruction	2,200	2	2	3	46	10	184	43	600	220 14	133	1
Manufactarring	JQ.	1		1		1	12	21	12		12	
Wholesale trade Lating and dunking places Retail trade ever esting and armking places.	77 519		1	1	1 6	2,	52	17	169	10	35	1 :
Retail trade eve esting and armking places. Other industries and not reported)	822 490	2	2	1	18	30	67	220	219	09	58 16	
	0.00	!		1	1			-		1		1
Clerical and kindred workers . Bookkee, ers	£ 208	ÿ	3"	57	110	402	322	559	-68	112	84	
Med carriers	546	1	1		6 47	126	106	130	3 81	32	15	
Other cleucal and kindred workers	1,761	9	36	56	257	271	211	-20	304	50	69	
Sales workers	1,749	72	93	73	10	184	الد ا	86د	343	129	28	
Insurance agents and brokers Real es ate agents and brokers Other specified "ales workers	444		1	4	31	43 8	37	109	111	52	- 30	
Other specified sales workers	381	58	37 37	21	22	27	31 82	67	00	11	41	
Salesmen and sales clerks (n.c.o) _ Manufasturing Wholesale trade _	890	14	37	48	94	106	82	201	166	62	38	
Wholesale trade _ Retar trade	48 746	11	34	44	2 78	89	69	21 1j6	1 137	57	37	
Other industres inci not reported)	W.	1	34	44	5	7	59	14	1 8	1 21	1 3,	
Craftsman foremen and kindred workers	096رد۔	17	51	224	1,230	1,728	1,61/	3 620	2,85"	859	247	,
Bacers	419	1	5	16	68	63	65	107			6	
Blacksmiths, organic and hammermen	_44 26	1	1	1	2	6	11 2	36	70 38 10	16 22 3	18	
Cannetmakers and patternmakers	172	1	2	2	21	24	20.	50	3.	10	2	1
connus tota and typosetters	3,343	1	73	45	271	49	رت. 5	83.4	743	333	224	1
Grandmen houstmen & const machinery operators	395	1	2	6	31	44	61	125	89	2.	2	
foreman in e.c.	297	1	-		11	15	22	84	107	31	34	
Manufacturing durable goods	48	1			1	1	3 5	1.3	14	10	3 5	
Manufacturing durable goods M g nondurable goods (incl. no. spec mfg) Nonmanufacturing industries (incl. not rptd .	186	1		1	3	10	14	50	74	10	16	
Linemen & servicemen, t greph t'shone, & power	109		-	-	22	12	12	27	21	2	4	
Losomotive engineers	155		i		8	10	11.	39	53	13	1 15	1
Machinists and job setters Masons, tile setters and stone cutters	100 802	1 2	2	11	114	134	16 94	23 182	25 155	44	6 35	
decomples and repairmen airplane.	6	1	1	,	1	1	300	2	1			
Mechanics and repairmen automobile Mechanics and repairmen radio and television	1,752	2	5	37	12	301 15 148	300 14 122	900 24 334	243 13	29	13	-
Other mechanics and repairmen, and loom fixers	.,03 '	1	4	9	8"			334	202	60	23	
Millwaghts	29	1		1	-	2	6	12	8	3		
	1,257	9	4	13	83	158	160	377	283	85	44	
Painters construct on), paperhangers & glamers. Plasters e ard coment finishers. Plumbers and type fitters. Printing craftmen, em. compositors & typesetters. Shoemakers and repairers except factory. Statemark company.	945 407	1	1 1	13	62	-03 50	97	280	255 93	70 22 3	39 14	
Printing craftsmen, and compositors & typesetters	31 215	1	1 2	3	14	4	1 2	123 7 42	93	3	1	
Shoemakers and repairers except factory	215 105	2	2	16	14	37 10	13	42 26	30	14	6	
Struc-ural metal workers	37				6	17	13	g 20	10	4 2	1	
	97	l .	1	1	12	17	10	3	21 5	1 =	4 2	
Tinemiths copperamiths and sheet metal workers Toolmakers, and the makers and siters	928	,	1	10	93	127	100	239	207	73	45	
Other crastamen and kindred workers	458		, "	. 1-	, ,,,,,,,,,,,,,,,,,,,,,,,,,,,,,,,,,,,,,	1 447			-01			

Table 76—AGE OF EMPLOYED PERSONS, BY OCCUPATION, COLOR, AND SEX, FOR THE STATE AND FOR STANDARD MPTROPOLITAN AREAS OF 250,000 OR MORE 1950—Con

s en occuration (C.), the sex	Total 4 years old and over	4 and 10	16 and 17 Tears	bang 19 years	20 to 24 years	-5 to 29	30 to 34 years	35 to 44 38279	45 to 54 years	о5 то 59 уеага	60 to 64 years	65 and over
PES ASSENCES												
Male-Con								8.132	5 096	1 288	70c	يو.
Operatives and kindsed workers	-2-37	A		97	4	4 - 2	-,10	20 277		1	1	2
Apprentice Aftendarts tuto service and parking	1, "	7	47	<i>27</i>	2	3€.	20€ 53	277	113 71	22	30	2
Brakemen and swate men, railroad. Bus drivers	200	,		4	.3	2-	37	99	51.	18	6	3
Furnacemen smerternen and heaters	7.		-		3	A.	1_	17	0	3	32	
	1 122	7	-	ν.	-11	289	28	5 LJ 83	30 45	16	14	13
Meat of tiers except slaughter and packing house Mine operations and laborers (near)	13	-	7	25	-	777	8-	9-	1	3*	10	8
brotormen street subway and elevated radway		i	4		4	_0	زار	ar.	21	- 7	4	. 2
Pam.e.s except construction and main enance Power stat on operators.	٠			-			يَّد ا	٠,1	9.	8	14	6
Sauvers	440		17.	8	4	1,0	85	307	100	41	30	14
EDINDERs and Weaters sexule _	67"				,é	43	46	46	230	88	63	35
Sationary fi emen Taxicab drivers and chauffours	1,209	1	3	-72	1.5	198	170	3,04.	287	29 240	24	13
Truck drivers and reliverymer Welders and flame-cutters	-1,700	250	43	5	1,74	40	-1672 -U	47	13	9	3	
Other specified operatives and kindred workers	4.0	-	-5	47	4-	f4		زدد	75	23 535	23	-71
Operatives and kindred works s (s.e.c.) Manufacaring _	,484	25	-72	20	1,419	1,433	1,281	2,7	1,338	35"	908	-47
Durable goods	3,29	-7		14	479 36-	478	4Co 244	402	43_	165 108	105 76	36 37
Furniture are, fixtures	726	2		-4	29	34	28	7	22 50	7	4	4
Stone clay and class produce	120				45	24 15	15	41	1	6	1	
Pumary metal inclustries Fabric'd metal in (incl not spec metal) Vachinery except ele reai	3	-	1 1	4	2	15 _5	10	-9 35	17	7	7	1
Biectrical machinery equipment desupplies	2				_		1	2 3	1	1		
Motor chicles and motor vehicle equipment Transp. ristion equip. exc. motor vehicle	80				1.	25	14	.2	20	i s	2 3	1 4
Other curable goods	98			ē	1+		12	23	4	188	102	
Nondurable goods	1,874	6	78	10*	574 106	377	255	-,133 445	732 295	82	50	3.
Yarn thread and fabra rais	57 (1		1 2	В	3	1	17	11	2	1	
Knit ing and other partie mill products Apparel & other facticated textile products	22		1	9	42	37	20	60	33	3	. 2	2
Apparel & other factions textile products Paper and allied products Chemicals and allied products	8 7 1 684		,	12	96 89	131	113	253 224	170	42	18	8
Leather and leather products Other nondurable goods	6 398		4	8	29	37	49	1.29	97	26	16	3
Not specified manufacturing indus nes	26		1	1	2	5	7	1.	7		16	
Nonmanufacturing industries und not rptd) -	3,048 850	.2	9	136 17	62	372	367 85	764 242	98	202 80	105	64
Transport., commun., & other public utilities Wholesale and retail trade	1,058	6	34	04	159	15	1.7	235	173	53	26 35	26 18 20
Other industries (incl. not reported	1,_40	5	a	28	158	141	145	30%	211	69	35	
Private household warkers	1,410	46	28	33	120	101	140	299	270	- 8r	34	Pl
Service workers except private household Harbers, beautitans, and mariounite	±6,34±	193	203	797	2,001	, 6°%	£1677	3,688	3,170	1,152	72	56.
Charwomen, janutors, and porters _	9,462	200	231	396	1,127	_,001	924	2,149	1,997	⁵²	45 466	248
Cooks, except private household Elevator operators Firemen fire protection	1,013		2.	45	132	200	236 12	41^	309	81 16	42	2.
Firemen fire protection Guards and watchmen	10	1	1	,	12	9	19	02	95	50	43	32
Policemen, sheriffs, and marshals Waiters partenders, and counter workers	346 12 1,753		42	n	24-	225	186	4C3	256	19	48	26
Other service warners except private household	2,614	-48	250	206	425	297	215	443	343	124	59	2/
Farm laborers and foremen	20,945	أ 752 ر	3 237	3,222	4,222	2,:79	1,819	5,621	3,050	1,289	954	1,194
Farm laborers unpaid analy workers	6,822	_, 28n	1,74	1,20,	1 319	344	.38	7e0	109	44	W.	1.06
Farm lasorers except unpaid, and farm foremen	20,123	0.12	1,492	1 719	2,903	2,0,55	1,681	3 431	2,947	1,245	910	1,088
Laborers except farm and mine	50,291	205	804	1,865	7,978	6 089	,013	12,750	10,375	3 134	1,855	1,32
Fishermen and oys ermen Longshoremen and s-cvedores	3,736	2	45	54 23	123	370	88 4%	195 1,208 721	1,079	42 c13	2) 116	18
Lumbermen raftsmen and wood choppers Other specified laborers	3,171	14	97	19.	394	351 38a	309 327	721 C32	643 523	180 207	_112 _41	46 205
Laborers (n.c., j.	39,454	347	273	2,436	4,780	4,881	4,733	9.934	8,004	2,489	1,459	±.018
Manufactung _ Durable goods _	7,594	23	-65	557	2,045	-,964 932	1,754	3,768	2.7.7	813	428	226
Purniture new & plan's mills muse more per	5,870	10	79	272	960	682	876	1,800	1,495 1,176	504 4_3 30	274 232	132 117
Stone, clay and gase products Primary metal industries Fabrie'd metal ind (in.l not spec metal) — Machinery including electrical Transportation equipment —	549 304		8	41 2	57	11/ 50	86 57	7.00	115 65	30	10	7 2
Fabris'd metal ind (in.l not spec metal) _ Machiners including electrical	177		2	3	22	24	26	34	26 21	8 5	6 2	1
Transportation equipment Other duable goods	470	1	- 1	2	41	53	77	145	86	34	19	4
Vondurable goods Vondurable goods Food and kindred products.	7,014	.2	73	210	895	1,025	970	1,958	1,206	32"	193	96
	2,578	9	55	120	415	354	296	024 73	431 30	131	82	96 *3
Chemicals and allied products Other nondurable goods	1,241 3,026	1 2	9	32	158	200	199	353	215	42	- 24	8
No specified manuscrining industries.	36	1	1	1	5 5	453	425 8	925	580	145	59 1	277
Nonmanufacturing industries (incl not ptd)	24,808	124	408	885	2,735	2,917	2,879	6,466	5,247	1,6,6	1,001	~90
Construction Rail.oads and railway express service	8 409 4,350	1.	4	332	1,070	1,150 364	1,075	2,141 1,332	1,281	495 325	258 237	123
Transportation except railroad Toucommunications, & utilities & sanitary serv	1 24.	1	24	20 31	198	233	227	429 322	384	110	50	25 47
Wholesale and re-ail trade. Other industries (incl. not reported)	r., 339	34	129	253	359	.95	-20	982	751	205	126	85
	4,741	0.0	141	185	427	442	441	760	678	431	309	418
Occupation not reported	2,424	59	98	14	342	369	242	473	349	125	26	140

Table 76.—AGE OF EMPLOYED PERSONS, BY OCCUPATION, COLOR, AND SEX, FOR THE STATE AND FOR STANDARD METROPOLITAN AREAS OF 250,000 OR MORE 1950—Con

Area, occupation, color and sex	Total, 14 years old and over	14 and 15 years	16 and 17 years	18 and 19 vears	20 to 24 years	25 to 29 years	30 to 34 vears	35 to 44 years	45 to 84 years	55 to 59 years	60 to 64 years	65 and over
"HE STATENONVITE												
Female, employed.	88,705	1,179	2,287	3,670	1:,136	12,318	_1,219	24,000	25.84	4,03,	2,334	1,68
Professional, rechargal, and kindred workers.	5,275	,		2,070	850							
Accountants and auditors	5	-		1 1		9,30	824	-1075	693	16,2	95	- 6
actresses dancers and entertainers (n.e.e)	24			1	1 4 2	1 7 6	4	2	2	1	1	
nubors editors and reporters hemists and natural scientists (n e c.)	2		100		2	1	2	1			2 4	
oliege presidents, prof'rs, & instructors (n.e.c.) eagners and draitsmen actitions and nutritionists	87		7	1	15	55	12	29	5		1	
netitians and nutritionists	27		3.7	5	4	2	4	7	1 5		0.9	
awvers and judges	4.		- 1			10	7	13	4			
fusicians and music teachers	120			1	30	10	1-	25.	e3	5	2	
urses, professional urses saudent professional	251 8			6	55	32	27	76	33	8	5	
hysicians and surgeons	10	1			,	4	. ,	1 4	2			
onal, welfare and recreation workers	68 4,174		4	42	688	738	11	20	.ī	. 2	3	4
echnicians, medical and dental	31		^	2	988	738	709	69درد 7	508	130	78	
her professional technical and kindred workers	12 -90		1		27	27	26	49	3 37	14	2	
Farmers and farm managers	2,008	12		71	92	116	1 48_	29	259	203	141	,,,
Managers, officials, & proprietors ext. farm	1,456	1	4	1	48	-						12
set.fied managers and officials anagers officials & propr s (n.e.c '-salaned	62		3	2 5	7	121	100	549 21	385	76	47	4
	276 163		1	5 2	12	28 16	25	84 50	15 75 9	13	8 3	
Other industries (inc) not reported) gra. officials & propr's (n.e.c.)—self-employed	113		,	3 4	29	12 85	19	444	26 295	5	5	
Eating and drinking places Wholesale & retail trade extresting & drinking pl	501	1	1	3	12	43	127	210	126	63	12	3
Other industries (incl. not reported,	464 132			3	14	34	52 -1	185	127	32	18	-
Clerical and kindred workers	1,179	2	1.	96	338	224	90	183	98		16	
okkeeper	24			5	26 25	_3 24	:.5 23	16	8	1	10.1	
shiers	124 366	P. 11	2 2	10 33	25 143	74 75	23 50	30 34 5	9 24		3	
dephone operators her derical and kindred workers.	45 ⇒60	2	8	20	16	100	3 99	96	57	1	12	
Sales workers	1,21.	5	3C	67	164	160		3-2	199	39	28	
surance and real extate agents and broken	226	-			18	28	46	96	41	9	11	
	35 863	5	1 3 24	2	128	117	10	227	146	2 28	14	1
esmen and sales clerks (n.e.c.) retail trade esmen and sales clerks (n.e.c.), exc retail trade_	27	1	2	4	12	10	6	14	5	20	3	_
Craftsmen foremen and kindred workers	339	2	3	6	39	49	48	34	70	21	5	
her crartemen and kindred workers	16	2	- 3	;	38	1 /8	3 42	6 88	66	21	5	
		1	1-12				42		100000			
Operatives and kindred workers resamakers and seamstresses except factory	8,363	-7	252	396	1,386	1,286	1,141	2,292	1,232	262	38	2
	3,777	7	59	168	037	610	512	1,081	514	115	45	2
her specified operatives and kindred workers.	273	3 7	11	18	.62	41	42	6,	2"	4	7	
mers and weavers, textile— mers and weavers, textile— her specified operatives and kindred workers— peratives and kindred workers (n e c)— Manufacturing Durable goods	3,688	3	81 20	207 176	642 544	595 506	533 453	96º 828	50. 43. 20	73 73 5	35	1
	187		. 3	,	26	3. 3	45	46	20	5	5	
Machinery, including electrical O her durable goods	160		3	5	24	30	39	41	19		1	
Nondurable goods	2,915	5	66 59	170 88	521	472 190	406	777	189	Ret	3ء	
Food and kindred products	1,295	5	59 1	88 10	193	6	177	310	195	47	25	
Textile unil products, except knitting	66 1,269		5	61	8	10	188	26 350	120	3	2	
Textile unil products, except knitting Apparel & other fabricated textile products Leather and leather products	7			1	3	2	1	1				
Not specified manufacturing industries	19	1	1	8	17	26	22	72	67	5		
Nonmanufacturing industries (incl not rptd.)	367	2	11	11	- 86	89	60	141	90	20	11	
Private household workers	19,595	330	900	1,363	4,052	* 420 49	7,849	11 113	8,242	2, 38	1,298	890
avate household workers—hvmg mavate household workers—hvmg out	39,075	2 328	888	_,342	3,984	4,371	4,792	10,999	8 100	2,097	1,271	853
Service workers, except private household	17,634	77	320	757	2,547	2 7/6	2,491	4,957	۷,706	574	283	176
tendants, hospital and other institution	454	1	9	22 13	96 116	63 208	59 210	12/ 357	60	23	5	
arwomen, jamitors, and porters	1,056	10	18 3/	28	92	12/	156	359	225	66	29	3:
arwomen, jamtors, and porters oks, except private household wisekeeps & stawards exc private household	4,738	. 8	-	132	527	683	696	1,522	897 32	162	67	20
notical nurses and midwives	1,798	6 8	60 60	25 139	65 431	77 430	240	243 32 ₁	176	24	37	3
her service workers, except private household.	7,518	40	190	427	1,212	1,150	1,021	2,075	1,071	225	110	6'
Farm laborers and foremen	9,149	_656	765	″ъ0_	1.274	1,0%	882	1,737	1,223	438	203	208
m laborers, unpaid family workers	4 348	434	467 299	422 338	635	409 595	372 510	801 936	496 725	_62 276	78 125	70 136
	4,801		4,,,	1				308	168	46	28	28
Laborers except farm and mine	1,1,7	16	19	52	156	152	174					
Occupation not reported	1,377	58	60	78	7.0€	140	193	28_	244	00	54	59

Table 76.—AGE OF EMPLOYED PERSONS, BY OCCUPATION, COLOR, AND SEX, FOR THE STATE AND FOR STANDARD METROPOLITAN AREAS OF 250,000 OR MORE: 1950—Con.

Area, occupation, color, and sex	Total, 14 years old and over	14 and 15 years	16 and 17 years	18 and 19 years	20 to 24 years	25 to 29 years	30 to 34 years	35 to 44 years	45 to 54 years	55 to 59 years	60 to 64 years	65 and over
NEW ORLEANS—TOTAL												
Female, employed	80,452	126	1,124	4,134	12,180	10,638	9,046	20,621	14,367	4,015	2,504	1,728
Professional, technical, and kindred workers	9,698		24	413	1,950	1,352	1,058	2,334	1,394	534	300	279
Accountants and auditors	279			8	47	43	27	85	51	15	3	2
Actresses, dancers, and entertainers (n.e.c.)	124		1	9	41	24	22	17	8		2	
Artists and art teachers	[illegible]			2	10	20	17	32	16	6	3	5
Authors, editors, and reporters	122			1	24	25	15	24	23	2	3	5
Chemists and natural scientists (n.e.c.)	113				47	29	11	13	9	4		
College presidents, prof'rs, & instructors (n.e.c.)	148				16	14	21	46	29	17	3	4
Designers and draftsmen	99			5	29	19	12	17	12	3	1	1
Dietitians and nutritionists	120		·	5	21	34	9	23	18	5	4	1
Lawyers and judges	30				3	6	2	7	7	1	1	3
Librarians	190			-	23	20	21	62	32	10	8	8
Musicians and music teachers	280			8	40	42	25	54	49	16	21	25
Nurses, professional	2,213			13	476	389	281	561	287	106	47	53
Nurses, student professional	828		14	366	397	34	9	5	1	1		1
Physicians and surgeons	[illegible]				15	41	17	22	[illegible]	7	1	5
Social scientists	36		·	1	11	1	2	13	5	2		1
Social welfare and recreation workers	435		·	3	91	65	44	114	74	22	17	5
Teachers (n.e.c.)	3,325		7	33	380	334	408	1,020	596	265	160	122
Technicians, medical and dental	344			6	139	82	31	50	21	7	4	2
Therapists and healers (n.e.c.)	32				2	5	4	6	10	3		2
Other professional, technical, and kindred workers	717		1	10	108	120	80	167	133	42	22	34
Farmers and farm managers	28				1	1		10	7	2	2	5
Managers, officials, & proprietors, exc. farm	3,773	2	9	32	144	250	383	1,260	1,024	285	185	199
Specified managers and officials	509		1	7	43	38	57	161	142	40	33	22
Managers, officials, & propr's (n.e.c.)—salaried	1,210	1	4	17	67	105	135	385	307	87	52	50
Wholesale and retail trade	555	1	1	8	31	53	74	200	122	32	18	15
Other industries (incl. not reported)	655	·	3	9	36	52	61	185	185	55	34	35
Mgrs., officials, & propr's (n.e.c.)—self-employed	1,998	1	4	8	34	107	191	694	574	158	100	177
Eating and drinking places	463			1	9	27	57	86	127	24	19	13
Wholesale & retail trade, exc. eating & drinking pl.	1,115	1	3	5	17	57	100	377	332	92	56	75
Other industries (incl. not reported)	420		1	2	8	23	34	131	115	42	25	39
Clerical and kindred workers	23,419	9	238	2,081	5,565	3,839	2,359	4,785	3,229	690	410	214
Bookkeepers	1,850		7	124	381	332	214	433	260	52	30	17
Cashiers	1,599	3	41	110	268	224	183	397	279	46	26	22
Stenographers, typists, and secretaries	9,093		64	837	2,363	1,675	945	1,749	1,057	154	114	75
Telephone operators	1,856	2	2	164	484	291	165	342	311	55	29	11
Other clerical and kindred workers	9,021	4	124	626	2,069	1,317	852	1,864	1,322	343	211	89
Sales workers	7,272	28	375	479	813	741	744	1,923	1,366	413	248	144
Insurance and real estate agents and brokers	369	1	2	10	33	39	40	99	80	31	20	14
Other specified sales workers	132		8	3	19	11	14	36	21	14	2	3
Salesmen and sales clerks (n.e.c.), retail trade	6,366	23	351	452	718	651	648	1,690	1,167	334	211	121
Salesmen and sales clerks (n.e.c.), exc. retail trade	405	3	12	14	43	40	42	98	98	34	15	6
Craftsmen, foremen, and kindred workers	982		7	21	79	100	107	310	232	53	48	25
Foremen (n.e.c.)	267	·		4	6	18	30	107	65	14	15	8
Other craftsmen and kindred workers	715		7	17	73	82	77	203	167	39	33	17
Operatives and kindred workers	10,391	13	147	364	1,213	1,295	1,237	2,946	1,994	587	373	222
Dressmakers and seamstresses, except factory	1,197		1	8	47	48	67	266	326	166	137	131
Laundry and dry cleaning operatives	1,724	2	20	48	215	248	224	511	302	80	47	27
Spinners and weavers, textile	210				12	12	22	85	56	11	9	3
Other specified operatives and kindred workers	409	1	11	23	61	53	49	108	77	17	7	2
Operatives and kindred workers (n.e.c.)	6,841	10	115	285	878	934	875	1,976	1,233	313	163	59
Manufacturing	5,948	8	97	250	762	816	765	1,757	1,060	256	131	46
Durable goods	430		3	9	51	70	78	101	75	29	5	9
Metal industries	168			4	22	31	35	39	28	8		1
Machinery, including electrical	12			2	2	1	4	-	2			
Other durable goods	250		3	3	27	39	39	61	45	21	5	8
Nondurable goods	5,474	8	92	240	702	743	677	1,643	980	226	126	37
Food and kindred products	1,515	3	48	71	180	192	198	431	264	74	47	7
Knitting mills	217		6	15	18	20	20	78	43	12	5	
Textile mill products, except knitting	258			5	22	29	31	80	70	11	6	4
Apparel & other fabricated textile products	2,698	5	19	111	415	405	362	827	407	84	51	12
Leather and leather products	13				2	2	-	4	2	2		
Other nondurable goods	773		19	38	65	95	65	223	194	43	17	14
Not specified manufacturing industries	44		2	1	9	3	10	13	5	1		
Nonmanufacturing industries (incl. not rptd.)	893	2	18	35	116	118	110	219	173	57	32	13
Private household workers	11,634	36	110	183	754	1,189	1,339	3,490	2,879	793	527	334
Private household workers—living in	528		3	14	52	56	41	98	97	57	51	59
Private household workers—living out	11,106	36	107	169	702	1,133	1,298	3,392	2,782	736	476	275
Service workers, except private household	11,505	21	187	436	1,440	1,649	1,609	3,115	1,886	555	355	250
Attendants, hospital and other institution	672		11	35	97	72	82	180	125	38	22	10
Barbers, beauticians, and manicurists	1,056		5	19	105	169	226	346	146	24	13	3
Charwomen, janitors, and porters	769	1	6	7	35	54	86	230	175	81	47	47
Cooks, except private household	1,138	1	6	12	78	144	161	364	269	64	28	11
Housekeepers & stewards, exc. private household	462	1		4	36	46	20	63	109	74	63	46
Practical nurses and midwives	733	1	1	5	46	63	76	215	184	62	47	33
Waitresses, bartenders, and counter workers	2,958	5	90	179	589	601	479	681	259	48	17	10
Other service workers, except private household	3,717	12	68	177	454	500	479	1,036	619	164	118	90
Farm laborers and foremen	115	2	2	3	13	11	10	25	30	13	6	
Farm laborers, unpaid family workers	31				3	2	3	8	9	4	2	
Farm laborers, except unpaid, and farm foremen	84	2	2	3	10	9	7	17	21	9	4	
Laborers, except farm and mine	800	7	10	24	91	106	87	237	158	46	21	13
Occupation not reported	835	7	17	36	117	105	83	186	168	44	29	43

Table 76.—AGE OF EMPLOYED PERSONS, BY OCCUPATION, COLOR, AND SEX, FOR THE STATE AND FOR STANDARD METROPOLITAN AREAS OF 250,000 OR MORE 1950—Con

Area occupation, color and sex	Total, 14 years old and over	14 and 15 sears	16 and 17 years	8 and 10 years	20 to 24 years	25 to 29 years	30 to 34 years	35 to 44 3 cars	45 to 54 years	of to of	60 to 64 Years	65 and over
NEW CRLEANS-TOTAL												
Male-Con		1 2									1	
Operatives and kindred workers	29,792	113	50.3	1,011	4,022	4,812	4, 47	7,540	4,955	1,34	801	204
Attendanta, auto service and parking	496 038	3 6	23	61	177	_31	5. 123	36	11 804		1 30	2
Bus drivers	.03			4	199 52	167	123	188 158	162	25	23	15
	997. 88		3	1	52 28 7	127	21.7	426	2/	25	. 6	3
Furnacemen, smeltermen, and heave s	58 950			1.5	16	25	6	15	1 2	8 2	7	12
Filers granders, and pounters, metal primacemen, smeltermen, and haute s Laundry and dry cleaning operatures. Mear cutters, except slaughter and packing house when operatives and laborers (ne.)	678	4	13	41	122	142	-27 83	255	182	30 46	24	10
Mine operatives and laborers (n.e.,) Motormen, street, subway, and elevated ailway	702		1	13	142	7	24	179	60	9	32	2.
Painters, except construction and maintenance	298	1			3	29	31	46	79	_9	17	3
Power s stion operators Sailors and deck hands	56	1	1	11	44	40	50	69	46 15	19	14	8
	1,340		8 2	27	253 14	2A9 19	160	34.0 27	24	/3	25 23	13
puners and weavers textile	45		_ ~		17	4	27	22	13	4	- 7	3
Parieso drivers and chauffeurs -	2,374 7,700		1	12	17	35 3±7	27 383	87	238 214	124	52 41	40
Frunk dravers and deliverymen.	7,700	85	335 1	343	16º 987	-,324 173	1,114	-,999 325	-,119 119	219	440	24 59
Other specified operatives and kindred workers	-,104	1	-8	27	55 152	165	216 132	275	185	22 72	2 50	23
Operatives and kindred workers (n.e.o.) _	9,529	1.4	352	385	1,485	-,493	1,188	2,114	640	484	3,2	242
Manuscturing Durable goods	6,2.5	5	16	257 81	1,622	_,C57	806	1,393	1,026	255	190	12.
Durable goods. Sawmills plan ng mills, & mise wood prod Furniture and fixtures	330	í	5 4	1.2	307 43	402	305	473	330 37	135	80	48
Stone clay, and class products	235		4	16 14	26 66	26	26	61	35	10	21	10
Stone clay, and glass products Primary me at industries	399		1	4	14 80	11	71	77 40	49 21	1-7	12 1 7	9 2
Fabrio d metal ind incl not spec metal). Marhinery except electrical Electrical macrimery, equipment, & supplies	459 -17 18	1	1	17	80 2	27	76 -7	90 22	19	13	7 8	5
Electrical macrimery, equipment, & supplies Motor vehicles and motor vehicle equipment	18		0.00	2	3	3 7	6	2		1	1	
Transportation equip exc motor vehicle	268		i	3	27	40	38	69	1 00	16	10	
Other durable goods	166		4	9	27	31	18	37	33	12	, E	9
Nondurable goods Food and kindred products Yarn threed and fabric rulls Kintlang, and other taxtile mill products Apparel & other fauncated textile products	4,030	3	66	175	710	644	490	912	692	15C	109	73 43
Yam thread and fabric rulls_	235	,	49	79	323 36	307	236	407	336 +9	69 13	51 g	43
Knit ang, and other textile mill products.	77		1 1 5	33	36 10	4	8	66 10	5	2	2	1 7
Paper and alhed products	4.9		3	26	79 465	59 146	106	108	129	11	10	7
Chemicals and a lied products Leather and leather products	247 24	1	1	3 5	37	32	36	68	45	20 15	7	3
Leather and leather products. Other nondurable goods Not specified manufacturing industries	306		1 5	.9	60	29	48	87	5 57	16	11	1,
	36		3	1	5	٦	5	8	/		1	
Nonmanufacturing industries unel not rptd) Transport commun & other public utalities	3,314	9	69	26 17	4c3 124	436 142	382	721 259	6/- 250	229 83	142 56	121
Transport commun & other public utalities Wholesale and retail trade	1,194	7	47	81	187	1:0	134	233	191	63	49	39 52
Other industries (incl not reported) Private household workers	1,033	-	17	30	152	37	137	229	173	83	27	30
Service workers arcapt private household.	16,598	69	258	417	1,496	1,8.2	1,693	3,818	3,564	1,467	1,048	956
Barbers heartement and management	046		1	3	63	88	91	263	382	177	79	62
Charwomen, janitors and porters	4,839	10	91	165	524	214 140	456	1,099	1,076	443	278	223
Elevator operators.	386		ŝ	15	64 27	24	145 25	306 61	250 90	58	45	24 50 12
Firemen fire protect.on Guards and watchmen	878 1,727		1	2	-58 37	126	119 63	285 2.5	200 440	48 296	28 275	12
Policemen, shanffs, and marshale	2,652		1.0		96	200,	182	334	362	147	69	352 64 73
Watere, bartenders and counter workers. Other service workers except private household.	2,652	12	107	147	316 341	346 326	348 253	722 533	445 419	161	111	73 93
	424	10	26	40	51.	10000	39	69	14	25		
Farm laborers and foremen Farm laborers unpaid family workers _	60	3	12	11	12	32	-	4			30	58
Farm laborers except unpaid, and farm foremen.	364	7	14	29	39	28	38	65	5 69	23	28	24
Laborers, except farm and mine	24,080	74	349	772	2,622	2,973	2,855	e,C95	5,189	1,553	994	605
Fishermen and oystermen Longshoremen and stevedores.	1,092	25 2	63	52	224	151 478	92	250	197	248	33	21
Lumbermen raftsmen and wood choppers	4,510			23		5	562 3	1,561	1,2.8	1	0.00	48
Other specified laborers	1,146	11	_9	38	108	118	117	245	248	94	58	80
Laborers (n.e c.)	17,296	36	259	655	2,145	2,221	2,082	4,029	3,520	1,142	753	454
Manufactums, Durable goods.	5,089 _,748	3	11	202 65	793 228	734 228	6u7 242	1,205	889 340	283	173 72	30
Furniture saw & plan's mills mise wood pr	227	1	7	28	83 38	58 62	71 54	107	100	29 16	28	5
Stone, cisy and glass products. Primary metal industries.	329 109	1		3	1.0	12	13	20	34	7	3	î
Panned metal and (mel not mee metal)	236		2	14	45	32	30 11	53 10	41 7	10	9	
Machinery including electroal. Transportation equipment.	470	1	2	5	38	58	65	136	105	37	18	. 8
	3,322	3	32	137	561	504	423	174	546	176	100	66
Nondurable goods Food and kindred products	1,451 250	3	23	71	233	204	469	319	251	83	54	31
Textue mill products and apparel. Chemicals and alited products	250 299		4	8	35 42	26 37	21 36	63	52 61	20 24	in in	10
Other nondurable goods.	1.322		5	54	257	237	197	308	172	49	24	25 1
Not specified manufacturing industries.	19				4	2	2	0 101	3	859	580	
Nonmanufacturing industries (incl. not rptd.) Construction	12,207 3,710	29	21.6 69	405	1,352	1,487	1,415	2,824	2,631	859 220 159	135	65
Railroads and railway express service	1 924	1 2	1	9	99 163	181	202	503 356	575 346 240	159	124	73
Transportation, except sailroad Jelecommunications & utilities & sanitary serv	1,512	1	3	43 11	80	198 90	126	21.2		89	58	30
Wholesale and retail trade.	2,439 1,660	21 7	101	15s 46	342 175	319	276 169	594 355	420	120	100	73 30 50 54 85
	1.66C	1 7	24	40	T.13	734	763	333	350	auri)	****	44
Other industries (incl not reported)	1,674	18	24	52	203	234	168	386	303	119	70	77

Table 76.—AGE OF EMPLOYED PERSONS, BY OCCUPATION, COLOR, AND SEX, FOR THE STATE AND FOR STANDARD METROPOLITAN AREAS OF 250,000 OR MORE 1950—Com

stee nonenot, contrated ex	Total 14 years old and over	14 and lo years		18 and .9 years	20 to 24 years	25 to 29 years	30 to 34 years	35 to 44 vears	4o to 54 vests	55 to of years	60 to 64 years	65 and over
E. CaleansTota												
Female, employed	80,452	.24	.,.24	4,134	_2,2&	10,638	2,046	20,621	_4,367	4,0.5	2,504	1,72
P-ofessional, *chnical, and amound workers	,,098		24	4,3	1,950	1,052	1,058	2,334	1,394	534	300	2
Accountants and auditors	279	1		8	47	43	27	د8	5	د د	3 2	
etresses dancers and entertainers 'n c e \	124		1	9 2	41	24 20	22 _7	17 32	16	6	3	
uthors editors, and reporters	142				24 47	25 29	7	24 13	23 9	2 4	3	
hemiste mo nat al scientists (r e.e.) olioge presidents, profits, & instructors (n.e.e., congress and draftsmen	148				-6	14	21	17	29 12	17	3	
setitians and nutriconusts	99 125	1		5	29 21	34	9	23	18	5	1 4	
awyers and udges	90 190				3	6 2.j	21	62	32	10	8	
fusterans and music leachers.	28			8	40	42 389	25 201	54 56	49 287	16	21	
urses profess.mal	2,213		14	13 366	397	34	9		1	±	1	
hva.cions and surgeons ocial scientists	36			_	10	41	17	22 13	-5	2		
ocial welfare and recreation workers	435		7	3	91	65	44 408	114	74 59a	22 265	17 160	1
'eschers (n.e.c.) 'echnicians med.cal and dental	3.4		,	6	380 139	82	31	50	21	7 3	4	
Therapists and healers (n.e.c.) Therapists and healers (n.e.c.)	32 717		1	10	108	120	an an	167	133	42	22	
Farmers and rarm managers	28					1		10	7	2	2	
Managers, officials & properetors exc. farm	3,773	2	g	32	144	250	383	4,760	1,024	285	185	1
necified managers and officials	5-5			7 1	43	38	ا7د	_61	140	40	33	
Maragers, officials, & propr's (1e.c /—salarred Wholesale and retail trade	1,210	î	4	17	67 31	135	135	385 200	307 122	87 32	52 18	
Other industries (incl. no reported)	0.55		3 4	9	36	52 107	74 61 121	694	185 574	55	34 100	,
dgra., oificia.» & pro.jr's in e.c. ;—self-employed. Eaung and drinking places Wholesale&n.a., trade, exc eating & drinking pl	1,998			1	24 9	27	52	86 377	127 332	24 92	19 56	1
Other industries (incl. not reported)	-,115 420	1	3	5 2	17	23	34	-31	115	42	25	
Clerical and kindred workers	23,449	9	238	2,081	5,265	3 839	2,359	4,785	3,229	690	410	-
Sookkeepers	,8,0		7	124	381	332	214	433 347	260	52	30	
ashiers enographers, typists, and secretaries	9,093	3	64	827	2,363	1,675	1.83 945	1,749	1,057	46 -54 55	26	
Telephone operators	9,021	2	124	164	2.009	1,317	165 852	342 1,864	1,322	55 343	29	
	7,272	26	373	479	81.3	74_	744	1,923	1,366	413	248	1
neurrance and real estate age; to and brokers	369	1		10	33	39	44	99	80	31	20	
the. specified sales workers elesmen and sales clerks (n.e.c.), retail 'rade elesmen and sales clerks (n.e.c.), exc. retail trade	1.32 6,366	23	2 9 35_	452	718	651	648	36 1,69C	21,267	334	2 2 2	
alesmen and sales derks (n e c), exc retail trade.	405	3	12	14	43	40	42	98	98	34	15	
Craftsmen foremen and kindred workers	952		7	21	79	100	107	310	232	53	18	
Poremen (a e.c.)	267		7	17	73	18 82	30 77	207	65	39	.5 33	
	10,394	13	147	364	1,213	1,295	1,237	2,946	⊥,994	587	373	
Operatives and kindred workers resemakers and seams resses, except factory		- 1	1	8	47	48	67	266	326	166	137	1
aundry and dry cleaning operatives	1,197 1,724 210	2	20	48	215	248	224	51_	302 56	80	47	-
pinners and weavers textile the, specified operatives and kindred workers.	449	1	41	23	61	53	49	108	77	17	7	
Deratives and kindred workers (2 e.c.)	0,841	10	97	285 250	878 762	934 816	875 765	1,976	1,060	33 256	163	
Manufacturing. Durane goods Meral industries Machiners, including electrical Other durable goods	430 168		3	9 4	51 22	70 31	78 35	101	75 28	29 8	5	
Machiners, including electrical	250		3	2 3	2 27	39	39	-	2	21		
Nonduranie goods	5,47/	8	92	240	702	743	677	1.643	45 980	226	.26	
Nondurable goods Food and kindred products	217	3	48	15	180	192	198	431	264	74	-26 47	
Knitting mills. Textus mill products, except knitting.	258		- 1	5	⊥8 22	2C 29	3_	80	43 70	12 11	6	
Apparel & other fabricated textile products_ Leather and leather products	2,696	2	19	111	445	405	362	827	407	84	51.	
Other nondurable goods	773		19	36	65	95	65 10	223 13	194	43 1	17	
Nonmanuseturing industries (incl not rptd	893	2	18	35	116	118	110	≥19	173	57	34	
Prayste household workers	1.,634	36	130	183	754	1,189	1,330	3,490	2,879	793	527	3.
Private household workers—Lving in	528 14,106	36	_3 _37	14	52 702	36	1,298	98	97	57	51.	
The state of the s	1,505	21	187	436	1,440	1,133		3,392	2,782	736	476	2
Service workers, except private household	6/2		11	35	97	72	1,609	3,115	1,886	555	355	2
arbers beauticians, and maniourists	1,050		5	19	105	169	226 .	346	146	24	23	
looks, except private household	1.138	-	6	12	35 78	144	86 161	23° 364	175 269	81 64	47 28	
Cooks, except private household Jousekeepers d stewards, exc private household Partical nurses and minuwives	462 733	-	1	4 5	30 46	63	161 20 76	63 215	109	64 14 62	63 47	
Wastresses bartenders, and counter workers	2,958 3,717	12	90	179	589 454	601 500	479 479	681	£59	48	17	
Farm laborers and foremen	115	2	2	3	13	300		±,036	61.9	164	118	
Farm laborers and foremen	31		- 2	- 3	3		10	25	30	13	. 6	
farm lacorers, except unpaid, and farm foremen	84	2	2	3	10	9	7	17	21	9	2	
Laborers, except farm and mine	800	7	40	24	91	106	87	237	158	46	21	
	835	7		-			-					

DETAILED CHARACTERISTICS

Table 76—AGE OF EMPLOYED PERSONS, BY OCCUPATION, COLOR, AND SEX, FOR THE STATE AND FOR STANDARD METROPOLITAN AREAS CF 250,000 OR MORE 1950—Con

Area, occupation color and sex	Total 14 years old and over	14 and 15 years	46 and 17 years	18 and 19 years	20 to 24 years	25 to 20 Vears	d0 to 34 Veals	35 to 44 vears	45 to 54 Years	55 to 59 years	60 to 54 years	65 and over
NL* QULL NS -NON-VITE						. 1				1		
Male employed	43,273	148	600	_ 1-0		- 663				2 68,		
Professional rechancal and kindred workers.	1,763	240			4,309		5,214	11,43	9,762		4 408	1,053
Accountants and aucu ors	1,763		2	-2	75	35	1	298	229	78	46	
Architec.s Artists and art teachers.	8			1	-	ī		4			1	Sec.
Authors editors, and reporters					2	2	2 3	4	3		2 1	10.00
lergymen -	251					6	à	>8	1 80	39	2	مُ
College residents profits & instructors (n.e.c.).	32 16				2	. 8	5	10	6	1 4	2	
Designers and draftsmen	3			-	-		1		۰	•		
Engineers electrical	. 1				-			-	2	1		700
Engineers mechanical Other technical engineers.	5	- P			1		1			٠.	2	
Lawyers and judges Musicians and music teachers	127		1	5	22	76	19	35	18	. 4	3	2
Natural suentists (n.e.o.)	20					7	2 2	3	1 5	1	1	4.7
Physica and auregons	53			1	3	9	1	9	14	3		11
Social scientists	17			1	1	3	i	10	2			
	277				.~	~ 7	49	- 00	4.2	9	8	6
lerhnicians medical and dertal Other processional, technical, and kindred workers	83			3	3	26	23	55	33	12	5	7
Farmers and farm managers	96	,	-	2	4	,		22	24	12	6	
Managors, officials & proprietors exc. farm	1,267			4								11
Officials of inspectors, State & local administration Other specified managers and officials	2,007			- 4	33	70			373	⊥25	68	58
	73 2>7		1	1	3	16		2 0 74	30	6	5	
Minuracturag Whoirsale and retail trade	14		1	1	11 2	1			80	.9 3	13	1
Finance insurance and real estate	9 54			-	5	8	10	30	24	8 2	6	1
Other industries (incl not reported). Mgrs, officials, & propr's (n e.c.)—self employed.	98 923		1	2	17	48	11	12 28 303	277	6	50	66 48 5 1
Construction	93			-	-3	5	83 8 2	28	22	.00 12	9	3
Manufacturing Wholessle trade	60	1			_	2 4	6	5 .2 85	19	ģ	3	8
Eating and drinking places Re all trade exc eating and drinking places Other industries (incl. nor reported)	220 274		1	1 1	5	13	23	-89	81	15	10	21
	264	ĺ		-	8	18	51	⊥05	73		1.2	7
Clerical and kindred workers	1,520		20	28	193	279		3:2	260	73	53	20
Bookgespers Mail carners	20 448				2 36	:0.	88	1.2	72	27	11	1
Other clones and kindred works.s	1 052	2	20	26	255	1.75	142	233	186	45	42	24
bales workers	753	2/	3	23	60	90	77	180	2.59	57	28	26
Inturance agents and brokers Real estate agents and prokers	224	1	1	2	19	29	18	-9 3	49	29	17	12
Other specified sales workers	244	21		12	_6 25	20 36	25 28	74	49 61	19	4 7	9
Manufacturing Wholesale trade	276 23 27	a a	9	1 1 1 1 1	3	1	2 4	8	4	2	· · · ·	
Retail "Tade	196		7	9	19	28	20	44	43	17	7	3
Other industries (inc) not reported,	30	1	1		3	3	2	-1	8		7.5	2
Caframen foremen and kindred workers.	4,704	5	22	60	416	618		- 284	1 086	327	205	121
Blacksmiths, forgemen, and hammermen	2.8	8	2	6	30	34	32	24	42	11 3	5 3	3
Boilermakers Cabinetmakers and patternmakers	15 62	l		1	2 7	6	7	23	5	3 4		2 6
Comentare	1,112	1	4	11	96	142	110	277	252	104	76	34
Compositors and typeserters	-04			i	6	2	11	36	27	8	3	5
Electricians Foremer 'n.e.c.)	748	1	1		2	5 6	1 8	-9	36	10	4	3
Manufacturing durable goods Mig, nondu.able goods (incl. not spec. mfg.) Nonmanufacturing industries (incl. not rptd.)	26	1					1	6 7	3	6 3	1	1
	70		1	1	1	, ,	6	26	26	3	3	1 2
Linemer & servicemen, t graph t phone & power	13		1 :		1	1	1	4	4			
Locometa /* firemen	29 35	1	1	١,	2	2	,	7 9	13	1	3	3
Locometry engineers Locometry firemen Machinis s and job setters Viscon tile sitem, and stone cutters	338	2	1	. 3	39	52	38	77	69	26	.9	12
Mechanics and repairmen a rpiane Mechanics and repairmen, automobile Mechanics and repairmen, radio and television	463	1	1 3	3	54	80	88	_40	80	. 8	5	2
Mechanics and repairmen, radio and television Other mechanics and repairmen, and loom nicers	47	1			5 32	35	8 39	12	10	20	6	4
Millwrights	4	1	1 '		_		1	2 5	1			
Millwinghts Molders meral	563	1	1 ,	17	30.	73			.40	33	2	11
Painters (construction , paperbangers, & glaziers Plaste ers and cement finishers	496	1	1 3	6		45	36	164 157 21	140	34	27	11 15
Plumbers and pipe fitters - Printing craftsmen, exe compositors d typesetters	57 6	1			1	1	1	2	3		1	
Ohannalasm and sanaware meant fanton	88	1 .	-]	2	1 -		9	1.3	8	7 6	3	1 2
Shoemakers and repairers except factory												
Structural metal workers	19	1	1	1	1 2			2	12	2	7	
Stationary engines					3	7	1 7	10		1 ~	2	ĩ

Table 76.—AGE OF EMPLOYED PERSONS, BY OCCUPATION COLOR, AND SEX, FOR THE STATE AND FOR STANDARD METROPOLITAN AREAS OF 250,000 OR MORE 1950—Con

Area occupanou cafor sin sex	Trial A years old and over	44 abu 15	.6 and 17	id and 19	20 to 24 70ars	25 to 20	3C to 94 years	35 to 44 years	40 to 54 years	55 to o9 years	60 to 64 years	65 and over
" JUZANG-NUME Z						1						
Male—Con		43	25.	ي 54		1,502	1,218	2,490	1,684	3/6	207	111
Approp	14-بر7 د8	43	7		25	16	8	8	7	1		
Attendants, auto service an passing Brakemen and switchmer railroad	366	2 1	4	20	83	73	53	75	41 6	8 5	1 4	7
Hadri ers	30			i	2	5	6 2	9 3	5 2	3	. 1	
Filtractmen smeltermen and heaters	787			i 22	ثی ا	2 2	102	222	-47	23	16	7
Laundry and dry cleaning operatives. Mea' out on, except shuighter and packing house Mine operatives and laborers (n e.c.	63		, ,		1	16	3	20	13	3 2	٦.	7
Mine operatives and laborers (n e.c Motormen attes sunway and elevated ranway	5.5			3	17		8	-7				
Para-ere except cons rue ion and maintenance.	70			2	7	В	-4	24	7	4	2	2
Power siz 'on operators Sations and neck rands	369			3	34	78 6	43	107	74	15	10	;
Sawyurs	54	li		3	6		i	1 18	1 10			
Spinners and weavers textile. Stationary firemen Taxicab drivers and chauffeurs	127				3 5	202	94	218	177	34	16	10
Truck drivers and c'ehverymen Wesders and name out ere.	3 637	40	16_	171	408	6.2	207 8	988	575 10	93 5	43	19
Other specified operatives and kindred workers	36 .23		5	4	1.	23	15	23	22	1.	11	2
Opers are and kindred workers in e.e., Manufacturing Dirable goods Sawmills, planing mile & mise wood prod Furni ure and fixtures	2,836	4	45 19	93	404 263	424 288	210	716 410	534 287	59 59	75 35	50 27
Durable goods	56	î	1	16	01	,6 25	85	149	94 25	30 7	±7 8	27 .3 3
Furm ure and fixtures	432 406	1		8	16 14 13	24	_5 28	29 35	10	6 5	3	3
Stone, day and glass products. Primary meta, industries Fabric'd metal ind (incl. not spec. metal)	33 57		_	4	2 4	1	3 7	13	6	3	1	2
Machinery except electrical.	14	1			1	8 5		3	4	1		20
Me or thicks and motor vehicle equipment	3				1	+	1		.,,	4	1	
Makhmery except efectorial. Electrica, machmers, equipment, & supplies Me or whicles and most vehicle equipment Transportation equip, exe motor venicle. Other duratle goods.	56 28			2	6 4	6	1 2	14	13	,	1	2
Nondurable goods	1 084	1	18	7.9	202 104	-86	12. 61	£∪2 90	192 51	29 _5	.3 8	-4 6
Nondurable goods Food and kindred products Lern thread and fabric miles	498 46	1	1"	1	6	68	6	15	10	2	1	
Crn trees and some mis- Knitting and other textile mil products - Apparel & othe fabrosited textile products Paper and alled products Chemicals and alled products.	10		1	9	3 37	34	18	58	30	2	2	2
Paper and allied products Chemicals and allied products	152		- 2	1	15	10 20	17 _0	25	36 15	4	7	3
	79			3	1,5	,	10	2 26	17	1 2	4	1
Other nondurable goods No specified manufacturing industries	1				50%	4	5	3	1		1	
Nonmanufacturing incustries (incl. not rp.d.)	1 180	2 1	26	3P	141 29	1,€	134 28	306 91	93	87 29	40 17	23 11
Nonmanufacturing incustries (incl not rp.4.) - Transport, commun & other public utilities Wholesaie and retail wade Other incustries (incl not reported)	342	1	19	25 6	29 78 34	63 40	62 44	114	88 65	25 33	±7	6
Private household workers	432		9	10	39	31	49	116	96		24	22
Service workers except private household	7,457	39	172	274	851	884	7777	:,608	1,512	535	345	2.0
Barbers beautymans, and mamourasts Charwomen, sautors, and porters.	297 4,487	8	1 83	160	508	35 489	34	1,033	6.3 981	16 384	18 229	21 171
Cooks, except private household	642		3	7 7	42 6	13	85	208	-4-	36 10 2	20	11 2
Firemen, firs protection _	78 4 91					-	3	1 46	18	16	10	17
Policemen sheriffs and marshals Warters, bartenders, and counter workers	10		9	23	3	101	89	247	4	2	27	11
Other service workers except private household	1,152	31	76	77	184	456	117	226	785	54	33	16
Farm labore.s and foremen	196	2	5	11	22	14	23	33	44	16	25	1/
Farm labore's, unusud amily workers Farm laborers except unpaid, and farm foremen	10	2	5	10	3	13	23	32	40	15	14	ڎ
Laporers, except farm and mine.	15,828	24	40	356	1,473	1,958	1,972	4,334	3.0°D	1,002	506	343
Fishermen and cystermen	60		2	2	5	6	8	-3	13	5	103	3 35
Lumbermen, raftsmen, and wood choppers	3,/93 10	2	*	17	.45 1	145 3 78	424	1,201	1,0	202		
Other specified laborers	716	5	1.	27	73		7 ₄	163	159	55	32 457	41
Laburers (n.e.c.) Manufacturing Durable goods	3,2.4	17	23	310 87	1,249	1 52¢ 47≥	443	2,953 826	2,499 584	719 175	101	264 53
Furniture, saw & plan's mills, mise, wood pr	406		7 5	27 16	33 68	157	139 61	320 83	252 62	74 17	47 17	21 13 4
Stone, clay, and gleer products Primary metal industries Fabric'd metal ind (incl. not spec metal)	256			7	23	49	42	7.	30	16	0 2	. 4
Fabric'd metal md (mel not spec me'al)	90 23		_		12	9	.4	27	19	4	1	
Viachnery moluting electroni	366		_	3	24	44,	>5	143	18	30	15	3
Other durable goods Nondurable goods Food and kindred produsts Textile mil products and apparel Chemicals and allied products.	1,976	2 2	16	60 38	314	314	252	502	330	101	53	32
Textile mil products and apparel	120	z l	В	38	148 15 25	11	90 45 26	-98 4- 61	21 45	53 4	30 5	14
Other nondurable goods Not specified manufacturing industries	205 768		3	18	126	23 .46	121	202	101	15 26	13	12
	11				1	1	,	4			1	
Nonmanufacturing industries (inel not rpid) Construction	8,389 2,669	15	28	223 87	801 279	1,054 365	1,023	2 _27	1 915	564 161 133	356 90	38 60
Railroads and railway express service Transportation except railroad	1,609	1 2	.2	6 24	69 115	143	16 .	431	512 291	133 87	93 45	19
Transportation except railroad Telecommunications & utilities & senitar, serv Wholesale and retail trade	288 1,658		2	24 4 76	26 212	45 45 2.5	204	63 404	62 305	19 84	15	10
Other industries (inel not reported)	986	7	14	26	100	135	25	235	192	90	4	45
	~53	2	7	13	5C	77	5	116	83	28	14	12

DETAILED CHARACTERISTICS

 $Table\ 76.\text{--}AGE\ OF\ EMPLOYED\ PERSONS,\ BY\ OCCUPATION,\ COLOR,\ AND\ SEX,\ FOR\ THE\ STATE\ AND\ FOR\ STANDARD\ METROFOLITAN\ AREAS\ OF\ 250,000\ OR\ MORE\ 1950---Con$

Area occupation color an l sex	Total, 14 years old and over	14 and 15 years	16 and 7 years	18 and 19 years	20 to 24 years	25 to 29 /ears	30 to 34 years	So to 44 years	40 00 54 Years	55 to 59 vears	60 to 64 years	65 and
NEW OPT CANS-RONWEITF	P. 10		41.53						- 5			
Female, employed	25 85.	46	265	712	2,862				e 010	100	706	
Professional recharal and kindred workers		40.	262		2,662	3,462	3,46,	7,693	5,039	+,190		
everytants and puditors	1,299			19	2.8	21.	134	3+3	469	41	30	
ciresses dancers, and entertainers (n.e.c.)	15		5	1	4		3 2	1	1			
there and are seasons those so.tors, and reporters hemists and natural scientists (n.e.c.) bliggs presidents prof'rs. & instructors (n.e.o.) sugners and draftsmen	25		- 1			1	2	1		N 1 1 1 1 1 1 1 1 1 1 1 1 1 1 1 1 1 1 1	1	
ollege presidents profrs. & insuructors (n e c)	1	1 3			3	1 4	2	3	. 2	10 10 10	73 100	
	22			. 5	3	1	4		ā	1 - 3	Sec. 190	200
wyers and judges	73	1			2	3	3			2		
usidans and music teachers	58	ĺ		1	.6	0	4	12	20	2	2	27 1 1
mes, professional	160			5	35	23	18	53	17	7	2	
yescams and surgeons cal scientists	3				,	i		1	1			
mal welfare, and recreation workers	6.3					12	1.	19	10	2	3	
achers (n.e c) chrsesans medical and dental	19		-	8 2	-27	125	136	2º6	10/		1 22	
her professional, technical and kindred workers	69				9	.0	6	15	16	1 6		
Farmers and farm managers	7		}					4	,			
	5,2										-	
Managers officials & proprietors, exc farm	5,2	-	1	7	16	50	75	181		21	17	-
ecified managers and officials anagers, officials & propris (n.e.c.)—salamed Wholesale and retail t.ace.	50		-	3		14	23	24	29 15	7	4	
Wholesale and retail trace. Other industries (inc. not reported	64	1		1 2	1 3	8	40 E4	12	1- 91	5	3	-
Other adustries (inc. not eported inc. officials & propris (n.e.c.) self-employed. Esting and drinking places	372 159	1		4	8 4	ננ	5 ₁ 28	146	32	14	-2	- 1
Wholesale & retail trade exc eating & drinking pl. Otour industries (incl. not reported)	145 68	1		3	3	14	18	53 26	40 19	6	1	
Clerical and kindred workers	649	١,	,	51	178	124	1.7	103	52	5	8	
okkeepers	38			1	14	3	11	6				_
shiers	60 209		,	3 25	14 71 7	12 40	10	17	3 3		2	
ephone operators	_7	1	-	20	7	6	1	1			and the same	
	325		٤		72	63	65	57	30	5	6	
Sales workers.	440		1	26	'/0	72	20	120	34	12	11	-
surance and real estate agents and brokers ber specified sales workers	14		2	3	10)	2	40	3	2	100	-
esmen and sales clerks (n.e.c.) retail trade lesmen and sales clerks (n.e.c.), oxc. retail trade	277	1	-0	22	48	52	29	66	34	6	6	
Craftsmen foremen, and kindred workers.	181	1	2	3	22	21	28	54	37			
remon (n.e.e.)	13	1	_	-	1 21	1 20	3 25	- 1	33	-	-	-
ber craftsmen and kindred workers	168	1	2	3	21	20	25	50	33	8	5	190
Operatives and kindred workers	4,383	4	40	-7	687	698	603	1,277	674	_34	74	
esmakers and scamstresses except factors	1,390	1	10	35	189	221	25 189	99 4_9	67 236	28 52	12 27	1
nners and weavers textile	13	1	3	9	27	2	2	25	5 6		1	1
her specified operatives and kindred workers. cratives and kindred workers in e.c.)	2,558	3	33	311	447	434	370	730	J40	53	31	2. 1
Manufacturing Durable goods	2,235	2	58	101	402	373	324 15	640	291	4	2-	100
Metal industries Machinery, including electrical	11	1			2	3	3 2	3	1			
Other durable goods	45	Į.		1	5	5	10	3	8	D		-
Nondurable goods Food and kindred products	2,160 613	2	27 20	3T 00	389	365 97	307 91	6_9 170	281 97	43	24 18	
	52	1 1	1	7,0	12	6	8	13	3	3		1
Textile mill products, except knifting	61 -,236	1	5	59	285	228	184	343	114	13	4	
Leather and leather products Other nondurable goods Not specified mantifacturing industries	188	į.		6	13	23	3	64	63	3	2	
Not specified manufacturing industries	16	(1 2	1 10	45	61	2 46	5 90	49	9	7	138
Noomanufacturing industries (incl not rptd.)	323	-		172	729	1 160	1,310	3 394	2,739	700	453	1
Private household workers	11,015	20	93	172	39	32	34	66	54	25	19	-
ivate household workers—iving in	10,709	20	90	_63	690	1,.08	1,276	3,328	2,085	682	454	
Service workers except private household	6,581	15	96	252	842	1,035	986	1,942	1,037	220	89	-
tendants hospital and other institution	352 461		7	16	37	\$°	49 103	102 163	53	11 7	4 2	
arwomen janitors, and porters			4	3	28	44	69	171	53 102 210	36	8	1
arwomen jamtors, and porters oks, except private household busekeepers & stewards, eve private household	963	1	4	1 11	7.	140	145	321 9	18 77	40	15	
sctreal nurses and midwives	360 852	1	21	57	28	48 212	50 123	126 154	63	14	3	1
astresses, bartenders and counter workers her strvice workers, except private household	3,053	10	59	157	404	446	4377	896	467	96	45	
Farm laborers and foremen	69	2	1	2	8	7	7	15	14	10	3	-
erm laborers, unpend family workers	5	2	1	2	7	7	1 6	14	14	8	3	

ann laborers except unpaid, and issue foremen .	64	1.	1		1	1	0	1	88	20	7	i
Laborers, except farm and mine	500	2	-	14	60	76	-	lo.		7 7 7 7 7 7 7 7 7 7 7 7 7 7 7 7 7 7 7 7	9	
Occupation nor reported	412	2	5	9	32	26	26	49	38	ند		L .

Table 77—RACE AND CLASS OF WORKER OF EMPLOYED PERSONS, BY OCCUPATION AND SEX, FOR THE STATE AND FOR STANDARD METROPOLITAN AREAS OF 100,000 OR MORE 1950

				The St		-	-			Bator I	louge St	andar.	Metropolita	m Area	-	***************************************
		1	Race	THE OF		Class of	PURKET			7	Bace			less of	worker	
Occupation and sex	Total, 14 years old and over	White	Vegro	Other races	Private wage and makers workers	Govern- ment work	Self em p.oyed workers	Lapsid family work ers	Total, 14 years old and over	РЪне	Vegro	O her	Private wage and salary workers	Govern- ment work- ers	Self em ployed workers	Unpaid family work- ers
			-	-			MOTRETA		-							
Male employed	6+6 782	-0.,723	_	1,008		5 ,5.3	-	_4 .64	38 961	28,218	10,735	- 8	30,457	4,426	4,003	75
Professional technical, and kindred workers. Accountants and auditors	3.997	37 83/	,,394 17	34	22 550 2,852	709	o 728	14	4 454	4,099	353	- 2	2,459	4487	29	
Architects	300 301 595 843	275 289 305 828	10 2' 13	2	177 470 672	17 40 40	156 84 75		441 37 20 238	37 19 71 236	1 1 2		18 11 49 21/	1 5 18 24 1	18	
C.ergymen College presidents profirs, & instructors (n.e.e.) Dent.sts Dent.sts	1 4_2 280 93o	1,254 34c 932	,000 قب پر پر	5	2,905 614 74 735	20 /91 37	251 769 27		173 449 54	104 393 59 101	69 55 5	1	169 56 60	393 1 37	37 57	
Engineers, seronautral Engineers, cruli Engineers, control Engineers mechanics Other technical engineers	2,991 9,8 9,8 2,263	1,97 915 1,280 2,257	12 2	2 1 1	1,108 1,930	373 98 126 234	23 54 99		254 103 170 427	251 103 170 426	1		98 90 1,58 385	-43 9 9 34	13 4 3 8	
Lawyen and judger Museanns and muse teachers Natural scientists "Le c Pharmacists Physicians and surgeons, Social succities Social, welfare and recreation workers	2 138 -, 76 969 1 111 2 838 177	2,192 803 9*4 1,668 2,748 16° 300	21. 15 43 85 0	. 5	474 7:25 6:80 579 589 89	28c 159 234 28 759 76 216	1,438 15 554 1,490 12	1	187 98 105 86 175 29	185 73 104 75 -65 28	25 1 11 10 10		36 59 34 51 32 8	29 26 58 2 15 2	120 13 33 128	
Surveyors Teachers (n a.e.) Technicians, medical and denta. Other professional technical, and kindred workers	323 701 2,392 536 0 976	300 752 4,_54 508 6,479	1 235 28 488	2 9	102 374 1 0_0 356 4 745	348 4,317 134 2,072	39 58 30 845	10	39 22 302 40 816	35 22 207 42 756	94 4 60		12 10 77 38 518	12 219 7 242	6 1 55	1
Farmers and facts managers	80 , e8	53,492	32,855	33	F79	45	85 656	-	647	326	321		7	. 6	634	
Managers, officials & proprietors, exc farm Officials & inspectors, State & local auministration	63,407	60, 195 1, 814	2 613	99	27 780	1,834	32,319	37	4,157	3,895	201		1,974	170	1.849	3
Character is miscours; and called a commenced colors and commenced colors and commenced colors and commenced colors and commenced colors and co	7,623 23,210 4,068 9,551 2,973 7,218 30,6.0 2,356 2,356	7,510 22,563 4,026 9,266 2,285 6,996 28,711 2,215 2,54	126 c30 51 277 88 214 2,034 140 48	17 17 1 3 8 65 1	5,341 22,439 4,059 9,486 2,274 6,620	2,766 771 9 53 99 598	30,778 2,355 2,204	32	412 1,736 313 707 199 517 1,839 264 83	1,677 312 682 194 489 1,653 250 81	3 59 1 25 3 28 136 14 2	1	312 1,662 312 705 192 450	87 74 1 2 67	1,894 263 63	3 1
Wholesale trade Rating and thraking places. Retail trade, exe estaing and dranking places Other industries (incl. not reported) Clerical and kindred workers	2,153 3,399 15,112 5,586	2,070 2,680 24,290 5,096 13 036	76 509 806 450 2 325	10 16 35	25,768	9,202	2,153 3,395 15 088 5,583 386	24 3 16	99 192 867 331 2 405	97 153 775 297 2,230	2 42 92 34 169	,	1,667	719	99 195 865 331	2
Bookkeepers Mail carriers Other clerics, and kindred workers.	3,741 1,872 29 761	3,710 1,326 28,000	28 545 . 752	1 9	3,981 22,387	255 1,872 7 U75	103 283	.16	241 143 2,021	241 89 1,906	>4 5		214 1 453	20 143 556	7 1	
Sales workers Lisurance agents and brokers	35 909	34,150	1,730	20	31,280	9,3	4,328	208	2,449	2,322	26	-	2,240	7	109	3
Real estate agents and brozers Other specified sales workers. Salesmen and sales elerks (n.e.o.) Manufacturing Wholessie trade. Other industries (incl. not reported)	1,021 2 223 28,539 2 931 6,000 18,363 1,245	957 2,842 27,649 2,879 2,952 17 617 1,201	34 377 874 52 47 732 43	1 14 1	2,824 2,627 2,627 1,095	54 22 28 38	435 410 5,117 105 368 7,534 110	199	107 142 1,874 181 359 1,270 64	1.01 125 1,796 173 356 1,204 63	78 8 3 66 1		57 130 1,743 .77 334 1,180 52	1 4	11 124 4 4: 86	3
Craftsmen foremen, and knadred workers	98 973	85,877 990	13,049 417	47	1 294	6,785	9 944	83	9,646	7,270	1,373	3	7,843	304	491	8
Backmantis rogrenes and haemorrenen. Boolernakers Boolernakers Cahmetmakers and osternmakers Campenter Compositors and typesetiens. Compositors and typesetiens. Better man. B	727 7*7 1 042 18,6-3 1,283 3,799 3,922 9,51 1,276 2,582 5,293	573 731 910 15,300 1,242 3,404 3,853 8,854 1,228 2,219 2,107	25 171 3,330 41 393 68 295 48 61 186	23	419 739 772 15,066 1,16° 2,853 3,237 8,194 1,271 2,580 4,343	36 13 74 723 19 863 314 957 5	271 5 233 2,810 97 83 371	3	24 .49 68 1,195 127 157 518 1,025 54 650 321	14 147 50 831 20 134 515 1,002 54 645 303	10 2 18 364 23 23 23	•	21. 149 0. 1,043 19 135 487 986 54 650 282	38 5 16 22 39	110 3	4
Lansmo d'esrvecenen i'groph, t'phone, d' power Locomorte suppness. Locomorte suppness. Locomorte suppness. Locomorte suppness. Locomorte suppness. Locomorte suppness. Machanis and allo settere Macana sule estrem, and stone estrem Machanis and reparrent, arphane Mochanie sond reparrent, arphane Mochanie sond reparrent arbaneliste suppness. Mochanie sond reparrent and foom faxers Millergias Millergias	3,327 846 672 3,535 1,784 283 9 901 885 10,185 638 136	2,918 820 517 3,435 982 277 8,149 847 9,148 599	109 16 155 100 800 5 1,751 1,000 39	27 1 1 1 2 7	2,860 834 665 3,302 1,586 1A5 8,598 500 8,447 614 1,14	167 12 7 13- 36 12 40. 85 1,200	102 161 6 1,388 300 275	12	261 69 47 441 257 6 582 56 867 40	25/ 666 22 436 121 6 450 52 791 39	7 3 2 5 135 126 4 70	1	260 69 48 435 227 499 41 790 40	1 4 4 15 4 50	2 26 58 11 27	
Pantiers (construction), paperhangers, 6. gianars Pantiers and cunsar impliers Pantiers and cunsar impliers Pantiers and cunsar impliers Panting confidence, encompanion & typosetter Shooma consumers of the construction Shooma consumers of the construction Shooma consumers of the consumers of Shootman in the Workers . Thomatia copporantila, and asset metal workers . Todankers, and de makers and setters Other continuous and kunded workers	0,739 1,250 4,903 522 720 3,793 851 368 1,185 64 5,921	2,482 304 4,496 91 505 3,688 8:4 272 4,155 60 4,993	1,253 946 404 31 215 135 37 97 30 4 923	3	4,771 1,100 4,0.2 494 308 3,423 831 247 1,003 57 4 967	409 41 280 8 11 354 8 17 50 2 417	1,547 109 610 10 400 15 104 1.5 5 535	12 1 1 1 1 1 1 1 1 1 1	555 167 867 47 56 292 95 27 106 1	419 29 795 46 33 289 91 11 103 1	36 138 71 1 23 3 4 1b 3	1	415 157 815 45 34 269 93 23 98 1	31. 3 21 1 29	.08 7 31 22 1 4 7	1 1 1

Table 77.—RACE AND CLASS OF WORKER OF EMPLOYED PERSONS, BY OCCUPATION AND SEX, FOR THE STATE AND FOR STANDARD METROPOLITAN AREAS OF 100,000 OR MORE: 1950—Con.

Occupation and sex	The State: Total, 14 years old and over	Race: White	Race: Negro	Race: Other races	Class of worker: Private wage and salary workers	Class of worker: Government workers	Class of worker: Self-employed workers	Class of worker: Unpaid family workers	Baton Rouge Standard Metropolitan Area: Total, 14 years old and over	Race: White	Race: Negro	Race: Other races	Class of worker: Private wage and salary workers	Class of worker: Government workers	Class of worker: Self-employed workers	Class of worker: Unpaid family workers
Female, employed	229,125	140,420	88,559	146	167,338	34,932	16,903	9,952	17,003	10,229	6,766	8	12,312	3,717	797	177
Professional, technical and kindred workers	29,169	23,894	5,253	22	10,221	17,662	1,175	111	2,432	1,881	550	1	868	1,472	90	2
Accountants and auditors	532	527	4	1	370	139	20	3	110	109	1		35	72	2	1
Actresses, dancers, and entertainers (n.e.c.)	214	190	24	.	129	5	78	2	16	14	2		9		7	.
Artists and art teachers	225	213	12		127	46	49	3	23	22	-		6	11	6	
Authors, editors and reporters	296	294	2	.	232	23	38	3	46	46			28	15	3	
Chemists and natural scientists (n.e.c.)	195	187	6	2	108	86	1		35	34	1		24	11		
College presidents, prof's & instructors (n.e.c.)	512	425	86	1	307	205	2		145	102	43		40	105		.
Designers and draftsmen	173	172	1		127	32	14	.	25	25			11	13	1	
Dietitians and nutritionists	272	245	27	.	144	128			30	28	2		14	16		
Lawyers and judges	57	57		.	13	10	34		4	4			1		3	
Librarians	658	617	41		154	501	2	1	104	93	11		12	92		
Musicians and music teachers	968	788	180	.	611	224	129	4	87	68	19		31	38	18	
Nurses, professional	4,891	4,640	247	.	3,340	1,311	234	6	373	356	17		308	38	27	
Nurses, student professional	1,027	1,019	2	6	580	447			26	26			26			
Physicians and surgeons	163	159	3	1	53	54	55	1	7	7			2	3	2	
Social scientists	71	61	10	.	42	27	2		17	14	3		6	11		
Social, welfare, and recreation workers	1,135	1,067	68	.	219	915	1		67	65	2		13	54		
Teachers (n.e.c.)	15,451	11,077	4,372	2	2,561	12,709	126	55	1,072	651	421		171	891	10	
Technicians, medical and dental	598	567	29	2	430	163	5		34	32	2		33	1		
Therapists and healers (n.e.c.)	72	60	12	.	27	34	11		8	5	3		4	2	2	
Other professional, technical, and kindred workers	1,727	1,537	187	3	964	546	184	33	203	180	22	1	94	99	9	1
Farmers and farm managers	2,963	955	2,005	3	30	4	2,927	2	42	22	20		2		40	
Managers, officials, & proprietors, exc. farm	10,645	9,187	1,447	11	3,415	968	5,939	323	700	561	139		298	74	312	16
Specified managers and officials	1,433	1,368	64	1	675	641	114	3	112	107	5		70	39	3	
Managers, officials, & prop's (n.e.c.)—salaried	3,067	2,791	274	2	2,740	327			263	238	25		228	35		
Wholesale and retail trade	1,528	1,365	162	1	1,497	31			146	126	20		139	7		
Other industries (incl. not reported)	1,539	1,426	112	1	1,243	296			117	112	5		89	28		
Mgrs., officials, & prop'rs (n.e.c.)—self-employed	6,145	5,028	1,109	8			5,825	320	325	216	109				309	16
Eating and drinking places	1,564	1,063	499	2			1,462	102	104	53	51				99	5
Wholesale & retail trade exc. eating & drinking pl.	3,571	3,087	482	2			3,399	172	174	123	51				166	8
Other industries (incl. not reported)	1,010	878	128	4			964	46	47	40	7		.		44	3
Clerical and kindred workers	49,762	48,583	1,166	13	38,769	9,973	573	447	5,007	4,861	145	1	3,240	1,682	41	44
Bookkeepers	6,058	5,974	83	1	5,336	371	200	151	624	613	11		505	96	10	13
Cashiers	3,394	3,270	121	3	3,121	77	108	88	317	306	10	1	280	17	9	11
Stenographers, typists, and secretaries	18,408	18,042	362	4	13,724	4,509	105	70	2,062	2,006	56	.	1,170	873	10	9
Telephone operators	4,473	4,428	44	1	4,271	197	4	1	292	281	11		267	25		
Other clerical and kindred workers	17,429	16,869	556	4	12,317	4,819	156	137	1,712	1,655	57		1,018	671	12	11
Sales workers	20,291	19,080	1,206	5	16,763	69	2,010	1,449	1,328	1,230	97	1	1,188	1	82	57
Insurance and real estate agents and brokers	780	524	256		679	5	93	3	55	36	19		49		5	1
Other specified sales workers	274	239	35	.	254	2	16	2	19	18	1	.	18		1	
Salesmen and sales clerks (n.e.c.), retail trade	18,381	17,518	858	5	15,099	21	1,857	1,404	1,208	1,132	75	1	1,082		72	54
Salesmen and sales clerks (n.e.c.), exc. retail trade	856	799	57		751	21	44	40	46	44	2		39	1	4	2
Craftsmen, foremen, and kindred workers	1,872	1,533	337	2	1,638	63	151	20	133	105	27	1	120	3	7	3
Foremen (n.e.c.)	372	356	16	.	360	10		2	19	18	1		19			
Other craftsmen and kindred workers	1,500	1,177	321	2	1,278	53	151	18	114	87	26	1	101	3	7	3
Operatives and kindred workers	20,269	11,906	8,328	35	18,393	554	1,159	163	1,042	457	585		890	85	58	9
Dressmakers and seamstresses, except factory	2,504	1,893	609	2	1,544	55	899	6	149	95	54		100	2	47	
Laundry and dry cleaning operatives	5,373	1,596	3,772	5	4,998	190	125	60	589	148	441		557	25	5	2
Spinners and weavers, textile	218	204	14		216		2		1		1		1			
Other specified operatives and kindred workers	1,206	933	272	1	906	204	56	40	104	82	22		56	41	2	5
Operatives and kindred workers (n.e.c.)	10,968	7,280	3,661	27	10,729	105	77	57	199	132	67		176	17	4	2
Manufacturing	9,369	6,248	3,097	24	9,298	11	47	13	113	80	33		108	2	3	
Durable goods	693	506	186	1	674	2	13	4	11	8	3		9		2	
Metal industries	176	162	14		175			1								
Machinery, including electrical	17	13	4		17											
Other durable goods	500	331	168	1	482	2	13	3	11	8	3		9		2	
Nondurable goods	8,618	5,703	2,892	23	8,567	9	33	9	100	70	30		97	2	1	
Food and kindred products	3,024	1,729	1,280	15	2,999	5	13	7	77	50	27		76	1		
Knitting mills	220	162	58		219		1									
Textile mill products, except knitting	266	200	65	1	265	.	1		1		1		1			
Apparel & other fabricated textile products	3,184	1,915	1,262	7	3,170	1	11	2	3	2	1		2		1	
Leather and leather products	18	11	7	.	16		2		1		1		1			.
Other nondurable goods	1,906	1,686	220		1,898	3	5		18	18			17	1		
Not specified manufacturing industries	58	39	19		57	.	1		2	2			2			
Nonmanufacturing industries (incl. not rptd.)	1,599	1,032	564	3	1,431	94	30	44	86	52	34		68	15	1	2
Private household workers	42,257	2,662	39,575	20	41,596		627	34	3,500	95	3,403	2	3,483		17	
Private household workers—living in	1,087	567	517	3	1,080		4	3	38	22	16		38			
Private household workers—living out	41,170	2,095	39,058	17	40,516		623	31	3,462	73	3,387	2	3,445		17	
Service workers, except private household	33,523	15,889	17,619	15	25,445	5,443	2,231	404	2,440	864	1,575	1	1,907	366	146	21
Attendants, hospital and other institution	1,443	989	453	1	652	780	5	6	70	61	9		55	14		1
Barbers, beauticians, and manicurists	2,832	1,776	1,056		1,373	12	1,440	7	222	113	109		112		110	
Charwomen, janitors, and porters	1,623	484	1,139		1,057	553	3	10	120	7	113		72	47		1
Cooks, except private household	6,243	1,505	4,737	1	4,373	1,709	105	56	364	22	342		308	49	3	4
Housekeepers & stewards, exc. private household	1,003	884	118	1	662	330	9	2	104	91	13		60	42	2	
Practical nurses and midwives	2,544	1,732	811	1	2,112	245	177	10	186	79	107		168	9	7	2
Waitresses, bartenders, and counter workers	8,509	6,711	1,791	7	7,740	361	233	175	618	366	251	1	553	45	12	8
Other service workers, except private household	9,326	1,808	7,514	4	7,476	1,453	259	138	756	115	641		579	160	12	5
Farm laborers and foremen	12,604	3,455	9,143	6	5,644	21	17	6,922	104	20	84		64	15	1	24
Farm laborers, unpaid family workers	6,922	2,574	4,346	2	.			6,922	24	9	15					24
Farm laborers, except unpaid, and farm foremen	5,682	881	4,797	4	5,644	21	17		80	11	69		64	15	1	.
Laborers, except farm and mine	1,881	764	1,110	7	1,657	110	73	41	71	18	53		63	6	1	1
Occupation not reported	3,889	2,512	1,370	7	3,747	85	21	36	204	115	88	1	189	13	2	

Table 77—RACE AND CLASS OF WORKER OF EMPLOYED PERSONS, BY OCCUPATION AND SEX, FOR THE STATE AND FOR STANDARD METROPOLITAN AREAS OF 100,000 OR MORE -1950—Con.

				The St	ate	9.0	100		15. 150	38502	Rouge St	andard	Matropolit	_		
			Race			Class of	worker			-	Race		(lass of v	worker	
'ясирацюю and sex	Total, 14 years old suu over	White	\egro	Other races	Private wage and salary workers	Govern- ment work- era	Self- em- ployed workers	Unpaid family work- era	Total 14 years old and over	White	Negro	Other races	Private wage and salary workers	ment work- ers	Self- em ployed workers	Unpaid family work- ers
Female, employed	229,125	.40,420	88,554	146	-67,338	34,932	.6,903	9,952	17,003	10,229	6,76C	ε	12,312	3,717	791	177
Professional, technical and kindred workers.	29,.69	23,894	5,253	22		17 662	4,175	111	2,432	1,881	550	1	868	1,472	90	;
recurtants and auditors	572	527	1 4	1	370	139	20	3	1.0	109	1 2		35	72	2 7	
stresses cancers, and entertainers (n.a.c.)	2.4	.90 213	24		129	46	78 49	2 3	23	22	-		6	11	6	
nunors, editors and reporters	296 195	294	12	;	232	23 80	38	3	46 35	46 34	1		28	15 11 105	3	
ollege presidents, prof rs & instructors (n.e.e.)	20'	4-	85	2	437	205	2 14		145 25	102	43		40 11	105 13		
netitians and nutrition.ets	272	172 245 57	27		144	128			30	28	2		1/	16	3	
brarians	-7 658	617	7-		13 154	10	34 2 3_9	1	204	93	1		12	92		
	4,891	788	.20		3 340	1,31.	3_9 234	6	87 373	68 356	19 17		3 308	38	1.8	
urses, professional urses student professional	1.027	4,64C 1,019	2-7	6 1	580	447			26	26	- "		26	3	2	
hysicians and surgeons	163	159 61	10	1	53 42	54 27	55	1	-7	14	3		6	11	-	100
ocial welfare, and recreation workers eachers (n e c.)	1,135	1,607	4,372	.,	219 2,561	12,709	.26	55	1,072	65 651	421		171	54 891	10	
eachers (n e c.) ecrucians, medical and dental herapists and healers (n.e.c.)	25,421 598 72	567 60	29	2	430	163 34	1,		34	32	2		33	1 2	2	
ther professional technica, and kindred workers.	1,727	1,53,	187	3	964	546	184	33	203	180	22	1	9/	99	2 9	147
Farmers and farm managers	2,963	925	2 (10)	3	30	4	2,927	2	42	22	20		2		40	
Managers, officials, & proprietors, exc. farm	10,645	9,187	1,447	11	3 415	968	5,939	323	700	502	139		298	74	312	1
pecified managers and officials.	1 433	1,368	64 274	2	675 2.740	641 327	114	3	263	1.07 238	25		70 228	39 35	3	
anagers, officials, & propes (n.e.c —salamed Wholesale and retail trade	1,528	1 365	162	1	2,740 1,497 1 243	31.			.46 117	126	20		1.39	28		l
Igrs., officials, & propr's (n.e.c.)—self-employed.	6,145 1,564	1,426	1,109	8 2	1 243	296	5,825	320	325	216	109	1	67	**	309 99	1
wholesals and relationated to the midistries (in a not reported) tyre, officials, & propr's (n.e.c.)—self-employed. Esting and draining places Wholesals & re-all trade are eaung & draining pl	3,271	1,063 3,087	499 482	2 4			1,462	102	104	53 123	51 51 7	1			106	
Other industries mer det reported)	1,010	878	128				964	46		40		1			44	
Clerical and kindred workers	49,762 6,058	48,583	1,166	13	38 769 3 336	9 973	573	151	5,007	4,8Cl 6:3	145		3 240	1 682	10	4
ashiere rendea	3,394	5,974 3,270	124	3	3 121	77	1,08	88	31.7	306	10	1	280	17	9	1
tanographers typusta, and secretaries	4,473 17 429	18,042	362 44	4	13,72/ 4,271	4,509 197	105	1	2 062 292	2,006 281	56 1.		1,,70	873 25	10	
Other certeal and kindred workers		16,869	556	4	12,317	4 819	156	237	1,712	1,655	57		1,018	67_	7.2	1
Sales workers	20 291	19,080	1,206	5	46, re3	7.9	2,010	. 449	1 328	1 230	97		1,188	1	82	5
nsurance and real estate agents and brokers other specified sales workers	760 274	524 239	256 35		679 254	5 2	93 46	3 2	55 19	36 18	19 1 75	i	49 18		5	
other specified sales workers. a.esmen and sales clerks (n.e.c.), retail trade elesmen and sales clerks (n.e.o.) exo retail trade	18,381 856	17,518	858 57	5	15,099 751	21	1,857	1,404	1,208	1,132	75	,	1,082	- 1	72	5
Crafismen foremen, and kindred workers	1,872	1,533	337	2	4,638	63	151	20	1,33	105	27	, 1	120	3	-	
oremen ,n.e.c.)	272	156	16	. 2	360	10		2	0.0	18	1		39	74		975
ther craftanen and kindred workers	1,500	1,177	321		1,278	53	15L	18	1.4	87	20	1		3	7	
Operatives and kindred workers	20,269	11,906	8,328	35	18,303	554	1,159	.63 6	1,042	457	585		890	85	58 47	-
sunory and dry cleaning operatives	2,504 5,373	1,893 2,596 204	3,772	2 5	4,998	190	125	60	589	148	54 441	1	100 557	25	5	
Spinners and weavers textile Other specified operatives and kindred workers Operatives and kindred workers (n.e.c.)	1,206 1,968	933	272	1	216	204	56 56	40	10	82	55	1	56	41	2	
Manufacturing	9,369	7,280 6,248	3,661	27 24	_0 729 9 298	1.05	77 47	57 13	199 1,3	132	33		176	17	4 3	
Durable goods	693 126	506	186	1	674	2	13	4	ų	8	33	1	9	- C	2	
Machinery including electrical Other durable goods	17	162 13 331	168	1	-75 17 482	2	13		100	8	3		9	2.		
Nondurable goods	8,618	5,703	2,892	23 15	8,507	9 5	33	9 7	100	70 50			97	2	1	١.
Nondurable goods Food and kinared products knutting mills	3,024	1,729	1,280	15	2,999 219	3	13	7	~	50	27	1	70	1		
Textale mill products except knitting	266 3 184	200 91.5	1,262	1 7	265 3,170	٠,	11	2	1 3	2	1		1 2			3
	18	11	7		16	3	2 5	-	1 18	18	î		1			
Other nondurable goods Not specified manufacturing industries Nonmanufacturing industries (incl. not rptd.)	1,906 58	1,686	19		1,898		1 2		2	2			17	1		
	1 599	1,032	564	3	1 43	94	30	44	38	52	34		68	15		8
Private nousehold workers	1,087	2 662	39,575 517	20	1,080		627	34	3,500	95	3,403	- 2	3,483		17	_
'nvate household workers—hvmg m 'nvate household workers—hvmg out	41,170	2,095	39,058	17	40,516	1	623	33	3,462	73	3,387	2	3,445	1	⊥ 7	
Service workers, except private household	33,523	15,889	17,619	15.	25,445	5,443	2,231	404	2,440	864	1,575	1		306	146	.5
ttendants, hospital and other institution	1,443	989	453	1	622	780 12	,	6 7	70	61.	9		55	14	4	
arbers, beauticians, and manicunsts harwomen, janitors, and porters	1,623	1,776	1,006		1,373	553	1,440	10	222	1,3	109		1.2	47	110	
ooks except private household lousekeepers & stewards exc private household	6,243	1,505	4,737	1	4,373 662	1,709 330 245	105	36 2 10	364 104 186	22 91	1,3		308 60	49 42	3 2	
Variences hartenders and counter workers	8,509	1,732	1 791	1 1 7	2,112	361	177 233	175	618	79 366	107 251	1	168	45	7	
Other service workers except private household	9,326	1,808	1,514	4	7,476	1,453	259	138	756	115	641		579	160	12	
Farm laborers and foremen -	12,604	3,455	9,143	6	5,644	21	17	6,922	104	20	84		64	15	1	2
Farm laborers, unpaid family workers Farm laborers except inpaid and farm foremen	6,922 5,682	2,574	4,346	2	5,64	21	17	6,922	. 24 80	9	15	Toyle	64	15	1	2
Laborers except farm and mine	1,881	764	1,110	7	1,657	110	7,5	41	71	18	53		63	6	1	
1	3,889	2,512	1,370	7	3,747	85	21		204	115		_		-		-
Occupation not reported	3,009	2,012	1,3/0	- 7	3,747	83	41	36	204	115	88	1	189	13	2	l

Table 77—RACE AND CLASS OF WORKER OF EMPLOYED PERSONS, BY OCCUPATION AND SEX, FOR THE STATE AND FOR STANDARD METROPOLITAN AREAS OF 100,000 OR MORE 1950—Con

The state of the s		hew 0	leans 3	tanderd	Metropol	*an Are				Jhre.	repor a	70(8"	*Atropo	te · Ares	-	CHES PROPERTY
	Total,		Race	200		Class or	worker	-			Race			Class of		-
Occupation and sex	14 years old and over	White	Negro	Other	Private wage and salary workers	Govern- ment work ers	Self era- ployed workers	family work- ers	Total 14 years old and	White	\egro	Other races	Private wags and	overn- ment work	Belf erg ploved	Capaco faznily work-
Male, employed	174,498	132,225					7	45				-	worker.	er.	workers	tra
Professional technical and kindred workers.			+2,045	30"	812, دد_	19,782	20 084	2.10	44 648	30,376	14,23"	.5	14 20-	3,758	6,804	263
Arec intents and auditors	14,908	2 065	1,024	29	8 975	3,395	2 638	_	372	3,631	281		4,279	6.1	-21	
Architects Artists and art teachers.	163	160 201	2	1 2	65	383 12	190 86	-	486	e83	3	1	358	27	25	
Authors, editors and reporters. Chemists	201 279	288	7,		132 478 163	1.8	297		29 60	26 15 44	5		55 53	6 3	8	-
	713	774 462 444	201		u62	109	25		47 250	-43	110		225	6 2	2b	
College presidents prof'rs, & instructors (n.e.c.) Dentists	476 349	333	26	4	425	46 30	4		34 86	32 80	4	1	31	7	78	
Designers and draftsmen Engineers, aerona.stical	476	479	4	1	351	1	14		:62	102		1	15.	6	5	
Segment, civil	701 4 5	696 414	3	2	38,	27	41		179	179	١.	1	128	43		
Ingmeers, mechanical Other echnical engineers	558 683	543 683	4	-	354 459	54 74	25		_01 124	1.0	,		95	5	2	
	960	966	,		224	98	-03		301 269	301 268			26. 73	34	165	
awys.s and judges fusicians and music teachers fatural secontests in e.e.)	269	377	125	2	418	140 23 05	602 63		76	65	11		45	16	14	
harmonets	1.231	413	20 48		244 375	1 1 2	176		2 ³ 9 82	238 P1	1 1		203	9	28 29	
hysicians and surgeons outsi s entis s outsi welface and reclasion workers	102	97		1	375 51 46	569 40	587		249 20	245			40	61	_48	
incressors.	130	107	1"	2.7	60	78	17		63	15 63	î		10	1 .	,	1
eachers (n.e.,) ea. atcans, medical and dental the professional technical, and kinared workers	915 286	638	2,6	4	386	503	26		26°	175	94	1	42 68 43	195	3	1
Othe professional technical, and kinared workers	2,218	2,055	-75	8	1 464	502	272		460	57 430	30		287	100	73	
Farmers and farm managers	530	434	95	1		3	>21		1,904	J.	1 300		2	2	1,879	
Managers officials, & proprietors exc farm	23,884	22,6.7	1,199	69	11,480	٨,600	10,787	11	5,750	5 523	219	7-	-	251	/ 710	-
offi has de uspectors, citale de lecal administration the specifier intanapers and offic also disasses, so flussis, de proper as e.e. — salaried. Manufac c. s.g. — Molosale and rotal trade. Finarre untulative, and real batate. — Other gird, serves (i.e. not reported).	522	5) 3	9	-		522			99	97	2		-	99		-
lanage s, officials, & propr s in e.c - salaried.	3,726	3 553 8,735	ف 249	10	2,7 <u>1</u> 7 8 753	822	152	1	2,445	2,394	8	ł	377	18	35	
Wholesale and rotail trade	3,587	1,508 3,4°6	14	1	1,019	26			369	-69 924	17		2,477 768 9-7	1		
F name insulance, and real estate	1,122	1 068	91 877		1,080	42			230	722	8		229	, ,		
igis, one-ties, is propes there) sen employed .	13,544	9,716	977	51	z 603	138	10,635	9	2,619	2,52	165		BC.	36	2,678	
Constructoring	742	561 725	93	2			95/ 742		272	26* 178	5		1	100	272 183 308	
Wrosesale trade	1 074	1 018	744	2			1.435	4	208	207	34		}		308	
Retail wade and eating and dinning places Other miliatures (incl not reported)	2,158	3,950	208	2 2 6 -3			1,435	4 4 1	1,063	1 001	34 62 56	١.			1,012	
Clerical and kindred workers	17 805	6,335	1 510	10	13 076	4 645	בי.	1	-,334	2 173	1.59	1		694		
nok courses	,294	1.274	1.6	2	1,143	123	-2		36,	360			2,609	16	30	-
las carriers ber olereal and kindred workers	15,898	215	1,045	1	11, 936	663	100		2,,02	2,642	2 8 149	1	2,267	409	25	
Salas workurs	13 294		2,045	1	12,033	31	1 175	55	3 620	3,4,8	162		3,267	4.09	337	
burane agents and blokers	1,797	17,54	224		12,033	12	1 1 2		3 620	3,4.8	31		3,267	4	337	
eal estate agents and brokers.	1.080	508	240		35×	1	200	1	140	115	5	1	39	1	6	
demon and salan corbs (. e c)	9,900	9,624	69	7	0 _74	1 2 -6	658	52	2,872	2,768	42 84		2,646	5	215	
Manufacturing _ Wholesale trade	1,430	2.622	36	1	2 511		54		74.	37L 736	5	1	370	1	31	
Retail trade	5,656 5 285 5.9	5,089	90	0	4,808	:2	424	51	1 606	1 531	75		1,431	1 2	168	
Craftsmen foremen, and kindred workers	30,977	26,267	4,08.	23	26,000	2,500	2,464	7	7 88"	6,729	1,158		6,787	414	685	
akers.	700	482	216	2	069	- 0	24	-	143	71			177	2	5 3	-
lacksmuths forgamen and ammermed	209	90	20 1.4		83	-4 9 14 218	13		26	23	32 12 3		21 26	^	3	
al metmakers and patternmakers	51.5	274 453 3,447	1,110	1	3 747	218	70 592	2	26 73 207	57 995	15		1,043	10	18	
ompositors and typeseiters	601	581	50	1	97	158	36 8 77	1	137	110	30		101	1 24	34	
canemen hoistmen, & const machinery ope ators	76	1,333	108 108	4	1,1,5	140	77		236	232		1	202	24 66	20	
recrians we men (n.e.o) Manufacturing aurable goods Mg, nonfurable goods (incl. no. spec. mfg Vo.manufacturing addistree (incl. not rpto.)	2,542	2 434	⊥2		2 738	306 3			738	726	22		1.04	66		
Mg., nondurable goods (incl no spec mfg:	628 498	4,428	26 70		1 '96	302			100 533	9p 521	12		00 468	6.		
nemen & surroomen, t graph tiphone, & power	986	973	1,3		956	30			274	268	111 1700	i	270	4		
peomotive engineers	209	253	20	1	249				121	19	22		121			
achinists and job setters	1,345	2,320	20 337	,	526	86	45		312 165	288 122	24	1	292	8	10	
seons the staters and stone cutters echartes and recarmen, surplane	133	241 ±27	2)	1	96	34			33 790	57	195		12 676	42	102	
echanics and repairmen, automobile	2,520	2,057	403 49	4	226	156 40 900	254 (53		53	54	4	4	34 697	20	15	
asons the silvers and stone entirers cehar.cs and repairmen, automobile cehar.cs and repairmen, radio and television cehar.cs and repairmen, radio and television liverights	3,727	3 421	330	6	3 076	300	2		829	707	122	1	13	80	52	
olders, metal	52	44	8		51		î		20	21	8		29			1
unters (construction), paperhangers, & glamers	2,471	1,908	490	3	1,829	204	435	3	707	265	41		312 113	32	163	-
inters (construction), paperhangers, & glassers insterers and namen't insiders interested in the fitters inting disferment exercompositors & typesetters committee and repeaters, except (settery stepper committee).	1,227	76 - 1230	57		3 036	122	148	7	322	281	5 <u>1</u>	.J	281	19	32	
inting claff-men exc compositors & typesetters compake a and repairers, extent factory	257	268 169	86	1	119	6	134		64	60 39			40	4	30	
ationary engineers	855 330	81*	40 19		583 323	158	3		390	-77 56	13 2 10	1	367	20	3	
	204	163 501	41/		144	4 4	36 38		30	26 120	10		26	7	9	
insmiths coppersmiths and sheet metal workers. colmakers, and die makers and setters ther craftsmen and kindred workers	41	43	42		30	,	3	1	8	8			0	1 1	1	
ber craftsmen and kondred workers	2,361	1 914	4.2	3	1,970	188	202	1	540	467	73	i	469	18	,3	

Table "7—RACH NND CLASS OF WORKER OF EMPLOYED PERSONS, BY OCCUPATION AND SEX, FOR THE STATE AND FOR STANDARD METROPOLITAN AREAS OF 100,000 OR MORE 1950—Con

				972-176	ret-cpo		-	1	- 1	Shae		thecard	Metronela	-		
Output to a second	Tota	-	Rau			-	-orker	-	To-el,	-	Race		-	Clars of		
Оегиральна апс не.	4 Vents old and over	While	Vegro	Other races	wage and salary workers	Mork- err	Self- em- ployed workers	family work ers	.4 years old and over	Whate	Negro	Other	Private wage and salar; workers	ment work ars	Self em ployed workers	Lapas family work ers
ofale—on Oper rives and kindred wo kers	41,716	An3	9 350	6-	2 he	1,60	_,C_3	.5	7 921	4 890	3,030	1	7,454	276	.86	
toprer sees Attendants o service and persong Stakenren and sar romen railroad Bus driven. Her- grunders and poisseers mail	4,3 0,8 7,	413 72 61- 96	365 14	5	924	4 49 40	12 6 13	1	96 275 242 94 25	14_ 160 87	13/ 01 7 4		25 404 241 80 19	13	1	
uers graders and possess ortal unacerns sudieraer and casers aumited and or casers aumited and or grades are sudieraers as a sudieraers and packing house time operatives and innovers near, doorwing the artists of the party and exysted salway.	950 #78 702 78	- 1 - 1 - 1 - 1 - 1 - 1 - 1 - 1 - 1 - 1	-4.1 30	4-	85_ 72 50 577 571 693 205	21.	.74	-	10 169 175 9 8	21 7 29 14 910 153	3 140 34 68		1,9 172 95s _28	1 1 25	-0 22 -8	
numbers ex on och the thin and maintenance . cwer statuon opera > 2. a.ors and deel hands . aryers pinners and weavers lexite	246 5n 1 3/6	726 44 9~ % 41	237 51.	32	25 46 1,229 124 -3	6 30 116	17	-	87 11 6 83	/0 11 46	37		8: 5 82		1	
tationary firenen ascent divers and chauffeur rusk curves and deliverymen welders and flame-outers ther specified of ratives and kindred workers	46° 2 374 7,777 920 1 134 9,529	233 2,639 4 (63 304 976 6 633	127 715 ,(35 56 121	2 10	36' 1,950 6,965 878 941 8 9 6	124 455 25 26 467	300 376 13 21	4	252 2,394 27,175 2 325	1,077 251 151	36 29 1,316 25 24	1	76 2,4 2,193 248 165 2,213	125	4 2_ 3 13	;
pera, ire ann Ludied workers (n.e.c.) Yandisterrap; Durald: group Bas mills planing mills de nase wood prod Furniture ann fintures Store clas, and plase to oducts Funary near drugstee Funary near drugstee Andelmery, etc. p. vertand alectross maximers soupment de applies More "abeliese and moter volume equipment"	6,215 2,149 330 255 399 4 -59 117 18 21	4,559 1,588 1,98 1,29 2t 71 4C6 1C3 14	1,647 559 132 100 132 23 5- 11	2	6,14* 2,1.6 327 232 .92 113 455 1.7 .8	1	27	2	2,443 942 193 39 465 35 64	925 64 15 421 1e 37 35	508 315 179 24 19		2,213 4,476 931 190 38 465 35	2	13 8 2 1	1
Transportation equip exe motor vensile Othe durable goods Nonaurable goods Food and kindred products has the good and one recult and products has tog and one recult and products Appured & rither tab oated textile products. Fayer sau allied virousely.	268 4 Jal 913 235 47 419 779 247	2,9-4 1,415 29 37 226 617 168	1, 777 40; 46 9 193 104	7 6	263 178 3 997 1,893 35 46 416 779 244	5 3	25	2	532 22.7 2 24 16	29C 95 1	-9 244 -22 1 6 7		66 428 216 2 21 _6 93		3	
Leather and leaser products Other non-urable goods Not peanly disanfacturing industries ormanufacturing industries (incl. not rptd., Fransport commun. & other public utables.	3/2 30 3 714 1 087	20 27% 25 2 1.5 746	92 11 1,170 341		19 362 35 2,784 871	45¢ 212	1 1 68		17, 19	138 8 439	393 119		77 17 277 277	74	1 20	1
Wholesale and "etail trade Other industries (mel not reported)	1 033	691	344	1	-, 180	241	12	3	292	104	146		212	60	19	1
Private household workers	*68	56	4.0	- 2	482	-	6	-	-1/2	11	-61	_	165		7	
Serice workers, except private boushold archer, pessitionis, and financiaries and opticate between several persons and opticate object except private boushold elevant operators increase fire protection except and wat hines because shorted and wat hines because the except and wat hines because the except persons except and water between the except private nutrated and according to the except persons of the except pe	16, 498 1,046 4,869 1,051 186 878 1 727 1,456 2,652 2,543	9 1.1 7-9 409 908 874 -,63x 1,416 1,926	7,-15 297 46/ 507 77 4 88 10 713 1,1-5	30 1	12,197 465 4,54 952 990 2,1,351 227 2,472 2,472	3,532 7 121 90 87 8 5 370 1,186 25 382	959 774 13 9 13 40 104	1 12	3,063 244 1,593 210 54 51 156 235 230 390	1,0.8 181 57 62, 43 151 779 2,2 96	2,341 60 1,J36 445 31 49 49	3	2,322 162 1,261 84 50 132 6 217 340	596 4 149 22 101 26 226 4 30	113 78 3 ,	2
Farm L.borers and foremen arm laborers, unpast, family workers arm laborers, except unpast and farm foremen	60 364	228 20 178	191 191 181	3	351	6	6	52 60 1	242 1,49	27	21,532	\dashv	1,447	2	2	242
Laborers except farm and mine	24,081		15 87	10	20,638	4,360	1,035	44	4,732	81>	3,915	- 1	4,193	415	:42	,
shermen and oys-ermen ong-horemen and str-edores unbermen raf-smen, and wood choppers ther specified laborers	1 092 4,210 34 -,148	1,032 1,017 18 432	51. 3,491 16 716	9	269 4 /12 28 26/	2 2 2 2	796 2 3 152	20	47 5 109 391	40 1 19 37	7 4 90 324		13 •5 90	3 17	34	
borres (n. e. c.) Manuheturus ar pasa grada grada masa wood pr Purstatte sawa grasa grada masa wood pr Brone can and digan products Pramay mesla industria. Pramay mesla industria. Pramay mesla industria. Tramportation equipment. Other curshes goods. Tother curshes goods. Food and sandowl products. Food and sandowl products. Textile multi prancies and money.	17, 290 5 389 -, 748 527 339 179 236 47 - 70	5,693 1,875 *21 -21 7° 32 140 24 104 21	11,796 3 214 1,227 476 256 77 90 23 366	2	15 165 5,076 1 742 525 529 1(6 215 47 77 30	2,03=	83 4 2 2	16	4,180 905 575 315 160 16 25 24	718 154 98 20 0	3 462 751 477 295 106 16 18 28		3,733 899 572 3,3 166 16 25 14	395	30	
Conductable goods Food and kindred products Textle mull products and appeared Chemitals and allied products Other mondurable goods Vit specified manusaturing industries	3,322 1,451 2:0 209 1,322	1,340 568 130 94 254	1,974 883 120 404 767	1 1	3,315 1,447 250 297 ± 321	2	2,		17 318 108 112 92 12	5 5 25 29	263 90 4 106 6.3		33.5 108 112 100	3,		
Nonmanusacturing industries (inst not rptd) Construction. Radroads and ailway express service Transportation except radroad Telecommunications, duillisted assuitary serv. Wooksale and retail trade	12 207 -,710 1,926 1,5-2 960 2,439	3,818 1,041 317 333 672	8,384 2,009 1,609 1,179 286	5	1,009 1,545 1,694 1,438	2,025 344 32 66 697	76	1	382 13° 21.	1 264 246 42 28 61	2,71, 1,095 340 111		2,834 2,834 2,212 382 133 84	392 122 4 121	4/6	2
Occubation not reborted	1,660	781 674 1 221	983 45°	3	2,406 747 1 530	874 129	10 36	10	486 712 637	94	393 618		482 941	135	36	

DETAILED CHARACTERISTICS

Table 77—RACE AND CLASS OF WORKER OF EMPLOYED PERSONS, BY OCCUPATION AND SEX, FOR THE STATE AND FOR STANDARD METROPOLITAN AREAS OF 100,000 OR MORE 1950—Con.

	2-6-	New Ox	leans e	braner	Matropo,	ar wres				Sare	abor	.r.d :	'- cho	314 4	9	-
			Race	out to		has of			1		Race			lass of		
Occupation and sex	Potal, 14 years old and over	White	Vagro	Other zaces	-	Govern- ment work- ers		Uppard family work- ers	Total, 4 years old and over	Whrte	\egro	Other		Govern- ment work- ers	belf- em- ployed workers	Unpaid family work- ers
Female, employed .	60,452	54,599	25,78.	62	o5 06.	10,3,3	4 3-4	202	27 288	12,438	10 24-	-	17,817	2,430	1,040	+3
Professional, technical, and kindred workers	9 698	8 399	1,28_	18	4,807	4,-2.	468		2 444	2,936	4.0	_		-12-2	137	
ocountants and suditors.	500	270	,	1	515	55	8	1	5	577	7.0	-	5	3	3	- day in
state and art tocourse	141	_09 133	43	1	97	18	24	2	6 1	12	1		1_4	4		1
hemists and natural scientists (n e.c.)		108	3	2	47		24 _9 1	. 1	21	?5]	22	3	3	
ollege president prof'rs & instructors 'n e.c.)	48	13o	1		141	17	. 0		21	e.,	1	Jane 1	1 2	7		
newtens and nutritionals awyers and judges	220	98	-62		74	4,	15		2	. 3		-	1	9	-	
biar ans fusic ans and music teachers	190	1,8	28		95	91	61		51 102	5 42 32	13	100	1/	36	,	endle.
urses, projes ional	4 2.3	2.053	156	4	1.33	445	LC5	,	2.7	520	12	1	-26	84	22	
hisicians and surgeons	8.8	8.0	2	6	383	47	34	,	308	108	_		409	1 1	5	
	36 435	372	c3	1	132	302	-	-	7	3	1		17	60	1	
ocal sciences and recreation workers - bechare (a e.c.) bechare (a e.c.)	3,32"	1 494 325	830	1 2	1,134	2,120	44	27	1,134	674	440		_32 59	987	11	
ther notessions technical and kindred workers	32	27	2	1	231 16	300	4		1,	10	3	1	6 88			
		648	63	1	487	152		8	1	119	100		88	28	12	
Farmers and farm managers	28	21.	- 6	-	1	-	27	-	21.,	18	179	-		-	2,4	_
Managers officials & proprietors exc. farm	3,77>	1,26_	504	9	1,510	.25		72		783	140	1	340			-
Specified m.ragers and officials Managers officials a prop. s (n.e.o. —salaried , Wholesele and 16ts-11 trails	1,210	1 09,	36 1.3	1	1 102	977 3R	סי		75	73	24		1 796	1 40		
	553	,0, 591	,0 6 t	,	552	35			129	149 -62 339	13		156	3	1	1
More of cals, & rope's (i.e.)—self-employed Lating and dimining places Wholesale & r. all rade exc eating & dirring pl	1,398	1,620	365	1 3		-	1,327	71	10	336	125	1	1		505 1.C.	1
Wholesale & r. all rade exc eating & durking pl Other industries (mel not reported)	420	304 370 352	197	1 4			1 074	10	297	242	22	1			229	
Clesical and kindred workers	23,-49	22,70	A50		10,141	4,00-	161	1113	1	5,087	. 04	1	4 450	6.1	7	
Bookseeper	1 850	1,312	31		1,703	9	27	25	5662	600	-	5	601	20	30	1
Senters two Lts. and scoretaries	1,599	8,66	205		1 1,517	29	29	. 4	60	2,40	1	2	330	31	1.7	
Telephone opera ora Other elemnal and Lindred nonkers	2,021	1.85	17	1	1,5,1		1	1	1 402	2,473	1 :	L	38:	23	1	
Sales workers	7,272	6,827	444				1	363		1,00	1		1,49		1	1
Insurance and real estate agents and prokers	360	244			341	1	2			7			9			
O nei spemfied sales workers Salesmen and sales clerka noc) retail trade	1,.06	1.8	274	11	5,709	1	27	350		1,392		5	1,30	6	1.	100
Salesmer and saics c.erks (n e c) exc re all trade	405	3/6	2		3"	9	14	1	72	8		5	6.	3	14	
Craftsmen, foremen and kindred workers	982	801	100	1	890		53		181	14.	2	9	1.5	-	1	
Foreme. (n.e.) Other trafismen and kindred workers	26 710	254	1	1 .	24.	22	5:	,	160	22		0	13	9	6 1	2
Operatives and kindred workers	⊥C, 3°a⊥	6 305	-, °6e	1	9 808	1 44	1 704		1 477	733	74	4	1.4	5 300	g! 9	
Dresamakers and seamstresses except actory.	-,197	984	343	3	96		30		24	100		5	_5		5, "1	
Laundry and ity cleaning operatives Spinners and year ers textile	7.0	334	_ 388	3	2 1,609 208 378	61	1 2	20	1	14	>		1 64	21	-	
Other specified overs wes and kindred workers Ope a ves and kindred workers (n.e.c Manufaering	6,841	4.283	2 343	1	378 p 763	35	22	1	122	310	10	7) 91	1 44	9 4		-
Manufae .ring	5,948	4,283 3 713 371	. 22	3 12	*,019	1	1		334	233	10	0	34	3	1	
Durable gords Metal ricus ries	168	157	1 4		160		-		3	1 . 7	•	i		3	1	1
Mashnery including destricts Other durable goods	-50	203	4	4 .	24				2 72	2.	4	9	1 7		1 7	
Food and kindred produc s	5,47	3,314	2 140	1.	5,45	1	1		7 249	201	1 4	8	7.		1 3	2
hn. tmg mille	217	15	50	B	21	7					1	1	1			
Textule min products, excep, kniting Apparel & of ser fabricated textule products	۸ 098	1,46		9 '	2 69	1.	1	5	1 1-8	130	1	8	- 4	7	1 :	L)
Control of the contro	13	585	181	R	7.	0	1	i	25.	1		1	2	8		
Not specified mana.turing industries A mmanus sturing industries (incl. not rptd.)	H44 193	570	1 320		84		3.6	1 .	1 148	75		2	12		5	1
Privace household workers	12,674	6.1	01:	3	11,58	1	0		2 4,217	L20	1		4,09	6	22	0
Private household workers— ving at	>28	22	. 30:	91	28	4.	1		4 60 5 57	2.	3 406	2	4,13		220	
Private household workers— ving our	11 106	39'	10 70	1	1 11,04		6:		1		100			1	2015	
Service workers, except private household	12,405	4 924			9 (9					130	2 2		1 9	5 5	6	-
A tendants hospital and other historian Barbe s, beautimans, and maniturests	1,056	29:	46	1	50 46	1	2 49.	3	322	201	1.	-	20	2	111	3
Claruchin and ore and por ers Cooks except priva c household Housekeepers & stewards ext pileate household	750 1,138	291	96	2	1	5 13	4 2	1	657	1 3	64		1 21	12	7 1	2
Housekeepers & stewards expulzate household	462 733	1 5	6	0	36	11 8	2	4	283	23	9 4		23	7 14	5 2	
Practical nurses and m.dwives Was reses bartanders and counter we were Othe service works except n vate accusehold	2,958	2,100	84		2,73	11.	10	6		61.		9	1,02	4 14	2 2	
	115	1							1 808	1	1	15. 14	49		H.O. T.	3
Farm laborers unpaid am.l. workers		4 2	_				-	1	1 3,2	-	5 0	71	49		1	3.
Farm laborers unpaid amily workers. Farm laborers except appaid er a farm foremer	84	2	1		8			2	406	1	8 48	8	1		1. '	
Laborers excep farm and mine	800	.00	-0	-	74	2 4	0	ci-	5 103		9 7	4	1 - 6	-	5 4	2
Оссиранов пот герогнед .	835	f2	3 2	1	1 9	5 2	6	2	8 402	20	1 20	4	1 19	4	5	3
	I		-		-				-			_				-

Table 78.—INCOME IN 1945 OF THE EXPERIENCED CIVILIAN LABOR FORCE, BY OCCUPATION AND SEX, FOR THE STATE AND FOR STANDARD METROPOLITAN AREAS OF 250,000 OR MORE 1950

Fer totaus by occupation from Aripusto co.m' see table ?? Now means not assembere classified. Percent not abown where less than 0.1 percent and memory to above a bure base in less than 0.00]

Tets. .4 yesra odd and over ('praces perrons without income) not re-ported \$7 000 \$10,000 Medis a income (dol.) \$4,500 to \$4,999 \$2,500 3,300 \$3,500 \$5,000 \$8,000 \$1 to | \$.000 \$1,500 \$099 t. to or 1088 S 499 \$1,399 82,000 Ares recupation and sex 96,999 \$8,999 to \$4,499 80,999 E2 499 to to TE 87.7E 630, دا 245 9,675 .445 1,902 32 025 6" 6 Male, exp civ abor force, 2,970 7° 3 2,7.0 1,745 2,805 3,696 42,-, 8, J, 37C 3 00 Profess a techn L kind ed wars 4 49 Accountants and audi one Arcusters -arists and art eachers Authors, ed. ors, and reporters 4.5 3 95a 65 560 345 490 30 20 80 63 230 50 275 260 15 40 45 170 115 45 15 120 150 165 75 30 35 80 105 45 15 10 15 45 210 60 31 85 4 94 4 5 min N 76 9 61 0 89 0 56 2 85 7 85 8 4,019 4 018 1 779 4,610 6,389 3,306 103 75 75 75 : " 40 40 1,43 215 10 Designers and drafteman
Engineers, aeronautical
Engineers civil
Engineers electrical
Engineers trechanical
Other technical engineers 85 5 5 150 195 60 70 95 4,300 ,192 4 188 4,673 35 70 145 50 13 125 65 °C 70 100 60 92 225 1.6 1.00 230 160 -15 -30 210 3.0 190 195 435 200 65 100 275 120 80 90 60 515 70 525 3-145 1,245 80 577 40 60 95 935 6 396 2,087 4 325 4,361 6,750 355 c0 455 50 240 1,000 1,010 835 1,010 1,010 1,000 1, 345 32 85 125 235 10 10 20 65 20 20 20 20 86 5 45 3 82 2 89 2 85 1 Lawyers and Judges
Musicians and music teachers
Natural scientists (Le c.)
Pharmacians
Phrynians and surgeons
Social accounts to 500 1-200 1-200 200 40 635 65 110 85 60 127 127 137 630 8,770 75 80 95 20 50 70 715 20 58p 150 2 305 1,455 1 40 15,690 160 330 600 7,875 7,305 12000 388882113333 240 35 105 125 100 50 20 30 295 15 45 10 25 13 305 90 600 110 25 243 70 545 20 205 205 30 640 5 0,618 3,4.3 2 639 3,167 10 35 Surreyors
Teachers in e.c.)
Technicians medical and deutal
Other process! ech kindred wkrs 80 5 5J0 230 75 2 8: 380 77,43. ,.O 43. 8 .40 5, 74. 2 335 2,140 030 890 3/0 600 445 590 730 954 4,060 600 Resumes and form managers
Mgrs. sols appepts, see, Came.
Offic. & compectors. Seate 6. local
Other spencion managers is offinated.
Mgrs. offic. group in co.d. instance
McMandacturage.
McMandacturage.
Finance manuraces, & real estace.
Offinance manuraces, & real estace.
Officer industriace (mcl. not proj.)
Mgr. off. proptin ex.)—endicaspioped
Wagnotte. reale.
Wagnotte. reale.
Wagnotte. reale.
Wagnotte. reale.
Wagnotte. reale.
Wagnotte. reale.
Wagnotte. reale.
Wagnotte. reale.
Wagnotte. reale.
Wagnotte. reale.
Wagnotte. reale.
Wagnotte. reale.
Wagnotte. reale.
Wagnotte. reale.
Wagnotte. reale.
Wagnotte. reale.
Wagnotte. reale.
Wagnotte. reale.
Wagnotte. reale.
Wagnotte. reale.
Wagnotte. reale.
Wagnotte. reale.
Wagnotte. reale.
Wagnotte. reale.
Wagnotte. reale.
Wagnotte. reale.
Wagnotte. reale.
Wagnotte. reale.
Wagnotte. reale.
Wagnotte. reale.
Wagnotte. reale.
Wagnotte. reale.
Wagnotte. reale.
Wagnotte. reale.
Wagnotte. reale.
Wagnotte. reale.
Wagnotte. reale.
Wagnotte. reale.
Wagnotte. reale.
Wagnotte. reale.
Wagnotte. reale.
Wagnotte. reale.
Wagnotte. reale.
Wagnotte. reale.
Wagnotte. reale.
Wagnotte. reale.
Wagnotte. reale.
Wagnotte. reale.
Wagnotte. reale.
Wagnotte. reale.
Wagnotte. reale.
Wagnotte. reale.
Wagnotte. reale.
Wagnotte. reale.
Wagnotte. reale.
Wagnotte. reale.
Wagnotte. reale.
Wagnotte. reale.
Wagnotte. reale.
Wagnotte. reale.
Wagnotte. reale.
Wagnotte. reale.
Wagnotte. reale.
Wagnotte. reale.
Wagnotte. reale.
Wagnotte. reale.
Wagnotte. reale.
Wagnotte. reale.
Wagnotte. reale.
Wagnotte. reale.
Wagnotte. reale.
Wagnotte. reale.
Wagnotte. reale.
Wagnotte. reale.
Wagnotte. reale.
Wagnotte. reale.
Wagnotte. reale.
Wagnotte.
Wagnotte. reale.
Wagnotte. reale.
Wagnotte. reale.
Wagnotte. reale.
Wagnotte. reale.
Wagnotte. reale.
Wagnotte. reale.
Wagnotte. reale.
Wagnotte. reale.
Wagnotte. reale.
Wagnotte. reale.
Wagnotte. reale.
Wagnotte. reale.
Wagnotte. reale.
Wagnotte. reale.
Wagnotte. reale.
Wagnotte. reale.
Wagnotte. reale.
Wagnotte. reale.
Wagnotte.
Wagnotte. reale.
Wagnotte. reale.
Wagnotte.
Wagnot 3,-25 105 530 1,515 310 480 750 22,70, 3 345 9 250 2 370 7 140 30 UIC 3,825 4,72. 5,620 4 530 4,005 2,885 5 034 4,105 5,825 3,6 3 - 760 88 3 56,125 3,860 5 100 250 (611 200 852 147 4,830 160 180 125 1,164 470 230 885 2,141 340 941 210 1 5 720 2,050 350 610 230 155 717 1,775 345 640 245 1,660 7,1-2 23,678 3,645 6,265 26,403 1,840 1,840 1,840 1,840 1,840 1,840 1,840 1,840 755 250 783 753 450 252 2,770 180 200 1,390 165 339 1,054 105 45 359 2,270 189 115 115 125 1,225 360 205 545 1,665 265 565 12 415 2,400 130 130 130 130 130 130 130 30 30 30 30 8: 620 95 865 250 385 720 280 70 540 1,877 470 575 1,620 90 150 175 370 25,055 +40 765 305 345 3,395 3,795 3,795 1,710 810 3 174 4,005 4 13° 4,59° 1,64. 4,773 4,267 3,180 3,536 3,536 3,614 7,526 2,960 3,587 90 350 4,480 65 60 1"-480 245 225 31-1,205 80 89 5 82 1 90 7 91 2 90 3 95 0 88 0 72 7 81 9 87 2 85 7 91 4 9 250 2 370 7 140 30 010 2,350 2 180 2,10 3 281 14,675 5,350 865 1,820 145 145 150 170 860 350 2,3,5 230 160 85 220 1,240 430 1,695 1,695 155 140 85 15, 875 3,5 1,450 460 735 55 50 50 95 910 175 575 975 70 145 65 450 165 165 140 830 200 Clerical and kindred workers 370 2 17 2.5 34,545 32 125 2 850 .,847 ه 1ه 3 78 1 245 4 920 <.255 245 535 415 ..595 315 9* 2,440 2 020 2 020 -4.5 90 2,590 530 190 3 %5 oC5 275 3,665 565 347 4,010 137 40 1,030 140 30 1,07> 85 435 35 10 370 2 795 3 _83 2 617 79 9 d6 1 81 5 1,925 28 685 1,850 235 155 1 865 195 4 475 2 865 4,00 3,475 3,865 , 415 1,785 920 2,030 79 1 Sales workers . .. 3€ 745 2 500 2,000 885 2 "22 Sase workers ...

Lustrace, agents and brokers
Real estate agents and brokers.
Uther not considered to the control of the cont 290 70 40 1,500 235 900 755 110 20,730 20,730 3,000 6,045 18,360 1 2-5 25 25 245 4,370 105 235 1,935 280 43 85 525 90 90 1.85 50 45 185 700 25 3,312 4 286 945 3,825 830 4 795 75 75 414 100 170 100 730 730 200 300 300 81 C 83 1 60 9 83 7 83 7 77 7 250 1,540 26,110 2 805 3 85 16,593 3 4.5 285 665 2,340 165 3,160 390 495 1 795 120 2,1,0 945 2 634 3,381 5,339 2 307 3,021 3,610 220 325 2,96 1,20 -,910 365 67-. 82-105 935 100 332 400 30 1,440 185 270 650 95 1,000 685 220 295 40 92 100,505 97,805 0 315 185 120 40 11,795 85.5 12,045 / 195 350 4,755 555 370 190 255 135 120 120 140 150 470 520 1 13, 170 255 710 1 465 725 870 1 -05 19 175 1 195 3, 2, 4,235 9,130 1 205 2,455 5,470 1 375 825 2,045 48,1-0 1 150 3,705 2,985 8 760 4 150 2 375 5,235 100 -/5 30 40 -,120 -,120 215 240 215 45 40 330 1/10 20 35 155 45 *60 185 245 465 980 -60 255 565 20 5 20 2 373 1 750 3,448 2 096 1 977 3,548 2 765 3,521 3,647 3,132 4,309 3 477 30 40 25 45 655 40 165 215 300 75 67 70 0 7 59 64 9 63 2 3 87 1 63 3 5 5 90 100 195 2 875 240 580 330 950 175 255 620 70 12 55 10 25 180 415 665 81 150 421 10 65 20 240 136 240 415 1,020 45 430 45 180 3 270 65 500 285 603 80 55 470 cers akers a d patternmakers 165 2 870 60 265 173 215 60 20 135 135 2,010 75 505 445 1,010 170 435 905 55 1,030 10-365 530 900 270 560 45 30 65 1,0 20 25 305 490 50 25 45 70 430 145 250 10 15 10 55 50 ectresses nomen (n.e.c.) Manufacturing durable goods Mg, nondurable (incl. not spec.) Nonmanufacturing (mel. not spec.) Vennandeketuring und netroid)

Linemen di viprionem i, graph ele
Loomentive signimenti
Cocomotive firmane
Machiniste and job ne stere
Machiniste and job ne stere
Machiniste and job ne stere
Machiniste and job ne stere
Mechanies a lor repairment, aurilane
Mechanies and repairment auto
Mechanies de rocali racio di seave in
Mechanies de opsir de looir fixes
Mill wright a
Mill wright a
Mill wright a 215 20 16* 210 205 25 235 240 20 1 530 125 1,075 20 405 15 25 415 215 20 740 1575 70 20 495 110 110 540 400 1,280 1,220 25 3,048 4,569 3,95e 3,250 2,534 83 4 70 0 67 9 70 2 39 0 3 755 925 700 5,500 1,935 285 10 47* 1,000 10,465 650 85 2 915 875 975 3,45 1 830 260 9,900 9,940 6-,3* 430 45 55 220 30 1,505 1,505 1,50 85 420 90 85 750 130 750 955 85 175 155 100 220 90 30 150 4.0 65 70 80 85 95 10 190 20 400 80 10 10 125 25 100 75 25 445 33 380 55 55 ا ا 272 20 752 35 10 30 5 100 5 50 •5 80 5 Noders metal .

Paun est contai) paperhips glarm.

Rasteurs and semant finis.est
Plumber and pupe fitten.

Print, raft; son, compos & sypeset
Stoomakors & repairer exo. fat.fory
Stationary : sgiteers
Structum heal workers
Taglors and furners.
Trosimits oppman shestmetal with
Toolimakers, & die maker & settee
Other ractifumes and landeré were 1,38° 23.5° 330 15 140 143 70 130 250 5>5 73 85 470 440 64 165 7,300 1,510 2,315 505 685 3 795 1 015 366 1,275 35 6 490 1,985 2,145 3,205 3,375 1,677 3,86 3,003 6,/55 1,435 4,97* 500 615 3 810 970 31c 1,100 905 -83 365 15 -25 -65 40 44 105 1,120 225 450 15 120 185 125 25 105 705 580 580 40 240 120 25 185 5 370 585 55 25 25 130 20 165 45 620 65 420 55 15 205 50 20 20 15 20 70 120 35 5 30 65 15 55 405 253 253 25 20 140 45 35 65 79 2 85 6 49 2 2,706

225

2 483 305

Table 78.—INCOME IN 1949 OF THE EXPERIENCED CIVILIAN LABOR FORCE, BY OCCUPATION AND SEX, FOR THE STATE AND FOR STANDARD METROPOLITAN AREAS OF 250 000 OR MORE 1950—Con.

[Based on 20-percent sample For totals by occupation from complete count, see table 73 "N.e.c." means not elsewhere classified Percent not shown where less than 0.1, percent and median not shown where base is less than 500]

Area, occupation, and sex	Total, 14 years old and over (includes persons without income)	Persons with income: Total	$1 to $999 or loss	$1 000 to $1 499	$1,500 to $1 999	$2 000 to $2,499	$2,500 to $2,999	$3,000 to $3 499	$3 500 to $3 999	$4 000 to $4,499	$4,500 to $4,999	$5,000 to $5 999	$6,000 to $6,999	$7,000 to $9 999	$10,000 and over	Median income (dol.)	Income not reported	Worked in 1949 — Percent with 50 to 52 weeks
THE STATE																		
Male—Con																		
Operatives and kindred workers	1??,?85	109,030	??,730	1?,525	17,??5	17 005	?0,695	9,?65	[illegible]	?,520	?,485	3,0??	[illegible]	?85	?0	[illegible]	4 1?0	67 0
Apprentices	1 230	1 1?0	2?5	175	135	200	145	3?	6?	9?	15					1,935	50	53 5
Attendants auto service & parking	4,070	3 ?55	[illegible]	775	895	490	60	75	40	75	15	30	5	10	10	1,?87	100	65 3
Brakemen and switchmen railroad	?,315	?,840	7?	65	105	230	140	3?	3?	?00	130	95	10	5		3 515	65	73 7
Bus drivers	3,470	3 095	2?	?5	395	610	540	420	3??	20	15	40	5	5		2 512	70	63 4
Filers, grinders & polishers metal	490	465	8	80	60	75	15	50	35	40		5					20	
Furnacemen smeltermen & heaters	75	75	15	5	15	5	25			5								
Laundry and dry cleaning operatives	2 880	2 730	540	275	630	525	145	1?5	50	25	2?	15	5	5	10	1,68?	115	72 6
Meat cutters exc slaughter & pack	2 145	1,770	235	215	335	430	330	19?	75	75	2?	35	15	10	5	2 188	125	78 9
Mine operatives & laborers (n.e.c.)	12,150	11,620	?55	710	700	?60	970	1,420	1 ?15	1 440	870	?85	75	240	5	1,466	435	65
Motormen, street, subway, & elev rwy	375	35?				70	15	15?	85	10	5	10					20	
Painters exc const & maintenance	895	8?5	75	45	145	170	110	30	60	70	25	35	5	5		2,404	30	77 5
Power station operators	2?0	225	5		5	?0	40	40	45	25	10	20					5	
Sailors and deck hands	2,990	2,?90	33?	?00	44?	500	?5?	?1?	1?5	110	55	40	4?	10		?190	16?	41 3
Sawyers	2,055	1 955	490	?5	360	255	9	[illegible]	80	20	20	15				1 431	?0	47 8
Spinners and weavers textile	[illegible]	[illegible]	5	15	15	20												
Stationary firemen	1 930	1,870	190	155	345	300	225	255	125	8?	75	35	10	5		3 342	50	69 6
Taxicab drivers and chauffeurs	4,035	3,833	720	915	765	7?5	36?	190	80	7?	15	2?	1?		5	1 683	130	72 7
Truck drivers and deliverymen	30,060	27 940	6 ?40	5,060	5 84?	4,?75	2 170	1 645	9?5	510	280	335	100	80	90	1,?70	1 090	65 6
Welders and flame cutters	4,045	3 910	215	185	365	500	145	695	420	385	185	350	110	50	5	3 ?76	95	65 0
Other spec. operat. & kindred wkrs	4 280	3 995	470	415	525	715	440	570	[illegible]	185	115	80	10	10	10	2,411	2?0	65 ?
Operatives & kindred wkrs (n.e.c.)	36 890	34,770	5,325	4 ?05	5,495	5,660	5 845	3 165	1,770	1,935	1 ?80	1 065	200	150	45	2 ?82	1 225	69 8
Manufacturing	27 370	25 890	3 545	3,100	3 900	4,090	2 325	2,435	1 ?70	1 660	1 260	1 005	160	120	40	2,?86	850	71 6
Durable goods	8,050	7 495	1 585	1 440	1,740	1,115	90	385	220	80	75	100	[illegible]	2?	5	1,706	305	6? ?
Saw & pl'g mills misc wood p.	4,045	3,70?	1,04?	5?5	900	430	18?	95	5?	25		10	10		5	1 41?	175	56 3
Furniture and fixtures	430	380	90	85	200	75	10	10	5				5				35	
Stone clay & glass products	1,?10	1 150	135	175	180	195	110	105	5?	110	40	45	10	5		2,372	35	69 ?
Primary metal industries	28?	275	15	40	35	45	15	25	30	5	10	5					5	
Fab'd metal (incl not spec)	69?	680	95	50	180	115	120	35	25	5	20	15				2 065	5	65 0
Machinery except electrical	44?	420	70	60	110	90	25	15	1?	15		10		5			20	
Electrical mach'y, equip. sup	3?	30	5				5	10	5	5							5	
Motor vehicles & mtr veh eqp	80	80		10	25	5	10	20	5	5								
Transp. equip. exc motor veh.	4?	385	55	40	65	100	70	25	10	10		5		5			1?	
Other durable goods	410	395	75	70	85	70	35	25	15		5	10					10	
Nondurable goods	19 12?	18,210	1,945	1,685	2 140	2 ?25	2,330	2,025	1,345	1 ?80	1 17?	895	13?	95	35	2,?88	540	76 0
Food and kindred products	5 74?	5 415	2,100	945	1,070	915	680	440	1?5	65	20	20	5	10	20	?810	160	64 ?
Yarn thread, & fabric mills	28?	27?	30	20	85	100	3?	10		5							5	
Knit'g & other textile mill pr.	9?	80	10	5	10	30	10					5					10	
Apparel & other fab'd tex. pr.	?80	?55	80	6?	145	90	40	30									5	
Paper and allied products	5,?55	4 835	145	270	7?5	1,150	1,075	755	385	200	160	90	10	20		2,601	14?	79 ?
Chemicals and allied products	3,010	2 900	195	345	390	390	2??	365	300	385	295	110	5	20	5	3 078	80	74 8
Leather and leather products	[illegible]	45	20	10	5	5	5											
Other nondurable goods	4 ?20	4,205	15?	125	105	745	135	465	495	820	760	670	115	45	10	4 194	1?5	89 ?
Not specified mfg industries	195	185	1	20	20	50	5	15		20	?7	10		5			5	
Nonmanufacturing (incl not rptd)	9,?20	8,880	1,780	1,345	1 5?5	1 570	920	7?5	400	2?5	120	?0	50	30	5	1,912	375	64 5
Trans commun. other pub util	2 970	2,825	295	275	250	550	425	365	205	135	60	35	10	10		2,357	110	72 4
Wholesale and retail trade	2,620	2 ?10	585	465	475	445	160	115	70	35	20	10		10		1,665	7?	65 2
Other ind (incl not rptd)	3 930	3,645	[illegible]	605	670	375	335	250	125	65	70	35	20	10	5	1,737	190	57 0
Private household workers	1 ?80	1 190	7?5	200	125	55	20	5	10	[illegible]	5				5	788	80	58 0
Service wkrs. exc priv. hshld	38 ?60	35,585	? 230	? 675	6,765	5,770	3,?30	2,050	935	535	245	295	[illegible]	115	85	1 699	1,300	72 3
Barbers, beauticians, & manicurists	?,255	3,000	465	?05	710	555	310	295	115	110	75	45	15	10	2?	2,018	19?	78 8
Charwomen, janitors, and porters	11,030	10 930	2 765	2,970	2 ?40	1,445	570	285	60	25	15	15	5	5	10	1,4?5	295	74 0
Cooks, except private household	2 750	2 395	[illegible]	42	435	440	22?	180	9?	50	[illegible]					1,794	75	67 8
Elevator operators	?70	525	100	175	145	60	20	20	5							1,464	10	75 0
Firemen fire protection	1 66?	1 600	35	25	130	540	4?5	2?5	120	40	15	45		10		2,58?	55	91 4
Guards and watchmen	?00	4,095	630	805	1 025	745	375	210	65	7?	25	25		30		1 799	130	69 3
Policemen sheriffs, and marshals	3,?05	2,985	170	175	255	715	655	55	130	7?0	65	55	4?	35	20	2 ?01	85	88 0
Waiters, bartenders & counter wkrs.	5 ?55	?,855	1 52?	?60	680	730	135	330	100	45	15	65	10	20	20	1 632	255	65 ?
Other service wkrs exc priv hshld	5,910	5,?10	2 230	?40	[illegible]	?40	345	190	137	45	40	45	20	15	15	1 ?9?	2?0	62 3
Farm laborers and foremen	[illegible]	34,485	25,035	5,005	2 055	8?5	285	240	100	100	20	40	40	50	20	673	2,100	40 0
Farm laborers unpaid family wkrs	?,680	?,810	4,975	475	175	80	30	25	20	20				5	5	84	615	42 ?
Farm laborers, exc unpaid & foremen	32,5?5	28,675	20,?00	4 530	1 500	815	255	215	80	80	20	40	40	45	15	69?	?,485	47 1
Laborers except farm and mine	88,855	82 300	?5 400	17,880	17,575	11 ?05	4 590	?,835	?,0?5	585	240	270	[illegible]	8?	35	1 440	3,270	53 ?
Fishermen and oystermen	7,5?0	6,740	? 8?0	1 290	85?	685	415	130	110	75	3?	65	25	15	20	1 ? 3	315	46 7
Longshoremen and stevedores	[illegible]	[illegible]	835	345	1,32?	1 045	570	340	190	70	45	[illegible]	15	15	5	1,896	210	41 2
Lumbermen raftsmen woodchoppers	?,750	[illegible]	2,?2?	1 280	840	355	60	105	20	70		20	10	10	20	1 044	260	39 1
Other specified laborers	?,050	4 ?8?	1 ?0?	1,12?	935	445	150	45	10	5	10	10	15	10	35	1 19?	215	57 1
Laborers (n.e.c.)	6?,955	60 445	17,920	13 240	13,955	?,035	3,295	1 945	725	435	150	145	40	35	35	1,?87	2,270	54 2
Manufacturing	22 76?	21,315	[illegible]	[illegible]	5 ?35	3 575	1,405	955	355	190	80	?5	[illegible]	10	10	[illegible]	810	60 1
Durable goods	10 ?35	10,195	? 205	2 785	2 525	1,115	350	150	45	15	20	15	5	5		1,340	400	52 ?
Furn saw & pl'g mills & wd pr	? 410	7,810	?,74?	?,?90	1 955	535	180	75		5	10	10				1,254	335	50 ?
Stone clay, & glass products	305	730	125	170	215	190	5?	[illegible]		[illegible]	5			5		1 721	10	63 ?
Primary metal industries	[illegible]	340	5?	65	85	75	50	20	5								10	
Fab'd metal (incl not spec)	?95	370	50	55	75	110	40	15	10				5				15	
Machinery, incl electrical	140	125	40	25	15	30						5					10	
Transportation equipment	?20	680	170	140	160	1?5	55	35	10	5						1 59?	15	44 8
Other durable goods	100	90	20	40	10	10		5									5	
Nondurable goods	11 750	11,090	2 010	1 635	2 47?	2 46?	1,070	805	330	17?	60	40	10	5	10	1,884	400	67 5
Food and kindred products	4,585	4,340	1 130	80?	1 170	650	28?	100	45		5	15	5		5	1,566	135	57 5
Textile mill prod. & apparel	360	355	75	50	135	50	30										5	
Chemicals and allied products	1,900	1,705	335	265	370	335	115	115	60	40	10					1 84?	55	67 0
Other nondurable goods	4,985	4,595	4?0	?70	845	1,3?5	635	525	225	135	45	25	5	5	5	2 226	205	76 6
Not specified mfg industries	93	80	20	35	20		5										10	
Nonmanufacturing (incl not rptd)	4?,19?	39 090	12,085	8 ?95	8 940	5 460	1,990	1 010	370	215	70	90	25	25	25	1,424	1,460	54 1
Construction	16,9??	15 980	5 020	5,790	3,550	?,895	640	325	135	85	45	40	25	15	15	1 365	660	44 2
Railroads & railway express serv.	?,5?0	5 340	[illegible]	[illegible]	1 260	1,6?5	60?	?05	10?	35	5	5		5		1,986	165	69 8
Transportation, except railroad	2,705	2 545	615	600	635	375	17?	100	35	15		5				1,246	100	55 7
Telecommun. util. & sanit serv	2 670	2,515	540	580	600	370	[illegible]	[illegible]	[illegible]	30				5		1,586	?0	69 1
Wholesale and retail trade	6,390	5 645	1,005	1,595	1,470	635	265	145	65	2?	10	25			5	1,401	180	59 8
Other ind (incl not rptd)	8,000	7,255	3,560	1,510	1,215	470	155	100	35	25	10	10			5	1,022	305	53 ?
Occupation not reported	15,875	12 785	4,715	2,090	1 595	1,320	810	805	395	320	140	275	120	90	110	1,401	1 540	41 9

Table 78.—INCOME IN 1949 OF THE EXPERIENCED CIVILIAN LABOR FORCE, BY OCCUPATION AND SEX, FOR THE STATE AND FOR STANDARD METROPOLITAN AREAS OF 250,000 OR MORE 1950—Con

[Based on 20-percent sample. For totals by occupation from complete count see table 78. "N.e.c." means not elsewhere classified. Percent not shown where less than 0.1 percent and median not shown where base is less than 500]

Area, occupation, and sex	Total 14 years old and over (includes persons without income)	Persons with income: Total	$1 to $999 or loss	$1,000 to $1,499	$1,500 to $1,999	$2,000 to $2,499	$2,500 to $2,999	$3,000 to $3,499	$3,500 to $3,999	$4,000 to $4,499	$4,500 to $4,999	$5,000 to $5,999	$6,000 to $6,999	$7,000 to $9,999	$10,000 and over	Median income (dol.)	Income not reported	Worked in 1949 — Percent with 50 to 52 weeks
THE STATE																		
Female, exp. civ labor force	2[illegible],22[illegible]	[illegible]92,[illegible]	[illegible]930	28,[illegible]	[illegible],[illegible]80	[illegible]860	17 5[illegible]	[illegible] [illegible]5	3,[illegible]55	[illegible] 545	780	945	485	54[illegible]	39[illegible]	995	10,745	57 [illegible]
Profess'l techn'l, kindred wkrs	2[illegible],[illegible]25	25 080	[illegible]	2,[illegible]	[illegible],[illegible]45	4 [illegible] 5	[illegible]565	[illegible],330	1 510	[illegible]20	350	305	130	135	65	2 329	1,395	38 0
Accountants and auditors	[illegible]0[illegible]	[illegible]65	4[illegible]	20	8	—	60	[illegible]	65	15	15	20		10			15	
Actresses dancers entert (n.e.c.)	[illegible]65	2[illegible]	[illegible]0	30	1[illegible]	20	10	15		5			[illegible]	5			40	
Artists and art teachers	[illegible]	22[illegible]	[illegible]0	3[illegible]	4[illegible]	40	25	20	15	10	15				5		[illegible]5	
Authors editors and reporters	2[illegible]	[illegible]	[illegible]	25	[illegible]	45	15		45	15		-		5			5	
Chemists & natural scientists (n.e.c.)	260	20[illegible]	[illegible]	1[illegible]	25	30	5	55	30	25	5	5			5		50	
College pres prof'rs instr's (n.e.c.)	54[illegible]	4[illegible]	[illegible]	1[illegible]	4[illegible]	15	15	65	55	45	45	35	15				30	45 0
Designers and draftsmen	2[illegible]5	1[illegible]0	30	15	2[illegible]	15	35	[illegible]5	10	5	5	-					35	
Dietitians and nutritionists	[illegible]80	2[illegible]	65	45	40	70	20	15	5	10							20	
Lawyers and judges	25	25	5			5					15							
Librarians	40[illegible]	[illegible]45	100	55	[illegible]0	70	6[illegible]	65	30	35	5	—	15	10	5	2,268	40	57 7
Musicians and music teachers	[illegible]95	745	345	95	75	40	2[illegible]	90	10	30	5	10	10	5		1,[illegible]45	40	39 5
Nurses professional	4,820	4,[illegible]90	715	475	490	990	615	[illegible]05	160	95	5[illegible]	30	25	20	5	2,[illegible]82	260	60 1
Nurses, student professional	1,[illegible]	66[illegible]	50[illegible]	45	[illegible]	5						5		10		559	5	75 3
Physicians and surgeons	1[illegible]5	[illegible]4[illegible]	[illegible]0	-		20	5	5	5	5		10	0	10	25			
Social scientists	6[illegible]	5[illegible]	5		[illegible]	5	10	[illegible]	10								5	
Social welfare & recreation workers	1,175	1,075	185	110	130	240	45	105	75	45	20	15	5			2 234	50	70 1
Teachers (n.e.c.)	15,49[illegible]	13,565	2,220	[illegible],130	[illegible]120	2,[illegible]70	2,185	3 225	300	31[illegible]	120	100	35	35	15	2,[illegible]33	610	17 [illegible]
Technicians medical and dental	655	590	9[illegible]	8[illegible]	[illegible]	1[illegible]0	115	70	15	20	[illegible]	5				2,205	20	70 3
Therapists and healers (n.e.c.)	60	50	5	10		10	5		10	10								
Other prof'l tech'l, kindred wkrs	1,720	1,[illegible]10	545	160	140	190	170	130	110	40	40	45	10	25	5	4,[illegible]58	155	67 6
Farmers and farm managers	3 070	2 250	1,740	200	110	50	25	20	10	5		20	20	10	10	647	195	42 3
Mgrs., offs. & props., exc. farm	[illegible]0,660	8,275	2,[illegible]3	1,300	475	925	635	600	550	200	165	205	125	180	185	[illegible],69[illegible]	755	80 7
Specified managers and officials	[illegible] 4[illegible]	1 265	240	145	200	175	125	115	100	25	35	45	25	25	10	2,136	105	86 [illegible]
Mgrs. offs., props. (n.e.c.)—salaried	2 990	2 525	645	595	310	53[illegible]	290	195	130	60	35	45	30	40	30	[illegible],859	150	74 9
Wholesale and retail trade	1,40[illegible]	1 [illegible]7[illegible]	370	155	100	135	120	65	45	20	25	25	10	25	5	[illegible],056	80	78 2
Other industries (incl. not rptd.)	1,585	1 355	275	130	150	200	150	130	85	45	10	20	20	1[illegible]	25	2 05[illegible]	70	72 0
Mgr. off., prop. n.e.c.—self employed	[illegible],225	4 485	1,56[illegible]	76[illegible]	405	415	240	290	100	110	95	115	70	115	145	[illegible],446	500	82 3
Eating and drinking places	[illegible],600	1,15[illegible]	495	200	115	90	45	75	45	5	15	15	10	20	25	[illegible],2[illegible]	130	78 8
Wh. & ret. trade, exc. eat. & drink	3,515	2,490	835	405	2[illegible]5	275	160	75	40	65	60	80	35	7[illegible]	70	[illegible],510	290	84 8
Other industries (incl. not rptd.)	[illegible] 11[illegible]	840	2[illegible]5	1[illegible]	95	90	35	60	15	40	30	40	25	20	30	[illegible],626	80	83 5
Clerical and kindred workers	50 280	44,2[illegible]	[illegible] 660	6,675	10,390	10 030	5 010	2 [illegible]95	1 025	420	140	140	[illegible]10	90	60	[illegible] 875	2 215	7[illegible] 3
Bookkeepers	6,350	5,790	775	820	1,250	1,345	665	295	170	60	20	35	25	25	5	[illegible],96[illegible]	31[illegible]	80 0
Cashiers	[illegible],55[illegible]	[illegible],020	1 010	840	670	[illegible]5	95	80	10	[illegible]5		5	5	15		[illegible] 298	175	66 [illegible]
Stenographers, typists, secretaries	18,[illegible]5	16,45[illegible]	2,260	1,905	5,875	4,220	2,205	1,115	380	195	75	45	35	45	40	2,0[illegible]2	750	76 7
Telephone operators	4,650	4,240	605	600	1,245	[illegible],170	355	175	6[illegible]	10	10	5				[illegible],867	195	76 5
Other clerical and kindred workers	17,[illegible]90	15 040	3,010	2,[illegible]10	[illegible] 550	2 990	1,630	860	400	140	35	50	45	5	15	[illegible],799	785	73 4
Sales workers	20,455	13,57[illegible]	7 055	4,050	2,[illegible]10	1,075	445	240	95	60	45	90	45	55	50	[illegible],093	890	62 8
Insur. & real est. agents & brokers	790	660	170	1[illegible]0	150	60	60	30	20	15		15	15	15		1,667	50	70 9
Other specified sales workers	365	195	100	50	35	[illegible]	5	5	5								20	
Salesmen & sales clerks (n.e.c.) retail	18 545	14,1[illegible]5	[illegible],450	3,[illegible]85	1,985	970	330	285	70	30	40	70	25	40	35	1 080	765	62 8
Salesmen & sales cl. (n.e.c.) exc. retail	855	60[illegible]	315	105	40	30	50	20		15	5	5	5		15	960	60	54 3
Craftsmen, foremen, kindred wkrs	[illegible],870	1,64[illegible]	440	255	[illegible] 0	205	115	135	25	40	15	35	10	5		1,669	125	63 6
Foremen (n.e.c.)	585	360	60	55	90	65	25	30	5		5	10	5				15	
Other craftsmen and kindred workers	[illegible],485	[illegible],280	380	2[illegible]0	450	140	[illegible]0	105	20	40	10	25	5	5		1,[illegible]00	110	6[illegible] [illegible]
Operatives and kindred workers	21,320	18,315	9 3[illegible]5	4,[illegible]8	2,550	1 065	235	80	35	15	15	40	5	3[illegible]	10	980	900	53 2
Dressmakers & seamstr. exc. factory	2,[illegible]85	2,145	1 235	515	245	120	5	[illegible]		5		5	5	5		868	100	5[illegible] 4
Laundry and dry cleaning operatives	5,780	4 865	2,985	1,400	340	85	25	70	10			10		10		818	285	63 9
Spinners and weavers, textile	220	205	2[illegible]	35	110	3[illegible]											5	
Other spec. operat. & kindred wkrs	1,230	965	415	205	155	100	30	25	10	10		5		10		[illegible],[illegible]65	80	52 3
Operatives & kindred wkrs (n.e.c.)	11,605	10 115	4,685	2,730	[illegible]700	725	175	30	15		15	20		10	10	1 018	430	47 6
Manufacturing	9,760	8,580	3,940	2,280	1,530	625	115	20	15		15	20		10	10	1,077	330	45 8
Durable goods	705	605	255	175	105	6[illegible]						5				1 136	45	47 9
Metal industries	185	165	[illegible]0	[illegible]0	40	45											20	
Machinery incl. electrical	35	[illegible]0	10	5	10	[illegible]											5	
Other durable goods	485	[illegible]10	185	150	55	15						5					20	
Nondurable goods	9 020	7 945	3 [illegible]0	2 095	[illegible],420	560	1[illegible]5	20	15		15	15		10	10	1 072	280	45 6
Food and kindred products	3,300	2,885	[illegible],085	495	340	110	35	5			5	5			5	765	75	34 0
Knitting mills	225	195	95	60	25	10								5			15	
Textile mill prod. exc. knit	300	260	40	70	[illegible]15	2[illegible]	10										25	
Apparel & other fab'd text. pr.	3 145	2,765	1 050	975	530	190	35	5	10							1,[illegible]50	145	49 0
Leather and leather products	15	15	10		5													
Other nondurable goods	2,035	1 825	[illegible]50	49[illegible]	405	29[illegible]	35	10	5		10	10		5	5	1 366	20	54 7
Not specified mfg industries	55	50	1[illegible]	10	5												5	
Nonmanufacturing (incl. not rptd.)	1,825	1,535	745	450	170	100	50	10								1,025	1[illegible]0	57 1
Private household workers	45,050	38,165	35 005	2,425	445	100	50	55	10	15	10	15	15	15	5	545	1,400	55 8
Private household wkrs—living in	995	875	690	150	25		5						5			634	25	76 [illegible]
Private household wkrs—living out	44,055	37,290	34,315	2,275	420	100	45	50	10	15	10	15	10	15	5	543	1 375	55 3
Service wkrs. exc. priv. hshld.	34,900	26 750	[illegible]9,605	5,450	2 060	865	335	205	85	45	25	55	15	10	5	733	1,5[illegible]0	54 3
Attendants hospital & other instn.	1,575	1,225	530	470	165	30	15		5	5		5				1,088	105	65 4
Barbers, beauticians & manicurists	3,020	2,530	1,360	[illegible]35	270	240	65	65	40	20	5	30	5		5	930	190	59 3
Charwomen, janitors and porters	1,695	1,445	935	315	110	65		10		5	5					773	70	69 3
Cooks except private household	6,37[illegible]	5,360	4,125	[illegible]35	235	15	30	15			5					650	260	47 9
Housekprs & stewards, exc. pr. hshld	[illegible],040	900	345	225	175	65	50	30	5					5		1,233	45	63 6
Practical nurses and midwives	2,845	2,460	1 [illegible]60	545	295	150	65	15	20	5		5				904	120	49 4
Waitresses, bartenders, counter wkrs	8 [illegible]00	6,7[illegible]0	[illegible],750	1,260	430	175	50	20	5		5	5	5	5		706	380	45 2
Other service wkrs. exc. priv. hshld.	9,090	8,130	6,200	1,265	380	125	60	50	10	10	5	20	5			656	340	60 8
Farm laborers and foremen	1[illegible],4[illegible]5	6,020	5,735	17[illegible]	50	30		10	5			5	5	5		525	690	22 1
Farm laborers unpaid family wkrs	7 105	1,500	[illegible],395	50	25	15		[illegible]	[illegible]					5		538	315	27 7
Farm labor. exc. unpaid & foremen	6 310	[illegible],[illegible]20	4,340	125	2[illegible]	15		5				5	5			521	375	17 0
Laborers, except farm and mine	[illegible] 855	1,540	760	315	265	125	50	10		5		10				1,016	95	52 8
Occupation not reported	5,700	3,050	2 070	345	220	175	65	65	15	20	15	25	5	5	5	732	575	34 1

Table 78.—INCOME IN 1949 OF THE EXPERIENCED CIVILIAN LABOR FORCE, BY OCCUPATION AND SEX, FOR THE STATE AND FOR STANDARD METROPOLITAN AREAS OF 250,000 OR MORE 1950—Con

[Based on 20 percent sample. For totals by occupation from complete count, see table 73. "N.e.c." means not elsewhere classified. Percent not shown where less than 0.1, percent and median not shown where base is less than 500]

Area, occupation, and sex	Total 14 years old and over (includes persons without income)	Persons with income: Total	$1 to $999 or loss	$1,000 to $1,499	$1,500 to $1,999	$2,000 to $2,499	$2,500 to $2,999	$3,000 to $3,499	$3,500 to $3,999	$4,000 to $4,499	$4,500 to $4,999	$5,000 to $5,999	$6,000 to $6,999	$7,000 to $9,999	$10,000 and over	Median income (dol.)	Income not reported	Worked in 1949—Percent with 50 to 52 weeks
NEW ORLEANS																		
Male, exp civ labor force	185,445	169,025	21,470	18,425	24,1[illegible]	26,[illegible]85	18,700	7,585	11,655	7,725	4,850	[illegible]650	3,[illegible]	3,720	4,665	[illegible]	9,110	72.5
Profess'l, techn'l, kindred wkrs	15,285	13,645	930	765	785	1,065	1,085	1,475	1,145	1,050	895	1,380	670	955	1,245	3,7[illegible]7	1,1[illegible]5	80.8
Accountants and auditors	2,085	1,910	45	80	60	170	140	215	290	145	165	265	145	75	75	3,835	130	90.[illegible]
Architects	155	145	10	5	5	15	5	5		5	10	25		20	40		10	
Artists and art teachers	265	240	55	15	20	15	40	35	10	15	15	10	5	15	10		20	
Authors, editors and reporters	330	320	15	20	5	15	20	20	35	35	20	45	35	30	25		10	
Chemists	275	275	15	15	25	10	25	35	55	25	15	15		20				
Clergymen	715	580	145	120	45	40	60	25	35	30	10	25	25	15		1,778	50	87.0
College pres., prof's, instr's (n.e.c.)	450	3[illegible]		30	30	25	20	40	55	30	35	40	30	15	25		15	
Dentists	390	340	10	5	10	20	15	10	25	25	15	40	25	60	80		50	
Designers and draftsmen	455	405	10	15	30	65	40	40	75	45	55	25	10	15			35	
Engineers, aeronautical	5	5											5					
Engineers, civil	685	640	25	15		35	35	40	70	9[illegible]	60	115	25	90	35	4,542	40	81.6
Engineers, electrical	415	380	25	20	5	25	25	20	50	35	60	65	25	2[illegible]			10	
Engineers, mechanical	555	525	25	15		30	55	50	60	60	45	90	50	15	30	4,229	30	85.4
Other technical engineers	795	740	20	15	35	30	15	110	70	65	65	120	50	85	60	4,577	45	82.6
Lawyers and judges	1,005	830	25	25	15	35	45	35	35	55	5	150	50	145	230	6,200	165	89.6
Musicians and music teachers	530	485	95	70	45	40	35	35	30	5[illegible]	30	10	5	25	10		40	
Natural scientists (n.e.c.)	240	180	10	10	10	5	5		25	1[illegible]	20	40	10	15	15		55	
Pharmacists	415	410	10	15	20	45	70	45	25	40	3[illegible]	50	2[illegible]	35	35		[illegible]	
Physicians and surgeons	1,5[illegible]0	1,410	165	85	125	120	50	105	35	40	35	35	60	115	430	4,125	115	83.9
Social scientists	85	80	10	5		5	5	5	10	10	5	20		5				
Social welfare & recreation workers	130	115	20	15	15		10	5	20	10	5	15					15	
Surveyors	140	135	5		15	20	20	20	15	1[illegible]	5			15	10			
Teachers (n.e.c.)	865	725	30	40	70	100	30	165	100	70	45	50	15	10		3,280	30	61.5
Technicians, medical and dental	300	280	[illegible]	30	35	45	70	4[illegible]	15	10		5		10			15	
Other profess'l, tech, kindred wkrs	2,450	2,095	15[illegible]	100	155	170	300	270	205	125	145	145	80	110	135	3,31[illegible]	250	77.5
Farmers and farm managers	530	420	190	40	70	30	20	15	20			[illegible]	5	10	15		80	
Mgrs, offs, & propr's, exc farm	23,820	21,575	1,235	995	1,220	1,775	1,6[illegible]5	2,29[illegible]	1,855	1,560	1,190	2,145	1,300	1,605	2,695	3,937	1,8[illegible]0	88.9
Offs & inspectors, State & local	560	47[illegible]	5	15	45	65	40	70	[illegible]	2[illegible]	35	10	40	25	15		25	
Other specified managers & officials	3,820	3,635	105	85	130	160	245	445	390	380	345	515	330	345	160	4,339	160	81.7
Mgrs., offs, props (n.e.c.)—salaried	8,[illegible]45	8,230	240	140	320	605	600	825	875	570	555	975	570	790	1,105	4,381	585	91.9
Manufacturing	1,450	1,345	10	25	20	65	80	90	130	145	90	185	100	190	2[illegible]5	5,1[illegible]6	90	93.8
Wholesale and retail trade	3,630	3,280	135	60	180	285	340	330	350	220	220	335	210	225	390	3,943	250	90.3
Finance, insurance, & real estate	1,215	1,115	[illegible]	20	20	85	65	110	150	70	105	125	75	115	190	4,750	95	9[illegible].3
Other industries (incl not rptd)	2,650	2,490	90	35	100	170	135	295	265	235	140	350	185	220	290	4,372	150	90.7
Mgr., off, prop (n.e.c.)—self-employed	[illegible]0,555	9,235	885	755	725	945	760	955	545	485	255	605	360	545	1,4[illegible]5	3,287	1,100	89.0
Construction	1,025	910	105	55	75	[illegible]	50	105	45	70	25	60	30	50	175	3,500	95	78.4
Manufacturing	[illegible]	640	45	45	25	45	35	65	20	10	30	65	50	55	170	5,000	105	87.7
Wholesale trade	1,070	930	115	55	55	60	50	40	35	50	30	55	75	90	220	4,583	130	90.0
Eating and drinking places	1,280	1,110	130	100	110	105	135	100	70	85	30	80	40	45	80	2,907	110	90.4
Retail trade, exc eat'g & drink'g	4,205	3,720	360	315	320	450	320	450	265	205	70	235	145	175	410	3,106	[illegible]25	91.4
Other industries (incl not rptd)	2,2[illegible]5	1,925	130	185	140	220	170	195	110	65	70	110	40	130	360	3,301	235	88.3
Clerical and kindred workers	16,825	15,[illegible]5	1,245	1,130	1,615	2,595	2,430	2,430	1,730	850	485	[illegible]70	185	170	80	2,741	825	82.9
Bookkeepers	1,385	1,265	90	65	130	215	270	190	95	65	50	55	2[illegible]		5	2,7[illegible]5	80	84.[illegible]
Mail carriers	675	655	35	10	30	90	130	165	160	15	10	5		5		3,098	10	84.0
Other clerical and kindred workers	14,765	13,[illegible]95	1,120	1,055	1,455	2,290	2,030	2,075	1,475	770	415	510	160	165	75	2,716	35	82.7
Sales workers	13,535	12,195	1,630	875	945	1,445	1,280	1,575	1,[illegible]5	845	505	7[illegible]5	360	445	400	2,9[illegible]0	815	79.4
Insurance agents and brokers	1,865	1,750	85	90	150	205	180	230	255	155	75	100	90	85	80	[illegible]	100	85.0
Real estate agents and brokers	480	420	40	15	25	55	15	60	10	35	20	40	1[illegible]	55	55		50	
Other specified sales workers	1,155	92[illegible]	410	165	100	40	40	40	55	30	20	10	5		10	1,159	70	61.4
Salesmen and sales clerks (n.e.c.)	10,035	[illegible],090	1,095	605	670	1,145	1,045	1,245	835	62[illegible]	390	605	250	125	235	2,993	595	79.8
Manufacturing	1,395	1,280	20	45	40	110	155	210	120	110	80	80	65	70	75	3,405	70	82.1
Wholesale trade	2,650	2,430	135	110	120	260	320	395	290	225	135	200	80	95	65	3,342	180	87.2
Retail trade	5,505	4,930	81[illegible]	415	485	725	520	585	370	250	165	285	75	140	105	2,529	310	75.9
Other industries (incl not rptd)	485	450	30	35	25	10	50	55	55	40	10	40	30	20	10		35	
Craftsmen, foremen, kindred wkrs	35,055	3[illegible],220	3,000	2,640	3,680	4,920	4,635	4,370	3,085	1,980	1,140	1,045	[illegible]70	[illegible]70	85	2,648	1,285	67.2
Bakers	710	660	40	45	75	145	205	80	35	15	15			5		2,[illegible]61	35	78.4
Blacksmiths, forgemen, hammermen	130	130	15	20	20	[illegible]0	2[illegible]	20	5									
Boilermakers	400	375	20	40	5	5	65	55	20	50	10	10	5	10			10	
Cabinet makers and patternmakers	455	435	20	40	55	95	100	65	35	10	5	15					15	
Carpenters	4,940	4,685	710	590	800	795	680	130	290	150	55	45	5	15	20	2,153	[illegible]55	41.6
Compositors and typesetters	565	550	30	35	25	75	40	60	55	75	50	65	25	1[illegible]		3,591	10	84.4
Cranemen, hoist'n, const mach oper	875	825	35	5	80	170	16[illegible]	110	120	60	20	55	5	5		2,883	45	69.6
Electricians	1,600	1,520	90	55	95	130	240	130	240	175	115	110	35	[illegible]		3,326	65	67.2
Foremen (n.e.c.)	2,445	2,345	55	55	135	205	290	410	305	240	220	165	80	85	10	[illegible],418	90	89.6
Manufacturing, durable goods	370	350	15	5	10	30	50	65	50	45	40	25	10	25			20	
Mfg., nondurable (incl not spec.)	580	565	10	5	15	85	120	12[illegible]	80	35	30	30	15	10	5	[illegible],190	10	91.2
Nonmanufacturing (incl not rptd)	1,495	1,430	30	45	110	180	120	220	195	160	150	110	55	50	5	3,526	60	88.5
Linemen & servicemen, t'graph, etc.	[illegible]	955	15	50	75	125	140	155	160	130	60	20	5			3,169	50	86.5
Locomotive engineers	270	260		5		5	5	20	45	65	55	35	25				5	
Locomotive firemen	195	190	15	5		15	20	25	30	50	25	15						
Machinists and job setters	1,360	1,310	55	65	110	240	230	230	205	105	15	35	5	10	5	2,902	25	67.9
Masons, tile setters, stone cutters	585	560	90	65	90	85	65	45	35	20	30	15	15	5		2,205	10	40.9
Mechanics and repairmen, airplane	105	95			5	5	10	25	5	25	15	5					10	
Mechanics and repairmen, auto	2,67[illegible]	[illegible],545	290	290	355	410	410	385	240	65	50	30	10	5	5	2,412	90	7[illegible].6
Mechanics & repair, radio & telev'n	395	375	85	35	35	45	55	45	25	5	30	10		5			20	
Other mech & repair & loom fixers	3,900	3,705	185	260	460	640	620	650	365	210	110	130	25	40	10	2,[illegible]48	135	82.3
Millwrights	100	100		5		25	15	25	15	5		5		5				
Molders, metal	30	30		5	10	10		5										
Painters (const), paperhgrs., glaziers	2,810	2,595	450	330	430	515	340	305	135	35	20	15	[illegible]	5	10	2,085	165	44.8
Plasterers and cement finishers	635	[illegible]95	125	95	95	115	40	25	35	40	15	10				1,908	35	40.7
Plumbers and pipe fitters	1,370	1,280	55	85	145	195	190	210	150	105	60	50	10	5	15	2,934	65	65.1
Print craft, exc compos & typeser	275	25[illegible]	15	5	10	35	15	35	30	2[illegible]	35	25	10	15			15	
Shoemakers & repairers exc factory	285	25[illegible]	70	55	50	35	20	20	[illegible]		[illegible]							
Stationary engineers	965	915	25	10	60	145	145	140	65	95	55	7[illegible]	50	15	5	3,259	35	87.1
Structural metal workers	395	380	35	15	60	55	55	55	50	25	15		15				15	
Tailors and furriers	205	180	50	30	5	35	15	5	10			20		5	5		20	
Tinsmiths, copsm, sheet metal wkrs	640	595	60	50	60	70	95	90	100	50	10	5		5		2,803	35	65.9
Toolmakers & die makers & setters	15	1[illegible]					10	5										
Other craftsmen and kindred wkrs	2,7[illegible]5	2,50[illegible]	345	300	305	325	340	305	235	170	50	80	40	10		2,465	120	73.[illegible]

Table 78.—INCOME IN 1949 OF THE EXPERIENCED CIVILIAN LABOR FORCE, BY OCCUPATION AND SEX, FOR THE STATE AND FOR STANDARD METROPOLITAN AREAS OF 250,000 OR MORE: 1950—Con.

[Based on 20-percent sample. For totals by occupation from complete count, see table 73. "N.e.c." means not elsewhere classified. Percent not shown where less than 0.1 percent and median not shown where base is less than 500]

Area, occupation, and sex	Total, 14 years old and over (includes persons without income)	Persons with income: Total	$1 to $999 or loss	$1,000 to $1,499	$1,500 to $1,999	$2,000 to $2,499	$2,500 to $2,999	$3,000 to $3,499	$3,500 to $3,999	$4,000 to $4,499	$4,500 to $4,999	$5,000 to $5,999	$6,000 to $6,999	$7,000 to $9,999	$10,000 and over	Median income (dol.)	Income not reported	Worked in 1949—Percent with 50 to 52 weeks
NEW ORLEANS																		
Male—Con.																		
Operatives and kindred workers	[illegible]	23,390	[illegible]	[illegible]	[illegible]	[illegible]	[illegible]	3,075	[illegible]	[illegible]	420	420	[illegible]	100	40	[illegible]	1,035	68.6
Apprentices	550	[illegible]	5	65	65	170	75	70	20	5	5						20	
Attendants, auto service & parking	430	895	105	170	170	145	30	15	5	10	5	5		5		1,634	45	63.1
Brakemen and switchmen, railroad	70	[illegible]		25	5	150	65	120	130	100	50	55	10			3,293	15	76.4
Bus drivers	[illegible]	[illegible]	[illegible]	25	30	[illegible]	120	[illegible]	145	95	50	5	5			3 269	10	89.9
Filers, grinders, & polishers, metal	[illegible]	[illegible]	5	25		20	25	10	5								5	
Furnacemen, smeltermen & heaters	[illegible]	55	10	5	15		5	5		5								
Laundry and dry cleaning operatives	[illegible]	[illegible]	[illegible]	125	[illegible]	[illegible]	40	45	15		5		5	5		1,699	46	68.7
Meat cutters, exc. slaughter & pack.	[illegible]	[illegible]	55	60	[illegible]	[illegible]	145	80	30	20	15	15	10		5	[illegible]	25	[illegible]
Misc. operatives & laborers (n.e.c.)	700	670	[illegible]	70	40	55	35	[illegible]	85	110	30	70	45	35		[illegible]	30	[illegible]
Motormen, street, subway & elev. rwy.	200	200				20	5	70	45	5		10						
Painters, exc. const. & maintenance	[illegible]	[illegible]	20	45	40	90	45	20	15	5	5	15					10	
Power station operators	60	60					5	10	15	10		15						
Sailors and deck hands	[illegible]	[illegible]	[illegible]	[illegible]	[illegible]	295	270	130	80	75	45	40	25	5		2 284	125	[illegible]
Sawyers	135	135	10	20	35	[illegible]	[illegible]			5	5							
Spinners and weavers, textile	30	30		5	15	[illegible]												
Stationary firemen	430	415	10	10	[illegible]	[illegible]	[illegible]	100	10	[illegible]	5	10					10	
Taxicab drivers and chauffeurs	[illegible]	2,080	325	415	485	430	230	110	[illegible]	20	10	5				1 809	75	[illegible]
Truck drivers and deliverymen	[illegible]	7,225	[illegible]	[illegible]	[illegible]	1,525	[illegible]	480	255	120	80	55	25	10	25	1,876	240	72.0
Welders and flame-cutters	[illegible]	1 080	60	45	[illegible]	195	150	240	110	65	40	50	20	10		[illegible]	45	65.6
Other spec. operat. & kindred wkrs	[illegible]	[illegible]	[illegible]	[illegible]	115	240	125	[illegible]	[illegible]	10	35	20				[illegible]	60	64.3
Operatives & kindred wkrs (n.e.c.)	[illegible]	[illegible]	1 390	1 105	[illegible]	[illegible]	[illegible]	935	[illegible]	200	[illegible]	60	25	25	10	2,089	290	69.0
Manufacturing	[illegible]	[illegible]	840	635	[illegible]	[illegible]	955	[illegible]	[illegible]	[illegible]	40	40	20	15	10	2,126	185	70.2
Durable goods	[illegible]	2,130	275	230	565	[illegible]	300	160	60	30	20	20	10	5		1,990	55	64.0
Saw & pl'g mills, misc. wood pr.	[illegible]	[illegible]	70	50	100	50	[illegible]	15				5	5				20	
Furniture and fixtures	[illegible]	[illegible]	30	40	55	[illegible]	[illegible]	10	5				5				5	
Stone, clay, & glass products	[illegible]	[illegible]	45	[illegible]	85	100	65	50		10	5						10	
Primary metal industries	140	135	5	15	55	55	[illegible]	[illegible]										
Fab'd metal (incl. not spec.)	500	490	[illegible]	30	[illegible]	95	[illegible]	35	15	5	15	10					5	
Machinery, except electrical	95	90	10	5	[illegible]	25		5	10	5				5			5	
Electrical mach'y, equip., sup.	[illegible]	15						5	5	5								
Motor vehicles & mt. veh. eqp.	[illegible]	25		5	15		5											
Transp. equip., exc. mo. or veh.	300	[illegible]	35	35	[illegible]	[illegible]	[illegible]	10	10	5							10	
Other durable goods	195	190	20	20	[illegible]	35	[illegible]	15	15									
Nondurable goods	[illegible]	[illegible]	555	400	[illegible]	[illegible]	[illegible]	450	155	85	20	15	10	10	10	[illegible]	[illegible]	73.9
Food and kindred products	1,990	1,840	[illegible]	165	290	360	335	245	80	45	5	5	5	10	10	[illegible]	[illegible]	[illegible]
Yarn, thread, & fabric mills	245	245	20	15	[illegible]	[illegible]	25	5		5								
Knitting & other textile mill pr.	80	[illegible]	10	5	10	2	[illegible]					5					10	
Apparel & other fab'd text. pr.	440	415	5	[illegible]	170	85	40	[illegible]		5							[illegible]	
Paper and allied products	570	[illegible]	80	[illegible]	115	[illegible]	170	130	25		10					[illegible]	[illegible]	76.8
Chemicals and allied products	220	210	[illegible]	25	40	[illegible]	[illegible]	[illegible]	10	5	5							
Leather and leather products	40	40	15	10	[illegible]	5	5											
Other nondurable goods	410	[illegible]	[illegible]	55	20	90	[illegible]	35	40	25		5	[illegible]				15	
Not specified mfg. industries	60	[illegible]	10	5	5	[illegible]	5					5					5	
Nonmanufacturing (incl. not rptd.)	[illegible]	[illegible]	[illegible]	470	655	[illegible]	[illegible]	325	[illegible]	85	15	10	[illegible]	10		[illegible]	105	66.8
Trans., commun., & other pub. util.	1 195	1,170	80	105	75	270	175	180	80	50		[illegible]		10		2,389	30	[illegible]
Wholesale and retail trade	1 310	1,220	[illegible]	230	260	230	95	55	30	20	[illegible]					[illegible]	40	64.9
Other ind. (incl. not rptd.)	1,095	1 045	[illegible]	135	220	265	90	90	35	10	10	5	5			[illegible]	35	59.0
Private household workers	500	[illegible]	230	70	70	30	15	5	15								30	
Service wkrs., exc. priv. hshld.	[illegible]	[illegible]	2,970	3,070	3,350	[illegible]	1 815	[illegible]	380	[illegible]	105	115	[illegible]	50	40	1,794	[illegible]	[illegible]
Barbers, beauticians, & manicurists	[illegible]	[illegible]	145	180	[illegible]	215	75	85	25	25	20	25			10	2,006	[illegible]	79.2
Charwomen, janitors, and porters	[illegible]	4,695	950	1,415	1,290	625	245	115	25	10	5			5	10	1 494	[illegible]	74.0
Cooks, except private household	1,050	[illegible]	[illegible]	150	210	210	[illegible]	80	30	15	10					[illegible]	40	74.3
Elevator operators	[illegible]	415	75	125	135	50	15	15									5	
Firemen, fire protection	865	835	15	5	45	380	235	70	40	20	10	15				[illegible]	30	[illegible]
Guards and watchmen	1,845	1 765	250	[illegible]	475	410	160	70	65	20	5			[illegible]		[illegible]	35	65.9
Policemen, sheriffs, and marshals	1,410	1 370	45	55	150	[illegible]	[illegible]	[illegible]	55	45	10	15	20	15	5	2 607	[illegible]	[illegible]
Waiters, bartenders, & counter wkrs.	[illegible]	2,435	585	400	[illegible]	375	275	[illegible]	55	[illegible]	10	[illegible]			10	1,728	[illegible]	[illegible]
Other service wkrs., exc. priv. hshld.	[illegible]	[illegible]	780	445	400	[illegible]	230	130	85	60	35	40	15	10	5	[illegible]	100	62.0
Farm laborers and foremen	590	455	230	80	75	40	[illegible]	10					5				65	
Farm laborers, unpaid family wkrs.	65	25	10	5				5										
Farm labor., exc. unpaid, & foremen	525	430	[illegible]	[illegible]	70	40	15	5					5				65	
Laborers, except farm and mine	[illegible]	24 390	[illegible]	[illegible]	[illegible]	4,730	1,880	980	380	150	55	[illegible]	35	[illegible]	20	[illegible]	870	56.8
Fishermen and oystermen	1,105	950	410	[illegible]	[illegible]	[illegible]	[illegible]	[illegible]		10						1,155	60	44.9
Longshoremen and stevedores	5,025	4,745	795	880	[illegible]	935	505	375	175	60	45	25	15	[illegible]	5	1,881	180	[illegible]
Lumbermen, raftsmen, woodchoppers	35	[illegible]	10	[illegible]	10													
Other specified laborers	1,230	1 145	[illegible]	255	[illegible]	[illegible]	[illegible]	[illegible]					5		5	1,456	50	[illegible]
Laborers (n.e.c.)	[illegible]	17 520	[illegible]	[illegible]	4,870	[illegible]	[illegible]	[illegible]	205	80	10	45	15	5	10	[illegible]	580	61.0
Manufacturing	5 575	[illegible]	825	855	[illegible]	[illegible]	440	210	[illegible]	15	5	[illegible]	5			1,811	[illegible]	55.2
Durable goods	1,930	[illegible]	350	[illegible]	[illegible]	400	[illegible]	55	[illegible]			[illegible]	5			[illegible]	60	59.0
Furn., saw & pl'g mills, w'd pr.	[illegible]	[illegible]	120	150	185	80	[illegible]	10								[illegible]	20	[illegible]
Stone, clay, & glass products	340	335	50	40	105	110	30											
Primary metal industries	[illegible]	95	[illegible]	20	20	35											5	
Fab'd metal (incl. not spec.)	[illegible]	285	30	[illegible]	60	[illegible]	40	[illegible]	10				[illegible]				10	
Machinery, exc. electrical	45	40	15	[illegible]	5	10						5					[illegible]	
Transportation equipment	[illegible]	[illegible]	110	[illegible]	15	75	40	25	5								[illegible]	
Other durable goods	35	25	5	5	[illegible]		5	5									[illegible]	
Nondurable goods	[illegible]	[illegible]	475	495	1,045	895	[illegible]	[illegible]	60	15		10				1 864	90	[illegible]
Food and kindred products	[illegible]	1,570	[illegible]	240	420	330	170	100	[illegible]		5	10				[illegible]	40	63.2
Textile mill prod. & apparel	[illegible]	295	40	40	130	[illegible]	35	5									5	
Chemicals and allied products	[illegible]	305	40	[illegible]	115	85	15	5										
Other nondurable goods	[illegible]	1 290	140	170	380	[illegible]	[illegible]	45	20	15						1 941	[illegible]	73.5
Not specified mfg. industries	25	25		10	15													
Nonmanufacturing (incl. not rptd.)	[illegible]	12,225	2,650	[illegible]	3,315	2 300	[illegible]	360	130	[illegible]	5	30	10	5	10	1,643	[illegible]	[illegible]
Construction	4 150	3 790	1 050	890	[illegible]	[illegible]	145	25	25	10		5	10	5	5	[illegible]	160	[illegible]
Railroads & railway express serv.	[illegible]	[illegible]	170	335	[illegible]	560	[illegible]	145	30	20						2,053	40	71.0
Transportation, except railroad	[illegible]	1 550	325	[illegible]	415	260	[illegible]	55	30	[illegible]		5				1,620	75	55.7
Telecommun., util., & sanit. serv.	[illegible]	[illegible]	120	110	385	180	35	15	10	[illegible]						1,766	5	72.5
Wholesale and retail trade	2 490	[illegible]	565	450	[illegible]	335	150	[illegible]	25	10	5	[illegible]			5	[illegible]	65	62.9
Other ind. (incl. not rptd.)	[illegible]	[illegible]	420	340	430	[illegible]	[illegible]	40	10	[illegible]		5				1,561	[illegible]	67.4
Occupation not reported	[illegible]	[illegible]	730	[illegible]	[illegible]	[illegible]	435	445	[illegible]	175	[illegible]	145	40	[illegible]	45	2,267	465	49.2

Table 78.—INCOME IN 1949 OF THE EXPERIENCED CIVILIAN LABOR FORCE, BY OCCUPATION AND SEX, FOR THE STATE AND FOR STANDARD METROPOLITAN AREAS OF 250,000 OR MORE 1950—Con.

[Based on 20 percent sample. For totals by occupation from complete count, see table 73. "N.e.c." means not elsewhere classified. Percent not shown where less than 0 percent and median not shown where base is less than 500]

Area, occupation, and sex	Total 14 years old and over (includes persons without income)	Persons with income: Total	$1 to $999 or loss	$1,000 to $1,499	$1,500 to $1,999	$2,000 to $2,499	$2,500 to $2,999	$3,000 to $3,499	$3,500 to $3,999	$4,000 to $4,499	$4,500 to $4,999	$5,000 to $5,999	$6,000 to $6,999	$7,000 to $9,999	$10,000 and over	Median income (dol.)	Income not reported	Worked in 1949—Percent with 50 to 52 weeks
NEW ORLEANS																		
Female, exp. civ labor force	83,075	70,510	27,330	13,180	10,885	8,570	4,650	2 920	1,140	620	335	330	230	175	145	1,301	3,905	65.4
Profess'l, techn'l, kindred wkrs	9,755	7,875	1,935	685	695	1,350	985	1,065	485	285	130	125	60	45	30	2,231	550	54.0
Accountants and auditors	275	255	30	10	15	70	45	15	25	5	10	10					10	
Actresses dancers, entert (n.e.c.)	180	135	70	25	10	10		10		5							30	
Artists and art teachers	170	160	10	25	25	35	25	5	10	5	15			5			10	
Authors, editors, and reporters	95	85	15	10	10	20	10		10	10								
Chemists & natural scientists (n.e.c.)	145	130	5	5	15	25	5	40	15	15					5		15	
College pres., prof'rs, instr's (n.e.c.)	170	115	25	10	5	10	10	20	5		5	10	15					
Designers and draftsmen	130	100	10	15	15	10	20	10	10	5	5						20	
Dietitians and nutritionists	110	95	25	10	10	20	15	5	5	5							5	
Lawyers and judges	10	10									10							
Librarians	195	165	30	10	15	45	30	15	10	5							15	
Musicians and music teachers	315	255	125	30	25	15	10	25		15		5	5				20	
Nurses professional	2,250	1,920	300	195	230	455	345	190	85	65	30	20		5		2,258	125	62.7
Nurses, student professional	815	525	510	5								5		5		515	5	79.2
Physicians and surgeons	95	90	25	5		10	5	5	5			5	5	10	15			
Social scientists	25	25	5		5	5	5		5									
Social, welfare, & recreation workers	480	435	85	45	50	95	55	30	35	25	5	5	5				25	
Teachers (n.e.c.)	3,220	2,490	475	180	160	375	295	575	215	105	30	40	20	15	5	2,593	200	27.6
Technicians medical and dental	360	325	50	45	40	65	55	50	5	5	5	5					10	
Therapists and healers (n.e.c.)	35	30	5			5	5		10	5								
Other profess'l tech kindred wkrs	680	530	135	60	45	80	50	70	35	10	15	20	5	5		2,156	60	73.2
Farmers and farm managers	35	30	20		5		5										5	
Mgrs., offs & propr's, exc. farm	3,815	3,070	795	445	400	320	230	265	135	100	85	70	75	60	90	1,869	285	83.2
Specified managers and officials	585	495	55	75	65	65	35	50	45	20	20	20	25	15	5		65	
Mgrs, offs., props (n.e.c.)—salaried	1,205	1,015	205	140	150	145	125	95	45	35	10	25	10	10	20	2,043	85	77.9
Wholesale and retail trade	500	430	100	50	60	55	60	30	10	20	5	15	10	10	5		45	
Other industries (incl not rptd)	705	585	105	90	90	90	65	65	35	15	5	10			15	2,042	40	75.8
Mgr., off., prop (n.e.c.)—self-employed	2,025	1,560	535	230	185	110	70	120	45	45	55	25	40	35	65	1,541	135	83.9
Eating and drinking places	455	365	140	50	35	15	5	50	25		10	10	10	5	10		25	
Wh & ret trade, exc eat. & drink	1,145	895	290	115	110	80	55	55	15	30	35	15	25	25	45	1,693	65	86.7
Other industries (incl not rptd.)	425	300	105	65	40	15	10	15	5	15	10		5	5	10		45	
Clerical and kindred workers	23,750	21,415	2,990	3,125	5,345	5,095	2,770	1,245	440	180	80	45	65	30	5	1,930	1,035	78.1
Bookkeepers	2,065	1,835	180	245	440	560	235	100	50	10	...	5	10			2,047	90	83.4
Cashiers	1,670	1,460	370	440	390	155	55	20	5	15			5	5		1,409	65	71.8
Stenographers typists, secretaries	8,955	8,165	855	810	2,045	2,225	1,250	605	185	70	55	20	20	25		2,084	380	79.9
Telephone operators	1 900	1 775	225	175	460	565	210	25	50	5	5	5				2,024	90	77.2
Other clerical and kindred workers	9 160	8,180	1,360	1,455	2 010	1 590	1,020	445	150	80	20	15	30		5	1 817	410	76.4
Sales workers	7,265	5,755	2 125	1,725	920	475	240	135	35	25	25	25	20		5	1,218	300	62.9
Insur & real est agents & brokers	355	295	70	40	85	30	35	5	5	10		10	5				20	
Other specified sales workers	140	110	45	20	25	10	5	5									10	
Salesmen & sales clerks (n.e.c.), retail	6,350	5,040	1,845	1,600	800	425	170	120	30	5	20	10	15			1,211	250	63.3
Salesmen & sal cl (n.e.c.) exc retail	420	310	165	65	10	10	30	5		10	5	5			5		20	
Craftsmen, foremen, kindred wkrs	965	845	200	135	245	110	65	55	10			15	5	5		1,679	75	69.7
Foremen (n.e.c.)	230	215	25	30	75	50	5	15	5			5	5				15	
Other craftsmen and kindred workers	735	630	175	105	170	60	60	40	5			10		5	...	1,603	60	67.9
Operatives and kindred workers	10,995	9,575	4,030	2 995	1 750	600	115	25	10	5		20		15	10	1,126	490	55.5
Dressmakers & seamstr, exc. factory	1,180	1,000	445	320	160	60				5		5		5		1,086	65	56.2
Laundry and dry cleaning operatives	1,925	1,650	975	500	105	40	10	10	5			5				846	90	62.6
Spinners and weavers, textile	215	205	25	35	110	35											5	
Other spec operat & kindred wkrs	395	315	100	70	90	40	5	5			...			5			20	
Operatives & kindred wkrs (n.e.c.)	7,280	6,405	2,485	2,070	1,265	425	100	10	5			10		5	10	1,173	310	52.5
Manufacturing	6 245	5,550	2,160	1 750	1 155	375	70	10	5			10		5	10	1,176	230	50.8
Durable goods	470	415	165	95	90	60						5					35	
Metal industries	185	165	60	20	40	45											20	
Machinery incl electrical	25	20	5	5	5	5											5	
Other durable goods	260	230	100	70	45	10						5					10	
Nondurable goods	5 730	5,110	1 980	1 650	1,060	315	70	10	5			5		5	10	1 174	190	50.9
Food and kindred products	1,655	1,465	705	375	265	80	25	5				5			5	1,037	35	46.9
Knitting mills	225	195	95	60	25	10								5			15	
Textile mill prod exc knit.	285	245	30	65	115	25	10										25	
Apparel & other fab'd text pr	2,640	2,345	900	830	465	110	30	5	5							1,164	105	48.7
Leather and leather products	15	15	10		5													
Other nondurable goods	940	845	240	320	185	90	5								5	1,285	10	56.9
Not specified mfg industries	45	25	15	5	5												5	
Nonmanufacturing (incl. not rptd.)	1,035	855	325	320	130	50	30									1,160	80	63.0
Private household workers	12,240	10,410	8,820	1 290	220	40	15	10					5	10		590	405	58.7
Private household wkrs—living in	490	440	305	125	10												20	
Private household wkrs—living out	11,750	9,970	8 515	1,165	210	40	15	10					5	10		585	385	57.5
Service wkrs, exc priv hshld	12,020	9,995	5,735	2,490	1,010	420	165	90	25	20	5	30		5		871	505	60.7
Attendants hospital & other instn	715	600	185	265	100	30	10		5			5				1,217	25	72.0
Barbers, beauticians, & manicurists	1 195	1,005	465	205	120	125	35	25	10	10		10				1,091	95	66.2
Charwomen janitors, and porters	815	710	330	230	80	65		5								1,054	30	75.7
Cooks, except private household	1,195	965	605	260	90		5				5					798	45	59.2
Housek'prs & stewards, exc. pr hshld	475	425	135	105	100	25	30	20	5					5			15	
Practical nurses and midwives	800	700	360	165	85	30	35	10	5	5		5				972	45	47.1
Waitresses, bartenders, counter wkrs	2,980	2,310	1,455	545	230	65	10	5								794	100	48.0
Other service wkrs, exc priv hshld	3,845	3 280	2,200	715	205	80	40	25		5		10				745	150	64.8
Farm laborers and foremen	170	110	90	10	5									5			30	
Farm laborers unpaid family wkrs	25	10	5											5				
Farm labor, exc unpaid, & foremen	145	100	85	10	5												30	
Laborers, except farm and mine	840	730	240	170	195	90	30	5								1,368	55	63.8
Occupation not reported	1,225	700	350	110	95	70	30	25		5	10				5	1,000	170	44.1

Table 79.—DETAILED INDUSTRY OF THE EXPERIENCED CIVILIAN LABOR FORCE AND OF EMPLOYED PERSONS, BY SEX, FOR THE STATE AND FOR STANDARD METROPOLITAN AREAS AND CITIES OF 100,000 OR MORE 1950

Detailed industry	The State				Standard metropolitan areas							
					Baton Rouge				New Orleans			
	Experienced civilian labor force		Employed		Experienced civilian labor force		Employed		Experienced civilian labor force		Employed	
	Male	Female	Male	Female	Male	Female	Male	Female	Male	Female	Male	Female
Total, 14 years old and over	679,402	238,4[illegible]	646 782	229,125	4[illegible],243	17,588	48,961	17,003	186,529	87,225	174,498	80,452
Agriculture, forestry and fisheries	146,405	16 328	144 480	15 950	1,321	165	1 281	161	2,628	194	2 495	182
Agriculture	137 354	16 106	135 665	15 740	1,301	153	1,261	150	1,435	168	1 341	156
Forestry	1,195	101	1,172	99	13	12	13	11	50	9	49	9
Fisheries	7,856	121	7,643	111	7		7		1,143	17	1,105	17
Mining	23,754	1,183	23,031	1 170	267	15	258	14	1,956	173	1,893	171
Metal mining	39		31		4		3		8		5	
Coal mining	70	4	62	4					27	2	23	2
Crude petroleum and natural gas extraction	21,429	1,082	20,776	1,074	214	13	208	12	1,857	156	1,806	154
Nonmetallic mining and quarrying, except fuel	2,216	97	2,162	92	49	2	47	2	64	15	59	15
Construction	69,548	1,646	63,377	1,575	6,[illegible]36	[illegible]23	5,366	340	20,042	628	17,914	599
Manufacturing	120,297	17,921	115,358	17 091	12,942	950	12,709	936	31,913	10,129	30,277	9,573
Durable goods	48,924	2,511	46 600	2 404	1,421	103	1,355	100	12,284	1,336	11,418	1,268
Lumber and wood products except furniture	29 164	793	27,960	752	331	14	303	12	1,674	231	1,566	218
Logging	5,985	52	5,775	49	40		36		38	3	36	3
Sawmills planing mills, and mill work	21,226	495	20,348	476	281	14	259	12	1,118	114	1 063	109
Miscellaneous wood products	1 953	246	1,843	227	10		8		518	114	467	106
Furniture and fixtures	1,624	309	1,544	296	34	6	30	6	929	165	874	155
Stone clay and glass products	3,470	162	3,368	156	175	19	167	19	1,435	86	1,383	81
Glass and glass products	933	35	923	34	14	3	12	3	89	15	83	14
Cement and concrete gypsum, and plaster products	986	43	946	43	134	13	129	13	421	15	403	15
Structural clay products	545	22	523	22	25		24		67	7	62	7
Pottery and related products	73	7	71	7		3		3	64		62	
Misc nonmetallic mineral and stone products	933	55	905	50	2		2		797	49	773	45
Metal industries	4 901	488	4,679	478	671	27	651	27	2,655	387	2,536	378
Primary metal industries	1,534	59	1 528	56	378	13	372	13	538	25	513	22
Blast furnaces steel works and rolling mills	198	9	185	9	10	1	9	1	70	6	66	6
Other primary iron and steel industries	889	31	853	28	38	2	38	2	422	15	404	12
Primary nonferrous industries	507	19	490	19	330	10	325	10	46	4	43	4
Fabricated metal industries (incl not spec metal)	3,307	429	3 151	422	293	14	279	14	2,117	362	2,023	356
Fabricated steel products	2,594	380	2,478	373	193	10	183	10	1,749	328	1,683	322
Fabricated nonferrous metal products	651	48	614	48	88	4	85	4	341	33	315	33
Not specified metal industries	62	1	59	1	12		11		27	1	25	1
Machinery except electrical	3 141	229	2,996	226	100	15	98	15	1,216	116	1,120	114
Agricultural machinery and tractors	249	14	249	14	7	2	7	2	46	4	46	4
Office and store machines and devices	131	26	127	26	19	3	19	3	76	19	72	19
Miscellaneous machinery	2,761	189	2,620	186	74	10	72	10	1,094	93	1 002	91
Electrical machinery equipment, and supplies	4[illegible]7	71	393	64	22	3	22	3	237	49	223	42
Transportation equipment	5,025	184	4,519	171	33	5	30	5	3,317	147	3 126	136
Motor vehicles and motor vehicle equipment	444	30	430	27	12	2	12	2	170	18	163	16
Aircraft and parts	36	3	29	2	6		6		17	1	11	
Ship and boat building and repairing	4,472	142	3,992	133	8	2	6	2	3,287	122	2,910	114
Railroad and misc transportation equipment	73	9	68	9	7	1	6	1	43	6	42	6
Professional and photographic equipment, and watches	243	79	238	77	23	7	22	7	134	39	130	38
Professional equipment and supplies	174	44	170	44	19	3	18	3	99	29	96	29
Photographic equipment and supplies	34	13	34	13	1	2	1	2	16	4	16	4
Watches clocks, and clockwork-operated devices	35	22	34	20	3	2	3	2	19	6	18	5
Miscellaneous manufacturing industries	939	196	897	184	32	7	32	6	487	116	460	106
Nondurable goods	70,737	15,258	68,164	14,547	11,496	841	11,331	830	19,413	8,695	18,661	8 216
Food and kindred products	22,586	5,074	21,163	4,703	923	148	887	144	8 460	2,594	8,064	2,391
Meat products	2,034	323	1,966	310	75	4	74	4	945	203	909	192
Dairy products	1,130	205	1 098	197	115	14	114	13	399	106	385	100
Canning & preserving fruits, vegetables, & sea foods	1,795	2,124	1,662	1,898	10	10	10	8	521	841	467	741
Grain-mill products	2,437	163	2,099	149	53	5	45	5	247	26	228	23
Bakery products	3,174	581	3,072	560	351	71	339	71	1,304	304	1,259	290
Confectionery and related products	220	295	213	274	6	5	6	5	152	247	148	228
Beverage industries	3 842	230	3,681	274	196	20	187	20	2,396	179	2,285	165
Misc food preparations and kindred products	7,702	979	7,132	934	102	18	97	17	2,313	590	2,210	560
Not specified food industries	252	114	240	107	15	1	15	1	183	98	173	92
Tobacco manufactures	145	691	142	647	1		1		115	594	112	550
Textile mill products	1,169	931	1 113	895	14	3	13	3	951	884	907	851
Knitting mills	134	267	127	260	2	1	2	1	100	256	94	249
Dyeing and finishing textiles, except knit goods	21	9	20	9					17	9	16	9
Carpets, rugs, and other floor coverings	16	8	15	8	2	1	2	1	7	4	6	4
Yarn thread and fabric mills	811	583	770	557	8	1	7	1	736	569	704	546
Miscellaneous textile mill products	187	64	181	61	2		2		92	46	67	43
Apparel and other fabricated textile products	1,335	3,865	1,276	3,695	14	5	13	5	1,153	3,279	1,096	3,125
Apparel and accessories	720	3 169	693	3 042	3	2	3	2	619	2,649	593	2,536
Miscellaneous fabricated textile products	615	696	583	653	11	3	10	3	534	630	503	589
Paper and allied products	13 118	1,596	12 833	1,569	21		19		2,827	337	2 767	324
Pulp paper, and paperboard mills	11,115	756	10,883	747	17		15		2,456	146	2,422	143
Paperboard containers and boxes	1,004	312	972	303	1		1		309	142	285	136
Miscellaneous paper and pulp products	999	528	978	519	3		3		62	49	60	45
Printing publishing and allied industries	5 451	1,202	5 326	1,183	467	119	453	118	2,781	536	2,708	521
Chemicals and allied products	10,677	817	10,387	787	3,089	172	3,064	170	1,521	236	1,454	225
Synthetic fibers	16		15						2		2	
Drugs and medicines	199	128	189	116	13	2	13	2	66	30	63	27
Paints, varnishes, and related products	239	45	237	45	9		9		181	27	180	27
Miscellaneous chemicals and allied products	10,223	644	9,946	626	3,067	170	3,042	168	1,272	179	1,209	171
Petroleum and coal products	15,452	987	15,140	977	6,788	382	6,705	378	1,475	185	1,427	181
Petroleum refining	14,626	941	14,339	931	6,786	382	6,703	378	809	144	783	140
Miscellaneous petroleum and coal products	826	46	801	46	2		2		666	41	644	41
Rubber products	691	62	676	60	171	10	168	10	57	25	54	24
Leather and leather products	113	33	108	31	8	2	8	2	73	25	72	24
Leather tanned curried, and finished	26	6	22	6	3	1	3	1	14	4	14	4
Footwear except rubber	44	15	44	15	3	1	3	1	28	11	28	11
Leather products, except footwear	43	12	42	10	2		2		31	10	30	9
Not specified manufacturing industries	636	152	594	140	25	6	23	6	216	98	198	89

Table 79.—DETAILED INDUSTRY OF THE EXPERIENCED CIVILIAN LABOR FORCE AND OF EMPLOYED PERSONS, BY SEX, FOR THE STATE AND FOR STANDARD METROPOLITAN AREAS AND CITIES OF 100,000 OR MORE: 1950—Con.

<table>
<tr><th rowspan="4">Detailed industry</th><th colspan="4">The State</th><th colspan="8">Standard metropolitan areas</th></tr>
<tr><th colspan="2" rowspan="2">Experienced civilian labor force</th><th colspan="2" rowspan="2">Employed</th><th colspan="4">Baton Rouge</th><th colspan="4">New Orleans</th></tr>
<tr><th colspan="2">Experienced civilian labor force</th><th colspan="2">Employed</th><th colspan="2">Experienced civilian labor force</th><th colspan="2">Employed</th></tr>
<tr><th>Male</th><th>Female</th><th>Male</th><th>Female</th><th>Male</th><th>Female</th><th>Male</th><th>Female</th><th>Male</th><th>Female</th><th>Male</th><th>Female</th></tr>
<tr><td>Transport, communication, & other public utilities</td><td>69,389</td><td>9 810</td><td>66 024</td><td>9,667</td><td>2,886</td><td>570</td><td>2 788</td><td>567</td><td>34,902</td><td>4,846</td><td>32,601</td><td>4,753</td></tr>
<tr><td>Transportation</td><td>53,772</td><td>3 338</td><td>50,760</td><td>3,265</td><td>1 779</td><td>144</td><td>1,709</td><td>143</td><td>29,289</td><td>2 074</td><td>27,094</td><td>2,023</td></tr>
<tr><td>Railroads and railway express service</td><td>17 907</td><td>787</td><td>17,712</td><td>769</td><td>706</td><td>30</td><td>688</td><td>30</td><td>7,172</td><td>431</td><td>6,996</td><td>422</td></tr>
<tr><td>Street railways and bus lines</td><td>4,896</td><td>527</td><td>4 850</td><td>522</td><td>255</td><td>54</td><td>250</td><td>54</td><td>2,079</td><td>166</td><td>2,083</td><td>182</td></tr>
<tr><td>Trucking service</td><td>6,615</td><td>281</td><td>6,186</td><td>273</td><td>331</td><td>21</td><td>309</td><td>21</td><td>2 652</td><td>[illegible]</td><td>2,45[illegible]</td><td>126</td></tr>
<tr><td>Warehousing and storage</td><td>1,839</td><td>179</td><td>1,747</td><td>175</td><td>65</td><td>5</td><td>64</td><td>5</td><td>1,167</td><td>94</td><td>1,097</td><td>88</td></tr>
<tr><td>Taxicab service</td><td>3,640</td><td>198</td><td>3,491</td><td>194</td><td>137</td><td>17</td><td>127</td><td>16</td><td>2 110</td><td>91</td><td>2,018</td><td>91</td></tr>
<tr><td>Water transportation</td><td>15,719</td><td>906</td><td>14 112</td><td>880</td><td>149</td><td>4</td><td>138</td><td>4</td><td>12 879</td><td>856</td><td>11 227</td><td>832</td></tr>
<tr><td>Air transportation</td><td>1,050</td><td>222</td><td>1,033</td><td>215</td><td>25</td><td>6</td><td>25</td><td>6</td><td>716</td><td>180</td><td>706</td><td>175</td></tr>
<tr><td>Petroleum and gasoline pipe lines</td><td>1 149</td><td>100</td><td>1,103</td><td>99</td><td>64</td><td>2</td><td>61</td><td>2</td><td>94</td><td>1</td><td>87</td><td>1</td></tr>
<tr><td>Services incidental to transportation</td><td>757</td><td>118</td><td>728</td><td>138</td><td>47</td><td>5</td><td>47</td><td>5</td><td>450</td><td>106</td><td>427</td><td>106</td></tr>
<tr><td>Telecommunications</td><td>3,423</td><td>5 081</td><td>3 351</td><td>5,025</td><td>283</td><td>302</td><td>279</td><td>301</td><td>1,635</td><td>2 302</td><td>1 595</td><td>2,267</td></tr>
<tr><td>Telephone (wire and radio)</td><td>2,865</td><td>4,844</td><td>2 824</td><td>4 792</td><td>262</td><td>285</td><td>259</td><td>284</td><td>1,274</td><td>2 163</td><td>1,257</td><td>2,130</td></tr>
<tr><td>Telegraph (wire and radio)</td><td>558</td><td>237</td><td>[illegible]2</td><td>233</td><td>21</td><td>17</td><td>20</td><td>17</td><td>361</td><td>139</td><td>338</td><td>137</td></tr>
<tr><td>Utilities and sanitary services</td><td>12,194</td><td>1,391</td><td>11,913</td><td>1,377</td><td>824</td><td>124</td><td>800</td><td>123</td><td>3 985</td><td>470</td><td>3,912</td><td>463</td></tr>
<tr><td>Electric light and power, and electric-gas utilities</td><td>5,462</td><td>884</td><td>5,349</td><td>876</td><td>548</td><td>87</td><td>531</td><td>86</td><td>1,874</td><td>376</td><td>1,837</td><td>372</td></tr>
<tr><td>Gas and steam supply systems</td><td>2,661</td><td>307</td><td>2,580</td><td>302</td><td>81</td><td>6</td><td>78</td><td>6</td><td>118</td><td>13</td><td>116</td><td>11</td></tr>
<tr><td>Water supply</td><td>1,287</td><td>89</td><td>1 261</td><td>88</td><td>107</td><td>21</td><td>104</td><td>21</td><td>634</td><td>29</td><td>627</td><td>28</td></tr>
<tr><td>Sanitary services</td><td>2,352</td><td>46</td><td>2,298</td><td>46</td><td>81</td><td>4</td><td>80</td><td>4</td><td>1,281</td><td>32</td><td>1,256</td><td>31</td></tr>
<tr><td>Other and not specified utilities</td><td>432</td><td>65</td><td>425</td><td>65</td><td>7</td><td>6</td><td>7</td><td>6</td><td>78</td><td>21</td><td>76</td><td>21</td></tr>
<tr><td>Wholesale and retail trade</td><td>117,161</td><td>58,411</td><td>113,547</td><td>56 606</td><td>7,902</td><td>4 005</td><td>7 602</td><td>3,893</td><td>44,720</td><td>23 416</td><td>42 827</td><td>22 415</td></tr>
<tr><td>Wholesale trade</td><td>27,674</td><td>5,051</td><td>26,927</td><td>4 944</td><td>1,370</td><td>184</td><td>1,329</td><td>183</td><td>13,465</td><td>3,316</td><td>13,049</td><td>3,237</td></tr>
<tr><td>Motor vehicles and equipment</td><td>685</td><td>110</td><td>672</td><td>105</td><td>27</td><td>3</td><td>27</td><td>3</td><td>319</td><td>69</td><td>241</td><td>65</td></tr>
<tr><td>Drugs, chemicals, and allied products</td><td>1 248</td><td>341</td><td>1,210</td><td>336</td><td>54</td><td>10</td><td>51</td><td>10</td><td>705</td><td>222</td><td>680</td><td>218</td></tr>
<tr><td>Dry goods and apparel</td><td>724</td><td>229</td><td>710</td><td>222</td><td>30</td><td>7</td><td>30</td><td>7</td><td>442</td><td>18</td><td>431</td><td>175</td></tr>
<tr><td>Food and related products</td><td>8,572</td><td>1,411</td><td>8 324</td><td>1 364</td><td>484</td><td>47</td><td>469</td><td>47</td><td>3 813</td><td>886</td><td>3,706</td><td>852</td></tr>
<tr><td>Electrical goods, hardware, and plumbing equipment</td><td>2,292</td><td>530</td><td>2 235</td><td>572</td><td>123</td><td>20</td><td>119</td><td>20</td><td>1,474</td><td>422</td><td>1,428</td><td>415</td></tr>
<tr><td>Machinery, equipment, and supplies</td><td>2 687</td><td>426</td><td>2,633</td><td>422</td><td>133</td><td>27</td><td>132</td><td>27</td><td>1 370</td><td>257</td><td>1 335</td><td>255</td></tr>
<tr><td>Petroleum products</td><td>3 353</td><td>634</td><td>3 286</td><td>624</td><td>105</td><td>17</td><td>105</td><td>17</td><td>1,332</td><td>439</td><td>1 301</td><td>432</td></tr>
<tr><td>Farm products—raw materials</td><td>1,284</td><td>183</td><td>1,234</td><td>180</td><td>39</td><td>2</td><td>38</td><td>2</td><td>531</td><td>115</td><td>568</td><td>113</td></tr>
<tr><td>Miscellaneous wholesale trade</td><td>5 753</td><td>680</td><td>5,571</td><td>665</td><td>336</td><td>47</td><td>326</td><td>46</td><td>2,767</td><td>543</td><td>2,681</td><td>533</td></tr>
<tr><td>Not specified wholesale trade</td><td>1,076</td><td>255</td><td>1,052</td><td>252</td><td>36</td><td>4</td><td>32</td><td>4</td><td>592</td><td>182</td><td>577</td><td>179</td></tr>
<tr><td>Retail trade</td><td>89,487</td><td>53,360</td><td>86,620</td><td>51 662</td><td>6,533</td><td>3,821</td><td>6,273</td><td>3,710</td><td>31,255</td><td>20,100</td><td>29,778</td><td>19,178</td></tr>
<tr><td>Food stores, except dairy products</td><td>20,402</td><td>9,109</td><td>19 866</td><td>8,976</td><td>1 181</td><td>513</td><td>1,152</td><td>505</td><td>6,711</td><td>2,944</td><td>6,429</td><td>2,880</td></tr>
<tr><td>Dairy products stores and milk retailing</td><td>1,514</td><td>181</td><td>1,458</td><td>178</td><td>99</td><td>19</td><td>93</td><td>18</td><td>585</td><td>83</td><td>566</td><td>80</td></tr>
<tr><td>General merchandise stores</td><td>5,667</td><td>9,538</td><td>5,508</td><td>9,278</td><td>442</td><td>728</td><td>432</td><td>722</td><td>2,309</td><td>4,925</td><td>2 197</td><td>4 747</td></tr>
<tr><td>Five and ten cent stores</td><td>429</td><td>1,834</td><td>414</td><td>1,761</td><td>26</td><td>106</td><td>24</td><td>103</td><td>145</td><td>773</td><td>138</td><td>727</td></tr>
<tr><td>Apparel and accessories stores, except shoe stores</td><td>2,236</td><td>4 225</td><td>2 164</td><td>4 102</td><td>146</td><td>310</td><td>142</td><td>305</td><td>1,144</td><td>1,884</td><td>1,087</td><td>1,806</td></tr>
<tr><td>Shoe stores</td><td>909</td><td>387</td><td>884</td><td>381</td><td>74</td><td>36</td><td>72</td><td>35</td><td>448</td><td>156</td><td>435</td><td>154</td></tr>
<tr><td>Furniture and house furnishings stores</td><td>3,472</td><td>927</td><td>3,370</td><td>913</td><td>301</td><td>83</td><td>290</td><td>80</td><td>1,220</td><td>337</td><td>1,174</td><td>328</td></tr>
<tr><td>Household appliance and radio stores</td><td>2,350</td><td>564</td><td>2,296</td><td>551</td><td>200</td><td>52</td><td>191</td><td>52</td><td>857</td><td>233</td><td>827</td><td>224</td></tr>
<tr><td>Motor vehicles and accessories retailing</td><td>8 409</td><td>960</td><td>8 234</td><td>939</td><td>690</td><td>84</td><td>66</td><td>82</td><td>2,364</td><td>321</td><td>2,254</td><td>311</td></tr>
<tr><td>Gasoline service stations</td><td>7,550</td><td>335</td><td>7,361</td><td>324</td><td>639</td><td>46</td><td>615</td><td>45</td><td>1,677</td><td>56</td><td>1,577</td><td>56</td></tr>
<tr><td>Drug stores</td><td>3,203</td><td>2 512</td><td>3 067</td><td>2 445</td><td>278</td><td>186</td><td>265</td><td>182</td><td>1,333</td><td>1,025</td><td>1,246</td><td>987</td></tr>
<tr><td>Eating and drinking places</td><td>13,700</td><td>16,990</td><td>12,956</td><td>16,147</td><td>845</td><td>1,197</td><td>818</td><td>1 131</td><td>6,591</td><td>5,336</td><td>6 150</td><td>4 915</td></tr>
<tr><td>Hardware and farm implement stores</td><td>2 828</td><td>475</td><td>2,783</td><td>468</td><td>228</td><td>41</td><td>221</td><td>41</td><td>608</td><td>134</td><td>595</td><td>129</td></tr>
<tr><td>Lumber and building material retailing</td><td>5,835</td><td>592</td><td>5,655</td><td>583</td><td>502</td><td>50</td><td>490</td><td>49</td><td>1,593</td><td>209</td><td>1,524</td><td>205</td></tr>
<tr><td>Liquor stores</td><td>1,229</td><td>280</td><td>1,189</td><td>267</td><td>118</td><td>23</td><td>113</td><td>23</td><td>305</td><td>113</td><td>287</td><td>103</td></tr>
<tr><td>Retail florists</td><td>359</td><td>409</td><td>351</td><td>406</td><td>41</td><td>28</td><td>41</td><td>27</td><td>170</td><td>117</td><td>163</td><td>116</td></tr>
<tr><td>Jewelry stores</td><td>940</td><td>555</td><td>926</td><td>543</td><td>64</td><td>44</td><td>62</td><td>42</td><td>418</td><td>243</td><td>410</td><td>236</td></tr>
<tr><td>Fuel and ice retailing</td><td>1 960</td><td>136</td><td>1 983</td><td>163</td><td>154</td><td>21</td><td>144</td><td>21</td><td>619</td><td>45</td><td>585</td><td>44</td></tr>
<tr><td>Miscellaneous retail stores</td><td>4,417</td><td>1 847</td><td>4 319</td><td>1 805</td><td>344</td><td>145</td><td>334</td><td>143</td><td>1,821</td><td>829</td><td>1,774</td><td>807</td></tr>
<tr><td>Not specified retail trade</td><td>1 984</td><td>1 469</td><td>1,936</td><td>1,428</td><td>111</td><td>109</td><td>109</td><td>106</td><td>379</td><td>337</td><td>360</td><td>323</td></tr>
<tr><td>Finance, insurance, and real estate</td><td>13,879</td><td>8,282</td><td>13,542</td><td>8 173</td><td>1,021</td><td>713</td><td>1,010</td><td>707</td><td>7 13[illegible]</td><td>4 357</td><td>6,947</td><td>4,282</td></tr>
<tr><td>Banking and credit agencies</td><td>3 890</td><td>3 276</td><td>3,842</td><td>3,256</td><td>280</td><td>352</td><td>278</td><td>352</td><td>1,948</td><td>1,516</td><td>1,878</td><td>1 504</td></tr>
<tr><td>Security & commodity brokerage, & investment companies</td><td>775</td><td>282</td><td>761</td><td>278</td><td>25</td><td>7</td><td>25</td><td>7</td><td>516</td><td>187</td><td>506</td><td>185</td></tr>
<tr><td>Insurance</td><td>6 000</td><td>3,206</td><td>5,925</td><td>3,157</td><td>497</td><td>271</td><td>493</td><td>266</td><td>2 866</td><td>1 819</td><td>2,820</td><td>1,783</td></tr>
<tr><td>Real estate (incl. real estate-insurance-law offices)</td><td>3 214</td><td>1 518</td><td>3,115</td><td>1,482</td><td>219</td><td>83</td><td>214</td><td>82</td><td>1,811</td><td>835</td><td>1,745</td><td>810</td></tr>
<tr><td>Business and repair services</td><td>19,055</td><td>1,876</td><td>18,328</td><td>1,822</td><td>1,185</td><td>139</td><td>1,136</td><td>135</td><td>6,640</td><td>953</td><td>6,235</td><td>921</td></tr>
<tr><td>Advertising</td><td>675</td><td>324</td><td>324</td><td>317</td><td>55</td><td>12</td><td>54</td><td>10</td><td>425</td><td>261</td><td>408</td><td>255</td></tr>
<tr><td>Accounting, auditing, and bookkeeping services</td><td>1,018</td><td>314</td><td>997</td><td>310</td><td>77</td><td>23</td><td>76</td><td>23</td><td>532</td><td>128</td><td>519</td><td>127</td></tr>
<tr><td>Miscellaneous business services</td><td>2 232</td><td>681</td><td>2,154</td><td>662</td><td>176</td><td>60</td><td>172</td><td>59</td><td>1,347</td><td>391</td><td>1,29[illegible]</td><td>376</td></tr>
<tr><td>Automobile repair services and garages</td><td>9,870</td><td>293</td><td>9,484</td><td>280</td><td>559</td><td>17</td><td>530</td><td>17</td><td>2 55[illegible]</td><td>84</td><td>2 380</td><td>77</td></tr>
<tr><td>Miscellaneous repair services</td><td>5,290</td><td>264</td><td>5 069</td><td>256</td><td>318</td><td>27</td><td>304</td><td>27</td><td>1,783</td><td>89</td><td>1,680</td><td>86</td></tr>
<tr><td>Personal services</td><td>20,165</td><td>61,087</td><td>19 468</td><td>58 376</td><td>1,342</td><td>5,192</td><td>1,284</td><td>4,983</td><td>7,137</td><td>18,592</td><td>6,600</td><td>17,510</td></tr>
<tr><td>Private households</td><td>6,078</td><td>46 104</td><td>5 631</td><td>43 834</td><td>354</td><td>3,809</td><td>325</td><td>3,636</td><td>1,285</td><td>2 984</td><td>1,203</td><td>12,145</td></tr>
<tr><td>Hotels and lodging places</td><td>3,256</td><td>3 750</td><td>3,092</td><td>3 612</td><td>174</td><td>310</td><td>165</td><td>299</td><td>1,774</td><td>1 662</td><td>1,659</td><td>1,579</td></tr>
<tr><td>Laundering, cleaning, and dyeing services</td><td>5,355</td><td>6,493</td><td>5 180</td><td>6,285</td><td>391</td><td>717</td><td>380</td><td>697</td><td>2,169</td><td>2,195</td><td>2,081</td><td>2 096</td></tr>
<tr><td>Dressmaking shops</td><td>46</td><td>1,046</td><td>44</td><td>1,015</td><td>3</td><td>62</td><td>3</td><td>61</td><td>23</td><td>363</td><td>22</td><td>346</td></tr>
<tr><td>Shoe repair shops</td><td>1,016</td><td>80</td><td>979</td><td>75</td><td>95</td><td>9</td><td>92</td><td>9</td><td>381</td><td>27</td><td>360</td><td>23</td></tr>
<tr><td>Miscellaneous personal services</td><td>4 614</td><td>3 514</td><td>4,542</td><td>3,555</td><td>327</td><td>285</td><td>319</td><td>281</td><td>1,507</td><td>1 361</td><td>1,475</td><td>1,321</td></tr>
<tr><td>Entertainment and recreation services</td><td>7,119</td><td>2,437</td><td>6,692</td><td>2,359</td><td>369</td><td>175</td><td>352</td><td>168</td><td>3,725</td><td>1,155</td><td>3,416</td><td>1,111</td></tr>
<tr><td>Radio broadcasting and television</td><td>626</td><td>197</td><td>614</td><td>191</td><td>71</td><td>28</td><td>70</td><td>27</td><td>260</td><td>72</td><td>253</td><td>70</td></tr>
<tr><td>Theaters and motion pictures</td><td>1 784</td><td>1,471</td><td>1,715</td><td>1,440</td><td>99</td><td>108</td><td>94</td><td>105</td><td>706</td><td>634</td><td>666</td><td>615</td></tr>
<tr><td>Bowling alleys and billiard and pool parlors</td><td>524</td><td>36</td><td>497</td><td>32</td><td>34</td><td></td><td>32</td><td></td><td>128</td><td>23</td><td>120</td><td>20</td></tr>
<tr><td>Miscellaneous entertainment and recreation services</td><td>4,185</td><td>733</td><td>3,866</td><td>706</td><td>165</td><td>39</td><td>156</td><td>36</td><td>2,629</td><td>426</td><td>2,377</td><td>406</td></tr>
<tr><td>Professional and related services</td><td>29,460</td><td>43 398</td><td>29,030</td><td>42 984</td><td>3,114</td><td>3 685</td><td>3,064</td><td>3 651</td><td>9 945</td><td>14,737</td><td>9 748</td><td>14 525</td></tr>
<tr><td>Medical and other health services, except hospitals</td><td>3 899</td><td>4,553</td><td>3,862</td><td>4 478</td><td>276</td><td>315</td><td>274</td><td>314</td><td>1,524</td><td>1,726</td><td>1 505</td><td>1,688</td></tr>
<tr><td>Hospitals</td><td>4,913</td><td>10,721</td><td>4,797</td><td>10 560</td><td>206</td><td>597</td><td>203</td><td>586</td><td>2,640</td><td>5,660</td><td>2 571</td><td>5,572</td></tr>
<tr><td>Legal services</td><td>1,894</td><td>1 124</td><td>1,886</td><td>1 104</td><td>160</td><td>101</td><td>158</td><td>100</td><td>817</td><td>475</td><td>813</td><td>466</td></tr>
<tr><td>Educational services, government</td><td>9,209</td><td>19 197</td><td>9,103</td><td>19,118</td><td>1,704</td><td>2,042</td><td>1,675</td><td>2,032</td><td>1,107</td><td>3,194</td><td>1,081</td><td>3,167</td></tr>
<tr><td>Educational services, private</td><td>3 170</td><td>5,100</td><td>3 170</td><td>5,063</td><td>298</td><td>411</td><td>289</td><td>408</td><td>1,670</td><td>2,394</td><td>1 641</td><td>2,370</td></tr>
<tr><td>Welfare and religious services</td><td>3,976</td><td>1 822</td><td>3,944</td><td>1,800</td><td>232</td><td>104</td><td>230</td><td>107</td><td>1,018</td><td>863</td><td>1 005</td><td>846</td></tr>
<tr><td>Nonprofit membership organizations</td><td>942</td><td>539</td><td>920</td><td>525</td><td>97</td><td>79</td><td>97</td><td>76</td><td>479</td><td>231</td><td>465</td><td>225</td></tr>
<tr><td>Engineering and architectural services</td><td>1,139</td><td>173</td><td>1,098</td><td>172</td><td>124</td><td>18</td><td>121</td><td>18</td><td>49[illegible]</td><td>97</td><td>480</td><td>97</td></tr>
<tr><td>Miscellaneous professional and related services</td><td>318</td><td>169</td><td>310</td><td>164</td><td>17</td><td>14</td><td>17</td><td>13</td><td>195</td><td>97</td><td>189</td><td>94</td></tr>
<tr><td>Public administration</td><td>25,567</td><td>8,913</td><td>24,553</td><td>8,807</td><td>1,769</td><td>1,236</td><td>1,733</td><td>1,221</td><td>11,982</td><td>3,459</td><td>11,371</td><td>3,378</td></tr>
<tr><td>Postal service</td><td>4,719</td><td>911</td><td>4,630</td><td>903</td><td>322</td><td>28</td><td>320</td><td>27</td><td>2,066</td><td>99</td><td>1 999</td><td>96</td></tr>
<tr><td>Federal public administration</td><td>7 920</td><td>3,902</td><td>7,254</td><td>3,837</td><td>257</td><td>206</td><td>240</td><td>205</td><td>4,571</td><td>2 267</td><td>4,168</td><td>2,221</td></tr>
<tr><td>State public administration</td><td>3 335</td><td>1,935</td><td>3,269</td><td>1,919</td><td>607</td><td>806</td><td>599</td><td>795</td><td>937</td><td>403</td><td>911</td><td>399</td></tr>
<tr><td>Local public administration</td><td>9,593</td><td>2 165</td><td>9,400</td><td>2,148</td><td>583</td><td>196</td><td>574</td><td>196</td><td>4,408</td><td>670</td><td>4 293</td><td>662</td></tr>
<tr><td>Industry not reported</td><td>17,403</td><td>6 852</td><td>9,251</td><td>4,535</td><td>488</td><td>390</td><td>378</td><td>224</td><td>3,823</td><td>1,606</td><td>1 926</td><td>1,032</td></tr>
</table>

Table 79.—DETAILED INDUSTRY OF THE EXPERIENCED CIVILIAN LABOR FORCE AND OF EMPLOYED PERSONS, BY SEX, FOR THE STATE AND FOR STANDARD METROPOLITAN AREAS AND CITIES OF 100,000 OR MORE: 1950—Con.

Detailed industry	Standard metropolitan areas—Con.				Cities											
	Shreveport				Baton Rouge				New Orleans				Shreveport			
	Experienced civilian labor force		Employed		Experienced civilian labor force		Employed		Experienced civilian labor force		Employed		Experienced civilian labor force		Employed	
	Male	Female	Male	Female	Male	Female	Male	Female	Male	Female	Male	Female	Male	Female	Male	Female
Total, 14 years old and over	[illegible]	22,9[illegible]	4[illegible]	22,2[illegible]	33,[illegible]	[illegible]	32,03[illegible]	[illegible]	157,986	74,786	144,581	[illegible]	34,188	19,180	33,073	18,6[illegible]3
Agriculture, forestry, and fisheries	[illegible]	[illegible]	3,[illegible]	[illegible]	23[illegible]	54	2[illegible]4	52	1,079	123	994	115	450	62	429	54
Agriculture	2,94[illegible]	[illegible]	2,[illegible]	1,[illegible]	218	43	190	42	798	104	732	96	42[illegible]	58	400	50
Forestry	[illegible]	1	16	–	14	11	11	10	22	9	22	9	[illegible]		5	
Fisheries	[illegible]	[illegible]	[illegible]	3	–		4		259	10	240	10	25	4	24	4
Mining	[illegible]	62[illegible]	3,[illegible]	62[illegible]	2[illegible]	1[illegible]	20[illegible]		81[illegible]	[illegible]41	779	[illegible]39	2,090	614	2,051	611
Metal mining	1				4		3		[illegible]		[illegible]					
Coal mining	–	1	3	[illegible]			[illegible]		18	2	16	2	1	1	1	1
Crude petroleum and natural gas extraction	3,[illegible]	620	3,175	625	19[illegible]	13	18[illegible]	12	750	127	723	125	2,059	613	2,031	610
Nonmetallic mining and quarrying, except fuel	24		22		16	1	[illegible]	1	42	12	38	12	20		19	
Construction	[illegible],481	[illegible]37	[illegible],236	[illegible]5	5,073	332	4,393	222	16,468	551	14,631	525	4,142	120	3,966	118
Manufacturing	6,737	954	6,601	940	10,[illegible]9	88[illegible]	10,228	870	23,955	8,452	22,617	7,973	5,085	833	4,9[illegible]	820
Durable goods	[illegible],54[illegible]	267	[illegible],485	264	932	9[illegible]	9[illegible]	90	9,605	[illegible],059	8,88[illegible]	1,005	2,610	222	2,[illegible]09	219
Lumber and wood products, except furniture	[illegible]	58	1,054	5[illegible]	190	[illegible]	177	11	1,025	131	970	146	685	45	668	44
Logging	11	1	112	1	6		4		20	3	19	3	3[illegible]	[illegible]	35	[illegible]
Sawmills, planing mills, and mill work	8[illegible]	44	738	44	194	11	169	11	698	74	657	73	539	32	526	32
Miscellaneous wood products	1[illegible]	1[illegible]	154	12	[illegible]		4		337	74	294	70	109	12	107	11
Furniture and fixtures	132	54	129	54	30	5	27	5	853	155	798	147	112	45	110	45
Stone, clay, and glass products	907	25	974	25	128	17	121	17	1,239	75	1,193	71	652	22	651	22
Glass and glass products	775	17	773	14	11	2	9	2	81	14	77	13	570	13	570	1[illegible]
Cement, and concrete, gypsum, and plaster products	4[illegible]	3	[illegible]1	3	106	13	101	13	378	13	363	13	37	3	36	[illegible]
Structural clay products	64	5	64	5	9		9		61	6	59	6	24	5	2[illegible]	5
Pottery and related products	[illegible]	3	3	3		2		2	54		52		1	1	1	1
Miscellaneous nonmetallic mineral and stone products	2[illegible]		23		2		2		665	42	642	39	20		20	
Metal industries	593	42	540	42	443	20	427	20	2,002	272	1,908	264	468	38	455	38
Primary metal industries	189	[illegible]	183	[illegible]	23[illegible]	13	226	13	422	21	400	18	139	[illegible]	133	[illegible]
Blast furnaces, steel works, and rolling mills	71	2	69	2	[illegible]	1	7	1	46	5	42	5	54	2	52	2
Other primary iron and steel industries	91	5	87	5	24	2	24	2	137	12	122	[illegible]	6[illegible]	3	57	3
Primary nonferrous industries	27	2	2	[illegible]	199	10	195	10	39	4	36	4	2[illegible]	1	2[illegible]	1
Fabricated metal industries (incl. not spec. metal)	3[illegible]	3[illegible]	357	[illegible]	212	13	20[illegible]	13	1,580	251	1,508	246	32[illegible]	32	322	32
Fabricated steel products	276	28	273	28	163	10	154	10	1,249	219	1,202	214	244	2[illegible]	241	2[illegible]
Fabricated nonferrous metal products	84	5	80	5	39	3	38	3	306	31	283	31	81	5	77	5
Not specified metal industries	4		4		10		9		25	1	23	1	4		4	
Machinery, except electrical	55[illegible]	43	549	43	94	13	93	13	1,000	100	916	98	440	35	436	35
Agricultural machinery and tractors	18		18		5	–	5	1	41	4	41	4	14		14	
Office and store machines and devices	14	[illegible]	14	3	19	3	19	3	67	18	63	18	13	2	13	2
Miscellaneous machinery	523	40	517	40	70	9	69	9	892	78	812	75	413	33	409	33
Electrical machinery, equipment, and supplies	[illegible]	9	5[illegible]	9	2[illegible]	2	22	2	194	42	182	36	39	8	39	8
Transportation equipment	[illegible]	6	[illegible]	[illegible]	32	5	29	5	2,695	122	2,378	112	46	5	44	4
Motor vehicles and motor vehicle equipment	38	4	38	3	12	2	12	2	142	14	13[illegible]	12	3[illegible]	4	35	[illegible]
Aircraft and parts	2		2		6		6		16	1	10		1			
Ship and boat building and repairing	13	[illegible]	11	1	7	2	5	2	2,500	107	2,197	94	8		6	
Railroad and misc. transportation equipment	3	–	3	1	[illegible]	1	6	1	37	6	36	6	[illegible]	1	[illegible]	1
Professional and photographic equipment and watches	41	8	41	8	22	6	21	6	114	38	111	37	33	7	33	7
Professional equipment and supplies	35	[illegible]	3[illegible]	3	18	3	1[illegible]	3	87	28	85	28	29	2	29	2
Photographic equipment and supplies	[illegible]	1	2	1	1	2	1	2	11	4	11	[illegible]	2	1	2	1
Watches, clocks, and clockwork-operated devices	4	4	4	4	–	1	3	1	16	6	[illegible]	3	2	4	2	4
Miscellaneous manufacturing industries	16[illegible]	22	15[illegible]	21	26	6	26	[illegible]	43[illegible]	104	428	[illegible]	135	17	133	16
Nondurable goods	3,117	673	3,040	662	9,407	784	9,2[illegible]6	774	14,16[illegible]	7,307	[illegible],562	6,890	2,47[illegible]	598	2,307	588
Food and kindred products	1,043	164	1,025	[illegible]1	817	12[illegible]	780	120	7,1[illegible]7	1,886	6,781	1,726	[illegible]	14[illegible]	904	141
Meat products	21[illegible]	44	208	44	66	3	65	3	812	168	790	157	163	36	180	36
Dairy products	[illegible]	[illegible]	61	6	89	10	88	[illegible]	312	95	301	90	67	6	65	6
Canning & preserving fruits, vegetables, & sea foods	12	1	12		10	8	10	[illegible]	291	307	259	303	10		10	
Grain-mill products	37	3	36	[illegible]	42	[illegible]	35	[illegible]	219	23	20[illegible]	20	34	[illegible]	33	3
Bakery products	3[illegible]4	62	310	60	327	59	317	59	1,163	268	1,121	255	280	54	2[illegible]	52
Confectionery and related products	[illegible]8	12	18	12	4	2	4	2	128	2[illegible]6	12[illegible]	197	15	12	15	12
Beverage industries	222	16	214	1[illegible]	1[illegible]3	20	165	20	2,088	1[illegible]8	1,98[illegible]	144	21[illegible]	15	202	15
Misc. food preparations and kindred products	139	18	[illegible]9	18	94	16	9[illegible]	15	1,964	503	1,876	47[illegible]	115	15	115	16
Not specified food industries	[illegible]	2	7	[illegible]	14	1	1[illegible]	1	140	88	133	84	7	1	7	1
Tobacco manufactures	7		7		1		1		97	[illegible]	94	[illegible]10			[illegible]	
Textile mill products	7	[illegible]	17	5	[illegible]	2	10	2	80[illegible]	758	765	732	11	4	11	4
Knitting mills	[illegible]		6		2	1	2	1	91	251	86	24[illegible]	[illegible]		–	
Dyeing and finishing textiles, except knit goods	[illegible]		1						[illegible]	[illegible]	15	[illegible]	1		[illegible]	
Carpets, rugs, and other floor coverings	[illegible]	3	[illegible]	[illegible]	1		1		6	4	6	4		[illegible]		[illegible]
Yarn, thread, and fabric mills	8	[illegible]	8	[illegible]	7	1	6	1	6[illegible]	453	585	436	5	1	5	[illegible]
Miscellaneous textile mill products	1		1		1		1		[illegible]	43	[illegible]	40				
Apparel and other fabricated textile products	57	162	57	177	12	4	[illegible]	4	1,657	3,015	[illegible],009	2,865	52	160	52	155
Apparel and accessories	32	164	32	159	3	1	3	1	542	2,450	767	2,338	31	144	31	139
Miscellaneous fabricated textile products	25	18	25	18	9	[illegible]	8		4[illegible]	6[illegible]	442	527	21	16	21	16
Paper and allied products	[illegible]	25	66	25	1[illegible]		[illegible]		851	225	793	212	54	24	53	24
Pulp, paper, and paperboard mills	45	10	42	10	31		9		55[illegible]	64	522	63	31	10	30	10
Paperboard containers and boxes	22	12	22	12	1		1		238	122	219	116	22	[illegible]	22	12
Miscellaneous paper and pulp products	[illegible]	3	2	[illegible]	2		2		56	[illegible]	[illegible]	3[illegible]	1	2	1	2
Printing, publishing, and allied industries	577	1[illegible]	568	133	440	1[illegible]7	420	116	2,459	491	2,393	4[illegible]6	541	125	532	124
Chemicals and allied products	391	35	3[illegible]5	34	2,394	161	2,373	159	940	196	848	187	3[illegible]1	29	32[illegible]	28
Synthetic fiber									1		1					
Drugs and medicines	10	2	10	2	11	2	11	2	37	28	3[illegible]	25	10	2	10	2
Paints, varnishes, and related products	6	2	5	2	9		9		140	[illegible]	139	25	4	2	3	2
Miscellaneous chemicals and allied products	37[illegible]	[illegible]	360	30	2,[illegible]74	159	2,353	157	742	145	704	139	327	25	316	24
Petroleum and coal products	932	123	901	123	5,386	368	5,317	365	748	145	718	141	496	109	465	109
Petroleum refining	827	120	797	120	5,384	368	5,315	365	454	118	438	114	401	107	377	107
Miscellaneous petroleum and coal products	105	3	104	[illegible]	2		2		294	27	280	27	89	[illegible]	88	2
Rubber products	15	3	15	[illegible]	12[illegible]	8	12[illegible]	8	4[illegible]	21	44	21	8	3	8	2
Leather and leather products	[illegible]	2	9	2	[illegible]		7		60	21	6[illegible]	20	8	[illegible]	8	1
Leather: tanned, curried, and finished		[illegible]	1	1	2		2		14	4	14	4		[illegible]	1	1
Footwear, except rubber	[illegible]		5		3		[illegible]		27	8	27	8	5		5	
Leather products, except footwear	3	1	[illegible]	1	2		2		25	[illegible]	24	8	2		2	
Not specified manufacturing industries	78	14	76	[illegible]	20	6	19	6	1[illegible]6	86	171	78	47	13	43	13

Table 79.—DETAILED INDUSTRY OF THE EXPERIENCED CIVILIAN LABOR FORCE AND OF EMPLOYED PERSONS, BY SEX, FOR THE STATE AND FOR STANDARD METROPOLITAN AREAS AND CITIES OF 100,000 OR MORE: 1950—Con.

Detailed industry	Standard metropolitan areas—Con.				Cities											
	Shreveport				Baton Rouge				New Orleans				Shreveport			
	Experienced civilian labor force		Employed		Experienced civilian labor force		Employed		Experienced civilian labor force		Employed		Experienced civilian labor force		Employed	
	Male	Female	Male	Female	Male	Female	Male	Female	Male	Female	Male	Female	Male	Female	Male	Female
Transport, communication, & other public utilities	5,422	954	5,346	947	2,4?5	719	2,384	5?3	49,8?4	4,227	27,723	4,138	4,4?4	83?	4,?59	82?
Transportation	3,833	341	3,769	338	1,498	175	1,432	1?4	25,?18	1,842	25,098	1,796	3,178	284	3,123	281
Railroads and railway express service	2,059	91	2,027	90	637	29	?25	2?	5,789	332	5,641	3?8	1,687	83	1,65?	82
Street railways and bus lines	417	27	41?	26	20?	?2	[illegible]	?2	1,755	165	1,741	161	365	29	36?	28
Trucking service	598	??	588	50	28?	19	?6	19	2,254	119	2,?75	113	49?	?8	49?	48
Warehousing and storage	110	16	107	16	??	?	52	?	1,07?	83	1,0?4	81	102	15	?91	?5
Taxicab service	168	?	165	?	122	17	1?2	16	9?2	85	1,96?	85	144	?	14?	5
Water transportation	29	8	29	8	20?	4	29	4	11,496	7?	9,?02	?5?	16	2	16	2
Air transportation	95	16	95	16	??	4	22	4	397	129	390	126	82	?5	82	?5
Petroleum and gasoline pipe lines	339	82	327	8?	?6	2	44	?	27	1	24	1	276	82	26?	81
Services incidental to transportation	18	?	18	?	31	3	-	?	381	90	360	9?	15	?	15	?
Telecommunications	316	41?	3?6	408	267	288	263	287	1,380	1,997	1,3?3	1,963	283	371	283	369
Telephone (wire and radio)	276	392	276	390	248	272	2?5	27?	1,05?	1,872	1,038	1,8?0	244	355	244	354
Telegraph (wire and radio)	40	19	40	18	19	16	18	15	327	125	305	123	39	16	39	15
Utilities and sanitary services	1,273	149	1,251	198	710	116	689	115	3,345	384	3,282	379	973	176	963	175
Electric light and power, and electro-gas utilities	388	62	388	61	479	80	463	79	1,506	310	1,47?	308	274	58	274	57
Gas and steam supply systems	597	123	592	12?	70	5	68	5	80	10	79	8	448	106	444	106
Water supply	127	10	124	10	96	21	94	21	592	2?	527	20	112	9	110	9
Sanitary services	156	4	152	4	59	4	58	-	1,?08	28	1,171	28	135	3	131	3
Other and not specified utilities	5		5		6	6	6	5	61	1?	59	1?	4		4	
Wholesale and retail trade	10,180	5,446	10,003	5,355	7,026	3,561	6,746	3,456	36,627	20,64?	36,924	19,715	8,825	4,750	8,656	4,655
Wholesale trade	2,726	469	2,688	465	1,267	177	1,227	175	11,668	2,918	11,296	2,847	2,451	435	2,397	429
Motor vehicles and equipment	94	14	91	14	26	3	26	3	285	51	278	48	87	15	86	13
Drugs, chemicals, and allied products	123	41	121	41	52	9	49	9	622	209	632	205	115	40	113	40
Dry goods and apparel	97	16	95	16	29	7	29	7	413	169	404	164	93	16	91	16
Food and related products	641	73	632	73	447	45	432	45	3,440	760	3,331	728	579	66	571	66
Electrical goods, hardware, and plumbing equipment	240	52	238	51	119	30	115	23	1,289	37?	1,250	364	216	50	215	49
Machinery, equipment, and supplies	453	79	446	79	146	27	125	27	1,076	223	1,047	221	409	74	403	74
Petroleum products	223	52	220	51	98	17	98	17	1,064	387	1,036	380	172	41	169	42
Farm products—raw materials	75	10	75	10	39	2	38	2	510	105	490	105	59	8	59	8
Miscellaneous wholesale trade	728	112	716	110	301	43	289	42	2,471	485	2,345	477	666	104	655	102
Not specified wholesale trade	54	20	54	20	30	4	26	4	528	158	513	155	35	19	35	19
Retail trade	7,454	4,977	7,315	4,890	5,759	3,384	5,519	3,280	26,959	17,723	25,628	16,868	6,394	4,317	6,259	4,236
Food stores, except dairy products	1,390	646	1,367	620	1,046	4??	1,017	409	5,779	2,477	5,529	2,419	1,127	471	1,106	465
Dairy products stores and milk retailing	257	18	249	18	65	?7	79	16	459	72	[illegible]	69	224	15	217	15
General merchandise stores	332	631	3??	674	409	680	400	674	2,100	4,427	1,992	4,2??	274	551	267	546
Five and ten cent stores	37	191	36	187	24	97	22	94	134	719	127	673	24	167	33	163
Apparel and accessories stores, except shoe stores	231	574	228	562	143	295	140	289	1,059	1,756	1,006	1,684	223	548	220	539
Shoe stores	126	52	128	52	72	35	70	34	411	14?	398	141	122	50	122	50
Furniture and house furnishings stores	468	171	45?	170	280	78	269	75	1,089	305	1,044	294	426	164	415	163
Household appliance and radio stores	226	48	227	47	186	47	178	47	724	20?	696	194	194	42	193	41
Motor vehicles and accessories retailing	878	101	867	98	606	74	582	74	1,937	260	1,874	252	761	89	752	86
Gasoline service stations	612	31	60?	31	543	42	53?	41	1,323	46	1,238	46	475	22	465	22
Drug stores	272	330	268	325	254	178	242	174	1,196	697	1,1??	660	255	300	245	295
Eating and drinking places	778	1,630	753	1,586	61?	1,00?	740	943	5,455	7,637	5,259	7,279	676	1,400	653	1,360
Hardware and farm implement stores	172	38	170	38	158	35	191	35	487	107	475	104	144	30	142	30
Lumber and building material retailing	526	69	518	68	3??	46	363	45	1,356	185	1,298	182	461	65	453	64
Liquor stores	170	31	165	30	1?2	21	10?	21	276	100	262	90	157	28	152	27
Retail florists	43	39	43	39	33	26	33	26	141	110	134	109	38	34	38	34
Jewelry stores	99	58	96	59	57	47	57	42	375	219	367	212	95	53	94	53
Fuel and ice retailing	174	26	170	26	127	21	117	2?	544	39	515	38	142	20	138	20
Miscellaneous retail stores	532	208	523	205	312	137	304	135	1,600	736	1,557	716	483	188	475	185
Not specified retail trade	121	105	119	101	84	90	82	87	314	287	295	275	81	80	79	78
Finance, insurance, and real estate	1,382	878	1,371	871	967	667	956	661	6,30?	3,961	6,155	3,889	1,270	811	1,259	805
Banking and credit agencies	359	326	359	324	270	330	268	330	1,739	1,340	1,701	1,328	332	298	332	296
Security & commodity brokerage, & investment companies	77	40	77	39	23	?	23	3	469	172	460	171	72	37	72	36
Insurance	590	284	584	283	477	252	469	247	2,457	1,659	2,414	1,625	549	259	543	258
Real estate (incl. real estate-insurance-law offices)	356	226	351	225	201	80	196	79	1,644	790	1,580	765	317	2??	312	215
Business and repair services	1,690	246	1,657	243	1,03?	132	992	129	5,696	856	5,367	825	1,378	220	1,354	217
Advertising	61	30	60	29	5?	11	51	9	381	245	?6	237	53	29	52	28
Accounting, auditing, and bookkeeping services	123	54	122	54	70	21	70	21	462	11?	450	112	117	5?	116	51
Miscellaneous business services	21?	84	207	83	164	56	160	55	1,192	356	1,140	341	188	80	185	79
Automobile repair services and garages	865	36	851	36	480	7	4??	17	2,168	70	2,0?1	63	677	25	668	25
Miscellaneous repair services	43?	42	417	41	264	27	250	27	1,493	?4	1,40?	72	343	35	333	34
Personal services	2,070	7,294	2,021	7,100	1,40?	4,384	1,147	4,2?1	6,4?4	17,191	6,157	16,212	1,?14	6,29?	1,?68	6,115
Private households	740	5,?30	720	5,361	297	3,149	271	3,010	1,165	11,978	1,09?	11,2?8	552	4,66?	534	4,51?
Hotels and lodging places	406	454	354	4?6	165	291	156	281	1,630	1,558	1,521	1,487	338	401	332	393
Laundering, cleaning, and dyeing services	400	809	388	797	248	630	237	581	1,966	2,05?	1,882	1,959	359	757	348	747
Dressmaking shops	1	78	1	75	2	54	2	53	22	341	21	32?		75		73
Shoe repair shops	98	5	94	5	89	8	86	8	351	2	332	2?	86	6	84	5
Miscellaneous personal services	43?	417	422	416	300	26?	295	253	1,340	1,240	1,31?	1,204	379	385	370	384
Entertainment and recreation services	457	223	442	220	145	167	339	163	2,879	1,??2	2,615	991	373	198	360	195
Radio broadcasting and television	91	32	89	32	70	28	69	27	244	64	207	62	71	30	70	30
Theaters and motion pictures	110	130	108	128	89	102	85	99	589	572	554	554	94	116	89	114
Bowling alleys, and billiard and pool parlors	52	1	49	1	32		30		110	18	103	17	46	1	43	1
Miscellaneous entertainment and recreation services	204	60	196	59	154	37	145	34	1,966	378	1,751	358	165	51	158	50
Professional and related services	2,085	3,708	2,055	3,683	2,688	3,149	2,642	3,116	8,997	13,259	8,846	13,069	1,783	3,305	1,756	3,284
Medical and other health services, except hospitals	393	511	389	505	261	291	259	286	1,376	1,533	1,339	496	350	485	347	480
Hospitals	259	1,061	281	1,048	159	515	156	504	2,416	5,176	2,390	5,098	266	985	259	972
Legal services	204	113	203	112	154	98	152	97	755	428	752	419	19?	108	190	107
Educational services, government	393	1,364	389	1,361	1,529	1,756	1,510	1,746	962	2,751	938	2,778	300	1,13?	29?	1,132
Educational services, private	185	357	181	355	363	284	357	282	1,326	2,194	1,308	2,17?	167	326	163	326
Welfare and religious services	333	182	330	182	102	99	101	99	935	786	922	770	265	159	263	159
Nonprofit membership organizations	126	83	122	81	91	75	71	72	427	212	412	207	99	74	95	72
Engineering and architectural services	132	19	130	19	13	18	13	18	416	88	406	88	11?	16	116	16
Miscellaneous professional and related services	30	20	30	20	16	13	1?	??	174	91	169	90	27	18	27	18
Public administration	2,087	642	2,059	636	1,55?	1,169	1,518	1,156	10,770	3,340	10,206	2,945	1,817	571	1,774	565
Postal service	443	37	441	36	288	18	286	17	1,841	70	1,776	67	373	14	3?2	1?
Federal public administration	817	385	786	381	230	192	216	191	3,998	2,027	3,635	1,987	745	36?	715	359
State public administration	129	77	128	77	553	775	5?5	764	835	358	810	314	104	71	103	71
Local public administration	692	143	687	142	480	184	471	184	4,096	585	3,985	577	592	123	584	122
Industry not reported	1,197	749	676	467	547	275	287	177	3,072	1,316	1,598	868	840	578	452	551

Table 80.—DETAILED INDUSTRY OF EMPLOYED PERSONS, BY SEX, FOR THE STATE: 1950 AND 1940

[Continued. 1940 figures revised where necessary to conform to 1950 classification]

Detailed industry	Male 1950	Male 1940	Female 1950	Female 1940
Employed 14 years old and over	546 782	[illegible]	[illegible]	[illegible]
Agriculture, forestry, and fisheries	[illegible]	[illegible]	[illegible]	[illegible]
Agriculture	[illegible] 625	225,176	15,740	23,960
Forestry	[illegible],172	[illegible]	99	80
Fisheries	7 [illegible]	5,983	11	72
Mining	[illegible]	14 524	[illegible]	345
Metal mining	1	[illegible]	•	2
Coal mining	12	[illegible]	4	
Crude petroleum and natural gas extraction	20 7[illegible]	12 [illegible]	1 07[illegible]	276
Nonmetallic mining and quarrying, except fuel	2 162	1,[illegible]	92	67
Construction	[illegible]	[illegible]	1 [illegible]	[illegible]
Manufacturing	[illegible]	87,318	[illegible]	[illegible]
Durable goods	46,600	[illegible],593	2 404	1,249
Lumber and wood products, except furniture	2[illegible],[illegible]65	27,019	752	453
Logging	5 775	[illegible],397	4[illegible]	2[illegible]
Sawmills, planing mills, and mill work	20 3[illegible]8	19 859	476	298
Miscellaneous wood products	1 8[illegible]	1 [illegible]3	227	128
Furniture and fixtures	1,54[illegible]	1 52[illegible]	296	156
Stone, clay, and glass products	3 [illegible]68	[illegible],632	156	95
Glass and glass products	9[illegible]3	721	34	28
Cement and concrete, gypsum, and plaster products	[illegible]40	[illegible],082	43	28
Structural clay products	523	[illegible]	22	15
Pottery and related products	7[illegible]	29		6
Miscellaneous nonmetallic mineral and stone products	9[illegible]5	366	[illegible]0	18
Metal industries	[illegible],6[illegible]9	3,093	478	280
Blast furnaces, steel works, and rolling mills	[illegible]85	169	9	8
Other primary iron and steel industries				
Fabricated steel products	[illegible] 331	2,207	401	241
Primary nonferrous industries				
Fabricated nonferrous metal products	1,[illegible]	[illegible]	6	2[illegible]
Not specified metal industries	59	[illegible]06	1	[illegible]
Machinery, except electrical	2,59[illegible]	1,821	226	124
Agricultural machinery and tractors	2[illegible]9	261	14	16
Office and store machines and devices	[illegible]27	1[illegible]0	26	21
Miscellaneous machinery	[illegible] 620	[illegible] 420	86	87
Electrical machinery, equipment, and supplies	[illegible]	272	64	25
Transportation equipment	4,[illegible]19	2 523	171	[illegible]7
Motor vehicles and motor vehicle equipment	430	48	27	1[illegible]
Aircraft and parts	29	9	2	[illegible]
Ship and boat building and repairing	3,99[illegible]	[illegible],979	[illegible]33	18
Railroad and misc. transportation equipment	68	52	9	1
All other durable goods	1,135	693	261	129
Professional equipment and supplies				
Photographic equipment and supplies	2[illegible]	86	[illegible]7	29
Watches, clocks, and clockwork-operated devices				
Miscellaneous manufacturing industries	931	607	204	100
Nondurable goods	68,164	46,[illegible]59	14,547	[illegible]0 [illegible]76
Food and kindred products	21 183	17,772	4,7[illegible]	[illegible],908
Meat products	1,956	1,030	[illegible]10	19[illegible]
Dairy products	1,098	621	197	[illegible]0
Canning & preserving fruits, vegetables, & sea foods	1,652	[illegible],094	1,898	1,032
Grain mill products	2 [illegible]	1,868	[illegible]49	[illegible]
Bakery products	3 [illegible]	2 [illegible]04	[illegible]60	[illegible]0
Confectionery and related products	[illegible]	26[illegible]	274	249
Beverage industries	3,[illegible]	2,[illegible]	274	237
Misc. food preparations and kindred products				
Not specified food industries	[illegible],[illegible]72	[illegible] 797	1,04[illegible]	[illegible]
Tobacco manufactures	142	238	6[illegible]7	1,015
Textile mill products	1,1[illegible]	1,7[illegible]	895	1,[illegible]98
Knitting mills	127	228	260	[illegible]62
Dyeing and finishing textiles, except knit goods	20	[illegible]2	[illegible]	3
Carpets, rugs, and other floor coverings	15	15	8	[illegible]
Yarn, thread, and fabric mills	770	[illegible]53	557	[illegible]6[illegible]
Miscellaneous textile mill products	181	[illegible]15	[illegible]1	[illegible]
Apparel and other fabricated textile products	1,276	[illegible],[illegible]60	3,69[illegible]	2 [illegible]20
Apparel and accessories	69[illegible]	[illegible]	3 042	2 [illegible]
Miscellaneous fabricated textile products	[illegible]83	5[illegible]2	[illegible]	576
Paper and allied products	1[illegible],833	7,161	1,[illegible]69	8[illegible]6
Pulp, paper, and paperboard mills	10,88[illegible]	6,[illegible]	74[illegible]	427
Paperboard containers and boxes	972	47[illegible]	[illegible]03	170
Miscellaneous paper and pulp products	978	325	519	2[illegible]
Printing, publishing, and allied industries	5 326	4 049	1,183	67[illegible]
Chemicals and allied products	10 387	[illegible],[illegible]05	787	[illegible]
Synthetic fibers	15	3		1
Paints, varnishes, and related products	237	217	[illegible]5	[illegible]6
Drugs and medicines				
Miscellaneous chemicals and allied products	10,[illegible]35	5,685	742	33[illegible]
Petroleum and coal products	15,[illegible]40	[illegible],449	9[illegible]	[illegible]42
Petroleum refining	14,339	7,[illegible]54	9[illegible]	429
Miscellaneous petroleum and coal products	[illegible]01	[illegible]	4[illegible]	[illegible]
Rubber products	[illegible]7[illegible]	109	[illegible]0	[illegible]9
Leather and leather products	[illegible]08	8[illegible]	3[illegible]	9
Leather: tanned, curried, and finished	22	8	6	1
Footwear, except rubber	44	36	1[illegible]	[illegible]
Leather products, except footwear	[illegible]2	39	[illegible]0	5
Not specified manufacturing industries	[illegible]94	566	1[illegible]	19[illegible]
Transportation, communication & other public utilities	66,[illegible]	40,[illegible]79	9 66[illegible]	4 238
Transportation	50,760	37 770	3 265	1,068
Railroads and railway express service	[illegible]7 512	1[illegible] 169	7[illegible]9	[illegible]7
Street railways and bus lines	[illegible],85[illegible]	2,866	[illegible]22	[illegible]
Trucking service	6 1[illegible]6	4,922	273	[illegible]44
Transport., commun., & other public utilities—Con.				
Transportation—Con.				
Warehousing and storage	[illegible],745	1,7[illegible]	1[illegible]	80
Taxicab service	[illegible],491	1,390	1[illegible]	28
Water transportation	[illegible]4 1[illegible]	11 40[illegible]	880	376
Air transportation	1,033	183	215	1[illegible]
Petroleum and gasoline pipe lines	1,103	72[illegible]	9[illegible]	19
Services incidental to transportation	728	4[illegible]0	[illegible]38	2[illegible]
Telecommunications	3,[illegible]51	[illegible],126	[illegible],[illegible]25	2,621
Telephone (wire and radio)	2,62[illegible]	1,39[illegible]	[illegible],[illegible]92	2,391
Telegraph (wire and radio)	[illegible]27	734	233	2[illegible]0
Utilities and sanitary services	[illegible],[illegible]	6,583	1,37[illegible]	549
Electric light and power and electric-gas utilities	[illegible],774	2,581	941	285
Other and not specified utilities				
Gas and steam supply systems	2,580	1,511	302	192
Water supply				
Sanitary services	3,[illegible]	2,431	3[illegible]	7[illegible]
Wholesale and retail trade	1[illegible],[illegible]47	[illegible]3,[illegible]03	56,606	29,297
Wholesale trade	26,[illegible]	1[illegible],52[illegible]	4,944	2,13[illegible]
Motor vehicles and equipment				
Drugs, chemicals, and allied products				
Dry goods and apparel				
Food and related products				
Electrical goods, hardware, and plumbing equipment	26,92[illegible]	[illegible]6,[illegible]27	[illegible] 944	2,131
Machinery, equipment, and supplies				
Petroleum products				
Farm products—raw materials				
Miscellaneous wholesale trade				
Not specified wholesale trade				
Retail trade	86,620	66 9[illegible]6	51,662	27,166
Food stores, except dairy products	19,860	18,104	8,976	4 812
Dairy products stores and milk retailing	[illegible] 458	[illegible],0[illegible]	[illegible]78	12[illegible]
General merchandise stores	5 508	4,8[illegible]8	9,278	5,5[illegible]8
Five and ten cent stores	414	191	[illegible],761	579
Apparel and accessories stores, except shoe stores	2,164	[illegible],[illegible]71	4 102	2 [illegible]74
Shoe stores	88[illegible]	730	38[illegible]	84
Furniture and house furnishings stores	3 370	2,[illegible]29	913	4[illegible]5
Household appliance and radio stores	2,296	[illegible],082	5[illegible]	178
Motor vehicles and accessories retailing	8,234	[illegible],[illegible]23	939	3[illegible]1
Gasoline service stations	7,361	5,942	331	165
Drug stores	[illegible],067	3 [illegible]38	[illegible],44[illegible]	999
Eating and drinking places	[illegible]2 [illegible]56	10 09[illegible]	16 [illegible]44	8,31[illegible]
Hardware and farm implement stores	2,[illegible]8[illegible]	1,544	468	20[illegible]
Lumber and building material retailing	[illegible],655	[illegible],544	583	280
Liquor stores	1,[illegible]89	[illegible]18	26[illegible]	[illegible]9
Retail florists	35[illegible]	30[illegible]	406	204
Jewelry stores	926	637	543	216
Fuel and ice retailing	1 803	1,806	163	53
Miscellaneous retail stores	[illegible]	2,596	1,805	968
Not specified retail trade	1,936	[illegible],730	1,428	769
Finance, insurance, and real estate	[illegible]3,643	11,086	8 [illegible]73	3,948
Banking and credit agencies				
Security & commodity brokerage, & investment companies	4,603	4,098	3 534	[illegible],483
Insurance	5 925	4,619	3,157	1,555
Real estate (incl. real estate-insurance-law offices)	3,[illegible]15	2,369	[illegible] 482	910
Business and repair services	[illegible]8,328	10,889	[illegible],822	649
Advertising	624	490	3[illegible]	8[illegible]
Accounting, auditing, and bookkeeping services				
Miscellaneous business services	[illegible],15[illegible]	1,[illegible]77	972	356
Automobile repair services and garages	[illegible],484	[illegible],[illegible]36	280	[illegible]39
Miscellaneous repair services	[illegible],369	2,[illegible]36	256	71
Personal services	[illegible]9,468	19,5[illegible]3	58,376	73,526
Private households	[illegible] 631	7,131	43,834	60 904
Hotels and lodging places	3,092	[illegible],303	3,612	3,522
Laundering, cleaning, and dyeing services	5 [illegible]80	[illegible],93[illegible]	6 28[illegible]	3,52[illegible]
Dressmaking shops				
Shoe repair shops	5,5[illegible]5	5,3[illegible]9	[illegible],645	5,578
Miscellaneous personal services				
Entertainment and recreation services	[illegible],692	4 894	2,[illegible]	1,3[illegible]
Radio broadcasting and television	614	210	191	46
Theaters and motion pictures	1,71[illegible]	1,291	1,440	722
Bowling alleys, and billiard and pool parlors				
Miscellaneous entertainment and recreation services	[illegible] 363	3,393	738	568
Professional and related services	29,0[illegible]0	19,084	[illegible]2 984	26,65[illegible]
Medical and other health services, except hospitals				
Hospitals	8 [illegible]59	[illegible],577	15 038	7,644
Educational services, government	9,103	6,347	19,1[illegible]3	[illegible]3,705
Educational services, private	3 [illegible]10	1,380	[illegible] 063	2,972
Welfare and religious services				
Nonprofit membership organizations	4,864	[illegible],403	2,3[illegible]5	[illegible],[illegible]29
Legal services				
Engineering and architectural services	[illegible],294	[illegible],3[illegible]	1,440	1,[illegible]52
Miscellaneous professional and related services				
Public administration	[illegible]4,55[illegible]	[illegible]4,327	8,807	4,407
Postal service	4 630	2,683	90[illegible]	604
Federal public administration	[illegible],254	3 012	3 837	1,229
State public administration				
Local public administration	[illegible]2,[illegible]69	8,632	4,06[illegible]	2,624
Industry not reported	9,251	[illegible],786	4 535	2,[illegible]55

(Table 81 of the standard series is omitted as there are no cities of 50,000 to 100,000 in the State)

Table 82—AGE OF EMPLOYED PERSONS, BY INDUSTRY AND SEX, FOR THE STATE AND FOR STANDARD METROPOLITAN AREAS OF 250,000 OR MORE 1950

Area industry and sex	Fotal, 14 years old and over	1 and 15	16 and 17 years	years 19	20 to 24 years	25 to 29 veers	30 to 34 years	3o to 44 years	45 to 54 years	oō to 59 years	60 to 64 years	65 and over
THE STATE Male, employed	646,782	5 103				G y s				100		
Agriculare forestry and faneres	144,480	-	3,2.8	21,301	72,062	82,838	79,674	158,9-1	_19 397	40 348	27 627	25 31
Agricultu e		3,509	6 940	7 4 70	14,993	2 572	-3,852	30 568	25 507	10,238	7,993	9,73
Forestry and usbenes	-35,665 8 81.5	3,361	431	f ,980 490	13,798	J 500	12 864	28,585	23 970 2 537	9,753 485	7,478	9,59
Mining	23,031	11	72	394	3 121	4, 66	2 81.2	3,6.6	3 675	7:7	376	43
bude pe role and natural gas extraction fining and quarrying except fuel	20,776	10	1 59 12	339	2 847 2.6	3, /8	3,-81	2° 4 946	10 3,269 3%	536	322	11
Construction	63,377	27	474	1 672	127	6,390	3.0	17 271	12,052	1.21 3 563	2 470	
Manufacturing	115,358	*00	1 352	3 437	967	15 951	15 -98	10 663	20,960	6 420	-	4,19
Durable goods	45 600	93 40	508	4,6-6	- , 600	6.52	-,844 636	11 727		2,888	1,875	1,1-
Sawru'ls, planing mills and mill work	5,775 23 348	28	254	297 821	866 2,729	2 307 219	2.1-2	1,41. 4 883	8 887 1,087 4 201	345	209	9 55
Miscellaneous wood products. Furniture and fixtures.	1,843	2 2	\$0 26	67 72	232	219 21	2,1-2	448 371	3 ₀ 6	132	90	5
Glass and glass p oducts Stone and clay p oducts Primary iron and steel industries	920	2	16	72	323	1.1	370	2.5	179	r2	33	3
	1,038	2	4	96	102	12.	156	319	202	50	66	2
Fabricated metal industries (incl not spec metal)	3,151	4	0	93	424	560	913 44	-38 797	470	12	108	5
Electrical machinery equipment and supplies Motor vehicles and motor vehicle equipment	393	,	3 5	11	3.4 55	/95 65	76	83	500	163	102	6
Ai creft and parts	430 29			-	43	80 7	76	129	59	21	n	1
Ai creft and parts Sh.p and boat building and repairing Railroau and misc transportation equipment	3,992	1	7	46	288 12	508	598	1,187	839	27	143	9
Al other diranle goods	1,135	2	18	54	-71	174	138	259	-93	25	35	4
ondurable goods Mest progress	68,164 1 966	602	%1 11	± 778	7,930	9 841	9,572	18,7(8	11,982	3 502	2,102	1 24
Bakery products Other food industries	3,072	20	64 243	149 606	472 2 053	2 046	452 1,913	775 3 987	438	121	50 82	3
	142		3	12	14	24	11	23	34	1,002	708 9	*6
Am ting mills Yam thread and fabric muls	773	1	4	-6	12	96	63	27 226	19 180	1e 50	38	2
Other textile mul products Apparel and other fabricated textile product	216 1 276	3 5 3	15	66	32 188	173	28 126	47 301	40 231	20	11	4-7
Paper and allied products Printing publishing and allied industries Chemicals and allied products	12,933	146	48 404	325	1 782	2 048 605	1,916	3,691	2 013 784	522 267	302 171	-7
Chem.cals and alind products	15, 40	6	30	1.83	1,226	1 812	1,807	3 027 4,891	1 546 3 252	396 910	234 41_ 17	16
Rusber products Lortwerr exceps abber	676		1	4	62	2 055	101	225	137	21	17	
Mather and leaths products except lootwear for specified manufas furing industries	54 394		2	13	8 72	85	83	11 13 165	97	30	3	1
Transport communication, & other public sudines.	65 024	A7	308	1 142	7,060	8,631	9,294	17,167	14 295	4,540	2,946	1,59
auroads and railway express service	4,8 0 7 931	7 3	15	1.25	1,306	1 671	1,780	4,115	4 736 1.067	1 797	1 354	3
rucking service and watehousing after trans, ortation	7 931 -4, 12	12	73	203 274	1 012	1 154	1 242	2,2.8	1,350	335	202	1.5
r transpor atros	1,003	3	3	19	101	1,781	2,676	4,037	3,103 92	864	504 17	30
elecommunications	3,351		40 73	116	686	782	756 448	1 252	935 492	2/3	130	7.
ater alphi sanitary services, and other unlines	7 929 3,984	5 2	19	169) 197 298	1 318	1,081	2 DC2	1 407	356	192	263
Wholesale and retail trade	113,54/	844	2,852	4,510	1, 860	- ,613	24 413	27 656	19 449	6,163	4,098	3 890
Vho.essue trade	26,927 21 324	34 414	201	761	3,320 2,351	4,118 2 258	3,764 2 287	6,944	4 680 3 523	1 4_1	897	827
ood and dairy products stores and milk retailing inneral merchandise and five and ten cent stores poarel and accessories stores	5,922 3,048	33 16 7	755	460	/28	750	651	1,354	1 25	367	995	1 039
writ_re, home fi mishings, and equipment stores lotor venicles and accessories retailing	5 466	7	29	146	779	389 989	309 830	-,457	599 919	196	133	152
asoune service stations	8,23/ 7 36.	48	272	498	998	1 472	1 353	2 252	256	296	109	96
rug stores sting and drinking places	3,067	1.27	378	486	1,539	276	256	3.337	302	177	_01 216	127
ardware farm implement, & olds; material retailing.	8,438 10 604	99	60	230	043	1 221	1 182	2 149	1,409	472 652	288	283
Emance insurance and real estate	13 643	9	38	240	1,245	1,754	1,504	2,247	2 944	1.083	79/	455
anking and other finance	4,603	4	17	147	578	620	4.6	1,078	921	317	222	243
Busines and retails	9,040	7	287	/32	2 274	2,033	2,700	2 064 4 861	2 023	766	572	645
Business and repair services Osmess services	3 775	,	30	65	2 274	2,033	2,700	4 861 880	3,027	304	194	201
Atomobile repair services and garages Astellaneous repair services	7,484 2,069	18 9	107	2.7	1,311	1 661 740	1 543 738	2,662	477 809	245 268	130	201 72 198
Personal services	19,468	184	4.4	667	1,95/	J 963	1 808	4,497	4,00	1,461	1,104	1,284
lotels and lodging places	>,631 3 092	110	204	488 434	3°6 342	380	262	_,133 658	1,232	278	422 225	65°
aundering dicaning and dyeing services	5,180 5,365	21 41	87	139	741 495	727 562	686 493	1,388	4,310	220 456	322	320
Entertainment and recreation services	6,694	158	328	330	872	918	748	1 451	1,117	361	217	192
Professional and related services	29,030	40	1-6	/43	2,609	4,372	4 003	7,130	5,245	1,937	1,432	1 651
edeal and other realth services	8,659	8	51.	130	-30	1,350	1,218	2,040	1,545	591	/69	548
dusational services private disational services private differ religious and membership organizations	9 103 3,110	19	29 22 24	168 50 53	353	1,495	1 360 449	2,258 763	468	549 153	383 123	257
elfare rengious, and membership organizations - gal engineering, and mise professional services.	4 864 3,294	11	10	53 42	231 241	422 522	51al 460 ₁	1,230	1,160	428 2_6	312 145	477
Public administration -	24,553	9	54	235	2,125	3 446	3 403	5,879	4,958	2 107	1,274	1,056
sta service	4,630 7,254	1	14	2.	448	767	713	1,087	862	410	1.86	97
ederal public administration . tate and local public administration .	12,069	4	11 29	5e 154	1,007	1,263	1,425	1 870 2,322	1,285 2 810	1 193	224 864	116
Industry not reported	9,251	194	299	324	1,_55	1,233	987	1 913	. 53L	601	404	63.0

The 82—AGE OF EMPLOYED PERSONS, BY INDUSTRY AND SEX, FOR THE STATE AND FOR STANDARD METROPOLITAN AREAS OF 250,000 OR MORE 1950—Cor

A visionity and a v	" : 'MI'S ("fanci "rears	f Lod 1"	years 12	20 to 2:	20 to 29 VGB.Tu	3J to 3- years	35 to 4± vosrs	45 to 54 years	of to 56	60 to 64 years	65 and over
.TE 77 73								- 100	38.777	10,76/	6,320	4,504
Female, employed	- 11-1	1 45	3,27	12, ~2	324	29 _2,	, 6 458 : 568	27,893 3,274	2 '41	956	521	707
Agriculture forestry and & peries	1,900	144	1 19	. 13-	1 240	1 171	- 74		2 544	9. 3	216	
Agrici's P. Forestry and "Mail 199	- 74. - 7	75.	- 72	. 02	1 812	1 2.4	25	1,330 44 24_	۶۰۰۶ ۶ قد 44	31 24	5	493 4
Violing		-1			~2]	252	164					1 3
Corn ning. Cride pet of um is unat gas extraction ing in tarrying once it is of	, 3	•;	3	20	229	239	12	214	8.	23	31	
Lansitur on	-		1	A.	333	53.	18"	354 4 509	2 5 18	18 586	325	155
Manufacturing		2"	271	96 0	2 922	2,554	2 176	603	2720	95	45	
Dareh! goo.	2 -7-	- 1	6	113	-14-	413	8	.1	6		1	4
Togans Save III. panns nills and nill vok Issee III. panns nills and nill vok Issee III. panns nills and nill vok Issee III. panns nills and nill vok	-4°7	ż	3	32	2C	85 1	20	.24 1.7 90	65 34	14	2 9	
Tyrritare ar 1 by ures	227		4	1	3.7 12	-8 3	*0	90	41	16		
tipes and giass ordue s Stem and east produc's	12.	,		3	23	72	8	32		6 5	6	
Primary from Langue and interestrates				1	3	22 8 8	3	4	1		3.11	
Pat c. tea or a adustree me not spe. me al) .	422	1		20	82	9C	65 33	95 45	28 23	16 2	3 2	. :
Mathematical except the trical	226		1	1.5	€3 14	7	10	17	7 4		3	
ofator rene and more very ke equipment	2				7	5	1	6				
the cancers every traversal and surplies both the mark via eq. prient and surplies which relieves and miles with equipment at critical and at a slip into boat harding and repairing. Randal and large transportative equipment better durch poods.	- 1				24	35	11	27	2>	4	2	
) the during the campoon in equipment	3-1	4	4	q	54	23	27	75	,2	19	_	1
\ indable_progs -	4 547	2.	5. 4	% <u>-1</u> 2∪	5 '95	2 230	1,802	3,867 وي	2,2	488	278	-1
Meat produce:	.60	3;	.19 _32	-9	74	62	6+	92 130	98	2_	1.0	
Other food in tustros	1 733	1 1	_32 2.1	2	785 59	58	453	1,000	646 169	14/	18	2
ting mil.	261		3	45	28	20 20 11	22 6d	91 18:	48 140	16	18	
to ting mil- lar bread and fabric mills (other extremall products	78			9	13	11	1	25	-8		3	
	3 695	2	37	1,22	36.7 3⊸3	237	492 246	± 106 408	527	20	67	1
Pager and allied products. The ray rule, hing and allied meastrics (homeiss and allied products	1 -83	2	23	84	23 180	1'	119	262 179	16b	25 49 15	37	1
	977		13	74	26.2	20.	133	- 4/2	81.	18	1	
Puber vol.cis For wear, extert subcr	€1 15	i		1	18	10	0		6	1 1	1	
Lat (1 and leather products except too wear	11		6		19	18	1 24	39	1 22	1 3	2	1
Not sp valit 12 manufacturing and astrice	5 CG		35	Ro	2 343	1,22/	959	1,776			137	. 5
T ansport communication & o.bs public unbines P the d- and culva express **-100	769	2	- 3,	8	32		97	204	_73	38	39	
- TC russy, and hus line-	522		5	- 45	80 109	110 79 54	73	141	63	16	0	
Flucking a ring and warehousing. Water cranspolistor	901		5	51	200	122	86	199	_ = = = = =	31	26	1
Air tra ports ich	215		13	8 22	71.	76	57	28 93	1 1	16	1 9	
	1,178	1	33	650 12o	1 700	776 22#	107	18:	408 92	90	32	
Flactry and got white es. Water surple sure large streets, and o her unlittee	1,109	1	-	10	124	12	21	44	30	8	9	
Wrolesa,e and retuil rade	Do 60a	292	1 901	/ 047	8 '406	7 213	6 693					
Where he track bond and darry products s ores and mile retaining	4,944	65	54 214	40× 450	1,030	797	1,171	2 /57	676	140	81 252	4
Aspan and during 1 not are a store and and recoming	9,154	51	01 99	1 004	1,776	1-2	⊥.100	2.623	721	485	322	1.0
Furniture hom . urnishnigs and equipment stores	/,483 454	4	99 17 13	263 10,	235	420 227	430 176	1,263	938	256	100	1
Vi for "placers and accessories retailing Casolin service state as	939	1	13	9	247 48	15_		221	7	17	13	
	2 4-3 16,44	17	647	28C 1,024	2,643	326	3.0 230 2,2,4	*27	306	71	27	1 :
Drus store. La ing na innaing places dardwin fami inplement & bidg ma eras reta ing. All other retail trade	/ 51	3	10	72	227	147	11.3	4,120 259	146	54.	18	10
	4 /12 8 ±73	13	100	301 945	626 2 032	*29	727	1,177	R28	1		
Finance insurance and real estate. Banking and other filanos.	3,534	1	34	940	2 032	1,134	724	1,543				
Insurance and real estate	4 C39	- 5	40	406	978	370		941				
Business and "opa.r services	1 822	2	10	26	371	278	219	414				
Autom shale repair services and garages	1 284	2	9	29 11	29 45	204	135		170	3		
Miscellaneous repair services	256	1 1		10	32	32	40	78	2	3		
Personal strates	€,376	449	1,297	2 089	6 26.	6,043	7 143	15,98	1_,68	3 299	2 084	_ 4"
P ste horscholds . Hote s a m lodging pla co	43 93-	431	1 114	1,547	4 364	4,733	5,148 366	11,951	9 224	2 -69	1 613	1 14
Leundering cleaning and dyeing services All other personal se vices.	6,285	9	127	204	90*	43± 865	82c 773	1,816	96	220	114) .
	4 645 2 369	26	19	10	528 40a	51.4 292			1	5 258	173	10
Estertunment and recreation services	42,984	44					-	-	-	-	56	
Professional and related services.		3	122	1,065	6,04,	> 423	4,910					
Educa sonal services government	1,,038 1º 1.8	20	122 3r 28	.7.	3,138 2 42± 792	2,14.	1,683 2 291 562	3,400 5,98	3,73	1 114	464	2
Edura onal services government Educa onal services private Median, re, neus and membership organizations - Legal ong neering and misc professional services.	5,063	5	28	138	792	63 ² 273	562 210	1 23.	86	311	220	2
Legal ang neer ng _nd misc professional services_	1 440		11 9	132	320	252	157	309				
Public administration	8,807	2	18	1/2	1,534	1,361	1,06			2 41	20.	
Postal service. Federal public administration State and local public administration	303		5	9	£31	65 765	107	241	2.5	9:	45	
	4,067	5	13	243	848	765 331	440	993	, n	12:		
Industry not reported.	4 535	137	151	27_	502	520	472	934	78.	2.0	56	1

Table 82.—AGE OF EMPLOYED PERSONS, BY INDUSTRY AND SEX, FOR THE STATE AND FOR STANDARD METROPOLITAN AREAS OF 250,000 OR MORE: 1950—Con.

Area, industry, and sex	Total, 14 years old and over	14 and 15 years	16 and 17 years	18 and 19 years	20 to 24 years	25 to 29 years	30 to 34 years	35 to 44 years	45 to 54 years	55 to 59 years	60 to 64 years	65 and over
THE STATE												
Female, employed	[illegible]	1 [illegible]	3,2[illegible]	12,[illegible]	3[illegible]	2[illegible]	[illegible] 458	[illegible]7,893	38,777	10,78[illegible]	6,320	4,504
Agriculture, forestry, and fisheries	[illegible]	[illegible]	[illegible]	[illegible]	1 [illegible]	1 [illegible]	[illegible] 568	3,[illegible]	2,[illegible]	956	571	[illegible]
Agriculture	[illegible]	[illegible]	[illegible]72	[illegible]02	1 [illegible]	1 [illegible]	[illegible]	[illegible],330	2,[illegible]	9[illegible]	[illegible]16	493
Forestry and fisheries	[illegible]	[illegible]		[illegible]	[illegible]	25	25	44	[illegible]3	11	5	4
Mining	[illegible]	[illegible]	[illegible]	[illegible]	[illegible]	252	164	24[illegible]	34	24	9	4
Coal mining	[illegible]					1	1					1
Crude petroleum and natural gas extraction	[illegible]		3	[illegible]	[illegible]	239	[illegible]	214	8[illegible]	23	[illegible]	3
Mining and quarrying, except fuel	[illegible]	4			[illegible]	2	12	27	[illegible]	1	1	
Construction	[illegible]	[illegible]	1	[illegible]	333	23[illegible]	18[illegible]	[illegible]64	228	58	31	23
Manufacturing	[illegible]	2[illegible]	2[illegible]1	[illegible]	2 922	2,[illegible]	2 1[illegible]6	4 509	2 5[illegible]8	586	325	155
Durable goods	2 [illegible]	[illegible]	6	11[illegible]	[illegible]	410	[illegible]10	60[illegible]	[illegible]	95	[illegible]	42
Logging	[illegible]	[illegible]		[illegible]	[illegible]	3	8	[illegible]1	6		1	2
Sawmills, planing mills, and millwork	[illegible]	2	3	33	21	85	[illegible]	24	6[illegible]	[illegible]4	[illegible]1	7
Miscellaneous wood products	227				20	4[illegible]	[illegible]	[illegible]7	34		2	[illegible]
Furniture and fixtures	2[illegible]		4	[illegible]	[illegible]	[illegible]8	[illegible]0	80	41	16	9	3
Glass and glass products	[illegible]			4	12	3	3	7	[illegible]			1
Stone and clay products	12[illegible]			[illegible]	23	22	8	32	[illegible]	6	6	1
Primary iron and steel industries	[illegible]			1	8	8	3	8	4	5		
Primary nonferrous industries	[illegible]9			2	[illegible]	8	[illegible]	4				
Fabricated metal ind. (incl. not spec. metal)	422			20	82	[illegible]	65	95	[illegible]8	16	3	[illegible]
Machinery, except electrical	226		3	[illegible]	[illegible]	36	30	45	23	2	2	6
Electrical machinery, equipment, and supplies	[illegible]		1	[illegible]	14	7	[illegible]0	17	7	2	3	1
Motor vehicles and motor vehicle equipment	2[illegible]				[illegible]	5	4	8	4	1		
Aircraft and parts	[illegible]						1	[illegible]				
Ship and boat building and repairing	[illegible]				24	35	11	27	25	4	2	
Railroad and misc. transportation equipment	[illegible]			[illegible]	[illegible]	1	1	2	1			
Other durable goods	[illegible]	[illegible]	4	[illegible]	29	23	27	75	[illegible]2	19	[illegible]	1[illegible]
Nondurable goods	[illegible]4 5[illegible]7	2[illegible]	2[illegible]9	[illegible]	2 [illegible]82	2 23[illegible]	1,802	[illegible],867	2,[illegible]2	488	278	[illegible]19
Meat products	[illegible]		6	20	5[illegible]	4[illegible]	47	92	33	[illegible]	3	3
Bakery products	[illegible]60	3	19	[illegible]9	74	82	64	130	98	2[illegible]	1[illegible]	5
Other food industries	1 [illegible]33	[illegible]	[illegible]32	2[illegible]	[illegible]	[illegible]	45[illegible]	1,000	646	14[illegible]	[illegible]9	22
Tobacco manufactures	[illegible]		21	[illegible]	59	58	40	188	169	37	18	10
Knitting mills	26[illegible]		3	[illegible]	28	2[illegible]	22	91	48	16	[illegible]	[illegible]
Yarn, thread, and fabric mills	5[illegible]			9	4[illegible]	[illegible]0	66	18[illegible]	140	29	[illegible]8	8
Other textile mill products	[illegible]8			1	13	11	[illegible]	25	[illegible]8	[illegible]	3	
Apparel and other fabricated textile products	3 [illegible]95	[illegible]	3[illegible]	188	[illegible]	[illegible]	492	1 106	577	[illegible]	67	[illegible]
Paper and allied products	1 969	2	12	8[illegible]	[illegible]	297	246	408	179	25	[illegible]	6
Printing, publishing, and allied industries	1 [illegible]83	[illegible]	23	8[illegible]	23	1[illegible]	119	262	166	49	3[illegible]	28
Chemicals and allied products	[illegible]87		13	4	180	[illegible]48	[illegible]07	179	[illegible]9	15	11	8
Petroleum and coal products	977		1	34	26[illegible]	2[illegible]	133	[illegible]2	81	[illegible]8	[illegible]	
Rubber products	6[illegible]				18	10	6	15	6	1	1	
Footwear, except rubber	15			1	2	2		[illegible]		1		
Leather and leather products, except footwear	1[illegible]				3	2	1	[illegible]	1	1		
Not specified manufacturing industries	[illegible]4[illegible]		6	[illegible]	19	18	24	39	22	3	2	1
Transportation, communication, & other public utilities	5 [illegible]66	[illegible]	[illegible]5	[illegible]	2 343	1,[illegible]	959	1,776	1,[illegible]32	23[illegible]	137	52
Railroads and railway express service	769	2	[illegible]	8	38	11[illegible]	97	204	[illegible]73	38	39	8
Street railways and bus lines	522		5	45	80	78	73	14[illegible]	94	16	[illegible]	2
Trucking service and warehousing	44[illegible]	1	[illegible]	4[illegible]	109	54	46	108	63	12	3	8
Water transportation	[illegible]		3	51	200	122	86	199	[illegible]0	31	26	12
Air transportation	215			8	71	73	22	28	8	2	1	1
Other transportation	4[illegible]		13	22	87	[illegible]6	57	93	[illegible]1	16	9	4
Telecommunications	[illegible]25	1	33	650	1 [illegible]60	[illegible]76	450	777	408	90	32	8
Electric and gas utilities	1,1[illegible]8		6	12[illegible]	404	22[illegible]	107	18[illegible]	9[illegible]	20	1[illegible]	4
Water supply, sanitary services, and other utilities	[illegible]99	1	[illegible]	1[illegible]	44	[illegible]	21	4[illegible]	3[illegible]	8	9	5
Wholesale and retail trade	[illegible]6 60[illegible]	29[illegible]	1 96[illegible]	[illegible] 0[illegible]7	8 [illegible]06	7 21[illegible]	6 69[illegible]	14 [illegible]34	8 808	2,241	1,206	79[illegible]
Wholesale trade	4,944	4	54	40[illegible]	1,030	797	566	[illegible] 093	676	[illegible]40	81	48
Food and dairy products stores and milk retailing	9,[illegible]54	65	274	450	[illegible]	[illegible]	1,171	2 [illegible]57	[illegible]	[illegible]	252	[illegible]01
General merchandise and five and ten cent stores	1[illegible]	5[illegible]	[illegible]	1 0[illegible]	[illegible]	[illegible]	[illegible],100	2,623	[illegible]	485	322	188
Apparel and accessories stores	[illegible],483		99	263	545	420	430	1,263	938	256	100	102
Furniture, home furnishings, and equipment stores	464	4	1[illegible]	10[illegible]	235	277	176	[illegible]97	[illegible]01	53	2[illegible]	19
Motor vehicles and accessories retailing	939	1	10	9	247	15[illegible]	[illegible]09	221	7[illegible]	1[illegible]	13	2
Gasoline service stations	131	2	4	10	48	54	5[illegible]	97	4[illegible]	9	8	2
Drug stores	2 4[illegible]	17	1[illegible]	280	[illegible]92	326	23[illegible]	[illegible]27	[illegible]08	7[illegible]	27	[illegible]3
Eating and drinking places	16,[illegible]44	1[illegible]	64[illegible]	1,024	2,643	2 48[illegible]	2,2[illegible]4	4,120	2,1[illegible]7	43[illegible]	[illegible]98	9[illegible]
Hardware, farm implement, & bldg. material retailing	[illegible]51	3	10	78	227	147	11[illegible]	259	146	[illegible]4	18	16
All other retail trade	4 [illegible]12	13	100	301	626	[illegible]29	[illegible]27	1,177	828	240	[illegible]	104
Finance, insurance, and real estate	8 [illegible]73	[illegible]	[illegible]9	9[illegible]5	2 032	1,134	722	[illegible],543	[illegible],1[illegible]	272	207	147
Banking and other finance	3,534	1	34	[illegible]89	[illegible] 0[illegible]4	50[illegible]	2[illegible]5	[illegible]96	360	63	53	2[illegible]
Insurance and real estate	4 639	[illegible]	4[illegible]	4[illegible]6	978	37[illegible]	42[illegible]	947	46	209	15[illegible]	122
Business and repair services	1 822	2	10	[illegible]	371	278	21[illegible]	414	268	54	35	2[illegible]
Business services	1 286		9	28	29	204	138	258	[illegible]76	3[illegible]	23	1[illegible]
Automobile repair services and garages	[illegible]80	2	[illegible]	11	45	42	[illegible]8	78	49	8	[illegible]	
Miscellaneous repair services	256			10	32	32	40	78	43	9	6	6
Personal services	[illegible]8,376	449	1,297	2 089	6 26[illegible]	6,[illegible]43	7 1[illegible]3	15,98[illegible]	1[illegible],682	[illegible] 299	2 084	[illegible] 4[illegible]6
Private households	43 93[illegible]	431	1 114	1,[illegible]47	4 36[illegible]	4,733	5,148	11,951	9 224	2 [illegible]69	1 613	1 143
Hotels and lodging places	[illegible]12	4	3[illegible]	128	40[illegible]	4[illegible]	366	[illegible]33	[illegible]	2[illegible]	18[illegible]	165
Laundering, cleaning, and dyeing services	6,2[illegible]3	9	12[illegible]	[illegible]04	9[illegible]	865	820	[illegible],8[illegible]	969	220	114	[illegible]
All other personal services	4 645	[illegible]	19	1[illegible]0	528	614	773	[illegible] 281	[illegible]86	258	171	100
Entertainment and recreation services	2 369	28	9[illegible]	[illegible]63	40[illegible]	292	252	528	4[illegible]0	1[illegible]4	56	33
Professional and related services	42,984	44	2[illegible]	1 [illegible]8[illegible]	6,[illegible]	[illegible] 423	4,910	11 455	7,62[illegible]	2 308	1 2[illegible]0	976
Medical and other health services	1[illegible],038	3	122	1,065	3,138	2,1[illegible]	1,681	3,400	2 [illegible]91	[illegible]47	349	240
Educational services, government	1[illegible] 1[illegible]8	20	[illegible]	[illegible]	2 42[illegible]	2,074	2 291	5,98[illegible]	3,[illegible]	[illegible] 114	464	287
Educational services, private	5,063	[illegible]	28	138	[illegible]92	63[illegible]	562	1 23[illegible]	86[illegible]	317	220	266
Welfare, religious, and membership organizations	2 325	5	11	80	[illegible]	273	219	531	465	182	129	[illegible]
Legal, engineering, and misc. professional services	1 440		9	132	320	232	197	309	[illegible]0	46	28	2[illegible]
Public administration	8,807	2	18	[illegible]2	1,534	1,36[illegible]	[illegible],0[illegible]	2 [illegible]78	1,[illegible]82	418	20[illegible]	[illegible]03
Postal service	90[illegible]			9	[illegible]5	65	137	241	2[illegible]3	93	48	32
Federal public administration	[illegible],8[illegible]		5	93	[illegible]1	765	549	993	[illegible]	125	47	12
State and local public administration	4,067	2	13	24[illegible]	848	[illegible]31	4[illegible]0	944	[illegible]12	20[illegible]	108	59
Industry not reported	4 [illegible]35	137	151	27[illegible]	602	520	472	934	78[illegible]	2[illegible]4	56	21[illegible]

Table 82.—AGE OF EMPLOYED PERSONS BY INDUSTRY AND SEX, FOR THE STATE AND FOR STANDARD METROPOLITAN AREAS OF 250,000 OR MORE: 1950—Con.

Area, industry, and sex	Total, 14 years old and over	14 and 15 years	16 and 17 years	18 and 19 years	20 to 24 years	25 to 29 years	30 to 34 years	35 to 44 years	45 to 54 years	55 to 59 years	60 to 64 years	65 and over
NEW ORLEANS												
Female, employed	[illegible]	125	1,124	4,134	12,180	10,038	9,016	20,621	14,367	4,015	2,504	1,728
Agriculture, forestry, and fisheries	82	7	2	4	19	22	19	41	41	18	9	5
Agriculture	156	2	2	4	15	16	13	37	36	17	9	5
Forestry and fisheries	21				4	6	6	4	3	1		
Mining	171		1	5	35	54	28	31	11	5		1
Coal mining	2											1
Crude petroleum and natural gas extraction	154		–	2	3	52	27	28	8	5		
Mining and quarrying, except fuel	15				4	–	1	3	3		.	
Construction	599	5	2	20	105	96	77	149	98	23	14	7
Manufacturing	[illegible]	7	130	139	1,406	1,351	1,141	2,696	1,679	393	220	104
Durable goods	1,268	1	1	57	216	215	162	304	203	61	22	21
Logging	3			1				1	1			
Sawmills, planing mills, and mill work	109			8	2	20	11	25	15	5	1	3
Miscellaneous wood products	106	.		1	14	23	14	30	19	3	1	1
Furniture and fixtures	15		2	1	17	19	28	42	30	11	7	3
Glass and glass products	14				5		2	2	4			1
Stone and clay products	67			3	17	14	2	18	8	2	3	
Primary iron and steel industries	18			1	5	3	1	6		2		
Primary nonferrous industries	4			2		1	1					
Fabricated metal industries (incl. not spec. metal)	556			12	64	67	57	80	51	19	1	3
Machinery, except electrical	114		1	8	28	17	15	21	19	1	1	3
Electrical machinery, equipment, and supplies	42		1	2	11	6	6	10	3	1	2	
Motor vehicles and motor vehicle equipment	16				2	3	1	7	2	1		
Aircraft and parts												
Ship and boat building and repairing	154			4	19	20	9	24	23	4	2	
Railroad and misc. transportation equipment	6			3	–		1	1				
All other durable goods	144	1	2	5	17	13	14	37	28	16	4	7
Nondurable goods	8,216	8	121	380	1,175	1,128	961	2,367	1,462	355	196	83
Meat products	192		3	13	25	29	29	59	26	4	2	2
Bakery products	290		11	24	33	34	30	69	59	18	9	3
Other food industries	1,909	5	41	81	265	166	229	523	343	81	57	15
Tobacco manufactures	550		17	27	37	49	37	172	156	34	14	11
Knitting mills	249		7	15	24	22	22	86	48	16	5	1
Yarn, thread, and fabric mills	546			9	43	49	67	178	145	29	18	8
Other textile mill products	56			1	10	9	3	18	13	2		
Apparel and other fabricated textile products	3,125	5	22	137	482	472	416	946	465	103	59	18
Paper and allied products	324		4	1	66	57	36	81	51	11	2	5
Printing, publishing, and allied industries	521		8	37	99	64	42	122	93	21	20	15
Chemicals and allied products	225		1	17	32	32	28	62	30	6	7	6
Petroleum and coal products	181		–	5	49	35	20	34	28	7	2	
Rubber products	27			2	7	4	1	6	2	1	1	
Footwear, except rubber	11			1		2	.	4	3	1		
Leather and leather products, except footwear	13				3	1	1	7		1		
Not specified manufacturing industries	89		3	4	15	8	18	25	14	2	2	
Transportation, communication, & other public utilities	4,753	1	27	184	1,330	758	483	883	641	132	91	28
Railroads and railway express service	422				42	72	53	11	99	21	26	5
Street railways and bus lines	182		3	2	45	39	25	31	22	5	3	
Trucking service and warehousing	214			1	50	30	18	55	35	7	3	5
Water transportation	852		2	46	193	112	81	191	141	29	26	11
Air transportation	175		1	7	55	67	16	19	7	2	1	
All other transportation	198		5	15	38	28	25	41	32	9	6	1
Telecommunications	2,267	1	10	264	759	343	221	354	257	42	13	3
Electric and gas utilities	383		1	30	133	75	34	56	37	11	6	
Water supply, sanitary services, and other utilities	80			4	15	12	10	12	11	6	7	3
Wholesale and retail trade	22,415	49	629	1,458	3,305	2,979	2,580	5,145	3,703	986	595	386
Wholesale trade	3,237	2	28	256	696	562	545	707	453	104	56	10
Food and dairy products stores, and milk retailing	2,060	14	86	118	258	305	154	899	582	107	97	80
General merchandise and five and ten cent stores	5,474	9	307	506	802	562	505	1,276	925	274	195	113
Apparel and accessories stores	1,960	2	32	107	228	185	187	541	418	127	82	51
Furniture, home furnishings, and equipment stores	532		11	47	43	84	63	148	71	20	9	6
Motor vehicles and accessories retailing	311		4	25	72	50	35	87	30	4	8	
Gasoline service stations	56		1	2	9	12	–	13	9	1	1	1
Drug stores	987	3	10	81	162	136	133	251	149	36	13	13
Eating and drinking places	4,915	14	99	200	726	854	701	1,322	693	145	60	41
Hardware, farm implement, & bldg. material retailing	324	1	4	13	33	50	37	95	58	14	6	6
All other retail trade	1,629	4	27	103	206	179	180	406	315	94	70	45
Finance, insurance, and real estate	4,282	2	49	455	1,012	588	355	853	617	151	117	83
Banking and other finance	1,689		26	205	458	262	145	316	208	28	37	14
Insurance and real estate	2,593	2	23	250	554	326	220	537	409	123	80	69
Business and repair services	921		6	71	193	144	98	208	144	28	17	12
Business services	758		6	64	168	121	75	165	114	23	14	10
Automobile repair services and garages	77			3	13	12	11	20	13	3	2	
Miscellaneous repair services	86			4	12	11	12	25	17	2	1	2
Personal services	17,51[illegible]	42	153	317	1,340	1,937	2,099	5,164	4,015	1,142	786	5[illegible]3
Private households	12,14[illegible]	38	111	187	779	1,236	1,376	3,623	3,021	842	569	360
Hotels and lodging places	1,379	2	8	37	149	180	162	433	310	118	[illegible]	83
Laundering, cleaning, and dyeing services	2,096	2	27	65	260	297	282	608	376	87	78	34
All other personal services	1,690		9	31	152	224	279	494	308	95	62	36
Entertainment and recreation services	1,112	4	20	60	193	142	137	260	203	44	31	17
Professional and related services	14,525	4	82	785	2,542	1,887	1,497	3,475	2,375	874	516	488
Medical and other health services	7,260	2	54	618	1,608	1,058	774	1,324	1,014	532	167	149
Educational services, government	3,167	2	9	34	293	292	375	1,002	653	262	141	104
Educational services, private	2,370		9	64	393	303	245	552	405	153	119	129
Welfare, religious, and membership organizations	1,071		3	23	167	114	96	241	214	104	73	86
Legal, engineering, and misc. professional services	657		7	46	131	120	49	156	89	23	16	20
Public administration	3,378		10	80	561	543	399	884	628	160	[illegible]	34
Postal service	60				5	6	14	36	19	8	5	3
Federal public administration	2,221		4	33	264	416	283	590	404	80	5	10
State and local public administration	1,061		6	47	192	121	102	258	205	60	43	21
Industry not reported	1,032	9	10	51	138	137	103	232	212	54	29	50

Table 83.—RACE AND CLASS OF WORKER OF EMPLOYED PERSONS, BY INDUSTRY AND SEX, FOR THE STATE AND FOR STANDARD METROPOLITAN AREAS OF 100,000 OR MORE: 1950

Area and industry	Male, 14 years old and over: Total	Male: Race: White	Male: Race: Negro	Male: Race: Other races	Male: Class of worker: Private wage & salary workers	Male: Class of worker: Government workers	Male: Class of worker: Self-employed workers	Male: Class of worker: Unpaid family wkrs.	Female, 14 years old and over: Total	Female: Race: White	Female: Race: Negro	Female: Race: Other races	Female: Class of worker: Private wage & salary workers	Female: Class of worker: Government workers	Female: Class of worker: Self-employed workers	Female: Class of worker: Unpaid family wkrs.
THE STATE																
Employed	646,782	461,713	184,061	1,008	475,952	55,913	150,753	14,164	229,175	140,420	88,559	146	167,338	37,932	16 903	9,952
Agriculture, forestry, and fisheries	144,480	81,360	62,599	521	38,641	1,057	91,294	13,438	15 950	4,652	11,286	12	5 942	84	2,981	6,943
Agriculture	135,665	73,591	61,980	94	35,231	504	86,625	13,305	15,740	4,531	11,201	8	5,828	33	2,944	6,935
Forestry and fisheries	8,815	7,769	619	427	3,460	553	4,669	133	210	121	85	4	114	51	37	8
Mining	23,031	22,225	788	18	22,399	30	600	2	1,170	1,153	17		1,156	2	12	
Coal mining	62	49	13		50	4	7	1	4	3	1		3		1	
Crude petroleum and natural gas extraction	20,776	20,366	392	18	20,212	24	539	1	1,074	1,062	12		1,063	1	10	
Mining and quarrying, except fuel	2,193	1,810	383		2,137	2	54		92	88	4		90	1	1	
Construction	63,377	46,655	16,691	31	46,978	8,366	7,945	88	1,575	1,389	185	1	1,022	426	94	33
Manufacturing	115,358	81 188	34,090	80	111,167	237	3,889	65	17,091	13,156	3,905	30	16,713	37	274	67
Durable goods	46,600	27,938	18,628	34	44,098	101	2,357	44	2,404	1,971	430	3	2,290	8	87	19
Logging	5,775	2,974	2,792	9	5,213	5	546	11	49	30	19		47	1	1	
Sawmills, planing mills, and mill work	20,348	9,505	10,827	16	19,616	5	706	21	476	350	126		464		8	4
Miscellaneous wood products	1,843	992	850	1	1,801		40	2	227	142	85		227			
Furniture and fixtures	1,544	1,032	512		1,392	2	150		296	189	106	1	279	1	12	4
Glass and glass products	923	797	126		903	1	19		34	32	2		33		1	
Stone and clay products	2,445	1,293	1,152		2,331	2	112		122	110	12		111		11	
Primary iron and steel industries	1,038	683	355		1,001	2	35		37	32	5		36		1	
Primary nonferrous industries	490	278	212		478	1	10	1	19	18	1		19			
Fabricated metal ind. (incl. not spec. metal)	3,151	2,726	425		2,973	16	162		422	396	26		415		5	2
Machinery, except electrical	2,996	2,692	303	1	2,759	4	231	2	226	219	7		215		6	5
Electrical machinery, equip., and supplies	393	357	36		364		27	2	64	56	8		60	1	1	2
Motor vehicles & motor vehicle equipment	430	387	43		417	1	12		27	25	2		20		7	
Aircraft and parts	29	27	2		25	2	2		2	2			1		1	
Ship and boat building and repairing	3,992	3,206	780	6	3,775	50	163	4	133	129	4		129	1	3	
Railroad & misc. transportation equipment	68	61	7		66	1	1		9	7	2		8		1	
All other durable goods	1,135	928	206	1	984	9	141	1	251	234	25	2	220	4	35	2
Nondurable goods	68,164	52,778	15,340	46	66,514	135	1,495	20	14 547	11,077	3,443	27	14,287	29	184	47
Meat products	1,966	1 413	553		1,879	13	74		310	272	38		306		4	
Bakery products	3,072	2,408	662	2	2,934	8	128	2	560	444	116		528		21	11
Other food industries	16,125	11,072	5,020	33	15,578	17	520	10	3,833	2,470	1,345	18	3,761	9	48	15
Tobacco manufactures	142	115	27		138		4		647	512	135		646		1	
Knitting mills	127	122	5		116	7	-		260	192	68		254	3	3	
Yarn, thread, and fabric mills	770	617	153		763	1	6		557	441	116		552		4	1
Other textile mill products	216	144	71	1	185	1	29	1	78	39	38	1	75		3	
Apparel & other fabricated textile products	1,276	906	370		1,178	2	96		3,695	2,329	1,359	7	3,668	3	22	2
Paper and allied products	12,833	9,752	3,079	2	12,783		49		1,569	1,487	82		1,563	1	4	1
Printing, publishing, and allied industries	5,326	4,879	447		4,935	6	384	1	1,183	1,151	32		1,097	7	62	17
Chemicals and allied products	10,387	7,933	2,448	6	10,227	12	114	4	787	714	73		776	3	8	
Petroleum and coal products	15,140	12,825	2,313	2	15,056	16	67	1	977	950	26	1	974	2	1	
Rubber products	676	509	167		651	22	3		60	55	5		58	1	1	
Footwear, except rubber	44	35	9		38		6		15	10	5		14		1	
Leather & leather products, exc. footwear	64	48	16		53		11		16	11	5		15		1	
Not specified manufacturing industries	594	472	122		555		37	1	140	108	32		136		3	1
Transport., commun., & other public util.	66,024	48,066	17,828	110	56,558	6,648	2,795	23	9,667	9,041	624	2	9,134	421	95	17
Railroads and railway express service	17,512	11,310	6,198	4	17,267	231	13	1	769	590	179		759	10		
Street railways and bus lines	4,850	4,360	490		3,122	1,592	135	1	522	452	70		354	152	12	4
Trucking service and warehousing	7,931	4,874	3,053	4	6,382	74	1,465	10	448	376	72		399	6	35	8
Water transportation	14,112	9,146	4,868	98	13,070	820	218	4	880	787	93		815	54	11	
Air transportation	1,033	866	166	1	914	96	23		215	202	13		207	7	1	
All other transportation	5,322	4,389	933		4,380	75	864	3	431	365	66		391	9	26	5
Telecommunications	3,351	3,081	270		3,302	33	14	2	5,025	4,928	95	2	4,987	31	7	
Electric and gas utilities	7,929	6,932	995	2	7,198	700	30	1	1,178	1,154	24		1,115	60	3	
Water supply, sanitary services, & other util.	3,984	3,128	855	1	923	3,027	33	1	199	187	12		107	92		
Wholesale and retail trade	113,547	90,150	23,292	105	85,785	228	27,123	411	56,606	45,595	10,986	25	46,379	243	7,619	2,365
Wholesale trade	26,927	21,791	5,123	13	23,766	83	3,066	12	4,944	4,571	370	3	4,741	13	137	53
Food & dairy prod. stores, & milk retailing	21,324	17,546	3,761	17	12,299	53	8,753	219	9,154	7,925	1,225	4	7,634	12	3,282	1,226
General merchandise & five & ten cent stores	5,922	5,116	799	7	4,695	15	1,194	18	11,039	10,459	577	3	10,411	24	472	132
Apparel and accessories stores	3,048	2,618	429	1	2,349	1	694	4	4,483	3,969	514		3,997		433	53
Furniture, home furnishings, & equip. stores	5,666	4,754	909	3	4,578	5	1,075	8	1,464	1,338	126		1,294		122	48
Motor vehicles and accessories retailing	8,234	7,223	1,010	1	7,095	4	1,128	7	939	924	15		867		42	30
Gasoline service stations	7,361	5,198	2,161	2	5,536	13	1,785	27	331	301	30		180	1	88	62
Drug stores	3,067	2,346	721		2,345	3	713	6	2,445	2,137	306	2	2,230	2	155	58
Eating and drinking places	12,956	8,679	4,232	45	8,760	30	4,099	67	16,144	8 749	7,384	11	13,544	174	1,916	510
Hardware, farm implem't, & bldg. mater'l ret.	8,438	6,233	2,203	2	7,119	1	1,309	9	1,051	1,009	41	1	913	3	95	40
All other retail trade	10,604	8,646	1,944	14	7,243	20	3,307	34	4,612	4,213	398	1	3,568	14	877	153
Finance, insurance, and real estate	13,643	11,737	1,904	2	10,974	774	1,890	5	8,173	7,236	936	1	7,386	435	326	26
Banking and other finance	4,603	4,230	372	1	3,765	451	386	1	3,534	3,451	83		3,158	348	24	4
Insurance and real estate	9,040	7,507	1,532	1	7,239	323	1,504	4	4,639	3,785	853	1	4,228	87	302	22
Business and repair services	18,328	15,334	2,988	6	12,9 2	143	5,241	32	1,822	1,732	89	1	1,509	20	236	57
Business services	3,775	3,564	211		2,627	49	1,099		1,286	1,254	32		1,118	18	147	3
Automobile repair services and garages	9,484	7,279	2,203	2	7,346	66	2,051	21	280	241	38	1	227	2	30	21
Miscellaneous repair services	5,069	4,491	574	4	2,939	28	2,091	11	256	237	19		164		59	33
Personal services	19,468	9,239	10,170	59	15,117	53	4,254	44	58,376	10,546	47,794	36	54,063	65	4,019	229
Private households	5,631	855	4,771	5	5,359		245	27	43,834	3,490	40,324	20	43,001		788	45
Hotels and lodging places	3,092	1,839	1,253		2,712	27	345	8	3,612	1,742	1,869	1	3,114	32	433	33
Laundering, cleaning, and dyeing services	5,180	2,773	2,356	51	4,040	16	1,118	6	6,285	2,403	3,869	13	5,802	28	350	105
All other personal services	5,565	3,772	1,790	3	3,006	10	2,546	3	4,645	2,911	1,732	2	2,146	5	2,448	46
Entertainment and recreation services	6,697	5,221	1,450	21	5,722	190	767	13	2,369	2,004	363	2	2,112	77	163	17
Professional and related services	29,030	22,637	6,367	26	11,221	12,928	4,855	26	42,984	32,425	10,534	25	17,529	24,280	1,019	156
Medical and other health services	8,659	6,896	1,754	9	2,512	3,636	2,509	2	15,038	12,096	2,924	18	9,643	4,964	394	37
Educational services, government	9,103	6,895	2 203	5		9,103			19,118	13,234	5,880	4		19,118		
Educational services, private	3,110	2,284	821	5	2,955		148	7	5,063	3,852	1,210	1	4,518		475	70
Welfare, religious, & membership organiz'ns	4,864	3,331	1,530	3	4,463	96	289	16	2,325	1,846	477	2	2,081	174	33	37
Legal, engineering, & misc. professional serv.	3,294	3,231	59	4	1,291	93	1,909	1	1,440	1,397	43		1,287	24	117	12
Public administration	24,553	21,792	2,746	15		24,553			8,807	8,497	307	3		8,807		
Postal service	4,630	3,584	1,043	3		4,630			903	844	58	1		903		
Federal public administration	7,254	6,476	766	12		7,254			3,837	3,755	82			3,837		
State and local public administration	12,669	11,732	937			12,669			4,067	3,898	167	2		4,067		
Industry not reported	9,251	6,089	3,148	14	8,428	706	100	17	4,535	2,994	1,533	8	4,393	35	65	42

Table 83.—RACE AND CLASS OF WORKER OF EMPLOYED PERSONS, BY INDUSTRY AND SEX, FOR THE STATE AND FOR STANDARD METROPOLITAN AREAS OF 100,000 OR MORE: 1950—Con.

Area and industry	Male, 14 years old and over: Total	Male: Race: White	Male: Race: Negro	Male: Race: Other races	Male: Class of worker: Private wage & salary workers	Male: Class of worker: Government workers	Male: Class of worker: Self-employed workers	Male: Class of worker: Unpaid family wkrs	Female, 14 years old and over: Total	Female: Race: White	Female: Race: Negro	Female: Race: Other races	Female: Class of worker: Private wage & sal ary workers	Female: Class of worker: Government workers	Female: Class of worker: Self-employed workers	Female: Class of worker: Unpaid family wkrs
[illegible]																
Employed	[illegible]	[illegible]	[illegible]	6	[illegible]	[illegible]	[illegible]	75	[illegible]	10 229	6,760	8	12 312	3 717	797	177
Agriculture, forestry, and fisheries	[illegible]	53[illegible]	[illegible]		476	[illegible]21	659	4[illegible]	161	56	105		66	28	43	24
Agriculture	[illegible]	[illegible]	751		454	107	655	4	150	45	105		66	17	43	24
Forestry and fisheries	[illegible]	20			2	14	4		11	[illegible]				11		
Mining	25[illegible]	2[illegible]	4		24[illegible]		[illegible]		14	14			14			
Coal mining																
Crude petroleum and natural gas extraction	2[illegible]	[illegible]	-		[illegible]99		9		12	12			12			
Mining and quarrying, except fuel	5[illegible]	4[illegible]	-		46		7		2	2			2			
Construction	[illegible]66	[illegible],422	[illegible] 9[illegible]		4 [illegible]	5[illegible]6	[illegible]73	6	340	319	21		149	179	4	6
Manufacturing	[illegible],[illegible]09	1[illegible],1[illegible]3	2,56[illegible]	[illegible]	1[illegible] [illegible]	23	4[illegible]	5	936	861	7[illegible]	1	9[illegible]1	8	14	[illegible]
Durable goods	1 [illegible]	[illegible]	54[illegible]		[illegible]	3	[illegible]	1	100	93	7		94		6	
Logging	3[illegible]	1	29		29		[illegible]									
Sawmills, planing mills, and mill work	4[illegible]9	[illegible]	[illegible]		345		14		12	10	2		12			
Miscellaneous wood products	8	2	6		[illegible]											
Furniture and fixtures	[illegible]	[illegible]	10		25		[illegible]		6	4	2		5		1	
Glass and glass products	[illegible]	[illegible]	[illegible]		[illegible]		1		3	3			2		1	
Stone and clay products	[illegible]	56	90		149		[illegible]		16	14	2		15		1	
Primary iron and steel industries	4[illegible]	31	1[illegible]		4[illegible]		3		3	3			3			
Primary nonferrous industries	325	160	165		324			1	10	10			10			
Fabricated metal ind. (incl. not spec. metal)	279	218	61		262	[illegible]	16		14	14			14			
Machinery, except electrical	98	[illegible]	14		88		10		15	15			14		1	
Electrical machinery, equipment, and supplies	22	20	2		[illegible]		[illegible]		3	3			3			
Motor vehicles & motor vehicle equipment	[illegible]	[illegible]	[illegible]		[illegible]	[illegible]			2	2			2			
Aircraft and parts	[illegible]	6			5		1									
Ship and boat building and repairing	[illegible]	[illegible]	2		4		2		2	2			2			
Railroad & misc. transportation equipment	6	6			6				1	1			1			
All other durable goods	54	48	6		45	[illegible]	8		13	12	1		11		2	
Nondurable goods	[illegible] 331	9 3[illegible]	2,[illegible]4	2	[illegible] 241	25	62	3	830	762	67	-	811	8	8	3
Meat products	[illegible]4	4[illegible]	27		[illegible]5	7	2		4	4			[illegible]			
Bakery products	339	234	105		330		9		71	49	22		69		1	1
Other food industries	4[illegible]	200	184		459		15		69	45	24		66	1	1	1
Tobacco manufactures		[illegible]			1											
Knitting mills	2	2			[illegible]				1	[illegible]			1			
Yarn, thread, and fabric mills	7	6	1		7				1		1		1			
Other textile mill products	[illegible]	[illegible]	[illegible]		4				1		1		1			
Apparel & other fabricated textile products	13	11	2		11		2		5	4	1		3		2	
Paper and allied products	19	13	6		18		1									
Printing, publishing, and allied industries	45[illegible]	41[illegible]	38		435	2	15	[illegible]	118	11[illegible]	[illegible]		108	5	4	1
Chemicals and allied products	3 364	2,[illegible]94	370		3 053	7	[illegible]	1	170	166	4		170			
Petroleum and coal products	6,[illegible]05	[illegible] 4[illegible]9	[illegible] 214	2	6,686	4	14	1	378	366	11	1	376	2		
Rubber products	[illegible]8	108	[illegible]		162	5	1		10	10			10			
Footwear, except rubber	[illegible]	2	1		[illegible]				[illegible]		1		1			
Leather & leather products, exc. footwear	5	[illegible]	[illegible]		5				1		1		1			
Not specified manufacturing industries	2[illegible]	20			19		[illegible]	1	6	6			6			
Transportation, commun., & other public util.	2 788	1,933	854	[illegible]	2 [illegible]12	164	11[illegible]		567	536	31		514	45	[illegible]	2
Railroads and railway express service	688	472	215	1	68[illegible]		1		30	[illegible]	2		30			
Street railways and bus lines	250	180	70		201	37	12		54	50	4		17	37		
Trucking service and warehousing	37[illegible]	15[illegible]	216		30[illegible]		69		26	22	4		23		1	[illegible]
Water transportation	138	92	46		123	13	2		4	[illegible]			3	1		
Air transportation	25	22	3		20	4	1		6	5	1		5	1		
All other transportation	235	154	81		214	1	20		23		14		22			
Telecommunications	279	253	26		278	1			301	295	6		301			
Electric and gas utilities	609	506	103		592	15	2		92	92			89	[illegible]	1	
Water supply, sanitary services, & other util.	191	97	94		92	93	6		31	3[illegible]			2[illegible]	8		
Wholesale and retail trade	[illegible],60[illegible]	5,38[illegible]	2 214	1	6,194	16	1,400	12	3 89[illegible]	2,890	1,001	2	3,376	22	385	110
Wholesale trade	1 329	1,021	307	1	1,194	1	1[illegible]4		[illegible]03	72	31		170		9	[illegible]
Food & dairy prod. stores & milk retailing	1 245	896	349		859	1	380	[illegible]	52[illegible]	400	123		326	1	143	53
General merchandise & five & ten cent stores	456	358	98		41[illegible]		39		825	766	59		809		11	5
Apparel and accessories stores	214	182	32		184		30		338	300	38		316		22	
Furniture, home furnishings & equip. stores	481	386	95		405		76		132	121	11		125		7	3
Motor vehicles and accessories retailing	665	555	110		590		75		82	79	3		79			2
Gasoline service stations	615	348	2[illegible]		485	1	128	1	45	39	6		26		11	8
Drug stores	265	189	76		215		50		182	147	34	1	171		8	3
Eating and drinking places	818	445	373		586	11	216	5	1,131	455	675	1	963	19	125	24
Hardware, farm implem't, & bldg. mater'l retail	711	433	278		628		83		90	88	2		84		4	2
All other retail trade	80[illegible]	5[illegible]	229		611	[illegible]	189	1	362	323	39		307	2	47	6
Finance, insurance, and real estate	1 0[illegible]	888	122		849	[illegible]	138		707	656	51		669	16	17	5
Banking and other finance	303	278	25		271	9	23		359	351	[illegible]		344	9	5	1
Insurance and real estate	[illegible]07	610	97		[illegible]78	14	115		348	305	43		325	7	12	4
Business and repair services	1,136	887	248	1	834	10	291	1	136	126	10		116	1	15	4
Business services	302	270	[illegible]		205	6	91		92	87	5		81		10	1
Automobile repair services and garages	530	359	170	[illegible]	418	3	108	1	17	15	2		12	1	1	3
Miscellaneous repair services	304	258	46		21[illegible]	[illegible]	92		27	24	3		23		4	
Personal services	1,284	558	726		1,047	[illegible]	230	4	4,983	706	4,275	2	4 722	20	225	16
Private households	325	25	300		109		14	2	3 636	148	3,486	2	3,610		23	3
Hotels and lodging places	165	33	82		149	[illegible]	14	1	299	152	147		257	14	24	4
Laundering, cleaning, and dyeing services	380	198	182		328	2	50		697	233	464		674	6	13	4
All other personal services	414	252	162		261		152	1	351	173	178		181		165	5
Entertainment and recreation services	35[illegible]	24[illegible]	108		29[illegible]	2[illegible]	35		168	142	26		150	7	9	2
Professional and related services	3,064	2,199	864	1	888	1,782	393	1	3,651	2,595	1 054	2	1,403	2,163	82	[illegible]
Medical and other health services	477	381	96		378	[illegible]5	[illegible]0		901	749	150	1	737	125	37	1
Educational services, government	1 675	1,184	490	1		1,675			2 032	1,368	663	1		2,032		
Educational services, private	289	134	155		269		20		408	207	201		375		33	
Welfare, religious, & membership organiz'ns	427	308	119		311	9	6	1	180	142	38		172	6	[illegible]	2
Legal, engineering, & misc. professional serv.	296	292	4		130	3	163		131	129	2		120		11	
Public administration	1,733	1,523	210			1 733			1,223	1,200	23			1,223		
Postal service	320	246	74			320			27	26	1			27		
Federal public administration	240	226	14			240			205	202	3			205		
State and local public administration	1,173	1,051	122			1,173			991	972	19			991		
Industry not reported	378	240	137	1	361	7	9	1	224	129	95		222	1		

Table 83—RACE AND CLASS OF WORKER OF EMPLOYED PERSONS, BY INDUSTRY AND SEX, FOR THE STATE AND FOR STANDARD METROPOLITAN AREAS OF 100,000 OR MORE 1950—Con

	-			- years	cld and ove						female,	14 year	s old and ov	er		
Aice and miliates			Race			Class of w	orker				Race	1 934		Class of w	orker	
paraglaria (Total	White	Negro	Other	Private wage & rai- ary wothers	Govern- ment vorkers	Self em- played workers	Inpa.d	Total	White	Negro	Other	Priva e wage & sal ar, workers	Govern- u.en workers	wo kers	family
NEW ORL FAMS	1					-	_					-		-		-
Employed	17/,490	131,225	42,90€	307	133,672	15,782	30,484	220	80,4 2	5-,599	25,703	40	65,063	30,343	4,744	. 20
Agriculture forestry and fisheries	2,495	1,926	553	10	926	42	-,447	. 81	_A2	108	11		101	16	32	
menture metry and naheries	1,2/_	843	492	6	637	19 23	024	61	1,0	⊌€	7.		90	5	30	-
Mining		1,083	6_	10	289	23	923	14		22	4	1	1		2	-
al mining	1,893	1,826			J. 852		30	_	171	168	3	-	163	1	2	_
ude per oleum and natural gas extraction	T 804	1,743	42 16	٠.	4n	:	2.		154	1:3	2		153		1	37
ming and qua rying except fuel	u4	40			61		3		5	14	1		14	1		Variation
Children and Child	17,34	_11,809	6,008		13,784	1,651	2,456	13	590	526	62	1	40%		32	
Manufacturing.	30,477	23,275	A,980		29,.19	75	1 078		9,273	6.9.3	2,645	1>	9 438	7	103	
Logging	36	8,823 24 77	2 588	7	10,304	40	467	2	1,268	1,129	136	و	1,234	3	22	135 1
ogging swmills, planing mill., and mill work Miscellaneous wood products.	467	276	487		1 011	1	51		_C9	#2	17		102		3	1
A raiture and fixtures Class and glass products	874	583 77	291		42L 817	1	13 56		_0e _25	30	16 53	1	166			
Glass and glass products Stone and day products	83	77 815	4p3		1 207	. 1	1		14	1/ 1/	5	_	14	:		3.5
Primary iron and steel noustries	470	324	146		462		8		67 18	52 16	2		18	:	2	
Primary nonferrous industries Febric d me al ind (inc. not spec metal)	2.023	1,808	21.		39	1	83		350	332		- 1	4	- 1	- 12	
fuchines a except electrical	1 120	(.55	64	1	1,057	2	61		.14	-10	57	•	351	:	4	
lectrical manunery equip and supplies fotor vehicles & motor vehicle equipment	222	202	21		157		8	1	42	36 15	6		41 15		1	
ircraft and parts hp and boat building and repairing	11	10	1						2000			:	1		-	
alroad & mass transportation equipment.	2 212	2,318	580	6	2,813	34	63		174	120	4		غد	1	_	
	290	>31	29		520	4	66		144	1,35	7	2	131	. 2	10	
durable good feat products	18,061	_4,301 689	4,34	15	18,032	30	.96 23	3	8,216	5,718	2,486	12	8,116	4	8.	
skery products ther food industries	1 459	343	284	,	1 207	3	49		290	1 n8 234	24 56		191 282		ä	
sher food industries	5,890	4,330 87	256	د ا	5,730	6	158	2	1,909	1,272	533	4	1,876	1	23	
nuting mills.	9/	93	4		20 27 S	3	1		550 249	181	1.5 58	:	549 246	1	2	l
arn, thread and more miles	704	5°2 85	-32	,	699		5		546	-12 36	114		542		1	ĺ
oparel & otae: appreated textule products	1.096	2,018	33.778		1.000	1	8 70	1	3,125	1.795	1,323	7	ده چندرد		12	1
sper and alised produc s	2,767	2,018 2,488	7-8	1	2,750 2,518 1,391 1,417		17		324 521	²⁷¹ 497	53 24		320		3	1
rinting publishing and allied indistries harmesis and allied products	1,427	1.063	390	1	1,391	11	188 51 9	1	225 161	203 173	22		218	2	20	1
retroleum and roal products	1,427	1,039	388 10		1,417	1	9		161	173 23	8		181	-	1	
Conver except rubber seather & leather products exc footwear - t specified manufact ring industries	54 28	44 22	6		2/		1		24 11 13	9	2 4		23 11 12		1	
eather & leather products exc footwear	-24 -98	37 151	47		36 183		15		E1 08	9 66	23		12		4	ĺ
Transport commun & other public util	32,600	22,769	9.7-2	90	28,740		1,002		4,753	4,358	394					İ
ulroads and raily ay express scryice.	5,596	4,835	2,159	- 20	6 855	136		- 2	422	279		-	4,568	144	3b	-
ee' railways and bus lines	2,083	1,570	781		1,854	194	35 419		Y85	1.44	±43 ⇒8	1	413 172	5	5	
usking ser zire and wa whousing . ale: uransportation	11,227	6,642	4,499	86	13,374	-62	89	2	63¢	743	39 89		196	48	22	1
transportation	2,534	2 001	104 532		C55	48 -02 42 18	9		175	167	.0		170	5		j
ecommunications offic and gas utilities	1,795	4.313	82		2,08/ , 584 1 793	9	432		2,267	2,233	31 31 3- 7		182 2,258	2 7	12	
etric and gas utilities ter supply sarriary services & other util.	1 950	1,670	283		1 793 252	159	10		383	376 76	7 4		366	15	5	100
Wholesale and retail trade					-		10			1. 100		1	.72	48	200.0000	
slevele trade	12,827	10,629	2,413	- £1 7	14,098 14,666	85	1,338	202	22,415	18,437 2 979	3,964	14	19,725	45	2,065	_ 51
d & darv prod stores & milk retailing.	£.994	5,575	377	4	4,356	20	2,201	48	3,237 2,460 5,474		906,	2	3 1.3	1	802	
arai morthandise & five & ten cent stores	2,335 1,522	-,964 -,281	371 240		2,170 1,236	3	160	48 2	1,960	2,393	342 301	2	1,814	11	123	
parel and an essoures stores . n.ture home rursishings & coup stores for teh.cles and accessories retailing	4,004	1.651	34.0	- 2	1.686	3	309	4	542	501	17	4.27	511 297	and the second	33	
oune service stay ons	-,254	1,990	264	2	1,1998	,	255 389	3	311	30o 49	2		297 40		12	
	1 240	699	367		1.004	1 7	240	27	987	831	155	6	917	. +	12	1
ing and dimking places dware, farm implem t & bldg mater'l ret	6,250	1,574	1,880	3,3	4 51C 1,753		1 606	27 6 8	4,115	2 007	2,302	6	4,204	15	346 29	1
other retail wrade	3,279	1,57± 4,839	728	12	1,753 2,525	6	1,240	8	1,029	1,463	159	1	1,.74	6	29	3
Finance insurance and real estate	6,94"	,,60'	1,078	2	5, 36	51.2	74	4	4,252	3,790	492		3,82	30.4	137	
iking and other finance	2,384 ددد 4	2,168 3 699	2±5 863	1	1,936 3,780	305	1/5 57C	1	1,689 2,593	1,65° 2,131	30 462		2,420 2,401	2o1 53	130	
Business and repair services	6,280		945	1			1,584	- 1	921	889		1	804	9		
Business and repair services	2,220	2,334	98	- 4	1,640	21	506		758		14		677	9	96 70	_ 2
omosile repair services and garages.	2,383	2,172	611		⊥ 859	24	498	2	77	68 77	8	1	67		8	
cellaneous repair se vices	1,590	1,473	20.5	4	T 058	71	580	1		2.0			63		18	
Personal services	- 500	3,535	3,014)l	رد 1. 46	19	1,557	3	17,510	3,312	14,184	14	15,170	- 2	1,275	_ :
als and Iodana place		1,091	568 070	- 1	1, 46 1,530	14	114	1	1.:79	802	976	4	1,409	7 5	150	
ndaring cleaning and dveing services	2,081	1,055	070	47	1,634	4	441 945	-	2,096	696 960	1,389	1	1,915	5 2	139	- 2
other personal services	-,		1	. 1		1			1,050			,				
Entertainment and recreation services	3,410	2,531	701	15	2,049	97	267	-3	1,-11	943	107	1	1,006	43	61	-
Professional and related services	9,743	7,354	2,173	17	4,848	2,947	979	2	7,260	11,168	3,340	17	7,877	6,217	376	5
deal and other health services.	1,084	749	330	2	1,310	1,770		2	3,167	2,092	-,075		4,134	2,548	-	
cational services, government cational services private fare religious & menue ship o gamz'ns.	1,64.	1 240 969	397		1 572		69		2,370	1,892	47"	1	2,188	85	150	. 3
fare religious & men ne ship o gamz'ns al engineeting & nusc professional serv	1,482	1 452	497 26	4	_,385 572	42 48	41 862		657	835 638	235	- 1	58-	47	50	
Poblic administration	11,071	9,704	1,655	15	-/-	11.37_			3,378	1.,94	181	2		.378		
tal service	1.999	1,148	848			1,999			96	58	38,			96		
deral public administration	4,168	3,612	544	12		4,168			2,221	2,_54	67	2		2,22	100	
te and local public administration	5,204	1,94_	263			5,204			1,061			2	1	1,001	1897 m m	•
Industry out reported	1, -26	٨, .56	76b	_ 4	_,839	72	1,5		1,032	782	248	- 2	988	7	26	

Tabe 83 —RACE AND CLASS OF WORKER OF EMPLOYED PERSONS, BY INDUSTRY AND SEX, FOR THE STATE AND FOR STANDARD METROPOLITAN AREAS OF 100,000 OR MORE 1950—Con.

			Мже .	1 years	ol and aver			54					vo bna blo e	lass of w	n ke	-
			Lare			Class of w					Rate		-			
) is rd industry	Total	white	legro	C .icr	Private Augt & Su ary workers	Govern- ment worken	Self em- ployed norkers	Unpaid family vikes	Total	White	Negro	Other	Private wage & sal ary workers	ment	Pelf-e 1- ployed workers	fami wars
9-PUBYEFOP's						3.358	6 100	262	22,288	_2,038	LQ 246	4	±7,617	2 430	1,610	4.
bayelqm4	44,628	3,376	-42 7		1.75	3,338	4,963	240	1 268	16	1,010		532	3	219	3
Agriculty e forestry and fishere	3, 32	852	3 .20		732	- 0	1,,33	240	1,062	54	1,008		530	1	217	
prestri un fideries .	3, 1	.93	. 70		19	13	36		6	4	2		2	2	2	
Mining -	3,201	3,029	1.2	1	2 394	1	166		626	624	2		619	-	/	-
cal torning		3			2		4		625	623	2		6.8		,	
In og and quarring except mes	3 17 1	ي.ر. اه	C		2,872	1	302		622	620	-		020		1	
1					100		670		132	1.4	21		1.2	9	14	
Construction	5 230	3,408	545		-,252	312		-	640	776	164		914	1	92	
Manufacti ing	6,601	4,405	1 443		3,1.5	12	274 164	2	264	1.80	75		252		8	_
Joseph	3 48	2,2-2	67		+6	- "	10 18		1 44 12	1 30 5	34		43		1	1
Logging.	112 743	203	725 90		147		18	1	12	30	14		12			1
Miscellaneous wood produces	-29	62	6		1.		10	1	51	17	37		52		2	1
Olass and glass products Stone and also products	-29 772	659	114		~~1 1.14		10 2 7		54 14 11 7	11 5 2	- 2		10		1	
Primary iron and steel industries	21 156	58 109	13 47		145		11		7	- 5	2	-	6 2		1	
Primary nonferrous industries.	156	46	,		22		21		2		3		32		1	
Vachnery except electrical	35%	245 434	72		334 514	2	3/	1	33 45 9	1/2	3	1	42	1		
Electrical machiners enuity and supplies_	55	47	8		51		4		9	9			1 3			
Motor vehicles & motor vehicle equipment	38	34	. 4		30	1	1			1 3		1	1 '			
Ship and boat building and repairing.	11		4		5	1 -	6		1	1	,				1 1	1
Railroad & nusc manmortation equipment. All other durable goods.	200	131	62		128	1	21		29	21	8		2.9		1	
ondurable goods	3 D40	2 203	83 .		2 928	7	±04	1	662	576	86		645	1	-	
Meat products	80%	111	97		205		3	1	44	19	19	1	>6		2	
Bakery products. Other food adustics	3_0	2+5 299	65 ∠08		,74 481		25	1	60 57	40	17	1	52		2 5	
Tobacco navifactures	7	-	200		7									1		1
Yary thread and fabric mills	8	5	- 4	9	4 7	2	1		2	2			1		1	
Other textue null products Apparel & other fabricated title products	3	4 3		100	3				3	1	2	1	176		١,	
	57	4 -	12 29		48 63	1	8		177 25	157	20	1	25	1	,	1
Paper and allied products Printing publishing and allied industries Chemicals and allied products	268	494	74		538	1	2		133	17 130	8	1	128	1	4	1
Chemicals and alited products	372 90. 	494 159 770	216 104	3 9	370 875	1 2	24		34 123	23	11	1	123		1	
Rubby r products	200	15			_5	~	-		2	2	1	1	7	1		
Footwear, except rubber	5	,			5		١,	- 1	2	2		1	1 2			1
o abouted manufactural industries	ic	43	. 3		63	1	6		14	12	3	1	1			
I remand to commun. & other public uni	5,246	4,015	1,334		4, 900	315	1,00	1	944	909	35		877	53	14	
Rauroads and railway express service Street railways and bus lines	2 027	1,_70	0.7		2,015	2	4		944	86	4		90	36		
Street railways and bus lines	413 695	263 415	50 280		365 597	/2	97		66 66	60 57	9	1	30	36	6	
Prinking service and warehousing	20	2*	4	8	21 75	1 16	6	- 1	8	8		1	1 2		6	
Air frai sportation _	95 510	58	46		75	16	4	-	16	16	,		15	3		1
Ali other transportation	31.6	464 281	.52		502 334	1	2 4	-	408	+00	3		407			
relecommunications Electric and gas utilities	980 281	872 157	108		₹96 47	10	4 2	15-00	184	182	2		183			1
Water supply summary wavees & other util					1 (21								1			1
Wholesale and retail trade	2 688	2,085	2,692	11	8,126	14	1 852		5,355 4€ >	4,035	1,319	-	4,600	22	1 14	-
Wholesale trade Food & darry prod stores & milk retailing	1 (75	1.183	413		2,440	1 3		4	638	509	129		36.	1		
General merchandise & fivo & ten cent stores	361 356	293 295	68 61			- 5	52	2	813	7o2	51 90	1	78.		2/	
Apparel and accessmes stores Furniture home furnishings & equip stores	684	558	145	1	284 571		72		617	J39	28		200	2	4	-
Motor vehicles and accessories retailing	869	26	153		774	١.,	94 136 41	1	98 3.	94	4	-	14	1	4 4 9	
Gasoline service stations.	502 268	317 174	285		464 227	1 *	41	-	325	25	>5		3.	1 13		
Saung and drinking places	753 688	350 496	384 191	9	539 577	3	209	2	1,586	688	897	1	1,420	13	134	
Dag stores Saung and druking places Hardware farm implem t & bldg mater i ret Al other rotal trade.	1 118	853	265	1	80a	1	311	1	459	416	43	6	36	7	7"	1
Finance, insurance and real estate	371	1,473	198		1 102	27	242		871	719	152		823		31	
Banking and other finance	436	416	20	-	372	9	55		36.3	34.1	le		35.	2 8	1	
neurance and real estate .	93.	757	178		730	18	187		504	372	376	1	177	4	48	3
Busmess and repair services	1 057	1,283	374		1 -72	1.	474	1	243	224	19	-	_9		35	3
	389	359	30 282		242 680	2	145		166	162	10	1	14.	1	4	4
Business services			62	Z	249	5	162	1	41	36	5	ś	2	6	1 4	3
Business services Automobile is pair services and garages.	851	3.5				6	298	2	7,100	954	6.145		6 56	,	529	
Business services Automobile is pair services and garages.	4.	3.5		4	1.75		-	2	5 36+	228	>,133		5,12		239	9
Susiness services Lutamobile is pair services and garages. Miscellaneous repair services Personal services	2.021	3.5 710	.,307	- 4	1,715		4.3								. 35	5
Business services Lutamobile in pair services and garages. Miscellaneous repair services Personal services Private househoode. Hetch and Johnne places.	4.	710 33 158	587 236	4	675 358	2	34		446	169	27		40	7 4	10	
Business services Lutamobile in pair services and garages. Miscellaneous repair services Personal services Private househoode. Hetch and Johnne places.	2,021 720 394	3.5 710	.,307	3 1	1,715 675 358 320 362	2	34 6s 153		446 797 496	250 307	5/6 189	5	1 74	6	205	
Seancia service Liutimobil - n pair services and garages. Miscellaneous repair services Personal services Provate househood - Gotels and lodging place. Lumdering distanting and dvaing services all other personal services.	720 594 388 519	333 710 33 158 211 308	.,307 236 174 2.0	3	675 358 320	2 4 28	68		797	250 307	189		1 74 28	6		5
Sunness services (utsimble) + npar services and garages. Miscollaneous repair services Personal services frivate household	2,021 720 394 388 519 442	333 710 33 158 211 308	,307 236 174 2,0 153	3 1	675 358 320 362 370	-	60 123 44		797 496 220	250 307 174	189	5	1 74 28 19	7 6 9 d	205	2
Sounces services tuckinoble is past services and gazagea. Miscellaneous repara services Private househords fictoria and longing place. Laundaring cleaning and divening services the object of the control of the control of the Einstitutions and receivance are Einstitutions and receivance Energianes and receivance Professionals and related services	2,021 720 394 388 519 442 2,055	325 710 33 158 241 308 289 1,473	.,307 687 236 174 2.0 153 582	3 1	675 358 320 362	263 166	575 256	1	797 496 220 3,683 1,553	250 307 174 2,587	169	5	1 740 20 19	7 1 676	136	2
Stateness nervices tacktionable in past services and garages. Miscellaneous repair services Provate househoods ficteds and lodging places. Laundering cleaning and diveng services Laundering cleaning and diveng services. Entercutances and receiption of the Entercutances and receiption of Professional and related services Medical and other heads services.	2,021 720 394 388 519 442 2,055 670 389	710 33 158 211 308 289 1,472 503 225	.,307 687 236 174 2.0 153 582 1e7 164	3 1	675 358 320 362 370 976 248	263 164 389	515 256	1	797 496 220 3,683 1,553 1,361	169 250 307 174 2,587 1 232 722	1 095 1 095 1 095 1 095	5	1 28 28 19 1 2,86 1 1,21	7 1 676	205 125 136 45	6
Stateness nervices tacktionable in past services and garages. Miscellaneous repair services Provate househoods ficteds and lodging places. Laundering cleaning and diveng services Laundering cleaning and diveng services. Entercutances and receiption of the Entercutances and receiption of Professional and related services Medical and other heads services.	2,021 720 594 388 519 442 2,055 670 389	333 710 33 158 241 908 289 1,472 503 225	.,307 236 174 2.0 153 582 167 164 63	3 1	675 358 320 362 370 976 248	263 164 389	515 256	1	797 496 220 3,683 1,553 1,361 355	169 250 307 174 2,587 1 232 722 264	1 095 1 1 095 1 095 1 095 1 095 1 095 1 095	5	1 40°74' 20° 19 1 7,86° 1 1,21 28° 28° 28° 28° 28° 28° 28° 28° 28° 28°	7 1 679 7 1 679 2 294 1,365	205 125 136 43	6
Stances services Lucimobile is past services and garages. Miscellaceous repair services Fersonal services Fersonal services Lucimobinos Lucim	2,021 720 394 388 519 442 2,055 670 389	710 33 158 211 308 289 1,472 503 225	.,307 687 236 174 2.0 153 582 1e7 164	3 1	675 358 320 362 370	263 164 389	575 256	1	797 496 220 3,683 1,553 1,361	169 250 307 174 2,587 1 232 722	1 092 1 1 092 1 1 092 1 1 092 1 1 092 1 1 092 1 1 1 1 1 1 1 1 1 1 1 1 1 1 1 1 1 1 1	5	1 28 28 19 1 2,86 1 1,21	7 1 679 7 1 679 2 294 1,361	205 125 136 43	6
Stateness nervices tacktudinals in page services and garagos. Miscellaneous repair services Private homehods ficteds and lodging places Laundering cleaning and diveng services Laundering cleaning and diveng services. Entectuaries and recreasion services. Professionals and related services Professionals and related services Discontinual services government Medical and other leads of the Medical and other leads of the Medical and other leads of the Medical and other leads of the Medical and other leads of the Medical and other leads of the Medical and other leads of the Medical and other leads of the Medical and other leads of the Medical and other leads of the Medical and other leads of the Medical and other leads of the Medical and Medical Medica	2,021 720 394 388 519 442 2,052 670 389 481 452	710 33 158 211 308 289 1,473 503 225 118 208	.,307 236 174 2.0 153 582 167 164 63 184	3 1	575 358 320 362 370 976 248 1/66	365 369 8	515 256	1	797 496 220 3,683 1,553 1,361 355 263 151	169 250 307 174 2,587 1 232 722 264 200 149	1 095 1 095 1 095 1 095 1 095 1 095 1 095	5	1 40° 74, 28° 19 1 7,86° 1 1,21 28° 23°	7 1 676 2 294 1,361	205 136 136 141 151 166 171	6
Stances services Lickimobile is past services and gazagea, Miscellaneous repair services - Private househord* - Private househord* - Great and dogung place, Londdring elisating and diveng services He interpretation services Entertaines and recentation services Medical and of other heads services Medical and of other heads services Medical and of other heads services Medical and of other heads services Medical and of other heads services Medical and of other heads services Medical and of other heads services Medical and of other heads services Medical and of other heads of the services Medical and of other heads of the services Medical and other heads of the services Medical services M	2,021 720 388 519 442 7,052 670 389 481 452 363 2,039	710 33 158 241 308 289 1,472 503 225 418 206 307	-,307 -,307 -,236 -,174 -,210 -,153 -,582 -,164 -,63 -,184 -,4 -,4 -,221 -,44		575 358 320 362 370 976 248 1/66	369 389 8	515 256 14 30 215	1	797 496 220 3,683 1,553 1,361 355 263 151 636	169 250 307 174 2,587 1 232 722 264 200 149 606	1 095 1 095	55	1 40° 74, 28° 19 1 7,86° 1 1,21 28° 23°	7 1 679 2 299 1,363 5 6 23	209 1 12 5 139 4 4 5 1 6 1 6 1 1 7	6
Stances services untermobile page services and garages. Miscellaneous reputs services review to bousehouts footels and lodging place. Laundering cleaning and dvening services - Laundering cleaning and dvening services - Entercutiones and recreation services Forfervonals and related services. Medical and of other heads its services Medical and of other heads services Medical and of other heads services Medical and of other heads services Medical and of other heads services Medical and of other heads services Medical and of other heads services Medical and of other heads services Medical and of other heads services Medical and of other heads Medical	2,021 720 394 388 519 442 7,052 670 389 481 452 363	710 33 158 211 308 289 1,473 503 225 118 206 309	-,307 		575 358 320 362 370 976 248 1/66	365 369 8	515 256 14 30 215	1	797 496 220 3,683 1,553 1,361 355 263 151 636	169 250 307 174 2,587 1 232 722 264 200 149	1 092 1 092 300 63° 91 63°	5 5 5 5 5 5 5 5 5 5 5 5 5 5 5 5 5 5 5 5	1 40° 74, 28° 19 1 7,86° 1 1,21 28° 23°	7 1 679 2 299 1,360	209 3 139 5 139 6 43 1 64	6

Table 84—MAJOR OCCUPATION GROUP OF EMPLOYED PERSONS, BY INDUSTRY AND SEX, FOR THE STATE AND FOR STANDARD METROPOLITAN AREAS OF 250,000 OR MORE 1950

THE STATE Male, employed Ag reulture forestry and asherses	1227	workers	proprietors incl farm	kindred workers	workers	foremen and kindred workers	kindred workers	mul private	mune	Occupation not reported
Ag sculture forestry and inheries	1000	1000		1177		WOILERS	workers	potnenoto		
	046,782	41 202	149 887	35,274	3.,979	48,9.3	114 790	38,210	.27 1.4℃	3 280
	144,460	38	8o ~92	161	63	740	2,464	13	53,224	40
Agriculture Forestry and fishe ies.	135,665	333	26,607	-35	4"	6 147	2,.52	18	45,579	
Mining	23,031	2,4.0			70	and the second of			7,600	32 8
Coal mining	62	4	4 4 - 3	4,270	94	7,237	13,902	4.0	30	- 55
Crude putroleum and natural gas extraouon_ M.ning and quarryang except fuel	20,776	7,32~	1,2	- 176 92	80 14	4,966 552	12,480	361 38	-9	48
Construct on	o3 37r	2 4.1	4,000	+0+	81	34,602	٤,023	440	14 903	126
Manufacturing Durab A goods	1.5, 158	907	6,750	5 684	4,3~	42,43	40,368	2,858	27,577	570
	46,400 5,~75	61	2,142	1,501	2 7	8 ×58 .77	14,010	91.7 22	4,510	200
Miscellaneous wood products	20,348 -,843 1 544	88 16	e54 85	508	10	2,184	7,497	349	8 655 586	140 17 7
Glass and glass products	1 544	11	120	56	10 24 14	204 441 91	504	19	204	7
Assemils, planing mils and mil work Missellaneous wood products Furniture and fixth. es Glass and glass products Frimary iron and stees undustries	2,44.5	78	.C5	200	44	338	925	47 30	698	10
Primary nonferrous industries Fabricated metal industries (incl. not spec metal)	490	23	50 20	17	18 40 152	102	393 lel	25	198	2 9
Machinery or ept electrical Electrical machinery coupment and supplies	2 996	120	در. 298	161 1C3	24	93	1,090 782	59	365 20 29	10
Me or vendes and motor vehicle compinent	393 730 29	27	42	25	r3	_0r	147	10	2ª 18	2
tireraft and parts Ship and boat building and repairing	.992	8 95	_86	1 27		16 872	390	-13	2	
Railroad and mass ransportation equipment All other durable goods	68	30	139	3 50	118	16	23 449	3	3.5b 6	9
SondLiable goods	68. 104 1	3 960	4 097	1,_51	118	2,1	21.157	13	1184	
Meat p oducts	3,072	33 14	1 8	201	272 227	116	914	51	194	346
Bakers product. Othe force and astates Tobacco manufactures	142	420	1,498	944	722	2,256	,9 7	454	3 84	78
hritting mills	75 770	1 1	. 9	15	22	20	34	8	7	
Yarn, thread and faunc mills Other textule mill products Apparel and other fabricated textule products	216	9	25	29 11	25	184	321	46	158	1
	1,276	339	162	130	102	2,077	5%1 6,161	128	54 I 90	1 3
Printing publishing and allied industries	5 326 20 387	7.58 685	625	416	76 1,442 2 8 108	2 17	407	328	2 70/ 53 1,735	91
Pe role in and soal products. Rubbe products	15 140	1 738	220 473	+.022	108	3,970	5.104	53,	2 093	5,
Footwear except rubber	44	50	42 7	17	16	110	254	44	117	2
Footwear except rubber Leather and leather products except cootwear Not meediff. manufacturing industries.	594	34	41	49	57	142	24 201	24	8	2 5
Iransport. communication & other public stiltnes	66,024	2,103	2,958	/ 14-	230	-2,092	20 171	2,683	14 000	253
Railroads and railway express service	17,412	-76	910	2,91/	14	4,314	3,4,3	_,005	4.719	47
Tru_cing service and wa enouging	4,850 7,931	90 912	291	24c 593	32	406	4 310	153	1,669	7
Water transportation	1,033 5 322	212 237 487	2,612	200	21	816	2,909	262	5.140	12 75
All cher transportation Telecommunications	5 322 3 3 1	186	387 357	475	12	1,5-6	3,510	124	72 272 .38	12
Heetric and gas utilities Water supply sanitary services and other utilities.	3,984	801 149	51.3 189	908 235	107	3 .13	1,343	193	900	51 24
Wholesale and remail rade	113 54/	2,507	32,177	7,144	22.19.	8,525	19,295		2 :51	
Wholesale trade	26,321	874	5,584	3,652	6,065	1,708	5, 023	10,710	7,834 841	387 65
Food and darry products stores, and milk retaing. Several merchandise and five and ten cent stores	5,922	55 50	2,012	649 4°0	1,848	428 108	396	139	841 206	172
Apparel and accessories stores furniture home furnishings and equipment stores. Motor vehicles and accessories retailing	3 048	26 52	968	138	1,4/3	921	108	2+7	34 670	1 8
Motor vehicles and accessories retailing Gaso'ine ervice statione	8,234	62	2,030	484	2,718 70	1,804	3,6	415	675	15
Orug stores.	≥ 067 =≥1956	1,049	347 4 275 1,788	274	283	42 80	609	332	45	15 21 4 26
fardwire, tarm implement & bldg. material retailing	8,438	95	1,788	644	1.773	1.154	1,431	176	1,348	39 26
	10,604	210		41.	3,005	1,142		232		
Finance insurance and real estate	4 603	215	1,696	2 544	4 994	420	107	1,182	31.7	3/
nsurence and wal estate	9,040	254	1,680	738	4,894	344	7	758	291	12
Business and repair services	18 328	1,27	2,000	642	40.	10,277	2,287	129	876	23
utomobile repai services and garages	9,484	1 178	507 934	433 _33	233	1,24	201 440ر ـ	525 75	99	11
Asserlance is repair services	5 060	56	559	76	22	3 238	962	15	133	8
Personal services	19,468	26	_ /65 30	432	21.5	1,23%	4,4/5	6,780 1,420	3,674	23
lotels and lodging piaces	5,63 ₁	50	491	29 ₀	11	±67 ≤16	10.2	1,420	3,490 77 77	5
Aundening cleaning and dyeing services ill other personal services	5,180	772	1,03C 228	79 42	60	685	3,561 30e	3,440	30	12
Entermoment and recreamon services	3,692	1,> 8	1,220	880	18∠	708	174	1,821	339	26
Processional and related services	29,030	18 365	1,046	1 072	50	1,791	1,101	4, 123	^80	72
deciral and other health services	8,65ª 9,103	4,5°7 5,585	797 155	348	11	613 823	433	2,.07	242	30
ducational services pri ate defare, religious and membership organisations	4 864	1,902	380	454 214	14	222 75	8-71	457	130	6
egal, engineering and misc professional services.	3,294	2,883	380	91	15	58	108	3_	32	2
Pablic administration	24,553	2,822	3,031	7,568	36	2,012	1,361	5,403	2,027	294
ostal per rice	4,5%0 7 25/	1,220	/17 , ₄ 13	2,311	11	50 844	55 40-	415	196 395	2.1
	12 669	1,760	4 501	1 508	85	4, 479	932	1,853	1,4,6	75
ederal punko administration tate and local public administration	9,251	765	403	240	120	229	192	151	1,_69	6,377

Table 84 —MA'OR OCCUPATION GROUP OF EMPLOYED PERSONS BY INDUSTRY AND SEX, FOR THE STATE AND FOR STANDARD METRCPOLITAN AREAS OF 250,0% OR MORE 1950—Con.

Founds employed Agrushus foresty and fisheres to sur to the control of the con	0 fz * /5	3-11-								
Agriculture foresty and fisheries For time fire to and fisherie M ung il myung il myung uid , if one m and nistitut gas extraction mag and quartyring encept he Construction		2-1-							-4 48 5	
ru dire try und fab. 1 e Missag Al stringer of malifal gas extraction Long and quarrying deept file Cossistences				974	2,9	1,870	a, 269	75 780	12,041	3,58
M ung al munq ud _sf one m and natural gas extraction ul _sf one m and natural gas extraction ulong an _quarrying except file Construction		-	7 .		_9	10	-6-	84	12 518	
al triung id , at one m and mantai gas extraction ning an a quarrange except five Construction	-	1 · · · · · · · · · · · · · · · · · · ·	-	4	2	11	25 65	5	120	
id _ s* a.e m and natiful gas extraction		-		- 7			1			
Construction	د, ج ع-		- 1	70		04	46 48	6	105	
	. ",	,	-	. 71-	14	4	- '-	47		
Man factoring	-, -		-,	4 2. !	40	509	9,778	2"2	71,	1
rabic goods	1.4	, ,		1 - 1	2.	3 1	3	8	2,	
Logung awmils planing mi's an, mill work Miscellaneous wood products	574	4	- 1	4	2	14	14.	5	33	
Tirt are and hyture	47i 34		0	47	1	401	1"1	1	1 5	
Carta are and hytares. (lass and glass products	34	4	-c	74	2	-	20	5	5	
Printary ron and the industries	10			25		1 1	1.8		19	
sebree and me a autotres (nel not spec metal)	1.7	4	-,	9.	?	8.		3	1	
lectrical machinery on ipment and supplies	2"	•	4	.9. .9.	^ ,	1 1	5 7		0	
Am raft and parts Sup and boat building and repairing Rullwad and raws t anspor ation equipment	در_	,	3	30		1 51	14	5	3	1
Rulroad and muse t anspor ation equipment	5.	r4	3-	2		10	204	6	6 493	
nguraor gocus	± 4+"	- 4.	2	ب <i>ر</i> بر فہ	22	40.	8,949 178	210	17 15	1
Men products Bakers products	1.0	34	6.5	.c. .c.	51	82	261	50	206 17	
Other road indust set	2, 37 40	, ,	1	7 1	1	8	6.2	4	17	
Yarn tureau and fabric nulls_	-0	- 4	2	1r -2	,	9	426 46	2"	54 16	i i
Other extile mill p oquets	7,	-	1,2	12	-4	11	2 227	26	4 57	
Other estile mill p oquets Apparel and other tab. Latin textile products Paper and all. ed or educts	676.	45		348 579	9.	11 29	4,057	19 10	1	1
Printing, 1 whilso he and allied in ust les	1 183	-90	3.5	4:8	35	164	136	19	41	1
Pe role im and cost products	47" e0	97	5 2	796 30			*5	15	2	
Carte and annual melibrar	_5		-	2	ï		12	1 5	4	
Lather and eather products except footwear at spec fielt manufacturing industries	140		0	-3	6	2	60	5	4	
I ransport communication & other public unities.	9 +67	12"	7, 5	ಕ,್ರ32	44	145	374	402	272	
alroads and railway express service	,69 ,22	6	14	52 · 239	2 4	16	20 179	4	1.6	
ucking service and warehousing	449 280	20	33 30	-92	3	7 8	47	29 46	61	
ster transports un	431	5	6	120	5	1	3 45	75 1"	7	1
other ansportation	5.025	13	ř.,	4,57		82	4	30	6	ì
se we and gas lightes ater supply sam any services, and other utilities	199	52	4	1 029	-/-	18	14	47	15	1
Wholesale and retait trade	56,606	J36	7,173	11 498	18,789	232	2,484	15,240	282	
closels trade	4.94/	67	22.	3,617	238	39	599 248	75	"4 60	<u> </u>
od and darry products stores and milk retailing meral merenandise and hye and en cent stores	4 154	110	2,572	1,956	6.87	95	565	629 232	34	
parel and accessors stores initure home furnishings and equipment stores	4,483	20	978 139	6:1 6:5	2,150 403	148	68 / 120	92	8	
oto vehicles and accessories retailing .	939	13	40 68	751 _02	15	-1 2	70	-1	5 4	1
	2 445	140	1,084	3c8	1 2.70	30	26	13,191	2	
ng stores ting and dunking places tridware farm implement & bldg material retailing to be retail trade	16,144 1,051 4,012	1.5	103	654	228	114	17	25 21.8	45 7 38	
	4,012	40 88	821	5,120	2,.91	_6	3.2		19	ì
Finance, insurance and rust estate	8,273	35	153		10	-6	17	136	1	-
surance and real estate_	4,639	قر	224	3,171	7"8	12	15	483	:8	
Business and repair services	_ 822	163	127	1,18_	38	125	175	79	3	
isinest services itomobile repair services and garages	± 286 280	150	84 18	907 1ce	2A 3	40	12	37 19	5	9864
isce aneous repair services	255	3	25	±C8	3 7	40 58	49	3	3	- 1
Personal services	56, 0,85	305	798	1 399	14	97	6,50"	40,865	239	
rvate households . otesa and lodging places undering deaning and dyeing services	43,834 د 61.2	37	252	528	13	9 9	108	45,30	1.8	
undering deaning and dyeing services	6 285 4,645	1/0	125	598 598	41 42	28	5 098	2,901	.04	1
Enterrainment and recreation services	2,369	338	20"	991	-51	35	100	52/	12	
Protessional and related services	42,984	20,615	>95	0 ^ 32	41	64	564	2,180	90	
edical and other health services	15 038	6,790	_44	2,042	-1	24	126	4,754 3 LSB	23	
ducational services government ducations services private	19,1_8	3,049	25	1,304	9	1/	112	690	29 24	100
dications serv v.s private elfar, rchgous, and mombership organisations gal engineering and mise professional services	5,06, 2,25 1,440	814 174	98 17	778 1,202	14	2	67	547 3d	12	1
Pub ic administration	8.602	1.21	593	(,008	11	11	66		25	1
outal service	*00	4	342	>0a	1		66	316	25	+
ederal public administration	4 06	216	49 202	3,452	4	7	37	55	15	
are and local public admunistration				-,	-					

Table 84.—MAJOR OCCUPATION GROUP OF EMPLOYED PERSONS, BY INDUSTRY AND SEX, FOR THE STATE AND FOR STANDARD METROPOLITAN AREAS OF 250,000 OR MORE 950—Con.

Area industry and sex	1 otal 14 years old and over	Professional sechnical, and kindred workers	Vanagers oficials, and proprietors, and farm	snd kindred workers	Sales workers	foremer and kindred workers	Operatives and kindred workers	Servee work.rs md private bousehold	except mine	Occupation no. reported
NGV CRLEAMS				7012010	_	WOLKERS	WOLKELE	D-2UNEDORG		
Male employed	174 498	14,900	24,4.4	-7,055	LI ak	30.97.	2" 792	17,586	24 504	
Agriculture forestry and asheries	2,492	90	541	19	9	24	-1:	27,386	1,68.	4,00
Agriculture Forestry and insheries	1,34	66	524 17	1	7	17	23	24		
Migrog	1,154	24		4	2			-	592 2,029	
	1 893	490	1	156	1.	2/2	3.0	- 3		4 1
cal mining. Fuds petroleum and ne ure gas extraction dining and quarrying except fiel	1 806 64	473 7	-17 1e	147	±0 5	346	54 23	37	1	
Construction	_7,914	91,	2 495	3%	14	0 743	, 3y7	147	3 ~2	
Manufacturing	20,271	1,342	2,44.	2 251	1 9-7	7 488	8 197	799	2 465	1.
Irable goods Logging Sawmills planing miles and mill work	11,418	423	804	650	40"	3,-19	3,374	_69	- 91 21	
Sawmills planing mile, and mill work Miscellaneous wood products. Firmitive and fixtures	1,063	48	79	62	18	/01	315	22	301	
Furniture and fixtures	874	41	26	38 1	اد 10	271	185 329	9 1	.10	
Glass and g.ass products Stone and elay products Primary iron and steel incustries	1,300	58	1 08	6	10 26 7	237	4.2	33	328	
Primary nonferrous industries	470	1,	19	2	7 8	_20	20	59	1,0	
Phiricated metal industries (inci not spec. metal). Machinery except electrical	2,023 1 120	75 1 74	1.7	-14	8 97 86	601	690	45	239	
Morey vehicles and motor which courses	223	38	18	2.	37	3c	34	16	239 24 15	
Aircraf and part	163	ا و	26	2.	19	50	33	3	3	
Ship and boat building and repairing. Ra_road a 1 rass transportation equipment	2,910	82	130	±50 2	6	1 356	609	39	472	
All o Per durable goods	0÷0	20	75	ton	50	_34	210	-2	30	
ondurable goods Meat produca	_8 u61 509	904	1,625	1,583	1,030	1 497	5.5°8	20	3,354	
Bakery product 4 Other road indus ries	2 896	210	518	454	87 315	475	2 04	197	1 200	
Tobacco manufactures Enitting mus	111	1 5	14	7.7	10	10	40	2	1,304	
Other textue mill produts	704	7	20	28	54	24 273	20 295	13	148	
Apparel and other abreated textile products	109	2 27	-38 1	123	10	18	38 448	42	148 18 80	
Paper and allies products Prin ing publishing and allied industries Chemicals and allied products	2,767	27 73 246	356	226 247	55 635	419 919	327	46	900	
Chemicals and alued products	4,44	104	187	132	145	174	350	47	28 305	
Petrocum and soal products Fubber products	-,447	193	91 13	155	277 22	2.4	322	20	387	
Tootuear everent rubter Leather and leather products except footwear of spectred manusacturing industries	28 44	3	2	4	8	3 2	19	1	3	
	196	18	24	12	٥د	32		13	20	
Transport communication & other public stilities	-2 601	1,0%	3,008	4,122	-02	4,041	8,7-9	1,44	8,488	1.0
ni oads and railway express service reet railways and out mee. Joking ad ree and warehousing	6 996 2,083	61 26 28	290 85	1,372	2	1,653 201	1 358 465	673 63 103	1 565	
ater runsports tion	3,548	284	312	268 1 171	13	20- 671	1 465 1 541 1,703	103 764	968 4 730	
ir transportation Il other trai sportation	11,227 706 2,534	284 208	1,°30 54 200	200	11	-00:	1,82	97 40	3o 131	
ele ommunications	1 551	17	.82	272	12	පිංති	38	56	29	
lectro and gas with the rater supply, sant sary services and other utilities	1 953	260 79	104	3.42	1	399	460	86 22	-97 771	
Wholesale and retail trade	42,827	1,472	14,351	3,963	8,513	3 354	5 225	2,098	-,720	2.1
holesae trace	13,049	610	4 728 4,542	2,342	2,-92	585 375	2 0 34	200	1 364 328	8
ood and dairy products stores, and milk retailing eneral merubunduse and five and ten cent stores	6,9°5 2 3 15 1,522	8 21	420	276	1,345 585 588	243	233	319	120	
perel and soursonus stores. inniur, home furnishings, and equipment stores ofor vehicles and accessories recolling	2 301	32	46b	98	596	33/	24	144 5J 76	18	
	2 254	33								
aso) ne service stations	1,577	4	515	178	76U	4±7 155	71	14	103	
asol ne service stations rug stores	1,577 1,246	357	515 133	14		155	7 1	14	103	
asol ne service stations rug stores	6 150	357 165 43	133 1 684 5.4	14 50 178 199	188 159 464	155 46 49 234	24, 27, 1 20, 80 299	14 165 1 598 48	103 116 13 29 315	
asol ne service stations rug stores sting and dirinking places atma and dirinking places andware tarm implement, & bldg material e'ailing I other retail trade	6 150 2,_19 3 579	357 169 43 95	515 133 1 684 5.4 4 090	14 50 178 199	188 159 464 943	155 45 45 234 464	299 427	14 165 3 598 48 192	103 116 13 29 315 190	
and he service stations up stores to my stores up stores up and drinking places after and drinking places are store to are implement, & bldg material e'ading lother retail trade Finance, 'assurance and real estate sublem and other finance.	6 150 2,119 3 579 5,94	357 169 43 95 32	515 133 1 o84 5.4 2 090 2 695	14 52 178 199 176 1,490	2,205	255 46 46 254 464 283	299 427 43	14 165 3 598 48 192 751	103 116 13 20 315 190 145	
and he swuce stataons rigg stores rigg and drinking piaces rigg and drinking piaces right and drinking piaces right and drinking piaces right and right and right and right right and right right and right	6 150 2,119 3 579 5,94° 2 38' 4 563	357 169 43 95 32.	515 133 1 o84 5.4 2 090 2 695	14 52 178 199 1,490 1 039 451	188 159 464 943 2,235	255 26 46 254 464 283 41 242	299 427 43 23	14 165 1558 48 102 751 253 498	103 116 13 29 315 190 145	
and he service statuons trust statuons trust states string and drinking places string and drinking places and are tarn implement, & blidg material drailing of other retail tends of the frameon, insurance and state states and the frameon transparence and real extate. Baumers and repair services	6 150 2,119 3 579 6,04 2 39 4 563 6,283	377 169 41 95 32 147 174 396	515 133 1 o84 5.4 4 090 4 695 820 875	14 52 178 199 1,490 1,490 1 039 451 346	2,205 48 2,205 48 4 .57	155 20 45 2.4 404 283 41 242 2,737	299 427 43 23 21 763	14 165 3 598 48 1°2 75_ 253 498 478	103 116 13 29 315 190 145	
and he service stataons (vug thorse stataons (vug thorse stataons (vug thorse stataons (vug thorse stataons (vug thorse stataons)). The control of the stataons (vug thorse stata	6 150 2, 119 3 579 5, 047 4 553 6, 283 2 22 2, 383	37 169 43 95 32 147 174 396 652 14	51.5 133 1 684 5 .4 2 090 2 695 820 875 897	14 52 178 199 1,490 1 039 451 346 229 47	188 159 464 943 2,235 48 4 .57 167 136 22	255 26 46 2,54 464 283 41 242 2,777	299 427 43 23 21 763	14 165 3 558 48 1°2 752 253 498 478	103 116 12 29 315 190 145	
Mol he service statuons (rug stored string and drinking holes stips and drinking holes stips and drinking holes stips and color relatification of the status of the status and real essate saking and other finance around a status of the statu	6 150 2,19 3 579 5,94 4 553 6,283 2 22 2,383 1 686	4 357 165 43 95 32 147 174 390 652 14 30	51.5 133 1 684 5.4 0 90 2 695 830 875 897 296 330 271	14 52 178 190 16 1,490 1 039 451 346 220 47 40	188 159 464 943 2,235 48 4.57 167	1.55 46 2.54 464 2.83 41 2.42 2,737 2.61 1,436	299 427 43 23 21 763 48 3 7 238	14 165 1588 48 102 752 253 498 478 759	103 116 13 29 315 190 145 28 197	
and he service statuons to the control of the contr	6 150 2, 19 3 579 5, 94° 2 59' 4 553 6, 283 2 22, 2, 383 1 680 6 800	357 165 43 95 37 147 174 396 652 14 30 309	512 133 1 084 5 2 090 695 875 897 296 330 271	14 52 178 199 1,490 1 039 451 346 229 47	188 159 464 943 2,235 48 4 .57 167 136 22	155 46 254 464 283 41 242 2,777 201 1,430	299 427 43 23 21 763 148 3 7 238	14 165 1588 48 102 751 253 498 478 739 22,695	103 116 13 29 315 190 145 20 124 44 49°	
and he service statuons to the control of the contr	6 150 2, 119 3 579 b, 94° 2 39° 4 553 6, 283 2 22, 2, 383 1 680 6 800	377 169 47 95 32 147 174 396 652 14 30 309	512 133 1 884 5.4 2 990 1 695 820 875 897 296 130 271 735 18	14 52 178 199 1,490 1 039 451 346 229 47 40 231 2	188 159 464 945 2,205 48 4 .57 167 22 9	155 26 46 234 464 283 41 242 2,777 261 1,430 1,740 205 27	299 427 43 23 24 763 448 3.7 2.38 4,744 446 64	14 165 1588 48 102 75_ 233 498 478 77 2,695 499	103 116 13 20 313 190 145 26 26 24 44 497	
Moch is envice statuous yet stored in the control of the control o	6 150 2,19 3 779 b,047 2 597 4 563 6,283 2 12. 2,383 1 680 6 800	377 162 47 95 32 147 174 174 174 174 175 174 175 174 175 175 175 175 175 175 175 175 175 175	512 133 1 84 5 2 090 2 695 820 875 897 296 330 271 735	14 52 178 199 190 1 039 451 346 229 47 40 231	188 159 464 943 2,235 48 4.57 167	155 46 254 464 283 41 242 2,777 201 1,430	299 427 43 23 21 763 148 3 7 238	14 165 1588 48 102 75_ 253 498 478 27 7 2,695	103 116 12 20 315 190 145 -38 197 20 124 44 497	
and in a service statuons rugs stored with a service statuons rugs stored with a self-statuon status and statu	6 150 2,119 3 579 b, 94" 2 595 6,283 2 22. 2,383 1 68. 6 800 	377 169 41 95 32 147 174 396 652 14 30 309 11 44	912 133 1 084 5.4 5.9 695 820 875 897 296 130 271 735 18 180 423	14 52 178 199 1,490 1 039 451 346 229 47 40 231 2	1.88 1.59 464 943 2,225 48 4.37 1.67 1.36 22 9 1.08	155 26 27 24 46 283 41 242 2,777 201 1,430 1,430 1,430 1,430 1,430 1,430 1,430 1,430 1,430 1,430 1,430 1,430 1,444 2,544 1,54	299 427 43 23 24 763 448 3 7 7 2 28 4,744 46 64 4,333	14 165 598 48 102 75_ 253 478 478 79 2 7 2,65 499 4,02	103 116 13 29 315 190 145 38 94 44 44 44 497 416 29 44	
and in a service statuon rugs force under the control of an including losses stops and drinking places to get an including losses and real estate asking and other finative or control or delete state asking and other finative or sentence and real estate sentence and real estate asking and estate asking	6 150 2,119 3 579 4 553 6,283 2 22 2,383 1 686 6 800 1,203 1,003 1	37, 169, 43, 43, 95, 32, 147, 174, 296, 652, 14, 30, 309, 11, 4, 1, 1, 2/4, 749	512 133 1 684 5 5.4 4 090 4 695 897 296 330 271 735 180 423 1.9	14 52 178 199 190 199 1039 1039 1451 346 229 47 40 231 160 49 18	188 159 464 2,205 48 4 37 167 36 22 9 108	155 46 234 464 283 41 242 2,777 261 1,430 1,740 305 27 127 27 27 27 27 27	299 427 43 23 24 763 448 3.7 2.18 4.7 4.4 64 4.3 3.3 7 2.18	14 165 1598 48 102 75_ 253 478 478 77 2,695 2,695 1,002 1,130	103 116 13 29 315 190 145 	
and he service statuons rugs forces of control of an implements, de bidg maternal of alling stope and past estate and maternal of alling liber relations and control of an extraction and control out of each	6 130 2,119 3 579 4 553 6,283 2 22 2,383 1 68 6 800 -,203 7,748 37,748	377 169 47 92 32 147 174 396 654 14 30 309 11 4 4 749 6, 17	512 133 1 684 2 695 806 875 897 298 130 271 735 180 423 1.09	14 52 178 199 199 190 109 451 109 451 47 40 231 160 49 18 279 452 47 40 49 160 162 163	1.88 1.59 4.64 94.3 2,225 4.8 2.37 1.67 1.36 2.2 9 1.08	155 46 47 254 464 283 41 242 2,747 261 1,430 1,740 1,630 1,740 1,630 1,	299 427 43 23 24 763 448 3 7 7 2 338 2,7 44 426 44 1,330 94 107	14 165 1598 48 102 75_ 213 498 478 77 2,695 459 1,130 960 1599	103 116 12 29 315 190 145 28 26 44 49 27 28 28 20 20 21 22 22 22 27	
and he service statuons (reg stores	6 1300 2,119 3 579 b, q4" 2 39' 4 550 6,283 2 22- 2,383 1 68- 6 800 -,203' 1,009 2,081 87' 3,416 7,748 - 076 - 076 - 076	37, 169 41 39 41 39 41 39 61 30 30 30 91 11 47 1 27 49 6, 17 2,276	515 133 1 984 5.4 1 990 693 820 875 897 296 330 271 735 180 423 1.9 4-57 4-7 4-7 4-7 4-7 4-7 4-7 4-7 4-7 4-7 4-	14 55 178 199 109 10 1,490 1059 451 345 47 40 231 25 47 40 29 49 49 49 49 49 49 49 49 49 49 49 49 49	188 159 4664 943 2,205 26 22 29 108 119 24 4	155 49 49 49 49 49 49 49 49 49 49 49 49 49	299 427 43 23 763 448 5 7 7 228 4,744 4,330 94 107 495	14 165 159 48 102 75_ 253 498 478 79 22 7 2,695 499 1,002 4,130 960 1,599 1,942 1,942 1,942 1,944 1,94	103 116 129 3119 190 145 191 192 194 194 197 198 199 199 199 199 199 199 199 199 199	
and he service statuons regularly glosses and real drawing looks and drawing places and real example and real drawing lother retail traditions, to bidg material drawing lother retail traditions of colors retail traditions and real example and retails are retails.	6 130 2,119 3 579 5,94" 1 197 4 553 6,283 2 12,2 2,383 1 68,6 6 800 -,203 2,031 877 3,416 7,748 -076 -071 -0	4 377 165 1 47 1 165 1 47 1 174 1 165 1 16	512 133 1 084 5 2, 4 090 699 200 207 203 203 203 203 203 203 203 203 203 203	14 55 178 199 - 16 1,490 1 039 451 346 229 47 47 40 231 2 160 49 18 2 2 2 4 3 4 4 4 4 4 4 4 4 4 4 4 4 4 4 4	188 159 444 944 944 2205 20 20 20 20 20 20 20 20 20 20 20 20 20	159 44 44 44 44 44 44 44 44 44 44 44 44 44	299 299 2427 43 221 763 5.7 7 238 6.37 44 1,330 94 100 100 100 100 100 100 100 100 100 10	14. 145 158 48 102 75. 233 476 476 476 478 478 478 478 478 478 478 478 478 478	103 116 139 311 190 145 145 20 20 44 44 49° 411 28 20 20 20 21 20 20 20 20 20 20 20 20 20 20 20 20 20	
such in service statuons rugs stored string and drinking places string and drinking places string and drinking places string and drinking places string and drinking places string and drinking string	6 1300 2,19 3 579 5,04" 2 49 4 569 6,283 2 2.2,383 1 68.0 4,203 4,203 4,203 7,748 7,748 1 076 1,438	377 165 1 41 32 32 32 32 147 144 306 652 146 30 96 652 146 30 96 652 146 30 96 652 147 147 147 147 147 147 147 147 147 147	512 133 1 084 5 2, 2 000 1 080	14 52,78 199 199 1,480 1 039 1	188 159 464 94.1 2,205 26 168 168 179 168 168 179 168 179 168 179 168 179 179 179 179 179 179 179 179 179 179	155 de de 155 de	297 43 21 763 48 5.7 7 238 4.7 46 6.5 4.7 4.1 107 4.7 107 4.7 107 4.7 107 4.7 107 107 107 107 107 107 107 107 107 10	14- 165- 168- 168- 172- 173- 233- 468- 478- 478- 478- 478- 478- 478- 478- 47	103 116 129 3119 190 145 191 192 194 194 197 198 199 199 199 199 199 199 199 199 199	
sach in service statuces recycle transcent of the control of the c	6 120 2 121 3 79 4 50 50 50 50 50 50 50 50 50 50 50 50 50	377 165 1 41 37 32 32 32 147 147 148 396 652 148 30 9 652 148 148 148 148 148 148 148 148 148 148	512 133 1 684 2 695 2 695 3 695 3 695 3 70 2 70 2 70 2 70 2 70 2 70 2 70 2 70 2	14 52,78 199 199 1,480 1 039 1	188 1.59 1.464 1.59 1.464 1.59 1.467 1.67 1.67 1.67 1.67 1.67 1.67 1.67 1.	155	297 43 21 23 21 24 36 37 63 37 44 33 44 43 30 107 49 407 407 408 407 409 409 409 409 409 409 409 409 409 409	14: 14: 15: 15: 15: 16: 16: 16: 16: 16: 16: 16: 16: 16: 16	103 115 12 12 12 12 12 19 19 10 145 19 10 145 10 10 10 10 10 10 10 10 10 10 10 10 10	10.
Moch to service statuous up stored in the up stored of a continuous continuou	6 130 2,19 3 579 5 04" 2 39' 4 553 6 283 2 2,283 1 680 -,203 2 ,203 2 ,203 1 680 -,203 2 ,203 2 ,203 1 680 -,203 1 ,20	377 165 1 41 32 32 32 32 147 144 306 652 146 30 96 652 146 30 96 652 146 30 96 652 147 147 147 147 147 147 147 147 147 147	512 133 1 644 5 50 2 000 693 200 201 201 201 201 201 201 201 201 201	14 53: 178: 199: 1,480 1 (39: 145) 346: 229: 40: 231: 240: 250: 260: 279: 279: 281: 281: 281: 281: 281: 281: 281: 281	188 159 464 94.1 2,205 26 168 168 179 168 168 179 168 179 168 179 168 179 179 179 179 179 179 179 179 179 179	155	297 43 21 763 45 57 63 64 57 64 64 64 64 64 64 64 64 64 64 64 64 64	14: 16: 16: 16: 16: 16: 16: 16: 16: 16: 16	103 115 129 29 29 190 140 140 20 44 449 440 440 441 26 27 28 38 38 38 38 38 38 38 38 38 38 38 38 38	10.

Table 84—MAJOR OCCUPATION GROUP OF EMPLOYED PERSONS, BY INDUSTRY AND SEX, FOR THE STATE AND FOR STANDARD METROPOLITAN AREAS OF 250,000 OR MORE 1950—Con

Area industry and ev	Total, 14 jears ora and over	Processionseconocal and kindred worsers	Managers officials and proprietors and farm	Clerica. and amdred workers	Sales workers	Crafumen, foremen and sindred workers	Operatives and kindred workers	Service workers mel. nnvate household	Laborers, except mine	Occupation not reported
KEN CEPTRANS					7,272	942	3,391	23, 239	915	835
Percale, employed	8. 452	34a t	3,80.	23,419		3	8	2	105	2
Agaiculture forestry and fishenes	7.2	3	29	29	1	3		1	97	2
Agriculture Forest v and fisheries	150	-	28	.2		3	7 1		8	
Mining		- 2	ر			1		-		
Coal mining Cruce petroleum and natural gas extraction Viring and quarrying except fuel	-4	14	2	12° 14		2	1	ī		
Солестичиоп	504		25	422	6	56	12	1.8	22	
Manuactarang .	3,553	J-12	2	2,380	-11	3.3	0,242	117	325	34
⊃urable goods	12.8	33	4-	251	_0	62	46_	16	87 2	-
Sawmil's planing milis, and mill work	.09	,	9	24	2	3	3⊥		7	
Misrefaneous wood products	10a 155	1	2	21		2 25	69	1	10	
Furniture and fixtures Glass and glass products Stone and clay products	14		1	24 11		1	2 2 2	2	3	
	e7 _8		3	15		-	2	-	1	
Primary nonferrous industries.	4		100	1.9	2	10	171	6	38	
Primary nonferrous industries. Fabricated weta' industries income no spec metaly Machinery, except electrical. Fabrical machiner, comment and simples	356	4 2	4	5, 20,	2	/	9	6	1	
Mo or velices and a oto vehicle equipment	42	2 2	-	2′	-	3	5		_	
Aircra t and narts			18.3	74			د	,	3	,
Ship and boat building and repairing Railroad and Just Mangaor atton equipment	-14	9	4	4		î			-	1 3
Railroad and cose dansper stack equipment. All other durable goods	144	8	10	50	,	U	61	1	236	2-
Andurable goods _	8 246	⊥35	139	2,505 64	98 1	271	5,°,6 113	99	9	-
Mest p oriusts Bakery products Other good industries	2.40		5	5° 452	17	2 34 40	162 1 256	19	8 70	9
	1,909	1,	38	7	3		516		17	9
Kniting mills. Yarn thread and sabre milis	249	2	2	10	1	7 9	219 421	20	2 36	2
Other textile mill producte	56		2	12 171		94	39	20 1	2	7
Other textule mill products Apparel and other fabricated saxiale products	3 125	19	11 2	104	9 7	9	176	2 7	13	. 2
Appare and one root este status products Paper and a ned proof est Pon ug publishing and alloid industries Chem. ests and a last products Petroleum and one products Ruiber products	*21	74	74	104 27 140	37	44	34 29	7	11	4
Chem cals and a lied products	225 181	8 9	_6 1	154			7	3	6	
Rubber products	24	1	2	-5	1		9		1	
Leathe and leather products except footwear	*3			33	ī		45	2	4 2	
ot specified manuscruring industries .	89	2	2		,	6t	118	232	215	
Transport. communication & other public milities	4 753	116	93	3,893	1		21	34	413	
Railroads and railway express service	182	1	7 :	2-6	2	3		17	21	
Street railways and bus sines Trucking service and warchousing Water transportstion	214 832		12	147 6*1	1	6	20 38	39 "5	12 59	1
Air transportation .	175	18	3	90	3			5		-
All other transportation Telecommunications	.98	59	38	2,081	5	37	4	39	2	3
Electric and gas utilities Water supply sanitary services, and other utilities	c.B	24	4	3.5	5 2	1	4	7 2	7	2
		35*	2 404	6 404	6 592	318	1,471	4 943	-13	25
Wholesale and retail trade Wholesale trade	3 237	135		2 39"	125	35	423	48	37	
General merchanduse and five and ten cent stores	< .960	84	114 753	558	4 397	27 69	1,4 364	67 432	29 21	8
	1,960	19	201	1,189	2,943 768	-m	422 37	99	3	1
Apparet and accessomes stores Furniture hour furnishings and equipment stores. Motor "shicles and accessories retailing	352 311	1'	52 10	288 254	108	16	37	33	3	(
Gasoline service stations -	56	1	10	30 179	4	1 2	6	1	2	1
Drug stores	987 4,915	8. 61.	24 598	266	مر م	11	_9 22	261 3,892	2	5
Hardware farm implement & bldg. material retailing.	1,09	24	40 273	200 447	6, 68u	47		11 95	2 8	
	4,282	6.	248	3,200	Jen	8	17	359	4	. 5
Finance, insurence and real estate Banking and other finance	1 689	20	52	1,524	4		7	69		1
Insurance and real estate	2 59	4C	196	1 606	377	. 7	10	390	5	1 4
Business and repair services	921	105	68	620	21		43	22	3	2
Business services Automobile repair services and garages	758 77	98	48	329 45	ı î	12 11	31	3	2	2
Mucelianeous repair services and garages	86	5 2	6 14	46	3	14	5 7	,	,	
Personal services	10,010	136	330	648	50	46	2,081	14,160	61	9
Presta housenolds	2,143	49	5	10 271	4	1	94 66	11 999	21	2 3
Hotels and lodging places Laundering cleaning, and dveing services	2 006	2	124	256	20	3	±,576	1,081	33	3
All other personal services	1,690	67	>5	99	21	6	375	1,07	1	1
Enter stament and recreation services	1,411	16/	72	479	70	29	86	200	6	4
Professional and related services	24,525	8 10-	235	2,931	_3	2.*	260	2,909	14	12
Medical and other health services	7,260 3 167	3 596 2,368	59 60	1,520 204	3	13	177	1,8~1	11	R 3
Educational services government Educational services private Welfarc, singous and membership organisations Legal, engines ing and miss professional services	2,370	2,506 2,626 43.6	64	341	100	6	27	292	11	1
Weifarc, sligious and membership organizations. Legal, enginee .ng and miss professional services.	1,071	41.6 100	38	335 531	3	1	45	2.32	1	1
Public administration	3,378	403	76	2 687		4	26	136		13
Postal service	96	2	12	47			1		1	2
Tederal public administration State and local public administration	2,221	154 247	32	1,948	1	3	21	42 77	6	10

	± 032	247	27	14	2		100			
Industry ant reported	z 032	22	. 27	14.	2	24	26	25	4	7_9

Table 85 —WEEKS WORKED IN 1949 BY THE EXPERIENCED CIVILIAN LABOR FORCE, BY INDUSTRY AND SEX, FOR THE STATE AND FOR STANDARD MFTROPOLITAN AREAS OF 250,030 OR MORE 1950 (Besed on 20-percent sample For totals by adustry run (200) pid 60-abt sec table 79

The state of the s	N. P. S. D. S.	700	_	-	s old and		00000		120		Fema	ie, 14 yea	s oud an	d over		- Control of the
Aier and incustry	Potal	Did not	T,	orked 12	1949 (nur	nber of w	veks)	A STOR		Did no	R	otked in	1949 (nu.	nber of w	nekm i	Work u
		in 1949	1 to 13	14 to 28	27 039	-0 to 49	50 .o 52	949 not reported	Total	work un 1949	1 to 13		_	40 to 49	a0 to 52	1949 no reported
THE STATE Experienced civilian labor force		1						3.400							w/1	
Agriculture forestry and fisheres	144 775	36,060	25,310	4,255	20,660	70,475	403,9/0		237,525	30,900	16,260	22,860	24,865	20,165	1_2,905	9,86
Agriculti a		16,650	6,520	9 755	12,54"	2,600	u8,795	8,915	16,795	4,760	2,300	2,910		1 195	2,995	87
Forest's and fisheries	135,6-5 9,130	675	300	1,110	0,940	20,325	64,800 3,995	8,500	16 610	4,730	2,340	2,885	1,68,	2,490	2,915	86
Mining	12,80	545	390	1,160	1,390	2,700	15,820	840	1,105	60	_5	70	55	775	775	5
rude pet oleum and natural gas extraction	20,570	460	300	1,020	1.	2,455	45	1C	995	50						
Coal mining Pride petroleum and natural gas extraction Mining and quarrying, except fuel	2,180	85	40	125	140	244	1,495	25	140	10	5	55 15	50	60	715	5
Construction	68,005	2 540	2,840	7,690	9,135	14,335	30,805	2,0.0	2,66>	.30	50	150	ر 105	125	4,000	7
Dura bla moda	1_9,285	3,75	3,060	7,135	8,200	13,770	79,070	4,290	17,735	-,545	1,180		4,590	1,850	8,965	77
Logung having mile and mill work. Miscellaneous wood products. Furniture and fixtu es	48, 265 5,770	255	-, 250 22,	4,075	4,830 775	7,505	26,720	2,175	2,485	175	120	210	205 5	2,0	., 315	20
Miscellaneous wood products_	21,200	875 65	70 ₀ 85	215	2,270	دية,ك 242	2,275 10,755 1,285	375 91.5 60	480 120	25 35	20	70 25	/5	60	250	1
	9,5,5	35	90	100	220	245 170	965	55	320	30	20	40	20	30	-80	1
Stone and clay products Prinary iror and steel industries	2,345	15	50 20 15	30 105	200	100 275	1,5/0 73U	95	1.0	ە.	10		4	2	20 85	
Prinary for and steel industries Prinary nonferrous industries Pabric d meta and (int) no spec metal Machinery, except electrical Electrical machinery (dup and supplies Machinery and behavior of the principles	445	25	15	65 40 170	90	150 50 395	73U 275	60 15	40 10				20 11/2	15	85 20 10	
Machinery, exceps electrical	3,390 2,975	80	50 50	170	210	395 260	2,370	_15 _20	400	10	-53	30 15	45	65	221	ı
	470	الم	5	10	15	25 40	305	25	100	1 1	10	15	5	50	130	1
Aircra't and parts	2.	3		-		5	370	10	30	2		,	100000		20	"
Rai "old & mist transportation agricment	-,450 70	130	145	495	575	690	2,245	160	_30	1,	ا ا		20	5	85	
Au other durable goods ordurable good	1,210	2,015	60	40	100	150	72	100	400	35	30	15	40	15	140	12
Meat products Bakery proquets		€0	1,500 45 60	3,005	340 100	6,180	1,345	2,00	-5,095 320	1,350	1,045 20	1,600	-,380 25	-,600 30	7,587	>4
Other food industries	3,150	115 590	60 195	1,095	1,285	285	2,430	60	.9.	80	30	15 35	25	aO.	370	2
Toos.co manufactures Knitting muls	17,240			5	20	5	_00	265 5	4,155	435 60	540 30	?~0 60	485 55 30	120	1,4/0	10
Notice male mile State mile Otler tex de mile products	825	20	45	45	35	20 90	95 580	20	260	رد دد	5	20	30	35 65	125	20 22 4
Appealed & ther fab unted tax le produces	00ء 265ء عالرادا	70	30	20 85	3. 30	10	960	20	3,720	5 290	±90	40C	35 25	10	55	- 4
Paper and alised produce: Printing publishing and allied industries Cheru als and allied produces	13,1.1	539	190	285	220 53	4,155	10 060	20 350	1.540	125 115	90	40C	110	510 170	1,730	15.
Chemi als and allied products Petrol-ur and coal products	2,410	240	160	445 275	53.	325	3 680 7,065 13,200	21.5 255	1,135	120	50	95 95	75 30	65 05	690	15. 3 2 7
	5,490	250	_05	275	3.0	950	13,200	400	95	35	15	2>	25	45	825	2
Fortwear except rubber . Leather & leather products, exc footwear	20 05			10	10		35	15	10	1			1		30	
not specified in anutal timing industries	700	35	10	50	30	85	440	45	-55	20	,	15	- 1	5	70	30
Transport. commun., & other public util	65,±70 18,095	1,675	21.5	4,090	5,010	7,565	45,335	2,435	9,810	540	295	510	520	625	7,050	אייכ
lairoads and railway express service.	4,695 8,295	85	35	670 l	895 290	2,290	13,320 3,385 7,045	590 190	795 500	25 35	20	25 65	ئد: ئاد:	65 25	605	15
ater transportation	15,440	275 450	495	1,545	755	2,290	7,700	295 743	460 90:	30 40	25	65	35	10	325	
Il other ransports ion	5,205	25	20	30 310	430	490	3,450	65	220	10	10	.0	10	40 20	160	20
elecommunications	3.145	80	CA OA	715	125 325	170	2,485	90	5,235	45 285	170	201	10	2C 390	31.5	13
lecture and was utilities ater supply, sanitary services & other util	3,865	195 BJ	120	300 220	325	310	2,860	200 85	1,090	32 15	35	25	35	35	833 120	50
Wholesale and retail trade.	144,11	5,100	,390	6,16>	5,450	7,975	81,255	-,075	57,135	7,250	2.985	5, 222	3,630	4.280	30,570	2,165
holesale trade ood & dary rod stores, & milk retailing	27,315 21,720	780	500 735	1,305	1,250	2 035	20,562	880	4,805 9,135	360	180	310	260	295	3,245	155
eneral merchandise di five & ten cent stores	2,,720 5,900 3,.20	235	175	1,170	835	1,-10	4 955	715	11.605	1,745	390	1,015	365 645	570 765	6,435	205
pparel and a ressories sores	3, 20	135	130	200	160	200	2,210	*C4	1,400	145	370	385	265 90	90	2,34<	490
otor vehicles and accessories retailing	8,25 7,425	295 320	325	325 505	350	590	0,235	340	880 320	65	151	0.5	35	65	010	25
nig stores sting and drinking places	3,232	265	±70	225	425 135	455	4,910 2,120	165	2,445	360	25	25	215	100	1,275	80
ardware farm implem" & bldg mater'l ret	8,600	790 310	230 170	985 375	930	995	5,310	3.5	1,140 4 435	2,645	1,225	2,065	1,480	-,532	6,980	640 50 170
l other etail trade_	10,525	455	380	57.	450	620	7,695	340		240	340	370	210	340	2,465	170
Finance insurance and real estate	13, ~ 0 4,525	460	215	56. 160	475	76a 260	3,460	130	8,090	9775	295	455 190	200	470	5,580	270
surance and real estate	9 240	300	165	400	380	200	7,160	335	4,445	39.J	185	265	340	225	2,625	115
Business and repair services	18,920	761	525	955	1,120	1,815	13,020	205	1,885	160	125	275	120	97	1,135	75
utiness services utomobile repair services and garages.	3,700 9,860	150	85 i 260 .	165 505	245	300 905	2,590	16° 350	1,290	95 40	95	125	80	60 20	780	55 10
erellaneous repair services	5,360	2/.5	180	28.5	435	610	3,415	190	285	25	20	25	30	15	100	10
Personal services	20,290	1,185	995	1,290	4,440	1,790	12,575	715	64,145	8,36.	-,720	0,840	4,705	5,820	29,49;	2,205
nvate households	5,390 3,050 5,490 5,560	550 175	790 E41	520	605 245	580 300	2,480	195 120	46,830 3,890	6,495	3,760	5,420	3,695	4,405	21,340	1,665
sundering cleaning and dyeing services	5,490	185 275	140	270	285	390 520	4,020	200	6,580 4,840	750 600	380	580	2C	625	2,240	225
Entertainmen and recreation services	7 . 20	440	424	290	58.	575	4,180	325	2,305	21.5	190	240	185	160	1,260	200
Professional and related services	-8,295	1,200	780	1,605	2,290	2,510	18 545	1,360	43,315	3,685	1,895	3,340	-0,995	4,772	_6,830	1,795
ledical and other heal-h services	6 105	253	150	420	375	500	8.365	390	LJ.370		745	1.410	1,020	1,200	8.835	615
du atonal services government	3,015	485 140	320	615	1,450	1,125	4,410 1,770 3 p.0	320 140	19,085 5,115 2,335	1,545	780 160	1,340 360 130 95	8,435 1,340	2,785	3,800	700
dustional se vices government dustional services, private elfar religious & member-hip organiz'ns egal, engineering & misc professional ser-	4,770 3,380	200	135	200	کید طبا 135	20.		305	2,335	26U	145	130	15C	1201	1,420	110
Public administration		10 5	95 365	785	900	270	2 390	2C5	8,795	75	65 480	95	39C	405		70
ostal service	24,640	60	45	80	105	290	3.755	432	1,000	65	480	55	390	50	5,845	2/5
ederal public administration	4,475 7 500	415	115	245	275	385	5,800	265	3,770	665	245	160	235	150	2,295	120
tate and local public adminis-ration Industry not reported	12,665	2,785	1,3/0	460	1,720	715	10,000	2 145	4,025	2 490	675	490 615	425		2,840	110
Industry not reported	«O,15»	7,755	1,310	2,000	1,720	1,685	8,460	2,145	6,965	2,690	0.13	0	423	290	1,355	915

Table 85 —WELKE WORKED IN 1549 BY THE EXPERIENCED CIVILIAN LABOR FORCE, BY INDUSTRY AND SEX, FOR THE STATE AND FOR STANDARD METROPOLITAN AREAS OF 250,000 OR MORE 1950—Con

Based on 20-p.n. at salie." For te alsow industry rem complete count see table 79]

	-	and the section of the section of	310.0	14 veer	s ord a. l	01-*	_				Femal	le, 14 yea	rs old and	over		
to out a source		Dio no.			1649 (prn		nek s.	We'k in		Dad not	77	orkea in 1	249 'num	ber of w	seka)	Work 12
4 ea and moustry	‴o sa	F Foll .	_				50 to 52	1949 not reported	Total	work in 1949	1 to 13	14 to 26	27 to 39	40 to 49	50 to 53	1949 not
		14-4	. 20 18	14 10 29	2" t · 39	40 10 40	30 10 02	7 aporteos		-	_					
NEW CONTRACT		4 1							83 075	8,695	4,375	970ء	6 700	6,605	46,645	3,_0:
Exper enced c value labor force	.23 44;	7 2-5	5 . 5	-1 524	12,575	.6 525	123,240	o 93C	83 075	30	15	30	_5	10	105	1
Agurante, forester and fi hones	2,005	2.5	0		3.0	.45	1,3.0	70	165	3	15	30	-5	10	80	
Agrica Tre Pores variable e.	- 242	1. 15	&. 30	200	50.	15	445	60	30						25	
Mining.	± 870	-0		75	~ :	20	1,470	-5	185	-		_ 10		10	125	
Cruss petrole, and partit, gas extraction	1.065	35		nđ	வ்	_35	1,4 5	45	.65			10	5	5	140	
Cruca petrole and naturage extraction	",	5		-0	5	10	35	5	20 "25	40	15	40	45	25	525	2
Construction	لدعرف	.85	75	2,.50	2 525	170	9 37>	920	9,990	800	-90	975	945	1 440	5 240	4
Manutacturing	21,075	325	365	755	2 340	3,.00	21 975	443	1,330	90	55	.10	95	150	760	1
Coggreg calls, and malwork have lancous wood products Figure and fixtures	-,035	15	20	.5	83	-1.	25	60	120		1	25	_0	25	65	
At wellaneous wood products	53.0	201	25	15	6	80	380	25	90	20	10	20	-0	20	*00 50	. :
Fig. ure and fixti res	8,	201	40	25	45	10	55 65	5 35	15	-					±5 e0	
Grass and glass products Stone and class products	+ 25	20	15	50	1	90 10 90 70	a65 350	35	61 15	1		5		,	9	
Primary nomerrous inci-tine.	2 170	1	5	115	5 135	270	1,520	1 1	360	10	10	37	45	55	200	
Stone and class products. Primary nonnerrous industries. Primary nonnerrous industries. Fashed netal ind unes not spec metal). Machinery everpt electrics. Floring numbers haping and supplies. Motor while are most use of excountment.	05	35	30	45	70	BC.	705	20 85 5	36 80	10	13			15	50 55 45	
Motor scholes a moto vet de equipment	570			5	15	- 2	115	ە_ ە	20	5	,	5				
Ship and Loat building and repairing Railroad & muse ranspo ta iou equiprient	3,490	ã	ودن	345	450	490	1,680	140	110	15			_0	2	75	
Railroad & muse ranspo ta ioù equipment All other durable goods	6.0	.*0	35	ط	35	70	40 395	30	10 200	15	15		201	10	95	:
Nongu able good.	_9 5°0	AFU	4eu 20	- 00	970	1 075	1~ 235	260 35	8,545	705	-25	855	84.5	980 20	1,425	31
Meat poducts Bake-y products Other food industries	930 4,140 6,25*	25	36	60 20 25	45 75	20 _20	1,020	25	21.5 31.5	50	15	2.	20	20	200	
Other food industries	6,25*	185	120	-05	385 10	r65	4,410	182	2,005	190	160 25	275 50 20	210	210	895 305	1 4
hnitting mills	120	20	30	45	30	15 75	80 25	15	755 590	20 35	25 5 2	20	30 35 15	35	120	3
Ya'n the ead and fubric mills O hir textile m'il products Apparel & otler fobrication textus products	145		30	.0	5	10	_05 840	198	70	240	135	-	15 405	415	1,475	,
	2,580	65	60	125	130	250	2,220	J0c	3,145	15	_5	34 ₄ 30 40	20	15	255 295	1
Printing publishing and slied industries Chemica s an allied products. Petroleum and coal products.	2 825	220	14.	135	1.0	.45 55	1,040	±20 40	4 5 250	60 15	20	27	30	30	135	1 2
Petroleum and coal produ s Rubber products	1,125	25	70	60	75	-10	1,_93	40	18,	10		>		30 20 10	150 20	
Footnear except rubber	40		20		-0		25	1 5	13					5	_0	
ot specified manuac uring rdustries	2310	15	3.	_0 15	20	żo	135	10 15	110	15	5	مَد	5	IL.	55	1
Transport commun., & other public util	3°,505	84>	735	2,235	2,900	1,645	21,875	1,205	4,740	±90	125	2100	2,00	275	3 660	9
Rudroads and rai way exploss service. Stiest railways and bus lines	7,275	100	95	295	36C 35	605 A10	5,560 1 580	081 CB	4.5 175	3	۵	20	25 40	25 10	345 105	
T-ucking service and warenousing Water transportation	12,40	125	410	330	265	1,910	2,300	120	865	25 35	20	50	20	10 35	165 680	,
Air transportation	305	10	10	30	205	35	1 520	50	185	20	5	10	5 10	20	140	
All other transportation lelecommunications	1.435	40	65 25	49	50	50	1,6%	50 45	2,295	80	90	80	95	150	1,75*	4
Flectric and gas utilities Water supply sar tary services & o her util	2,020	999	25 35	50 55	60	80	1,000	60 30	55	10		5	10	2.	40	-
Wholesale and retail trade	43,140	2,080	± ±65	2,475	2 215	2,740	30,935	1,390	22,490	7,345	1 4.0	2,000	1,365	.,520	12,870	5
Wholesale trade	13,280 6,765	405 460	24.5 24.5	630 3u5	515 330	8 5 465	10,285	390 190	3,077	190 455	125	190	170	150 155	2,145 1,910 3,460	9
Food & dairy prod stores & mile retailing. General increhandise & two & ten cent stores	2,295	90	10.	365 130 85 75	120 90	120	1,677	70 40 70	5,600	465 215	555 145	230 179	3,0 130	,30 ,60	3,400	24
Apparel and accessories stores Furniture home furnishings & equip stores. Mctor vehicles and accessories etalling	1,990	90 65 150	55	75	150	140	1,490	70	230 285	55 15		65 20	25 15	35 5	215	2
Gasolina service stations	1.00	75 125 370	55 60 95 80 235	11,	105	150 35 49	1,050	80	25	10	.0 5	65	75	65	10	1
Drug a ores hading and drinking places	1,255	370	235	435	70 430	49_	805 2,695	90 245	575 5,000 325	140 815	295	620	4351	505	2,155	
Facdware, farn implem t & bldg mater l ret All other retail trade	2,165 3,385	110	135	120	110	95 175	2,700	165	1,520	30 155	120	135	25	20	225 870	4
because insurance and real estate	7,200	250	90	285	195	165	5,810	21.5	4,360	2BC	155	250	235	200	3,060	2
Banking and other finan e Insurance and real estate	2,375 4,035	85 165	15 75	75 230	30 165	145 220	1,96.	50	2,535	80	15	90 160	100 _35	120 -40	1,710	3
But-ness and repair services	6,555	3Co	10	365	475	595	4,145	-75	950	65	50	65	65	35	025	4
Business services	2 240	64		85	175	220	1,560	85	795	35 10	55	55	45	30	520	3
Automobile repair services and garages Miscellaneous repair services	2 240 2,5_5 _,800	125	50 97 55	100	130 170	225 150	1,705	60	80	10		-0	5 15		50	
Personal services	6,865	205	195	535	455	560	4.665	190	18 640	2,355	1 4.5	1,900	.485	1 600	9,4,5	56
Private households	-,140	80	55 55	175 105	90 145	80 165	0.5	2	12,770	1,720	905	1,400	1,005	1.,30	6,130	42
Hotels and lodging places Launder ig cleaning and dying services All other personal -ervices	2,275	75 45	60	135	160	175	2,075	70 45 50	2,295	245 190	1.0	200 185	100 170	220	1,005	7
All other pursonal -e-vies Entertainment and recreation services	-,850 3,680	45 200	240	130	80	315	1 370	170	_,820	190 85			100	40	945	
Professional and related services	9,595	380	250	520	465	725	2,090	405	14 0.5	1,440	570	1,075	2.020	1,445	7,545	24
Megual and other health services	4.050	1.60		250	110	245 30	3,080	165	14,615 1,361 3 090	790	320	600	2,030	530	7,545	16
Educational services governmen Educational services private Welfare religious & membership organisms	1,000	50 60	70 30 50 45	-10	125	30د 00ء	480	. 25 65	3 090 2,420	225	10	230 105	1 050	595 255	1,010	11
Weifare reignas & membership organiz as Legal engineering & mise professional serv	1,450	60	45 60	65	35	60	1,120	65	1,100	125	60	75	54	10	685	
Public administration .	1_,360	410	145	290	320	545	9,275	375	3,390	230		35	10	25	480	
Postal service	1,900	30	3C 05	C	55 110	110	1,595	50	90		95	<u></u>	140	125	2,510	
Fede.a. public administration State and local public administ ation	2,205 5,195	572	5C	145	110	355	3,440 4 240	140 18°	2 260 1,020	200 30	75	85 80	80 60	65 55	1,700	3
Indus.ry not reported.	5,705	600	2.5	395	300	145	3,170	480	1,680	635	125	125	70	Co	3.50	33
		-				-										

Table 86.—INCOME IN 1949 OF THE EXPERIENCED CIVILIAN LABOR FORCE, BY INDUSTRY AND SEX, FOR THE STATE AND FOR STANDARD METROPOLITAN AREAS OF 250,000 OR MORE: 1950

[Based on 20-percent sample. For totals by industry from complete count, see table 79. Median not shown where base is less than 500]

Area, industry, and sex	Total (includes persons without income)	Persons with income: Total	$1 to $499 or loss	$500 to $999	$1,000 to $1,499	$1,500 to $1,999	$2,000 to $2,499	$2,500 to $2,999	$3,000 to $3,499	$3,500 to $3,999	$4,000 to $4,499	$4,500 to $4,999	$5,000 to $5,999	$6,000 to $9,999	$10,000 and over	Median income (dol.)	Income not reported
THE STATE																	
Male experienced civilian labor force	610,740	608,725	61,900	65,120	86 960	78,250	72 910	49 660	48,315	[illegible],690	26,590	[illegible],630	21 24[illegible]	20,930	11,445	1,982	32 025
Agriculture forestry and fisheries	144,775	123,090	32,910	37 765	20,705	12,2[illegible]0	7,535	3 175	2 850	1 290	1,120	460	980	1,225	815	879	6,470
Agriculture	135 645	114,970	31,700	35,750	19,080	1[illegible]	6 680	2 700	2 480	1,140	1,035	385	910	1 170	790	860	6,090
Forestry and fisheries	9,130	8,160	1,230	2 015	1 125	1,130	855	475	370	150	85	75	70	55	25	1 257	380
Mining	22 850	21,600	480	890	1,015	1,100	1 940	1 760	2,510	3,345	2,785	1,035	1,790	1 840	450	3,665	370
Coal mining	100	80	15	15	10		5	15	10		0						20
Crude petroleum and natural gas extraction	20,570	19,470	385	705	800	320	1 555	1,420	2,275	3,245	2,695	1,605	1,755	1 775	440	3 777	840
Mining and quarrying except fuel	2,180	2,050	85	175	200	280	380	325	225	100	80	90	35	65	10	2,375	110
Construction	68,335	63,640	4,350	7 545	7,710	10,880	8,830	5 910	8 090	3 370	2 720	1 545	2,055	1 500	695	1 969	5 045
Manufacturing	119 285	111,890	6,330	10 845	13,900	15,820	15 460	10,595	11,155	7,201	6,525	4,740	5,240	3,625	1,420	2 293	4,720
Durable goods	48 265	45,145	5,335	6,785	8,155	8,295	5 830	3,460	2,840	1,805	1,320	670	885	895	520	1,740	2,130
Logging	5,770	5 245	770	1 47	1 195	805	435	155	110	65	55	15	40	45	60	1 158	330
Sawmills planing mills and mill work	21,250	19 740	1,750	3,725	5,010	4,245	2,170	1,005	715	385	250	90	130	130	135	1,439	835
Miscellaneous wood products	2,115	2 015	145	550	365	465	325	140	80	55	20	20		30	20	1,655	85
Furniture and fixtures	1,525	1,425	100	150	235	350	250	90	100	65	15	10	25	25	10	1,825	65
Glass and glass products	940	880	40	30	55	45	105	75	130	120	110	55	75	35	5	3,345	55
Stone and clay products	2,345	2,205	70	225	350	765	410	245	145	40	80	35	45	35	20	1 997	90
Primary iron and steel industries	1 140	1,065	15	40	115	280	185	85	95	60	65	20	35	25	20	2,169	60
Primary nonferrous industries	445	425	25	10	60	80	60	35	40	45	10	15	25	5	15		15
Fabricated metal ind (incl not spec metal)	3 390	3,195	95	165	250	445	540	425	325	290	245	115	165	155	60	2,679	140
Machinery except electrical	2,975	2,760	75	130	195	330	395	430	360	145	160	95	120	75	85	2,797	165
Electrical machinery equip., and supplies	405	345	20	20	10	25	55	20	60	40	25	30	15	20	25		45
Motor vehicles & motor vehicle equipment	470	425		10	25	65	55	35	85	55	30	15	10	75	15		35
Aircraft and parts	25	25					5	10	5		5						
Ship and boat building and repairing	4,420	4,190	160	340	400	545	725	590	455	285	245	95	135	130	35	2,448	130
Railroad & misc. transportation equipment	70	70		5		5	5	15	15	15	5		5				
All other durable goods	1,210	1,105	50	110	180	145	160	125	130	35	30	40	70	45	15	2,2[illegible]	60
Nondurable goods	70,020	66,170	2 975	4,035	5 340	7,455	9 515	7 085	7,235	5,305	5 185	4,060	4 320	2 705	895	2,766	2 525
Meat products	1 895	1,770	65	150	205	305	390	260	135	50	80	35	55	35	5	2,305	65
Bakery products	3,165	3,000	130	150	285	380	505	490	320	245	75	100	115	75	35	2,751	85
Other food industries	17,240	16,310	1,085	1,815	2 395	2 955	2,545	1 705	1 540	850	425	275	285	250	215	1,991	615
Tobacco manufactures	135	115	5	5	30	20	5	15	10	5	5	5	5		5		10
Knitting mills	145	130	5	10	10	15	30	30		15				10	5		15
Yarn, thread and fabric mills	825	795	15	35	60	250	205	90	45	35	15	15	5	15	10	2,116	20
Other textile mill products	230	215		50	10	35	30	15	30	15		10	10		5		10
Apparel & other fabricated textile products	1,225	1,180	65	85	140	235	195	115	85	45	35	35	25	55	55	2,192	45
Paper and allied products	12,920	12,530	195	570	765	1,350	2,690	2,060	1 685	1,040	760	435	450	275	55	2 620	390
Printing publishing and allied industries	5,040	4,775	185	345	375	515	455	320	480	315	365	245	360	285	130	2,676	265
Chemicals and allied products	10,335	9 850	420	580	735	985	1 295	930	1,155	980	1,045	650	685	390	160	3,078	355
Petroleum and coal products	15,490	14,815	575	715	540	585	1,085	980	1 690	1 675	2,185	2,145	2,265	1,275	200	4,152	350
Rubber products	630	565	5	15	15	35	65	60	50	100	85	70	50	15		3,688	60
Footwear except rubber	50	40	5			10	10	5	5					5			10
Leather & leather products exc footwear	95	80	20	10	15		15	10	5						5		15
Not specified manufacturing industries	700	605	20	25	105	75	115	30	80	35	50	10	35	25	-	2 35[illegible]	65
Transport. commun & other public util	68 170	64 310	2 040	4,315	6,920	8,790	10,280	7,425	7,880	5,555	4 000	2,300	2,340	1,885	580	2 491	2 930
Railroads and railway express service	18,395	17 370	340	575	1 240	1,835	2 945	2,110	2 760	1 865	1,565	900	765	410	30	2 911	605
Street railways and bus lines	4,895	4,575	85	220	360	510	780	760	860	595	285	85	40	25	20	2 752	185
Trucking service and warehousing	8,295	7 765	445	950	1,255	1,480	1,200	830	650	500	210	90	120	110	125	1,916	360
Water transportation	15,440	14 355	440	1,190	1 685	2,190	2,390	1,565	1,550	990	635	445	405	685	185	2 350	780
Air transportation	1,140	1,040	35	35	75	75	120	165	140	100	95	65	10	75	50	3,054	95
All other transportation	5,165	4,845	240	565	910	750	670	425	295	255	250	130	160	135	60	2,972	220
Telecommunications	3,145	2 930	85	120	215	225	295	270	375	340	310	265	270	145	15	3,240	145
Electric and gas utilities	8,110	7,635	170	320	505	795	1 060	930	1,760	1,025	605	300	475	290	80	3,017	415
Water supply sanitary services & other util	3 885	3,725	200	340	675	330	820	370	170	85	45	20	45	10	15	1 848	125
Wholesale and retail trade	110,115	104,015	7 320	10,250	15,320	14,580	13,770	10,315	9,190	6,060	4,220	2,595	4 255	4,970	3 510	2,239	5,935
Wholesale trade	27 315	25 365	965	1,675	2,520	3,490	3,360	2,555	2,650	1,875	1,385	895	1,330	1,545	1,120	2,6[illegible]	1,405
Food & dairy prod stores, & milk retailing	21,220	19,030	2 075	2,505	2 995	2,585	2,505	1 880	1,490	935	705	295	450	550	300	1,922	965
General merchandise & five & ten cent stores	5,900	5 415	265	475	640	710	770	595	480	390	240	135	230	235	275	2,399	485
Apparel and accessories stores	3 120	2,870	165	220	215	350	305	275	250	115	110	80	220	255	210	2,645	170
Furniture home furnishings & equip stores	5,275	4,800	105	285	460	640	675	560	540	320	225	155	255	310	220	2,665	330
Motor vehicles and accessories retailing	8,255	7,540	310	375	620	785	1,000	925	1,025	740	310	710	415	395	350	2,868	520
Gasoline service stations	7,425	6 790	665	825	1,305	1,370	990	440	230	145	195	65	120	15	65	1,749	85
Drug stores	3,235	2,860	435	375	250	250	270	125	230	135	100	100	160	235	135	2,722	165
Eating and drinking places	13,105	11 795	1,210	1,925	1 870	1,775	1,590	935	750	355	365	195	350	310	185	1,749	685
Hardware farm implem't & bldg mater'l ret	8,650	7,980	305	630	1,085	1 400	1 170	820	680	425	280	175	300	400	110	2,247	495
All other retail trade	10 525	9,575	730	1,160	1 360	1,245	1,135	835	765	575	335	190	425	580	340	2 173	570
Finance insurance, and real estate	13,770	12 530	320	525	1,105	1,345	1 320	1,340	1 315	1 135	875	580	825	1,165	980	3,232	1,100
Banking and other finance	4,525	4,070	75	115	355	425	445	480	425	375	285	220	255	385	330	3,282	70
Insurance and real estate	9 245	8,460	245	410	750	920	875	660	890	760	590	360	570	780	650	3 208	830
Business and repair services	18 920	17,605	945	1 640	2,320	2,600	2 610	2 105	1,755	1,065	720	350	570	570	335	2,249	870
Business services	3,700	3,355	135	175	270	400	320	470	385	235	210	160	220	335	240	3 140	255
Automobile repair services and garages	9 860	9 210	490	840	1,420	1 590	1,535	1,235	815	525	235	120	205	130	70	2,086	455
Miscellaneous repair services	5,360	5,040	320	625	630	610	755	600	555	305	275	70	145	105	45	2 221	260
Personal services	20,290	18 605	7,565	3,640	3,275	2,815	2,440	1,200	985	505	295	180	270	250	185	1 474	900
Private households	5 890	5 380	1,675	1 895	975	500	170	70	45	10	5		5	5	25	768	185
Hotels and lodging places	3,030	2,780	200	530	580	460	315	260	125	75	20	20	5	35	25	1 491	130
Laundering, cleaning and dyeing services	5,490	5 115	25	500	870	985	1,000	365	385	240	130	65	100	140	60	1,973	460
All other personal services	5,860	5,330	345	720	850	875	955	505	430	185	140	5	115	70	75	1 935	335
Entertainment and recreation services	7,120	6,315	835	915	910	725	685	490	750	280	225	205	230	215	145	1,847	805
Professional and related services	28,795	25 685	1,430	2,400	3,280	2,890	2,360	1,905	2,235	1,745	1,360	940	1 400	1,630	1,915	2,374	1,515
Medical and other health services	8 405	7,650	365	660	970	875	920	555	520	285	220	175	275	555	1,175	2,527	545
Educational services government	8,725	8,250	455	575	1,030	1,050	745	595	835	835	650	520	520	385	60	2 731	285
Educational services private	3 015	2,530	195	255	365	310	250	170	310	225	140	90	120	115	45	2,400	180
Welfare religious, & membership organiz ns	4,770	4,320	375	765	725	480	455	300	325	285	180	80	155	155	40	1 807	210
Legal, engineering, & misc professional serv	3,380	2,935	100	150	190	175	190	185	245	110	170	75	330	420	595	4 360	395
Public administration	24,645	23,335	645	985	1,810	2 275	3,805	3,500	2 950	2,590	1,540	835	1,005	910	260	2 757	895
Postal service	4,475	4,285	85	95	125	145	385	710	845	1,150	450	160	90	30	15	3 342	140
Federal public administration	7,500	7,050	170	315	455	265	845	880	875	860	505	440	620	460	65	3,175	260
State and local public administration	12,665	12,000	390	575	1,230	1,845	2,580	2,010	1,230	585	405	255	295	420	180	2 380	495
Industry not reported	20,135	16,105	2,145	3 440	2,490	1,870	1,675	940	1,015	545	375	185	285	235	135	1 593	2,150

$T_able~86-INCOME$ In 1949 of the experienced civilian labor force, by industry and Sex, for the state and for standard metropolitan areas of 250,000 or more 1950—Con

ne For trails by industry from complete cours see table 79 Median not shown where base is less than 600]

	Total							Persons	with me	ome							Inco
Area inquistry, and sex	(_ndudes persons without income,	Total	\$1 to \$499 or some	\$000 to \$999	\$1,000 to \$1,499	\$1,500 to \$1,999	82,000 to 32,499	\$2,500 to \$2,999	\$8,000 to \$3,499	\$3,000 to \$3,999	\$4,000 to \$4,499	\$4,506 to \$4,999	\$5,000 to \$5,999	\$6 000 to \$9,999	\$10,000 and over	Median in come (dol)	-
'HF STA''E												-40		1 030	395	995	10
Female, experienced civilian labor force	23",825	154,87	52,4-5	14 485	28,400	2 ,930	_8 860	10,500	8,345	3,_55	- 545	780	945	40	10		10
Agriculture torestry and fineries	_b 795	8 575	5 980	,640	435	2	_45	40	35 30	20	0	-	25	40	10		
graculture	105	8,455	5,72	1,u15 25	427	194	±35 10	35 5	5	20	5		3		7160		
Mining.	.23	_ 305	5	47	8.3	130	295	160	_10	80	3.	5	70		. 5	2,343	_
hal nining	1				75	100	275	155	100	80	35	5	, ,		,	2,382	
true petroleum and natural gas extracuon .	1_0	9.0	40	37.	13	20	20	175	10				2				
Construction	4 625	00	1.0	. 60	155	295	275	21.0	1.35	_0	1.5		1.5	10	10		_
Manufacturing -	1" "5-	-5,4-0	2 631	2,475	200، ود	2,950	2,01.	720	570	280	170	70	65	55	50	1,379	-
hyrable goods	2 -8	2,775	2-4	290	391	420	43~	85	85	50	~ 0	15	-			1,640	
Logging	30 -80	30 435	40	9.	100	65	70	70	_5	20	70	,	70				
Miscellaneous wood products	1,40 32J	150 285	45 20	40	115	20 40	5 20		-5 5	5			5				
Sawmins, basing his aid to Miscellaneous wood nood ets Furn: ure and "xtures	-0	10	2 5	1			15 25	1.5	10				ر ا				
Stone and clay products	0 40	30 40	5	5	10	20	.0		100								
Primary nonferrous in ustries	400	ار 10د	50	60	55	90	دد	.5 .5	10	5			-		100		
	.90	175	15	15	25	45	50 35	5	20	5	5	3	-0				
Electrical machinery equip, and supplies Motor venides & motor vehicle equipment	-00	85 85	5	5	5	1.5	,,,,	10	20	5	5	1	10	,	i		
Aircraft and parts. Ship and boat building and repairing.	5	70	ź		,	35	۰۰0	-	10	5				-	5		
Railroad & misc 'ransportation equipment.' All other curable goods	10	5	40	. 5	25	55	40	10	,				5				
	15,093	230	2.375	2,370	2,775	2 510	1,575	630	470	225	.45 5	25	30	25	22		
Mest products	327	292	35	40	65	70	53 40	15	10		5			5	10	1	
Bakery products Other food industries	995	>,630	1 340	70	125 585	-10 430	31.0	35 85	45	5	15	5	5	30		843	
Tobacco manufactures	755 260	700 225	21	_45 80	295	130	50 10			5		5		5	5		
Kmtung mills Yarn thread, and raune mills.	605	545	30	15	140	270	70	14	-	-						1,562	
Other textile mill products _ Apparel & other fabricated textile products.	3,730	3,295	25	770	10	25 694	15 210	0	30	10					2	1,139	
Paper and allied products.	1,135	1,390	110	160	210	340 d0.	370 120	130	30 50	25	43	10	10	20	5	1,816	
Paper and allied products. Printing, publishing, and allied industries Chemicals and allied products	830	945 655	100	165	42	90	124	105	50	40 125	25	2	5			2,094	
Petroleum and coal products	995	930 45	15	25	40 15	100	-95 10	115 5	225	125	50	25	2		. 3	2,870	
Footwear except rubber	55	1.)		- 5		5						į.					100
Leather & leather products ext footwear of spenfied manu acturing industries	157	10	5	15	15	20	i	5	15	5	,	ĺ					
Transport. commun., & other public util	7,810	8,045	200	~2v	1,020	2 030	2 265	1,170	525	250	55	30	30	25	1.5	2 0>8	
ulmade and railway express service	795	740	27	50	55 55	9º 75	175	125	145	37 10	25	-0		5	101	2,429	
rect raiws s and Lus lines cking service and warehousing	500 460	435 300	35	40	55	80	1.00	40	1	10				1	1.5		1
ater transportation.	905	825 205	40	20 45	100	220	240 50	125	35		5		5	10		2, 05	
r transportation	445	30,	25	45	70	35	90	60 *3 545	45	10 _15	5	20		10		_,982	į
elecommunications	5,235	4,785	2.55	355	100	180	355	1-5	230	70	10	20	10	1		2,190	
ater supply samuary services, & other util.	3.00	150	20	-5	25	35	30	15	5					5			١.
Wholesale and retail trade	of 155	45 500	9 860	10 790	9,925	6,385	3,935	_, 765	1,130		240	190		355		1,106	-
holesale trade	4,805	4,255 C. 140	165 4 320	1,385	1,410	955	980 535	/55 190	250 190	"0	51	30	1 43	70	50	1,894	1
ood & darry prod stores, & milk retailing eneral merchandise & five & ten cent stores	4 400	9.885	1,875	1 995	2,753	1,585	840 375	305	185	1_0	40	45	70	65	20	1,195	
pparel and accessories stores irrniture home furnishings, & equip stories ofor vehicles and accessories retailing	1,400	3, 00	675 155	150	850 270	465	12.	65	135	10	1.0		1	1 5		1 1,435	
lotor vehicles and accessories retailing	880	76,	40	75 35	140	220	15C	°C 20	20	5	5			10	1	1,790	1
ug stores	2,445	1,970	355	460	2,292	325	305	44	25	25 55	5	30	40	10	25	1, 42	
ating and drinking places ardware, farm implem t, & bldg mater" res. d other retail trade	16 970	940	4 235	4,750	±30	C8.	_85	160	35	30	1.5	1	1	30		83	
	4,435	3,560	685	665	800	630	3_0	741	82	30	13				20		
Finance, insurance, and real estate	8,790 3,645	7,200	245	706	1,120	1,870	1,460	360	170	-	30	30		-			\vdash
anking and other finance istrance and real estate	4 445	3,30 3,895	405	505	625	920	675	45	170		35	10	25	70	2	1 895	
Business and repair services	1,885	1,580	1.85	230	2.0	355	283	140	45	20	40		1	25		1 704	
UMITERS SCIVICES	1,290 31J	235	10,	1/,0	-5c 45	290 40	202	9.5 20	30	50	40	10	1	25	1	1,784	
utomobile repair corvices and garages	285	235	4.	50	35	25	35	25	10	1	1	1	1 '				1
Personal services	62 145	52,650	2/ 510	19,3.5	1,420	1,772	745	275	215	80	105	- 30	7:	9"	10	547	
en ete households	46 830	39 675	21,370	34 835	2 575	103	ـ ≥5	8>	65	25	15	10	1:	31	:		
otels and lodging places	5,899 6,980	3,310 5,505	995	2,00	1,265	330 54J	_45 170	65	45	15	23		10	10		925	1
d other personal services	4,840	4,100	1,430	1,075	700	395	275	80	65	30	35		30	35	1 :	802	1
Entertainment and recreation services .	2,355	2,050	480	590	290	201	225	80	85					1;		952	
Professional and related services	43,315	37,000	2,385	6,175	5 .95	4,185	4,990	3,840	4,255								
durational services, government	19 370 _9,085	12,925 17 340	1,950	2,390	2,665	1,725	1,700	2,330	3,.30	245	420	65	7:	100	1 2	2.268	2.
	5,115	3,700	4,025	745	490	395	32.0	215	3,530 27,5 50 45	90		50	3	1 50		1.082	1
elfare rehgious & membership organis ne egal engineering, & mist, professional serv	2,335	1 1,800	350 90	415 120	335 .50	275 225	200 345	-20	45	90 55 45	15				10	1 246	1
Public administration -	8,795	7 ~20	275	080	800	1,20	1,700	1,265	850			1	5	1			
ostal acrylos	1.000	925	70	125	16"	90	120	130	215	65	1.0	15	1		1	2 750	
ederal public administration .	3,770	3,000	24.	495 300	220 495	255 865	91.5	7-5	290		85	30	2	2		2,462	1

DETAILED CHARACTERISTICS

 $T_{\rm bble}$ 86—INCOME IN 1949 OF THE EXPERIENCED CIVILIAN LABOR FORCE, BY INDUSTRY AND SEX, FOR THE STATE AND FOR STANDARD METROPOLITAN AREAS OF 250,000 OR MORE 1950—Con.

[Based on 20-percent sample For totals by industry from complete count, see table 79 Median not shown where base is less than 500]

	Total (uncludes	-						Person	with in	ome				100	(Internal	19.0	Inpon
Area industry and sex	persons withou income)	[otal	\$1 to \$459 or loss	\$500 to 8999	\$1,000 \$1,499	\$1,500 to \$1,999	\$2,000 \$2,499	\$2,500 to \$2,999	83,000 to 83 499	\$3 500 to 88,999	\$=,000 to \$4,499	\$4,500 to \$4,999	\$5,000 to \$5,999	\$6,000 to 89 999	\$10,000 and over	Median income (dol.)	re perte
NEW CALEANS	18. No.																
Male experienced civilian labor force	183,445	169,02-	3,440	13,40	18,425	24 .15	26,285	18,700	17,585	11,050	1, 45	4,850	6,65	6,400	4 665	2,390	9.1
Agricultu e forestry and fishenes	2,005	2,295	420	>25	423	430	200	12:		15	10	10	45	30	-	1,229	
grandture creatry and fisheries	1,340	1,735	233	300 23s	210	250	-30	5	45 10	1_	1.	1.0	4	£	30	1,315	1
Mining	1.870	1,800	10	433	80	7817	100	20							1100	1,143	
ol milane	35	25	-	73	_O		120	- 80	2-4	215	250	-4-	250	450		4,150	
rude petroleum and natural gas extraution.	1,76	1,715	10	42	10	40	105	ar	20	215	240	140	245	240	80	4, 193	
Construction	1 5	16,230	1,046	2,020	2,350	-								1 0 5		100	
Manufacturing.	34,690	29, 10	1,000	2.73		2,050	2,905	1,735	1,540	0د0رد	1,275	44,	550	4"5	325	2,11.	
nraha moda	, 955	11,270	4-5	585	2,560	4,02"	190	3,852	3,230	700	240	31.0	1,005	1,025	645 220	2,408	1,
Legging Sawmills, planing mills, and mill work Missellaneous wood products	1,03	970	20	25	1.0	180	3.55	110	20	20	35	20	25	25		2,000	
Miscellaneous wood products Furniture and fixtures	_80	550	25	40	1.0	150	: 25	65	15	-0		1.5		-5	45	1.783	
Gless and closs products	990	85	4C 2C	50	-15	450	-55	15	65 20	51	5	30	10	10	10	1,915	
Stone and clay products_ rumary iron and s eel industries	1,200	1,155 5_0	25 15	80 20	45	24° 135	200	1°5	115 55	20 35	30	2,	30 15	20	15	2,26	
Primary nonferrous industries	50	25		20	15 130	1.5	5						5	13	15		
Fabric d metal ind (ind not spec metal)	2,170	2,075	55 25	34	130	300 35	155	33C	195	150	130	75 23	70 35	1^5	45 25	2,625	
Electrical marninery equip and supplies Motor velacies & motor vehicle equipment	210 150	185 130	2	10		30	15	15	رد 0د	25	10	20	-5	10	10	.,	
crors t and nare-	10				,		1	10			1	,	, ,		-		
hip and box building and repairing	29f	3,1.5	95	230	30>	375	5_5	460	340	240	403	8,	-45	132	25	2,332	
la from de mise ransportation somprert	670	-70	20	/0	93	95	cs	BC.	72	20	40	2.	30	10	10	2,531	
rdı allı goods fest procurts	.9, 33L 9₅C	18,260 870	925 30	1,075	2,505	2,700	3,460	2 310	2,070	1,290 15	725 45	53°	u10	590 20	405	2,414 2 33C	
akery products	4,31.	1.225	40	70	110	_30	225	215	145	110	6.5	25	37	20	25	2,587	
obacco manufactures	b 255	5.900 3C	325	343	2±0 45	930	975	730	820	480	205	_35	19	1.25	1.0	2,428	
Can thread and fabric mile	120	105	. 5	5	+0	15	20	25		10	5						
arn thread and factor this other textule mill products pparel & other fabricated textue products	145	710	15	30	50	230	195 20 175	35 10	30 ∡0	0.0	10	10	15	70	-0	2,103	
	2,880	2,750	50	120	120	210	725	_10	40 75 34≤	40 152	30 70	30 61	20	20	55	2,186 2,333 2,72, 2 432	
nating, publishing, and alked industries the most and assed products	2,880	2,757	274	230	240	1e0	273	70	215	190	160	140	180		80	2,72	
he mos a and a med products	1,445	1,360	4C	65	135	170	19°2	185	135	5	45 80	35 60	180 50 55	100	55 25	2,79	
tubber products	40	-0	1	5	5		303	10	10	5		5	1 2		~	.,,,	
Conwear except rubber	4C 65	30 55	12	5	10	,	-0	10	5					5			
eather & leather products exc cotwear, a specified manufacturing industries.	210	180	- 5	1	40	30	30	2	که	5	10		1.5				
Transport commun & other public uni	32,500	7 0.5	8-5	1,540	3,295	4,590	5,205	3 645	1,050	2,827	1,790	4,037	1,045	995	285	2,490	1
drosos and rail vay express service	1,885	1 775	120	35	430 80	665		8' 5	1,340	910	280 150	300	250	135	13	3,005 3,154	
ter transportation	12,400	3 335	3-5	390 965	340	76u	5P5 1 860	320	230	90	95	25 400	30	35 563	50 125	1,870	
transportatior	805	745	105	20	401	60	75	100	120	81.0	510 65	401	1/2 1/1	70	-5	3,240	
other transportation	2,2,5	2,250 1,340	9L 30	40	4c0	465	70ر 132	280	110	195	1/0	20	40	35	10	1,897	
ter supply sanitary services & other util	2,020	T,900	32 50	99 60	1/0	19-	230	20	200	295	_60	65	120 160	75	1.5	3,455	
Wholesale and rettil trade		1,655				485	505	200	90	3.	25	10	25	10	3	2,072	
classia trodu	43,14C 13,28C	39,080	2,480	6 15	4,350	1 652	1,685	4,000	3,720	2,43.5	±,630	1,095	2 805 730	1,940	1,405	2,363	. 2
d & dairy prod sto as, & muk retailing ners merchandise & five & ter cent stores	0,755	6,035	335	655	815	705	1 685 795	575	1,2-5	375	225	105	1/5	_85	-25	2,737	
parel and accessories stores	€ دور د	1.395	75	120	300	350	375 160	100	125	170	80 55	50 35	75	50	110	2,737	
m ne home furnishings & equip stores tor vehicles and accessomes retailing.	2,380	2 055	92	-0,	155	245 180	250	195 245	1/1>	60 90	95	45	95	145	90	2,46.	
soline service stations	1,670	-,505 1,115	150 750	150	217	340	270	105	ددو دند 70	32	85 55	95 40	120	25	2	3,0.1	
ig stores.	6,245	5,555	195	130]	285	1.005	200	40	70 355	45	70 140	4C 85	160	70 1:0	45 105	1,970	
ing and drinking places da re from implem t, & bldg mater liret.	2 155	1,950	125	_35	150	1,005	:05	180	220	180 -70 -70	45	45	115	110	75	2,314	
otder retail traine	35ء , ف	1,23,	245	3751	415	.0.5		320	280	- 1		400	155	215	145		
Finance, insurance and real estate	2,37>	2,105	145	245	570	785	795 285	575 20J	230	205	385	265	380	135	210	3,083	
king and othe nnance	4 815	4,-30	115	183	410	535	,20	370	420	305	293	105	275	100	365	3,038	
Business and repair services	6,0.0	5,155	280	425	815	9:0	920	725	685	300	225	150	205	220	1*5	2,330	
medi day year	2,240	2,075	4.5	9:	200	320	230	170	2401	140	103	85	130	100	130	2 934	_
omobile repair services and garages cedaneous repair services	4,515	2 _95	1./5 100	190 140	240	450	404 285	240	205	155	82	30 35	45 30	30	20	2,059	
Personal services	0,805	6,355	582	982	1,255	1 20	1,080	525	375	155	80	70	85	85	50	+.70-	
a e househo.g•	1,,46	1.040	5:0	330	195	190	65 465	20	10	10				5		970	_
tels and lodging picces indening cleaning and dyeing services	2,600	1,480 2,145	160	220	31.5	385	200	170	70 145	25 75	10.	35	25	15 55	2.5	2,003	
other personal services	1,850	1,690	95	200	280	270	350	150	130	40	25	23	45	10	30	1,935	
Entertainment and recreation services	3,630	3,235	3:0	342	480	305	435	292	320	440	145	205	140	125	130	2,_93	
Professional and related services	9,590	8,61.	395	565	2,205	. 5 يان ر ـ	1,000	- p8>	790	475	400	260	445	e30	830	2,651	_
ics and other health services.	4.080	3,735	180	260	405	485	,00 155	345	270	250	85	75	110	200	120	2,478	_
nections services, government nectional services private.	1,000	960 1,330 1,290	30 i	90	70	OB_	140	02	150	105	-5	5C	65	15 85	25 40 15	2-47	
lfare religious, & membership organiz as	1,45C	1,290	45	150	≥°5	1.0	105	75	95	90	70 75	35	70 170	20:	250	4 582	
gal, enguncering & mise professional serv		1,300							-			- 1					
Public administration	1,350	10.740	275	250	560	-,135	2,055	1,925	1,425	1,125	280	342	Jeb .	48C	100	3 261	-
seral public administration.	4,255	4,010	70	120	165	*30	48"	535	5.20	677	32.5	2	440	125	35	3,288	
te an I local public administration	5,195	4 885	70	_00	345	750	1,36.	1 000	460	195	110	75		150		2 429	
Industry not reported .	5,700	4,600	4_0	520	53_	222	720	520	5.05	300	175	80	_35	0.5	50	2,_%	_

Table 86.—INCOME IN 1949 OF THE EXPERIENCED CIVILIAN LABOR FORCE, BY INDUSTRY AND SEX, FOR THE STATE AND FOR STANDARD METROPOLITAN AREAS OF 250,000 OR MORE: 1950—Con.

[Based on 20-percent sample. For totals by industry from complete count, see table 79. Median not shown where base is less than 500]

Area, industry, and sex	Total (includes persons without income)	Persons with income: Total	$1 to $499 or loss	$500 to $999	$1,000 to $1,499	$1,500 to $1,999	$2,000 to $2,499	$2,500 to $2,999	$3,000 to $3,499	$3,500 to $3,999	$4,000 to $4,499	$4,500 to $4,999	$5,000 to $5,999	$6,000 to $9,999	$10,000 and over	Median income (dol.)	Income not reported
NEW ORLEANS																	
Male experienced civilian labor force	183,445	169,02[illegible]	8,440	13,000	18,425	24,115	26,285	18,700	17,585	11,055	7,245	4,850	6,655	6,400	4,665	2,390	9,110
Agriculture, forestry, and fisheries	2,665	2,295	420	325	420	430	200	125	55	15	10	10	15	30	30	1,229	170
Agriculture	1,340	1,335	235	300	210	250	130	65	45	15		10	15	30	30	1,315	100
Forestry and fisheries	1,325	960	185	235	210	180	70	60	10		10					1,143	70
Mining	1,870	1,800	10	50	80	55	120	85	245	215	250	145	250	250	20	4,150	60
Coal mining	35	25			10		5	5			5						10
Crude petroleum and natural gas extraction	1,765	1,715	10	45	60	40	105	80	210	215	240	145	245	240	80	4,195	45
Mining and quarrying, except fuel	70	60		5	10	15	10				5		5	10			10
Construction	19,800	18,230	1,040	2,020	2,380	3,050	2,905	1,735	1,540	1,050	80	445	555	475	325	2,113	910
Manufacturing	31,695	29,510	1,345	1,775	2,660	4,625	5,400	3,855	3,230	1,995	1,275	845	1,005	1,025	645	2,408	1,200
Durable goods	11,955	11,270	455	685	1,095	1,895	1,910	1,540	1,135	700	540	310	380	455	220	2,404	420
Logging	70	40	5	5	5	5	5		5	5			5				
Sawmills, planing mills, and mill work	1,035	970	80	75	150	180	155	110	70	20	35	20	15	25	25	2,000	50
Miscellaneous wood products	580	550	25	40	65	150	125	65	15	10		15		25	5	1,283	15
Furniture and fixtures	890	825	40	50	115	450	155	50	65	50	5	10	15	10	10	1,915	50
Glass and glass products	90	85	20		10		5	15	20				10	5			5
Stone and clay products	1,200	1,155	25	80	110	245	260	175	115	20	30	25	30	20	15	2,246	25
Primary iron and steel industries	540	520	15	20	45	135	140	40	55	35	30	5	15	10	15	2,182	20
Primary nonferrous industries	55	55			15	15	5						5		15		
Fabricated metal ind. (incl. not spec. metal)	2,170	2,075	55	95	130	300	355	330	195	150	130	75	70	175	45	2,625	65
Machinery, except electrical	1,050	960	25	35	45	95	155	180	125	60	60	25	35	65	25	2,847	70
Electrical machinery, equip., and supplies	210	185	5	10		15	15	15	35	25	10	20	15	10	10		15
Motor vehicles & motor vehicle equipment	150	130		5	5	30	10	20	10	10	10	5	5	10	10		10
Aircraft and parts	10	10						10									10
Ship and boat building and repairing	3,290	3,155	95	230	305	375	555	460	340	240	200	85	125	100	25	2,335	90
Railroad & misc. transportation equipment	45	45				5	5	10	10	5	5		5				
All other durable goods	610	570	25	70	55	95	65	80	75	20	20	25	30	10	10	2,531	25
Nondurable goods	19,530	18,260	925	1,075	1,565	2,700	3,460	2,310	2,070	1,290	725	535	610	590	405	2,414	760
Meat products	950	870	30	65	50	135	235	130	75	15	45	10	35	20	5	2,330	40
Bakery products	1,310	1,225	40	70	110	130	225	215	145	110	65	25	35	20	25	2,587	55
Other food industries	6,255	5,900	325	340	520	930	975	730	820	480	205	135	18	125	110	2,428	140
Tobacco manufactures	105	90	5		45	15	5	15	5	5	5		5		5		5
Knitting mills	120	105	5	5	10	15	25	25		10	5				5		10
Yarn, thread, and fabric mills	750	710	15	30	90	220	195	85	30	50	10	10	15	10	10	2,103	10
Other textile mill products	145	130		5		30	20	10	20	5	5	10	10		5		10
Apparel & other fabricated textile products	1,115	1,040	50	65	120	210	175	110	75	40	30	30	20	50	55	2,186	40
Paper and allied products	2,880	2,755	85	120	225	465	725	445	345	155	70	65	20	[illegible]	5	2,333	70
Printing, publishing, and allied industries	2,825	2,490	270	230	240	160	270	70	215	190	160	140	180	185	80	2,721	150
Chemicals and allied products	1,445	1,360	40	65	105	215	395	185	135	30	45	35	50	45	55	2,432	60
Petroleum and coal products	1,525	1,465	40	60	85	170	300	145	185	135	80	60	55	100	25	2,7[illegible]9	50
Rubber products	45	40		5	5			10	10	5		5					
Footwear, except rubber	40	30	5			5	5	5	5					5			10
Leather & leather products, exc. footwear	65	55	15	5	10		10	10	5								10
Not specified manufacturing industries	210	180	5	1	40	30	30	5	45	5	10		15				20
Transport., commun., & other public util.	35,505	34,050	845	1,645	3,295	4,590	5,205	3,645	1,350	2,825	1,790	1,035	1,045	995	285	2,490	1,435
Railroads and railway express service	7,275	7,015	120	165	430	665	1,270	875	1,340	910	580	300	250	135	5	3,005	205
Street railways and bus lines	1,885	1,775	15	35	80	75	205	310	455	330	150	45	5	5	15	3,184	85
Trucking service and warehousing	3,575	3,335	140	390	575	760	585	320	230	90	95	35	30	35	50	1,870	180
Water transportation	12,400	11,535	345	965	1,340	1,795	1,860	1,215	1,350	810	550	400	955	565	125	2,326	615
Air transportation	805	745	20	20	40	60	75	100	120	80	65	40	10	70	45	3,240	55
All other transportation	2,375	2,250	90	215	420	465	370	280	115	80	65	20	40	35	15	1,897	85
Telecommunications	1,435	1,340	30	40	80	90	135	145	165	195	170	115	120	75	10	3,455	65
Electric and gas utilities	2,020	1,900	35	55	130	195	230	200	295	295	160	65	260	65	15	3,178	105
Water supply, sanitary services, & other util.	1,735	1,655	50	60	140	485	505	200	80	35	25	15	25	10	5	2,072	60
Wholesale and retail trade	43,140	39,080	2,480	7,350	4,350	5,470	5,400	4,000	3,720	2,415	1,630	1,095	1,805	1,940	1,405	2,363	2,360
Wholesale trade	13,280	12,295	410	655	1,130	1,655	1,685	1,335	1,245	305	660	480	730	815	610	2,737	715
Food & dairy prod. stores, & milk retailing	6,755	6,035	355	655	815	765	795	675	615	375	225	105	375	185	125	2,143	320
General merchandise & five & ten cent stores	2,295	2,155	100	150	300	350	375	220	195	170	80	50	75	50	80	2,237	70
Apparel and accessories stores	1,530	1,395	75	115	145	215	160	100	135	60	55	35	115	75	110	2,461	90
Furniture, home furnishings, & equip. stores	1,990	1,785	85	105	155	245	255	195	185	90	95	45	95	145	90	2,622	145
Motor vehicles and accessories retailing	2,380	2,055	120	90	115	180	270	245	335	215	85	95	120	100	65	3,011	225
Gasoline service stations	1,670	1,505	120	160	215	340	280	105	135	35	55	15	45	25	5	1,879	105
Drug stores	1,255	1,115	195	130	115	125	120	40	70	45	70	40	50	70	45	1,970	35
Eating and drinking places	6,225	5,555	450	800	785	1,005	755	585	355	180	140	85	160	150	105	1,869	310
Hardware, farm implement, & bldg. material ret.	2,165	1,950	125	135	160	345	305	180	220	170	65	45	115	110	75	2,514	170
All other retail trade	3,585	3,235	245	375	415	315	400	320	280	170	100	100	155	215	145	2,354	205
Finance, insurance, and real estate	7,210	6,555	145	245	620	785	795	575	680	570	385	265	380	535	575	3,083	515
Banking and other finance	2,375	2,125	30	65	210	250	285	205	230	235	90	105	105	135	210	3,038	195
Insurance and real estate	4,835	4,430	115	180	410	535	510	370	450	365	295	160	275	400	365	3,106	320
Business and repair services	6,555	6,155	280	425	815	950	920	725	685	395	225	150	205	225	175	2,330	290
Business services	2,240	2,075	45	95	200	320	230	170	240	140	100	85	130	190	130	2,934	135
Automobile repair services and garages	2,515	2,395	135	190	375	450	405	315	205	155	40	30	45	30	20	2,059	80
Miscellaneous repair services	1,800	1,685	100	140	240	180	285	240	240	100	85	35	30	5	5	2,320	75
Personal services	6,805	6,355	585	985	1,155	1,120	1,080	525	375	155	80	70	85	85	55	1,702	100
Private households	1,140	1,040	210	330	195	190	65	25	10	10				5		970	45
Hotels and lodging places	1,600	1,480	160	220	315	275	165	170	70	25	10	10	25	15	20	1,582	60
Laundering, cleaning, and dyeing services	2,275	2,145	120	205	360	385	500	180	165	75	45	35	15	55	5	2,003	105
All other personal services	1,850	1,690	95	250	285	270	350	150	130	45	25	25	45	10	30	1,935	90
Entertainment and recreation services	3,680	3,335	310	345	480	305	435	295	320	140	145	105	140	135	100	2,193	185
Professional and related services	9,595	8,615	395	585	1,165	1,015	1,000	685	790	475	400	260	445	630	830	2,651	570
Medical and other health services	4,080	3,735	180	260	465	485	500	345	270	150	125	75	110	200	520	2,478	240
Educational services, government	1,000	960	30	20	70	150	155	60	350	80	85	60	30	15	25	2,806	20
Educational services, private	1,375	1,330	65	90	215	180	140	80	180	105	15	50	65	85	40	2,411	75
Welfare, religious, & membership organiz'ns	1,450	1,290	75	150	275	150	105	95	95	90	70	35	70	65	15	1,983	60
Legal, engineering, & misc. professional serv.	1,490	1,300	45	65	80	50	100	75	95	30	75	40	170	205	250	4,588	175
Public administration	11,360	10,740	175	250	560	1,135	2,055	1,925	1,625	1,125	580	345	365	480	100	2,810	400
Postal service	1,900	1,845	35	30	50	50	245	325	645	455	135	55	40	5		3,261	10
Federal public administration	4,265	4,010	70	120	165	330	485	535	520	475	315	215	420	325	35	3,288	140
State and local public administration	5,195	4,885	70	100	345	755	1,365	1,070	460	195	110	75	135	150	65	2,429	230
Industry not reported	5,705	4,605	410	520	33	555	720	525	505	300	175	80	135	95	50	2,196	715

Table 86.—INCOME IN 1949 OF THE EXPERIENCED CIVILIAN LABOR FORCE, BY INDUSTRY AND SEX, FOR THE STATE AND FOR STANDARD METROPOLITAN AREAS OF 250,000 OR MORE 1950—Con.

[Based on 20-percent sample. For totals by industry from complete count see table 79. Median not shown where base is less than 500]

Area, industry, and sex	Total (includes persons without income)	Persons with income: Total	$1 to $499 or loss	$500 to $999	$1,000 to $1,499	$1,500 to $1,999	$2,000 to $2,499	$2,500 to $2,999	$3,000 to $3,499	$3,500 to $3,999	$4,000 to $4,499	$4,500 to $4,999	$5,000 to $5,999	$6,000 to $9,999	$10,000 and over	Median income (dol.)	Income not reported
NEW ORLEANS																	
Female, experienced civilian labor force	[illegible]	[illegible]	11,3[illegible]	15,41[illegible]	13,[illegible]80	10,885	8,570	4,650	2,920	1,140	620	355	330	405	145	1,301	3 905
Agriculture, forestry, and fisheries	[illegible]	[illegible]	6[illegible]	30	20	20	15	10	-	-	5			5			[illegible]
Agriculture	[illegible]	140	[illegible]	25	15	[illegible]	10	10						5			5
Forestry, and fisheries	[illegible]	25	-	[illegible]	5	[illegible]	[illegible]		-		5						5
Mining	18[illegible]	170		5	10	[illegible]	65	35	35	10				5			[illegible]
Coal mining																	
Crude petroleum and natural gas extraction	[illegible]	150			10		60	35	30	10				5			15
Mining and quarrying, except fuel	[illegible]	[illegible]		[illegible]		5	5		5								
Construction	715	605	20	55	50	115	140	130	80	5	5		5			2,223	65
Manufacturing	9 990	9 825	1 [illegible]	1,5[illegible]5	2,215	2,075	1,11[illegible]	295	190	60	55	15	20	20	35	1,380	[illegible]
Durable goods	[illegible] 35	[illegible] 65	100	140	220	285	270	60	40	1[illegible]	10	5	10		10	1 715	95
Logging	5	5						5									
Sawmills, planing mills, and mill work	125	120	5	20	30	20	20	10	-	5			5		5		5
Miscellaneous wood products	90	[illegible]	25	10	20	15											10
Furniture and fixtures	155	1[illegible]	15	20	75	25	5		10								
Glass and glass products	15	[illegible]				5	5		5								
Stone and clay products	65	55		[illegible]		20	25	5	5								
Primary iron and steel industries	15	1[illegible]			5	10											
Primary nonferrous industries						-											
Fabric'd metal ind. (incl. not spec. metal)	[illegible]0	[illegible]	20	60	[illegible]0	80	1[illegible]5	10	5	5							20
Machinery, except electrical	80	75	5	10	10	20	20		5								
Electrical machinery, equip., and supplies	80	65	5		[illegible]	1[illegible]	25	5	5		5						10
Motor vehicles & motor-vehicle equipment	25	20		5				10			5						
Aircraft and parts																	
Ship and boat building and repairing	110	9[illegible]			5	30	25	5	5	5					5		5
Railroad & misc. transportation equipment	1[illegible]			5													5
All other durable goods	200	145	25	10	20	45	30	10					5				40
Nondurable goods	[illegible] 545	7 58[illegible]	1 [illegible]35	1 [illegible]30	1,985	1,77[illegible]	835	2[illegible]5	140	40	40	10	10	20	25	1,334	[illegible]
Meat products	215	200	15	20	50	45	45	5	30		5				5		5
Bakery products	[illegible]5	255	25	35	90	85	5	10	-						5		10
Other food industries	2 0[illegible]	1 76[illegible]	425	370	36[illegible]	285	200	65	25	5	10		5	10		1 120	70
Tobacco manufactures	325	275	55	95	250	120	[illegible]0								5	1,275	10
Knitting mills	25[illegible]	220	30	30	60	30	10					5		5			15
Yarn, thread, and fabric mills	[illegible]90	390	30	15	125	220	70	15	5							1,676	30
Other textile mill products	70	65		15	5	25	15		5								5
Apparel & other fabricated textile products	3,145	2,8[illegible]	[illegible]85	640	90[illegible]	620	190	95	20	5					5	1 21[illegible]	135
Paper and allied products	360	34[illegible]	20	40	70	105	[illegible]0	20	10				[illegible]	5			5
Printing, publishing, and allied industries	475	38[illegible]	35	60	40	[illegible]	65	40	20	10	20	5			5		45
Chemicals and allied products	250	220	30	40	10	[illegible]0	[illegible]0	15	5	10							10
Petroleum and coal products	185	170		5	5	45	50	10	40	10	5						5
Rubber products	35	30		5	15	5	-										
Footwear, except rubber	10	10		[illegible]		5											
Leather & leather products exc. footwear	10	10	5	5													
Not specified manufacturing industries	110	80	10	15	10	13	10		10	5	5						10
Transport., commun., & other public util.	4,7[illegible]0	4,[illegible]93	180	2[illegible]5	380	1,000	1,405	720	230	150	15	1[illegible]	15	10		2,129	205
Railroads and railway express service	415	400	15	[illegible]0	20	50	105	75	[illegible]0	25		5		5			10
Street railways and bus lines	175	155	25	20	10	45	30	20		5							20
Trucking service and warehousing	2[illegible]5	18[illegible]		20	20	55	60	20	10								10
Water transportation	86[illegible]	790	30	45	95	220	24[illegible]	115	30	5	5		5			2,010	[illegible]0
Air transportation	185	175	5	20		20	50	55	20			-		5			5
All other transportation	195	170	5	10	70	15	40	25		5							15
Telecommunications	2,295	2,140	90	120	140	525	[illegible]30	355	80	[illegible]	10	10	5			2,1[illegible]	85
Electric and gas utilities	340	325		5	20	60	135	50	15	35			5				10
Water supply, sanitary services, & other util.	55	55	10	5	[illegible]	10	15	5	5								
Wholesale and retail trade	22,490	18,695	2,920	3,690	4,[illegible]40	3,305	2,000	870	560	175	110	9[illegible]	110	150	70	1,295	960
Wholesale trade	3 070	2,805	220	210	470	660	67[illegible]	275	170	40	[illegible]5	20	10	15	5	1 881	80
Food & dairy prod. stores, & milk retailing	2,97[illegible]	2,200	305	400	550	405	245	105	60	25	35	2[illegible]	5	25	15	1,359	105
General merchandise & five & ten cent stores	5,870	5,105	830	910	1,553	89[illegible]	440	210	115	50	10	15	35	30	15	1,261	300
Apparel and accessories stores	1,89[illegible]	1,595	240	320	420	260	185	45	60	10	5	15	10	15	10	1,283	90
Furniture, home furnishings, & equip. stores	[illegible]50	4[illegible]0	55	65	13[illegible]	95	60	15	25								20
Motor vehicles and accessories retailing	28[illegible]	260	10	25	35	75	60	45	5				5				15
Gasoline service stations	2[illegible]	15			10			5									-
Drug stores	9[illegible]5	78[illegible]	140	120	255	170	50	20	15	5						1,250	45
Eating and drinking places	[illegible],020	3,910	905	1,390	855	425	110	35	70	[illegible]	5	15	25	30	10	878	240
Hardware, farm implem't, & bldg. mater'l ret.	[illegible]25	275	30	25	35	50	50	30	10	10	5		5	15	10		10
All other retail trade	1,320	1,295	185	225	300	275	125	85	30	10	15	5	15	20	5	1 390	55
Finance, insurance, and real estate	4,360	[illegible],940	320	390	635	1,060	8[illegible]0	385	150	75	35	20	10	40		1,[illegible]95	215
Banking and other finance	1,825	1,705	115	100	22[illegible]	465	435	175	95	55	15	15		10		1 944	65
Insurance and real estate	2 [illegible]35	2,235	205	290	410	395	385	210	55	20	20	5	10	30		1,679	150
Business and repair services	950	825	60	70	120	230	150	95	25	[illegible]	30	10	5	10	5	1,853	45
Business services	795	70[illegible]	60	65	90	195	130	6[illegible]	20	15	30	10	5	10	5	1,846	40
Automobile repair services and garages	80	55			15	20	10	10									5
Miscellaneous repair services	[illegible]5	70		5	15	15	10	20	5								
Personal services	18,640	15,905	5 080	6 675	2 660	855	290	150	80	20	40		30	25		715	[illegible]
Private households	12 770	10 875	[illegible] 165	4,975	1,345	255	35	35	20	5	5			15		628	[illegible]
Hotels and lodging places	1,[illegible]55	1 490	260	570	340	205	45	35	20		10		5			925	90
Laundering, cleaning, and dyeing services	2 235	1,965	215	745	635	220	75	40	20	5	5		5			[illegible]18	110
All other personal services	1,820	1 575	440	385	340	75	115	40	20	10	20		20	10		95[illegible]	105
Entertainment and recreation services	1,12[illegible]	995	160	245	135	155	150	45	45	10	20	5		[illegible]		1,269	35
Professional and related services	14,[illegible]15	12,990	1,635	1,995	1,935	1 765	1,640	1 160	1,055	185	2[illegible]5	145	125	110	25	1,6[illegible]7	685
Medical and other health services	7,365	6,230	955	1,065	1,270	870	815	600	300	135	80	35	60	35	10	1,431	2[illegible]0
Educational services, government	[illegible],090	2,755	185	360	225	190	395	525	640	245	1[illegible]0	55	40	20	5	[illegible]	135
Educational services, private	2,420	1,605	305	340	255	205	170	105	95	35	10	25	15	40	5	1,309	190
Welfare, religious, & membership organiz'ns	1,105	850	155	190	130	105	90	65	30	35	15	20		5	5	1,308	6[illegible]
Legal, engineering, & misc. professional serv.	[illegible]3	550	35	40	[illegible]	9[illegible]	1[illegible]0	65	20	35		40	10		5	2,147	65
Public administration	3,370	3,065	90	185	255	440	695	710	430	125	80	20	10	20	5	2,405	115
Postal service	90	85	5	15	20	10	10	10	[illegible]0		5						5
Federal public administration	2,260	2 035	50	95	40	160	435	590	355	100	65	20	10	10	5	2,617	65
State and local public administration	1,020	945	35	75	95	270	250	110	65	25	10			10		1,99[illegible]	45
Industry not reported	1,660	955	225	215	125	160	85	45	40	10	10	10		5	5	1,110	345

THE STATE												-	4,44,	13,010		00.000	l ste	- un	-
Total -	1 30' 160	47_ 100	736,e50	230,340	129 >25	3- 599	1.2,2,5	99,50	64 42.	5./ 125	39 ,45	29 "	46,490	23, ~~	4 ,2,5	ar 27		7,200	2 ,
Vegro	2 o35	2,2°0.	305 810	117 550 235	114 320	52,780 245	76,250 36 135 30	2-,-111	55,120 5,75J 55	5~,5°0 C20 c5	38, 2 1,825	28 ECC 20	.8,055 415 20	720 570	10 493	220	-2 845 90 25	1,7.7 73	55,
Male	777 715 2/2, 45 1 570	230 230	730 ~65 510,990 219 262 1,210	48 .75 48 .75 45 250 190	26 .83 71,345 64,420 385	98,355 56, 25 4-,705 227	35,5-4 52 - 8 J 32,745 120	57 -8J 19,49J	52 370 44,995 7 725 50	57 230 46,35 4 1 20	30 005	27 395 28,6.1 725 20	19,445 -7 3 to 360	23 455	10 39 13,2.5 17.	20,925	12,79	2,228	12,
Female in e egro her races	9,0 560 659,445 304 051 1,065	542,7.4 30- 505 112,33.	373,045 225 W 	13n 33, u3 990 72,303	-13 600 -8,180 ,370	40 225 29, 10 1. 075	27 350 43,5°0 3,7°0	22, 57 20 mg	12 055 11,12* 725	9 695 P 695 1 0J0	3 505 275	2,_20	298 98 25	± 635 ,5 0 90	855 775 60	,C 5 980 65	1 20	721 222 544	37,
URBAN AND RURAL NONHARM	,					-													
Total -	1,052,275	500 · 94	914 970				97 Oca	8a 00	.8 845	55,_15		27,255	.7,265	2_ 025	10,420	1 .65		1 441	92
egro	442,970	3°_, 00 128,175 920	624 395 289 355 1,270	87 900 82,7.0 190	99 285 93,620 387	68,99° -4 320 235	64 305 32 635 _25	19 815 75	5 . 1±0 7 650 55	50 497 -,6,5 70	72 270 - 743 15	20 49J 74J 20	-6,897	41 745 -70 10	-0 205 210	10, e0 200 5	11,955	1,536 831 1 CC	60
Male hite egro _ ther races _	7.1 °30 509 855 302,450 1 -25	79 690 7-,790 25,100 200	586 ±00 420,450 164 65 1,105	58 345 32,440 25 745 160	48,655 44,090 3,5	75 910 -1 780 33,930 22u	1,125 840 29,190	49,440 7,94	47 420 • 0,5-5 € 825	45 950 42,205 2 75	33 c70 32,_74 _ +8J	25,405 44,550 645	46,300 14,472 345	20,725 23,435 380	9 a.0 9,475 1.0	10 175	120 120	1,962 2 460 1 _04	25
Female Inte	793,870 552 ~20 240,599	21,005 317,2_0 103 075 720	328 813 203 945 12- 750	112 -15 >5 460 57,12>	10,165 5-590 49 330	37,620 27,215 10,390	25 940 22 485 3,445	20,950 19,00 1,87	10 645 820	9 les 8 185 930	3,0+C 3,398 265	2 000	985 ^25 55	1,500	31.3 7.0 80	83C 33C	1,025	727 960 554	31 12
RURAL FARM	,				1		4	,	,	41			,			7		-	
Total _	362 990 224,885	155,725	189 84.V	59,490	30 240	25,030	45 B30	11,31.	* 536	4,810	2 615	5 560	1,205	ı >45	825	922	940	309	_9
egro ther axes	.38 845 280	55,095 125	112 2JS 76,45J 130	24 665 34 780 -5	30 240 25,200 55	16 560 8 460 10	3 900 3 900 5	9,545 1 755	*,930 600	4,440	2 535 80	2 170 90	45	1,465	725	935 20	900	±,0∪? 366	-2
Malebute ogrother aces .	.84 130 117 8-0 70,295	34 0.5 21 170 12,83*	40,505 40,540 53,960 105	35 670° 16,100 19,005	43,060 22 es0 20,360 50	22,425 14 643 7 775	-4 420 -3,860 1 995	10 105 3,5.6 1 205 10	4 950 4 45-) 500	4,260 1,930 345	2 405 2 335 70	2 140 2, %J gn	1, LOC 45	1,365 75	780 740 40	965 15	905 865 40	925 1 22. 684	963
Female	175,690 107,025 68,530	191 710 70,355 42 -601	21,7±2 21,7±2 22 9° 22	23,820 8,.30 15 275	7,435 7,590 5,8/0	4,603 1,915 68:	,065 ,201	1 40:	>80 ~£0 100	*30 510 21	200 210	110 10	60 60	100	43	75 70 5	3> 35	633 368	9 5
TANDARD METROPOL							i	. 10				4,			-	٧.	2		j
2000F 1074E	12,010	34 905	69 1%	11,643	10,990	7 560	6,175	5 00	3,850	4,700	3 68>	3,630	2,875	3,700	٠,44٠	1,3-0	. 355	1,823	7,
tute egro tiler ares	76,345 30,400 64	5, ع60 فيد, 11 0	46,1/5 22,905 10	4,780 € 055 10	4,780 5 2 0	4 Out 3 555	340 2,030	3 45	3 015	3 780 920	3 335 350	3 500 130	2,820	3,615 85	3C	1,310	1,030 25	2,622	4,
Male hite	54 915 37 87 1 17 C.00	6 125 -, 723 -, 183 -, 183	45,320 31,805 1° 445 10	4 030 2 415 1 8C3	5 065 2 310 2,735	2,75 2,75	7,105 1 *30 2,275	4,005 2,235 4,770	3,005 2 165 8-0	3,750 2,960 7-0	3,245 4,510 355	7,321 125	2,755 2,710 45	3 55 3 480 75	1,395 1,360	1 243 1 225 20	950 20	2 618 3,508 1,420	3 2
Female hite eggo ther ages	58 095 3°, 75 15 400 20	30,580 21 *35 3 *35 10	23,830 14,310 9,720	7 815 3 563 4 250	5 952 2,470 3 425	2 815 2,83, 930	2,370	1,710 18'	950 8>C 100	950 820 130	440 420 10	175 175 5	120 10	45 10	45 40 5	95 85 10	85 80 5	846 1,305 574	3,
MEA OFLEANS	511,←5	168,175	3.6 540	45 050	>7,890	٠٠, ٥٥٥	39,260	3~ ~00	24,915	24,.35	13 485	8,800	כסכ כ	7,490	3,850	4,310	5 315	1,680	25
hite eg o ther races	369 780 141 480 645	124,400 43,600	2,4,665 91 542 380	26 275 18,760	29 747 28,065 85	25 120 -6,040 45	13,340	28,545 8,837 55	2:,71. 7 170 35	19 710	12,710 75; 1u	8,220	5.270	7,340 10	3,783 60 5	4,250	5,265 35 15	2,0°0 981	20,
Male_ hute eg o ther races	238 053 173 795 63,830	20 47* 1º /30 8 °00	197,300 144,790 52,380 330	10,765 8 475 5,475	23 075 .2,260 10,710	23,090 12,755 10 800	26,505 14,895 1 580	27,910 17,900 7 960	17,740 -4,815 2,893 30	18 2-0 15,575 1,020 45	12 075 11,410 650	7 985 7 735 230	4 940 4 955	9,915 6 795 113 10	3,465	3,45	4,860. 610 30	2 206 2,-21 1 / 59	11 2
Female - hite eg o	273 335 195,985 77,350 240	1/1 °00 106,470 15 100	119,0°0 79 875 39 165	31 085 1° 400 13,285	34 845 7,480 - 345 20	17 *15 12,325 5 180	12,875 1, 13C 1, 4u	8,790 8 943 843	3 17° 4,835 2°5	3 795 3 135 260	1,410	815 765 60	455 430 20	37, 343, 30	352 340 25	365 333 30	455 450 5	909 1 189 682	12 9,
	720	ادفد	90			10	2	3	3									-	
SHPEVE COT	*2 385 +4,231 65	27,910 27,325 10,560 25	80,225 48,625 91,380 20	35 610 5 963 9,643	-7,150 6,235 10 915	8 850 4,605	7,225 3,925 3,235	6,7°5 4,°75 1,790	4,810 4,105 625	5,310 4 9nr 405	7,535 ,-40 95	2,825	1 74 15	2 -40 2,275 62	1,40	1,275	4,-00 4 85 15	2 397	8,
Male hite egro	28 63- 38, 40 20 05. 40	5,690 3 43, 2 24,1	47,950 31,305 -0 600	4,830 1,831 3 (25	2,570 2,530 4,420	5 "55 2 01" 3,540	2,095 2,095 2,√8℃	4,435 , 855 1,580	3,570 3 015 555	7 200 3 935 265	3,_50 3 075 75	2,500	- 590 571	2 455 2,205 50	1,095 1,065 30	1,160	1,270	2,1'0 3 166 . 121	3
Female Thie eggo	68, 45 43,845 24,474	32 220 23,800 8,315	32,275	10,736 4, 25 6,605	10,200 3,705 6,495	3,291	2, 145 ,830 311	2 320 2 420 200	1,240 170 70	1 .10 970 140	285 965 20	265 253 10	70	185 170 12	8- 75	115	130 -25 5	755 187 567	2

Table 87—INCOME IN 1949 OF PIRONS, BY RACE AND SEX, FOR THE STATE, FARM AND NONFARM, AND FOR STANDARD METROPOLITAN AREAS AND CITIES OF 100,000 OR MORE

1950—Con

Based on Xi-percuat sage ob. evaluous complete-count data in scales 25 35 and 36. Median not covern where base in less that. SOI]

	Total								Pers	one with	incon_e								
Area farm residence race and ser	A years old and over	Persons without income	Total	91 to 499 or 068	\$300 5999	\$1 000 to \$1 499	\$1,500 51,999	32,000 to 82 499	R2 J00 to \$2,999	88,000 88 499	\$8,500 to \$3 999	\$1 000 to \$1 499	\$4,500 to \$4,399	\$5,000 to \$5,999	48,000 to -6,999	\$7,000 to \$9,999	\$10,000 and over	Median neome (do.)	
C*TIES							1												
BaTJ + JOP	9.,21.	J8,3°C	מדי יי	9,390	2,720	0,085	1,555	4,045	1,430	4 430	1 175	3 380	2,475	,320	1,240	4,250	972	_ 923	30
White - Negro - Other races	46,240 47 922 5.	21, ~U 1,840 31	40,343 -6,76	0,275 7,165 0	-,200 520	2,6.0	2 4C5 2,200	3 490 1,455	2,705	3 225 U35	2 52. 255	2,080	-,443 30	3,270 0	1,320	1,225	20	2 53> 967	2 77
Male While \egro O her races	2,73v 1,405 45	4, 25 ,040 1,275 2.	37,175 27 315 9 .50 10	2,025 98. 10	1,900	3 -5 1,805 1,800	3,.60 .,50; .,055	3 1d5 1,855 1 350	2,355 1 ±0° 65°	3,±/5 2,02, -50	2,755 2,510 245	4,910 2,810 00	2,370 2,345 25	3,185 3,145 40	1,300 10	1 160 150 10	508 588 508	2,808 3,545 1 .40	2 3 1 87 62 1
Female White Negro Other record	4',_90 33,490 13,490	27,005 18 4e0 5,565 10	20 .95 180 ca 7,415	0,175 190 195 185	5 05. 2,40 2 81-	2 :0 1,650 800	2 195 1, 300 295	1,635 1,635 125	875 800 75	851 770 85	420 4_0 1.0	170	.35 30 3	13* 125 10	40 35 5	90 85 5	70	888 1 352 190	2 56 1,85
NEW TRUELIS	/ 3,280	38 835	271, 300	.s8 230	51,340	36,50	34,425	31 885	20,790	1~ 805	095	7 235	4,485	0,120	٥,150	3,570	4 000	_ 639	23,14
N bite Negro Other maces	103 19 129, 20 565	48 61.0 40,06~ 40C	26 930 84 950 320		26,175	21,56, 14 875 40	42,23, 12 2,3 35	23,855 7,985 45	1 / 790 2 980 25	1,78° 1,78° 45	10,360 72.	6,965	4,295	975 13- 10	3 082 60 2	3 525 45	4 550 35 _5	2 05± 986	17,65 5,40
Male htte egro hter a es	20.,0X.0 44. 54., 53 140 560	27,330 14,415 7,880 35	165,665 17,710 27,680 275	11,720 5,925 4,;80	19,890 10,065 9,280	20,000 10,620 4,885 35	23,0,0 12,4,2 10,475 .0	23 255 15,995 7,22 40	3,445 2,715 20	14,795 13,220 1,230 45	9,805	6,500 6,275 225	4 065 3 900 150 15	5,585 5,470 105 10	2,615	3,240 3,245 25	4 185 4,140 30 15	2,163 4 603 1,469	12,04 9,41 2,58
remale	233,240 161,655 71,380 205	16,505 84,195 32,185 125	105,635 69 220 30,370 45	26 5_0 14,085 12,825	31,45. 45,0.5 46,372	1, 900 10,905 -, 990	-1,4.5 9,810 1,640	8,630 7,860 765 5	4,6_5 / 345 265 5	3,010 2,755 255	1 290 1 180 1:0	735 690 ^5	420 395 20 5	535 50° 30	315 310 25	330 310 20	415 410 5	91.8 1,22° 694	2,82 2,82
SHREVEPORT	94,550	2/,1.0	61,0-5	10,490	12,360	7 _50	5,80	5 580	3,900	4,16	2,805	2,265	1,455	£,090	1,0/5	,,50	1,315	_ 57C	5,77
White Vegro Other races	54,76 29 940 60	40,715 6,415 20	9 295 22,37J 20	4 685 - 795 10	4 570 7, J90	3 505	3,220 2,6+5 5	1,409	510	3 97"	2,7:2	2 210 50 5	1,4-5 _0	2 040	1,020	1, ·40 20	1,305	2,433 850	4,79
Male White Negro Other races.	42,672 29,910 12,925 40	2,46, 1,420	35,740 24 525 1.,195	2, 25	2,240 2,710 2,510	4,325 560 2 705	2,750 1 565 2,380	3 505 2 200 -,304	2,7.C 2 305 445	3,215 2 985 230	4 450 2,380 70	2 -55 2,005 45	1,365	1,735 1,900 35	980 965 15	1,040	1,191 1 190 5	2,378 3,244 1,311	3,4a 2,92
Femsle White	21 890 24,855 17 J15	23 480 18,250 5,215	20,900 14 '30 14,175	7,765 3 340 4,425	8,140 2 960 5 180	2,825 1 945 880	1,920 2 655 265	2,075 1 895 180	1,135	9.50 80.5 235	3.3 335 20	-10 200	70 70	157 440 15	64 3.5 10	100	20 45 5	819 1,274 612	2,50 1,87

Table 88—INCOME IN 1949 OF PERSONS, BY COLOR AND SEX, FOR THE STATE, URBAN AND RURAL 1950 [Based on 20 percent sample available, compute counts cast in abiles 28 and 28 Modum not shown where base is less than 500]

	Total,	Persons							Pe	sons with	income								
A.cs, color and sex	14 years old and over	without	Total	\$1 to \$499 or loss	\$200 10 8999	\$1,000 to \$1,499	\$1,500 to \$1,999	82,000 to 82 499	\$2,500 to \$2,999	\$3,000 to \$3,499	83.500 to 83.999	\$4,000 to \$4,499	\$4 500 to \$4 999	85 000 to 85 999	%6,000 to %6,999	97 000 to 99 999	5 0,000 and over	Median income (dol.,	
THE STATE		100								10.4	7,							1.3	
Total	1,871,590	655,820	1 _73,611	230, 250	249,780	1,28,280	₁ 12 895	90,110	64,425	59 925	39 245	29.515	₄₈ 420	e3 770	11 2/	12,120	13 060	1 250	111 960
Male Female	902,730 969,560	1.3 108	730 765		130,18C 113 000		85 *45 27,350	77,555	22,055	50,20 9,690	36,775 3,870	27,395 2,120	1,040	22,165	±0,290 815	1,075	11,970	د,"ك.ه 121	58,160 53,800
Nonwhite Male Female	*64,450 2/4,3.5 10,1.1	184,315 30,104 46,153	367,100 219,775 1-7,3%	117 785 45,440 72,345		41 930	32,865 32,865 3,800	41,657 19 577 2,080	1,100 7 375 930	-,000 2,000	1,8-0 1,560 275	855 745 140	435 375 60	560 465 95	257 172 80	225 160 65	205 100 30	77/7 99/7 314	16,375 16,580
Urban Male Female	1 076,295 501,005 57 ,290	343,444 52,615 490,830	670,050 416,055 254,005	1.4,730 -5 .75 79,-55	127,095 52 735 74,357	50 435	73,805 51 US 22 700	8,445 50 135 48,450	4 ,030 30 730 9 900	43,795 30 195 7,600	29,125 25 960 3,165	2_ 625 10 890 _ 735	11,280 665	18,800 17 545 1,275	8,250 8,250 570		10,735 9,780 955	2,573 2,185 819	62 790 32,335 30,455
Nonwhite Male	141,010 172 655	69 0,5 17,710 71 325	208,840 010,010 73,230	54,240 15,185 3° 005	6,595 25,400 38,495	عرفد 24,657 8 995	26 07u 23,060 3,010	14,780	6,48, 5 790 690	3,255 BL2	1,310 21*	630 250 80	280 40	395 315 60	160 110 30	165 115 50	125 110 15	88° 1 335 548	15,990 7,690 8,400
Rural nonfarm. Male Fernale	431,305 212,725 240 580	156,030 26,475 130,179	27,910 190,195 74,835	23,170 23,270 260	66 40 385 25 80	31,181 25,495 5 00	23,260 26,020 3 240	19,7., 17,2 5 2 500	13,265 20,690 1,575	1,20	8 2C> 7, 10 495	5 630 5,365 265	3,145 3 020 120	3,425 3 200 22)	1,500 1,360 140	1 >20 1 375 125	285 285 100	1,000 1,422 58A	29,745 16,145 19,600
Nonwhite Male	131 460 62 865 68,245	40,060 7,240 32,470	81,735 10,100 31,63*	28,720 10,720 _8,000		10,°10 1,700 1,710	6,690 r 24° 443	3 ~75 3 25 245	1,095	655 490 165	235 165 50	135 1 20	73 23 23	35 75 13	55 25 30	10	25 10	70' 891 439	9,665 2 175 4,490
Rura form - Male	368 300 175,620	1°2,725 34 G.5 121,710	188 840 144,605 44,23°	59,49 35 670 23,820	43,Cf0	25,030 22,425 4,605	,830 .4,-20	16,135	1,530 4,950 580	4,8:3 4,280 530	2 4C5 210	2 260 2,140 120	1,205 1,145 60	1,545 1,440 105	825 780 45		940 905 35	809 925 764	19,425 9,680 9,745
Male Female	134, 05 /0 440 08 655	55,220 12 865 42,355	76,585 57,065 22,52	34,825 19 31 15,240	20,420	8 470 -,780 690	3 905 1,560 3/3	1 703 1 565 20L	600 -00 100	370 330 20	80° 70°	90 50 10	45 45	80 75 5	40 40	20 15 5		560 581 350	7 900 3,51° 3,790

DETAILED CHARACTERISTICS

 $T_{\rm 2blc}$ 89.—INCOME IN 1949 OF PERSONS, BY AGE AND SLX, FOR THE STATE, FARM AND NONFARM, AND FOR STANDARD METROPOLITAN AREAS OF 250,000 OR MORE 1950

Based on 20 percen, sample available complete-count data in tables ... and 33 Means not snown where used is ess than 500)

Ame town touderes	Total	Persons							Pers	ons with	Licome				-		_		Incom
Area narm readence age, and sex	old and	without income	Total	\$1 to \$499 or .088	\$600 8999	\$1,000 to \$1,499	\$1 500 .0 \$1,999	\$2 000 to \$2,499	\$2,500 to \$2,999	\$3 000 to \$3 499	\$3 500 to \$3,999	\$4 000 to \$4 499	\$4,500 to \$4,999	95,000 to So 999	\$5.000 \$6,999	\$7 000 10 19 999	a10,000 ind over	Median ricome 'dol	not re
THE STATE						-	1 74	y 12 0				- 8	Amor	1 - 13	100				î.
Male	977,030	13,105	730,765	94,015	٥,180	08,055	8-,5%	77,500	52,270	50,230	36,375	2,395	17,440	22,165	10,390	11.07	1,970	1.75	58
4 to 19 years 0 to 24 years 5 to 34 years 5 to 34 years 5 to 54 years 5 to 64 years 5 to 64 years 6 years 6 years	74,445 79,795 191,910 175,105 136,572 89,910 83,290	69,020 10,090 7 045 2,770 6,705 6,735 8,640	4,080 83,070 -7,886 53,190 121,80% 77,73% 70,025	26,270 11,790 10,980 11,25 11 795 12,155 9,770	9,~;C 17,120 18,750 18,455 17,535 15,560 39,020	4,930 14 200 23,715 20,030 15,995 10,565 6,320	2,265 -2,260 23 450 -9,640 15,200 2,720 5,210	1,135 13,175 23,150 19,355 13,740 7,255 2,755	5,700 17,805 13,720 8,425 4,710 1,55	4,345 17,380 13 725	2,035 12,700 10,305 6,715 3,01 9,5	85 1,335 9 0.0 8,045 5 360 1,295 665	10 680 5,245 2 905 3,5% 1,4±0	35 600 6 015 7,455 -,763 2,365	25 155 2, 125 3 225 2 915 -, 190 455	20 _52 1,725 3,730 3,635 1,670 540	10 165 1,360 3,445 3,725 2,275 970	429 1,390 2,12 2,264 2,014 ,534 823	10,: 6,: 11,: 11,: 8,: 5,:
Female	969,500	542,515	373,745	_36 335	112,600	40,225	27,250	22 .5.	12,0	y, 0°5	3,870	2,120	1,045	1,505	85o	1, 145	١,09٠	72_	53,
4 to 19 years 1 to 24 years 5 to 34 years 5 to 34 years 5 to 34 years 5 to 64 years 5 to 64 years 5 years and over	1:0,560 1:1,285 209,830 1:8,030 1:1,410 (2,925 (5,220	90,845 55,445 126,545 107,225 79,145 50,915 28,595	28,910 46,460 73,390 71,815 57,910 36,770 50,800	19,705 17,295 25,765 24,765 20,225 25,94, 3,235	4,920 10,060 17,125 17,075 .3,855 9,950 -0 ~5	2,450 6,24L 2,545 9,225 (,190 3 610 2,895	1 61J 5,800 6,845 7,850 4 0_5 2,000 1,200	4, 4751 6, 345 5, 360 2, 430 1 545 840	100 2,500 3,750 3,465	45 555 2,44, 3,,25 2, -2	210 83, 7,280 840 540	20 70 365 650 495 315 _05	10 40 45 315 295 -70	30 80 230 350 450 250 200	10 30 90 205 175 45 200	15 70 230 260 260 240	5 35 105 245 3.0 165 225	370 795 819 827 761 622	10,1 5,3 9,3 9,3 7,3 5,3
URBAN AND RURAL NONFARM											161				-				
Male	1.3,720	79,^90	58:, 6)	58,345	#3,120	7, 930	71,125	17 400	4 ,420		33,50		عر,300	20,725	~,6_0	10,1+2	11,060	1,902	48,4
4 to 19 years 0 to 24 years 5 to 34 years 5 to 34 years 5 to 54 years 5 to 64 years 5 to 64 years	87,21, 87,8-0 62,344 -(2,31) -08 125 68,9-5 62,935	7,435 4,950 4,120 4,600 4,775 6 730	33,210 68,740 147,45 128,487 90,270 59,705 52,495	17,825 7,775 0,765 0,000 0,290 7,125 6,565	7,290 10,767 2,640 11,220 10,740 9,90 28,190	4,195 13,260 1°,585 14,255 11,595 1,595 1,905 2,235	1, %5 10, 845 19, 435 10, 375 12 460 7,095 3,260	1, 110 23, 460 11, 745 11, 745 2, 25 2,330	255 2,410 10,3°5 12,1-2 7,500 4,250 1,465	2,250 7,850 3,940 1,230	2,227 12,053 1,500 6,210 2,745 880	4,855 2,095 4,855 2,095	5,720 5,720 5,48° 3,340 1,360 480	5,750 5,750 6,970 4,705 2,10	20 140 1,965 3 270 2,720 1,115 380	105 1805 1,435 2,780 1,550 490	30 155 1,220 3,185 3,480 2,140 855	4,6 1,513 2,387 2,497 2,300 1,845 849	7,- 5,0 10, 9,0 7, 4,0 3,0
Female	793,870	4_1,000	328,810	1,2,515	100, 4	37,620	25,540	20,050	11,45	€,165	3,060	2,000	985	1,500	810	.770	1,053	759	44,0
4 to 19 years) t. 2n years 5 to 44 years 5 to 54 years 6 to 54 years 6 to 64 years 9 years 10 to 64 years	96 e ⁵ 0 94,800 154,415 114,625 72,660 79,500	48,035 48,035 102,835 82,370 60,090 39,115 23,875	23,775 42,215 64,940 64,380 48,525 22,230 30,745	14,607 2-,776 20,515 16,565 13,225 10,905	4,425 9,351 16 075 11,500 12,535 8,840 33,160	2,260 2,55 9,740 8,760 2,715 3,350 2,640	2, 45 2, 615 1, 525 5, 525 3, 750 1, 930 1, 100	425 4,320 5,45 3,045 3,253 1,38	3,645 2,-05 4,035 900 395	45 2,310 2,355 1,980 930 370	25 190 785 1,205 785 520 150	20 42 625 470 285 185	32 130 295 285 166 65	30 70 220 335 425 230 190	190 190 140 185	10 60 130 150 250 170 200	245 245 260 260 260	398 848 854 875 807 807 903 717	8, 8, 7, 6, 4, 4
RUBAL PARM																			
Male	180,30	500 ر /د	_44,603	35,670	40,060	20,425	4,420	17,104	4,400	4,280	2,40	2,140	1,145	1,440	780	880	900	925	9,
4 to 9 years 7/2 24 years to 34 years 1/2 34 years 1/2 5 to 64 years 5 to 64 years 5 to 64 years 5 to 64 years	7,73 17,945 26,555 33,790 28,450 20,975 20,335	22,600 2,655 1,665 -,020 - 605 -,960 1,910	11,870 17,320 26 615 30,755 -5,535 18,030 17,530	8,445 4,015 4,215 5,255 5,505 5,030 3,200	2,150 4,360 6,060 7,235 6,795 5,630 10,80	3,640 4,830 5,75 4,400 2,600 1,785	300 1,415 4,220 3,570 2,740 1,625 550	140 2, 395 4, 875 1, 950 1,000 130	340 1,440 1,575 925 460 1°0	240 1,055 1,445 880 490	5 670 805 260 260	200 200 200 200 200 200 200 200 200 200	5 70 243 420 230 130 45	35 265 485 360 225 80	5 15 10 200 195 75 75	20 295 295 205 -C	10 140 250 245 235 145	35_ 8_ 1,314 1,261 1,055 854 757	2, 1, 1,
Female .	מנס, כלו	121,713	44,235	23,820	ى3,43	2,64;	1,410	1,205	- 8^	>37	210	120	Cu	105	5	73	35	464	2,
4 o 19 years 0 to 24 years 10 to 24 years 10 to 34 years 5 to 44 years 5 to 64 years 5 to 64 years 5 vears and ove.	33,91, 16,438 31,040 -3,915 26,785 17,255 15,720	26,160 1,410 2°,710 24,855 19,055 1,800 4,720	2,1° 4,2/5 6,450 7,435 0,385 4,53 10,055	4 270 2,095 3,995 4 250 3 660 2,720 2,230	495 705 1,050 1,465 1,320 1,110 7,270	230 385 505 525 475 260 255	1.5 185 320 325 245 100 100	2) 330 315 210 130 50	50 200 200 200 200 200 200 200 200 200	10 ±05 ±70 ±35 45 35	5 20 5 5 5 20 20	15 25 25 30 20	15 20 10	10 10 15 25 30	15 15	15 15 20 10	10	301 394 404 437 436 416 692	1,6
TANDARD METROPOL ITAN ARTAS															2				200
NE ORLEANS																			
Male to 19 years	238,050	20,475	8,045	3,830	23,075	23,690	26,500	27, 111	19,740	13,240	12,√75	7,085	5,120	6,915	3,485	3,94	+,860	2,206	14,
to 14 years to 34 years to 34 years to 34 years to 54 years to 54 years years and over	25,905 54,750 49,030 49,030 24,955 48,515	2,700 1,700 1,600 1,800 1,695 2,240	21,635 50,075 44,510 75,570 21,795 15,220	2,200 1,920 1,920 ,450 ,460 -,535	3,380 3,405 2,950 2,740 2,490 2,970	4,095 5,665 4,260 3,530	3,845 6,67 5,845 4,775 3,090 - 575	3,385 8,125 9,675 1,310 2,970 1 155	2,050 6,00 0,075 3,00 1,965 680	1,370 6 315 4,675 3,430 1,845 570	3,930 3,440 2,555 1,385 370	300 2,445 2,425 1,715 805 260	115 1,405 1,665 1,245 455 220	1,700 2,245 1,755 800 180	50 675 1,220 -,300 390 140	15 655, -,260 1,130 67; -/10	465 1 205 1,285 1,095 432	2,6,2 2,4,5 2,594 2,498 2,205 1 327	1, 2, 2, 1, 1
Female	555, د27	_41,700	119,390	1,085د	34,815	17,515	12,875	9,790	5,175	£, °95	1,410	815	455	575	305	360	435	909	12,
4 to 19 , ears 0 to 24 /ears 5 to 34 /ears 5 to 34 /ears 5 to 44 years 5 to 44 years 5 to 44 years 5 to 64 , ears 5 years and over	27,670 30,585 60,89- 55,740 42,645 28,003 24,015	18,54° 14,045 33,195 28,335 22,650 14,95 9 975	0,090 15,250 25,185 25,230 10,240 1.,740 16,485	3,440 +,105 6,220 5,010 4,460 3,390 3,050	6.110	2,395 4,085 4,280 2,700 1,865 1,195	730 2, 485 3, 21.5 2, 885 2, 000 ., 73.5 52.5	1,98* 2,780 2,345 1,495 650 2°0	40 575 1,450 1,485 980 465 180	20 -95 895 1,000 605 440 150	330 425 320 205 70	30 95 290 175 130 95	10 50 155 1 ₂₀ 90 32	10 75 125 130 140 80	30 40 80 70 60 85	33 45 65 400 55 65	5 35 80 140 60	517 1,046 1,052 1,08 1,08 974 890	2, 2, 2, 1, 1, 1,

Table 90.—INCOME IN 949 OF PERSONS, BY FAMILY STATUS AGE AND SEX, FOR THE STATE, FARM AND NONFARM, AND FOR STANDARD METROPOLITAN AREAS OF 250,000 OR MORE 1950

[Based on As Devect's Saltale - Medicar not above white a base is less take 000;

	Lotal	1.			-	-		-A	Pen	ons with	incomi			2.5			-		
family sta is age and sex	i4 veats ow and over	Persons w-thout preame	Total	\$1 to \$499 or .068	\$:00 to \$999	\$1 000 to \$1,499	\$1 300 to \$1 999	\$2 000 to \$2 -99	\$2,500 to \$2,999	\$3,000 to \$3 499	\$8,500 to \$3,999	84,000 to 54,499	\$4,00f to \$4,999	\$5,000 to \$5,989	\$6,030 to \$6,999	\$7 000 to \$9,999	and over	Median incorre (dol	Income not re- norted
THE STATE		i																	
Ms e	1.4, FEU 7.4, FEU 7.7, FEU 47.5, FEU 1.4, FEU 1.4, FEU 1.4, FEU 1.5,	113 2 3 19, 22 19, 22 20, 20 6, 20 10, 21 2,3-, 7,7-1 1 050	20,84	24,270 24,270 24,270 24,270 26,240 27,824	17,2°5 83,161 70 92 3,243 8,155 17,265 0,2°0 18,434	85,075 67,73, 4 895 2,885 20,315	2,325 15 C20 1,745 -2,305	77,575 2 790 3,510 1,510 1,410 775 10,500 4,40 125	12,3% 49,43° 42,775 41,620 1,139 6,-60 6,390 95 2,90 30	20, 230 47, 425 42, 705 41, 230 2, 230 90 7,945 95 2, 770 30	34,350 54,350 51,435 30,800 635 2015 40 2,805 70 1,690	27,795 26,2e0 24,060 390 1,810 40 1,725 25 1,130	17,44 16 515 15 85 15,440 205 9-0 10 900 20 520 00	20,025	7,525 9,370 -55 -03 20 355	10,600 10,135 10,155 140 405 20	1, 450	1,785 2,051 2,051 2,089 1,151 93, 402 1,053 1,053 1,00 891	28,_50 42,875 22,085 23,070 1,815 7,190 8,740 7,770 680 7,271 8 0.15
Female In families Hesd Wire of head _ Other relative or head _ to 19 years 20 to 84 years 65 _ ears and over Urrelated ind viduals numates of institutions	924 900 8,460 594,015 257,725 257,725 257,725 257,725 257,725 257,725 257,725 257,725 257,725 257,725	54_,75 7/ 800 16,34,35 134,35 7,720 7,720 7,720 4,410	57,765 153,770 107,117 20,28-	11-7,905 15,040 6°,025 5 780 14,3°0 19,500 3,440 14,23°	90,275 23,220 24,460 30,521 3,370 13,340 -1,7.2 22,785	45,465 6 425 15,830 40,500 4, 45 5,700 50,400 7	27,3.0 23,455 3 471 -1,495 8,495 1,115 7,100 280 3 820	22 155 18,810 2 735 9,465 6,610 6,45 122 3,340	12,655 9,930 1,555 5,25 3 120 80 2,00 90 2 120	9,695 7,965 -,510 /,010 2,4-5 30 2,3-0 75 1,7-2	3,890 730 1,325 1,00° 20 740 47 810	2,126 452 452 690 410 5 370 35 525	1 0,5 700 240 ,57 460 5 42 10 475	1,275 570 680 225 25 155 45	120 5 30	320 320 375 155 15 100 40 195	1 090 845 203 485 460 12° 40 245	721 703 789 6°4 717 36 930 705 704 665	53,800 4, 945 3,950 23,510 6,483 9,035 5,880 4,570 5,265
URBAN AND RURAL NOVIARM																		1	
Male In families Head Viarried vilepresent Other markel status Relauve of bead 14 to 19 years 20 to 64 years 65 years and over arelated individuals Introtes of institutions	71 - 730 3 - 75 457, 295 433 31 17, -62 -23, -36 78 230 72 625 9, 225 69, 79, 10, -0	79,04, 71,055 13,445 11,800 1,63, 57,0,0 4-,20 11,513 1,330 1,330 1,345 1,0,0	28 420 418 420 418 420 402,540 15,970 109 740 27,930 74,715 0,395 50 445	56,3/5 47,725 21,800 10,795 2,00, 27,927 10,700 1,005 8,145	7: 453 1,425 47,410 / 325 25,060 (,265 14,250 16,085 540	75,930 60,220 44,825 47,655 2,100 ab,395 3,540 12,845 9,400 3,0	7) 2 ⁴ (^ 280 51 7 5 4 ⁹ , 50 1,385 12,4- 1,465 10 925 20,50	67,450 72,515 52,515 52,517 1,555 9,810 155 7,510 120	47,42c 44,36) 38,393 37,585 1,310 5,933 140 5,740 8* 2,825	43,950 43,180 38,565 37,545 1 000 4,625 75 4,445 95 4,735 35	30,6°C 31,9°70 29,335 28,750 385 2,644 35 2,740 65 1 600 35	25,2,5 24,13: 22,505 22,160 34,1 1,033 1,555 40 1,115	16,300 12,48° 14,680 14,495 185 805 20 805	20,525 18,720 18,720 230 200 200 20 20 20 20 20 20 20 20 20 20	9,610 8,794 8 655 140 955 15 310 30 455	10,195 9,730 9,380 9,245 35 37 10 32 43 445	1.,065 10,185 10,185 3,995 190 380 .0 100 20 200	1,°62 2,058 2,20 2,060 1,380 1,057 4.1 1,483 769 1,204 891	48,460 33,870 20,975 19,485 1,497 12,82, 6,125 0,200 500 6,665
Female in families Fend Wife of head. Other relative of road ls to 19 means 20 to 64 veans. 55 years and over- unreasted mid-rhaby umates of institutions	793,870 712 845 70,745 444,235 197 850 76,270 96,775 25,210 74,000 6,33	42_ 00; 406,860 1: 2.0 292,45: 99,10; 090 36 905: 8,940 15,640 >05	328, 83 n 271, 00 52, 40 130 365 86, 2, 5 16 480 54, 88 15 00 50 715 545	1 2,515 97,140 3 760 34,542 99,385 10,507 15,505 3,175 15,180 135	100,1.5 78,210 21 140 31 66. 25,415 2,975 11 920 10 53° 21,64. 310	3",620 "1,395 5 375 14 095 10,042 2 432 8, M0 520 5 452	25,940 3,230 10,870 6 (05) 1 0,00 6 710 200 3,870	20 °50 17,685 2 °47 2,353 6 °32 265 5,760 177 3,260	11,475 9,390 1,535 4,910 2,940 65 2,790 85 2,080	9, 6 7,440 1,445 3,70 2,267 30 3,45 70 1,700	3,550 2,520 5 5 1,240 927 20 360 40 805	2,000 1,485 47, 530 380 380 340 35, 5.5	90J 730 235 355 40 40 125 10 235	1 500 1,180 33. C30 2,5 2,5 1/5 45 380	810 195 270 115 90 25 250	970 775 295 345 135 10 90	1,055 £10 #85 462 160 120 40 245	759 747 802 690 772 388 967 706 804 665	8,015 44,055 34,485 3,4-5 18,325 12,665 1,730 4,825 1,210 4,305 1,265
RURAL PARM												C.	3 "		***		a h		
Male n families feat feat feat Marned wriepresent (the mar is status Relaw to fiscal feat feat feat feat feat feat feat feat	183,300 181,785 116,990 111,365 2,615 64 805 36 006 25,69 3,015 0,217	34,015 33,265 5 680 0,27,410 .7,585 22,345 4,475 65	144,c05 139,445 106,590 101,710 4,880 52,855 1, 135 19,450 2,770 5,1ec	33,99u 19 9c0 18,6s0 1 300 14 030 8,030 5,560 790 1,280	43,064 40,710 31,730 29,810 1,920 6,980 1,304 5,335 1,747 2,350	22,425 21,805 17,9 5 17 240 1,920 1,70 3,17 65	14 400 14,210 11,835 11,424 2,375 280 2,070 25 210	10,_0; 9,975 8,455 8,220 235 1,520 115 1,385 20,	4,950 4,877 4,72 4,05 143 695 5 6/0 .0 75	4,280 4,245 3,730 2 190 40 510 15 500	2,405 2,375 2,100 2 050 30 275 5 265 5 30	2,140 2,125 1,945 1,900 40 40 5 170 5 170	1,145 1,130 1,00,1 983 20 12, 140 15	1 420 1,305 1 275 30 110 5	780 780 730 745 25 27 20 5	850 810 810 5 35 10 2>	875 875 825 20 40 40 40	539 1,040 269 797 633 345 890 700 61	9 680 2,072 4,710 4,382 272 4,365 2 645 1 570 180 60
Textale n families Head Whe of head Other relative of head 1 to 19 years 20 to 64 years 65 years and ever n-negato undwid-als nms'e. of institutions	1"2 690 1"7,055 7,43 109,780 54,840 29,840 29,840 5,760 3,635	20,710 20,940 -,735 94,060 ->,115 73,030 10,755 1,30	44 235 41,655 5,2-5 20,3.3 -3,035 4,405 7,393 4,100 2,580	27,820 22 765 1,780 12,400 8,455 3,705 4,025 765 1,055	13,432 12,292 2,360 4,800 5 -15 4.5 1,470 3 250 1,140	2,637 2,460 4,70 1,:35 8,55 1,30 640 65 14,	1 410 1 3 0 245 625 490 85 990 15	1,203 1,120 95 Clo 41,2 25 305	580 540 500 300 75 15 15 15	5.0 505 260 260 260 273 5 25	.7.0 205 3- 85 85 85	140 140 20 60 -0	50 60 5 35 20 20	105 335 50 40 40	45 25 15 5 20	75 2. 30 40 31	35 35 15 20	464 45° 7.77 411 468 297 422 692 603	9 /60 455 ,185 3,320 2,405 1,055 330 285
STANDARD METROPOLITAN AREAS												. !							
Male n numbes . Head Merred, wife present. Other marrial status Relative of head 14 to 19 years . 20 .0 69 years and over intelated findwiduls intelated findwiduls ima ee of insutritions	238,050 210,515 45,785 139,090 " 495 00,730 22, Nu 37,680 3,345 75,145 1,390	26, '5 23,630 4,460 3,775 68- 1° 170 13 940 4,513 715 2,485 360	197, xi0 175,741 173,225 6,71,1 40,300 175,255 6,71,1 40,300 175,255 40,300 175,255 460 44,275 485	13,9e5 11,645 4,660 4,040 560 7,045 3,475 3,25 345 200 120	_8,125 _0,480		26,50° 21,3° 17,430 10,440 5,9 540 5,220 105 3,105 45	23 750 20,815	18,360	1/,0,0	12,0°; 11 42: 10 175 9,895 280 1,250 30 645	7 547 6,91 6,770 145 625 10 595 20 445	5,210 4,85 4,480 4,420 30 30 325	6,915 6,500 0,045 5,962 80 453 10 453 10 453	3,255 3 115 3,000 25 140 10 120 22*	3,945 3,720 3,575 3 530 45 145 125 20 225	2,310 25 170 5 160		14,07: 11,14: (,885 6,200 5,4,260 1,62: 2,465 170 2,38: 54:

Tible 90 —INCOME IN 1949 OF PERSONS, BY FAMILY STATCS, AGL, AND SFX, FOR THE STATE, FARM AND NONFARM, AND FOR STANDARD METROPOLITAN AREAS OF 250000 OR MORE 1950—Con

Based on M percent sample Diedra n Ashown went loss sam all,

Area 'arm residence	To al	Persons						1 200	200	לורא פר	ne .mc								
famil, status age	old and	without	Total	\$1 to \$100 or loss	\$000 \$096	\$1,00° \$1,499	\$1 .00 \$1 999	\$2 000 \$2 100	42,500 53 90	\$3 000 \$3 199	73 ,67 co 27 949	44 000 44 99	4 .07	\$2,000 \$2,999	SE 000 56 999	57 00°0 ≈9 999	-10.0 Kg	-C-LAND	not re-
STANDARD METROPOL- ITAN AREAS—Cor						1									1 10 m				
NEW ORLEANSC. D			. Se				100				e de		o fee	1					1
Female -	273, 255	14_,700	13,090	31,035	34,8,5	_7,51	44,875	y '90	2,475	3,395	2,4 0	915	منه.	57	.60	2.5	455	909	12 76
In families Heau Wife or read Oner relative of head 14 to 19 years	244 675 26,195 -41,765 76,715 23,.00	93,1.0 93,1.0 96,790	90,900 16,880 43 375 35,41, 3,150	2: 9.0 3,62 -4,54 8,66 2 -70	7,230 7,130 10,0 5 10,0 5	2,723	1,02 -,042 4 ren 4,63u 580	5 345 -,545 1,5 1	4 180 780 1,260 1,540	1,080	3,25 320 00 4,5		/25	205	82		5	908 908 85u 350 536	1,24 2,08 2,08
20 to 64 years 60 years and or er. (inrelated individuals Immates of institutions.	-2, :20 14, :35 27, ~70 -,140	4,505 5,36, 140	24,420 0 14, 20,790 330	4,7:0 1,460 4,15f 100	4, ±00 3 ±55 7 4_3 95	4 250 295 3,245 25	3,990 129 1 800 5	2,295	1,455 25 995	1,J^^	285	20 285	30 5 125	30 11:2	50 15 -0°	35.5	55		2,50 48 1,63

Table 91—INCOME IN 1949 OF PERSONS, BY WEEKS WORKED IN 1949 AND SEX FOR THE STATE, FARM AND NONFARM, AND FOR STANDARD METROPOLITAN AREAS OF 250,000 OR MORE 1950

[Based on 26-percent sample | Median not show where base is less than 500]

			-	[Disco	. ou 20-p	ercent sa	muse "	edian not s	-	-	_	. 5001	with Research	***************************************			_		-
Arca 'arm rescence weeks worked.	Total, 14 years	Persons without		\$1 to	\$o00	\$1,000	\$1,500	\$2 000	\$2,500	SS OOO	33,000	S4 000	84,,(2)	85,000	S6 000	87 000°	>10,000	\andınn	Income act re-
and sex	old and over	income	Total	\$499 or	to 8999	to \$1,-99	to 51,999	to \$2 -99	to 52,999	to \$3,499	to \$3,999	to 94 .99	to 94,999	Ru 999	to \$6,999	to 59,999	and	(gol)	
THE STATE												1						3-4	
Tota	1,874,590		ي81, د1, 10				.12,895	99,710	64,425	59,925	39,945	29 5.5	48,430	23 770		12,12		1,459	111,900
Did not work in 1949 Worked in 1949 - 1 to 13 weeks - 14 to 20 works - 27 to 89 weeks - 50 to 52 weeks - Work in 1940 not rptd.	93,15* 930,820 89,865 97,855 90,420 106,085 552,595 111 *12	6.3,955 10,320 -,300 6,095 3,245 2,965 12,715 -1,545	394,825 83a,305 83,405 89,965 85,540 101,105 522,570 26,680	56,2.5 168,1.0 53,900 38,830 :6,013 13,000 36,303 9,725	20,700 11,775 27,245 27,245 27,390 29,707 31,725 6,390	18,205 -16,425 -4,165 11,315 15,895 18 74J 60,485 3,880	6,363 103 920 1,623 5,670 9,935 14,400 72 295 2 59,	3,920 93,720 640 3,075 7,511 1,485 71,001 2,070	2 040 61 175 320 1,255 4,745 6,870 48 01 1,210	1 640 57,035 230 950 4 665 5,500 45 260 1 230	1,030 38,.10 .55 -15 1,77> 3,39> 32,,70	28,100 120 385 913 2,670 24,010 620	17,640 40 120 533 4,335 15,380	910 22,-05 85 190 485 1,650 12,955 425	50	11,005 65 2,5 300 620 9,703 440	170 170	1,1,9	1,460 1,775 1,615 2,015 17 310 73,300
Male	902,030	11,100	730 765	94,015	136,180	98,355	85,245	77,525	52,300	0 230	30,00	27,390	17,40	22,.60	10,190	11,075	1,970	2,72	58 160
Did not work in 1949 Weiked in 1949 1 to 19 weeks 14 to 26 weeks 27 to 59 weeks 40 to 49 weeks 50 to 52 weeks Work in 1949 not uptd	185,88 58,650 40,31* 54,815 56,335 81,330 425,985 57,495	97,600 -3,010 -380 1,965 1,370 1,030 6,415 2,495	84,7.5 627,145 37,995 51,715 54,10. 77,915 405,445 18,865	17,325 73,450 23 720 14,240 7,020 7,595 20,855 3 240	44,82, 87,235 8,120 -7,895 -1,785 -3,295 3-1,240 4 20	11,49° 83,885 3,405 8,65, 11,485 14,675 47,665 7,980	3,845 79 669 1,420 4,880 7,095 11,880 53,790 2,030	2,750 73,680 545 2,755 5,410 9,610 55,360 1,645	1,215 30,160 230 1,090 3,005 5,885 39,950 995	2,265 -,009 40,060	6+0 34 955 115 365 1,300 2,990 29,985 680	400 26,430 95 325 (25 4,335 22,940 565	340 16,785 25 	21,340 5 50 410 1,560 19,175 395	175 700 8,855 215	285 10,400 30 175 270 575 9,350 390	520 10,310 290	1,348	3,530 18,495 640 1,155 1,050 1,555 14,155 36 135
Female	969,560	542,725	3/3,54.	139, 3,95	1 600	40 425	27,050	22,,25	2,055	9,095	3,870	2 -<0	-,045	1,605	855	390	615	721	10,845
Did not work in 1940 - Workod in 1949 - 1 to 13 weeks 14 to 26 weeks 27 to 39 weeks - 40 to 49 weeks - 50 to 52 weeks Work in 1949 not rptd -	637,270 278,170 49,850 43,040 53 915 24 755 126,510 54,120	5-6, 155 -7,310 3 920 4,130 1,875 7,085 6,300 9 050	1,C,C70 255,160 45,110 38,270 31,435 23,_90 117,1,5 7,815	38,830 9-,660 40,180 2/,593 8,984 5,405 -5,500 4,785	35,925 55,40,3 655 9,350 8,605 6,410 27,385 2,270	640 2,660 2,660 4,410 4,062 20,815 900	200 790 2,240 2,530	1 670 20,040 92,20 2,103 1,875 15,645 445	8:5 11,015 90 1,740 955 8,065 215	760 8,720 55 110 2,-00 255 5 200 215	390 3,355 40 50 475 4C3 2,385 25	395 1,670 25 40 200 315 -,070 55	250 857 1 20 125 8, 610 35	480 1 065 40 40 75 90 820 60	4/5 10 5 25 45	605 35 80 30 45 4.5	4.0 10 30 20 20 23	6-4 797 281 389 891 983 1,377 747	820 640 605 460 3,155 37,255
URBAN AND RURAL NONFARM														-				. "	
l otal	1,507 600	500,095	914,970	170,800	1,3,285	.13,550	97 005	88,400	58,895		30دو27	27,255	17,285				12,120		92,535
Did not work in 1949 Worked in 1949 1 to 18 weeks 14 to 29 weeks 27 to 39 weeks 40 to 49 weeks to 62 weeks Work in 1949 not spid	649,220 769,970 70,710 77,75 72,27 80,465 459,24* 78,4_0	1 3/5 1,185 240 290 6,725	738,610 68,175 74,640 70,200 73,065 447,530 18,780	122,262 54,340 20,990 11,165 6,992 22,075	9,620 23,445 17,675 13,090	95,835 3,420 9,995 -4,005 -3,955	1,375 5,040 8,710 12,075 62,865	3,120 83 675 495 2 805 6,490 9,840 64,075 1,605	1,120 4 235 6,080 44,430	163 850 4,_90 3,405 42,070	1,590 1,590 3,140 30,440	2,420 42,385 525	430 46,540 35 105 485 1,220 14,000 715	780 21, 045 75 420 1, 524 48, 600 400	85 175 645 8,710 230	210 26 505 9,13 335	14, 155 46, 9,980 30,	1 740 326 556 1,227 1,677 2,320 1,3_1	00,400
Male	713,730	_		58,340				67,450	47,420		_		16 -00	20,725		-	11,005		2 67
Drd no work in 1949 Worked in 1949 1 to 13 weeks 14 to 25 weeks 27 to 39 weeks 40 to 49 weeks 50 to 52 weeks Work in 1949 not rotd	140,585 528,780 51,100 44,020 4,890 350,820 44,765	4,025 -95 460 275 390 4,-05	30,100 42,625 42,765 56,935 336,405	18,730 10 545 3,880 2,525 8,520	56 477 6 390 4, 382 9, 860 7, 250 -7, 990	2,825 7,500 9,755 10,92 34,060	66,900 1,185 4,315 6,745 9,695	1,640 64,620 4.5 2,503 4,720 8,07 43,910	45,625 180 985 2 685 5,_00 36,585	44, 110 750 2 045 4, 505 37 000	25 1,165 2 765 28,155	24,430 80 265 650 2,110 71,325	15,°30 20 85	20 030 35 130 350	9,175 80 150 600 9,330 185	9 005 20 140 240 460 8,745 350	10,395 55 1.3 133 445 9,645 270	2,171 402 862 1,392 1,911 2 508 1,077	15,-7° 48: 93: 8:0 1,19: 12 010 20,3:0
Female	793,870	423, 005	328,81	12,515		37,62	-	20,950		-		-	985	1,500			-	7*9 652	8.88.
Did not work in 1949 Worked in 1949 1 to 13 weeks 14 to 25 weeks 27 to 19 weeks 40 to 49 weeks 50 to 52 weeks Work in 1949 not rptd	508, 035 241, 590 29, 580 39, 255 26, 385 2, 945 118, 425 43 645	3,760 850 725 463 430 7,320	27,435 21,_30 1,1,_25	33 610 19,445 7,285 4,470 43,555	3 230 8,560 8,560 81* 5,940	30,850 :95 2,49: 4,04: 3,440 19,87:	23,165 190 725 1,965 2,380 17,905	_5 163	10,510 90 135 1,550 890 7,845	8,270 5,100 2 145 900 5,070	3, 80 40 45 42: 37: 2,29:	1,635 25 4, 310 1,060	15 20 100 85 590	40 40 73 90 773	465 10 2 2 45 380	565 35 70 25 45 390	420 30 20 20 340	855 283 412 912 1,020 1,406	5,100 705 485 415 2,780

 $T_{able~91}\hbox{--INCOME~IN~1949~OF~PERSONS, BY~WEEKS~WORKED~IN~1949~AND~SEX, FOR~THE~STATE, FARM~AND~NONFARM, AND~FOR~STANDARD~METROPOLITAN~AREAS~OF~250,000~OR~MORE~1950\hbox{---}Con$

[Based on 20-percent sample Median not shown where base is less than 500]

			_	ш		percent so	and the second	odan noe	-							_	and the later of	-	
Area, farm equence, weeks worked, and sex	Total, 14 veers old and over	P	Persons with accome														Income		
		Persons withou medic	"nta:	\$1 c 499 or 1088	%000 to 4999	\$1 000 to \$1 499	\$1,500 TO \$ 999	\$2,000 to \$2,499	\$2,500 to \$2,999	\$3,000 to \$3,499	\$3,500 to \$3,999	\$4,000 to \$4,499	\$4,500 to \$4,999	\$5,000 to \$5,999	\$6,000 to \$6,999	\$7,000 to \$9,999	510,000 end overo	income	not re-
RURAL FARM																			
Tom	300,000	52,725	138, 340	29,490	50,490	عب بدو	0-8,5	٦_د,_٥	5,550	4,810	2,615	_	1,200	1,545	820	945	940	809	19,425
Did not work in 1949 Worked in 1949 1 to 13 weeks 4 to 26 weeks 27 to 39 weeks 40 to 49 weeks 50 to 52 weeks Work in 1949 not rptd	.70,4,5 160,850 19,55 20,10 21,45 22,620 13,250 23,205	2,500 2,535 2,500 2,500 2,500 2,75 2,950 2,010	37,245 142,695 4,950 25,45 12,340 25,040 75,040 ,900	40,345 -1,366 8,846 4,850 C,305	19,085 34,940 2,5 3,800 4,71 6,025 2,470	3,270 20,660 645 -,320 2,090 4,075 12 -25 1,200	245 60 2,325 60 2,325 4.0	200 20,045 270 1,025 1,675 e 930 465	335,000 50 135 510 700 3,785	35 100 475 555 3, 90	2,430 25 45 185 255 1,920	2,005 15 75 70 250 250 95	1 100 5 25 50 40	130 1,360 20 65 130 -,135	80 705 25 20 25 100 535 40	75 835 10 45 -5 115 630 45	20 790 5 20 15 75 675 30	684 876 323 434 799 017 1,223 828	2,81° 270 325 300 405 2,320 12,990
Mate	.98,56	ر4,01	J4,605	35,670	4.,060	22 420	14 420	10, 105	4,950	4,280	2,405	2,140	1,245	1,440	780	880	905	925 753	°,680
Did not work in 1949 Worked in 1949 I to 12 weeks 4 to 26 weeks 27 to 39 weeks 40 to 49 weeks 50 to 52 weeks Work in 1949 not riptd	45,.00 50,4% 6,865 10,7°5 12,615 -2,810 75,165 12,730	24, 365 8, 985 885 -, 507 1, 07 4, 010 647	20,060 118,265 7,845 9,090 11,340 20,980 64,010 9 280	4,815 29,250 4,790 3,695 3,500 5,070 12,345 -,565	10,210 30,960 1,720 3,010 3,925 6,145 10,150 1,890	2 450 18,900 580 1,155 -,730 3,850 1,585 1,075	985 12,765 230 565 950 2,185 8,850 670	610 5,060 130 250 690 1,40 6,450 435	275 4,035 50 105 ,00 695 3,365 140	3,905 3,905 35 30 220 500 3,060	2,255 25 40 25 225 1,850	2,000 12 60 60 245 1,615 85	1,055 25 25 26 305 890 30	1,310 10 20 60 130 1,090	695 25 20 25 400 525 30	795 10 32 30 113 605 40	780 5 20 15 75 665 20	983 393 641 821 941 1,259 917	855 -,020 155 200 180 340 -,142 -, 805
Fema_e	_"5,690	٦٠,٦٥	-4,235	23,820	435,د_	2,505	1,410	1,200	590	530	210	120	- 60	105	45	75	35	464	9,745

Did not work in 1949 — Worked in 1949 — 1 to 13 weeks — 14 to 26 weeks — 27 to 39 weeks — 40 to 49 weeks — 50 to 02 weeks — Work in 1949 not rptd —	128 635 36 580 10,270 9,785 5,530 2,820 8,-85	109,490 10,550 3,070 3,435 1,420 685 1,980 1,970	17 185 25 430 7,085 r,255 4,000 2,000 6,000	0,760 10,295 0,570 5,145 1,700 935 1,945	8,975 ,980 425 790 470 470 580	723 1,760 55 160 365 225 940 125	275 1,090 10 e5 275 40 600 45	190 965 15 20 335 135 480 30	505 505 505 190 55 220	450 450 2,5 55 30	35 175 5 50 30 90	15 5 5 10 10 10 10 10 10 10 10 10 10 10 10 10	3. % s	55 50 50	10	30 40 10 5 25	.5 .0 	603 390 270 304 690 601 855 539	1,960 600 115 120 120 60 _75 7,185
STANDARD METRO- POLITAN AREAS																		- 1	
NEW CRIBANS	5,605	168 175	ر16,590	/5 080	57,890	/1 20s	30 300	37,700	24,915	21,635	_3,485	8,800	2,565	7,490	3,850	4,310	5,3,2	1,080	26,840
Total Did not work in 1949 Worked in 1949 - 1 to 13 weeks 14 to 26 weeks 27 to 39 weeks 40 to 49 weeks 5 to 52 weeks Work in 1949 not rptd -	214,605 272,5,5 19,795 25,345 25,340 25,310 178,915 24,445	161,675 2,335 405 255 240 180 2,255 3,165	49,240 261,270 15,990 24,595 22,495 24,585 170,905 0,080	25,050 15,695 30,320 13,875 8 200 2,175 1,215 Å,855 1,035	23,680 33,160 3,040 8,425 8,425 8,2305 1,050	5,335 34,825 .,120 3,660 3,235 4,840 10,070 843	39,380 1,880 36,785 455 4,960 3,475 4,530 26,365 T5	1,240 37,850 185 1,040 2,.40 3,845 28,440 610	680, 23,775 95, 450, 2,245 2,295 19,690 460	20,660 60 370 1,045 1,840 1°,345 380	345 -2,910 -45 -135 -425 -865 11,440 -230	260 8,375 35 75 245 560 7,460 165	160 5,300 5 40 290 4,785	280 7,06* 20 70 105 290 6,580 140	21.0 3,505 10 25 5, 125 3 320 105	215 3,950 30 85 75 180 3,580 145	405 4,760 15 00 70 145 4,470 90	731 -,9,9 342 74,310 -,795 2,383 -,277	3,690 7,950 400 495 450 540 6,055 15,200
Male	238,050	26,475	197, -00	13,965	2,075	25,090	26,505	27,010	.9,740	18,240	12,075	7,980	5,1:0	6,915	3,485	3,945	4,860	2,200	14,075
Did not work in 1949 Worked in 1949 1 to 13 weeks 14 to 25 weeks 27 to 39 weeks 40 to 49 weeks 50 to 52 weeks Work in 1949 not rptd	42,9% 182,900 8,580 4,115 14,250 17,550 126,405 12,175	24,660 1,170 120 125 75 85 76,640	17,540 175,060 8,305 13,675 13 905 17,065 123,010 4,000	3, 20 10,370 4,690 2,630 7:0 330 1,965 475	8,393 14 235 1,935 4,655 2,505 1,360 3,780 450	2,990 20,1.5 920 2,680 3,460 2,952 10,070 285	990 25,035 .65 1,660 2,680 	580 26,905 150 935 1,910 3,150 20,755 425	335 19,020 70 385 980 1,990 -5,595 385	295 17,615 50 350 680 1,530 -5,005	180 11,695 25 115 340 735 10,480 200	1_0 7,720 25 25 1°0 520 5,930	90 4,920 140 263 4 493 100	1.0 0,090 5 45 90 260 6,290 115	3,300 3,300 25 45 95 3,130	75,735 15 55 70 155 3,440 135	180 4,605 25 55 65 145 4,325 75	837, 2,339, 442, 952, 1,544, 2,050, 2,762, 2,312	775 6,770 155 315 270 400 4,6.0 7,2.0
Female -	273,255	141,700	1.9,090	31,085	34,815	17,515	12,875	9,790	5,175	3,395	1,410	815	435	57>	305	355	455	909	12,705
Did not work in 1949 - Worked in 1949 1 to 18 weeks - 14 to 26 weeks - 27 to 39 weeks - 40 to 49 weeks - 50 to 52 weeks - Work in 1949 not rptd -	171,630 89,655 11,215 11,230 8,940 7,760 50,510 12,270	137,015 2,165 285 130 165 95 1,490 2,520	31,700 85,310 .0,585 10,520 8,590 7,520 47,595 2,080	10,575 19,950 9,180 5,570 1,425 885 2 390 560	15,290 18,925 1,105 3,770 3,320 2,205 8,525 600	2,545 14,710 270 980 1,775 1,88° 9,900 260	89C 11,750 90 300 705 955 9,01C 233	650 8,945 35 105 430 690 3,635	345 4,755 25 65 265 305 4,095 75	300 3,045 10 20 362 210 2 340 50	165 1,215 20 20 85 150 960 30	50 655 10 20 55 40 5_0	70 380 5 10 40 30 295	270 375 15 25 25 20 290	15 235 5 10 30 190	140 215 15 30 5 25 40	285 155 5 5 145 15	672 -,128 291 400 9,2 1,178 1,629 900	2,915 2 180 245 180 185 145 1,425 7,670

Table 92 - INCOME IN 1949 OF PERSONS, BY CLASS OF WORKER AND SEX, FOR THE STATE, FARM AND NONFARM, AND FOR STANDARD METROPOLITAN AREAS OF 250,000 OR MORE 1950

[Based on 20-percent sample. Median not shown with a base in less than .09?

Area farm residence class of	Tota zneludes	cludes														Incox		
worker and ser	persons without income)	Tosa	\$1 .0 \$439 or loss	\$000 to \$999	\$1,000 to \$1,499	\$1 500 to \$1,999	\$2 000 to \$2 499	\$2,500 to \$2,999	\$3,000 to \$3 499	\$3,999 \$3,999	\$4,000 \$4,499	84,500 to \$4,999	\$5,000 to \$5,999	88,000 to \$6 999	\$7 000	810,000 and over	Median income (dol)	pore
THE STATE			100.00			200	9.0	4	100	11/2			10.0	- 177		89		
Total, 14 years old and over memenced ovultan 'abou torce Private wag, and salar, workers Government workers Self employed workers Unpaid family workers to in exper civilin labor force.	908,565 623,570 91,490 108 355 25,150 963,025	\$01.620 559,733 84,795 148,735 6,360 302,190	230,3.0 115,345 78,845 5,495 25,795 5,240 115,005	249 780 129 603 89,020 7,505 31,355 1,725 120,175	138,58° 109,360 76,720 9,760 22,1'5 705 29,220	112 895 100,210 72,215 11,960 15,755 280 12,665	99,710 91,770 02,355 13,480 12,770 165 7 940	64 425 60, 9 42,070 10,770 7 285 65 4,2:5	59,925 56,660 39,405 9,980 7,220 55 3,205	39 945 7,845 27,670 9 935 4,190 50 2,100	29 515 28,135 21,165 3 340 3,000 30 1,380	17,410 13,615 2,045 1,740 10 1,080	23,770 22 190 15,885 2,465 4,110 1 1,580	11,245 10,155 0,940 950 2,290 1,090	12,120 10,000 6,280 925 3,590 10 1,215	15,060 11 840 -,605 -,60 10 1,220	1,259 1,732 1,744 2,265 1,388 399 650	111 28 20 1
Male 14 years old and over persenced civilian labor force Private wage and salary workers Jovernment workers Sel. employed workers Unpaid family workers it in exper civilian labor force	902,030 670 740 448,775 36 213 151 160 4 660 23,,290	730,765 608,725 413,846 53,250 135,430 6 205 122,040	94,015 02,900 35,355 2,050 41,655 1,860 31,115	36 180 85,120 51,830 3,51 28,4_5 1,360 51,060	98,055 80,960 54,0.0 6,140 20,290 520 17,390	85,545 76,230 95,125 8,240 14,655 210 7 215	77,555 72,910 52,513 8,410 11,480 105 4,645	52,370 49,460 36,270 5,515 6,820 50 2,710	50,230 48,315 36,190 5,410 6,490 25 1 915	36,075 34,640 26,250 4,410 4,000 30 1,385	27,395 26,390 20,475 2,703 3,385 25 805	7,445 46,630 2,220 1,763 1 620	22,165 21,245 15,440 1,940 3 855	10,390 9,670 6,685 850 2,125	11,079 10,360 6,725 849 3,-85	11,970 4,445 4,470 435 0,335 5	1,715 1,982 2,101 2,397 1 435 402 795	58 32 20 1 9
Female, 14 years old and over penented civilina labor force rivate wage and salary workers lovertment workers workers lamily workers the expert (vulan labor force	969 560 237,825 174 865 39,275 7 95 10,490 721,735	373,0.5 192,895 1.5,890 31,.45 13,.00 255 180,.50	2,445 43,480 3,445 4,140 1,380 80,890	123,600 44,485 37 190 3 990 2,940 365 69 122	40,225 28,400 22,710 3,62 1,555 185 13,875	27,350 21 960 17,090 3 720 1,100 70 5,370	42,155 18 860 12,840 5,000 990 60 3,295	12,055 10,530 5,8.0 4 2.5 465 10 1 525	9,695 8,345 3,215 4,570 530 30 1,350	3,870 3,105 -,420 1 520 -90 20 7-5	2,120 3,545 690 605 21,5 5	1,045 780 395 260 120 5 265	1,605 545 4-2 245 24,10 650	855 485 225 100 107 107 3	1,045 545 255 80 205 5	2,090 395 25 70 70 225 5	721 995 89- 2,096 927 390 54*	53 10 7 1
URBAN AND RURAL NONFARM				7										- 6		100		
Total 14 years old and over menenoid c vinan labo force. Private ware, and salary works a Government ware.com Self-employed workers "Impaid family workers on a usper civilian labor force	738,205 569,690 83 300 79 9,5 5,260 769,395	914 970 661,870 513,220 77,210 69,845 1,585 253 100	78 630 66,300 4 835 7,230 565 91 950	93,905 77 415 6,530 9,557 445 400,380	123,_50 #7 350 69,975 8 740 8 375 260 26 200	97 0c5 85,545 67 730 10,595 7,105 15 11,50	81,50 61,830 12 190 7,140 96,7 150	58,395 54,945 40,070 20 045 4 795 35 3 950	50,1.5 52,080 37,755 9,295 5,020 30 3,035	37 330 35,360 27 600 5,525 200 35 1,970	27,255 26,0,5 20,095 3, 95 2,720 15 1,240	17,285 16,275 -2,975 - 930 1,360 10 1,010	22,225 20,790 15,340 2,095 3,345 10 1,435	9,395 6,650 910 1,8°0	10,045 5,065 685 3,090 5 1,120	12, 20 10,989 4,450 4,50 9,080 1,135	1,4_1 1 919 1,817 2 J2- 2,256 761 672	92 35 25 6 57
Male 14 years old and over- penened civilian labor torce Priva e wage and salari Covernment workers Self-employed vorkers Unpaid family workers t in expe. civilian labor force	713,730 >24,570 +05 325 3. 125 66,295 1,725 189,160	584,160 483 360 374 88, 48,450 59, 80 845 102,800	28,745 32,750 27,355 1,750 4,45 300 24,585	93,120 51,260 41,695 3,015 6,395 255 41,860	75,930 60,940 48,000 9,440 6,763 120 15,610	71 -25 64 425 50,975 7,205 6,18 65 6,700	67,450 63,260 49 2., 7,635 6,350 40 4,190	47,420 44,885 34,375 6,110 4,375 22 2 535	45,950 44,160 34,585 5,040 4,530 5 2,790	33 670 32,345 25,710 4,300 3,CL5 20 1,325	25,255 24,49° 19,40, 2,565 2,510 10 765	46,300 -5 535 -2,585 1,695 1 250 5	20,725 19,875 14,905 1,860 3,110	9 010 2,930 6,425 810 -,695	10 195 9,520 5,820 805 2,895	11,005 10,605 4 315 420 1,870	1,967 2 252 2,19° 2,446 2,475 740 820	48 25 18 1
Femals, 14 years old and over gwrenceu c un lann foru, Private wage and salari workens Govinnman workers Self-employed workers Linaud family workers in evpc eivilian labor force	793,870 213,635 164,365 32,175 13,560 3,535 580 235	326 810 378 510 138,345 28,760 10,665 740 150,370	12,515 45,180 38,945 3,085 2,885 265 57,335	100 165 41 645 35,720 3 5 5 2,260 150 98,520	37,620 27,030 21,975 3,300 1,615 140 1° 59c	25,9-0 21,120 16,755 3,390 925 50 4,820	20,950 17,990 12,535 4,555 790 50 2,960	11,475 10 060 5,695 3,935 420 1,41	9,165 7,920 3 150 4,255 490 25 1,245	3,660 3,0.5 1 390 1,425 485 15 64	2,000 1,525 990 620 210 5	985 740 390 235 110 5 245	1,700 915 405 202 235 0 585	810 465 225 100 37 5 345	970 525 2/5 80 195 5	1,055 380 335 30 2.0 5 675	75° 1,04° 92 2,120 1,058 850 560	7
RUBAL FARM																	11.7	
Total, 14 years old and over conented civilian abor force Priva e wage and salary workers too trament workers sel-employed workers to make a virial abor for e	363 793 175,365 53,880 8,190 88 400 _9,690 193,650	188,840 139,750 46,500 7,585 78,890 6,775 49,090	59,490 36 415 12 5.5 660 18,565 4,675 23,075	36,499 36,709 11 605 975 42 800 1,320 17,795	2,030 22,000 6,745 020 13,800 445 3,020	15,830 14,665 4,485 1 305 8,650 465 1,165	11,310 10,520 3,525 1,290 5,630 70 790	5 *30 5 245 2,000 725 2,490 30 285	4,610 4,580 1,670 985 2,200 20 20	2 615 4,485 4,000 410 990 15 430	2,360 2 120 1,070 155 880 25 140	1,135 640 1_0 360	1,745 1,700 5/5 90 735	825 200 400 460 460	955 860 215 40 600 5	855 145 15 680 5 85	956 963 1,917 958 362 577	19 7 2 4
Male 14 years old and over opener ced on the "abor force. Prival wage and salary workers Government workers belf employed workers Unpaid family workers Unpaid family workers of its even exists abor orce.	188 300 140 170 43,380 5,090 84 765 12 935 42,130	144,602 122,362 38,955 4,800 76,250 2,360 19,240	35 670 29,150 1,980 3(3) 17,310 3 560 6,520	43 060 33,860 10,135 500 22,120 1,175 9,200	22,425 20,640 6,010 700 10,530 400 400	14,420 3 805 4,150 1,035 8 47, 1/5 615	10,105 9,650 3,280 775 5,430 65 455	4,920 4,775 1,895 4C5 2 445 30 175	4,280 4 155 -,605 -,605 -,600 20 20 125	2,405 2 345 1,640 31.0 985 10	2,140 2,100 1 070 140 875	1,145 1,095 635 90 370	1,440 1,370 535 80 750	780 740 250 40 440	880 840 203 70 595 40	90> 840 155 15 963 5	925 995 1 - 3 1,935 991 370 668	1
Femsie, 14 years old and over penence i civilian labor force fuvaire mage and saurry workers Government workers Self-employed workers Umpad family workers in exper civilian labor force	275,690 27,190 20,500 3,177 3,635 6,955	44,233 14,385 7,745 2,785 2,640 1,415 29,850	43,840 7,265 4,535 360 1,257 2,115 16,555	2 840 1,470 475 680 215 10,595	2,605 1,370 735 320 270 43 1,237	1 410 860 335 330 175 20 550	1,205 870 245 5.5 1.00 1.00 335	550 470 103 320 45	530 425 65 315 40 5	21.0 14.0 100 100 5 70	120 2^ 15	60 40 5 25 10	105 3C 10 10 10	45 20 20 23	75 20 10 10	35 15 15 20	464 495 416 2660 548 317 454	1 3
ANDARD METROPOLITAN AREAS														ni.			(4	
Foral 14 years old and over perienced of this labor orce Private Wage an i salary workers Government workers Self-emprosed sockers Unpaid fam, www.kers timexpressible labor force	511,605 266,520 20° e/0 30,640 25 150 1,130 245,085	316,50 23°,535 188 315 28,566 2,920 240 77,055	45,050 20 355 17,145 1 260 1,875 75 24,605	57,890 28,4-5 24,460 ,685 2,270 30 2~,445	41,205 31,605 26,730 2,313 2,510 55 9,600		34,85, 27,075 5,45 2,320 2,845	24 915 29,330 17,330 4,515 7 495 10 4,565	21,635 20,503 15,1°0 3,85 1,45 15	13,485 12,795 9,680 2,090 1,020 5	8,800 8,345 6 235 4,25 855 450	5,505 5 ±85 4,035 676 475 5	7,490 6,980 4,905 895 1,200	3,850 3,410 2,430 340 635 5	4,310 3 695 2,425 430 1 0.5 5	5,315 4,810 2,1,5 205 2,450	2 063 1,950 2,473 2 46± 735	1
Male, 14 years old and over persenced it linan inhor torce Private wage and salary workers. Government vorkers. Self exployed workers Unpaid tamily workers Unpaid tamily workers Unit oxport arvitain labor to ee	258,050 283,445 242,110 20,225 20,820 290 54,605	197,500 16°,0.5 131,3-5 19,185 18,415 80 28,475	13 965 8,440 6,880 430 1,100 30 5,525	23,075 13 030 10,765 745 1,540 10,045	23,690 18,425 15 2.0 1 260	26,535 24,115 19,540 2,740	27,910 26,285 20,400 3,805 2,080	19,740	_8,240 _7 585 _3,790 2 280 1,110	12,075 11 655 9,095 1,600 955	7,925 7,725 5,040 1,025 750	5,110 4,850 3,855 985 410 260	6,915 6,650 4,800 910 1,040	3,485 3,180 2,300 310 570	2,335 400 985	4,860 4 665 2,105 195 2,365	2,206 2,390 2,325 2,606 2,769	14
Female 14 years old and over open-sued divinan labor force. Priva e vage and salary workers Government workers. Sel emplo of workers Unpe d family workers Unpe d family workers of in exper critism abor force	273,555 83,075 67,490 11,415 4,330 840 190,480	29 0°0 70 3,0 27,470 9 375 3 502 160 48,580	31 C6. 11,915 10,26: 830 77: 4.	34 815 15,415 15,695 970 730 40 19,400	17,515 13,160 11,520 1,050 570 40	12,875 10,685 9 400 1 135 245	7,790 8 5°0 6 675 1 640 240 12	5,170 4,650 3,010 1,485 145 10 525	3 3°- 2,920 1,30°- 20°- 40	1 410 1,140 585 490 65	40.5	455 335 480 85 65	975 330 185 80 60	365 230 _30 30 95 5	365 175 90 30 50	145 145 10 10 8 ₂	1 301 1,307 2,2,/ 1 217	12 3

Table 93.—INCOME IN 1949 OF PERSONS, BY TYPE OF INCOME AND SEX, FOR THE STATE, FARM AND NONFARM, AND FOR STANDARD METROPOLITAN AREAS OF 250,000 OR MORE: 1950

[Based on 20-percent sample. Median not shown where base is less than 500]

Area, farm residence, type of income, and sex	Total persons with income	$1 to $499 or loss	$500 to $999	$1,000 to $1,499	$1,500 to $1,999	$2,000 to $2,499	$2,500 to $2,999	$3,000 to $3,499	$3,500 to $3,999	$4,000 to $4,499	$4,500 to $4,999	$5,000 to $5,999	$6,000 to $6,999	$7,000 to $9,999	$10,000 and over	Median income (dol.)
THE STATE																
Total, 14 years old and over	1,103,810	220,370	289,780	138,580	112,895	93,710	64,425	59,925	33,945	29,515	18,490	22,770	11,245	14,120	13,060	1,259
Earnings only	[illegible]	269,550	125,230	98,040	85,460	76,150	75,230	42,710	27,550	20,265	12,440	15,520	7,105	7,070	6,880	1,783
Wages or salary only	[illegible]25,030	235,500	96,865	73,885	74,445	66,100	39,690	30,830	20,955	17,355	11,000	11,965	5,185	7,215	2,450	1,439
Self-employment income only	[illegible]	26,815	21,885	19,945	8,935	8,075	4,310	4,695	2,690	2,293	970	2,760	1,440	2,220	4,170	1,139
Wages or salary and self-employment income	29,360	7,205	6,540	4,140	2,540	1,975	1,300	1,155	905	710	470	795	460	635	480	1,113
Earnings and income other than earnings	181,765	10,210	25,015	24,095	21,940	20,820	17,910	16,470	11,790	8,765	5,790	7,675	3,870	4,580	5,390	2,248
Wages or salary and other income	139,875	6,420	17,855	17,760	16,130	16,395	15,175	13,845	10,020	7,310	4,845	5,930	2,540	2,785	2,160	2,335
Self-employment income and other income	36,385	4,310	6,710	5,540	4,940	3,570	2,210	1,920	1,260	1,085	660	1,265	805	1,430	2,645	1,864
Wages or salary, self-empl. income, & oth. income	8,150	395	1,050	1,045	870	860	595	405	510	370	245	480	325	365	585	2,387
Other income, no earnings	176,770	50,570	98,535	16,405	5,735	2,735	1,285	1,045	605	490	300	575	470	470	790	649
Male, 14 years old and over	730,765	94,015	136,180	98,335	85,345	77,755	52,370	50,230	36,075	27,395	17,445	22,165	10,390	11,075	12,970	1,755
Earnings only	497,660	72,660	74,445	68,030	63,385	57,535	35,530	35,275	24,995	19,105	11,915	14,740	6,780	6,700	6,335	1,766
Wages or salary only	385,950	49,405	50,455	54,380	53,280	48,675	30,520	30,010	21,680	16,420	10,600	11,375	5,005	4,000	2,145	1,884
Self-employment income only	86,495	18,225	18,185	11,900	7,745	7,740	3,820	4,170	2,485	2,065	890	2,635	1,315	2,100	3,890	1,287
Wages or salary and self-employment income	25,265	5,170	5,795	1,750	2,360	1,820	1,190	1,055	830	620	425	730	460	600	260	1,222
Earnings and income other than earnings	156,290	5,780	17,995	19,860	19,290	18,575	16,155	14,545	10,795	8,100	5,335	7,215	3,335	4,175	5,075	2,410
Wages or salary and other income	117,210	3,570	11,715	14,500	13,905	14,565	13,550	12,410	9,180	6,795	4,535	5,620	2,370	2,590	2,045	2,420
Self-employment income and other income	31,755	1,600	5,405	4,875	4,575	3,215	2,055	1,700	1,143	980	585	1,160	720	1,245	2,500	1,937
Wages or salary, self-empl. income, & oth. income	7,325	510	875	985	810	795	550	375	475	325	215	435	205	340	530	2,429
Other income, no earnings	76,815	15,575	43,770	10,465	2,670	1,475	685	410	285	190	195	210	215	200	600	761
Female, 14 years old and over	373,045	126,355	153,600	40,245	27,350	22,135	12,055	9,695	3,870	2,120	1,045	1,605	855	1,045	1,090	721
Earnings only	242,175	96,890	50,815	29,390	22,535	18,615	9,700	7,435	2,555	1,155	525	780	325	370	285	717
Wages or salary only	219,080	86,235	40,350	27,505	21,165	17,425	9,100	6,780	2,275	875	400	490	180	255	85	752
Self-employment income only	18,800	8,620	5,720	2,095	1,190	1,015	490	525	205	190	80	225	125	120	180	605
Wages or salary and self-employment income	4,095	2,035	745	390	180	175	110	130	75	90	45	65	20	35	20	508
Earnings and income other than earnings	28,145	4,430	7,620	4,235	2,650	2,250	1,755	1,025	995	665	415	460	275	405	315	1,238
Wages or salary and other income	22,660	3,620	6,140	3,460	2,225	1,830	1,555	1,375	840	515	310	310	170	195	115	1,227
Self-employment income and other income	4,630	725	1,305	665	365	355	155	220	120	105	75	105	85	185	145	1,190
Wages or salary, self-empl. income, & oth. income	825	85	175	110	60	65	45	30	35	45	30	15	20	25	55	842
Other income, no earnings	102,955	34,995	55,165	6,000	2,165	1,290	600	635	320	300	105	365	255	270	490	649
URBAN AND RURAL NONFARM																
Total, 14 years old and over	914,970	170,880	193,285	113,[illegible]	97,065	88,400	58,895	55,115	37,330	27,255	17,285	21,225	10,420	11,165	12,120	1,411
Earnings only	608,415	120,925	93,260	80,370	75,045	68,220	41,520	39,160	25,795	18,665	11,640	14,480	6,575	6,485	6,315	1,564
Wages or salary only	543,810	110,950	84,070	72,860	69,275	62,195	37,610	35,020	22,995	16,395	10,535	11,630	5,065	4,110	2,140	1,530
Self-employment income only	52,900	9,105	7,455	6,165	4,870	5,135	3,140	3,385	2,245	1,780	780	2,265	1,150	1,865	3,760	1,839
Wages or salary and self-employment income	11,745	1,870	1,735	1,345	1,100	930	770	755	555	490	325	585	360	510	415	1,949
Earnings and income other than earnings	156,245	7,820	18,960	18,715	17,435	17,725	16,205	14,990	10,965	8,155	5,375	7,215	3,385	4,240	5,060	2,429
Wages or salary and other income	130,690	6,445	15,870	15,945	14,955	15,405	14,380	13,330	9,625	7,015	4,685	5,760	2,470	2,735	2,100	2,395
Self-employment income and other income	20,395	1,205	2,625	2,250	2,035	1,825	1,400	1,390	975	845	520	1,030	655	1,205	2,425	2,988
Wages or salary, self-empl. income, & oth. income	5,160	170	455	550	445	495	425	270	365	295	170	425	260	300	535	3,074
Other income, no earnings	150,270	42,115	81,065	14,465	4,585	2,455	1,170	965	570	435	270	530	460	440	745	64[illegible]
Male, 14 years old and over	586,160	58,345	93,120	75,930	71,125	67,450	47,420	45,950	35,670	25,255	16,300	20,725	9,610	10,195	11,065	1,969
Earnings only	393,595	42,260	40,455	52,150	53,560	50,610	32,280	32,130	23,390	17,575	11,140	13,775	6,275	6,150	6,045	2,044
Wages or salary only	343,445	30,285	20,035	46,175	48,430	5,535	28,875	28,375	20,815	15,550	10,145	11,110	7,885	3,910	2,060	1,998
Self-employment income only	40,810	7,870	5,085	4,985	3,750	4,265	2,705	2,310	2,070	1,610	705	2,080	1,045	1,760	3,590	2,273
Wages or salary and self-employment income	9,620	1,105	1,335	1,090	980	810	700	645	505	415	290	525	355	480	395	2,185
Earnings and income other than earnings	130,645	4,000	12,260	14,875	14,435	15,595	14,540	13,460	10,010	7,495	4,985	6,765	3,125	3,865	4,755	2,626
Wages or salary and other income	109,110	3,155	10,070	12,600	2,780	13,610	12,885	12,005	8,820	6,505	4,385	5,450	2,305	2,545	1,985	2,591
Self-employment income and other income	16,985	735	1,825	1,780	1,755	1,535	1,270	1,200	855	740	445	935	580	1,045	2,285	2,840
Wages or salary, self-empl. income, & oth. income	4,550	110	365	475	400	450	385	255	335	250	155	380	440	275	485	3,184
Other income, no earnings	61,920	12,085	34,405	8,925	2,530	1,245	600	60	270	185	175	185	210	180	265	772
Female, 14 years old and over	328,810	112,515	100,165	37,620	25,940	20,950	11,475	9,165	1,660	2,000	985	1,500	810	970	1,055	759
Earnings only	214,560	78,665	46,805	28,220	21,385	17,610	9,240	7,030	2,405	1,090	500	705	300	335	270	806
Wages or salary only	200,365	73,460	44,035	26,385	20,345	16,620	8,735	6,440	2,180	855	390	460	180	200	80	803
Self-employment income only	12,070	4,435	2,370	1,580	920	870	435	475	175	170	75	185	105	105	170	838
Wages or salary and self-employment income	2,125	765	400	255	120	120	70	110	50	75	35	60	15	30	20	872
Earnings and income other than earnings	25,600	3,820	6,700	3,900	3,000	2,130	1,665	1,530	955	660	390	450	260	375	305	1,255
Wages or salary and other income	21,380	3,290	5,800	3,315	2,175	1,795	1,495	1,315	805	510	300	310	165	190	115	1,226
Self-employment income and other income	3,410	470	810	410	280	290	130	190	120	105	75	95	75	160	140	1,452
Wages or salary, self-empl. income, & oth. income	810	60	90	75	45	45	40	25	30	45	15	45	20	25	50	2,389
Other income, no earnings	88,650	30,030	46,660	5,540	2,555	1,210	570	605	300	250	95	345	250	260	480	653
RURAL FARM																
Total, 14 years old and over	188,840	55,490	96,495	25,030	15,830	11,310	5,530	4,810	2,615	2,260	1,205	1,545	825	955	940	809
Earnings only	131,180	48,625	31,970	17,650	10,875	7,930	3,710	3,550	1,755	1,595	800	1,040	530	585	565	760
Wages or salary only	61,220	25,550	12,735	7,025	5,170	3,045	2,010	1,810	960	930	465	335	120	105	90	699
Self-employment income only	52,345	17,740	14,430	7,830	4,265	2,940	1,170	1,310	745	475	190	495	290	355	410	792
Wages or salary and self-employment income	17,615	5,335	4,810	2,795	1,440	1,045	530	430	350	220	145	210	120	125	65	831
Earnings and income other than earnings	28,160	2,410	6,635	5,380	4,105	3,100	1,705	1,180	845	610	375	460	285	340	330	1,466
Wages or salary and other income	9,180	1,345	1,985	1,545	1,175	990	725	515	335	295	160	170	70	50	60	1,506
Self-employment income and other income	15,990	1,140	4,075	3,290	2,905	1,745	810	530	285	240	140	235	150	225	220	1,442
Wages or salary, self-empl. income, & oth. income	2,990	225	595	545	425	365	170	135	145	75	75	55	65	65	50	1,653
Other income, no earnings	29,500	8,455	17,870	2,000	450	280	115	80	35	55	30	45	10	30	45	676
Male, 14 years old and over	144,605	35,970	43,060	22,425	14,420	10,105	4,950	4,280	2,405	2,140	1,145	1,440	780	880	905	925
Earnings only	103,765	30,400	27,960	15,880	9,725	6,925	3,250	3,145	1,605	1,530	775	965	505	550	550	884
Wages or salary only	42,505	12,780	10,420	5,905	4,350	3,140	1,645	1,475	865	870	455	305	120	90	85	907
Self-employment income only	45,645	13,355	13,090	7,315	3,995	2,775	1,125	1,260	415	455	185	455	270	340	400	854
Wages or salary and self-employment income	15,645	4,265	4,460	2,660	1,380	1,010	490	410	325	205	135	205	115	120	65	921
Earnings and income other than earnings	25,645	1,780	5,735	5,005	4,355	2,980	1,625	1,085	785	605	350	450	270	310	320	1,515
Wages or salary and other income	8,100	715	1,645	1,400	1,125	955	605	455	360	290	150	70	65	45	60	1,649
Self-employment income and other income	14,770	865	3,580	3,095	2,820	1,680	785	500	285	250	140	225	140	200	215	1,475
Wages or salary, self-empl. income, & oth. income	2,775	200	510	510	410	345	165	130	140	75	60	55	65	65	45	1,704
Other income, no earnings	15,195	3,790	9,365	1,540	340	200	85	50	15	5	20	25	5	20	35	719
Female, 14 years old and over	44,235	27,820	13,435	2,605	1,410	1,205	580	530	210	120	60	105	45	75	35	464
Earnings only	27,415	18,225	4,010	1,770	1,150	1,005	460	405	150	65	35	75	25	35	15	376
Wages or salary only	18,715	12,770	2,315	1,120	820	805	365	335	95	30	10	30		15	5	366
Self-employment income only	6,730	4,185	1,350	515	270	165	55	50	50	20	5	40	20	15	10	402
Wages or salary and self-employment income	1,970	1,270	345	135	60	35	40	20	25	15	10	5	5	5		388
Earnings and income other than earnings	2,515	630	920	375	150	120	90	95	40	5	25	10	15	30	10	841
Wages or salary and other income	1,080	330	340	145	80	35	60	60	35	5	10		5	5		809
Self-employment income and other income	1,220	275	495	195	65	65	25	30				10	10	25	5	838
Wages or salary, self-empl. income, & oth. income	215	25	85	35	15	20	5	5	5		15				5	
Other income, no earnings	14,305	4,965	8,505	460	110	80	30	30	20	30	10	20	5	10	10	629

Fem.lat, it years old and ove

En map only

Wages or a.ary only

Sid-eraployment income only

Sid-eraployment income only

Map or a.ary only

Wages or solary and other than carungs

Wages or solary and other income

Enfarth proposers it rooms and other income

Wages or solary and other income

Wages or solary and only

Other more in orange

Other more in orange

Other more in orange 27,820 18,225 12,770 4,185 1,270 930 275 275 275 13,425, 4,010, 2,315, 1,350, 345, 340, 495, 8,505 2 605 1,7°C 1,20 515 1,5 375 145 125 35 44,255 27,415 -8,715 6,70 2,515 1,080 1,220 215 360 360 55 40 90 90 25 30 21° 150 95 25 35 1 205 1,005 805 465 35 120 35 65 530 405 335 30 95 60 30 5 120 65 30 20 15 60 25 10 25 10 25 1,150 820 270 60 50 65 15 105 75 30 40 5 464 376 366 402 388 841 809 818 20 3 10

ي.

5 5

40

10

CPSIA information can be obtained at www.ICGtesting.com
Printed in the USA
BVHW030103240822
645287BV00004B/68

9 781378 864296